Contents

Helping you to pass

BPP Learning Media – ACCA Approved Content Provider

As ACCA's **Approved Content Provider**, BPP Learning Media gives you the **opportunity** to use study materials reviewed by the ACCA examination team. By incorporating the examination team's comments and suggestions regarding the depth and breadth of syllabus coverage, the BPP Learning Media Study Text provides excellent, **ACCA-approved** support for your studies.

The PER alert!

Before you can qualify as an ACCA member, you not only have to pass all your exams but also fulfil a three year **practical experience requirement** (PER). To help you to recognise areas of the syllabus that you might be able to apply in the workplace to achieve different performance objectives, we have introduced the '**PER alert**' feature. You will find this feature throughout the Study Text to remind you that what you are **learning to pass** your ACCA exams is **equally useful to the fulfilment of the PER requirement**.

Your achievement of the PER should be recorded in your online *My Experience* record.

Tackling studying

Studying can be a daunting prospect, particularly when you have lots of other commitments. The **different features** of the Study Text, the **purposes** of which are explained fully on the **Chapter features** page, will help you whilst studying and improve your chances of **exam success**.

Developing exam awareness

Our Study Text are completely **focused** on helping you pass your exam.

Our advice on **Studying F6** outlines the **content** of the paper and the **necessary skills** you are expected to be able to demonstrate and any **brought forward knowledge** you are expected to have.

Exam focus points are included within the chapters to highlight when and how specific topics were examined, or how they might be examined in the future.

Testing what you can do

Testing yourself helps you develop the skills you need to pass the exam and also confirms that you can recall what you have learnt.

We include **Questions** – lots of them – both within chapters and in the **Practice Question Bank**, as well as **Quick Quizzes** at the end of each chapter to test your knowledge of the chapter content.

Chapter features

Each chapter contains a number of helpful features to guide you through each topic.

Topic list	Tells you what you will be studying in this chapter and the relevant section numbers, together with ACCA syllabus references.
Introduction	Puts the chapter content in the context of the syllabus as a whole.
Study Guide	Links the chapter content with ACCA guidance.
Exam Guide	Highlights how examinable the chapter content is likely to be and the ways in which it could be examined.
FAST FORWARD	Summarises the content of main chapter headings, allowing you to preview and review each section easily.
Examples	Demonstrate how to apply key knowledge and techniques.
Key terms	Definitions of important concepts that can often earn you easy marks in exams.
Exam focus points	Tell you when and how specific topics were examined, or how they may be examined in the future.
Formula to learn	Formulae that are not given in the exam but which have to be learnt.
PER alert	Gives you a useful indication of syllabus areas that closely relate to performance objectives in your Practical Experience Requirement (PER).
Question	Gives you essential practice of techniques covered in the chapter.
Chapter Roundup	A full list of the Fast Forwards included in the chapter, providing an easy source of review.
Quick Quiz	A quick test of your knowledge of the main topics in the chapter.
Practice Question Bank	Found at the back of the Study Text with more comprehensive chapter questions. Cross referenced for easy navigation.

Topic list example:

Topic list	Syllabus reference

Studying F6

As the name suggests, this paper examines the **basic principles of taxation**. This is a very important area for certified accountants as many areas of practice involve a consideration of taxation issues. It also provides a **foundation for P6: Advanced Taxation** which will be chosen by those who work in a tax environment.

Members of the F6 examination team have written **several technical articles** including two on Inheritance Tax, two on chargeable gains, one on groups, two on VAT, one on benefits, one on motor cars, one on adjustment of profit and one on Finance Act 2016. All these articles are available on the ACCA website. Make sure you read them to gain further insight into what the F6 examination team is looking for.

1 What F6 is about

You are introduced to the rationale behind – and the functions of – **the tax system**. The syllabus then considers the **separate taxes** that an accountant would need to have a detailed knowledge of, such as **income tax from self-employment**, **employment and investments**, the **corporation tax** liability of individual companies and groups of companies, the **national insurance contribution** liabilities of both employed and self employed persons, the **value added tax** liability of businesses, the **chargeable gains** arising on disposals of investments by both individuals and companies, and the **inheritance tax** liabilities arising on chargeable lifetime transfers and on death.

You will be expected to have a **detailed knowledge** of these taxes, but **no previous knowledge is assumed**. You should **study the basics** carefully and **learn the pro forma computations**. It then becomes straightforward to complete these by slotting in figures from your detailed workings.

As well as being able to calculate tax liabilities, you may be required to **explain the basis of the calculations**, **apply tax planning techniques** for individuals and companies and **identify the compliance issues** for each major tax through a variety of business and personal scenarios and situations.

2 What skills are required?

- Be able to **integrate** knowledge and understanding from across the syllabus to enable you to complete detailed computations of tax liabilities.
- Be able to **explain** the underlying principles of taxation by providing a simple summary of the rules and how they apply to the particular situation.
- Be able to **apply** tax planning techniques by identifying available options and testing them to see which has the greater effect on tax liabilities.

3 How to improve your chances of passing

- There is no choice in this paper, all questions have to be answered. You must therefore study the **entire syllabus**, there are no short-cuts.
- The first section of the paper consists of 15 **objective test questions**, worth two marks each. These will inevitably cover a **wide range of the syllabus**.
- The second section of the paper also consists of 15 **objective test questions,** worth two marks each. However, they are linked to a scenario. You must make sure you **understand the scenario** before attempting the questions.
- Practising longer questions set in the third section of the paper under **timed conditions** is essential. BPP's **Practice & Revision Kit** contains 10 mark and 15 mark questions on all areas of the syllabus.
- **Answer all parts** of the question. Even if you cannot do all of the calculation elements, you will still be able to gain marks in the discussion parts.

- **Answer selectively** – the examination team will expect you to consider carefully what is relevant and significant enough to include in your answer. Don't include unnecessary information.
- Keep an eye out for **articles** as the **examination team** will use **Student Accountant** to communicate with students.

The exam paper

Computer-based exams

ACCA have commenced the launch of computer based exams (CBE's) for F5–F9. They have been piloting computer-based exams in limited markets since September 2016 with the aim of rolling out into all markets internationally over a five year period. Paper-based examinations will be run in parallel while the CBEs are phased in and BPP materials have been designed to support you, whichever exam option you choose.

Exam duration

The Skills module examinations F5–F9 contain a mix of objective and longer type questions with a duration of three hours for 100 marks. For paper-based exams there is an extra 15 minutes to reflect the manual effort required.

As ACCA increase their offering of F5–F9 session CBEs, they will be introducing seeded content to guarantee all exams are equivalent and fair. When the seeded content is introduced, students will be given more time to complete the exams – increasing to 3 hours and 20 minutes to take into account the inclusion of additional seeded content.

For more information on these changes and when they will be implemented, please visit the ACCA website. http://www.accaglobal.com/uk/en/student/changes-to-exams/f5-f9-session-cbe.html

Format of the exam

The exam format is the same irrespective of the mode of delivery and will comprise three exam sections:

Section	Style of question type	Description	Proportion of exam, %
A	Objective test (OT)	15 questions × 2 marks	30
B	Objective test (OT) case	3 questions × 10 marks Each question will contain 5 subparts each worth 2 marks	30
C	Constructed Response (Long questions)	1 question × 10 marks 2 questions × 15 marks	40
Total			100

Section A and B questions will be selected from the entire syllabus. The paper version of these objective test questions contains multiple choice only and the computer-based versions will contain a variety. The responses to each question or subpart in the case of OT cases are marked automatically as either correct or incorrect by computer.

The 10 mark Section C questions can come from any part of the syllabus. The 15 mark Section C questions will mainly focus on the following syllabus areas but a minority of marks can be drawn from any other area of the syllabus:

- Income tax (syllabus area B)
- Corporation tax (syllabus area E)

The responses to these questions are human marked.

Syllabus and Study Guide

The complete F6 syllabus and study guide can be found by visiting the exam resource finder on the ACCA website: http://www.accaglobal.com/uk/en/student/exam-support-resources.html

PART A

UK tax system

1

Introduction to the UK tax system

Topic list	Syllabus reference
1 The overall function and purpose of taxation in a modern economy	A1(a)
2 Different types of taxes	A1(b), (c)
3 Principal sources of revenue law and practice	A2(a)-(c), (e), (f)
4 Tax avoidance and tax evasion	A2(d), (g)

Introduction

We start our study of tax with an introduction to the UK tax system.

First, we consider briefly the purpose of raising taxes, focussing on economic, social and environmental factors. We next consider the specific UK taxes, both revenue and capital, and also direct and indirect.

We see how the collection of tax is administered in the UK, and where the UK tax system interacts with overseas tax jurisdictions.

Finally, we highlight the difference between tax avoidance and tax evasion and explain the need for a professional and ethical approach in dealing with tax. In particular, we look at the situation where a client has failed to disclose information to the tax authorities.

When you have finished this chapter you should be able to discuss the broad features of the tax system. In the following chapters we will consider specific UK taxes, starting with income tax.

Study guide

		Intellectual level
A1	**The overall function and purpose of taxation in a modern economy**	
(a)	Describe the purpose (economic, social etc) of taxation in a modern economy.	1
(b)	Explain the difference between direct and indirect taxation.	2
(c)	Identify the different types of capital and revenue tax.	1
A2	**Principal sources of revenue law and practice**	
(a)	Describe the overall structure of the UK tax system.	1
(b)	State the different sources of revenue law.	1
(c)	Describe the organisation of HM Revenue & Customs (HMRC) and its terms of reference.	1
(d)	Explain the difference between tax avoidance and tax evasion, and the purposes of the General Anti-Abuse Rule (GAAR).	1
(e)	Appreciate the interaction of the UK tax system with that of other tax jurisdictions.	2
(f)	Appreciate the need for double taxation agreements.	2
(g)	Explain the need for an ethical and professional approach.	2

Exam guide

You may be asked a question on a specific topic from this part of the syllabus in either Section A or Section B. An example would be to identify sources of revenue law. You are unlikely to be asked a whole Section C question on this part of the syllabus. You may, however, be asked to comment on one aspect, such as the difference between tax avoidance and tax evasion or how to act if a client has failed to disclose information to the tax authorities, as part of a question.

1 The overall function and purpose of taxation in a modern economy

FAST FORWARD

Economic, social and environmental factors may affect the government's tax policies.

1.1 Economic factors

In terms of economic analysis, government **taxation represents a withdrawal from the UK economy** while its expenditure acts as an injection into it. So the government's net position in terms of taxation and expenditure, together with its public sector borrowing policies, has an effect on the level of economic activity within the UK.

The government favours longer-term planning, and regularly sets out proposed plans for expenditure. These show the proportion of the economy's overall resources which will be allocated by the government and how much will be left for the private sector.

This can have an effect on demand for particular types of goods, eg health and education on the one hand, which are predominately the result of public spending, and consumer goods on the other, which results from private spending. Changing demand levels will have an impact on employment levels within the different sectors, as well as on the profitability of different private sector suppliers.

Within that overall proportion left in the private sector, **the government uses tax policies to encourage and discourage certain types of activity**.

It **encourages**:

(a) **Saving** on the part of the individual, by offering tax incentives such as tax-free Individual Savings Accounts (ISAs) and tax relief on pension contributions

(b) **Donations to charities** through the Gift Aid scheme

(c) **Entrepreneurs** who build their own business, through reliefs from capital gains tax

(d) **Investment in plant and machinery** through capital allowances

(e) **Marriage and civil partnerships** through the transferable personal allowance (marriage allowance). Civil partners are members of a same sex couple which has registered as a civil partnership under the Civil Partnerships Act 2004. Same sex couples can also marry in England, Wales and Scotland (but not Northern Ireland).

It **discourages**:

(a) **Smoking** and **alcoholic drinks**, through the duties placed on each type of product

(b) **Motoring**, through fuel duties

Governments can and do argue that these latter taxes and duties to some extent mirror the extra costs to the country as a whole of such behaviours, such as the cost of coping with smoking related illnesses. However, the Government needs to raise money for spending in areas where there are no consumers on whom the necessary taxes can be levied, such as defence, law and order, overseas aid and the cost of running the government and Parliament.

1.2 Social factors

Social justice lies at the heart of politics, since what some think of as just is regarded by others as completely unjust. Attitudes to the redistribution of wealth are a clear example.

In a free market some individuals generate greater amounts of income and capital than others and once wealth has been acquired, it tends to grow through the reinvestment of investment income received. This can lead to the rich getting richer and the poor poorer, with economic power becoming concentrated in relatively few hands.

Some electors make the value judgement that these trends should be countered by **taxation policies which redistribute income and wealth** away from the rich towards the poor. This is one of the key arguments in favour of some sort of capital gains tax and inheritance tax, taxes which, relative to the revenue raised, cost a great deal to collect.

Different taxes have different social effects:

(a) **Direct taxes** based on income and profits (income tax), gains (capital gains tax) or wealth (inheritance tax) **tax only those who have these resources.**

(b) **Indirect taxes** paid by the consumer (VAT) **discourage spending** and encourage saving. Lower or nil rates of tax can be levied on essentials, such as food.

(c) **Progressive taxes** such as income tax, where the proportion of the income or gains paid over in tax increases as income/gains rise, **target those who can afford to pay**. Personal allowances and the rates of taxation can be adjusted so as to ensure that those on very low incomes pay little or no tax.

(d) Taxes on capital or wealth ensure that people cannot avoid taxation by having an income of zero and just living off the sale of capital assets.

Almost everyone would argue that taxation should be **equitable** or 'fair', but there are many different views as to what is equitable.

An **efficient tax** is one where the costs of collection are low relative to the tax paid over to the government. The government publishes figures for the administrative costs incurred by government departments in operating the taxation systems, but there are also compliance costs to be taken into account. Compliance costs are those incurred by the taxpayer, whether they be the individual preparing tax returns under the self assessment system or the employer operating the PAYE system to collect income tax or the business collecting value added tax. Some of the more equitable taxes may be less efficient to collect.

1.3 Environmental factors

The taxation system accommodates environmental concerns to a certain extent, especially concerns about renewable and non-renewable sources of energy and global warming.

Examples of tax changes which have been introduced for environmental reasons are:

(a) The **climate change levy**, raised on businesses in proportion to their consumption of energy. Its claimed purpose is to encourage reduced consumption.

(b) The **landfill tax** levied on the operators of landfill sites on each tonne of rubbish/waste processed at the site. Its claimed purpose is to encourage recycling by taxing waste which has to be stored.

(c) The changes to rules on the **lease or purchase of cars**, and taxation of **cars and private fuel provided for employees** to be dependent on CO_2 emissions. Its claimed purpose is to encourage the manufacture and purchase of low CO_2 emission cars to reduce emissions into the atmosphere caused by driving.

Only the last of these will be directly felt by individuals, even if the other taxes are passed on by being factored into a business's overheads.

2 Different types of taxes

FAST FORWARD

Central government raises revenue through a wide range of taxes. Tax law is made by statute.

2.1 Taxes in the UK

Central government raises revenue through a wide range of taxes. Tax law is made by **statute**.

The main taxes, their incidence and their sources, are set out in the table below.

Tax	Suffered by	Source
Income tax	**Individuals** **Partnerships**	Capital Allowances Act 2001 (CAA 2001); Income Tax (Earnings and Pensions) Act 2003 (ITEPA 2003); Income Tax (Trading and Other Income) Act 2005 (ITTOIA 2005); Income Tax Act 2007 (ITA 2007)
Corporation tax	**Companies**	CAA 2001 as above, Corporation Tax Act 2009 (CTA 2009), Corporation Tax Act 2010 (CTA 2010)
Capital gains tax	**Individuals** **Partnerships** **Companies** (which pay tax on capital gains in the form of corporation tax)	Taxation of Chargeable Gains Act 1992 (TCGA 1992)
Inheritance tax	**Individuals** **Trustees**	Inheritance Tax Act 1984 (IHTA 1984)
Value added tax	**Businesses**, both incorporated and unincorporated	Value Added Tax Act 1994 (VATA 1994)

You will also meet National Insurance. **National insurance is payable by employers, employees and the self employed.**

Further details of all these taxes are found later in this Study Text.

The other taxes referred to in the previous section, such as landfill tax, are not examinable at F6.

Finance Acts are passed each year, incorporating proposals set out in the **Budget**. They make changes which apply mainly to the tax year ahead. **This Study Text includes the provisions of the Finance Act 2016.** This is the **Finance Act examinable** in the sessions in June 2017, **September 2017, December 2017 and March 2018**.

2.2 Revenue and capital taxes

Revenue taxes are those charged on income. In this Study Text we cover:

(a) **Income tax**
(b) **Corporation tax** (on income profits)
(c) **National insurance**

Capital taxes are those charged on capital gains or on wealth. In this Study Text we cover:

(a) **Capital gains tax**
(b) **Corporation tax** (on capital gains)
(c) **Inheritance tax**

2.3 Direct and indirect taxes

Direct taxes are those charged on **income, gains and wealth. Income tax, national insurance, corporation tax**, **capital gains tax** and **inheritance tax** are **direct taxes**. Direct taxes are collected directly from the taxpayer.

Indirect taxes are those **paid by the consumer to the supplier** who then passes the tax to the Government. **Value added tax** is an indirect tax.

3 Principal sources of revenue law and practice

FAST FORWARD

Tax is administered by HM Revenue and Customs (HMRC).

3.1 The overall structure of the UK tax system

3.1.1 Her Majesty's Treasury

Her Majesty's Treasury formally imposes and collects taxation. The management of the Treasury is the responsibility of the Chancellor of the Exchequer.

3.1.2 Her Majesty's Revenue and Customs (HMRC)

The administrative function for the collection of tax is undertaken by Her Majesty's Revenue and Customs (HMRC).

The HMRC staff are referred to in the tax legislation as **'Officers of Revenue and Customs'**. They are responsible for supervising the self-assessment system and raising queries about tax liabilities.

3.1.3 Crown Prosecution Service (CPS)

The **Crown Prosecution Service (CPS)** provides legal advice and institutes and conducts criminal prosecutions in England and Wales where there has been an investigation by HMRC.

3.1.4 Tax Tribunal

Tax appeals are heard by the **Tax Tribunal** which is made up of **two tiers**:

(a) **First Tier Tribunal**
(b) **Upper Tribunal**

The **First Tier Tribunal deals with most cases** other than complex cases. The **Upper Tribunal deals with complex cases** which either involve an important issue of tax law or a large financial sum. The Upper Tribunal **also hears appeals** against decisions of the First Tier Tribunal. We look at the appeals system in more detail later in this Study Text.

3.2 Different sources of revenue law

FAST FORWARD

The sources of revenue law are Acts of Parliament, Statutory Instruments and case law.

As stated above, taxes are imposed by statute. This comprises not only **Acts of Parliament** but also regulations laid down by **Statutory Instruments**. Statute is interpreted and amplified by **case law**.

HMRC also issue:

(a) **Statements of practice**, setting out how they intend to apply the law

(b) **Extra-statutory concessions**, setting out circumstances in which they will not apply the strict letter of the law where it would be unfair

(c) A wide range of **explanatory leaflets**

(d) **Revenue and Customs Brief.** This is gives HMRC's view on specific points.

(e) The **Internal Guidance**, a series of manuals used by HMRC staff

(f) **Agent Update**, for tax practitioners.

A great deal of information and HMRC publications can be found on the HM Revenue and Customs pages of the UK Government website (www.gov.uk).

Although the HMRC publications do not generally have the force of law, some of the VAT notices do where power has been delegated under regulations. This applies, for example, to certain administrative aspects of the cash accounting scheme.

3.3 The interaction of the UK tax system with that of other tax jurisdictions

3.3.1 The European Union

FAST FORWARD

UK membership of the European Union has a significant effect on UK taxes, in particular value added tax (VAT). This will continue until the UK leaves the European Union.

Membership of the European Union has a significant effect on UK taxes although there is no general requirement imposed on the EU member states to move to a common system of taxation nor to harmonise their individual tax systems. The states may, however, agree jointly to enact specific laws, known as '**Directives**', which provide for a common code of taxation within particular areas of their taxation systems.

The most important example to date is **Value Added Tax (VAT)**, where the UK is obliged to pass its laws in conformity with the rules laid down in the European legislation. The VAT Directives still allow for a certain amount of flexibility between member states, eg in setting rates of taxation. There are only limited examples of Directives in the area of Direct Taxes, generally concerned with cross-border dividend and interest payments and corporate reorganisations.

However, under the EU treaties, member states are also obliged to permit freedom of movement of workers, freedom of movement of capital and freedom to establish business operations within the EU. These treaty provisions have '**direct effect**', ie a taxpayer is entitled to claim that a UK tax provision is ineffective because it **breaches one or more of the freedoms** guaranteed under European Law.

The European Court of Justice has repeatedly held that taxation provisions which discriminate against non-residents (ie treat a non-resident less favourably than a resident in a similar situation) are contrary to European Law, unless there is a very strong public interest justification.

There are provisions regarding the **exchange of information** between European Union Revenue authorities.

The long term implications of the **UK referendum in June 2016 to leave the European Union** are not fully known. However, until the UK has gone through the process of ceasing its membership, **European Union rules will continue to apply to the UK**.

3.3.2 Other countries

In general, the rules of tax jurisdictions of other countries do not have a direct interaction with UK tax. However, the UK has entered into **double tax agreement** with various countries, as discussed below.

3.4 Double taxation agreements

FAST FORWARD

Double taxation agreements are designed to protect against the risk of double taxation where the same income or gains are taxable in two countries.

Double Taxation agreements between two countries are primarily designed to protect against the risk of double taxation where the same income or gains are taxable in two countries.

For example, an individual may have a **source of income which is taxed in the country in which the income arose** but **is also taxed in the individual's country of residence**. The agreement could provide that the **income is only to be taxed in one country** or that **credit is to be given for tax arising in one country against the tax charge in the other country**.

Double taxation agreements may also include **non-discrimination provisions** which prevent a foreign national from being treated more harshly than a national of a country.

Double taxation agreements also usually include rules for the **exchange of information** between the different Revenue authorities.

4 Tax avoidance and tax evasion

PER alert

One of the competencies you require to fulfil Performance Objective 17 Tax planning and advice of the PER is to advise clients responsibly about the differences between tax planning, tax avoidance and tax evasion. You can apply the knowledge you obtain from this section of the Study Text to help to demonstrate this competence.

FAST FORWARD

Tax avoidance is the legal minimisation of tax liabilities; tax evasion is illegal.

4.1 Tax evasion

Tax evasion consists of seeking to pay too little tax by deliberately misleading HMRC by either:

(a) **Suppressing information to which they are entitled** (eg failing to notify HMRC that you are liable to tax, understating income or gains or omitting to disclose a relevant fact, eg that business expenditure had a dual motive), or

(b) **Providing them with deliberately false information** (eg deducting expenses which have not been incurred or claiming capital allowances on plant that has not been purchased).

Tax evasion is illegal. Minor cases of tax evasion have generally been settled out of court on the payment of penalties. However, there is now a **statutory offence of evading income tax**, which enables such matters as deliberate failure to operate PAYE to be dealt with in magistrates' courts.

Serious cases of tax evasion, particularly those involving fraud, will continue to be the subject of **criminal prosecutions** which may lead to **fines and/or imprisonment on conviction**.

4.2 Tax avoidance

Tax avoidance is more difficult to define.

In a very broad sense, it could include **any legal method of reducing your tax burden**, eg taking advantage of tax shelter opportunities explicitly offered by tax legislation such as ISAs. However, the term is more commonly used in a more narrow sense, to denote complex arrangements designed to produce unintended tax advantages for the taxpayer.

The effectiveness of tax avoidance schemes has often been examined in the courts. Traditionally the tax rules were applied to the legal form of transactions, although this principle was qualified in later cases. It was held that the Courts could disregard transactions which were preordained and solely designed to avoid tax.

Traditionally, the response of HMRC has been to seek to mend the **loopholes** in the law as they come to their attention. In general, there is a presumption that the effect of such changes should not be backdated.

There are **disclosure obligations** on promoters of certain tax **avoidance schemes**, and on taxpayers, to provide details to HMRC of any such schemes used by the taxpayer. This enables HMRC to introduce anti avoidance measures at the earliest opportunity.

4.3 The distinction between avoidance and evasion

The **distinction between tax evasion and tax avoidance should generally be clear cut**, since tax avoidance is an entirely legal activity and does not entail misleading HMRC. However, some tax avoidance arrangements may be subject to the General Anti-Abuse Rule discussed below.

Care should also be taken in giving advice in some circumstances. For example, a taxpayer who does not return income or gains because he wrongly believes that he has successfully avoided having to pay tax on them may, as a result, be accused of tax evasion.

4.4 General anti-abuse rule (GAAR)

FAST FORWARD

There is a general anti-abuse rule (GAAR) which enables HMRC to counteract tax advantages arising from abusive tax arrangements.

Tax avoidance is usually targeted with legislation which applies in specific circumstances. **The GAAR provides additional means for HMRC to 'counteract' tax advantages arising from abusive 'tax arrangements'**, ie arrangements that involve obtaining a **tax advantage** as (one of) their main purpose(s).

Arrangements are **abusive** if they **cannot be regarded as a reasonable course of action**, for example, where they **lead to unintended results involving one or more contrived or abnormal steps and exploit any shortcomings in the tax provisions**.

Examples of abusive arrangements include those that result in:

(a) Significantly less income, profits or gains
(b) Significantly greater deductions or losses, or
(c) A claim for the repayment or crediting of tax that has not been, and is unlikely to be, paid

A 'tax advantage' includes:

(a) Relief or increased relief from tax
(b) Repayment or increased repayment of tax
(c) Avoidance or reduction of a charge to tax
(d) Avoidance of a possible assessment to tax
(e) Deferral of a payment of tax or advancement of a repayment of tax
(f) Avoidance of an obligation to deduct or account for tax

HMRC may counteract tax advantages arising by, for example, increasing the taxpayer's tax liability. HMRC must follow certain procedural requirements and, if it makes any adjustments, these must be on a 'just and reasonable' basis.

4.5 The need for an ethical and professional approach

FAST FORWARD

If a client makes a material error or omission in a tax return, or fails to file a tax return, and does not correct the error, omission or failure when advised, the accountant should cease to act for the client, inform HMRC of this cessation and make a money laundering report.

Under self assessment, all taxpayers (whether individuals or companies) are responsible for disclosing their taxable income and gains and the deductions and reliefs they are claiming against them.

Many taxpayers arrange for their accountants to prepare and submit their tax returns. **The taxpayer is still the person responsible for submitting the return and for paying whatever tax becomes due**: the accountant is only acting as the taxpayer's agent.

The practising accountant often acts for taxpayers in their dealings with HMRC and situations can arise where the accountant has concerns as to whether the taxpayer is being honest in providing information to the accountant for onward transmission.

How the accountant deals with such situations is a matter of **professional judgement**, but in deciding what to do, the accountant will be expected to uphold the standards of the Association of Chartered Certified Accountants. He must act **honestly** and **objectively**, with **due care and diligence**, and showing the highest standards of **integrity**.

If an accountant learns of a material error or omission in a client's tax return or of a **failure to file a required tax return**, the accountant has a responsibility to **advise the client of the error, omission or failure** and **recommend that disclosure be made to HMRC**.

If the client, after having had a reasonable time to reflect, does not correct the error, omission or failure or authorise the accountant to do so on the client's behalf, the accountant should **inform the client in writing that it is not possible for the accountant to act for that client.**

The accountant should also **notify HMRC that the accountant no longer acts for the client but should not provide details of the reason for ceasing to act**.

An accountant whose client refuses to make disclosure to HMRC, after having had notice of the error, omission or failure and a reasonable time to reflect, **must also report the client's refusal and the facts surrounding it to the Money Laundering Reporting Officer within the accountancy firm or to the appropriate authority (National Crime Agency) if the accountant is a sole practitioner.**

Accountants who suspect or are aware of tax evasion activities by a client may themselves commit an offence if they do not report their suspicions. The accountant must not disclose to the client, or any one else, that such a report has been made if the accountant knows or suspects that to do so would be likely to prejudice any investigation which might be conducted following the report as this might constitute the criminal offence of 'tipping-off'.

Exam focus point

You may be asked to explain how you, as a trainee Chartered Certified Accountant, should deal with a situation where a client is evading tax, for example by not disclosing income or gains to HMRC.

Chapter Roundup

- Economic, social and environmental factors may affect the government's tax policies.
- Central government raises revenue through a wide range of taxes. Tax law is made by statute.
- Tax is administered by HM Revenue and Customs (HMRC).
- The sources of revenue law are Acts of Parliament, Statutory Instruments and case law.
- UK membership of the European Union has a significant effect on UK taxes, in particular value added tax (VAT). This will continue until the UK leaves the European Union.
- Double taxation agreements are designed to protect against the risk of double taxation where the same income or gains are taxable in two countries.
- Tax avoidance is the legal minimisation of tax liabilities; tax evasion is illegal.
- There is a general anti-abuse rule (GAAR) which enables HMRC to counteract tax advantages arising from abusive tax arrangements.
- If a client makes a material error or omission in a tax return, or fails to file a tax return, and does not correct the error, omission or failure when advised, the accountant should cease to act for the client, inform HMRC of this cessation and make a money laundering report.

Quick Quiz

1 What is the difference between a direct and an indirect tax?

2 What is an Extra Statutory Concession?

3 How might a double taxation agreement benefit a UK taxpayer who has income arising in a country which has such an agreement with the UK?

4 Tax avoidance is legal. True/False?

5 When may HMRC use the general anti-abuse rule (GAAR)?

Answers to Quick Quiz

1 A direct tax is one charged on income or gains; an indirect tax is paid by a consumer to the supplier, who then passes it to HMRC.

2 An Extra Statutory Concession is a relaxation by HMRC of the strict rules where their imposition would be unfair.

3 The agreement could provide that the income is only to be taxed in one country or that credit is to be given for tax arising in one country against the tax charge in the other country.

4 True. Tax avoidance is legal; tax evasion is illegal.

5 The GAAR may be used by HMRC where a taxpayer has used abusive tax arrangements to obtain a tax advantage.

Now try the question below from the Practice Question Bank

Number	Type	Marks	Time
Q1	Section A	2	4 mins
Q2	Section A	2	4 mins
Q3	Section A	2	4 mins

PART B

Income tax and national insurance contributions

2 Computing taxable income and the income tax liability

Topic list	Syllabus reference
1 Scope of income tax	B1(a)
2 Computing taxable income	B5(a)
3 Types of income	B4(f), B5(a)
4 Tax exempt income	B4(g), B7(c)
5 Deductible interest	B5(e)
6 Personal allowance	B5(b)
7 Computing income tax liability and income tax payable	B4(f), B5(d)
8 Accrued income scheme	B4(h)
9 Gift aid	B5(f)
10 Child benefit income tax charge	B5(g), B7(c)
11 Transferable personal allowance	B5(c), B7(c)
12 Married couples and couples in a civil partnership	B5(h), B7(b),(c)

Introduction

In the previous chapter we considered the UK tax system generally. Now we look at income tax, which is the tax applied on the income individuals make from their jobs, their businesses and their savings and investments. We consider the scope of income tax and see how to collect together all of an individual's income in a personal tax computation, and we also see which income can be excluded as being exempt from tax.

Next, we look at the circumstances in which interest paid can be deducted in the income tax computation.

Each individual is entitled to a personal allowance and only if that is exceeded will any tax be due. We then learn how to work out the income tax liability on taxable income and how much tax remains to be paid in cash.

We consider how the accrued income scheme applies to interest on UK Government securities (gilts). We see how donations to charity under the gift aid scheme can save tax. We also look at the income tax charge in relation to child benefit. We then consider the relief given by the transferable amount of the personal allowance between spouses/civil partners. Finally we consider how married couples or civil partners are subject to income tax and how they can minimise their tax liabilities.

In the next chapter we look at employment income.

Study guide

		Intellectual level
B1	**The scope of income tax**	
(a)	Explain how the residence of an individual is determined.	1
B4	**Property and investment income**	
(f)	Compute the tax payable on savings and dividends income.	2
(g)	Recognise the treatment of individual savings accounts (ISAs) and other tax exempt investments.	1
(h)	Understand how the accrued income scheme applies to UK Government securities (gilts).	1
B5	**The comprehensive computation of taxable income and income tax liability**	
(a)	Prepare a basic income tax computation involving different types of income.	2
(b)	Calculate the amount of personal allowance available.	2
(c)	Understand the impact of the transferable amount of personal allowance for spouses and civil partners.	2
(d)	Compute the amount of income tax payable.	2
(e)	Explain the treatment of interest paid for a qualifying purpose.	2
(f)	Understand the treatment of gift aid donations and charitable giving.	1
(g)	Explain and compute the child benefit tax charge.	1
(h)	Understand the treatment of property owned jointly by a married couple, or by a couple in a civil partnership.	1
B7	**The use of exemptions and reliefs in deferring and minimising income tax liabilities**	
(b)	Understand how a married couple or a couple in a civil partnership can minimise their tax liabilities.	2
(c)	Basic income tax planning.	2

Exam guide

Section A questions on the topics in this chapter may include identification of different types of income or calculation of the personal allowance. They could also include a simple computation of income tax liability on one type of income, or a computation of the child benefit income tax charge. Section B questions on the topics in this chapter could focus on tax implications of various types of income and the treatment of married couples/civil partners.

It is likely that you will have to prepare a full computation of income tax liability (and possibly income tax payable) in a Section C question, in a 15 mark question or a 10 mark question. You should familiarise yourself with the layout of the computation, and the three types of income: non-savings, savings and dividends. It is then a simple matter of slotting the final figures into the computation from supporting workings for the different types of income.

Gift aid donations could feature in a question in any section. You will come across the technique of increasing the basic rate and higher rate limits again when you deal with pensions later in this Study Text.

Throughout this chapter, you should be aware of basic income tax planning such as investing in sources of exempt income. We will also deal with some tax planning for spouses/civil partners in capital Section 12.

1 Scope of income tax

1.1 Residence

1.1.1 Statutory residence test

FAST FORWARD

An individual will automatically not be UK resident if he meets any of the automatic overseas tests. An individual, who does not meet any of the automatic overseas tests, will automatically be UK resident if he meets any of the automatic UK tests. An individual who has not met any of the automatic overseas tests nor any of the automatic UK tests will be UK resident if he meets the sufficient ties test.

A taxpayer's **residence** has important consequences in establishing the **tax treatment of his UK and overseas income and capital gains. Statute sets out a test to determine whether or not an individual is UK resident in a tax year.**

The **operation of the test** can be summarised as follows.

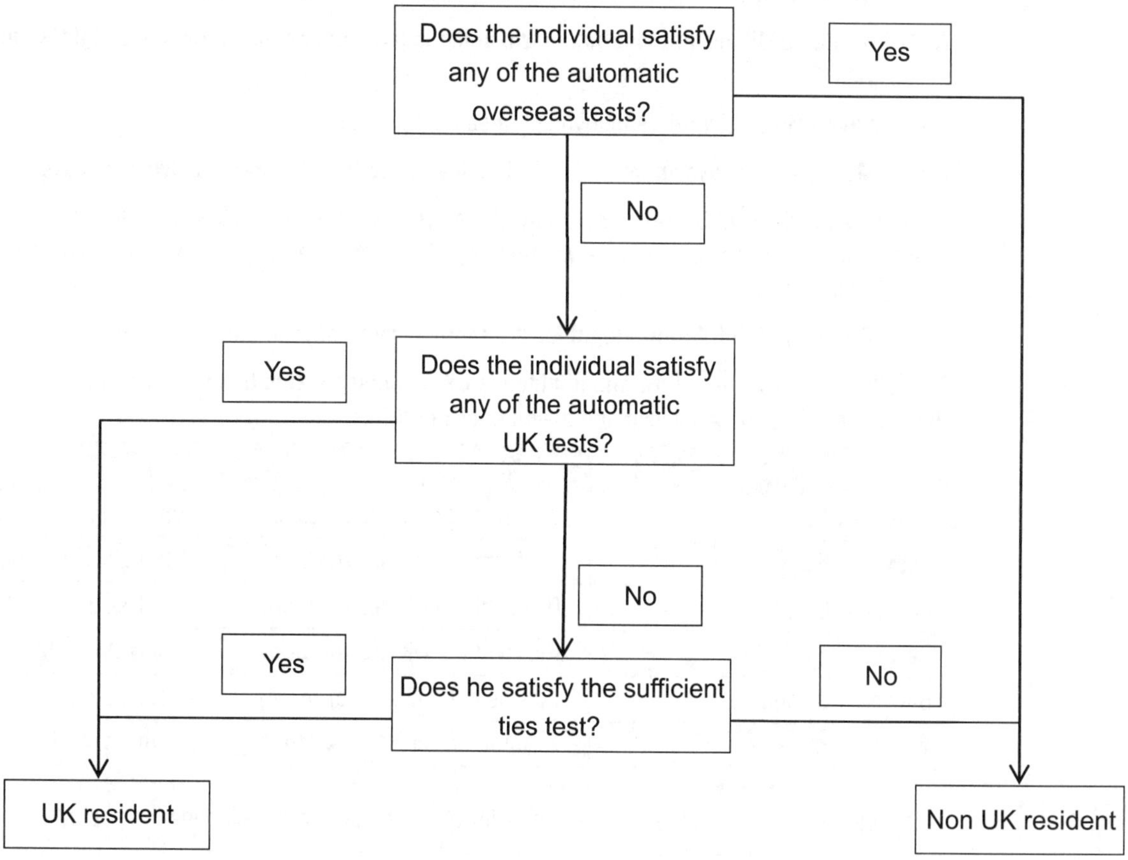

1.1.2 Automatic overseas tests

The automatic overseas tests must be considered first.

The **automatic overseas tests** treat an individual as **not resident in the UK in a tax year** if that individual:

(a) **Spends less than 16 days in the UK in that tax year** and **was resident in the UK for one or more of the three previous tax years** (typically someone who is leaving the UK); or

(b) **Spends less than 46 days in the UK in that tax year** and **was not resident in the UK for any of the previous three tax years** (typically someone who is arriving in the UK); or

(c) **Works full-time overseas throughout that tax year** and **does not spend more than 90 days in the UK during that tax year**

1.1.3 Automatic UK tests

If **none of the automatic overseas tests are met**, then the **automatic UK tests are considered.**

The **automatic UK tests treat an individual as UK resident in a tax year** if that individual:

(a) **Spends 183 days or more in the UK** during that tax year; or
(b) Has a **home in the UK** and **no home overseas**; or
(c) **Works full-time in the UK** during that tax year

1.1.4 Sufficient UK ties tests

If the **individual meets none of the automatic overseas tests and none of the automatic UK tests**, the **'sufficient ties' test** must be considered.

The **sufficient ties test** compares the **number of days spent in the UK** and the **number of connection factors or 'ties' to the UK.**

An **individual who was not UK resident in any of the previous three tax years** (typically someone who is arriving in the UK) must determine whether any of the following ties apply:

(a) **UK resident close family** (eg spouse/civil partner, child under the age of 18)

(b) **Available UK accommodation in which the individual spends at least one night during the tax year**

(c) **Substantive UK work** (employment or self-employment)

(d) **More than 90 days spent in the UK in either or both of the previous two tax years**

An **individual who was UK resident in any of the previous three tax years** (typically someone who is leaving the UK) must also determine whether any of the ties in (a) to (d) above apply plus whether an additional tie applies:

(e) **Present in the UK at midnight for the same or more days** in that tax year than in any other country

The following table shows **how an individual's UK residence status is found** by comparing **the number of days in the UK** during a tax year and the **number of UK ties**:

Days in UK	Previously resident	Not previously resident
Less than 16	Automatically not UK resident	Automatically not UK resident
Between 16 and 45	Resident if 4 UK ties (or more)	Automatically not UK resident
Between 46 and 90	Resident if 3 UK ties (or more)	Resident if 4 UK ties
Between 91 and 120	Resident if 2 UK ties (or more)	Resident if 3 UK ties (or more)
Between 121 and 182	Resident if 1 UK tie (or more)	Resident if 2 UK ties (or more)
183 or more	Automatically UK resident	Automatically UK resident

Exam focus point

This table will be given in the tax rates and allowances section of the examination paper.

1.1.5 Days spent in UK

Generally, **if a taxpayer is present in the UK at the end of a day (ie midnight)**, that **day counts as a day spent by the taxpayer in the UK.**

Exam focus point

The detailed rules in the statutory residence test are quite complex (and have been simplified here), especially those in regard to work and having a home in the UK or overseas. **These more complex aspects are not examinable in Paper F6 (UK).**

1.1.6 Examples

(a) James spent 40 days in the UK during the tax year 2016/17. He had not previously been resident in the UK. James did not work during 2016/17.

James is arriving in the UK. He satisfies one of the automatic overseas tests since he spent less than 46 days in the UK in 2016/17 and was not resident in the UK for any of the previous three tax years. James is therefore not UK resident for the tax year 2016/17.

(b) Caroline had not previously been resident in the UK before she arrived on 6 April 2016. She spent 60 days in the UK during the tax year 2016/17. She did not work during 2016/17. Her only home during 2016/17 is in the UK.

Caroline is arriving in the UK. She does not satisfy any of the automatic overseas tests since she spends 46 days or more in the UK and does not work overseas. She satisfies one of the automatic UK tests since her only home is in the UK. Caroline is therefore UK resident for the tax year 2016/17.

(c) Miranda had always been resident in the UK before the tax year 2016/17 and has previously spent more than 90 days in the UK in every tax year. Miranda does not work during 2016/17. Miranda is married to Walter who is UK resident in 2016/17. They own a house in the UK which is available to them for the whole of 2016/17. On 6 April 2016, Miranda bought an overseas apartment where she spent 285 days during 2016/17. The remaining 80 days were spent in her UK house.

Miranda is leaving the UK. She does not satisfy any of the automatic overseas tests since she spends 16 days or more in the UK and does not work overseas. She does not satisfy any of the automatic UK tests since she spends less than 183 days in the UK, has an overseas home and does not work in the UK. The 'sufficient ties' test is therefore relevant. Miranda has three UK ties:

(i) Close family resident in the UK (spouse)
(ii) Available accommodation in the UK in which she spends at least one night in the tax year
(iii) More than 90 days spent in the UK in both of the previous two tax years

Miranda spends between 46 and 90 days in the UK in 2016/17. These three ties are therefore sufficient to make her UK resident in 2016/17.

(d) Norman has not been resident in, or visited, the UK in any tax year before 2016/17. On 6 April 2016, he bought a house in the UK and spent 160 days in the UK during the tax year 2016/17. Norman also has an overseas house in which he spent the remainder of the tax year 2016/17. Norman did not work in 2016/17 and his close family are not UK resident in 2016/17.

Norman is arriving in the UK. He does not satisfy any of the automatic overseas tests since he spends 46 days or more in the UK and does not work overseas. He does not satisfy any of the automatic UK tests as he spent less than 183 days in the UK, has an overseas home and does not work in the UK. The 'sufficient ties' test is therefore relevant. Norman spends between 121 and 182 days in the UK during 2016/17 and so he would need two UK ties to be UK resident for that tax year. Since Norman has only one tie with the UK in 2016/17 (available accommodation), he is therefore not UK resident for the tax year 2016/17.

1.2 Tax consequences of residence

FAST FORWARD

An individual who is UK resident is taxed on worldwide income.

Generally, a **UK resident is liable to UK income tax on his UK and overseas income** whereas a **non-UK resident is liable to UK income tax only on income arising in the UK**. We deal with the capital gains tax consequences later in this Study Text.

Exam focus point

The taxation of the overseas income of a UK resident and the taxation of non-UK residents is outside the scope of the F6(UK) syllabus.

2 Computing taxable income

FAST FORWARD

> In a personal income tax computation, we bring together, for each tax year, income from all sources, splitting the sources into non-savings, savings and dividend income.

An individual's income from all sources is brought together (aggregated) in a personal tax computation for each tax year.

Key terms

> The **tax year**, or **fiscal year**, or **year of assessment** runs from 6 April to 5 April. For example, the tax year 2016/17 runs from 6 April 2016 to 5 April 2017.

In the computation, three columns are needed to distinguish between non-savings income, savings income and dividend income. Here is an example. All items are explained later in this Study Text.

RICHARD: INCOME TAX COMPUTATION 2016/17

	Non-savings income	*Savings income*	*Dividend income*	*Total*
	£	£	£	£
Income from employment	48,150			
Building society interest		1,400		
Dividends			6,000	
Total income	48,150	1,400	6,000	
Less interest paid	(2,000)			
Net income	46,150	1,400	6,000	53,550
Less personal allowance	(11,000)			
Taxable income	35,150	1,400	6,000	42,550

	£
Income tax	
Non savings income	
£32,000 × 20%	6,400
£3,150 (35,150 – 32,000) × 40%	1,260
Savings income	
£500 × 0%	0
£900 (1,400 – 500) × 40%	360
Dividend income	
£5,000 × 0%	0
£1,000 (6,000 – 5,000) × 32.5%	325
Tax liability	8,345
Less tax suffered	
PAYE tax on salary (say)	(7,750)
Tax payable	595

Key terms

> **Total income** is all income subject to income tax. Each of the amounts which make up total income is called a component. **Net income** is total income after deductible interest and trade losses. **Taxable income** is net income less the personal allowance.

Income tax is charged on **taxable income**. Non-savings income is dealt with first, then savings income and then dividend income. We look at how to compute the income tax liability later in this chapter.

2.1 The complete proforma for computing taxable income

Here is a complete proforma computation of taxable income. It is probably too much for you to absorb at this stage, but refer back to it as you come to the chapters dealing with the types of income shown. You will also see how trading losses fit into the proforma later in this Study Text.

	Non-savings income	*Savings income*	*Dividend income*	*Total*
	£	£	£	£
Trading income	X			
Employment income	X			
Pension income	X			
Property business income	X			
Bank/building society interest		X		
Other interest (eg gilt interest)		X		
Dividends	–	–	X	
Total income	X	X	X	
Less interest paid	(X)	(X)	(X)	
Net income	X	X	X	X
Less personal allowance	(X)	(X)	(X)	
Taxable income	X	X	X	X

3 Types of income

FAST FORWARD

Income must be classified according to the nature of the income as different computational rules apply to different types of income.

PER alert

One of the competencies you require to fulfil Performance Objective 15 Tax computations and assessments of the PER is to extract and analyse data from financial records and filing information relevant to the preparation of tax computations and related supporting documents. You can apply the knowledge you obtain from this section of the Study Text to help to demonstrate this competence.

3.1 Classification of income

All income received must be **classified** according to the nature of the income. This is because different computational rules apply to different types of income. Income can then be further classified as non-savings, savings or dividend income. The main types of income are:

(a) **Income from employment (employment income, non-savings income)**
(b) **Pension income (non-savings income)**
(c) **Profits of trades, professions and vocations (trading income, non-savings income)**
(d) **Income from property letting (property business income, non-savings income)**
(e) **Interest income (savings income)**
(f) **Dividends (dividend income)**

3.2 Non-savings income

The rules for computing **employment income**, **trading income** and **property business income** will be covered in later chapters. These types of income are **non-savings income**. **Pension income** is also non-savings income.

3.3 Savings income

Savings income is interest. Interest is paid on bank and building society accounts, most National Savings & Investments (NS&I) products, on Government securities (gilts) such as Treasury Stock, and on company loan stock.

Exam focus point

Certain types of savings income are paid after deduction of basic rate tax (paid net) but these are **not examinable** in F6 (UK). **All savings income in F6(UK) is paid without deduction of basic rate tax** (paid gross). This includes interest paid on bank and building society accounts.

3.4 Dividend income

Dividend income consists of **dividends** received as a result of ownership of shares. Dividends are paid without deduction of tax (paid gross).

4 Tax exempt income

FAST FORWARD

Income from certain investments, such as those held in Individual Savings Accounts (ISAs), is exempt from income tax.

4.1 Types of tax exempt investments

PER alert

One of the competencies you require to fulfil Performance Objective 17 Tax planning and advice of the PER is to mitigate and/or defer tax liabilities through the use of standard reliefs, exemptions and incentives. You can apply the knowledge you obtain from this section of the Study Text to help to demonstrate this competence.

Income from certain investments is exempt from income tax. They are therefore useful for tax planning to minimise tax from investments.

Exam focus point

In the examination you may be given details of exempt income in a Section C question. You should state in your answer that the income is exempt to show that you have considered it and have not just overlooked it, otherwise the relevant marks will not be awarded.

4.2 Individual savings accounts

Key term

ISAs are tax efficient savings accounts. There are two types of ISA.

- Cash ISA (which only has a cash component)
- Stocks and shares ISA (which primarily has a stocks and shares component, although cash may be held in a stocks and shares ISA if the provider allows this)

The annual subscription limit **for ISAs is £15,240 per tax year (2016/17)**. This can be invested in cash, stocks and shares, or any combination of the two. An individual can **withdraw money from a cash ISA** and **replace it in the same tax year without the replaced cash counting towards the ISA subscription limit**.

Exam focus point

The ISA limit will be given to you in the Tax Rates and Allowances in the examination paper.

Dividend income and interest received from ISAs is exempt from income tax, whether it is paid out to the investor or retained and reinvested within the ISA. Similarly, **capital gains made within a ISA are exempt from capital gains tax**. The introduction of the savings income nil rate band and the dividend nil rate band (see later in this chapter) means that ISAs are not as advantageous as they were previously. However, **additional rate taxpayers and individuals who have already used their savings income nil band will still benefit from using a cash ISA**. The **main benefit of using a stocks and shares ISA** is the **capital gains tax exemption** where an individual already uses the annual exempt amount (see later in this Study Text).

Exam focus point

The help-to-buy ISA and the innovative finance ISA are **not examinable** in F6(UK).

4.3 Savings certificates

Savings certificates are issued by National Savings and Investments (NS&I). They may be fixed rate certificates or index linked and are for fixed terms of between two and five years. On maturity the profit is tax exempt. This profit is often called interest.

4.4 Premium bonds

Prizes received from premium bonds are exempt from tax.

4.5 Child benefit

Child benefit is a benefit paid to people responsible for caring for at least one child. It is usually paid to the mother of the child.

Child benefit is usually exempt from income tax. However, an **income tax charge** applies if a taxpayer receives child benefit (or their partner receives child benefit) and has **adjusted net income over £50,000 in a tax year**. This charge is covered later in this chapter.

5 Deductible interest

FAST FORWARD

Deductible interest is given tax relief by being deducted from total income to compute net income.

An individual who pays interest on a loan in a tax year is entitled to relief in that tax year if the loan is for one of the following purposes:

(a) **Loan to buy plant or machinery for partnership use.** Interest is allowed for three years from the end of the tax year in which the loan was taken out. If the plant or machinery is used partly for private use, the allowable interest is apportioned.

(b) **Loan to buy plant or machinery for employment use.** Interest is allowed for three years from the end of the tax year in which the loan was taken out. If the plant or machinery is used partly for private use, the allowable interest is apportioned.

(c) **Loan to buy interest in employee-controlled company.** The company must be an unquoted trading company resident in the UK with at least 50% of the voting shares held by employees.

(d) **Loan to invest in a partnership.** The investment may be a share in the partnership or a contribution to the partnership of capital or a loan to the partnership. The individual must be a partner (other than a limited partner) and relief ceases when he ceases to be a partner.

(e) **Loan to invest in a co-operative.** The investment may be shares or a loan. The individual must spend the greater part of his time working for the co-operative.

Tax relief is given by deducting the interest from total income to calculate net income for the tax year in which the interest is paid. For F6(UK) purposes it is deducted from **non-savings income first, then from savings income and lastly from dividend income**.

Exam focus point

There are some situations where this order of set off will not be the most beneficial but such a scenario **will not be examined** in F6(UK).

Question — Deductible interest

In 2016/17, Frederick has taxable trading income of £45,000, savings income of £4,320 and dividend income of £6,000. Frederick pays interest of £1,370 in 2016/17 on a loan to invest in a partnership. What is Frederick's net income for 2016/17?

Answer

	Non-savings income	*Savings income*	*Dividend income*	*Total*
	£	£	£	£
Total income	45,000	4,320	6,000	55,320
Less interest paid	(1,370)			
Net income	43,630	4,320	6,000	53,950

6 Personal allowance

FAST FORWARD

All individuals are entitled to a personal allowance. It is deducted from net income, first against non savings income, then against savings income and lastly against dividend income. The personal allowance is reduced by £1 for every £2 that adjusted net income exceeds £100,000 and can be reduced to nil.

Once income from all sources has been aggregated and any deductible interest deducted, the remainder is the taxpayer's net income. An allowance, the **personal allowance,** is **deducted from net income**. Like deductible interest, for F6(UK) purposes it reduces **non-savings income first, then savings income and lastly dividend income**.

Exam focus point

There are some situations where this order of set off will not be the most beneficial but such a scenario **will not be examined** in F6(UK).

All individuals (including children) **are entitled to a personal allowance of £11,000.**

However, if the **individual's adjusted net income exceeds £100,000,** the **personal allowance is reduced by £1 for each £2 by which adjusted net income exceeds £100,000 until the personal allowance is nil (which is when adjusted net income is £122,000 or more)**.

Key term

Adjusted net income is net income less the gross amounts of personal pension contributions and gift aid donations.

We will look at personal pension contributions and gift aid donations later in this Study Text and revisit this topic again then. At the moment, we will look at the situation where net income and adjusted net income are the same amounts.

Question — Personal allowance

In 2016/17, Clare receives employment income of £95,000, bank interest of £8,000 and dividends of £7,500. Calculate Clare's taxable income for 2016/17.

Answer

	Non-savings income	Savings income	Dividend income	Total
	£	£	£	£
Employment income	95,000			
Bank interest		8,000		
Dividends			7,500	
Net income (N)	95,000	8,000	7,500	110,500
Less personal allowance (W)	(5,750)			
Taxable income	89,250	8,000	7,500	104,750

Working	£
Net income	110,500
Less income limit	(100,000)
Excess	10,500
Personal allowance	11,000
Less half excess £10,500 × ½	(5,250)
	5,750

Note. Where there is no deductible interest, so that total income is the same as net income, it is acceptable just to state the net income at this stage of the computation.

Where an individual has an adjusted net income between £100,000 and £122,000, the effective rate of tax on the income between these two amounts will usually be 60%. This is calculated as 40% (the higher rate on income) plus 40% of half (ie 20%) of the excess adjusted net income over £100,000 used to restrict the personal allowance. The individual should consider **making personal pension contributions and/or gift aid donations to reduce adjusted net income to below £100,000**.

7 Computing income tax liability and income tax payable

FAST FORWARD

To work out the income tax liability on the taxable income, first compute the tax on non-savings income, then on savings income and, finally, on dividend income. To work out tax payable, deduct tax paid under Pay As You Earn (PAYE). If tax deducted under PAYE exceeds the tax liability, the excess will be repayable.

PER alert

One of the competencies you require to fulfil Performance Objective 15 Tax computations and assessments of the PER is to prepare or contribute to the computation or assessment of tax computations for individuals. You can apply the knowledge you obtain from this section of the Study Text to help to demonstrate this competence.

Key terms

The **income tax liability** is the amount of tax charged on the individual's taxable income. **Income tax payable** is the balance of the income tax liability still to be settled in cash.

7.1 Introduction

Income tax payable is computed on an individual's taxable income using the proforma in shown earlier in this chapter. The tax rates are applied to taxable income first to non-savings income, then to savings income and finally to dividend income. We will start by looking at taxpayers who only have non-savings income, then to taxpayers who have both non-savings and savings income and, finally, to taxpayers who have non-savings income, savings income, and dividend income.

7.2 Computations with non-savings income only

Taxpayers with non-savings income only may pay income tax at basic rate, higher rate and additional rate.

7.2.1 Basic rate on non-savings income

The **basic rate of tax** on non-savings income is **20%** for 2016/17. The **basic rate limit** for 2016/17 is **£32,000**.

7.2.2 Higher rate on non-savings income

The **higher rate of tax** on non-savings income is **40%** for 2016/17. The **higher rate limit** for 2016/17 is **£150,000**.

Question — **Basic rate and higher rate on non-savings income**

In 2016/17 Jem has trading income of £41,000 and property business income of £8,500. Calculate Jem's tax liability for 2016/17.

Answer

	Non-savings income
	£
Trading income	41,000
Property business income	8,500
Net income	49,500
Less personal allowance	(11,000)
Taxable income	38,500

Income tax

	£
Non-savings income	
£32,000 × 20%	6,400
£6,500 (38,500 – 32,000) × 40%	2,600
Tax liability	9,000

7.2.3 Additional rate on non-savings income

The **additional rate of tax** on non-savings income is **45%** for 2016/17. **This rate applies to non-savings income in excess of the higher rate limit which is £150,000 in 2016/17.**

Question — **All rates of tax on non-savings income**

In 2016/17 Milo has employment income of £145,000 and property business income of £10,800. Calculate Milo's tax liability for 2016/17.

Answer

	Non-savings income
	£
Employment income	145,000
Property business income	10,800
Net income/taxable income (no PA available as net income exceeds £122,000)	155,800
Income tax	
	£
Non-savings income	
£32,000 × 20%	6,400
£118,000 (150,000 – 32,000) × 40%	47,200
£5,800 (155,800 – 150,000) × 45%	2,610
Tax liability	56,210

7.3 Computations with non-savings income and savings income only

7.3.1 Savings income starting rate

There is a **tax rate of 0% for savings income up to £5,000 (the savings income starting rate limit)**. This rate is called the **savings income starting rate. The savings income starting rate only applies where the savings income falls wholly or partly below the starting rate limit.**

Remember that income tax is charged first on non-savings income. So, in most cases, an individual's non-savings income will exceed the savings income starting rate limit and the savings income starting rate will not be available on savings income.

7.3.2 Savings income basic, higher and additional rates

The **basic rate of tax** for savings income is **20%** for 2016/17. The **higher rate of tax** for savings income is **40%** for 2016/17. The **additional rate of tax** for savings income is **45%** for 2016/17.

7.3.3 Savings nil rate band

There is a **tax rate of 0%** for **savings income** within the **savings income nil rate band.** The savings income nil rate band for 2016/17 is **£1,000** if the individual is a **basic rate taxpayer** and **£500** if the individual is a **higher rate taxpayer.** There is **no savings income nil rate band** for **additional rate taxpayers**.

The **savings income nil rate band** counts towards the **basic rate limit of £32,000.**

Exam focus point

> The detailed rules for establishing whether an individual is a higher rate or additional rate taxpayer for the purpose of computing the availability of the savings income nil rate band are quite complicated and are **not examinable** in F6(UK). Therefore, in any question involving the savings income nil rate band, it will be quite clear which tax rate is applicable.

Question

Savings income starting rate and savings nil rate band

In 2016/17 Alicia has trading income of £13,600 and bank interest of £8,000. Calculate Alicia's tax liability for 2016/17.

Answer

	Non-savings income £	Savings income £	Total £
Trading income	13,600		
Bank interest		8,000	
Net income	13,600	8,000	21,600
Less personal allowance	(11,000)		
Taxable income	2,600	8,000	10,600
Income tax			£
Non-savings income			
£2,600 × 20%			520
Savings income			
£2,400 (5,000 – 2,600) × 0% (savings starting rate)			0
£1,000 × 0% (savings nil rate band)			0
£4,600 (8,000 – 2,400 – 1,000) × 20%			920
Tax liability			1,440

Question

Savings nil rate, basic rate and higher rate with savings income

In 2016/17 Joe has employment income of £39,800 and bank interest of £5,200. Calculate Joe's tax liability for 2016/17.

Answer

	Non-savings income £	Savings income £	Total £
Employment income	39,800		
Bank interest		5,200	
Net income	39,800	5,200	45,000
Less personal allowance	(11,000)		
Taxable income	28,800	5,200	34,000
Income tax			£
Non-savings income			
£28,800 × 20%			5,760
Savings income			
£500 × 0% (savings nil rate band – higher rate taxpayer)			0
£2,700 (32,000 – 28,800 – 500) × 20%			540
£2,000 (5,200 – 500 – 2,700) × 40%			800
Tax liability			7,100

Question

All rates of tax with savings income

In 2016/17 Maddie has trading income of £146,800 and building society interest of £6,700. Calculate Maddie's tax liability for 2016/17.

Answer

	Non-savings income £	Savings income £	Total £
Trading income	146,800		
Building society interest		6,700	
Net income/taxable income (no PA available)	146,800	6,700	153,500

Maddie is not entitled to the personal allowance as her net income exceeds £122,000.

Income tax	£
Non-savings income	
£32,000 × 20%	6,400
£114,800 (146,800 – 32,000) × 40%	45,920
Savings income	
£3,200 (150,000 – 146,800) × 40%	1,280
£3,500 (6,700 – 3,200) × 45%	1,575
Tax liability	55,175

No savings nil rate band is available because Maddie is an additional rate taxpayer.

7.4 Computations with non-savings, savings and dividend income

7.4.1 Dividend income basic, higher and additional rates

The **basic rate of tax** for dividend income is **7.5%** for 2016/17. The **higher rate of tax** for dividend income is **32.5%** for 2016/17. The **additional rate of tax** for dividend income is **38.1%** for 2016/17.

7.4.2 Dividend nil rate band

There is a **tax rate of 0%** for **dividend income** within the **dividend income nil rate band.** The dividend income nil rate band is **£5,000** for **all taxpayers**.

The **dividend income nil rate band** counts towards the **basic rate limit of £32,000 and the higher rate limit of £150,000**.

Question — Dividend nil rate, basic rate and higher rate with dividend income

In 2016/17 Margery has employment income of £33,450, building society interest of £1,600 and dividends of £15,000. Calculate Margery's tax liability for 2016/17.

Answer

	Non-savings income £	Savings income £	Dividend income £	Total £
Employment income	33,450			
BSI		1,600		
Dividends			15,000	
Net income	33,450	1,600	15,000	50,050
Less personal allowance	(11,000)			
Taxable income	22,450	1,600	15,000	39,050

Income tax	
	£
Non-savings income	
£22,450 × 20%	4,490
Savings income	
£500 × 0% (savings nil rate band – higher rate taxpayer)	0
£1,100 (1,600 – 500) × 20%	220
Dividend income	
£5,000 × 0% (dividend nil rate band)	0
£2,950 (32,000 – 22,450 – 1,600 – 5,000) × 7.5%	221
£7,050 (15,000 – 5,000 – 2,950) × 32.5%	2,291
Tax liability	7,222

Question

All rates of tax with dividend income

In 2016/17 Julian has employment income of £148,000, bank interest of £6,250 and dividends of £20,000. Calculate Julian's tax liability for 2016/17.

Answer

	Non-savings income £	*Savings income* £	*Dividend income* £	*Total* £
Employment income	148,000			
Bank interest		6,250		
Dividends			20,000	
Net income/taxable income (no PA available)	148,000	6,250	20,000	174,250

Julian is not entitled to the personal allowance as his net income exceeds £122,000.

Income tax	
Non-savings income	
£32,000 × 20%	6,400
£116,000 (148,000 – 32,000) × 40%	46,400
Savings income	
£2,000 (150,000 – 148,000) × 40%	800
£4,250 (6,250 – 2,000) × 45%	1,912
Dividend income	
£5,000 × 0%	0
£15,000 (20,000 – 5,000) × 38.1%	5,715
Tax liability	61,227

No savings nil rate band is available because Julian is an additional rate taxpayer.

Exam focus point

ACCA's article on Finance Act 2016, written by a member of the F6(UK) examination team, contains further examples of **the computation of the income tax liability**.

7.5 Steps in computing the income tax liability and income tax payable

We now summarise the **steps required to compute the income tax liability**.

Step 1 **The first step in preparing a personal tax computation is to set up three columns**
One column for non-savings income, one for savings income and one for dividend income. Add up income from different sources. The sum of these is known as 'total income'. Deduct deductible interest and trade losses to compute 'net income'. Deduct the personal allowance to compute 'taxable income'.

Step 2 **Deal with non-savings income first**
Any non-savings income up to the basic rate limit of £32,000 is taxed at 20%. Non-savings income between the basic rate limit and the higher rate limit of £150,000 is taxed at 40%. The maximum non-savings income to which the higher rate applies is therefore £(150,000 – 32,000) = £118,000. Any further non-savings income is taxed at 45%.

Step 3 **Now deal with savings income**
Savings income below the savings income starting rate limit of £5,000 is taxed at the savings income starting rate of 0%. Then tax savings income covered by the savings nil rate band (for basic rate and higher rate taxpayers) at 0%. Any remaining savings income up to the basic rate limit of £32,000 is taxed at 20%. Savings income between the basic rate limit and the higher rate limit of £150,000 is taxed at 40%. Any further savings income is taxed at 45%.

Step 4 **Lastly, tax dividend income**
The first £5,000 is within the dividend nil rate band and is taxed at 0%. Other dividend income below the basic rate limit of £32,000 is taxed at 7.5%. Dividend income between the basic rate limit and the higher rate limit of £150,000 is taxed at 32.5%. Any further dividend income is taxed at 38.1%.

Step 5 **Add the amounts of tax together.** This will usually be the **income tax liability**.

The following **additional step** is needed to compute income tax payable when the income tax liability has been calculated.

Step 6 **Deduct tax paid under Pay As You Earn** (PAYE).

Question — Calculation of income tax payable

In 2016/17, Michael has employment income of £56,300 (PAYE deducted £5,800), bank interest of £4,250 and dividends of £7,500. He pays deductible interest of £3,000. How much income tax is payable by Michael in 2016/17?

Answer

	Non-savings income	*Savings income*	*Dividend income*	*Total*
	£	£	£	£
Employment income	56,300			
Bank interest		4,250		
Dividends			7,500	
Total income	56,300	4,250	7,500	
Less interest paid	(3,000)			
Net income	53,300	4,250	7,500	65,050
Less personal allowance	(11,000)			
Taxable income	42,300	4,250	7,500	54,050

	£
Income tax	
Non-savings income	
£32,000 × 20%	6,400
£10,300 × 40%	4,120
Savings income	
£500 × 0% (savings nil rate band – higher rate taxpayer)	0
£3,750 (4,250 – 500) × 40%	1,500
Dividend income	
£5,000 × 0%	0
£2,500 (7,500 – 2,500) × 32.5%	812
Tax liability	12,832
Less PAYE	(5,800)
Tax payable	7,032

8 Accrued income scheme

FAST FORWARD

The accrued income scheme ensures that a taxpayer who sells a gilt is taxed on any interest income included in the proceeds. Similarly, relief is given to the purchaser of the gilt for the interest included in the price paid.

8.1 Introduction

If the **owner of UK Government securities (known as gilt-edged securities or 'gilts')** sells them before a particular date, **that individual will not be entitled to the next interest payment**. The new owner will receive it. However, **the sale proceeds received by the seller includes interest accrued to the date of sale**. Since gilts are exempt from capital gains tax (see later in this Study Text), this would be a way of avoiding tax on this interest without the special rules of the accrued income scheme described in this section.

However, if securities are sold on or after a particular date, they are sold **excluding interest** and the **original owner is entitled to the whole of the next interest payment and will be taxed on it under the usual income tax rules**. However, **the sale proceeds will exclude interest accruing after the date of sale so that this accrued interest effectively goes to the purchaser**. Again, the usual tax rules do not reflect the actual receipt of interest and so the accrued income scheme applies to reflect the situation.

The **accrued income scheme only applies** where the seller **holds securities with a nominal value exceeding £5,000** during the tax year in which the interest period ends.

8.2 How the accrued income scheme works

Under the **accrued income scheme**, where **gilts are transferred at a price which includes interest, the accrued interest reflected in the value of gilts is taxed as savings income on the seller**. This is because **the seller is treated as entitled to the proportion of interest which has accrued since the last interest payment. The buyer is entitled to relief against the interest they receive equal to the amount taxable on the seller.**

Conversely, **where the transfer is excluding interest, the seller will receive the whole of the next interest payment. They will be entitled to relief for the amount of interest assessed on the purchaser. The purchaser is treated as entitled to the proportion of the interest accrued between the sale and the next payment date and it is taxed as savings income.**

Exam focus point

The accrued income scheme also applies to securities other than gilts, such as corporate bonds. However, in F6(UK), **any question on the accrued income scheme will be confined to gilts**.

Question — Accrued income scheme

Owen owned £10,000 (nominal value) 5% UK Government Loan Stock. Interest was payable on 30 June and 31 December each year. Owen sold the loan stock to Yvonne on 30 November 2016 for sale proceeds of £11,208 including accrued interest of £208 for the period between 1 July 2016 and 30 November 2016 (£10,000 × 5% × 5/12). What are the amounts taxable on Owen and Yvonne as savings income in respect of the loan stock for 2016/17?

Answer

Owen

	£
Interest received 30.6.16	
£10,000 × 5% × 6/12	250
Accrued interest deemed received 31.12.16	
£10,000 × 5% × 5/12	208
Total taxable as savings income	458

Yvonne

	£
Interest received 31.12.16	
£10,000 × 5% × 6/12	250
Less relief for accrued interest (amount taxable on Owen)	
£10,000 × 5% × 5/12	(208)
Total taxable as savings income (ie 1 month of interest £10,000 × 5% × 1/12)	42

Exam focus point

The accrued income scheme rules may seem complicated but remember that the aim is to tax each taxpayer on the interest they actually receive either as an interest payment or as part of the price of the gilt.

9 Gift aid

FAST FORWARD

Increase the basic rate limit and the higher rate limit by the gross amount of any gift aid payment to give tax relief at the higher and additional rates.

9.1 Gift aid donations

Key term

One-off and regular charitable gifts of money qualify for tax relief under the **gift aid scheme** provided the donor gives the charity a gift aid declaration.

Gift aid declarations can be made in writing, electronically through the internet or orally over the phone. A declaration can cover a one-off gift or any number of gifts made after a specified date (which may be in the past).

The gift must not be repayable and must not confer any more than a minimal benefit on the donor.

9.2 Tax relief for gift aid donations

A gift aid donation is treated as though it is paid net of basic rate tax (20%). This gives basic rate tax relief when the payment is made. For example, if you would like your charity to receive a donation of £1,000, you would only need to make a payment to them of £800. The charity reclaims the 20% tax relief that you have received, resulting in a gross gift of £1,000.

Additional tax relief for higher rate and additional rate taxpayers is given in the personal tax computation by increasing the donor's basic rate limit and higher rate limit by the gross amount of the gift. To arrive at the gross amount of the gift you must multiply the amount paid by 100/80. In the above example, the gross amount would be the amount paid of £800 × 100/80 = £1,000. The effect of increasing the basic rate limit is to increase the amount on which basic rate tax is payable. This is sometimes called 'extending the basic rate band'.

The effect of increasing the higher rate limit is simply to preserve the amount of taxable income on which higher rate tax is payable.

No additional relief is due for basic rate taxpayers. Increasing the basic rate limit is irrelevant as taxable income is below this limit.

Question — Gift aid with higher rate relief

In 2016/17, James has employment income of £67,135. This is his only income for the tax year. In September 2016 he paid £8,000 (net) under the gift aid scheme. Compute James' income tax liability for 2016/17.

Answer

		Non-savings Income
		£
Employment income/Net income		67,135
Less personal allowance		(11,000)
Taxable income		56,135
Income tax	£	£
Basic rate	42,000 (W) × 20%	8,400
Higher rate	14,135 × 40%	5,654
	56,135	14,054

Working

Basic rate limit £32,000 + (£8,000 × 100/80) = £42,000

Question — Gift aid with additional rate relief

In 2016/17, Matt has trading income of £182,000. This is his only income for the tax year. In January 2017, he made a gift aid donation of £12,000 (net). Compute Matt's income tax liability for 2016/17.

Answer

		Non-savings Income
		£
Taxable income (no personal allowance as income over £122,000)		182,000
Income tax	£	£
Basic rate	47,000 (W1) × 20%	9,400
Higher rate	118,000 (W2) × 40%	47,200
Additional rate	17,000 × 45%	7,650
	182,000	64,250

Workings

1 Basic rate limit £32,000 + (£12,000 × 100/80) = £47,000

2 Higher rate limit £150,000 + (£12,000 × 100/80) = £165,000. The higher rate band is therefore £(165,000 – 47,000) = £118,000 ie the same as the usual £(150,000 – 32,000).

9.3 Adjusted net income

Key term

Adjusted net income is net income less the gross amounts of personal pension contributions and gift aid donations.

The restrictions on the personal allowance are calculated in relation to adjusted net income.

Question — Adjusted net income

Margaretta earns a salary of £110,000 in 2016/17. In January 2017, she made a gift aid donation of £5,000. Compute Margaretta's income tax liability for 2016/17.

Answer

		Non-savings income
		£
Employment income/Net income		110,000
Less personal allowance (W1)		(9,125)
Taxable income		100,875
Income tax	£	£
Basic rate (W2)	38,250 × 20%	7,650
Higher rate	62,625 × 40%	25,050
	100,875	32,700

Workings

1 Personal allowance

	£
Net income	110,000
Less: gift aid donation £5,000 × 100/80	(6,250)
Adjusted net income	103,750
Less income limit	(100,000)
Excess	3,750
Personal allowance	11,000
Less half excess £3,750 × ½	(1,875)
	9,125

2 Basic rate limit £32,000 + (£5,000 × 100/80) £38,250

10 Child benefit income tax charge

FAST FORWARD

There is an income tax charge to recover child benefit if the recipient or their partner has adjusted net income over £50,000 in a tax year.

An **income tax charge** applies if a taxpayer receives child benefit (or their partner receives child benefit) and the taxpayer has **adjusted net income over £50,000 in a tax year. Adjusted net income is defined in**

the same way as for the restriction of the personal allowance described earlier in this chapter. The effect of the charge is to recover child benefit from taxpayers who have higher incomes.

A 'partner' is a **spouse**, a **civil partner,** or an **unmarried partner** where the couple are **living together as though they were married or were civil partners**.

If the taxpayer has **adjusted net income over £60,000,** the charge is equal to the **full amount of child benefit received**.

If the taxpayer has **adjusted net income between £50,000 and £60,000**, the charge is **1% of the child benefit amount for each £100 of adjusted net income in excess of £50,000. The calculation**, at all stages, **is rounded down to the nearest whole number.**

Exam focus point

> This information will be given in the tax rates and allowances in the examination paper.

If **both partners have adjusted net income in excess of £50,000**, the **partner with the higher adjusted net income** is liable for the charge.

The child benefit income tax charge is collected through the self-assessment system (dealt with later in this Study Text). This includes the need for **taxpayers to submit tax returns,** which can be time consuming and costly. To avoid this, **taxpayers can opt not to receive child benefit at all** so that the income tax charge does not apply.

Question

Child benefit income tax charge

Samantha is divorced and has two children aged ten and six. She has net income of £56,000 in 2016/17. Samantha made personal pension contributions of £4,500 (gross) during 2016/17. She receives child benefit of £1,788 in 2016/17. Calculate Samantha's child benefit income tax charge for 2016/17.

Answer

	£
Net income	56,000
Less personal pension contributions (gross)	(4,500)
Adjusted net income	51,500
Less threshold	(50,000)
Excess	1,500
÷ £100	15
Child benefit income tax charge: 1% × £1,788 × 15	268

Tutorial note

If Samantha had made an extra gross personal pension contribution of £1,500 during 2016/17, her adjusted net income would not have exceeded £50,000 and she would not have been subject to the child benefit income tax charge.

11 Transferable personal allowance

FAST FORWARD

An individual is permitted to transfer £1,100 of their personal allowance to their spouse/civil partner, in certain circumstances, giving a tax reducer of £220.

11.1 Transferable personal allowance

An individual can elect to transfer £1,100 of their personal allowance to their spouse/civil partner if certain conditions are met. This is sometimes known as the marriage allowance.

Exam focus point

The transferable amount of personal allowance will be given to you in the tax rates and allowances in the examination paper.

11.2 Conditions

Neither the spouse/civil partner making the transfer nor the spouse/civil partner receiving the transfer can be a higher rate or additional rate taxpayer.

11.3 Method of giving relief

The spouse/civil partner receiving the transfer does not have an increased personal allowance. **Instead, they are entitled to a tax reducer of £1,100 × 20% = £220. The tax reducer reduces the individual's tax liability.** If the individual has a tax liability of less than £220, the tax reducer reduces the tax liability to nil.

Question — Transferable personal allowance

Alec and Bertha are a married couple. In the tax year 2016/17, Alec has net income of £7,000 and Bertha has net income of £25,000. All their income is non-savings income. Alec has made an election to transfer part of his personal allowance to Bertha. Show Alec and Bertha's taxable income for 2016/17 and compute Bertha's income tax liability.

Answer

Alec

	Non-savings Income
	£
Net income	7,000
Less personal allowance £(11,000 – 1,100)	(9,900)
Taxable income	0

Bertha

	Non-savings Income
	£
Net income	25,000
Less personal allowance	(11,000)
Taxable income	14,000

Income tax	
£14,000 × 20%	2,800
Less marriage allowance tax reducer £1,100 × 20%	(220)
Income tax liability	2,580

11.4 Election

The election for transfer of the personal allowance is made to HMRC online by the spouse/civil partner making the transfer.

For the tax year 2016/17, if the election is made before 6 April 2017 it will have effect for 2016/17 and subsequent tax years unless it is cancelled by the transferor spouse/civil partner or circumstances change (eg divorce or a tax reduction is not actually obtained). **If the election for the tax year 2016/17 is made on or after 6 April 2017 it must be made within four years of the end of the tax year (ie by 5 April 2021) and will only apply for the tax year 2016/17.**

The couple, as a whole, will save tax through the election if the net income of the transferor is below £11,000.

12 Married couples and couples in a civil partnership

FAST FORWARD

Spouses and civil partners are separate taxpayers but should ensure that each spouse/civil partner uses their savings nil rate band and dividend nil rate band. Income on property held jointly by married couples and civil partners is treated as if it were shared equally unless they make a joint declaration of the actual shares of ownership.

PER alert

One of the competencies you require to fulfil Performance Objective 17 Tax planning and advice of the PER is to review the situation of an individual or entity advising on any potential tax risks and/or additional tax minimisation measures. You can apply the knowledge you obtain from this section of the Study Text to help to demonstrate this competence.

12.1 Spouses and civil partners

Spouses and civil partners are taxed as two separate people. Each spouse/civil partner is entitled to a personal allowance depending on their income. Spouses and civil partners should ensure, where possible, that **each spouse/civil partner uses their savings nil rate band and dividend nil rate band**.

12.2 Example: income tax planning for spouses/civil partners (1)

Liam and Joe are a married couple. In 2016/17, Liam has trading profits of £180,000 and receives building society interest of £300 and Joe has a salary of £88,000 and receives dividends of £11,000. Since Liam is an additional rate taxpayer, he is not entitled to the savings nil rate band but he has not utilised his dividend nil rate band. Joe has not utilised his savings nil rate band of £500 (higher rate taxpayer) and has exceeded his dividend nil rate band of £5,000. Liam should therefore transfer his building society funds to Joe thus saving income tax of £300 × 45% = £135. Joe should transfer shares producing £5,000 of dividends to Liam thus saving income tax of £5,000 × 32.5% = £1,625.

12.3 Joint property

When spouses/civil partners jointly own income-generating property, it is assumed that they are entitled to equal shares of the income.

If the spouses/civil partners are not entitled to equal shares in the income-generating property, they may make a joint declaration to HMRC, specifying the proportion to which each is entitled. These proportions are used to tax each of them separately, in respect of income arising on or after the date of the declaration.

12.4 Example: income tax planning for spouses/civil partners (2)

Brian is a higher rate taxpayer who owns a rental property producing £26,000 of property income on which he pays tax at 40%, giving him a tax liability of £10,400. His spouse, Mary, has no income. If Brian transfers only 5% of the asset to Mary, they will be treated as jointly owning the property and will each be taxed on 50% of the income. Brian's tax liability will be reduced to £5,200.

Mary's liability is then calculated as follows:

	£
Net income	13,000
Less personal allowance	(11,000)
Taxable income	2,000
Tax on £2,000 × 20%	400

This gives an overall tax saving of £(5,200 – 400) = £4,800. This could alternatively be calculated as £11,000 × 40% = £4,400 plus £2,000 × 20% = £400 giving the total saving of £4,800.

Chapter Roundup

- An individual will automatically not be UK resident if he meets any of the automatic overseas tests. An individual, who does not meet any of the automatic overseas tests, will automatically be UK resident if he meets any of the automatic UK tests. An individual who has not met any of the automatic overseas tests nor any of the automatic UK tests will be UK resident if he meets the sufficient ties test.
- An individual who is UK resident is taxed on worldwide income.
- In a personal income tax computation, we bring together, for each tax year, income from all sources, splitting the sources into non-savings, savings and dividend income.
- Income must be classified according to the nature of the income as different computational rules apply to different types of income.
- Income from certain investments, such as those held in Individual Savings Accounts (ISAs), is exempt from income tax.
- Deductible interest is given tax relief by being deducted from total income to compute net income.
- All individuals are entitled to a personal allowance. It is deducted from net income, first against non savings income, then against savings income and lastly against dividend income. The personal allowance is reduced by £1 for every £2 that adjusted net income exceeds £100,000 and can be reduced to nil.
- To work out the income tax liability on the taxable income, first compute the tax on non-savings income, then on savings income and, finally, on dividend income. To work out tax payable, deduct tax paid under Pay As You Earn (PAYE). If tax deducted under PAYE exceeds the tax liability, the excess will be repayable.
- The accrued income scheme ensures that a taxpayer who sells a gilt is taxed on any interest income included in the proceeds. Similarly, relief is given to the purchaser of the gilt for the interest included in the price paid.
- Increase the basic rate limit and the higher rate limit by the gross amount of any gift aid payment to give tax relief at the higher and additional rates.
- There is an income tax charge to recover child benefit if the recipient or their partner has adjusted net income over £50,000 in a tax year.
- An individual is permitted to transfer £1,100 of their personal allowance to their spouse/civil partner, in certain circumstances, giving a tax reducer of £220.
- Spouses and civil partners are separate taxpayers but should ensure that each spouse/civil partner uses their savings nil rate band and dividend nil rate band. Income on property held jointly by married couples and civil partners is treated as if it were shared equally unless they make a joint declaration of the actual shares of ownership.

Quick Quiz

1 If an individual meets none of the automatic overseas tests and none of the automatic UK tests of residence in a tax year, what determines whether the individual is resident in the UK?

2 Give one type of savings income that is received by individuals net of 20% tax.

3 What are the tax advantages of holding investments in an Individual Savings Account (ISA)?

4 Income tax on non-savings income is charged at _ % below the basic rate limit, at _% between the basic rate limit and the higher rate limit, and at _% above the higher rate limit. Fill in the blanks.

5 How is dividend income taxed?

6 Ingrid owned £30,000 (nominal value) 4% UK Government Loan Stock. Interest was payable on 31 March and 30 September each year. Ingrid sold the loan stock on 31 July 2016 including interest. What is the amount of savings income taxable on Ingrid in respect of the loan stock for 2016/17?

7 If Dennis has taxable income of £32,700 and makes gift aid payments of £400, on how much of his income will he pay higher rate tax?

8 Mike and Matt are a married couple. Mike owns 25% of an investment property and Matt owns 75%. How will the income be taxed?

Answers to Quick Quiz

1 The number of ties the individual has to the UK and the number of days spent in the UK that year. Whether the individual is leaving the UK or arriving in the UK also determines how many ties are to be satisfied for UK residence.

2 Bank (or building society) interest.

3 Dividend income and interest received from ISAs are exempt from income tax. Capital gains made within an ISA are exempt from capital gains tax.

4 Income tax on non-savings income is charged at **20%** below the basic rate limit, at **40%** between the basic rate limit and the higher rate limit, and at **45%** above the higher rate limit.

5 Dividend income within the dividend nil rate band is taxed at 0%. Any remaining dividend income below the basic rate limit is taxed at 7.5%, at 32.5% between the basic rate limit and the higher rate limit, and at 38.1% above the higher rate limit.

6 Accrued interest to date of sale £30,000 × 4% × 4/12 (1 April to 31 July) = £400. This is an application of the accrued income scheme.

7 The basic rate limit is increased by £400 × 100/80 = £500 to £32,500. Dennis will be liable to higher rate tax on £32,700 – £32,500 = £200.

8 Mike and Matt will each be taxed on 50% of the income from the investment property unless they make a joint declaration to specify the actual proportions in which case Mike will be taxed on 25% of the income and Matt on 75%.

Now try the questions below from the Practice Question Bank

Number	Type	Marks	Time
Q4	Section A	2	4 mins
Q5	Section A	2	4 mins
Q6	Section A	2	4 mins
Q7	Section A	2	4 mins
Q8	Section A	2	4 mins
Q9	Section C	10	20 mins
Q10	Section C	15	29 mins
Q11	Section C	15	29 mins

3

Employment income

Topic list	Syllabus reference
1 Employment and self employment	B2(a)
2 Basis of assessment for employment income	B2(b), B2(c)
3 Allowable deductions	B2(c), B2(d)
4 Statutory approved mileage allowances	B2(c), B2(e)
5 Charitable donations under the payroll deduction scheme	B5(f)

Introduction

In the previous chapters we saw how to construct the income tax computation. Now we start to look in greater detail at the different types of income that people may receive so that the income can be slotted into the computation.

Many people earn money by working. We look at the important distinction between employment and self employment, so that we can consider the way in which people are taxed on the wages or salaries from their jobs.

Sometimes the employee may incur expenses when carrying out his job. We look at the rules determining when these can be deducted from employment income for tax purposes. We also look at the rules covering mileage payments made by employers to employees who use their own cars for business journeys. Finally employees can make tax efficient contributions to charity under the payroll giving scheme.

In the next chapter we look at how benefits received as a result of employment are taxed and at how tax is deducted from employment income under the PAYE system.

Study guide

		Intellectual level
B2	**Income from employment**	
(a)	Recognise the factors that determine whether an engagement is treated as employment or self-employment.	2
(b)	Recognise the basis of assessment for employment income.	2
(c)	Recognise the income assessable.	2
(d)	Recognise the allowable deductions, including travelling expenses.	2
(e)	Discuss the use of the statutory approved mileage allowances.	2
B5	**The comprehensive computation of taxable income and income tax liability**	
(f)	Understand the treatment of charitable giving.	1

Exam guide

You are very likely to be asked a question concerning at least one aspect of employment taxation in your exam. This could range from identifying the date on which earnings are received in Section A or Section B to a discussion of the distinction between employment and self employment in Section C, either as part of a 15 mark question or a 10 mark question.

1 Employment and self employment

FAST FORWARD

Employment involves a contract of service whereas self employment involves a contract for services. The distinction between employment and self employment is decided by looking at all the facts of the engagement.

1.1 Employment income

Employment income includes income arising from an employment under a **contract of service**.

Some people, however, set themselves up in business and carry out work for customers under a **contract for services**.

Before we can calculate employment income, we must be sure that the individual is employed rather than self employed. This can only be decided by looking at all the facts of the engagement.

1.2 Employment and self employment

Exam focus point

Many of the tax rules have come about as a result of legal cases. In the exam you are not required to know the relevant cases. However we have included the case names in the Study Text for your information.

It can be difficult to distinguish between employment (receipts taxable as earnings) and self employment (profits taxable as trading income). Employment involves a contract of service, whereas self employment involves a contract for services. Taxpayers tend to prefer self employment, because the rules on deductions for expenses are more generous.

Factors which may be of importance include:

- The degree of control exercised over the person doing the work (a high level of control indicates employment)
- Whether the worker must accept further work (if yes, indicates employment)
- Whether the person who has offered work must provide further work (if yes, indicates employment)
- Whether the worker provides his own equipment (if yes, indicates self-employment)
- Whether the worker is entitled to employment benefits such as sick pay, holiday pay and pension facilities (entitlement indicates employment)
- Whether the worker hires his own helpers (if yes, indicates self-employment)
- What degree of financial risk the worker takes (if high risk, indicates self-employment)
- What degree of responsibility for investment and management the worker has (if most of responsibility is the worker's, indicates self-employment)
- Whether the worker can profit from sound management (if can do so, indicates self-employment)
- Whether the worker can work when he chooses (if can do so, indicates self-employment)
- Whether the worker works for a number of different people or organisations (working for just one person or organisation indicates employment)
- The wording used in any agreement between the worker and the person for whom he performs work (but not conclusive about the actual legal relationship between them)

Relevant cases include:

(a) *Edwards v Clinch 1981*

A civil engineer acted occasionally as an inspector on temporary unplanned appointments.

Held: there was no ongoing office which could be vacated by one person and held by another so the fees received were from self employment not employment.

(b) *Hall v Lorimer 1994*

A vision mixer was engaged under a series of short-term contracts.

Held: the vision mixer was self employed, not because of any one detail of the case but because the overall picture was one of self-employment.

(c) *Carmichael and Anor v National Power plc 1999*

Individuals engaged as visitor guides on a casual 'as required' basis were not employees. An exchange of correspondence between the company and the individuals was not a contract of employment as there was no provision as to the frequency of work and there was flexibility to accept work or turn it down as it arose. Sickness, holiday and pension arrangements did not apply and neither did grievance and disciplinary procedures.

A worker's status also affects national insurance contributions (NIC). The self-employed generally pay less than employees. National insurance contributions are covered later in this Study Text.

2 Basis of assessment for employment income

FAST FORWARD

General earnings are taxed in the year of receipt. Money earnings are generally received on the earlier of the time payment is made and the time entitlement to payment arises.

2.1 Outline of the charge

Employment income includes income arising from an employment under a contract of service and the income of office holders, such as directors. The term 'employee' is used in this Study Text to mean anyone who receives employment income (ie both employees and directors).

General earnings are an employee's earnings (see key term below) plus the 'cash equivalent' of any taxable non-monetary benefits.

Key term

'Earnings' means any salary, wage or fee, any gratuity or other profit or incidental benefit obtained by the employee if it is money or money's worth (something of direct monetary value or convertible into direct monetary value) or anything else which constitutes a reward of the employment.

Taxable earnings from an employment in a tax year are the general earnings received in that tax year.

2.2 When are earnings received?

2.2.1 General earnings consisting of money

General earnings consisting of money are treated as received at the earlier of:

- **The time when payment is made**
- **The time when a person becomes entitled to payment of the earnings**

If the employee is a **director** of a company, earnings from the company are received on the **earliest** of:

- The earlier of the two alternatives given in the general rule (above)
- The time when the amount is **credited in the company's accounting records**
- **The end of the company's period of account** (if the amount was determined by then)
- The **time the amount is determined** (if after the end of the company's period of account)

Question

Receipt of money earnings

Josephine and Vincent are employed by D plc. Josephine is a director of D plc. Vincent is not a director of D plc. D plc makes up its accounts to 31 March each year.

Bonuses were awarded by D plc as follows:

Josephine: £5,000. This amount was determined by the directors on 28 February 2017 and credited to Josephine's director's account on 10 March 2017, subject to a condition that she was could not draw down the bonus until 15 April 2017, on which date she became entitled to payment of the bonus. Josephine was actually paid the bonus on 28 April 2017.

Vincent: £3,000. Vincent became entitled to be paid this bonus on 31 March 2016, but agreed that payment should be delayed due to D plc's cash flow problems. He was actually paid the bonus on 30 April 2016.

Explain when each of the bonuses is received for the purposes of employment income and so determine the tax year in which it will be taxed.

Answer

Josephine

Josephine is a director and so her bonus is received for the purposes of employment income on the earliest of:

Time payment made:	28 April 2017
Time of entitlement:	15 April 2017
Credited in records	10 March 2017
End of period of account	31 March 2017 (amount determined before end of period)

The earliest of these dates is 10 March 2017 and so this is the date of receipt of the bonus. The tax year in which the bonus is taxed is therefore 2016/17.

Vincent

Vincent is not a director so his bonus is received for the purposes of employment income on the earlier of:

Time payment made:	30 April 2016
Time of entitlement:	31 March 2016

The earlier of these dates is 31 March 2016 and so this is the date of receipt of the bonus. The tax year in which the bonus is taxed is therefore 2015/16.

2.2.2 General earnings consisting taxable benefits

Taxable benefits (see next chapter) are generally treated as received when they are provided to the employee.

2.2.3 Pension income

The receipts basis does not apply to pension income. Pension income is taxed on the amount accruing in the tax year, whether or not it has actually been received in that year.

2.3 Net taxable earnings

Total taxable earnings less total allowable deductions (see below) **are net taxable earnings of a tax year.** Deductions cannot usually create a loss: they can only reduce the net taxable earnings to nil. If there is more than one employment in the tax year, separate calculations are required for each employment.

3 Allowable deductions

FAST FORWARD

Deductions for expenses are extremely limited. Relief is available for the costs that an employee is obliged to incur in travelling in the performance of his duties or in travelling to the place he has to attend in performance of his duties. Relief is **not** available for normal commuting costs.

3.1 The general rules

Deductions for expenses are extremely limited and are notoriously hard to obtain. Although there are some specific deductions, which are covered below, the general rule is that relief is limited to:

- **Qualifying travel expenses**
- **Other expenses the employee is obliged to incur and pay as holder of the employment which are incurred wholly, exclusively and necessarily in the performance of the duties of the employment**

3.2 Travel expenses

3.2.1 Qualifying travel expenses

Tax relief is not available for an employee's normal commuting costs. This means relief is not available for any costs an employee incurs in getting from home to his normal place of work. However **employees are entitled to relief for travel expenses that they are obliged to incur and pay in travelling in the performance of their duties or travelling to or from a place which they have to attend in the performance of their duties (other than a permanent workplace).**

Question — **Relief for travelling costs (1)**

Judi is an accountant. She often travels to meetings at the firm's offices in Scotland returning to her office in Leeds after the meetings. What tax relief is available for Judi's travel costs?

Answer

Relief is available for the full cost of these journeys as the travel is undertaken in the performance of Judi's duties.

Question — **Relief for travelling costs (2)**

Zoe lives in Wycombe and normally works in Chiswick. Occasionally she visits a client in Wimbledon and travels direct from home. Distances are shown in the diagram below:

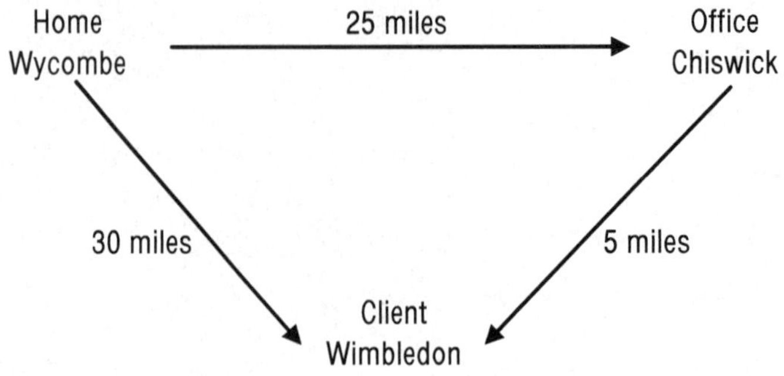

What tax relief is available for Zoe's travel costs?

Answer

Zoe is not entitled to tax relief for the costs incurred in travelling between Wycombe and Chiswick since these are normal commuting costs. However, relief is available for all costs (30 miles) that Zoe incurs when she travels from Wycombe to Wimbledon to visit her client.

To prevent manipulation of the basic rule normal commuting will not become a business journey just because the employee stops during the journey to perform a business task (eg to send an email). Nor will relief be available if the journey is essentially the same as the employee's normal journey to work.

Question

Relief for travelling costs (3)

Jeremy is based in an office in Birmingham City Centre. One day he is required to attend a 9.00 am meeting with a client whose premises are around the corner from his Birmingham office. Jeremy travels from home directly to the meeting. What tax relief is available for Jeremy's travel costs?

Answer

Since the journey is substantially the same as Jeremy's ordinary journey to work, tax relief is not available.

3.2.2 Site based employees

Site based employees (eg construction workers, management consultants etc) **who do not have a permanent workplace, are entitled to relief for the costs of all journeys made from home to wherever they are working.** This is because these employees do not have an ordinary commuting journey or any normal commuting costs.

3.2.3 Temporary workplace

If an employee is seconded to work at another location for some considerable time, then the question arises as to whether the journey from home to that workplace can become normal commuting. There is a 24 month rule.

Tax relief is available for travel, accommodation and subsistence expenses incurred by an employee who is working at a temporary workplace on a secondment expected to last up to 24 months. If a secondment is initially expected not to exceed 24 months, but it is extended, relief ceases to be due from the date the employee becomes aware of the change.

When looking at how long a secondment is expected to last, HMRC will consider not only the terms of the written contract but also any verbal agreement by the employer and other factors such as whether the employee buys a house etc.

Question

Relief for travelling costs (4)

Philip works for Vastbank at its Newcastle City Centre branch. Philip is sent to work full-time at another branch in Morpeth for 20 months at the end of which he will return to the Newcastle branch. Morpeth is about 20 miles north of Newcastle. What tax relief is available for Philip's travel costs?

Answer

Although Philip is spending all of his time at the Morpeth branch it will not be treated as his normal work place because his period of attendance will be less than 24 months. Thus Philip can claim relief in full for the costs of travel from his home to the Morpeth branch.

3.3 Other expenses

Relief is given for other expenses incurred **wholly, exclusively and necessarily in the performance of the duties** of the employment. The word 'exclusively' strictly implies that the expenditure must **give no private benefit at all**. If it does, none of it is deductible. In practice HMRC may ignore a small element of private benefit or make an apportionment between business and private use.

Whether an expense is 'necessary' is not determined by what the employer requires. The test is **whether the duties of the employment could not be performed without the outlay**.

The following cases illustrate how the requirements are interpreted. Remember you are not expected to know the case names, they are given for information only.

- *Sanderson v Durbridge 1955*

  The cost of evening meals taken when attending late meetings was not deductible because it was not incurred in the performance of the duties.

- *Blackwell v Mills 1945*

  As a condition of his employment, an employee was required to attend evening classes. The cost of his text books and travel was not deductible because it was not incurred in the performance of the duties.

- *Lupton v Potts 1969*

  Examination fees incurred by a solicitor's articled clerk were not deductible because they were incurred neither wholly nor exclusively in the performance of the duties, but in furthering the clerk's ambition to become a solicitor.

- *Brown v Bullock 1961*

  The expense of joining a club that was virtually a condition of an employment was not deductible because it would have been possible to carry on the employment without the club membership, so the expense was not necessary.

- *Elwood v Utitz 1965*

  A managing director's subscriptions to two residential London clubs were claimed by him as an expense on the grounds that they were cheaper than hotels.

  The expenditure was deductible as it was necessary in that it would be impossible for the employee to carry out his London duties without being provided with appropriate accommodation. The residential facilities (which were cheaper than hotel accommodation) were given to club members only.

- *Lucas v Cattell 1972*

  The cost of business telephone calls on a private telephone is deductible, but **no part of the line or** telephone **rental charges is deductible**.

- *Fitzpatrick v IRC 1994; Smith v Abbott 1994*

  Journalists could not claim a deduction for the cost of buying newspapers which they read to keep themselves informed, since they were merely preparing themselves to perform their duties.

The cost of clothes for work is not deductible, except for certain trades requiring protective clothing where there are annual deductions on a set scale.

An employee required to work at home may be able to claim a deduction for the additional costs of working from home, such as an appropriate proportion of expenditure on lighting and heating. Employers can pay up to £4 per week (or £18 per month for monthly paid employees) without the need for supporting evidence of the costs incurred by the employee. Payments above the £4 (or £18) limit require evidence of the employee's actual costs.

3.4 Other deductions

Some expenditure is specifically deductible in computing net taxable earnings:

(a) **Contributions to registered occupational pension schemes**

(b) **Subscriptions to professional bodies** on the list of bodies issued by the HMRC (which includes most UK professional bodies such as the ACCA), if relevant to the duties of the employment

(c) Payments for certain liabilities relating to the employment and for insurance against them (see below)

Employees may also claim capital allowances on plant and machinery (other than cars or other vehicles) necessarily provided for use in the performance of those duties. The computation of capital allowances is discussed later in this Study Text.

3.5 Liabilities and insurance

If a director or employee incurs a liability related to his employment or pays for insurance against such a liability, the cost is a deductible expense. If the employer pays such amounts, there is no taxable benefit.

A liability relating to employment is one which is imposed in respect of the employee's acts or omissions as employee. Thus, for example, liability for negligence would be covered. Related costs, for example the costs of legal proceedings, are included.

For insurance premiums to qualify, the insurance policy:

(a) Must cover only liabilities relating to employment, vicarious liability in respect of liabilities of another person's employment, related costs and payments to the employee's own employees in respect of their employment liabilities relating to employment and related costs

(b) Must not last for more than two years (although it may be renewed for up to two years at a time), and the insured person must not be required to renew it

4 Statutory approved mileage allowances

FAST FORWARD

Employers may pay a mileage allowance to employees who use their own car on business journeys. Payments up to the statutory limits are tax free, any excess is taxable, and a deduction can be claimed if the payment is lower.

A single approved mileage allowance for business journeys in an employee's own vehicle applies to all cars and vans. There is no income tax on payments up to this allowance and employers do not have to report mileage allowances up to this amount. The allowance for 2016/17 is **45p per mile on the first 10,000 miles** in the tax year with **each additional mile over 10,000 miles at 25p per mile.**

The authorised mileage allowance for **employees using their own motor cycle is 24p per mile**. For **employees using their own pedal cycle it is 20p per mile.**

If employers pay less than the statutory approved mileage allowance, employees can claim tax relief up to that level.

The statutory approved mileage allowance does not prevent employers from paying higher rates, but any excess will be subject to income tax. There is a similar (but slightly different) system for NICs, covered later in this Study Text.

Employers can make income tax and NIC free payments of up to 5p per mile for each fellow employee making the same business trip who is carried as a passenger. If the employer does not pay the employee for carrying business passengers, the employee cannot claim any tax relief.

Question

Mileage allowance

Sophie uses her own car for business travel. During 2016/17, Sophie drove 15,400 miles in the performance of her duties. Sophie's employer paid her a mileage allowance. How is the mileage allowance treated for tax purposes assuming that the rate paid is:

(a) 40p a mile?
(b) 25p a mile?

Answer

(a)

	£
Mileage allowance received (15,400 × 40p)	6,160
Less tax free [(10,000 × 45p) + (5,400 × 25p)]	(5,850)
Taxable benefit	310

£5,850 is tax free and the excess amount received of £310 is a taxable benefit.

(b)

	£
Mileage allowance received (15,400 × 25p)	3,850
Less tax free amount [(10,000 × 45p) + (5,400 × 25p)]	(5,850)
Allowable deduction	(2,000)

There is no taxable benefit and Sophie can claim a deduction from her employment income of £2,000.

5 Charitable donations under the payroll deduction scheme

FAST FORWARD

Employees can make tax deductible donations to charity under the payroll deduction scheme. The amount paid is deducted from gross pay.

Employees can make charitable donations under the payroll deduction scheme by asking their employer to make deductions from their gross earnings. The deductions are then passed to a charitable agency which will either distribute the funds to the employees' chosen charities on receipt of their instructions, or provide the employee with vouchers that can be redeemed by the recipient charities.

The donation is an allowable deduction from the employee's earnings for tax purposes. Tax relief is given at source as the employer must deduct the donation from gross pay before calculating PAYE.

Exam focus point

Make sure you understand the difference between how tax relief is given for gift aid donations and how tax relief is given through the payroll deduction scheme.

Chapter Roundup

- Employment involves a contract of service whereas self employment involves a contract for services. The distinction between employment and self employment is decided by looking at all the facts of the engagement.
- General earnings are taxed in the year of receipt. Money earnings are generally received on the earlier of the time payment is made and the time entitlement to payment arises.
- Deductions for expenses are extremely limited. Relief is available for the costs that an employee is obliged to incur in travelling in the performance of his duties or in travelling to the place he has to attend in performance of his duties. Relief is **not** available for normal commuting costs.
- Employers may pay a mileage allowance to employees who use their own car on business journeys. Payments up to the statutory limits are tax free, any excess is taxable, and a deduction can be claimed if the payment is lower.
- Employees can make tax deductible donations to charity under the payroll deduction scheme. The amount paid is deducted from gross pay.

Quick Quiz

1 On what basis are earnings taxed?

2 In order for general expenses of employment to be deductible, they must be incurred _____, _____ and _____ in the performance of the duties of the employment. Fill in the blanks.

3 In what circumstances can the cost of home to workplace travel be a qualifying travel expense?

4 What relief can Karen claim if she is paid 40p for each mile that she drives her own car on company business and she drives 5,000 miles in 2016/17?

A £250
B £1,750
C £2,000
D £2,250

5 Could Karen claim any extra relief if she was accompanied by a work colleague for 1,000 of those miles?

Answers to Quick Quiz

1 Earnings are taxed on a receipts basis.

2 In order for general expenses of employment to be deductible, they must be incurred **wholly, exclusively** and **necessarily** in the performance of the duties of the employment.

3 Home to workplace travel will be a qualifying travel expense if the employee travels to a temporary workplace on a secondment expected to last up to 24 months.

4 A. Karen could claim relief of 5,000 × (45 – 40)p = £250. The 40p per mile received would not be taxable.

5 Karen could not claim any extra relief if she was accompanied by a work colleague for 1,000 of those miles. If her employer had made extra payments of up to 5p per mile for those journeys the extra payment would have been tax free.

Now try the questions below from the Practice Question Bank

Number	Type	Marks	Time
Q12	Section A	2	4 mins
Q13	Section A	2	4 mins
Q14	Section A	2	4 mins
Q15	Section B	2	4 mins
Q16	Section B	2	4 mins
Q17	Section B	2	4 mins
Q18	Section B	2	4 mins
Q19	Section B	2	4 mins

4

Taxable and exempt benefits. The PAYE system

Topic list	Syllabus reference
1 Taxable benefits	B2(g)
2 Exempt benefits	B2(g)
3 The PAYE system	B2(f), (h)

Introduction

In the previous chapter we discussed when a worker was an employee and when he was self employed. We then considered the taxation of salaries and wages and the deduction of expenses and charitable donations.

In this chapter we look at benefits provided to employees. Benefits are an integral part of many remuneration packages, but the tax cost of receiving a benefit must not be overlooked. Special rules apply to fix the taxable value of certain benefits.

Finally, we look at how tax is deducted from employment income under the PAYE system. Tax is deducted on cash payments and some benefits. Other benefits are dealt with through the PAYE code.

In the next chapter we look at how employees can save for their retirement through pension provision and the tax reliefs available.

Study guide

		Intellectual level
B2	**Income from employment**	
(f)	Explain the PAYE system, how benefits can be payrolled, and the purpose of form P11D.	1
(g)	Explain and compute the amount of benefits assessable.	2
(h)	Recognise the circumstances in which real time reporting late filing penalties will be imposed on an employer and the amount of penalty which is charged.	2

Exam guide

Benefits are a very important part of employment income and you are likely to come across them in your exam in any of Sections A, B or Section C, in a 15 mark question or a 10 mark question. If you come across exempt benefits in a Section C question, note this in your answer to show that you have considered each item.

The PAYE system is a system of deduction of tax at source. You should be able to explain how it collects tax. The forms for the PAYE system are important, as are the dates for submission.

Exam focus point

ACCA's article Benefits, written by a member of the F6(UK) examination team states that benefits feature regularly in the F6 (UK) exam, and this article mainly covers those **aspects of benefits** that have been **examined in previous sittings** of F6 (UK).

1 Taxable benefits

FAST FORWARD

Employees are taxed on benefits under the benefits code.

1.1 Vouchers

If an employee:

(a) receives cash vouchers (vouchers exchangeable for cash)
(b) uses a credit token (such as a credit card) to obtain money, goods or services, or
(c) receives exchangeable vouchers (such as book tokens), also called non-cash vouchers

the employee is taxed on the **cost to the employer of providing the benefit**, less any amount the employee pays the employer for providing the benefit.

1.2 Accommodation

FAST FORWARD

The benefit in respect of accommodation is its annual value. There is an additional benefit if the property cost over £75,000.

1.2.1 Annual value charge

The taxable value of accommodation provided to an employee is the rent that would have been payable if the premises had been let at their annual value (sometimes called 'rateable value'). **If the premises are rented** rather than owned by the employer, then **the taxable benefit is the higher of the rent actually paid and the annual value.**

1.2.2 Additional benefit charge

If a property was bought by the employer for a cost of more than £75,000, an additional amount is chargeable as follows:

(Cost of providing the living accommodation – £75,000) × the official rate of interest at the start of the tax year. The official rate of interest at the start of the 2016/17 tax year is 3%.

Exam focus point

> The 'official rate' of interest will be given to you in the exam.

Thus with an official rate of 3%, the total benefit for accommodation costing £95,000 and with an annual value of £2,000 would be £2,000 + £(95,000 – 75,000) × 3% = £2,600.

The 'cost of providing' the living accommodation is the total of the cost of purchase and the cost of any improvements made before the start of the tax year for which the benefit is being computed. It is therefore not possible to avoid the charge by buying an inexpensive property requiring substantial repairs and improving it.

Where the property was acquired more than six years before first being provided to the employee, the **market value when first so provided plus the cost of subsequent improvements** is used as the **cost of providing the living accommodation.** However, unless the actual cost plus improvements up to the start of the tax year in question exceeds £75,000, the additional charge cannot be imposed, however high the market value.

1.2.3 Job related accommodation

There is no taxable benefit in respect of job related accommodation. Accommodation is job related if:

(a) Residence in the accommodation is necessary for **the proper performance of the employee's duties (as with a caretaker)**

(b) The accommodation is provided **for the better performance of the employee's duties** and the employment is of a kind in which it is customary for accommodation to be provided (as with a policeman), or

(c) The **accommodation is provided as part of arrangements in force because of a special threat to the employee's security**.

Directors can only claim exemptions (a) or (b) if:

(i) They have no **material interest** ('material' means over 5%) in the company.
(ii) Either they are **full time working directors** or the company is **non-profit making or is a charity**.

1.2.4 Contribution by employee

Any contribution paid by the employee is deducted from the annual value of the property and then from the additional benefit.

Question — **Accommodation**

Quinton was provided with a company flat in January 2016. The rateable value of the flat is £1,200. The property cost his employer £125,000, but was valued at £150,000 in January 2016. Quinton paid rent of £500 pa.

What is the taxable benefit for 2016/17 assuming:

(a) His employer purchased the property in 2014

(b) His employer purchased the property in 2008, or

(c) Quinton was required to live in the flat as he was employed as the caretaker for the company premises (of which the flat was part).

Answer

		£
(a)		
	Annual value	1,200
	Less rent paid	(500)
		700
	Additional amount £(125,000 – 75,000) × 3%	1,500
	Taxable benefit	2,200
(b)		£
	Annual value	1,200
	Less rent paid	(500)
		700
	Additional amount £(150,000 – 75,000) × 3%	2,250
	Taxable benefit	2,950
	As Quinton first moved in more than six years after the company bought the flat, the value at the date he moved in is used.	
(c)	Job related accommodation: taxable benefit	£ nil

1.3 Expenses

1.3.1 General business expenses

If business expenses, on such items as travel or hotel stays, are reimbursed by an employer, the basic rule is that the reimbursed amount is a taxable benefit for employees and, to avoid being taxed on this amount, **an employee must then make a claim to deduct it as an allowable deduction** as explained earlier in this Study Text.

However, **such reimbursed expenses will be automatically treated as exempt, provided that the amount of the deduction is at least equal to the amount of the expense**. The exemption applies to actual expenses incurred and to flat rate payments such as allowances for travel or meals.

1.3.2 Private incidental expenses

When an individual has to spend one or more nights away from home, his employer may reimburse expenses on items incidental to his absence (for example laundry and private telephone calls). **Such incidental expenses are exempt** if:

(a) The expenses of travelling to each place where the individual stays overnight, throughout the trip, are incurred necessarily in the performance of the duties of the employment (or would have been, if there had been any expenses).

(b) The total (for the whole trip) of incidental expenses not deductible under the usual rules is **no more than £5 for each night spent wholly in the UK** and **£10 for each other night**. If this limit is exceeded, all of the expenses are taxable, not just the excess. The expenses include any VAT.

This incidental expenses exemption applies to expenses reimbursed, and to benefits obtained using credit tokens and non-cash vouchers.

1.3.3 Expenses related to living accommodation

In addition to the benefit of living accommodation itself, **employees are taxed on related expenses paid by the employer**, such as:

(a) **Heating, lighting or cleaning the premises**
(b) **Repairing, maintaining or decorating the premises**
(c) **The provision of furniture (the annual value is 20% of the cost)**

If the accommodation is 'job related', however, the **taxable amount is restricted to a maximum of 10% of the employee's 'net earnings'.** For this purpose, net earnings comprises the total employment income, net of expenses and pension contributions, but excluding these related expenses.

Council tax and water or sewage charges paid by the employer are taxable in full as a benefit unless the accommodation is 'job-related'.

1.4 Cars

Exam focus point

ACCA's article Motor cars, written by a member of the F6(UK) examination team explains the implications of acquiring, running, or having the use of a motor car for income tax, corporation tax, value added tax (VAT) and national insurance contribution (NIC).

FAST FORWARD

Employees who have a company car are taxed on a % of the car's list price which depends on the level of the car's CO_2 emissions. The same % multiplied by £22,200 determines the benefit where private fuel is also provided.

1.4.1 Cars provided for private use

A car provided by reason of the employment to an employee or member of his family or household for private use gives rise to a taxable benefit. 'Private use' includes home to work travel.

A tax charge arises whether the car is provided by the employer or by some other person. The benefit is computed as shown below, even if the car is taken as an alternative to another benefit of a different value.

The starting point for calculating a car benefit is the list price of the car (plus accessories). **The percentage of the list price that is taxable depends on the car's CO_2 emissions.**

1.4.2 Taxable benefit

For cars that emit **CO_2 of 95 g/km (2016/17), the taxable benefit is 16% of the car's list price. This percentage increases by 1% for every 5g/km (rounded down to the nearest multiple of 5) by which CO_2 emissions exceed 95g/km up to a maximum of 37%.** Therefore the 16% rate also applies to cars with emissions between 96g/km and 99g/km as these are rounded down to 95g/km. Then, for cars with emissions between 100g/km and 104g/km, the relevant percentage will be 16 + ((100 – 95)/5) = 17% etc.

Exam focus point

The CO_2 baseline figure of 95g/km and the baseline percentage of 16% will be given to you in the tax rates and allowances section of the exam paper.

For cars that emit CO_2 between 76g/km and 94g/km, the taxable benefit is 15% of the car's list price.
For cars that emit CO_2 between 51g/km and 75g/km, the taxable benefit is 11% of the car's list price.
For cars that emit CO_2 of 50 g/km or less, the taxable benefit is 7% of the car's list price.

Exam focus point

The percentages for cars which emit CO_2 of 94g/km or less will be given to you in the tax rates and allowance section of the exam paper.

Diesel cars have a supplement of 3% of the car's list price added to the taxable benefit. The maximum percentage, however, remains 37% of the list price.

1.4.3 List price

The price of the car is the sum of the following items:

(a) **The list price of the car** for a single retail sale at the time of first registration, including charges for delivery and standard accessories. The manufacturer's, importer's or distributor's list price must be used, even if the retailer offered a discount. A notional list price is estimated if no list price was published.

(b) **The price (including fitting) of all optional accessories provided when the car was first provided** to the employee, excluding mobile telephones and equipment needed by a disabled employee. The extra cost of adapting or manufacturing a car to run on road fuel gases is not included.

(c) **The price (including fitting) of all optional accessories fitted later** and costing at least £100 each, excluding mobile telephones and equipment needed by a disabled employee. Such accessories affect the taxable benefit from and including the tax year in which they are fitted. However, accessories which are merely replacing existing accessories and are not superior to the ones replaced are ignored. Replacement accessories which *are* superior are taken into account, but the cost of the old accessory is then deducted.

There is a special rule for **classic cars**. If the car is at least 15 years old (from the time of first registration) at the end of the tax year, and its market value at the end of the year (or, if earlier, when it ceased to be available to the employee) is over £15,000 and greater than the price found under the above rules, that market value is used instead of the price. The market value takes account of all accessories (except mobile telephones and equipment needed by a disabled employee).

Capital contributions made by the employee in that and previous tax years up to a maximum of £5,000 are deducted from the list price. Capital contributions are payments by the employee in respect of the price of the car or accessories for the same car. Contributions beyond the maximum are ignored.

Question — **Car benefit (1)**

Nigel is provided with a diesel car which had a list price of £22,000 when it was first registered. The car has CO_2 emissions of 153g/km.

You are required to calculate Nigel's car benefit for 2016/17.

Answer

Car benefit £22,000 × 30% (16% + (150 – 95)/5 + 3%) = £6,600

Note that 153 is rounded down to 150 to be exactly divisible by 5.

Question — **Car benefit (2)**

Robyn is provided with a petrol car which had a list price of £18,000 when it was first registered. The car has CO_2 emissions of 90 g/km.

You are required to calculate Robyn's car benefit for 2016/17.

Answer

Car benefit £18,000 × 15% = £2,700

1.4.4 Reductions in the benefit

The benefit is reduced on a time basis where a car is first made available or ceases to be made available during the tax year or is incapable of being used for a continuous period of not less than 30 days (for example because it is being repaired).

The benefit is reduced by any payment the user must make for the private use of the car (as distinct from a capital contribution to the cost of the car). The benefit cannot become negative to create a deduction from the employee's income.

Question

Time apportioning benefits

Vicky starts her employment on 6 January 2017 and is immediately provided with a new petrol car with a list price of £25,000. The car was more expensive than her employer would have provided and she therefore made a capital contribution of £6,200. The employer was able to buy the car at a discount and paid only £23,000. Vicky contributed £100 a month for being able to use the car privately. CO_2 emissions are 228g/km.

You are required to calculate her car benefit for 2016/17.

Answer

	£
List price *	25,000
Less capital contribution (maximum)	(5,000)
	20,000

	£
£20,000 × 37%** × 3/12 ***	1,850
Less contribution to running costs (£100 × 3)	(300)
Car benefit	1,550

* The discounted price is not relevant

** 16% + (225 – 95) × 1/5 = 42% restricted to 37% max

*** Only available for three months in 2016/17

1.4.5 Pool cars

Pool cars are exempt. A car is a pool car if **all** the following conditions are satisfied:

(a) It is used by more than one employee and is not ordinarily used by any one of them to the exclusion of the others.

(b) Any private use is merely incidental to business use.

(c) It is not normally kept overnight at or near the residence of an employee.

1.4.6 Ancillary benefits

There are many ancillary benefits associated with the provision of cars, such as insurance, repairs, vehicle licences and a parking space at or near work. No extra taxable benefit arises as a result of these, with the exception of the cost of providing a driver.

1.5 Fuel for cars

1.5.1 Introduction

Where fuel is provided there is a further benefit in addition to the car benefit.

No taxable benefit arises where either

(a) **All the fuel provided was made available only for business travel, or**

(b) **The employee is required to make good, and has made good, the whole of the cost of any fuel provided for his private use.**

Unlike most benefits, a reimbursement of only part of the cost of the fuel available for private use does not reduce the benefit.

1.5.2 Taxable benefit

The taxable benefit is a percentage of a base figure. The base figure for 2016/17 is £22,200. The percentage is the same percentage as is used to calculate the car benefit (see above).

Exam focus point

> The fuel base figure will be given to you in the tax rates and allowances section of the exam paper.

1.5.3 Reductions in the benefit

The fuel benefit is reduced in the same way as the car benefit **if the car is not available for 30 days or more.**

The fuel benefit is also reduced if private fuel is not available for part of a tax year. However, if private fuel later becomes available in the same tax year, the reduction is not made. If, for example, fuel is provided from 6 April 2016 to 30 June 2016, then the fuel benefit for 2016/17 will be restricted to just three months. This is because the provision of fuel has permanently ceased. However, if fuel is provided from 6 April 2016 to 30 June 2016, and then again from 1 September 2016 to 5 April 2017, then the fuel benefit will not be reduced since the cessation was only temporary.

Question — **Car and fuel benefit**

Brian was provided by his employer with a new car with a list price of £15,000 on 6 April 2016. The car emits 141g/km of CO_2. During 2016/17 the employer spent £900 on insurance, repairs and a vehicle licence. The firm paid for all petrol, costing £1,500, without reimbursement. Brian paid the firm £270 for the private use of the car. Calculate the taxable benefits for private use of the car and private fuel.

Answer

Round CO_2 emissions figure down to the nearest 5, ie 140g/km.

Amount by which CO_2 emissions exceed the baseline:

(140 – 95) = 45g/km

Divide by 5 = 9

Taxable percentage = 16% + 9% = 25%

	£
Car benefit £15,000 × 25%	3,750
Less contribution towards use of car	(270)
	3,480
Fuel benefit £22,200 × 25%	5,550
Total benefits	9,030

If the contribution of £270 had been towards the petrol the benefit would have been £(3,750 + 5,550) = £9,300 since partial reimbursement of private use fuel does not reduce the fuel benefit.

Note there is no additional benefit for the insurance, repairs and licence costs. The car benefit is deemed to cover all these expenses incurred by the employer.

1.6 Vans and heavier commercial vehicles

If a van (of normal maximum laden weight up to 3,500 kg) **is made available for an employee's private use, there is an annual scale charge of £3,170.** The scale charge covers ancillary benefits such as insurance and servicing. The benefit is scaled down if the van is not available for the full year (as for cars) and is reduced by any payment made by the employee for private use.

There is, however, **no taxable benefit where an employee takes a van home** (ie uses the van for home to work travel) but is not allowed any other private use.

Where private fuel is provided, there is an additional charge of £598. If the van is unavailable for part of the year, or fuel for private use is only provided for part of the year, the benefit is scaled down.

If a commercial vehicle of normal maximum laden weight over 3,500 kg is made available for an employee's private use, but the employee's use of the vehicle is not wholly or mainly private, no taxable benefit arises except in respect of the provision of a driver.

1.7 Beneficial loans

FAST FORWARD

Cheap loans are charged to tax on the difference between the official rate of interest and any interest paid by the employee.

1.7.1 Taxable benefit

Employment related loans to employees and their relatives give rise to a benefit equal to:

(a) **Any amounts written off** (unless the employee has died)

(b) The excess of the interest based on an official rate prescribed by the Treasury, over any interest actually charged ('taxable cheap loan'). Interest payable during the tax year but paid after the end of the tax year is taken into account.

The following loans are normally not treated as taxable cheap loans for calculation of the interest benefits (but are taxable for the purposes of the charge on loans written off).

(a) A loan on normal commercial terms made in the ordinary course of the employer's money-lending business.

(b) A loan made by an individual in the ordinary course of the lender's domestic, family or personal arrangements.

1.7.2 Calculating the interest benefit

There are two alternative methods of calculating the taxable benefit. The simpler **'average' method** automatically applies unless the taxpayer or HMRC elect for the alternative **'strict' method**. **The taxpayer should make the election for the 'strict' method** if this results in a **lower taxable benefit,** as this will give a **lower charge to income tax**. **HMRC normally only make the election** where it appears that the **'average' method** is **being deliberately exploited.** In both methods, the benefit is the interest at the official rate minus the interest payable.

For the purposes of the F6 (UK) exam, the official rate of interest is assumed to be 3% throughout 2016/17.

The 'average' method averages the balances at the beginning and end of the tax year (or the dates on which the loan was made and/or repaid if it was not in existence throughout the tax year) and applies the official rate of interest to this average. If the loan was not in existence throughout the tax year only the number of complete tax months (from the 6th of the month) for which it existed are taken into account.

The 'strict' method is to compute interest at the official rate on the actual amount outstanding on a daily basis. However, for exam purposes, it is acceptable to work on a monthly basis.

Question — **Loan benefit**

Carole is employed by B plc at a salary of £50,000 a year. B plc made a taxable cheap loan of £40,000 to Carole in January 2016. At 6 April 2016 the whole of the loan was outstanding. Carole repaid £15,000 of the loan on 6 December 2016. The remaining balance of £25,000 was outstanding at 5 April 2017. Carole paid interest to B plc of £550 on the loan during 2016/17. What is Carole's taxable benefit under both the 'average' and the 'strict' methods for 2016/17?

Answer

Average method

	£
$3\% \times \frac{40,000+25,000}{2}$	975
Less interest paid	(550)
Benefit	425

Strict method

	£
£40,000 × $\frac{8}{12}$ (6 April – 5 December) × 3%	800
£25,000 × $\frac{4}{12}$ (6 December – 5 April) × 3%	250
	1,050
Less interest paid	(550)
Benefit	500

HMRC could elect for the 'strict' method, although this is unlikely given the difference between the methods is relatively small and it does not appear that the 'average' method is being deliberately exploited.

Note. You must always show the workings for the average method. If it appears likely that the taxpayer should or HMRC might elect for the 'strict' method you will need to show those workings as well.

1.7.3 The de minimis test

The interest benefit is not taxable if the total of all non-qualifying loans to the employee did not exceed £10,000 at any time in the tax year.

A qualifying loan is one on which all or part of any interest paid would qualify for tax relief (see further below).

When the £10,000 threshold is exceeded, a benefit arises on interest on the whole loan, not just on the excess of the loan over £10,000.

1.7.4 Qualifying loans

If the whole of the interest payable on a qualifying loan is eligible for tax relief as deductible interest (as seen earlier in this Study Text), then no taxable benefit arises. If the interest is only partly eligible for tax relief, then the employee is treated as receiving earnings because the actual rate of interest is below the official rate. He is also treated as paying interest equal to those earnings. This **deemed interest paid may qualify as a business expense or as deductible interest in addition to any interest actually paid**.

Question

Beneficial loans

Anna has an annual salary of £30,000, and two loans from her employer:

(a) A season ticket loan of £8,300 at no interest
(b) A loan, 90% of which was used to buy a partnership interest, of £54,000 at 0.5% interest

What is Anna's tax liability for 2016/17?

Answer

	£
Salary	30,000
Season ticket loan (non-qualifying): not over £10,000	0
Loan to buy partnership interest (qualifying): £54,000 × (3 – 0.5 = 2.5%)	1,350
Earnings/Total income	31,350
Less deductible interest deemed paid (£54,000 × 3% × 90%)	(1,458)
Net income	29,892
Less personal allowance	(11,000)
Taxable income	18,892
Income tax	
Tax liability £18,892 × 20%	3,778

1.8 Private use of other assets

FAST FORWARD

20% of the value of assets made available for private use is taxable.

When assets are made available for private use to employees or members of their family or household, the taxable benefit is the higher of 20% of the market value when first provided as a benefit to any employee and the rent paid by the employer. The 20% charge is time-apportioned when the asset is provided for only part of the year. The charge after any time apportionment is reduced by any contribution made by the employee.

There is an additional taxable benefit of any other amounts that the employer pays during the tax year relating to the provision of the asset such as running costs.

Bicycles provided for journeys to work, as well as being available for private use, are exempt from the private use benefit rules.

If an asset made available is subsequently acquired by the employee, **the taxable benefit on the acquisition is the greater of:**

- The **current market value minus the price paid by the employee**
- The **market value when first provided minus any amounts already taxed (ignoring contributions by the employee) minus the price paid by the employee**

This rule prevents tax free benefits arising on rapidly depreciating items through the employee purchasing them at their low second-hand value.

There is an exception to this rule for bicycles which have previously been provided as exempt benefits (see later in this chapter). The taxable benefit on acquisition is restricted to current market value, minus the price paid by the employee.

1.9 Example: assets made available for private use

A suit costing £400 is purchased by an employer for use by an employee on 6 April 2015. On 6 April 2016 the suit is purchased by the employee for £30, its market value then being £50.

The benefit in 2015/16 is £400 × 20% = £80.

The benefit in 2016/17 is £290, being the *greater* of:

		£
(a)	Market value at acquisition by employee	50
	Less price paid	(30)
		20
(b)	Original market value	400
	Less taxed in respect of use	(80)
		320
	Less price paid	(30)
		290

Question — Bicycles

Rupert is provided with a new bicycle by his employer on 6 April 2016. The bicycle is available for private use as well as commuting to work. It cost the employer £1,500 when new. On 6 October 2016 the employer transfers ownership of the bicycle to Rupert when it is worth £800. Rupert does not pay anything for the bicycle. What is the total taxable benefit on Rupert for 2016/17 in respect of the bicycle?

Answer

Use benefit	Exempt
Transfer benefit (use MV at acquisition by employee only)	
MV at transfer	£800

1.10 Scholarships

If scholarships are given to members of an employee's family, the **employee is taxable on the cost** unless the scholarship fund's or scheme's payments by reason of people's employments are not more than 25% of its total payments.

1.11 Childcare

FAST FORWARD

Workplace childcare is an exempt benefit. Employer-supported childcare and childcare vouchers are exempt up to £55 per week. Maximum tax relief is limited to £11 per week (the equivalent of £55 × 20%).

The cost of running a **workplace nursery or playscheme is an exempt benefit (without limit)**.

Otherwise a certain amount of childcare is tax free if the employer contracts with an approved childcarer or provides childcare vouchers to pay an approved childcarer. The childcare must usually be available to all employees and the childcare must either be registered or approved home-childcare.

A **£55 per week limit applies to basic rate employees** who use employer-supported childcare schemes or receive childcare vouchers. The amount of tax relief for a basic rate taxpayer is therefore £55 × 20% = £11 per week.

Higher rate and additional rate employees have their tax relief restricted so that it is the equivalent of that received by a basic rate taxpayer. Higher and additional rate employees can therefore receive vouchers tax-free up to £28 per week and £25 per week respectively, each giving £11 of tax relief which is the same amount a basic rate taxpayer would receive.

Exam focus point

Whether an employee is considered basic rate, higher rate or additional rate for these purposes, is determined by the level of his earnings only (and not other income). However, the examination team has stated that in an exam question involving childcare, it will be quite clear at what rate a taxpayer is paying tax.

Question

Archie is employed by M plc and is paid a salary of £80,000 in 2016/17. He starts receiving childcare vouchers from M plc worth £50 per week for his daughter in June 2016 and receives them for 26 weeks during 2016/17. What is Archie's employment income for 2016/17?

Answer

	£
Salary (higher rate employee)	80,000
Childcare vouchers £(50 – 28) × 26 weeks	572
Employment income 2016/17	80,572

Exam focus point

In early 2017, a new tax free childcare scheme for working families will be introduced. This scheme will eventually replace the existing tax relief on employer-supported childcare. However, since the existing arrangements will continue to be available until April 2018, the new tax free child scheme is **not examinable** in F6(UK) for the exams in June 2017, September 2017, December 2017 and March 2018.

1.12 Other benefits

FAST FORWARD

There is a residual charge for other benefits, usually equal to the cost to the employer of the benefits.

We have seen above how certain specific benefits are taxed. **There is a sweeping up charge for all other benefits. Under this rule the taxable value of a benefit is the cost of the benefit less any part of that cost made good by the employee to the persons providing the benefit.**

The residual charge applies to any benefit provided for an employee or a member of his family or household, by reason of the employment. There is an exception where the employer is an individual and the provision of the benefit is made in the normal course of the employer's domestic, family or personal relationships.

1.13 Example: other benefits

A private school offers free places to the children of its staff. The marginal cost to the school of providing the place is £2,000 pa, although the fees charged to other pupils is £5,000 pa.

The taxable value of the benefit to the staff is the actual cost of £2,000 per pupil, not the full £5,000 charged to other pupils.

2 Exempt benefits

FAST FORWARD

There are a number of exempt benefits including removal expenses, sporting facilities, and workplace parking.

Various benefits are exempt from tax. These include:

(a) **Reimbursed expenses** (see earlier in this chapter)

(b) **Entertainment provided to employees by genuine third parties** (eg seats at sporting/cultural events), even if it is provided by giving the employee a voucher

(c) **Gifts of goods** (or vouchers exchangeable for goods) from third parties (ie not provided by the employer or a person connected to the employer) if the total cost (incl. VAT) of all gifts by the same donor to the same employee in the tax year is £250 or less. If the £250 limit is exceeded, the full amount is taxable, not just the excess.

(d) **Non-cash awards for long service** if the period of service was at least 20 years, no similar award was made to the employee in the past ten years and the cost is not more than £50 per year of service

(e) **Awards under staff suggestion schemes** if:

(i) There is a formal scheme, open to all employees on equal terms.

(ii) The suggestion is outside the scope of the employee's normal duties.

(iii) Either the award is not more than £25, or the award is only made after a decision is taken to implement the suggestion.

(iv) Awards over £25 reflect the financial importance of the suggestion to the business, and either do not exceed 50% of the expected net financial benefit during the first year of implementation or do not exceed 10% of the expected net financial benefit over a period of up to five years.

(v) Awards of over £25 are shared on a reasonable basis between two or more employees putting forward the same suggestion.

If an award exceeds £5,000, the excess is always taxable.

(f) **The first £8,000 of removal expenses** if:

(i) The employee does not already live within a reasonable daily travelling distance of his new place of employment, but will do so after moving.

(ii) The expenses are incurred or the benefits provided by the end of the tax year following the tax year of the start of employment at the new location.

(g) **Some childcare** (see earlier in this Chapter)

(h) **Sporting or recreational facilities available to employees generally and not to the general public**, unless they are provided on domestic premises, or they consist of an interest in or the use of any mechanically propelled vehicle or any overnight accommodation. Vouchers only exchangeable for such facilities are also exempt, but membership fees for sports clubs are taxable.

(i) **Assets or services used in performing the duties of employment** provided any private use of the item concerned is insignificant. This exempts, for example, the benefit arising on the private use of employer-provided tools.

(j) **Welfare counselling** and similar minor benefits if the benefit concerned is available to employees generally

(k) **Bicycles or cycling safety equipment** provided to enable employees to get to and from work or to travel between one workplace and another. The equipment must be available to the employer's employees generally. Also, it must be used mainly for the aforementioned journeys.

(l) **Workplace parking**

(m) **Up to £15,480 a year paid to an employee who is on a full-time course lasting at least a year,** with average full-time attendance of at least 20 weeks a year. If the £15,480 limit is exceeded, the whole amount is taxable.

(n) **Work related training** and related costs. This includes the costs of training material and assets either made during training or incorporated into something so made.

(o) **Air miles** or car fuel coupons obtained as a result of business expenditure but used for private purposes

(p) **The cost of work buses and minibuses or subsidies to public bus services**

A works bus must have a seating capacity of 12 or more and a works minibus a seating capacity of nine or more but not more than 12 and be available generally to employees of the employer concerned. The bus or minibus must mainly be used by employees for journeys to and from work and for journeys between workplaces.

(q) **Transport/overnight costs where public transport is disrupted by industrial action,** late night taxis and travel costs incurred where car sharing arrangements unavoidably breakdown

(r) The private use of one **mobile phone, which can be a smartphone**. Top up vouchers for exempt mobile phones are also tax free. If more than one mobile phone is provided to an employee for private use only the second or subsequent phone is a taxable benefit valued using the rules for assets made available to employees.

(s) **Employer provided uniforms** which employees must wear as part of their duties

(t) The cost of **staff parties** which are open to staff generally provided that the **cost per head per year (including VAT) is £150 or less**. The £150 limit may be split between several parties.

(u) **Private medical insurance premiums paid to cover treatment when the employee is outside the UK in the performance of his duties.** Other medical insurance premiums are taxable as is the cost of medical diagnosis and treatment except for routine check ups. Eye tests and glasses for employees using VDUs are exempt.

(v) **Cheap loans that do not exceed £10,000** at any time in the tax year (see above)

(w) **Job related accommodation** (see above)

(x) **Employer contributions towards additional household costs incurred by an employee who works wholly or partly at home.** Payments up to £4 a week (£18 per month for monthly paid employees) may be made without supporting evidence (see earlier in this Study Text).

(y) **Personal incidental expenses** (see earlier in this Study Text)

(z) **Recommended medical treatment** costing up to £500 per employee per tax year paid for by an employer. The treatment must be recommended in writing by a health professional (eg doctor, nurse) and the purpose of the treatment must be to assist the employee to return to work after a period of injury or ill-health lasting at least 28 days. If the payments exceed £500 in a tax year, they are wholly taxable.

(aa) **Trivial benefits costing up to £50 per employee per tax year** provided these are not in the form of cash or a cash voucher. Examples of exempt trivial benefits include providing an employee with a Christmas or birthday present and sending flowers to an employee on the birth of a baby.

Where a voucher is provided for a benefit which is exempt from income tax the provision of the voucher itself is also exempt.

3 The PAYE system

FAST FORWARD

Most tax in respect of employment income is deducted under the PAYE system. The objective of the PAYE system is to collect the correct amount of tax over the year. An employee's PAYE code is designed to ensure that allowances etc are given evenly over the year.

3.1 Introduction

3.1.1 Cash payments

The objective of the PAYE system is to deduct the correct amount of income tax and national insurance contributions from employees over the year. Its scope is very wide. It applies to most cash payments, other than reimbursed business expenses, and to certain non cash payments.

In addition to wages and salaries, PAYE applies to round sum expense allowances and payments instead of benefits. It also applies to any readily convertible asset.

A readily convertible asset is any asset which can effectively be exchanged for cash. The amount subject to PAYE is the amount that would be taxed as employment income. This is usually the cost to the employer of providing the asset.

Tips paid direct to an employee are normally outside the PAYE system (although still assessable as employment income).

It is the employer's duty to deduct income tax and national insurance contributions from the pay of his employees, whether or not he has been directed to do so by HMRC. **If he fails to do this he** (or sometimes the employee) **must pay over the tax which he should have deducted and the employer may be subject to penalties.**

3.1.2 Benefits

PAYE must be applied to a taxable non-cash voucher if at the time it is provided:

(a) The voucher is capable of being exchanged for readily convertible assets; or
(b) The voucher can itself be sold, realised or traded.

PAYE must normally be operated on cash vouchers and on each occasion when a director/employee uses a credit-token (eg a credit card) to obtain money or goods which are readily convertible assets. However, a cash voucher or credit token which is used to pay expenses is not subject to PAYE.

Other taxable benefits may be included within the payroll if the employer chooses to do so. Otherwise they will be reported on Form P11D (see later in this chapter) and the employee's PAYE code will be adjusted to collect the income tax due on these benefits.

3.2 How PAYE works

Employers must report PAYE information to HMRC under the Real Time Information (RTI) system.

Under RTI, **an employer is required to submit information to HMRC electronically**. This can be done by:

(a) Using commercial payroll software

(b) Using HMRC's Basic PAYE Tools software (designed for use by an employer who has up to nine employees)

(c) Using a payroll provider (such as an accountant or payroll bureau) to do the reporting on behalf of the employer

The employer reports payroll information electronically to HMRC, on or before any day when the employer pays someone (ie in 'real time'). This report will normally be carried out by the payroll software (or the payroll provider) at the same time that the payments are calculated and is called **a Full Payment Submission (FPS)**. The FPS includes details of:

(a) The amounts paid to employees
(b) Deductions made under PAYE such as income tax and national insurance contributions
(c) Details of employees who have started employment or left employment since the last FPS

The software works out the amount of PAYE tax to deduct on any particular pay day by using the employees' code numbers (see below). Tax is normally worked out on a cumulative basis. This means that with each payment of earnings the running total of tax paid is compared with tax due on total earnings to that date. The difference between the tax due and the tax paid is the tax to be deducted on that particular payday.

National insurance contributions are also calculated by the software in relation to the earnings period (see later in this Study Text).

3.3 Payment under the PAYE system

Under PAYE, income tax and national insurance is normally paid over to HMRC monthly, 17 days after the end of the tax month (if paid electronically) or 14 days after the end of the tax month (if paid by cheque). Large employers (with 250 or more employees) must make electronic payments. **A tax month**

runs from 6th of one calendar month to the 5th of the following calendar month. For example, for the tax month from 6 June 2016 to 5 July 2016, payment must be made by 22 July 2016 (electronically) or 19 July 2016 (cheque).

If an employer's average monthly payments under the PAYE system are less than £1,500, the employer may choose to pay quarterly, within 17 or 14 days (depending on the method of payment) **of the end of each tax quarter**. Tax quarters end on 5 July, 5 October, 5 January and 5 April. Payments can continue to be made quarterly during a tax year even if the monthly average reaches or exceeds £1,500, but a new estimate must be made and a new decision taken to pay quarterly at the start of each tax year.

3.4 PAYE codes

An employee is normally entitled to various allowances. Under the PAYE system an amount reflecting the effect of a proportion of these allowances is set against his pay each pay day. To determine the amount to set against his pay the allowances are expressed in the form of a code.

An employee's code may be any one of the following:

L Tax code for people entitled to the full personal allowance
M Tax code for people who are receiving £1,100 of personal allowance from a spouse or civil partner
N Tax code for people who are giving £1,100 of personal allowance to a spouse or civil partner

The codes BR, DO and OT are generally used where there is a second source of income and all allowances have been used in a tax code which is applied to the main source of income. The BR code means that basic rate tax will be deducted without any allowances.

Generally, a tax code number is arrived at by deleting the last digit in the sum representing the employee's tax free allowances. Every individual is entitled to a personal tax free allowance of £11,000. The code number for an individual who is entitled to this but no other allowance is 1100L.

The code number may also reflect other items. For example, **it will be restricted to reflect benefits, small amounts of untaxed income** and **unpaid tax on income from earlier years**. If an amount of tax is in point, it is necessary to gross up the tax in the code using the taxpayer's estimated marginal rate of income tax.

Question — PAYE codes

Adrian is entitled to the full personal allowance (suffix letter L) and earns £15,000 each tax year. He has benefits of £1,160 and his unpaid tax for 2014/15 was £58. Adrian is entitled to a tax free personal allowance of £11,000 in 2016/17. Adrian is a basic rate taxpayer. What is Adrian's PAYE code for 2016/17?

Answer

	£
Personal allowance	11,000
Benefits	(1,160)
Unpaid tax £58 × 100/20	(290)
Available allowances	9,550

Adrian's PAYE code is 955L.

Codes are determined and amended by HMRC. They are normally notified to the employer on a code list. The employer must act on the code until amended instructions are received from HMRC, even if the employee has appealed against the code.

When the payroll is run, an employee is generally given 1/52nd or 1/12th of his tax free allowances against each week's/month's pay. However because of the cumulative nature of PAYE, if an employee is first paid in, say, September, that month he will receive six months' allowances against his gross pay. In cases where the employee's previous PAYE history is not known, this could lead to under-deduction of tax. To avoid this, codes for the employees concerned have to be operated on a 'week 1/month1' basis, so that only 1/52nd or 1/12th of the employee's allowances are available each week/month.

3.5 PAYE forms

FAST FORWARD

Employers must complete forms P60, P11D and P45 as appropriate. Form P60 is a year end return. A P45 is needed when an employee leaves. Form P11D records details of benefits.

At the end of each tax year, the employer must provide each employee with a form P60. This shows total taxable earnings for the year, tax deducted, code number, NI number and the employer's name and address. **The P60 must be provided by 31 May following the year of assessment.**

Following the end of each tax year, the employer must submit to HMRC by 6 July:

(a) **Forms P11D** (benefits which are not payrolled)
(b) **Forms P11D(b)** (return of Class 1A NICs (see later in this Study Text))

A copy of the form P11D must also be provided to the employee by 6 July. The details shown on the P11D include the full cash equivalent of all taxable benefits (other than those which are payrolled), so that the employee may enter the details on his self-assessment tax return.

When an employee leaves, a form P45 (particulars of Employee Leaving) must be prepared. This form shows the employee's code and details of his income and tax paid to date and is handed to the employee. One of the parts is the employee's personal copy. If the employee takes up a new employment, he must hand another part of the form P45 to the new employer. The details on the form are used by the new employer to calculate income tax due under PAYE when the payroll is next run.

3.6 Interest and penalties

Daily interest is charged on late payments of income tax and NICs under PAYE by taking the number of days by which a payment is late and applying the relevant late payment interest rate. HMRC make the charge after the end of the tax year.

Late payment penalties may be charged on PAYE amounts that are not paid in full and on time. Employers are not charged a penalty for the first late PAYE payment in a tax year, unless that payment is over six months late. The amounts of the penalties on subsequent late payments in the tax year depend on how much is late each time and the number of times payments are late in a tax year. The maximum penalty is 4% of the amount that is late in the relevant tax month and applies to the 11th (or more) late payment that tax year. **Where the tax remains unpaid at six months, the further penalty is 5% of tax unpaid**, with a further 5% if tax remains unpaid at 12 months, even if there is only one late payment in the year.

There are also penalties for making late returns under RTI which are imposed on a monthly basis. The first late submission of the tax year is ignored. Further late submissions will attract penalties based on the **number of employees** as follows:

Number of employees	Monthly penalty
1 to 9	£100
10 to 49	£200
50 to 249	£300
250 or more	£400

If the return is **more than three months late**, there is an **additional penalty** due of 5% of the tax and NIC due.

Exam focus point

> HMRC allows a return to be up to three days late before imposing a penalty. However, the examination team has specifically stated this aspect is **not examinable** in F6(UK). There are also various other relaxations to the penalty rules which may apply but you should assume that the rules set out in above apply when answering a F6(UK) examination question.

Penalties for inaccurate returns are subject to the common penalty regime for errors (see later in this Study Text).

3.7 PAYE settlement agreements

PAYE settlement agreements (PSAs) are arrangements under which employers can make single payments to settle their employees' income tax liabilities on expense payments and benefits which are minor, irregular or where it would be impractical to operate PAYE.

Chapter Roundup

- Employees are taxed on benefits under the benefits code.
- The benefit in respect of accommodation is its annual value. There is an additional benefit if the property cost over £75,000.
- Employees who have a company car are taxed on a % of the car's list price which depends on the level of the car's CO_2 emissions. The same % multiplied by £22,200 determines the benefit where private fuel is also provided.
- Cheap loans are charged to tax on the difference between the official rate of interest and any interest paid by the employee.
- 20% of the value of assets made available for private use is taxable.
- Workplace childcare is an exempt benefit. Employer-supported childcare and childcare vouchers are exempt up to £55 per week. Maximum tax relief is limited to £11 per week (the equivalent of £55 × 20%).
- There is a residual charge for other benefits, usually equal to the cost to the employer of the benefits.
- There are a number of exempt benefits including removal expenses, sporting facilities, and workplace parking.
- Most tax in respect of employment income is deducted under the PAYE system. The objective of the PAYE system is to collect the correct amount of tax over the year. An employee's PAYE code is designed to ensure that allowances etc are given evenly over the year.
- Employers must complete forms P60, P11D and P45 as appropriate. Form P60 is a year end return. A P45 is needed when an employee leaves. Form P11D records details of benefits.

Quick Quiz

1 What accommodation does not give rise to a taxable benefit?

2 Mike is provided with a petrol-engined car by his employer throughout 2016/17. The car has a list price of £15,000 (although the employer actually paid £13,500 for it) and has CO_2 emissions of 105g/km. Mike's taxable car benefit is:

A £2,430
B £2,700
C £4,050
D £4,500

3 When may an employee who is provided with fuel by his employer avoid a fuel benefit?

4 To what extent are qualifying removal expenses paid for by an employer taxable?

5 Give an example of a PAYE code.

Answers to Quick Quiz

1 Job related accommodation

2 B. Amount by which CO_2 emissions exceed the baseline is (105 – 95) = 10 ÷ 5 = 2 + 16%
= 18% × £15,000
= £2,700

3 There is no fuel benefit if:

(a) All the fuel provided was made available only for business travel, or
(b) The full cost of any fuel provided for private use was completely reimbursed by the employee.

4 The first £8,000 of qualifying removal expenses are exempt. Any excess is taxable.

5 1100L.

Now try the questions below from the Practice Question Bank

Number	Type	Marks	Time
Q20	Section A	2	4 mins
Q21	Section A	2	4 mins
Q22	Section A	2	4 mins
Q23	Section B	2	4 mins
Q24	Section B	2	4 mins
Q25	Section B	2	4 mins
Q26	Section B	2	4 mins
Q27	Section B	2	4 mins
Q28	Section C	10	20 mins

Pensions

5

Topic list	Syllabus reference
1 Types of pension scheme and membership	B7(a)
2 Contributing to a pension scheme	B7(a)
3 Receiving benefits from pension arrangements	B7(a)

Introduction

In the previous two chapters we have discussed the taxation of employment income. Most employers are now required to make pension contributions for most of their employees, often using an occupational pension scheme to which employees also contribute. Employees may choose instead (by opting out), or in addition, to take out a personal pension scheme run by a financial institution such as a bank or building society.

Self-employed or non-working individuals can only make provision for a pension using a personal pension scheme.

Whichever type of scheme is chosen the amount of tax relief available is the same. However, the method for giving the relief can be different: contributions to occupational schemes are usually deducted from gross pay before PAYE is calculated whilst contributions to personal pensions are paid net of basic rate tax and further tax relief is given through the personal tax computation. We cover both methods of giving tax relief in detail in this chapter.

Study guide

		Intellectual level
B7	**The use of exemptions and reliefs in deferring and minimising income tax liabilities**	
(a)	Explain and compute the relief given for contributions to personal pension schemes and to occupational pension schemes.	2

Exam guide

Pension contributions can be paid by all individuals and you may come across them as part of an income tax question in Section C. In Section C you may also be required to discuss the types of pension schemes available and the limits on the tax relief due, or you may have to deal with them in an income tax computation. Pensions may be tested in a 15 mark question or a 10 mark question. Section A or B questions might test a specific aspect of pensions such as the amount of the annual allowance.

You must be sure that you know how to deal with the two ways of giving relief – contributions to occupational schemes are deducted from earnings whilst contributions to personal pensions are paid net of basic rate tax and further tax relief is given by increasing the basic rate and higher rate limits.

1 Types of pension scheme and membership

FAST FORWARD

An employee may be a member of his employer's occupational pension scheme. Any individual whether a member of an occupational pension scheme or not, can take out a 'personal pension' plan with a financial institution such as an insurance company, bank or building society.

1.1 Introduction

An individual is encouraged by the Government to make financial provision to cover his needs when he reaches a certain age. There are state pension arrangements which provide some financial support, but the Government are keen for individuals to make their own pension provision to supplement their state pensions.

Automatic enrolment is being introduced so that employers must automatically enrol most employees into a workplace pension scheme (although employees can then opt out of the scheme). Under automatic enrolment, **there are minimum contributions to the workplace pension scheme required by law** (up to 30 September 2017 usually equal to 2% of earnings of which a minimum amount equal to 1% of earnings must be contributed by the employer).

Alternatively, individuals (employees, self-employed and those who are not working) may make their own pension provision through a personal pension provider such as an insurance company.

Tax relief is given for both employer pension provision and personal pension provision. This includes both relief for contributions paid into pension schemes during an individual's working life and an exemption from tax on income and gains arising in the pension fund itself.

1.2 Pension arrangements

An individual may make pension provision in a number of ways.

1.2.1 Occupational pension scheme

Key term

Employers may set up an **occupational pension scheme**. The employer may use the services of an insurance company (an insured scheme) or may set up a totally self administered pension fund.

There are two kinds of occupational pension scheme – earnings-related (**defined benefits arrangements**) and investment-related (**money purchase arrangements**). In a **defined benefits arrangements** the pension is generally based on employees' earnings either at retirement (a **final salary** scheme) or throughout their employment (a **career average** scheme) and linked to the number of years they have worked for the employer.

A **money purchase pension** – also known as a **defined contribution scheme** – does not provide any guarantee regarding the level of pension which will be available. The individual invests in the pension scheme and the amount invested is used to build up a pension.

1.2.2 Personal pensions

Key term

Personal pensions are money purchase schemes, which are provided by banks, insurance companies and other financial institutions.

Stakeholder pensions are a particular type of personal pension scheme. They must satisfy certain rules, such as a maximum level of charges, ease of transfer and so on.

Any individual (whether employed or not) may join a personal pension scheme.

1.2.3 More than one pension arrangement

An individual may make a number of different pension arrangements depending on his circumstances. For example, he may be a member of an occupational pension scheme and also make pension arrangements independently with a financial provider. If the individual has more than one pension arrangement, the rules we will be looking at in detail later apply to all the pension arrangements he makes. For example, **there is a limit on the amount of contributions that the individual can make in a tax year. This limit applies to all the pension arrangements that he makes, not each of them.**

The rules below apply to registered pension schemes, ie those registered with HMRC.

2 Contributing to a pension scheme

FAST FORWARD

Anyone can contribute to a personal pension scheme, even if they are not earning, subject to the contributions threshold of £3,600 (gross).

2.1 Contributions by a scheme member

Any individual **under the age of 75 can make tax relievable pension contributions** in a tax year.

The maximum amount of contributions attracting tax relief made by an individual in a tax year is the higher of:

(a) **The individual's relevant UK earnings chargeable to income tax in the year**
(b) **The basic amount (set at £3,600 for 2016/17)**

These figures are gross contributions (see further below) and apply whether the individual pays into an occupational scheme, a personal pension scheme or both.

Relevant UK earnings are broadly employment income, trading income and income from furnished holiday lettings (see later in this Study Text).

If the individual does not have any UK earnings in a tax year, the maximum pension contribution he can obtain tax relief on is £3,600.

Where an individual contributes to more than one pension scheme, the aggregate of his contributions will be used to give the total amount of tax relief.

2.2 Methods of giving tax relief

FAST FORWARD

Contributions to personal pension plans are paid net of basic rate tax. Higher/additional rate relief is given through the personal tax computation. Contributions to occupational pension schemes are usually paid under the net pay scheme.

2.2.1 Pension tax relief given at source

This method will be used where an individual makes a contribution to a pension scheme run by a personal pension provider such as an insurance company.

Relief is given at source by the contributions being deemed to be made net of basic rate tax. This applies whether the individual is an employee, self-employed or not employed at all and whether or not he has taxable income. HMRC then pay an amount of basic rate tax to the pension provider.

Further tax relief is given if the individual is a higher rate or additional rate taxpayer. The relief is given by increasing the basic rate limit and the higher rate limit for the year by the gross amount of contributions for which the taxpayer is entitled to relief. You will recognise this method as the same way in which relief is given for gift aid donations.

Exam focus point

Make sure your workings show clearly how you have increased the basic rate and higher rate limits. Note the difference between this method and that used for net pay arrangements (see below).

Question — **Pension tax relief given at source**

Joe has earnings of £60,000 in 2016/17. He pays a personal pension contribution of £7,200 (net). He has no other taxable income.
Show Joe's tax liability for 2016/17.

Answer

	Non-savings Income
	£
Earnings/Net income	60,000
Less PA	(11,000)
Taxable income	49,000

Tax

	£
£41,000 (W) × 20%	8,200
£8,000 × 40%	3,200
49,000	11,400

Basic rate limit £32,000 + (£7,200 × 100/80) = £41,000

Remember that **gross personal pension contributions** are also used to compute **adjusted net income** and that **the restriction on the personal allowance** is calculated in relation to adjusted net income.

2.2.2 Net pay arrangements

An occupational scheme will normally operate net pay arrangements.

In this case, the employer will deduct gross pension contributions from the individual's earnings before operating PAYE. The individual therefore obtains tax relief at his marginal rate of tax automatically.

Question — **Net pay arrangements**

Maxine has taxable earnings of £60,000 in 2016/17. Her employer deducts a pension contribution of £9,000 from these earnings before operating PAYE. She has no other taxable income.

Show Maxine's tax liability for 2016/17.

Answer

	Non-savings Income
	£
Earnings/Total income	60,000
Less pension contribution	(9,000)
Net income	51,000
Less PA	(11,000)
Taxable income	40,000

Tax

	£
£32,000 × 20%	6,400
£8,000 × 40%	3,200
40,000	9,600

This is the same result as Joe in the previous example. Joe had received basic rate tax relief of £(9,000 – 7,200) = £1,800 at source, so his overall tax position was £(11,400 – 1,800) = £9,600.

2.3 Contributions not attracting tax relief

An individual can also make contributions to his pension arrangements which do not attract tax relief, for example out of capital. The member must notify the scheme administrator if he makes contributions in excess of the higher of his UK relevant earnings and the basic amount.

Such contributions do not count towards the annual allowance limit (discussed below) but will affect the value of the pension fund for the lifetime allowance.

2.4 Employer pension contributions

Where the active scheme member is an employee, their **employer will often make contributions to their pension scheme** and under automatic enrolment are required by law to make at least minimum contributions to a workplace pension scheme. Employer pension contributions to any type of pension scheme are **exempt benefits** for the employee.

There is **no limit** on the amount of the contributions that may be made by an employer but **they always count towards the annual allowance** and will also affect the value of the pension fund for the lifetime allowance (see further below).

All contributions made by an employer are made gross and the employer will usually obtain tax relief for the contribution by deducting it as an expense in calculating trading profits for the period of account in which the payment is made.

2.5 Annual allowance

FAST FORWARD

There is an overriding limit on the amount that can be paid into an individual's pension scheme for each tax year. This is called the annual allowance. The annual allowance is reduced if an individual has adjusted income in excess of £150,000. Unused annual allowance can be carried forward for up to three years.

2.5.1 Introduction

The annual allowance effectively restricts the amount of tax relievable contributions that can be paid into an individual's pension scheme each year. The annual allowance for 2014/15, 2015/16 and 2016/17 is £40,000. The amount of the annual allowance for 2013/14 was £50,000.

Exam focus point

These amounts will be shown in the tax rates and allowances in the exam. There were some complex transitional rules which meant that for 2015/16 the annual allowance could have been more than £40,000 for some individuals depending on when contributions were made in the year. These transitional rules are **not examinable** in F6(UK) and you should assume that in any exam question involving pensions the timing of the contributions means that only an annual allowance of £40,000 was available for 2015/16. This assumption also applies in relation to carry forward of unused annual allowance to future years.

2.5.2 Reduced annual allowance

From the tax year 2016/17, **individuals who have adjusted income in excess of £150,000 have a reduced annual allowance.**

The annual allowance is reduced by £1 for every £2 that the individual's adjusted income exceeds £150,000, subject to a **minimum annual allowance of £10,000**. The minimum annual allowance will apply where the individual has adjusted income of £210,000 or more since £(40,000 – [210,000 – 150,000]/2) = £10,000.

Adjusted income for the self-employed is the same as net income (ie total income less loss relief against general income and deductible interest). This is because the individual will only have made pension contributions with tax relief by deduction at source (see 2.2.1) which does not affect the computation of net income.

Adjusted income for employees is net income plus pension contributions to occupational pension schemes under net pay arrangements (see Section 2.2.2) (as these will have been deducted in computing net income) **plus employer contributions to occupational pension schemes and/or personal pension schemes.** If the employee has made personal pension contributions with tax relief by deduction at source, these are not relevant in computing adjusted income.

Exam focus point

There is a threshold level of income below which tapering does not apply but this is **not examinable** in F6(UK).

Question — **Reduced annual allowance**

In the tax year 2016/17, Bella was a member of a partnership and had a partnership trading profit of £168,000. During the tax year, Bella paid deductible interest of £5,000 on a loan to invest in the partnership She also had property business income of £13,500 for 2016/17. What is Bella's reduced annual allowance for 2016/17?

Answer

First work out Bella's adjusted income. This will be equal to her net income since she is self-employed and so has made pension contributions with tax relief by deduction at source.

	Non-savings income
	£
Trading income from partnership	168,000
Property business income	13,500
Total income	181,500
Less interest paid	(5,000)
Net income = adjusted income	176,500

Then compute the reduced annual allowance:

	£
Adjusted income	176,500
Less threshold	(150,000)
Excess	26,500
Annual allowance	40,000
Less half excess £26,500 × ½	(13,250)
Reduced annual allowance	26,750

2.5.3 Carry forward of unused annual allowance

Where **an individual is a member of a registered pension scheme** but **does not make contributions of at least the annual allowance in a tax year**, the individual can **carry forward the unused amount of the annual allowance for up to three years**. In any year for which the individual is not a member of a pension scheme, the annual allowance does not apply and so there can be no carry forward.

The annual allowance in the current tax year is treated as being used first, then any unused annual allowance is brought forward from earlier years, using the earliest tax year first. Where the annual allowance has been reduced as described in Section 2.5.2, the reduced amount will be carried forward to later years.

Question

Carry forward of annual allowance

Ted is a sole trader. His gross contributions to his personal pension scheme have been as follows:

2013/14	£26,000
2014/15	£36,000
2015/16	£25,000

In 2016/17 Ted will have taxable trading profits of about £100,000 and wishes to make a large pension contribution in January 2017. He has no other sources of income.

(a) What is the maximum gross tax relievable pension contribution Ted can make in January 2017, taking into account any brought forward annual allowance?

(b) If Ted makes a gross personal pension contribution of £43,000 in January 2017, what are the unused annual allowances he can carry forward to 2017/18?

Answer

(a)

	£
Annual allowance 2016/17	40,000
Annual allowance unused in 2013/14 £(50,000 – 26,000)	24,000
Annual allowance unused in 2014/15 £(40,000 – 36,000)	4,000
Annual allowance unused in 2015/16 £(40,000 – 25,000)	15,000
Maximum gross pension contribution in 2016/17	83,000

(b)

	£
Annual allowance 2016/17 used in 2016/17	40,000
Annual allowance unused in 2013/14 used in 2016/17	3,000
Contribution in 2016/17	43,000

The remaining £(24,000 – 3,000) = £21,000 of the 2013/14 annual allowance cannot be carried forward to 2017/18 since this is more than three years after 2013/14. The unused annual allowances are therefore £4,000 from 2014/15 and £15,000 from 2015/16 and these are carried forward to 2017/18.

2.5.4 Contributions in excess of annual allowance

FAST FORWARD

An annual allowance charge arises if tax-relievable contributions exceed the available annual allowance.

If tax-relievable pension contributions exceed the annual allowance, there is a charge to income tax based on the individual's taxable income. This will occur if the taxpayer has relevant earnings in excess of the available annual allowance and makes a contribution in excess of the available annual allowance (including any brought forward annual allowance). **The taxpayer is primarily liable for the tax on the excess contribution.**

The annual allowance charge is calculated by taxing the excess contribution as an extra amount of income received by the taxpayer. The calculation therefore claws back the tax relief given on the pension contribution.

Question

Annual allowance charge

Jaida had employment income of £240,000 in 2016/17. She made a gross personal pension contribution of £70,000 in December 2016. She does not have any unused annual allowance brought forward. What is Jaida's income tax liability for 2016/17?

Answer

	Non-savings Income £
Taxable income (no personal allowance available)	240,000

Tax

	£
£102,000 (W1) × 20%	20,400
£118,000 × 40%	47,200
£220,000 (W2)	
£20,000 × 45%	9,000
£240,000	
£60,000 (W3) × 45%	27,000
Tax liability	103,600

Workings

1 Basic rate limit £32,000 + £70,000 = £102,000

2 Higher rate limit £150,000 + £70,000 = £220,000

3 Excess pension contribution £(70,000 – 10,000 minimum as adjusted income exceeds £210,000) = £60,000

3 Receiving benefits from pension arrangements

PER alert

One of the competencies you require to fulfil Performance Objective 17 Tax planning and advice of the PER is to assess the tax implications of proposed activities or plans of an individual or entity with reference to relevant and up to date legislation. You can apply the knowledge you obtain from this section of the Study Text to help to demonstrate this competence.

3.1 Pension benefits

FAST FORWARD

An individual can start to receive pension benefits from the age of 55. Under flexi-access drawdown, a tax-free lump sum of 25% of the pension fund can be taken and the remainder reinvested to give taxable pension income as required.

After reaching the minimum pension age of 55, an individual can start to receive pension benefits with complete flexibility to access their personal pensions.

There are a number of common ways in which an individual can receive benefits from personal pension schemes. One is **flexi-access drawdown** where the individual usually takes a **tax-free lump sum of 25%** of the pension fund. The **rest of the pension fund** is then reinvested to provide **taxable pension income** as required by the individual. Previously individuals usually had to buy an annuity with the balance (which is still an option).

Exam focus point

There is an anti-avoidance annual allowance limit which applies when an individual starts to receive pension benefits flexibly but is also entitled to make further contributions to the pension fund. This annual allowance limit is **not examinable** in F6(UK).

3.2 The lifetime allowance

FAST FORWARD

An individual is not allowed to build up an indefinitely large pension fund. There is a maximum value for a pension fund called the lifetime allowance.

The amount of the **lifetime allowance for 2016/17 is £1,000,000**. This limit applies to the total funds built up in an individual's pension funds.

If the pension fund exceeds the lifetime allowance, this will give rise to an income tax charge on the excess value of the fund when the individual receives pension benefits from the fund. The rate of the charge is 55% if the excess value is taken as a lump sum, or 25% if the funds are used to provide a pension income.

Chapter Roundup

- An employee may be a member of his employer's occupational pension scheme. Any individual whether a member of an occupational pension scheme or not, can take out a 'personal pension' plan with a financial institution such as an insurance company, bank or building society.
- Anyone can contribute to a personal pension scheme, even if they are not earning, subject to the contributions threshold of £3,600 (gross).
- Contributions to personal pension plans are paid net of basic rate tax. Higher/additional rate relief is given through the personal tax computation. Contributions to occupational pension schemes are usually paid under the net pay scheme.
- There is an overriding limit on the amount that can be paid into an individual's pension scheme for each tax year. This is called the annual allowance. The annual allowance is reduced if an individual has adjusted income in excess of £150,000. Unused annual allowance can be carried forward for up to three years.
- An annual allowance charge arises if tax-relievable contributions exceed the available annual allowance.
- An individual can start to receive pension benefits from the age of 55. Under flexi-access drawdown, a tax-free lump sum of 25% of the pension fund can be taken and the remainder reinvested to give taxable pension income as required.
- An individual is not allowed to build up an indefinitely large pension fund. There is a maximum value for a pension fund called the lifetime allowance.

Quick Quiz

1 Martha has UK earnings of £3,000 in 2016/17. What is the maximum actual amount of pension contribution she can pay in 2016/17 to a personal pension?

A £2,400
B £2,880
C £3,000
D £3,600

2 Fern joined a registered pension scheme in 2014/15 and made a gross contribution of £14,000. She had not been a member of registered pension scheme before this time. She did not make any contribution in 2015/16. Fern has relevant earnings of £125,000 in 2016/17 and no other sources of income. What is the maximum gross pension contribution Fern can make in 2016/17 (contribution to be made in February 2017) without incurring an annual allowance charge, taking into account any brought forward annual allowance?

3 Jim became a member of a pension scheme for the first time in 2016/17. His only income in 2016/17 is trading income of £163,000. What is Jim's annual allowance for 2016/17?

4 What are the consequences of the total of employee and employer pension contributions exceeding the annual allowance?

5 What are the consequences of exceeding the lifetime allowance?

Answers to Quick Quiz

1 B. The maximum gross contribution that Martha can pay is the higher of her relevant earnings (£3,000) and the basic amount (£3,600). She will actually pay £3,600 × 80% = £2,880 to the pension provider.

2 Fern will not be able to use any unused personal allowance from 2013/14 as she was not a member of a registered pension scheme in this year. She has £(40,000 – 14,000) = £26,000 unused from 2014/15 and £40,000 from 2015/16. Her total maximum contribution in February 2017 without incurring an annual allowance charge is therefore £(26,000 + 40,000 + 40,000) = £106,000.

3

	£
Adjusted income = net income	163,000
Less threshold	(150,000)
Excess	13,000
Annual allowance	40,000
Less half excess £13,000 × ½	(6,500)
Reduced annual allowance	33,500

4 The excess is subject to the annual allowance charge primarily chargeable on the employee.

5 If the lifetime allowance is exceeded the excess is charged at 55% (if taken as a lump sum) or 25% (if taken as a pension).

Now try the questions below from the Practice Question Bank

Number	Type	Marks	Time
Q29	Section A	2	4 mins
Q30	Section A	2	4 mins
Q31	Section A	2	4 mins
Q32	Section B	2	4 mins
Q33	Section B	2	4 mins
Q34	Section B	2	4 mins
Q35	Section B	2	4 mins
Q36	Section B	2	4 mins

6

Property income

Topic list	Syllabus reference
1 Property business income	B4(a)
2 Furnished holiday lettings	B4(b)
3 Rent a room relief	B4(c)
4 Premiums on leases	B4(d)
5 Property business losses	B4(e)

Introduction

We have finished looking at an individual's employment income and can turn our attention to other income to be slotted into the tax computation.

We are now going to look at the computation and taxation of the profits of a property letting business. First we see how to work out the profit (you may like to return to this section once you have studied Chapters 7 and 8).

Next we look at the special conditions which must be satisfied if a letting is to be treated as a furnished holiday let and at the extra tax reliefs available if it is.

We then consider the special relief available to taxpayers who let out rooms in their own homes, rent a room relief.

Finally we see how part of a premium for granting a short lease is taxed as income, and briefly consider how to deal with property business losses.

In the following chapters we shall turn our attention to the profits of an actual trade, profession or vocation.

Study guide

		Intellectual level
B4	**Property and investment income**	
(a)	Compute property business profits.	2
(b)	Explain the treatment of furnished holiday lettings.	1
(c)	Understand rent-a-room relief.	1
(d)	Compute the amount assessable when a premium is received for the grant of a short lease.	2
(e)	Understand how relief for a property business loss is given.	2

Exam guide

You are likely to be required to compute property income as part of a 10 or 15 mark question in Section C. You may find it in the context of income tax or corporation tax – the basic computational rules are the same (apart from interest paid which is not included as an expense when computing property income for corporation tax purposes). Specific aspects of property income such as lease premiums may be tested in Section A or Section B questions. Rent a room relief is an important relief for individuals (it does not apply to companies), and the special rules for furnished holiday lettings will only be examined in an income tax context. Remember that property income is non-savings income even though a property portfolio is usually regarded as an investment.

1 Property business income

FAST FORWARD

Property business profits are calculated on an accruals basis.

1.1 Profits of a property business

Income from land and buildings in the UK is taxed as non-savings income.

The profits of the UK property business are computed for tax years. Each tax year's profit is taxed in that year.

1.2 Computation of profits

A taxpayer with UK rental income is treated as running a business, his 'UK property business'. All the rents and expenses for all properties are pooled, to give a single profit or loss. Profits and losses are computed in the same way as trading profits are computed for tax purposes, on an **accruals basis**. A loss from a UK property business is carried forward to set against the **first future profits from the UK property business**.

Expenses will often include rent payable where a landlord is himself renting the land which he in turn lets to others. For individuals, interest on loans to buy or improve properties is treated as an expense (on an accruals basis).

Relief is available for irrecoverable rent as an impairment loss.

1.3 Capital allowances

FAST FORWARD

If a residential property is let furnished replacement of domestic items relief can be claimed. Capital allowances are not available.

Capital allowances are given on plant and machinery used in the UK property business in the same way as they are given for a trading business with an accounting date of 5 April (we will study capital allowances in greater detail later in this Study Text). However, **capital allowances are not normally available on plant or machinery used in a dwelling but someone who lets a furnished property used as a dwelling (residential property) can instead claim replacement of domestic items relief.**

1.4 Replacement of domestic items relief

No relief is given for the **initial cost** of providing domestic items. **Relief is given** if a domestic item is **replaced**.

Domestic items are defined as furniture, furnishings, household appliances and kitchenware. Examples include beds, televisions, fridges, freezers, washing machines, carpets and other floor coverings, curtains, crockery and cutlery. It does not include fixtures which become part of the property including boilers and radiators.

The **amount of the relief** is the **expenditure on the new replacement asset less any proceeds** from selling the old asset which has been replaced. If the **new asset is not the same, or substantially the same, as the old asset, only the cost of an equivalent asset is given relief.**

Question — Property business income

Over the last few years, Peter has purchased several properties in Manchester as 'buy to let' investments.

5 Whitby Ave is let out furnished at £500 per month. A tenant moved in on 1 March 2016 but left unexpectedly on 1 May 2017 having paid rent only up to 31 December 2016. The tenant left no forwarding address.

17 Bolton Rd has been let furnished to the same tenant for a number of years at £800 per month.

A recent purchase, 27 Turner Close has been let unfurnished since 1 August 2016 at £750 per month. Before then it was empty whilst Peter redecorated it after its purchase in March 2016.

Peter's expenses during 2016/17 are:

	No 5	*No 17*	*No 27*
	£	£	£
Insurance	250	250	200
Letting agency fees	–	–	100
Repairs	300	40	–
Redecoration	–	–	500
Curtains	130	–	–
Washer-dryer	–	600	–
Dining table and chairs	–	350	–

No 27 was in a fit state to let when Peter bought it but he wanted to redecorate the property as he felt this would allow him to achieve a better rental income.

The new curtains for No 5 were replacements for old curtains. Peter sold the old curtains for £15.

The washer-dryer for No 17 was a replacement for a washing machine without a dryer. If Peter had bought a new washing machine without a dryer, similar to the old machine, it would have cost him £475. The old washing machine was scrapped with no proceeds. Peter had not previously provided a dining table and chairs in No 17.

Peter made a UK property business loss in 2015/16 of £300.

What is Peter's taxable property income for 2016/17?

Answer

2016/17	*No 5* £	*No 17* £	*No 27* £
Accrued income			
12 × £500	6,000		
12 × £800		9,600	
8 × £750			6,000
Less:			
Insurance	(250)	(250)	(200)
Letting agency fees			(100)
Impairment loss (irrecoverable rent)			
3 × £500	(1,500)		
Repairs	(300)	(40)	
Redecoration (N)			(500)
Replacement domestic items relief			
Curtains £(130 -15)	(115)		
Washer dryer (limited to cost of washing machine without dryer)		(475)	
Dining table and chairs (no relief for initial expenditure)		(0)	
Property Income	3,835	8,835	5,200

	£
Total property income	17,870
Less loss b/fwd	(300)
Taxable property income for 2016/17	17,570

Note: The redecoration of No.27 is an allowable expense. This is an example of the application of the case of *Odeon Associated Theatres Ltd v Jones 1971* (covered in more detail later in this Study Text) which showed that the cost of initial repairs to remedy normal wear and tear of a recently acquired asset was an allowable expense. This contrasts with the case of *Law Shipping v. CIR 1921* where the cost of initial repairs to improve an asset recently acquired to make it fit to earn profits was disallowable capital expenditure. The key point in relation to No. 27 is that it was in a fit state to let when acquired.

2 Furnished holiday lettings

FAST FORWARD

Special rules apply to income from furnished holiday lettings. Whilst the income is taxed as normal as property business income, the letting is treated as if it were a trade. Capital allowances are available on the furniture and the income is relevant earnings for pension purposes. However, only carry forward trade loss relief is available.

2.1 Introduction

There are special rules for furnished holiday lettings (FHLs). The letting is treated as if it were a trade. This means that, although the income is taxed as income from a property business, the provisions which apply to actual trades also apply to furnished holiday lettings.

(a) **Capital allowances are available on furniture instead of replacement domestic items relief.**

(b) The income qualifies as **relevant earnings for pension relief** (see earlier in this Study Text).

(c) **Capital gains tax rollover relief, entrepreneurs' relief and relief for gifts of business assets are available** (see later in this Study Text).

However, losses from FHLs are not treated as trade losses for relief against general income, early years loss relief and terminal loss relief. If a loss arises on a FHL, the only trade loss relief available is carry forward loss relief by deduction from the first available future profits of the same FHL business. Trading loss reliefs are dealt with later in this Study Text.

2.2 Conditions

Exam focus point

A FHL must be situated in the UK or in another state within the European Economic Area. However, **only FHLs situated within the UK are within the F6(UK) syllabus.**

The letting must be of furnished accommodation made on a **commercial basis with a view to the realisation of profit**. The property must also satisfy the following three conditions.

(a) **The availability condition** – the accommodation is available for commercial let as holiday accommodation to the public generally, for **at least 210 days during the year**.

(b) **The letting condition** – the accommodation is commercially let as holiday accommodation to members of the public for **at least 105 days during the year**.

If the **landlord has more than one FHL**, at least one of which satisfies the 105 day rule ('qualifying holiday accommodation') and at least one of which does not, ('the underused accommodation'), he may elect to **average the occupation of the qualifying holiday accommodation and any or all of the underused accommodation**. If the average of occupation is at least 105 days, the under-used accommodation will be treated as qualifying holiday accommodation.

Exam focus point

It is possible to make an election so that a rental property continues to qualify as a furnished holiday letting for up to two years after the 105 day test ceases to be met. This election is **not examinable** in F6(UK).

(c) **The pattern of occupation condition – not more than 155 days in the year** fall during periods of longer term occupation. Longer term occupation is defined as a **continuous period of more than 31 days during which the accommodation is in the same occupation** unless there are abnormal circumstances.

If someone has furnished holiday lettings and other lettings, **draw up two income statements as if they had two separate property businesses**. This is so that the profits and losses can be identified for the special rules which apply to FHLs.

3 Rent a room relief

FAST FORWARD

Rents received from letting a room in the taxpayer's home may be tax free under the rent a room scheme.

3.1 The exemption

If an individual lets a room or rooms, furnished, in his main residence as living accommodation, then a special exemption may apply under the rent a room scheme.

The limit on the exemption is gross rents (before any expenses or capital allowances) of £7,500 in a tax year (2016/17). This limit is halved if any other person (eg spouse/civil partner) also received income from renting accommodation in the property.

If gross rents are not more than the limit, the rents are wholly exempt from income tax and expenses are ignored. However, the taxpayer may claim to ignore the exemption, for example to generate a loss by taking into account both rent and expenses.

Exam focus point

> If you are asked to calculate property income in an exam don't overlook rent a room relief, but be sure to state whether the relief applies.

3.2 Alternative basis

If gross rents exceed the limit, the taxpayer will be taxed in the ordinary way, ignoring the rent a room scheme, unless he elects for the 'alternative basis'. If he so elects, he will be taxable on gross receipts less £7,500 (or £3,750 if the limit is halved), with no deductions for expenses.

3.3 Election

An election to ignore the exemption (if gross rents are below £7,500), or an election for the alternative basis (if gross rents exceed £7,500) must be made by the 31 January which is 22 months from the end of the tax year concerned. An election to ignore the exemption applies only for the tax year for which it is made, but an election for the alternative basis remains in force until it is withdrawn or until a year in which gross rents do not exceed the limit.

Question — Rent a room relief

Sylvia owns a house near the sea in Norfolk. She has a spare bedroom and during 2016/17 this was let to a chef working at a nearby restaurant for £148 per week which includes the cost of heating and electricity.

Sylvia estimates that her lodger costs her an extra £150 on gas, £125 on electricity, and £50 on buildings insurance each year. What is Sylvia's property income for 2016/17?

Answer

Sylvia's gross rents are above the rent a room limit. Therefore she has the following choices:

(1) Under the normal method (no election needed), she can be taxed on her actual profit:

	£
Rental income £148 × 52	7,696
Less expenses (150 + 125 + 50)	(325)
	7,371

(2) Under the 'alternative basis' (elect for rent a room relief):

Total rental income of £7,696 exceeds £7,500 limit, so taxable income is £196 (ie 7,696 – 7,500) if rent a room relief claimed.

Sylvia should claim rent a room relief and so be taxed on the 'alternative basis'.

4 Premiums on leases

FAST FORWARD

> A premium received on the grant of a lease may be partly taxable as property income.

When a premium or similar consideration is received on the grant (that is, by a landlord to a tenant) **of a short lease (50 years or less), part of the premium is treated as property income received in the year of grant.**

The premium taxed as property income is the whole premium, less 2% of the premium for each complete year of the lease, except the first year.

This rule does not apply on the **assignment** of a lease (one tenant selling his entire interest in the property to another).

4.1 Example: income element of premium

Janet granted a lease to Jack on 1 March 2017 for a period of 40 years. Jack paid a premium of £16,000. How much of the premium received by Janet is taxed as property income?

	£
Premium received	16,000
Less 2% × (40 –1) × £16,000	(12,480)
Taxable as property income	3,520

Note that if Janet **owned a 40 year lease and assigned it to Jack**, no part of the amount received would be taxed as property income.

4.2 Premiums paid by traders

FAST FORWARD

If the premium is paid by a trader, a deduction can be made in computing taxable trading profits.

Where a trader pays a premium for a lease he may deduct an amount when computing his taxable trading profits in each year of the lease. The amount deductible is the figure taxed as property income on the landlord divided by the number of years of the lease.

You may want to look at this point again once you have studied trade profits later in this Study Text.

4.3 Example: deduction for premium paid by trader

On 1 July 2016 Bryony, a trader, pays Scott, the landlord, a premium of £30,000 for a ten year lease on a shop. Bryony makes up accounts to 31 December each year.

Scott is taxable on property income in 2016/17 of £30,000 – (£30,000 × (10 – 1) × 2%) = £24,600.

Bryony can therefore deduct £24,600/10 = £2,460 in each of the ten years of the lease. She starts with the accounts year in which the lease starts (year ended 31 December 2016) and apportions the relief to the nearest month. Her deduction for 2016/17 is therefore:

1 July 2016 to 31 December 2016: 6/12 × £2,460	£1,230

5 Property business losses

FAST FORWARD

A loss on a property letting business is carried forward to set against future property business profits.

A loss from a UK property business is carried forward to set against the **first future profits from the UK property business**. It may be carried forward until the UK property business ends, but it must be used as soon as possible.

As explained above, however, FHL losses are dealt with under special rules so that **losses from a FHL business must be kept separate and can only be used against profits of the same FHL business**.

Chapter Roundup

- Property business profits are calculated on an accruals basis.
- If residential property is let furnished replacement of domestic items relief can be claimed. Capital allowances are not available.
- Special rules apply to income from furnished holiday lettings. Whilst the income is taxed as normal as property business income, the letting is treated as if it were a trade. Capital allowances are available on the furniture and the income is relevant earnings for pension purposes. However, only carry forward trade loss relief is available.
- Rents received from letting a room in the taxpayer's home may be tax free under the rent a room scheme.
- A premium received on the grant of a lease may be partly taxable as property income.
- If the premium is paid by a trader, a deduction can be made in computing taxable trading profits.
- A loss on a property letting business is carried forward to set against future property business profits.

Quick Quiz

1 For what period is property business income computed?

2 How is capital expenditure relieved for furnished lettings?

3 In order for property to be a furnished holiday letting it must be:

(a) Available for letting for at least _____ days during the year

(b) Actually let for at least _____ days during the year

(c) Not let as longer term accommodation for more than _____days in the year (longer term occupation is a continuous period of more than _____days in the same occupation)

Fill in the blanks.

4 How much income per annum is tax free under the rent a room scheme?

A £3,750
B £7,500
C £10,000
D £11,000

5 Laura owns a property which qualifies as a furnished holiday letting (FHL) on which she made a profit in 2015/16 and a loss in 2016/17. She also lets out another property, which is not a FHL, on which she has a profit in 2016/17. How can Laura relieve the loss on the FHL?

A Against the other property profit of 2016/17
B Carry forward against all future property business income
C Carry back against the FHL profit of 2015/16
D Carry forward against profits of the same FHL business

Answers to Quick Quiz

1 Property business income is computed for tax years (6 April to 5 April).

2 Except for furnished holiday lettings where capital allowances are available for the cost of furniture, capital expenditure on furnishings is relieved through replacement of domestic items relief.

3 In order for property to be a furnished holiday letting it must be:

(a) Available for letting for at least **210** days during the year

(b) Actually let for at least **105** days during the year

(c) Not let as longer term accommodation for more than **155** days in the year (longer term occupation is a continuous period of more than **31** days in the same occupation)

4 B. £7,500

5 D. Carry forward against profits of the same FHL business

Now try the questions below from the Practice Question Bank

Number	Type	Marks	Time
Q37	Section A	2	4 mins
Q38	Section A	2	4 mins
Q39	Section A	2	4 mins
Q40	Section C	10	20 mins

7

Computing trading income

Topic list	Syllabus reference
1 The badges of trade	B3(b)
2 The adjustment of profits	B3(c)
3 Cash basis of accounting for small businesses	B3(d)
4 Pre-trading expenditure	B3(e)

Introduction

The final figure to slot into the income tax computation is income from self employment (trading income).

We are therefore going to look at the computation of profits of unincorporated businesses. We work out a business's profit as if it were a separate entity (the separate entity concept familiar to you from basic bookkeeping) but, as an unincorporated business has no legal existence apart from its trader, we cannot tax it separately. We have to feed its profit into the owner's personal tax computation.

Later chapters will consider capital allowances, which are allowed as an expense in the computation of profits, the taxation of business profits, and how trading losses can be relieved. We will then extend our study to partnerships, ie to groups of two or more individuals trading together.

Study guide

		Intellectual level
B3	**Income from self-employment**	
(b)	Describe and apply the badges of trade.	2
(c)	Recognise the expenditure that is allowable in calculating the tax-adjusted trading profit.	2
(d)	Explain and compute the assessable profits using the cash basis for small businesses.	2
(e)	Recognise the relief that can be obtained for pre-trading expenditure.	2

Exam guide

Section A questions on computing taxable trading income may test two or three particular adjustments such as the restriction for motor cars with high CO_2 emissions. You may also be required to deal with a number of adjustments in a Section B question. You may be required to compute trading profits in a Section C question. The computation may be for an individual, a partnership or a company. In each case the same principles are applied. You must however watch out for the adjustments which only apply to individuals, such as private use expenses. You may also be asked to explain the badges of trade in a Section C question. These topics may be tested as part of a 15 mark or a 10 mark question.

1 The badges of trade

FAST FORWARD

The badges of trade are used to decide whether or not a trade exists. If one does exist, the accounts profits need to be adjusted in order to establish the taxable profits.

Key term

A trade is defined in Income Tax Act 2007 only as 'any venture in the nature of trade'. Further guidance about the scope of this definition is found in a number of cases which have been decided by the Courts. This guidance is summarised in a collection of principles known as the **'badges of trade'**. These are set out below. They apply to both corporate and unincorporated businesses.

Exam focus point

You are not expected to know case names – we have included these below for your information only.

1.1 The subject matter

Whether a person is trading or not may sometimes be decided by examining the subject matter of the transaction. Some assets are commonly held as investments for their intrinsic value: an individual buying some shares or a painting may do so in order to enjoy the income from the shares or to enjoy the work of art. A subsequent disposal may produce a gain of a capital nature rather than a trading profit. But **where the subject matter of a transaction is such as would not be held as an investment** (for example 34,000,000 yards of aircraft linen (*Martin v Lowry 1927*) or 1,000,000 rolls of toilet paper (*Rutledge v CIR 1929*)), **it is presumed that any profit on resale is a trading profit**.

1.2 The frequency of transactions

Transactions which may, in isolation, be of a capital nature will be interpreted as **trading transactions where their frequency indicates the carrying on of a trade.** It was decided that whereas normally the purchase of a mill-owning company and the subsequent stripping of its assets might be a capital transaction, where the taxpayer was embarking on the same exercise for the fourth time he must be carrying on a trade (*Pickford v Quirke 1927*).

1.3 Existence of similar trading transactions or interests

If there is an **existing trade**, then a **similarity to the transaction which is being considered** may point to that transaction having a trading character. For example, a builder who builds and sells a number of houses may be held to be trading even if he retains one or more houses for longer than usual and claims that they were held as an investment (*Harvey v Caulcott 1952*).

1.4 The length of ownership

The courts may infer a venture in the nature of trade where **items purchased are sold soon afterwards**.

1.5 The organisation of the activity as a trade

The courts may infer that a trade is being carried on if the transactions are **carried out in the same manner as someone who is unquestionably trading**. For example, an individual who bought a consignment of whiskey and then sold it through an agent, in the same way as others who were carrying on a trade, was also held to be trading (*CIR v Fraser 1942*). On the other hand, if an **asset has to be sold in order to raise funds in an emergency, this is less likely to be treated as trading**.

1.6 Supplementary work and marketing

When work is done to make an asset more marketable, or **marketing steps are taken to find purchasers**, the Courts will be more ready to ascribe a trading motive. When a group of accountants bought, blended and recasked a quantity of brandy, they were held to be taxable on a trading profit when the brandy was later sold (*Cape Brandy Syndicate v CIR 1921*).

1.7 A profit motive

The absence of a profit motive will not necessarily preclude a tax charge as trading income, but its presence is a strong indication that a person is trading. The purchase and resale of £20,000 worth of silver bullion by the comedian Norman Wisdom, as a hedge against devaluation, was held to be a trading transaction (*Wisdom v Chamberlain 1969*).

1.8 The way in which the asset sold was acquired

If goods are acquired deliberately, trading may be indicated. If goods are acquired unintentionally, for example by gift or inheritance, their later sale is unlikely to be trading.

1.9 Method of finance

If the **purchaser has to borrow money to buy an asset such that he has to sell that asset quickly to repay the loan**, it may be inferred that trading was taking place. This was a factor in the *Wisdom v Chamberlain* case as Mr Wisdom financed his purchases by loans at a high rate of interest. It was clear that he had to sell the silver bullion quickly in order to repay the loan and prevent the interest charges becoming too onerous. On the other hand, taking out a long term loan to buy an asset (such as a mortgage on a house) would not usually indicate that trading is being carried on.

1.10 The taxpayer's intentions

Where a transaction is clearly trading on objective criteria, **the taxpayer's intentions are irrelevant**. If, however, a transaction has (objectively) a dual purpose, the taxpayer's intentions may be taken into account. An example of a transaction with a dual purpose is the acquisition of a site partly as premises from which to conduct another trade, and partly with a view to the possible development and resale of the site.

This test is not one of the traditional badges of trade, but it may be just as important.

2 The adjustment of profits

Exam focus point

ACCA's article Adjustment of profit, written by a member of the F6(UK) examination team gives advice on attempting exam questions on adjustment of profit, with a working example of a question in a recent F6 (UK) exam.

FAST FORWARD

The net profit in the statement of profit or loss must be adjusted to find the taxable trading profit.

2.1 Illustrative adjustment

Exam focus point

The rules relating to profits from trades apply equally to profits from all professions and vocations.

Although the **net profit** shown in the statement of profit or loss is the starting point in computing the taxable trade profits, many adjustments may be required to calculate the taxable amount.

Exam focus point

Only international accounting standard terminology is used when presenting accounting information contained within an examination question. This applies for companies, sole traders and partnerships.

Here is an illustrative adjustment of a statement of profit or loss:

		£	£
Net profit			140,000
Add:	expenditure charged in the accounts which is not deductible from trading profits	50,000	
	income taxable as trading profits which has not been included in the accounts	30,000	
			80,000
			220,000
Less:	profits included in the accounts but which are not taxable as trading profits	40,000	
	expenditure which is deductible from trading profits but has not been charged in the accounts (eg capital allowances)	20,000	
			(60,000)
Adjusted taxable trading profit			160,000

You may refer to deductible and non-deductible expenditure as allowable and disallowable expenditure respectively. The two sets of terms are interchangeable.

Exam focus point

An examination question requiring adjustment to profit will direct you to start the adjustment with the net profit of £XXXX and to deal with all the items listed, indicating with a zero (0) any items which do not require adjustment. Marks will not be given for relevant items unless this approach is used. Therefore students who attempt to rewrite the statement of profit or loss will be penalised.

2.2 Accounting policies

The fundamental concept is that the profits of the business must be calculated in accordance with generally accepted accounting principles. These profits are subject to any adjustment specifically required for income tax purposes.

2.3 Deductible and non-deductible expenditure

FAST FORWARD

Disallowable (ie non-deductible) expenditure must be added back to the net profit in the computation of the taxable trading profit. Any item not deducted wholly and exclusively for trade purposes is disallowable expenditure. Certain other items, such as depreciation, are specifically disallowable.

2.3.1 Introduction

Certain expenses are specifically disallowed by the legislation. These are covered below. If however a deduction is specifically permitted this overrides the disallowance.

2.3.2 Payments contrary to public policy and illegal payments

Fines and penalties are not deductible. However, **HMRC usually allow employees' parking fines incurred in parking their employer's cars while on their employer's business. Fines relating to traders, however, are never allowed.**

A payment is not deductible if making it constitutes an offence by the payer. This covers protection money paid to terrorists, and also bribes. Statute also prevents any deduction for payments made in response to blackmail or extortion.

2.3.3 Capital expenditure

Capital expenditure is not deductible. This means that depreciation is non-deductible.

Profits and losses on the sale of non-current assets must be deducted or added back respectively. Chargeable gains or allowable losses may be dealt with under capital gains tax (see later in this Study Text).

The most contentious items of expenditure will often be repairs (revenue expenditure) **and improvements** (capital expenditure).

- **The cost of restoration of an asset by, for instance, replacing a subsidiary part of the asset is revenue expenditure.** Expenditure on a new factory chimney replacement was allowable since the chimney was a subsidiary part of the factory (*Samuel Jones & Co (Devondale) Ltd v CIR 1951*). However, in another case a football club demolished a spectators' stand and replaced it with a modern equivalent. This was held not to be repair, since repair is the restoration by renewal or replacement of subsidiary parts of a larger entity, and the stand formed a distinct and *separate* part of the club (*Brown v Burnley Football and Athletic Co Ltd 1980*).
- **The cost of initial repairs to improve an asset recently acquired to make it fit to earn profits is disallowable capital expenditure.** In *Law Shipping Co Ltd v CIR 1923* the taxpayer failed to obtain relief for expenditure on making a newly bought ship seaworthy prior to using it.
- **The cost of initial repairs to remedy normal wear and tear of recently acquired assets is allowable revenue expenditure.** *Odeon Associated Theatres Ltd v Jones 1971* can be contrasted with the *Law Shipping* judgement. Odeon were allowed to charge expenditure incurred on improving the state of recently acquired cinemas.

Capital allowances may, however, be available as a deduction for capital expenditure from trading profits (see later in this Study Text).

Two exceptions to the 'capital' rule are worth noting.

(a) **The costs of registering patents and trade marks are deductible.**

(b) **Incidental costs of obtaining loan finance**, or of attempting to obtain or redeeming it, are deductible, other than a discount on issue or a premium on redemption (which are really alternatives to paying interest).

2.3.4 Expenditure not wholly and exclusively for the purposes of the trade

Expenditure is not deductible if it is not for trade purposes (the remoteness test), or if it reflects more than one purpose (the duality test). The private proportion of payments for motoring expenses, rent, heat and light and telephone expenses of a trader is non-deductible. If an exact apportionment is possible, relief is given on the business element. Where the payments are to or on behalf of employees, the full amounts are deductible but the employees are taxed under the benefits code (see earlier in this Study Text).

The remoteness test is illustrated by the following cases.

- *Strong & Co of Romsey Ltd v Woodifield 1906*
  A customer injured by a falling chimney when sleeping in an inn owned by a brewery claimed compensation from the company. The compensation was not deductible: 'the loss sustained by the appellant was not really incidental to their trade as innkeepers and fell upon them in their character not of innkeepers but of householders'.
- *Bamford v ATA Advertising Ltd 1972*
  A director misappropriated £15,000. The loss was not allowable: 'the loss is not, as in the case of a dishonest shop assistant, an incident of the company's trading activities. It arises altogether outside such activities'.
- Expenditure which is wholly and exclusively to benefit the trades of several companies (for example in a group) but is not wholly and exclusively to benefit the trade of one specific company is not deductible *(Vodafone Cellular Ltd and others v Shaw 1995).*
- *McKnight (HMIT) v Sheppard (1999)* concerned expenses incurred by a stockbroker in defending allegations of infringements of Stock Exchange regulations. It was found that the expenditure was incurred to prevent the destruction of the taxpayer's business and that as the expenditure was incurred for business purposes it was deductible. It was also found that although the expenditure had the effect of preserving the taxpayer's reputation, that was not its purpose, so there was no duality of purpose.

The **duality test** is illustrated by the following cases.

- *Caillebotte v Quinn 1975*
  A self-employed carpenter spent an average of 40p per day when obliged to buy lunch away from home but just 10p when he lunched at home. He claimed the excess 30p. It was decided that the payment had a dual purpose and was not deductible: a taxpayer 'must eat to live not eat to work'.
- *Mallalieu v Drummond 1983*
  Expenditure by a lady barrister on black clothing to be worn in court (and on its cleaning and repair) was not deductible. The expenditure was for the dual purpose of enabling the barrister to be warmly and properly clad as well as meeting her professional requirements.
- *McLaren v Mumford 1996*
  A publican traded from a public house which had residential accommodation above it. He was obliged to live at the public house but he also had another house which he visited regularly. It was held that the private element of the expenditure incurred at the public house on electricity, rent, gas, etc was not incurred for the purpose of earning profits, but for serving the non-business purpose of satisfying the publican's ordinary human needs. The expenditure, therefore had a dual purpose and was disallowed.

However, the cost of overnight accommodation when on a business trip may be deductible and reasonable expenditure on an evening meal and breakfast in conjunction with such accommodation is then also deductible.

2.3.5 Impairment losses (bad debts)

Only impairment losses where the liability was incurred wholly and exclusively for the purposes of the trade are deductible for taxation purposes. For example, **loans to employees written off are not deductible** unless the business is that of making loans, or it can be shown that the writing-off of the loan was earnings paid out for the benefit of the trade.

Under generally accepted accounting principles, a review of all trade receivables should be carried out to assess their fair value at the balance sheet date and any impairment losses written off. **The tax treatment follows the accounting treatment so no adjustment is required for tax purposes.** General provisions (ie those calculated as a percentage of total trade receivables, without reference to specific receivables) will now rarely be seen. In the event that they do arise, increases or decreases in a general provision are not allowable /taxable and an adjustment will need to be made.

Where a tax deduction has been taken for an impairment loss, but the relevant debt is later recovered, the recovery is taxable so no adjustment is required to the amount of the recovery shown in the statement of profit or loss.

Exam focus point

When this topic was tested in a F6 (UK) examination, the examination team commented that there was a consistent problem with the revenue received in respect of a previously written off impairment loss. Most candidates did not appreciate that no adjustment was necessary.

Think carefully about this point – an impairment loss equal to the receipt had been deducted in a previous accounting period, but this amount has now been received. This is part of the current period trading profit. Since this is how the receipt is shown in the statement of profit or loss, no adjustment needs to be made.

2.3.6 Unpaid remuneration and employee benefit contributions

If earnings for employees are charged in the accounts but are not paid within nine months of the end of the period of account, the cost is only deductible for the period of account in which the earnings are paid. When a tax computation is made within the nine month period, it is initially assumed that unpaid earnings will not be paid within that period. The computation is adjusted if they are so paid.

Earnings are treated as paid at the same time as they are treated as received for employment income purposes.

Similar rules apply to employee benefit contributions.

2.3.7 Entertaining and gifts

The general rule is that expenditure on entertaining and gifts is non-deductible. This applies to amounts reimbursed to employees for specific entertaining expenses and gifts, and to round sum allowances which are exclusively for meeting such expenses. There is no distinction between UK and overseas customer entertaining for income tax and corporation tax purposes (you will find out later in this Study Text that a different rule applies for value added tax).

There are specific exceptions to the general rule:

- **Entertaining for and gifts to employees are normally deductible** although where gifts are made, or the entertainment is excessive, a charge to tax may arise on the employee under the benefits legislation.
- Gifts to customers not costing more than £50 per donee per year are allowed if they carry a conspicuous advertisement for the business and are not food, drink, tobacco or vouchers exchangeable for goods.
- **Gifts to charities may also be allowed** although many will fall foul of the 'wholly and exclusively' rule above (see further later in this Chapter). If a gift aid declaration is made by an individual in respect of a gift, tax relief will be given under the gift aid scheme, not as a trading expense. If a qualifying charitable donation is made by a company, it will be given tax relief by deduction from total profits (we deal with companies later in this Study Text).

2.3.8 Lease charges for cars with CO_2 emissions exceeding 130g/km

Exam focus point

ACCA's article Motor cars, written by a member of the F6(UK) examination team explains the implications of acquiring, running, or having the use of a motor car for income tax, corporation tax, value added tax (VAT) and national insurance contribution (NIC).

There is a restriction on the leasing costs of a car with CO_2 emissions exceeding 130 g/km. 15% of the leasing costs will be disallowed in the adjustment of profits calculation.

Question Restriction for car leasing costs

Mandy is a sole trader. In May 2016 she leased a car for use in her business. The leasing costs for 2016/17 were £4,000. The car had CO_2 emissions of 141g/km.

What is the amount of the leasing costs that will be disallowed in the adjustment of profits calculation?

Answer

Since the car has CO_2 emissions exceeding 130 g/km, 15% of the leasing costs will be disallowed ie £4,000 × 15% = £600. This disallowed amount will be added back to the net profit assuming the full leasing cost of £4,000 has originally been deducted in calculating the net profit. If the leasing cost has not been deducted in calculating the net profit, then the allowable 85% of the leasing cost can be deducted.

2.3.9 Patent royalties and copyright royalties

Patent royalties and copyright royalties paid in connection with an individual's trade are deductible as trading expenses.

2.3.10 National insurance contributions

No deduction is allowed for any national insurance contributions **except for employer's contributions**. For your exam, these are Class 1 secondary contributions and Class 1A contributions (see later in this Study Text).

2.3.11 Penalties and interest on tax

Penalties and interest on late paid tax are not allowed as a trading expense. For the purpose of your exam, tax includes income tax, capital gains tax, corporation tax (for companies), and VAT.

2.3.12 Appropriations

Salary or interest on capital paid to a trader are not deductible. A salary paid to a member of the trader's family is allowed as long as it is not excessive in respect of the work performed by that family member.

The private proportion of payments for motoring expenses, rent, heat and light and telephone expenses of a trader is not deductible. Where the payments are to or on behalf of employees, the full amounts are deductible but are taxed on the employees as benefits for income tax.

Payments of the trader's income tax and national insurance contributions are not deductible.

Question

Here is the statement of profit or loss of John, a trader.

Statement of profit or loss for year ended 31 May 2016

	£	£
Gross profit		79,500
Other income		
Bank interest received		500
Expenses		
Wages and salaries (N1)	47,000	
Rent and rates	12,000	
Depreciation	1,500	
Motor expenses – cars owned by business (N2)	5,000	
Motor expenses – cost of leased car CO_2 emissions 150g/km (N4)	500	
Entertainment expenses – customers	750	
Office expenses	1,350	
		(68,100)
Finance costs		
Interest payable on overdraft		(1,500)
Net profit		10,400

Notes

1. Salaries include £10,000 paid to John's wife, Julie, who works part time in the business. If John had employed another person to do this work, John would have had to pay at least this amount.
2. Motor expenses on cars owned by the business are £3,000 for John's car used 20% privately and £2,000 for his part-time salesman's car used 40% privately.
3. Capital allowances are £860.
4. The lease of the car started on 1 May 2016. No private use on the leased car.

Compute the adjusted taxable trade profit for the year ended 31 May 2016. You should start with the net profit figure of £10,400 and indicate by the use of zero any items which do not require adjustment.

Answer

John – Adjusted taxable trading profit for year ended 31 May 2016

		£	£
Net profit			10,400
Add:	wages and salaries	0	
	rents and rates	0	
	depreciation	1,500	
	trader private motor expenses (£3,000 × 20%)	600	
	salesman's car	0	
	leased car cost disallowed (£500 × 15%)	75	
	entertainment expenses customers	750	
	office expenses	0	
	interest payable on overdraft	0	
			2,925
			13,325
Deduct:	bank interest received	(500)	
	capital allowances	(860)	
			(1,360)
Profit adjusted for tax purposes			11,965

Note. The employee's private motor expenses are allowable for the trader but the provision of the car will be taxed on the employee as an income tax benefit. The salary paid to Julie is allowed as it is reasonable remuneration for the work actually done.

2.3.13 Subscriptions and donations

The general 'wholly and exclusively' rule determines the deductibility of expenses. Subscriptions and donations are not deductible unless the expenditure is for the benefit of the trade. The following are the main types of subscriptions and donations you may meet and their correct treatments.

- Trade subscriptions (such as to a professional or trade association) are generally deductible.
- Charitable donations are generally deductible only if they are small and to local charities.
- Political subscriptions and donations are generally not deductible.
- When a business makes a gift of equipment manufactured, sold or used in the course of its trade to an educational establishment or for a charitable purpose, nothing need be brought into account as a trading receipt.

2.3.14 Legal and professional charges

Legal and professional charges relating to capital or non-trading items are not deductible. These include charges incurred in acquiring new capital assets or legal rights, issuing shares, drawing up partnership agreements and litigating disputes over the terms of a partnership agreement.

Professional charges are deductible if they relate directly to trading. Deductible items include:

- Legal and professional charges incurred defending the taxpayer's title to non-current assets
- Charges connected with an action for breach of contract
- Expenses of the **renewal** (not the original grant) of a lease for less than 50 years
- Charges for trade debt collection
- Normal charges for preparing accounts/assisting with the self assessment of tax liabilities

Accountancy expenses arising out of an enquiry into the accounts information in a particular year's return are not allowed where the enquiry reveals discrepancies and additional liabilities for the year of enquiry, or any earlier year, which arise as a result of negligent or fraudulent conduct.

Where, however, the enquiry results in no addition to profits, or an adjustment to the profits for the year of enquiry only and that assessment does not arise as a result of negligent or fraudulent conduct, the additional accountancy expenses are allowable.

2.3.15 Interest

Interest paid by an individual on borrowings for trade purposes is deductible as a trading expense on an accruals basis, so no adjustment to the accounts figure is needed.

Individuals cannot deduct interest on overdue tax.

2.3.16 Miscellaneous deductions

Here is a list of various other items that you may meet.

Item	Treatment	Comment
Educational courses for staff	Allow	
Educational courses for trader	Allow	If to update existing knowledge or skills, not if to acquire new knowledge or skills
Removal expenses (to new business premises)	Allow	Only if not an expansionary move

Item	Treatment	Comment
Travelling expenses to the trader's place of business	Disallow	*Ricketts v Colquhoun 1925*: unless an itinerant trader (*Horton v Young 1971*)
Counselling services for employees leaving employment	Allow	If qualify for exemption from employment income charge on employees
Pension contributions (to schemes for employees and company directors)	Allow	If paid, not if only provided for; special contributions may be spread over the year of payment and future years
Premiums for insurance: • Against an employee's death or illness • To cover locum costs or fixed overheads whilst the policyholder is ill	Allow	Receipts are taxable
Damages paid	Allow	If not too remote from trade: *Strong and Co v Woodifield 1906*
Improving an individual's personal security	Allow	Provision of a car, ship or dwelling is excluded

2.4 Income taxable as trading income but excluded from the accounts

The usual example is when a trader takes goods for his own use. In such circumstances the selling price of the goods if sold in the open market is added to the accounting profit. If the trader pays anything for the goods, this is left out of the account. In other words, the trader is treated for tax purposes as having made a sale to himself.

This rule does not apply to supplies of services, which are treated as sold for the amount (if any) actually paid (but the cost of services to the trader or his household is not deductible).

2.5 Accounting profits not taxable as trading income

FAST FORWARD

Receipts not taxable as trading profit must be deducted from the net profit. For example, rental income and interest received are not taxable as trading profit. The rental income is taxed instead as property business income, whilst the interest is taxed as savings income.

There are three types of receipts which may be found in the accounting profits but which must be excluded from the taxable trading profit computation. These are:

(a) **Capital receipts**
(b) **Income taxed in another way** (at source or as another type of income)
(c) **Income specifically exempt from tax**

However, compensation received in one lump sum for the loss of income is likely to be treated as income (*Donald Fisher (Ealing) Ltd v Spencer 1989*).

Income taxed as another type of income, for example rental income, is excluded from the computation of taxable trading profits but it is brought back into the income tax computation further down as property business income. Similarly capital receipts are excluded from the computation of taxable trading profits but they may be included in the computation of chargeable gains (see later in this Study Text).

2.6 Deductible expenditure not charged in the accounts

FAST FORWARD

Amounts not charged in the accounts that are deductible from trading profits must be deducted when computing the taxable trading income. An example is capital allowances.

Capital allowances (see the next Chapter) are an example of deductible expenditure not charged in the accounts.

A second example is **an annual sum which can be deducted by a trader that has paid a lease premium to a landlord who is taxable on the premium as property business income** (see earlier in this Study Text). Normally, the amortisation of the lease will have been deducted in the accounts and must be added back as an appropriation of profit.

Question

Adjustment of profits

Here is the statement of profit or loss of Steven, a trader, for the year ended 5 April 2017.

	£	£
Gross profit		90,000
Other income		
Bank interest received		860
c/f		90,860
	£	£
c/f		90,860
Expenses		
Wages and salaries	59,000	
Rent and rates	8,000	
Depreciation	1,500	
Impairment losses (trade)	150	
Entertainment expenses for customers	750	
Patent royalties paid	3,200	
Legal expenses on acquisition of new factory	250	
		(72,850)
Finance costs		
Bank interest paid		(300)
Net profit		17,710

Salaries include £15,000 paid to Steven's wife, Melanie, who works full time in the business.

Compute the adjusted taxable trade profit. You should start with the net profit figure of £17,710 and indicate by the use of zero (0) any items which do not require adjustment.

Answer

Steven – Adjusted taxable trading profit for year ended 5 April 2017

	£	£
Net profit		17,710
Add: wages and salaries (Melanie's salary not excessive for full time work)	0	
rent and rates	0	
depreciation	1,500	
impairment losses (trade)	0	
entertainment expenses for customers	750	
patent royalties	0	
legal expenses (capital)	250	
bank interest paid	0	
		2,500
		20,210
Less bank interest received		(860)
Profit adjusted for tax purposes		19,350

3 Cash basis of accounting for small businesses

3.1 Introduction

FAST FORWARD

An election can be made for an unincorporated business to calculate trading profits on the cash basis (instead of in accordance with generally accepted accounting principles) in certain circumstances.

Usually, **businesses prepare accounts using generally accepted accounting principles for tax purposes.** In particular, this means that **income and expenses are dealt with on an accruals basis**. This is referred to as **'accruals accounting'** in this section.

Certain small unincorporated businesses may elect to use cash accounting (known as 'the cash basis') rather than accruals accounting for the purposes of calculating their taxable trading income.

Exam focus point

The detailed cash basis rules are quite complex. These **more complex aspects are not examinable at Paper F6 (UK)**. In any examination question involving an unincorporated business, **it should be assumed that the cash basis is not relevant unless it is specifically mentioned**.

3.2 Which businesses can use the cash basis?

The cash basis can only be used by unincorporated businesses (sole traders and partnerships) **whose receipts for the tax year do not exceed the value added tax (VAT) registration threshold** (currently £83,000 – this figure is given in the Tax rates and Allowances available in the exam).

An election must be made for the cash basis to apply. The election is generally effective for the tax year for which it is made and all subsequent tax years.

However **a business must cease to use the cash basis** if:

(a) (i) **Receipts in the previous tax year exceeded twice the VAT registration threshold for that year** (the threshold in 2015/16 was £82,000), and

(ii) **Receipts for the current year exceed the VAT registration threshold for that year**; or

(b) Its **'commercial circumstances' change** such that the **cash basis is no longer appropriate** and **an election is made to use accruals accounting.**

3.3 Calculation of taxable profits under the cash basis

3.3.1 Introduction

The taxable trading profits under the cash basis are calculated as:

(a) **Cash receipts; less**
(b) **Deductible business expenses actually paid in the period.**

3.3.2 Cash receipts

Cash receipts include all amounts received relating to the business including cash and card receipts. They include **amounts received from the sale of plant and machinery, other than on the sale of motor cars.** We look at the definition of plant and machinery when we look at capital allowances later in this Study Text.

Receipts from the sale of motor cars and capital assets which are not classed as plant and machinery (eg land) are not taxable receipts.

3.3.3 Deductible business expenses

Under the cash basis, business expenses are deductible when they are paid.

Business expenses for the cash basis of accounting include capital expenditure on plant and machinery (except motor cars). Other capital expenses are not business expenses eg purchase of land, motor cars, and legal fees on such purchases.

The majority of the specific tax rules covered earlier in this chapter concerning the deductibility of business expenses also apply when the cash basis is used. It should be remembered, in particular, that only business expenses are tax deductible so that any private element must be disallowed. **Fixed rate expenses** for private use of motor cars and business premises used for private purposes may be used instead (see further below).

3.3.4 Fixed rate expenses

FAST FORWARD

Fixed rate expenses can be used in relation to expenditure on motor cars and business premises partly used as the trader's home.

Exam focus point

Although the **use of fixed rate expenses is optional**, in **any examination question involving the cash basis**, it should be assumed that, where relevant, **expenses are claimed on this basis.**

The option of claiming expenses on a fixed rate basis is also available to unincorporated businesses generally, but it will **only be examined in F6 (UK) within the context of the cash basis.**

Where a business elects to use the cash basis, for Paper F6 (UK) purposes, it will be assumed to use fixed rate expenses rather than make deductions on the usual basis of actual expenditure incurred.

For Paper F6 (UK) purposes, fixed rate expenses relate to:

(a) **Expenditure on motor cars**
(b) **Business premises partly used as the trader's home**

These are dealt with in detail in the following two subsections.

3.3.5 Fixed rate mileage expense

The fixed rate mileage (FRM) expense can be claimed in respect of **motor cars** which are **owned or leased by the business** and which are **used for business purposes by the sole trader/partner or an employee of the business.**

The FRM expense is calculated as the business mileage times the appropriate rate per mile. The appropriate mileage rates for motor cars are **45p per mile for the first 10,000 miles**, then **25p per mile thereafter**.

Exam focus point

These rates are the **same as the authorised mileage rates for employment income** given in the Tax rates and Allowances available in the exam.

3.3.6 Business premises used partly as trader's home

A fixed rate monthly adjustment can be made where a sole trader/partner uses part of the business premises as his home eg where a sole trader runs a small hotel or guesthouse and also lives in it. The adjustment is deducted from the actual allowable business premises costs to reflect the private portion of household costs, including food, and utilities (eg heat and light). It does not include mortgage interest, rent, council tax or rates: apportionment of these expenses must be made based on the extent of the private occupation of the premises.

The deductible fixed rate amount depends on **how many people use the business premises each month as a private home**:

Number relevant occupants	Non-business use amount
1	£350
2	£500
3 or more	£650

Exam focus point

These rates will be **given in the examination question**, if relevant.

Be careful when using these amounts – they are **not the deductible expense itself but the disallowable amount**.

3.4 Example

Larry started trading as an interior designer on 6 April 2016. The following information is relevant for the year to 5 April 2017.

Revenue was £65,000 of which £8,000 was owed as receivables at 5 April 2017.

A motor car was acquired on 6 April 2016 for £15,000. Larry drove 10,000 miles in the car during the year to 5 April 2017 of which 3,000 miles were for private journeys. The car qualifies for a capital allowance of £1,890, after taking account of private use. The motoring costs were £2,000. The fixed rate mileage expense for motoring is 45p per mile for the first 10,000 miles, then 25p per mile after that.

Machinery was acquired on 1 May 2016 for £4,000. The machinery qualifies for a capital allowance of £4,000.

Other allowable expenses were £12,000 of which £1,000 was owed as payables at 5 April 2017.

If Larry uses the accruals accounting basis and does not use fixed rate expenses, his trading profit will be calculated as follows:

	£	£
Revenue (accruals)		65,000
Less: capital allowance on motor car	1,890	
business motoring expenses £2,000 × 7,000/10,000	1,400	
capital allowance on machinery	4,000	
other allowable expenses (accruals)	12,000	
		(19,290)
Taxable trading profit		45,710

If Larry uses the cash basis of accounting and fixed rate expenses, his trading profit will be calculated as follows:

	£	£
Revenue (cash received £65,000 – £8,000)		57,000
Less: FRM on car 7,000 × 45p	3,150	
cost of machinery	4,000	
other allowable expenses (cash paid £12,000 – £1,000)	11,000	
		(18,150)
Taxable trading profit		38,850

3.5 Basis of assessment

A trader using the cash basis can, like any other trader, prepare his accounts to any date in the year. The basis of assessment rules which determine in which tax year the profits of an accounting period are taxed apply in the same way for accruals accounting and cash basis traders (see later in this Study Text).

3.6 Losses

A net cash deficit (ie a loss) can normally only be relieved against future cash surpluses (ie future trading profits). Cash basis traders cannot offset a loss against other income or gains. Trading losses for the accruals accounting traders are dealt with in detail later in this Study Text.

4 Pre-trading expenditure

FAST FORWARD

Pre-trading expenditure incurred within the seven years prior to the commencement of trade is allowable if it would have been allowable had the trade already started.

Expenditure incurred before the commencement of trade is deductible, if it is incurred within seven years of the start of trade and it is of a type that would have been deductible had the trade already started. **It is treated as a trading expense incurred on the first day of trading.**

Chapter Roundup

- The badges of trade are used to decide whether or not a trade exists. If one does exist, the accounts profits need to be adjusted in order to establish the taxable profits.
- The net profit in the statement of profit or loss must be adjusted to find the taxable trading profit.
- Disallowable (ie non-deductible) expenditure must be added back to the net profit in the computation of the taxable trading profit. Any item not deducted wholly and exclusively for trade purposes is disallowable expenditure. Certain other items, such as depreciation, are specifically disallowable.
- Receipts not taxable as trading profit must be deducted from the net profit. For example, rental income and interest received are not taxable as trading profit. The rental income is taxed instead as property business income, whilst the interest is taxed as savings income.
- Amounts not charged in the accounts that are deductible from trading profits must be deducted when computing the taxable trading income. An example is capital allowances.
- An election can be made for an unincorporated business to calculate trading profits on the cash basis (instead of in accordance with generally accepted accounting principles) in certain circumstances.
- Fixed rate expenses can be used in relation to expenditure on motor cars and business premises partly used as the trader's home.
- Pre-trading expenditure incurred within the seven years prior to the commencement of trade is allowable if it would have been allowable had the trade already started.

Quick Quiz

1 List the traditional badges of trade.

2 What are the remoteness test and the duality test?

3 No adjustment for taxation is required to the accounts for deduction of a trader's salary. True/False?

4 Sid is a sole trader. Included in his most recent statement of profit or loss are the following deductions:

£3,000 legal fees for acquiring a new 15-year lease of his business premises.

£180 car parking fines incurred by Sid whilst on business trips.

£40 interest for late payment of Sid's previous year's income tax.

How much must be added back to the net profit figure when calculating the tax adjusted profit figure?

A £3,180
B £3,220
C £220
D £3,040

5 Which ONE of the following items of expenditure will Leila, a fashion designer, be allowed to deduct in calculating her tax adjusted trading profit?

A The cost of building a new wall in front of her retail shop

B The cost of installing air conditioning in her workshop

C The cost of initial repairs to a recently acquired second-hand office building which was not usable until the repairs were carried out

D The cost of redecorating her retail shop

6 Which ONE of the following is an allowable trading expense for a sole trader?

A Gift of fleece jackets to customers with trade logo costing £60 each
B A subscription to a political party
C Legal fees in respect of employment contracts
D A Gift Aid donation

7 Which businesses can use the cash basis of accounting?

8 Pre-trading expenditure is deductible if it is incurred within ____ years of the start of trade and is of a type that would have been deductible if the trade had already started. Fill in the blank.

Answers to Quick Quiz

1 The subject matter
The frequency of transactions
Existence of similar trading transactions or interests
The length of ownership
The organisation of the activity as a trade
Supplementary work and marketing
Method of finance
A profit motive
The way in which the goods were acquired

2 Expenditure is not deductible if it is not for trade purposes (the remoteness test) or if it reflects more than one purpose (the duality test).

3 False. The trader's salary must be added back as it is an appropriation of profit.

4 B All three items are disallowed and must be added back.

5 D The cost of redecoration is an allowable expense in calculating trading profit. The other expenditure is capital expenditure and so is not allowable.

6 C Legal fees on employment contracts are an allowable income expense.

7 Unincorporated businesses (sole traders and partnerships) whose receipts for the tax year do not exceed the value added tax (VAT) registration threshold can elect to use the cash basis of accounting.

8 Pre-trading expenditure is deductible if it is incurred within **seven** years of the start of the trade and is of a type that would have been deductible if the trade had already started.

Now try the questions below from the Practice Question Bank

Number	Type	Marks	Time
Q41	Section A	2	4 mins
Q42	Section A	2	4 mins
Q43	Section A	2	4 mins
Q44	Section B	2	4 mins
Q45	Section B	2	4 mins
Q46	Section B	2	4 mins
Q47	Section B	2	4 mins
Q48	Section B	2	4 mins
Q49	Section C	15	29 mins

8

Capital allowances

Topic list	Syllabus reference
1 Capital allowances in general	B3(h)
2 Plant and machinery – qualifying expenditure	B3(h)(i)
3 The main pool	B3(h)(ii), (iii), (iv)
4 Special rate pool	B3(h)(ii), (iii), (vi)
5 Private use assets	B3(h)(ii), (iv)
6 Motor cars	B3(h)(iii)
7 Short life assets	B3(h)(v)

Introduction

We saw in the last chapter that depreciation cannot be deducted in computing taxable trade profits and that capital allowances may be given instead. In this chapter, we look at the rules for calculating capital allowances, starting with plant and machinery.

Our study of plant and machinery falls into three parts. First, we look at what qualifies for allowances: many business assets obtain no allowances at all.

Secondly, we see how to compute the allowances on the main pool and the special rate pool.

Lastly, we look at the special rules for assets with private use, motor cars and assets with short lives.

You may wish to return to this chapter while you are studying Chapter 19 on companies.

Study guide

		Intellectual level
B3	**Income from self-employment**	
(h)	Capital allowances	
(i)	Define plant and machinery for capital allowances purposes.	1
(ii)	Compute writing down allowances, first year allowances and the annual investment allowance.	2
(iii)	Compute capital allowances for motor cars.	2
(iv)	Compute balancing allowances and balancing charges.	2
(v)	Recognise the treatment of short life assets.	2
(vi)	Recognise the treatment of assets included in the special rate pool.	2

Exam guide

Section A questions on capital allowances may focus on one particular type of asset such as a motor car. You may also be asked to compute capital allowances on a variety of assets in a Section B question. In Section C, you may have to answer a whole question on capital allowances or a capital allowances computation may be included as a working in a computation of taxable trading profits. This may be as part of a 15 mark question or a 10 mark question. The computations may be for either income tax or corporation tax purposes; the principles are basically the same. Look out for private use assets; only restrict the capital allowances if there is private use by **traders**, never restrict capital allowances for private use by **employees**. This means that when you calculate capital allowances for a company there will never be any private use adjustments. Also watch out for the length of the period of account; you may need to scale WDAs and the AIA up (income tax only) or down (income tax or corporation tax).

1 Capital allowances in general

FAST FORWARD

Capital allowances are available to give tax relief for certain capital expenditure.

Capital expenditure is not deducted in computing taxable trade profits when using the accruals method of accounting, but it *may* attract capital allowances. Capital allowances are treated as a trading expense and are deducted in arriving at taxable trade profits. Balancing charges, effectively negative allowances, are added in arriving at those profits.

Capital expenditure on plant and machinery qualifies for capital allowances. Both unincorporated businesses (sole traders and partnerships) and companies are entitled to capital allowances. For completeness, in this Chapter we will look at the rules for companies alongside those for unincorporated businesses. We will look at companies in more detail later in this Study Text.

For the purposes of the F6 (UK) exam, if an unincorporated business uses the cash basis of accounting (as seen in the previous chapter), **capital allowances are not available.**

For unincorporated businesses, capital allowances are calculated for periods of account. These are simply the periods for which the trader chooses to prepare accounts. For companies, capital allowances are calculated for accounting periods (see later in this Study Text).

For capital allowances purposes, expenditure is generally deemed to be incurred when the obligation to pay becomes unconditional. This will often be the date of delivery, even if payment is actually required later than this date. For example, the sales contract may require payment to be made within four weeks of delivery but the obligation to pay still becomes unconditional on the delivery date. However, amounts due more than four months after the obligation becomes unconditional are deemed to be incurred when they fall due. Pre-trading expenditure is treated for capital allowances purposes as if it had been incurred on the first day on which the business is carried on.

2 Plant and machinery – qualifying expenditure

FAST FORWARD

There are various statutory rules on what does or does not qualify as plant.

2.1 Definition of plant and machinery

Capital expenditure on plant and machinery qualifies for capital allowances if the plant or machinery is used for a qualifying activity, such as a trade. 'Plant' is not fully defined by the legislation, although some specific exclusions and inclusions are given. The word 'machinery' may be taken to have its normal everyday meaning.

2.2 The statutory exclusions

2.2.1 Buildings

Expenditure on a building and on any asset which is incorporated in a building or is of a kind normally incorporated into buildings does not usually qualify as expenditure on plant. (There are exceptions to this (see Section 2.2.3 below) and also certain 'integral features' (see later in this chapter) are specifically treated as plant).

In addition to complete buildings, **the following assets count as 'buildings', and are therefore not plant (except if they qualify as 'integral features')**.

- Walls, floors, ceilings, doors, gates, shutters, windows and stairs
- Mains services, and systems, of water, electricity and gas
- Waste disposal, sewerage and drainage systems
- Shafts or other structures for lifts etc

2.2.2 Structures

Expenditure on structures and on works involving the alteration of land **does not qualify as expenditure on plant**, but see below for exceptions.

A 'structure' is a fixed structure of any kind, other than a building. An example is a bridge.

2.2.3 Exceptions

Over the years a large body of case law has been built up under which plant and machinery allowances have been given on certain types of expenditure which might be thought to be expenditure on a building or structure. Statute therefore gives a list of various assets which **may** still be plant. These include:

- Any machinery not within any other item in this list
- Gas and sewerage systems:
  - Provided mainly to meet the particular requirements of the trade, or
  - Provided mainly to serve particular machinery or plant used for the purposes of the trade
- Manufacturing or processing equipment, storage equipment, including cold rooms, display equipment, and counters, checkouts and similar equipment
- Cookers, washing machines, refrigeration or cooling equipment, sanitary ware and furniture and furnishings
- Hoists
- Sound insulation provided mainly to meet the particular requirements of the trade
- Refrigeration or cooling equipment
- Computer, telecommunication and surveillance systems

- Sprinkler equipment, fire alarm and burglar alarm systems
- Partition walls, where movable and intended to be moved
- Decorative assets provided for the enjoyment of the public in the hotel, restaurant or similar trades; advertising hoardings
- Movable buildings intended to be moved in the course of the trade
- Expenditure on altering land for the purpose only of installing machinery or plant

Items falling within the above list of exclusions will only qualify as plant if they fall within the meaning of plant as established by case law. This is discussed below.

2.2.4 Land

Land or an interest in land does not qualify as plant and machinery. For this purpose 'land' excludes buildings, structures and assets which are installed or fixed to land in such a way as to become part of the land for general legal purposes.

2.2.5 Integral features

The following **integral features of a building or structure** qualify for capital allowances as plant (in the special rate pool, see later in this chapter):

- Electrical systems (including lighting systems)
- Cold water system
- Space or water heating system, a powered system of ventilation, air cooling or air purification, and any floor or ceiling comprised in such a system
- Lift, an escalator or a moving walkway
- External solar shading

When a building is sold, the vendor and purchaser can make a joint election to determine how the sale proceeds are apportioned between the building and its integral features.

2.2.6 Computer software

Capital expenditure on computer software (both programs and data) **normally qualifies as expenditure on plant and machinery.**

2.3 Case law

FAST FORWARD

There are also cases on the definition of plant. To help you to absorb them, try to see the function/setting theme running through them.

Exam focus point

In this chapter we mention the names of cases where it was decided what was or wasn't 'plant'. You are **not** expected to know the names of cases for your examination. We have included them for your information only.

The original case law **definition of plant** (applied in this case to a horse) is **'whatever apparatus is used by a businessman for carrying on his business: not his stock in trade which he buys or makes for sale; but all goods and chattels, fixed or movable, live or dead, which he keeps for permanent employment in the business'** (*Yarmouth v France 1887*).

Subsequent cases have refined the original definition and have largely been concerned with the **distinction between plant actively used in the business (qualifying) and the setting in which the business is carried on (non-qualifying). This is the 'functional' test.** Some of the decisions have now been enacted as part of statute law, but they are still relevant as examples of the principles involved.

A barrister succeeded in his claim for his law library: 'Plant includes a man's tools of his trade. It extends to what he uses day by day in the course of his profession. It is not confined to physical things like the dentist's chair or the architect's table' (*Munby v Furlong 1977*).

Office partitioning was allowed. Because it was movable, it was not regarded as part of the setting in which the business was carried on (*Jarrold v John Good and Sons Ltd 1963*) (actual item now covered by statute).

At a motorway service station, false ceilings contained conduits, ducts and lighting apparatus. **They did not qualify because they did not perform a function in the business. They were merely part of the setting in which the business was conducted** (*Hampton v Fortes Autogrill Ltd 1979*).

Similarly, it has been held that when an attractive floor is provided in a restaurant, the fact that the floor performs the function of making the restaurant attractive to customers is not enough to make it plant. It functions as premises, and the cost therefore does not qualify for capital allowances (*Wimpy International Ltd v Warland 1988*).

Conversely, light fittings, decor and murals can be plant. A company carried on business as hoteliers and operators of licensed premises. The function of the items was the creation of an atmosphere conducive to the comfort and well being of its customers (*CIR v Scottish and Newcastle Breweries Ltd 1982*) (decorative assets used in hotels etc, now covered by statute).

General lighting in a department store was held not to be plant, as it was merely setting. Special display lighting, however, could be plant *(Cole Brothers Ltd v Phillips 1982)*. Note that changes in legislation mean that it is now possible to claim allowances on lighting as an integral feature (see earlier in this chapter), but the case is still a useful example of the distinction between setting and function.

3 The main pool

FAST FORWARD

With capital allowances computations, the main thing is to get the layout right. Having done that, you will find that the figures tend to drop into place.

3.1 Main pool expenditure

Most expenditure on plant and machinery, including expenditure on cars with CO_2 emissions of 130g/km or less, is put into a pool of expenditure (the main pool) on which capital allowances may be claimed. An addition increases the pool whilst a disposal decreases it.

Exceptionally the following items are not put into the main pool:

(a) Assets dealt with in the special rate pool
(b) Assets with private use by the trader
(c) Short life assets where an election has been made

These exceptions are dealt with later in this chapter.

Expenditure on plant and machinery by a person about to begin a trade is treated as incurred on the first day of trading. Assets previously owned by a trader and then brought into the trade (at the start of trading or later) are treated as bought for their market values at the times when they are brought in.

3.2 Annual investment allowance

PER alert

One of the competencies you require to fulfil Performance Objective 17 Tax planning and advice of the PER is to identify when to refer matters to someone with more specialist knowledge. You can apply the knowledge you obtain from this section of the Study Text to help to demonstrate this competence.

FAST FORWARD

Businesses are entitled to an annual investment allowance (AIA) of £200,000 for a 12 month period of account.

Businesses can claim an **annual investment allowance (AIA) on the first £200,000 spent each year on plant or machinery**, including assets in the main pool, but not including motor cars. Expenditure on motorcycles does qualify for the AIA.

Where the period of account is more or less than a year, the maximum allowance is proportionately increased or reduced.

After claiming the AIA, the balance of expenditure on main pool assets is transferred to the main pool immediately and is eligible for writing down allowances in the same period.

Exam focus point

The AIA limit changed to £200,000 on 1 January 2016. For exams in June 2017, September 2017, December 2017 and March 2018, **only this current limit is examinable** in F6(UK).

3.3 First year allowance for low emission cars

FAST FORWARD

A first year allowance (FYA) at the rate of 100% is available on new low emission cars. The FYA is not pro-rated in short or long periods of account.

Key term

A **low emission car** is one which has **CO_2 emissions of 75g/km or less**.

A 100% first year allowance (FYA) is available for expenditure incurred on new (ie unused and not second hand) **low emission motor cars.**

If the FYA is not claimed in full (for example if the trader does not want to create a loss – see later in this Study Text), the balance of expenditure is transferred to the main pool after any writing down allowance has been calculated on the main pool.

The FYA is not adjusted pro-rata in a short or long period of account, unlike the AIA and writing down allowances.

3.4 Writing down allowances

FAST FORWARD

Expenditure on plant and machinery in the main pool qualifies for a WDA at 18% every 12 months.

Key term

A **writing down allowance (WDA)** is given on main pool expenditure **at the rate of 18% a year** (on a reducing balance basis). The WDA is calculated on the tax written down value (TWDV) of pooled plant, after adding the current period's additions and taking out the current period's disposals.

When plant is sold, proceeds, limited to a maximum of the original cost, are taken out of the pool. Provided that the trade is still being carried on, the pool balance remaining is written down in the future by WDAs, even if there are no assets left.

3.5 Example

Elizabeth has tax written down value on her main pool of plant and machinery of £16,000 on 6 April 2016. In the year to 5 April 2017 she bought a car with CO_2 emissions of 110g/km for £8,000 (no non-business use) and she disposed of plant, which originally cost £4,000, for £6,000. The maximum capital allowances claim for the year is as follows.

	Main pool	*Allowances*
	£	£
TWDV b/f	16,000	
Addition (not qualifying for AIA)	8,000	
Less disposal (limited to cost)	(4,000)	
	20,000	
WDA @ 18%	(3,600)	3,600
TWDV c/f	16,400	
Maximum capital allowances claim		3,600

Question

Capital allowances

Julia is a sole trader preparing accounts to 5 April each year. At 5 April 2016, the tax written down value on her main pool is £12,500.

In the year to 5 April 2017, Julia bought the following assets:

1 June 2016	Machinery	£190,000
12 November 2016	Van	£17,500
10 February 2017	Car for salesman (CO_2 emissions 120g/km)	£9,000

She disposed of plant on 15 December 2016 for £12,000 (original cost £16,000).

Calculate the maximum capital allowances claim that Julia can make for the year ended 5 April 2017.

Answer

	AIA	*Main pool*	*Allowances*
	£	£	£
y/e 5 April 2017			
TWDV b/f		12,500	
Additions qualifying for AIA			
1.6.16 Machinery	190,000		
12.11.16 Van	17,500		
	207,500		
AIA	(200,000)		200,000
	7,500		
Transfer balance to pool	(7,500)	7,500	
Additions not qualifying for AIA			
10.2.17 Car		9,000	
Disposal			
15.12.16 Plant		(12,000)	
		17,000	
WDA @ 18%		(3,060)	3,060
TWDV c/f		13,940	
Maximum capital allowances			203,060

3.6 Short and long periods of account

WDAs are 18% × number of months/12:

(a) For unincorporated businesses where the period of account is longer or shorter than 12 months. For individuals, capital allowances computations are computed for periods of account not tax years.

(b) For companies where the accounting period is shorter than 12 months (a company's accounting period for tax purposes is never longer than 12 months), or where the trade concerned started in the accounting period and was therefore carried on for fewer than 12 months. For companies, capital allowances computations are computed for accounting periods, (we will be studying companies in detail later in this Study Text).

Question

Short period of account

Venus is a sole trader and has prepared accounts to 30 April each year. At 30 April 2016, the tax written down value of her main pool was £66,667. She decides to prepare her next set of accounts to 31 December 2016.

In the period to 31 December 2016, the following acquisitions were made:

1 May 2016	Plant	£146,666
10 July 2016	Car (CO_2 emissions 110 g/km)	£9,000
3 August 2016	Car (CO_2 emissions 65 g/km) – new	£11,000

Venus disposed of plant on 1 November 2016 for £20,000 (original cost £28,000).

Calculate the maximum capital allowances that Venus can claim for the period ending 31 December 2016.

Answer

	AIA	*FYA*	*Main pool*	*Allowances*
	£	£	£	£
p/e 31 December 2016				
TWDV b/f			66,667	
Additions qualifying for AIA				
1.5.16 Plant	146,666			
AIA £200,000 × 8/12	(133,333)			133,333
	13,333			
Transfer balance to pool	(13,333)		13,333	
Additions qualifying for FYA				
3.8.16 Car (new – low emission)		11,000		
Less: 100% FYA		(11,000)		11,000
Additions not qualifying for AIA or FYA				
10.7.16 Car			9,000	
Disposals				
1.11.16 Plant			(20,000)	
			69,000	
WDA @ 18% × 8/12			(8,280)	8,280
TWDVs c/f			60,720	
Maximum allowances claim				152,613

Note that the annual investment allowance and the writing down allowance are reduced for the short period of account, but the first year allowance is given in full.

Question

Long period of account

Oscar started trading on 1 July 2016 and prepared his first set of accounts to 31 December 2017. He bought the following assets:

10 July 2016	Plant	£130,000
1 October 2016	Car for business use only (CO_2 emissions 120g/km)	£11,000
12 February 2017	Plant	£235,000

Calculate the maximum capital allowances claim that Oscar can make for the period ended 31 December 2017. Assume that the rates of capital allowances in 2016/17 also apply in 2017/18.

Answer

	AIA	*Main pool*	*Allowances*
	£	£	£
p/e 31 December 2017			
Additions qualifying for AIA			
10.7.16 Plant	130,000		
12.2.17 Plant	235,000		
	365,000		
AIA £200,000 × 18/12	(300,000)		300,000
	65,000		
Transfer balance to main pool	(65,000)	65,000	
Additions not qualifying for AIA			
1.10.16 Car		11,000	
		76,000	
WDA @ 18% × 18/12		(20,520)	20,520
TWDV c/f		55,480	
Maximum capital allowances			320,520

Note that the annual investment allowance and the writing down allowance are increased for the long period of account.

3.7 Small balance on main pool

A writing down allowance equal to unrelieved expenditure in the main pool (after adjusting for current period acquisitions and disposals) can be claimed where this is **£1,000 or less for a 12 month period of account** (pro-rated for long or short period of account). If the maximum WDA is claimed, the main pool will then have a nil balance carried forward.

Question

Small balance on main pool

Alan has traded for many years, preparing accounts to 5 April each year. At 5 April 2016, the tax written down value of his main pool was £15,000. On 1 October 2016, he sold some plant and machinery for £14,200 (original cost £16,000).

Calculate the maximum capital allowances claim that Alan can make for the year ending 5 April 2017.

Answer

	Main pool	Allowances
	£	£
y/e 5 April 2017		
TWDV b/f	15,000	
Disposal	(14,200)	
	800	
WDA (small pool)	(800)	800
TWDV c/f	nil	
Maximum capital allowances		800

Exam focus point

Note the tax planning opportunities available. If plant is bought just before an accounting date, allowances become available as soon as possible. Alternatively, it may be desirable to claim less than the maximum allowances to even out annual taxable profits and avoid a higher rate of tax in later years. However, in the exam you should always claim the maximum available capital allowances unless you are told otherwise.

3.8 Balancing charges and allowances

Balancing charges occur when the disposal value deducted exceeds the balance remaining in the pool. The charge equals the excess and is effectively a negative capital allowance, increasing profits. Most commonly this happens when the trade ceases and the remaining assets are sold. It may also occur, however, whilst the trade is still in progress.

Balancing allowances on the main and special pools of expenditure arise only when the trade ceases. The balancing allowance is equal to the remaining unrelieved expenditure after deducting the disposal value of all the assets. Balancing allowances may also arise on single pool items (see later in this chapter) whenever those items are disposed of.

3.9 Interaction with value added tax (VAT)

We deal with VAT in Chapters 24 and 25. You may want to make a note to re-read this section when you study VAT.

Qualifying expenditure includes irrecoverable value added tax (VAT). The VAT may be irrecoverable because the trader is not VAT registered, or because it is type of expenditure on which the VAT is not recoverable (eg the acquisition of a car not used wholly for business purposes).

If the trader is VAT registered and can reclaim VAT on a purchase, only the expenditure net of VAT will be qualifying expenditure. Similarly, on a disposal of an asset on which capital allowances have been claimed, if VAT is charged by the trader on the disposal, **only the disposal proceeds net of VAT will be deducted**.

Not all capital allowances questions will require you to consider VAT. Take care, if the question mentions VAT inclusive or exclusive amounts or states that the trader is VAT-registered, that you make the appropriate VAT adjustments when performing capital allowances calculations.

3.10 Example

Frank is registered for VAT. He had the following transactions in capital assets during the year ended 5 April 2017:

Purchases:

12 May 2016	Plant for £42,000 (including VAT of £7,000)
4 October 2016	A car with CO_2 emissions of 115 g/km for £15,000 (including VAT of £2,500), 20% private use by one of Frank's employees.

Disposal:

30 September 2016	Machinery, which had originally cost £24,000 (including VAT of £4,000), was sold for £21,000 (including VAT of £3,500)

The tax written down value of Frank's main pool on 6 April 2016 was £70,000.

The maximum capital allowances that Frank can claim for the year ended 5 April 2017 are:

	AIA	*Main pool*	*Allowances*
	£	£	£
y/e 5 April 2017			
TWDV b/f		70,000	
Addition qualifying for AIA			
12.5.16 Plant			
£(42,000 – 7,000)	35,000		
AIA	(35,000)		35,000
Addition not qualifying for AIA			
4.10.16 Car (N)		15,000	
Disposal			
30.9.16 Machinery			
£(21,000 – 3,500)		(17,500)	
		67,500	
WDA @ 18%		(12,150)	12,150
TWDV c/f		55,350	
Maximum capital allowances			47,150

Note. The VAT on the car is irrecoverable because an employee uses it partly for private purposes (see Chapter 24). Whilst private use by the employee does not restrict the rate of capital allowances (as private use by Frank would), for VAT purposes **any** private use prevents the recovery of VAT.

3.11 Cessation of trade

For plant and machinery, **when a business ceases to trade, no AIAs, FYAs or WDAs are given in the final period of account** (unincorporated businesses) or accounting period (companies – see later in this Study Text). Each asset is deemed to be disposed of on the date the trade ceased (usually at the then market value). Additions (if any) in the relevant period are brought in and then the disposal proceeds (limited to cost) are deducted from the balance of qualifying expenditure. If the proceeds exceed the balance then a balancing charge arises. If the balance of qualifying expenditure exceeds the proceeds then a balancing allowance is given.

4 Special rate pool

FAST FORWARD

The special rate pool contains expenditure on thermal insulation, long life assets, features integral to a building and cars with CO_2 emissions over 130g/km. The AIA can be used against such expenditure except cars. The WDA is 8%.

4.1 Operation of the special rate pool

Expenditure on thermal insulation, long life assets, features integral to a building (see earlier in this chapter), **solar panels, and cars with CO_2 emissions over 130g/km is not dealt with in the main pool but in a special rate pool.**

The annual investment allowance can apply to expenditure on such assets except on cars. The taxpayer can decide how to allocate the AIA. It will be more tax efficient to set the allowance against special rate pool expenditure in priority to main pool expenditure where there is expenditure on assets in both pools in the period. Expenditure in excess of the AIA is added to the special rate pool and will be eligible for writing down allowance in the same period in which the expenditure is incurred.

The writing down allowance for the special rate pool is 8% for a 12 month period. As with the writing down allowance on the main pool, this is adjusted for short and long periods of account.

Where the **unrelieved expenditure in the special rate pool** (after adjusting for current period acquisitions and disposals) **is £1,000 or less for a 12 month period**, a writing down allowance can be claimed of up to £1,000. This amount is pro-rated for long and short periods. This is in addition to any similar claim in relation to the main pool (see earlier in this chapter).

4.2 Long life assets

Key term

Long life assets are assets with an expected working life of 25 years or more.

The **long life asset rules only apply to businesses whose total expenditure on assets with an expected working life of 25 years or more in a chargeable period is more than £100,000**. If the expenditure exceeds £100,000, the whole of the expenditure enters the special rate pool, not just the excess over £100,000. If the expenditure is £100,000 or less, the long life asset rules do not apply and the expenditure will be added to the main pool in the normal way. For this purpose all expenditure incurred under a contract is treated as incurred in the first chargeable period to which that contract relates.

The £100,000 limit is reduced or increased proportionately in the case of a chargeable period of less or more than 12 months.

The following are **not** treated as long life assets:

(a) **Plant and machinery in dwelling houses, retail shops, showrooms, hotels and offices**
(b) **Cars**

4.3 Example

Lucy has been trading for many years, preparing accounts to 5 April each year. The tax written down value of her main pool at 5 April 2016 was £110,000. In the year to 5 April 2017, Lucy had the following expenditure:

10 June 2016	General plant costing £45,000
12 December 2016	Lighting system in shop £50,000
15 January 2017	Car for business use only (CO_2 emissions 155 g/km) £25,000
26 January 2017	Delivery van £15,000
4 March 2017	Lifts £152,500

The maximum capital allowances claim that Lucy can make for the year to 5 April 2017 is as follows.

	AIA	Main pool	Special rate pool	Allowances
	£	£	£	£
y/e 5 April 2017				
TWDV b/f		110,000		
Additions for AIA (best use)				
12.12.16 Lighting	50,000			
4.3.17 Lifts	152,500			
	202,500			
AIA	(200,000)			200,000
	2,500			
Transfer balance to special rate pool	(2,500)		2,500	
Additions not given AIA				
10.6.16 Plant		45,000		
26.1.17 Van		15,000		
Additions not qualifying for AIA				
15.1.17 Car			25,000	
		170,000	27,500	
WDA @ 18%		(30,600)		30,600
WDA @ 8%			(2,200)	2,200
TWDVs c/f		139,400	25,300	
Allowances				232,800

5 Private use assets

FAST FORWARD

An asset which is used privately by a trader is dealt with in a single asset pool and the capital allowances are restricted.

An asset which is used partly for private purposes by a sole trader or a partner is put into its own pool (single asset pool).

Capital allowances are calculated on the full cost. However, only the business use proportion of the allowances is allowed as a deduction from trading profits. This restriction applies to the AIA, FYAs, WDAs, balancing allowances and balancing charges.

An asset with some private use by an employee (not the owner of the business) suffers no such restriction. The employee may be taxed under the benefits code (see earlier in this Study Text) so the business receives capital allowances on the full cost of the asset.

Exam focus point

Capital allowances on assets with some private use is a common exam topic. Check carefully whether the private use is by the owner of the business or by an employee.

Question — **Capital allowances on private use asset**

Jacinth has been in business as a sole trader for many years, preparing accounts to 31 March.
On 1 November 2016 she bought computer equipment for £2,700 which she uses 75% in her business and 25% privately. She has already used the AIA against other expenditure in the year to 31 March 2017.

Calculate the maximum capital allowance that Jacinth can claim in respect to the computer equipment in the year to 31 March 2017.

Answer

	Computer equipment £	Allowances @ 75% £
y/e 31 March 2017		
Acquisition	2,700	
WDA @ 18%	(486)	365
TWDV c/f	2,214	
Maximum capital allowance on computer equipment		365

6 Motor cars

Exam focus point

ACCA's article Motor cars, written by a member of the F6(UK) examination team explains the implications of acquiring, running, or having the use of a motor car for income tax, corporation tax, value added tax (VAT) and national insurance contribution (NIC).

FAST FORWARD

Motor cars are generally dealt with in the main pool or the special rate pool (cars emitting over 130g/km), unless there is private use by the trader in which case the car is held in a single asset pool.

As we have already seen, motor cars are categorised in accordance with their CO_2 emissions:

(a) **Cars emitting over 130g/km**: expenditure is added to the special rate pool

(b) **Cars emitting between 76 and 130 g/km**: expenditure is added to the main pool

(c) **Cars emitting 75 g/km or less**: expenditure on new cars eligible for 100% first year allowance, if allowance not claimed in full, excess added to main pool; expenditure on second hand cars is added to main pool

Cars with an element of private use are kept separate from the main and special pools and are dealt with in single asset pools. Such cars are entitled to a WDA of 18% (car with CO_2 emissions between 76 and 130 g/km) or 8% (car with CO_2 emissions over 130 g/km).

Question — Capital allowances on private use car

Quodos started to trade on 1 July 2016, preparing accounts to 31 December 2016 and each 31 December thereafter. On 1 August 2016 he bought a car for £17,000 with CO_2 emissions of 110 g/km. The private use proportion is 10%. The car was sold in July 2019 for £4,000. Quodos has no other assets which qualify for capital allowances.

Calculate the capital allowances, assuming:

(a) The car was used by an employee; or

(b) The car was used by Quodos.

and that the capital allowances rates in 2016/17 apply throughout.

Answer

(a)

	Main pool	Allowances
	£	£
1.7.16 – 31.12.16		
Purchase price	17,000	
WDA 18% × 6/12 × £17,000	(1,530)	1,530
	15,470	
1.1.17 – 31.12.17		
WDA 18% × £15,470	(2,785)	2,785
	12,685	
1.1.18 – 31.12.18		
WDA 18% × £12,685	(2,283)	2,283
	10,402	
1.1.19 – 31.12.19		
Proceeds	(4,000)	
	6,402	
WDA 18% × £6,402	(1,152)	1,152
TWDV c/f	5,250	

The private use of the car by the employee has no effect on the capital allowances due to Quodos. The car will be placed in the main pool. No balancing allowance is available on the main pool until trade ceases even though the car has been sold.

(b)

	Car	Allowances 90%
	£	£
1.7.16 – 31.12.16		
Purchase price	17,000	
WDA 18% × 6/12 x £17,000	(1,530)	1,377
	15,470	
1.1.17 – 31.12.17		
WDA 18% × £15,470	(2,785)	2,507
	12,685	
1.1.18 – 31.12.18		
WDA 18% × £12,685	(2,283)	2,055
	10,402	
1.1.19 – 31.12.19		
Proceeds	(4,000)	
Balancing allowance	6,402	5,762

The car is placed in a single asset pool because of the private use by the trader, Quodos. Only 90% of the WDAs and balancing allowance are available as a result of this private use.

7 Short life assets

FAST FORWARD

Short life asset elections can bring forward the allowances due on an asset.

A trader can elect that specific items of plant, which are expected to have a short working life, be kept separately from the main pool.

Key term

Any asset subject to this election is known as a **'short life asset'**, and the election is known as a 'de-pooling election'.

The election is irrevocable. For an unincorporated business, the time limit for electing is the 31 January which is 22 months after the end of the tax year in which the period of account of the expenditure ends. (For a company, it is two years after the end of the accounting period of the expenditure.) **Short life asset treatment cannot be claimed for any motor cars, or plant used partly for non-trade purposes.**

The short life asset is kept in a single asset pool. Provided that the short life asset is disposed of **within eight years of the end of the accounting period** in which it was bought, a balancing charge or allowance arises on its disposal.

If the asset is not disposed of within this time period, its tax written down value is added to the main pool at the beginning of the next period of account (accounting period for companies). This will be after allowances have been claimed nine times on the asset; once in the period of acquisition and then each year for the following eight years.

The election should therefore be made for assets likely to be sold for less than their tax written down values within eight years. It should not usually be made for assets likely to be sold within eight years for more than their tax written down values. There is no requirement to show from the outset that the asset will actually have a 'short life', so it is a matter of judgment whether the election should be made.

The annual investment allowance can be set against short life assets. The taxpayer can decide how to allocate the AIA. It will be more tax efficient to set the allowance against main pool expenditure in priority to short life asset expenditure.

Question

Short life assets

Caithlin bought a machine for business use on 1 May 2016 for £9,000 and elected for de-pooling. She did not claim the AIA in respect of this asset. Her accounting year end is 30 April.

Calculate the capital allowances due if:

(a) The asset is scrapped for £300 in August 2024
(b) The asset is scrapped for £200 in August 2025

and assuming that the capital allowances rates in 2016/17 apply throughout.

Answer

(a)

	£
Year to 30.4.17	
Cost	9,000
WDA 18%	(1,620)
	7,380
Year to 30.4.18	
WDA 18%	(1,328)
	6,052
Year to 30.4.19	
WDA 18%	(1,089)
	4,963
Year to 30.4.20	
WDA 18%	(893)
	4,070
Year to 30.4.21	
WDA 18%	(733)
	3,337
Year to 30.4.22	
WDA 18%	(601)
	2,736
Year to 30.4.23	
WDA 18%	(492)
	2,244
Year to 30.4.24	
WDA 18%	(404)
	1,840
Year to 30.4.25	
Disposal proceeds	(300)
Balancing allowance	1,540

(b) If the asset is still in use at 30 April 2024, WDAs up to 30.4.24 will be as above. In the year to 30.4.25, a WDA can be claimed of 18% × £1,840 = £331. The tax written down value of £1,840 – £331 = £1,509 will be added to the main pool at the beginning of the next period of account. The disposal proceeds of £200 will be deducted from the main pool in that period's capital allowances computation. No balancing allowance will arise and the main pool will continue.

Chapter Roundup

- Capital allowances are available to give tax relief for certain capital expenditure.
- There are various statutory rules on what does or does not qualify as plant.
- There are also cases on the definition of plant. To help you to absorb them, try to see the function/setting theme running through them.
- With capital allowances computations, the main thing is to get the layout right. Having done that, you will find that the figures tend to drop into place.
- Businesses are entitled to an annual investment allowance (AIA) of £200,000 for a 12 month period of account.
- A first year allowance (FYA) at the rate of 100% is available on new low emission cars. The FYA is not pro-rated in short or long periods of account.
- Expenditure on plant and machinery in the main pool qualifies for a WDA at 18% every 12 months.
- The special rate pool contains expenditure on thermal insulation, long life assets, features integral to a building and cars with CO_2 emissions over 130g/km. The AIA can be used against such expenditure except cars. The WDA is 8%.
- An asset which is used privately by a trader is dealt with in a single asset pool and the capital allowances are restricted.
- Motor cars are generally dealt with in the main pool or the special rate pool (cars emitting over 130g/km), unless there is private use by the trader in which case the car is held in a single asset pool.
- Short life asset elections can bring forward the allowances due on an asset.

Quick Quiz

1 Writing down allowances are pro-rated in a six month period of account. True/False?

2 Lucas makes up accounts for a 15 month period to 30 June 2016. What Annual Investment Allowance is he entitled to?

A £50,000
B £150,000
C £200,000
D £250,000

3 Is a first year allowance on a low emission car pro-rated in a six month period of account?

4 When may balancing allowances arise?

5 An asset must be disposed of within ____ years of the end of the accounting period (or period of account) in which it was acquired in order for it to be advantageous to treat it as a short life asset. Fill in the blank.

6 Paula makes up accounts to 5 April each year. She buys a car in August 2016 costing £20,000 for use in her business. Her private use of the car is 30%. The CO_2 emissions of the car are 150g/km.

What WDA is available on the car for the year ended 5 April 2017?

A £1,120
B £1,600
C £2,520
D £3,600

Answers to Quick Quiz

1 True. In a six month period, writing down allowance are pro-rated by multiplying by 6/12.

2 D. £200,000 × 15/12 = £250,000.

3 No. A first year allowance is given in full in a short period of account.

4 Balancing allowances may arise in respect of main or special rate pool expenditure only when the trade ceases. Balancing allowances may arise on single pool assets whenever those assets are disposed of.

5 An asset must be disposed of within **8** years of the end of the accounting period (or period of account) in which it was acquired in order for it to be advantageous to treat it as a short life asset.

6 A. £20,000 × 8% (CO_2 emissions of the car exceed 130g/km) = £1,600. WDA is £1,600 × 70% = £1,120.

Now try the questions below from the Practice Question Bank

Number	Type	Marks	Time
Q50	Section A	2	4 mins
Q51	Section A	2	4 mins
Q52	Section A	2	4 mins
Q53	Section B	2	4 mins
Q54	Section B	2	4 mins
Q55	Section B	2	4 mins
Q56	Section B	2	4 mins
Q57	Section B	2	4 mins
Q58	Section C	15	29 mins

9

Assessable trading income

Topic list	Syllabus reference
1 Recognise the basis of assessment	B3(a)
2 Commencement and cessation	B3(f)
3 The choice of an accounting date	B3(g)

Introduction

In the previous two chapters we have seen how to calculate the taxable trading profits after capital allowances. We are now going to look at how these are taxed in the owner's hands.

Businesses do not normally prepare accounts for tax years so we look at the basis of assessment which is the method by which the taxable trading profits of periods of account are allocated to tax years. As well as the normal rules for a continuing business we need special rules for the opening years of a trade, and again in the closing years.

A business may choose its accounting date and this may have an effect on when the tax is payable on profits.

In the next chapter we will look at the tax reliefs available should the business make a loss.

Study guide

		Intellectual level
B3	**Income from self-employment**	
(a)	Recognise the basis of assessment for self-employment income.	2
(f)	Compute the assessable profits on commencement and on cessation.	2
(g)	Recognise the factors that will influence the choice of accounting date.	2

Exam guide

You are likely to have to deal with a tax computation for an unincorporated business in any of Sections A, B or C. It may be a simple computation for a continuing business, or you may have to deal with a business in its opening or closing years, including computing taxable trading profits and allocating them to tax years. You must be totally familiar with the rules and be able to apply them in the exam. These topics may be tested in a 15 mark question or a 10 mark question in Section C. A specific point, such as computing an amount of overlap profits, may be tested in Sections A or B.

1 Recognise the basis of assessment

FAST FORWARD

Basis periods are used to link periods of account to tax years. Broadly, the profits of a 12 month period of account ending in a tax year are taxed in that year (current year basis).

1.1 Basis periods and tax years

A tax year runs from 6 April to 5 April, but most businesses do not have periods of account ending on 5 April. **Thus there must be a link between a period of account of a business and a tax year**. The procedure is to **find a period to act as the basis period for a tax year. The profits for a basis period are taxed in the corresponding tax year.** If a basis period is not identical to a period of account, the profits of periods of account are time-apportioned as required on the assumption that profits accrue evenly over a period of account. We will apportion to the nearest month for exam purposes.

The same rules apply to link periods of account to tax years regardless of whether the normal accruals method of accounting or the cash basis is used.

The general rule is that **the basis period is the year of account ending in the tax year**. This is known as the **current year basis of assessment**. For example, if a trader prepares accounts to 31 December each year, the profits of the year to 31 December 2016 will be taxed in the tax year 2016/17.

This general rule does not apply in the opening or closing years of a business. This is because in the first few years the business has not normally established a pattern of annual accounts, and very few businesses cease trading on the annual accounting date.

Apart from the first tax year of trade and the last tax year of trade, HMRC will expect to see 12 months of profits showing in the income tax computation each year. As the periods of account may not be 12 months long in the opening and closing years, the current year basis may be impossible to apply, therefore special rules need to be applied to establish which 12 months should be allocated to which tax year.

2 Commencement and cessation

FAST FORWARD

In the first tax year of trade actual profits of the tax year are taxed. In the second tax year, the basis period is either the first 12 months, the 12 months to the accounting date ending in year two or the actual profits from April to April. Profits of the 12 months to the accounting date are taxed in year three.

2.1 The first tax year

The first tax year is the year during which the trade commences. For example, if a trade commences on 1 June 2016 the first tax year is 2016/17.

The **basis period for the first tax year runs from the date the trade starts to the next 5 April** (or to the date of cessation if the trade does not last until the end of the tax year).

So continuing the above example a trader commencing in business on 1 June 2016 will be taxed on profits arising from 1 June 2016 to 5 April 2017 in 2016/17, the first tax year.

2.2 The second tax year

(a) **If the accounting date falling in the second tax year is at least 12 months after the start of trading, the basis period is the 12 months to that accounting date.**

(b) **If the accounting date falling in the second tax year is less than 12 months after the start of trading, the basis period is the first 12 months of trading.**

(c) **If there is no accounting date falling in the second tax year, because the first period of account is a very long one which does not end until a date in the third tax year, the basis period for the second tax year is the year itself (from 6 April to 5 April).**

The following flowchart may help you determine the basis period for the second tax year.

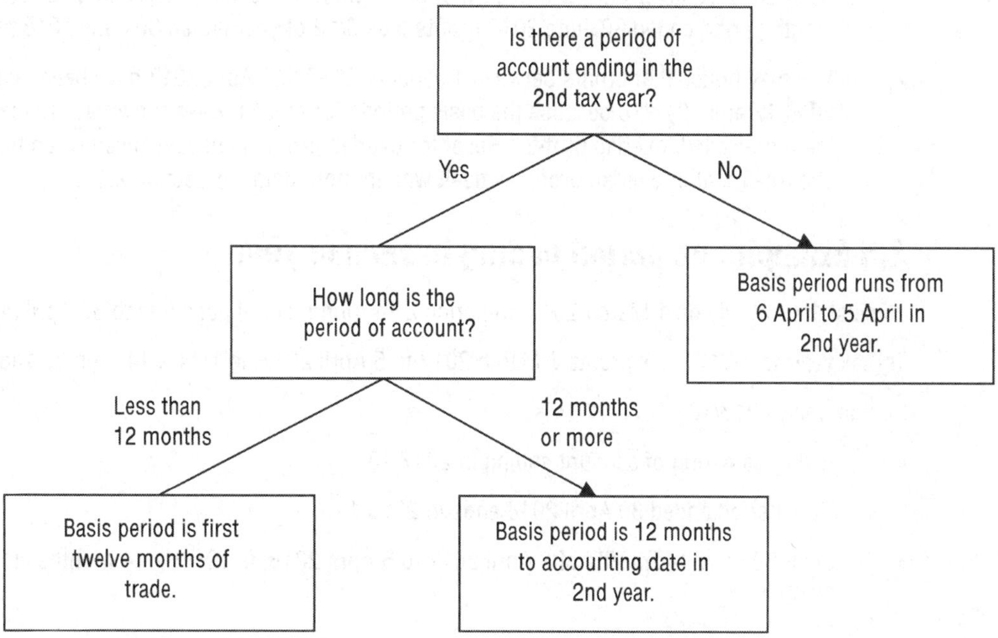

2.3 Example: period of 12 months or more ending in second year

John starts to trade on 1 January 2017 preparing accounts to 31 December 2017.

1st tax year: 2016/17 – tax profits 1 January 2017 to 5 April 2017, ie 3/12 × year ended 31 December 2017

2nd tax year: 2017/18

- Is there a period of account ending in 2017/18?

  Yes – year ended 31 December 2017 ends in 2017/18.

- How long is the period of account?

  12 months or more, ie 12 months (exactly) to 31 December 2017.

- So in 2017/18 tax profits of 12 months to 31 December 2017.

2.4 Example: short period ending in second year

Janet starts to trade on 1 January 2017 preparing accounts as follows:

- Six months to 30 June 2017
- 12 months to 30 June 2018

1st tax year: 2016/17 – tax profits 1 January 2017 to 5 April 2017, ie 3/6 × 6 months ended 30 June 2017

2nd tax year: 2017/18

- Is there a period of account ending in 2017/18?

  Yes – period ended 30 June 2017 ends in 2017/18.

- How long is the period of account?

  Less than 12 months

- So in 2017/18 tax profits of first 12 months of trade ie 1 January 2017 to 31 December 2017, ie 6 month period ended 30 June 2017 profits plus 6/12 of year ended 30 June 2018 profits.

- You may notice that profits between 1 January 2017 to 5 April 2017 have been taxed in both 2016/17 and 2017/18 because the basis periods for these tax years overlap. These profits are therefore called 'overlap profits'. Relief for overlap profits is usually given when the trade ceases. The treatment of overlap profits is dealt with in more detail in Section 2.11.

2.5 Example: no period ending in second year

Jodie starts to trade on 1 March 2017 preparing a 14 month set of accounts to 30 April 2018.

1st tax year: 2016/17 – tax profits 1 March 2017 to 5 April 2017, ie 1/14 × 14 months ended 30 April 2018

2nd tax year: 2017/18

- Is there a period of account ending in 2017/18?

  No – period ended 30 April 2018 ends in 2018/19.

- So in 2017/18 tax profits of 6 April 2017 to 5 April 2018, ie 12/14 × 14 months ended 30 April 2018.

2.6 The third tax year

(a) **If there is an accounting date falling in the second tax year, the basis period for the third tax year is the 12 month period of account ending in the third tax year (current year basis).**

(b) If there is no accounting date falling in the second tax year, the basis period for the third tax year is the 12 months to the accounting date falling in the third tax year.

2.7 Example: accounting date in second year

Wilma starts to trade on 1 October 2016. She made taxable profits of £9,000 for the first nine months to 30 June 2017 and £30,000 for the year to 30 June 2018.

The taxable profits for the first three tax years are as follows:

Year	*Basis period*	*Working*	*Taxable profits* £
2016/17	1.10.16 – 5.4.17	£9,000 × 6/9	6,000
2017/18	1.10.16 – 30.9.17	£9,000 + £30,000 × 3/12	16,500
2018/19	1.7.17 – 30.6.18 (period of account ending in 3rd year)		30,000

2.8 Example: no accounting date in the second year

Thelma starts to trade on 1 March 2017. Her first accounts, covering the 16 months to 30 June 2018 show a profit of £36,000. The taxable profits for the first three tax years are as follows.

Year	*Basis period*	*Working*	*Taxable profits* £
2016/17	1.3.17 – 5.4.17	£36,000 × 1/16	2,250
2017/18	6.4.17 – 5.4.18	£36,000 × 12/16	27,000
2018/19	1.7.17 – 30.6.18 (12 months to the accounting date in 3rd year)	£36,000 × 12/16	27,000

2.9 Later tax years

For later tax years, except the year in which the trade ceases, the normal current year basis of assessment applies, ie the basis period is the 12 month period of account ending in the tax year (see above).

Question — Basis periods

Peter commenced trading on 1 September 2012 preparing accounts to 30 April each year with the following results.

Period	*Profit* £
1.9.12 – 30.4.13	8,000
1.5.13 – 30.4.14	15,000
1.5.14 – 30.4.15	9,000
1.5.15 – 30.4.16	10,500

Show the profits to be taxed in each year from 2012/13 to 2016/17.

Answer

Year	*Basis period*	*Working*	*Taxable Profits* £
2012/13	1.9.12 – 5.4.13	£8,000 × 7/8	7,000
2013/14	1.9.12 – 31.8.13	£8,000 + (£15,000 × 4/12)	13,000
2014/15	1.5.13 – 30.4.14		15,000
2015/16	1.5.14 – 30.4.15		9,000
2016/17	1.5.15 – 30.4.16		10,500

2.10 The final year

FAST FORWARD

On a cessation the basis period runs from the end of the basis period for the previous tax year.

(a) If a trade starts and ceases in the same tax year, the basis period for that year is the whole lifespan of the trade.

(b) If the final year is the second year, the basis period runs from 6 April at the start of the second year to the date of cessation. This rule overrides the rules that normally apply for the second year.

(c) If the final year is the third year or a later year, **the basis period runs from the end of the basis period for the previous year to the date of cessation**. This rule overrides the rules that normally apply in the third and later years.

Question — **Ceasing to trade**

Harriet, who has been trading since 2001, ceases her trade on 31 March 2017.

Her results for recent years were:

Year ended 31 December	£
2014	10,000
2015	14,000
2016	21,000
Period ended 31 March 2017	4,000

Show the taxable trade profits for the last three tax years of trading.

Answer

Trade ceases in 2016/17.

Year	*Basis period*	*Working*	*Assessment*
			£
2014/15	Y/e 31.12.14		10,000
2015/16	Y/e 31.12.15		14,000
2016/17	1.1.16 – 31.3.17	Y/e 31.12.16 plus p/e 31.3.17	25,000

2.11 Overlap profits

Key term

Profits which have been taxed more than once are called **overlap profits**.

When a business starts, some profits may be taxed twice because the basis period for the second year includes some or all of the period of trading in the first year or because the basis period for the third year overlaps with that for the second year, or both.

Overlap profits are relieved when the trade ceases by being deducted from the final year's taxable profits. Any deduction of overlap profits may create or increase a loss. The usual loss reliefs (covered later in this Study Text) are then available.

Exam focus point

A business with a 31 March year end will have no overlap profits as its accounting year coincides with the tax year. A business with a 31 December year end, for example, will have three months of overlap profit as its accounting year ends three months before the end of the tax year. Use this rule of thumb to check your calculation of overlap profits.

2.12 Examples: overlap profits

(a) John starts to trade on 1 January 2017 preparing accounts to 31 December 2017. Show the overlap period.

Tax year	*Basis period*
2016/17	1.1.17 – 5.4.17
2017/18	1.1.17 – 31.12.17
2018/19	1.1.18 – 31.12.18

Overlap period: 1.1.17 – 5.4.17 (three months)

(b) Janet starts to trade on 1 January 2017 preparing accounts as follows:

6m to 30 June 2017
12m to 30 June 2018

Show the overlap period.

Tax year	*Basis period*
2016/17	1.1.17 – 5.4.17
2017/18	1.1.17 – 31.12.17
2018/19	1.7.17 – 30.6.18

Overlap period: 1.1.17 – 5.4.17 plus 1.7.17 – 31.12.17 (nine months)

(c) Jodie starts to trade on 1 March 2017 preparing a 14 month set of accounts to 30 April 2018. Show the overlap period.

Tax year	*Basis period*
2016/17	1.3.17 – 5.4.17
2017/18	6.4.17 – 5.4.18
2018/19	1.5.17 – 30.4.18

Overlap period: 1.5.17 – 5.4.18 (11 months)

Question — Ceasing to trade and overlap profits

Jenny trades from 1 July 2011 to 31 December 2016, with the following results.

Period	*Profit*
	£
1.7.11 – 31.8.12	7,000
1.9.12 – 31.8.13	12,000
1.9.13 – 31.8.14	15,000
1.9.14 – 31.8.15	21,000
1.9.15 – 31.8.16	18,000
1.9.16 – 31.12.16	5,600
	78,600

Calculate the taxable trade profits to be taxed from 2011/12 to 2016/17, the overlap profits and state when these overlap profits can be relieved.

Answer

The profits to be taxed in each tax year from 2011/12 to 2016/17 and the total of these taxable profits are calculated as follows.

Year	*Basis period*	*Working*	*Taxable profit*
			£
2011/12	1.7.11 – 5.4.12	£7,000 × 9/14	4,500
2012/13	1.9.11 – 31.8.12	£7,000 × 12/14	6,000
2013/14	1.9.12 – 31.8.13		12,000
2014/15	1.9.13 – 31.8.14		15,000
2015/16	1.9.14 – 31.8.15		21,000
2016/17	1.9.15 – 31.12.16	£(18,000 + 5,600 – 3,500)	20,100
			78,600

The overlap profits are those in the period 1 September 2011 to 5 April 2012, a period of seven months. They are £7,000 × 7/14 = £3,500. Overlap profits are deducted from the final year's taxable profit when the business ceases.

Exam focus point

Over the life of the business, the total taxable profits equal the total actual profits.

3 The choice of an accounting date

FAST FORWARD

The choice of an accounting date may affect when tax is payable on trading profits. It may also create overlap profits and help or hinder tax planning.

A new trader should consider which accounting date would be best. There are **a number of factors to consider** from the point of view of taxation.

- **If profits are expected to rise, a date early in the tax year** (such as 30 April) will delay the time when rising accounts profits feed through into rising taxable profits, whereas a date late in the tax year (such as 31 March) will accelerate the taxation of rising profits. This is because with an accounting date of 30 April, the taxable profits for each tax year are mainly the profits earned in the previous tax year. With an accounting date of 31 March the taxable profits are almost entirely profits earned in the current year.
- If the accounting date in the second tax year is less than 12 months after the start of trading, the taxable profits for that year will be the profits earned in the first 12 months. If the accounting date is at least 12 months from the start of trading, they will be the profits earned in the 12 months to that date. **Different profits may thus be taxed twice**, and if profits are fluctuating this can make a considerable difference to the taxable profits in the first few years.
- **The choice of an accounting date affects the profits shown in each set of accounts**, and this may affect the taxable profits.
- **An accounting date of 30 April gives the maximum interval between earning profits and paying the related tax liability.** For example if a trader prepares accounts to 30 April 2017, this falls into the tax year 2017/18 with payments on account being due on 31 January 2018 and 31 July 2018, and a balancing payment due on 31 January 2019 (details of payment of income tax are dealt with later in this Study Text). If the trader prepares accounts to 31 March 2017, this falls in the tax year 2016/17 and the payments will be due one year earlier (ie on 31 January 2017, 31 July 2017 and 31 January 2018).

- **Knowing profits well in advance of the end of the tax year makes tax planning much easier.** For example, if a trader wants to make personal pension contributions and prepares accounts to 30 April 2017 (2017/18), he can make contributions up to 5 April 2018 based on those relevant earnings. If he prepares accounts to 31 March 2017, he will probably not know the amount of his relevant earnings until after the end of the tax year 2016/17, too late to adjust his pension contributions for 2016/17.
- **However, a 31 March or 5 April accounting date means that the application of the basis period rules is more straightforward and there will be no overlap profits.** This may be appropriate for small traders.
- **With an accounting date of 30 April, the assessment for the year of cessation could be based on up to 23 months of profits.** For example, if a trader who has prepared accounts to 30 April ceases trading on 31 March 2017 (2016/17), the basis period for 2016/17 will run from 1 May 2015 to 31 March 2017. This could lead to larger than normal trading profits being assessable in the year of cessation. However, this could be avoided by carrying on the trade for another month so that a cessation arises on 30 April 2017 so that the profits from 1 May 2015 to 30 April 2016 are taxable in 2016/17 and those from 1 May 2016 to 30 April 2017 are taxable in 2017/18. Each case must be looked at in relation to all relevant factors, such as other income which the taxpayer may have and loss relief – there is no one rule which applies in all cases.

Question

The choice of an accounting date

Christine starts to trade on 1 December 2014. Her monthly profits are £1,000 for the first seven months, and £2,000 thereafter. Show the taxable profits for the first three tax years with each of the following accounting dates (in all cases starting with a period of account of less than 12 months).

(a) 31 March
(b) 30 April
(c) 31 December

Answer

(a) *31 March*

Period of account	*Working*	*Profits*
		£
1.12.14 – 31.3.15	£1,000 × 4	4,000
1.4.15 – 31.3.16	£1,000 × 3 + £2,000 × 9	21,000
1.4.16 – 31.3.17	£2,000 × 12	24,000

Year	*Basis period*	*Taxable profits*
		£
2014/15	1.12.14 – 5.4.15	4,000
2015/16	1.4.15 – 31.3.16	21,000
2016/17	1.4.16 – 31.3.17	24,000

(b) *30 April*

Period of account	*Working*	*Profits*
		£
1.12.14 – 30.4.15	£1,000 × 5	5,000
1.5.15 – 30.4.16	£1,000 × 2 + £2,000 ×10	22,000

Year	*Basis period*	*Working*	*Taxable profits*
			£
2014/15	1.12.14 – 5.4.15	£5,000 × 4/5	4,000
2015/16	1.12.14 – 30.11.15	£5,000 + £22,000 × 7/12	17,833
2016/17	1.5.15 – 30.4.16		22,000

(c) *31 December*

Period of account	*Working*	*Profits*
		£
1.12.14 – 31.12.14	£1,000 × 1	1,000
1.1.15 – 31.12.15	£1,000 × 6 + £2,000 × 6	18,000
1.1.16 – 31.12.16	£2,000 × 12	24,000

Year	*Basis period*	*Working*	*Taxable profits*
			£
2014/15	1.12.14 – 5.4.15	£1,000 + £18,000 × 3/12	5,500
2015/16	1.1.15 – 31.12.15		18,000
2016/17	1.1.16 – 31.12.16		24,000

Chapter Roundup

- Basis periods are used to link periods of account to tax years. Broadly, the profits of a 12 month period of account ending in a tax year are taxed in that year (current year basis).
- In the first tax year of trade actual profits of the tax year are taxed. In the second tax year, the basis period is either the first 12 months, the 12 months to the accounting date ending in year two or the actual profits from April to April. Profits of the 12 months to the accounting date are taxed in year three.
- On a cessation the basis period runs from the end of the basis period for the previous tax year.
- The choice of an accounting date may affect when tax is payable on trading profits. It may also create overlap profits and help or hinder tax planning.

Quick Quiz

1 What is the normal basis of assessment?

2 Isabella started trading on 1 September 2016. She prepares her first set of accounts to 31 December 2017. The basis period for the year of commencement is:

A 1 September 2016 to 31 December 2016
B 1 September 2016 to 5 April 2017
C 1 September 2016 to 31 August 2017
D 1 September 2016 to 31 December 2017

3 Ernie started trading on 1 January 2016. He decided to prepare accounts to 31 October each year. His taxable trading profits is as follows:

p/e 31.10.16	£3,000
y/e 31.10.17	£23,760

What are Ernie's overlap profits?

A £900
B £2,880
C £3,960
D £4,860

4 Gita ceased trading on 31 March 2017. Her taxable trading profits were:

y/e 31.12.16	£5,600
p/e 31.3.17	£4,500

Gita had £2,300 of unused overlap profits.

What is her taxable trading profit for 2016/17?

A £10,100
B £7,800
C £6,400
D £2,200

5 How are overlap profits relieved?

Answers to Quick Quiz

1 The normal basis of assessment is that the profits for a tax year are those of the 12 month accounting period ending in the tax year.

2 B. 1 September 2016 to 5 April 2017 ie the actual tax year.

3 D £4,860

First tax year (2015/16)
Actual basis
Basis period 1.1.16 to 5.4.16

Second tax year (2016/17)
Period of account in 2nd year less than 12 months
Basis period 1.1.16 to 31.12.16

Third tax year (2017/18)
Current year basis
Basis period 1.11.16 to 31.10.17

Overlap profits
Period of overlap 1.1.16 to 5.4.16 and 1.11.16 to 31.12.16

Overlap profits

	£
3/10 × £3,000	900
2/12 × £23,760	3,960
	4,860

4 B £7,800

Last tax year (2016/17) Basis period 1.1.16 to 31.3.17

	£
y/e 31.12.16	5,600
p/e 31.3.17	4,500
	10,100
Less overlap profits	(2,300)
	7,800

5 On the cessation of a business by deduction from the final year's taxable profits.

Now try the questions below from the Practice Question Bank

Number	Type	Marks	Time
Q59	Section A	2	4 mins
Q60	Section A	2	4 mins
Q61	Section A	2	4 mins
Q62	Section C	15	29 mins
Q63	Section C	15	29 mins

10

Trading losses

Topic list	Syllabus reference
1 Losses	B3(i)
2 Carry forward trade loss relief	B3(i)(i)
3 Trade loss relief against general income	B3(i)(ii), (i)(v)
4 Losses in the early years of a trade	B3(i)(iii)
5 Terminal trade loss relief	B3(i)(iv)

Introduction

We have seen how to calculate taxable trading profits and how to allocate them to tax years so that they can be slotted into the income tax computation.

Traders sometimes make losses rather than profits. In this chapter we consider the reliefs available for losses. A loss does not in itself lead to getting tax back from HMRC. Relief is obtained by setting a loss against trading profits, against general income or against capital gains (which are covered later in this Study Text), so that tax need not be paid on them. There are restrictions on how much loss relief can be claimed in a tax year.

An important consideration is the choice between different reliefs. The aim is to use a loss to save as much tax as possible, as quickly as possible.

In the next chapter we will see how the rules on trading profits and losses for sole traders are extended to those trading in partnership.

Study guide

		Intellectual level
B3	**Income from self-employment**	
(i)	Relief for trading losses	
(i)(i)	Understand how trading losses can be carried forward.	2
(i)(ii)	Understand how trading losses can be claimed against total income and chargeable gains, and the restriction that can apply.	2
(i)(iii)	Explain and compute the relief for trading losses in the early years of a trade.	1
(i)(iv)	Explain and compute terminal loss relief.	1
(i)(v)	Recognise the factors that will influence the choice of loss relief claim.	2

Exam guide

Section A questions on loss relief may deal with a specific aspect such as the cap on loss relief against general income. You may also have to deal with a number of aspects of loss relief in a Section B question. Section C could have a detailed computational question involving the carry back and carry forward of losses for a sole trader. Ensure you know the rules for ongoing trades and the additional relief in the early years of trading. On cessation, terminal loss relief may be used. Once you have established the reliefs available look to see which is most beneficial.

PER alert

One of the competencies you require to fulfil Performance Objective 17 Tax planning and advice of the PER is to mitigate and/or defer tax liabilities through the use of standard reliefs, exemptions and incentives. You can apply the knowledge you obtain from this chapter of the Study Text to help to demonstrate this competence.

1 Losses

FAST FORWARD

Trading losses may be relieved against future profits of the same trade, against general income and against capital gains.

1.1 Introduction

When computing taxable trade profits, profits may turn out to be negative, meaning a loss has been made in the basis period. **A loss is computed in exactly the same way as a profit**, making the same adjustments to the accounts profit or loss.

If there is a loss in a basis period, the taxable trade profits for the tax year based on that basis period are nil.

This chapter considers how losses are calculated and how a loss-suffering taxpayer can use a loss to reduce his tax liability.

The rules in this chapter apply only to individuals, trading alone or in partnership. They do not apply to a business using the cash basis. Loss reliefs for companies are completely different and are covered later in this Study Text.

1.2 The computation of the loss

The trade loss for a tax year is the trade loss in the basis period for that tax year.

1.3 Example: computation of trade loss

Here is an example of a trader with a 31 December year end who has been trading for many years.

Period of account	*Loss*
	£
Y/e 31.12.16	9,000
Y/e 31.12.17	24,000

Tax year	*Basis period*	*Trade loss for the tax year*
		£
2016/17	Y/e 31.12.16	9,000
2017/18	Y/e 31.12.17	24,000

1.4 How loss relief is given

Loss relief is given by deducting the loss from total income to calculate net income. Carry forward loss relief and terminal loss relief can only be set against the trading profits of the same trade. Other loss reliefs may be set against general income (ie any component of total income).

2 Carry forward trade loss relief

FAST FORWARD

Trading losses may be relieved against future profits of the same trade. The relief is against the first available profits of the same trade.

2.1 The relief

A trade loss not relieved in any other way will be **carried forward to set against the first available trade profits of the same trade** in the calculation of net trading income. Losses may be carried forward for any number of years unless they have been entirely used up.

Carry forward trade loss relief is the only trade loss relief which applies to furnished holiday lettings (see earlier in this Study Text).

2.2 Example: carrying forward losses

Brian has the following results.

Year ending	£
31 December 2014	(6,000)
31 December 2015	5,000
31 December 2016	11,000

Brian's net trading income, assuming that he claims carry forward loss relief only are:

	2014/15		*2015/16*		*2016/17*
	£		£		£
Trade profits	0		5,000		11,000
Less carry forward loss relief	(0)	(i)	(5,000)	(ii)	(1,000)
Net trading income	0		0		10,000

Loss memorandum		£
Trading loss, y/e 31.12.14		6,000
Less: claim in y/e 31.12.15 (15/16)	(i)	(5,000)
claim in y/e 31.12.16 (balance of loss) (16/17)	(ii)	(1,000)
		0

3 Trade loss relief against general income

FAST FORWARD

A trading loss may be set against general income in the year of the loss and/or the preceding year. Personal allowances may be lost as a result of a claim. Once a claim has been made in any year, the remaining loss can be set against net chargeable gains.

3.1 The relief

Instead of carrying a trade loss forward against future trade profits, a claim may be made to relieve it against general income.

3.2 Relieving the loss

Relief is against the income of the tax year in which the loss arose. In addition or instead, relief may be claimed **against the income of the preceding year.**

If there are losses in two successive years, and relief is claimed against the first year's income both for the first year's loss and for the second year's loss, relief is given for the first year's loss before the second year's loss.

A claim for a loss must be made by the 31 January which is 22 months after the end of the tax year of the loss: thus by 31 January 2019 for a loss in 2016/17.

The taxpayer cannot choose the amount of loss to relieve: thus the loss may have to be set against income part of which would have been covered by the personal allowance or taxed at 0% in the savings income nil rate band or the dividend nil rate band. However, the taxpayer can choose whether to claim full relief in the current year and then relief in the preceding year for any remaining loss, or the other way round.

When calculating the income tax liability, the **loss is usually set against non-savings income, then against savings income and finally against dividend income.**

Exam focus point

There are some situations where this order of set off will not be the most beneficial but such a scenario will **not be examined** in F6(UK).

Question — **Loss relief against general income**

Janet has a loss in her period of account ending 31 December 2016 of £37,000. Her other income is dividend income of £30,000 a year, and she wishes to claim loss relief against general income for the year of loss and then for the preceding year. Her trading income in the previous year was £nil. Show her taxable income for each year, and comment on the effectiveness of the loss relief. Assume that tax rates and allowances for 2016/17 have always applied.

Answer

The loss-making period ends in 2016/17, so the year of the loss is 2016/17.

	2015/16	*2016/17*
	£	£
Total income	30,000	30,000
Less loss relief against general income	(7,000)	(30,000)
Net income	23,000	0
Less personal allowance	(11,000)	(11,000)
Taxable income	12,000	0

In 2016/17, £(11,000 + 5,000) = £16,000 of the loss has been wasted because that amount of income would have been covered by the personal allowance and the dividend nil rate band. If Janet just claims loss relief against general income, there is nothing she can do about this waste of loss relief.

3.3 Capital allowances

The trader may adjust the size of the loss relief claim by not claiming all the capital allowances he is entitled to: a reduced claim will increase the balance carried forward to the next year's capital allowances computation. This may be a useful **tax planning point to preserve the personal allowance or where the effective rate of relief for capital allowances in future periods will be greater than the rate of tax relief for the loss relief.**

Question

Capital allowances and loss relief

Mario is a sole trader making up accounts to 31 December each year. In the year to 31 December 2016, he makes a trading loss, before taking capital allowances into account, of £7,500. Mario has a tax written down value on his main pool at 1 January 2016 of £12,000. He does not make any additions or disposals in the year to 31 December 2016 and does not intend to make any additions or disposals in the year to 31 December 2017.

Mario has property income of £19,000 in 2016/17 and wishes to use trade loss relief against general income in 2016/17 only (ie without any carry back to 2015/16). He expects to make a trading profit of £30,000 in the year to 31 December 2017.

What advice would you give Mario?

Answer

Mario should make a reduced capital allowance claim so that the loss relief claim will preserve his personal allowance in 2016/17.

The maximum capital allowances claim that Mario could make in 2016/17 is £12,000 × 18% = £2,160. He should only claim £(19,000 – 7,500 – 11,000) = £500. The tax written down value of the pool at 1 January 2017 will then be £(12,000 – 500) = £11,500 on which Mario can claim the maximum allowance at 18% for relief in 2017/18.

3.4 Trading losses relieved against capital gains

Where relief is claimed against general income of a given year, the taxpayer may include **a further claim to set the loss against his chargeable gains for the year** less any allowable capital losses for the same year or for previous years. This amount of net gains is computed ignoring the annual exempt amount (see later in this Study Text).

The trading loss is first set against general income of the year of the claim, and only any excess loss is set against capital gains. The taxpayer cannot specify the amount to be set against capital gains, so the annual exempt amount may be wasted. We include an example here for completeness. You will study chargeable gains later in this Study Text and we suggest that you come back to this example at that point.

Question — Loss relief against income and gains

Sibyl had the following results for 2016/17.

	£
Loss available for relief against general income	27,000
Income	19,500
Capital gains less current year capital losses	15,000
Annual exempt amount for capital gains tax purposes	11,100
Capital losses brought forward	9,000

Show how the loss would be relieved against income and gains.

Answer

	£
Income	19,500
Less loss relief against general income	(19,500)
Net income	0
Capital gains	15,000
Less loss relief: lower of £(27,000 – 19,500) = £7,500 (Note 1) and £(15,000 – 9,000) = £6,000 (Note 2)	(6,000)
	9,000
Less annual exempt amount (restricted)	(9,000)
	0

Notes

1 This equals the loss left after the loss relief claim against general income.

2 This equals the gains left after losses b/fwd but ignoring the annual exempt amount.

A trading loss of £(7,500 – 6,000) = £1,500 is carried forward. Sibyl's personal allowance and £(11,100 – 9,000) = £2,100 of her capital gains tax annual exempt amount are wasted. Her capital losses brought forward of £9,000 are carried forward to 2017/18. Although we deducted this £9,000 in working out how much trading loss we were allowed to use in the claim, we do not actually need to use any of the £9,000 as the remaining gain is covered by the annual exempt amount.

3.5 Restrictions on trade loss relief against general income

3.5.1 Commercial basis

FAST FORWARD

Loss relief cannot be claimed against general income unless the loss-making business is conducted on a commercial basis.

Relief cannot be claimed against general income unless the loss-making business is conducted on a commercial basis with a view to the realisation of profits throughout the basis period for the tax year.

3.5.2 Relief cap

FAST FORWARD

An individual taxpayer can only deduct the greater of £50,000 and 25% of adjusted total income when making a claim for loss relief against general income.

There is a **restriction on certain deductions which may be made by an individual from total income for a tax year**. For F6 (UK) purposes, the restricted deduction concerns **trade loss relief against general income, whether claimed for the tax year of the loss or the previous year**.

The total deductions in a tax year cannot exceed the greater of:

(a) **£50,000**; and
(b) **25% of the taxpayer's adjusted total income for the tax year.**

Key term

For F6 (UK) purposes, **adjusted total income** is total income less the gross amounts of personal pension contributions.

If a claim is made for relief against general income in the previous year, there is no restriction on the amount of loss that can be used against trading income (of the same trade). The restriction only applies to the other income in that year. Any restricted loss can still be carried forward against future profits from the same trade.

The limits apply in each year for which relief is claimed. If a current year and a prior year claim are made, the relief in the current year is restricted to the greater of £50,000 and 25% of the adjusted total income in the current year. The relief in the prior year is restricted to the greater of £50,000 and 25% of the adjusted total income in the prior year.

Question

Restriction on loss relief

Grace has been trading for many years, preparing accounts to 5 April each year. Her recent results have been as follows:

	Profit/(loss)
	£
Year to 5 April 2016	20,000
Year to 5 April 2017	(210,000)

Grace also owns a number of investment properties and her property business income is £130,000 in 2015/16 and £220,000 in 2016/17.

Show Grace's taxable income for the tax years 2015/16 and 2016/17 assuming that she claims relief for her trading loss against general income in both of those years.

Answer

	2015/16	*2016/17*
	£	£
Trading income	20,000	0
Property business income	130,000	220,000
Total income	150,000	220,000
Less loss relief against general income	(70,000)	(55,000)
Net income	80,000	165,000
Less personal allowance	(11,000)	(0)
Taxable income	69,000	165,000

Loss relief for 2016/17 is capped at £(220,000 × 25%) = £55,000 since this is greater than £50,000. The personal allowance is not available as adjusted net income exceeds £122,000.

In 2015/16, the loss relief claim is not capped against the trading profit of £20,000. Relief against other income is capped at £50,000 since this is greater than £(150,000 × 25%) = £37,500. The total loss relief claim is therefore £(20,000 + 50,000) = £70,000. The balance of the loss is £(210,000 – 55,000 – 70,000) = £85,000 is carried forward against future profits of the same trade.

Note that the restriction on loss relief means that the loss has been relieved at the additional rate in 2016/17 and at the higher rate in 2015/16. The personal allowance has also been restored for 2015/16.

3.6 The choice between loss reliefs

FAST FORWARD

It is important for a trader to choose the right loss relief, so as to save tax at the highest possible rate and so as to obtain relief reasonably quickly.

When a trader has a choice between loss reliefs, he should aim to obtain relief both quickly and at the highest possible tax rate. However, do consider that losses relieved against income which would otherwise be covered by the personal allowance are wasted. Consideration also needs to be given to any restriction on loss relief.

Another consideration is that a trading loss cannot be set against the capital gains of a year unless relief is first claimed against general income of the same year. It may be worth making the claim against income and wasting the personal allowance in order to avoid a CGT liability.

Question — The choice between loss reliefs

Felicity's trading results are as follows.

Year ended 30 September	*Trading profit/(loss)*
	£
2014	3,900
2015	(21,000)
2016	14,000

Her other income (all non-savings income) is as follows.

	£
2014/15	6,800
2015/16	33,500
2016/17	18,000

Show the most efficient use of Felicity's trading loss. Assume that the personal allowance has been £11,000 throughout.

Answer

Relief could be claimed against general income for 2014/15 and/or 2015/16, with any unused loss being carried forward. Relief in 2014/15 would be against general income of £(3,900 + 6,800) = £10,700, all of which would be covered by the personal allowance anyway, so this claim should not be made.

A claim against general income should be made for 2015/16 as this saves tax quicker than a carry forward claim in 2016/17.

The final results will be as follows:

	2014/15	*2015/16*	*2016/17*
	£	£	£
Trading income	3,900	0	14,000
Less carry forward loss relief	(0)	(0)	(0)
	3,900	0	14,000
Other income	6,800	33,500	18,000
	10,700	33,500	32,000
Less loss relief against general income	(0)	(21,000)	(0)
Net income	10,700	12,500	32,000
Less personal allowance	(11,000)	(11,000)	(11,000)
Taxable income	0	1,500	21,000

Exam focus point

> Before recommending loss relief against general income consider whether it will result in the waste of the personal allowance. Such waste is to be avoided if at all possible.

4 Losses in the early years of a trade

4.1 The computation of the loss

Under the rules determining the basis period for the first three tax years of trading, there may be periods where the basis periods overlap. If profits arise in these periods, they are taxed twice but are relieved later, usually on cessation. However, a loss in an overlap period can only be relieved once. It must not be double counted.

If basis periods overlap, **a loss in the overlap period is treated as a loss for the earlier tax year only**.

4.2 Example: losses in early years

Here is an example of a trader who starts to trade on 1 July 2016 and makes losses in opening periods.

Period of account	*Loss*
	£
P/e 31.12.16	9,000
Y/e 31.12.17	24,000

Tax year	*Basis period*	*Working*	*Trade loss for the tax year*
			£
2016/17	1.7.16 – 5.4.17	£9,000 + (£24,000 × 3/12)	15,000
2017/18	1.1.17 – 31.12.17	£24,000 less loss already used in 2016/17 (£24,000 × 3/12 = 6,000)	18,000

4.3 Example: losses and profits in early years

The rule against using losses twice also applies when losses are netted off against profits in the same basis period. Here is an example, with a commencement on 1 July 2016.

Period of account	*(Loss)/profit*
	£
1.7.16 – 30.4.17	(10,000)
1.5.17 – 30.4.18	24,000

Tax year	*Basis period*	*Working*	*Trade (Loss)/Profit*
			£
2016/17	1.7.16 – 5.4.17	£(10,000) × 9/10	(9,000)
2017/18	1.7.16 – 30.6.17	£24,000 × 2/12 + £(10,000) × 1/10	3,000

4.4 Early trade losses relief

FAST FORWARD

> In opening years, a special relief involving the carry back of losses against general income is available. Losses arising in the first four tax years of a trade may be set against general income in the three years preceding the loss making year, taking the earliest year first.

Early trade losses relief is available for **trading losses incurred in the first four tax years of a trade**.

Relief is obtained by **setting the allowable loss against general income in the three years preceding the year of loss**, applying the loss to the earliest year first. Thus a loss arising in 2016/17 may be set off against income in 2013/14, 2014/15 and 2015/16 in that order.

A claim for early trade losses relief applies to all three years automatically, provided that the loss is large enough. The taxpayer cannot choose to relieve the loss against just one or two of the years, or to relieve only part of the loss. However, the taxpayer could reduce the size of the loss by not claiming the full capital allowances available to him. This will result in higher capital allowances in future years.

Claims for the relief must be made by the 31 January which is 22 months after the end of the tax year in which the loss is incurred.

Early trade losses relief is an alternative to using trade loss relief against general income or using carry forward loss relief. The advantage of early trade losses relief is that it enables losses to be carried back for three years and so gives relief earlier than the other loss reliefs. Whether that is advantageous or not depends on the particular circumstances of the trader, for example whether the trader has any other income and whether there are different rates of tax in the tax years which might be affected by a particular loss relief claim.

Question — Early trade losses relief

Albert is employed as a part time refuse collector until 1 January 2015. On that date he starts up his own business as a scrap metal merchant, making up his accounts to 30 June each year. His earnings as a refuse collector are:

	£
2011/12	5,000
2012/13	6,000
2013/14	7,000
2014/15 (nine months)	6,000

His trading results as a scrap metal merchant are:

	Profit/ (Loss) £
Six months to 30 June 2015	(3,000)
Year to 30 June 2016	(1,500)
Year to 30 June 2017	(1,200)

Assuming that loss relief is claimed as early as possible, show the net income for each of the years 2011/12 to 2017/18 inclusive.

Answer

Since reliefs are to be claimed as early as possible, early trade loss relief is applied. The losses available for relief are as follows.

	£	£	*Years against which relief is available*
2014/15 (basis period 1.1.15 – 5.4.15)			
Three months to 5.4.15 £(3,000) × 3/6		(1,500)	2011/12 to 2013/14
2015/16 (basis period 1.1.15 – 31.12.15)			
Three months to 30.6.15			
(omit 1.1.15 – 5.4.15: overlap) £(3,000) ×3/6	(1,500)		
Six months to 31.12.15 £(1,500) × 6/12	(750)		
		(2,250)	2012/13 to 2014/15
2016/17 (basis period 1.7.15 – 30.6.16)			
Six months to 30.6.16			
(omit 1.7.15 – 31.12.15: overlap) £(1,500) × 6/12		(750)	2013/14 to 2015/16
2017/18 (basis period 1.7.16 – 30.6.17)			
12 months to 30.6.17		(1,200)	2014/15 to 2016/17

The net income is as follows.

	£	£
2011/12		
Original	5,000	
Less 2014/15 loss	(1,500)	
		3,500
2012/13		
Original	6,000	
Less 2015/16 loss	(2,250)	
		3,750
2013/14		
Original	7,000	
Less 2016/17 loss	(750)	
		6,250
2014/15		
Original	6,000	
Less 2017/18 loss	(1,200)	
		4,800

The taxable trade profits for 2014/15 to 2017/18 are zero because there were losses in the basis periods.

5 Terminal trade loss relief

FAST FORWARD

On the cessation of trade, a loss arising in the last 12 months of trading may be set against trade profits of the tax year of cessation and the previous three years, taking the latest year first.

5.1 The relief

Trade loss relief against general income will often be insufficient on its own to deal with a loss incurred in the last months of trading. For this reason there is a special relief, **terminal trade loss relief, which allows a loss on cessation to be carried back for relief against taxable trading profits in previous years.**

5.2 Computing the terminal loss

A terminal loss is **the loss of the last 12 months of trading**.

It is built up as follows.

		£
(a)	The actual trade loss for the tax year of cessation (calculated from 6 April to the date of cessation)	X
(b)	The actual trade loss for the period from 12 months before cessation until the end of the penultimate tax year	X
Total terminal trade loss		X

If the result of either (a) or (b) is a profit rather than a loss, it is treated as zero.

Any unrelieved overlap profits are included within (a) above.

If any loss cannot be included in the terminal loss (eg because it is matched with a profit) it can be relieved instead against general income.

5.3 Relieving the terminal loss

The loss is relieved against trade profits only.

Relief is given in the tax year of cessation and the three preceding years, later years first.

Question — **Terminal loss relief**

Set out below are the results of a business up to its cessation on 30 September 2016.

	Profit/(loss)
	£
Year to 31 December 2013	2,000
Year to 31 December 2014	400
Year to 31 December 2015	300
Nine months to 30 September 2016	(1,950)

Unrelieved overlap profits were £450.

Show the available terminal loss relief, and suggest an alternative claim if the trader had had other non-savings income of £14,000 in each of 2015/16 and 2016/17. Assume that 2016/17 tax rates and allowances apply to all years.

Answer

The terminal loss comes in the last 12 months, the period 1 October 2015 to 30 September 2016. This period is split as follows.

2015/16 Six months to 5 April 2016
2016/17 Six months to 30 September 2016

The terminal loss is made up as follows.

Unrelieved trading losses		£	£
2016/17			
6 months to 30.9.16	£(1,950) × 6/9		(1,300)
Overlap relief	£(450)		(450)
2015/16			
3 months to 31.12.15	£300 × 3/12	75	
3 months to 5.4.16	£(1,950) × 3/9	(650)	
			(575)
			(2,325)

Taxable trade profits will be as follows.

Year	*Basis period*	*Profits*	*Terminal loss relief*	*Final taxable Profits*
		£	£	£
2013/14	Y/e 31.12.13	2,000	1,625	375
2014/15	Y/e 31.12.14	400	400	0
2015/16	Y/e 31.12.15	300	300	0
2016/17	1.1.16 – 30.9.16	0	0	0
			2,325	

If the trader had had £14,000 of other income in 2015/16 and 2016/17 we could consider loss relief claims against general income for these two years, using the loss of £(1,950 + 450) = £2,400 for 2016/17.

The final results would be as follows. (We could alternatively claim loss relief in 2016/17, but a claim in either year would save income tax at the same (basic) rate, so the preference is to save tax earlier rather than later.)

	2013/14	2014/15	2015/16	2016/17
	£	£	£	£
Trade profits	2,000	400	300	0
Other income	0	0	14,000	14,000
	2,000	400	14,300	14,000
Less loss relief against general income	0	0	(2,400)	0
Net income	2,000	400	11,900	14,000

Another option would be to make a claim for terminal loss relief (as above) and a claim against general income for the balance of the loss not relieved as a terminal loss £(2,400 – 2,325) = £75 in either 2015/16 or 2016/17.

However, as there is only taxable income (after the personal allowance) in 2015/16 and 2016/17 the terminal loss relief claim in fact saves no tax in earlier years, and the full claim against general income is more tax efficient.

Chapter Roundup

- Trading losses may be relieved against future profits of the same trade, against general income and against capital gains.
- Trading losses may be relieved against future profits of the same trade. The relief is against the first available profits of the same trade.
- A trading loss may be set against general income in the year of the loss and/or the preceding year. Personal allowances may be lost as a result of the claim. Once a claim has been made in any year, the remaining loss can be set against net chargeable gains.
- Loss relief cannot be claimed against general income unless the loss-making business is conducted on a commercial basis.
- An individual taxpayer can only deduct the greater of £50,000 and 25% of adjusted total income when making a claim for loss relief against general income.
- It is important for a trader to choose the right loss relief, so as to save tax at the highest possible rate and so as to obtain relief reasonably quickly.
- In opening years, a special relief involving the carry back of losses against general income is available. Losses arising in the first four tax years of a trade may be set against general income in the three years preceding the loss making year, taking the earliest year first.
- On the cessation of trade, a loss arising in the last 12 months of trading may be set against trade profits of the tax year of cessation and the previous three years, taking the latest year first.

Quick Quiz

1 Against what income can trade losses carried forward be set off?

A General income
B Non-savings income
C Any trading income
D Trading income from the same trade

2 When a loss is to be relieved against general income, how are losses linked to particular tax years?

3 Against which years' general income may a loss be relieved, for a continuing business which has traded for many years?

4 Maggie has been trading as a decorator for many years. In 2015/16, she made a trading profit of £10,000. She has savings income of £16,000 each year. She makes no capital gains.

Maggie makes a loss of £(48,000) in 2016/17 and expects to make either a loss or smaller profits in the foreseeable future. How can Maggie obtain loss relief?

5 Marie has total income of £230,000 in 2016/17, consisting of employment income. She has also carried on a sole trade for many years, preparing accounts to 31 December. For the year to 31 December 2016, the sole trade business made a loss of £80,000. What is the maximum amount of the loss that Marie can relieve in 2016/17 under loss relief against general income?

6 Joe starts trading on 6 April 2016, having previously been employed for many years. He makes a loss in his first year of trading. Against income of which years can he set the loss under early trade loss relief?

7 Terminal loss relief can be given in the year of _____ and then in the _____ preceding years, _____ years first. Fill in the blanks.

Answers to Quick Quiz

1 D. Against trading income from the same trade.

2 The loss for a tax year is the loss in the basis period for that tax year. However, if basis periods overlap, a loss in the overlap period is a loss of the earlier tax year only.

3 The year in which the loss arose and/or the preceding year.

4 Maggie can make a claim to set the loss against general income of £16,000 in 2016/17. She can also claim loss relief against general income of £(10,000 + 16,000) = £26,000 in 2015/16. The remaining £(48,000 – 16,000 – 26,000) = £6,000 will be carried forward and set against the first available trading profits of her decorating trade.

5 Greater of £50,000 and (25% × £230,000) = £57,500.

6 Loss incurred 2016/17: set against general income of 2013/14, 2014/15 and 2015/16 in that order.

7 Terminal loss relief can be given in the year of **cessation** and then in the **three** preceding years, **later** years first.

Now try the questions below from the Practice Question Bank

Number	Type	Marks	Time
Q64	Section A	2	4 mins
Q65	Section A	2	4 mins
Q66	Section A	2	4 mins
Q67	Section C	10	20 mins

11

Partnerships and limited liability partnerships

Topic list	Syllabus reference
1 Assessment of partnerships to tax	B3(j)(i)
2 Change in profit sharing ratios	B3(j)(ii)
3 Change in membership of partnership	B3(j)(iii)
4 Loss reliefs for partners	B3(j)(iv)

Introduction

We have covered sole traders, learning how to calculate taxable trading profits after capital allowances and allocate them to tax years and how to deal with losses.

We now see how the income tax rules for traders are adapted to deal with business partnerships. On the one hand, a partnership is a single trading entity, making profits as a whole. On the other hand, each partner has a personal tax computation, so the profits must be apportioned to the partners. The general approach is to work out the profits of the partnership, then tax each partner as if he were a sole trader running a business equal to his slice of the partnership (for example 25% of the partnership).

This chapter concludes our study of the income tax computation. In the next chapter we will turn our attention to national insurance.

Study guide

		Intellectual level
B3	**Income from self-employment**	
(j)	Partnerships and limited liability partnerships	
(j)(i)	Explain and compute how a partnership is assessed to tax.	2
(j)(ii)	Explain and compute the assessable profits for each partner following a change in the profit sharing ratio.	2
(j)(iii)	Explain and compute the assessable profits for each partner following a change in the membership of the partnership.	2
(j)(iv)	Describe the alternative loss relief claims that are available to partners.	1

Exam guide

Section A questions on partnerships may involve allocation of profits to partners, possibly involving salaries and/or interest on capital. You may also have to deal with a number of partners in a Section B question. A Section C question, which may be for 15 marks or 10 marks, may involve changes in partnerships such as a partner joining or leaving. As long as you remember to allocate the profits between the partners according to their profit sharing arrangements for the period of account, you should be able to cope with any aspect of partnership tax. Remember that each partner is taxed as a sole trader, and you should apply the opening and closing year rules and loss reliefs as appropriate to that partner.

1 Assessment of partnerships to tax

FAST FORWARD

A partnership is simply treated as a source of profits and losses for trades being carried on by the individual partners.

1.1 Introduction

A partnership is **a group of individuals who are trading together**. They will agree amongst themselves how the business should be run and how profits and losses should be shared. Most partnerships have **unlimited liability** for the partners for the debts of the partnership. A **partnership** is **not treated as a separate entity from the partners for tax purposes** (in contrast to a company).

It is possible to set up a **limited liability partnership** (LLP) where the liability of the partners for debts of the partnership is limited. A LLP is a legal person in its own right (similar to a company). However, LLPs and their partners are generally taxed on the same basis as unlimited partnerships, as described in the rest of this chapter.

1.2 Computing partnership profits

A business partnership is treated like a sole trader for the purposes of computing its profits. Partners' salaries and interest on capital are not deductible expenses and must be added back in computing profits, because they are a form of drawings.

Where the partners own assets (such as their cars) individually, capital allowances must be calculated in respect of such assets (not forgetting any adjustment for private use). **The capital allowances must go into the partnership's tax computation as they must be claimed by the partnership, not by the individual partner.**

Question — Partnership with asset owned by individual partner

Gustav and Melanie have been in partnership for many years, preparing accounts to 31 March each year. They share profits in the ratio 3:2. In the year to 31 March 2017, the partnership's trading profit is £60,000. The partnership does not own any assets which qualify for capital allowances but Gustav owns a car (which he acquired for £22,000 in May 2016) which he uses 75% for the business of the partnership. The car has CO_2 emissions of 150 g/km.

Show the trade profits allocated to each partner for the period of account to 31 March 2017, assuming that the partnership makes the maximum capital allowances claim.

Answer

	Total	*Gustav*	*Melanie*
	£	£	£
Partnership profit	60,000		
Less capital allowance on car £22,000 × 8% × 75%	(1,320)		
Trade profits allocated to partners (3:2)	58,680	35,208	23,472

1.3 Allocating partnership profits between partners

FAST FORWARD

Divide profits or losses between the partners according to the profit sharing arrangements in the period of account concerned. If any of the partners are entitled to a salary or interest on capital, apportion this first, not forgetting to pro-rate in periods of less than 12 months.

Once the partnership's profits for a period of account have been computed, they are shared between the partners according to the profit sharing arrangements for that period of account.

Question — Allocating profits

Steve and Tanya have been in partnership for many years, preparing accounts to 31 October each year. For the year ended 31 October 2016, taxable trading profits were £70,000. Steve is allocated an annual salary of £12,000 and Tanya's salary is £28,000. The profit sharing ratio is 2:1.

Show the trade profits allocated to each partner for the period of account ended 31 October 2016.

Answer

Allocate the profits for the period of account ended 31 October 2016.

	Total	*Steve*	*Tanya*
	£	£	£
Profit	70,000		
Salaries	40,000	12,000	28,000
Balance (2:1)	30,000	20,000	10,000
Trade profits allocated to partners	70,000	32,000	38,000

1.4 The tax positions of individual partners

Each partner is taxed like a sole trader who runs a business which:

- Starts when he joins the partnership
- Finishes when he leaves the partnership
- Has the same periods of account as the partnership (except that a partner who joins or leaves during a period will have a period which starts and/or ends part way through the partnership's period)
- Makes profits or losses equal to the partner's share of the partnership's profits or losses

Exam focus point

Partners are effectively taxed in the same way as sole traders with just one difference. Before you tax the partner you need to take each set of accounts (as adjusted for tax purposes) and divide the trade profit (or loss) between each partner.

Then carry on as normal for a sole trader – each partner is treated in the same way as a sole trader in respect of his trade profits for each period of account.

Question

Taxing partnership profits

Ursula and Victor have been in partnership for many years, preparing accounts to 30 April each year. For the year ended 30 April 2016, taxable trading profits were £45,000. Victor is allocated an annual salary of £5,000 and the remaining profits are then shared between Ursula and Victor in the ratio 3:1. Neither Ursula nor Victor have any other sources of income.

Compute the taxable income for Ursula and Victor for the tax year 2016/17.

Answer

First, allocate the profits for the period of account ended 30 April 2016.

	Total	*Ursula*	*Victor*
	£	£	£
Profit	45,000		
Salary to Victor	5,000	0	5,000
Balance (3:1)	40,000	30,000	10,000
Trade profits allocated to partners	45,000	30,000	15,000

Then compute the taxable income for the tax year 2016/17. The current year basis of assessment applies so the partnership income is the share of profits for each partner for the period of account ended 30 April 2016. It is important to note that Victor's 'salary' is not taxable as employment income but is part of his trading income.

	Ursula	*Victor*
	£	£
Trading income	30,000	15,000
Less personal allowance	(11,000)	(11,000)
Taxable income	19,000	4,000

2 Change in profit sharing ratios

If the **profit sharing arrangements change part way through the period of account**, the **profits, salaries and interest** for the period of account must be **pro-rated** accordingly.

Question — Change in profit sharing arrangements

Sue and Tim have been in partnership for many years, preparing accounts to 31 December each year. For the year ended 31 December 2016, taxable trading profits were £50,000. Sue is allocated an annual salary of £10,000 and Tim's salary is £15,000.

The profit sharing ratio was 1:1 until 31 August 2016 when it changed to 1:2 with no provision for salaries.

Show the trade profits allocated to each partner for the period of account ended 31 December 2016.

Answer

Allocate the profits for the period of account ended 31 December 2016.

	Total	*Sue*	*Tim*
	£	£	£
Profit	50,000		
1 January – 31 August (8 months)	33,333		
Salaries (8/12 × £10,000/£15,000)	16,667	6,667	10,000
Balance (1:1)	16,666	8,333	8,333
	33,333		
1 September – 31 December (four months)	16,667		
Salaries	Nil	–	–
Balance (1:2)	16,667	5,556	11,111
	16,667		
Trade profits allocated to partners	50,000	20,556	29,444

Note. Since the profit sharing arrangements changed part way through the period of account, the profits and salaries for the period of account must be pro-rated accordingly.

3 Change in membership of partnership

FAST FORWARD: Commencement and cessation rules apply to partners individually when they join or leave.

When a trade continues but partners join or leave (including cases when a sole trader takes in partners or a partnership breaks up leaving only one partner as a sole trader), **the special rules for basis periods in opening and closing years do not apply to the people who were carrying on the trade both before and after the change. They carry on using the period of account ending in each tax year as the basis period for the tax year (ie the current year basis). The commencement rules only affect joiners, and the cessation rules only affect leavers.**

Question — Partner joining partnership

Daniel and Ashley have been in partnership for many years preparing accounts to 31 December each year and sharing profits in the ratio 2:1.

On 1 June 2016, Kate joined the partnership. From that date, profits were shared Daniel 50% and Ashley and Kate 25% each.

The partnership profits for the year ended 31 December 2016 were £72,000 and for the year ended 31 December 2017 were £90,000.

Compute the partnership profits taxable on Daniel, Ashley and Kate for 2016/17 and 2017/18 and the overlap profits for Kate on commencement.

Answer

Allocation of partnership profits

	Total	Daniel	Ashley	Kate
y/e 31.12.16	£	£	£	£
1.1.16 – 31.5.16				
Profits (5/12) 2:1	30,000	20,000	10,000	n/a
1.6.16 – 31.2.16				
Profits (7/12) 50:25:25	42,000	21,000	10,500	10,500
Profit allocation	72,000	41,000	20,500	10,500
y/e 31.12.17				
Profits 50:25:25	90,000	45,000	22,500	22,500

Taxable partnership profits for 2016/17 and 2017/18

	Daniel	Ashley	Kate
	£	£	£
2016/17			
CYB y/e 31.12.16	41,000	20,500	
First year – actual basis			
1.6.16 – 31.12.16			10,500
1.1.17 – 5.4.17			
3/12 × £22,500			5,625
			16,125
2017/18			
CYB y/e 31.12.17	45,000	22,500	
Second year – 12 months to 31.12.17			22,500

Overlap profits

Kate has overlap profits for the period 1.1.17 to 5.4.17 of £5,625.

Question — Partner leaving partnership

Maxwell, Laura and Wesley traded in partnership for many years, preparing accounts to 30 September. Each partner was entitled to 5% interest per annum on capital introduced into the partnership. Each partner had introduced £60,000 of capital on the commencement of the partnership. From that date, profits were shared in the ratio 50% to Maxwell, 30% to Laura and 20% to Wesley.

On 1 May 2016, Wesley left the partnership. From that date profits were shared equally between the two remaining partners and no interest was paid on capital. The partnership taxable trading income for the year to 30 September 2016 was £120,000. Wesley had overlap profits on commencement of £5,000.

Compute the partnership profits taxable on Maxwell, Laura and Wesley for 2016/17.

Answer

Allocation of partnership profits

	Total	Maxwell	Laura	Wesley
	£	£	£	£
1.10.15 – 30.4.16				
Interest 7/12 × £60,000 × 5% each	5,250	1,750	1,750	1,750
Profits (7/12) 50:30:20	64,750	32,375	19,425	12,950
	70,000	34,125	21,175	14,700
1.5.16 – 30.9.16				
Profits (5/12) 1:1	50,000	25,000	25,000	n/a
Profits allocated for year	120,000	59,125	46,175	14,700

Taxable partnership profits for 2016/17

	Maxwell	Laura	Wesley
	£	£	£
2016/17			
CYB y/e 30.9.16	59,125	46,175	
Final year			
1.10.15 – 30.4.16			14,700
Less: overlap relief			(5,000)
			9,700

When no-one carries on the trade both before and after the change, as when a partnership transfers its trade to a completely new owner or set of owners, the **cessation rules apply to the old owners** and the **commencement rules apply to the new owners.**

4 Loss reliefs for partners

FAST FORWARD

Partners are individually entitled to loss relief in the same way as sole traders.

4.1 Entitlement to loss relief

Partners are entitled to the same loss reliefs as sole traders. The reliefs are:

(a) **Carry forward against future trading profits.**

(b) **Set off against general income of the same and/or preceding year.** This claim can be extended to set off against capital gains. The restriction on loss relief (see earlier in this Study Text) applies.

(c) **For a new partner, losses in the first four tax years of trade can be set off against general income of the three preceding years.** This is so even if the actual trade commenced many years before the partner joined.

(d) **For a ceasing partner, terminal loss relief is available** when he is treated as ceasing to trade. This is so even if the partnership continues to trade after he leaves.

Different partners may claim loss reliefs in different ways.

Question

Partnership losses

Mary and Natalie have been trading for many years sharing profits equally. On 1 January 2017 Mary retired and Oliver joined the partnership. Natalie and Oliver share profits in the ratio of 2:1. Although the partnership had previously been profitable it made a loss of £24,000 for the year to 31 March 2017. The partnership is expected to be profitable in the future.

Calculate the loss accruing to each partner for 2016/17 and explain what reliefs are available.

Answer

We must first share the loss for the period of account between the partners.

	Total	Mary	Natalie	Oliver
	£	£	£	£
y/e 31.3.17				
1.4.16– 31.12.16				
Total £24,000 × 9/12	(18,000)	(9,000)	(9,000)	
1.1.17 – 31.3.17				
Total £24,000 × 3/12	(6,000)		(4,000)	(2,000)
Total for y/e 31.03.17	(24,000)	(9,000)	(13,000)	(2,000)

Mary

For 2016/17, Mary has a loss of £9,000. She may claim relief against general income of 2016/17 and/or 2015/16 and may extend the claim to capital gains.

Mary has ceased trading and may instead claim terminal loss relief. The terminal loss will be £9,000 (a profit arose in the period 1.1.16 – 31.3.16 which would be treated as zero) and this may be set against her taxable trade profits for 2016/17 (£nil), 2015/16, 2014/15 and 2013/14.

Natalie

For 2016/17, Natalie has a loss of £13,000. She may claim relief against general income of 2016/17 and/or 2015/16 and may extend the claim to capital gains. Any loss remaining unrelieved may be carried forward against future income from the same trade.

Oliver

Oliver's loss for 2016/17 is £2,000. He may claim relief for the loss against general income (and gains) of 2016/17 and/or 2015/16. As he has just started to trade he may claim relief for the loss against general income of 2013/14, 2014/15 and 2015/16. Any loss remaining unrelieved may be carried forward against future income from the same trade.

Chapter Roundup

- A partnership is simply treated as a source of profits and losses for trades being carried on by the individual partners.
- Divide profits or losses between the partners according to the profit sharing arrangements in the period of account concerned. If any of the partners are entitled to a salary or interest on capital, apportion this first, not forgetting to pro-rate in periods of less than 12 months.
- Commencement and cessation rules apply to partners individually when they join or leave.
- Partners are individually entitled to loss relief in the same way as sole traders.

Quick Quiz

1 How are partnership trading profits divided between the individual partners?

2 Janet and John are partners sharing profits 60:40. For the years ended 30 June 2016 and 2017 the partnership made profits of £100,000 and £150,000 respectively. John's taxable trading profits in 2016/17 are:

A £30,000
B £40,000
C £50,000
D £60,000

3 Yolanda and Yan are in partnership sharing profits 80:20. For the year ended 31 December 2016 the business makes a loss of £40,000. Yan decides to use his share of the loss against general income.

Yolanda must also use her share of the loss against general income. True/False?

4 Pete and Doug have been partners for many years, sharing profits equally. On 1 January 2016 Dave joins the partnership and it is agreed to share profits 40:40:20. For the year ended 30 June 2016 profits are £100,000.

Doug's share of these profits is:

A £42,500
B £45,000
C £47,500
D £50,000

5 What loss reliefs are partners entitled to?

Answers to Quick Quiz

1 Profits are divided in accordance with the profit sharing arrangements that existed during the period of account in which the profits arose.

2 B. £40,000.

2016/17: y/e 30 June 2016

£100,000 × 40% = £40,000.

3 False. Yolanda has a choice of loss reliefs:

Loss relief against general income or carry forward loss relief.

Her loss relief claim is unaffected by Yan's.

4 B. £45,000

	Pete	Doug	Dave
Y/e 30 June 2016	£	£	£
1.7.15 – 31.12.15			
6m × £100,000			
£50,000 50:50	25,000	25,000	
1.1.16 – 30.6.16			
6m × £100,000			
£50,000 40:40:20	20,000	20,000	10,000
	45,000	45,000	10,000

5 Partners are entitled to the same loss reliefs as sole traders. These are loss relief against general income, early years trade loss relief, carry forward loss relief and terminal loss relief.

Now try the questions below from the Practice Question Bank

Number	Type	Marks	Time
Q68	Section A	2	4 mins
Q69	Section A	2	4 mins
Q70	Section A	2	4 mins
Q71	Section B	2	4 mins
Q72	Section B	2	4 mins
Q73	Section B	2	4 mins
Q74	Section B	2	4 mins
Q75	Section B	2	4 mins

National insurance contributions

12

Topic list	Syllabus reference
1 Scope of national insurance contributions (NICs)	B6
2 Class 1 and Class 1A NICs for employed persons	B6(a)(i), (b)
3 Class 2 and Class 4 NICs for self-employed persons	B6(a)(ii)

Introduction

In the previous chapters we have covered income tax for employees and for the self-employed.

We look at the national insurance contributions payable under Classes 1 and 1A in respect of employment and under Classes 2 and 4 in respect of self-employment.

In the next chapter we will turn our attention to the taxation of chargeable gains.

Study guide

		Intellectual level
B6	**National insurance contributions for employed and self-employed persons**	
(a)	Explain and compute national insurance contributions payable	
(i)	Class 1 and Class 1A NIC.	2
(ii)	Class 2 and Class 4 NIC.	2
(b)	Understand the annual employment allowance.	2

Exam guide

National insurance contributions may be tested in Sections A or B or as part of a 15 mark or 10 mark question in Section C. You must be absolutely clear who is liable for which class of contributions; only employers, for example, pay Class 1A.

1 Scope of national insurance contributions (NICs)

Four main classes of national insurance contribution (NIC) exist, as set out below.

(a) **Class 1**. This is divided into:

  (i) **Primary Class 1**, paid by employees
  (ii) **Secondary Class 1**, **Class 1A** and **Class 1B** paid by employers

(b) **Class 2**. Paid by the self-employed
(c) **Class 3**. Voluntary contributions (paid to maintain rights to certain state benefits)
(d) **Class 4**. Paid by the self-employed

Exam focus point

Class 1B and Class 3 contributions are outside the scope of your syllabus.

The National Insurance Contributions Office (NICO), which is part of HM Revenue and Customs, examines employers' records and procedures to ensure that the correct amounts of NICs are collected.

2 Class 1 and Class 1A NICs for employed persons

2.1 Class 1 NICs

FAST FORWARD

Class 1 NICs are payable by employees and employers on earnings.

Both **employees** and **employers pay NICs** related to the employee's earnings. NICs are not deductible from an employee's gross salary for income tax purposes. However, employers' contributions are deductible trade expenses.

2.1.1 Earnings

'Earnings' broadly comprise gross pay, excluding benefits which cannot be turned into cash by surrender (eg holidays). Earnings also include payments for use of the employee's own car on business over the approved amount of 45p per mile (irrespective of total mileage). Therefore, where an employer reimburses an employee using his own car for business mileage, the earnings element is the excess of the mileage rate paid over 45 per mile. This applies even where business mileage exceeds 10,000 miles in a tax year.

Certain payments are exempt. In general the income tax and NIC exemptions mirror one another. For example, payment of personal incidental expenses covered by the £5/£10 a night income tax de minimis exemption are excluded from NIC earnings. Relocation expenses of a type exempt from income tax are also excluded from NIC earnings but without the income tax £8,000 upper limit (although expenses exceeding £8,000 are subject to Class 1A NICs as described below).

An expense with a business purpose is not treated as earnings. For example, if an employee is reimbursed for business travel or for staying in a hotel on the employer's business this is not normally 'earnings'. Again the NIC rules for travel expenses follow the income tax rules.

One commonly met expenses payment is telephone calls. If an employee is reimbursed for his own telephone charges the reimbursed cost of private calls (and all reimbursed rental) is earnings.

In general, non cash vouchers are subject to Class 1 NICs. However, the following are exempt.

- Childcare vouchers up to the amount exempt from income tax (see earlier in this Study Text)
- Any other voucher which is exempt from income tax

An employer's contribution to an employee's occupational or private registered pension scheme is excluded from the definition of 'earnings'.

2.1.2 Rates of Class 1 NICs

The rates of contribution for 2016/17, and the income bands to which they apply, are set out in the Tax Rates and Allowance Tables in this Study Text.

Employees pay main primary contributions of 12% of earnings between the primary threshold of £8,060 and the upper earnings limit (UEL) of £43,000 or the equivalent monthly or weekly limit (see below). They also pay additional primary contributions of 2% on earnings above the upper earnings limit.

Where the employee is aged 21 or over, employers pay secondary contributions of 13.8% on earnings above the secondary threshold of £8,112, or the equivalent monthly or weekly limit. There is no upper limit.

Exam focus point

There are different rules for secondary contributions if the employee is aged under 21 and for apprentices aged under 25. These rules are **not examinable** in F6(UK). You should therefore assume that all employees are aged 25 or over in questions.

If an individual has more than one job then NIC is calculated on the earnings from each job separately and independently. However there is an overall annual maximum amount of Class 1 NIC any individual will be due to pay. If the total NIC paid from those different jobs exceeds the maximum that individual can claim a refund of the excess.

2.1.3 Earnings period

NICs are calculated in relation to an earnings period. This is the period to which earnings paid to an employee are deemed to relate. Where earnings are paid at regular intervals, the earnings period will generally be equated with the payment interval, for example a week or a month. An earnings period cannot usually be less than seven days long.

Exam focus point

In the exam NICs will generally be calculated on an annual basis.

Question — **Class 1 contributions**

Sally works for Red plc. She is paid £4,000 per month.

Show Sally's primary contributions and the secondary contributions paid by Red plc for 2016/17. Ignore the employment allowance (see Section 2.1.4 later in this chapter).

Answer

Primary threshold £8,060
Secondary threshold £8,112
Upper earnings limit £43,000
Annual salary £4,000 × 12 = £48,000

Sally	
Primary contributions	£
£(43,000 – 8,060) = £34,940 × 12% (main)	4,193
£(48,000 – 43,000) = £5,000 × 2% (additional)	100
Total primary contributions	4,293
Red plc	£
Secondary contributions	
£(48,000 – 8,112) = £39,888 × 13.8%	5,505

Special rules apply to company directors, regardless of whether they are paid at regular intervals or not. Where a person is a director at the beginning of the tax year, his earnings period is the tax year, even if he ceases to be director during the year. **The annual limits as shown in the Tax Tables apply.**

Question

Employees and directors

Bill and Ben work for Weed Ltd. Bill is a monthly paid employee. Ben who is a director of Weed Ltd, is also paid monthly. Each is paid an annual salary of £40,800 in 2016/17 and each also received a bonus of £3,000 in December 2016.

Show the primary and secondary contributions for both Bill and Ben, using a monthly earnings period for Bill. Ignore the employment allowance (see Section 2.1.4 later in this chapter).

Answer

Bill
Primary threshold £8,060/12 = £672
Secondary threshold £8,112/12 = £676
Upper earnings limit £43,000/12 = £3,583
Regular monthly earnings £40,800/12 = £3,400

Primary contributions	
	£
11 months	
£(3,400 – 672) = £2,728 × 12% × 11 (main only)	3,601
1 month (December)	
£(3,583 – 672) = £2,911 × 12% (main)	349
£(3,400 + 3,000 – 3,583) = £2,817 × 2% (additional)	56
Total primary contributions	4,006
Secondary contributions	
	£
11 months	
£(3,400 – 676) = £2,724 × 13.8% × 11	4,135
1 month (December)	
£(3,400 + 3,000 – 676) = £5,724 × 13.8%	790
Total secondary contributions	4,925

Ben
Total earnings £(40,800 + 3,000) = £43,800

Primary contributions

	£
Total earnings exceed UEL	
£(43,000 – 8,060) = £34,940 × 12% (main)	4,193
£(43,800 – 43,000) = £800 × 2% (additional)	16
Total primary	4,209
Secondary contributions	
£(43,800 – 8,112) = £35,688 × 13.8%	4,925

Because Ben is a director an annual earnings period applies. The effect of this is that increased primary contributions are due.

2.1.4 Employment allowance

FAST FORWARD

The employment allowance enables an employer to reduce its total Class 1 secondary contributions by up to £3,000 per tax year.

An employer can make a claim to **reduce its total Class 1 secondary contributions** by an **employment allowance equal to those contributions**, subject to a **maximum allowance of £3,000 per tax year.**

Some employers are **excluded employers** for the purposes of the employment allowance. These include **companies** where the **only employed earner for whom the company pays Class 1 secondary contributions is a director of the company**, employers who employ **employees for personal, household or domestic work**, **public authorities** and employers who **carry out functions either wholly or mainly of a public nature** such as provision of National Health Service services.

Question — Employment allowance

Blue plc is a trading company which has two employees, one who earns £25,000 per year and the other who earns £20,000 per year. Each employee is paid in equal monthly amounts and so an annual computation of Class 1 computation can be made.

Calculate the Class 1 secondary contributions payable by Blue plc for 2016/17.

Answer

	£
Employee 1: £(25,000 – 8,112) = 16,888 × 13.8%	2,331
Employee 2: £(20,000 – 8,112) = 11,888 × 13.8%	1,641
	3,972
Less employment allowance (maximum)	(3,000)
Secondary contributions 2016/17	972

2.2 Class 1A NICs

Exam focus point

ACCA's article Motor cars, written by a member of the F6(UK) examination team explains the implications of acquiring, running, or having the use of a motor car for income tax, corporation tax, value added tax (VAT) and national insurance contribution (NIC).

FAST FORWARD

Class 1A NICs are payable by employers on benefits provided for employees.

Employers must pay Class 1A NIC at 13.8% in respect of most taxable benefits. Taxable benefits are calculated in accordance with income tax rules. There is no Class 1A in respect of any benefits already treated as earnings for Class 1 purposes (eg non cash vouchers). Tax exempt benefits are not liable to Class 1A NIC.

Question — **Class 1A NIC**

James has the following benefits for income tax purposes

	£
Company car	5,200
Living accommodation	10,000
Medical insurance	800

Calculate the Class 1A NICs that the employer will have to pay.

Answer

Total benefits are £16,000 (£10,000 + £5,200 + £800)

Class 1A NICs:

13.8% × £16,000 = £2,208

2.3 Miscellaneous points

Class 1 contributions are collected under the PAYE system described earlier in this Study Text.

Class 1A contributions are collected annually in arrears. If the payment is made electronically, payment must reach HMRC's bank account no later than 22 July following the end of the tax year. Payment by cheque must reach HMRC no later than 19 July following the end of the tax year.

It is important to note that Class 1 and 1A contributions broadly apply to amounts which are taxable as employment income. They do not apply to dividends paid to directors and employees who are also shareholders in the company. This means that it may be more tax-efficient for an employee/shareholder to receive payment from a company in the form of dividends. We look at this situation when we consider the company's liability to corporation tax later in this Study Text.

3 Class 2 and Class 4 NICs for self-employed persons

FAST FORWARD

The self-employed pay Class 2 and Class 4 NICs. Class 2 NICs are paid at a flat weekly rate. Class 4 NICs are based on the level of the individual's profits.

3.1 Class 2 contributions

The self-employed (sole traders and partners) pay NICs in two ways.

Class 2 contributions are payable at a flat rate. The Class 2 rate for 2016/17 is £2.80 a week. No Class 2 contributions are payable if the individual's taxable trading profits are less than the small profits threshold which is £5,965 (2016/17).

Class 2 NICs are payable under the self assessment system but payments on account are not required. For 2016/17, Class 2 NICs are payable by 31 January 2018.

3.2 Class 4 contributions

Additionally, **the self-employed pay Class 4 NICs,** based on the level of the individual's taxable trading profits.

Main rate Class 4 NICs are calculated by applying a fixed percentage (9% for 2016/17) to the individual's profits between the lower profits limit (£8,060 for 2016/17) and the upper profits limit (£43,000 for 2016/17). Additional rate contributions are 2% (for 2016/17) on profits above that limit.

3.3 Example: Class 4 contributions

If a sole trader had profits of £16,915 for 2016/17 his Class 4 NIC liability would be as follows.

	£
Profits	16,915
Less lower profits limit	(8,060)
	8,855

Class 4 NICs = 9% × £8,855 = £797 (main only)

3.4 Example: additional Class 4 contributions

If an individual's profits are £47,000, additional Class 4 NICs are due on the excess over the upper profits limit. Thus the amount payable in 2016/17 is as follows.

	£
Profits (upper limit)	43,000
Less lower limit	(8,060)
	34,940
Main rate Class 4 NICs 9% × £34,940	3,145
Additional rate Class 4 NICs £(47,000 – 43,000) = £4,000 × 2%	80
	3,225

Class 4 NICs are collected by HMRC through the self assessment system. They are paid at the same time as the associated income tax liability and so are part of payments on account and balancing payments. We look at the self assessment system in detail later in this Study Text.

Chapter Roundup

- Class 1 NICs are payable by employees and employers on earnings.
- The employment allowance enables an employer to reduce its total Class 1 secondary contributions by up to £3,000 per tax year.
- Class 1A NICs are payable by employers on benefits provided for employees.
- The self-employed pay Class 2 and Class 4 NICs. Class 2 NICs are paid at a flat weekly rate. Class 4 NICs are based on the level of the individual's profits.

Quick Quiz

1 What national insurance contributions are payable by employers and employees?

2 Purple Ltd has one employee, Frank, who is also a director of the company. In 2016/17, Purple Ltd pays Frank an annual salary of £37,000. What are the Class 1 secondary contributions payable by Purple plc for 2016/17?

A £987
B £5,106
C £3,987
D £2,106

3 On what are Class 1A NICs based?

4 Class 2 NICs are paid by an employer. True/False?

5 How are Class 4 NICs calculated?

Answers to Quick Quiz

1 Employees – Class 1 primary contributions

Employers – Class 1 secondary contributions
Class 1A contributions

2 C. £(37,000 – 8,112) = 28,888 × 13.8% = £3,987. The employment allowance is not available Frank is the sole employed earner and a director of Purple Ltd.

3 Class 1A NICs are based on taxable benefits paid to employees.

4 False. Class 2 contributions are paid by the self-employed.

5 The main rate is a fixed percentage (9% in 2016/17) of an individual's tax profits between an upper profits limit and lower profits limit. The additional rate (2%) applies above the upper profits limit.

Now try the questions below from the Practice Question Bank

Number	Type	Marks	Time
Q76	Section A	2	4 mins
Q77	Section A	2	4 mins
Q78	Section A	2	4 mins
Q79	Section B	2	4 mins
Q80	Section B	2	4 mins
Q81	Section B	2	4 mins
Q82	Section B	2	4 mins
Q83	Section B	2	4 mins
Q84	Section C	15	29 mins

P A R T C

Chargeable gains for individuals

13

Computing chargeable gains

Topic list	Syllabus reference
1 Chargeable persons, disposals and assets	C1(a), (b)
2 Computing a gain or loss	C2(a), (b)
3 The annual exempt amount	C5(a)
4 Capital losses	C2(b)
5 CGT payable by individuals	C5(a), C6(b)
6 Transfers between spouses/civil partners	C2(c), C6(b)
7 Part disposals	C2(d)
8 The damage, loss or destruction of an asset	C2(e)

Introduction

Now that we have completed our study of the income tax and national insurance liabilities we turn our attention to the capital gains tax computation. We deal with individuals in this chapter. Chargeable gains for companies are dealt with later in this Study Text.

We look at the circumstances in which a chargeable gain or allowable loss may arise. Then we look at the detailed calculation of the gain or loss on a disposal of an asset.

We then consider the annual exempt amount and look at the relief for capital losses, including the interaction between capital losses brought forward and the annual exempt amount. This enables us to compute CGT payable by individuals.

Following on from this, we start to identify the different types of disposals you may be presented with in the exam. We look first at part disposals. If only part of an asset has been disposed of we need to know how to allocate the cost between the part disposed of and the part retained.

Finally, for this chapter we consider the damage or destruction of an asset and the receipt of compensation or insurance proceeds, and look at the reliefs available where the proceeds are applied in restoring or replacing the asset.

In the following chapters we look at further rules, including those for disposals of shares, and various CGT reliefs that may be available.

Study guide

		Intellectual level
C1	**The scope of the taxation of capital gains**	
(a)	Describe the scope of capital gains tax.	2
(b)	Recognise those assets which are exempt.	1
C2	**The basic principles of computing gains and losses**	
(a)	Compute and explain the treatment of capital gains.	2
(b)	Compute and explain the treatment of capital losses.	2
(c)	Understand the treatment of transfers between a husband and wife or between a couple in a civil partnership.	2
(d)	Understand the amount of allowable expenditure for a part disposal.	2
(e)	Recognise the treatment where an asset is damaged, lost or destroyed, and the implications of receiving insurance proceeds and reinvesting such proceeds.	2
C5	**The computation of capital gains tax**	
(a)	Compute the amount of capital gains tax payable.	2
C6	**The use of exemptions and reliefs in deferring and minimising tax liabilities arising on the disposal of capital assets**	
(b)	Basic capital gains tax planning.	2

Exam guide

Section A questions on the topics in this chapter may include dealing with losses or computing the amount of capital gains tax payable. You may have to deal with a number of disposals in a Section B question. You might have to prepare a detailed capital gains computation for either an individual or company in Section C. Learn the basic layout, so that slotting in the figures becomes automatic. Then in the exam you will be able to turn your attention to the particular points raised in the question. The A/(A+B) formula for part disposals must be learnt.

Exam focus point

ACCA's article Chargeable gains, written by a member of the F6(UK) examination team, in Part 1 looks at **chargeable gains** in either a **personal or corporate context**. Part 2 focuses on **shares**, **reliefs**, and the way in which **gains made by limited companies are taxed**.

1 Chargeable persons, disposals and assets

FAST FORWARD

A gain is chargeable if there is a chargeable disposal of a chargeable asset by a chargeable person.

Key term

For a chargeable gain to arise there must be:

- A **chargeable person**; and
- A **chargeable disposal**; and
- A **chargeable asset**.

otherwise no charge to tax occurs.

1.1 Chargeable persons

FAST FORWARD

Capital gains are chargeable on individuals and companies.

The following are chargeable persons.

- **Individuals**
- **Companies**

UK resident individuals are chargeable persons in relation to the disposal of assets situated anywhere in the world. Residence is defined for CGT in the same way as for income tax (see Section 1.1 in Chapter 2).

Exam focus point

The computation of capital gains arising on overseas assets is **not examinable** in F6 (UK).

We will look at the taxation of chargeable gains on companies later in this Study Text. Note that individuals pay capital gains tax (CGT) on capital gains, whilst companies bring chargeable gains into their corporation tax computation and pay corporation tax on them.

1.2 Chargeable disposals

The following are chargeable disposals.

- **Sales of assets or parts of assets**
- **Gifts of assets or parts of assets**
- **The loss or destruction of assets**

A chargeable disposal occurs on the date of the contract (where there is one, whether written or oral), or the date of a conditional contract becoming unconditional. This may differ from the date of transfer of the asset. However, when a capital sum is received for example on the loss or destruction of an asset, the disposal takes place on the day the sum is received.

Where a disposal involves an acquisition by someone else, the date of acquisition for that person is the same as the date of disposal.

Transfers of assets on death are exempt disposals.

1.3 Chargeable assets

All forms of property, wherever in the world they are situated, are chargeable assets unless they are specifically designated as exempt (see further below).

1.4 Exempt assets

The following are exempt assets.

- **Motor vehicles** suitable for private use
- **National Savings and Investments certificates** and **premium bonds**
- **Gilt-edged securities (treasury stock)**
- **Qualifying corporate bonds (QCBs)**
- **Certain chattels**
- **Investments held in individual savings accounts (ISAs)**
- Foreign currency bank accounts held by individuals
- Decorations for bravery where awarded, not purchased
- Damages for personal or professional injury
- Debts (except debts on a security)

If an asset is an exempt asset any gain is not chargeable and any loss is not allowable.

Exam focus point

In the exam, if you think that an asset is exempt just state this – don't waste time working out a gain or loss.

2 Computing a gain or loss

FAST FORWARD

A gain or loss is computed by taking the proceeds and deducting the cost. Incidental costs of acquisition and disposal are deducted together with any enhancement expenditure reflected in the state and nature of the asset at the date of disposal.

2.1 Basic calculation

A gain (or an allowable loss) is generally calculated as follows.

	£
Disposal consideration	45,000
Less incidental costs of disposal	(400)
Net proceeds	44,600
Less allowable costs	(21,000)
Gain	23,600

Usually the disposal consideration is the proceeds of sale of the asset, but a disposal is deemed to take place at market value:

- **Where the disposal is not a bargain at arm's length**
- **Where the disposal is made for a consideration which cannot be valued**
- **Where the disposal is by way of a gift**

Special valuation rules apply for shares (see later in this Study Text).

Incidental costs of disposal may include:

- Valuation fees
- Estate agency fees
- Advertising costs
- Legal costs

Allowable costs include:

- The original cost of acquisition
- Incidental costs of acquisition
- Capital expenditure incurred in enhancing the asset

Enhancement expenditure is capital expenditure which enhances the value of the asset and is reflected in the state or nature of the asset at the time of disposal, or expenditure incurred in establishing, preserving or defending title to, or a right over, the asset. Excluded from this category are:

- Costs of repairs and maintenance
- Costs of insurance
- Any expenditure deductible from trading profits
- Any expenditure met by public funds (for example council grants)

Question **Calculating the gain**

Joanne bought a piece of land as an investment for £20,000. The legal costs of purchase were £250. Joanne spent £2,000 on installing drainage pipes on the land which enhanced its value.

Joanne sold the land on 12 December 2016 for £35,000. She incurred estate agency fees of £700 and legal costs of £500 on the sale.

Calculate Joanne's gain on sale.

Answer

	£
Proceeds of sale	35,000
Less costs of disposal £(700 + 500)	(1,200)
	33,800
Less costs of acquisition £(20,000 + 250)	(20,250)
costs of enhancement	(2,000)
Gain	11,550

3 The annual exempt amount

FAST FORWARD

An individual is entitled to an annual exempt amount for each tax year.

There is an annual exempt amount for each tax year. For each individual for 2016/17 it is £11,100.

The annual exempt amount is deducted from the **chargeable gains** for the year after the deduction of losses and other reliefs. The resulting amount is the individual's **taxable gains**.

An individual who has gains taxable at more than one rate of tax may deduct the annual exempt amount for that year in the way that produces the lowest possible tax charge.

4 Capital losses

FAST FORWARD

Losses are set off against gains of the same year and any excess carried forward. Brought forward losses are only set off to reduce net gains down to the amount of the annual exempt amount.

4.1 Allowable losses of the same year

Allowable capital losses arising in a tax year are deducted from gains arising in the same tax year.

An individual who has gains taxable at more than one rate of tax may deduct any allowable losses in the way that produces the lowest possible tax charge.

Any loss which cannot be set off is carried forward to set against future gains. Losses must be used as soon as possible (but see below).

4.2 Allowable losses brought forward

Allowable losses brought forward are only set off to reduce net current year gains to the annual exempt amount. No set-off is made if net chargeable gains for the current year do not exceed the annual exempt amount.

Net current year gains are current year gains less current year allowable losses. Note that if a claim is made to set trading losses against capital gains in any tax year (as we saw earlier in this Study Text), they will be set off before capital losses brought forward. Unlike capital losses brought forward, trading losses cannot be restricted to preserve the annual exempt amount.

4.3 Example: the use of losses

(a) George has gains for 2016/17 of £13,000 and allowable losses of £6,000. As the losses are **current year losses** they must be fully relieved against the £13,000 of gains to produce net gains of £7,000 despite the fact that net gains are below the annual exempt amount.

(b) Bob has gains of £15,000 for 2016/17 and allowable losses brought forward of £6,000. Bob restricts his loss relief to £3,900 so as to leave net gains of £(15,000 – 3,900) = £11,100, which will be exactly covered by his annual exempt amount for 2016/17. The remaining £2,100 of losses will be carried forward to 2017/18.

(c) Tom has gains of £10,500 for 2016/17 and losses brought forward from 2015/16 of £4,000. He will not use any of his brought forward losses in 2016/17 and instead will carry forward all of his losses to 2017/18. His gains of £10,500 are covered by his annual exempt amount for 2016/17.

5 CGT payable by individuals

FAST FORWARD

Capital gains tax is usually payable at the rate of 10% or 20% depending on the individual's taxable income.

PER alert

One of the competencies you require to fulfil Performance Objective 15 Tax computations and assessments of the PER is to prepare or contribute to the computation or assessment of tax computations for individuals. You can apply the knowledge you obtain from this section of the Study Text to help to demonstrate this competence.

5.1 Rates of tax on most taxable gains

Taxable gains on gains, other than those on residential property, are usually chargeable to capital gains tax at a rate depending on the individual's taxable income. The basic rate band is treated as being used first by income. Gains are taxed at 20% if the individual's taxable income exceeds the basic rate limit (ie they are a higher rate or additional rate taxpayer). If the individual's taxable income falls below the basic rate limit (ie they are a basic rate taxpayer), gains are taxed at 10% up to the basic rate limit and 20% above the limit.

The following diagram shows you how to apply these rules:

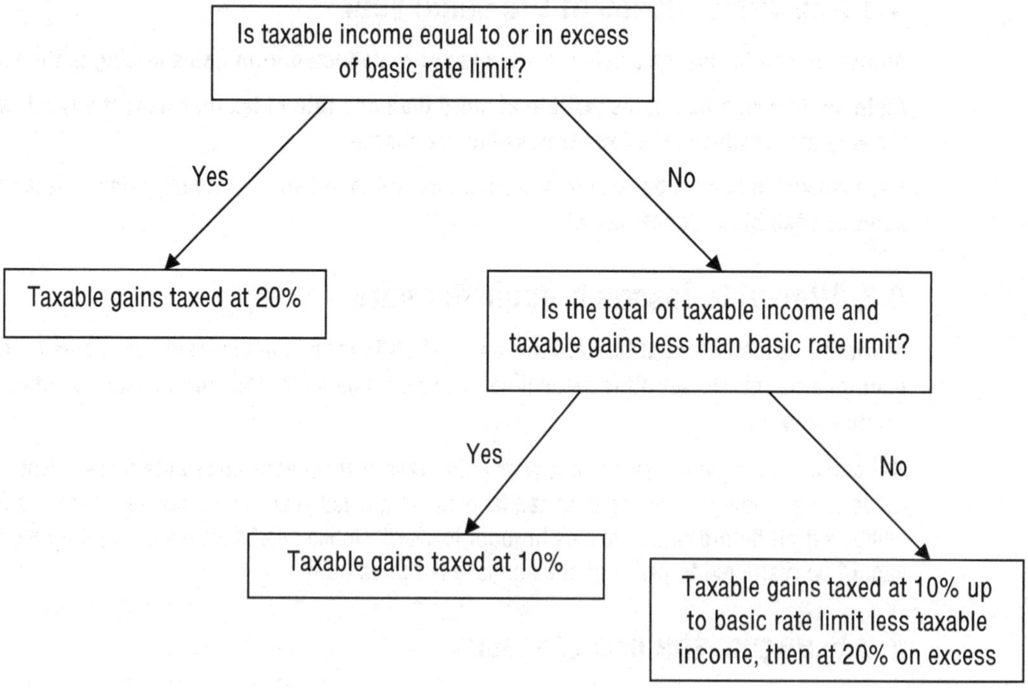

Remember that the basic rate band limit will usually be £32,000 for 2016/17 but the limit will be increased by the gross amount of gift aid donations and personal pension contributions.

Question

Mo has taxable income of £22,630 in 2016/17. He made personal pension contributions of £242 (net) per month during 2016/17. In December 2016, he makes a chargeable gain of £29,000 on the disposal of some shares. The gain does not qualify for entrepreneurs' relief (see later in this Study Text).

Calculate the CGT payable by Mo for 2016/17.

Answer

	£
Chargeable gain	29,000
Less annual exempt amount	(11,100)
Taxable gain	17,900
Basic rate limit	32,000
Add personal pension contributions £(242 × 12) = £2,904 × 100/80	3,630
Increased basic rate limit	35,630
CGT	
£(35,630 – 22,630) = £13,000 @ 10%	1,300
£(17,900 – 13,000) = £4,900 @ 20%	980
Total CGT payable	2,280

5.2 Rates of tax on residential property gains

FAST FORWARD

Capital gains tax is payable at the rate of 18% or 28% on residential property gains depending on the individual's taxable income.

Residential property includes an interest in a dwelling such as a house or flat. It also includes an interest in a contract acquired 'off-plan' where the property has not yet been constructed.

Taxable gains on residential property which are not fully exempt under principal private residence relief (see later in this Study Text) **are chargeable to capital gains tax at the rate of 18% or 28% depending on the individual's taxable income for the tax year.** Residential property gains within the basic rate band are taxed at 18% and those in excess of the basic rate limit (adjusted as described in the previous section) are taxed at 28%.

If an individual has a mixture of residential property gains and gains on other assets (other than those qualifying for entrepreneurs' relief – see later in this Study Text), **the annual exempt amount and allowable losses should be deducted first from residential property gains and secondly from gains on other assets.**

Where the individual has unused basic rate band, it does not matter whether the residential property gains or the other gains are taxed first. This is because the differential between the rates in both cases is 10%.

Question — **Rates of CGT on mixture of gains**

Fran has taxable income of £23,000 in 2016/17. In August 2016, she makes a chargeable gain of £15,500 on the sale of some shares. In March 2017, she makes a chargeable gain of £19,000 on the disposal of a residential property which is not covered by principal private residence relief. Calculate the CGT payable by Fran for 2016/17.

Answer

	Other gain	*Residential property*
	£	£
Shares	15,500	
Residential property		19,000
Less annual exempt amount (best use)		(11,100)
Taxable gains	15,500	7,900
CGT		
If tax residential property gain first		
£7,900 @ 18%		1,422
£1,100 (32,000 – 23,000 – 7,900) @ 10%		110
£14,400 (15,500 – 1,100) @ 20%		2,880
Total CGT		4,412
If tax other gain first		
£9,000 (32,000 – 23,000) @ 10%		900
£6,500 (15,500 – 9,000) @ 20%		1,300
£7,900 @ 28%		2,212
Total CGT		4,412

Exam focus point

In the exam, **you only need to compute the CGT payable in one way** eg residential property gains then other gains. It is **not necessary** to show that the same amount of CGT is payable if the gains are taxed the other way around.

5.3 CGT on entrepreneurs' relief gains

There is also a special 10% rate of tax for gains for which the taxpayer claims entrepreneurs' relief. We will look at this situation later in this Study Text.

5.4 Payment date for capital gains tax

Capital gains tax is payable by 31 January following the end of the tax year (ie by 31 January 2018 for the tax year 2016/17). We look at payment of capital gains tax in more detail later in this Study Text.

5.5 Basic capital gains tax planning

FAST FORWARD

Basic capital gains tax planning involves maximising the use of the annual exempt amount, ensuring the lowest rate of tax applies and timing of payment of tax.

Basic capital gains tax planning usually involves three considerations.

The first consideration is that an individual should make use of the annual exempt amount. For example, if there is a gain which already uses the annual exempt amount in the tax year, it may be advisable to delay making another gain until the next tax year.

The second consideration is the rate of tax in relation to the individual's taxable income. Where possible, gains should be made in the tax year in which the individual has the lowest amount of taxable income, in particular where they have part of the basic rate band unused.

The third consideration is the timing of the payment of capital gains tax. It may be better to make a gain early in a tax year rather than late in a tax year to give the longest gap between receiving the proceeds and paying the tax due.

6 Transfers between spouses/civil partners

FAST FORWARD

Disposals between spouses or members of a civil partnership are made on a no gain no loss basis and do not give rise to a chargeable gain or allowable loss.

Spouses/civil partners are taxed as two separate people. Each has an annual exempt amount, and losses of one spouse/civil partner cannot be set against gains of the other.

Disposals between spouses/civil partners living together give rise to no gain or loss, whatever actual price (if any) was charged by the transferor. **This means that there is no chargeable gain or allowable loss, and the transferee takes over the transferor's cost.** This is not the same as the disposal being exempt from CGT.

Since transfers between spouses/civil partners are on a no gain no loss basis, it may be beneficial to transfer the whole or part of an asset to the spouse/civil partner with an unused annual exempt amount or with taxable income below the basic rate limit.

Question — Inter spouse transfer

Harry is a higher rate taxpayer who always makes gains of at least £20,000 each year on disposals of investments. His wife, Margaret, has taxable income of £2,130 each year and has no chargeable assets.

Harry bought a plot of land for £150,000 in 2012. He gave it to Margaret when it was worth £180,000 on 10 May 2015. Margaret sold it on 27 August 2016 for £190,000. The land does not qualify for entrepreneurs' relief and is not residential property.

Calculate any chargeable gains arising to Harry and Margaret and show the tax saving arising from the transfer between Harry and Margaret, followed by the disposal by Margaret, instead of a disposal in August 2016 by Harry.

Answer

The disposal from Harry to Margaret in May 2015 is a no gain no loss disposal. Harry has no chargeable gain, and the cost for Margaret is Harry's original cost.

The gain on the sale by Margaret in August 2016 is:

	£
Proceeds of sale	190,000
Less cost	(150,000)
Gain	40,000

If Harry had made the disposal in August 2016, the whole of the gain would have been taxed at 20%.

Margaret's gain will be reduced by her annual exempt amount, saving tax at 20% on that amount compared with the situation where Harry makes the disposal.

Margaret also has £(32,000 – 2,130) = £29,870 of her basic rate band remaining. She will be taxed at 10% on the gain within the basic rate band, instead of 20% if Harry makes the disposal.

The tax saving is therefore:

	£
Tax saved on annual exempt amount £11,100 @ 20%	2,220
Tax saved at basic rate £(40,000 – 11,100) = £28,900 @ (20 – 10)%	2,890
Tax saving on disposal by Margaret instead of Harry	5,110

7 Part disposals

FAST FORWARD

On a part disposal, the cost must be apportioned between the part disposed of and the part retained.

The disposal of part of a chargeable asset is a chargeable event. The chargeable gain (or allowable loss) is computed by deducting a fraction of the original cost of the whole asset from the disposal value. The balance of the cost is carried forward until the eventual disposal of the remaining part of the asset.

Exam formula

The fraction is:

$$\text{Cost} \times \frac{A}{A+B} = \frac{\text{value of the part disposed of}}{\text{value of the part disposed of} + \text{market value of the remainder}}$$

In this fraction, A is the proceeds **before** deducting incidental costs of disposal.

The part disposal fraction should not be applied indiscriminately. Any expenditure incurred wholly in respect of a particular part of an asset should be treated as an allowable deduction in full for that part and not apportioned. An example of this is incidental selling expenses, which are wholly attributable to the part disposed of.

Question

Part disposal

Hedley owns a four hectare plot of land which originally cost him £150,000. He sold one hectare in July 2016 for £60,000. The incidental costs of sale were £3,000. The market value of the three hectares remaining is estimated to be £180,000. What is the gain on the sale of the one hectare?

Answer

The amount of the cost attributable to the part sold is

$$\frac{60,000}{60,000+180,000} \times £150,000 = £37,500$$

	£
Proceeds	60,000
Less disposal cost	(3,000)
Net proceeds of sale	57,000
Less cost (see above)	(37,500)
Gain	19,500

8 The damage, loss or destruction of an asset

FAST FORWARD

The gain which would otherwise arise on the receipt of insurance proceeds may, subject to certain conditions, be deferred.

8.1 Destruction or loss of an asset

If an asset is destroyed any compensation or insurance monies received will normally be brought into an ordinary CGT disposal computation as proceeds.

If all the proceeds are applied for the replacement of the asset within 12 months, any gain can be deducted from the cost of the replacement asset. The replacement asset should have a similar function to the destroyed asset and be a similar type of asset.

If only part of the proceeds are used, the gain immediately chargeable can be limited to the amount not used. The rest of the gain is then deducted from the cost of the replacement.

Question — Asset destroyed

Fiona bought a painting for £25,000. It was destroyed in July 2016. Insurance proceeds were £34,000, and Fiona spent £30,500 on a replacement painting in January 2017. Compute the gain immediately chargeable and the base cost of the new painting.

Answer

	£
Proceeds	34,000
Less cost	(25,000)
Gain	9,000
Gain immediately chargeable £(34,000 – 30,500)	(3,500)
Deduction from base cost	5,500

The base cost of the new painting is £(30,500 – 5,500) = £25,000.

8.2 Damage to an asset

If an asset is damaged then the receipt of any compensation or insurance monies received will normally be treated as a part disposal.

If all the proceeds are applied in restoring the asset the taxpayer can elect to disregard the part disposal. The proceeds will instead be deducted from the cost of the asset.

Question — Asset damaged

Frank bought an investment property for £100,000 in May 2016. It was damaged two and a half months later. Insurance proceeds of £20,000 were received in November 2016, and Frank spent a total of £25,000 on restoring the property. Prior to restoration the property was worth £120,000. Compute the gain immediately chargeable, if any, and the base cost of the restored property assuming Frank elects for there to be no part disposal.

How would your answer differ if no election were made?

Answer

As the proceeds have been applied in restoring the property Frank has elected to disregard the part disposal.

The base cost of the restored property is £(100,000 – 20,000 + 25,000) = £105,000.

If no election were made, the receipt of the proceeds would be a part disposal in November 2016:

	£
Proceeds	20,000
Less cost £100,000 × 20,000/(20,000 + 120,000)	(14,286)
Gain	5,714

The base cost of the restored asset is £(100,000 – 14,286 + 25,000) = £110,714.

Assuming this is Frank's only disposal in the tax year, the gain is covered by the annual exempt amount. It may therefore be preferable not to make the election.

Chapter Roundup

- A gain is chargeable if there is a chargeable disposal of a chargeable asset by a chargeable person.
- Capital gains are chargeable on individuals and companies.
- A gain or loss is computed by taking the proceeds and deducting the cost. Incidental costs of acquisition and disposal are deducted together with any enhancement expenditure reflected in the state and nature of the asset at the date of disposal.
- An individual is entitled to an annual exempt amount for each tax year.
- Losses are set off against gains of the same year and any excess carried forward. Brought forward losses are only set off to reduce net gains down to the amount of the annual exempt amount.
- Capital gains tax is usually payable at the rate of 10% or 20% depending on the individual's taxable income.
- Capital gains tax is payable at the rate of 18% or 28% on residential property gains depending on the individual's taxable income.
- Basic capital gains tax planning involves maximising the use of the annual exempt amount, ensuring the lowest rate of tax applies and timing of payment of tax.
- Disposals between spouses or members of a civil partnership are made on a no gain no loss basis and do not give rise to a chargeable gain or allowable loss.
- On a part disposal, the cost must be apportioned between the part disposed of and the part retained.
- The gain which would otherwise arise on the receipt of insurance proceeds may, subject to certain conditions, be deferred.

Quick Quiz

1. Give some examples of chargeable disposals.
2. On what assets does a UK resident pay CGT?
3. What is enhancement expenditure?
4. To what extent must allowable losses be set against chargeable gains?
5. At what rate or rates do individuals pay CGT on gains which are not residential property gains and do not qualify for entrepreneurs' relief?
6. Ten acres of land are sold for £15,000 out of 25 acres. Original cost for the 25 acres was £9,000. Costs of sale are £2,000. Rest of land valued at £30,000. What is the total amount deductible from proceeds?

   A £2,000
   B £2,872
   C £5,000
   D £5,600

7. Emma drops and destroys a vase. She receives compensation for £2,000 from her insurance company. How can she avoid a charge to CGT arising?

Answers to Quick Quiz

1 The following are chargeable disposals

- Sales of assets or parts of assets
- Gifts of assets or parts of assets
- Receipts of capital sums following the loss or destruction of an asset

2 All assets, whether situated in the UK or abroad, unless specifically exempt.

3 Enhancement expenditure is capital expenditure enhancing the value of the asset and reflected in the state/nature of the asset at disposal, or expenditure incurred in establishing, preserving or defending title to asset.

4 Current year losses must be set off against gains in full, even if this reduces net gains below the annual exempt amount. Losses brought forward are set off to bring down gains to the level of the annual exempt amount.

5 Individuals pay CGT at the rate of 10% or 20% on most taxable gains depending on their taxable income.

6 C. $\frac{15{,}000}{15{,}000 + 30{,}000} \times £9{,}000 = £3{,}000 + £2{,}000$ (costs of disposal) = £5,000

7 Emma can avoid a charge to CGT on receipt of the compensation by investing at least £2,000 in a replacement asset within 12 months.

Now try the questions below from the Practice Question Bank

Number	Type	Marks	Time
Q85	Section A	2	4 mins
Q86	Section A	2	4 mins
Q87	Section A	2	4 mins
Q88	Section C	10	20 mins

14

Chattels and the principal private residence exemption

Topic list	Syllabus reference
1 Chattels	C3(a), (b)
2 Wasting assets	C3(a), (b)
3 Private residences	C3(c), C6(b)

Introduction

In the previous chapter we have considered the basic rules for the capital gains computation and the calculation of CGT payable by an individual, together with the rules for part disposals and assets damaged or destroyed.

We now turn our attention to specific assets, starting with chattels. Where there is a disposal of low value assets, the chattels rules may apply to restrict the gain or allowable loss. The gain may even be exempt in certain circumstances. We look at the detailed rules.

The highest value item that an individual is likely to sell is his home. We look at the rules to see when the gain may be wholly or partly exempt.

In the next chapter we will consider the reliefs specifically available on business assets, and later we will turn our attention to the special rules for shares.

Study guide

		Intellectual level
C3	**Gains and losses on the disposal of movable and immovable property**	
(a)	Identify when chattels and wasting assets are exempt.	1
(b)	Compute the chargeable gain when a chattel or a wasting asset is disposed of.	2
(c)	Calculate the chargeable gain when a principal private residence is disposed of.	2
C6	**The use of exemptions and reliefs in deferring and minimising tax liabilities arising on the disposal of capital assets**	
(b)	Basic capital gains tax planning	2

Exam guide

You are quite likely to come across a question on either chattels or the reliefs available on the disposal of a principal private residence in any of Sections A, B or C.

With chattels always look for the exemption for wasting chattels, a restriction of the gain if proceeds exceed £6,000, or a restriction of loss relief if proceeds are less than £6,000. The rules for chattels apply to companies as well as individuals, but watch out for assets on which capital allowances have been given.

On the disposal of a principal private residence if there has been any non-occupation or business use make a schedule of the relevant dates before you start to calculate the gain in case it turns out to be wholly exempt.

1 Chattels

1.1 What is a chattel?

Key terms

A **chattel** is tangible moveable property.

A **wasting asset** is an asset with an estimated remaining useful life of 50 years or less.

Plant and machinery, whose predictable useful life is always deemed to be less than 50 years, is an example of a wasting chattel (unless it is immoveable, in which case it will be wasting but not a chattel). Machinery includes, in addition to its ordinary meaning, motor vehicles (unless exempt as cars), railway and traction engines, engine-powered boats and clocks.

1.2 Wasting chattels

FAST FORWARD

Gains on most wasting chattels are exempt and losses are not allowable.

Wasting chattels are exempt (so that there are no chargeable gains and no allowable losses).

There is one exception to this: assets used for the purpose of a trade, profession or vocation in respect of which capital allowances have been or could have been claimed. This means that items of plant and machinery used in a trade are not exempt merely on the grounds that they are wasting (see below). However, cars are always exempt.

1.3 Gains on non-wasting chattels

FAST FORWARD

When a non-wasting chattel is sold for less than £6,000, any gain is exempt. There is marginal relief for gains where sale proceeds exceed £6,000.

If a chattel is not exempt under the wasting chattels rule, any gain arising on its disposal will still be exempt if the asset is sold for gross proceeds of £6,000 or less, even if capital allowances were claimed on it.

If sale proceeds exceed £6,000, any gain is limited to a maximum of 5/3 × (gross proceeds – £6,000).

Question

Chattels: gains

Adam purchased a Chippendale chair for £1,800. On 10 October 2016 he sold the chair at auction for £6,300 (which was net of the auctioneer's 10% commission). What is the gain?

Answer

	£
Proceeds (£6,300 × 100/90)	7,000
Less incidental costs of sale	(700)
Net proceeds	6,300
Less cost	(1,800)
Gain	4,500

The maximum gain is 5/3 × £(7,000 – 6,000) = £1,667.

The chargeable gain is the lower of £4,500 and £1,667, so it is £1,667.

1.4 Losses on non-wasting chattels

FAST FORWARD

A loss on the sale of a non-wasting chattel is restricted where proceeds are less than £6,000.

Where a chattel which is not exempt under the wasting chattels rule is sold for less than £6,000 and a loss arises, the allowable loss is restricted by assuming that the chattel was sold for gross proceeds of £6,000. This rule cannot turn a loss into a gain, only reduce the loss, perhaps to zero.

Question

Chattels: losses

Eve purchased a rare first edition for £8,000 which she sold in October 2016 at auction for £2,700 (which was net of 10% commission). Compute the gain or loss.

Answer

	£
Proceeds (assumed)	6,000
Less incidental costs of disposal (£2,700 × 10/90)	(300)
	5,700
Less cost	(8,000)
Allowable loss	(2,300)

1.5 Chattels and capital allowances

FAST FORWARD

The CGT rules are modified for assets eligible for capital allowances.

The wasting chattels exemption does not apply to chattels on which capital allowances have been claimed or could have been claimed. The chattels rules based on £6,000 do apply.

Where a chattel on which capital allowances have been obtained is sold at a loss, the allowable cost for chargeable gains purposes is reduced by the lower of the loss and the net amount of allowances given (taking into account any balancing allowances or charges). **The result is no gain and no loss.** This is because relief for the loss has already been given through the capital allowances computation.

If the chattel is sold at a gain the cost is not adjusted for capital allowances. This is because the capital allowances will have been clawed back through the balancing charge.

2 Wasting assets

FAST FORWARD

When a wasting asset is disposed of its cost must be depreciated over its estimated useful life.

2.1 Introduction

A wasting asset is one which has an estimated remaining useful life of 50 years or less and whose original value will depreciate over time. Examples of such assets are copyrights and registered designs.

2.2 The computation

The normal capital gains computation is amended to reflect the anticipated depreciation over the life of the asset.

The cost is written down on a straight line basis, and it is this depreciated cost which is deducted in the computation.

Thus if a taxpayer acquires a wasting asset with a remaining life of 40 years and disposes of it after 15 years, so that 25 years of useful life remain, only 25/40 of the cost is deducted in the computation.

Any enhancement expenditure must be separately depreciated.

2.3 Example: wasting asset

Harry bought a copyright on 1 July 2012 for £20,000. The copyright is due to expire in July 2032. He sold it on 1 July 2016 for £22,000.

Harry's gain is:

	£
Proceeds of sale	22,000
Less depreciated cost £20,000 × 16/20	(16,000)
Gain	6,000

2.4 Capital allowances

If capital allowances have been given on a wasting asset its cost is not depreciated over time.

3 Private residences

FAST FORWARD

There is an exemption for gains on principal private residences, but the exemption may be restricted because of periods of non-occupation or because of business use.

3.1 General principles

A gain arising on the sale of an individual's only or main private residence (sometimes called his **principal private residence or PPR**) **is exempt from CGT.** The exemption covers total grounds, including the house, of up to half a hectare. The total grounds can exceed half a hectare if the house is large enough to warrant it, but if not, the gain on the excess grounds is taxable.

For the exemption to be available the taxpayer must have occupied the property as a residence rather than just as temporary accommodation.

3.2 Occupation

The gain is wholly exempt where the owner has occupied the whole of the residence throughout his period of ownership. Where occupation has been for only part of the period, the proportion of the gain exempted is

$$\textbf{Total gain} \times \frac{\text{Period of occupation}}{\text{Total period of ownership}}$$

The **last 18 months of ownership are always** treated as **a period of occupation**, if at some time the residence has been the taxpayer's main residence, even if within those last 18 months the taxpayer also has another house which is his actual principal private residence.

Where a loss arises and all, or a proportion of, any gain would have been exempt, all or the same proportion of the loss is not allowable.

3.3 Deemed occupation

The **period of occupation is also deemed to include certain periods of absence, provided the individual had no other exempt residence at the time and the period of absence was at some time both preceded and followed by a period of actual occupation.** The last 18 months rule (see above) takes precedence over this rule.

These periods of **deemed occupation** are:

(a) **Any period** (or periods taken together) of absence, **for any reason, up to three years**, and

(b) **Any periods** during which the owner was **required by his employment** (ie employed taxpayer) **to live abroad**, and

(c) **Any period** (or periods taken together) **up to four years** during which the owner was **required to live elsewhere due to his work** (ie both employed and self employed taxpayer) so that he could not occupy his private residence.

It does not matter if the residence is let during the absence.

Exempt periods of absence must normally be preceded and followed by periods of actual occupation. This rule is relaxed where an individual who has been required to work abroad or elsewhere (ie (b) and (c) above) is unable to resume residence in his home because the terms of his employment require him to work elsewhere.

Question — Principal private residence relief

Abel purchased a house on 1 April 1991 for £88,200. He lived in the house until 31 December 1992. He then worked abroad for two years before returning to the UK to live in the house again on 1 January 1995. He stayed in the house until 30 June 2011 before retiring and moving out to live with friends in Spain until the house was sold on 31 December 2016 for £170,000.

Calculate Abel's capital gains tax payable for 2016/17 assuming that this is the only disposal that he makes in the tax year and that he is a higher rate taxpayer.

Answer

	£
Proceeds	170,000
Less cost	(88,200)
Gain before PPR exemption	81,800
Less PPR exemption (working)	
$\frac{261}{309} \times £81,800$	(69,093)
Chargeable gain	12,707
Less annual exempt amount	(11,100)
Taxable gain	1,607
CGT on £1,607 @ 28% (residential property rate)	450

Working

Exempt and chargeable periods

Period		Total months	Exempt months	Chargeable Months
(i)	April 1991 – December 1992 (occupied)	21	21	0
(ii)	January 1993 – December 1994 (working abroad)	24	24	0
(iii)	January 1995 – June 2011 (occupied)	198	198	0
(iv)	July 2011 – June 2015 (see below)	48	0	48
(v)	July 2015 – December 2016 (last 18 months)	18	18	0
		309	261	48

No part of the period from July 2011 to June 2015 can be covered by the exemption for three years of absence for any reason because it is not followed at any time by actual occupation.

Exam focus point

To help you to answer questions such as that above it is useful to draw up a table showing the period of ownership, exempt months (actual/deemed occupation) and chargeable months (non-occupation) similar to that in the working.

3.4 Business use

Where part of a residence is used exclusively for business purposes throughout the entire period of ownership, the gain attributable to use of that part is taxable. The 'last 18 months always exempt' rule does not apply to that part.

Question — Business use of PPR

Smail purchased a property for £35,000 on 31 May 2010 and began operating a dental practice from that date in one quarter of the house. He closed the dental practice on 31 December 2016, selling the house on that date for £130,000.

Compute the gain arising.

Answer

	£
Proceeds	130,000
Less cost	(35,000)
Gain before PPR exemption	95,000
Less PPR exemption 0.75 × £95,000	(71,250)
Gain	23,750

Exemption is lost on one quarter throughout the period of ownership (including the last 18 months) because of the use of that fraction for business purposes.

If part of a residence was used for business purposes for only part of the period of ownership, the gain is apportioned between chargeable and exempt parts. If the business part was **at some time** used as part of the residence, the gain apportioned to that part **will** qualify for the last 18 months exemption.

3.5 Letting relief

The principal private residence exemption is extended to any gain accruing while the property is let, up to a certain limit. The two main circumstances in which the letting exemption applies are:

(a) When the owner is absent and lets the property, where the absence is not a deemed period of occupation.

(b) When the owner lets part of the property while still occupying the rest of it. The absence from the let part cannot be a deemed period of occupation, because the owner has another residence (the rest of the property). However, the let part will qualify for the last 18 months exemption **if** the let part has **at some time** been part of the only or main residence.

In both cases the letting must be for residential use. **The extra exemption is restricted to the lowest of:**

(a) The amount of the total **gain** which is already **exempt under the PPR provisions**
(b) The gain accruing during the letting period (the **letting part of the gain**)
(c) **£40,000** (maximum)

Letting relief cannot convert a gain into an allowable loss.

If a lodger lives as a member of the owner's family, sharing their living accommodation and eating with them, the **whole** property is regarded as the owner's main residence.

Question

Letting relief (1)

Ovett purchased a house in Truro on 5 October 2002 and sold it on 5 April 2017 making a gain of £290,000.

On 5 July 2005 he had been sent to work in Edinburgh, and he did not return to his own house until 6 January 2015. The property was let out during his absence, and he lived in a flat provided for him by his employer. What is the gain arising?

Answer

	£
Gain before PPR exemption	290,000
Less PPR exemption (working)	
£290,000 × 144/174	(240,000)
	50,000
Less letting exemption: Lowest of:	
(a) gain exempt under PPR rules: £240,000	
(b) gain attributable to letting: £290,000 × $\frac{30}{174}$ = £50,000	
(c) £40,000 (maximum)	(40,000)
Gain	10,000

Working

Period	Notes	Total ownership months	Exempt months	Chargeable Months
5.10.02 – 4.7.05	Actual occupation	33	33	0
5.7.05 – 4.7.09	Four years absence working in the UK	48	48	0
5.7.09 – 4.7.12	Three year of absence for any reason	36	36	0
5.7.12 – 5.1.15	Absent – let	30	0	30
6.1.15 – 5.4.17	Occupied (includes last 18 months)	27	27	0
		174	144	30

Question

Letting relief (2)

Celia purchased a house on 31 March 2002 for £90,000. She sold it on 31 August 2016 for £340,000. In 2007 the house was redecorated and Celia began to live on the top floor renting out the balance of the house (constituting 60% of the total house) to tenants between 1 July 2007 and 1 January 2016. On 2 January 2016 Celia put the whole house on the market but continued to live only on the top floor until the house was sold. What is the gain arising?

Answer

	£
Proceeds	340,000
Less: cost	(90,000)
Gain before PPR exemption	250,000
Less PPR exemption (working)	
£250,000 × $\frac{117.8}{173}$	(170,231)
	79,769
Less letting exemption: Lowest of:	
(a) gain exempt under PPR rules: £170,231	
(b) gain attributable to letting: £250,000 × $\frac{55.2}{173}$ = £79,769	
(c) £40,000 (maximum)	(40,000)
Gain	39,769

Working

Period	Notes	Total ownership months		Exempt months	Chargeable months
1.4.02 – 30.06.07	100% of house occupied	63		63	0
1.7.07 – 28.2.15	40% of house occupied	92	{	36.8	
	60% of house let				55.2
1.3.15 – 31.8.16	Last 18 months treated as 100% of house occupied	18		18	0
		173		117.8	55.2

Note. The gain on the 40% of the house always occupied by Celia is fully covered by PPR relief. The other 60% of the house has not always been occupied by Celia and thus any gain on this part of the house is taxable where it relates to periods of time when Celia was not actually (or deemed to be) living in it.

Even if Celia reoccupied all floors prior to the sale, she cannot claim exemption for part of the period of letting under the 'three year absence for any reason' rule since during this time she has a main residence which qualifies for relief (ie the rest of the house). However, she can claim exemption for the whole of the house for the last 18 months since the let part was part of her only residence prior to the letting.

Chapter Roundup

- Gains on most wasting chattels are exempt and losses are not allowable.
- When a non-wasting chattel is sold for less than £6,000, any gain is exempt. There is marginal relief for gains where sale proceeds exceed £6,000.
- A loss on the sale of a non-wasting chattel is restricted where proceeds are less than £6,000.
- The CGT rules are modified for assets eligible for capital allowances.
- When a wasting asset is disposed of its cost must be depreciated over its estimated useful life.
- There is an exemption for gains on principal private residences, but the exemption may be restricted because of periods of non-occupation or because of business use.

Quick Quiz

1 How are gains on non-wasting chattels sold for more than £6,000 restricted?

2 How are losses on non-wasting chattels sold for less than £6,000 restricted?

3 Leonie bought a copyright on 1 December 2010 for £30,000. The copyright had a life of 25 years when she bought it. She sold the copyright on 1 December 2016. What is her allowable cost for computing the gain on sale?

4 For what periods may an individual be deemed to occupy his principal private residence?

5 The maximum letting exemption is

A £30,000
B £40,000
C £60,000
D £80,000

Answers to Quick Quiz

1 Gain restricted to 5/3 × (gross proceeds – £6,000)

2 Allowable loss restricted by deeming proceeds to be £6,000

3 £30,000 × 19/25 = £22,800. The copyright has a life of 19 years when it is sold.

4 Periods of deemed occupation are:

- Last 18 months of ownership
- Any period of absence up to three years
- Any period during which the owner was required by his employment to work abroad
- Any period up to four years during which the owner was required to live elsewhere due to his work (employed or self employed) so that he could not occupy his private residence

5 B. £40,000

Now try the questions below from the Practice Question Bank

Number	Type	Marks	Time
Q89	Section A	2	4 mins
Q90	Section A	2	4 mins
Q91	Section A	2	4 mins
Q92	Section B	2	4 mins
Q93	Section B	2	4 mins
Q94	Section B	2	4 mins
Q95	Section B	2	4 mins
Q96	Section B	2	4 mins

15

Business reliefs

Topic list	Syllabus reference
1 Entrepreneurs' relief	C5(b), C6(b)
2 The replacement of business assets (rollover relief)	C6(a)(i), C6(b)
3 Gift relief (holdover relief)	C6(a)(ii), C6(b)

Introduction

Having discussed the general rules for capital gains we now turn our attention to specific reliefs for businesses.

Entrepreneurs' relief is a very important relief. It applies on the sale of a business and certain trading company shares. The rate of tax payable is 10% on such disposals regardless of the taxpayer's taxable income.

Another important relief is rollover relief, which enables a gain on the disposal of a business asset to be rolled over if a new asset is purchased for business use. This enables the payment of tax to be deferred until the business has actually retained the proceeds of sale uninvested so that it can meet the liability. This is the only relief that is available to both individuals and companies.

Finally, we consider the relief for gifts of business assets. This relief allows an entrepreneur to give away his business during his lifetime and pass any gains to the donee.

In the next chapter we will cover the computation of capital gains on the disposal of shares.

Study guide

		Intellectual level
C5	**The computation of capital gains tax**	
(b)	Explain and apply entrepreneurs' relief.	2
C6	**The use of exemptions and reliefs in deferring and minimising tax liabilities arising on the disposal of capital assets**	
(a)	Explain and apply capital gains tax reliefs:	
(i)	Rollover relief.	2
(ii)	Holdover relief for the gift of business assets.	2
(b)	Basic capital gains tax planning	2

Exam guide

Business reliefs are an important part of the F6 exam and may be tested in any of Sections A, B or C. Rollover relief may be met in either an unincorporated business or a company context, and as it is an extremely important relief for all businesses it is likely to be examined. If you are required to compute a gain on a business asset look out for the purchase of a new asset, but carefully check the date and cost of the acquisition. Do not be caught out by the purchase of an investment property. The relief for gifts of assets is only available to individuals, and effectively passes the gain to the donee. Entrepreneurs' relief is only available to individuals but is a particularly valuable relief as it reduces the rate of capital gains tax to 10%.

PER alert

One of the competencies you require to fulfil Performance Objective 17 Tax planning and advice of the PER is to mitigate and/or defer tax liabilities through the use of standard reliefs, exemptions and incentives. You can apply the knowledge you obtain from this chapter of the Study Text to help to demonstrate this competence.

1 Entrepreneurs' relief

FAST FORWARD

Entrepreneurs' relief applies on the disposal of a business and certain trading company shares. Gains on assets qualifying for the relief are taxed at 10%.

1.1 Conditions for entrepreneurs' relief

Entrepreneurs' relief is available where there is a **material disposal of business assets**.

A **material disposal** of **business assets** is:

- A disposal of the **whole or part of a business** which has been **owned by the individual** throughout the period of **one year** ending with the date of the disposal
- A disposal of **one or more assets in use for the purposes of a business at** the time at which the business **ceases to be carried on** provided that:
  - The business was owned by the individual throughout **the period of one year** ending with the date on which the business ceases to be carried on**; and**
  - The date of cessation is within **three years** ending with the date of the disposal.
- A disposal of **shares or securities of a company where** the company is the individual's **personal company;** the company is either a **trading company** or the **holding company of a trading group;**

the individual is an **officer or employee** of the company (or a group company) and these conditions are met either:

- Throughout the period of **one year** ending with the date of the disposal**; or**
- Throughout the period of **one year** ending with the date on which the company (or group) **ceases to be a trading company (or trading group)** and that date is within the period of **three years** ending with the date of the disposal.

For the first category to apply, there has be a **disposal of the whole or part of the business as a going concern**, not just a disposal of individual assets. A business includes one carried on as a partnership of which the individual is a partner. The business must be a **trade, profession or vocation** conducted on a **commercial basis with a view to the realisation of profits**. Note that gains on all business assets on such a disposal are eligible for entrepreneurs' relief, provided the business has been owned for more than a year. This is the case regardless of how long the assets themselves have been owned.

In relation to the third category, a **personal company** in relation to an individual is one where:

- The individual holds **at least 5% of the ordinary share capital;** and
- The individual can exercise **at least 5% of the voting rights in the company** by virtue of that holding of shares.

For both the first and second category, relief is only available on **relevant business assets**. These are assets **used for the purposes of the business** and **cannot include shares and securities** or **assets held as investments**.

1.2 The operation of the relief

Where there is a material disposal of business assets which results in both gains and losses, losses are netted off against gains to give a single chargeable gain on the disposal of the business assets.

The rate of tax on this chargeable gain is 10% regardless of the level of the individual's taxable income.

An individual may use losses on assets not qualifying for entrepreneurs' relief and the annual exempt amount in the most beneficial way. This will be achieved if these amounts are set off in the following order:

(1) **Residential property gains**
(2) **Other gains not qualifying for entrepreneurs' relief**
(3) **Entrepreneurs' relief gains**

The chargeable gain qualifying for entrepreneurs' relief is always treated as the lowest part of the amount on which an individual is chargeable to capital gains tax. This means chargeable gains qualifying for entrepreneurs' relief will use up any unused basic rate band before those gains that do not qualify for the relief. Although this does not affect the tax on the gain qualifying for entrepreneurs' relief (which is always at 10%), it may have an effect on the rate of tax on other taxable gains.

1.3 Example

Simon sells his business, all the assets of which qualify for entrepreneurs' relief, in September 2016. The chargeable gain arising is £10,000.

Simon also made a chargeable gain of £25,000 in December 2016 on an asset which did not qualify for entrepreneurs' relief and is not residential property.

Simon has taxable income of £15,000 in 2016/17.

The CGT payable for 2016/17 is calculated as follows:

	Gains	CGT
	£	£
Gain qualifying for entrepreneurs' relief		
Taxable gain	10,000	
CGT @ 10%		1,000
Gain not qualifying for entrepreneurs' relief		
Gain	25,000	
Less annual exempt amount (best use)	(11,100)	
Taxable gain	13,900	
CGT on £(32,000 – 15,000 – 10,000)		
= 7,000 @ 10%		700
CGT on £(13,900 – 7,000) = 6,900 @ 20%		1,380
CGT 2016/17		3,080

Note that the £10,000 gain qualifying for entrepreneurs' relief is deducted from the basic rate limit for the purposes of computing the rate of tax on the gain not qualifying for entrepreneurs' relief.

1.4 Lifetime limit

There is a lifetime limit of £10 million of gains on which entrepreneurs' relief can be claimed.

Question — Limit on entrepreneurs' relief

Maureen sells a shareholding in January 2017 realising a gain of £9,300,000. The conditions for entrepreneurs' relief are satisfied for this disposal and Maureen makes a claim for the relief to apply. Maureen had already made a claim for entrepreneurs' relief in an earlier tax year in respect of gains totalling £900,000. Maureen also makes an allowable loss of £(20,000) in 2016/17 on an asset not qualifying for entrepreneurs' relief. Her taxable income for 2016/17 is £200,000.

Calculate the CGT payable by Maureen for 2016/17.

Answer

	Gains	CGT
	£	£
Gain qualifying for entrepreneurs' relief		
£(10,000,000 – 900,000)	9,100,000	
CGT @ 10% on £9,100,000		910,000
Gain not qualifying for entrepreneurs' relief		
£(9,300,000 – 9,100,000)	200,000	
Less allowable loss (best use)	(20,000)	
Net gain	180,000	
Less annual exempt amount (best use)	(11,100)	
Taxable gain	168,900	
CGT @ 20% on £168,900		33,780
Total CGT due		943,780

Exam focus point

The entrepreneurs' relief lifetime limit of £10,000,000 and rate of tax of 10% will be given in the tax rates and allowances section of the examination paper.

1.5 Claim

PER alert

One of the competencies you require to fulfil Performance Objective 16 Tax compliance and verification of the PER is to identify available claims, or the need to object to/appeal an assessment, ensuring that they are submitted within the required time limits. You can apply the knowledge you obtain from this section of the Study Text to help to demonstrate this competence.

An individual must claim entrepreneurs' relief: it is not automatic. The claim deadline is the first anniversary of 31 January following the end of the tax year of disposal. For a 2016/17 disposal, the taxpayer must claim by 31 January 2019.

1.6 Investors' relief

FAST FORWARD

Investors' relief will apply from 2019/20 for disposals of qualifying shares in unlisted trading companies of which the investor is not an officer or employee. The rate of tax on gains qualifying for investors' relief will be 10%.

Investors' relief is a similar relief to entrepreneurs' relief. It will apply to gains on qualifying shares from 2019/20.

Qualifying shares must satisfy the following conditions:

(a) They must be **new ordinary shares** in an **unlisted trading company** (or unlisted holding company of a trading group) which have been **subscribed for** by the **individual making the disposa**l.

(b) The shares must have **been issued by the company on or after 17 March 2016 and held continuously** by that individual usually for **at least three years** from **the date of the issue of the shares** until **the date of disposal**. However, where the shares were issued between 17 March 2016 and 5 April 2016, the three-year period is extended by the period between the issue of the shares and 5 April 2016.

There is **no minimum shareholding** requirement.

The individual (and connected persons) **must not be an officer or employee of the company** (nor any connected company).

The **rate of tax** on investors' relief gains **will be 10%**. There will be a **£10 million lifetime limit of gains on which investors' relief can be claimed** separate from the limit for entrepreneurs' relief.

Exam focus point

As a result of this three year holding period, investors' relief will not be available on disposals until the tax year 2019/20. You need to be aware of the tax advantages of investors' relief and the qualifying conditions. However, computational aspects will **not be examined** in F6 (UK) until such time as the relief is available on disposals.

FAST FORWARD

2 The replacement of business assets (rollover relief)

Rollover relief is available to all businesses that reinvest in qualifying assets in the period commencing one year before and ending 36 months after the disposal concerned.

2.1 Conditions

A gain may be 'rolled over' (deferred) where the proceeds received on the disposal of a business asset are spent on a replacement business asset. This is **rollover relief**. A claim cannot specify that only part of a gain is to be rolled over.

All the following conditions must be met.

(a) **The old asset sold and the new asset bought are both used only in the trade** or trades carried on **by the person claiming rollover relief.** Where part of a building is in non-trade use for all or a substantial part of the period of ownership, the building (and the land on which it stands) is treated as two separate assets, the trade part (qualifying) and the non-trade part (non-qualifying). This split cannot be made for other assets.

(b) **The old asset and the new asset both fall within one** (but not necessarily the same one) **of the following classes.**

   (i) Land and buildings (including parts of buildings) occupied as well as used only for the purpose of the trade

   (ii) Fixed (that is, immovable) plant and machinery

   (iii) Goodwill

(c) **Reinvestment of the proceeds received on the disposal of the old asset** takes place in a period beginning one year before and ending three years after the date of the disposal.

(d) **The new asset is brought into use in the trade on its acquisition** (not necessarily immediately, but not after any significant and unnecessary delay).

The new asset can be used in a different trade from the old asset.

A claim for the relief must be made by the later of four years of the end of the tax year in which the disposal of the old asset takes place and four years of the end of the tax year in which the new asset is acquired.

2.2 Operation of relief

FAST FORWARD

A rolled over gain is deducted from the base cost of the replacement asset acquired.

Deferral is obtained by deducting the chargeable gain from the cost of the new asset. For full relief, the whole of the proceeds must be reinvested. Where only part is reinvested, a gain equal to the amount not reinvested or the full gain, if lower, will be chargeable to tax immediately.

The new asset will have a base cost for chargeable gains purposes of its purchase price less the gain rolled over.

Question

Rollover relief

A freehold factory was purchased by Zoë for business use in August 2007. It was sold in December 2016 for £70,000, giving rise to a gain of £17,950. A replacement factory was purchased in June 2017 for £60,000. Compute the base cost of the replacement factory, taking into account any possible rollover of the gain from the disposal in December 2016.

Answer

	£
Gain	17,950
Less rollover relief (balancing figure)	(7,950)
Chargeable gain: amount not reinvested £(70,000 – 60,000)	10,000
Cost of new factory	60,000
Less rolled over gain	(7,950)
Base cost of new factory	52,050

2.3 Non-business use

Where the old asset has not been used in the trade for a fraction of its period of ownership, the amount of the gain that can be rolled over is reduced by the same fraction. When considering proceeds not reinvested the restriction on rollover relief is based on the proportion of proceeds relating to the part of the asset used in the trade or the proportion relating to the period of trade use.

Exam focus point

Look out for both the old and the new asset having some non-business use. You must compare the proceeds of the business use proportion with the amount reinvested in the business use portion of the new asset.

Question — Assets with non-business use

John bought a factory for £150,000 on 11 January 2012, for use in his business. From 11 January 2013, he let the factory out for a period of two years. He then used the factory for his own business again, until he sold it on 10 July 2016 for £225,000. On 13 January 2017, he purchased another factory for use in his business. This second factory cost £100,000.

Calculate the chargeable gain on the sale of the first factory and the base cost of the second factory.

Answer

Gain on first factory

	Non business	*Business*
	£	£
Proceeds of sale (24:30) (W1)	100,000	125,000
Less cost (24:30)	(66,667)	(83,333)
Gain	33,333	41,667
Less rollover relief		(16,667)
Chargeable gain (W2)	33,333	25,000

Base cost of second factory

	£
Cost	100,000
Less gain rolled over	(16,667)
Base cost c/f	83,333

Workings

1 *Use of factory*

Total ownership period:

11.1.12 – 10.07.16 = 54 months

Attributable to non business use:

11.1.13 – 10.1.15 = 24 months

Attributable to business use (balance: 54m – 24m) = 30 months

2 *Proceeds not reinvested*

	£
Proceeds of business element	125,000
Less cost of new factory	(100,000)
Not reinvested	25,000

2.4 Depreciating assets

FAST FORWARD

When the replacement asset is a depreciating asset, the gain on the old asset is 'frozen' rather than rolled over.

Where the replacement asset is a depreciating asset, the gain is not rolled over by reducing the cost of the replacement asset. Rather it is deferred until it crystallises on the earliest of:

(a) The disposal of the replacement asset

(b) The date the replacement asset ceases to be used in the trade (but the gain does not crystallise on the taxpayer's death)

(c) Ten years after the acquisition of the replacement asset (maximum)

Key term

An asset is a **depreciating asset** if it is, or within the next ten years will become, a wasting asset. Thus, any asset with an expected life of 60 years or less is covered by this definition. Plant and machinery is always treated as depreciating.

Question — Gain deferred into depreciating asset

Norma bought a freehold shop for use in her business in June 2015 for £125,000. She sold it for £140,000 on 1 August 2016. On 10 July 2016, Norma bought some fixed plant and machinery to use in her business, costing £150,000. She then sells the plant and machinery for £167,000 on 19 November 2018. Show Norma's gains in relation to these transactions.

Answer

2016/17 – Gain deferred

	£
Proceeds of shop	140,000
Less cost	(125,000)
Gain	15,000

This gain is deferred in relation to the purchase of the plant and machinery as all the proceeds have been reinvested.

2018/19 – Sale of plant and machinery

	£
Proceeds	167,000
Less cost	(150,000)
Gain	17,000

Total gain chargeable on sale in 2018/19 (gain on plant and machinery plus deferred gain)
£(15,000 + 17,000) = £32,000

Where a gain on disposal is deferred against a replacement depreciating asset it is possible to transfer the deferred gain to a non-depreciating asset provided the non-depreciating asset is bought before the deferred gain has crystallised.

3 Gift relief (holdover relief)

FAST FORWARD

Gift relief can be claimed on gifts of business assets.

3.1 The relief

If an individual gives away a qualifying asset, the transferor and the transferee can jointly claim within four years of the end of the tax year of the transfer, that the transferor's gain be reduced to nil. The transferee is then deemed to acquire the asset for market value at the date of transfer less the transferor's deferred gain.

If a disposal involves actual consideration rather than being an outright gift, but is still not a bargain made at arm's length (so that the proceeds are deemed to be the market value of the asset), this is known as a sale at undervalue. **Any excess of actual consideration over actual cost is chargeable immediately and only the balance of the gain is deferred.** The amount chargeable immediately is limited to the full gain.

Exam focus point

The asset need only be a business asset in the hands of the donor. It is immaterial if the donee does not use it for business purposes.

3.2 Qualifying assets

Gift relief can be claimed on gifts or sales at undervalue on transfers of **business assets.** The definition of a business asset for gift relief is **not** the same as for entrepreneurs' relief.

Business assets are:

(a) Assets used in a trade, profession or vocation carried on:

  (i) By the donor

  (ii) By the donor's personal company (ie one where the individual holds at least 5% of the voting rights)

  If the asset was used for the purposes of the trade, profession or vocation for only part of its period of ownership, the gain to be held over is the gain otherwise eligible × period of such use/total period of ownership.

  If the asset was a building or structure only partly used for trade, professional or vocational purposes, only the **part of the gain attributable to the part so used is eligible for gift relief**.

(b) **Shares and securities in trading companies**

  (i) The shares or securities are **not listed on a recognised stock exchange** (but they may be on the AIM); or

  (ii) If the donor is an individual, the company concerned is his **personal company** (defined as above)

  If the company has chargeable non-business assets at the time of the gift, and point (b)(ii) above applied at any time in the last 12 months, **the gain to be held over is:**

Exam formula

$$\text{Gain} \times \frac{\text{the market value of the chargeable business assets (CBA)}}{\text{the market value of the chargeable assets (CA)}}$$

Question

Gift relief

On 6 May 2016 Angelo sold to his son Michael a freehold shop valued at £200,000 for £50,000, and claimed gift relief. Angelo had originally purchased the shop from which he had run his business for £30,000. Michael continued to run a business from the shop premises but decided to sell the shop in March 2017 for £195,000. Compute any chargeable gains arising.

Answer

(a) *Angelo's gain*

	£
Proceeds (market value)	200,000
Less cost	(30,000)
Gain	170,000
Less gain deferred (balance)	(150,000)
Chargeable gain £(50,000 – 30,000) (actual proceeds less actual cost)	20,000

(b) *Michael's gain*

	£
Proceeds	195,000
Less cost £(200,000 – 150,000) (MV less deferred gain)	(50,000)
Gain	145,000

Question

Gift of shares – CBA/CA restriction

Morris gifts shares in his personal company to his son Minor realising a gain of £100,000. The market values of the assets owned by the company at the date of the gift are:

	£
Freehold factory and offices	150,000
Leasehold warehouse	80,000
Investments	120,000
Current assets	200,000

Show the gain qualifying for hold-over relief and the chargeable gain.

Answer

Gain qualifying for hold-over relief:

$$£100{,}000 \times \frac{\text{Chargeable business assets (CBA)}}{\text{Chargeable assets (CA)}} = £100{,}000 \times \frac{150+80}{150+80+120}$$

$$= £100{,}000 \times \frac{230}{350}$$

$$= \underline{£65{,}714}$$

The gain which is not held-over (ie chargeable in current year) is £100,000 – £65,714 = £34,286

Chapter Roundup

- Entrepreneurs' relief applies on the disposal of a business and certain trading company shares. Gains on assets qualifying for the relief are taxed at 10%.
- Investors' relief will apply from 2019/20 for disposals of qualifying shares in unlisted trading companies of which the investor is not an officer or employee. The rate of tax on gains qualifying for investors' relief will be 10%.
- Rollover relief is available to all businesses that reinvest in qualifying assets in the period commencing one year before and ending 36 months after the disposal concerned.
- A rolled over gain is deducted from the base cost of the replacement asset acquired.
- When the replacement asset is a depreciating asset, the gain on the old asset is 'frozen' rather than rolled over.
- Gift relief can be claimed on gifts of business assets.

Quick Quiz

1 Patrick has been running a trading business for five years. In 2016/17 he sold the business to Andrew realising gains of £75,000. Patrick has already used his annual exempt amount for 2016/17 against other gains. He had not made any previous claim for entrepreneurs' relief. What is Patrick's CGT liability?

2 On 10 July 2016, Olivia subscribes for 5,000 new ordinary shares in X Ltd, a trading company. She is not an employee or officer of the company. What is the earliest date that Olivia can dispose of her shares and claim investors' relief?

3 Alice sells a factory for £500,000 realising a gain of £100,000. She acquires a factory two months later for £480,000. How much rollover relief is available?

A £20,000
B £60,000
C £80,000
D £100,000

4 What deferral relief is available when a business asset is replaced with a depreciating business asset?

5 Which disposals of shares qualify for gift relief?

Answers to Quick Quiz

1 CGT @ 10% on £75,000 £7,500

2 10 July 2019 (three years)

3 C. Amount not reinvested £(500,000 – 480,000) = £20,000. Rollover relief £(100,000 – 20,000) = £80,000.

4 The gain is frozen on the acquisition of a depreciating asset until the earliest of: disposal of that asset; the date the asset is no longer used in the trade; ten years after the acquisition of replacement asset.

5 Shares which qualify for gift relief are those in trading companies:

- Which are not listed on a recognised stock exchange; or
- Which are in the individual's personal company ie the individual holds at least 5% of the voting rights

Now try the questions below from the Practice Question Bank

Number	Type	Marks	Time
Q97	Section A	2	4 mins
Q98	Section A	2	4 mins
Q99	Section A	2	4 mins
Q100	Section B	2	4 mins
Q101	Section B	2	4 mins
Q102	Section B	2	4 mins
Q103	Section B	2	4 mins
Q104	Section B	2	4 mins
Q105	Section C	10	20 mins

16

Shares and securities

Topic list	Syllabus reference
1 Valuing quoted shares	C4(a)
2 The matching rules for individuals	C4(b)
3 The share pool	C4(c)
4 Bonus and rights issues	C4(d)
5 Reorganisations and takeovers	C4(d)
6 Gilts and qualifying corporate bonds	C4(e)

Introduction

We have now covered most aspects of the capital gains computation apart from shares and securities.

Shares and securities need special rules because an individual may hold several shares or securities in the same company, bought at different times for different prices but otherwise identical. We need to identify the shares which are disposed to compute the gain or loss.

We also discuss bonus and rights issues, takeovers and reorganisations.

In the next chapter we will conclude our study of personal taxation by considering administration.

Study guide

		Intellectual level
C4	**Gains and losses on the disposal of shares and securities**	
(a)	Recognise the value of quoted shares where they are disposed of by way of a gift.	2
(b)	Explain and apply the identification rules as they apply to individuals including the same day and 30 day matching rules.	2
(c)	Explain and apply the pooling provisions.	2
(d)	Explain and apply the treatment of bonus issues, rights issues, takeovers and reorganisations.	2
(e)	Identify the exemption available for gilt-edged securities and qualifying corporate bonds.	1

Exam guide

The valuation rules for gifts of quoted shares may be tested in either Section A or B. The disposal of shares and securities are likely to form at least part of a question on capital gains in Section C. You must learn the identification rules as they are crucial in calculating the gain correctly. The identification rules for companies are covered later in this Study Text. Takeovers and reorganisations are important; remember to apportion the cost across the new holding.

1 Valuing quoted shares

FAST FORWARD

Where quoted shares are disposed of by way of a gift, the market value of the shares is the lower of the two prices shown in the Stock Exchange Daily Official List plus one-half of the difference between those two prices.

Where quoted shares are disposed of by way of a gift, the market value of these shares is needed as 'proceeds' in order to calculate the chargeable gain or allowable loss.

Quoted shares are valued as the lower of the two prices shown in the Stock Exchange Daily Official List plus one-half of the difference between those two prices.

Question — CGT value of shares

Shares in A plc are quoted at 100–110p. What is the market value for CGT purposes?

Answer

The value is 100 + ½ × (110 – 100) = 105p.

2 The matching rules for individuals

FAST FORWARD

There are special rules for matching shares sold with shares purchased. Disposals are matched first with shares acquired on the same day, then within the following 30 days and finally with the share pool.

Quoted and unquoted shares and securities present special problems when attempting to compute gains or losses on disposal. For instance, suppose that Ivy buys some quoted shares in X plc as follows.

Date	*Number of shares*	*Cost*
		£
5 May 2010	220	150
17 August 2016	100	375

On 15 August 2016, Ivy sells 120 of the shares for £1,450. To determine the chargeable gain, we need to be able to work out which shares out of the two original holdings were actually sold.

We therefore need **matching rules**. These **allow us to decide which shares have been sold and so work out what the allowable cost on disposal should be**.

At any one time, we will only be concerned with shares or securities of the same class in the same company. If an individual owns both ordinary shares and preference shares in X plc, we will deal with the two classes of share entirely separately, because they are distinguishable.

Below 'shares' refers to both shares and securities.

For individuals, share disposals are matched with acquisitions in the following order.

(a) **Same day acquisitions**

(b) **Acquisitions within the following 30 days** (known as the 'bed and breakfast rule'); if more than one acquisition, use a 'first in, first out' (FIFO) basis

(c) **Any shares in the share pool (see below)**

The 'bed and breakfast' rule stops shares being sold to crystallise a capital gain or loss, usually to use the annual exempt amount, and then being repurchased a day or so later. Without the rule a gain or loss would arise on the sale, since it would be 'matched' to the original acquisition.

Exam focus point

Learn the 'matching rules' because a crucial first step to getting a shares question right is to correctly match the shares sold to the original shares purchased.

3 The share pool

3.1 Composition of pool

We treat any shares acquired (other than those acquired on the same day or within the next 30 days) as a 'pool' which grows as new shares are acquired and shrinks as they are sold.

In making computations which use the share pool, we must keep track of:

(a) The **number** of shares
(b) The **cost** of the shares

3.2 Disposals from the share pool

In the case of a disposal the cost attributable to the shares disposed of are deducted from the amounts within the share pool. The proportion of the cost to take out of the pool should be computed using the A/(A + B) fraction that is used for any other part disposal. However, we are not usually given the value of the remaining shares (B in the fraction). We just use numbers of shares.

Question — The share pool

In August 2006 Oliver acquired 4,000 shares in Twist plc at a cost of £10,000. Oliver sold 3,000 shares on 10 July 2016 for £17,000. Compute the gain and the value of the share pool following the disposal.

Answer

The gain is computed as follows:

	£
Proceeds	17,000
Less cost (working)	(7,500)
Gain	9,500

Working – share pool

	No of shares	*Cost* £
Acquisition – August 2006	4,000	10,000
Disposal – July 2016	(3,000)	
Cost $\frac{3,000}{4,000} \times £10,000$		(7,500)
	1,000	2,500

Question — Matching rules

Anita acquired shares in Kent Ltd as follows:

1 July 1996	1,000 shares for £2,000
11 April 2001	2,500 shares for £7,500
17 July 2016	400 shares for £1,680
10 August 2016	500 shares for £2,000

Anita sold 4,000 shares for £16,400 on 17 July 2016.

Calculate Anita's net gain on sale.

Answer

First match the disposal with the acquisition on the same day:

	£
Proceeds $\frac{400}{4,000} \times £16,400$	1,640
Less cost	(1,680)
Loss	(40)

Next match the disposal with the acquisition in the next thirty days:

	£
Proceeds $\frac{500}{4,000} \times £16,400$	2,050
Less cost	(2,000)
Gain	50

Finally, match the disposal with the shares in the share pool:

	£
Proceeds $\frac{3,100}{4,000} \times £16,400$	12,710
Less cost (working)	(8,414)
Gain	4,296
Net gain £(50 + 4,296 – 40)	4,306

Working

	No. of shares	*Cost* £
1.7.96 Acquisition	1,000	2,000
11.4.01 Acquisition	2,500	7,500
	3,500	9,500
17.7.16 Disposal	(3,100)	(8,414)
c/f	400	1,086

4 Bonus and rights issues

FAST FORWARD

Bonus shares are shares acquired at no cost. Rights issue shares are acquired for payment.

4.1 Bonus issues

Bonus shares are shares issued by a company in proportion to each shareholder's existing holding. For example, a shareholder may have 1,000 shares. If the company makes a 2 shares for each 1 share held bonus issue (called a '2 for 1 bonus issue'), the shareholder will receive 2 bonus shares for each 1 share held. So the shareholder will end up with 1,000 original shares and 2,000 bonus shares making 3,000 shares in total.

When a company issues bonus shares all that happens is that the size of the original holding is increased. Since bonus shares are issued at no cost there is no need to adjust the original cost.

4.2 Rights issues

In a rights issue the company offers shareholders rights issue shares in proportion to their existing shareholdings.

The difference between a bonus issue and a rights issue is that in a rights issue the new shares are paid for by the shareholder and this results in an adjustment to the original cost.

Question — **Rights issue**

Simon had the following transactions in S Ltd.

1.10.97	Bought 10,000 shares for £15,000
1.2.10	Took up rights issue 1 for 2 at £2.75 per share
14.10.16	Sold 2,000 shares for £6,000

Compute the gain arising in October 2016.

Answer

Share pool

	Number	*Cost*
		£
1.10.97 Acquisition	10,000	15,000
1.2.10 Rights issue (1 for 2)	5,000	13,750
	15,000	28,750
14.10.16 Sale	(2,000)	(3,833)
c/f	13,000	24,917

Gain

	£
Proceeds	6,000
Less cost	(3,833)
Gain	2,167

5 Reorganisations and takeovers

FAST FORWARD

The costs of the original holding are allocated to the new holdings pro rata to their values on a takeover or reorganisation.

5.1 Reorganisations

A reorganisation takes place where new shares or a mixture of new shares and debentures are issued in exchange for the original shareholdings. The new shares take the place of the old shares. The problem is how to apportion the original cost between the different types of capital issued on the reorganisation.

If the new shares and securities are quoted, then the cost is apportioned by reference to the market values of the new types of capital on the first day of quotation after the reorganisation.

Question

Reorganisations

Devon has an original quoted shareholding of 3,000 shares which is held in a share pool with a cost of £13,250.

In 2016 there is a reorganisation whereby each ordinary share is exchanged for two 'A' ordinary shares (quoted at £2 each) and one preference share (quoted at £1 each). Show how the original cost will be apportioned.

Answer

Share pool

	New holding	*MV*	*Cost*
		£	£
Ords 2 new shares	6,000	12,000	10,600 (W)
Prefs 1 new share	3,000	3,000	2,650 (W)
Total		15,000	13,250

Working

$^{12}/_{15} \times$ £13,250 = cost of ordinary shares

$^{3}/_{15} \times$ £13,250 = cost of preference shares

5.2 Takeovers

A chargeable gain does not arise on a 'paper for paper' takeover. The cost of the original holding is passed on to the new holding which takes the place of the original holding.

The takeover rules apply where the company issuing the new shares ends up with **more than 25%** of the ordinary share capital of the old company or the majority of the voting power in the old company, or the company issuing the new shares makes a general offer to shareholders in the other company which is initially made subject to a condition which, if satisfied, would give the first company control of the second company.

The exchange must take place for bona fide commercial reasons and does not have as its main purpose, or one of its main purposes, the avoidance of CGT or corporation tax.

Question — Takeover (1)

Simon held 20,000 £1 shares in D plc out of a total number of issued shares of one million. They were bought in 2002 for £2 each. In 2016 the board of D plc agreed to a takeover bid by S plc under which shareholders in D plc received three ordinary S plc shares plus one preference share for every four shares held in D plc. Immediately following the takeover, the ordinary shares in S plc were quoted at £5 each and the preferences shares at 90p. Show the base costs of the ordinary shares and the preference shares.

Answer

The total value due to Simon on the takeover is as follows.

		£
Ordinary	20,000 × 3/4 × £5	75,000
Preference	20,000 × 1/4 × 90p	4,500
		79,500

The base costs are therefore:

	£
Ordinary shares: 75,000/79,500 × 20,000 × £2	37,736
Preference shares: 4,500/79,500 × 20,000 × £2	2,264
	40,000

If part of the takeover consideration is cash then a gain must be computed.

Question — Takeover (2)

In May 2005 Rosanna bought 50,000 £1 shares in P plc (a 1% holding) for £2.10 each. In 2016 P plc was taken over by L plc and shareholders in P plc received two ordinary shares in L plc plus £2 in cash for each five shares held in P plc. Immediately following the takeover, the ordinary shares in L plc were quoted at £6 each. Calculate the gain arising on the takeover and show the base cost of the ordinary shares in L plc.

Answer

The total value due to Rosanna on the takeover is as follows.

		£
Ordinary	50,000 × 2/5 × £6	120,000
Cash	50,000 × 1/5 × £2	20,000
		140,000

The cost of the original shares is therefore apportioned between the ordinary shares and the cash as follows.

	£
Ordinary shares: 120,000/140,000 × 50,000 × £2.10	90,000
Cash: 20,000/140,000 × 50,000 × £2.10	15,000
	105,000

The gain on the takeover relates to the cash received.

	£
Proceeds	20,000
Less cost	(15,000)
Gain	5,000

6 Gilts and qualifying corporate bonds

FAST FORWARD

Gilts and qualifying corporate bonds held by individuals are exempt from CGT. You should never waste time computing gains and losses on them.

Key term

Gilts are UK Government securities issued by HM Treasury as shown on the Treasury list. You may assume that the list includes all issues of Treasury Loan, Treasury Stock, Exchequer Loan, Exchequer Stock and War Loan.

Disposals of gilt edged securities (gilts) and qualifying corporate bonds by individuals are exempt from CGT.

Key term

A **qualifying corporate bond (QCB)** is a security (whether or not secured on assets) which satisfies all of the following conditions:

(a) Represents a **'normal commercial loan'**. This excludes any bonds which are convertible into shares (although bonds convertible into other bonds which would be QCBs are not excluded), or which carry the right to excessive interest or interest which depends on the results of the issuer's business.

(b) Is **expressed in sterling** and for which no provision is made for conversion into or redemption in another currency

(c) Was **acquired** by the person now disposing of it **after 13 March 1984**

(d) Does not have a redemption value which depends on a published index of share prices on a stock exchange

Chapter Roundup

- Where quoted shares are disposed of by way of a gift, the market value of the shares is the lower of the two prices shown in the Stock Exchange Daily Official List plus one-half of the difference between those two prices.
- There are special rules for matching shares sold with shares purchased. Disposals are matched first with acquisitions on the same day, then within the following 30 days and finally with the share pool.
- Bonus shares are shares acquired at no cost. Rights issue shares are acquired for payment.
- The costs of the original holding are allocated to the new holdings pro rata to their values on a takeover or reorganisation.
- Gilts and qualifying corporate bonds held by individuals are exempt from CGT. You should never waste time computing gains and losses on them.

Quick Quiz

1 In what order are acquisitions of shares matched with disposals for individuals?

2 In July 2006 Rick acquired 1,000 shares in X plc. He acquired 1,000 more shares on each of 15 January 2008 and 15 January 2017. He sells 2,500 shares on 10 January 2017. How are the shares matched on sale?

3 How are bonus issues dealt with?

4 Sharon acquired 10,000 shares in Z plc in 2007. She takes up a 1 for 2 rights offer in May 2016. How many shares does Sharon have in her share pool after the rights offer?

5 What is a qualifying corporate bond?

Answers to Quick Quiz

1 The matching of shares sold is in the following order:

(a) Same day acquisitions
(b) Acquisitions within the following 30 days
(c) Shares in the share pool

2 January 2017 1,000 shares (following 30 days)
Share pool 1,500 shares

3 Number of shares increased. No adjustment to cost.

4 10,000 + 5,000 = 15,000 shares

5 A qualifying corporate bond is a security which:

- Represents a normal commercial loan
- Is expressed in sterling
- Was acquired after 13 March 1984
- Is not redeemable in relation to share prices on a stock exchange

Now try the questions below from the Practice Question Bank

Number	Type	Marks	Time
Q106	Section A	2	4 mins
Q107	Section A	2	4 mins
Q108	Section A	2	4 mins
Q109	Section C	10	20 mins

PART D

Tax administration for individuals

17

Self assessment and payment of tax by individuals

Topic list	Syllabus reference
1 The self assessment system	A3(a)
2 Tax returns and keeping records	A4(a), (d)
3 Self assessment and claims	A4(a)
4 Payment of income tax and capital gains tax	A4(b)
5 HMRC powers	A5(a)
6 Interest and penalties	A6(a)
7 Disputes and appeals	A5(b)

Introduction

In the earlier chapters we have learned how to calculate an individual's liability to income tax, capital gains tax and national insurance.

In this chapter we see how individuals (including partners) must 'self assess' their liability to income tax, capital gains tax and Class 4 NICs.

We also look at how HMRC enforces compliance with tax law, including compliance checks and imposing penalties and interest.

In the remaining chapters we will consider the other taxes within the syllabus: inheritance tax, corporation tax and VAT.

Study guide

		Intellectual level
A3	**The systems for self-assessment and the making of returns**	
(a)	Explain and apply the features of the self assessment system as it applies to individuals.	2
A4	**The time limits for the submission of information, claims and payment of tax, including payments on account**	
(a)	Recognise the time limits that apply to the filing of returns and the making of claims.	2
(b)	Recognise the due dates for the payment of tax under the self-assessment system and compute payments on account and balancing payments/repayments for individuals.	2
(d)	List the information and records that taxpayers need to retain for tax purposes.	1
A5	**The procedures relating to compliance checks, appeals and disputes**	
(a)	Explain the circumstances in which HM Revenue & Customs can make a compliance check into a self assessment tax return.	2
(b)	Explain the procedures for dealing with appeals and First and Upper Tier Tribunals.	2
A6	**Penalties for non-compliance**	
(a)	Calculate late payment interest and state the penalties that can be charged.	2

Exam guide

Section A or B questions on the topics in this chapter might relate to the dates for filing returns or the amount of interest or penalties. In Section C you might be asked to explain an aspect of the self assessment system, such as the filing of a return, the payment of tax or compliance checks by HMRC. Your knowledge should include the penalties used to enforce the self assessment system.

1 The self assessment system

PER alert

One of the competencies you require to fulfil Performance Objective 16 Tax compliance and verification of the PER is to explain tax filing and payment requirements and the consequences of non-compliance to clients. You can apply the knowledge you obtain from this section of the Study Text to help to demonstrate this competence.

1.1 Introduction

The self assessment system relies upon the taxpayer completing and filing a tax return and paying the tax due. The system is enforced by a system of penalties for failure to comply within the set time limits, and by interest for late payment of tax.

Many taxpayers have very simple affairs: receiving a salary under deduction of tax through PAYE, with a small amount of investment income which can be dealt with through the PAYE code. These individuals will not normally have to complete a tax return. Self-employed taxpayers, company directors and individuals with complicated affairs will have to complete a tax return.

Individuals within the self assessment system are required to complete and file a return every year unless HMRC recognise that their affairs have become sufficiently straightforward for no return to be required.

Conversely, individuals whose affairs become more complicated so that they are likely to owe tax must notify HMRC that they should be brought within the self assessment system.

1.2 Notification of liability to income tax and CGT

FAST FORWARD

Individuals who do not receive a tax return must notify their chargeability to income tax or CGT.

Individuals who are chargeable to income tax or CGT for any tax year and who have not received a notice to file a return are required to give notice of chargeability to an Officer of the Revenue and Customs within six months from the end of the year ie by 5 October 2017 for 2016/17.

A person who has no chargeable gains and who is not liable to higher rate tax does not have to give notice of chargeability if all his income:

(a) Is taken into account under PAYE

(b) Is from a source of income not subject to tax under a self assessment

(c) Has had (or is treated as having had) income tax deducted at source, or

(d) Is savings income and/or dividend income falling within the savings nil rate band and the dividend nil rate band.

A penalty may be imposed for late notification (see later in this chapter).

2 Tax returns and keeping records

PER alert

One of the competencies you require to fulfil Performance Objective 16 Tax compliance and verification of the PER is to verify and question client submissions and ensure timely submission of all relevant information to the tax authorities by the due date. You can apply the knowledge you obtain from this section of the Study Text to help to demonstrate this competence.

FAST FORWARD

Tax returns must usually be filed by 31 October (paper) or 31 January (electronic) following the end of the tax year.

2.1 Tax returns

The tax return comprises a basic six-page return form, **together with supplementary pages for particular sources of income**. Taxpayers are sent a return and a number of supplementary pages depending on their known sources of income, together with a Tax Return Guide and various notes relating to the supplementary pages. Taxpayers with new sources of income may have to ask for further supplementary pages. Taxpayers with simple tax returns may be asked to complete a short four-page tax return. If a return for the previous year was filed electronically the taxpayer may be sent a notice to file a return, rather than the official HMRC form.

The taxpayer must sign a declaration that the information given on the tax return and any supplementary pages is **correct and complete to the best of the taxpayer's knowledge and belief** and a statement that the **taxpayer understands** that he may have to **pay financial penalties and face prosecution if he gives false information**.

Partnerships must file a separate return which includes a Partnership Statement showing the firm's profits, losses, proceeds from the sale of assets, tax suffered, tax credits, and the division of all these amounts between partners. Each partner must then include his share of partnership profits on his personal tax return.

A partnership return must include a declaration of the name and tax reference of each partner, as well as the usual declaration that the return is correct and complete to the best of the signatory's knowledge. There is a warning on the form that if false information is given or any of the partnership's income or gains is concealed, the partners may be liable to financial penalties and/or HMRC may prosecute them.

2.2 Time limit for submission of tax returns

Key term

The **latest filing date** for a personal tax return for a tax year (Year 1) is:

- **31 October** in the next tax year (Year 2), for a **non-electronic return** (eg a paper return)
- **31 January** in Year 2, for an **electronic return** (eg made via the internet)

There are **two exceptions to this general rule.**

The **first exception applies if the notice to file a tax return is issued by HMRC to the taxpayer after 31 July in Year 2, but on or before 31 October in Year 2**. In this case, the **latest filing date is:**

- **The end of three months following the notice, for a non-electronic return.**
- **31 January in Year 2, for an electronic return.**

The second exception applies **if the notice to file the tax return is issued to the taxpayer after 31 October in Year 2**. In this case, **the latest filing date is the end of three months following the notice**.

Question — Submission of tax returns

Advise each of the following clients of the latest filing date for her personal tax return for 2016/17 if the return is:

(a) Non-electronic
(b) Electronic

Norma	Notice to file tax return issued by HMRC on 6 April 2017
Melanie	Notice to file tax return issued by HMRC on 10 August 2017
Olga	Notice to file tax return issued by HMRC on 12 December 2017

Answer

	Non-electronic	*Electronic*
Norma	31 October 2017	31 January 2018
Melanie	9 November 2017	31 January 2018
Olga	11 March 2018	11 March 2018

A partnership return may be filed as a non-electronic return or an electronic return. **The general rule and the exceptions to the general rule for personal returns apply also to partnership returns.**

2.3 Keeping records

All taxpayers must retain all records required to enable them to make and deliver a correct tax return.

Records must be retained until the later of:

(a) (i) Five **years after the 31 January following the tax year where the taxpayer is in business** (as a sole trader or partner or letting property). Note that this applies to all of the records, not only the business records; or

(ii) One **year after the 31 January following the tax year otherwise**; or

(b) Provided notice to deliver a return is given before the date in (a):

  (i) **The time after which a compliance check enquiry by HMRC into the return can no longer be commenced; or**

  (ii) **The date any such compliance check enquiry has been completed.**

HMRC can specify a shorter time limit for keeping records where the records are bulky and the information they contain can be provided in another way.

Where a person receives a notice to deliver a tax return after the normal record keeping period has expired, he must keep all records in his possession at that time until no compliance issues can be raised in respect of the return or until such a compliance check enquiry has been completed.

Taxpayers can keep 'information', rather than 'records', but must show that they have prepared a complete and correct tax return. The information must also be able to be provided in a legible form on request. Records can be kept in electronic format.

HMRC can inspect 'in-year' records, ie *before* a return is submitted, if they believe it is reasonably required to check a tax position.

3 Self assessment and claims

FAST FORWARD

If a paper return is filed the taxpayer can ask HMRC to compute the tax due. Electronic returns have tax calculated automatically.

3.1 Self assessment

Key term

A **self assessment** is a calculation of the amount of taxable income and gains after deducting reliefs and allowances, a calculation of income tax and CGT payable after taking into account tax deducted at source.

If the taxpayer is filing a **paper return (other than a Short Tax Return), he may make the tax calculation on his return or ask HMRC to do so on his behalf.**

If the taxpayer wishes HMRC to make the calculation for Year 1, a paper return must be filed:

- **On or before 31 October in Year 2; or**
- **If the notice to file the tax return is issued after 31 August in Year 2, within two months of the notice**

If the taxpayer is filing an **electronic return, the calculation of tax liability is made automatically when the return is made online.**

3.2 Amending the self assessment

The taxpayer may amend his return (including the tax calculation) for Year 1 within twelve months after the filing date. For this purpose the filing date means:

- **31 January of Year 2; or**
- **Where the notice to file a return was issued after 31 October in Year 2, the last day of the three month period starting with the issue**

A return may be amended by the taxpayer at a time when a compliance check enquiry is in progress into the return. The amendment does not restrict the scope of a compliance check enquiry into the return but may be taken into account in that enquiry. If the amendment is made during a compliance check enquiry to the amount of tax payable, the amendment does not take effect while the enquiry is in progress.

A return may be amended by HMRC to correct any obvious error or omission in the return (such as errors of principle and arithmetical mistakes) or anything else that an officer has reason to believe is incorrect in the light of information available. The correction must be usually be made within nine months after the day on which the return was actually filed. The taxpayer can object to the correction but must do so within 30 days of receiving notice of it.

3.3 Claims

All claims and elections which can be made in a tax return must be made in this manner if a return has been issued. A claim for any relief, allowance or repayment of tax must be quantified at the time it is made. **In general, the time limit for making a claim is four years from the end of tax year.** Where different time limits apply, these have been mentioned throughout this Study Text.

3.4 Recovery of overpaid tax

If a taxpayer discovers that he has overpaid tax, for example because he has made an error in his tax return, he can make a claim to have the overpaid tax repaid to him. The claim must be made within four years of the end of the tax year to which the overpayment relates.

4 Payment of income tax and capital gains tax

PER alert

One of the competencies you require to fulfil Performance Objective 16 Tax compliance and verification of the PER is to determine the incidence (timing) of tax liabilities and their impact on cash flow/financing requirements. You can apply the knowledge you obtain from this section of the Study Text to help to demonstrate this competence.

FAST FORWARD

Two payments on account and a final balancing payment of income tax and Class 4 NICs are due. All capital gains tax and Class 2 NICs are due on 31 January following the end of the tax year.

4.1 Payments on account and final payment

4.1.1 Introduction

The self assessment system may result in the taxpayer making three payments of income tax and Class 4 NICs.

Date	Payment
31 January in the tax year	1st payment on account
31 July after the tax year	2nd payment on account
31 January after the tax year	Final payment to settle the remaining liability

HMRC issue payslips/demand notes in a credit card type 'Statement of Account' format, but there is no statutory obligation for it to do so and **the onus is on the taxpayer to pay the correct amount of tax on the due date**.

4.1.2 Payments on account

Key term

Payments on account are usually required where the income tax and Class 4 NICs due in the previous year exceeded the amount of income tax deducted at source; this excess is known as **'the relevant amount'**. Income tax deducted at source for F6 (UK) is tax deducted under Pay As You Earn.

The payments on account are each equal to 50% of the relevant amount for the previous year.

Exam focus point

Payments on account of Class 2 NICs and capital gains tax are never required.

Question

Payments on account

Sue is employed and paid tax for 2015/16 as follows:

		£
Total amount of income tax charged		11,100
This included:	Tax deducted under PAYE	3,200
She also paid:	Capital gains tax	4,800

How much are the payments on account for 2016/17 and by what dates are they due?

Answer

		£
Income tax:		
Total income tax charged for 2015/16		11,100
Less tax deducted for 2015/16 under PAYE		(3,200)
'Relevant amount'		7,900
Payments on account for 2016/17:		
31 January 2017	£7,900 × 50%	3,950
31 July 2017	£7,900 × 50%	3,950

There is no requirement to make payments on account of capital gains tax.

Exam focus point

A question set involving payments on account for the tax year 2016/17 based on 2015/16 figures **will not be set** in F6 (UK) involving tax deducted at source from savings income or dividend income in that year.

Payments on account are not required if the relevant amount falls below a de minimis limit of £1,000. Also, payments on account are not required from taxpayers who paid 80% or more of their tax liability for the previous year through PAYE or other deduction at source arrangements.

4.1.3 Reducing payments on account

Payments on account are normally fixed by reference to the previous year's tax liability but if a taxpayer expects his liability to be lower than this **he may claim to reduce his payments on account to:**

(a) **A stated amount; or**
(b) **Nil**

The claim must state the reason why he believes his tax liability will be lower, or nil.

If the taxpayer's eventual liability is higher than he estimated he will have reduced the payments on account too far. Although the payments on account will not be adjusted, the taxpayer will suffer an interest charge on late payment.

A penalty of the difference between the reduced payment on account and the correct payment on account may be levied if the reduction was claimed fraudulently or negligently.

4.1.4 Balancing payment

The balance of any income tax and Class 4 NICs together with all CGT due for a year, is normally payable on or before the 31 January following the year. Class 2 NICs for 2016/17 will also be payable on or before 31 January 2018.

Question

Giles made payments on account for 2016/17 of £6,500 each on 31 January 2017 and 31 July 2017, based on his 2015/16 liability. He then calculates his total income tax and Class 4 NIC liability for 2016/17 at £15,250. No tax was deducted at source or under PAYE in 2015/16. In addition he calculated that his CGT liability for disposals in 2016/17 is £5,120 and his Class 2 NIC for 2016/17 is £146.

What is the final payment due for 2016/17?

Answer

Income tax and Class 4 NIC: £15,250 – £6,500 – £6,500 = £2,250. CGT = £5,120. Class 2 NIC = £146.

Final payment due on 31 January 2018 for 2016/17: £2,250 + £5,120 + £146 = £7,516

In one case the due date for the final payment is later than 31 January following the end of the year. **If a taxpayer has notified chargeability by 5 October but the notice to file a tax return is not issued before 31 October, then the due date for the payment is three months after the issue of the notice.**

Tax charged in an amended self assessment is usually payable on the later of:

(a) The normal due date, generally 31 January following the end of the tax year
(b) The day following 30 days after the making of the revised self assessment

5 HMRC powers

PER alert

One of the competencies you require to fulfil Performance Objective 16 Tax compliance and verification of the PER is to correspond appropriately and in a professional manner with the relevant parties in relation to both routine and specific matters/enquiries. You can apply the knowledge you obtain from this section of the Study Text to help to demonstrate this competence.

5.1 Compliance check enquiries

FAST FORWARD

A compliance check enquiry into a return, claim or election can be started by an officer of HMRC within a limited period.

5.1.1 Starting compliance check enquiry

HM Revenue and Customs has powers to make compliance check enquiries into returns, claims or elections which have already been submitted.

Some returns, claims or elections are **selected for a compliance check enquiry at random, others for a particular reason**, for example, if HM Revenue and Customs believes that there has been an **underpayment of tax** due to the taxpayer's failure to comply with tax legislation.

An officer of HM Revenue and Customs has a limited period within which to commence a compliance check enquiry on a return or amendment. The officer must give written notice of his intention by:

(a) **The first anniversary of the actual filing date, if the return was delivered on or before the due filing date;** or

(b) **The quarter day following the first anniversary of the actual filing date, if the return is filed after the due filing date. The quarter days are 31 January, 30 April, 31 July and 31 October.**

If the taxpayer amends the return after the due filing date, the compliance check enquiry 'window' extends to the quarter day following the first anniversary of the date the amendment was filed. Where the compliance check enquiry was not started within the limit which would have applied had no amendment been filed, the enquiry is restricted to matters contained in the amendment.

The officer does not have to have, or give, any reason for starting a compliance check enquiry. In particular, the taxpayer will not be advised whether he has been selected at random for an audit. Compliance check enquiries may be full enquires, or may be limited to 'aspect' enquiries.

5.1.2 During the compliance check enquiry

In the course of the compliance check enquiry **the officer may require the taxpayer to produce documents, accounts or any other information required. The taxpayer can appeal to the Tax Tribunal against such a requirement.**

5.1.3 Completion of a compliance check enquiry

An officer must issue a notice that the compliance check enquiry is complete.

The officer cannot then make a further compliance check enquiry into that return. HMRC may, in limited circumstances, raise a discovery assessment if they believe that there has been a loss of tax.

5.2 Determinations

If notice has been served on a taxpayer to submit a return but the return is not submitted by the due filing date, an officer of HMRC may make a determination of the amounts liable to income tax and CGT and of the tax due. Such a determination must be made to the best of the officer's information and belief, and is then treated as if it were a self assessment. This enables the officer to seek payment of tax, including payments on account for the following year and to charge interest.

A determination must be made within four years following the end of the relevant tax year.

5.3 Discovery assessments

If an officer of HMRC discovers that profits have been omitted from assessment, that any assessment has become insufficient, or that any relief given is, or has become excessive, an assessment may be raised to recover the tax lost.

If the tax lost results from an error in the taxpayer's return but the return was made in accordance with prevailing practice at the time, no discovery assessment may be made.

A discovery assessment may only be raised where a return has been made if:

(a) There has been **careless or deliberate understatement** by the taxpayer or his agent; or

(b) At the time that compliance check enquiries on the return were completed, or could no longer be made, the officer **did not have information** to make him aware of the loss of tax.

Information is treated as available to an officer if it is contained in the taxpayer's return or claim for the year or either of the two preceding years, or it has been provided as a result of a compliance check enquiry covering those years, or it has been specifically provided.

The time limit for raising a discovery assessment is four years from the end of the tax year but this is extended to six years if there has been careless understatement and 20 years if there has been deliberate understatement. The taxpayer may appeal against a discovery assessment within 30 days of issue.

5.4 Dishonest conduct of tax agents

FAST FORWARD

> HMRC can investigate dishonest conduct by a tax agent and issue a civil penalty of up to £50,000 where there has been dishonest conduct.

HMRC can investigate whether there has been dishonest conduct by a tax agent (ie an individual who, in the course of business, assists clients with their tax affairs). Dishonest conduct occurs when a tax agent does something dishonest with a view to bringing about a loss of tax.

HMRC can issue a civil penalty of up to £50,000 where there has been **dishonest conduct and the tax agent fails to supply the information or documents that HMRC has requested**.

6 Interest and penalties

PER alert

One of the competencies you require to fulfil Performance Objective 16 Tax compliance and verification of the PER is to explain tax filing and payment requirements and the consequences of non-compliance to clients. You can apply the knowledge you obtain from this section of the Study Text to help to demonstrate this competence.

6.1 Interest on late paid tax

FAST FORWARD

Interest is chargeable by HMRC on late payment of tax.

Interest is chargeable on late payment of both payments on account and balancing payments. Late payment interest is charged from the due date for payment until the day before the date on which payment is made.

Exam focus point

You will be given the rate of interest to use in the exam.

Interest is charged from 31 January following the tax year (or the normal due date for the balancing payment, in the rare event that this is later), even if this is before the due date for payment on:

(a) Tax payable following an amendment to a self assessment
(b) Tax payable in a discovery assessment
(c) Tax postponed under an appeal, which becomes payable

Since a determination (see above) is treated as if it were a self assessment, interest runs from 31 January following the tax year.

If a taxpayer claims to reduce his payments on account and there is still a balancing payment to be made, interest is normally charged on the payments on account as if each of those payments had been the lower of:

(a) The reduced amount, plus 50% of the balancing payment
(b) The amount which would have been payable had no claim for reduction been made

Question — Interest

Herbert's payments on account for 2016/17 based on his income tax liability for 2015/16 were £4,500 each. However when he submitted his 2015/16 income tax return in January 2017 he made a claim to reduce the payments on account for 2016/17 to £3,500 each. The first payment on account was made on 29 January 2017 and the second on 12 August 2017.

Herbert filed his 2016/17 tax return in December 2017. The return showed that his tax liabilities for 2016/17 (before deducting payments on account) were income tax and Class 4 NIC: £10,000, capital gains tax: £2,354, Class 2 NIC: £146. Herbert paid the balance of tax due of £5,500 on 19 February 2018.

For what periods and in respect of what amounts will Herbert be charged interest?

Answer

Herbert made an excessive claim to reduce his payments on account, and will therefore be charged interest on the reduction. The payments on account should have been £4,500 each based on the original 2015/16 liability (not £5,000 each based on the 2016/17 liability). Interest will be charged as follows:

(a) First payment on account

   (i) On £3,500 – nil – paid on time
   (ii) On £1,000 from due date of 31 January 2017 to day before payment date, 18 February 2018

(b) Second payment on account

(i) On £3,500 from due date of 31 July 2017 to day before payment date, 11 August 2017
(ii) On £1,000 from due date of 31 July 2017 to day before payment date, 18 February 2018

(c) Balancing payment (£1,000), capital gains tax (£2,354) and Class 2 NIC (£146) = £3,500

(i) On £3,500 from due date of 31 January 2018 to day before payment date, 18 February 2018

Where interest has been charged on late payments on account but the final balancing settlement for the year produces a repayment, all or part of the original interest is repaid.

6.2 Repayment of tax and repayment supplement

FAST FORWARD

Interest (repayment supplement) is payable by HMRC on overpayment of tax.

Tax is repaid when claimed unless a greater payment of tax is due in the following 30 days, in which case it is set-off against that payment.

Interest is paid on overpayments of:

(a) **Payments on account**

(b) **Final payments** of income tax and Class 4 NICs and CGT, including tax deducted at source or tax credits on dividends

(c) **Penalties**

Repayment supplement runs from the original date of payment (even if this was prior to the due date), until the day before the date the repayment is made. Income tax deducted at source and tax credits are treated as if they were paid on the 31 January following the tax year concerned.

Repayment supplement is tax free.

For the purpose of F6 (UK) exams in June 2017, September 2017, December 2017 and March 2018, the assumed rate of interest on underpaid tax is 3% and the assumed rate of interest on overpaid tax is 0.5%.

6.3 Penalties for errors

FAST FORWARD

There is a common penalty regime for errors in tax returns, including income tax, NICs, corporation tax and VAT. Penalties range from 30% to 100% of the Potential Lost Revenue. Penalties may be reduced.

A common penalty regime for errors in tax returns for income tax, national insurance contributions, corporation tax and value added tax.

A penalty may be imposed where **a taxpayer makes an inaccurate return** if he has:

- Been **careless** because he has not taken reasonable care in making the return or discovers the error later but does not take reasonable steps to inform HMRC; or
- Made a **deliberate error** but **does not make arrangements to conceal it**; or
- Made a **deliberate error** and **has attempted to conceal it** eg by submitting false evidence in support of an inaccurate figure.

Note that **an error which is made where the taxpayer has taken reasonable care** in making the return and which he **does not discover later, does not result in a penalty**.

In order for a penalty to be charged, the **inaccurate return must result in**:

- **An understatement of the taxpayer's tax liability**; or
- **A false or increased loss for the taxpayer**; or
- **A false or increased repayment of tax to the taxpayer**.

If a return contains more than one error, a penalty can be charged for each error.

The rules also extend to **errors in claims for allowances and reliefs** and in **accounts submitted in relation to a tax liability**.

Penalties for error also apply where **HMRC has issued an assessment estimating a person's liability** where:

- A **return has been issued to that person and has not been returned**; or
- The taxpayer was **required to deliver a return to HMRC but has not delivered it**.

The taxpayer will be charged a penalty where:

- The **assessment understates the taxpayer's liability** to income tax, capital gains tax, corporation tax or VAT; and
- **The taxpayer fails to take reasonable steps within 30 days of the date of the assessment** to tell HMRC that there is an under-assessment.

The amount of **the penalty for error is based on the Potential Lost Revenue (PLR)** to HMRC as a result of the error. For example, if there is an understatement of tax, this understatement will be the PLR.

The maximum amount of the penalty for error depends on the type of error:

Type of error	Maximum penalty payable
Careless	30% of PLR
Deliberate not concealed	70% of PLR
Deliberate and concealed	100% of PLR

Question

Penalty for error

Alex is a sole trader. He files his tax return for 2016/17 on 10 January 2018. The return shows his trading income to be £60,000. In fact, due to carelessness, his trading income should have been stated to be £68,000. State the maximum penalty that could be charged by HMRC on Alex for his error.

Answer

The Potential Lost Revenue as a result of Alex's error is:

£(68,000 – 60,000) = £8,000 × [40% (income tax) + 2% (Class 4 NIC)]	£3,360

Alex's error is careless so the maximum penalty for error is:

£3,360 × 30%	£1,008

A penalty for error may be reduced if the taxpayer tells HMRC about the error – this is called a disclosure. The reduction depends on the **circumstances of** the disclosure and the **help that the taxpayer gives to HMRC in relation to the disclosure**.

An **unprompted disclosure is one made at a time when the taxpayer has no reason to believe HMRC has discovered, or is about to discover, the error**. Otherwise, the disclosure will be a **prompted disclosure**. The **minimum penalties** that can be imposed are as follows:

Type of error	Unprompted	Prompted
Careless	0% of PLR	15% of PLR
Deliberate not concealed	20% of PLR	35% of PLR
Deliberate and concealed	30% of PLR	50% of PLR

Question

Reduction of penalty

Sue is a sole trader. She files her tax return for 2015/16 on 31 January 2017. The return shows a loss for the year of £(80,000). In fact, Sue has deliberately increased this loss by £(12,000) and has submitted false figures in support of her claim. HMRC initiate a review into Sue's return and in reply Sue then makes a disclosure of the error. Sue is a higher rate taxpayer due to her substantial investment income and she has made a claim to set the loss against general income in 2016/17.

State the maximum and minimum penalties that could be charged by HMRC on Sue for her error.

Answer

The potential lost revenue as a result of Sue's error is:

£12,000 × 40%	£4,800

Sue's error is deliberate and concealed so the maximum penalty for error is:

£4,800 × 100%	£4,800

Sue has made a prompted disclosure so the minimum penalty for error is:

£4,800 × 50%	£2,400

The help that the taxpayer gives to HMRC relates to when, how and to what extent the taxpayer:

- **Tells HMRC about the error,** making full disclosure and explaining how the error was made
- **Gives reasonable help** to HMRC to enable it **to quantify the error**
- **Allows access to business and other records** and other relevant documents

A taxpayer can appeal to the First Tier Tax Tribunal against:

- The **penalty being charged**
- The **amount of the penalty**

6.4 Penalties for late notification of chargeability

FAST FORWARD

A common penalty regime also applies to late notification of chargeability.

A common penalty regime also applies to certain taxes for failures to notify chargeability to, or liability to register for, tax that result in a loss of tax. The taxes affected include income tax, NICs, PAYE, CGT, corporation tax and VAT. Penalties are behaviour related, increasing for more serious failures, and are based on the 'potential lost revenue'.

The minimum and maximum penalties as percentages of PLR are as follows:

Behaviour	Maximum penalty	Minimum penalty with unprompted disclosure		Minimum penalty with prompted disclosure	
Deliberate and concealed	100%	30%		50%	
Deliberate but not concealed	70%	20%		35%	
		≥12m	<12m	≥12m	<12m
Careless	30%	10%	0%	20%	10%

Note that there is no zero penalty for reasonable care (as there is for penalties for errors on returns – see above), although the penalty may be reduced to 0% if the failure is rectified within 12 months through unprompted disclosure. The penalties may also be reduced at HMRC's discretion in 'special circumstances'. However, inability to pay the penalty is not a 'special circumstance'.

The same penalties apply for failure to notify HMRC of a new taxable activity.

Where the taxpayer's failure is not classed as deliberate, there is no penalty if he can show he has a 'reasonable excuse'. Reasonable excuse does not include having insufficient money to pay the penalty. Taxpayers have a right of appeal against penalty decisions to the First Tier Tribunal.

6.5 Penalties for late filing of tax return

FAST FORWARD

A penalty can be charged for late filing of a tax return based on how late the return is and how much tax is payable.

An individual is liable to a penalty where a tax return is filed after the due filing date. The penalty date is the date on which the return will be overdue (ie the date after the due filing date).

The initial penalty for late filing of the return is £100.

If the failure continues after the end of the period of three months starting with the penalty date, HMRC may give the individual notice specifying that a daily penalty of £10 is payable for a maximum of 90 days. The daily penalty runs from a date specified in the notice which may be earlier than the date of the notice but cannot be earlier than the end of the three month period.

If the failure continues after the end of the period of six months starting with the penalty date, a further penalty is payable. This penalty is the greater of:

- **5% of the tax liability** which would have been shown in the return
- **£300**

If the failure continues after the end of the period of 12 months starting with the penalty date, a further penalty is payable. This penalty is determined in accordance with the taxpayer's conduct in withholding information which would enable or assist HMRC in assessing the taxpayer's liability to tax. **The penalty is computed as follows:**

Type of conduct	Penalty
Deliberate and concealed	Greater of: • 100% of tax liability which would have been shown on return • £300
Deliberate not concealed	Greater of: • 70% of tax liability which would have been shown on return • £300
Any other case (eg careless)	Greater of: • 5% of tax liability which would have been shown on return • £300

6.6 Penalty for late payment of tax

FAST FORWARD

A penalty is chargeable where tax is paid after the due date based on the amount of unpaid tax. Up to 15% of that amount is payable where the tax is more than 12 months late.

A penalty is chargeable where tax is paid after the penalty date. The penalty date is 30 days after the due date for the tax. Therefore no penalty arises if the tax is paid within 30 days of the due date.

The penalty chargeable is:

Date of payment	Penalty
Not more than five months after the penalty date	5% of tax which is unpaid at the penalty date.
More than five months after the penalty date but not more than 11 months after the penalty date	5% of tax which is unpaid at the end of the five month period. This is in addition to the 5% penalty above.
More than 11 months after the penalty date	5% of tax which is unpaid at the end of the 11 month period. This is in addition to the two 5% penalties above.

Penalties for late payment of tax apply to:

(a) **Balancing payments of income tax and Class 4 NICs and any CGT under self assessment or a determination**

(b) Tax due on the amendment of a self assessment

(c) Tax due on a discovery assessment

Penalties for late payment do not apply to late payments on account.

6.7 Penalty for failure to keep records

The maximum penalty for each failure to keep and retain records is £3,000 per tax year/accounting period. This penalty can be reduced by HMRC.

7 Disputes and appeals

PER alert

One of the competencies you require to fulfil Performance Objective 16 Tax compliance and verification of the PER is to identify available claims, or the need to object to/appeal an assessment, ensuring that they are submitted within the required time limits. You can apply the knowledge you obtain from this section of the Study Text to help to demonstrate this competence.

FAST FORWARD

Disputes between taxpayers and HMRC can be dealt with by an HMRC internal review or by a Tribunal hearing.

7.1 Internal reviews

For direct taxes, appeals must first be made to HMRC, which will assign a 'caseworker'.

For indirect taxes, appeals must be sent directly to the Tax Tribunal, although the taxpayer can continue to correspond with his caseworker where, for example, there is new information.

At this stage the taxpayer may be offered, or may ask for, an **'internal review'**, which will be made by an objective HMRC review officer not previously connected with the case. This is a less costly and more effective way to resolve disputes informally, without the need for a Tribunal hearing. An appeal to the Tax Tribunal cannot be made until any review has ended.

The taxpayer must either accept the review offer, or notify an appeal to the Tax Tribunal within 30 days of being offered the review, otherwise the appeal will be treated as settled.

HMRC must usually carry out the review within 45 days, or any longer time as agreed with the taxpayer. The review officer may decide to uphold, vary or withdraw decisions.

After the review conclusion is notified, **the taxpayer has 30 days to appeal to the Tax Tribunal**.

7.2 Tribunal hearings

If there is no internal review, or the taxpayer is unhappy with the result of an internal review, the case may be heard by the Tax Tribunal. The person wishing to make an appeal (the appellant) must send a notice of appeal to the Tax Tribunal. The Tax Tribunal must then give notice of the appeal to the respondent (normally HMRC).

The Tax Tribunal is made up of two 'tiers':

(a) A First Tier Tribunal
(b) An Upper Tribunal

The case will be allocated to one of four **case 'tracks'**:

(a) **Complex cases**, which the Tribunal considers will require lengthy or complex evidence or a lengthy hearing, or involve a complex or important principle or issue, or involves a large amount of money. Such cases will usually be heard by the Upper Tribunal.

(b) **Standard cases, heard by the First Tier Tribunal**, which have detailed case management and are subject to a more formal procedure than basic cases

(c) **Basic cases, also heard by the First Tier Tribunal**, which will usually be disposed of after a hearing, with minimal exchange of documents before the hearing

(d) **Paper cases, dealt with by the First Tier Tribunal**, which applies to straightforward matters such as fixed filing penalties and will usually be dealt with in writing, without a hearing

A decision of the First Tier Tribunal may be appealed to the Upper Tribunal.

Decisions of the Upper Tribunal are binding on the Tribunals and any affected public authorities. A decision of the Upper Tribunal may be appealed to the Court of Appeal.

Chapter Roundup

- Individuals who do not receive a tax return must notify their chargeability to income tax or CGT.
- Tax returns must usually be filed by 31 October (paper) or 31 January (electronic) following the end of the tax year.
- If a paper return is filed the taxpayer can ask HMRC to compute the tax due. Electronic returns have tax calculated automatically.
- Two payments on account and a final balancing payment of income tax and Class 4 NICs are due. All capital gains tax and Class 2 NICs are due on 31 January following the end of the tax year.
- A compliance check enquiry into a return, claim or election can be started by an officer of HMRC within a limited period.
- HMRC can investigate dishonest conduct by a tax agent and issue a civil penalty of up to £50,000 where there has been dishonest conduct.
- Interest is chargeable by HMRC on late payment of tax.
- Interest (repayment supplement) is payable by HMRC on overpayment of tax.
- There is a common penalty regime for errors in tax returns, including income tax, NICs, corporation tax and VAT. Penalties range from 30% to 100% of the Potential Lost Revenue. Penalties may be reduced.
- A common penalty regime also applies to late notification of chargeability.
- A penalty can be charged for late filing of a tax return based on how late the return is and how much tax is payable.
- A penalty is chargeable where tax is paid after the due date based on the amount of unpaid tax. Up to 15% of that amount is payable where the tax is more than 12 months late.
- Disputes between taxpayers and HMRC can be dealt with by an HMRC internal review or by a Tribunal hearing.

Quick Quiz

1 A taxpayer who has not received a tax return must give notice of his chargeability to capital gains tax due in 2016/17 by_______. Fill in the blank.

2 By when must a taxpayer normally file a paper tax return for 2016/17?

A 31 October 2017
B 31 December 2017
C 31 January 2018
D 5 April 2018

3 What are the normal payment dates for income tax?

4 What penalty is due in respect of income tax payments on account that are paid two months after the due date?

5 What is the maximum penalty for failure to keep records?

6 Which body hears tax appeals?

Answers to Quick Quiz

1 A taxpayer who has not received a tax return must give notice of his chargeability to capital gains tax due in 2016/17 by **5 October 2017**.

2 A. 31 October 2017

3 Two payments on account of income tax are due on 31 January in the tax year and on 31 July following. A final balancing payment is due on 31 January following the tax year.

4 None. The penalty for late paid tax does not apply to late payment of payments on account.

5 £3,000

6 The Tax Tribunal which consists of the First Tier Tribunal and the Upper Tribunal.

Now try the questions below from the Practice Question Bank

Number	Type	Marks	Time
Q110	Section A	2	4 mins
Q111	Section A	2	4 mins
Q112	Section A	2	4 mins
Q113	Section B	2	4 mins
Q114	Section B	2	4 mins
Q115	Section B	2	4 mins
Q116	Section B	2	4 mins
Q117	Section B	2	4 mins

PART E

Inheritance tax

18

Inheritance tax: scope and transfers of value

Topic list	Syllabus reference
1 Chargeable persons	D1(a)
2 Transfers of value	D1(b), (c)
3 Exemptions	D3(a), D3(b)
4 Calculation of tax on lifetime transfers	D1(d), D2(a), D3(b)
5 Calculation of tax on death estate	D1(d), D2(b)
6 Transfer of unused nil rate band	D2(c)
7 Basic inheritance tax planning	D3(b)
8 Payment of inheritance tax	D4(a)

Introduction

In this chapter we introduce inheritance tax (IHT). IHT is primarily a tax on wealth left on death. It also applies to gifts within seven years of death and to certain lifetime transfers of wealth.

The tax is different from income tax and CGT, where the basic question is: how much has the taxpayer made? With IHT, the basic question is, how much has been given away? We tax the amount which the taxpayer has transferred – the amount by which he is worse off. If the taxpayer pays IHT on a lifetime gift, he is worse off by the amount of the gift plus the tax due, and we have to take that into account. Some transfers are, however, exempt from IHT.

We will see that the first £325,000 of transfers is taxed at 0% (the 'nil rate band'), and is therefore effectively tax-free. To stop people from avoiding IHT by, for example, giving away £1,625,000 in five lots of £325,000, we need to look back seven years every time a transfer is made to decide how much of the nil rate band is available to set against the current transfer.

Next, we will see how to bring together all of a deceased person's assets at death, and compute the tax on the estate. Finally, we look at the administration and payment of IHT.

In the next chapter we will start our study of corporation tax.

Study guide

		Intellectual level
D1	**The basic principles of computing transfers of value**	
(a)	Identify the persons chargeable.	2
(b)	Understand and apply the meaning of transfer of value, chargeable transfer and potentially exempt transfer.	2
(c)	Demonstrate the diminution in value principle.	2
(d)	Demonstrate the seven year accumulation principle taking into account changes in the level of the nil rate band.	2
D2	**The liabilities arising on chargeable lifetime transfers and on the death of an individual**	
(a)	Understand the tax implications of lifetime transfers and compute the relevant liabilities.	2
(b)	Understand and compute the tax liability on a death estate.	2
(c)	Understand and apply the transfer of any unused nil rate band between spouses.	2
D3	**The use of exemptions in deferring and minimising inheritance tax liabilities**	
(a)	Understand and apply the following exemptions:	
(i)	Small gifts exemption.	2
(ii)	Annual exemption.	2
(iii)	Normal expenditure out of income.	2
(iv)	Gifts in consideration of marriage.	2
(v)	Gifts between spouses.	2
(b)	Basic inheritance tax planning.	2
D4	**Payment of inheritance tax**	
(a)	Identify who is responsible for the payment of inheritance tax and the due date for payment of inheritance tax.	2

Exam guide

Inheritance tax (IHT) may be the subject of a 10 mark question in Sections B or C and you may also find specific aspects being tested in Section A such as tax on a single transfer of value. You will need to know when IHT is charged: transfers of value (basically gifts) and chargeable persons. The concepts of potentially exempt transfers (PETs), chargeable lifetime transfers (CLTs) and the seven year accumulation principle are all fundamental to an understanding of IHT. Once you have worked out the amount of a transfer of value, you need to be able to work out the IHT liability on it. This could be payable during the donor's lifetime and/or on death for a lifetime transfer and on death for a death estate. There are a number of exemptions which may be used to reduce IHT liability such as gifts between spouses/civil partners. Finally, you need to have an understanding of how IHT is paid and who pays it.

Exam focus point

ACCA's article Inheritance tax, written by a member of the F6(UK) examination team, in Part 1 considers the **scope of inheritance tax, transfers of value, rates of tax** and **exemptions**. Part 2 covers the more difficult aspects of **lifetime transfers**, the calculation of the **value of a person's estate**, and the **payment of inheritance tax**.

1 Chargeable persons

FAST FORWARD

IHT is a tax on gifts made by individuals to other individuals or trustees.

Inheritance tax is a tax on gifts or '**transfers of value**' made by **chargeable persons**. This generally involves a transaction as a result of which wealth is transferred by one individual to another, either directly or via a trust.

Individuals are chargeable persons for inheritance tax.

Spouses and civil partners are taxed separately under inheritance tax although there is an exemption for transfers between the couple (dealt with later in this chapter).

The general principle is that all transfers of value of assets made by individuals, whether during lifetime or on death, are within the charge to IHT.

2 Transfers of value

FAST FORWARD

IHT applies to lifetime transfers of value and transfers of value made on death.

2.1 Introduction

There are **two main chargeable occasions** for inheritance tax:

(a) Transfers of value made in the lifetime of the donor (**lifetime transfers**)
(b) Transfers of value made on death, for example when property is left in a Will (**death estate**)

An example of a transfer of value is a **gift by an individual** to **another individual**.

Another example of a transfer of value is a **gift by an individual** to **trustees**. **A trust is a legal structure where one person (the settlor) gives property to one or more people (the trustees) to be held for the benefit of one or more people (the beneficiaries).**

2.2 Transfers of value

2.2.1 What is a transfer of value?

IHT cannot arise unless there is a transfer of value.

A transfer of value is any gratuitous disposition (eg a gift) made by a person which results in his being worse off, that is, he suffers a diminution (ie reduction) in the value of his estate. An individual's estate is basically all the assets which he owns.

Exam focus point

The examination team has stated that, as far as Paper F6 is concerned, the terms 'transfer' and 'gift' can be taken to mean the same thing and that a transfer of value will always be a gift of assets.

2.2.2 Gratuitous intent

Transfers where there is no gratuitous intent are not chargeable to IHT. An example would be selling a painting for £1,000 at auction which later turns out to be worth £100,000 or other poor business deals.

2.2.3 Diminution in value

In many cases the diminution in value of the donor's estate will be the same as the increase in the value of the donee's estate, for example if there is a cash gift or the gift of a house. However, sometimes the two will not be the same. Typically this is the situation where unquoted shares are gifted.

The measure of the transfer for inheritance tax purposes is always the loss to the donor (the diminution in value of his estate), not the amount gained by the donee.

2.2.4 Example

Audrey holds 5,100 of the shares in an unquoted company which has an issued share capital of 10,000 shares. Currently Audrey's majority holding is valued at £15 per share.

Audrey wishes to give 200 shares to her son, Brian. However, the shares are worth only £2.50 each to Brian, since Brian will have only a small minority holding in the company. After the gift Audrey will hold 4,900 shares and these will be worth £10 each. The value per share to Audrey will fall from £15 to £10 per share since she will lose control of the company.

The diminution in value of Audrey's estate is £27,500, as follows.

	£
Before the gift: 5,100 shares × £15	76,500
After the gift: 4,900 shares × £10	(49,000)
Diminution in value	27,500

Brian has only been given shares with a market value of 200 × £2.50 = £500. Remember, a gift is also a deemed disposal at market value for CGT purposes and it is this value that will be used in any CGT computation. IHT, however, uses the principle of diminution in value which can, as in this case, give a much greater value than the market value of the asset transferred.

2.3 Chargeable transfers and potentially exempt transfers

Inheritance tax is chargeable on a **chargeable transfer**. This is any transfer of value which is not an exempt transfer (see later in this Study Text).

Key terms

A **potentially exempt transfer (PET)** is a **lifetime transfer** (other than an exempt transfer) **made by an individual to another individual**. Any other lifetime transfer by an individual (eg a gift to trustees) which is not an exempt transfer is a **chargeable lifetime transfer (CLT)**.

A **potentially exempt transfer (PET)** is exempt from IHT when made and will remain exempt if the donor survives for at least seven years from making the gift. If the donor dies within seven years of making the PET, the transfer will become chargeable to IHT.

A **chargeable lifetime transfer (CLT)** is immediately chargeable to IHT when made.

On death, an individual is treated as if he had made a transfer of value of the property comprised in his estate immediately before death. This is a **chargeable transfer** to the extent that it is not covered by an exemption.

3 Exemptions

FAST FORWARD

Exemptions may apply to make transfers or parts of transfers non chargeable. Some exemptions only apply on lifetime transfers (annual, normal expenditure out of income, marriage/civil partnership), but the spouse/civil partner exemption applies on both life and death transfers.

PER alert

One of the competencies you require to fulfil Performance Objective 17 Tax planning and advice of the PER is to mitigate and/or defer tax liabilities through the use of standard reliefs, exemptions and incentives. You can apply the knowledge you obtain from this section of the Study Text to help to demonstrate this competence.

3.1 Introduction

There are various exemptions available to eliminate or reduce the chargeable amount of a lifetime transfer or property passing on an individual's death.

The lifetime exemptions apply to PETs as well as to CLTs. Only the balance of such gifts after the lifetime exemptions have been taken into account is then potentially exempt.

3.2 Exemptions applying to lifetime transfers only

3.2.1 The small gifts exemptions

Outright gifts to individuals totalling £250 or less per donee in any one tax year are exempt. If gifts total more than £250 the whole amount is chargeable. A donor can give up to £250 each year to each of as many donees as he wishes. The small gifts exemption cannot apply to gifts into trusts.

3.2.2 The annual exemption (AE)

The first £3,000 of value transferred in a tax year is exempt from IHT. The annual exemption is used only after all other exemptions (such as for transfers to spouses/civil partners (see below)). If several gifts are made in a year, the £3,000 exemption is applied to earlier gifts before later gifts. The annual exemption is used up by PETs as well as CLTs, even though the PETs might never become chargeable.

Exam focus point

> Where CLTs and PETS are made in the same year the CLTs should be made first to use any available annual exemptions. If used up against the PETs the exemption(s) will be wasted if the PET never becomes chargeable.

Any unused portion of the annual exemption is carried forward for one year only. Only use it the following year **after** that year's own annual exemption has been used.

Question — **Annual exemptions**

Frank has no unused annual exemption brought forward at 6 April 2015.

On 1 August 2015 he makes a transfer of £600 to his son Peter.
On 1 September 2015 he makes a transfer of £2,000 to his nephew Quentin.
On 1 July 2016 he makes a transfer of £3,300 to a trust for his grandchildren.
On 1 June 2017 he makes a transfer of £5,000 to his friend Rowan.

Show the application of the annual exemptions.

Answer

2015/16	£
1.8.15 Gift to Peter	600
Less AE 2015/16	(600)
	0

	£
1.9.15 Gift to Quentin	2,000
Less AE 2015/16	(2,000)
	0

The unused annual exemption carried forward is £3,000 – £600 – £2,000 = £400.

2016/17		£	£
1.7.16 Gift to trust			3,300
Less:	AE 2016/17	3,000	
	AE 2015/16 b/f	300	
			(3,300)
			0

The unused annual exemption carried forward is zero because the 2016/17 exemption must be used before the 2015/16 exemption brought forward. The balance of £100 of the 2015/16 exemption is lost, because it cannot be carried forward for more than one year.

2017/18	£
1.6.17 Gift to Rowan	5,000
Less AE 2017/18	(3,000)
	2,000

3.2.3 Normal expenditure out of income

Inheritance tax is a tax on transfers of capital, not income. A transfer of value is exempt if:

(a) It is made as part of the normal expenditure of the donor
(b) Taking one year with another, it was made out of income
(c) It leaves the donor with sufficient income to maintain his usual standard of living

As well as covering such things as regular presents **this exemption can cover regular payments out of income such as a grandchild's school fees or the payment of life assurance premiums on a policy for someone else.**

3.2.4 Gifts in consideration of marriage/civil partnership

Gifts in consideration of marriage/civil partnership are exempt up to:

(a) **£5,000 if from a parent of a party to the marriage/civil partnership**
(b) **£2,500 if from a remoter ancestor or from one of the parties to the marriage/civil partnership**
(c) **£1,000 if from any other person**

The limits apply to gifts from any one donor for any one marriage/civil partnership. The exemption is available only if the marriage/civil partnership actually takes place.

3.3 Exemption applying to both lifetime transfers and transfers on death

3.3.1 Transfers between spouses/civil partners

Any transfers of value between spouses/civil partners are exempt. The exemption covers lifetime gifts between them and property passing under a will or on intestacy.

Question

Exemptions

Dale made a gift of £153,000 to her son on 17 October 2012 on the son's marriage. Dale gave £100,000 to her spouse on 1 January 2016. Dale gave £70,000 to her daughter on 11 May 2016. The only other gifts Dale made were birthday and Christmas presents of £100 each to her grandchildren. Compute the amount of the transfers of value after exemptions for each of these gifts.

Answer

17 October 2012

	£
Gift to Dale's son	153,000
Less: ME	(5,000)
AE 2012/13	(3,000)
AE 2011/12 b/f	(3,000)
PET	142,000

1 January 2016

	£
Gift to Dale's spouse	100,000
Less spouse exemption	(100,000)
	0

11 May 2016

	£
Gift to Dale's daughter	70,000
Less: AE 2016/17	(3,000)
AE 2015/16 b/f	(3,000)
PET	64,000

The gifts to the grandchildren are covered by the small gifts exemption.

4 Calculation of tax on lifetime transfers

PER alert

One of the competencies you require to fulfil Performance Objective 15 Tax computations and assessments of the PER is to prepare or contribute to the computation or assessment of tax computations for individuals. You can apply the knowledge you obtain from this section of the Study Text to help to demonstrate this competence.

FAST FORWARD

The tax on a chargeable transfer is calculated with reference to chargeable transfers in the previous seven years.

There are two aspects of the calculation of tax on lifetime transfers:

(a) Lifetime tax on CLTs

(b) Additional death tax on CLTs and death tax on PETs, in both cases where the donor dies within seven years of making the transfer

Exam focus point

You should always calculate the lifetime tax on any CLTs first, then move on to calculate the death tax on all CLTs and PETs made within seven years of death.

4.1 Lifetime tax

FAST FORWARD

IHT is charged on what a donor loses. If the donor pays the IHT on a lifetime gift he loses both the asset given away and the money with which he paid the tax due on it. Grossing up is required.

4.1.1 Donee pays tax

Lifetime inheritance tax on lifetime transfers is chargeable at two rates of tax: a 0% rate (the 'nil rate') and 20%. The nil rate is chargeable where accumulated transfers do not exceed the nil rate band limit. The excess is chargeable at 20%.

When a CLT is made and the donee (ie the trustees) pays the lifetime tax, follow these steps to work out the lifetime IHT on it:

Step 1 Look back seven years from the date of the transfer to see if any other CLTs have been made. If so, these transfers use up the nil rate band available for the current transfer. This is called **seven year accumulation**. Work out the value of any nil rate band still available.

Step 2 Compute the gross value of the CLT. You may be given this in the question or you may have to work out the diminution of value or deduct exemptions (such as the annual exemption).

Step 3 Any part of the CLT covered by the nil rate band is taxed at 0%. Any part of the CLT not covered by the nil rate band is charged at 20%.

Exam focus point

The nil band and the lifetime rate will be given in the rates and allowances section of the exam paper. Where nil rate bands are required for previous years, these will be given in the question.

Question — Donee pays the lifetime tax

Eric makes a gift of £336,000 to a trust on 10 July 2016. The trustees agree to pay the tax due.

Calculate the lifetime tax payable by the trustees if Eric has made:

(a) A lifetime chargeable transfer of value of £100,000 in August 2008
(b) A lifetime chargeable transfer of value of £100,000 in August 2009
(c) A lifetime chargeable transfer of value of £350,000 in August 2009

Answer

(a) **Step 1** No lifetime transfers in seven years before 10 July 2016 (transfers after 10 July 2009). Nil rate band of £325,000 available.

Step 2 Value of CLT is £336,000 less £3,000 (AE 2016/17) and £3,000 (AE 2015/16) = £330,000.

Step 3

	IHT
	£
£325,000 × 0%	0
£5,000 × 20%	1,000
£330,000	1,000

(b) **Step 1** Lifetime transfer of value of £100,000 in seven years before 10 July 2016 (transfers after 10 July 2009). Nil rate band of £(325,000 – 100,000) = £225,000 available.

Step 2 Value of CLT after exemptions is £330,000.

Step 3

	IHT
	£
£225,000 × 0%	0
£105,000 × 20%	21,000
£330,000	21,000

(c) **Step 1** Lifetime transfer of value of £350,000 in seven years before 10 July 2016 (transfers after 10 July 2009). No nil rate band available as all covered by previous transfer.

Step 2 Value of CLT after exemptions is £330,000.

Step 3

	IHT
	£
£330,000 @ 20%	66,000

4.1.2 Donor pays tax

Where IHT is payable on a CLT, the **primary liability to pay tax is on the donor,** although the donor may agree with the donee (as in the above example) that the donee is to pay the tax instead.

If the donor pays the lifetime IHT due on a CLT, the total reduction in value of his estate is the transfer of value plus the IHT due on it. The transfer is therefore a net transfer and must be grossed up in order to find the gross value of the transfer. **We do this by working out the tax as follows.**

Formula to learn

$$\textbf{Chargeable amount (ie not covered by nil band)} \times \frac{20\text{ (rate of tax)}}{80\text{ (100 minus the rate of tax)}}$$

When a CLT is made and the donor pays the lifetime tax, follow these steps to work out the lifetime IHT on it:

Step 1 Look back seven years from the date of the transfer to see if any other CLTs have been made. If so, these transfers use up the nil rate band available for the current transfer. Work out the value of any nil rate band still available.

Step 2 Compute the net value of the CLT. You may be given this in the question or may have to work out the diminution of value or deduct exemptions (such as the annual exemption).

Step 3 Any part of the CLT covered by the nil rate band is taxed at 0%. Any part of the CLT not covered by the nil rate band is taxed at 20/80.

Step 4 Work out the gross transfer by adding the net transfer and the tax together. You can check your figure by working out the tax on the gross transfer.

Question — **Donor pays the lifetime tax**

James makes a gift of £336,000 to a trust on 10 July 2016. James will pay the tax due.

Calculate the lifetime tax payable, if James has made:

(a) A lifetime chargeable transfer of value of £100,000 in August 2008
(b) A lifetime chargeable transfer of value of £100,000 in August 2009
(c) A lifetime chargeable transfer of value of £350,000 in August 2009

Answer

(a) **Step 1** No lifetime transfers in seven years before 10 July 2016 (transfers after 10 July 2009). Nil rate band of £325,000 available.

Step 2 Net value of CLT is £336,000 less £3,000 (AE 2016/17) and £3,000 (AE 2015/16) = £330,000.

Step 3

	IHT
	£
£325,000 × 0%	0
£5,000 × 20/80	1,250
£330,000	1,250

Step 4 Gross transfer is £(330,000 + 1,250) = £331,250.

Check: Tax on the gross transfer would be:

	IHT
	£
£325,000 × 0%	0
£6,250 × 20%	1,250
£331,250	1,250

(b) **Step 1** Lifetime transfer of value of £100,000 in seven years before 10 July 2016 (transfers after 10 July 2009). Nil rate band of £(325,000 – 100,000) = £225,000 available.

Step 2 Net value of CLT is £330,000.

Step 3

	IHT
	£
£225,000 × 0%	0
£105,000 × 20/80	26,250
£330,000	26,250

Step 4 Gross transfer is £(330,000 + 26,250) = £356,250.

Check: Tax on the gross transfer would be:

	IHT
	£
£225,000 × 0%	0
£131,250 × 20%	26,250
£356,250	26,250

(c) **Step 1** Lifetime transfer of value of £350,000 in seven years before 10 July 2016 (transfers after 10 July 2009). No nil rate band available as all covered by previous transfer.

Step 2 Net value of CLT is £330,000.

Step 3

	IHT
	£
£330,000 × 20/80	82,500

Step 4 Gross transfer is £(330,000 + 82,500) = £412,500.

Check: Tax on the gross transfer would be:

	IHT
	£
£412,500 × 20%	82,500

Question — Effect of different nil rate bands

Trevor made a cash gift to a trust of £300,000 on 9 December 2006. This was his first transfer of value. The nil rate band in 2006/07 was £285,000.

He then made a gift to the trust of shares worth £206,000 on 15 November 2011. The nil rate band in 2011/12 was £325,000.

Trevor paid the lifetime tax due on the December 2006 transfer but the trustees paid the lifetime tax due on the November 2011 transfer.

Compute:

(a) The lifetime tax payable by Trevor on the lifetime transfer in December 2006
(b) The lifetime tax payable by the trustees on the lifetime transfer in November 2011

Answer

Lifetime tax on December 2006 transfer

Step 1 No lifetime transfers in seven years before 9 December 2006. Nil rate band of £285,000 available.

Step 2

	£
Gift	300,000
Less: AE 2006/07	(3,000)
AE 2005/06 b/f	(3,000)
Net CLT	294,000

Step 3

	IHT £
£285,000 × 0%	0
£9,000 × 20/80	2,250
£294,000	2,250

Step 4 Gross transfer is £(294,000 + 2,250) = £296,250. **Check:** Tax on the gross transfer would be:

	IHT £
£285,000 × 0%	0
£11,250 × 20%	2,250
£296,250	2,250

Lifetime tax on November 2011 transfer

Step 1 Lifetime transfer of value of £296,250 in 7 years before 15 November 2011 (transfers after 15 November 2004). Nil rate band of £(325,000 – 296,250) = £28,750 available.

Step 2

	£
Gift	206,000
Less AE 2011/12	(3,000)
AE 2010/11 b/f	(3,000)
	200,000

Step 3

	IHT
	£
£28,750 × 0%	0
£171,250 × 20%	34,250
£200,000	34,250

4.2 Death tax on chargeable lifetime transfers

FAST FORWARD

Death tax is chargeable on chargeable lifetime transfers if the donor dies within seven years of making the transfer. Taper relief reduces the death tax if the donor survives between three and seven years.

Death inheritance tax on lifetime transfers is chargeable if the donor dies within seven years of making the lifetime transfer. It is chargeable at two rates: 0% and 40%. The nil rate is chargeable where accumulated transfers do not exceed the nil rate band limit at the date of death. The excess is chargeable at 40%.

The longer the donor survives after making a gift, the lower the death tax. This is because taper relief applies to lower the amount of death tax payable as follows:

Years before death	% reduction
Over three but less than four years	20
Over four but less than five years	40
Over five but less than six years	60
Over six but less than seven years	80

Exam focus point

The taper relief table will be given in the tax rates and allowances section of the examination paper.

Death tax on a lifetime transfer is **always** payable by the donee, so grossing up is not relevant.

Follow these steps to work out the death tax on a CLT:

Step 1 Look back seven years from the **date of the transfer** to see if any other chargeable transfers were made. If so, these transfers use up the nil rate band available for the current transfer. Work out the value of any nil rate band remaining.

Step 2 Compute the value of the CLT. This is the gross value of the transfer that you worked out for computing lifetime tax.

Step 3 Any part of the CLT covered by the nil rate band is taxed at 0%. Any part of the CLT not covered by the nil rate band is charged at 40%.

Step 4 Reduce the death tax by taper relief (if applicable).

Step 5 Deduct any lifetime tax paid. The death tax may be reduced to nil, but there is **no repayment of lifetime tax**.

Exam focus point

The nil band and the death rate will be given in the rates and allowances section of the exam paper. Where nil rate bands are required for previous years, these will be given in the question.

Question — Lifetime tax and death tax on CLTs

Look back at the question Effect of different nil rate bands in Section 4.1 earlier in this chapter.

Trevor's lifetime chargeable transfers were 9 December 2006 £296,250 and 15 November 2011 £200,000 (lifetime tax paid £34,250).

Trevor died in August 2016. Compute the death tax payable on the lifetime transfer in November 2011.

Answer

Death tax on November 2011 transfer

Step 1 Lifetime transfer of value of £296,250 in 7 years before 15 November 2011 (transfers after 15 November 2004). Nil rate band of £(325,000 [nil rate band in 2016/17] – 296,250) = £28,750 available.

Step 2 Value of CLT is £200,000.

Step 3

	IHT
	£
£28,750 × 0%	0
£171,250 × 40%	68,500
£200,000	68,500

Step 4 Death more than 4 years but less than 5 years after transfer

	£
Death tax	68,500
Less: taper relief @ 40%	(27,400)
Death tax left in charge	41,100

Step 5 Tax due £(41,100 – 34,250) 6,850

4.3 Death tax on potentially exempt transfers

FAST FORWARD

Death tax is chargeable on potentially exempt transfers if the donor dies within seven years of making the transfer. Taper relief reduces the death tax if the donor survives between three and seven years. Grossing up is never required on PET because the death tax is payable by the donee.

If the donor dies within seven years of making a PET it will become chargeable to death tax in the same way as a CLT. There will be no lifetime tax paid, so Step 5 above will not apply.

We will now work through an example where there is both a PET and a CLT.

Exam focus point

Calculate lifetime tax on CLTs first. Then move on to death tax, working through all CLTs and PETs in chronological order. Remember: on death, PETs become chargeable so must be taken into account when calculating the death tax on later CLTs.

Question

Lifetime tax and death tax on CLTs and PETs

Louise gave £346,000 to her son on 1 February 2013. This was the first transfer that Louise had made.

On 10 October 2016, Louise gave £376,000 to a trust. The trustees paid the lifetime IHT due.

On 11 January 2017, Louise died.

Compute:

(a) The lifetime tax payable by the trustees on the lifetime transfer made in 2016
(b) The death tax payable on the lifetime transfer made in 2013
(c) The death tax payable on the lifetime transfer made in 2016

Answer

(a) Lifetime tax – 2016 CLT

Step 1 There are no chargeable lifetime transfers in the seven years before 10 October 2014 because the 2013 transfer is a PET and therefore exempt during Louise's lifetime. Nil rate band of £325,000 available.

Step 2 Value of CLT £376,000 less £3,000 (AE 2016/17) and £3,000 (AE 2015/16) = £370,000.

Step 3

	IHT
	£
£325,000 × 0%	0
£ 45,000 × 20%	9,000
£370,000	9,000

(b) Death tax – 2013 PET becomes chargeable

Step 1 No lifetime transfers of value in seven years before 1 February 2013 (transfers after 1 February 2006). Nil rate band (at date of death) of £325,000 available.

Step 2 Value of PET £346,000 less £3,000 (AE 2012/13) and £3,000 (AE 2011/12) = £340,000.

Step 3

	IHT
	£
£325,000 × 0%	0
£ 15,000 × 40%	6,000
£340,000	6,000

Step 4 Transfer over three but less than four years before death

	£
Death tax	6,000
Less taper relief @ 20%	(1,200)
Death tax due	4,800

(c) Death tax – 2016 CLT additional tax

Step 1 Lifetime transfer of value of £340,000 in seven years before 10 October 2016 (transfers after 10 October 2009). Note that as the PET becomes chargeable on death, its value is now included in calculating the death tax on the CLT. No nil rate band available.

Step 2 Value of CLT is £370,000 as before

Step 3

£370,000 @ 40%

Step 4 Transfer within three years before death so no taper relief.

Step 5 Tax due £(148,000 – 9,000)

4.4 Advantages of making lifetime transfers

PER alert

One of the competencies you require to fulfil Performance Objective 17 Tax planning and advice of the PER is to review the situation of an individual or entity advising on any potential tax risks and/or additional tax minimisation measures. You can apply the knowledge you obtain from this section of the Study Text to help to demonstrate this competence.

There are a number of inheritance tax advantages of making lifetime transfers:

(a) **If the donor makes a potentially exempt transfer and survives seven years, he has reduced his estate for IHT but the transfer is exempt.** No inheritance tax is payable on the transfer and it does not form part of the seven year cumulation for later transfers.

(b) **If the donor makes a chargeable lifetime transfer and survives seven years, he has reduced his estate for IHT and the only inheritance tax payable is that on the lifetime transfer at lifetime rates.** However, note that the chargeable lifetime transfer remains in cumulation and affects the calculation of tax on transfers made in the seven years after it.

(c) If the donor does not survive seven years, IHT is payable on lifetime transfers at death rates at the date of death but **taper relief reduces the death tax if the donor survives between three and seven years**.

(d) **The values of lifetime transfers cannot exceed the transfer of value when made.** Therefore, **it is good tax planning to give away assets which are likely to increase in value such as land and shares**.

However, there is one situation where **it may not be advantageous for the donor to make a lifetime transfer** in terms of overall tax liability. This is where a **gift of an asset would result in a large chargeable gain (either immediately chargeable or deferred under gift relief)**. In this case, it may be better for the donor to retain the asset until death as there is a tax-free uplift in value on death for capital gains tax purposes so that the donee will receive the asset at market value at the date of the donor's death. This is particularly relevant if the donor is unlikely to survive three years from the date of a lifetime gift and so death rates without the benefit of taper relief would apply to a lifetime transfer.

5 Calculation of tax on death estate

PER alert

One of the competencies you require to fulfil Performance Objective 15 Tax computations and assessments of the PER is to prepare or contribute to the computation or assessment of tax computations for individuals. You can apply the knowledge you obtain from this section of the Study Text to help to demonstrate this competence.

FAST FORWARD

When someone dies, we must bring together all their assets to find the value of their death estate and then charge inheritance tax on it (to the extent that it is not exempt) taking account of transfers made in the seven years before death.

h estate?

nsists of all the property he owned immediately before death (such as ther investments, cars and cash) **less debts and funeral expenses**.

ything received as a result of death, for example the proceeds of a life on the individual's death. The value of the policy immediately before the

ssets are not in the syllabus. Values will be provided in the question

...eral expenses

The rules on debts are as follows.

(a) **Debts incurred by the deceased can be deducted** if they can be **legally enforced** as they are either **imposed by law** or they are a debt for which the deceased received **consideration**. Specific examples of the application of these rules include:

- (i) **Taxes** – deductible as imposed by law
- (ii) **Electricity and gas bills** – deductible as incurred for consideration
- (iii) **Gambling debts** – deductible if relates to legal gambling (eg in a licensed casino or betting shop), not deductible if relates to illegal gambling or any gambling in Northern Ireland as not legally enforceable
- (iv) **Promise to pay an amount to a relative** – not deductible as no consideration received
- (v) **Oral agreement for sale of interest in land** – not deductible as not legally enforceable since contracts for such sales must be evidenced in writing

(b) **Debts incurred by the deceased but payable after the death may be deductible under the above rules,** but the amount should be discounted because of the future date of payment.

(c) **Rent and similar amounts which accrue day by day should be accrued up to the date of death.**

(d) **If a debt is charged on a specific property it is deductible primarily from that property.** For example, a mortgage secured on a house is deductible from the value of that house.

This does not include endowment mortgages as these are repaid upon death by the life assurance element of the mortgage.

Repayment mortgages and interest-only mortgages are deductible (although there may be separate life assurance policies which become payable at death and which will effectively cancel out the mortgage).

Reasonable funeral expenses may also be deducted:

(a) What is reasonable depends on the deceased's condition in life.
(b) Reasonable costs of mourning for the family are allowed.
(c) **The cost of a tombstone is deductible.**

Question

Zack died on 19 June 2016.

Zack's assets at the date of his death consisted of the following:

10,000 shares in A plc valued at £8,525
Cash in bank £9,280
Freehold property valued at £150,000 subject to a repayment mortgage of £45,000

Zack's debts due at the date of his death were as follows:

Electricity £150
Council tax £300

Zack had also told his daughter on 10 June 2016 that he would pay £1,000 towards the cost of her summer holiday and that he would pay her this amount on 1 July 2016.

Zack's executors paid reasonable funeral expenses of £2,000 (including the cost of a tombstone) on 1 September 2016.

Calculate Zack's death estate for IHT purposes.

Answer

	£	£
A plc shares		8,525
Cash in bank		9,280
Freehold property	150,000	
Less repayment mortgage	(45,000)	
		105,000
Gross estate		122,805
Less: debts and funeral expenses		
electricity (incurred for consideration)	150	
council tax (imposed by law)	300	
amount towards holiday for daughter (gratuitous promise)	0	
funeral expenses	2,000	
		(2,450)
Death estate		120,355

5.2 Computing death tax on the death estate

Inheritance tax on the death estate is chargeable at two rates: 0% and 40%. The nil rate is chargeable where accumulated transfers do not exceed the nil rate band limit. The excess is chargeable at 40%.

In order to calculate the tax on the death estate, use the following steps:

Step 1 Look back seven years from the date of death to see if any CLTs or PETs which have become chargeable have been made. If so, these transfers use up the nil rate band available for the death estate. Work out the value of any nil rate band still available.

Step 2 Compute the value of the death estate.

Step 3 Deduct any amount covered by the spouse exemption to leave the chargeable death estate.

Step 4 Any part of the chargeable death estate covered by the nil rate band is taxed at 0%. Any part of the death estate not covered by the nil rate band is charged at 40%.

Exam focus point

From 6 April 2017 an additional nil rate band (the main residence nil rate band) will be available when residential property is inherited by direct descendents of the deceased. Some aspects of this additional nil rate band apply from 8 July 2015 but the additional nil rate band is **not examinable** in F6(UK) in exams in June 2017, September 2017, December 2017 and March 2018.

Question — Tax on death estate

Laura dies on 1 August 2016, leaving a death estate valued at £500,000. Laura left £100,000 to her husband and the remainder of her estate to her son. Laura had made a gift of £171,000 to her sister on 11 September 2015.

Compute the tax payable on Laura's death estate.

Answer

Death tax

Note. There is no death tax on the September 2015 PET which becomes chargeable as a result of Laura's death, as it is within the nil rate band at her death. However, it will use up part of the nil rate band, as shown below.

Step 1 Lifetime transfer of value of £171,000 less £3,000 (AE 2015/16) and £3,000 (AE 2014/15) = £165,000 in seven years before 1 August 2016 (transfers after 1 August 2009). Nil rate band of £(325,000 – 165,000) = £160,000 available.

Step 2 Value of death estate is £500,000.

Step 3 Chargeable death estate is £(500,000 – 100,000) = £400,000.

Step 4

	IHT
	£
£160,000 × 0%	0
£240,000 × 40%	96,000
£400,000	96,000

6 Transfer of unused nil rate band

FAST FORWARD

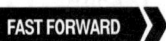

If one spouse or civil partner does not use up the whole nil rate band on death, the excess may be transferred to the surviving spouse/civil partner.

6.1 How the transfer of unused nil rate band works

If:

- **An individual ('A') dies**; and
- **A had a spouse or civil partner ('B') who died before A**; and
- **A and B were married or in a civil partnership immediately before B's death**; and
- **B had unused nil rate band (wholly or in part) on death**

then a **claim may be made to increase the nil rate band maximum at the date of A's death by B's unused nil-rate band in order to calculate the IHT on A's death.**

The revised nil rate band will apply to the calculation of additional death tax on CLTs made by A, PETs made by A and death tax on A's death estate.

6.2 Example

Robert and Claudia were married for many years until the death of Robert on 10 April 2016. In his will, Robert left his death estate valued at £100,000 to his sister. He had made no lifetime transfers.

Claudia died on 12 January 2017 leaving a death estate worth £850,000 to her brother. Claudia had made a chargeable lifetime transfer of £50,000 in 2013.

The inheritance tax payable on the death of Claudia, assuming that a claim is made to transfer Robert's unused nil rate band, is calculated as follows:

Step 1 (a) Lifetime transfer of value of £50,000 in seven years before 12 January 2017 (transfers after 12 January 2010).

(b) Nil rate band at Claudia's death is £325,000. Nil rate band is increased by claim to transfer Robert's unused nil rate band at death £(325,000 – 100,000) = £225,000. The maximum nil rate band at Claudia's death is therefore £(325,000 + 225,000) = £550,000 and the available nil rate band for working out the tax on her estate is £(550,000 – 50,000) = £500,000.

Step 2 Value of Claudia's death estate is £850,000.

Step 3

	IHT
	£
£500,000 × 0%	0
£350,000 × 40%	140,000
£850,000	140,000

6.3 Changes in nil rate band between deaths of spouses/civil partners

If the nil rate band increases between the death of B and the death of A, the amount of B's unused nil rate band must be scaled up so that it represents the same proportion of the nil rate band at A's death as it did at B's death.

For example, if the nil rate band at B's death was £300,000 and B had an unused nil rate band of £90,000, the unused proportion in percentage terms is therefore 90,000/300,000 × 100 = 30%. If A dies when the nil rate band has increased to £325,000, B's unused nil rate band is £325,000 × 30% = £97,500 and this amount is transferred to increase the nil rate band maximum available on A's death.

The increase in the nil rate band maximum cannot exceed the nil rate band maximum at the date of A's death eg if the nil rate band is £325,000, the increase cannot exceed £325,000, giving a total of £650,000.

Question — Transfer of nil rate band

Jenna and Rebecca were civil partners until the death of Jenna on 19 August 2008.

Jenna made no lifetime transfers. Her death estate was £240,000 and she left it to her mother. The nil rate band at Jenna's death was £300,000.

Rebecca died on 24 February 2017. Her death estate was £550,000 and she left her entire estate to her brother. She had made no lifetime transfers.

Calculate the inheritance tax payable on the death of Rebecca, assuming that any beneficial claims are made.

Answer

Step 1

(a) No lifetime transfers of value in seven years before 24 February 2017.

(b) Nil rate band at Rebecca's death is £325,000. Nil rate band is increased by claim to transfer Jenna's unused nil rate band at death. Unused proportion was £(300,000 – 240,000) = 60,000/300,000 × 100 = 20%. The adjusted unused proportion is therefore £325,000 × 20% = £65,000. The maximum nil rate band at Rebecca's death is therefore £(325,000 + 65,000) = £390,000 and this is also the available nil rate band for her estate.

Step 2 Value of Rebecca's death estate is £550,000.

Step 3

	IHT
	£
£390,000 × 0%	0
£160,000 × 40%	64,000
£550,000	64,000

6.4 Claim to transfer unused nil rate band

The claim to transfer the unused nil rate band is usually made by the personal representatives of A. The time limit for the claim is two years from the end of the month of A's death (or the period of three months after the personal representatives start to act, if later) or such longer period as an officer of HMRC may allow in a particular case.

If the personal representatives do not make a claim, a claim can be made by any other person liable to tax chargeable on A's death within such later period as an officer of HMRC may allow in a particular case.

7 Basic inheritance tax planning

PER alert

One of the competencies you require to fulfil Performance Objective 17 Tax planning and advice of the PER is to assess the tax implications of proposed activities or plans of an individual or entity with reference to relevant and up to date legislation. You can apply the knowledge you obtain from this section of the Study Text to help to demonstrate this competence.

FAST FORWARD

Basic planning may reduce or eliminate inheritance tax payable. Where appropriate, donors should use exemptions, make gifts early in life, make use of the nil rate band in relation to gifts to trusts, and consider making gifts to grandchildren, rather than children.

7.1 Use exemptions

Donors should ensure that **use is made of exemptions in relation to lifetime gifts**, in particular the **annual exemption**, the **marriage/civil partnership exemption**, the **normal expenditure out of income exemption** and the **spouse/civil partner exemption**.

When considering how to pass on assets in the **death estate**, the **spouse/civil partner exemption may be used to ensure that no inheritance tax is payable when the first spouse/civil partner dies**. Remember that an election can be made to ensure that unused nil rate band of the first spouse/civil partner is available to be used against the estate of the surviving spouse/civil partner.

7.2 Make gifts early in life

The earlier that a gift is made in lifetime which is, or may become, a chargeable transfer, the more likely it is that the donor will survive seven years from making it.

If a **gift is made shortly before death**, there will be **little or no inheritance tax benefit** as the gift will be chargeable on the death of the donor. In addition, if the **gift is of a chargeable asset for capital gains tax** (eg shares, land) there will be a **chargeable disposal at market value which may result in a chargeable gain**, whereas **transfers of chargeable assets on death are exempt disposals**.

7.3 Make use of the nil rate band

Gifts to trusts are chargeable transfers. If the gift is **within the nil rate band**, however, there will be **no inheritance tax payable when the gift is made**.

Transfers are only cumulated for seven years and therefore, after that time has elapsed, a **further gift within the nil rate band can be made to a trust**, again without incurring any immediate payment of inheritance tax.

7.4 Skip a generation

Donors may consider giving assets to their children, either during lifetime or on death. Such assets may then be passed by those children to their own children, the grandchildren of the donor.

If the **donor's children already have sufficient assets for their financial needs, it may be beneficial to skip a generation** so that **gifts are made to grandchildren, rather than children**. This **avoids a further charge to inheritance tax on the death of the children** so that gifts will then only be taxed once before being inherited by the grandchildren, rather than twice.

8 Payment of inheritance tax

PER alert

One of the competencies you require to fulfil Performance Objective 16 Tax compliance and verification of the PER is to determine the incidence (timing) of tax liabilities and their impact on cash flow/financing requirements. You can apply the knowledge you obtain from this section of the Study Text to help to demonstrate this competence.

8.1 Liability for IHT

FAST FORWARD

The liability to pay IHT depends on the type of transfer and whether it was made in lifetime or on death.

The donor is primarily liable for the tax due on chargeable lifetime transfers. However the donee (ie the trustees) may agree to pay the tax out of the trust assets.

On death, liability for payment is as follows.

(a) **Tax on the death estate is paid by the deceased's personal representatives (PRs)** out of estate assets.

(b) **Tax on a PET that has become chargeable is paid by the donee.**

(c) **Additional liabilities on a CLT is paid by the donee.**

8.2 Due dates

(a) **For chargeable lifetime transfers the due date is the later of:**

(i) **30 April just after the end of the tax year of the transfer**

(ii) **Six months after the end of the month of the transfer**

(b) **Tax arising on the death estate: the due date is six months from the end of the month of death.** However, if the personal representatives **submit an account of the death estate** within the six month period, they must **pay the IHT due on the death estate on the submission of the account.**

(c) **Tax arising on death in respect of PETs and CLTs: the due date for additional tax is six months from the end of the month of death.**

Question

Payment of inheritance tax

Lisa gave some shares to a trust on 10 July 2012. She gave a house to her daughter on 12 December 2014. Lisa died on 17 May 2016 leaving her death estate to her son.

For each of these transfers of value, state who is liable to pay any inheritance tax due and the due date for payment.

Answer

10 July 2012

Chargeable lifetime transfer. Lifetime tax payable by Lisa (unless trustees agree to pay tax), due later of 30 April 2013 and 31 January 2013 ie 30 April 2013. Death tax payable by trustees, due 30 November 2016.

12 December 2014

Potentially exempt transfer – no lifetime tax. Death tax payable by daughter, due 30 November 2016.

17 May 2016

Death tax payable by personal representatives out of death estate, due on earlier of submission of account and 30 November 2016.

Chapter Roundup

- IHT is a tax on gifts made by individuals to other individuals or trustees.
- IHT applies to lifetime transfers of value and transfers of value made on death.
- Exemptions may apply to make transfers or parts of transfers non chargeable. Some exemptions only apply on lifetime transfers (annual, normal expenditure out of income, marriage/civil partnership), but the spouse/civil partner exemption applies on both life and death transfers.
- The tax on a chargeable transfer is calculated with reference to chargeable transfers in the previous seven years.
- IHT is charged on what a donor loses. If the donor pays the IHT on a lifetime gift he loses both the asset given away and the money with which he paid the tax due on it. Grossing up is required.
- Death tax is chargeable on chargeable lifetime transfers if the donor dies within seven years of making the transfer. Taper relief reduces the death tax if the donor survives between three and seven years.
- Death tax is chargeable on potentially exempt transfers if the donor dies within seven years of making the transfer. Taper relief reduces the death tax if the donor survives between three and seven years. Grossing up is never required on a PET because the death tax is payable by the donee.
- When someone dies, we must bring together all their assets to find the value of their death estate and then charge inheritance tax on it (to the extent that it is not exempt) taking account of transfers made in the seven years before death.
- If one spouse or civil partner does not use up the whole nil rate band on death, the excess may be transferred to the surviving spouse/civil partner.
- Basic planning may reduce or eliminate inheritance tax payable. Where appropriate, donors should use exemptions, make gifts early in life, make use of the nil rate band in relation to gifts to trusts, and consider making gifts to grandchildren, rather than children.
- The liability to pay IHT depends on the type of transfer and whether it was made in lifetime or on death.

Quick Quiz

1 What is a transfer of value?

2 What type of transfer by an individual is a potentially exempt transfer?

3 To what extent may an unused annual exemption be carried forward?

4 Don gives some money to his daughter on her marriage. What marriage exemption is applicable?

5 Why must some lifetime transfers be grossed up?

6 What is taper relief?

7 Greg dies leaving the following debts:

(a) Grocery bill
(b) HM Revenue and Customs – income tax to death
(c) Mortgage on house
(d) Illegal gambling debt

Which are deductible against his death estate and why?

8 Mark and Hilary had been married for many years. Mark died on 11 May 2016 leaving his estate to Hilary. He had made a chargeable lifetime transfer of £160,000 in July 2013. If Hilary dies in February 2017, what is the maximum nil rate band on her death?

9 When is lifetime inheritance tax on a chargeable lifetime transfer due for payment?

Answers to Quick Quiz

1 A transfer of value is any gratuitous disposition by a person resulting in a diminution of the value of his estate.

2 A potentially exempt transfer is a lifetime transfer made by an individual to another individual.

3 An unused annual exemption can be carried forward one tax year.

4 The marriage exemption for a gift to the donor's child is £5,000.

5 Where the donor pays the lifetime tax due it must be grossed up to calculate the total reduction in value of the estate.

6 Taper relief reduces death tax where a transfer is made between three and seven years before death.

7 (a) Grocery bill – deductible as incurred for consideration
(b) Income tax to death – deductible as imposed by law
(c) Mortgage – deductible, will be set against value of house primarily
(d) Illegal gambling debt – not deductible as not legally enforceable

8 Hilary's nil rate band is £325,000. Mark's unused nil rate band is £(325,000 – 160,000) = £165,000. The nil rate band maximum on Hilary's death is therefore £490,000.

9 The due date for lifetime tax on a chargeable lifetime transfer is the later of:

(a) 30 April just after the end of the tax year of the transfer
(b) Six months after the end of the month of transfer

Now try the questions below from the Practice Question Bank

Number	Type	Marks	Time
Q118	Section A	2	4 mins
Q119	Section A	2	4 mins
Q120	Section A	2	4 mins
Q121	Section B	2	4 mins
Q122	Section B	2	4 mins
Q123	Section B	2	4 mins
Q124	Section B	2	4 mins
Q125	Section B	2	4 mins
Q126	Section C	10	20 mins

PART F

Corporation tax

19

Computing taxable total profits and the corporation tax liability

Topic list	Syllabus reference
1 The scope of corporation tax	E1(a)–(c)
2 Taxable total profits	E2(j)
3 Trading income	E2(a)–(c)
4 Property business income	E2(d)
5 Loan relationships (interest income)	E2(h)
6 Miscellaneous income	E2(j)
7 Qualifying charitable donations	E2(i)
8 Long periods of account	E2(j)
9 Computing the corporation tax liability	E4(a)
10 Choice of business medium	E4(a)

Introduction

Now that we have completed our study of personal tax we turn our attention to corporation tax, ie the tax that a company must pay on its profits.

First we consider the scope of corporation tax and we see that a company must pay tax for an 'accounting period' which may be different from its period of account.

We then learn how to calculate taxable total profits. This involves first calculating total profits by adding together income from different sources, such as trading income, interest and property income, and capital gains, and then deducting trading and property losses and qualifying charitable donations. You have learnt the general rules for calculating income in your earlier studies, but here we see where there are special rules for companies.

You will then learn how to compute the corporation tax liability on taxable total profits.

Finally, we investigate choice of business medium by comparing the tax effects of trading as a sole trader and through a company.

In the next chapter we will deal with chargeable gains for companies.

Study guide

		Intellectual level
E1	**The scope of corporation tax**	
(a)	Define the terms 'period of account', 'accounting period', and 'financial year'.	1
(b)	Recognise when an accounting period starts and when an accounting period finishes.	1
(c)	Explain how the residence of a company is determined.	2
E2	**Taxable total profits**	
(a)	Recognise the expenditure that is allowable in calculating the tax-adjusted trading profit.	2
(b)	Recognise the relief which can be obtained for pre-trading expenditure.	1
(c)	Compute capital allowances (as for income tax).	2
(d)	Compute property business profits and understand how relief for a property business loss is given.	2
(h)	Recognise and apply the treatment of interest paid and received under the loan relationship rules.	1
(i)	Recognise and apply the treatment of qualifying charitable donations.	2
(j)	Compute taxable total profits.	2
E4	**The comprehensive computation of corporation tax liability**	
(a)	Compute the corporation tax liability	2

Exam guide

One of the 15 mark questions in Section C will focus on corporation tax. Corporation tax may also be tested in 10 mark questions in Sections B or C. You should also expect to see one or more questions on corporation tax in Section A. When dealing with a corporation tax question in Section C you must first be able to identify the accounting period(s) involved; watch out for long periods of account. You must also be able to calculate taxable total profits; learn the standard layout so that you can easily slot in figures from your workings.

1 The scope of corporation tax

FAST FORWARD

Companies pay corporation tax on their taxable total profits.

1.1 Companies

Companies must pay corporation tax on their **taxable total profits** for each **accounting period**. We look at the meaning of these terms below.

Key term

A **company** is any corporate body (limited or unlimited) or unincorporated association, eg sports club.

1.2 Accounting periods

FAST FORWARD

An accounting period cannot exceed 12 months in length so a long period of account must be split into two accounting periods. The first accounting period of a long period of account is always 12 months in length.

Corporation tax is chargeable in respect of accounting periods. It is important to understand the difference between an accounting period and a period of account.

Key term

A **period of account** is any period for which a company prepares accounts; usually this will be 12 months in length but it may be longer or shorter than this.

Key term

An **accounting period** is the period for which corporation tax is charged and cannot exceed 12 months. Special rules determine when an accounting period starts and ends.

An accounting period starts on the earliest of:

- When a company starts to trade
- When the company otherwise becomes liable to corporation tax (eg it opens a bank account which pays interest)
- Immediately after the previous accounting period finishes

An accounting period finishes on the earliest of:

- 12 months after its start
- The end of the company's period of account
- The company starting or ceasing to trade
- The company entering/ceasing to be in administration
- The commencement of the company's winding up
- The company's ceasing to be resident in the UK
- The company's ceasing to be liable to corporation tax

If a company has a period of account exceeding 12 months (a long period of account), it is split into two accounting periods: the first 12 months and the remainder.

Question — **Accounting periods**

For each of the following companies, identify the accounting period(s).

(a) J Ltd, which has been trading for many years, prepares accounts for the twelve months to 30 September 2016.

(b) K plc is incorporated on 1 April 2016. On 1 June 2016, K plc starts to trade and makes up its first set of accounts to 31 August 2016.

(c) L Ltd, which has been trading for many years preparing accounts to 31 December each year, prepares accounts for the eleven months to 30 November 2016.

(d) M Plc, which has been trading for many years preparing accounts to 31 July each year, prepares accounts for the sixteen months to 30 November 2016.

Answer

(a) 1 October 2015 (immediately after previous accounting period finishes) to 30 September 2016 (12 months after start of accounting period and also the end of period of account).

(b) 1 June 2016 (company starts to trade) to 31 August 2016 (end of period of account).

(c) 1 January 2016 (immediately after previous accounting period finishes) to 30 November 2016 (end of period of account).

(d) First accounting period: 1 August 2015 (immediately after previous accounting period finishes) to 31 July 2016 (12 months after start).

Second accounting period: 1 August 2016 (immediately after previous accounting period finishes) to 30 November 2016 (end of period of account).

1.3 Financial year

FAST FORWARD

Tax rates are set for financial years.

The rates of corporation tax are fixed for financial years.

Key term

A financial year runs from 1 April to the following 31 March and is identified by the calendar year in which it begins. For example, the year ended 31 March 2017 is the Financial year 2016 (FY 2016). This should not be confused with a tax year, which runs from 6 April to the following 5 April.

1.4 Residence of companies

FAST FORWARD

A company is UK resident if it is incorporated in the UK or if it is incorporated overseas and its central management and control are exercised in the UK.

A company incorporated in the UK is resident in the UK. A company incorporated abroad is resident in the UK if its central management and control are exercised here. Central management and control are usually treated as exercised where the board of directors meet.

Question

Residence of a company

Supraville SARL is a company incorporated in France. It has its head office in London where the board of directors meet monthly. It trades throughout the European Union.

Is Supraville SARL resident in the UK?

Answer

Yes, Supraville SARL is resident in the UK.

The central management and control of Supraville SARL is in London (ie the UK) where the board of directors meet.

2 Taxable total profits

FAST FORWARD

Taxable total profits comprises the company's income and chargeable gains (total profits) less some losses and qualifying charitable donations. It does not include dividends received from other companies.

PER alert

One of the competencies you require to fulfil Performance Objective 15 Tax computations and assessments of the PER is to extract and analyse data from financial records and filing information relevant to the preparation of tax computations and related supporting documents. You can apply the knowledge you obtain from this section of the Study Text to help to demonstrate this competence.

2.1 Proforma computation

FAST FORWARD

Income includes trading income, property income, income from non-trading loan relationships (interest) and miscellaneous income.

A company may have both income and gains. As a general rule income arises from receipts which are expected to recur regularly (such as the profits from a trade) whereas chargeable gains arise on the sale of capital assets which have been owned for several years (such as the sale of a factory used in the trade).

A company may receive income from various sources. All income received must be classified according to the nature of the income as different computational rules apply to different types of income. The main types of income for a company are:

- Profits of a trade
- Profits of a property business
- Interest income from non-trading loan relationships
- Miscellaneous income

The computation of chargeable gains for a company is dealt with later in this Study Text. At the moment, you will be given a figure for chargeable gains in order to compute taxable total profits. We also deal with losses in detail later in this Study Text so, at the moment, you just need to know that some losses are given tax relief by being deducted from total profits.

A company's taxable total profits are arrived at by aggregating its various sources of income and its chargeable gains and then deducting losses and qualifying charitable donations. Here is a pro forma computation.

	£
Trading profits	X
Property business income	X
Interest income from non-trading loan relationships	X
Miscellaneous income	X
Chargeable gains	X
Total profits	X
Less losses deductible from total profits	(X)
Less qualifying charitable donations	(X)
Taxable total profits for an accounting period	X

Exam focus point

It would be of great help in the exam if you could learn the above proforma. When answering a corporation tax question you could immediately reproduce the proforma and insert the appropriate numbers as you are given the information in the question.

Dividends received from other companies (UK resident and non-UK resident), for the purposes of the F6 exam, are usually exempt and so not included in taxable total profits.

3 Trading income

3.1 Adjustment of profits

FAST FORWARD

The adjustment of profits computation for companies broadly follows that for computing business profits subject to income tax. There are, however, some minor differences.

The trading income of companies is derived from the profit before taxation figure in the statement of profit or loss, just as for individuals, adjusted as follows.

		£	£
Profit before taxation			X
Add expenditure not allowed for taxation purposes			X
			X
Less:	income not taxable as trading income	X	
	expenditure not charged in the accounts but allowable for the purposes of taxation	X	
	capital allowances	X	
			(X)
Profit adjusted for tax purposes			X

Exam focus point

An examination question requiring adjustment to profit will direct you to start the adjustment with the profit before taxation of £XXXX and deal with all the items listed indicating with a zero (0) any items which do not require adjustment. Marks will not be given for relevant items unless this approach is used. Therefore students who attempt to rewrite the statement of profit or loss will be penalised.

The adjustment of profits computation for companies broadly follows that for computing business profits subject to income tax. There are, however, some minor differences. There is no disallowance for 'private use' for companies; instead the director or employee will be taxed on the benefit received.

Qualifying charitable donations are added back in the calculation of adjusted profit. They are treated instead as a deduction from total profits.

Investment income including rents is deducted from profit before taxation in arriving at trading income but brought in again further down in the computation (see below).

Exam focus point

When adjusting profits as supplied in a statement of profit or loss confusion can arise as regards whether figures are net or gross. Properly drawn up company accounts should normally include all income gross. However, some examination questions include items 'net'. Read the question carefully.

3.2 Pre-trading expenditure

Pre-trading expenditure incurred by the company within the seven years before trade commences is treated as an allowable expense incurred on the first day of trading provided it would have been allowable had the company been trading when the expense was actually incurred.

3.3 Capital allowances

The calculation of capital allowances follows income tax principles.

For companies, however, there is never any reduction of allowances to take account of any private use of an asset. The director or employee suffers a taxable benefit instead. As shown above capital allowances must be deducted in arriving at taxable trading income.

A company's accounting period can never exceed 12 months. If the period of account is longer than 12 months it is **divided into two**; one for the first 12 months and one for the balance. **The capital allowances computation must be carried out for each period separately.**

Exam focus point

> The calculation of trading income should be undertaken as a first step to the calculation of taxable total profits. However, it is important to realise that these are two distinct aspects when calculating a company's liability to corporation tax and you should not attempt to present them in one calculation.

4 Property business income

Rental income is deducted in arriving at trading income but brought in again further down in the computation as property business income.

The calculation of property business income follows income tax principles. The income tax rules for property businesses were set out earlier in this Study Text. In summary all UK rental activities are treated as a single source of income calculated in the same way as trading income.

However **interest paid by a company on a loan to buy or improve property is not a property business expense**. The **loan relationship rules apply** instead (see below).

5 Loan relationships (interest income)

5.1 General principle

If a company borrows or lends money, including issuing or investing in debentures or buying gilts, it has a loan relationship. This can be a creditor relationship (where the company lends or invests money) **or a debtor relationship** (where the company borrows money or issues securities). Loan interest paid or received is dealt with on a receivable (accruals) basis.

5.2 Treatment of trading loan relationships

If the company is a party to a **loan relationship for trade purposes, any debits – ie interest paid or other debt costs – charged through its accounts are allowed as a trading expense** and are therefore deductible in computing trading income. An example of a trading loan relationship is a loan to buy plant and machinery to use in the trade.

Similarly **if any credits – ie interest income or other debt returns – arise on a trading loan these are treated as a trading receipt and are taxable as trading income**. This is not likely to arise unless the trade is one of money lending.

5.3 Treatment of non-trading loan relationships

If a loan relationship is not one to which the company is a party for trade purposes any debits or credits must be pooled. A net credit on the pool is chargeable as interest income. Examples of non trading loan relationships would be cash on deposit at the bank (creditor relationship), or a loan to purchase a property that is rented out (debtor relationship).

Interest charged on underpaid tax is allowable and interest received on overpaid tax is assessable under the rules for non-trading loan relationships.

Exam focus point

> You will not be expected to deal with net deficits (ie losses) on non-trading loan relationships in your exam.

5.4 Accounting methods

Debits and credits must be brought into account using the UK generally accepted accounting practice (GAAP) or using the International Accounting Standards (IAS). This will usually be the **accruals basis**.

5.5 Incidental costs of loan finance

Under the loan relationship rules expenses ('debits') are allowed if incurred directly:

(a) To bring a loan relationship into existence
(b) Entering into or giving effect to any related transactions
(c) Making payment under a loan relationship or related transactions or
(d) Taking steps to ensure the receipt of payments under the loan relationship or related transaction

A related transaction means 'any disposal or acquisition (in whole or in part) of rights or liabilities under the relationship, including any arising from a security issue in relation to the money debt in question'.

The above categories of incidental costs are also allowable even if the company does not enter into the loan relationship (ie abortive costs). Costs directly incurred in varying the terms of a loan relationship are also allowed.

5.6 Other matters

It is not only the interest costs of borrowing that are allowable or taxable. Capital costs are treated similarly.

6 Miscellaneous income

Patent royalties received which do not relate to the trade are taxed as miscellaneous income. Patent royalties which relate to the trade are included in trading income normally on an accruals basis.

7 Qualifying charitable donations

FAST FORWARD

Qualifying charitable donations are deducted from total profits when computing taxable total profits.

Qualifying charitable donations are deductible from total profits when computing taxable total profits.

Almost all donations of money to charity by a company can be qualifying charitable donations whether they are single donations or regular donations. There is no need for a claim to be made in order for a payment to be treated as a qualifying charitable donation (compare with gift aid donations where a declaration is required).

Donations to local charities which are incurred wholly and exclusively for the purposes of a trade are deducted in the calculation of the tax adjusted trading profits.

Marlborough Ltd is a UK resident trading company. The company's statement of profit or loss for the year ended 31 March 2017 is as follows:

	£	£
Gross profit		700,000
Other income		
Loan stock interest (note 1)		14,500
Rental income (note 2)		18,000
Expenses		
Salaries	76,000	
Depreciation	37,900	
Loss on sale of non-current asset	1,400	
Impairment losses (all trade)	2,800	
Professional fees (note 3)	12,900	
Repairs and renewals (note 4)	17,100	
Other expenses (note 5)	25,600	
		(173,700)
Finance costs		
Loan interest (note 6)		(12,000)
Profit before taxation		546,800

Notes

(1) *Loan stock interest*

The loan stock interest is in respect of loan stock held by Marlborough Ltd as an investment. The amount of £14,500 is the amount received and accrued to 31 March 2017.

(2) *Rental income*

The rental income is in respect of a warehouse which is held as an investment and is let out to an unconnected company. The rental received of £18,000 is also the amount accrued to 31 March 2017.

(3) *Professional fees*

Professional fees are as follows:

	£
Accountancy and audit fees	4,600
Debt collection of trade debts	5,000
Legal fees in connection with renewing a 25 year lease	1,300
Legal fees in connection with director's motoring offences	2,000
	12,900

(4) *Repairs and renewals*

Repairs and renewals include:

	£
Extension to factory	7,988
Repainting exterior of company's offices	6,000

(5) *Other expenses*

Other expenses include:

	£
100 pens with an advertisement for company, given to customers	2,100
Qualifying charitable donation	5,000

(6) *Loan interest*

The loan interest relates to the warehouse let out (see note (2)). The amount shown is the amount paid and accrued to 31 March 2017.

(7) *Plant and machinery*

On 1 April 2016 the tax written down value of the main pool was £22,500. The following transactions took place during the year ended 31 March 2017:

		Cost/(Proceeds)
		£
10 June 2016	Purchased general plant	20,200
25 January 2017	Sold a van (original cost £17,000)	(11,500)
15 March 2017	Purchased a motor car CO_2 emissions 128g/km	10,600

The motor car purchased on 15 March 2017 is used by the company's sales manager: 30% of the mileage is for private journeys.

(a) What are Marlborough Ltd's trading profits for the year ended 31 March 2017? Start with the profit before taxation figure of £546,800 and list all of the items in the statement of profit or loss indicating by the use of a zero (0) any items that do not require adjustment.

(b) What are Marlborough Ltd's taxable total profits for the year ended 31 March 2017?

Answer

(a) **Marlborough Ltd – trading profits for y/e 31 March 2017**

	£	£
Profit before taxation		546,800
Add:		
Salaries (trade)	0	
Depreciation (capital)	37,900	
Loss on sale of non-current asset (capital loss)	1,400	
Impairment losses (trade)	0	
Accountancy and audit fees	0	
Debt collection (trade)	0	
Legal fees – renewal of short lease	0	
Legal fees – motoring offences (not trade)	2,000	
Repairs and renewals: extension (capital)	7,988	
Repairs and renewals: repainting (revenue)	0	
Other expenses: pens (<£50, advertisement)	0	
Other expenses: qualifying charitable donation	5,000	
Loan interest (non-trading loan relationship)	12,000	
		66,288
Deduct:		
Loan stock interest (non-trading loan relationship)	14,500	
Rental income (property business income)	18,000	
Capital allowances (W)	24,088	
		(56,588)
Profit adjusted for tax purposes		556,500

Working

Capital allowances on plant and machinery

	AIA	*Main pool*	*Allowances*
	£	£	£
TWDV b/f		22,500	
Additions qualifying for AIA			
10.6.16 General plant	20,200		
AIA	(20,200)		20,200
Additions not qualifying for AIA			
15.3.17 Car		10,600	
Disposal			
25.1.17 Van		(11,500)	
		21,600	
WDA @ 18%		(3,888)	3,888
TWDV c/f		17,712	
Allowances			24,088

Note. The private use of the car by the employee is not relevant for capital allowance purposes. No adjustment is ever made to a company's capital allowances to reflect the private use of an asset.

(b) **Marlborough Ltd – taxable total profits for y/e 31 March 2017**

	£	£
Trading profit (part (a))		556,500
Non-trading loan relationship credit (loan stock)	14,500	
Less non-trading loan relationship debit (warehouse loan)	(12,000)	
		2,500
Property business income		18,000
Total profits		577,000
Less qualifying charitable donation		(5,000)
Taxable total profits		572,000

8 Long periods of account

FAST FORWARD

Long periods of account are split into two accounting periods: the first 12 months and the remainder.

As we saw earlier in this chapter, if a company has a long period of account exceeding 12 months, it is split into two accounting periods: the first 12 months and the remainder.

Where the period of account differs from the corporation tax accounting periods, profits are **allocated to the relevant periods** as follows:

- **Trading income** before capital allowances and **property income** are apportioned on a **time basis.**
- **Capital allowances** and balancing charges are **calculated for each accounting period**.
- **Other income is allocated to the period to which it relates** (eg interest accrued). Miscellaneous income, however, is apportioned on a time basis.
- **Chargeable gains and losses** are allocated to the **period in which they are realised**.
- **Qualifying charitable donations** are deducted in the accounting **period in which they are paid**.

Question — Long period of account

Xenon Ltd makes up an 18 month set of accounts to 30 September 2017 with the following results.

	£
Trading income (no capital allowances claimed)	180,000
Interest income	
18 months @ £500 accruing per month	9,000
Capital gain (1 August 2017 disposal)	250,000
Less qualifying charitable donation (paid 31 March 2017)	(50,000)
	389,000

What are the taxable total profits for each of the accounting periods based on the above accounts?

Answer

The 18 month period of account is divided into:

Year ending 31 March 2017
6 months to 30 September 2017

Results are allocated:

	Y/e 31.3.17	*6m to 30.9.17*
	£	£
Trading income 12:6	120,000	60,000
Interest income		
12 × £500	6,000	
6 × £500		3,000
Capital gain (1.8.17)		250,000
Total profits	126,000	313,000
Less qualifying charitable donation (31.3.17)	(50,000)	
Taxable total profits	76,000	313,000

9 Computing the corporation tax liability

PER alert

One of the competencies you require to fulfil Performance Objective 15 Tax computations and assessments of the PER is to prepare or contribute to the computation or assessment of tax computations for single companies, groups or other entities. You can apply the knowledge you obtain from this section of the Study Text to help to demonstrate this competence.

9.1 Rate of corporation tax

FAST FORWARD

There is a single rate of corporation tax which is applied to a company's taxable total profits to compute the corporation tax liability.

For financial years 2015 and 2016, there is a single rate of corporation tax (the main rate) which is 20%. This rate is applied to the company's taxable total profits to compute the corporation tax liability.

Question — **Corporation tax liability**

A Ltd had taxable total profits of £1,142,000 in the year to 31 March 2017. Compute A Ltd's corporation tax liability.

Answer

£1,142,000 × 20%	£228,400

9.2 Accounting period in more than one financial year

An accounting period **may fall within more than one financial year. If the rates for corporation tax are the same in both financial years, tax can be computed for the accounting period as if it fell within one financial year.**

However, **if the rates for corporation tax are different in the financial years, taxable total profits are time apportioned between the financial years.**

10 Choice of business medium

FAST FORWARD

An individual can choose between trading as a sole trader or trading through a company. Trading through a company may reduce the overall tax and national insurance liability.

10.1 Trading as a sole trader or through a company

An individual starting in business must decide whether to trade as a sole trader or as a company. If a company is used, the individual can be both a director and a shareholder of the company.

A sole trader pays **income tax on trading income** and also **Class 2 and Class 4 national insurance contributions**.

A company pays corporation tax on its taxable total profits. Any director's salary and its associated Class 1 secondary national insurance contributions are deducted in computing those profits. The employment allowance is not available if the director is the only employee. An amount equal to the **remaining profits after corporation tax** can then be **paid out to shareholders as a dividend**. The **individual as a director pays income tax on employment income** and **Class 1 primary contributions** on cash earnings. The **individual as a shareholder pays income tax on dividend income**. There are **no national insurance contributions on dividends**.

10.2 Example: sole trader or company?

Sharif is starting a new business and expects to make profits of £42,000 before tax and national insurance.

Sharif wants to know how much net income he would receive from the business if he trades as a sole trader or, alternatively, through a company of which he would be the sole shareholder, director and employee, with the company paying him a salary of £8,200 (in order to maintain Class 1 national insurance contributions) and then an amount equal to the company's remaining profits (after corporation tax) as a dividend. Sharif has no other income.

As a sole trader

	£
Profits	42,000
Less personal allowance	(11,000)
Taxable income	31,000
Income tax on £31,000 at 20%	6,200
National Insurance Classes 2 (52 × £2.80) and 4 (£(42,000 – 8,060) × 9%)	3,201
	9,401
Net income £(42,000 – 9,401)	32,599

Through a company

	£
Profits	42,000
Less director's salary	(8,200)
Less employer's secondary Class 1 contributions (8,200 – 8,112) × 13.8%	(12)
Taxable profits	33,788
Less corporation tax 20% × £33,788	(6,758)
Net profits	27,030

The employment allowance is not available as Sharif is the only employee of the company and a director of the company.

A dividend of £27,030 can be paid to Sharif.

	Non-savings income	*Dividend income*	*Total*
	£	£	£
Earnings	8,200		
Dividend		27,030	
Net income	8,200	27,030	30,430
Less personal allowance	(8,200)	(2,800)	
Taxable income	0	24,230	24,230
Dividend income			
£5,000 × 0%			0
£19,230 (24,230 – 5,000) × 7.5%			1,442
Income tax liability			1,442

		£	£
Net income			
Salary			8,200
Dividend			27,030
			35,230
Less:	income tax	1,442	
	employee's primary Class 1 contributions £(8,200 – 8,060) × 12%	17	
			(1,459)
Net income			33,771

If Sharif trades through a company, he will receive £(33,771 – 32,599) = £1,172 more net income from the business than if he trades as a sole trader.

Chapter Roundup

- Companies pay corporation tax on their taxable total profits.
- An accounting period cannot exceed 12 months in length so a long period of account must be split into two accounting periods. The first accounting period of a long period of account is always 12 months in length.
- Tax rates are set for financial years.
- A company is UK resident if it is incorporated in the UK or if it is incorporated overseas and its central management and control are exercised in the UK.
- Taxable total profits comprises the company's income and chargeable gains (total profits) less some losses and qualifying charitable donations. It does not include dividends received from other companies.
- Income includes trading income, property income, income from non-trading loan relationships (interest) and miscellaneous income.
- The adjustment of profits computation for companies broadly follows that for computing business profits subject to income tax. There are, however, some minor differences.
- Qualifying charitable donations are deducted from total profits when computing taxable total profits.
- Long periods of account are split into two accounting periods: the first 12 months and the remainder.
- There is a single rate of corporation tax which is applied to a company's taxable total profits to compute the corporation tax liability.
- An individual can choose between trading as a sole trader or trading through a company. Trading through a company may reduce the overall tax and national insurance liability.

Quick Quiz

1 When does an accounting period end?

2 What is the difference between a period of account and an accounting period?

3 Zed Ltd has been trading for many years, preparing accounts to 31 October. It decides to prepare accounts for the fifteen month period ending 31 January 2017. What are Zed Ltd's accounting period(s) for the long period of account?

A 1 November 2015 to 31 January 2017
B 1 November 2015 to 31 October 2016 and 1 November 2016 to 31 January 2017
C 1 November 2015 to 31 January 2016 and 1 February 2016 to 31 January 2017
D 1 November 2015 to 31 March 2016 and 1 April 2016 to 31 January 2017

4 Should interest paid on a trading loan be adjusted in the trading income computation?

5 How is trading income (before capital allowances) of a long period of account divided between accounting periods?

A On a receipts basis
B On an accruals basis
C On a time basis
D On any basis the company chooses

6 What is the rate of corporation tax for financial year 2016?

Answers to Quick Quiz

1. An accounting period ends on the earliest of:

   (a) 12 months after its start
   (b) The end of the company's period of account
   (c) The commencement of the company's winding up
   (d) The company ceasing to be resident in the UK
   (e) The company ceasing to be liable to corporation tax

2. A period of account is the period for which a company prepares accounts. An accounting period is the period for which corporation tax is charged. If a company prepares annual accounts the two will coincide.

3. B. 1 November 2015 to 31 October 2016 and 1 November 2016 to 31 January 2017. The first accounting period of a long period of account is always 12 months in length.

4. Interest paid on a trading loan should not be adjusted in the trading income computation as it is an allowable expense, computed on the accruals basis.

5. C. Trading income (before capital allowances) is apportioned on a time basis.

6. The corporation tax rate for financial year 2016 is 20%.

Now try the questions below from the Practice Question Bank

Number	Type	Marks	Time
Q127	Section A	2	4 mins
Q128	Section A	2	4 mins
Q129	Section A	2	4 mins
Q130	Section B	2	4 mins
Q131	Section B	2	4 mins
Q132	Section B	2	4 mins
Q133	Section B	2	4 mins
Q134	Section B	2	4 mins
Q135	Section C	15	29 mins

Chargeable gains for companies

20

Topic list	Syllabus reference
1 Corporation tax on chargeable gains	E3(a)
2 Indexation allowance	E3(b)
3 Disposal of shares by companies	E3(d)–(f)
4 Relief for replacement of business assets (rollover relief)	E3(g)

Introduction

We studied chargeable gains for individuals earlier in this Study Text. In this chapter, we will consider the treatment of chargeable gains for companies.

Companies pay corporation tax on their chargeable gains, rather than capital gains tax. The computation of gains for companies is slightly more complicated than for individuals because companies are entitled to indexation allowance.

We also consider the matching rules for companies which dispose of shares in other companies. Again, these rules are slightly more complicated than for individuals.

Finally, we look at how the relief for replacement of business assets applies to companies.

In the next chapters we will deal with losses and groups.

Study guide

		Intellectual level
E3	**Chargeable gains for companies**	
(a)	Compute and explain the treatment of chargeable gains.	2
(b)	Explain and compute the indexation allowance available.	2
(d)	Understand the treatment of disposals of shares by companies and the identification rules including the same day and nine day matching rules.	2
(e)	Explain and apply the pooling provisions.	2
(f)	Explain and apply the treatment of bonus issues, rights issues, takeovers and reorganisations.	2
(g)	Explain and apply rollover relief.	2

Exam guide

There will be a 15 mark question on corporation tax in Section C. This may include the gains of a company so it is important that you can deal with the aspects covered in this chapter. Corporation tax may also be tested in 10 mark questions in Sections B or C. A Section A question may test a specific point such as computation of the indexation allowance.

Exam focus point

ACCA's article Chargeable gains, written by a member of the F6(UK) examination team, in Part 1 looks at **chargeable gains** in either a **personal or corporate context**. Part 2 focuses on **shares**, **reliefs**, and the way in which **gains made by limited companies are taxed**.

1 Corporation tax on chargeable gains

FAST FORWARD

Chargeable gains for companies are computed in broadly the same way as for individuals, but indexation allowance applies and there is no annual exempt amount.

Companies do not pay capital gains tax. Instead their chargeable gains are included in the calculation of taxable total profits.

A company's capital gains or allowable losses are computed in a similar way to individuals but with a few major differences:

- There is relief for inflation called the indexation allowance
- **No annual exempt amount** is available
- Different matching rules for shares apply if the shareholder is a company

2 Indexation allowance

FAST FORWARD

The indexation allowance gives relief for the inflation element of a gain.

The purpose of having an indexation allowance is to remove the inflation element of a gain from taxation.

Companies are entitled to indexation allowance from the date of acquisition until the date of disposal of an asset. It is based on the movement in the Retail Price Index (RPI) between those two dates.

For example, if J Ltd bought a painting on 2 January 2004 and sold it on 19 November 2016 the indexation allowance is available from January 2004 until November 2016.

Exam formula

The indexation factor is:

$$\frac{\text{RPI for month of disposal} - \text{RPI for month of acquisition}}{\text{RPI for month of acquisition}}$$

The calculation is expressed as a decimal and is rounded to three decimal places.

Indexation allowance is available on the allowable cost of the asset from the **date of acquisition** (including incidental costs of acquisition). It is also available on **enhancement expenditure from the month in which such expenditure becomes due and payable. Indexation allowance is not available on the costs of disposal.**

Question

The indexation allowance

An asset is acquired by a company on 15 February 2003 (RPI = 179.3) at a cost of £5,000. Enhancement expenditure of £2,000 is incurred on 10 April 2004 (RPI = 185.7). The asset is sold for £15,500 on 20 December 2016 (assumed RPI = 263.4). Incidental costs of sale are £500. Calculate the chargeable gain arising.

Answer

The indexation allowance is available until December 2016 and is computed as follows.

	£
$\frac{263.4 - 179.3}{179.3} = 0.469 \times £5,000$	2,345
$\frac{263.4 - 185.7}{185.7} = 0.418 \times £2,000$	836
	3,181

The computation of the chargeable gain is as follows.

	£
Proceeds	15,500
Less incidental costs of sale	(500)
Net proceeds	15,000
Less allowable costs £(5,000 + 2,000)	(7,000)
Unindexed gain	8,000
Less indexation allowance (see above)	(3,181)
Indexed gain	4,819

Indexation allowance cannot create or increase an allowable loss. If there is a gain before the indexation allowance, the allowance can reduce that gain to zero but no further. If there is a loss before the indexation allowance, there is no indexation allowance.

If the indexation allowance calculation gives a negative figure, treat the indexation as nil: do not add to the unindexed gain.

3 Disposal of shares by companies

FAST FORWARD

There are special rules for matching shares sold by a company with shares purchased. Disposals are matched with acquisitions on the same day, the previous nine days and the FA 1985 share pool.

3.1 The matching rules

We have discussed the share matching rules for individuals earlier in this Study Text. We also need special rules for companies.

For companies the matching of shares sold is in the following order.

(a) Shares acquired on the **same day**

(b) Shares acquired in the **previous nine days**, if more than one acquisition on a 'first in, first out' (FIFO) basis

(c) Shares from the **FA 1985 pool**

The composition of the FA 1985 pool in relation to companies which are shareholders is explained below.

Exam focus point

Learn the 'matching rules' because a crucial first step to getting a shares question right is to correctly match the shares sold to the original shares purchased.

3.2 Example: share matching rules for companies

Nor Ltd acquired the following shares in Last plc:

Date of acquisition	*No of shares*
9.11.02	15,000
15.12.04	15,000
11.7.16	5,000
15.7.16	5,000

Nor Ltd disposed of 20,000 of the shares on 15 July 2016.

We match the shares as follows:

(a) Acquisition on same day: 5,000 shares acquired 15 July 2016
(b) Acquisitions in previous 9 days: 5,000 shares acquired 11 July 2016
(c) FA 1985 share pool: 10,000 shares out of 30,000 shares in FA 1985 share pool (9.11.02 and 15.12.04)

3.3 The FA 1985 share pool

Exam focus point

The examination team has stated that a detailed question will not be set on the pooling provisions. However, work through the examples below as you are expected to understand how the pool works.

The FA 1985 pool comprises the following shares of the same class in the same company.

- **Shares held by a company on 1 April 1985 and acquired by that company on or after 1 April 1982**
- **Shares acquired by that company on or after 1 April 1985**

We must keep track of:

(a) The **number** of shares
(b) The **cost** of the shares ignoring indexation
(c) The **indexed cost** of the shares

The first step in constructing the FA 1985 share pool is to calculate the value of the pool at 1 April 1985 by indexing the cost of each acquisition before that date up to April 1985.

3.4 Example: the FA 1985 pool

Oliver Ltd bought 1,000 shares in Judith plc for £2,750 in August 1984 and another 1,000 for £3,250 in December 1984. RPIs are August 1984 = 89.9, December 1984 = 90.9 and April 1985 = 94.8. The FA 1985 pool at 1 April 1985 is as follows.

	No of shares	*Cost*	*Indexed Cost*
		£	£
August 1984 (a)	1,000	2,750	2,750
December 1984 (b)	1,000	3,250	3,250
	2,000	6,000	6,000
Indexation allowance			
$\frac{94.8-89.9}{89.9} = 0.055 \times £2,750$			151
$\frac{94.8-90.9}{90.9} = 0.043 \times £3,250$			140
Indexed cost of the pool at 1 April 1985			6,291

Disposals and acquisitions of shares which affect the indexed value of the FA 1985 pool are termed **'operative events'. Prior to reflecting each such operative event within the FA 1985 share pool, a further indexation allowance (an 'indexed rise') must be computed up to the date of the operative event concerned from the date of the last such operative event** (or from the later of the first acquisition and April 1985 if the operative event in question is the first one).

Indexation calculations within the FA 1985 pool (after its April 1985 value has been calculated) **are not rounded to three decimal places**. This is because rounding errors would accumulate and have a serious effect after several operative events.

If there are several operative events between 1 April 1985 and the date of a disposal, the indexation procedure described above will have to be performed several times over.

Question — **Value of FA 1985 pool**

Following on from the above example, assume that Oliver Ltd acquired 2,000 more shares on 10 July 1986 at a cost of £4,000. Recalculate the value of the FA 1985 pool on 10 July 1986 following the acquisition. RPI July 1986 = 97.5.

Answer

	No of shares	*Cost*	*Indexed cost*
		£	£
Value at 1.4.85 b/f	2,000	6,000	6,291
Indexed rise $\frac{97.5-94.8}{94.8} \times £6,291$			179
	2,000	6,000	6,470
Acquisition	2,000	4,000	4,000
Value at 10.7.86	4,000	10,000	10,470

In the case of a disposal, following the calculation of the indexed rise to the date of disposal, the cost and the indexed cost attributable to the shares disposed of are deducted from the amounts within the FA 1985 pool. The proportions of the cost and indexed cost to take out of the pool should be computed by using the proportion that the shares disposed of bear to the total number of shares held.

The indexation allowance is the indexed cost taken out of the pool minus the cost taken out. As usual, the indexation allowance cannot create or increase a loss.

Question

Continuing the above exercise, suppose that Oliver Ltd sold 3,000 shares on 10 July 2016 for £24,000. Compute the gain, and the value of the FA 1985 pool following the disposal. Assume RPI July 2016 = 261.5.

Answer

	No of shares	*Cost*	*Indexed cost*
		£	£
Value at 10.7.86	4,000	10,000	10,470
Indexed rise			
$\frac{261.5-97.5}{97.5} \times £10,470$			17,611
	4,000	10,000	28,081
Disposal	(3,000)		
Cost and indexed cost $\frac{3,000}{4,000} \times £10,000$ and £28,081		(7,500)	(21,061)
Value at 10.7.16	1,000	2,500	7,020

The gain is computed as follows:

	£
Proceeds	24,000
Less cost	(7,500)
Unindexed gain	16,500
Less indexation allowance £(21,061 – 7,500)	(13,561)
Indexed gain	2,939

3.5 Bonus and rights issues

When **bonus issue shares are issued**, all that happens is that **the size of the original holding is increased.** Since **bonus issue shares are issued at no cost** there is **no need to adjust the original cost** and there is **no operative event for the FA 1985 pool** (so no indexation allowance needs to be calculated).

When **rights issue shares are issued**, the **size of the original holding is increased** in the same way as for a bonus issue. So if the original shareholding was part of the FA 1985 pool, the rights issue shares are added to that pool. This might be important for the matching rules if a shareholding containing the rights issue shares is sold shortly after the rights issue.

However, in the case of a rights issue, the **new shares are paid for and this results in an adjustment to the original cost**. For the purpose of **calculating the indexation allowance, expenditure on a rights issue is taken as being incurred on the date of the issue** and not the date of the original holding.

3.6 Example: bonus and rights issue

S Ltd bought 10,000 shares in T plc in May 2000 (RPI = 170.7) at a cost of £45,000.

There was a 2 for 1 bonus issue in October 2002.

There was a 1 for 3 rights issue in June 2006 (RPI = 198.5) at a cost of £4 per share. S Ltd took up all of its rights entitlement.

S Ltd sold 20,000 shares in T plc for £120,000 in January 2017 (assumed RPI = 263.5).

FA 1985 share pool

		No. of shares	Cost	Indexed cost
			£	£
5.00	Acquisition	10,000	45,000	45,000
10.02	Bonus 2:1	20,000		
		30,000		
6.06	Indexed rise			
	$\frac{198.5-170.7}{170.7} \times £45,000$			7,329
	Rights 1:3	10,000	40,000	40,000
		40,000	85,000	92,329
1.17	Index rise			
	$\frac{263.5-198.5}{198.5} \times £92,329$			30,234
				122,563
	Disposal	(20,000)	(42,500)	(61,282)
c/f		20,000	42,500	61,281

The gain is:

	£
Proceeds	120,000
Less cost	(42,500)
Unindexed gain	77,500
Less indexation allowance £(61,282 – 42,500)	(18,782)
Indexed gain	58,718

3.7 Reorganisations and takeovers

The rules on reorganisation and takeovers apply in a similar way for company shareholders as they do for individuals.

In the case of a **reorganisation, the new shares or securities take the place of the original shares. The original cost and the indexed cost of the original shares is apportioned between the different types of capital issued on the reorganisation.**

Where there is a takeover of shares which qualifies for the 'paper for paper' treatment, the cost and indexed cost of the original holding is passed onto the new holding which take the place of the original holding.

Question — Takeover

J Ltd acquired 20,000 shares in G Ltd in August 1990 (RPI = 128.1) at a cost of £40,000. It acquired a further 5,000 shares in December 2006 (RPI = 202.7) at a cost of £30,000.

In September 2016, G Ltd was taken over by K plc and J Ltd received one ordinary share and two preference shares in K plc for each one share held in G Ltd. Immediately following the takeover, the ordinary shares in K plc were worth £4 per share and the preference shares in K plc were worth £1 per share.

(a) Show the cost and indexed cost of the ordinary shares and the preference shares in K plc.

(b) Calculate the gain arising if J Ltd sells 10,000 of its ordinary shares in K plc for £42,500 in February 2017 (assumed RPI = 263.8).

Answer

(a) *G Ltd FA 1985 share pool*

		No. of shares	Cost	Indexed cost
			£	£
8.90	Acquisition	20,000	40,000	40,000
12.06	Indexed rise			
	$\frac{202.7-128.1}{128.1} \times £40,000$			23,294
	Acquisition	5,000	30,000	30,000
		25,000	70,000	93,294

Note that the takeover is not an operative event because the pool of cost is not increased or decreased and so it is not necessary to calculate an indexed rise to the date of the takeover.

Apportionment of cost/indexed cost to K plc shares

	No. of shares	MV	Cost	Indexed cost
		£	£	£
Ords × 1	25,000	100,000	46,667	62,196
Prefs × 2	50,000	50,000	23,333	31,098
Totals		150,000	70,000	93,294

(b) *K plc ordinary shares FA 1985 share pool*

		No. of shares	Cost	Indexed cost
			£	£
12.06	Acquisition (deemed)	25,000	46,667	62,196
2.17	Indexed rise			
	$\frac{263.8-202.7}{202.7} \times £62,196$			18,748
				80,944
	Disposal	(10,000)	(18,667)	(32,378)
		15,000	28,000	48,566

Note that the indexation allowance on the ordinary shares is calculated from the December 2006, not from the date of the takeover.

The gain is:

	£
Proceeds	42,500
Less cost	(18,667)
Unindexed gain	23,833
Less indexation allowance £(32,378 – 18,667)	(13,711)
Indexed gain	10,122

4 Relief for replacement of business assets (rollover relief)

FAST FORWARD

Rollover relief for replacement of business assets is available to companies to defer gains arising on the disposal of business assets.

4.1 Conditions for relief

As for individuals, **a gain may be deferred by a company where the proceeds on the disposal of a business asset are spent on a replacement business asset under rollover relief**.

The conditions for the relief to apply to company disposals are:

(a) The old assets sold and the new asset bought are both used only in the trade of the company (apportionment into business and non-business parts available for buildings).

(b) The old asset and the new asset both fall within one (but not necessarily the same one) of the following classes.

  (i) **Land and buildings** (including parts of buildings) occupied as well as used only for the purposes of the trade

  (ii) Fixed plant and machinery

(c) Reinvestment of the proceeds received on the disposal of the old asset takes place in a period beginning one year before and ending three years after the date of the disposal.

(d) The new asset is brought into use in the trade on its acquisition.

Note that goodwill is not a qualifying asset for the purposes of corporation tax.

A claim for the relief must be made by the later of four years of the end of the accounting period in which the disposal of the old asset takes place and four years of the end of the accounting period in which the new asset is acquired.

4.2 Operation of relief

Deferral is obtained by deducting the indexed gain from the cost of the new asset. For full relief, the whole of the proceeds must be reinvested. If only part is reinvested, a gain equal to the amount not invested, or the full gain, if lower, will be chargeable to tax immediately.

The new asset will have a base cost for chargeable gains purposes of its purchase price less the gain rolled over.

Question — Rollover relief

D Ltd acquired a factory in April 2000 (RPI = 170.1) at a cost of £120,000. It used the factory in its trade throughout the period of its ownership.

In August 2016 (assumed RPI = 261.9), D Ltd sold the factory for £220,000. In November 2016, it acquired another factory at a cost of £190,000.

Calculate the gain chargeable on the sale of the first factory and the base cost of the second factory.

Answer

Chargeable gain on sale of first factory

	£
Proceeds	220,000
Less cost	(120,000)
Unindexed gain	100,000
$\frac{261.9 - 170.1}{170.1} = 0.540 \times £120,000$	(64,800)
Indexed gain	35,200
Less rollover relief (balancing figure)	(5,200)
Chargeable gain: amount not reinvested £(220,000 – 190,000)	30,000

Base cost of second factory

	£
Cost of second factory	190,000
Less rolled over gain	(5,200)
Base cost	184,800

4.3 Depreciating assets

The relief for investment into depreciating assets works in the same way for companies as it does for individuals.

The indexed gain is calculated on the old asset and is deferred until the gain crystallises on the earliest of:

(a) The disposal of the replacement asset
(b) The date the replacement asset ceases to be used in the trade
(c) Ten years after the acquisition of the replacement asset

Chapter Roundup

- Chargeable gains for companies are computed in broadly the same way as for individuals, but indexation allowance applies and there is no annual exempt amount.
- The indexation allowance gives relief for the inflation element of a gain.
- There are special rules for matching shares sold by a company with shares purchased. Disposals are matched with acquisitions on the same day, the previous nine days and the FA 1985 share pool.
- Rollover relief for replacement of business assets is available to companies to defer gains arising on the disposal of business assets.

Quick Quiz

1 A company is entitled to an annual exempt amount against its chargeable gains. True/False?

2 Indexation allowance runs from the date of _______ to date of ______. Fill in the blanks.

3 What are the share matching rules for company shareholders?

4 J Ltd bought 10,000 ordinary shares for £20,000 in K Ltd in December 2015 (RPI 260.6). In October 2016 (RPI 262.8), there was a 2 for 1 rights issue in K Ltd at £2.50 per share and J Ltd took up all its rights issue shares. What is the indexed cost of the FA 1985 share pool immediately after the rights issue?

5 H Ltd sells a warehouse for £400,000. The warehouse cost £220,000 and the indexation allowance available is £40,000. The company acquires another warehouse ten months later for £375,000. What is the amount of rollover relief?

Answers to Quick Quiz

1. False. A company is not entitled to an annual exempt amount against its chargeable gains.
2. Indexation allowance runs from the date of **acquisition** to date of **disposal**.
3. The matching rules for shares disposed of by a company shareholder are:
   (a) Shares acquired on the same day
   (b) Shares acquired in the previous nine days
   (c) Shares from the FA 1985 pool
4. *FA 1985 share pool*

		No. of shares	Indexed cost
			£
12.15	Acquisition	10,000	20,000
10.16	Indexed rise		
	$\frac{262.8 - 260.6}{260.6} \times £20{,}000$		169
	Rights 2:1 @ £2.50	20,000	50,000
		30,000	70,169

5. The gain on the sale of first warehouse is:

	£
Proceeds	400,000
Less cost	(220,000)
Unindexed gain	180,000
Less indexation allowance	(40,000)
Indexed gain	140,000
Less rollover relief (balancing figure)	(115,000)
Chargeable gain: amount not reinvested £(400,000 – 375,000)	25,000

Now try the questions below from the Practice Question Bank

Number	Type	Marks	Time
Q136	Section A	2	4 mins
Q137	Section A	2	4 mins
Q138	Section A	2	4 mins
Q139	Section B	2	4 mins
Q140	Section B	2	4 mins
Q141	Section B	2	4 mins
Q142	Section B	2	4 mins
Q143	Section B	2	4 mins
Q144	Section C	10	20 mins

21

Losses

Topic list	Syllabus reference
1 Trading losses – overview	E2
2 Carry forward trade loss relief	E2(e)
3 Trade loss relief against total profits	E2(f)
4 Choosing loss reliefs and other planning points	E2(g)
5 Other losses	E2(d), E3(c)

Introduction

In the previous three chapters we have seen how a company calculates its taxable total profits and the corporation tax payable.

We now look at how a company may obtain relief for losses.

In the next chapter we will look at groups, and in particular how losses can be relieved by group relief.

Study guide

		Intellectual level
E2	**Taxable total profits**	
(d)	Compute property business profits and understand how relief for a property business loss is given.	2
(e)	Understand how trading losses can be carried forward.	2
(f)	Understand how trading losses can be claimed against income of the current or previous accounting periods.	2
(g)	Recognise the factors that will influence the choice of loss relief claim.	2
E3	**Chargeable gains for companies**	
(c)	Explain and compute the treatment of capital losses.	1

Exam guide

Losses could form part of a 15 mark question or a 10 mark question in Section C. They may also be included in Section A or B questions, for example dealing with carry forward loss relief. Dealing with losses involves a methodical approach: first establish what loss is available for relief, second identify the different reliefs available, and third evaluate the options. Do check the question for specific instructions; you may be told that loss relief should be taken as early as possible.

1 Trading losses – overview

FAST FORWARD

Trading losses may be relieved by deduction from current total profits, from total profits of earlier periods or from future trading income.

In summary, the following reliefs are available for trading losses incurred by a company:

(a) Claim to deduct the loss from current total profits

(b) Claim to deduct the loss from earlier total profits

(c) Make no claim and automatically carry forward the loss to be deducted from future trading profits of the same trade

These **reliefs may be used in combination**. The options open to the company are:

(a) Do nothing, so that the loss is automatically carried forward against future trading profits

(b) Claim to deduct the loss from current total profits, then automatically carry forward any remaining unrelieved loss to be deducted from future trading profits

(c) Claim to deduct the loss from current total profits, then claim to carry any unused loss back and deduct from earlier total profits, and then automatically carry any remaining unrelieved loss forward to be deducted from future trading profits.

The reliefs are explained in further detail later in this chapter.

Exam focus point

Remember that total profits is income and gains before the deduction of qualifying charitable donations. This may lead to qualifying charitable donations becoming unrelieved.

2 Carry forward trade loss relief

FAST FORWARD

Trading losses carried forward can only be deducted from future trading profits arising from the same trade.

A company must deduct a trading loss which is carried forward against trading profits from the same trade in future accounting periods (unless it has been otherwise relieved by making a claim to deduct it from total profits). **Relief is against the first available profits.**

Question

Carry forward trade loss relief

A Ltd has the following results for the three years to 31 March 2017.

		Year ended	
	31.3.15	*31.3.16*	*31.3.17*
	£	£	£
Trading profit/(loss)	(8,550)	3,000	6,000
Property income	0	1,000	1,000
Qualifying charitable donation	300	1,400	1,700

Calculate the taxable total profits for all three years showing any losses available to carry forward at 1 April 2017 and the amounts of any qualifying charitable donations which become unrelieved.

Answer

		Year ended	
	31.3.15	*31.3.16*	*31.3.17*
	£	£	£
Trading profits	0	3,000	6,000
Less carry forward loss relief		(3,000)	(5,550)
	0	0	450
Property income	0	1,000	1,000
Total profits	0	1,000	1,450
Less qualifying charitable donation	0	(1,000)	(1,450)
Taxable total profits	0	0	0
Unrelieved qualifying charitable donation	300	400	250

Note that the trading loss carried forward is deducted from the trading profit in future years. It cannot be deducted from the property income.

Loss memorandum

	£
Loss for y/e 31.3.15	8,550
Less used y/e 31.3.16	(3,000)
Loss carried forward at 1.4.16	5,550
Less used y/e 31.3.17	(5,550)
Loss carried forward at 1.4.17	0

3 Trade loss relief against total profits

FAST FORWARD

Loss relief by deduction from total profits is given before qualifying charitable donations and so qualifying charitable donations may become unrelieved.

3.1 Current year relief

A company may claim to deduct a trading loss incurred in an accounting period from total profits. This may make qualifying charitable donations unrelieved because such donations are deducted from total profits after this loss relief to compute taxable total profits.

3.2 Carry back relief

FAST FORWARD

Loss relief by deduction from total profits may be given by deduction from current period profits and from the previous 12 months.

Such a loss may then be carried back and deducted from total profits of an accounting period falling wholly or partly within the 12 months prior to the start of the period in which the loss was incurred. Again, this may cause qualifying charitable donations to be unrelieved.

FAST FORARD

A claim for current period loss relief can be made without a claim for carry back relief. However, if a loss is to be carried back, a claim for current period relief must have been made first.

Any possible loss relief claim for the period of the loss must be made before any excess loss can be carried back to a previous period.

Any carry back is to more recent periods before earlier periods. Relief for earlier losses is given before relief for later losses.

Any loss remaining unrelieved after any loss relief claims against total profits is automatically carried forward to be deducted from future profits of the same trade.

Question — Loss relief against total profits

Helix Ltd has the following results.

	y/e 30.11.15	*y/e 30.11.16*
	£	£
Trading profit/(loss)	22,500	(19,500)
Bank interest received	500	500
Chargeable gains	0	4,000
Qualifying charitable donation	250	250

Calculate the taxable total profits for both years affected assuming that loss relief by deduction from total profits is claimed. Show the amount of any qualifying charitable donations which become unrelieved.

Answer

	y/e 30.11.15	*y/e 30.11.16*
	£	£
Trading profit	22,500	0
Investment income	500	500
Chargeable gains	0	4,000
Total profits	23,000	4,500
Less current period loss relief	0	(4,500)
	23,000	0
Less carry back loss relief	(15,000)	(0)
	8,000	0
Less qualifying charitable donation	(250)	0
Taxable total profits	7,750	0
Unrelieved qualifying charitable donation		250
Loss memorandum		
Loss incurred in y/e 30.11.16		19,500
Less used: y/e 30.11.16		(4,500)
y/e 30.11.15		(15,000)
Loss available to carry forward		0

If a period falls partly outside the prior 12 months, loss relief is limited to the proportion of the period's profits (before qualifying charitable donations) equal to the proportion of the period which falls within the 12 months.

Question — **Short accounting period and loss relief**

Tallis Ltd had the following results for the three accounting periods to 31 December 2016.

	y/e 30.9.15	*3 months to 31.12.15*	*y/e 31.12.16*
	£	£	£
Trading profit (loss)	20,000	12,000	(39,000)
Building society interest received	1,000	400	1,800
Qualifying charitable donations	600	500	0

Calculate the taxable total profits for all years and show any qualifying charitable donations which become unrelieved. Assume loss relief is claimed by deduction from total profits where possible.

Answer

	y/e 30.9.15	*3 months to 31.12.15*	*y/e 31.12.16*
	£	£	£
Trading profit	20,000	12,000	0
Interest income	1,000	400	1,800
Total profits	21,000	12,400	1,800
Less current period loss relief			(1,800)
	21,000	12,400	0
Less carry back loss relief	(15,750)	(12,400)	
	5,250	0	0
Less qualifying charitable donations	(600)		0
Taxable total profits	4,650	0	0
Unrelieved qualifying charitable donations	0	500	0

Loss memorandum	£
Loss incurred in y/e 31.12.16	39,000
Less used y/e 31.12.16	(1,800)
Less used p/e 31.12.15	(12,400)
Less used y/e 30.9.15 £21,000 × 9/12 (max)	(15,750)
C/f	9,050

Notes

1 The loss can be carried back to set against total profits of the previous 12 months. This means total profits in the y/e 30.9.15 must be time apportioned by multiplying by 9/12.

2 Losses remaining after the loss relief claims against total profits are carried forward to set against future trading profits.

3.3 Claims

A claim for relief by deduction from current or earlier period total profits must be made within two years of the end of the accounting period in which the loss arose. Any claim must be for the *whole* loss (to the extent that profits are available to relieve it). The loss can however be reduced by not claiming full capital allowances, so that higher capital allowances are given (on higher tax written down values) in future years (see later in this chapter).

3.4 Interaction with losses brought forward

A trading loss carried back is relieved after any trading losses brought forward have been offset.

Question — **Losses carried forward and back**

Chile Ltd has the following results.

	Year ended 30.11.15	30.11.16	30.11.17
	£	£	£
Trading profit/(loss)	21,000	(20,000)	40,000
Bank interest received	1,000	1,500	500
Chargeable gains	0	2,000	0
Qualifying charitable donations	500	500	500

Chile Ltd had a trading loss of £16,000 carried forward at 1 December 2014.

Compute the taxable trading profits for all the years affected assuming that loss relief by deduction from total profits is claimed. Show the amount of any qualifying charitable donations which become unrelieved.

Answer

The loss of the year to 30 November 2016 is relieved by deduction from current year total profits and from total profits of the previous twelve months. The trading loss brought forward at 1 December 2014 is relieved in the year ended 30 November 2015 before the loss brought back.

	Year ended 30.11.15	30.11.16	30.11.17
	£	£	£
Trading profit	21,000	0	40,000
Less carry forward loss relief	(16,000)	0	(10,500)
	5,000	0	29,500
Interest income	1,000	1,500	500
Chargeable gains	0	2,000	0
Total profits	6,000	3,500	30,000
Less current period loss relief	0	(3,500)	0
	6,000	0	30,000
Less carry back loss relief	(6,000)	0	0
	0	0	30,000
Less qualifying charitable donation	0	0	(500)
Taxable total profits	0	0	29,500
Unrelieved qualifying charitable donations	500	500	

	£
Loss memorandum (1)	
Loss brought forward at 1 December 2014	16,000
Less used y/e 30.11.15	(16,000)
	0

	£
Loss memorandum (2)	
Loss incurred in y/e 30.11.16	20,000
Less used: y/e 30.11.16	(3,500)
y/e 30.11.15	(6,000)
	10,500
Less used: y/e 30.11.17	(10,500)
C/f	0

3.5 Terminal trade loss relief

FAST FORWARD

Trading losses in the last 12 months of trading can be carried back and deducted from total profits of the previous three years.

For trading losses incurred in the 12 months up to the cessation of trade the carry back period is extended from 12 months to three years, later years first.

Question — **Terminal losses**

Brazil Ltd had the following results for the accounting periods up to the cessation of trade on 30 September 2016.

	y/e 30.9.13	*y/e 30.9.14*	*y/e 30.9.15*	*y/e 30.9.16*
	£	£	£	£
Trading profits	60,000	40,000	15,000	(180,000)
Gains	0	10,000	0	6,000
Property income	12,000	12,000	12,000	12,000

You are required to show how the losses are relieved assuming the maximum use is made of loss relief by deduction from total profits.

Answer

	y/e 30.9.13	*y/e 30.9.14*	*y/e 30.9.15*	*y/e 30.9.16*
	£	£	£	£
Trading profits	60,000	40,000	15,000	0
Property income	12,000	12,000	12,000	12,000
Gains	0	10,000	0	6,000
Total profits	72,000	62,000	27,000	18,000
Less current period loss relief				(18,000)
				0
Less carry back loss relief	(72,000)	(62,000)	(27,000)	
Taxable total profits	0	0	0	0

Loss memorandum	
Loss in y/e 30.9.16	180,000
Less used y/e 30.9.16	(18,000)
Loss of y/e 30.9.16 available for 3 year carry back	162,000
Less used y/e 30.9.15	(27,000)
	135,000
Less used y/e 30.9.14	(62,000)
	73,000
Less used y/e 30.9.13	(72,000)
Loss remaining unrelieved	1,000

4 Choosing loss reliefs and other planning points

FAST FORWARD

When selecting a loss relief, consider the timing of the relief and the extent to which relief for qualifying charitable donations might be lost.

PER alert

One of the competencies you require to fulfil Performance Objective 17 Tax planning and advice of the PER is to mitigate and/or defer tax liabilities through the use of standard reliefs, exemptions and incentives. You can apply the knowledge you obtain from this section of the Study Text to help to demonstrate this competence.

4.1 Alternative loss reliefs

Several alternative loss reliefs may be available. In making a choice consider:

- **How quickly relief will be obtained**: loss relief against total profits is quicker than carry forward loss relief and so generally preferable to carrying forward the loss.
- **The extent to which relief for qualifying charitable donations might be lost.**

Question — **The choice between loss reliefs**

M Ltd has had the following results.

	Year ended 31 March			
	2015	*2016*	*2017*	*2018*
	£	£	£	£
Trading profit/(loss)	2,000	(500,000)	200,000	138,000
Chargeable gains	35,000	250,000	0	0
Qualifying charitable donations	30,000	20,000	20,000	20,000

Recommend appropriate loss relief claims, and compute the corporation tax for all years based on your recommendations. Assume that future years' profits will be similar to those of the year ended 31 March 2018 and that the rate of corporation tax is 20% throughout.

Answer

A loss relief against total profits claim for the year ended 31 March 2016 will obtain relief quickly. However, it will waste the qualifying charitable donations.

Taxable total profits in the previous year are £7,000 (£35,000 + £2,000 – £30,000). Carry back would waste qualifying charitable donations of £30,000 and would use £37,000 of loss to save tax on £7,000.

If no current period loss relief claim is made, £200,000 of the loss will be carried forward and will obtain relief in the year ended 31 March 2017, with £20,000 of qualifying charitable donations being wasted. The remaining £300,000 of the loss, would be carried forward to the year ended 31 March 2018 and later years.

To conclude, a loss relief claim by deduction from total profits should be made for the year of the loss but not in the previous year. £20,000 of qualifying charitable donations would be wasted in the current year, but relief on £250,000 would be obtained quickly. Carrying the loss back would mean that £30,000 of qualifying charitable donations would become unrelieved. Therefore it would be more advantageous to carry the loss forward.

The final computations are as follows:

	Year ended 31 March			
	2015	*2016*	*2017*	*2018*
	£	£	£	£
Trading income	2,000	0	200,000	138,000
Less carry forward loss relief	0	0	(200,000)	(50,000)
	2,000	0	0	88,000
Chargeable gains	35,000	250,000	0	0
Total profits	37,000	250,000	0	88,000
Less current period loss relief	0	(250,000)	0	0
	37,000	0	0	88,000
Less qualifying charitable donations	(30,000)	0	0	(20,000)
Taxable total profits	7,000	0	0	68,000
CT at 20%	1,400	0	0	13,600
Unrelieved qualifying charitable donations	0	20,000	20,000	0

4.2 Capital allowances and loss relief

A company with losses should consider claiming less than the maximum amount of capital allowances available. This will result in a higher tax written down value to carry forward and therefore higher capital allowances in future years.

Reducing capital allowances in the current period reduces the loss available for relief against total profits. As this relief, if claimed, must be claimed for all of a loss available, a reduced capital allowance claim could be advantageous where qualifying charitable donations may be wasted in the current (or previous) period if the maximum claim is made. Also a large loss cannot be used in the current (or previous) accounting period if there is no other income or gains, but would have to be carried forward. In that case, it may be advantageous to make a reduced capital allowance claim so that any loss in future accounting periods is greater. An increased loss in a future accounting period can be used against other income and gains in that period (compared with a brought forward loss that can only be used against trading income of the same trade) or can be group relieved (see later in this Study Text).

5 Other losses

5.1 Capital losses

FAST FORWARD

Capital losses can only be set against capital gains in the current or future accounting periods.

Capital losses can only be set against capital gains in the same or future accounting periods, never against income. Capital losses must be set against the first available gains and cannot be carried back.

5.2 Property business losses

FAST FORWARD

Property business losses are set off first against total profits in the current period and then carried forward against future total profits.

Property business losses are first deducted from the company's total profits of the current accounting period. Any excess is then:

(a) **Carried forward to the next accounting period** and treated as a loss made by the company in that period; or

(b) Available for surrender as **group relief** (see later in this Study Text).

Chapter Roundup

- Trading losses may be relieved by deduction from current total profits, from total profits of earlier periods or from future trading income.
- Trading losses carried forward can only be deducted from future trading profits arising from the same trade.
- Loss relief by deduction from total profits is given before qualifying charitable donations and so qualifying charitable donations may become unrelieved.
- Loss relief by deduction from total profits may be given by deduction from current period profits and from profits of the previous 12 months.
- A claim for current period loss relief can be made without a claim for carry back relief. However, if a loss is to be carried back, a claim for current period relief must have been made first.
- Trading losses in the last 12 months of trading can be carried back and deducted from total profits of the previous three years.
- When selecting a loss relief, consider the timing of the relief and the extent to which relief for qualifying charitable donations might be lost.
- Capital losses can only be set against capital gains in the current or future accounting periods.
- Property business losses are set off first against total profits in the current period and then carried forward against future total profits.

Quick Quiz

1 Against what profits may trading losses carried forward be set?

A Against all trading profits
B Against total profits
C Against profits from the same trade
D Against trading profits and gains

2 To what extent may losses be carried back?

3 Why might a company make a reduced capital allowances claim?

4 W plc made a chargeable gain of £40,000 in the year ended 31 March 2015 and a capital loss of £8,000 in the year ended 31 March 2016. Can W plc carry back the £8,000 loss against the gain of £40,000?

5 What loss reliefs are available to a company, which is not in a group, that has a property business loss?

Answers to Quick Quiz

1 C. Against profits from the same trade.

2 A loss may be carried back and set against total profits of the previous 12 months. The loss carried back is the trading loss left unrelieved after a claim to deduct the loss from total profits of the loss making accounting period has been made. A loss arising on the final 12 months of trading can be carried back and deducted from profits arising in the previous 36 months.

3 Reducing capital allowances in the current accounting period reduces the loss available for relief by deduction from total profits. Such a loss relief claim means that all of the available loss is utilised, possibly making qualifying charitable donations unrelieved. Reducing capital allowances reduces the size of the available loss and so may preserve relief for qualifying charitable donations. It may also generate a larger trading loss in future accounting periods which can be set against other income and gains (rather than a carried forward loss which can only be set against trading profits of the same trade) or group relieved.

4 No. Capital losses cannot be carried back.

5 Deduct from the company's total profits of the current accounting period. Excess carried forward the next accounting period and treated as a loss made by the company in that period.

Now try the questions below from the Practice Question Bank

Number	Type	Marks	Time
Q145	Section A	2	4 mins
Q146	Section A	2	4 mins
Q147	Section A	2	4 mins
Q148	Section C	10	20 mins

22

Groups

Topic list	Syllabus reference
1 Group relief	E5(a), E6
2 Chargeable gains group	E5(b), E6

Introduction

In the previous chapters in this section we have covered corporation tax on single companies, including the reliefs for losses.

In this chapter we consider the extent to which tax law recognises group relationships between companies. Companies in a group are still separate entities with their own tax liabilities, but tax law recognises the close relationship between group companies. They can, if they meet certain conditions, share their losses and also pass assets between each other without chargeable gains.

In the next chapter we consider administrative aspects of corporation tax.

Study guide

		Intellectual level
E5	**The effect of a group corporate structure for corporation tax purposes**	
(a)	Define a 75% group, and recognise the reliefs that are available to members of such a group.	2
(b)	Define a 75% chargeable gains group, and recognise the reliefs that are available to members of such a group.	2
E6	**The use of exemptions and reliefs in deferring and minimising corporation tax liabilities**	

Exam guide

Section A questions on groups could include the identification of members of a 75% group relief group or a 75% chargeable gains group. Groups may also feature in your examination as part of the 15 mark corporation tax question in Section C or in a 10 mark question in that Section or in Section B. Your first step in dealing with any group question must be to establish the relationship between the companies and identify what group or groups exist. You may find it helpful to draw a diagram. You must be aware that 75% group relief groups and 75% chargeable gains groups do not always coincide.

PER alert

One of the competencies you require to fulfil Performance Objective 15 Tax computations and assessments of the PER is to prepare or contribute to the computation or assessment of tax computations for single companies, groups or other entities. You can apply the knowledge you obtain from this chapter of the Study Text to help to demonstrate this competence.

Exam focus point

ACCA's article Groups, written by a member of the F6(UK) examination team states that it is important that F6 (UK) candidates know the **group relationship** that must exist for **reliefs to be available**. Working through the examples in this article will prepare you for anything that could be set in the exam.

1 Group relief

FAST FORWARD

Within a 75% group, current period trading losses, excess property business losses and excess qualifying charitable donations can be surrendered between UK companies. Group relief is available where the existence of a group is established through companies resident anywhere in the world.

1.1 Group relief provisions

The group relief provisions enable companies within a 75% group to transfer trading losses to other companies within the group, in order to set these against taxable total profits and reduce the group's overall corporation tax liability.

1.2 Definition of a 75% group

Key term

For one company to be a **75% subsidiary** of another, the holding company must have:

- At least 75% of the ordinary share capital of the subsidiary
- A right to at least 75% of the distributable income of the subsidiary
- A right to at least 75% of the net assets of the subsidiary were it to be wound up

Two companies are members of a 75% group where one is a 75% subsidiary of the other, or both are 75% subsidiaries of a third company.

Two companies are in a 75% group only if there is a 75% effective interest. Thus an 80% subsidiary (T) of an 80% subsidiary (S) is not in a 75% group with the holding company (H), because the effective interest is only 80% × 80% = 64%. However, S and T are in a 75% group and can claim group relief from each other. S **cannot** claim group relief from T and pass it on to H; it can only claim group relief for its own use.

A 75% group may include non-UK resident companies. **However, losses may generally only be surrendered between UK resident companies.**

Exam focus point

Relief for trading losses incurred by an overseas subsidiary is not examinable in your paper.

Illustration of a 75% group:

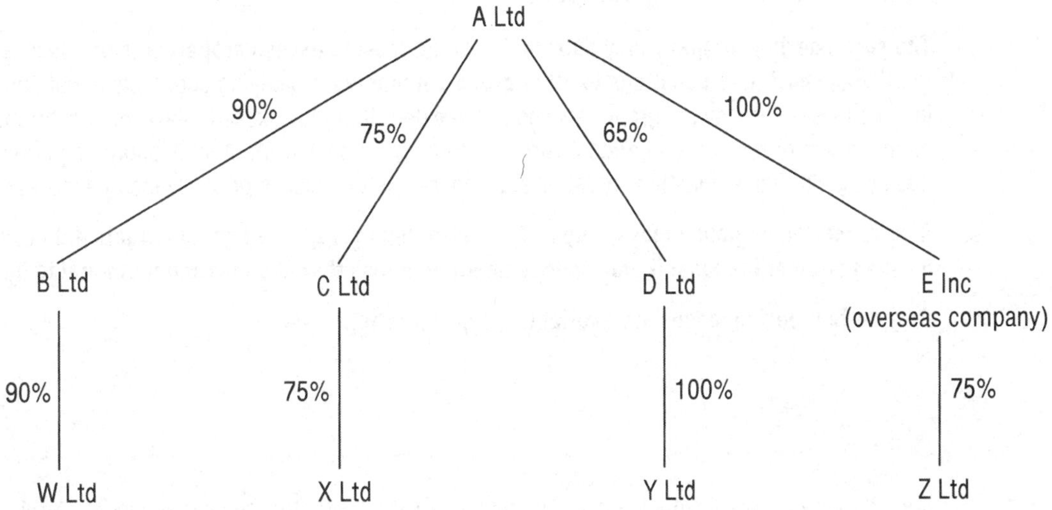

The companies in the 75% group are:

A Ltd
B Ltd
W Ltd (81% effective holding by A)
C Ltd
E Inc
Z Ltd (75% effective holding by A)

In addition C Ltd and X Ltd and also D Ltd and Y Ltd form their own separate mini-75% groups.

Note that a 75% group may also be called a 'group relief' group.

1.3 The relief

FAST FORWARD

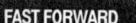

> A surrendering company can surrender any amount of its trading loss but a claimant company can only claim an amount up to its available taxable total profits.

1.3.1 Transfer of loss

A company which has made a loss (the surrendering company) may transfer its loss to another member of the 75% group (the claimant company).

1.3.2 The claimant company

A **claimant company** is **assumed to use its own current year losses** in working out the taxable total profits against which it may claim group relief, **even if it does not in fact claim relief for current losses against total profits.**

Furthermore, **group relief is set against taxable total profits after all other reliefs for the current period (for example qualifying charitable donations) or brought forward from earlier periods.**

Group relief is given before relief for any amounts carried back from later periods.

1.3.3 The surrendering company

The surrendering company may surrender trading losses, excess property income losses and excess qualifying charitable donations to other group companies. Qualifying charitable donations and property income losses can only be group relieved to the extent that they exceed total profits before taking account of any losses of the current period or brought forward or back from other accounting periods. Excess qualifying charitable donations must be surrendered before excess property income losses.

A surrendering company may group relieve a trading loss before setting it against its own total profits for the period of the loss. It may specify an amount less than the maximum amount to be surrendered.

Only current period losses are available for group relief.

Question

Group relief

K plc has one 75% subsidiary, L plc. The results for the group for the year ended 31 March 2017 are as follows:

	K plc	*L plc*
	£	£
Trading (loss)	(4,000)	(20,700)
Trading loss brought forward at 1 April 2016	0	(5,000)
Non-trading loan relationship income	10,000	2,900
Chargeable gain	15,000	0
Qualifying charitable donations	(2,000)	(3,200)

What is the maximum group relief that K plc can claim from L plc?

Answer

L plc can surrender losses under group relief as follows:

	£
Current year trading loss	20,700
Excess qualifying charitable donations £(3,200 – 2,900)	300
Total losses available for group relief	21,000

L plc cannot surrender its brought forward trading loss under group relief.

K plc has the following available taxable total profits:

	£
Non-trading loan relationship income	10,000
Chargeable gain	15,000
	25,000
Less current year trading loss	(4,000)
	21,000
Less qualifying charitable donations	(2,000)
Available taxable total profits	19,000
Maximum group relief that K plc can claim from L Ltd (lower of £21,000 and £19,000)	19,000

K plc must take account of its current year trading loss in working out available taxable total profits even if it does not actually make a claim for current year relief.

1.4 Corresponding accounting periods

FAST FORWARD

Profits and losses of corresponding accounting periods must be matched up.

Surrendered losses must be set against taxable total profits of a corresponding accounting period. If the accounting periods of a surrendering company and a claimant company are not the same this means that both the profits and losses must be apportioned so that only the results of the period of overlap may be set off. Apportionment is on a time basis. However, in the period when a company joins or leaves a group, an alternative method may be used if the result given by time-apportionment would be unjust or unreasonable.

Question

Corresponding accounting periods

	£
S Ltd incurs a trading loss for the year to 30 September 2016	(150,000)
H Ltd makes taxable total profits:	
for the year to 31 December 2015	200,000
for the year to 31 December 2016	100,000

What is the maximum group relief that H Ltd can claim from S Ltd?

Answer

H Ltd can claim group relief as follows.

	£
The lower of:	
For the year ended 31 December 2015 taxable total profits of the corresponding accounting period (1.10.15 – 31.12.15) are £200,000 × 3/12	50,000
Losses of the corresponding accounting period are £150,000 × 3/12	37,500

A claim for £37,500 of group relief may be made against H Ltd's taxable total profits for the year ended 31 December 2015.

	£
The lower of:	
For the year ended 31 December 2016 taxable total profits of the corresponding accounting period (1.1.16 – 30.9.16) are £100,000 × 9/12	75,000
Losses of the corresponding accounting period are £150,000 × 9/12	112,500

A claim for £75,000 of group relief may be made against H Ltd's taxable total profits for the year ended 31 December 2016.

If a claimant company claims relief for losses surrendered by more than one company, the total relief that may be claimed for a period that overlaps is limited to the proportion of the claimant's taxable total profits attributable to that period. Similarly, if a company surrenders losses to more than one claimant, the total losses that may be surrendered in a period that overlaps is limited to the proportion of the surrendering company's losses attributable to that period.

1.5 Claims

A claim for group relief is normally made on the claimant company's tax return. It is ineffective unless a notice of consent is also given by the surrendering company.

Groupwide claims/surrenders can be made as one person can act for two or more companies at once.

Any payment by the claimant company for group relief, up to the amount of the loss surrendered, is ignored for all corporation tax purposes.

1.6 Alternative loss reliefs

Several alternative loss reliefs may be available, including group relief. In making a choice consider:

- **How quickly relief will be obtained**: obtaining loss relief by using group relief is quicker than carry forward loss relief and so generally preferable to carrying forward the loss.
- **The extent to which relief for qualifying charitable donations might be lost:** group relief is deducted after qualifying charitable donations in the claimant company, so relief for these donations is not lost. By contrast, if the loss-making company claims relief for the loss against its own current year total profits, relief for qualifying charitable donations in that company may be wasted.

1.7 Capital allowances and group relief

Companies with profits may benefit by reducing their claims for capital allowances in a particular year. This may leave sufficient profits to take advantage of group relief which may only be available for the current year. The amount on which writing-down allowances can be claimed in later years is increased accordingly.

2 Chargeable gains group

FAST FORWARD

A chargeable gains group consists of the top company plus companies in which the top company has a 50% effective interest, provided there is a 75% holding at each level.

2.1 Definition

Companies are in a chargeable gains group if:

(a) At each level, there is a 75% holding
(b) The top company has an effective interest of over 50% in the group companies

If A holds 75% of B, B holds 75% of C and C holds 75% of D, then A, B and C are in such a group, but D is outside the group because A's interest in D is only 75% × 75% × 75% = 42.1875%. Furthermore, D is not in a group with C, because the group must include the top company (A).

The definition of a chargeable gains group is wider than that of a 75% group as only a effective 50% interest is needed compared to a 75% interest. However a company can only be in one chargeable gains group although it may be a member of more than one 75% group.

Illustration of a chargeable gains group:

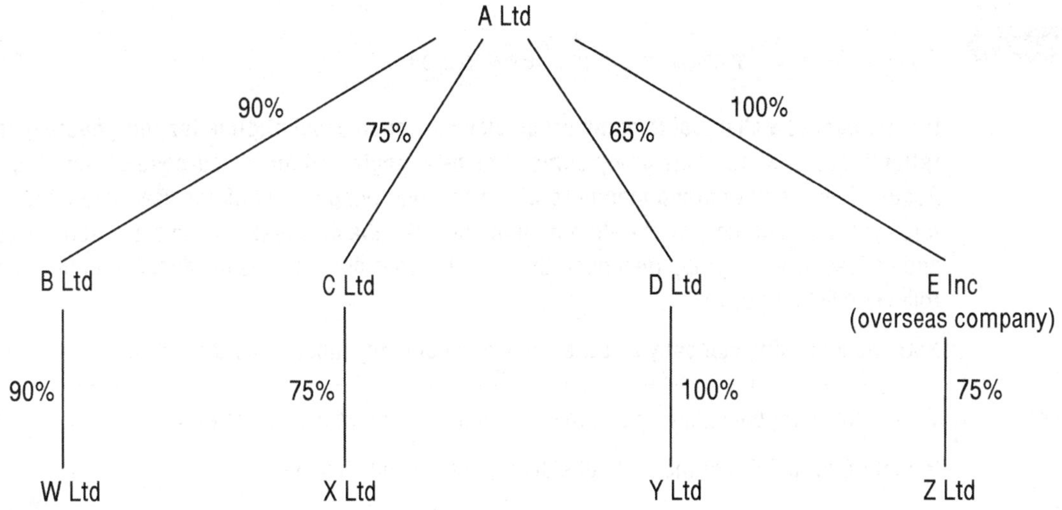

The companies in a group for chargeable gains purposes are:

A Ltd
B Ltd
W Ltd
C Ltd
X Ltd (75% subsidiary of 75% subsidiary, effective interest over 50%)
E Inc
Z Ltd

There is a separate chargeable gains group of D Ltd and Y Ltd.

2.2 Intra-group transfers

FAST FORWARD

Within a chargeable gains group, assets are transferred at no gain and no loss.

Companies in a chargeable gains group make intra-group transfers of chargeable assets without a chargeable gain or an allowable loss arising. No election is needed, as this relief is compulsory. The assets are deemed to be transferred at such a price as will give the transferor no gain and no loss (ie cost plus indexation allowance up to the date of transfer)

2.3 Matching group gains and losses

FAST FORWARD

Gains and losses can be matched within a group. This can be done by electing that all or part of any gain or loss is treated as transferred between group companies.

Two members of a chargeable gains group can elect to transfer a chargeable gain or allowable loss, or any part of a gain or loss, between them. This election must be made within two years of the end of the accounting period in which the gain or loss accrues in the company which is making the transfer.

Only current year losses can be transferred, not brought forward losses.

2.4 Rollover relief

FAST FORWARD

Rollover relief is available in a chargeable gains group.

If a member of a chargeable gains group disposes of an asset eligible for chargeable gains rollover relief it may treat all of the group companies as a single unit for the purpose of claiming such relief. Acquisitions by other group members within the qualifying period of one year before the disposal to three years afterwards may therefore **be matched with the disposal**. If an asset is transferred at no gain and no loss between group members, that transfer does not count as the acquisition of an asset for rollover relief purpose.

Both the disposing company and the acquiring company must make the claim.

Exam focus point

Try to remember the following summary – it will be of great help in the exam.

Parent Co **owns** 75% or more of subsidiary (directly and effectively)

- Surrender trading losses, excess property business losses, excess qualifying charitable donations to companies with some taxable total profits for same time period

Parent Co **owns** 75% or more of subsidiary and subsidiary owns 75% or more of its subsidiaries

- Transfer assets between companies automatically at no gain/no loss
- Chargeable gains and losses can be matched between group member companies
- All companies treated as one for rollover relief purposes

Chapter Roundup

- Within a 75% group, current period trading losses, excess property business losses and excess qualifying charitable donations can be surrendered between UK companies. Group relief is available where the existence of a group is established through companies resident anywhere in the world.
- A surrendering company can surrender any amount of its trading loss but a claimant company can only claim an amount up to its available taxable total profits.
- Profits and losses of corresponding accounting periods must be matched up.
- A chargeable gains group consists of the top company plus companies in which the top company has a 50% effective interest, provided there is a 75% holding at each level.
- Within a chargeable gains group, assets are transferred at no gain and no loss.
- Gains and losses can be matched within a group. This can be done by electing that all or part of any gain or loss is treated as transferred between group companies.
- Rollover relief is available in a chargeable gains group.

Quick Quiz

1 List the types of losses which may be group relieved.

2 N Ltd and M Ltd are in a group relief group. N Ltd prepared accounts for the year to 31 March 2017 and had taxable total profits of £96,000. M Ltd prepared accounts for the nine month period ended 31 December 2016 and had a trading loss of £80,000. How much of M Ltd's loss for the period ended 31 December 2016 can be group relieved against N Ltd's taxable total profits for the year to 31 March 2017?

3 G Ltd owns 85% of the ordinary share capital of H Ltd and 70% of the ordinary share capital of J Ltd. H Ltd owns 80% of the ordinary share capital of K Ltd. Which of the companies are in a chargeable gains group with G Ltd?

4 When may assets be transferred intra-group at no gain and no loss?

5 How can chargeable gains and losses within a group be matched with each other?

Answers to Quick Quiz

1 Trading losses, excess property business losses and excess qualifying charitable donations.

2 £72,000. Corresponding period is 1 April 2016 to 31 December 2016. Lower of N Ltd's taxable total profits of the period of £96,000 × 9/12 = £72,000 and M Ltd's loss of the period of £80,000.

3 H Ltd and K Ltd. There is at least a 75% interest at each level and G Ltd has an effective interest of at least 50% in K Ltd. J Ltd is not a member of the chargeable gains group as G Ltd does not have at least a 75% interest in it.

4 No gain no loss asset transfers are mandatory between companies in a chargeable gains group.

5 Two members of a gains group can elect that all or part of a gain or loss is transferred between them within two years of the end of the accounting period in which the gain or loss accrued. This election allows the group to match its gains and losses in one company.

Now try the questions below from the Practice Question Bank

Number	Type	Marks	Time
Q149	Section A	2	4 mins
Q150	Section A	2	4 mins
Q151	Section A	2	4 mins
Q152	Section C	10	20 mins

23

Self assessment and payment of tax by companies

Topic list	Syllabus reference
1 Corporation tax self assessment	A3(b)
2 Returns, records and claims	A4(a), (d)
3 Compliance checks, appeals and disputes	A5(a), (b)
4 Payment of corporation tax and interest	A4(b), (c), A6(a)
5 Penalties	A6(a)

Introduction

We now complete our corporation tax studies by looking at the self assessment system for corporation tax, under which companies must file returns and pay the tax due.

In the following chapters we will turn our attention to VAT, which applies to both incorporated and unincorporated businesses.

Study guide

		Intellectual level
A3	**The systems for self assessment and the making of returns**	
(b)	Explain and apply the features of the self assessment system as it applies to companies, including the use of iXBRL.	2
A4	**The time limits for the submission of information, claims and payment of tax, including payments on account**	
(a)	Recognise the time limits that apply to the filing of returns and the making of claims.	2
(b)	Recognise the due dates for the payment of tax under the self-assessment system.	2
(c)	Explain how large companies are required to account for corporation tax on a quarterly basis and compute the quarterly instalment payments.	2
(d)	List the information and records that taxpayers need to retain for tax purposes.	1
A5	**The procedures relating to compliance checks, appeals and disputes**	
(a)	Explain the circumstances in which HM Revenue & Customs can make a compliance check into a self assessment tax return.	2
(b)	Explain the procedures for dealing with appeals and First and Upper Tier Tribunals.	2
A6	**Penalties for non-compliance**	
(a)	Calculate late payment interest and state the penalties that can be charged.	2

Exam guide

Section A questions on corporation tax administration could include the identification of filing dates and the calculation of interest on late paid tax or penalties. You may also be tested on these aspects in a Section B question. In Section C you might be asked to explain an aspect of the tax administration system such as the appeals process.

1 Corporation tax self assessment

FAST FORWARD

A company that does not receive a notice requiring a return to be filed must, if it is chargeable to tax, notify HMRC within 12 months of the end of the accounting period.

1.1 Introduction

PER alert

One of the competencies you require to fulfil Performance Objective 16 Tax compliance and verification of the PER is to explain tax filing and payment requirements and the consequences of non-compliance to clients. You can apply the knowledge you obtain from this section of the Study Text to help to demonstrate this competence.

The self assessment system relies upon the company completing and filing a tax return and paying the tax due. The system is enforced by a system of penalties for failure to comply within the set time limits, and by interest for late payment of tax.

Dormant companies and companies which have not yet started to trade may not be required to complete tax returns. Such companies have a duty to notify HMRC when they should be brought within the self assessment system.

1.2 Notification of first accounting period

A company must notify HMRC of the beginning of its first accounting period (ie usually when it starts to trade) and the beginning of any subsequent period that does not immediately follow the end of a previous accounting period. The notice must be in the prescribed form and submitted within three months of the relevant date.

1.3 Notification of chargeability

A company that does not receive a notice requiring a return to be filed must, if it is chargeable to tax, **notify HMRC within twelve months of the end of the accounting period**.

2 Returns, records and claims

PER alert

One of the competencies you require to fulfil Performance Objective 16 Tax compliance and verification of the PER is to verify and question client submissions and ensure timely submission of all relevant information to the tax authorities by the due date. You can apply the knowledge you obtain from this section of the Study Text to help to demonstrate this competence.

FAST FORWARD

A company must, in general, file a tax return within 12 months of the end of an accounting period.

2.1 Returns

A company's tax return must be filed electronically and must include a self assessment of any tax payable. Limited companies are also required to file electronically a copy of their accounts. The filing of accounts must be done in inLine eXtensible Business Reporting Language (iXBRL).

iXBRL is a standard for reporting business information in an electronic form which uses tags that can be read by computers. HMRC supplies software which can be used by small companies with simple accounts. This software automatically produces accounts and tax computations in the correct format. Other companies can use:

(a) Other software that automatically produces iXBRL accounts and computations
(b) A tagging service which will apply the appropriate tags to accounts and computations
(c) Software that enables the appropriate tags to be added to accounts and computations

The tags used are contained in dictionaries known as taxonomies, with different taxonomies for different purposes. The tagging of tax computations is based on the corporation tax computational taxonomy, which includes over 1,200 relevant tags.

An obligation to file a return arises only when the company receives a notice requiring a return. A return is required for each accounting period ending during or at the end of the period specified in the notice requiring a return. A company also has to file a return for certain other periods which are not accounting periods (eg for a period when the company is dormant).

A notice to file a return may also require other information, accounts and reports. For a UK resident company the requirement to deliver accounts normally extends only to the accounts required under the Companies Act.

A return is due on or before the filing date. This is normally the later of:

(a) **12 months after the end of the period to which the return relates**
(b) **Three months from the date on which the notice requiring the return was made**

The relevant period of account is that in which the accounting period to which the return relates ends.

2.2 Amending a return

A company may amend a return within 12 months of the filing date.

HMRC may amend a return to correct obvious errors, or anything else that an officer has reason to believe is incorrect in the light of information available, within nine months of the day the return was filed, or if the correction is to an amended return, within nine months of the filing of an amendment. The company may amend its return so as to reject the correction. If the time limit for amendments has expired, the company may reject the correction by giving notice within three months.

2.3 Records

Companies must keep records until the latest of:

(a) **Six years from the end of the accounting period**
(b) **The date any compliance check enquiries are completed**
(c) **The date after which a compliance check enquiry may not be commenced**

All business records and accounts, including contracts and receipts, must be kept or information showing that the company has prepared a complete and correct tax return.

If a return is demanded more than six years after the end of the accounting period, any records or information which the company still has must be kept until the later of the end of a compliance check enquiry and the expiry of the right to start one.

2.4 Claims

Wherever possible claims must be made on a tax return or on an amendment to it and must be quantified at the time the return is made.

If a company believes that it has paid excessive tax, for example as a result of an error in its tax return, a claim may be made within four years from the end of the accounting period. An appeal against a decision on such a claim must be made within 30 days. A claim may not be made if the return was made in accordance with a generally accepted practice which prevailed at the time.

Other claims must be made by four years after the end of the accounting period, unless a different time limit is specified.

If HMRC amend a self assessment or issue a discovery assessment then the company has a further period to make, vary or withdraw a claim (unless the claim is irrevocable) even if this is outside the normal time limit. The period is one year from the end of the accounting period in which the amendment or assessment was made, or one year from the end of the accounting period in which the compliance check enquiry was complete if the amendment is the result of a compliance check enquiry. The relief is limited where there has been fraudulent or negligent conduct by the company or its agent.

3 Compliance checks, appeals and disputes

PER alert

One of the competencies you require to fulfil Performance Objective 16 Tax compliance and verification of the PER is to correspond appropriately and in a professional manner with the relevant parties in relation to both routine and specific matters/enquiries. You can apply the knowledge you obtain from this section of the Study Text to help to demonstrate this competence.

FAST FORWARD

HMRC can carry out compliance check enquiries on returns.

3.1 Compliance check enquiries

HM Revenue and Customs may decide to conduct a compliance check enquiry on a return, claim or election that has been submitted by a company, in the same way as for individuals.

The officer of HM Revenue and Customs must give written notice of his intention to conduct a compliance check enquiry. The notice must be given by:

(a) **The first anniversary of the due filing date** (most group companies) or **the actual filing date** (other companies), **if the return was delivered on or before the due filing date;** or

(b) **The quarter day following the first anniversary of the actual filing date, if the return is filed after the due filing date. The quarter days are 31 January, 30 April, 31 July and 31 October.**

If the company amends the return after the due filing date, the compliance check enquiry 'window' extends to the quarter day following the first anniversary of the date the amendment was filed. Where the compliance check enquiry was not started within the limit which would have applied had no amendment been filed, the enquiry is restricted to matters contained in the amendment.

3.2 Appeals and disputes

The procedure for HMRC internal reviews and appeals relating to individuals, discussed earlier in this Study Text, also applies to companies.

4 Payment of corporation tax and interest

PER alert

One of the competencies you require to fulfil Performance Objective 16 Tax compliance and verification of the PER is to determine the incidence (timing) of tax liabilities and their impact on cash flow/financing requirements. You can apply the knowledge you obtain from this section of the Study Text to help to demonstrate this competence.

FAST FORWARD

In general, corporation tax is due nine months and one day after the end of an accounting period but large companies must pay their corporation tax in quarterly instalments.

4.1 Companies which are not large companies

Corporation tax is due for payment by **companies which are not large companies** (see below), **nine months and one day after the end of the accounting period**. For example, if a company, which is not a large company, has an accounting period ending on 31 December 2016, the corporation tax for the period is payable on 1 October 2017.

4.2 Large companies

4.2.1 Payment in instalments

Large companies must pay their corporation tax in instalments.

4.2.2 What is a large company?

A large company is one whose profits exceed the profit threshold.

For this purpose profits (which may be referred to as **augmented profits**) **are the taxable total profits of the company plus dividends received from other companies.**

The exception to this rule is that any dividends received from a 51% subsidiary company (sometimes called 'group dividends') **are ignored and so are not included.**

Key term

A company (company B) is a **51% subsidiary** of company A if more than 50% of company B's ordinary shares are owned directly or indirectly by company A.

Question — Profits

Q plc had the following results for the year ended 31 March 2017.

	£
Taxable total profits	1,142,000
Dividend received 1 May 2016 from 40% subsidiary	278,000
Dividend received 1 August 2016 from 90% subsidiary	378,000

What are Q plc's profits for determining whether it is a large company?

Answer

	£
Taxable total profits	1,142,000
Dividend from 40% subsidiary	278,000
Profits	1,420,000

The dividend from the 90% subsidiary is ignored because this is from a company which is a '51% subsidiary' of Q plc.

The profit threshold is £1,500,000 for a 12 month accounting period.

Exam focus point

The profit threshold will be given in the tax rates and allowances in the exam.

The profit threshold is reduced in two circumstances:

(a) The company has a **short accounting period. In this case the threshold is scaled down**. For example, if a company has a three month accounting period, the threshold is (£1,500,000 × 3/12) = £375,000.

(b) The company has **related 51% group companies at the end of the immediately preceding accounting period**. The threshold is **divided by that number of related 51% group companies**, including the company itself.

Key term

A company (company B) is a related **51% group company** of another company (company A) if company A is a 51% subsidiary of company B or company B is a 51% subsidiary of company A or both company A and company B are 51% subsidiaries of another company. Non-UK resident company may be included as related 51% group companies. Companies which do not carry on a trade (dormant companies) are not related 51% group companies.

Question — Related 51% group companies

Y Ltd prepares accounts to 31 March each year. At 31 March 2016, Y Ltd had three wholly owned subsidiary companies – V Ltd, X Ltd and Z Ltd – and owned 45% of the ordinary shares of U Ltd. X Ltd did not carry on any trade or business during the year to 31 March 2016. Z Ltd is not resident in the UK.

Y Ltd acquired 75% of the ordinary shares of T Ltd on 1 July 2016.

What is the profit threshold for Y Ltd for determining corporation tax payment dates for the year ending 31 March 2017?

Answer

V Ltd and Z Ltd (residence not relevant) are related 51% group companies with Y Ltd so there are three related 51% group companies.

X Ltd is not a related 51% group company because it is dormant.

U Ltd is not a related 51% group company because it is not a 51% subsidiary of Y Ltd.

T Ltd was not a related 51% group company at the end of the previous accounting period and so does not reduce the profit threshold of Y Ltd in respect of the year ending 31 March 2017.

The profit threshold for Y Ltd for the year ending 31 March 2017 is therefore £(1,500,000/3) = £500,000.

4.2.3 Due dates for instalments

Instalments are due on the 14th day of the month, starting in the seventh month of the accounting period. Provided that the accounting period is 12 months long subsequent instalments are due in the tenth month during the accounting period and in the first and fourth months after the end of the accounting period. If an accounting period is less than 12 months long subsequent instalments are due at three monthly intervals but with the final payment being due in the fourth month of the next accounting period.

Question

Instalment due dates

D Ltd is a large company which has a 12 month accounting period which ends on 31 December 2016. What are the due dates for payment of D Ltd's instalments of corporation tax for this accounting period?

Answer

14 July 2016, 14 October 2016, 14 January 2017 and 14 April 2017.

4.2.4 Calculating the instalments

Instalments are based on the estimated corporation tax liability for the current period (not the previous period). **A company is therefore required to estimate its corporation tax liability before the end of the accounting period, and must revise its estimate each quarter.** It is extremely important for companies to forecast their tax liabilities accurately. Large companies whose directors are poor at estimating may find their companies incurring significant interest charges. **Companies can have instalments repaid if they later conclude the instalments ought not to have been paid.**

The amount of each instalment is computed by:

(a) **Working out 3 × CT/n** where CT is the amount of the estimated corporation tax liability payable in instalments for the period and n is the number of months in the period

(b) **Allocating the smaller of that amount and the total estimated corporation tax liability to the first instalment**

(c) **Repeating the process for later instalments until the amount allocated is equal to the corporation tax liability**

If the company has an accounting period of 12 months, there will be four instalments and each instalment should be 25% of the estimated amount due.

Question — **Instalments for 12 month accounting period**

B Ltd is a large company which has a corporation tax liability of £440,000 for the year ended 31 March 2017. Show when the corporation tax liability is due for payment.

Answer

Due date	*Amount*
	£
14 October 2016	110,000
14 January 2017	110,000
14 April 2017	110,000
14 July 2017	110,000
	440,000

The position is slightly more complicated if the company has an accounting period of less than 12 months, as is shown in the following question.

Question — **Instalments for short accounting period**

K plc is a large company which has a corporation tax liability of £880,000 for the eight month accounting period to 30 September 2016. Show when the corporation tax liability is due for payment.

Answer

£880,000 must be paid in instalments.

The amount of each instalment is $3 \times \frac{£880,000}{8}$ = £330,000

The due dates and the amounts payable are:

	£
14 August 2016	330,000
14 November 2016	330,000
14 January 2017	220,000 (balance)

4.2.5 Exceptions

A company is not required to pay instalments in the first year that it is a large company, unless its profits exceed £10 million. The £10 million threshold is reduced proportionately by the number of related 51% group companies (including the company in question) at the end of the previous accounting period.

Any company whose corporation tax liability does not exceed £10,000 need not pay by instalments.

4.3 Interest on late or overpaid tax

Interest runs from the due date on over/underpaid instalments. The position is looked at cumulatively after the due date for each instalment. HMRC calculate the interest position after the company submits its corporation tax return.

Companies which do not pay by instalments are charged interest if they pay their corporation tax after the due date, and will receive interest if they overpay their tax or pay it early.

Interest paid/received on late payments or over payments of corporation tax is dealt with as investment income as interest paid/received on a non-trading loan relationship.

For the purpose of F6 (UK) exams in June 2017, September 2017, December 2017 and March 2018, the assumed rate of interest on underpaid tax is 3% and the assumed rate of interest on overpaid tax is 0.5%.

5 Penalties

PER alert

One of the competencies you require to fulfil Performance Objective 16 Tax compliance and verification of the PER is to explain tax filing and payment requirements and the consequences of non-compliance to clients. You can apply the knowledge you obtain from this section of the Study Text to help to demonstrate this competence.

FAST FORWARD

Penalties may be levied for failure to notify the first accounting period, failure to notify chargeability, the late filing of returns, failure to keep records, and errors in returns.

5.1 Notification of first accounting period

Failure to notify, and provide information about, the first accounting period can mean a penalty of £300 plus £60 per day the information is outstanding, and a penalty of up to £3,000 for fraudulently or negligently giving incorrect information.

5.2 Notification of chargeability

The common penalty regime for late notification of chargeability discussed earlier in this Study Text in relation to individuals also applies to companies.

5.3 Late filing penalties

There is a £100 penalty for a failure to submit a return on time, rising to £200 if the delay exceeds three months. These penalties become £500 and £1,000 respectively when a return was late (or never submitted) for each of the preceding two accounting periods.

An additional tax geared penalty is applied if a return is more than six months late. The penalty is 10% of the tax unpaid six months after the return was due if the total delay is up to 12 months, and 20% of that tax if the return is over 12 months late.

There is a tax geared penalty for a fraudulent or negligent return and for failing to correct an innocent error without unreasonable delay. The maximum penalty is equal to the tax that would have been lost had the return been accepted as correct. HMRC can mitigate this penalty. If a company is liable to more than one tax geared penalty, the total penalty is limited to the maximum single penalty that could be charged.

5.4 Failure to keep records

Failure to keep records can lead to a **penalty of up to £3,000** for each accounting period affected.

5.5 Errors in returns

The common penalty regime for making errors in tax returns discussed earlier in this Study Text applies for corporation tax.

Chapter Roundup

- A company that does not receive a notice requiring a return to be filed must, if it is chargeable to tax, notify HMRC within 12 months of the end of the accounting period.
- A company must, in general, file a tax return within 12 months of the end of an accounting period.
- HMRC can carry out compliance check enquiries on returns.
- In general, corporation tax is due nine months and one day after the end of an accounting period, but large companies must pay their corporation tax in quarterly instalments.
- Penalties may be levied for failure to notify the first accounting period, failure to notify chargeability, the late filing of returns, failure to keep records, and errors in returns.

Quick Quiz

1 When must HMRC give notice to a non-group company that it is going to start a compliance check enquiry if the return was filed on or before the due filing date?

2 A plc has one wholly owned subsidiary, B plc which it has owned for many years. A plc prepared accounts for the nine-months to 31 December 2016. What is the profit threshold for this accounting period for A plc?

3 State the due dates for the payment of quarterly instalments of corporation tax for a 12 month accounting period.

4 Q plc submits its corporation tax return four months late. This is the first late return made by the company. What is the late filing penalty?

5 What is the maximum penalty if a company fails to keep records?

A £1,000
B £2,000
C £3,000
D £4,000

Answers to Quick Quiz

1 Notice must be given by the first anniversary of the actual filing date.

2 There are two related 51% group companies and a short accounting period. The profit threshold is therefore:

£1,500,000/2 × 9/12 = £562,500

3 14th day of:

(a) 7th month in AP
(b) 10th month in AP
(c) 1st month after AP ends
(d) 4th month after AP ends

4 £200 as the delay exceeds three months.

5 C. £3,000 for each accounting period affected.

Now try the questions below from the Practice Question Bank

Number	Type	Marks	Time
Q153	Section A	2	4 mins
Q154	Section A	2	4 mins
Q155	Section A	2	4 mins
Q156	Section B	2	4 mins
Q157	Section B	2	4 mins
Q158	Section B	2	4 mins
Q159	Section B	2	4 mins
Q160	Section B	2	4 mins
Q161	Section C	10	20 mins

PART G

Value added tax

An introduction to VAT

24

Topic list	Syllabus reference
1 The scope of VAT	F2
2 Zero-rated and exempt supplies	F2(f)
3 Registration	F1(a), (c)
4 Deregistration	F1(a)
5 Transfer of going concern	F2(a)
6 Pre-registration input tax	F1(b)
7 Accounting for and administering VAT	F2(a), (b)
8 The tax point	F2(c)
9 The valuation of supplies	F2(e)
10 The deduction of input tax	F2(g)
11 Relief for impairment losses	F2(h)

Introduction

The final topic in our studies is value added tax (VAT). We cover VAT in this and the next chapter.

VAT is a tax on turnover rather than on profits. As the name suggests, it is charged on the value added. The VAT is collected bit by bit along the chain of manufacturer, wholesaler, retailer, until it finally hits the consumer who does not add value, but uses up the goods.

In this chapter we look at the scope of VAT and then consider when a business must, or may, be registered for VAT. We also look at administration and accounting. VAT is a tax with simple computations but many detailed rules to ensure its enforcement. You may find it easier to absorb the detail if you ask yourself, in relation to each rule, exactly how it helps to enforce the tax.

Finally, we look at the rules regarding the deduction of input tax and relief for impairment losses on trade debts.

In the following chapter we will conclude our study of VAT and the F6 syllabus.

Study guide

		Intellectual level
F1	**The VAT registration requirements**	
(a)	Recognise the circumstances in which a person must register or deregister for VAT (compulsory) and when a person may register or deregister for VAT (voluntary).	2
(b)	Recognise the circumstances in which pre-registration input VAT can be recovered.	2
(c)	Explain the conditions that must be met for two or more companies to be treated as a group for VAT purposes, and the consequences of being so treated.	1
F2	**The computation of VAT liabilities**	
(a)	Calculate the amount of VAT payable/recoverable.	2
(b)	Understand how VAT is accounted for and administered.	2
(c)	Recognise the tax point when goods or services are supplied.	2
(e)	Explain and apply the principles regarding the valuation of supplies.	2
(f)	Recognise the principal zero rated and exempt supplies.	2
(g)	Recognise the circumstances in which input VAT is non-deductible.	2
(h)	Recognise the relief that is available for impairment losses on trade debts.	2

Exam guide

Section A questions on basic value added tax (VAT) topics could include identification of the date for registration and dealing with impairment losses. Section B questions could also include computing the amount of VAT payable or recoverable. In Section C, registration requirements may be examined in more detail; make sure that you know the difference between the historical test and the future test, and the dates by which HMRC must be notified and registration takes effect. Do not overlook pre-registration input VAT. You may also be required to calculate the VAT due for a return period; watch out for non deductible input tax and check the dates if there are impairment losses.

Exam focus point

ACCA's article Value added tax, written by a member of the F6(UK) examination team, in Part 1 considers **VAT registration and deregistration**, and **output and input** VAT.

1 The scope of VAT

FAST FORWARD

VAT is charged on turnover at each stage in a production process, but in such a way that the burden is borne by the final consumer.

1.1 The nature of VAT

VAT is a tax on turnover, not on profits. The basic principle is that the VAT should be borne by the final consumer. Registered traders may deduct the tax which they suffer on supplies to them (input tax) from the tax which they charge to their customers (output tax) at the time this is paid to HMRC. Thus, at each stage of the manufacturing or service process, the net VAT paid is on the value added at that stage.

1.2 Example: the VAT charge

A forester sells wood to a furniture maker for £100 plus VAT. The furniture maker uses this wood to make a table and sells the table to a shop for £150 plus VAT. The shop then sells the table to the final consumer for £300 plus VAT of 20%. VAT will be accounted for to HMRC as follows.

	Cost	Input tax 20%	Net sale price	Output tax 20%	Payable to HMRC
	£	£	£	£	£
Forester	0	0	100	20.00	20.00
Furniture maker	100	20.00	150	30.00	10.00
Shop	150	30.00	300	60.00	30.00
					60.00

Because the traders involved account to HMRC for VAT charged less VAT suffered, their profits for income tax or corporation tax purposes are based on sales and purchases net of VAT.

1.3 Taxable supplies

FAST FORWARD

VAT is chargeable on taxable supplies made by a taxable person in the course or furtherance of any business carried on by him. Supplies may be of goods or services.

Key term

A **taxable supply** is a supply of goods or services made in the UK, other than an exempt supply.

PER alert

One of the competencies you require to fulfil Performance Objective 15 Tax computations and assessments of the PER is to prepare or contribute to computations or assessments of indirect tax liabilities. You can apply the knowledge you obtain from this section of the Study Text to help to demonstrate this competence.

A taxable supply is either standard-rated or zero-rated. The standard rate is 20%.

Certain supplies, which fall within the classification of standard rate supplies, are charged at a reduced rate of 5%. An example is the supply of domestic fuel.

Zero-rated supplies are taxable at 0%. A taxable supplier whose outputs are zero-rated but whose inputs are standard-rated will obtain repayments of the VAT paid on purchases.

An exempt supply is not chargeable to VAT. A person making exempt supplies is unable to recover VAT on inputs. The exempt supplier thus has to shoulder the burden of VAT. Of course, he may increase his prices to pass on the charge, but he cannot issue a VAT invoice which would enable a taxable customer to obtain a credit for VAT, since no VAT is chargeable on his supplies.

1.4 Example: standard-rated, zero-rated and exempt supplies

Here are figures for three traders, the first with standard-rated outputs, the second with zero-rated outputs and the third with exempt outputs. All their inputs are standard-rated. The standard rate is 20%.

	Standard-rated	*Zero-rated*	*Exempt*
	£	£	£
Inputs	20,000	20,000	20,000
VAT	4,000	4,000	4,000
	24,000	24,000	24,000
Outputs	30,000	30,000	30,000
VAT	6,000	0	0
	36,000	30,000	30,000
Pay/(reclaim)	2,000	(4,000)	0
Net profit	10,000	10,000	6,000

VAT legislation lists zero-rated, reduced rate and exempt supplies. There is no list of standard-rated supplies. Therefore any supplies that do not appear on the zero-rated, reduced rate or exempt lists will be assumed to be standard-rated by default.

We look at the main categories of zero-rated and exempt supplies later in this chapter.

1.5 Supplies of goods

Goods are supplied if exclusive ownership of the goods passes to another person.

The following are treated as supplies of goods.

- The supply of any form of power, heat, refrigeration or ventilation, or of water
- The grant, assignment or surrender of a major interest (the freehold or a lease for over 21 years) in land
- Taking goods permanently out of the business for the non-business use of a taxable person or for other private purposes including the supply of goods by an employer to an employee for his private use
- Transfers under an agreement contemplating a transfer of ownership, such as a hire purchase agreement

Gifts of goods are normally treated as sales at cost (so VAT is due). **However, business gifts are not supplies of goods if:**

(a) **The total cost of gifts made to the same person does not exceed £50 in any 12 month period.** If the £50 limit is exceeded, output tax will be due in full on the total of gifts made. Once the limit has been exceeded a new £50 limit and new 12 month period begins.

(b) **The gift is a sample** (unlimited number of samples allowed).

1.6 Supplies of services

Apart from a few specific exceptions, **any supply which is not a supply of goods and which is done for a consideration is a supply of services.** A consideration is any form of payment in money or in kind, including anything which is itself a supply.

A supply of services also takes place if:

- Goods are lent to someone for use outside the business
- Goods are hired to someone
- Services bought for business purposes are used for private purposes

1.7 Taxable persons

The term 'person' includes individuals, partnerships (which are treated as single entities, ignoring the individual partners) and **companies. If a person is in business making taxable supplies, then the value of these supplies is called the taxable turnover. If a person's taxable turnover exceeds certain limits then he is a taxable person and should be registered for VAT** (see later in this Study Text).

2 Zero-rated and exempt supplies

FAST FORWARD

Some supplies are taxable (either standard-rated, reduced-rate or zero-rated). Others are exempt.

2.1 Types of supply

We have seen that a trader may make standard rated, reduced-rate, zero-rated or exempt supplies.

If a trader makes a supply we need to categorise that supply for VAT as follows:

Step 1 Consider the zero-rated list to see if it is zero-rated. If not:

Step 2 Consider the exempt list to see if it is exempt. If not:

Step 3 Consider the reduced rate list to see if the reduced rate of VAT applies. If not:

Step 4 The supply is standard rated.

Exam focus point

In the exam you will not be expected to categorise all the zero-rated and exempt supplies. The main supplies in each group are highlighted below.

2.2 Zero-rated supplies

The following are items on the **zero-rated list**.

(a) Human and animal food
(b) Sewerage services and water
(c) Printed matter used for reading (eg books, newspapers)
(d) Construction work on new homes or the sale of the freehold of new homes by builders
(e) Transport of goods and passengers
(f) Drugs and medicines on prescription or provided in private hospitals
(g) Clothing and footwear for young children and certain protective clothing eg motor cyclists' crash helmets

2.3 Exempt supplies

The following are items on the **exempt** list.

(a) Financial services
(b) Insurance
(c) Public postal services provided by the Royal Mail under its duty to provide a universal postal service (eg first and second class letters)
(d) Betting and gaming
(e) Certain education and vocational training
(f) Health services
(g) Burial and cremation services
(h) Sale of freeholds of buildings (other than commercial buildings less than 3 years old) and leaseholds of land and buildings.

2.4 Exceptions to the general rule

The zero-rated, exempt and reduced rate lists outline general categories of goods or services which are either zero-rated or exempt or charged at a rate of 5%. However, the VAT legislation then goes into great detail to outline exceptions to the general rule.

For example the zero-rated list states human food is zero-rated. However, the legislation then states that food supplied in the course of catering (eg restaurant meals, hot takeaways) is not zero-rated. Luxury items of food (eg crisps, peanuts, chocolate covered biscuits) are also not zero-rated.

In the exempt list we are told that financial services are exempt. However the legislation then goes on to state that this does not include credit management, except if the credit management is by the person who also granted the credit. Investment advice is also not exempt.

Land and buildings is a complex topic. Broadly, sales of new homes are zero-rated, sales of new commercial buildings are standard rated and most other transactions are exempt.

Thus great care must be taken when categorising goods or services as zero-rated, exempt or standard-rated. It is not as straightforward as it may first appear.

3 Registration

FAST FORWARD

A trader becomes liable to register for VAT if the value of taxable supplies in any past period up to 12 months exceeds £83,000 or if there are reasonable grounds for believing that the value of the taxable supplies will exceed £83,000 in the next 30 days alone. A trader may also register voluntarily.

3.1 Compulsory registration

3.1.1 Historical test

At the end of every month a trader must calculate his cumulative turnover of taxable supplies for the previous 12 months to date. Taxable supplies are the total of standard rated supplies and zero rated supplies, but not exempt supplies. **The trader becomes liable to register for VAT if the value of his cumulative taxable supplies** (excluding VAT) **exceeds £83,000**. The person is required to notify HMRC within 30 days of the end of the month in which the £83,000 limit is exceeded. HMRC will then register the person with effect from the end of the month following the month in which the £83,000 was exceeded, or from an earlier date if they and the trader agree.

Registration under this rule is not required if HMRC are satisfied that the value of the trader's taxable supplies (excluding VAT) in the year then starting will not exceed £81,000.

Question — **VAT registration**

Fred started to trade cutlery on 1 January 2016. Sales (excluding VAT) were £7,500 a month for the first nine months and £8,400 a month thereafter. From what date should Fred be registered for VAT?

Answer

	£	
Sales to 31 October 2016	75,900	
Sales to 30 November 2016	84,300	(exceeds £83,000)

Fred must notify his liability to register by 30 December 2016 (not 31 December) and will be registered and charge VAT from 1 January 2017.

3.1.2 Future test

A person is also liable to register **at any time** (not necessarily at the end of the month) if there are reasonable grounds for believing that his taxable supplies (excluding VAT) in the following 30 days will exceed £83,000. Only taxable turnover of that 30 day period is considered **not** cumulative turnover. HMRC must be notified by the end of the 30 day period and registration will be with effect from the beginning of that period.

Exam focus point

> Be sure you know the difference between the historic and future tests.

Question — Future test

Constant Ltd started to trade on 1 February 2016 with sales of goods as follows

	VAT status	*£ per month*
Goods A	standard-rated	7,000
Goods B	zero-rated	3,000

On 1 June 2016 Constant Ltd signed a contract to provide £40,000 of Goods A and £35,000 of Goods B to Unicorn plc by 25 June 2016. This is in addition to normal sales.

From which date should Constant Ltd be registered for VAT?

Answer

Goods A and B are taxable supplies.

Cumulative turnover at end of May 2016 is £40,000.

Cumulative turnover at end of June 2016 is £125,000.

But on 1 June 2016 the company signed a contract and so 'knew' that within the next 30 days it would supply £85,000 of taxable supplies – this meets the future test conditions. Therefore the company needs to notify HMRC of its need to register within 30 days of 1 June 2016, ie by 30 June 2016.

HMRC will then register the company from 1 June 2016.

The historic test is met at the end of June 2016 (this would require notification by 30 July 2016 and registration from 1 August 2016).

However when a trader satisfies both tests HMRC will use the test that gives the earlier registration date.

In this case the future test gives the earliest date, 1 June 2016.

3.1.3 Other registration issues

When determining the value of a person's taxable supplies for the purposes of registration, supplies of goods and services that are *capital assets* of the business are to be disregarded, except for non zero-rated taxable supplies of interests in land.

When a person is liable to register in respect of a past period, it is his responsibility to pay VAT. If he is unable to collect it from those to whom he made taxable supplies, the VAT burden will fall on him. A person must start keeping VAT records and charging VAT to customers as soon as he is required to be registered. However, VAT should not be shown separately on any invoices until the registration number is known. The invoice should show the VAT inclusive price and customers should be informed that VAT invoices will be forwarded once the registration number is known. Formal VAT invoices should then be sent to such customers within 30 days of receiving the registration number.

Notification of liability to register must be made on form VAT 1. This can be downloaded from the HMRC website, can be requested by telephone, or an application to register can be made online through the website. Simply writing to, or telephoning, a local VAT office is not enough. On registration the VAT office will send the trader a certificate of registration. This shows the VAT registration number, the date of registration, the end of the first VAT period and the length of the VAT periods. We will look at VAT periods later in this chapter.

If a trader makes a supply before becoming liable to register, but gets paid after registration, VAT is not due on that supply.

3.2 Voluntary registration

A person may decide to become registered even though his taxable turnover falls below the registration limit. Unless a person is registered he cannot recover the input tax he pays on purchases.

Voluntary registration is advantageous where a person wishes to recover input tax on purchases. However, charging VAT may make the supply less competitive if customers are not VAT registered and the trader may have to absorb the VAT output tax thus reducing his profit.

Therefore, consideration needs to be given to the situation of the customer. For example, consider a trader who has one input during the period which cost £1,000 plus £200 VAT at 20%; he works on the input which becomes his sole output for the year and he decides to make a profit of £1,000.

(a) If he is not registered he will charge £2,200 and his customer will obtain no relief for any VAT.

(b) If he is registered he will charge £2,000 plus VAT of £400. His customer will have input tax of £400 which he will be able to recover if he, too, is registered.

If the customer is a non-taxable person he will prefer (a) as the cost to him is £2,200. If he is taxable he will prefer (b) as the net cost is £2,000. Thus, a decision whether or not to register voluntarily may depend upon the status of customers.

The decision to register may also depend on the image of the business the trader wishes to project (registration may give the impression of a substantial business). The **administrative burden of registration** should also be considered.

3.3 Group registration

FAST FORWARD

Two or more companies under common control can register as a group for VAT purposes. A single VAT return and payment are then made by a representative member for a VAT period but all members of the group are jointly and severally liable for VAT due. There is no need to account for VAT on supplies between group members.

Two or more companies under common control may apply for group registration.

The **effects and advantages of group registration** are as follows.

- Each VAT group must appoint a representative member which must **account for the group's output tax and input tax, completing one VAT return and paying VAT on behalf of the group. Thus this simplifies VAT accounting, saving administrative costs,** and allows payments and repayments of VAT to be netted off. However, **all members of the group are jointly and severally liable for any VAT due from the representative member.**
- **Any supply of goods or services by a member of the group to another member of the group is, in general, disregarded for VAT purposes,** reducing the VAT accounting required.
- Any other supply of goods or services by or to a group member is in general treated as a supply by or to the representative member.
- Any VAT payable on the import of goods by a group member is payable by the representative member.

Two or more companies are eligible to be treated as members of a group provided each of them is either established in the UK or has a fixed establishment in the UK, and:

- **One of them controls each of the others; or**
- **One person** (which could be an individual or a holding company) **controls all of them**; or
- **Two or more persons carrying on a business in partnership control all of them.**

An application to create, terminate, add to or remove a company from a VAT group may be made at any time.

It is not necessary for each company, which meets the requirements, to join a particular VAT group. It may be beneficial, for example, in the case of a company making largely zero-rated supplies (and so receiving VAT repayments) to remain outside the group and benefit from cash flow repayments from completing monthly VAT returns (see later in this Study Text).

4 Deregistration

FAST FORWARD

A trader may deregister voluntarily if he expects the value of his taxable supplies in the following one year period will not exceed £81,000. Alternatively, a trader who no longer makes taxable supplies may be compulsorily deregistered.

4.1 Voluntary deregistration

A person is eligible for voluntary deregistration if HMRC are satisfied that the value of his taxable supplies (net of VAT and excluding supplies of capital assets) **in the following one year period will not exceed £81,000**. However, voluntary deregistration will not be allowed if the reason for the expected fall in value of taxable supplies is the cessation of taxable supplies or the suspension of taxable supplies for a period of 30 days or more in that following year.

HMRC will cancel a person's registration from the date the request is made or from an agreed later date.

4.2 Compulsory deregistration

A trader may be compulsorily deregistered if HMRC are satisfied that he is no longer making nor intending to make taxable supplies. Failure to notify a requirement to deregister within 30 days may lead to a penalty. Compulsory deregistration may also lead to HMRC reclaiming input tax which has been wrongly recovered by the trader since the date on which he should have deregistered.

4.3 The consequences of deregistration

FAST FORWARD

VAT is chargeable on all goods and services on hand at the date of deregistration.

On deregistration, VAT is chargeable on all stocks and capital assets in a business on which input tax was claimed, since the registered trader is in effect making a taxable supply to himself as a newly unregistered trader. If the VAT chargeable does not exceed £1,000, it need not be paid.

5 Transfer of going concern

FAST FORWARD

The transfer of a business as a going concern is outside the scope of VAT.

There is no VAT charge if a business (or a separately viable part of it) **is sold as a going concern to another taxable person** (or a person who immediately becomes a taxable person as a result of the transfer). Such a sale is **outside the scope of VAT**.

If a transfer of a going concern (TOGC) is from a VAT registered trader to a new owner who is not VAT registered, then it is possible to apply to transfer the registration number of the previous owner to the new owner. This would also transfer to the new owner the responsibility for the past VAT history of the old business. So, if the previous owner had committed any VAT misdemeanours the liability for those would transfer to the new owner of the business. As a result of this it may not be wise to apply to transfer the VAT registration number between old and new owners unless of course, it is a situation where there is a very close connection between the two.

If the VAT registration number is not transferred then the new owners do not have any responsibility for the VAT affairs of the previous owner of the business. This is probably a safer way to structure the transfer of a business.

6 Pre-registration input tax

FAST FORWARD

VAT incurred on goods and services before registration can be treated as input tax and recovered from HMRC subject to certain conditions.

6.1 Introduction

VAT incurred before registration can be treated as input tax and recovered from HMRC subject to certain conditions.

Input tax cannot be recovered if it is attributable to onward supplies made before the date of registration by the trader who is becoming VAT registered. This rule applies whether the input tax is treated as being incurred before or after the date of registration.

6.2 Pre-registration goods

If the claim is for input tax suffered on goods purchased prior to registration then the following conditions must be satisfied.

(a) The **goods were acquired for the purpose of the business** which either was carried on or was to be carried on by him at the time of supply.

(b) The **goods have not been supplied onwards or consumed before the date of registration** (although they may have been used to make other goods which are still held).

(c) The **VAT must have been incurred in the four years prior to the date of registration.**

6.3 Pre-registration services

If the claim is for input tax suffered on the supply of services prior to registration then the following conditions must be satisfied.

(a) The **services were supplied for the purposes of the business** which either was carried on or was to be carried on by him at the time of supply.

(b) **The services were supplied within the six months prior to the date of registration.**

7 Accounting for and administering VAT

7.1 Administration

FAST FORWARD

VAT is administered by HMRC. Appeals are heard by the Tax Tribunal.

7.1.1 Introduction

The administration of VAT is dealt with by HM Revenue and Customs (HMRC).

Local offices are responsible for the local administration of VAT and for providing advice to registered persons whose principal place of business is in their area. They are controlled by regional collectors.

From time to time a registered person will be visited by HMRC staff from a local office to ensure that the law is understood and is being applied properly. If a trader disagrees with any decision as to the application of VAT given by HMRC he can ask his local office to reconsider the decision. It is not necessary to appeal formally while a case is being reviewed in this way. Where an appeal can be settled by agreement, a written settlement has the same force as a decision by the Revenue and Customs Prosecution Office.

7.1.2 Assessments

HMRC may issue assessments of VAT due to the best of their judgement if they believe that a trader has failed to make returns or if they believe those returns to be incorrect or incomplete. The time limit for making assessments is normally four years after the end of a VAT period, but this is extended to 20 years in the case of fraud, dishonest conduct, certain registration irregularities and the unauthorised issue of VAT invoices.

HMRC sometimes write to traders, setting out their calculations, before issuing assessments. The traders can then query the calculations.

7.1.3 Appeals

A trader may appeal to the Tax Tribunal in the same way as an appeal may be made for income tax and corporation tax (see earlier in this Study Text). VAT returns and payments shown thereon must have been made before an appeal can be heard.

7.2 VAT periods

FAST FORWARD

VAT is accounted for on regular returns – most are submitted electronically. Extensive records must be kept.

The VAT period (also known as the tax period) is the period covered by a VAT return. It is usually three calendar months. The return shows the total input and output tax for the tax period.

HMRC allocate VAT periods according to the class of trade carried on (ending in June, September, December and March; July, October, January and April; or August, November, February and May), to spread the flow of VAT returns evenly over the year. When applying for registration a trader can ask for VAT periods which fit in with his own accounting year. It is also possible to have VAT periods to cover accounting systems not based on calendar months.

A registered person whose input tax will regularly exceed his output tax can elect for a one month VAT period, but will have to balance the inconvenience of making 12 returns a year against the advantage of obtaining more rapid repayments of VAT.

Certain small businesses may submit an annual VAT return (see later in this Study Text).

7.3 Electronic filing

Nearly all VAT registered businesses must file their VAT returns online and make payments electronically.

The time limit for submission and payment is one month plus seven days after the end of the VAT period. For example, a business which has a VAT quarter ending 31 March 2017 must file its VAT return and pay the VAT due by 7 May 2017.

7.4 Substantial traders

Once a trader's total VAT liability for the 12 months or less to the end of a VAT period exceeds £2,300,000, the trader must start making payments on account of each quarter's VAT liability during each quarter.

Two payments on account of each quarter's VAT liability must usually be made. The first is due one month before the end of the quarter and the second is due at the end of the month which is the final month of the quarter. The amount of each payment on account made during the quarter is 1/24 of the trader's annual VAT liability in the period in which the threshold is exceeded. For the purposes of calculating the payments on account (but not for the purposes of the £2,300,000 threshold for entry into the scheme), a trader's VAT due on imports from outside the EU is ignored.

If the VAT liability for the quarter exceeds the total of the payments on account, a balancing payment is due one month after the end of the quarter to bring the total payments for that quarter to the amount of the VAT liability. If the VAT liability for the quarter is less than the total of the payments on account, HMRC will make a repayment to the trader.

Payments must be made and the quarterly VAT return submitted by the last day of the relevant month ie there is no additional seven days. **Payments must be made electronically.**

The default surcharge (see later in this Study Text) applies to late payments.

Question

Substantial traders

Large Ltd is liable to make payments on account of VAT calculated at £250,000 each for the quarter ended 31 December 2016.

What payments/repayment are due if Large Ltd's VAT liability for the quarter is calculated as:

(a) £680,000?
(b) £480,000?

Answer

(a)

Date	Payment
30 November 2016	Payment on account of £250,000
31 December 2016	Payment on account of £250,000
31 January 2017	Balancing payment of £(680,000 – 250,000 – 250,000) = £180,000 with submission of VAT return for quarter

(b)

Date	Payment/repayment
30 November 2016	Payment on account of £250,000
31 December 2016	Payment on account of £250,000
31 January 2017	Repayment by HMRC of £(480,000 – 250,000 – 250,000) = £(20,000) on submission of VAT return for quarter

Once a trader is in the scheme, the payments on account are reviewed annually at a set time. However, **the trader can apply to reduce payments on account at any time if the total VAT liability for the latest four returns is less than 80% of the total on which the payments on account are currently based**, ie the VAT liability decreases by 20% or more. **Conversely, HMRC may increase the payments on account in between annual reviews if the trader's total 12 month VAT liability increases by 20% or more**, ie the VAT for the last four periods is at least 120% of the amount on which the payments on account are currently based.

A trader can apply to leave the scheme if his 12 month VAT liability is below £1,800,000. A trader whose VAT liability at the annual review was below £2,300,000 will be automatically removed from the scheme six months later.

A trader may elect to pay his actual VAT liability monthly instead of making payments on account. For example, the actual liability for January would be due at the end of February. The trader can continue to submit quarterly returns as long as HMRC is satisfied the trader is paying sufficient monthly amounts.

7.5 Refunds of VAT

There is a four year time limit on the right to reclaim overpaid VAT. This time limit does not apply to input tax which a business could not have reclaimed earlier because the supplier only recently invoiced the VAT, even though it related to a purchase made some time ago. Nor does it apply to overpaid VAT penalties.

If a taxpayer has overpaid VAT and has recovered excessive input tax by reason of the same mistake, HMRC can set off any tax, penalty, interest or surcharge due to them against any repayment due to the taxpayer and repay only the net amount. In such cases the normal four year time limit for recovering VAT, penalties, interest, etc by assessment does not apply.

HMRC can refuse to make any repayment which would unjustly enrich the claimant. They can also refuse a repayment of VAT where all or part of the tax has, for practical purposes, been borne by a person other than the taxpayer (eg by a customer of the taxpayer) except to the extent that the taxpayer can show loss or damage to any of his businesses as a result of mistaken assumptions about VAT.

8 The tax point

FAST FORWARD

The tax point is the deemed date of supply. The basic tax point is the date on which goods are removed or made available to the customer, or the date on which services are completed. If a VAT invoice is issued or payment is received before the basic tax point, the earlier of these dates becomes the actual tax point. If the earlier date rule does not apply, and the VAT invoice is issued within 14 days of the basic tax point, the invoice date becomes the actual tax point.

8.1 The basic tax point

The tax point of each supply is the deemed date of supply. The basic tax point is the date on which the goods are removed or made available to the customer, or the date on which services are completed.

The tax point determines the VAT period in which output tax must be accounted for and credit for input tax will be allowed. The tax point also determines which rate applies if the rate of VAT or a VAT category changes (for example when a supply ceases to be zero-rated and becomes standard-rated).

8.2 The actual tax point

If a VAT invoice is issued or payment is received before the basic tax point, the earlier of these dates automatically becomes the tax point. If the earlier date rule does not apply and if the VAT invoice is issued within 14 days after the basic tax point, the invoice date becomes the tax point (although the trader can elect to use the basic tax point for all his supplies if he wishes). This 14 day period may be extended to accommodate, for example, monthly invoicing; the tax point is then the VAT invoice date or the end of the month, whichever is applied consistently.

Question — Tax point

Julia sells a sculpture to the value of £1,000 net of VAT. She receives a payment on account of £250 plus VAT on 25 April 2016. The sculpture is delivered on 28 May 2016. Julia's VAT return period is to 30 April 2016. She issues an invoice on 4 June 2016.

Outline the tax point(s) and amount(s) due.

Answer

A separate tax point arises in respect of the £250 deposit and the £750 balance payable.

Julia should account for VAT as follows.

(a) Deposit

25 April 2016: tax at 20% × £250 = £50. This is accounted for in her VAT return to 30 April 2016. The charge arises on 25 April 2016 because payment is received before the basic tax point (which is 28 May 2016 – date of delivery).

(b) Balance

4 June 2016: tax at 20% × £750 = £150. This is accounted for on the VAT return to 31 July 2016. The charge arises on 4 June because the invoice was issued within 14 days of the basic tax point of 28 May 2016 (delivery date).

8.3 Miscellaneous points

Goods supplied on sale or return are treated as supplied on the earlier of adoption by the customer or 12 months after despatch.

Continuous supplies of services paid for periodically normally have tax points on the earlier of the receipt of each payment and the issue of each VAT invoice, unless one invoice covering several payments is issued in advance for up to a year. The tax point is then the earlier of each due date or date of actual payment. However, for connected businesses the tax point will be created periodically, in most cases based on 12 month periods.

9 The valuation of supplies

FAST FORWARD

In order to ascertain the amount of VAT on a supply, the supply must be valued. If a discount is offered for prompt payment, VAT is chargeable on the amount received.

9.1 Value of supply

The value of a supply is the VAT-exclusive price on which VAT is charged. The consideration for a supply is the amount paid in money or money's worth.

Thus with a standard rate of 20%:
Value + VAT = consideration
£100 + £20.00 = £120.00

The VAT proportion of the consideration is known as the 'VAT fraction'. It is:

$$\frac{\text{rate of tax}}{100+\text{rate of tax}} = \frac{20}{100+20} = \frac{1}{6}$$

Provided the consideration for a bargain made at arm's length is paid in money, the value for VAT purposes is the VAT exclusive price charged by the trader. If it is paid in something other than money, as in a barter of some goods or services for others, it must be valued and VAT will be due on the value.

If the price of goods is effectively reduced with money off coupons, the value of the supply is the amount actually received by the taxpayer.

9.2 Discounts

If the trader offers a discount for prompt payment, output VAT is charged on the actual amount received for the supply. The trader must either provide details of the discount on the sales invoice or issue an invoice for the full amount and then issue a credit note if the discount is taken up.

Question — **Discounts**

Melissa sells furniture. She makes a standard-rated supply to a customer, Chris, on 10 March 2017 for £5,000 plus VAT. However, the invoice states that Chris is entitled to a 10% discount if he pays within 14 days. What is the output tax payable on the supply if:

(a) Chris pays on 20 March 2017; or
(b) Chris pays on 30 March 2017?

Answer

(a) **Payment on 20 March 2017 (within 14 days)**

	£
Full amount	5,000
Less discount 10% × £5,000	(500)
Discounted amount	4,500
VAT @ 20% on £4,500	£900

(b) **Payment on 30 March 2017 (more than 14 days)**

	£
Full amount	5,000
VAT @ 20% on £5,000	1,000

9.3 Miscellaneous

For goods supplied under a hire purchase agreement VAT is chargeable on the cash selling price at the start of the contract.

When goods are permanently taken from a business for non-business purposes VAT must be accounted for on their market value. Where business services are put to a private or non-business use, the value of the resulting supply of services is the cost to the taxable person of providing the services. If services bought for business purposes are used for non-business purposes (without charge), then VAT must be accounted for on their cost, but the VAT to be accounted for is not allowed to exceed the input tax deductible on the purchase of the services.

10 The deduction of input tax

10.1 Input tax recovery

FAST FORWARD

Not all input VAT is deductible, eg VAT on most motor cars.

For input tax to be deductible, the payer must be a taxable person, with the supply being to him in the course of his business. In addition a VAT invoice must be held (except for payments of up to £25 including VAT which are for telephone calls, or car park fees, or which are made through cash operated machines).

Input tax recovery can be denied to any business that does not hold a valid VAT invoice and cannot provide alternative evidence to prove the supply took place.

10.2 Capital items

The distinction between capital and revenue which is important in other areas of tax **does not apply to VAT**. Thus a manufacturer buying plant subject to VAT will be able to obtain a credit for all the VAT immediately. The plant must of course be used to make taxable supplies, and if it is only partly so used only part of the VAT can be reclaimed. Conversely, if plant is sold second-hand then VAT should be charged on the sale and is output tax in the normal way.

10.3 Non-deductible input tax

Exam focus point

In the F6 (UK) exam students are **not required** to know actual cases where VAT decisions were made. They are included below for your information only.

The following input tax is not deductible even for a taxable person with taxable outputs.

(a) **VAT on motor cars not used wholly for business purposes**. VAT on cars is never reclaimable unless the car is acquired new for resale or is acquired for use in or leasing to a taxi business, a self-drive car hire business or a driving school (see further below).

(b) **VAT on business entertaining** where the cost of the entertaining is not a tax deductible trading expense, unless the entertainment is of overseas customers in which case the input tax is deductible.

If the items bought are used partly for non-deductible entertaining and partly for other purposes, an apportionment of the expenses is required. In *Ernst & Young v CCE* the Tribunal held that staff entertaining was wholly for business purposes and a full input tax recovery was allowed. HMRC accept this decision in respect of staff entertainment but maintain that following the case *KPMG v CCE* input tax on entertaining guests at a staff party is non-deductible.

(c) **VAT on expenses incurred on domestic accommodation for directors.**

(d) **VAT on non-business items passed through the business accounts.** However, when goods are bought partly for business use, the purchaser may:

(i) Deduct all the input tax, and account for output tax in respect of the private use; or
(ii) Deduct only the business proportion of the input tax

Where services are bought partly for business use, only method (ii) may be used. If services are initially bought for business use but the use then changes, a fair proportion of the input tax (relating to the private use) is reclaimed by HMRC by making the trader account for output tax.

(e) **VAT which does not relate to the** making of supplies by the buyer in the course of a **business**.

10.4 Irrecoverable VAT

Exam focus point

ACCA's article Motor cars, written by a member of the F6(UK) examination team explains the implications of acquiring, running, or having the use of a motor car for income tax, corporation tax, value added tax (VAT) and national insurance contribution (NIC).

Where all (as with many cars) or some (as for partial business use) of the input tax on a purchase is not deductible, the **non-deductible VAT is included in the cost for income tax, corporation tax, capital allowance or capital gains purposes. Deductible VAT is omitted from costs, so that only net amounts are included in accounts. Similarly, sales** (and proceeds in chargeable gains computations) **are shown net of VAT**, because the VAT is paid over to HMRC.

10.5 Motoring expenses

10.5.1 Cars

The VAT incurred on the purchase of a car not used wholly for business purposes is not recoverable (except as mentioned above). If accessories are fitted after the original purchase and a separate invoice is raised then the VAT on the accessories can be treated as input tax so long as the accessories are for business use. **If VAT is not recoverable on a car because it is not used wholly for business purposes, then VAT is not charged if the car is subsequently sold.**

If a car is used wholly for business purposes (including leasing, so long as the charges are at the open market rate), the input tax is recoverable but the buyer must account for VAT when he sells the car.

If a car is leased, the lessor recovered the input tax when the car was purchased and the lessee makes some private use of the car (for example private use by employees), **the lessee can only recover 50% of the input tax on the lease charges. A hiring of five days or less is assumed to be for wholly business use.**

If a car is used for business purposes then any VAT charged on repair and maintenance costs can be treated as input tax. No apportionment has to be made for private use.

10.5.2 Fuel

FAST FORWARD

If fuel is supplied for private purposes all input VAT incurred on the fuel is allowed and the business will normally account for output VAT using a set of scale charges.

If a business pays for fuel which is only used for business purposes, it can claim all the input tax paid on that fuel. However, many businesses will pay for fuel which is used for private motoring by employees.

If a business does provide fuel to an employee for private and business use but the employee reimburses the business the full cost of the private fuel, there is an actual taxable supply by the business valued at the amount received from that employee. The business can claim its input tax on all fuel, but then must account for output tax on the amount paid by the employee. HM Revenue and Customs will accept that the full cost of all private fuel has been reimbursed where a log is kept recording private miles and the employee pays a fuel-only mileage rate that covers the average fuel cost (on its website, HM Revenue and Customs publish a set of such rates for different sizes of engine).

If a business provides fuel to its employees for private use without charge or at a charge below the full cost, there is a deemed taxable supply. The business then has the following options for how to account for VAT on fuel:

(a) **Not to claim any input tax in respect of fuel** purchased by the business. **No output tax is charged**. In effect, the fuel is not brought into the VAT system at all.

(b) **Claim input VAT only on the fuel purchased for business journeys**. This requires the business to keep detailed mileage records of business and private use. **No output tax is charged in respect of private use.** In effect, the private fuel is not brought into the VAT system.

(c) **Claim input tax on all fuel purchased and charge output tax based either on the full cost of the private fuel supplied** (again, this requires detailed mileage records to be kept) **or the fuel scale charge which reflects the deemed output in respect of private use. The fuel scale charge is based on the CO_2 emissions of the car.**

Exam focus point

In the F6 (UK) exam, questions on the treatment of private use fuel will normally involve the use of the fuel scale charge.

The above rules apply **even where employees pay for the fuel themselves and the business reimburses them**: as long as the business obtains VAT invoices for the fuel, it can treat the fuel as its own purchase/input.

Question

Fuel scale charge

Iain is an employee of ABC Ltd. He has the use of a car with CO_2 emissions of 176 g/km for one month and a car with CO_2 emissions of 208 g/km for two months during the quarter ended 31 August 2016.

ABC Ltd pays all the petrol costs in respect of both cars without requiring Iain to make any reimbursement in respect of private fuel. Total petrol costs for the quarter amount to £360 (including VAT). ABC Ltd wishes to use the fuel scale charge as detailed records of private mileage have not been kept.

What is the VAT effect of the above on ABC Ltd?

VAT scale rates (VAT inclusive) for three month periods

CO_2 emissions	£
175	291
205	362

Answer

Value added tax for the quarter:

	£
Car 1	
£291 × 1/3 =	97
Car 2	
£362 × 2/3 =	241
	338
Output tax:	
1/6 × £338	£56
Input tax	
1/6 × £360	£60

11 Relief for impairment losses

FAST FORWARD

Relief for VAT on impairment losses is available if the debt is over six months old (measured from when the payment is due) and has been written off in the trader's accounts.

Where a supplier of goods or services has accounted for VAT on the supply and the customer does not pay, the supplier may claim a refund of VAT on the amount unpaid. **Relief is available for VAT for impairment losses (bad debts) on trade debts if the debt is over six months old (measured from when payment is due) and has been written off in the creditor's accounts.** Where payments on account have been received, they are attributed to debts in chronological order. If the debtor later pays all or part of the amount owed, a corresponding part of the VAT repaid must be paid back to HMRC.

Impairment loss relief claims must be made within four years of the time the impairment loss became eligible for relief (in other words, within four years and six months from when the payment was due). The creditor must have a copy of the VAT invoice, and records to show that the VAT in question has been accounted for and that the debt has been written off. The VAT is reclaimed on the creditor's VAT return as an amount of input tax.

A business which has claimed input tax on a supply, but which has not paid the supplier of the goods or services within six months of date of supply (or the date on which the payment is due, if later), must repay the input tax, irrespective of whether the supplier has made a claim for bad debt relief. The input tax will be repaid by making an adjustment to the input tax on the VAT return for the accounting period in which the end of the six months falls.

Exam focus point

Watch out for the six month rule when claiming relief for impairment losses.

Question

Impairment loss relief

Elixir Ltd has VAT accounting periods ending on 31 March, 30 June, 30 September and 31 December. The company sold standard rated goods to Ben on 1 July 2016. The VAT inclusive amount on the invoice was £2,000 and payment was due by 15 July 2016. Ben paid Elixir Ltd £500 as part payment on 1 October 2016 but then became untraceable and Elixir Ltd has written off the remaining debt.

State how much impairment loss relief can be claimed by Elixir Ltd and the earliest VAT return on which the claim can be made.

Answer

The amount of the loss is £(2,000 – 500) = £1,500.

The VAT on the loss is £1,500 × 1/6 = £250, so this amount can be claimed as impairment loss relief.

Payment was due on 15 July 2016 and so the six month period ended on 15 January 2017. The earliest VAT return on which an impairment loss relief claim is that for the quarter ending 31 March 2017.

Chapter Roundup

- VAT is charged on turnover at each stage in a production process, but in such a way that the burden is borne by the final consumer.
- VAT is chargeable on taxable supplies made by a taxable person in the course or furtherance of any business carried on by him. Supplies may be of goods or services.
- Some supplies are taxable (either standard-rated, reduced-rate or zero-rated). Others are exempt.
- A trader becomes liable to register for VAT if the value of taxable supplies in any period up to 12 months exceeds £83,000 or if there are reasonable grounds for believing that the value of the taxable supplies will exceed £83,000 in the next 30 days alone. A trader may also register voluntarily.
- Two or more companies under common control can register as a group for VAT purposes. A single VAT return and payment are then made by a representative member for a VAT period but all members of the group are jointly and severally liable for VAT due. There is no need to account for VAT on supplies between group members.
- A trader may deregister voluntarily if he expects the value of his taxable supplies in the following one year period will not exceed £81,000. Alternatively, a trader who no longer makes taxable supplies may be compulsorily deregistered.
- VAT is chargeable on all goods and services on hand at the date of deregistration.
- The transfer of a business as a going concern is outside the scope of VAT.
- VAT is administered by HMRC. Appeals are heard by the Tax Tribunal.
- VAT incurred on goods and services before registration can be treated as input tax and recovered from HMRC subject to certain conditions.
- VAT is accounted for on regular returns – most are submitted electronically. Extensive records must be kept.
- The tax point is the deemed date of supply. The basic tax point is the date on which goods are removed or made available to the customer, or the date on which services are completed. If a VAT invoice is issued or payment is received before the basic tax point, the earlier of these dates becomes the actual tax point. If the earlier date rule does not apply, and the VAT invoice is issued within 14 days of the basic tax point, the invoice date becomes the actual tax point.
- In order to ascertain the amount of VAT on a supply, the supply must be valued. If a discount is offered for prompt payment, VAT is chargeable on the amount received.
- Not all input VAT is deductible, eg VAT on most motor cars.
- If fuel is supplied for private purposes all input VAT incurred on the fuel is allowed and the business will normally account for output VAT using a set of scale charges.
- Relief for VAT on impairment losses is available if the debt is over six months old (measured from when the payment is due) and has been written off in the trader's accounts.

Quick Quiz

1. On what transactions will VAT be charged?
2. What is a taxable person?
3. What are the two advantages of group registration?
4. When may a person choose to be deregistered?
5. What is the time limit in respect of claiming pre-registration input tax on goods?
6. On what amount is VAT charged if a discount is offered for prompt payment?
7. What input tax is never deductible?
8. What relief is available for impairment losses?

Answers to Quick Quiz

1 VAT is charged on taxable supplies of goods and services made in the UK by a taxable person in the course or furtherance of any business carried on by him.

2 Any 'person' whose taxable turnover exceeds the registration limit. The term 'person' includes individuals, partnerships and companies.

3 The two advantages of group registration are:

- Saving on administrative costs: only one VAT return needs to be completed for the group
- No VAT on supplies between group members

4 A person is eligible for voluntary deregistration if HMRC are satisfied that the value of his taxable supplies in the following year will not exceed £81,000.

5 The VAT must have been incurred in the four years prior to the effective date of registration.

6 VAT is chargeable on the actual amount received for the supply.

7 VAT on:

- Motor cars
- UK business entertaining
- Expenses incurred on domestic accommodation for directors
- Non-business items passed through the accounts
- Items which do not relate to making business supplies

8 Where a supplier has accounted for VAT on a supply and the customer fails to pay, then the supplier may claim a refund of the VAT accounted for to HMRC but never actually collected from the customer.

Now try the questions below from the Practice Question Bank

Number	Type	Marks	Time
Q162	Section A	2	4 mins
Q163	Section A	2	4 mins
Q164	Section A	2	4 mins
Q165	Section B	2	4 mins
Q166	Section B	2	4 mins
Q167	Section B	2	4 mins
Q168	Section B	2	4 mins
Q169	Section B	2	4 mins
Q170	Section C	10	20 mins
Q171	Section C	10	20 mins

25

Further aspects of VAT

Topic list	Syllabus reference
1 VAT invoices and records	F2(d)
2 Penalties	F2(i)
3 Imports, exports, acquisitions and despatches	F2(j)
4 Special schemes	F3(a)(i)–(iii)

Introduction

In the previous chapter we looked at the scope of VAT and when businesses must, or may, register for VAT.

In this chapter we consider the contents of a valid VAT invoice and the main penalties used to enforce the VAT system.

VAT needs to be applied to imports, so that people do not have a tax incentive to buy abroad, and VAT is taken off many exports in order to encourage sales abroad. We see how this is achieved for transactions both within and outside the European Union.

Finally we look at the three special schemes which are intended to reduce the administrative burden for small businesses.

This chapter concludes our study of UK taxation and the F6 syllabus.

Study guide

		Intellectual level
F2	**The computation of VAT liabilities**	
(d)	List the information that must be given on a VAT invoice.	1
(i)	Understand when the default surcharge, a penalty for an incorrect VAT return, and default interest will be applied.	1
(j)	Understand the treatment of imports, exports and trade within the European Union.	2
F3	**The effect of special schemes**	
(a)	Understand the operation of, and when it will be advantageous to use, the VAT special schemes:	
(i)	Cash accounting scheme.	2
(ii)	Annual accounting scheme.	2
(iii)	Flat rate scheme.	2

Exam guide

The topics in this chapter could be examined in any of Sections A, B or C. Penalties are an important topic as they are used to enforce the VAT system, but the special schemes are designed to make life simpler for small businesses. You may be asked to advise on the VAT treatment of imports and exports outside the European Union (EU) and on trade within the EU. The flat rate scheme may also lead to a small extra profit for the business, depending on the flat rate percentage and the level of inputs.

Exam focus point

ACCA's article Value added tax, written by a member of the F6(UK) examination team, in Part 2 **VAT returns**, **VAT invoices**, **penalties**, **overseas aspects of VAT**, and **special VAT schemes**.

1 VAT invoices and records

1.1 VAT invoices

FAST FORWARD

A taxable person making a taxable supply to another registered person must supply a VAT invoice within 30 days.

A taxable person making a taxable supply to another VAT registered trader must supply a VAT invoice within 30 days of the time of supply, and must keep a copy. There is no requirement to supply a VAT invoice if the supply is exempt or if the supply is to a non-VAT registered customer.

The invoice must show:

(a) The supplier's name, address and registration number

(b) The date of issue, the tax point and an invoice number

(c) The name and address of the customer

(d) A description of the goods or services supplied, giving for each description the quantity, the unit price, the rate of VAT and the VAT exclusive amount

(e) The rate of any cash discount

(f) The total invoice price excluding VAT (with separate totals for zero-rated and exempt supplies)

(g) Each VAT rate applicable and the total amount of VAT

If an invoice is issued, and a change in price then alters the VAT due, a credit note or debit note to adjust the VAT must be issued.

Credit notes must give the reason for the credit (such as 'returned goods'), and the number and date of the original VAT invoice. If a credit note makes no VAT adjustment, it should state this.

A less detailed VAT invoice may be issued by a taxable person where the invoice is for a total including VAT of up to £250. Such an invoice must show:

(a) The supplier's name, address and registration number
(b) The date of the supply
(c) A description of the goods or services supplied
(d) The rate of VAT chargeable
(e) The total amount chargeable including VAT

Zero-rated and exempt supplies must not be included in less detailed invoices.

VAT invoices are not required for payments of up to £25 including VAT which are for telephone calls, or car park fees, or made through cash operated machines. In such cases, input tax can be claimed without a VAT invoice.

1.2 Records

FAST FORWARD

Every VAT registered trader must keep records for six years.

Every VAT registered trader must keep records for six years, although HMRC may sometimes grant permission for their earlier destruction. They may be kept on paper, on microfilm or microfiche or on computer. However, there must be adequate facilities for HMRC to inspect records.
All records must be kept up to date and in a way which allows:

- The calculation of VAT due
- Officers of HMRC to check the figures on VAT returns

The following records are needed.

- Copies of VAT invoices, credit notes and debit notes issued
- A summary of supplies made
- VAT invoices, credit notes and debit notes received
- A summary of supplies received
- A VAT account
- Order and delivery notes, correspondence, appointment books, job books, purchases and sales books, cash books, account books, records of takings (such as till rolls), bank paying-in slips, bank statements and annual accounts
- Records of zero-rated and exempt supplies, gifts or loans of goods, taxable self-supplies and any goods taken for non-business use

2 Penalties

2.1 The default surcharge

FAST FORWARD

A default occurs when a trader either submits his VAT return late, or submits the return on time but pays the VAT late. A default surcharge is applied if there is a default on payment during a default surcharge period.

A default occurs when a trader either submits his VAT return late, or submits the return on time but pays the VAT late. If a trader defaults, HMRC will serve a surcharge liability notice on the trader. The notice specifies a surcharge period running from the date of the notice to the anniversary of the end of the period for which the trader is in default.

If a further default occurs in respect of a return period ending during the specified surcharge period, the original surcharge period will be extended to the anniversary of the end of the period to which the new default relates. In addition, if the default involves the late payment of VAT (as opposed to simply a late return) **a surcharge is levied.**

The surcharge depends on the number of defaults involving late payment of VAT which have occurred in respect of periods ending in the surcharge period, as follows.

Default involving late payment of VAT in the surcharge period	Surcharge as a percentage of the VAT outstanding at the due date
First	2%
Second	5%
Third	10%
Fourth or more	15%

Surcharges at the 2% and 5% rates are not normally demanded unless the amount due would be at least £400 but for surcharges calculated using the 10% or 15% rates there is a minimum amount of £30 payable.

A trader must submit one year's returns on time and pay the VAT shown on them on time in order to break out of the surcharge liability period and the escalation of surcharge percentages.

Question

Default surcharge

Peter Popper has an annual turnover of around £300,000. His VAT return for the quarter to 31.12.14 is late. He then submits returns for the quarters to 30.9.15 and 31.3.16 late as well as making late payment of the tax due of £12,000 and £500 respectively.

Peter's VAT return to 31.3.17 is also late and the VAT due of £1,100 is also paid late. All other VAT returns and VAT payments are made on time. Outline Peter Popper's exposure to default surcharge.

Answer

A surcharge liability notice will be issued after the late filing on the 31.12.14 return outlining a surcharge period extending to 31.12.15.

The late 30.9.15 return is in the surcharge period so the period is extended to 30.9.16. The late VAT payment triggers a 2% penalty. 2% × £12,000 = £240. Since £240 is less than the £400 de minimis limit it is not collected by HMRC.

The late 31.3.16 return is in the surcharge period so the period is now extended to 31.3.17. The late payment triggers a 5% penalty. 5% × £500 = £25. Since £25 is less than the £400 de minimis limit it is not collected by HMRC.

The late 31.03.17 return is in the surcharge period. The period is extended to 31.03.18. The late payment triggers a 10% penalty 10% × £1,100 = £110. This is collected by HMRC since the £400 de minimis does not apply to penalties calculated at the 10% (and 15%) rate.

Peter will have to submit all four quarterly VAT returns to 31.3.18 on time and pay the VAT on time to 'escape' the default surcharge regime.

A default will be ignored for all default surcharge purposes if the trader can show that the return or payment was sent at such a time, and in such a manner, that it was reasonable to expect that HMRC would receive it by the due date. A default will also be ignored if the trader can demonstrate a reasonable excuse for the late submission or payment.

The application of the default surcharge regime to small businesses is modified. **A small business is one with a turnover below £150,000**. When a small business is late submitting a VAT return or paying VAT it will receive a letter from HMRC offering help. No penalty will be charged. If a further default occurs within 12 months a surcharge liability notice will be issued.

2.2 Penalties for errors

FAST FORWARD

There is a common penalty regime for errors in tax returns, including VAT. Errors in a VAT return up to certain amounts may be corrected in the next return.

2.2.1 Common penalty regime

The common penalty regime for making errors in tax returns discussed earlier in this Study Text applies for value added tax.

2.2.2 Errors corrected in next return

Errors on a VAT return not exceeding the greater of:

- **£10,000** (net under-declaration minus over-declaration)
- **1% x net VAT turnover for return period** (maximum £50,000)

may be **corrected on the next return.**

Other errors should be notified to HMRC in writing eg by letter.

In both cases, a penalty for the error may be imposed. Correction of an error on a later return is not, of itself, an unprompted disclosure of the error and fuller disclosure is required for the penalty to be reduced.

Default interest (see below) on the unpaid VAT as a result of the error is only charged where the limit is exceeded for the error to be corrected on the next VAT return.

2.3 Interest on unpaid VAT (default interest)

FAST FORWARD

Default interest is charged on unpaid VAT if HMRC raise an assessment of VAT or the trader makes a voluntary payment before the assessment is raised. It runs from the date the VAT should have been paid to the actual date of payment but cannot run for more than three years before the assessment or voluntary payment.

Interest (not deductible in computing taxable profits) **is charged on VAT which is the subject of an assessment** (where returns were not made or were incorrect), **or which could have been the subject of an assessment but was paid before the assessment was raised. It runs from the reckonable date until the date of payment.** This interest is sometimes called 'default interest'.

The reckonable date is when the VAT should have been paid (usually one month and seven days from the end of the return period), or in the case of VAT repayments, seven days from the issue of the repayment order. However, where VAT is charged by an assessment, interest does not run from more than three years before the date of the assessment; where the VAT was paid before an assessment was raised, interest does not run for more than three years before the date of payment.

In practice, interest is only charged when there would otherwise be a loss to the Exchequer. It is not, for example, charged when a company failed to charge VAT but if it had done so another company would have been able to recover the VAT.

3 Imports, exports, acquisitions and despatches

3.1 Introduction

The terms **import and export** refer to purchases and sales of goods with countries **outside the European Union (EU)**.

The terms **acquisition and despatch** refer to purchases and sales of goods with countries **in the EU**.

3.2 Trade in goods outside the European Union

FAST FORWARD

Imports of goods from outside the EU are subject to VAT and exports of goods to outside the EU are zero-rated.

3.2.1 Imports

Goods imported into the UK from outside the EU are effectively treated in the same way as goods that are purchased within the UK. This is because imports are chargeable to VAT if the same goods supplied in the home market by a registered trader would be chargeable to VAT. The rate of VAT is the same as that which would have applied if the supply had been made in the home market.

An importer of goods from outside the EU must calculate VAT on the value of the goods imported and account for it at the point of entry into the UK. He can then deduct the VAT payable as input tax on his next VAT return. HMRC issue monthly certificates to importers showing the VAT paid on imports. VAT is chargeable on the onward sale of the goods in the UK in the normal way.

If security (such as a bank guarantee) can be provided, the deferred payment system can be used whereby VAT is automatically charged to the importer's bank account each month rather than payment being made for each import when the goods arrive in the UK. Approved importers are able to provide reduced (and in some cases zero) security in respect of the deferred payment scheme. Such importers need to seek the approval of HMRC.

3.2.2 Exports

There is a general zero-rating where a UK VAT registered trader exports goods outside of the EU.

It is not sufficient merely to export goods. The zero-rating only applies if HMRC 'are satisfied' that the supplier has exported the goods. Evidence of the export must therefore be retained by the trader and must take the form specified by HMRC.

3.3 Trade in goods within the European Union

FAST FORWARD

Sales of goods to registered traders in other EU states are zero-rated. Taxable acquisitions of goods to the UK from other EU states are subject to VAT in the UK as both output tax and input tax.

3.3.1 Sales (despatches)

Where goods are sold by a UK registered trader to a customer in another EU member state, the supply is usually zero-rated if the supply is made to a VAT registered trader.

3.3.2 Purchases (acquisitions)

Goods acquired in the UK by a VAT registered trader from another EU member state are liable to UK VAT. Consequently, output tax has to be accounted for by that UK trader on the relevant VAT return. **The 'tax point' for such acquisitions is the earlier of:**

- **The fifteenth day of the month following the month of acquisition**
- **The date of issue of an invoice**

The transaction is entered on the UK trader's VAT return as an output and an input so the effect is usually neutral. Thus the UK trader is effectively in the same overall position as he would have been if he had acquired the goods from another UK VAT registered trader.

Although the end result is the same as with an import from outside the EU, the difference with an EU acquisition is that there is no need to actually pay the VAT subsequent to its recovery as input VAT.

3.4 Supplies of services

FAST FORWARD

Services supplied to a business customer are generally treated as being supplied in the country where that customer is situated. Therefore, if the customer is a UK VAT registered trader, output VAT is payable by that trader on the supply. Supplies of services by a UK VAT registered trader to business customers outside the UK are generally outside the scope of UK VAT.

3.4.1 Place of supply of services

Services supplied to a business customer are generally treated as **being supplied in the country where that customer is situated**. A 'business customer' is anyone carrying on a business anywhere in the world, not just VAT registered traders and not just customers in the EU.

3.4.2 Supplies of services to a UK business customer

Where a UK business customer receives services from outside the UK, the place of supply will be the UK. Therefore, if the business customer is a VAT registered trader**, output tax has to be accounted for by that UK trader on the relevant VAT return.**

The tax point for a supply of such services is the earlier of:

- **The time the service is completed**
- **The time the service is paid for**

The transaction is entered on the UK trader's VAT return as an output and an input so the effect is usually neutral. Thus the UK trader effectively in the same overall position as if the services have been supplied by another UK VAT registered trader.

3.4.3 Supplies of services by a UK trader

Supplies of services by a UK VAT registered trader to business customers outside the UK are generally outside the scope of UK VAT. This is because the place of supply is not in the UK.

Exam focus point

The rules on international services are complex. For F6 (UK) purposes, you only need to know the rules in outline as explained in this section.

4 Special schemes

FAST FORWARD

Special schemes include the cash accounting scheme, the annual accounting scheme and the optional flat rate scheme. These schemes can make VAT accounting easier and ease cash flow for certain types of trader.

PER alert

One of the competencies you require to fulfil Performance Objective 15 Tax computations and assessments of the PER is to explain the basis of tax calculations, and interpret the effect of current legislation and case law. You can apply the knowledge you obtain from this section of the Study Text to help to demonstrate this competence.

4.1 The cash accounting scheme

The cash accounting scheme enables businesses to account for VAT on the basis of cash paid and received. That is, the date of payment or receipt determines the return in which the transaction is dealt with. This means that the cash accounting scheme gives automatic impairment loss relief (bad debt relief) because VAT is not due on a supply until payment has been received.

The scheme can only be used by a trader whose taxable turnover (exclusive of VAT) for the 12 months starting on their application to join the scheme is not expected to exceed £1,350,000. A trader can join the scheme only if all returns and VAT payments are up to date (or arrangements have been made to pay outstanding VAT by instalments).

If the value of taxable supplies exceeds £1,600,000 in the 12 months to the end of a VAT period a trader must leave the cash accounting scheme immediately.

Businesses which leave the scheme (either voluntarily or because they have breached the £1,600,000 limit) can account for any outstanding VAT due under the scheme on a cash basis for a further six months.

4.2 The annual accounting scheme

The annual accounting scheme is only available to traders who regularly pay VAT to HMRC, not to traders who normally receive repayments. It is available for traders **whose taxable turnover (exclusive of VAT) for the 12 months starting on their application to join the scheme is not expected to exceed £1,350,000.**

Under the annual accounting scheme traders file annual VAT returns but throughout the year they must make payments on account of their VAT liability by direct debit. The year for which each return is made may end at the end of any calendar month. Unless HMRC agree otherwise, the trader must pay 90% of the previous year's net VAT liability during the year by means of nine monthly payments commencing at the end of the fourth month of the year. The balance of the year's VAT is then paid with the annual return. There is an option for businesses to pay three larger interim instalments.

Late payment of instalments is not a default for the purposes of the default surcharge.

An annual VAT return must be submitted to HMRC along with any balancing payment due within two months of the end of the year.

It is not possible to use the annual accounting scheme if input tax exceeded output tax in the year prior to application. In addition, all VAT payments must be up to date.

If the expected value of a trader's taxable supplies exceeds £1,600,000, notice must be given to HMRC within 30 days and he may then be required to leave the scheme. If the £1,600,000 limit is in fact exceeded, the trader must leave the scheme.

If a trader fails to make the regular payments required by the scheme or the final payment for a year, or has not paid all VAT shown on returns made before joining the scheme, he may be expelled from the scheme. HMRC can also prevent a trader using the scheme 'if they consider it necessary to do so for the protection of the revenue'.

Advantages of annual accounting:

- Only **one VAT return each year** so fewer occasions to trigger a default surcharge
- Ability to **manage cash flow** more accurately
- **Avoids need for quarterly calculations for input tax recovery**

Disadvantages of annual accounting:

- Need to **monitor future taxable supplies** to ensure turnover limit not exceeded
- **Timing of payments have less correlation to turnover** (and hence cash received) by business
- **Payments based on previous year's turnover may not reflect current year turnover** which may be a problem if the scale of activities has reduced.

4.3 Flat rate scheme

The optional flat rate scheme enables businesses to calculate VAT due simply by applying a flat rate percentage to their turnover.

Under the scheme, businesses calculate VAT by applying a fixed percentage to their **tax inclusive turnover**, ie the total turnover, **including all reduced rate, zero-rated and exempt income.** However, the businesses **cannot reclaim any input tax suffered.**

The percentage depends upon the trade sector into which a business falls. It ranges from 4% for retailing food, confectionery or newspapers to 14.5% for accountancy and bookkeeping services.

A 1% reduction off the flat rate % can be made by businesses in their first year of VAT registration.

Exam focus point

The flat rate percentage will be given to you in your examination.

Businesses using the scheme must issue VAT invoices to their VAT registered customers but they do not have to record all the details of the invoices issued or purchase invoices received to calculate the VAT due. Invoices issued will show VAT at the normal rate rather than the flat rate.

To join the flat rate scheme businesses must have a VAT exclusive annual taxable turnover of up to £150,000.

A business must leave the flat rate scheme if the total value of its VAT inclusive supplies in the year (excluding sales of capital assets) is more than £230,000.

4.4 Example: flat rate scheme

An accountant undertakes work for individuals and for business clients. In a VAT year, the business client work amounts to £35,000 and the accountant will issue VAT invoices totalling £42,000 (£35,000 plus VAT at 20%). Turnover from work for individuals totals £18,000, including VAT. Total gross sales are therefore £60,000. The flat rate percentage for an accountancy businesses is 14.5%.

VAT due to HMRC will be 14.5% × £60,000 (VAT inclusive amount) = £8,700

Under the normal VAT rules the output tax due would be:

	£
£35,000 × 20%	7,000
£18,000 × 1/6	3,000
	10,000

Whether the accountant is better off under the scheme depends on the amount of input tax incurred as this would be offset, under normal rules, from output tax due. The reduced VAT administration should also be taken into account.

Chapter Roundup

- A taxable person making a taxable supply to another registered person must supply a VAT invoice within 30 days.
- Every VAT registered trader must keep records for six years.
- A default occurs when a trader either submits his VAT return late, or submits the return on time but pays the VAT late. A default surcharge is applied if there is a default on payment during a default surcharge period.
- There is a common penalty regime for errors in tax returns, including VAT. Errors in a VAT return up to certain amounts may be corrected in the next return.
- Default interest is charged on unpaid VAT if HMRC raise an assessment of VAT or the trader makes a voluntary payment before the assessment is raised. It runs from the date the VAT should have been paid to the actual date of payment but cannot run for more than three years before the assessment or voluntary payment.
- Imports of goods from outside the EU are subject to VAT and exports of goods to outside the EU are zero-rated.
- Sales of goods to registered traders in other EU states are zero-rated. Taxable acquisitions of goods to the UK from other EU states are subject to VAT in the UK as both output tax and input tax.
- Services supplied to a business customer are generally treated as being supplied in the country where that customer is situated. Therefore, if the customer is a UK VAT registered trader, output VAT is payable by that trader on the supply. Supplies of services by a UK VAT registered trader to business customers outside the UK are generally outside the scope of UK VAT.
- Special schemes include the cash accounting scheme, the annual accounting scheme and the optional flat rate scheme. These schemes can make VAT accounting easier and ease cash flow for certain types of trader.

Quick Quiz

1 How long must a VAT trader keep records?

2 What is a default?

3 Dylan makes an error in his VAT for the quarter ending 31 March 2017 which results in a net under-declaration of £5,000. His net VAT turnover for the period is £150,000. How can Dylan correct the error?

4 Are goods despatched to the EU standard-rated or zero-rated?

5 Higgins is registered for VAT in the UK. Higgins is supplied with services by a French business on 1 September 2016. The value of the supply is £50,000. What are the VAT consequences of the supply?

6 How does the cash accounting scheme operate?

7 The turnover limits for the annual accounting scheme are not exceeding £________m to join the scheme and once turnover exceeds £________m the trader must leave the scheme. Fill in the blanks.

8 What is the optional flat rate scheme?

Answers to Quick Quiz

1 A VAT trader must keep records for six years.

2 A default occurs when a trader either submits his VAT return late or submits the return on time but pays the VAT late.

3 Dylan can correct the error in his VAT return for the quarter ending 30 June 2017. This is because the error of £5,000 is less than the greater of £10,000 and 1% of his net VAT turnover for the return period (£1,500).

4 In general, despatches to the EU are zero-rated.

5 Higgins will have to account for output tax of £50,000 × 20% = £10,000 on the supply and also £10,000 of input tax. The supply is therefore tax neutral for him.

6 The cash accounting scheme operates by a trader accounting for VAT on the basis of cash paid and received (rather than invoices). The date of payment or receipt determines the return in which the transaction is dealt with. The scheme gives automatic impairment loss relief because VAT on a supply is not due until payment is received.

7 The turnover limits for the annual accounting scheme are not exceeding **£1.35m** to join the scheme and once turnover exceeds **£1.6m** the trader must leave the scheme.

8 The optional flat rate scheme enables businesses to calculate VAT simply by applying a percentage to their tax-inclusive turnover. Under the scheme, businesses calculate VAT due by applying a flat rate percentage to their tax inclusive turnover, ie the total turnover generated, including all reduced-rate, zero-rated and exempt income. The percentage depends upon the trade sector in which a business falls.

Now try the questions below from the Practice Question Bank

Number	Type	Marks	Time
Q172	Section A	2	4 mins
Q173	Section A	2	4 mins
Q174	Section A	2	4 mins
Q175	Section B	2	4 mins
Q176	Section B	2	4 mins
Q177	Section B	2	4 mins
Q178	Section B	2	4 mins
Q179	Section B	2	4 mins
Q180	Section C	10	20 mins

Practice question and answer bank

Introduction to the UK tax system MCQs **4 mins each**

1 Which of the following are functions of HM Revenue and Customs (HMRC) in the UK tax system?

(1) Formally imposes taxation
(2) Produces a wide range of explanatory notes
(3) Provides advice on minimising tax liability
(4) Has the administrative function for collection of tax.

A 1 and 2
B 2 and 3
C 1 and 4
D 2 and 4 **(2 marks)**

2 Which of the following are NOT revenue taxes?

(1) Income tax
(2) Capital gains tax
(3) National insurance
(4) Inheritance tax

A 1 and 2
B 2 and 4
C 3 and 4
D 2 and 3 **(2 marks)**

3 You work for a firm of accountants. A few weeks ago, you prepared a tax return for Serena. Serena has now told you that she forgot to include some bank interest in the return but that she does not intend to tell HM Revenue and Customs (HMRC) of the omission.

Which of the following actions should you take?

(1) Inform Serena in writing that it is not possible for your firm to act for her.

(2) Inform HMRC that your firm is no longer acting for Serena.

(3) Inform HMRC about the details of Serena's omission.

(4) Report to your firm's Money Laundering Reporting Officer Serena's refusal to disclose the omission to HMRC and the facts surrounding it.

A 1, 2 and 3
B 2, 3 and 4
C 1, 2 and 4
D 1, 3 and 4 **(2 marks)**

Computing taxable income and the income tax liability MCQs

4 mins each

4 Which of the following types of income are exempt from income tax?

(1) Dividends from a company
(2) Interest received from an Individual Savings Account
(3) £50 Premium Bond prize
(4) Interest on NS&I Savings Certificates
(5) Interest on government securities (gilts)

A 1, 2 and 4
B 2, 3 and 5
C 2, 3 and 4
D 1, 4 and 5

(2 marks)

5 In 2016/17, Robert had property business income of £108,000. This was his only income in 2016/17. Robert also paid a gross personal pension contribution of £3,000 in December 2016.

What is the personal allowance available to Robert for the tax year 2016/17?

A £6,000
B £7,000
C £8,500
D £11,000

(2 marks)

6 Peter has taxable income for the tax year 2016/17 as follows:

Non-savings income	£2,000
Savings income	£6,410

What is Peter's income tax liability for the tax year 2016/17?

A £882
B £482
C £1,082
D £1,682

(2 marks)

7 Rhoda has taxable income of £175,000 in 2016/17 which is all employment income. PAYE of £40,000 was deducted.

What is Rhoda's income tax payable for the tax year 2016/17?

A £64,850
B £19,900
C £24,850
D £23,600

(2 marks)

8 John is a widower and has two children aged fourteen and twelve. He receives child benefit of £1,788 in 2016/17. John has net income of £53,400 in 2016/17 and he made a gift aid donation of £300 (gross) in January 2017.

What is John's child benefit income tax charge for the tax year 2016/17?

A £536
B £554
C £608
D £1,788

(2 marks)

9 Sandeep, Harriet and Romelu **20 mins**

(a) Sandeep had not previously been UK-resident prior to the tax year 2016/17. He arrived in the UK on 6 April 2016 and remained in the UK for 190 days. Sandeep does not work during 2016/17.

Required

Explain why Sandeep is UK resident in the tax year 2016/17. **(2 marks)**

(b) Harriet had always been UK-resident prior to the tax year 2016/17, but she has not spent more than 90 days in the UK in the two previous tax years. Harriet is self-employed and does substantive (but not full-time) work in the UK during 2016/17. She has no close family. Harriet owns a house in the UK. On 6 April 2016, she started to rent an overseas apartment in which she lived for 255 days. She then returned to the UK where she lived in her house for the remainder of the tax year 2016/17.

Required

Explain why Harriet is UK resident in the tax year 2016/17. **(4 marks)**

(c) Romelu had not previously been UK-resident prior to the tax year 2016/17 and has never spent more than 60 days in the UK in previous tax years. His wife is UK resident. Romelu arrived in the UK on 6 April 2016 and remained in the UK for 92 days during which time he lived in a rented flat. He also has a home outside the UK where he spent the rest of 2016/17. Romelu does not work during 2016/17.

Required

Explain why Romelu is non-UK resident in the tax year 2016/17. **(4 marks)**

(Total = 10 marks)

10 John and Helen **29 mins**

John and Helen are a married couple. They have a twelve year old son, Marcus. John and Helen received the following income in 2016/17.

	John	*Helen*
	£	£
Salary (before tax deducted)	66,090	23,000
PAYE tax deducted	15,636	2,400
Dividends	6,211	7,820
Bank deposit interest	1,000	1,095
Building society interest	990	525

Required

(a) Compute the tax payable by John and by Helen for 2016/17. **(13 marks)**

(b) Explain the tax implications if Helen had received child benefit of £1,076 during 2016/17. **(2 marks)**

(Total = 15 marks)

11 Michael and Josie **29 mins**

Michael and Josie are a married couple. They received the following income in 2016/17.

	Michael	*Josie*
	£	£
Salary (before tax deducted)	163,540	100,000
PAYE tax deducted	59,690	29,200
Dividends	17,111	7,820
Bank deposit interest	7,500	150
Building society interest	7,400	550

Josie made a gift aid donation of £1,600 in December 2016.

Required

Compute the tax payable by Michael and Josie for 2016/17. **(15 marks)**

Employment income MCQs — 4 mins each

12 Jacob works part time for Z Ltd at a salary of £8,000 a year. He is not a director of Z Ltd. On 30 November 2016, Jacob received a bonus of £1,800 in respect of Z Ltd's trading results for the year ended 31 October 2016. He expects to receive a bonus of £2,400 in November 2017 in respect of Z Ltd's results for the year ended 31 October 2017.

What is Jacob's employment income for the tax year 2016/17?

A £8,000
B £9,800
C £10,050
D £10,400 **(2 marks)**

13 You are a tax advisor for the following clients.

(1) Ben, who is a computer systems advisor. He works in the Bristol office one day a week and spends the rest of his time visiting clients in London and Manchester.

(2) Colin, who is a computer technician. He works two days a week at the Bristol workshop depot and three days a week at the Swindon workshop.

(3) Diane, who works for an accountancy firm. She is based in the Birmingham office but has been seconded to the Bristol office for 12 months.

(4) Erica, who works permanently in the same Birmingham office as Diane. She occasionally travels from home to visit a client in Bristol.

Which of your clients can claim tax relief for travelling expenses between home and Bristol?

A 1 and 2
B 2 and 3
C 3 and 4
D 1 and 4 **(2 marks)**

14 Sarah is employed by Y plc. She uses her own car for business purposes and is reimbursed 35p per mile by Y plc. In 2016/17, Sarah travelled 15,000 miles on business.

What is the employment income consequence of the reimbursement for business mileage?

A £5,250 taxable benefit
B £(500) allowable expense
C £(1,500) allowable expense
D £(5,750) allowable expense **(2 marks)**

Danni — 4 mins each

The following scenario relates to questions 15 to 19.

Danni joined a UK company, Clifton plc, as purchasing director on 1 July 2016, based at their Nottingham office.

Salary and bonus

Until 31 December 2016, Danni's monthly salary as a director was £6,000. From 1 January 2017, her salary increased by 2.5%.

Clifton plc awarded Danni a bonus of £10,000 in relation to a special purchasing project during Clifton plc's period of account ended 31 March 2017. This bonus was determined by the board of directors on 15 March 2017, credited in the company's accounts on 10 April 2017, which was also the date when Danni became entitled to payment of the bonus. The bonus was paid to Danni on 31 May 2017.

Travel to Clifton plc's offices

From 1 July 2016, Danni travelled to Clifton plc's office in Nottingham from home using the Nottingham Tram Network. Danni bought a monthly tram season ticket for each of the months from July 2016 to December 2016.

From 1 January 2017, Danni was seconded to Clifton plc's office in Manchester for a period of six months. Danni bought a monthly rail season ticket for each month of her secondment.

Travel to clients

Danni also used her own car for journeys to meet clients in Leicester, which is 24 miles from Nottingham. She made five return journeys between 1 July 2016 and 5 April 2017. Clifton plc paid Danni 30p per mile for these journeys.

Subscriptions

Danni is a member of the Chartered Institute of Purchasing and Supply (MCIP) and paid her annual membership fee on 31 December 2016. Danni is also a member of her local tennis club at which she sometimes meets potential suppliers for Clifton plc and paid her annual membership fee on 1 September 2016.

Payroll giving

Clifton plc has a payroll giving scheme. Danni made monthly contributions through the scheme from 31 December 2016.

15 What is the amount of Danni's employment income from her salary and bonus taxable in the tax year 2016/17?

A £64,000
B £54,450
C £64,450
D £54,000 **(2 marks)**

16 Which of the following of Danni's travel to Clifton plc's offices will be qualifying travel expenses?

(1) Travel from home to Clifton plc's office in Nottingham.
(2) Travel from home to Clifton plc's office in Manchester

A 1 only
B 2 only
C Both 1 and 2
D Neither 1 nor 2 **(2 marks)**

17 What are the employment income consequences of using her own car for journeys to meet clients in Leicester?

A £72 taxable benefit
B £108 allowable deduction
C £12 taxable benefit
D £36 allowable deduction **(2 marks)**

18 Which of the following of Danni's subscriptions will be deductible in computing her employment income?

(1) Chartered Institute of Purchasing and Supply (MCIP)
(2) Tennis club

A 1 only
B 2 only
C Both 1 and 2
D Neither 1 nor 2 **(2 marks)**

19 How is tax relief given for Danni's contributions through the payroll giving scheme?

	By whom	*How tax relief given*
A	Clifton plc	Deducting the donation from Danni's gross pay before calculating PAYE
B	Clifton plc	Increasing the basic rate tax limit when computing PAYE on Danni's gross pay
C	Danni	Making contributions net of basic rate tax
D	Danni	Making a claim in her self assessment tax return

(2 marks)

Taxable and exempt benefits. The PAYE system MCQs

4 mins each

20 Lenny is employed by B plc at a salary of £42,000 each tax year. He is provided with a car available for private use throughout 2016/17. The car has CO_2 emissions of 113 g/km and a list price of £20,000. B plc paid £18,000 for the car as a result of a dealer discount. The car has a diesel engine. No private fuel is provided.

What is Lenny's taxable car benefit for the tax year 2016/17?

A £3,800
B £4,400
C £3,960
D £3,420 **(2 marks)**

21 Bernie is employed by N Ltd. N Ltd provided Bernie with the use of free accommodation (not job related) from 6 April 2016 to 5 August 2016. The accommodation cost Bernie's employer £99,000 in February 2014 and was previously occupied by another employee. The accommodation had a market value of £123,000 in April 2016 and an annual value of £3,660.

What is Bernie's total taxable benefit in respect of the accommodation for the tax year 2016/17?

A £1,220
B £240
C £1,460
D £1,700 **(2 marks)**

22 Julia is employed by C plc at a salary of £20,000 each tax year. For the tax year 2016/17 C plc paid Julia's corporate gym membership at a cost of £1,200. Julia receives no other benefits from C plc. C plc does not payroll any of the benefits provided to employees.

Which form, if any, does C plc use to report this benefit to HM Revenue and Customs (HMRC) and by what date must it be submitted to HMRC?

	Form	*Date by when must be submitted to HMRC*
A	P11D	31 May 2017
B	P11D	6 July 2017
C	P60	31 May 2017
D	P60	6 July 2017

(2 marks)

Verdi

4 mins each

The following scenario relates to questions 23 to 27.

Verdi is setting up a business and will be employing twelve individuals. He understands that he will need to operate the Pay As You Earn (PAYE) system for income tax and national insurance contributions.

23 Which of the following methods can Verdi use to submit information electronically under the Real Time Information (RTI) system?

(1) Commercial payroll software
(2) HMRC's Basic PAYE Tools software
(3) Payroll provider

A 1 and 2
B 2 and 3
C 1 and 3
D 2 only **(2 marks)**

24 Which of the following information will be included in the first Full Payment Submission (FPS) made by Verdi?

(1) The amounts paid to employees
(2) Deductions made under PAYE
(3) Details of employees who have started employment

A 2 and 3
B 1 and 2
C 1 and 3
D 1, 2 and 3 **(2 marks)**

25 When must Verdi make his FPSs and when must he pay the corresponding PAYE if he does so electronically?

	Report	*Payment*	
A	End of tax month	14 days after end of tax month	
B	End of tax month	17 days after end of tax month	
C	On or before any day when he pays someone	14 days after end of tax month	
D	On or before any day when he pays someone	17 days after end of tax month	**(2 marks)**

26 Verdi makes both his first and second Full Payment Submission (FPS) each six weeks late.

What are the monthly penalties that HMRC will impose?

	First FPS	*Second FPS*	
A	Nil	£200	
B	£200	£200	
C	Nil	£100	
D	£100	£100	**(2 marks)**

27 At the end of the tax year, Verdi must provide each employee with a form showing total taxable earnings for the year, tax deducted, code number, NI number and the employer's name and address.

What is the name of this form and by when must it be provided?

	Name of form	*Date by when must be provided*	
A	P60	6 July following the end of the tax year	
B	P60	31 May following the end of the tax year	
C	P45	6 July following the end of the tax year	
D	P45	31 May following the end of the tax year	**(2 marks)**

28 Azure plc **20 mins**

The following items have been provided by a UK company, Azure plc.

(a) A loan of £16,000 at 0.75% a year to Andrew on 6 October 2016. The loan was not for a qualifying interest purpose.

(b) A flower arrangement costing £45 given to Penelope on 6 April 2016 on the occasion of her wedding.

(c) The loan of a TV to Charles from 6 June 2016, the asset having cost the company £800 in 2012 and having had a market value of £500 in June 2016.

(d) A long service award in December 2016 to Demelza, the company secretary, comprising a gold wrist watch costing £1,000. Demelza has been employed by the company since December 1989.

(e) Removal expenses of £9,500 to Janet in September 2016 who moved from Plymouth to Liverpool to take up a new position in the Liverpool office in July 2016.

(f) The provision of two mobile phones to Lawrence on 6 April 2016 both of which were available solely for private use. Azure plc paid £120 for the hire of each of the mobile phones for the tax year. The market value of each of the phones was £500. The cost of the calls made during the year was £300 for one of the phones and £400 for the other phone.

Required

State in detail how each of the above items would be treated for 2016/17, computing the amount of any taxable benefit. **(10 marks)**

Pensions MCQs **4 mins each**

29 In the tax year 2016/17, Treena earned £3,500 from part time work, trading income of £2,000 and gross bank interest of £500.

What is the maximum gross pension contribution that Treena could have made during the tax year 2016/17 on which there would have been tax relief?

A £3,500
B £5,500
C £3,600
D £6,000 **(2 marks)**

30 In the tax year 2016/17, Jemima earned a salary of £90,000 and she paid a contribution of £15,000 to her employer's occupational pension scheme. Jemima has no other sources of income.

What is Jemima's taxable income for the tax year 2016/17?

A £90,000
B £75,000
C £64,000
D £60,250 **(2 marks)**

31 Rio started in business as a sole trader on 6 April 2014 and had the following results:

2014/15	£20,000
2015/16	£30,000
2016/17	£85,000

Rio had not made any pension provision prior to 2015/16 but on 6 April 2015 he joined a personal pension scheme and made a contribution of £17,000 (gross) on that date. He now wishes to make a pension contribution in March 2017.

What is the maximum gross pension contribution that Rio can make in March 2017 on which there will be tax relief without incurring an annual allowance charge?

A £63,000
B £103,000
C £85,000
D £83,000 **(2 marks)**

Gary, George and Geraldine **4 mins each**

The following scenario relates to questions 32 to 36.

Gary

Gary has taxable income of £44,400 for 2016/17, all from employment income and after deduction of his personal allowance. He paid £4,000 (net) into his personal pension scheme in 2016/17.

George

George has trading income of £15,000 for 2016/17. In this tax year he also has property business income from a furnished holiday letting of £8,000 and gross bank interest of £1,200. George wants to know the tax consequences of accessing his pension fund of £500,000 when he reaches the age of 55 under flexi-access drawdown.

Geraldine

Geraldine had trading income of £60,000 in 2015/16. She paid £25,000 (net) into her personal pension scheme in 2015/16. This was the first year in which she had been a member of a registered pension scheme. She has trading income of £130,000 in 2016/17. She now wishes to make a personal pension contribution in March 2017. Geraldine hopes to build up a pension fund of £1,500,000 by the time she is aged 55 when she will start taking pension benefits. She will take the excess of the fund over the lifetime allowance as a lump sum.

32 What is Gary's income tax payable for the tax year 2016/17?

A £11,360
B £10,560
C £10,360
D £8,880 **(2 marks)**

33 What are George's relevant earnings for 2016/17?

A £3,600
B £15,000
C £23,000
D £24,200 **(2 marks)**

34 What are the tax consequences of George accessing his pension fund under flexi-access drawdown?

A Lump sum taxable at 55%, pension income taxable at 25%
B Tax-free lump sum of up to 25% of pension fund, remainder taxable as pension income
C Tax-free lump sum of up to 50% of pension fund, remainder taxable as pension income
D All withdrawals taxable as pension income **(2 marks)**

35 What is the maximum net personal pension contribution that Geraldine will be able to make in March 2017, obtaining tax relief and without resulting in a tax charge?

A £40,000
B £48,750
C £32,000
D £39,000 **(2 marks)**

36 What will Geraldine's tax position be if she takes the excess of the fund over the lifetime allowance as a lump sum?

A She will be subject to income tax at her marginal rate of tax on the lump sum
B She will be subject to income tax at the rate of 55% on the lump sum
C She will be subject to income tax at the rate of 25% on the lump sum
D She will not be subject to income tax on the lump sum **(2 marks)**

Property income MCQs — 4 mins each

37 Paul rents out a house which is fully furnished. The house does not qualify as a furnished holiday letting. Paul paid the following expenses in relation to the letting:

	£
New chairs for garden (not previously provided) bought July 2016	600
Replacement cooker (upgrade, similar cooker to original would have cost £650, no scrap value for old cooker) bought September 2016	900
Central heating breakdown cover premium paid 1 January 2017 for year to 31 December 2017 (not previously covered)	580

What is the amount of Paul's allowable expenses for calculating his property business income in the tax year 2016/17?

A £1,395
B £1,045
C £795
D £1,230 **(2 marks)**

38 Laura granted an 11 year lease on a property to a tenant for a premium of £30,000.

What is the amount of the premium on which will Laura be chargeable to income tax?

A £23,400
B £6,000
C £30,000
D £24,000 **(2 marks)**

39 Which TWO of the following statements about furnished holiday lettings are correct?

(1) The accommodation must be available for commercial let as holiday accommodation to the public generally for at least 105 days during the tax year.

(2) Replacement of domestic items relief may be claimed.

(3) The income from furnished holiday lettings qualifies as relevant earnings for pension contributions.

(4) If an individual has a furnished holiday letting and another letting, two income statements must be prepared in order to identify separate profits and losses.

A 1 and 2
B 3 and 4
C 1 and 3
D 2 and 4 **(2 marks)**

40 Rafe — 20 mins

On 1 May 2016, Rafe started to invest in rented properties. He bought two houses in the first three months, as follows.

House 1

Rafe bought house 1 for £62,000 on 1 May 2016. It needed a new roof before it was fit to be let out. Rafe paid £5,000 for the work to be done in May. He then let it unfurnished for £600 a month from 1 June to

30 November 2016. The first tenant then left, and the house was empty throughout December 2016. On 1 January 2017, a new tenant moved in. The house was again let unfurnished. The rent was £6,000 a year, payable annually in advance.

Rafe paid a buildings insurance premium of £480 for the period from 1 June 2016 to 31 May 2017.

House 2

Rafe bought house 2 for £45,000 on 1 July 2016. He spent £1,200 on routine redecoration and £5,300 on new furniture in July, and let the house fully furnished from 1 August 2016 for £7,800 a year, payable annually in advance. Rafe paid a buildings insurance premium of £920 for the period from 1 July 2016 to 30 June 2017 and a boiler insurance premium of £180 for the period from 1 August 2016 to 31 July 2017. In March 2017, the tenant damaged a sofa which was part of the furniture bought in July 2016 and Rafe bought an identical replacement sofa for £800. The damaged sofa was scrapped with no value.

During 2016/17 Rafe also rented out one furnished room of his main residence. He received £7,850 and incurred allowable expenses of £875.

Required

Compute Rafe's property business income for 2016/17. **(10 marks)**

Computing trading income MCQs **4 mins each**

41 Which TWO of the following items of expenditure will Walter NOT be allowed to deduct in calculating his tax-adjusted trading profit before capital allowances?

(1) Installing air conditioning in his workshop

(2) Repairing the central heating in his offices

(3) Redecorating his showroom

(4) Making initial repairs to a recently acquired second-hand office building which was not usable until the repairs were carried out

A 1 and 2
B 2 and 3
C 1 and 4
D 2 and 4 **(2 marks)**

42 Allie is a sole trader and has a profit of £160,000 on her statement of profit or loss for the year ended 31 December 2016. Included within this figure are these expenses:

(1) £3,000 legal fees in connection with renewing a 15-year lease of Allie's business premises
(2) £180 car parking fines incurred by Allie whilst visiting clients
(3) £40 hamper of food for customer

What is Allie's tax adjusted profit for the year ended 31 December 2016?

A £160,040
B £163,180
C £163,220
D £160,220 **(2 marks)**

43 Terry has been in business for many years preparing accounts to 5 April each year. On 6 July 2016 leased a car with CO_2 emissions of 155g. The leasing costs were £400 per month. In the period from 6 July 2016 to 5 April 2016, Terry drove 13,500 miles, of which 10,800 were on business.

What is the deductible expense for Terry in repect of the car for the year ended 5 April 2017?

A £2,880
B £2,448
C £3,060
D £3,600 **(2 marks)**

Margaret **4 mins each**

The following scenario relates to questions 44 to 48.

On 6 April 2016, Margaret acquired a country house called The Cedars and immediately started a sole trader guest house business in it. Two-thirds of The Cedars was used by guests and one-third by Margaret. The following information is relevant for the year to 5 April 2017.

(1) Revenue was £36,000 of which £500 was owed as receivables at 5 April 2017.

(2) Furniture for guest use was acquired for £2,500.

(3) A plot of land was acquired to provide parking solely for the use of guests for £7,500.

(4) Gas and electricity bills relating to the whole of The Cedars amounted to £7,400. Cleaning and gardening costs, again relating to the whole of The Cedars, amounted to £1,800. Margaret also spent £2,000 on providing food eaten by her and the guests. There were no amounts outstanding at 5 April 2017. The fixed rate adjustment for private use of business premises for one occupant is £350 per month.

(5) Margaret purchased a motor car on 6 April 2016. She drove 15,000 miles in the car during the year of which 12,000 miles were for journeys relating to the guest house business.

(6) Other allowable expenses were £2,000 of which £900 was owed as payables at 5 April 2017.

Margaret will elect to use the cash basis for accounting for the tax year 2016/17 and will use fixed rate expenses where available. She expects to make a loss in period of account ending 5 April 2018.

44 What is the amount of revenue that will be taxable in the tax year 2016/17 and the amount of other allowable expenses that will be allowable in that tax year?

	Revenue	*Other allowable expenses*
A	£36,000	£2,000
B	£36,000	£1,100
C	£35,500	£2,000
D	£35,500	£1,100

(2 marks)

45 What are the amounts which are allowable in relation to the furniture and the plot of land for guest parking?

	Furniture	*Land for guest parking*
A	£2,500	£7,500
B	£2,500	£Nil
C	£450	£7,500
D	£450	£Nil

(2 marks)

46 What is the amount of a household expenses in item (4) that are allowable under the cash basis?

A £11,200
B £7,467
C £7,000
D £5,000

(2 marks)

47 What is the amount of the allowable motoring expenses?

A £5,000
B £3,000
C £5,750
D £5,400

(2 marks)

48 How will Margaret be able to relieve the loss that she expects to make in the tax year 2017/18?

(1) Against general income of 2017/18
(2) Against general income of 2016/17
(3) Carry forward against future trading profits of the guest house business

A 1, 2 and 3
B 3
C 1 and 2
D 1 and 3

(2 marks)

49 Archie **29 mins**

Archie's statement of profit or loss for the year to 31 March 2017 was as follows.

	£	£
Gross profit		246,250
Other income		
Impairment trade losses recovered (previously written off)	373	
Profit on sale of office	5,265	
Building society interest	1,900	
		7,538
Expenses		
General expenses	73,611	
Repairs and renewals	15,000	
Legal and accountancy charges	1,200	
Subscriptions and donations	7,000	
Impairment losses (trade)	500	
Salaries and wages	30,000	
Travel	8,000	
Depreciation	15,000	
Rent and rates	1,500	
		(151,811)
Net profit		101,977

Notes

(1) *General expenses include the following.*

	£
Entertaining staff	1,000
Entertaining suppliers	600

(2) *Repairs and renewals include the following.*

	£
Redecorating existing premises	300
Renovations to new premises to remedy wear and tear of previous owner (the premises were usable before these renovations)	500

(3) *Legal and accountancy charges are made up as follows.*

	£
Debt collection service	200
Staff service agreements	50
Tax consultant's fees for advice on tax efficient personal investments	30
45 year lease on new premises	100
Audit and accountancy	820
	1,200

(4) *Subscriptions and donations include the following.*

	£
Donations under the gift aid scheme	5,200
Donation to a political party	500
Sports facilities for staff	600
Subscription to trade association	100

(5) Travel expenses included Archie's motoring expenses of £2,000. 25% of his use of his car was for private purposes.

(6) Capital allowances amounted to £2,200.

Required

Compute Archie's taxable trading profit for the accounting period to 31 March 2017. You should start with net profit figure of £101,977 and you should indicate by the use of zero (0) any items which do not require adjustment. **(15 marks)**

Capital allowances MCQs **4 mins each**

50 Which TWO of the following items COULD be plant which is eligible for capital allowances?

(1) Refrigerator for coffee shop
(2) Extension to office building
(3) Sound insulation in a recording studio
(4) A bridge

A 1 and 4
B 2 and 3
C 2 and 4
D 1 and 3 **(2 marks)**

51 Julian is a sole trader who prepares accounts to 5 April each year. He acquired a car for both business and private purposes on 1 October 2016. The car has a CO_2 emission rate of 165 grams per kilometre and cost £21,000. The private mileage for Julian's period of account to 5 April 2017 was 25% of the total mileage for that year.

What is the maximum amount of capital allowances that Julian can claim in respect of the car for the year ended 5 April 2017?

A £1,260
B £3,780
C £2,835
D £1,680 **(2 marks)**

52 Olive started trading on 1 October 2016 and prepared her first set of accounts to 31 December 2016. On 10 October 2016 she acquired machinery at a cost of £60,000.

What is the maximum amount of capital allowances that Olive can claim for the period ended 31 December 2016?

A £60,000
B £51,800
C £50,450
D £50,000 **(2 marks)**

Sylvester **4 mins each**

The following scenario relates to questions 53 to 57.

Sylvester is the sole proprietor of a small engineering business. He has previously prepared accounts annually to 5 April but has decided to prepare accounts for the nine-month period to 31 December 2016. The following tax written down values are brought forward on 6 April 2016:

Main pool	£56,800
Special rate pool	£500
Motor car for Sylvester's use (30% private use)	£6,000

The following disposals and additions were made during the period ended 31 December 2016.

Disposals:	20 April 2016	–	Plant £12,000 (original cost £10,000)
	21 May 2016	–	Motor car for Sylvester's own use £7,200 (original cost £8,923)
	20 June 2016	–	Plant £800 (original cost £3,000)
Additions:	21 May 2016	–	New motor car for Sylvester's own use £19,000 CO_2 emissions 150 g/km. Private use of this car is 20%.

Sylvester is considering buying a new motor car for use by sales representative in January 2017. He is considering two cars. Motor car [1] has CO_2 emissions of 70g/km. Motor car [2] has CO_2 emissions of 140g/km. The motor car will be the only acquisition in the year to 31 December 2017.

53 What is the balancing charge that arises on the disposal of Sylvester's car?

A £1,200
B £840
C £360
D £2,046 **(2 marks)**

54 What is the maximum writing down allowance on Sylvester's new car for the period to 31 December 2016?

A £912
B £1,520
C £1,140
D £1,216 **(2 marks)**

55 What is the maximum writing down allowance on the main pool for the period to 31 December 2016?

A £6,210
B £5,940
C £8,280
D £7,920 **(2 marks)**

56 What is the maximum writing down allowance on the special rate pool for the period to 31 December 2016?

A £68
B £40
C £500
D £30 **(2 marks)**

57 How will the purchase of the motor car for use by the sales representative be treated if Sylvester wishes to claim maximum capital allowances in the year to 31 December 2017?

(1) It will be given a 100% first year allowance
(2) It will be added to the main pool and given writing down allowances of 18% as part of the pool
(3) It will be added to the special rate pool and given writing down allowances of 8% as part of the pool

	Motor car [1]	*Motor car [2]*
A	1	2
B	2	3
C	2	1
D	1	3

(2 marks)

58 Tom **29 mins**

Tom prepares accounts to 30 June. Despite substantial investment in new equipment, business has been indifferent and he will cease trading on 31 December 2020. His last accounts will be prepared for the six months to 31 December 2020.

The tax written down values at 1 July 2016 were as follows.

	£
Main pool	33,500
Short life asset (acquired 1.5.15)	4,400

Additions and disposals have been as follows.

		£
20.9.16	Plant cost	27,000
15.7.17	Car for own use cost	13,400
14.7.19	Plant sold for	340
10.5.20	Short life asset sold for	2,900

Private use of the car was 20% for all years. The car emits CO_2 of 105g/km.

At the end of 2020, the plant will be worth £24,000 and the car £10,600.

Required

Calculate the capital allowances for the periods from 1 July 2016 to 31 December 2020, assuming the capital allowances rates for 2016/17 apply throughout. **(15 marks)**

Assessable trading income MCQs **4 mins each**

59 Frank started trading on 1 January 2016. He prepared his first set of accounts for the 13-month period to 31 January 2017. His tax adjusted trading profit for this period was £19,500.

What are Frank's overlap profits?

A £1,500
B £3,250
C £4,500
D £3,000

(2 marks)

60 Fredericka stopped trading on 31 March 2017. Her tax adjusted profits for the last two periods of account were:

y/e 31.1.17	£10,000
p/e 31.3.17	£2,500

Fredericka had £1,000 of overlap profit when she started trading.

What is Fredericka's taxable trading income for the tax year 2016/17?

A £12,500
B £11,500
C £9,833
D £1,500 **(2 marks)**

61 Renee commenced trading on 1 January 2016. She prepared her first set of accounts for the 18 month period to 30 June 2017.

What is Renee's basis period for the tax year 2016/17?

A 1 July 2016 to 30 June 2017
B 6 April 2016 to 5 April 2017
C 1 January 2016 to 31 December 2016
D 1 January 2016 to 5 April 2016 **(2 marks)**

62 Clive **29 mins**

Clive starts a business as a sole trader on 1 January 2017.

His business plan shows that his monthly profits are likely to be as follows.

January 2017 to June 2017 (inclusive)	£800	a month
July 2017 to December 2017 (inclusive)	£1,200	a month
Thereafter	£2,000	a month

Clive is considering two alternative accounting dates, 31 March and 30 April, in each case commencing with a period ending in 2017.

Required

Show the taxable trading profits which will arise for each of the first four tax years under each of the two alternative accounting dates, and recommend an accounting date. **(15 marks)**

63 Fiona **29 mins**

Fiona started to trade as a baker on 1 January 2017 and prepared her first accounts to 30 April 2018. Adjusted profits before capital allowances are as follows.

	£
Period to 30 April 2018	47,030
Year to 30 April 2019	24,787

Fiona incurred the following expenditure on plant and machinery.

Date	*Item*	£
1.1.17	Desk and other office furniture	2,625
4.1.17	General plant	8,070
1.3.17	Second-hand oven	5,300
25.3.17	Delivery van	5,450
15.4.17	General plant	8,555
15.5.17	Car for Fiona	6,600
30.1.19	General plant	10,000
30.4.19	Mixer	1,200

The private use of the car is 35%. The car has CO_2 emissions of 103g/km.

Required

Calculate the taxable profits for the first four tax years and the overlap profits carried forward. Assume that the capital allowances rates applicable in 2016/17 apply throughout. **(15 marks)**

Trading losses MCQs **4 mins each**

64 Which TWO of the following statements about trading loss relief for an individual are correct?

(1) A claim to set a trading loss against general income can be restricted so that the individual has enough net income to use the personal allowance.

(2) A trading loss carried forward must be set against the first available profits of the same trade.

(3) A trading loss carried forward can only be used in the following six tax years.

(4) A trading loss claim for relief against general income must be made by 31 January 22 months after the end of the tax year of the loss.

A 1 and 2
B 1 and 3
C 3 and 4
D 2 and 4 **(2 marks)**

65 Shelley has been a sole trader for many years, preparing accounts to 31 January each year. In the year to 31 January 2016 she made a profit of £9,000 and in the year to 31 January 2017 she made a loss of £24,000. In 2015/16 she had property business income of £4,000. She has no other income in 2016/17.

How much of the loss of the tax year 2016/17 remains to carry forward to the tax year 2017/18 if Shelley makes a loss relief claim against general income for the tax year 2015/16?

A £22,000
B £11,000
C £20,000
D £15,000 **(2 marks)**

66 William has been a sole trader for many years, preparing accounts to 31 March each year. In the year to 31 March 2016, William made a profit of £15,000 and in the year to 31 March 2017 he made a loss of £180,000. William has property business income of £260,000 in the tax year 2015/16. He has no other income in 2016/17.

What is the amount of the loss that William can set against his general income for the tax year 2015/16?

A £65,000
B £50,000
C £83,750
D £68,750 **(2 marks)**

67 Morgan **20 mins**

Morgan has been in business as a sole trader for many years. He has the following expected results.

Year ending 5 April		£
2017	Profit	15,000
2018	Loss	(40,000)
2019	Profit	45,000

In addition to his trading income, Morgan has savings income of £12,000 a year.

Required

(a) Outline the ways in which Morgan could obtain relief for his loss. **(5 marks)**

(b) Prepare a statement showing how the loss would be relieved assuming that relief were to be claimed as soon as possible. Assume that the rates and allowances applicable in 2016/17 apply in later years. Comment on whether this is likely to be the best relief.

(5 marks)

(Total = 10 marks)

Partnerships and limited liability partnerships MCQs

4 mins each

68 Jess and Kate have been in partnership for many years preparing accounts to 31 December each year. Laura joined the partnership on 1 January 2017. From this date, the profits were shared equally between the three partners. The partnership had a trading profit of £60,000 for the year ended 31 December 2017.

What is Laura's taxable trading income from the partnership for the tax year 2016/17?

A £15,000
B £5,000
C £20,000
D £10,000 **(2 marks)**

69 Quayle and Partridge have been in partnership for many years sharing profits equally and preparing accounts to 31 March each year. From 1 May 2016 the profits were divided 1 part to Quayle and 2 parts to Partridge. The partnership had a trading profit of £96,000 for the year ended 31 March 2017.

What is Quayle's taxable trading income from the partnership for the tax year 2016/17?

A £29,333
B £4,000
C £33,333
D £32,000 **(2 marks)**

70 Victor is a 50% partner in a partnership which prepares accounts to 5 April each year. In the year to 5 April 2017, the partnership makes a loss of £(180,000) and Victor has other income of £60,000 in 2016/17.

What is the amount of loss relief that Victor can claim against general income in 2016/17?

A £15,000
B £50,000
C £60,000
D £90,000 **(2 marks)**

Anne, Betty and Chloe

4 mins each

The following scenario relates to questions 71 to 75.

Anne and Betty had been in partnership since 1 January 2010. Anne was entitled to a salary of £6,000 per year and the remainder of the profits were shared 30% to Anne and 70% to Betty. On 30 September 2016 Betty resigned as a partner and was replaced on 1 October 2016 by Chloe. From that date, profits were shared 60% to Anne and 40% to Chloe with no salaries being payable.

The partnership's taxable trading profits/(losses) are as follows:

	£
Year ended 31 December 2016	60,000
Year ended 31 December 2017	42,000
Year ended 31 December 2018 (estimated)	(18,000)

As at 6 April 2016 Anne and Betty each had unrelieved overlap profits of £3,000.

71 What is Anne's taxable trading profit for the period between 1 January 2016 and 30 September 2016?

A £12,150
B £21,150
C £16,650
D £17,700 **(2 marks)**

72 What is Betty's taxable trading profit for the tax year 2016/17?

A £25,350
B £28,500
C £28,350
D £39,000 **(2 marks)**

73 What is Chloe's taxable trading profit for the tax year 2016/17?

A £4,200
B £6,000
C £16,800
D £10,200 **(2 marks)**

74 How can Anne relieve her trading loss for the tax year 2018/19?

(1) Against general income of 2018/19 and/or 2017/18
(2) Carry forward against future trading income of the partnership
(3) Carry back against trading income of 2017/18, 2016/17 and 2015/16 later years first
(4) Carry back against general income of 2015/16, 2016/17 and 2017/18 earlier years first

A 1 and 2
B 2 and 3
C 1, 2 and 3
D 1, 2 and 4 **(2 marks)**

75 How can Chloe relieve her trading loss for the tax year 2018/19?

(1) Against general income of 2018/19 and/or 2017/18
(2) Carry forward against future trading income of the partnership
(3) Carry back against trading income of 2017/18, 2016/17 and 2015/16 later years first
(4) Carry back against general income of 2015/16, 2016/17 and 2017/18 earlier years first

A 1, 2 and 4
B 1, 2 and 3
C 1 and 2
D 2 and 4 **(2 marks)**

National insurance contributions MCQs — 4 mins each

76 Natalie is a sole trader and has taxable trading profits of £42,000 for her period of account ended 31 August 2016.

What is the TOTAL amount of national insurance contributions (NIC) that Natalie has to pay for the tax year 2016/17?

A £3,055
B £3,049
C £3,201
D £3,926 **(2 marks)**

77 Nigel is an employee earning £36,000 a year, payable in equal monthly amounts. In February 2017 he received a bonus of £8,000.

What are Nigel's class 1 (primary) national insurance contributions (NIC) in respect of February 2017?

A £1,239
B £497
C £351
D £349 **(2 marks)**

78 Gina was paid an annual salary of £45,000 during 2016/17. In addition, her employer provided her with a computer for private use for which the taxable benefit is £300.

What are the national insurance contributions (NIC) liabilities?

A Class 1 primary and secondary contributions on £45,000

B Class 1 primary contributions on £45,000, Class 1 secondary contributions on £45,300

C Class 1 primary contributions on £45,300, Class 1 secondary contributions on £45,000, Class 1A contributions on £300

D Class 1 primary contributions on £45,000, Class 1 secondary contributions on £45,000, Class 1A contributions on £300 **(2 marks)**

Derek and Denise **4 mins each**

The following scenario relates to questions 79 to 83.

Derek

Derek is the sole employee of Rose, a sole trader. In the tax year 2016/17, Derek was paid a salary of £55,000. He was also provided with a car from 6 October 2016. The car was available for private use and had a list price of £12,000 and had CO_2 emissions of 66 g/km. Derek was not provided with any fuel.

Denise

Denise started business on 6 January 2017 as a designer dressmaker. She prepared her first set of accounts for the four month period to 5 May 2017 and had taxable profits of £15,000. There are 14 contribution weeks in the period from 6 January 2017 to 5 April 2017 and five contribution weeks in the period from 6 April 2017 to 5 May 2017.

79 What are the primary Class 1 national insurance contributions payable by Derek for 2016/17?

A £4,427
B £4,193
C £5,633
D £4,433 **(2 marks)**

80 What are the secondary Class 1 national insurance contributions payable by Rose for 2016/17?

A £3,471
B £2,627
C £6,471
D £3,478 **(2 marks)**

81 What are the Class 1A national insurance contributions payable by Rose for 2016/17?

A £124
B £91
C £58
D £182 **(2 marks)**

82 What are the Class 2 contributions payable by Denise in 2016/17 and by when are they payable?

A £39 by 31 January 2018
B £53 by 31 July 2017
C £39 by 31 July 2017
D £53 by 31 January 2018 **(2 marks)**

83 What are the Class 4 contributions payable by Denise in 2016/17?

A £625
B £383
C £287
D £1,012 **(2 marks)**

84 Sasha — 29 mins

Sasha is a computer programmer. Until 5 April 2016 she was employed by Net Computers plc, but since then has worked independently from home. Sasha's income for the year ended 5 April 2017 is £60,000. All of this relates to work done for Net Computers plc. Her expenditure for the year ended 5 April 2017 is as follows:

(1) The business proportion of light, heat and telephone for Sasha's home is £880.

(2) Computer equipment was purchased on 6 April 2016 for £4,000.

(3) A motor car was purchased by Sasha on 6 April 2016 for £10,000 with CO_2 of 115g/km. Motor expenses for the year ended 5 April 2017 amount to £3,500, of which 40% relate to journeys between home and the premises of Net Computers plc. The other 60% relate to private mileage.

Required

(a) List eight factors that will indicate that a worker should be treated as an employee rather than as self-employed. **(4 marks)**

(b) (i) Calculate the amount of taxable trading profits if Sasha is treated as self-employed during 2016/17.

(ii) Calculate the amount of Sasha's taxable earnings if she is treated as an employee during 2016/17. **(7 marks)**

(c) (i) Calculate Sasha's liability to Class 2 and Class 4 NIC if she is treated as self-employed during 2016/17.

(ii) Calculate Sasha's liability to Class 1 NIC if she is treated as an employee during 2016/17. **(4 marks)**

(Total = 15 marks)

Computing chargeable gains MCQs — 4 mins each

85 Which TWO of the following assets will ALWAYS be exempt from capital gains tax?

(1) A qualifying corporate bond (QCB)
(2) Investments held in individual savings accounts (ISAs)
(3) A plot of land
(4) A decoration for bravery

A 1 and 2
B 2 and 3
C 2 and 4
D 1 and 4 **(2 marks)**

86 Joe has chargeable gains of £16,500 and allowable capital losses of £3,000 in the tax year 2016/17. He also has allowable capital losses of £4,000 brought forward from the tax year 2015/16.

What is the correct use of these amounts for the tax year 2016/17?

A £16,500 – £3,000 (current year loss) – £4,000 (brought forward loss) = £9,500
B £16,500 – £3,000 (current year loss) – £2,400 (brought forward loss) = £11,100
C £16,500 – £4,000 (brought forward loss) – £1,400 (current year loss) = £11,100
D £16,500 – £3,000 (current year loss) = £13,500

(2 marks)

87 Melanie purchased a ten-acre plot of land for £80,000. In January 2017, she sold three of the acres for £36,000 with expenses of sale amounting to £1,000. The market value of the remaining seven acres of land in January 2017 was £90,000.

What is Melanie's chargeable gain on the disposal of the three acres of land in the tax year 2016/17?

A £12,600
B £13,600
C £13,143
D £12,143 **(2 marks)**

88 Peter 20 mins

Peter made the following disposals of assets during the tax year 2016/17.

30 June 2016

Residential investment property for £150,000 less costs of disposal £1,280. Acquired for £79,000.

27 July 2016

Part of a plot of land used for agricultural purposes. The proceeds of sale were £35,000. The costs of disposal were £700. The original cost of the land was £54,000. The remainder of the land is worth £70,000.

1 September 2016

A vase which was destroyed. It cost £12,000. Compensation of £20,000 was received on 30 September 2016. Peter bought a new vase as a replacement for £17,000 on 21 December 2016.

Peter had taxable income of £27,600 in 2016/17.

Required

Calculate Peter's capital gains tax payable for the year 2016/17. **(10 marks)**

Chattels and the principal private residence exemption MCQs 4 mins each

89 Edward purchased a painting for £1,500, incurring purchase costs of £75. In October 2016 he sold the painting for £7,000, incurring disposal costs of £350.

What is Edward's chargeable gain in the tax year 2016/17?

A £1,667
B £5,500
C £5,075
D £1,083 **(2 marks)**

90 Belinda purchased a necklace for £7,500, incurring purchase costs of £400. In January 2017 she sold the necklace for £4,000, incurring disposal costs of £200.

What is Belinda's allowable loss in the tax year 2016/17?

A £1,500
B £1,900
C £2,100
D £4,100 **(2 marks)**

91 Roger purchased a house on 1 January 1993 and lived in it until 31 December 2004. On 1 January 2005 Roger went to live with his parents and the house was unoccupied for six years. Roger then lived in the house from 1 January 2011 until it was sold on 31 December 2016.

How many years of Roger's period of ownership of the house will be chargeable to capital gains tax?

A Three years
B Six years
C 21 years
D 10 and a half years **(2 marks)**

John and Elsie **4 mins each**

The following scenario relates to questions 92 to 96.

John

John purchased a property in England on 1 August 2004 and lived in it until 31 July 2005 when he moved overseas to take up an offer of employment. He returned to the UK on 1 August 2010 and moved back into the house until 31 January 2011 when he moved out permanently and went to live with his mother. The house was let out between 1 February 2014 and 31 January 2016. The house was then put up for sale and was finally sold on 31 July 2016 realising a gain of £72,000.

Elsie

Elsie made the following disposals of assets during the tax year 2016/17.

(1) An oil painting for £5,000 (net of £400 commission). She had purchased the painting for £11,500.

(2) A vase for gross proceeds of £7,500. Elsie spend £75 advertising the vase for sale. She had purchased the vase for £4,000.

92 How many exempt months are there for the purposes of computing principal private residence relief on John's disposal?

A 84 months
B 132 months
C 144 months
D 96 months **(2 marks)**

93 How many extra exempt months would there have been if John had moved back into the house between 1 February 2016 and the date of sale?

A 6 months
B 48 months
C 36 months
D No extra months **(2 marks)**

94 How many months would be covered by letting relief assuming John did NOT move back into the house on 1 February 2016?

A No months
B 12 months
C 18 months
D 24 months **(2 marks)**

95 What is Elsie's allowable loss on the disposal of the oil painting?

A £6,500
B £10,833
C £5,900
D £5,500 **(2 marks)**

96 What is Elsie's chargeable gain on the disposal of the vase?

A £2,500
B £2,375
C £3,425
D £3,500 **(2 marks)**

Business reliefs MCQs **4 mins each**

97 Jane has two chargeable gains in the tax year 2016/17:

£10,000 – claim made for entrepreneurs' relief
£13,000 – no claim made for entrepreneurs' relief and not residential property

She has taxable income of £25,000 in the tax year 2016/17.

What is Jane's capital gains tax liability for the tax year 2016/17?

A £3,600
B £1,190
C £1,380
D £2,300 **(2 marks)**

98 Norman is a sole trader. He sold Shop A in July 2016 for £80,000, realising a chargeable gain of £25,000. Norman used the proceeds to buy a Shop B for £70,000 and used the remainder as working capital.

What is the cost of Shop B for capital gains tax purposes if Norman makes a claim for replacement of business assets (rollover) relief?

A £60,000
B £65,000
C £45,000
D £55,000 **(2 marks)**

99 On which TWO of the following gifts can a claim be made for gift relief?

(1) 10% shareholding in an unlisted investment company

(2) Factory owned by an individual and used in the trade of that individual's personal company

(3) Premises owned by a sole trader of which two thirds are used for trade purposes and one third is used for private purposes

(4) 2% shareholding in a trading company listed on the London Stock Exchange

A 1 and 2
B 2 and 3
C 2 and 4
D 1 and 4 **(2 marks)**

Roy and Graham **4 mins each**

The following scenario relates to questions 100 to 104.

Roy was a sole trader for many years. He had bought a factory for use in his trade on 10 July 2010 for £150,000. On 1 December 2016, Roy sold his sole trader business as a going concern to his son, Graham. The market value of the factory at that time was £260,000 and the consideration paid by Graham for the factory was £180,000.

Due to restructuring of the business, Graham let out the factory to an unconnected company from 1 December 2016. However, on 1 March 2017 he ceased trading and sold the factory to a developer for £320,000.

The factory is the only chargeable asset owned by either Roy or Graham. Both Roy and Graham are higher rate taxpayers.

100 What is the capital gains tax payable by Roy for the tax year 2016/17 if a claim is not made for gift relief?

A £1,890
B £11,000
C £27,692
D £9,990 **(2 marks)**

101 What is the capital gains tax payable by Graham for the tax year 2016/17 if a claim is not made for gift relief?

A £4,890
B £12,000
C £9,780
D £13,692 **(2 marks)**

102 What is the capital gains tax payable by Roy for the tax year 2016/17 if a claim is made for gift relief?

A £3,000
B £1,890
C £5,292
D £0 **(2 marks)**

103 What is the capital gains tax payable by Graham for the tax year 2016/17 if a claim is made for gift relief?

A £25,780
B £31,780
C £12,890
D £28,000 **(2 marks)**

104 Why is it beneficial for Roy and Graham not to make a claim for gift relief on the factory?

A The CGT liability would be payable earlier
B It enables Roy to use his annual exempt amount
C Graham would have to pay Roy more for the factory
D More of the gain is covered by a lower rate of CGT **(2 marks)**

105 Kai **20 mins**

Kai started in business as a sole trader in August 2010. He acquired a freehold shop for £105,000 and a warehouse for £150,000.

Kai sold his business as a going concern to Jibran in December 2016 and received £75,000 for goodwill, £90,000 for the shop and £180,000 for the warehouse. Kai also sold a plot of land to Jibran which he had not used in his business and is not residential property. The land cost £10,000 and Jibran paid £25,900 for it.

Other than those listed above, Kai had never undertaken any transactions which were relevant for capital gains tax purposes.

Kai's taxable income in 2016/17 was £20,000.

Required

Compute the capital gains tax payable by Kai for 2016/17, assuming that he makes any beneficial claims. State the date by which any claim must be made. **(10 marks)**

Shares and securities MCQs — 4 mins each

106 On 14 March 2017, Caroline gave her daughter 10,000 shares in A plc. On that date the shares were quoted at £2.20 – £2.22.

What is the value of gift for capital gains tax purposes?

A £22,100
B £22,000
C £22,200
D £22,050 **(2 marks)**

107 Bill bought 1,000 shares in B plc on 10 March 2010. He purchased a further 500 B plc shares on 31 July 2016 and 250 B plc shares on 10 August 2016. Bill sold 800 B plc shares on 31 July 2016.

How are the 800 B plc shares sold on 31 July 2016 matched?

A Against 250 of the shares acquired on 10 August 2016 and then against 550 of the shares acquired on 10 March 2010

B Against 500 of the shares acquired on 31 July 2016 and then against 300 of the shares acquired on 10 March 2010

C Against 500 of the shares acquired on 31 July 2016, then against 250 of the shares acquired on 10 August 2016 and then against 50 of the shares acquired on 10 March 2010

D Against 800 of the shares acquired on 10 March 2010 **(2 marks)**

108 Which TWO of the following statements about shares and securities owned by an individual are correct?

(1) A disposal of government securities ('gilts') by an individual is chargeable to capital gains tax.

(2) If a company makes a 2 for 1 bonus issue, each shareholder will receive 1 extra share for each 2 shares held without payment.

(3) In a rights issue the rights issue shares are paid for by the shareholder resulting in an adjustment to the cost of the shareholding.

(4) A chargeable gain does not usually arise on a takeover where new shares are exchanged for old shares.

A 1 and 3
B 3 and 4
C 2 and 4
D 1 and 2 **(2 marks)**

109 Melissa **20 mins**

Melissa bought shares in Fisher plc as follows:

12 July 2002	3,000 shares for £21,000
17 January 2005	Bonus issue 1 share for each 1 share held
14 December 2007	Rights issue 1 share for each 3 shares held at £3.25 per share
11 July 2016	4,000 shares for £16,000

She sold 10,000 shares for £42,000 on 2 July 2016.

Required

Compute Melissa's gain on sale. **(10 marks)**

Self assessment and payment of tax for individuals MCQs **4 mins each**

110 Steven and Rita wish to file their personal tax returns for 2016/17 electronically. The notice to file by HM Revenue and Customs (HMRC) to Steven was issued on 31 May 2017. The notice to file by HMRC to Rita was issued on 30 November 2017.

What is the latest filing date for each of Steven and Rita?

	Steven	*Rita*
A	31 October 2017	28 February 2018
B	31 October 2017	31 January 2018
C	31 January 2018	28 February 2018
D	31 January 2018	31 January 2018

(2 marks)

111 Tony is self-employed and his trading income is his only source of income. His income tax liabilities and Class 4 national insurance contributions (NIC) for 2015/16 and 2016/17 are as follows:

	2015/16	*2016/17*
	£	£
Income tax	10,000	12,500
Class 4 NIC	2,000	2,500
	12,000	15,000

How will Tony pay his income tax and Class 4 NIC for the tax year 2016/17?

A £15,000 on 31 January 2018
B £7,500 on 31 January and 31 July 2017
C £5,000 on 31 January 2017, 31 July 2017 and 31 January 2018
D £6,000 on 31 January and 31 July 2017, £3,000 on 31 January 2018 **(2 marks)**

112 Pepe has a trading loss of £30,000 for the tax year 2016/17. Due to carelessness he enters £38,000 on his tax return and makes a loss relief claim for £38,000 against his property business income for the tax year 2016/17. The property business income would otherwise have been taxed at 40%.

What is the maximum penalty that could be charged by HM Revenue and Customs (HMRC) in respect of the error?

A £3,200
B £960
C £2,400
D £640

(2 marks)

Ash

4 mins each

The following scenario relates to questions 113 to 117.

Ash is employed and also has a bank deposit account and owns some shares.

Ash's income tax liability for the tax year 2015/16 was £16,800. Of this £7,200 was paid under the PAYE system. Ash had made payments on account for the tax year totalling £3,600. On 31 March 2017, Ash filed his tax return for 2015/16. The late filing was due to Ash's carelessness and was not deliberate.

On 5 May 2017, HM Revenue and Customs issued a notice to Ash to file his tax return for the tax year 2016/17. Ash's income tax liability for the tax year 2016/17 was £22,000. £7,100 of this was paid under PAYE system. Ash did not make any claim in respect of his payments on account for 2016/17. On 30 April 2018, Ash paid the balancing payment for 2016/17.

113 What is the penalty for late filing of Ash's tax return for the tax year 2015/16?

A Greater of 100% of tax liability which would have been shown on return and £300
B Greater of 70% of tax liability which would have been shown on return and £300
C Greater of 5% of tax liability which would have been shown on return and £300
D £100 **(2 marks)**

114 What is the amount of the balancing payment for the tax year 2015/16?

A £16,800
B £6,000
C £13,200
D £9,600 **(2 marks)**

115 What is the amount of each of the payments on account (POAs) for the tax year 2016/17?

A £4,800
B £16,800
C £9,600
D £8,400 **(2 marks)**

116 What are the due dates for the payments on account for the tax year 2016/17?

	First POA	*Second POA*
A	31 July 2017	31 January 2018
B	14 July 2017	14 January 2018
C	31 January 2017	31 July 2017
D	5 April 2017	5 October 2017

(2 marks)

117 What is the penalty for late payment of the balancing payment of Ash's tax liability for the tax year 2016/17?

A £100
B 5% of the unpaid tax
C 10% of the unpaid tax
D 15% of the unpaid tax **(2 marks)**

Inheritance tax: scope and transfers of value MCQs

4 mins each

118 Bernard made a gross chargeable lifetime transfer of £260,000 in August 2012. In November 2016, he gave £420,000 to a trust for the benefit of his son and daughter. Bernard agreed to pay any lifetime IHT due.

How much inheritance tax will be payable by Bernard on transfer of value in November 2016?

A £87,250
B £69,800
C £88,750
D £22,500 **(2 marks)**

119 Andy and Hilda had been married for many years when Andy died in June 2007. 60% of Andy's nil rate band was unused on his death. The nil rate band at Andy's death was £300,000. Hilda died in December 2016. Her only lifetime transfers of value were cash gifts of £6,000 to her nephew in January 2016 and £10,000 to her niece in March 2016.

What is the maximum nil rate band available for use against Hilda's death estate?

A £504,000
B £520,000
C £510,000
D £495,000 **(2 marks)**

120 On 15 July 2016 Yvette gave £500,000 to a trust for the benefit of her grandchildren. Yvette died on 27 December 2016.

What are the due dates for inheritance tax to be paid on this transfer of value?

	Lifetime tax	*Death tax*	
A	31 January 2017	30 June 2017	
B	30 April 2017	30 June 2017	
C	31 January 2017	30 April 2017	
D	30 April 2017	30 April 2017	**(2 marks)**

Colin and Diane

4 mins each

The following scenario relates to questions 121 to 125.

Colin

Colin always used his annual exemption in April each year. On 21 January 2009 he gave cash of £352,000 to a trust. Colin paid the inheritance tax due. The nil rate band in 2008/09 was £312,000.

On 10 November 2011, Colin gave a further amount of cash to the trust. The trustees paid the inheritance due. Colin died on 15 June 2016. Additional inheritance tax was payable by the trustees as a result of his death.

Diane

Diane died on 20 December 2016. During her lifetime, she used her annual exemption in April each year and also made the following gifts.

Date	*Gift*	*Donee*
20.8.11	Shares worth £15,000	Daughter
19.6.12	Shares worth £360,000	Trustees (Trustees paid the IHT)

The nil rate band in both 2011/12 and 2012/13 was £325,000.

121 What was the amount of lifetime inheritance tax paid by Colin on the gift made by him on 21 January 2009?

A £8,500
B £10,000
C £6,750
D £8,000 **(2 marks)**

122 What were the due dates for payment of inheritance tax on the gift made by Colin on 10 November 2011?

	Lifetime tax	*Death tax*
A	30 April 2012	30 April 2017
B	31 May 2012	31 December 2016
C	30 April 2012	31 December 2016
D	31 May 2012	30 April 2017

(2 marks)

123 What was the amount of lifetime inheritance tax paid by the trustees on the gift made by Diane on 19 June 2012?

A £5,800
B £8,750
C £10,000
D £7,000 **(2 marks)**

124 What was the amount of taper relief which could be set against the inheritance tax payable on Diane's death on the gift made by her on 19 June 2012?

A £12,000
B £5,600
C £8,000
D £5,000 **(2 marks)**

125 Which one of the following is NOT an advantage of making a lifetime transfer of value?

A There is no capital gains tax on a lifetime transfer of value if the donor dies after seven years of making it.

B If the donor makes a chargeable lifetime transfer and survives seven years, he has reduced his estate for IHT and the only inheritance tax payable is that on the lifetime transfer at lifetime rates.

C The values of lifetime transfers cannot exceed the transfer of value when made.

D If the donor makes a potentially exempt transfer and survives seven years, he has reduced his estate for IHT but the transfer is exempt. **(2 marks)**

126 Simona 20 mins

Simona died on 19 January 2017, leaving the following assets:

	£
Shares in MS plc	320,000
Life assurance policy	see note
House	175,000
Household furniture	20,000
Cash in bank	97,750
Car	5,000

Simona also had the following debts at her death:

	£
Bank loan secured on house	10,000
Credit card bills	7,000
Income tax	3,000
Gas bill	250

Note

The value of the insurance policy immediately before Simona's death was £60,000. The proceeds payable as a result of Simona's death were £250,000.

The personal representative of Simona's estate paid funeral expenses of £2,500.

Simona had not made any lifetime gifts.

Simona was widowed in September 2007. Her husband left £20,000 to his sister and the rest of his estate to Simona. He had not made any lifetime gifts. The nil rate band for 2007/08 was £300,000. Simona remarried in April 2010.

In her will, Simona left her house to her second husband and the remainder of her estate to her children.

Required

(a) Compute Simona's chargeable death estate. **(6 marks)**

(b) Explain and compute the amount of the nil rate band available to be set against Simona's death estate, assuming any elections available are made. **(3 marks)**

(c) Using your answer to part (b), compute the inheritance tax payable on Simona's death estate. **(1 mark)**

(Total = 10 marks)

Computing taxable total profits and the corporation tax liability MCQs — 4 mins each

127 H Ltd started trading on 1 December 2015 and prepared its first set of accounts to 31 March 2017.

What are H Ltd's accounting period(s) for the period of account to 31 March 2017?

A 1 December 2015 to 31 March 2016 and 1 April 2016 to 31 March 2017
B 1 December 2015 to 5 April 2016 and 6 April 2016 to 31 March 2017
C 1 December 2015 to 30 November 2016 and 1 December 2016 to 31 March 2017
D 1 December 2015 to 31 March 2017 **(2 marks)**

128 L Ltd is a trading company which prepares accounts to 31 March each year. In its statement of profit or loss for the year to 31 March 2017, it has included a deduction of £3,200 in respect of the annual leasing cost for a car. The car has a recommended list price of £16,000 and CO_2 emissions of 140g/km.

What is the allowable expense in respect of the leasing cost for the accounting period ended 31 March 2017?

A £2,720
B £480
C £3,360
D £3,200 **(2 marks)**

129 Z Ltd is a trading company which prepared accounts to 30 June 2016. In addition to its trading activities, Z Ltd lets out an unfurnished house for an annual rent of £14,400 payable in monthly instalments. The tenant is due to pay each instalment in arrears on the last day of each month but did not pay the June 2016 instalment until 14 July 2016. There was interest of £7,500 accrued during the year to 30 June 2016 on a mortgage taken out by Z Ltd to acquire the house and Z Ltd also made capital repayments on the mortgage of £300 during that year.

How much must Z Ltd include in its taxable total profits as its property business income for the accounting period ended 30 June 2016?

A £13,200
B £6,900
C £5,400
D £14,400 **(2 marks)**

Red plc and Green plc — 4 mins each

The following scenario relates to questions 130 to 134.

Red plc

Red plc previously prepared accounts to 31 December. A decision has been made to change its year end to 31 March. The following information relates to the 15 month period of account from 1 January 2016 to 31 March 2017.

Red plc had a tax written down value of £24,000 on its main pool at 1 January 2016. It bought a car with CO_2 emissions of 120g/km for use by an employee in November 2016 at a cost of £12,000. It also bought some machinery in February 2017 at a cost of £290,000, and a new car with CO_2 emissions of 60g/km for £10,000 in March 2017.

Green plc

Green plc previously made its accounts up to 31 December. A decision has been made to change its year end to 31 May. The following information relates to the 17 month period of account from 1 January 2015 to 31 May 2016.

	£
Trading profits	391,000
Bank interest accrued and received	
31.5.15	15,000
31.12.15	6,000
31.5.16	2,500
Chargeable gain on property sold on	
1.9.15	5,000
Qualifying charitable donations paid	
28.2.15	15,000
31.8.15	15,000
28.2.16	40,000

130 What are the maximum capital allowances for Red plc for the first accounting period in the period of account to 31 March 2017?

A £16,320
B £4,320
C £2,700
D £6,480 **(2 marks)**

131 What is the maximum amount of the annual investment allowance which can be claimed on the expenditure on machinery in February 2017?

A £290,000
B £50,000
C £250,000
D £200,000 **(2 marks)**

132 What are the maximum capital allowances for Red plc in respect of the car purchased in March 2017 in the accounting period of purchase?

A £2,500
B £10,000
C £1,800
D £450 **(2 marks)**

133 What are the taxable total profits for Green plc for the first accounting period in the period of account to 31 May 2016?

A £272,000
B £130,000
C £302,000
D £115,000 **(2 marks)**

134 What are the taxable total profits for Green plc for the second accounting period in the period of account to 31 May 2016?

A £117,500
B £234,500
C £77,500
D £289,500 **(2 marks)**

135 Elderflower Ltd **29 mins**

Elderflower Ltd is a company which trades as a manufacturer of specialist soft drinks. The company's statement of profit or loss for the year ended 31 March 2017 is as follows:

	£	£
Gross profit		510,000
Other income		
Profit on disposal of office building (note 1)		54,000
Bank interest (note 2)		7,000
Expenses		
Depreciation	54,690	
Professional fees (note 3)	22,000	
Repairs and renewals (note 4)	29,700	
Other expenses (note 5)	24,400	
		(130,790)
Finance costs		
Interest payable (note 6)		(23,000)
Profit before taxation		417,210

Notes

(1) *Disposal of office building*

The profit of £54,000 is in respect of a freehold office building that was sold on 30 June 2016 for £380,000. The chargeable gain on sale has been computed to be £45,580.

(2) *Bank interest received*

The bank interest was received on 31 March 2017 and is the amount accrued to that date. The bank deposit is held for non-trading purposes.

(3) *Professional fees*

Professional fees are as follows:

	£
Accountancy and audit fee	5,900
Legal fees in connection with the issue of share capital	8,800
Legal fees in connection with the issue of loan notes (see note 6)	6,400
Legal fees in connection with fine for breach of health and safety legislation	900
	22,000

(4) *Repairs and renewals*

The figure of £29,700 for repairs includes £9,700 for constructing an extension to the company's manufacturing premises and £5,400 for repainting the interior of the company's offices.

(5) *Other expenses*

Other expenses include £2,310 for entertaining customers and a qualifying charitable donation of £500.

(6) *Interest payable*

Elderflower Ltd issued loan notes on 1 October 2016. The capital raised was used for trading purposes. Interest of £23,000 in respect of the first six months of the loan was paid on 31 March 2017.

(7) *Plant and machinery*

On 1 April 2016 the tax written down values of plant and machinery were as follows:

	£
Main pool	27,500
Special rate pool (consisting of car with CO_2 emissions of 176g/km)	14,700

The following transactions took place during the year ended 31 March 2017:

		Cost/(Proceeds)
		£
10 May 2016	Purchased plant	20,200
5 January 2017	Sold the special rate pool motor car	(9,700)
20 March 2017	Sold a delivery van	(11,600)
31 March 2017	Purchased a motor car CO_2 emissions 107g/km	9,600

The van sold on 20 March 2017 for £11,600 originally cost £18,500. The motor car purchased on 31 March 2017 is used by the sales manager: 25% of the mileage is for private journeys.

Required

(a) Calculate Elderflower Ltd's trading profit for the year ended 31 March 2017. Your answer should commence with the profit before taxation figure of £417,210 and should list all of the items in the statement of profit or loss indicating by the use of a zero (0) any items that do not require adjustment. You should assume that the company claims the maximum available capital allowances. **(12 marks)**

(b) Calculate Elderflower Ltd's taxable total profits for the year ended 31 March 2017. **(2 marks)**

(c) Calculate Elderflower Ltd's corporation tax liability for the year ended 31 March 2017. **(1 mark)**

(Total = 15 marks)

Chargeable gains for companies MCQs — 4 mins each

136 U Ltd acquires an asset in April 2002 (RPI = 175.7) for £12,000, incurring costs of acquisition of £800. U Ltd sells the asset in August 2016 (RPI = 261.9) for £17,500, incurring costs of disposal of £1,000.

What is the chargeable gain or allowable loss (if any) on the sale?

A £3,700 gain
B £(2,585) loss
C £(2,192) loss
D Neither a gain nor a loss **(2 marks)**

137 D Ltd sold a factory for £640,000 on 15 March 2017. It had paid £120,000 for the factory on 12 January 2012. D Ltd incurred expenses of £8,000 in buying the factory and £6,000 in selling the factory. The assumed indexation factor for the period January 2012 to March 2017 is 0.109.

What is D Ltd's chargeable gain on the disposal?

A £491,394
B £492,048
C £492,920
D £506,000 **(2 marks)**

138 F Ltd sells a factory for £200,000. The factory cost £110,000 and the indexation allowance available is £20,000. The company acquires another factory 15 months later for £187,500.

What is the amount of rollover relief which F Ltd can claim?

A £12,500
B £70,000
C £77,500
D £57,500 **(2 marks)**

Long Ltd, Tall Ltd and Short Ltd — 4 mins each

The following scenario relates to questions 139 to 143.

Long Ltd

On 16 October 2016, Long Ltd sold 6,000 £1 ordinary shares in Shallow Ltd for £45,000. Long Ltd had purchased 10,000 shares in Shallow Ltd on 21 May 2008 for £40,000.

Tall Ltd

Tall Ltd purchased 5,000 shares in Middle plc on 10 June 2002 for £14,000. On 28 October 2016, Middle plc made a 1 for 1 rights issue at £4 per share. Tall Ltd took up its full entitlement to rights issue shares.

Short Ltd

Short Ltd purchased 10,000 shares in Far plc on 20 June 2002 for £34,000. On 7 March 2017 Far plc was taken over by Deep plc. Short Ltd received two £1 ordinary shares and one £1 preference share in Deep plc for each £1 ordinary share held in Far plc. Immediately after the takeover each £1 ordinary share in Deep plc was quoted at £5 and each £1 preference share was quoted at £2.50.

RPIs (actual and assumed)

June 2002 = 176.2 May 2008 = 215.1 October 2016 = 262.8

139 Which TWO of the following statements about chargeable gains for companies are true?

(1) There is an annual exempt amount available to set against chargeable gains
(2) There is relief for inflation called the indexation allowance
(3) A company pays corporation tax on its gains at a rate of 10%
(4) A company is liable to corporation tax on its net chargeable gains as part of its total profits

A 1 and 3
B 1 and 4
C 2 and 4
D 2 and 3 **(2 marks)**

140 What is the correct order of matching share disposals for companies?

(1) Shares acquired on the same day
(2) Shares from the FA 1985 pool
(3) Shares acquired in the previous nine days

A 1, then 2, then 3
B 1, then 3, then 2
C 2, then 1, then 3
D 2, then 3, then 1 **(2 marks)**

141 What is the chargeable gain on the disposal by Long Ltd on 16 October 2016?

A £15,678
B £4,578
C £21,000
D £15,672 **(2 marks)**

142 What is the indexed cost of the Middle plc shares following the rights issue on 28 October 2016?

A £50,711
B £20,881
C £34,000
D £40,881 **(2 marks)**

143 What are the costs of the ordinary shares and the preference shares in Deep plc held by Short Ltd following the takeover on 7 March 2017?

	Ordinary shares	*Preference shares*
A	£22,667	£11,333
B	£27,200	£6,800
C	£20,000	£10,000
D	£100,000	£25,000

(2 marks)

144 Xeon Ltd — 20 mins

Xeon Ltd made the following disposals in the year ended 31 March 2017.

(a) On 31 May 2016, Xeon Ltd sold a warehouse used in its trade for £120,000. The company had bought the warehouse for £65,000 on 1 July 2003. Xeon Ltd had bought another warehouse for use in its trade for £100,000 on 1 July 2015.

(b) On 18 June 2016, Xeon Ltd sold two acres of land for £30,000. These two acres were part of a five acre plot of land which was purchased for £21,000 on 1 April 2000. The remaining three acres were valued at £40,000 in June 2016. Xeon Ltd spent £1,000 in December 2012 on improving the two acres of land sold in June 2016.

Xeon Ltd made any beneficial claims in respect of these gains.

Required

Compute Xeon Ltd's chargeable gains for the year ended 31 March 2017 and show the cost for chargeable gains purposes of the warehouse bought on 1 July 2015. **(10 marks)**

RPIs (actual and assumed)

April 2000 = 170.1
July 2003 = 181.3
December 2012 = 246.8
May 2016 = 260.8
June 2016 = 261.2

Losses

4 mins each

145 Which TWO of the following statements about loss reliefs for a company are correct?

(1) Property business losses of a company cannot be set against total profits of the same accounting period

(2) Trade losses of a company carried forward can only be used against profits of the same trade

(3) Trade loss relief may be given by deduction from current period total profits and those in the previous 12 months

(4) Capital losses made by a company can be used against chargeable gains of the previous accounting period

A 1 and 2
B 2 and 3
C 1 and 4
D 2 and 4

(2 marks)

146 E plc prepares accounts to 31 December each year. In the year ended 31 December 2015 E plc had total profits of £36,000 and it made a qualifying charitable donation of £1,000. In the year ended 31 December 2016 E plc made an adjusted trading loss of £40,000, had other taxable income of £10,000 and made a qualifying charitable donation of £3,000.

What is the loss that E plc can claim to carry back to the year ended 31 December 2015?

A £30,000
B £33,000
C £36,000
D £35,000

(2 marks)

147 The following information relates to T plc for the year ended 31 March 2017:

	£
Trading income	165,000
Income from non-trading loan relationships	27,000
Chargeable gain	14,000
Trading loss b/f at 1 April 2016	(170,000)
Capital loss b/f at 1 April 2016	(3,000)

What are T plc's taxable total profits for the year ended 31 March 2017?

A £33,000
B £27,000
C £41,000
D £38,000

(2 marks)

148 Ferraro Ltd

20 mins

Ferraro Ltd has the following results.

	y/e 31.3.15	*9m to 31.12.15*	*y/e 31.12.16*
	£	£	£
Trading profit (loss)	6,200	4,320	(100,000)
Bank deposit interest accrued	80	240	260
Rents receivable	1,420	1,440	1,600
Chargeable gain	0	7,680	0
Qualifying charitable donations	0	1,000	1,500

Required

Compute all taxable total profits, claiming loss reliefs as early as possible. State the amounts of any losses carried forward as at 31 December 2016. **(10 marks)**

Groups **4 mins each**

149 C Ltd had the following results for the year ended 31 March 2017:

	£
Trading income	(16,000)
Income from non-trading loan relationships	1,000
Capital loss	(5,000)

C Ltd paid a qualifying charitable donation of £4,000 on 2 February 2017.

What is the maximum amount that C Ltd can surrender for group relief?

A £16,000
B £20,000
C £19,000
D £21,000 **(2 marks)**

150 O Ltd owns 100% of P Ltd. In the year to 31 December 2016 O Ltd made a trading loss of £60,000. P Ltd had taxable total profits of £54,000 for the year to 31 March 2017.

What group relief can P Ltd claim from O Ltd which can be set against its taxable total profits for the year to 31 March 2017?

A £40,500
B £54,000
C £45,000
D £60,000 **(2 marks)**

151 A Ltd group has the following structure:

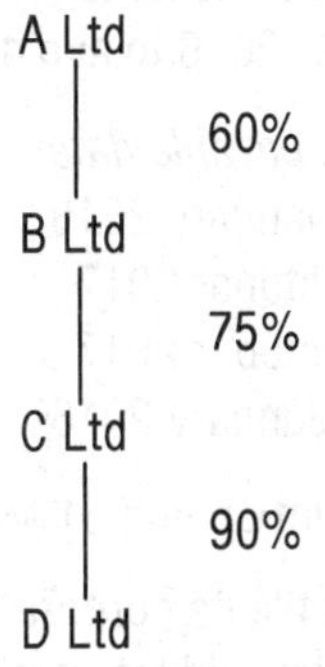

Which ONE of the following is a chargeable gains group?

A A Ltd, B Ltd and C Ltd
B B Ltd and C Ltd
C B Ltd, C Ltd and D Ltd
D C Ltd and D Ltd **(2 marks)**

152 P Ltd

20 mins

P Ltd owns the following holdings in ordinary shares in other companies.

Q Ltd	83%
R Ltd	77%
S Ltd	67%
M Ltd	80%
T Ltd	70%

The following are the results of the above companies for the year ended 31 March 2017.

	P Ltd	*Q Ltd*	*R Ltd*	*S Ltd*	*M Ltd*	*T Ltd*
	£	£	£	£	£	£
Trading profit	0	14,000	210,000	0	20,000	70,000
Trading loss	226,000	0	0	8,000	0	0
Property business income	6,000	4,000	0	0	0	0
Qualifying charitable donation paid	4,500	2,000	5,000	0	14,000	0

P Ltd and S Ltd are not expected to become profitable for several years and have no capacity to carry back losses.

Required

Compute the overall corporation tax payable for the above accounting period for the above companies. Assume that loss relief is claimed in the most beneficial manner.

(10 marks)

Self assessment and payment of tax by companies

4 mins each

153 N Ltd is not a large company and prepares accounts to 31 December every year.

What are the dates by which N Ltd must file its tax return and pay its corporation tax for the accounting period ended 31 December 2016 to avoid penalties and interest?

	Return date	*Tax payable date*
A	31 January 2018	31 January 2018
B	31 December 2017	1 October 2017
C	31 January 2018	1 October 2017
D	31 December 2017	31 January 2018

(2 marks)

154 Q plc has a 15-month period of account ending 31 March 2017.

What is the date by which Q plc must file its corporation tax return for the first accounting period in this period of account to avoid penalties and interest?

A 31 March 2018
B 30 June 2017
C 31 December 2017
D 1 October 2017

(2 marks)

155 M Ltd prepared accounts for the year ended 31 March 2017.

What is the earliest date until which M Ltd must retain its business records related to this year, assuming that no compliance check is made, and what is the maximum penalty for non-compliance?

(1) Retention date: 31 March 2019
(2) Retention date: 31 March 2023
(3) Maximum penalty: £2,000
(4) Maximum penalty: £3,000

A 1 and 3
B 2 and 3
C 1 and 4
D 2 and 4 **(2 marks)**

Skyblue Ltd and Turquoise plc — 4 mins each

The following scenario relates to questions 156 to 160.

Skyblue Ltd

Skyblue Ltd prepares accounts to 30 September each year. HM Revenue and Customs sent Skyblue Ltd a notice on 15 December 2016 requiring it to file a corporation tax return for the accounting period ended 30 September 2016. Skyblue Ltd is not a member of a group of companies.

Turquoise plc

Turquoise plc prepares accounts to 31 March each year. In its return for the year ending 31 March 2017, loss relief for £100,000 was claimed, resulting in a reduction of £20,000 in the company's corporation tax. In fact, the loss relief available was only £10,000. The error was deliberate but not concealed.

156 How must Skyblue Ltd file its corporation tax return for the year ended 30 September 2016 and what is the latest filing date?

	Return	*Filing date*
A	Paper return	31 January 2018
B	Electronic return	31 January 2018
C	Paper return	30 September 2017
D	Electronic return	30 September 2017

(2 marks)

157 What is the penalty charged on Skyblue Ltd if it files its return four months late, if either it has always submitted its returns on time or has submitted late returns for each of the preceding two accounting periods?

	On time	*Last two returns late*
A	£100	£200
B	£200	£500
C	£200	£1,000
D	£100	£500

(2 marks)

158 What is the latest date by which HM Revenue and Customs can give written notice to Skyblue Ltd of a compliance check on the return if it is filed either on the due date or four months late?

	Due date	*Four months late*
A	Quarter day following the first anniversary of the filing date	Quarter day following the first anniversary of the filing date
B	First anniversary of the filing date	Quarter day following the first anniversary of the filing date
C	Quarter day following the first anniversary of the filing date	First anniversary of the filing date
D	First anniversary of the filing date	First anniversary of the filing date

(2 marks)

159 What is the maximum penalty that may be imposed on Turquoise plc for its error?

A	£5,400
B	£18,000
C	£12,600
D	£7,000

(2 marks)

160 What is the minimum percentage of potential lost revenue that may be imposed as a penalty on Turquoise plc if it either makes an unprompted disclosure or a prompted disclosure of the error?

	Unprompted	*Prompted*
A	20%	35%
B	0%	15%
C	70%	100%
D	30%	50%

(2 marks)

161 Cyan plc and Crimson plc — 20 mins

Cyan plc

Cyan plc prepared its accounts to 31 March for many years. In May 2016, Cyan plc decided to change its accounting date to 31 December and so prepared accounts to 31 December 2016. Its taxable total profits for this nine-month period were £1,350,000. Cyan plc did not receive any dividends during the period and it has no related 51% group companies. In the year to 31 March 2016, Cyan plc had taxable total profits of £1,632,000.

Crimson plc

Crimson plc prepares accounts to 31 March each year. In the year ended 31 March 2017 it had taxable total profits of £450,000.

Crimson plc has owned 55% of the ordinary shares of Tangerine plc and 45% of the ordinary share capital of Russet plc for many years. Tangerine plc has owned 96% of the ordinary share capital of Rouge plc for many years.

Crimson plc bought 80% of the ordinary shares of Chestnut plc on 1 July 2016.

Crimson plc received a dividend of £30,000 from Russet plc on 1 February 2017 and a dividend of £50,000 from Tangerine plc on 1 March 2017.

Required

(a) Calculate the corporation tax payable by Cyan plc for the accounting period ended 31 December 2016. **(1 mark)**

(b) Show how the corporation tax liability in part (a) will be paid. **(4 marks)**

(c) Explain which companies are related 51% group companies with Crimson plc for the calculation of the profits threshold to determine whether Crimson plc is a large company in the year ended 31 March 2017. **(2 marks)**

(d) Using your answer to part (c), determine whether Crimson plc is a large company in the year ended 31 March 2017. **(3 marks)**

(Total = 10 marks)

An introduction to VAT MCQs **4 mins each**

162 Alec has been in business since 1 June 2016 making water bottles. He will prepare his first set of accounts for the 12 months ending 31 May 2017. Alec's total taxable turnover for the seven months ended 31 December 2016 amounted to £45,000. On 1 January 2017 he received an order for water bottles amounting to £82,500 to be delivered later that month. Alec registered for VAT only when he was required to do so.

From what date will HM Revenue and Customs (HMRC) register Alec for value added tax (VAT) purposes?

A 1 January 2017
B 1 February 2017
C 1 June 2017
D 1 March 2017 **(2 marks)**

163 B plc is registered for value added tax (VAT). In the quarter ended 31 October 2016 it made taxable supplies (before taking account of any discounts) of £60,000, exclusive of VAT. All supplies are standard rated. On each sales invoice, B plc offers a discount of 4% to all of its customers who settle their invoices within 30 days. Only 25% of all customers (representing a quarter of the £60,000 above) pay within this time.

How much output VAT should B plc show on its VAT return for the quarter ended 31 October 2016 in respect of the above supplies?

A £11,880
B £11,640
C £11,520
D £12,000 **(2 marks)**

164 K Ltd received an order for machine parts on 14 December 2016. K Ltd dispatched these to the customer on 18 December 2016. An invoice was issued on 31 December 2016 and full payment was received on 15 January 2017.

What is the tax point for the sale of the machine parts?

A 18 December 2016
B 31 December 2016
C 15 January 2017
D 14 December 2016 **(2 marks)**

Justin **4 mins each**

The following scenario relates to questions 165 to 169.

Justin has the following transactions in the quarter ended 31 December 2016. All amounts exclude any VAT unless otherwise stated.

	£
Purchases	
Furniture for resale	275,000
Restaurant bills: two-thirds for entertaining UK customers, one-third for entertaining non-UK customers	1,800
Petrol for car owned by Justin and used by an employee for business and private use (VAT inclusive)	600
Sales	
Furniture	490,000
Books on interior design	2,400

The employee uses the car provided by Justin 30% for private use. Justin has opted to use the fuel scale for the employee's car. The appropriate fuel scale charge for the quarter is £362 inclusive of VAT.

Justin is considering buying a car for his own use which will be used for both business and private purposes.

165 What is the output VAT payable on the sales of furniture and books?

A £81,667
B £98,480
C £98,000
D £82,067 **(2 marks)**

166 What is the net VAT payable or recoverable by Justin for petrol for the employee's car?

A £40 recoverable
B £60 recoverable
C £10 recoverable
D £60 payable **(2 marks)**

167 What is the amount of the input VAT recoverable on the restaurant bills?

A £240
B £120
C £360
D £Nil **(2 marks)**

168 When must Justin submit his VAT return for the quarter to 31 December 2016 and by when must he pay the associated VAT?

	Submission	*Payment*
A	31 January 2017	7 February 2017
B	14 February 2017	14 February 2017
C	7 February 2017	7 February 2017
D	31 January 2017	14 February 2017

(2 marks)

169 What will be the VAT treatment of the car purchased for use by Justin?

	Input tax	*Sale*
A	Full recovery of input VAT	Full charge to output tax on sale
B	No recovery of input VAT	Full charge to output tax on sale
C	Business use recovery of input VAT	Business use charge to output tax on sale
D	No recovery of input VAT	No charge to VAT on sale

(2 marks)

170 Newcomer Ltd and Au Revoir Ltd **20 mins**

(a) Newcomer Ltd commenced trading on 1 October 2016. Its forecast sales are as follows.

		£
2016	October	18,500
	November	19,900
	December	23,400
2017	January	22,300
	February	22,700
	March	19,200

The company's sales are all standard-rated, and the above figures are exclusive of VAT.

Required

Explain when Newcomer Ltd will be required to compulsorily register for VAT. **(6 marks)**

(b) Au Revoir Ltd has been registered for VAT for many years and its sales are all standard-rated. The company has recently seen a downturn in its business activities, and sales for the years ended 31 October 2016 and 2017 are forecast to be £75,000 and £73,500 respectively. Both of these figures are exclusive of VAT.

Required

Explain why Au Revoir Ltd will be permitted to voluntarily deregister for VAT, and from what date deregistration will be effective. **(4 marks)**

(Total = 10 marks)

171 Ongoing Ltd — 20 mins

Ongoing Ltd is registered for VAT, and its sales and purchases are all standard-rated. The following information relates to the company's VAT return for the quarter ended 30 April 2016:

(1) Standard-rated sales amounted to £120,000. Ongoing Ltd offers its customers a 5% discount for prompt payment, and this discount is taken by half of the customers. The discount is detailed on the sales invoice.

(2) Standard-rated purchases and expenses amounted to £35,640. This figure includes £480 for entertaining UK customers.

(3) On 15 April 2016 the company wrote off impairment losses (bad debts) of £2,100 and £840 in respect of invoices due for payment on 10 August 2015 and 5 December 2015 respectively.

(4) On 30 April 2016 the company purchased a motor car at a cost of £16,450 for the use of a salesperson, and machinery at a cost of £21,150. Both these figures are inclusive of VAT. The motor car is used for both business and private mileage.

(5) On 30 April 2016 the company sold a motor car for £12,000 which had been used for both business and private mileage.

Unless stated otherwise, all of the above figures are exclusive of VAT. Ongoing Ltd does not operate the cash accounting scheme.

Required

Calculate the amount of VAT payable by Ongoing Ltd for the quarter ended 30 April 2016.

(10 marks)

Further aspects of VAT MCQs — 4 mins each

172 Which TWO of the following statements about the value added tax (VAT) cash accounting scheme are correct?

(1) All VAT returns must be up to date before a trader can join the scheme.

(2) Trader must pay 90% of the previous year's net VAT liability during the year by means of nine monthly payments.

(3) Trader's taxable turnover (exclusive of VAT) in 12 months before application must not exceed £1,350,000.

(4) Scheme gives automatic impairment loss relief (bad debt relief).

A 1 and 2
B 2 and 3
C 1 and 4
D 2 and 4 **(2 marks)**

173 Iris is a UK value added tax (VAT) registered trader. She sold goods with a VAT exclusive price of £30,000 to Heinrich in February 2017. Heinrich runs a business in Germany and is VAT registered in that country. Iris quoted the Heinrich's VAT number on the invoice and has proof of delivery to him in Germany. The rate of VAT in Germany on the goods would be 19%.

What is the VAT that Iris must charge on this supply?

A £5,000
B £6,000
C £5,700
D £Nil **(2 marks)**

174 X plc is registered for value added tax (VAT) and uses the flat rate scheme. In its VAT quarter ended 30 June 2016 it had a tax inclusive turnover of £110,000. This comprises of standard rated sales of £80,000, zero-rated sales of £20,000 and exempt sales of £10,000. The flat rate scheme percentage for the company's trading sector is 9%.

What is the VAT payable to HMRC by X plc for the quarter ended 30 June 2016?

A £9,900
B £7,200
C £9,000
D £8,100 **(2 marks)**

Jason 4 mins each

The following scenario relates to questions 175 to 179.

Jason is a sole trader who has recently registered for value added tax (VAT). He buys and sells goods from and to other businesses situated elsewhere in the European Union (EU) and also, occasionally, businesses outside the EU. He also supplies services to business customers outside the EU.

Jason bought some goods from a trader in Germany on 20 July 2016. An invoice was issued by the German trader on 18 August 2016 and was paid by Jason on 28 August 2016.

175 How will the supplies of goods made by Jason be treated for UK VAT if made to a VAT registered trader in another EU state or to a customer outside the EU?

	EU registered trader	*Outside EU*
A	Standard rated	Zero rated
B	Zero rated	Zero rated
C	Standard rated	Outside the scope of VAT
D	Zero rated	Outside the scope of VAT

(2 marks)

176 How Jason will deal with the VAT implications of buying goods from Germany?

	Output tax	*Input tax*
A	Output tax at UK rate at point of entry	Input tax at UK rate in next VAT return
B	Output tax at UK rate on next VAT return	Input tax at German rate in next VAT return
C	Output tax at UK rate at point of entry	Input tax at German rate in next VAT return
D	Output tax at UK rate on next VAT return	Input tax at UK rate in next VAT return

(2 marks)

177 What is the tax point for the purchase by Jason of goods from Germany?

A 28 August 2016
B 18 August 2016
C 15 August 2016
D 20 July 2016 **(2 marks)**

178 How will Jason deal with the VAT implications of his occasional import of goods from outside the EU?

	Output tax	*Input tax*	
A	Output tax at UK rate at point of entry	No input tax	
B	Output tax at UK rate on next VAT return	No input tax	
C	Output tax at UK rate at point of entry	Input tax at UK rate in next VAT return	
D	Output tax at UK rate on next VAT return	Input tax at UK rate in next VAT return	**(2 marks)**

179 What is the VAT treatment of supplies of services by Jason to business customers outside the EU?

A Outside the scope of VAT
B Standard rated
C Zero rated
D Exempt **(2 marks)**

180 K Ltd and L Ltd 20 mins

(a) K Ltd is registered for value added tax (VAT). The directors of K Ltd have recently heard about the annual accounting scheme and asked you for advice on this matter.

Required

Prepare draft notes, for a meeting with the directors of K Ltd, outlining:

(i) The rules and qualifying conditions that the company must satisfy in order to join and continue to use the VAT annual accounting scheme. **(4 marks)**

(ii) The advantages and disadvantages of using the scheme. **(3 marks)**

(b) L Ltd carries on a business as a wholesale adult clothing outlet and is registered for VAT. In recent months, L Ltd has had difficulty in obtaining payment of its invoices from its customers which has led to cash flow problems.

The directors of L Ltd have heard that there is a VAT scheme which may be advantageous for L Ltd to use. It wishes to continue to submit quarterly VAT returns.

Required

State the VAT scheme which would be advantageous for L Ltd to use and advise the directors of the conditions to join the scheme. **(3 marks)**

(Total = 10 marks)

Introduction to the UK tax system MCQs

1 D 2 and 4

HM Revenue and Customs (HMRC) produces a wide range of explanatory notes and has the administrative function for collection of tax.

HM Treasury formally imposes taxation. Advice on minimising tax liability is provided by professional advisors such as accountants.

2 B 2 and 4

Inheritance tax and capital gains tax are capital taxes.

Income tax and national insurance are revenue taxes. Corporation tax is both a revenue tax (in respect of its income) and a capital tax (in respect of its chargeable gains).

3 C 1, 2 and 4

Inform Serena in writing that it is not possible for your firm to act for her, inform HMRC that your firm is no longer acting for Serena, and report Serena's refusal to disclose the omission and the facts surrounding it to your firm's Money Laundering Reporting Officer.

You are not required to inform HMRC about the details of Serena's omission.

Computing taxable income and the income tax liability MCQs

4 C 2, 3 and 4

Interest received from an Individual Savings Account, Premium Bond prizes, and interest on NS&I Savings Certificates are exempt from income tax.

Dividends from a company and interest on government securities (gilts) are chargeable to income tax.

5 C £8,500

	£
Net income	108,000
Less personal pension contribution	(3,000)
Adjusted net income	105,000
Less income limit	(100,000)
Excess	5,000
Personal allowance	11,000
Less half excess £5,000 × ½	(2,500)
Available personal allowance	8,500

6 A £882

	£
£2,000 × 20%	400
£(5,000 – 2,000) = 3,000 × 0% (savings starting rate band)	0
£1,000 × 0% (savings nil rate band)	0
£(6,410 – 3,000 – 1,000) = 2,410 × 20%	482
Tax liability	882

Non-savings income is taxed at 20%. Savings income is taxed at 0% where such income falls within the first £5,000 of taxable income and then at 0% on the amount of the savings nil rate band of £1,000. The remainder of the savings income is then taxed at 20%.

7 C £24,850

	£
£32,000 × 20%	6,400
£(150,000 – 32,000) = 118,000 × 40%	47,200
£(175,000 – 150,000) = 25,000 × 45%	11,250
Tax liability	64,850
Less PAYE deducted	(40,000)
Tax payable	24,850

8 B £554

	£
Net income	53,400
Less gift aid donation (gross)	(300)
Adjusted net income	53,100
Less threshold	(50,000)
Excess	3,100
÷ £100	31
Child benefit income tax charge: 1% × £1,788 × 31	554

9 Sandeep, Harriet and Romelu

Tutorial note. When answering a question on residence status, start by considering whether the individual is automatically non-UK resident. If this test is not satisfied, then consider whether the individual is automatically UK resident. Again, if this test is not satisfied, then consider whether the combination of days in the UK and sufficient UK ties makes the individual UK resident.

(a) Sandeep is not automatically non-UK resident for the tax year 2016/17 because he spends 46 days or more in the UK during that tax year and does not work full-time overseas (and, in any case, has spent more than 90 days in the UK for the tax year).

He is automatically UK resident for the tax year 2016/17 because he spends 183 days or more in the UK during that tax year.

(b) Harriet was previously resident in the UK. She does not satisfy any of the automatic overseas tests since she spends 16 days or more in the UK and does not work full-time overseas.

Harriet does not satisfy any of the automatic UK tests since she spends less than 183 days in the UK, during the tax year 2016/17, has an overseas home and does not work full-time in the UK.

The 'sufficient ties' test is therefore relevant. Harriet has two UK ties:

(i) Substantive work in the UK
(ii) Available accommodation in the UK in which she spends at least one night in the tax year

Harriet spends between 91 and 120 days in the UK in 2016/17. These two ties are therefore sufficient to make her UK resident for the tax year 2016/17.

(c) Romelu was not previously resident in the UK. He does not satisfy any of the automatic overseas tests since he spends 46 days or more in the UK during the tax year 2016/17 and does not work full-time overseas.

Romelu does not satisfy any of the automatic UK tests as he spent less than 183 days in the UK, has an overseas home and does not work in the UK.

The 'sufficient ties' test is therefore relevant. Romelu has two UK ties:

(i) UK resident close family (spouse)
(ii) Available accommodation in the UK in which he spends at least one night in the tax year

Romelu spends between 91 and 120 days in the UK in 2016/17 and so he would need three UK ties to be UK resident for that tax year. Since Romelu has only two ties with the UK, he is therefore non-UK resident for the tax year 2016/17.

10 John and Helen

Tutorial note. In part (a), John's dividend income is between the basic rate limit and the higher rate limit, so the excess over the dividend nil rate band is taxed at 32.5%. Helen's dividends in excess of the dividend nil rate band, however, fall below the basic rate limit and are consequently taxed at 7.5%. In part (b), John's adjusted net income is the same as his net income, since he has not made any personal pension contributions or gift aid donations in 2016/17.

(a) *John and Helen 2016/17*

	Non-savings income	*Savings income*	*Dividend income*	*Total*
John	£	£	£	£
Employment income	66,090			
Dividends			6,211	
Bank deposit interest		1,000		
Building society interest		990		
Net income	66,090	1,990	6,211	74,291
Less personal allowance	(11,000)			
Taxable income	55,090	1,990	6,211	63,291

	£
Non savings income	
£32,000 × 20%	6,400
£23,090 (55,090 – 32,000) × 40%	9,236
Savings income	
£500 × 0% (higher rate taxpayer)	0
£1,490 (1,990 – 500) × 40%	596
Dividend income	
£5,000 × 0%	0
£1,211 (6,211 – 5,000) × 32.5%	394
Tax liability	16,626
Less: PAYE	(15,636)
Tax payable	990

	Non-savings income	Savings income	Dividend income	Total
	£	£	£	£
Helen				
Employment income	23,000			
Dividends			7,820	
Bank deposit interest		1,095		
Building society interest		525		
Net income	23,000	1,620	7,820	32,440
Less personal allowance	(11,000)			
Taxable income	12,000	1,620	7,820	21,440

	£
Non-savings income	
£12,000 × 20%	2,400
Savings income	
£1,000 × 0% (basic rate taxpayer)	0
£620 (1,620 – 1,000) × 20%	124
Dividend income	
£5,000 × 0%	0
£2,820 (7,820 – 5,000) × 7.5%	211
Tax liability	2,735
Less PAYE	(2,400)
Tax payable	335

(b) John will be liable to the child benefit income tax charge for the tax year 2016/17 because his spouse has received child benefit during this tax year and he has adjusted net income in excess of £50,000 that is higher than that of Helen. Since John's adjusted net income exceeds £60,000, the child benefit income tax charge is the full amount of child benefit (£1,076) received by Helen in 2016/17. This charge will be collected under the self assessment system.

11 Michael and Josie

> **Tutorial note**. Michael is not entitled to a personal allowance because his net income is more than £122,000. Josie is entitled to a reduced personal allowance because her adjusted net income is between £100,000 and £122,000.

	Non-savings income	Savings income	Dividend income	Total
Michael	£	£	£	£
Employment income	163,540			
Dividends			17,111	
Bank deposit interest		7,500		
Building society interest		7,400		
Net income/Taxable income	163,540	14,900	17,111	195,551

	£
Non savings income	
£32,000 × 20%	6,400
£118,000 (150,000 – 32,000) × 40%	47,200
£13,540 (163,540 – 150,000) × 45%	6,093
Savings income	
£14,900 × 45%	6,705
Dividend income	
£5,000 × 0%	0
£12,111 (17,111 – 5,000) × 38.1%	4,614
	71,012
Less PAYE	(59,960)
Tax payable	11,052

No savings nil rate band available because Michael is an additional rate taxpayer.

	Non-savings income	Savings income	Dividend income	Total
	£	£	£	£
Josie				
Employment income	100,000			
Dividends			7,820	
Bank deposit interest		150		
Building society interest		550		
Net income	100,000	700	7,820	108,520
Less personal allowance (W1)	(7,740)			
Taxable income	92,260	700	7,820	100,780

	£	£
Non-savings income		
£34,000 (W2) × 20%		6,800
£58,260 (92,260 – 34,000) × 40%		23,304
Savings income		
£500 × 0% (higher rate taxpayer)		0
£200 (700 – 500) × 40%		80
Dividend income		
£5,000 × 0%		0
£2,820 (7,820 – 5,000) × 32.5%		916
Tax liability		31,100
Less: PAYE		(29,200)
Tax payable		1,900

Workings

1 Personal allowance

	£
Net income	108,520
Less gross gift aid donation £1,600 × 100/80	(2,000)
Adjusted net income	106,520
Less income limit	(100,000)
Excess	6,520

	£
Personal allowance	11,000
Less half excess £6,520 × ½	(3,260)
Revised personal allowance	7,740

2 Basic rate limit and higher rate limit

£32,000 + (£1,600 × 100/80)	£34,000
£150,000 + (£1,600 × 100/80)	£152,000

Employment income MCQs

12 B £9,800

	£
Salary	8,000
Bonus received 30 November 2016 (receipts basis)	1,800
Employment income 2016/17	9,800

13 C 3 and 4

Diane is employed in a temporary workplace for less than 24 months, so travel from home to her temporary workplace is allowable. Erica's journey from home to Bristol is travel in the performance of duties so travel from home to the client is allowable.

Ben has a permanent workplace in Bristol and is not entitled to deduct travelling expenses from home to his workplace. Colin has two permanent workplaces so he is not entitled to deduct travelling expenses to either of them.

14 B £(500) allowable expense

	£
Amount reimbursed 15,000 × 35p	5,250
Less: statutory allowance	
10,000 miles × 45p	(4,500)
5,000 miles × 25p	(1,250)
Allowable expense	(500)

Danni

Tutorial note. Tax relief is not available for an employee's normal commuting costs but relief is available where the employee has a temporary workplace where the secondment is expected to last up to 24 months.

15 C £64,450

	£
Salary	
1.7.16 – 31.12.16	
£6,000 × 6	36,000
1.1.17 – 31.3.17	
£(6,000 × 102.5%) × 3	18,450
Bonus	
31 March 2017 (receipts basis)	10,000
Taxable in tax year 2016/17	64,450

As Danni is a director of Clifton plc, bonus is received on the earliest of:

- The time when payment is made (31 May 2017)
- The time when she becomes entitled to payment of the bonus (10 April 2017)
- The time when the amount is credited in the company's accounting records (10 April 2017)
- The end of the company's period of account (as the amount was determined on 15 March 2017 which is within the period of account) (31 March 2017)

The earliest of these dates is provided by the last test and so the date of receipt is 31 March 2017.

16 B 2 only

Home to permanent workplace: not qualifying travel expenses
Home to temporary workplace expected to last less than 24 month: qualifying travel expenses

17 D £36 allowable deduction

24 miles × 2 (return journey) × 5 = 240 miles

Excess over statutory mileage allowance 240 × (0.45 – 0.30) = £(36) allowable deduction

18 A 1 only

Chartered Institute of Purchasing and Supply (MCIP): Subscription to professional body relevant to the duties of the employment

Tennis club: not incurred wholly, exclusively and necessarily in the performance of the duties of the employment

19 A By Clifton plc deducting the donation from Danni's gross pay before calculating PAYE

Taxable and exempt benefits. The PAYE system MCQs

20 B £4,400

CO_2 emissions are 113 g/km, round down to 100 g/km

Appropriate percentage: (110 – 95) = 15 g/km in excess of threshold

15/5 = 3%

16% + 3% + 3% = 22%

List price £20,000 × 22% = £4,400

21 C £1,460

	£
Annual value	3,660
Additional amount £(99,000 – 75,000) × 3%	720
	4,380
× 4/12	1,460

Accommodation provided for private use by an employer is taxed on the annual value plus an additional amount if the accommodation cost the company more than £75,000. The market value is only used if the accommodation was acquired more than six years prior to being provided. Both benefits are pro-rated for occupation for part of the tax year.

22 A Form P11D by 6 July 2017

Verdi

Tutorial note. Verdi cannot use the HMRC's Basic PAYE Tools software to report PAYE information electronically because he will have more than nine employees.

23 C 1 and 3

Verdi can use commercial payroll software or a payroll provider.

24 D 1, 2 and 3

The first FPS will contain the amounts paid to employees, deductions made under PAYE and details of employees who have started employment.

25 D Report on or before any day when he pays someone, payment 17 days after end of tax month if paid electronically

26 A First FPS nil, second FPS £200

The first late submission of the tax year is ignored. Further late submissions will attract penalties based on the number of employees. Since Verdi has between 10 and 49 employees, the penalty on the second FPS is £200.

27 B Form P60 by 31 May following the end of the tax year

28 Azure plc

Tutorial note. The calculation of benefits is particularly important for exam purposes. Ensure that you pro-rate the benefits if they are not available for the entire year.

(a) A taxable benefit must be computed for Andrew. The benefit will equal the difference between the interest which would have arisen at the official rate and the actual interest paid. The benefit for 2016/17 is therefore £16,000 × (3 – 0.75)% × 6/12 months = £180.

(b) The flower arrangement costing £45 given to Penelope is a trivial benefit, so the taxable benefit is nil.

(c) Charles will have a taxable benefit of the annual value of the TV, which will be computed as 20% of the value of the asset when first provided as a benefit to any employee. If the TV had been lent to an employee when it was bought, the benefit for 2016/17 would be £800 × 20% = £160 × 10/12 = £133. If the TV was first provided as a benefit in June 2016, the benefit would be £500 × 20% = £100 × 10/12 = £83.

(d) Long service awards of tangible property to employees with at least 20 years service are not taxed provided the cost to the employer does not exceed £50 for each year of service and no similar award has been made to the same person within the previous ten years. In Demelza's case the limit on value would be £50 × 25 = £1,250, so there will be no taxable benefit.

(e) The first £8,000 of removal expenses payable to Janet will be an exempt benefit because:

(i) She does not already live within a reasonable daily travelling distance of her new place of employment, but will do so after moving, and

(ii) The expenses are incurred or the benefits provided by the end of the tax year following the tax year of the start of employment at the new location.

Janet will be taxable on the excess removal expenses £(9,500 – 8,000) = £1,500.

(f) The private use of one mobile phone is an exempt benefit. The private use of the second phone is a taxable benefit. Lawrence can choose which phone is exempt and should therefore choose the one which has the higher phone charges.

The taxable benefit on the second phone is calculated as follows.

	£
Greater of:	
20% of market value (20% × £500 = £100)	
Hire charge £120	
ie	120
Cost of calls	300
Taxable benefit	420

Pensions MCQs

29 B £5,500

The maximum amount of contributions attracting tax relief which could be made by Treena in 2016/17 is the higher of:

(a) Relevant earnings which is the total of her employment income of £3,500 and her trading income of £2,000; and

(b) Basic amount of £3,600.

Bank interest is not relevant earnings.

30 C £64,000

	£
Earnings	90,000
Less occupational pension contribution	(15,000)
Net income	75,000
Less personal allowance	(11,000)
Taxable income	64,000

Under net pay arrangements (most occupational pension schemes) the gross contribution is deducted from earnings so that tax relief is given at all rates of tax. Under tax relief at source (most personal pension schemes), the payment is made net of basic rate tax and higher rate relief and additional rate relief are given by increasing the basic rate and higher rate limits in the tax computation.

31 A £63,000

	£
Annual allowance 2016/17	40,000
Annual allowance unused in 2015/14 £(40,000 – 17,000)	23,000
Maximum gross pension contribution in 2016/17	63,000

The annual allowance for 2014/15 is not available as Rio was not a member of a pension scheme in that year.

Gary, George and Geraldine

Tutorial note. In question 35, Geraldine's relevant earnings of £130,000 exceed the gross pension contributions of £48,750, so she can obtain tax relief on this contribution.

32 C £10,360

	£
£37,000 (W) × 20%	7,400
£7,400 × 40%	2,960
44,400	10,360

Working

Basic rate limit £32,000 + (£4,000 × 100/80) = 37,000

33 C £23,000

	£
Trading income	15,000
FHL property income	8,000
Relevant earnings	23,000

34 B Tax-free lump sum of up to 25% of pension fund, remainder taxable as pension income

35 D £39,000

In 2015/16, Geraldine had made a gross contribution of £(25,000 × 100/80) = £31,250. She therefore has an unused annual allowance of (40,000 – 31,250) = £8,750. This will be brought forward and added to her annual allowance of £40,000 for 2016/17, giving a total of £(8,750 + 40,000) = £48,750. The net equivalent (ie the amount she would actually pay) is £48,750 × 80% = £39,000.

36 B She will be subject to income tax at the rate of 55% on the lump sum.

The lump sum is in excess of the lifetime allowance of £1,000,000 and so it taxable at the rate of 55%.

Property income MCQs

37 C £795

	£
Chairs – no relief for new furniture	0
Cooker – cost of replacing original only	650
Central heating breakdown cover (accruals basis)	
£580 × 3/12	145
Allowable expenses	795

38 D £24,000

	£
Premium received	30,000
Less £30,000 × 2% × (11 – 1)	(6,000)
Amount chargeable to income tax	24,000

39 B 3 and 4

The income from furnished holiday lettings qualifies as relevant earnings for pension contributions, and if an individual has a furnished holiday letting and another letting, two income statements must be prepared in order to identify separate profits and losses.

The accommodation must be available for commercial let as holiday accommodation to the public generally for at least 210 days during the tax year. Capital allowances are available on furniture instead of replacement of domestic items relief.

40 Rafe

Tutorial note. Remember to accrue the rents receivable and expenses payable for the tax year. Where you disallow an expense, such as the new roof, note this in your computation to show that you have considered it.

	£	£
Rent		
House 1: first letting £600 × 6		3,600
House 1: second letting £6,000 × 3/12		1,500
House 2: £7,800 × 8/12		5,200
		10,300
Expenses		
House 1: new roof, disallowable because capital	0	
House 1: buildings insurance £480 × 10/12	400	
House 2: redecoration	1,200	
House 2: new furniture	0	
House 2: buildings insurance £920 × 9/12	690	
House 2: boiler insurance £180 × 8/12	120	
House 2: replacement domestic items relief on replacement sofa	800	
		(3,210)
Income from houses 1 and 2		7,090
Rent a room (W)		350
Total property business income		7,440

Working

Rafe should claim rent a room relief in respect of the letting of the furnished room in his main residence, since this is more beneficial than the normal basis of assessment (£7,850 – £875 = £6,975). This means that Rafe will be taxed on an additional £350 (£7,850 – £7,500) of property business income.

Computing trading income MCQs

41 C 1 and 4

Installing air conditioning in his workshop and making initial repairs to a recently acquired second-hand office building which was not usable until the repairs were carried out (see *Law Shipping Co Ltd v CIR 1923*) are capital expenditure. They are not allowable as expense in calculating trading profits.

Repairing the central heating in his offices and redecorating the showroom are allowable expenses in calculating trading profits.

42 D £160,220

	£
Profit per accounts	160,000
Add: parking fines	180
hamper	40
Tax-adjusted profit	160,220

The legal fees in relation to the short lease are allowable as this involves a renewal of a short lease rather than the grant of a new lease. Parking fines for the owner of a business are never allowable. Gifts of food are not allowable.

43 B £2,448

	£
Lease payments £400 × 9	3,600
Less 15% disallowed for high emission car	(540)
	3,060
Business use proportion 10,800/13,500 × 3,060	2,448

Margaret

Tutorial note. The fixed rate adjustment for the private use of a trader's business premises is not the amount which is allowable, but instead reduces the allowable amount.

44 D Revenue £35,500, other allowable expenses £1,100

Under the cash basis, revenue and expenses are recognised on the amounts actually received and paid in the period of account.

45 B Furniture £2,500, plot of land for guest parking £Nil

Business expenses for the cash basis of accounting include capital expenditure on plant and machinery such as furniture but not other capital expenses such as the acquisition of the land for guest parking.

46 C £7,000

	£
Gas and electricity	7,400
Cleaning and gardening	1,800
Food	2,000
	11,200
Less fixed rate private use proportion £350 × 12	(4,200)
Allowable household expenses	7,000

47 A £5,000

	£
First 10,000 miles @ 45p	4,500
Next 2,000 miles @ 25p	500
Allowable motoring expenses	5,000

48 B 3

A net cash deficit (ie a loss) under the cash basis can only be relieved against future cash surpluses (ie future trading profits). Cash basis traders cannot offset a loss against general income.

49 Archie

Tutorial note. You are extremely likely to be required to adjust accounts profit in your exam to arrive at taxable trading profits. The best way to familiarise yourself with the adjustments required is to practise plenty of questions like this.

	£	£
Net profit		101,977
Add: general expenses: entertaining staff	0	
general expenses: entertaining suppliers	600	
repairs and renewals: redecoration	0	
repairs and renewals: renovation	0	
legal and accountancy: debt collection	0	
legal and accountancy: staff service agreements	0	
legal and accountancy: tax consultancy (not for purposes of trade)	30	
legal and accountancy: grant of short lease on new premises	100	
legal and accountancy: audit and accountancy	0	
subscription and donations: gift aid donation	5,200	
subscription and donations: political donation	500	
subscription and donations: sports facilities for staff	0	
subscription and donations: trade association	0	
impairment losses (trade)	0	
salaries and wages	0	
travel: private travel expenses 25% × £2,000	500	
depreciation	15,000	
rent and rates	0	
		21,930
Less: profit on sale of office	5,265	
impairment losses recovered	0	
capital allowances	2,200	
building society interest	1,900	
		(9,365)
Taxable trading profit		114,542

Capital allowances MCQs

50 D 1 and 3

Refrigeration equipment and sound insulation (provided mainly to meet the particular requirements of the trade) are items which could be plant for the purposes of capital allowances.

Expenditure on a building such as an office extension could not qualify as plant. A bridge is a structure and is therefore also not plant.

51 A £1,260

	Car	Allowances 75%
	£	£
y/e 5 April 2017		
Addition	21,000	
WDA @ 8%	(1,680)	1,260
TWDV c/f	19,320	
Maximum capital allowances		1,260

52 C £50,450

	AIA	Main pool	Allowances
	£	£	£
p/e 31 December 2016			
Addition qualifying for AIA			
Machinery	60,000		
AIA £200,000 × 3/12	(50,000)		50,000
	10,000		
Transfer balance to main pool	(10,000)	10,000	
WDA @ 18% × 3/12		(450)	450
TWDV c/f		9,550	
Maximum capital allowances			50,450

Sylvester

Tutorial note. Balancing adjustments where there has been private use of the asset are restricted to the business use element.

53 B £840

	Sylvester's car (70%)		Allowances/ (charges)
	£		£
TWDV b/f	6,000		
Disposal	(7,200)		
Balancing charge	(1,200)	× 70%	(840)

54 A £912

	Sylvester's car (80%)		Allowances/ (charges)
Private use car	19,000		
WDA 8% × 9/12	(1,140)	× 80%	912
TWDV c/f	17,860		

55 A £6,210

	Main pool	Allowances/ (charges)
	£	£
TWDV b/f	56,800	
Disposals (10,000 + 800)	(10,800)	
	46,000	
WDA 18% × 9/12	(6,210)	6,210
TWDV c/f	39,790	

The disposal proceeds on the plant sold on 20 April 2016 are restricted to cost.

56 C £500

A writing down allowance equal to unrelieved expenditure in the special rate pool for a 9 month period of account can be claimed where this is £750 (£1,000 × 9/12) or less.

57 D Motor car [1] will be given a first year allowance, Motor car [2] will be added to the special rate pool and given writing down allowances of 8% as part of the pool.

A 100% first year allowance (FYA) is available for expenditure incurred on new low emission motor cars. A low emission car is one which has CO_2 emissions of 75g/km or less.

Expenditure on motor cars which emit over 130g/km is added to the special rate pool.

58 Tom

Tutorial note. The key to being able to deal with a capital allowances computation correctly is to get the layout right. Once you have done this, the figures should fall into place.

	AIA	Main pool	Private use car (80%)	Short life asset	Allowances
	£	£	£	£	£
1.7.16 – 30.6.17					
Brought forward		33,500		4,400	
Addition qualifying for AIA					
Plant	27,000				
AIA	(27,000)				27,000
	0				
WDA @ 18%		(6,030)		(792)	6,822
Carried forward		27,470		3,608	
Allowances					33,822
1.7.17 – 30.6.18					
Addition (not AIA)			13,400		
WDA @ 18%		(4,945)	(2,412) × 80%	(649)	7,524
Carried forward		22,525	10,988	2,959	
Allowances					7,524
1.7.18 – 30.6.19					
WDA @ 18%		(4,055)	(1,978) × 80%	(533)	6,170
Carried forward		18,470	9,010	2,426	
Allowances					6,170

	AIA	Main pool	Private use car (80%)		Short life asset	Allowances
	£	£	£		£	£
1.7.19 – 30.6.20						
Brought forward		18,470	9,010		2,426	
Disposals		(340)			(2,900)	
		18,130			(474)	
Balancing charge					474	(474)
WDA @ 18%		(3,263)	(1,622)	× 80%		4,561
Carried forward		14,867	7,388			
Allowances						4,087
1.7.20 – 31.12.20						
Disposals		(24,000)	(10,600)			
		(9,133)	(3,212)			
Balancing charges		9,133	3,212	× 80%		(11,703)

Tutorial note. The capital allowances are restricted as a result of the private use of an asset by the owner of the business.

Assessable trading income MCQs

59 D £3,000

First tax year (2015/16)
Actual basis
Basis period 1.1.16 to 5.4.16

Second tax year (2016/17)
Period of account in 2nd year at least 12 months so basis period is 12 months to that accounting date
Basis period 1.2.16 to 31.1.17

Overlap profits
Period of overlap 1.2.16 to 5.4.16 (two months)

2/13 × £19,500 £3,000

60 B £11,500

Last tax year (2016/17)
Basis period 1.2.16 to 31.3.17

	£
y/e 31.1.17	10,000
p/e 31.3.17	2,500
	12,500
Less overlap profits	(1,000)
	11,500

61 B 6 April 2016 to 5 April 2017

2016/17 is the second year of trading. There is no period of account ending in 2016/17, so the basis period is the tax year.

62 Clive

> **Tutorial note**. Significant cash flow advantages can be gained with a careful choice of accounting date.

Taxable profits for the four years 2016/17 to 2019/20

The accounts profits will be as follows.

Period ending in	*Working*	*Accounting date* *31 March*	*30 April*
		£	£
2017	3 × £800	2,400	
	4 × £800		3,200
2018	3 × £800 + 6 × £1,200 + 3 × £2,000	15,600	
	2 × £800 + 6 × £1,200 + 4 × £2,000		16,800
2019	12 × £2,000	24,000	24,000
2020	12 × £2,000	24,000	24,000

The taxable profits will be as follows.

		Accounting date *31 March*	*30 April*
		£	£
2016/17	Actual basis (1 January 2017 to 5 April 2017)	2,400	
	£3,200 × 3/4 (work to nearest month)		2,400
2017/18	Year to 31.3.18	15,600	
	First 12 months (1 January 2017 to 31 December 2017)		
	£3,200 + £16,800 × 8/12		14,400
2018/19	Year to 31.3.19	24,000	
	Year to 30.4.18		16,800
2019/20	Year to 31.3.20	24,000	
	Year to 30.4.19		24,000
		66,000	57,600

30 April is the better choice of accounting date as it will give a considerable cash flow advantage.

63 Fiona

> **Tutorial note**. In a question like this, work out the capital allowances for each period of account before you think about allocating profits to tax years.
>
> Writing down allowances and the annual investment allowance are time apportioned in a long period of account.

We must first work out the capital allowances.

	AIA	Main pool	Private use car (65%)	Allowances
	£	£	£	£
1.1.17 – 30.4.18				
Additions qualifying for AIA				
Desk and office furniture (1.1.17)	2,625			
General plant (4.1.17)	8,070			
Second-hand oven (1.3.17)	5,300			
Delivery van (25.3.17)	5,450			
General plant (15.4.17)	8,555			
	30,000			
AIA £200,000 × 16/12 = £266,667	(30,000)			30,000

	AIA	Main pool	Private use car (65%)	Allowances
	£	£	£	£
Addition not qualifying for AIA				
Car (15.5.17)			6,600	
WDA @ 18% × 16/12		—	(1,584) × 65%	1,030
Carried forward		0	5,016	
Allowances				31,030
1.5.18 – 30.4.19				
Additions qualifying for AIA				
General plant (30.1.19)	10,000			
Mixer (30.4.19)	1,200			
	11,200			
AIA	(11,200)			11,200
WDA @ 18%			(903) × 65%	587
Carried forward			4,113	
Allowances				11,787

Profits are as follows.

Period	*Profit*	*Capital allowances*	*Adjusted profit*
	£	£	£
1.1.17 – 30.4.18	47,030	31,030	16,000
1.5.18 – 30.4.19	24,787	11,787	13,000

The taxable profits are as follows.

Year	*Basis period*	*Working*	*Taxable profit*
			£
2016/17	1.1.17 – 5.4.17	£16,000 × 3/16	3,000
2017/18	6.4.17 – 5.4.18	£16,000 × 12/16	12,000
2018/19	1.5.17 – 30.4.18	£16,000 × 12/16	12,000
2019/20	1.5.18 – 30.4.19		13,000

The overlap profits are the profits from 1 May 2017 to 5 April 2018: £16,000 × 11/16 = £11,000.

Trading losses MCQs

64 D 2 and 4

A trading loss carried forward must be set against the first available profits of the same trade. A trading loss claim for relief against general income must be made by 31 January 22 months after the end of the tax year of the loss.

A claim to set a trading loss against general income cannot be restricted so that the individual has enough net income to use the personal allowance. A trading loss can be carried forward indefinitely.

65 B £11,000

	2015/16
	£
Trading income	9,000
Property business income	4,000
	13,000
Less loss relief against general income c/b from 2016/17	(13,000)
Net income	0

The trading loss available to carry forward to 2017/18 is £(24,000 – 13,000) = £11,000.

66 C £83,750

	2015/16
	£
Trading income	15,000
Property business income	260,000
Total income	275,000
Less loss relief against general income	(83,750)
Net income	191,250

In 2015/16, the loss relief cap does not apply to loss relief against the trading income of £15,000. However, the cap does apply to the loss relief against non-trading income. The cap is £275,000 × 25% = £68,750. The total loss relief claim for 2015/16 is therefore £(15,000 + 68,750) = £83,750.

67 Morgan

Tutorial note. Take care to consider all available reliefs. When deciding on the best relief you must consider both the rate of tax saved and the timing of the relief.

(a) Loss relief could be claimed:

(i) Against general income of the year of loss (2017/18), the savings income of £12,000

(ii) Against general income of the preceding year (2016/17). This would be trading profits of £15,000 plus savings income of £12,000

(iii) Against the first available future profits of the same trade. This would be trading profits of £45,000 in 2018/19

(b) **The quickest claim**

The quickest way to obtain relief would be for Morgan to use loss relief against general income in both years. The tax computations would then be as follows.

	2016/17	2017/18
	£	£
Trading profits	15,000	0
Savings income	12,000	12,000
Total income	27,000	12,000
Less loss relief against general income	(27,000)	(12,000)
Net income	0	0

The balance of the loss, £1,000, would be carried forward and relieved against future trading income in 2018/19.

Although this proposal produces loss relief quickly, it has the disadvantage of wasting Morgan's personal allowance and savings income nil rate band in both years. Morgan could, if he chose, delay his relief by carrying the loss forward. The loss would then be set off only against trading income, with the savings income using his personal allowance and the savings income nil rate band in 2018/19.

Partnerships and limited liability partnerships MCQs

68 B £5,000

y/e 31 December 2017

Profit share £60,000 × 1/3	£20,000

2016/17 basis period is 1 January 2017 to 5 April 2017 so 3/12 of this amount is taxable in 2016/17 ie £5,000.

69 C £33,333

y/e 31 March 2017

	£
1.4.16 – 30.4.16	
Profit share £96,000 × 1/12 × 1/2	4,000
1.5.16 – 31.3.17	
Profit share £96,000 × 11/12 × 1/3	29,333
	33,333

Current year basis applies as there is no commencement or cessation, simply a change in profit sharing ratios.

70 B £50,000

Victor's share of the loss is 50% ie £90,000. However, the amount of loss relief that Victor can claim against general income of £60,000 is restricted to the greater of £50,000 and 25% of Victor's adjusted total income (ie 25% × £60,000 = £15,000) ie £50,000.

Anne, Betty and Chloe

Tutorial note. Each partner can make a separate loss relief claim for her share of the partnership loss.

71 C £16,650

	£
1.1.16 – 30.9.16	
Salary £6,000 × 9/12	4,500
PSR £([60,000 × 9/12] - 4,500) × 30%	12,150
	16,650

72 A £25,350

	£
2016/17	
Basis period 1.1.16 – 30.9.16	
PSR £([60,000 × 9/12] - 4,500) × 70%	28,350
Less overlap profits relieved on cessation	(3,000)
	25,350

73 D £10,200

	£
2016/17	
Basis period 1.10.16 – 5.4.17	
1.10.16 – 31.12.16	
PSR £(60,000 × 3/12) × 40%	6,000
1.1.17 – 5.4.17	
PSR £(42,000 × 3/12) × 40%	4,200
	10,200

74 A 1 and 2

Against general income of 2018/19 and/or 2017/18 and against future trading profits.

75 A 1, 2 and 4

Against general income of 2018/19 and/or 2017/18, against future trading profits and against general income of 2015/16, 2016/17 and 2017/18 earlier years first (early years loss relief).

National insurance contributions MCQs

76 C £3,201

	£
Class 2	146
£2.80 × 52	
Class 4	
£(42,000 – 8,060) = 33,940 × 9%	3,055
Total NIC 2016/17	3,201

77 B £497

Total earnings received in February 2017 are £11,000 (£3,000 + £8,000)

The NIC primary limits for each month are £8,060/12 = £672 and £43,000/12 = £3,583.

NIC payable is therefore:

	£
£(3,583 – 672) = 2,911 × 12%	349
£(11,000 – 3,583) = 7,417 × 2%	148
NIC February 2017	497

78 D Class 1 primary contributions on £45,000, Class 1 secondary contributions on £45,000, Class 1A contributions on £300

Class 1 primary and secondary contributions are generally payable on cash earnings. Class 1A contributions are payable on non-cash benefits by the employer only.

Derek and Denise

Tutorial note. It is important that you can calculate and distinguish NICs for the self-employed and employed individuals.

79 D £4,433

	£
£(43,000 – 8,060) = 34,940 × 12%	4,193
£(55,000 – 43,000) = 12,000 × 2%	240
	4,433

80	A	£3,471	
			£
		£(55,000 – 8,112) = 46,888 × 13.8%	6,471
		Less Employment Allowance (only employee of sole trader)	(3,000)
			3,471
81	B	£91	
		£(12,000 × 11% × 6/12) × 13.8%	91

82 A £39 by 31 January 2018

14 × £2.80 = £39 payable under self assessment by 31 January following the end of the tax year.

83 C £287

Basis period for 2016/17 is 6.1.17 to 5.4.17 (3 months)

£([15,000 × 3/4] – 8,060) = 3,190 × 9% = £287

84 Sasha

Tutorial notes.

1. Strictly, expenses are only deductible in calculating net taxable earnings if they are incurred wholly, necessarily and exclusively in the performance of the duties. In practice, however, HM Revenue and Customs allow an apportionment between private and business use as here.
2. Capital allowances are available to an employee who provides plant and machinery necessarily for use in the performance of his duties, in the same way as a sole trader.
3. The use of the car for travel between home and work is ordinary commuting and not business use.
4. 'Earnings' for Class 4 NIC purposes are trading profits. However, earnings for Class 1 NIC purposes are gross earnings before the deductions of any expenses.

(a) Factors that will indicate that a worker should be treated as an employee rather than as self-employed are:

(i) Control by employer over employee's work
(ii) Employee must accept further work if offered (and employer must offer work)
(iii) Employee does not provide own equipment
(iv) Employee does not hire own helpers
(v) Employee does not take substantial financial risk
(vi) Employee does not have responsibility for investment and management of business and cannot benefit from sound management
(vii) Employee cannot work when he chooses but when an employer tells him to work
(viii) Described as an employee in any agreement between parties

(b) (i) *Income assessable as trading profits*

	£	£
Gross income		60,000
Less: business expenses on heating etc	880	
computer – AIA	4,000	
business expenses re car (£3,500 × 40%)	1,400	
WDA @ 18% on business car (CO_2 up to 130g/km)		
£10,000 × 18% × 40% (business proportion)	720	(7,000)
Assessable as trading profits		53,000

(ii) *Net taxable earnings*

	£	£
Gross income		60,000
Less: business expenses on heating etc	880	
computer – AIA	4,000	(4,880)
Net taxable earnings		55,120

If Sasha is an employee, car journeys between home and her place of work are treated as private motoring so there is no allowable deduction at all for the use of the car.

(c) (i) *Class 2 and Class 4 NIC*

		£
Class 2	£2.80 × 52	146
Class 4	£(43,000 – 8,060) = 34,940 × 9%	3,145
	£(53,000 – 43,000) = 10,000 × 2%	200
Total		3,491

(ii) *Class 1 NIC (Primary)*

	£
£(43,000 – 8,060) = 34,940 × 12%	4,193
£(60,000 – 43,000) = 17,000 × 2%	340
Total	4,533

Computing chargeable gains MCQs

85 A 1 and 2

Qualifying corporate bonds (QCBs) are exempt assets. Investments held in individual savings accounts (ISAs) are exempt assets.

A plot of land is a chargeable asset. Decorations for bravery are exempt assets only if awarded, not purchased.

86 B £16,500 – £3,000 (current year loss) – £2,400 (brought forward loss) = £11,100

Current year losses must always be used in full against the current year gains.

If losses are brought forward then they must be used against the first available gains after the current year losses and then only enough to reduce the current year's net gains to the annual exempt amount limit of £11,100.

Therefore in this case the £3,000 must be used first and only £2,400 of the brought forward figure needs to be used.

87 D £12,143

The amount of the cost attributable to the part sold is:

$$\frac{£36,000}{£36,000 + £90,000} \times £80,000 = £22,857$$

	£
Proceeds £(36,000 – 1,000)	35,000
Less cost (see above)	(22,857)
Gain	12,143

88 Peter

> **Tutorial note**. The first disposal is a basic computation. The second disposal tests the A/(A+B) formula and the third part tests compensation for the destruction of an asset.

Peter CGT payable 2016/17

Summary

	Residential property £	*Other gains* £
Residential investment property (W1)	69,720	
Non-residential land (W2)		16,300
Destroyed asset (W3)		3,000
	69,720	19,300
Less annual exempt amount (best use)	(11,100)	(0)
Taxable gains	58,620	19,300
CGT		
£(32,000 – 27,600) = £4,400 @ 18%	792	
£(58,620 – 4,400) = £54,220 @ 28%	15,182	
	15,974	
£19,300 @ 20%		3,860
CGT 2016/17 £(15,974 + 3,860)		19,834

Note: The same amount of tax would be payable if the other gains were taxed first:

	Residential property £	*Other gains* £
Taxable gains	58,620	19,300
CGT		
£(32,000 – 27,600) = £4,400 @ 10%		440
£(19,300 – 4,400) = £14,900 @ 20%		2,980
		3,420
£58,620 @ 28%	16,414	
CGT 2016/17 £(3,420 + 16,414)		19,834

Workings

1 *Investment property*

	£
Proceeds	150,000
Less cost of disposal	(1,280)
Net proceeds	148,720
Less cost	(79,000)
Gain	69,720

2 *Land*

	£
Proceeds	35,000
Less cost of disposal	(700)
Net proceeds	34,300
Less cost	
$£54{,}000 \times \dfrac{35{,}000}{35{,}000 + 70{,}000}$	(18,000)
Gain	16,300

3 *Vase*

	£
Proceeds	20,000
Less cost	(12,000)
Gain	8,000
Gain immediately chargeable £(20,000 – 17,000)	3,000

Remainder £(8,000 – 3,000) = £5,000 rolled into base cost of new vase.

Chattels and the principal private residence exemption MCQs

89 A £1,667

	£
Proceeds less disposal costs £(7,000 – 350)	6,650
Less cost and purchase costs £(1,500 + 75)	(1,575)
Gain	5,075

The maximum gain is 5/3 × £(7,000 – 6,000) = £1,667

The chargeable gain is the lower of £5,075 and £1,667 ie £1,667

90 C £2,100

	£
Proceeds (assumed)	6,000
Less disposal costs	(200)
	5,800
Less cost and purchase costs £(7,500 + 400)	(7,900)
Allowable loss	(2,100)

91 A Three years

		Exempt	*Chargeable*
1.1.93 – 31.12.04	Actual occupation	12	
1.1.05 – 31.12.07	Up to 3 years any reason	3	
1.1.08 – 31.12.10	Unoccupied		3
1.1.11 – 31.12.16	Actual occupation	6	–
Total		21	3

Any periods up to three years are exempt if the house is then reoccupied, so only the remaining three years of the period when Roger was staying with his parents are chargeable as Roger then went back to occupy his house.

John and Elsie

> **Tutorial note**. The last 18 months of ownership are always treated as a period of occupation, if at some time the residence has been the taxpayer's main residence.

92 D 96 months

	Exempt months
1.8.04 – 31.7.05 – actual residence	12
1.8.05 – 31.7.10 – employed abroad any period	60
1.8.10 – 31.1.11 – actual residence	6
1.2.15 – 31.7.16 – last 18 months ownership	18
	96

93 C 36 months

Because John had a period of actual occupation after a period of absence, he can claim 36 months deemed occupation for any reason during the period of absence from 1.2.11 to 31.1.15.

94 B 12 months

The property is let between 1.2.14 and 31.1.16. However, the period 1.2.15 to 31.1.16 is already covered by the last 18 months exemption. The remainder of the let period to be covered by letting relief is therefore 1.2.14 to 31.1.15 = 12 months.

95 C £5,900

	£
Proceeds (deemed)	6,000
Less costs of disposal	(400)
Net proceeds	5,600
Less cost	(11,500)
Loss	(5,900)

96 A £2,500

	£
Proceeds	7,500
Less costs of disposal	(75)
Net proceeds	7,425
Less cost	(4,000)
Gain	3,425
Cannot exceed £(7,500 – 6,000) × 5/3	2,500

Business reliefs MCQs

97 C £1,380

	£
Entrepreneurs' relief claimed	1,000
£10,000 × 10%	
No entrepreneurs' relief claimed	
£(13,000 – 11,100) = £1,900 × 20%	380
Total CGT	1,380

Gain on which entrepreneurs' relief is claimed is taxed at 10%. The other gain will be reduced by the annual exempt amount and then taxed at 20% because the entrepreneurs' relief gain is treated as using up the remainder of the basic rate band.

98 D £55,000

	£
Chargeable gain on Shop A	25,000
Less amount not reinvested £(80,000 – 70,000)	(10,000)
Amount eligible for rollover relief	15,000
Original cost of Shop B	70,000
Less rollover relief	(15,000)
Cost of Shop B for CGT	55,000

99 B 2 and 3

Gift relief can be claimed for the factory owned by an individual and used in the trade of that individual's personal company. It can also be claimed for premises owned by a sole trader of which two thirds are used for trade purposes and one third is used for private purposes (although the relief will be restricted to the business part of the premises).

Gift relief is not available on investment company shares. It is only available on listed trading company shares if the company is the individual's personal company: a 2% shareholding is too small to meet this test.

Roy and Graham

Tutorial note. When dealing with a sole trader, you should bear in mind that entrepreneurs' relief may apply to reduce the rate of tax on the gain. In questions 101 and 103, entrepreneurs' relief is not available for Graham's disposal because he has not used the factory in his own business.

100 D £9,890

	£
Market value	260,000
Less cost	(150,000)
Gain	110,000
Less annual exempt amount	(11,100)
Taxable gain	98,900
CGT payable @ 10% (entrepreneurs' relief claimed)	9,890

101 C £9,780

	£
Proceeds	320,000
Less cost	(260,000)
Gain	60,000
Less annual exempt amount	(11,100)
Taxable gain	48,900
CGT payable @ 20%	9,780

102 B £1,890

Partial gift relief is available as payment is made by Graham.

	£
Gain before gift relief	110,000
Less gift relief (balancing figure)	(80,000)
Gain after gift relief £(180,000 – 150,000) (cash gain)	30,000
Less annual exempt amount	(11,100)
Taxable gain	18,900
CGT payable @ 10%	1,890

103 A £25,780

	£
Proceeds	320,000
Less cost £(260,000 – 80,000)	(180,000)
Gain	140,000
Less annual exempt amount	(11,100)
Taxable gain	128,900
CGT payable @ 20%	25,780

104 D More of the gain is covered by a lower rate of CGT

If Roy and Graham make a claim for gift relief, the total tax payable is £(1,890 + 25,780) = £27,670. If they do not make a claim for gift relief, the total tax payable is £(9,890 + 9,780) = £19,670, which is £8,000 less than if a gift relief claim is made. This is due to the availability of entrepreneurs' relief for Roy and so more of the gain is covered by a lower rate of CGT.

105 Kai

Tutorial note. Gains qualifying for entrepreneurs' relief use up the basic rate band in priority to gains not qualifying for the relief.

		Gains	CGT
	£	£	£
Gains qualifying for entrepreneurs' relief			
Goodwill		75,000	
Shop	90,000		
Less cost	(105,000)		
Gain		(15,000)	
Warehouse	180,000		
Less cost	(150,000)		
Warehouse		30,000	
Taxable gains		90,000	
CGT @ 10% on £90,000			9,000
Gains not qualifying for entrepreneurs' relief			
Land	25,900		
Less cost	(10,000)		
Gain		15,900	
Less annual exempt amount (best use)		(11,100)	
Taxable gain		4,800	
CGT @ 20% on £4,800 (N)			960
Total CGT due			9,960

The claim for entrepreneurs' relief must be made by 31 January 2019.

Notes

1 Where there is a material disposal of business assets which results in both gains and losses, losses are netted off against gains to give a single chargeable gain on the disposal of the business assets.

2 The basic rate band is used first by income (£20,000), then by gains qualifying for entrepreneurs' relief (£90,000). The remaining gain is therefore above the basic rate limit and so taxable at 20%.

Shares and securities MCQs

106 A £22,100

$\frac{2.22-2.20}{2} + 2.20 = 2.21 \times 10{,}000$ £22,100

107 C Against 500 of the shares acquired on 31 July 2016, then against 250 of the shares acquired on 10 August 2016 and then against 50 of the shares acquired on 10 March 2010.

The matching rules are first against same day acquisitions, then shares in the following 30 days and then the share pool.

108 B 3 and 4

In a rights issue the rights issue shares are paid for by the shareholder resulting in an adjustment to the cost of the shareholding. A chargeable gain does not usually arise on a takeover where new shares are exchanged for old shares ('paper for paper' takeover).

A disposal of gilts by an individual is exempt from capital gains tax. If a company makes a 2 for 1 bonus issue, each shareholder will receive 2 extra shares for each 1 share held without payment.

109 Melissa

Tutorial note. The matching rules are very important and must be learnt.

First match the disposal with the acquisition in the next 30 days:

	£	£
Proceeds $\frac{4,000}{10,000} \times £42,000$	16,800	
Less cost	(16,000)	800

Next match the remaining shares with the share pool:

	£	£
Proceeds $\frac{6,000}{10,000} \times £42,000$	25,200	
Less cost (W)	(20,625)	4,575
Total gains		5,375

Working

	No. of shares	*Cost*
		£
12 July 2002 acquisition	3,000	21,000
17 January 2005 bonus issue 1 for 1	3,000	0
	6,000	21,000
14 December 2007 rights issue 1 for 3 @ £3.25 per share	2,000	6,500
	8,000	27,500
2 July 2016 disposal	(6,000)	(20,625)
c/f	2,000	6,875

Self assessment and payment of tax for individuals MCQs

110 C Steven 31 January 2018, Rita 28 February 2018

The latest filing date for a personal tax return is usually 31 January following the end of the tax year. However, if the notice to file the tax return is issued to the taxpayer after 31 October following the end of the tax year, the latest filing date is the end of 3 months following the notice.

111 D £6,000 on 31 January and 31 July 2017, £3,000 on 31 January 2018

Payments on account will be made on 31 January and 31 July 2017, with the balance being paid on 31 January 2018.

Payments on account for 2016/17 are payable based on 50% of the relevant amount (income tax plus Class 4 NIC) for 2015/16.

112 B £960

The maximum penalty for a careless error is 30% of the potential lost revenue (PLR). The PLR in this instance is 40% × £8,000 = £3,200. The penalty is therefore 30% × £3,200 = £960.

Ash

Tutorial note. In relation to a late payment penalty, the penalty date is 30 days after the due date for the payment of tax. For the late filing penalty, the penalty date is the date on which the return is overdue.

113 D £100

The penalty date for late filing of the tax return is the date on which the return will be overdue (ie 1 February 2017 which is the day after the filing date). The date of filing is not more than three months after the penalty date. The late payment penalty is therefore £100.

114 B £6,000

The balancing payment in respect of Ash's 2015/16 tax liability was calculated as follows:

	£
2015/16 income tax liability	16,800
Less: PAYE	(7,200)
	9,600
Less payments on account	(3,600)
Balancing payment	6,000

115 A £4,800

Ash's payments on account for 2016/17 are based on the excess of the 2015/16 tax liability over amounts deducted under the PAYE system:

	£
2015/16 tax liability	16,800
Less: PAYE	(7,200)
'Relevant amount'	9,600

The two payments on account for 2016/17 were therefore £4,800 (£9,600/2) each.

116 C First POA 31 January 2017, Second POA 31 July 2017

117 B 5% of the unpaid tax

The penalty date for late payment of tax is 30 days after the due date. The date of payment is therefore not more than five months after the penalty date. The late payment penalty is therefore 5% of the unpaid tax at the penalty date.

Inheritance tax: scope and transfers of value MCQs

118 A £87,250

	£
Gift	420,000
Less AEs 2016/17, 2015/16 b/f	(6,000)
Net chargeable transfer	414,000
Less nil band remaining £(325,000 – 260,000)	(65,000)
	349,000
IHT @ 20/80	87,250

The gross chargeable transfer in August 2012 is after any exemptions but the gift in November 2016 must have the annual exemptions deducted to find the net chargeable transfer.

119 C £510,000

	£
Andy's unused nil band	
60% × £325,000	195,000
Hilda's unused nil band	
£(325,000 – 10,000)	315,000
	510,000

The transfer by Hilda to her nephew is covered by her annual exemptions for 2015/16 and 2014/15 b/f.

120 B Lifetime tax 30 April 2017, death tax 30 June 2017

For chargeable lifetime transfers the due date is the later of 30 April just after the end of the tax year of the transfer and six months after the end of the month of the transfer. The due date for the tax arising on death is six months from the end of the month of death.

Colin and Diane

Tutorial note. In question 123, the PET is treated as exempt during Diane's lifetime so does not enter into cumulation whilst Diane is alive.

121 B £10,000

No chargeable transfers were made in the seven years prior to 21.1.09 so all of the nil band of £312,000 remained available for use.

			£
Net transfer of value			352,000
			£
IHT	£312,000	× 0% =	Nil
	£ 40,000	× 20/80 =	10,000
	£352,000		10,000

122 B Lifetime tax 31 May 2012, Death tax 31 December 2016

123 D £7,000

The trustees pay the IHT due so no grossing up is required.

			£
Gross transfer of value			360,000
			£
IHT	£325,000	× 0% =	Nil
	£ 35,000	× 20% =	7,000
	£360,000		7,000

124 C £8,000

The PET has come into charge so the available nil rate band is £(325,000 – 15,000) = £310,000.

			£
Gross transfer of value			360,000
			£
IHT	£310,000	× 0% =	Nil
	£ 50,000	× 40% =	20,000
	£360,000		20,000
Taper relief (4 to 5 years) 40% × £20,000			8,000

125 A There is no capital gains tax on a lifetime transfer of value if the donor dies after seven years of making it.

This statement is not true. There may be capital gains tax on the gift if this is of a chargeable asset, and the market value of the asset is such that a gain arises. The seven year period is only relevant for inheritance tax purposes.

126 Simona

Tutorial note. Where a deceased spouse's unused nil rate band is transferred on the death of the surviving spouse and the nil rate band has increased between the deaths of the spouses, the unused nil rate band is increased pro-rata.

(a) **Simona's death estate**

	£	£
Shares in MS plc		320,000
Life assurance policy (amount of proceeds payable as result of death)		250,000
House	175,000	
Less loan secured on house	(10,000)	
		165,000
Household furniture		20,000
Cash in bank		97,750
Car		5,000
Less: credit card bills	7,000	
income tax	3,000	
gas bill	250	
funeral expenses	2,500	(12,750)
Net death estate		845,000
Less spouse exemption (net value of house)		(165,000)
Chargeable death estate		680,000

(b) Simona's full nil rate band at death is available as she made no lifetime transfers.

Simona's first husband had an unused nil rate band of £(300,000 – 20,000) = £280,000. In terms of the nil rate band at Simona's death, the unused proportion is:

$$\frac{280,000}{300,000} \times £325,000 = £303,333$$

Simona's personal representatives can elect to transfer this unused nil rate band to Simona. The total nil rate band available to calculate death tax on Simona's death estate is therefore £(325,000 + 303,333) = £628,333.

(c) The IHT on Simona's death estate is:

£(680,000 – 628,333) = £51,667 @ 40% £20,667

Computing taxable total profits and the corporation tax liability MCQs

127 C 1 December 2015 to 30 November 2016 and 1 December 2016 to 31 March 2017

If a company has a long period of account it is divided into one accounting period of 12 months and one accounting period of the remainder.

128 A £2,720

	£
Leasing cost	3,200
Less £3,200 × 15% disallowable	(480)
Allowable deduction	2,720

129 D £14,400

Rent (accruals)	£14,400

The mortgage is a non-trading loan relationship and so the interest is a debit which must be set against credits from other non-trading loan relationships. Capital repayments are not relevant to the computation of property business income.

Red plc and Green plc

Tutorial note. Where a company has a long period of account, it has two accounting periods: first 12 months and then the remainder.

130 D £6,480

	Main pool £	*Allowances* £
12 months ended 31.12.16		
TWDV b/f	24,000	
Addition not qualifying for AIA		
11.16 Car	12,000	
	36,000	
WDA @ 18%	(6,480)	6,480

131 B £50,000

The purchase of the machinery takes place in the second accounting period from 1 January 2017 to 31 March 2017 which is three months long. The annual investment allowance is therefore £200,000 × 3/12 = £50,000.

132 B £10,000

This a new low emission car and so 100% FYA is available regardless of the length of the accounting period.

133 A £272,000

	1.1.15 - 31.12.15 (12m)
	£
Trading profits (12/17)	276,000
Investment income (15,000 + 6,000)	21,000
Chargeable gain	5,000
Total profits	302,000
Less qualifying charitable donations (15,000 + 15,000)	(30,000)
Taxable total profits	272,000

134 C £77,500

	1.1.16 - 31.5.16 (5m)
	£
Trading profits (5/17)	115,000
Investment income	2,500
Total profits	117,500
Less qualifying charitable donation	(40,000)
Taxable total profits	77,500

135 Elderflower Ltd

Tutorial notes. You must use the layout shown when adjusting profits for taxation. The notes have been added for tutorial purposes.

(a) **Trading profit for y/e 31 March 2017**

	£	£
Profit before taxation		417,210
Add:		
Depreciation	54,690	
Accountancy and audit	0	
Legal fees – share capital (N1)	8,800	
Legal fees – loan notes (N1)	0	
Legal fees – health and safety (N1)	900	
Repairs and renewals: extension (N2)	9,700	
Repairs and renewals: repainting (N2)	0	
Other expenses: entertaining customers	2,310	
Other expenses: qualifying charitable donation	500	
Interest payable (N3)	0	
		76,900
Deduct:		
Office building profit	54,000	
Bank interest	7,000	
Capital allowances (W)	25,190	
		(86,190)
Profit adjusted for tax purposes		407,920

Notes

1. Costs relating to share capital need to be added back as they relate to a capital expense. However, the fees relating to the loan notes are a loan relationship expense and thus deductible as a trading expense because the debenture is for trade purposes. Legal fees in relation to the fine are not deductible as the fine is a payment contrary to public policy.
2. The cost of the extension has been added back as a capital expense but the cost of repainting is allowable as it is a repair and therefore a revenue expense.
3. No adjustment is needed for the interest because it relates to a trade purpose loan.

Working

Capital allowances on plant and machinery

	AIA	*Main pool*	*Special rate pool*	*Allowances*
	£	£	£	£
TWDV b/f		27,500	14,700	
Additions qualifying for AIA				
10.5.16 Equipment	20,200			
AIA	(20,200)			20,200
Additions not qualifying for AIA				
31.3.17 Car (N1)		9,600		
Disposals				
5.1.17 Car			(9,700)	
			5,000	
20.3.17 Van		(11,600)		
		25,500		
WDA @ 18%		(4,590)		4,590
WDA @ 8% (N2)			(400)	400
TWDVs c/f		20,910	4,600	
Allowances				25,190

Notes.

1. The private use of the car by the employee is not relevant for capital allowance purposes. No adjustment is ever made to a company's capital allowances to reflect the private use of an asset.
2. Although the only asset in the special rate pool has been sold, the pool of expenditure continues to be written down. A balancing allowance on the special rate pool can only arise when the trade ceases.

(b) **Total taxable profits y/e 31 March 2017**

	£
Trading profit (part (a))	407,920
Chargeable gain	45,580
Investment income	7,000
Total profits	460,500
Less qualifying charitable donation	(500)
Taxable total profits	460,000

(c) **Corporation tax liability y/e 31 March 2017**

£460,000 × 20%	92,000

Chargeable gains for companies MCQs

136 D Neither a gain nor a loss

		£
Net proceeds £(17,500 – 1,000)		16,500
Less cost £(12,000 + 800)		(12,800)
Unindexed gain		3,700
Less indexation allowance $\frac{261.9-175.7}{175.7}$ = 0.491 × £12,800		(6,285)
Chargeable gain/allowable loss (indexation cannot create a loss)		0

137 B £492,048

	£
Net proceeds £(640,000 – 6,000)	634,000
Less cost £(120,000 + 8,000)	(128,000)
	506,000
Less indexation allowance 0.109 × £128,000	(13,952)
Chargeable gain	492,048

138 D £57,500

	£
Proceeds	200,000
Less cost	(110,000)
Unindexed gain	90,000
Less indexation allowance	(20,000)
Indexed gain	70,000
Less rollover relief (balancing figure)	(57,500)
Chargeable gain: amount not reinvested £(200,000 – 187,500)	12,500

Long Ltd, Tall Ltd and Short Ltd

139 C 2 and 4

There is relief for inflation called the indexation allowance and a company is liable to corporation tax on its net chargeable gains as part of its total profits.

140 B 1, then 3, then 2

Shares acquired on the same day, then shares acquired in the previous nine days and finally shares from the FA 1985 pool.

141 A £15,678

	£
Proceeds	45,000
Less cost £40,000 × 6,000/10,000	(24,000)
	21,000
Less indexation allowance $\frac{262.8-215.1}{215.1}$ × £24,000	(5,322)
Gain	15,678

142 D £40,881

	No. of shares	Indexed cost
		£
June 2002 Acquisition	5,000	14,000
October 2016 Indexed rise		
$\frac{262.8-176.2}{176.2} \times £14,000$		6,881
Rights 1:1 @ £4 per share	5,000	20,000
	10,000	40,881

143 B Ordinary shares £27,200, Preference shares £6,800

	No. of shares	MV	Cost
		£	£
Ordinary shares	20,000	100,000	27,200
Preference shares	10,000	25,000	6,800
	30,000	125,000	34,000

144 Xeon Ltd

Tutorial note. When using the part disposal formula, remember that it only applies to cost which relates to the whole of the original asset, not to expenditure incurred just on the part being sold (which is deductible in full).

Warehouse

	£
Proceeds	120,000
Less cost	(65,000)
	55,000
Less indexation allowance $\frac{260.8-181.3}{181.3}$ (0.438) × £65,000	(28,470)
Gain	26,530
Less rollover relief (balancing figure)	(6,530)
Gain left in charge £(120,000 – 100,000)	20,000

Cost of warehouse bought in July 2015

	£
Cost	100,000
Less rollover relief	(6,530)
Revised cost	93,470

Plot of land

	£
Proceeds	30,000
Less cost $\frac{30,000}{30,000+40,000} \times £21,000$	(9,000)
expenditure in December 2012	(1,000)
	20,000
Less indexation allowance	
$\frac{261.2-170.1}{170.1}$ (0.536) × £9,000	(4,824)
$\frac{261.2-246.8}{246.8}$ (0.058) × £1,000	(58)
	15,118

Losses MCQs

145 B 2 and 3

Trade losses of a company carried forward can only be used against profits of the same trade. Trade loss relief may be given by deduction from current period total profits and those in the previous 12 months.

Property business losses of a company are set against total profits of the same accounting period. Capital losses can only be set against chargeable gains in the same or future accounting periods.

146 A £30,000

E plc must make a current year loss claim against total profits if it wishes to make a claim to carry a loss back so the loss available for carry back is £(40,000 – 10,000) = £30,000.
E plc cannot keep sufficient income to cover the qualifying charitable donation. The carry back is against total profits (ie before qualifying charitable donations).

147 D £38,000

	£
Trading income	165,000
Less trading loss b/f	(165,000)
	0
Non-trading loan relationship income	27,000
Chargeable gain £(14,000 – 3,000)	11,000
Taxable total profits	38,000

148 Ferraro Ltd

Tutorial note. The pro forma for loss relief is important. If you learn the pro forma you should find that the figures slot into place. Note that the result of a losses claim may be that, as here, qualifying charitable donations become unrelieved.

	Accounting periods		
	12m to 31.3.15	*9m to 31.12.15*	*12m to 31.12.16*
	£	£	£
Trading profits	6,200	4,320	0
Investment income	80	240	260
Property business income	1,420	1,440	1,600
Chargeable gain	0	7,680	0
Total profits	7,700	13,680	1,860
Less current period loss relief	0	0	(1,860)
	7,700	13,680	0
Less carry back loss relief	(1,925)	(13,680)	(0)
Less qualifying charitable donations	(0)	(0)	(0)
Taxable total profits	5,775	0	0
Unrelieved qualifying charitable donations		1,000	1,500

Loss memo	£
Loss of y/e 31.12.16	100,000
Less used y/e 31.12.16	(1,860)
	98,140
Less used 9m/e 31.12.15	(13,680)
	84,460
Less used y/e 31.3.15 3/12 × £7,700	(1,925)
c/f against first available profits of the same trade	82,535

> **Tutorial note**. The loss is carried back to set against profits arising in the previous 12 months. This means that the set off in the y/e 31.3.15 is restricted to 3/12 × £7,700 = £1,925.

Groups MCQs

149 C £19,000

	£
Trading loss	16,000
Excess qualifying charitable donation £(4,000 – 1,000)	3,000
Amount available for group relief	19,000

150 A £40,500

The lower of:

P Ltd profits 1.4.16 – 31.12.16 £54,000 × 9/12	£40,500
O Ltd loss 1.4.16 – 31.12.16 £(60,000) × 9/12	£45,000

151 C B Ltd, C Ltd and D Ltd

B Ltd owns 75% of C Ltd and so is in a chargeable gains group with it. B Ltd also has an effective interest in D Ltd of 75% × 90% = 67.5%. As this is 50% or more, D Ltd is also in this gains group.

A Ltd does not own 75% or more of B Ltd and so cannot be in a chargeable gains group with B Ltd or its subsidiaries.

152 P Ltd

> **Tutorial note**. It is helpful to use a pro forma as shown in the answer to work out.

S Ltd and T Ltd are outside the P Ltd group for group relief purposes so the loss of S Ltd cannot be group relieved.

A claim by P Ltd against its own total profits would waste its qualifying charitable donation and carrying the loss forward against future profits of P Ltd would not obtain relief for several years.

A claim for group relief should therefore be made. P Ltd's trading loss of £226,000 could be surrendered under group relief to Q Ltd, R Ltd and M Ltd. The amount to be surrendered is after taking account of qualifying charitable donations.

The following is one possible use of group relief (the overall corporation tax liability will be the same regardless of which group company ends up with taxable total profits of £1,000):

	P Ltd	*Q Ltd*	*R Ltd*	*S Ltd*	*M Ltd*	*T Ltd*	*Overall CT*
	£	£	£	£	£	£	
Trading profits	0	14,000	210,000	0	20,000	70,000	
Property business income	6,000	4,000	0	0	0	0	
Total profits	6,000	18,000	210,000	0	20,000	70,000	
Less qualifying charitable donation	(4,500)	(2,000)	(5,000)	0	(14,000)	0	
	1,500	16,000	205,000	0	6,000	70,000	
Less group relief	0	(16,000)	(205,000)	0	(5,000)	0	
Taxable total profits	1,500	0	0	0	1,000	70,000	
Corporation tax (FY16) @ 20%							
Corporation tax payable	300	0	0	0	200	14,000	14,500

Self assessment and payment of tax by companies MCQs

153 B Return date 31 December 2017, tax payable date 1 October 2017

The return must be submitted within 12 months of the end of the accounting period and the tax paid nine months and one day after the end of the accounting period.

154 A 31 March 2018

The tax return must be filed within 12 months of the end of the period of account because it is not more than 18 months long. Therefore the return for the first accounting period which ends on 31 December 2016 must be submitted by 31 March 2018.

155 D Retention date: 31 March 2023, maximum penalty: £3,000

A company must keep its records for six years from the end of the accounting period, if no compliance check is made.

Failure to keep records can lead to a maximum penalty of £3,000 for each accounting period affected.

Skyblue Ltd and Turquoise plc

Tutorial note. In question 159 first calculate the potential lost revenue (PLR) as a result of the error as the penalty will be a percentage of this amount.

156 D Electronic return filed by 30 September 2017

157 C On time £200, last two returns late £1,000

158 B Due date: first anniversary of the filing date, four months late: quarter day following the first anniversary of the filing date

159 C £12,600

	£
£(100,000 – 10,000) = £90,000 × 20%	18,000
The maximum penalty for a deliberate, but not concealed, error is:	
£18,000 × 70%	12,600

160 A Unprompted 20%, prompted 35%

161 Cyan plc and Crimson plc

Tutorial note. Large companies must pay their CT liabilities in quarterly instalments. The profit threshold for determining whether a company is a large company must be adjusted for related 51% group companies and for short accounting periods.

(a) **Cyan plc – corporation tax payable p/e 31.12.16**

	£
Corporation tax £1,350,000 × 20%	270,000

(b) **Cyan plc – payments of corporation tax for p/e 31.12.16**

Profit limit £1,500,000 × 9/12	1,125,000

Cyan plc is therefore a large company for the period.

Cyan plc is required to pay its corporation tax liability in instalments because it is a large company and this is not the first year that it is large.

The amount of each instalment and the due dates are as follows:

$3 \times \frac{£270,000}{9} = \underline{£90,000}$ payable on 14 October 2016, 14 January 2017, 14 April 2017.

(c) **Crimson plc - related 51% group companies**

Tangerine plc – related 51% group company as more than 50% of Tangerine plc's ordinary shares are owned directly by Crimson plc.

Russet plc - not related 51% group company as more than 50% of Russet plc's ordinary shares are not owned directly by Crimson plc.

Rouge plc - related 51% group company as more than 50% of Rouge plc's ordinary shares are owned indirectly by Crimson plc (55% × 96% = 52.8%).

Chestnut plc - related 51% group company as more than 50% of Chestnut plc's ordinary shares are owned directly by Crimson plc. However, since this relationship did not exist on 31 March 2016, it is not relevant for determining whether Crimson plc is a large company for the year ended 31 March 2017.

(d) **Crimson plc – whether large company in the year ended 31 March 2017**

	£
Taxable total profits	450,000
Dividend from 45% subsidiary (Russet plc)	30,000
Profits	480,000

The dividend from Tangerine plc is not included in the calculation of profits as it is received from a related 51% group company.

The profit threshold of £1,500,000 must be divided by three which is the total number of related 51% group companies including the company itself (Tangerine plc, Rouge plc and Crimson plc), and so is £500,000.

Therefore Crimson plc is not a large company in the year ended 31 March 2017.

An introduction to VAT MCQs

162 A 1 January 2017

Alec is liable to register for value added tax (VAT) when he is aware that his taxable turnover during the next 30 days will exceed the VAT registration limit of £83,000 (the future test). Alec must then charge VAT from the first day of that 30-day period, in this case 1 January 2017.

163 A £11,880

VAT is charged on the amounts actually received. Therefore the VAT due is £[(60,000 × 25% × 96%) + 60,000 × 75%) × 20% = £11,880.

164 B 31 December 2016

The tax point is generally the earliest of: the date of delivery, the invoice date and the cash receipt date. However, if as in this case, the invoice is issued within 14 days of delivery, then the invoice date becomes the tax point.

Justin

Tutorial note. Note how the input and output VAT is accounted for in respect of petrol and that the VAT incurred on the entertaining for UK customers is blocked from recovery.

165 C £98,000

	£
Output VAT	
Furniture: £490,000 × 20% (standard rated)	98,000
Books: £2,400 × 0% (zero rated)	0
	98,000

166 A £40 recoverable

	£
Output VAT	
£362 × 1/6	60
Input VAT	
£600 × 1/6	(100)
Net VAT recoverable	(40)

167 B £120

Non-UK customers only: £1,800 × 1/3 × 20% = £120

168 C Submission 7 February 2017, payment 7 February 2017

169 D No recovery of input VAT, no charge to VAT on sale

170 Newcomer Ltd and Au Revoir Ltd

> **Tutorial note.** This question is a typical question on registration and deregistration. Note the importance of the dates.

(a) The registration threshold is £83,000 during any consecutive 12 month period.

This is exceeded in January 2017:

		£
2016	October	18,500
	November	19,900
	December	23,400
2017	January	22,300
		84,100

Therefore, Newcomer Ltd must notify HM Revenue and Customs within 30 days of the end of the month the threshold was exceeded, ie by 1 March 2017.

Newcomer Ltd will be registered from the end of the month following the month in which the registration threshold was exceeded ie from 1 March 2017, or an earlier date agreed between the company and HM Revenue and Customs.

(b) A person is eligible for voluntary deregistration if HM Revenue and Customs are satisfied that the amount of his taxable supplies (net of VAT) in the following one year period will not exceed £81,000. However, voluntary deregistration will not be allowed if the reasons for the expected fall in value of taxable supplies is the cessation of taxable supplies or the suspension of taxable supplies for a period of 30 days or more in that following year. HM Revenue and Customs will cancel a person's registration from the date the request is made or an agreed later date.

171 Ongoing Ltd

> **Tutorial notes.**
>
> 1 Where a discount is offered for prompt payment, VAT is chargeable on amount received.
>
> 2 VAT on business entertaining is generally not recoverable. However the cost of entertaining overseas customers is recoverable.
>
> 3 Impairment loss (bad debt) relief is only available for debts over six months old (measured from when the payment is due).
>
> 4 VAT incurred on the purchase of a car not used wholly for business purposes is not recoverable. However, the subsequent sale of the car is exempt from VAT.

	£	£
Output tax		
£[(120,000 × 50% × 95%) + (120,000 × 50%) = 117,000 × 20% (note 1, note 4)		23,400
Input tax		
£(35,640 – 480) = 35,160 × 20% (note 2)	7,032	
£(2,100 × 95%) = £1,995 × 20% (note 3)	399	
£21,150 × 1/6 (note 4)	3,525	(10,956)
VAT payable for quarter ending 30 April 2016		12,444

Notes

1 VAT is calculated after the deduction of the prompt payment discount taken up.

2 UK entertaining is not an expense on which input tax can be recovered.

3 The debt must be six months old to claim bad debt relief. The output tax accounted for on the supply was net of the 5% discount for prompt payment even though the discount was obviously not taken up. The same amount of input tax can therefore be recovered under bad debt relief.

4 Input tax on motor cars not used wholly for business purposes is irrecoverable. However, the sale of the car, on which input tax is irrecoverable, is exempt from VAT.

Further aspects of VAT MCQs

172 C 1 and 4

All VAT returns must be up to date before a trader can join the scheme and it gives automatic impairment loss relief (bad debt relief) because VAT is not due on a supply until payment has been received.

The turnover condition is that a trader can join the scheme if their taxable turnover (exclusive of VAT) for the 12 months starting on their application to join the scheme is not expected to exceed £1,350,000. The payment of VAT by monthly payments applies to the annual accounting scheme.

173 D £Nil

Where goods are sold to another EU member state, the supply is zero-rated if the supply is made to a registered trader.

174 A £9,900

The flat rate percentage is applied to the full tax inclusive turnover including all standard, zero and exempt supplies so the VAT liability is £110,000 × 9% = £9,900.

Jason

Tutorial note. Make sure that you are clear about the different procedures for dealing with VAT on goods acquired from outside and inside the EU. The overall effect will usually be the same, but there is an actual payment of VAT required for imports from outside the EU at the time of importation.

175 B EU registered trader zero rated, outside EU zero rated

176 D Output tax at UK rate in next VAT return, input tax at UK rate in next return

177 C 15 August 2016

The 'tax point' is the earlier of:

(a) The fifteenth day of the month following the month of acquisition

(b) The date of issue of an invoice

178 C Output tax at UK rate at point of entry, input tax at UK rate in next VAT return

179 A Outside the scope of VAT

Supplies of services by a UK VAT registered trader to business customers outside the EU are outside the scope of UK VAT as the place of supply is not in the UK.

180 K Ltd and L Ltd

Tutorial note. In part (a), it is a good idea to present your answer as bullet points where you are asked to prepare notes for a meeting. The main advantage of the cash accounting scheme is automatic impairment loss relief so you should have spotted that this was the relevant scheme in part (b).

(a) **K Ltd – notes for meeting on annual accounting scheme**

(i) *Rules and qualifying conditions*

- Must regularly pay VAT (rather than receive repayments) to HM Revenue & Customs (HMRC)
- Taxable turnover (excluding VAT) must not be expected to exceed £1,350,000 in next 12 months
- All VAT returns must be up-to-date
- Nine payments on account required, commencing at the end of the fourth month of the year
- Payments are made by direct debt
- Each payment is 10% of the net VAT payable for the previous year
- Option to pay three larger interim instalments
- Annual return must be submitted within two months of the VAT year-end and any balance paid
- If the expected value of taxable supplies by the end of a year exceeds £1,600,000, notice must be given to HMRC within 30 days and may then be required to leave the scheme
- If by the end of that year the £1,600,000 limit is in fact exceeded, must leave the scheme

(ii) *Advantages*

- Only one VAT return each year so fewer occasions to trigger a default surcharge
- Ability to manage cash flow more accurately
- Avoids need for quarterly calculations for input tax recovery

Disadvantages

- Need to monitor future taxable supplies to ensure turnover limit not exceeded
- Timing of payments are less related to turnover (and therefore cash flow received) by business
- Payments based on previous year's turnover may not reflect current year turnover which may be a problem if the scale of activities has reduced

(b) **L Ltd – cash accounting scheme**

The cash accounting scheme will provide automatic impairment loss relief. This is because L Ltd will account for VAT on the basis of cash paid and received and so the date of payment or receipt determines the return in which the transaction is dealt with. Therefore, VAT will not be due on a supply until payment has been received.

L Ltd can use the cash accounting scheme if its expected taxable turnover for the next 12 months does not exceed £1,350,000. L Ltd must also be up-to-date with its VAT returns and VAT payments.

Tax tables

SUPPLEMENTARY INFORMATION

1. Calculations and workings need only be made to the nearest £.
2. All apportionments may be made to the nearest month.
3. All workings should be shown in Section C.

TAX RATES AND ALLOWANCES

The following tax rates and allowances are to be used in answering the questions.

Income tax

		Normal rates	Dividend rates
Basic rate	£1 – £32,000	20%	7.5%
Higher rate	£32,001 to £150,000	40%	32.5%
Additional rate	£150,001 and over	45%	38.1%

Savings rate nil rate band	– Basic rate taxpayers	£1,000
	– Higher rate taxpayers	£500
Dividend nil rate band		£5,000

A starting rate of 0% applies to savings income where it falls within the first £5,000 of taxable income.

Personal allowance

	£
Personal allowance	11,000
Transferable amount	1,100
Income limit	100,000

Residence status

Days in UK	Previously resident	Not previously resident
Less than 16	Automatically not resident	Automatically not resident
16 to 45	Resident if 4 UK ties (or more)	Automatically not resident
46 to 90	Resident if 3 UK ties (or more)	Resident if 4 UK ties
91 to 120	Resident if 2 UK ties (or more)	Resident if 3 UK ties (or more)
121 to 182	Resident if 1 UK tie (or more)	Resident if 2 UK ties (or more)
183 or more	Automatically resident	Automatically resident

Child benefit income tax charge

Where income is between £50,000 and £60,000, the charge is 1% of the amount of child benefit received for every £100 of income over £50,000.

Car benefit percentage

The base level of CO_2 emissions is 95 grams per kilometre.

The percentage rates applying to petrol cars with CO_2 emissions up to this level are:

50 grams per kilometre or less	7%
51 grams to 75 grams per kilometre	11%
76 grams to 94 grams per kilometre	15%
95 grams per kilometre	16%

Car fuel benefit

The base figure for calculating the car fuel benefit is £22,200.

Individual savings accounts (ISAs)

The overall investment limit is £15,240.

Pension scheme limits

Annual allowance	– 2014/15 to 2016/17	£40,000
	– 2013/14	£50,000
Minimum allowance		£10,000
Income limit		£150,000

The maximum contribution that can qualify for tax relief without any earnings is £3,600.

Authorised mileage allowances: cars

Up to 10,000 miles	45p
Over 10,000 miles	25p

Capital allowances: rates of allowance

Plant and machinery

Main pool	18%
Special rate pool	8%

Motor cars

New cars with CO_2 emissions up to 75 grams per kilometre	100%
CO_2 emissions between 76 and 130 grams per kilometre	18%
CO_2 emissions over 130 grams per kilometre	8%

Annual investment allowance

Rate of allowance	100%
Expenditure limit	£200,000

Cap on income tax reliefs

Unless otherwise restricted, reliefs are capped at the higher of £50,000 or 25% of income.

Corporation tax

Rate of tax	20%
Profit threshold	£1,500,000

Value Added Tax (VAT)

Standard rate	20%
Registration limit	£83,000
Deregistration limit	£81,000

Inheritance tax: tax rates

£1 – £325,000		Nil
Excess	– Death rate	40%
	– Lifetime rate	20%

Inheritance tax: taper relief

Years before death	*Percentage reduction*
Over 3 but less than 4 years	20%
Over 4 but less than 5 years	40%
Over 5 but less than 6 years	60%
Over 6 but less than 7 years	80%

Capital gains tax

		Normal rates	Residential property
Rates of tax	– Lower rate	10%	18%
	– Higher rate	20%	28%
Annual exempt amount			£11,100
Entrepreneurs' relief	– Lifetime limit		£10,000,000
	– Rate of tax		10%

National insurance contributions

Class 1 Employee	£1 – £8,060 per year	Nil
	£8,061 – £43,000 per year	12%
	£43,001 and above per year	2%
Class 1 Employer	£1 – £8,112 per year	Nil
	£8,113 and above per year	13.8%
	Employment allowance	£3,000
Class 1A		13.8%
Class 2	£2.80 per week	
	Small profits threshold	£5,965
Class 4	£1 – £8,060 per year	Nil
	£8,061 – £43,000 per year	9%
	£43,001 and above per year	2%

Rates of Interest (assumed)

Official rate of interest	3%
Rate of interest on underpaid tax	3%
Rate of interest on overpaid tax	0.5%

Index

Note: Key Terms and their page references are given in **bold**

BPP LEARNING MEDIA

ew Form – Paper F6 (Taxation) Finance Act 2016 (10/16)

ase help us to ensure that the ACCA learning materials we produce remain as accurate and user-friendly s possible. We cannot promise to answer every submission we receive, but we do promise that it will be ead and taken into account when we update this Study Text.

Name: ______________________ **Address:** ______________________

____

____

How have you used this Study Text?
(Tick one box only)

☐ On its own (book only)
☐ On a BPP in-centre course ______________
☐ On a BPP online course
☐ On a course with another college
☐ Other ______________________

Why did you decide to purchase this Study Text? *(Tick one box only)*

☐ Have used BPP Study Texts in the past
☐ Recommendation by friend/colleague
☐ Recommendation by a lecturer at college
☐ Saw information on BPP website
☐ Saw advertising
☐ Other ______________________

During the past six months do you recall seeing/receiving any of the following?
(Tick as many boxes as are relevant)

☐ Our advertisement in *ACCA Student Accountant*
☐ Our advertisement in *Pass*
☐ Our advertisement in *PQ*
☐ Our brochure with a letter through the post
☐ Our website www.bpp.com

Which (if any) aspects of our advertising do you find useful?
(Tick as many boxes as are relevant)

☐ Prices and publication dates of new editions
☐ Information on Study Text content
☐ Facility to order books
☐ None of the above

Which BPP products have you used?

Study Text	☑	*Passcards*	☐	*Other*	☐
Kit	☐	*i-Pass*	☐		

Your ratings, comments and suggestions would be appreciated on the following areas.

	Very useful	*Useful*	*Not useful*
Introductory section	☐	☐	☐
Chapter introductions	☐	☐	☐
Key terms	☐	☐	☐
Quality of explanations	☐	☐	☐
Examples	☐	☐	☐
Exam focus points	☐	☐	☐
Questions and answers in each chapter	☐	☐	☐
Fast forwards and chapter roundups	☐	☐	☐
Quick quizzes	☐	☐	☐
Question Bank	☐	☐	☐
Answer Bank	☐	☐	☐
Index	☐	☐	☐

Overall opinion of this Study Text. *Excellent* ☐ *Good* ☐ *Adequate* ☐ *Poor* ☐

Do you intend to continue using BPP products? *Yes* ☐ *No* ☐

On the reverse of this page is space for you to write your comments about our Study Text. We welcome your feedback.

The BPP Learning Media author of this edition can be emailed at: accaqueries@bpp.com

Please return this form to: Head of ACCA and FIA Programmes, BPP Learning Media Ltd, FREEPOST, London, W12 8AA

TELL US WHAT YOU THINK

Please note any further comments and suggestions/errors below. For example, was the text accurate, readab concise, user-friendly and comprehensive?

UNLOCKING THE LAW

UNLOCKING
EU LAW

3rd edition

Tony Storey
Chris Turner

Series editors
Jacqueline Martin
& Chris Turner

UNLOCKING THE LAW

HODDER EDUCATION
AN HACHETTE UK COMPANY

Orders: please contact Bookpoint Ltd, 130 Milton Park, Abingdon, Oxon OX14 4SB.
Telephone: (44) 01235 827720. Fax: (44) 01235 400454. Lines are open from 9.00–5.00, Monday to Saturday, with a 24-hour message answering service.
You can also order through our website www.hoddereducation.co.uk

British Library Cataloguing in Publication Data
A catalogue record for this title is available from the British Library.

ISBN: 978 1 444 10914 6

First Edition Published 2005
Second Edition Published 2008
This Edition Published 2011

Impression number	10	9	8	7	6	5	4	3	2	1
Year	2015		2014		2013		2012		2011	

Cover photo © VCL/Bronwyn Kidd/Getty Images
Typeset by Phoenix Photosetting, Chatham, Kent
Printed in Italy for Hodder Education, an Hachette UK Company, 338 Euston Road, London NW1 3BH

Contents

Acknowledgements

The books in this series are a departure from traditional law texts and represent one view of a type of learning resource that we feel is particularly useful to students. The series editors would therefore like to thank the publishers for their support in making the project a reality. In particular we would also like to thank Alexia Chan for her continued faith in the project from its first conception, and also Colin Goodlad for subsequent development.

The publishers apologise if inadvertently any sources remain unacknowledged and will be glad to make the necessary arrangements at the earliest opportunity.

Guide to the book

In the Unlocking the Law books all the essential elements that make up the law are clearly defined to bring the law alive and make it memorable. In addition, the books are enhanced with learning features to reinforce learning and test your knowledge as you study. Follow this guide to make sure you get the most from reading this book.

AIMS AND OBJECTIVES

Defines what you will learn in each chapter.

SECTION

Highlights sections from Acts.

ARTICLE

Defines Articles of the EC Treaty or of the European Convention on Human Rights or other Treaty.

CLAUSE

Shows a Bill going through Parliament or a draft Bill proposed by the Law Commission.

CASE EXAMPLE

Illustrates the law in action.

JUDGMENT

Provides extracts from judgments on cases.

QUOTATION

Encourages you to engage with primary sources.

ACTIVITY

Enables you to test yourself as you progress through the chapter.

SAMPLE ESSAY QUESTIONS

Provide you with real-life sample essays and show you the best way to plan your answer.

SUMMARY

Concludes each chapter to reinforce learning.

Preface

The 'Unlocking' series is an entirely new style of undergraduate law textbooks. Many student texts are very prose dense and have little in the way of interactive materials to help a student feel his or her way through the course of study on a given module.

The purpose of this series then is to try to make learning each subject area more accessible by focusing on actual learning needs, and by providing a range of different supporting materials and features.

All topic areas are broken up into 'bite size' sections with a logical progression and extensive use of headings and numerous sub-headings. Each book in the series will also contain a variety of charts, diagrams and key facts summaries to reinforce the information in the body of the text. Diagrams and flow charts are particularly useful because they can provide a quick and easy understanding of the key points, especially when revising for examinations. Key facts charts not only provide a quick visual guide through the subject but are useful for revision purposes also.

The books have a number of common features in the layout. Important cases are separated out for easy access and have full citation in the text as well as the table of cases for ease of reference. The emphasis of the series is on depth of understanding much more than breadth. For this reason each text also includes key extracts from judgments where appropriate. Extracts from academic comment from journal articles and leading texts are also included to give some insight into the academic debate on complex or controversial areas. In both cases these are indented to make them clear from the body of the text.

Finally, the books also include much formative 'self-assessment', with a variety of activities ranging through subject-specific comprehension, application of the law, and a range of other activities to help the student gain a good idea of his or her progress in the course.

Many students feel nervous about studying the law of the European Union and, because of the way that it is sometimes presented, many also feel that it is hard to study. Nevertheless, it is important not only to gain a good understanding but also to enjoy the study of EU law because it is now a core subject in all qualifying law degrees. It is also important because so many other areas of law are now dependent on it. It would be difficult to teach or study contract law, employment law, company law or consumer law without a reasonable appreciation of the effects of EU law. In fact, the substantive law is both an exciting and a developing area of law. It highlights our ability to move freely about Europe, and much modern discrimination law has only developed because of our membership of the Union. It is therefore very relevant to everyday life.

The book is designed to cover all of the main topic areas on undergraduate and professional EU law syllabuses and help provide a full understanding of each. The new edition has been amended to include all important recent developments.

We hope that you will gain as much enjoyment in reading about the law of the European Union, and testing your understanding with the various activities in the book, as we have had in writing it, and that you gain much enjoyment and interest from your study of the law.

The law is stated as we believe it to be on 30 October 2010.

Chris Turner
Tony Storey

Table of cases

Chronological Cases before the Court of Justice and the General Court

Table of treaty articles and legislation

Directives

Regulations

Table of International Legislation

Table of Equivalents

EC Treaty pre and post Treaty of Amsterdam

Previous numbering	**New numbering**
PART ONE	PART ONE
Art 2	Art 2
Art 3	Art 3
Art 3a	Art 4
Art 3b	Art 5
Art 3g	Art 6
Art 4	Art 7
Art 5	Art 10
Art 6	Art 12
Art 6a (New Art)	Art 13
PART TWO	PART TWO
Art 8	Art 17
Art 8a	Art 18
PART THREE	PART THREE
Art 12	Art 25
Art 28	Art 26
Art 29	Art 27
Art 30	Art 28
Art 34	Art 29
Art 36	Art 30
Art 37	Art 31
TITLE II	TITLE II
Art 39	Art 33
Art 40	Art 34
Art 41	Art 35
Art 42	Art 36
TITLE III	TITLE III
Art 48	Art 39
Art 49	Art 40
Art 52	Art 43
Art 54	Art 44
Art 55	Art 45
Art 56	Art 46
Art 57	Art 47
Art 58	Art 48
Art 59	Art 49
Art 60	Art 50
Art 61	Art 51
Art 63	Art 52
Art 64	Art 53
Art 65	Art 54
Art 66	Art 55
Art 73b	Art 56
Art 73c	Art 57
Art 73d	Art 58
Art 73f	Art 59
Art 73g	Art 60
TITLE IV	TITLE V
Art 74	Art 70
Art 75	Art 71
Art 76	Art 72
Art 77	Art 73
Art 78	Art 74
Art 79	Art 75
Art 80	Art 76
Art 81	Art 77
Art 82	Art 78
Art 83	Art 79
Art 84	Art 80
TITLE V	TITLE VI
Art 85	Art 81
Art 86	Art 82
Art 87	Art 83
Art 88	Art 84
Art 89	Art 85
Art 90	Art 86
Art 92	Art 87
Art 93	Art 88
Art 94	Art 89
Art 95	Art 90
Art 96	Art 91
Art 98	Art 92
Art 99	Art 93
Art 100	Art 94
Art 100a	Art 95
Art 101	Art 96
Art 102	Art 97
	Art 100
	Art 101
	Art 102
Art 130r	
Art 119	Art 141
Art 128	Art 151
Art 129a	Art 153
TITLE XII	TITLE XV
Art 129b	Art 154
Art 129c	Art 155
Art 129d	Art 156
TITLE XIII	TITLE XVI
Art 130	Art 157
TITLE XV	TITLE XVIII
Art 130f	Art 163
Art 130g	Art 164
Art 130h	Art 165
Art 130i	Art 166
Art 130j	Art 167
Art 130k	Art 168
Art 130l	Art 169

EC Treaty and Treaty on the Functioning of the European Union pre and post Treaty of Lisbon

	Art 4
Art 3 (part)	Art 8
Art 4	Art 119
Art 5	
Art 6	Art 11
Art 153 (part)	Art 12
Art 7	
Art 10	
Art 12	Art 18
Art 13	Art 19
Art 17	Art 20
Art 18	Art 21
Art 19	Art 22
Art 20	Art 23
Art 21	Art 24
Art 22	Art 25
PART THREE	PART THREE
	Title I
Art 14	Art 26
Art 15	Art 27
Title I	Title II
Art 23	Art 28
Art 24	Art 29
Chapter 1	Chapter 1
Art 25	Art 30
Art 26	Art 31
Art 27	Art 32
Part Three, Title X	Chapter 2
Art 135	Art 33
Chapter 2	Chapter 3
Art 28	Art 34
Art 29	Art 35
Art 30	Art 36
Art 31	Art 37
Title II	Title III
Art 32	Art 38
Art 33	Art 39
Art 34	Art 40
Art 35	Art 41
Art 36	Art 42
Art 37	Art 43
Art 38	Art 44
Title III	Title IV
Chapter 1	Chapter 1
Art 39	Art 45
Art 40	Art 46
Art 41	Art 47
Art 42	Art 48
Chapter 2	Chapter 2
Art 43	Art 49
Art 44	Art 50
Art 45	Art 51
Art 46	Art 52
Art 47	Art 53
Art 48	Art 54
Art 294	Art 55
Chapter 3	Chapter 3
Art 49	Art 56
Art 50	Art 57
Art 51	Art 58
Art 52	Art 59
Art 53	Art 60
Art 54	Art 61
Art 55	Art 62
Chapter 4	Chapter 4
Art 56	Art 63
Art 57	Art 64
Art 58	Art 65
Art 59	Art 66
Art 60	Art 75
Title IV	Title V
	Chapter 1
Art 61	Art 67
	Art 68
	Art 69
	Art 70
	Art 71
Art 64	Art 72
	Art 73
Art 66	Art 74
Art 60	Art 75
	Art 76
	Chapter 2
Art 62	Art 77
Art 63 (part)	Art 78
Art 64 (part)	
Art 63 (part)	Art 79
	Art 80
Art 64	Art 72
	Chapter 3
Art 65	Art 81
Art 66	Art 74
Art 67	
Art 68	
Art 69	
	Chapter 4
	Art 82
	Art 83
	Art 84
	Art 85
	Art 86
	Chapter 5
	Art 87
	Art 88
	Art 89
Title V	Title VI
Art 70	Art 90
Art 71	Art 91
Art 72	Art 92
Art 73	Art 93
Art 74	Art 94
Art 75	Art 95
Art 76	Art 96
Art 77	Art 97
Art 78	Art 98
Art 79	Art 99
Art 80	Art 100
Title VI	Title VII
Chapter 1	Chapter 1

Section 1	Section 1
Art 81	Art 101
Art 82	Art 102
Art 83	Art 103
Art 84	Art 104
Art 85	Art 105
Art 86	Art 106
Section 2	Section 2
Art 87	Art 107
Art 88	Art 108
Art 89	Art 109
Chapter 2	Chapter 2
Art 90	Art 110
Art 91	Art 111
Art 92	Art 112
Art 93	Art 113
Chapter 3	Chapter 3
Art 95	Art 114
Art 94	Art 115
Art 96	Art 116
Art 97	Art 117
	Art 118
Title VII	Title VIII
Art 4	Art 119
Chapter 1	Chapter 1
Art 98	Art 120
Art 99	Art 121
Art 100	Art 122
Art 101	Art 123
Art 102	Art 124
Art 103	Art 125
Art 104	Art 126
Chapter 2	Chapter 2
Art 105	Art 127
Art 106	Art 128
Art 107	Art 129
Art 108	Art 130
Art 109	Art 131
Art 110	Art 132
Art 111 (part)	Art 219
Art 111 (part)	Art 138
	Art 133
Chapter 3	Chapter 3
Art 112	Art 283
Art 113	Art 284
Art 114	Art 134
Art 115	Art 135
	Chapter 4
	Art 136
	Art 137
Art 111 (part)	Art 138
Chapter 4	Chapter 5
Art 116	
	Art 139
Art 117 (part)	Art 141
Art 121	Art 140
Art 122	
Art 123	
Art 118	
Art 123,	Art 141
Art 117	
Art 124	Art 142
Art 119	Art 143
Art 120	Art 144
Art 121	Art 140
Art 121	
Art 122	
Art 122	Art 140
Art 123 (part)	Art 141 (part)
Art 123 (part)	Art 140 (part)
Art 124 (part)	Art 142
Title VIII	Title IX
Art 125	Art 145
Art 126	Art 146
Art 127	Art 147
Art 128	Art 148
Art 129	Art 149
Art 130	Art 150
Title IX	Part Five, Title II
Art 131	Art 206
Art 132	
Art 133	Art 207
Art 134	
Title X	Part Three, Title II, Chapter 2,
Art 135	Art 33
Title XI	Title X
Chapter 1	
Art 136	Art 151
	Art 152
Art 137	Art 153
Art 138	Art 154
Art 139	Art 155
Art 140	Art 156
Art 141	Art 157
Art 142	Art 158
Art 143	Art 159
Art 144	Art 160
Art 145	Art 161
Chapter 2	Title XI
Art 146	Art 162
Art 147	Art 163
Art 148	Art 164
Chapter 3	Title XII
Art 149	Art 165
Art 150	Art 166
Title XII	Title XIII
Art 151	Art 167
Title XIII	Title XIV
Art 152	Art 168
Title XIV	Title XV
Art 153 (part)	Art 169
Art 153 (part)	Art 12
Title XV	Title XVI
Art 154	Art 170
Art 155	Art 171
Art 156	Art 172
Title XVI	Title XVII
Art 157	Art 173

Title XVII	Title XVIII
Art 158	Art 174
Art 159	Art 175
Art 160	Art 176
Art 161	Art 177
Art 162	Art 178
Title XVIII	Title XIX
Art 163	Art 179
Art 164	Art 180
Art 165	Art 181
Art 166	Art 182
Art 167	Art 183
Art 168	Art 184
Art 169	Art 185
Art 170	Art 186
Art 171	Art 187
Art 172	Art 188
	Art 189
Art 173	Art 190
Title XIX	Title XX
Art 174	Art 191
Art 175	Art 192
Art 176	Art 193
	Title XXI
	Art 194
	Title XXII
	Art 195
	Title XXIII
	Art 196
	Title XXIV
	Art 197
Title XX	Part Five, Title III, Chapter 1
Art 177	Art 208
Art 178	
Art 179	Art 209
Art 180	Art 210
Art 181	Art 211
Title XXI	Part Five, Title III, Chapter 2
Art 181a	Art 212
PART FOUR	PART FOUR
Art 182	Art 198
Art 183	Art 199
Art 184	Art 200
Art 185	Art 201
Art 186	Art 202
Art 187	Art 203
Art 188	Art 204
	PART FIVE
	Title I
	Art 205
Part Three, Title IX	Title II
Art 131	Art 206
Art 133	Art 207
	Title III
Part Three, Title XX,	Chapter 1
Art 177	Art 208
Art 179	Art 209
Art 180	Art 210
Art 181	Art 211
Part Three, Title XXI,	Chapter 2
Art 181a	Art 212
	Art 213
	Chapter 3
	Art 214
	Title IV
Art 301	Art 215
	Title V
	Art 216
Art 310	Art 217
Art 300	Art 218
Art 111 (part)	Art 219
	Title VI
Arts 302 to 304	Art 220
	Art 221
	Title VII
	Art 222
PART FIVE	PART SIX
Title I	Title I
Chapter 1	Chapter 1
Section 1	Section 1
Art 189	
Art 190 (part)	Art 223
Art 191 (part)	Art 224
Art 192 (part)	Art 225
Art 193	Art 226
Art 194	Art 227
Art 195	Art 228
Art 196	Art 229
Art 197 (part)	Art 230
Art 198	Art 231
Art 199	Art 232
Art 200	Art 233
Art 201	Art 234
	Section 2
	Art 235
	Art 236
Section 2	Section 3l
Art 202	
Art 203	
Art 204	Art 237
Art 205 (part)	Art 238
Art 206	Art 239
Art 207	Art 240
Art 208	Art 241
Art 209	Art 242
Art 210	Art 243
Section 3	Section 4
Art 211	
	Art 244
Art 212	Art 249 (part)
Art 213	Art 245
Art 214	
Art 215	Art 246
Art 216	Art 247
Art 217 (part)	Art 248

Art 218 (part)	Art 249
Art 219	Art 250
Section 4	Section 5
Art 220	
Art 221 (part)	Art 251
Art 222	Art 252
Art 223	Art 253
Art 224	Art 254
	Art 255
Art 225	Art 256
Art 225a	Art 257
Art 226	Art 258
Art 227	Art 259
Art 228	Art 260
Art 229	Art 261
Art 229a	Art 262
Art 230	Art 263
Art 231	Art 264
Art 232	Art 265
Art 233	Art 266
Art 234	Art 267
Art 235	Art 268
	Art 269
Art 236	Art 270
Art 237	Art 271
Art 238	Art 272
Art 239	Art 273
Art 240	Art 274
	Art 275
	Art 276
Art 241	Art 277
Art 242	Art 278
Art 243	Art 279
Art 244	Art 280
Art 245	Art 281
	Section 6
	Art 282
Art 112	Art 283
Art 113	Art 284
Section 5	Section 7
Art 246	Art 285
Art 247	Art 286
Art 248	Art 287
Chapter 2	Chapter 2
	Section 1
Art 249	Art 288
	Art 289
	Art 290
	Art 291
	Art 292
	Section 2
Art 250	Art 293
Art 251	Art 294
Art 252	
	Art 295
Art 253	Art 296
Art 254	Art 297
	Art 298
Art 255	Art 15
Art 256	Art 299
	Chapter 3
	Art 300
Chapter 3	Section 1
Art 257	
Art 258 (part)	Art 301
Art 259	Art 302
Art 260	Art 303
Art 261	
Art 262	Art 304
Chapter 4	Section 2
Art 263 (part)	Art 305
Art 264	Art 306
Art 265	Art 307
Chapter 5	Chapter 4
Art 266	Art 308
Art 267	Art 309
Title II	Title II
Art 268	Art 310
	Chapter 1
Art 269	Art 311
Art 270	
	Chapter 2
	Art 312
	Chapter 3
Art 272 (part)	Art 313
Art 271	Art 316
Art 272 (part)	Art 313
Art 272 (part)	Art 314
Art 273	Art 315
Art 271	Art 316
	Chapter 4
Art 274	Art 317
Art 275	Art 318
Art 276	Art 319
	Chapter 5
Art 277	Art 320
Art 278	Art 321
Art 279	Art 322
	Art 323
	Art 324
	Chapter 6
Art 280	Art 325
	Title III
Arts 11 and 11a	Art 326
Arts 11 and 11a	Art 327
Arts 11 and 11a	Art 328
Arts 11 and 11a	Art 329
Arts 11 and 11a	Art 330
Arts 11 and 11a	Art 331
Arts 11 and 11a	Art 332
Arts 11 and 11a	Art 333
Arts 11 and 11a	Art 334
PART SIX	PART SEVEN
Art 281	
Art 282	Art 335
Art 283	Art 336
Art 284	Art 337
Art 285	Art 338
Art 286	Art 16

Art 287	Art 339
Art 288	Art 340
Art 289	Art 341
Art 290	Art 342
Art 291	Art 343
Art 292	Art 344
Art 293	
Art 294	Art 55
Art 295	Art 345
Art 296	Art 346
Art 297	Art 347
Art 298	Art 348
Art 299 (part)	Art 349
Art 299 (part)	Art 355
Art 300	Art 218
Art 301	Art 215
Art 302	Art 220
Art 303	Art 220
Art 304	Art 220
Art 305	
Art 306	Art 350
Art 307	Art 351
Art 308	Art 352 Art 353
Art 309	Art 354
Art 310	Art 217
Art 311	
Art 299 (part)	Art 355
Art 312	Art 356
Final Provisions	
Art 313	Art 357 Art 358

List of Figures

1

The origins and character of EC law

AIMS AND OBJECTIVES

After reading this chapter you should be able to:

- Understand the reasons for the development of a single Europe
- Understand the background to the Treaties and the idea of the Community
- Understand the main aims and objectives of the Treaties
- Understand the concept of supranationalism
- Understand how the Treaties have developed through subsequent Treaties
- Understand the principles and consequences of enlargement of territory and scope
- Understand the significance of the EU Constitution and the Reform Treaty
- Analyse the development of the EU
- Analyse the consequences of enlargement

1.1 The origins of and background to the Treaties

1.1.1 The background to the idea of a single Europe

One problem that appears to confront students of EU law is an apparent assumption in the United Kingdom that Europe is something foreign, that it refers to a place and to people across the English Channel that have nothing to do with the United Kingdom. This is, of course, not the truth, since the United Kingdom has been a member of the European Community (more recently the European Union) since signing the Treaties and ratifying membership in the European Communities Act 1972. The United Kingdom has been a member of the European Community since 1st January 1973. It has remained so after a majority vote for membership in a popular referendum in 1975 in which there was freedom for MPs of whatever party to support the campaign to deliver a 'yes' or a 'no' vote according to the way that their consciences and their commitment led them.

Nevertheless, Euro-scepticism is not uncommon within the country and it would not be unreasonable to suggest that this, in part at least, follows the encouragement of certain elements of the media. This Euro-scepticism seems to be founded in two critical misconceptions about the nature and the role of the Community (now the Union following the Treaty on European Union signed at Maastricht in 1992):

- That the idea of European unity is a new and modern political concept – in fact it is anything but. The idea is certainly as old as Europe itself and has been put into place before but in different political form.
- That the Community is based mainly on co-operation between the Member States that may or may not be followed. Again, this is not the truth. The Community legal order is

based on the objectives of the Treaties that have been agreed by all Member States, and it works towards the achievement of the single dominant purpose of the Community: the full economic integration of the Member States towards a truly united Europe.

In fact, it is unusually appropriate that the Treaty responsible for creating and framing the concept of the Community should be referred to commonly as the Treaty of Rome (this is, of course, the second Treaty of Rome, the first being the EURATOM Treaty). It is appropriate because it is possible to see the Roman Empire as the first real attempt to unify Europe. Of course, in this case it was by a colonial power and through military dictatorship. Nevertheless, the whole purpose of the empire was economic, increasing availability of resources and markets and control of trade.

Following the Romans, it is possible to identify a number of situations demonstrating the same aspiration of a united Europe:

- The original view of Christendom expounded by the Roman Catholic Church, or more precisely of the Papacy that led it, was very much a European ideal, and everything outside Europe was considered to be barbarian.
- Charlemagne moulded and reigned over the so-called 'Holy Roman Empire' which covered much of modern Europe. This was obviously a political empire and it soon fell apart after his death as it passed to his sons, becoming the principalities that form the basis of many of the modern nation states.
- Henry IV of France also tried very hard to create a Christian Commonwealth of Europe.
- More recently, Napoleon Bonaparte declared a stated ambition and policy for a European empire.
- More recently still, Hitler's expansionist philosophy was also aimed at a Reich that would control most of Europe.
- Even besides the above, there have been numerous philosophers, including Kant, Rousseau, Marx and Neitzsche, who have all presented a united Europe as an ideal, and this despite their representing the widest spectrum of political philosophy, from Fascism to Communism.

Historically, then, it is true to say that the so-called 'Euro-sceptics' are in a minority and that there has always been in the widest sense a European identity and the desire for European unity. In this way it is Euro-scepticism which is the recent phenomenon and indeed exists only in restricted elements of national feeling that are hostile to the idea of the Community. It clearly has a particular foothold in the United Kingdom.

The 'Euro-sceptics' have always shown hostility towards the concept of a federal Europe, despite the fact that in its foundations the Community looked towards an eventual political unity as well as an economic unity. The British hostility towards federalism is even stranger since the idea of a federal Europe originated in Britain. It was suggested by Winston Churchill (who was Prime Minister during the war years) before the Second World War and supported then because of the fear of a fascist Germany. In fact, Jean Monnet, who is accepted as being the 'intellectual father' of the concept of European Union, himself credited the origins of the ideal to the British.

A further point worth making when considering the origins of the concept is that whatever philosophy has ever been put forward for European union has always included incorporation of a binding legal order as well as any economic, social or political union.

1.1.2 The origins of the Community

It must be remembered that the idea of European unity is based on a very noble and worthwhile principle: the avoidance of war in Europe. War between various nation states, most notably France and Germany, had been an almost constant feature for several centuries before the absolute devastation in the two 'World Wars' of the twentieth century.

The late nineteenth and early twentieth centuries saw various attempts at European integration of different types with this object in mind. The French 'Briand Plan' of 1929–30 is a classic example.

Nevertheless, economic and political imperatives conspired to create even more disruptive conflicts. As a result, following the Second World War there was an even stronger recognition of the need to avoid future conflicts. Certain other key points were also recognised in the immediate post-war period:

- that the Treaty of Versailles, while devised to prevent German hostility, had actually been a total failure and had led in part to the rise of Nazi Germany
- that the only successful means of preventing war in Europe was not to repress the German state but to tie Germany into a European partnership.

Churchill (Prime Minister during the war) in fact encouraged the idea of a form of European unity. In a speech in Zurich in 1946, shortly after the close of the war, Churchill (by now the Leader of the Opposition) suggested that:

> 'We must build a kind of United States of Europe. In this way only will hundreds of millions of toilers be able to regain the simple joys and hopes which make life worth living ... The structure of the United States of Europe, if well and truly built, will be such as to make the material strength of a single state less important.'
>
> I Ward, *A Critical Introduction to European Law* (Butterworths, 1996), pp 6–7

It is worth noting that Churchill was not so much concerned with all nations losing power as he was with Germany losing power.

A European Union of Federalists was then established in 1946. Its supporters on the Continent argued that the way forward was the creation of 'supranational' bodies. In the Montreux Resolution of 1947 the group suggested that:

QUOTATION

> 'unification in Western Europe means escaping the risk of power politics. Federalists must declare without compromise that it is absolute sovereignty that must be abated ... a part of that sovereignty must be entrusted to a federal authority'.

A variety of intergovernmental conferences quickly followed at which agreements were reached to set up new organisations on either a global or merely a European scale. These organisations included:

- the **International Monetary Fund** (IMF)
- the **General Agreement on Tariffs and Trade** (GATT)
- the **Organisation for European Economic Co-operation** (OEEC) (this in effect was the creation of the United States through the 'Marshall Plan' of 1947 – the idea being to create an organisation that would administer the financial aid that was needed to repair the damage done to Europe during the Second World War)
- the **Council of Europe** (this was a most significant development for its creation of a European Convention on Human Rights and a European Court of Human Rights)
- the **BENELUX Union** (a union between the countries of Belgium, the Netherlands and Luxembourg – still among the smallest nations in the European Union – significantly, though, the origins of supranationalism can be seen in this organisation for economic co-operation).

If the institutional origins of European Unity began with the 'Marshall Plan' then the next major phase was the 'Schuman Plan'. Robert Schuman was the French Foreign Minister and Jean Monnet was another French politician with responsibility for economic planning, who actually drafted the plan for Schuman. Both men were strong supporters of the idea of European co-operation.

The basis of the plan was the integration of French and German coal and steel production under the control of what was referred to as a 'higher authority'. This is the narrow agenda of the plan. The broader agenda was that it should represent the first stage towards a federal state of Europe.

The plan then led to and formed the basis of the first Treaty: the European Coal and Steel Community Treaty (ECSC Treaty), formally signed as the Treaty of Paris in 1951. A significant point concerning all the various 'plans' for a united Europe is the concern to incorporate a legal order as well as economic and political union. This was demonstrated in the Treaty of Paris which created a Community with supranational institutions.

1.1.3 The creation of the Treaties

As a result of the Schuman Plan, the first of the Treaties creating the European Community, later to develop into the European Union, was the European Coal and Steel Community Treaty (ECSC Treaty) – the Treaty of Paris 1951.

Focusing on the production of steel and coal was not a random choice. The Treaty had as a distinct aim the prevention of further hostilities within Europe and the establishment of stable relations between countries that had formerly been at war. That both France and Germany had regions where steel and coal were a major factor in the economy was also an actual and potential cause of conflict between the two countries. Establishing close economic co-operation in these specific fields was a logical means of preventing conflict. Not surprisingly, Monnet was made the first President of the ECSC.

The Treaty in essence devised the institutional framework of all the Communities. At first this was based on the political institutions: a 'High Authority' (later to be the Commission) to act as the executive arm, controlling production, a political assembly of representative members from the various Member States, and a Special Council of Ministers, with a partly legislative and a partly consultative role. Of course, since it was always envisaged that economic integration must be backed by a legal order, a Court of Justice was also added later.

The Treaty was in the end signed by only six European nations:

- France
- Germany
- Italy
- Belgium
- The Netherlands and
- Luxembourg.

The last three were already closely linked through the BENELUX Union. The UK significantly declined the opportunity to join the Community. Britain had suffered a lot less devastation than many of the mainland European nations and political thinking of the time leaned towards the so-called 'special relationship' with the United States of America as having more to offer than membership of an economically integrated Europe, and it saw its main market as the Commonwealth.

However, economic integration was established with the Treaty although there were still setbacks in terms of achieving unity. For instance, another initiative aimed at preventing conflict, the European Defence Community, collapsed in 1953.

Nevertheless, the move towards greater economic integration continued. The Spaak Committee Report of 1952 recommended the placing of atomic energy under a single authority and also called for the creation of a 'Common Market':

QUOTATION

> 'a vast area with a common political economy which will form a powerful productive unit and permit a steady expansion, an increase in stability, a more rapid rise in the standard of living, and the development of harmonious relations between member states'.

The report led directly to the creation of two more Treaties. These were the two Treaties of Rome that were signed by all six members of the ECSC on the same day in 1957, the European Atomic Energy Community Treaty (EURATOM) and the European Economic Community Treaty (later to be re-named the EC Treaty).

From the start, the three Communities shared the Common Assembly and also the European Court of Justice (ECJ). Initially the High Authority of the ECSC and the two Commissions of the other two Communities remained separate.

1.2 The basic aims and objectives of EC law and the concept of supranationalism

The major aim of the Treaties was economic integration, but the Treaties also reflect the wider purpose behind that integration. In the preamble to the EC Treaty it is clearly stated that the central objective of the signatories to the Treaties was to 'lay the foundations of an ever closer union among the peoples of Europe [by] pooling their resources to preserve and strengthen peace and liberty'.

The union was to be achieved by integration of the Member States' economic and monetary policies for the creation of a Common Market free from internal barriers to trade. The objectives of the EC in seeking to attain this Common Market were quite simply stated in the EC Treaty itself and as it has later been amended and built on by the subsequent Treaties:

- to promote throughout the Community a harmonious development of economic activities
- a continuous, balanced expansion
- an increase in stability
- an accelerated raising of the standard of living and quality of life and closer relations between the states belonging to it and sustainable development of economic activities
- a high level of employment and of social protection
- equality between men and women
- sustainable and non-inflationary growth
- a high degree of competitiveness and convergence of economic performance
- a high level of protection and of improvement of the quality of the environment
- economic and social cohesion among the Member States.

The objectives dictated the structure of the Communities that were created in the Treaties. Key features of the structure can be identified in the EC Treaty:

- the introduction of four basic freedoms – freedom of movement of workers, the right to establish a trade or profession and to provide services freely, the free movement of goods, and the free movement of capital within the Community – all with a view to the removal of internal barriers to trade
- the progressive approximation of economic policies of the Member States and the harmonisation of national laws in key economic areas such as agriculture, transport and trade
- the creation of a Common Customs Tariff to regulate imports into the Community from other countries
- the creation of a Common Commercial Policy to regulate trade between Member States and other countries.

Inevitably, different Member States had different things to gain from the Treaties and the creation of the three Communities. As a result, from the start proper integration was always hampered by national self-interest. This ensured that development could only be 'incremental' and that, often, principle would be sacrificed to what was achievable.

In fact, even before the creation of the Treaties there was a division in attitudes between those who retained a full federalist ideal and those who preferred a more co-operative progress towards integration, this latter group often being referred to as the 'functualists':

- the **federalists** believed in the creation of a single supranational body that would in effect take over all of the functions of the individual Member States
- the **functualists** preferred to focus on individual areas of the economy and put these under joint management to improve efficiency and with the view that co-operation would then naturally spread from one economic area to another.

The ECSC was based on the attitudes of the functionalists. This gave way to 'neo-functualism' which is demonstrated in the broader principles of the EC Treaty, and which reflects the need to limit the power of national governments to legislate in certain areas. This is the basis of supranationalism.

One of the major problems in achieving integration is in defining the constitution of the Community and how it becomes part of the law of the individual Member States. It is of course possible to argue that the constitution of the EC is represented by what is laid down in the Treaties and the objectives that they contain. However, the EC constitution has the added complication of being founded in Treaty relationships that are then entered into by sovereign States.

In this way another problem concerns the way that the Treaties are incorporated into Member States' law because of the different natures of the constitutions of the different Member States. These are of two distinct types:

- **monist** constitutions: of the original six members these included both France and the Netherlands. In such constitutions the Treaty is automatically incorporated into the national legal system at the point of ratification
- **dualist** constitutions: of the original six these included Germany, Italy and Belgium. Significantly, of course, they also include the UK where the Treaty could only be incorporated into English law after enactment. In the case of the UK this was as the result of the passing of the European Communities Act 1972.

The result of the different methods of incorporation is that there can be a wide variance in how the Treaties are then interpreted and applied in the individual Member States. As a result, in order for the legal order of the Community to have any effect the Community institutions must be 'supranational' in character. In other words, in relation to those areas that are covered by Treaty obligations, the institutions and those Community obligations must take precedence over national law and institutions.

As a result of this the European Court of Justice (ECJ) has proved to be one of the most significant institutions both in administering and defining EC law, and also in developing the principle of 'supranationalism'. Both have been vital in ensuring the universal application of the Treaties.

Commentators have frequently accepted the importance of the court in furthering the objectives laid down in the Treaties.

> 'To avoid disparities arising out of different national approaches to the incorporation of EC law and to ensure uniformity in its application, the Court of Justice has developed its own jurisprudence on the Supremacy of EC law.'
>
> P Kent, *Law of the European Union* (Longman), p 55

> 'ECJ has uniformly and consistently been the most effective integration institution in the Community. Its role was established in A220 [Art 164]: "The Court shall ensure that in the interpretation and application of this Treaty the law is observed." From its very inception in the Treaty, the ECJ set about establishing its hierarchical authority as the ultimate court of constitutional review. In this area two areas in particular are important. First there is the role of the ECJ in controlling member state courts, and, second, there is the role of the Court in managing the incessant inter-institutional struggles.'
>
> I Ward, *A Critical Introduction to European Law* (Butterworths, 1996), p 52

1.3 The development of the Treaties (from the European Coal and Steel Community Treaty to the Treaty of Nice)

During the early years of the Community, between 1958 and 1965, there was some successful progress towards economic integration. The period in any case was one of economic boom. The creation of a 'Customs union' was underway, with the removal of tariffs. However, there was much less progress towards the creation of an actual Common Market. Some competition policy was put in place and there was some movement made to achieve the free movement of workers. Nevertheless, there was perhaps over prominence of the Common Agricultural Policy (CAP). The ECJ did, of course, do much even in these early years to define the character of the legal order.

Nevertheless, the Common Market should have been achieved within the so-called 'transitional period' referred to throughout the EC Treaty. This comprised three four-year periods or a total of 12 years from 1957, so the Common Market should have been in place by 1969.

However, in the 1960s even the neo-functualists faced problems with their proposed method of achieving integration. Much of this was the fault of France and in particular President De Gaulle. In 1965–66 De Gaulle created a crisis over qualified majority voting, with France withdrawing from participation in the Council. This was partly resolved by the Luxembourg Accords, which effectively created a sort of veto for the Member States on major issues. This compromise created what has been described as the **intergovernmentalist approach**. In effect, what it did was to shift more power to the council and away from the supranational bodies.

In any case the years between then and 1986 and the adoption of the Single European Act are commonly characterised as years of stagnation in terms of integration. It is possible to explain the lack of development during this time by the economic recession and also the retreat into national interest. This could particularly be said of the UK from 1979 to 1997.

There were, of course, other areas in which the Community did develop:

- by enlargement of the number of Member States
- by a broadening of policy both inside and outside the original Treaty objectives
- by the judicial activism of the ECJ (specifically in the development of the concept of supremacy, and by the development of the means of securing enforcement of the objectives of the Treaty through the processes of direct effect and its associated alternatives).

Another major development has been the creation of further Treaties developing and expanding the original Treaties. To start with, the Merger Treaty of 1965 established a single set of institutions to preside over all three Communities.

The Single European Act

The Single European Act (SEA) of 1986 represents the effective 're-launch' of the Community. A Commission White Paper of 1985 identified that there were a number of pressing problems facing the Community. One of the most critical of these was the fact that the Single Market had not yet been achieved even 16 years after it should have been in place. The Commission therefore proposed to set a new deadline for achieving this aim and to create the means of making it more attractive to the Member States. It was able to push forward for four main reasons:

- the dynamism of the then Commission President, Jacques Delors
- a commitment to further integration by key political figures within the Member States themselves, the most important among these being Chancellor Kohl of Germany and President Mitterand of France

- the relative economic prosperity at the time of many of the Member States, which meant that they also had fewer urgent national problems to deflect them from their Community objectives
- a growing realisation in any case that survival depended on an effective EC.

The result was the Single European Act 1986. This set a new time scale for the implementation of the Single Market of 31st December 1992.

Besides re-focusing on the principal aim of the original Treaty, the SEA also included constitutional and institutional reform:

- a new law-making process was devised – the co-operation procedure – that gave Parliament much greater involvement in certain measures and aimed to reduce the 'democratic deficit'
- the European Council was formally recognised and this provided for regular twice-yearly meetings of the heads of state
- a new Court of First Instance (CFI) was created to support the ECJ through its massively increased workload
- procedural changes also meant that there was an increase of qualified majority voting in Council to speed up the decision-making process
- there was also a move towards the idea of European political co-operation and Community competency was extended beyond pure economic objectives to include areas such as social policy and environmental policy.

Nevertheless, the SEA still had its critics who claimed that it had done nothing more than to begin again the process of integration that should have already been achieved and that it did nothing in effect to remove the veto of individual Member States.

The Treaty on European Union

Commonly referred to as the Maastricht Treaty, the Treaty on European Union (TEU) was signed at Maastricht in 1992. The Treaty was concluded following two intergovernmental conferences in 1989, the first concerning the Commission President's three-stage plan for European Monetary Union (EMU), and the second concerning political union.

The Treaty itself took a further year to gain force because of difficulties in the ratification process in certain of the Member States and objections to the federalist character of the word 'union'.

While the Treaty fell short of what many Member States wanted, it did include some major developments:

- it did create the Union by identifying all the states comprising the Community as being part also of the Union
- it also created the concept of European citizenship, although, unlike those rights enjoyed by workers, citizenship did not fall within the legal order
- some constitutional and institutional changes were achieved with the creation of a new co-decision procedure for legislating and the inclusion of a Parliamentary Ombudsman and a Committee of the Regions
- the objectives of the Community were amended to include EMU, environmental protection and social policy and the activities were to include research and technical development, trans-European networks, health, education, culture, consumer protection, energy, civil protection and tourism
- it also created the 'three-pillar' structure of the EU: added to the central pillar of the Communities would be a second pillar to cover co-operation in foreign policy and security, and a third pillar to cover co-operation in justice and home affairs.

At Maastricht 11 of the then 12 Member States also agreed on the Social Charter but the UK opted out, thus necessitating the Protocol procedure.

The Treaty of Amsterdam 1997

The Treaty of Amsterdam 1997 (ToA) was the result of intergovernmental conferences in 1996 and 1997. It was agreed in 1997 but did not gain force for another two years. One of the principal problems facing the EU at the time of the Treaty was future enlargement, but in fact the Treaty did very little on this. It is possibly seen as not being so wide-ranging as the TEU but there were a number of key developments:

- It broadened the objectives of the EU from pure economic aims to the inclusion of some social and political objectives. For instance, where the original Treaty prohibited discrimination based on nationality and Art 141 provides for limited controls in relation to sex discrimination, the Treaty of Amsterdam gave Council the power to introduce laws to prevent discrimination based on racial or ethnic origin, religion or belief, disability, age and sexual orientation. Fundamental human rights are also given greater protection under the Treaty of Amsterdam.
- The new UK Labour Government had accepted the Social Policy Agreement, so the Protocol on Social Policy from the TEU giving the UK an opt-out was repealed in the Treaty of Amsterdam.
- The Treaty repealed many of the Articles of the original Treaty that were now obsolete and it also grouped together the Articles as amended by the TEU and re-numbered them.
- Institutionally, there was some reform, with the co-decision procedure extended in scope so that only EMU matters fell under the co-operation procedure.
- There were also some changes to the pillar structure created in the TEU. Under the second pillar, on common foreign policy and security, the Council was given the power to make certain international agreements on behalf of the Member States. Under the third pillar many provisions were moved under the main pillar and the name of the pillar was changed to 'Police and Judicial Co-operation in Criminal Matters'.
- A concept of close co-operation was also introduced which allows Member States to co-operate and use the institutions and procedures on areas which are not yet the subject of legislation. This is aimed at reducing some of the tension that exists in certain policy areas.

The Treaty of Nice 2000

The Treaty of Nice (ToN) was agreed in December 2000 but did not gain force until 1st February 2003 because of difficulties in ratifying the Treaty in Ireland, where a referendum initially voted against ratification.

One of the major purposes of the Nice summit was to prepare the necessary Treaty amendments and institutional changes to deal with enlargement of the Union.

- Institutional changes included changes to the composition of the institutions, with a new allocation of seats in Parliament, an extension to the number of Commissioners and judges in the ECJ.
- They also incorporated changes to the voting procedures, with the extension of qualified majority voting in Council to account for a new 25-state Union.
- There was also change to the judicial system, with the creation of a 'Chamber' attached to the CFI.
- The Treaty also approved the Charter of Fundamental Human Rights, with provision for suspension of voting rights where there are breaches.
- Besides this, measures were introduced for the provision of 'enhanced co-operation'. This is the basic idea that some states can be at different levels of integration at the same time by agreeing on certain areas but opting out of others. An example of this would be both Greece and Denmark opting out of EMU. It is sometimes also referred to as 'variable geometry' or as 'multi-speed Europe'.

1.4 Enlargement

Enlargement of the EU has occurred and continues to occur in two ways, sometimes referred to as 'widening' and 'deepening'.

'Deepening' refers to the increasing scope of influence of the EU over its Member States. As has been seen above, the extension to the three-pillar structure of the EU has widened its influence. There has been a move gradually, through recent Treaties, to a social and political agenda well beyond the limited economic context of the original Treaties. There has been a widening and redistribution of the power of the different institutions and the creation of extra institutions. Besides this, the ECJ has steadily defined the scope and effect of EC law.

The current context of the word 'enlargement' is more towards the widening of the EU by territory. This has grown significantly since the original Treaties which were entered into by only six nations: Germany, France, Italy and the three BENELUX countries:

- in 1973 the 6 became 9, with the addition of the UK, Ireland and Denmark
- in 1981 Greece also joined, making for a Community of 10 countries
- in 1986 Portugal and Spain also joined, to make it 12
- in 1995 the EU was enlarged to a group of 15 with the accession of Austria, Finland and Sweden
- 2004 saw the biggest single expansion, with ten nations joining: the Czech Republic, Hungary, Poland, Slovakia, Slovenia, Estonia, Lithuania, Latvia, Malta and Cyprus
- Romania and Bulgaria joined the EU in 2007, while three other countries (Croatia, Turkey and Macedonia) are in various stages of negotiation for entry into the EU.

Between 1957 and 2007, then, the number of Member States has risen from 6 to 27 and this will increase again. The EU is already the largest trading bloc in the world and the population covered by the Union is now more than 450 million. Gaining membership is not as simple as just making an application.

Before a country can be considered for membership it must now meet three specific requirements:

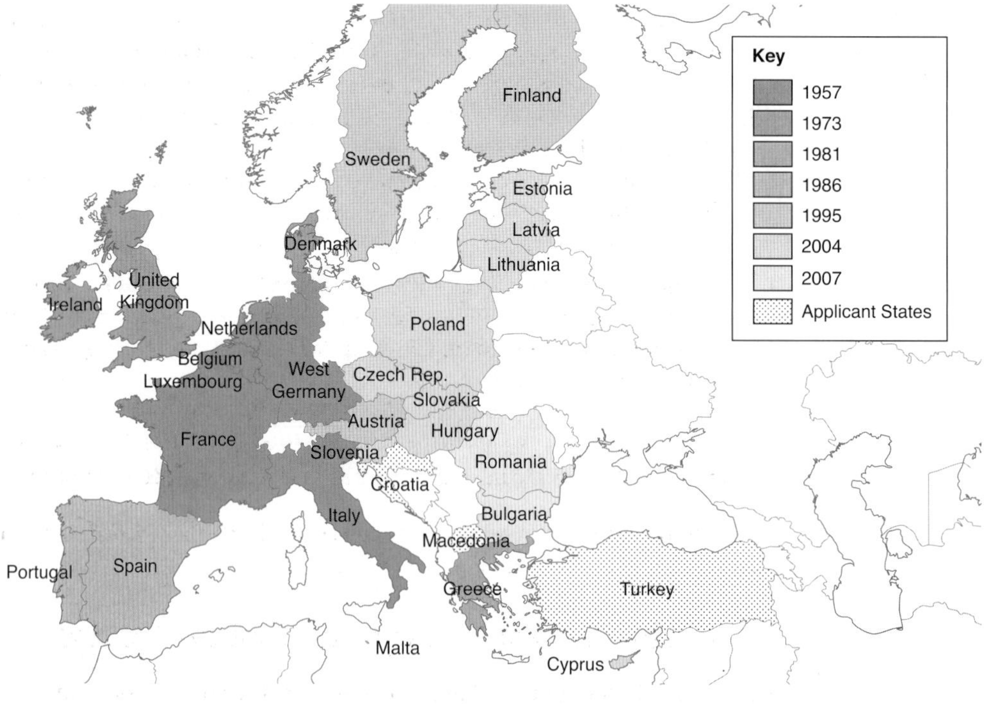

Figure 1.4 Member States of the European Union

- it must show that its institutions are democratic and guarantee the rule of law, protect human rights, and specifically are able to protect minorities
- it must show that it operates a market economy that is capable of surviving within the Single Market
- it must show that it is able to apply the laws of the EU and can meet the aims of economic, political and monetary union.

One significant point to make about the Union, when considering it in the context of one of the central aims of the devisers of the original Treaties, is that peace within the Member States has been maintained throughout that period.

1.5 The EU Constitution

1.5.1 The Constitutional Treaty

Recent Treaties, as well as the intergovernmental conferences, have focused on the difficulties of expanding the EU, and the impact that has on the institutions and the administration of the law. A year after the Nice Treaty was signed, at a meeting of the European Council in Laeken, a 'Declaration of the Future of the European Union' was adopted.

The Laeken Declaration committed the Union to becoming more democratic, more transparent and more effective, and therefore recognised the need to create a Constitution. The meeting also recognised that the traditional method for reviewing and developing the Treaties, through intergovernmental conferences of the heads of state, lacked transparency and democracy. A decision was taken to convene a Convention of representatives of governments of all the Member States and of the countries which had applied for membership as well as representatives from the institutions and the various committees: a convention of 105 members in total.

This Convention looked into the various problems associated with taking the Union forward and eventually prepared a Draft Constitution which was presented to the intergovernmental conference at Thessaloniki in June 2003. The Draft Constitution was subsequently agreed by the Member State governments, identified as the EU Constitution and was referred to the Member States for ratification. A number of Member States ratified the EU Constitution by parliamentary vote. Certain Member States, including founder members such as France, decided to ratify by a national referendum. The rejection of the EU Constitution in the French referendum in May 2005, followed by the Netherlands' rejection in June 2005, created doubts as to whether the EU could proceed with the EU Constitution at all.

One of the principal purposes of the EU Constitution was to put into a single document all of the existing Treaties so that it should be readable and clear. The Constitution itself was made up of four separate parts:

- The first part contained all of the provisions that related to the objectives, powers and decision-making processes of the Union and those relating to its institutions.
- The second part incorporated the Charter of Fundamental Rights agreed upon at Nice.
- The third part focused on the policies of the Union and incorporated many of the provisions already contained in the existing Treaties.
- The fourth part, as usual, was referred to as the Final Clauses and in this instance contained the procedures for adopting and reviewing the Constitution.

Many of the specific developments contained in the Constitution are indicated in later chapters of this book where relevant.

1.5.2 The Reform Treaty (the Lisbon Treaty)

Following the effective collapse of the Constitutional Treaty, the Brussels European Council in 2007 decided that the relative inertia resulting from this collapse, as well as the need to develop the institutional reforms begun in the Treaty of Nice 2001, meant that the position needed to be resolved and so the Treaty of Lisbon, the so-called Reform Treaty, was also drafted in 2007.

While argument has raged in UK politics on the question of whether the Lisbon Treaty is just the Constitutional Treaty in a different guise, there are significant differences, although many important aspects of the Treaty remain unchanged.

One of the most important changes for students of EU Law is in the different form and structure of the two Treaties:

- The Constitutional Treaty proposed in effect to create a single written constitution, incorporating but repealing all previous Treaties. Unfortunately, to overcome the objections to the Constitutional Treaty, the Lisbon Treaty follows the format of previous amending Treaties, keeping the other Treaties in place while amending them. As a result, significant cross-referencing is still required between all the various Treaties and the Lisbon Treaty.
- The proposed change to EU laws and EU framework laws in the Constitutional Treaty is not repeated in the Lisbon Treaty and the traditional legislation, regulations, directives and decisions remain.
- The Charter of Fundamental Rights would have been incorporated in the Constitutional Treaty while the Lisbon Treaty provides only that it should have the same legal value as the Treaties. However, a protocol allows that in the UK and Poland the Charter will create no justiciable rights beyond those already in existence within the national law of those two states.
- Institutional reforms remain mainly intact. Qualified Majority Voting is to be extended to other areas, as in the Constitutional Treaty. The introduction of Double Majority Voting remains, although its introduction will be delayed. Parliament is to be given increased powers, as in the Constitutional Treaty, with the extension of the co-decision procedure to a wider range of areas.
- Where the Constitutional Treaty proposed to abandon the rather complex three-pillar structure of the TEU, and place foreign affairs and justice and home affairs within the constitution, the existing structure in essence is to be retained.
- One contentious issue of the Constitutional Treaty, the creation of a flag, anthem and motto, has been abandoned in the Lisbon Treaty.

Originally the Treaty was rejected in an Irish referendum. A further successful referendum led to the Treaty being ratified by Ireland in 2009, and Poland also ratified the Treaty, so that it is now in force.

1.6 The future

1.6.1 Enlargement – nationally

Although the EU underwent its biggest expansion very recently, in May 2004, the Union is not yet at 'capacity'. Indeed, any nation satisfying the basic admission criteria for membership is entitled to apply for membership. At the time of writing, three European countries have submitted applications and are at various stages in the application process. They are:

- Croatia – first applied for membership in 2003 and formal accession negotiations commenced in 2005.
- Turkey – the country which has undergone the most complicated and protracted application process ever, is still at an early negotiating stage with the European Commission. Concerns about Turkey's human rights record remain. Nevertheless, there is presently a widely predicted, albeit tentative, admission date of 2015 for Turkey. The implications of Turkish accession are enormous. Not only would Turkey's population in 2015 make it the most populous country in the EU, but its geographical location, on the very edge of Europe, its predominantly Muslim population and largely agricul-

tural economy all pose significant (but not insurmountable) problems in terms of its successful integration. Nevertheless, Turkey is a member of NATO and its geopolitical significance, as the biggest predominantly Muslim state with a secular government in the world, is huge.

- Macedonia – applied for membership at the end of 2005.

Other countries which may consider applying to join the EU in the future are the remaining former Yugoslav states of Bosnia–Herzegovina and Serbia. The situation in Ukraine is extremely interesting. Following the dramatic events in December 2004, culminating in a second Presidential election (after the first was overturned by its Supreme Court because of widespread fraud), which was won by the Western-leaning and pro-European Yuschenko, Ukraine's prospects of EU membership have improved significantly. Ukraine is, like Turkey, a country of enormous geopolitical significance, positioned as it is between the present EU to the west (it borders Hungary, Poland and Slovakia), Romania to the south and Belarus and Russia to the north and east.

1.6.2 Enlargement – scope of legislation

Over the last 20 years, the scope of EU legislation has expanded significantly, taking in new topics such as discrimination on grounds of sexual orientation and race (discussed in Chapter 18 of this book) and environmental protection (see Chapter 19). It is unlikely that the EU has ceased expanding legally, as well as nationally.

1.6.3 Towards full union

As discussed in Chapter 10 of this book, the EU is already well on the way to achieving full economic and monetary union, with the single European currency, the Euro, successfully launched in 1999 (for electronic transactions) and in 2002 (for all other transactions), and the establishment of the European Central Bank. The next logical step would be for those participating states to hand over further control of their economic policies to a central European authority. This could in turn lead to the next step in integration terms – **political union** – which would probably involve conferring far greater powers on the Council and/or European Parliament at the expense of national Parliaments, especially in the fields of foreign policy and security.

The next step in integration terms would also be the ultimate step – **full union** – which entails the complete unification of all national economies. That would mean the end of such fiercely protected national policies as the setting of rates of income tax and, with it, national identities. The EU would then become a state in its own right, albeit a federal state with a certain amount of autonomy devolved to the former Member States, which would be re-classified as 'regions' of the EU, in accordance with the principle of subsidiarity. A name-change would then be necessary, the obvious contender being 'the United States of Europe'. The EU does, after all, have its own Constitution already!

ACTIVITY

Self-assessment questions

1. In what ways is it wrong to suggest that the idea of a united Europe is a new idea?
2. What was the main reason why the idea of an integrated Europe was so important and so desirable during the 1940s and 1950s?
3. What is the importance of the Marshall Plan?
4. What part did the Schuman Plan play in the creation of the EC?
5. What resulted from the Spaak Report?
6. What were the main objectives of the EC Treaty and how were they to be achieved?
7. What were the basic differences between the 'federalists' and the 'functionalists' and in what way were the 'neo-functionalists' a development?

8. What exactly is meant by the term 'supranationalism'?
9. In what ways did the SEA help to develop the original Treaties?
10. What institutional and constitutional reform was made in the SEA?
11. What were the main objectives of the TEU?
12. What major changes were made by the TEU?
13. What changes were made in the Treaty of Amsterdam?
14. What was the central purpose of the Treaty of Nice?
15. What further developments were made in the Treaty of Nice?
16. What precisely is the meaning of 'enlargement'?
17. To what extent has the EC been enlarged?
18. What are the problems associated with enlargement?
19. Why was it felt necessary to introduce a Draft Constitution?
20. What did the drafters wish to be the key features of the Draft Constitution?
21. What are the major differences between the Constitutional Treaty and the Reform Treaty (the Treaty of Lisbon)?

KEY FACTS

Origins	
Background	Many examples of desire for a united Europe: • early Roman Catholic Church • Charlemagne and the 'Holy Roman Empire' • Henry IV of France and the Christian Commonwealth of Europe • Napoleon Bonaparte declared ambition for a European empire • Hitler's expansionist philosophy • also, Kant, Rousseau, Marx and Neitzsche all advocated a united Europe.
Growth of organisations	IMF, GATT, OEC, Council of Europe, BENELUX Union.
Schuman Plan	Drafted by Jean Monnet – led to ECSC.
Spaak Report	Led to EURATOM.
Overall aim	No more wars in Europe.
Members	Six countries: France, Germany, Italy, Belgium, the Netherlands and Luxembourg.
Objectives of EC law	
Aim of EC Treaty	• To 'lay the foundations of an ever closer union among the peoples of Europe [by] pooling their resources to preserve and strengthen peace and liberty'. • To be achieved by integration of Member States' economic and monetary policies for creation of a common market free from internal barriers to trade.
Key objectives	• Introduction of 'Four Freedoms' – freedom of movement of workers, right to establish and provide services, free movement of goods, free movement of capital within the Community. • Progressive approximation of economic policies of Member States and harmonisation of national laws in eg agriculture, transport and trade. • Creation of Common Customs Tariff. • Creation of Common Commercial Policy.

Development of the Treaties	
ECSC	• Created the Communities and the legal order.
EURATOM, EC	• Created the institutions.
SEA	• Put in place the Common Market. • Introduced co-operation procedure for legislation. • Created European Council and Court of First Instance. • Extended qualified majority voting (QMV) in Council.
TEU	• Created the Union and the idea of citizenship. • Added two more pillars: foreign affairs and security, and justice and home affairs (based on co-operation). • Introduced co-decision procedure for legislation. • Introduced EMU. • Some institutional reform and extended QMV in Council. • Subsidiarity.
ToA	• Re-numbered original EC Treaty and repealed many obsolete Articles. • Some institutional reform and extension of QMV in Council. • Broadened objectives eg new discrimination law. • Introduced 'closer co-operation'.
ToN	Institutional reforms for enlargement in 2004.
Enlargement	
1973	UK, Ireland and Denmark.
1981	Greece.
1986	Portugal and Spain.
1995	Austria, Finland and Sweden.
2004	Czech Republic, Hungary, Poland, Slovakia, Slovenia, Estonia, Lithuania, Latvia, Malta and Cyprus.
2007	Romania and Bulgaria
Applications	Turkey, Croatia and Macedonia
The EU Constitution	
Purpose	Laeken Declaration committed Union to becoming more democratic, more transparent and more effective, so need to create a constitution (single document in readable form) – set up Convention for this purpose.
Form of Draft Constitution	• First part – objectives, powers and decision-making processes of the Union. • Second part incorporates the Charter of Fundamental Rights. • Third part – policies of the Union. • Fourth part – Final Clauses (includes procedures for adopting and reviewing Constitution.
The Reform Treaty (the Treaty of Lisbon)	Following failure to ratify Constitutional Treaty, Reform Treaty introduced – retains much of Constitutional Treaty but an amending Treaty not a single Constitution.

SUMMARY

- There are many examples of former attempts at a united Europe.
- The EU (formerly the EC) was created following the Second World War with its key aim being: To 'lay the foundations of an ever closer union among the peoples of Europe [by] pooling their resources to preserve and strengthen peace and liberty', and this was to be achieved by integration of Member States' economic and monetary policies for creation of a common market free from internal barriers to trade.
- The original 6 Member States has expanded to 27.
- A variety of Treaties have expanded the scope of the original Treaties.
- The Lisbon Treaty, while an amending treaty, introduces wide scale institutional reform.

Further reading

Articles

Meyring, B, 'Intergovernmentalism and Supranationality: Two Stereotypes for a Complex Reality' (1997) 22 ELR 221.

Wouters, J, 'Institutional and Constitutional Challenges for the European Union: Some Reflections in the Light of the Treaty of Nice' (2001) 26 ELR 342.

Books

Douglas-Scott, S, *Constitutional Law of the European Union* (Longman, 2002), Chapter 1.

Kent, P, *Law of the European Union* (3rd edn, Longman, 2001).

Ward, I, *A Critical Introduction to European Law* (Butterworths, 1996), Chapter 1.

Websites

More information on the European Union can be obtained on the website http://europa.eu

2

The development from Community to Union

AIMS AND OBJECTIVES

After reading this chapter you should be able to:

- Understand the basic legal order of the Community
- Understand the aims and objectives of the Community
- Understand the concept of European Union prior to the Treaty of Lisbon
- Understand the three-pillar structure of the Union and the reasons for it prior to the Treaty of Lisbon
- Understand why a new structure was needed

2.1 Introduction

Prior to the ratification of the Lisbon Treaty it was important to understand the different concepts of Community and Union. From the foundation of the original Treaties to the time of the Treaty on European Union (TEU) there was a Community, firstly the EEC and later the EC. The Treaties comprised not only the objectives of the Community but also the legal order. Following the TEU the EU was created. Between the TEU and the Lisbon Treaty there was both the EC and the EU at the same time. In very general terms the EC was founded in the Treaties, as amended, and was based on law and the EU, stemming from the agreements made at Maastricht, was based on co-operation. This was a cumbersome and unsatisfactory structure which has been reformed by the Treaty of Lisbon.

Because of this, books written between the TEU and ToL on the law of the European Union varied in their titles and it was sometimes difficult to understand the difference between EC law on the one hand and EU law on the other, or whether indeed the different titles were interchangeable. It may seem even more complex if the title merely refers to 'European law'. It was important, therefore, in studying the law of the European Union, to understand the difference between the European Community (EC) and the European Union (EU).

Academics identified and commented upon this problem.

> In this millenial time, both Europe's law, and Europe itself, lack a straightforward identity. For example, "European law" is a very unsatisfactory term – an expression used as shorthand for a variety of (sometimes) interlocking legal systems – namely, EC law (ie the law of the European Community); EU law (being wider and more intergovernmental than EC law, but often confused with the former … or most generally, a group term for the family of the legal systems in Europe, widely diverse as they are.'
>
> S Douglas-Scott, *Constitutional Law of the European Union* (Longman, 2002), p 3

In the simplest historical terms, the second Treaty of Rome in 1957 created the European Economic Community (EEC), a name which was later reduced to 'European Community' by the Maastricht Treaty as the scope and character of the Treaties changed. The EU, on the other hand, was a much later creation of that Maastricht Treaty, the Treaty on European Union (TEU) 1992.

There were significant differences between the two concepts and the differences had important consequences. This is why the TEU chose still, in creating the 'three-pillar' structure of the Union, to refer to one of those pillars as the 'Community' pillar.

The original three Treaties creating what collectively became the EC, as well as having specific economic objectives, put in place also certain decision-making processes and in effect created a legal order to ensure the achievement of the objectives. This is why we may refer to it as 'EC law'.

The TEU introduced a broader framework, with the addition of more social and political objectives to add to those economic ones that had the force of law. Because all Member States could not agree completely on how these broadened objectives should be achieved, the TEU introduced the concept of close co-operation between Member States on these matters. These did not have the force of law in the same way that the substantive provisions of the EC Treaty did. In particular, the other two pillars, Pillar 2, based on common foreign policy and security, and Pillar 3, originally based on co-operation in justice and home affairs and later changed to police and judicial co-operation in criminal matters, are based on co-operation and do not have the force of law. Besides these, the TEU also made the additions of Protocols where certain Member States were allowed to opt out of development of specific policies. An example of this was the social policy based on the Social Chapter, to which the UK would not originally agree.

It is useful, then, to have a basic idea of what came within the scope of the Community, and therefore could be enforced in the ECJ, and what was within the broader scope of the Union and could only be developed by co-operation of the Member States. Sections 2.2 and 2.3 below detail the different character of the Community and Union between the TEU and the Lisbon Treaty.

2.2 The Community and the basic legal order

The basic provisions of the Community legal order are to be found in the EC Treaty as subsequently amended by the TEU, re-numbered in the Treaty of Amsterdam, and with some amendments to the Articles in the Treaty of Nice.

The Treaty is divided in effect into a preamble and six parts:

- Part 1 contains the Community principles
- Part 2 refers to citizenship of the Union
- Part 3 contains the Community policies
- Part 4 concerns association with overseas countries
- Part 5 contains the rules governing the institutions of the Community
- Part 6 is what is known as the 'General and Final Provisions'.

The most significant of these in relation to the Community are Part 1, Part 2, Part 5 and, to an extent, Part 6.

2.2.1 The Community principles

In essence, these amounted to the 'tasks' or objectives of the Community (these are now found in Part 1 TFEU). According to Article 7, these tasks are entrusted to a European Parliament, a Council, a Commission, a Court of Justice and the Court of Auditors. All of these institutions may only act within the limits of the powers granted to it by the Treaty.

Article 2 identified in general terms the 'economic, social and political' tasks. The most immediate of these is the creation of a 'Common Market'. For this purpose this also includes 'the elimination of all obstacles to intra-Community trade in order to merge the national markets into a single market'. A further objective has been added by the TEU: the addition of an 'economic and monetary union'. Following amendments in the Treaty of Amsterdam, the new Art 2 read as follows:

ARTICLE

'The Community shall have as its task, by establishing a common market and an economic and monetary union and by implementing common policies or activities referred to in Articles 3 and 4, to promote throughout the Community a harmonious, balanced and sustainable development of economic activities, a high level of employment and of social protection, equality between men and women, sustainable and non inflationary growth, a high degree of competitiveness and convergence of economic performance, a high level of protection and improvement of the quality of the environment, the raising of the standard of living and quality of life, and economic and social cohesion and solidarity among Member States.'

Article 3, then, sets out the principal activities that Community law should engage in to achieve the objectives set out in Art 2:

- the elimination of customs duties, quantitative restrictions and other measures having equivalent effect
- the development of a Common Commercial Policy
- the creation of an Internal Market
- the implementation of measures to ensure the entry and movement of people within the Internal Market
- creation of Common Agriculture and Fisheries Policies
- creation of Common Transport Policies
- the implementation of measures, ensuring the prevention of anti-competitive practices
- the harmonisation of national laws in the Member States in order to allow a Common Market to function.

Article 3 also included a new task: 'the promotion of co-ordination between employment policies of the Member States with a view to enhancing their effectiveness by developing a co-ordinated strategy for employment'. It also provided that 'In all the activities referred to … the Community shall aim to eliminate inequalities, and to promote equality between men and women.'

Article 3 finally also seeks to ensure that the 'Community' acts within the limits of its powers and for the objectives assigned to it.

Article 10 significantly identified the obligations of the Member States, that they should '… take all appropriate measures … to ensure fulfillment of the objectives arising out of the Treaty …'. Furthermore, it provided that they should '… abstain from any measure which could jeopardise the attainment of the objectives …'.

For the furtherance of all these objectives Art 12 then provided for the basic principle of non-discrimination on the basis of nationality. Without this overarching principle, the four fundamental freedoms that make up the Common Market might otherwise be ineffective.

2.2.2 The Community policies

The Community policies are the basis of meeting the objective of creating a Common Market and are to be found in Part 3 of the EC Treaty'(and are in Part 3 TFEU also).

Clearly, the most important of the policies in this respect are what is commonly referred to as the 'Four Freedoms'. These are:

- **free movement of goods** (see Chapter 13) contained in Arts 28–31 (now Arts 34–37 TFEU). (This does not specifically include agriculture which appears as a special category under Arts 32–38.) (Now Arts 38–44 TFEU.) (It is of course supplemented by the rules on the Common Customs Union under Arts 25–27, now Arts 30–32 TFEU.)

- **free movement of workers** (see Chapter 12) contained in Arts 39–42 (now Arts 45–48 TFEU). (This refers only to workers but of course free movement of citizens is now guaranteed under Arts 17–22, now Arts 20–25 TFEU.)
- **the right to establish a trade or profession and to provide services freely** (see Chapter 13) contained in Arts 43–48 (now Arts 49–54 TFEU) (establishment) and Arts 49–55 (now Arts 56–62 TFEU) (services). (Again, transport has its own rules under Arts 70–80, now Arts 90– 00 TFEU.)
- **free movement of capital**, contained in Arts 56–60 (now Arts 63–66 TFEU) (supplemented by the rules on taxation in Arts 81–97, now Arts 110–118 TFEU).

The rules on free movement of goods provide for the elimination of all discriminatory Customs duties and the elimination of any quantitative restrictions (or measures having an equivalent effect) between Member States applied to products originating in Member States and products coming from non-Member States which are 'in free circulation'. There are exemptions which Member States may rely on, including the obvious ones such as protection of health.

The rules ensuring the free movement of persons or to establish a trade, business or profession or to provide services in another Member State are guaranteed under the Treaty in Arts 39, 43 and 49 respectively (now Arts 45, 49 and 56 TFEU). The rules extend rights to workers' families as well as workers and there are a number of procedural protections in secondary legislation. Again, there are a limited number of exemptions or derogations that Member States might plead in justification of a refusal of entry or even a deportation.

The rules guaranteeing free movement of capital traditionally focused on the elimination of discriminatory Customs duties and discriminatory taxation. Free movement of capital is now developed in the TEU. All restrictions on the movement of capital and payments are prohibited. Of course, following the TEU there is now a policy that is ultimately driven towards creating both economic and monetary union.

The 'Four Freedoms' are not the only policies. Other major policies also aimed at securing the Single Market include the rules on anti-competitive practices in Arts 81 and 82 (now Arts 101 and 102 TFEU) (see Chapter 16). Besides this there are also rules ensuring that men and women shall receive equal pay for equal work, in Art 141 (now Art 157 TFEU) (see Chapter 18). This basic principle has now been supplemented by a whole series of rules on social policy and discrimination.

A Common Transport Policy is also envisaged in the Treaty. Agriculture is subject to a complex set of rules and there is a Common Agricultural Policy (CAP) also in place which also provides for subsidies. As well as this, the Treaty now includes policies on research and technological development in Arts 163–173 (now Arts 179–190 TFEU), on consumer protection in Art 153 (now Art 169 TFEU), and on the environment in Arts 174–176 (now Arts 191–193 TFEU), as well as other areas.

2.2.3 Rules governing the institutions and procedure

Part 5 of the Treaty (and Part 5 TFEU) contains the rules that govern all of the major institutions, their composition and role. The rules are contained in Arts 189–280 (now Arts 223–334 TFEU). These rules are broken down as follows:

- Parliament is covered by Arts 189–201 (now Arts 224–236 TFEU)
- Council is covered by Arts 202–210 (now Arts 237–243 TFEU)
- the Commission is covered by Arts 211–219 (now Arts 244–250 TFEU)
- the ECJ is covered by Arts 220–245 (now Arts 251–284 TFEU).

There are also rules relating to the other major institutions, including the Court of Auditors in Arts 246–248 (now Arts 285–287 TFEU), the Economic and Social Committee in Arts 257–262 (now Arts 301–304 TFEU), the Committee of the Regions in Arts 263–265 (now Arts 305–307 TFEU), and the European Investment Bank in Arts 266–267 (now Arts 308–309 TFEU).

One of the most important procedural Articles in the Treaty is Art 249 (now Art 288 TFEU). This identifies and explains the different forms of legislation.

Besides this, the relationship with the Member States is at least partly defined in Art 234 (now Art 267 TFEU) which provides the reference mechanism for gaining preliminary rulings or interpretations of EC law from the ECJ.

2.2.4 The General and Final Provisions

These provisions identify among other things that the Community has a legal personality. On this basis, under Art 310 (now Art 217 TFEU) it can make arrangements with other international bodies.The Final Provisions also of course identify the potential liability of the Community institutions through Art 288 (now Art 340 TFEU).

Power is also given to Member States as a result of these Final Provisions to derogate from Treaty obligations in certain extreme circumstances. An example of this would be for security reasons or in the case of serious internal disturbance or threat of external conflict, and also possibly in the case of balance of payments crises.

Another interesting power identified in this part of the Treaty is the very broad power given to Council under Art 308 (now Art 352 TFEU) to legislate to do anything which is '… necessary to attain … an objective of the Community …'.

2.2.5 Comment

It in some ways was always possible to see the EC Treaty and its provisions as a form of constitution since it set out the basic policies and principles of the Community, the methods for introducing new law and the rules governing the political and legal institutions, as well as a body of substantive law.

Nevertheless, the Treaty and the Community it establishes fell somewhat short of a constitution in the sense that a constitution would exist in a federal structure. The Community (now EU) did carry with it its own legal order and the ECJ has been instrumental in ensuring that EC (now EU) law prevails and is enforceable by the ordinary citizens. Nevertheless, the Court of Justice and the other institutions still depend on the courts in the Member States also being prepared to enforce EC (now EU) law.

Besides this, a federal government would have the power to legislate in foreign affairs, would have its own defence policy, and would be in charge of criminal justice with its own police force, much the same as in the United States of America.

The EU did have an interest in these matters since the TEU but through co-operation of the Member States rather than with the force of law. The Constitutional Treaty was aimed at overcoming some of these difficulties but was not ratified. The Lisbon Treaty, while not representing a single constitutional document, has altered the structure of the EU that existed after the TEU.

2.3 The Treaty on European Union

2.3.1 The concept of a European Union

The European Union finally came into force in 1993, only after acceptance of the TEU by the Member States and following ratification. It followed two intergovernmental conferences and the growing recognition of the need to expand beyond the limitations of the original Treaties.

The TEU had six main purposes some of which interlink:

- to extend the scope of the Community and in that sense to extend the competencies of the decision-making processes
- to create a Union with a new structure incorporating not just the existing legal order represented by the Community but also a common foreign and defence policy and a common justice system

- to redistribute power among the institutions of the EC
- to create the concept of citizenship to extend rights to individuals in a much broader sense than was enjoyed under the existing Treaties
- to introduce monetary union
- to incorporate a Community Charter of Fundamental Social Rights.

Originally, most Member States were also concerned to extend the scope of environmental protection covered by EC law but this was among the casualties of the negotiated Treaty.

The TEU created an entirely new structure that would exist over and above that of the existing Community.

The Treaty did not radically alter but preserved the objectives of the original Treaties. In any case these had been modified and amended by the SEA before. The prime objective of the TEU, then, and thus of the Union, is still to achieve the basic objectives of the Community.

However, through the TEU, the Union has added objectives over and above those in the original Treaty. These include:

- closer co-operation on the administration of justice and in home affairs
- the assertion of a truly international identity through adoption of a common foreign policy and common security policy (including an EU defence policy)
- the promotion of social and economic progress which is balanced and sustainable by removing internal frontiers, strengthening economic and social cohesion, and establishing economic and monetary union (with a single currency to make this work more effectively)
- the strengthening of the protection of the rights and interests of nationals of the Member States through the introduction of a European citizenship
- the protection of fundamental human rights
- maintaining and building upon the *acquis communautaire* (EU law already in existence, whether from the founding Treaties or from the case law of the ECJ).

A number of factors go into making the TEU a poor compromise in contrast to the ambitions of those who believed that further integration was necessary for survival. The Thatcher Government in the UK was too *laissez-faire* to accept the approach taken by Delors. The collapse of Communism in Eastern Europe added extra complications. The resultant Treaty, then, was a lot less than many of its architects wished for and the structure created was unwieldy and left too much to the will of individual Member States. Therefore it has come in for much criticism.

> 'The Maastricht Treaty came under criticism from all angles. It seemed to be too much of a last minute compromise, patched together at the eleventh hour, with resulting Protocols and Declarations which had to be added to deal with specific member states' reservations. It also appeared to be a creature of chaos and fragmentation: what Curtin described as employing a "bricoleur's amateurism, in its renumbering and non-unitary structure". In so doing, there might have been attempts to "constitutionalise" the Treaties, but for those with a tidy frame of mind, this was unsatisfactory. In aiming to innovate, consolidate and redefine, it seemed only to confuse and disappoint.'
>
> S Douglas-Scott, *Constitutional Law of the European Union* (Longman, 2002), p 31

2.3.2 The three-pillar structure of the Union

The TEU introduced what is commonly known as the 'three-pillar' structure of the EU.

The three pillars are as follows:

- Pillar 1: comprises the legal order of original Treaties; this was amended and also added to by the inclusion of economic and monetary union. It is referred to as the 'Community Pillar'.

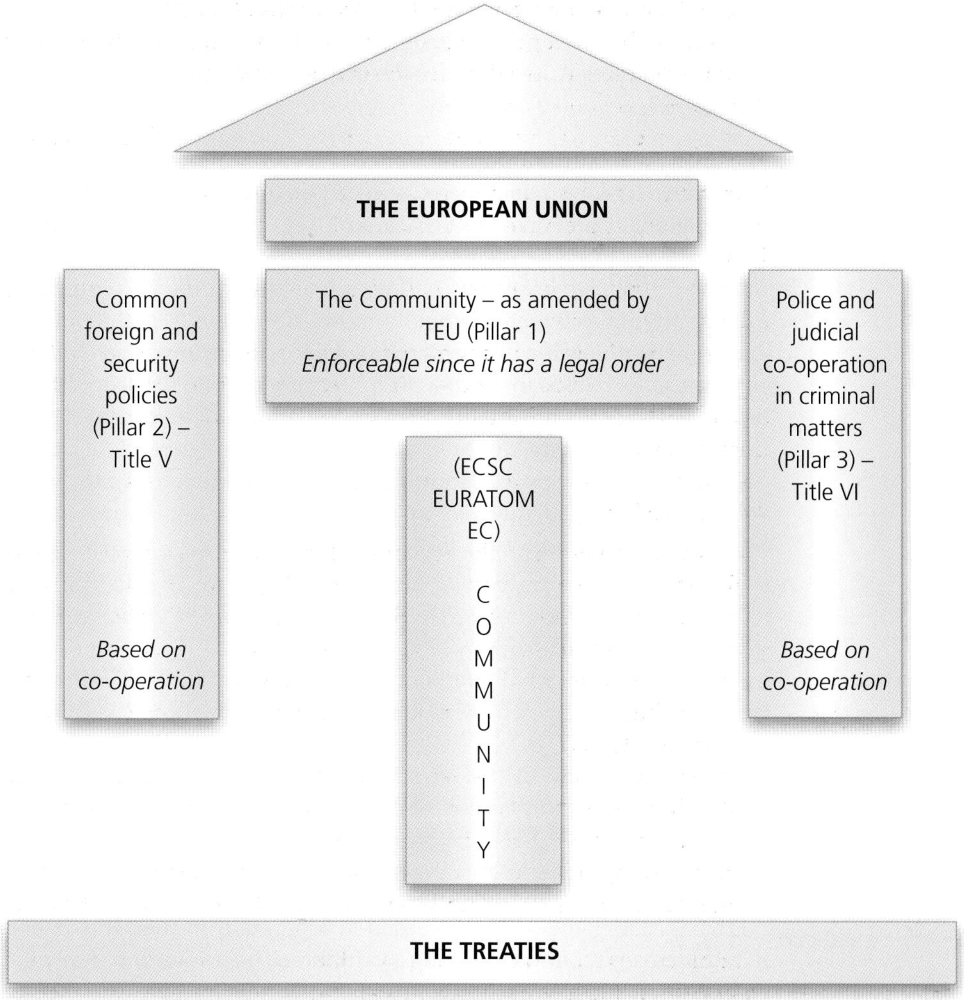

Figure 2.3.2 The three-pillar structure of the European Union after the TEU (and amendment to Pillar 3 in the Treaty of Amsterdam) prior to the merger of the three pillars in the Lisbon Treaty

- Pillar 2: co-operation towards common foreign and security policy.
- Pillar 3: co-operation towards common systems on justice and home affairs.

Official publications of the EU therefore represent the structure pictorially as in Figure 2.3.2.

Pillar 1

Pillar 1 represents all of the common provisions of the existing Community and while these are widened as above includes also all of the objectives of the original Treaties. It also sets out the basic aims of the newly formed Union.

The major amendments to the EC Treaty include:

- the introduction of a concept of Union citizenship. This is now defined in Art 17 after amendment by the Treaty of Amsterdam
- the adoption of the principle of 'subsidiarity' as a general principle of law. This is now in Art 5 following amendment by the Treaty of Amsterdam
- changes to the decision-making process. This included the co-operation procedure (see Chapter 5) and a changed role for the institutions, in particular an extension to qualified majority voting in Council and greater powers for Parliament including in some cases the right of veto

- new tasks and activities extra to those in the original EC Treaty and detailed in Arts 2 and 3 as indicated in section 2.2.1
- the introduction of European Monetary Union with the addition of a common currency.

The Treaty also introduced a number of Protocols allowing certain Member States to opt out of the decision-making process in certain areas. Notable among these were Protocols on social policy and on monetary union.

Pillar 2 and Pillar 3

Pillar 2 and Pillar 3 were originally inserted in Titles V and VI of the TEU respectively and were not specifically incorporated into the foundation Treaty as amended. The consequence of this is that these two pillars are beyond the scope of the Community legal order. As such they rely on the co-operation of the Member States for their development.

Pillar 2 concerned adoption of a common foreign and security policy. The basic objective of securing a common policy was stated as being to '... safeguard common values, fundamental interests & independence of the Union, to strengthen security, preserve peace and develop and consolidate democracy and the rule of law and respect for human rights and fundamental freedoms ...'. The general obligation on Member States then was one of 'loyalty and mutual solidarity and to refrain from any action contrary to those objectives'.

Any action to be taken under this pillar would be on the basis of a unanimous vote in Council. However, certain powers were left open to Council to reach decisions on a qualified majority and Council could decide when a 'common position' was necessary and also when joint action should be taken. Ultimately, though, even when Council reaches a unanimous decision, the Member States still have the final say. Generally, Parliament and the Commission have little involvement in this pillar and the ECJ was, until amendments in the Treaty of Amsterdam, specifically excluded from involvement in either of the two intergovernmental pillars.

Pillar 3 under the TEU concerned co-operation in justice and home affairs. Again, it is based on Council reaching unanimous decisions but with the Member States' co-operation still being required to act. Parliament and the Commission again have little involvement, and the ECJ was excluded from processes until the Treaty of Amsterdam.

This was the most controversial of the intergovernmental pillars because it concerned sensitive issues within the Member States, specifically immigration and asylum-seeking. This area has now been moved into the policies after the Treaty of Amsterdam under Title IV. Of course, judicial and police co-operation is also a sensitive area. One obvious problem is reconciling the different types of legal systems and the different criminal laws in the Member States.

As a result, the focus within the pillar is on co-operation and there is no actual mention of implementing policy. Following the Treaty of Amsterdam, some aspects of the third pillar have been made subject to ECJ jurisdiction.

Because of some of the difficulties with this pillar and following amendments in the Treaty of Amsterdam, the third pillar has now been re-named 'police and judicial co-operation in criminal matters'.

Obviously, certain Member State leaders felt that the two pillars would eventually be included within the Community structure. This, of course, did not happen until the Lisbon Treaty and was the reasoning behind the Draft Constitution.

It was inevitable that, with the effective collapse of the Constitutional Treaty, the EU would need to look again at constitutional reform. The Reform Treaty, the Treaty of Lisbon, attempts to revisit the constitutional reforms of the Constitutional Treaty while at the same time compromising to the objections raised by different Member States. The Reform Treaty lacks the simplicity and clarity of the Constitutional Treaty. While it incorporates most of the constitutional reforms, it is nevertheless an amending Treaty and so has to be cross-referenced with the other Treaty rather than providing a single written constitution.

2.4 The institutional and legal character of the EU

There was always inevitably debate over whether it was accurate to speak of EU law rather than EC law. The two extra pillars created by the TEU had no foundation in law but were based on co-operation. The most important bodies in the development of these two pillars were the European Council and the intergovernmental conferences. The legal order came from the EC Treaty, not the TEU, and it was probably most accurate then still to use the term 'EC law', and to use the term 'EU' to refer to the geographical unit formed by the Member States and to the broader base including both the legal order and those areas based on co-operation of the Member States.

Strictly speaking, the EU did not have an institutional framework in the same way that the Community did. Article 3 of the TEU did provide that 'The Union shall be served by a single institutional framework ...'. Article 5 of the TEU then went on to say that '... Parliament, the Council, the Commission, and the Court of Justice shall exercise their powers ... for the purposes provided ... on the one hand by the Treaties establishing the Communities ... and on the other hand by the other provisions of this Treaty ...'. In this way, the Union did make use of the institutions of the Community for its wider purposes for the fulfillment of the other two pillars but in a different and more limited respect.

The European Council, then, was extremely significant to the development of the Union. It has autonomy and there is little input from the other institutions. While the Commission is said to be 'fully associated', it has no power. Council was given the power to take decisions on Titles V and VI but with little internal effect and so usually these had to be backed up by ratification in the Member States. Parliament had no influence on Titles V and VI and the ECJ had no jurisdiction either. Following the Treaty of Amsterdam amendments there is little change to the role of these institutions in the case of Pillar 2. Because of the inclusion of certain areas from Pillar 3 into the Community policies there is involvement there. Also, the Treaty of Amsterdam gives a greater role to both Parliament and the ECJ in relation to Pillar 3.

The TEU in many ways can be seen as a surrender to national interests. There are obvious examples of this. The introduction of Protocols allowed certain Member States in effect to opt out of the necessary developments towards integration. The inclusion of the principle of subsidiarity also seems contradictory since a Union is a concept which implies a federal system.

The Treaty attempted to deal with many of the pressing issues and did make institutional changes. Nevertheless, the 'democratic deficit' was probably increased rather than decreased. The Commission is still powerful and still undemocratic and the resignation of the Commissioners in 1999 demonstrates the need for accountability. Parliament is increasingly democratic and was given much increased involvement but was still relatively ineffective. The Council remains a major power. The Union, or at least some of its significant objectives, remain based on cooperation rather than having the force of law and thus it could be argued that supranationalism was once again sacrificed for national interests.

National interests were at least in part the reason for the collapse of the Constitutional Treaty. The Reform Treaty, the Treaty of Lisbon, attempts to reintroduce the necessary constitutional reforms in a revised manner acceptable to Member States. Nevertheless, the UK and Poland have a partial exemption from the Charter of Fundamental Rights, and the Treaty has proved to be controversial with certain politicians in the UK, who argue that it is no different to the Constitutional Treaty.

Following the Lisbon Treaty, the three pillars of the EU formed by the TEU have been merged so that there is now a single European Union. Because of the various objections by various Member States special procedures still exist in the areas of foreign policy as well as in security and defence. Nevertheless, the very complex structure that existed between the TEU and the Lisbon Treaty has been simplified.

ACTIVITY

Self-assessment questions

1. What were the basic differences between the European Community and the European Union?
2. What are the basic parts of the EC Treaty (now TFEU), as amended by subsequent Treaties?
3. What are the principal tasks and activities as set out in Arts 2 and 3 of the EC Treaty (now TFEU)?
4. What are the main policies of the EC (now TFEU)?
5. What impact do Arts 352 and 217 TFEU have on the furtherance of the objectives of the EU?
6. How far is it true to say that the EC Treaty is the Constitution of the EC?
7. What are the major purposes of the Union?
8. In what ways has the TEU added to the objectives of the EC?
9. Why is the TEU criticised?
10. What was the 'three-pillar' structure of the EU?
11. How do the second and third pillars differ from the first pillar?
12. How did the third pillar change after the TEU?
13. How has the role of the different institutions changed since the creation of the Union?
14. What has been the effect on the so-called 'democratic deficit'?
15. Why was it more logical to refer to 'EC law' rather than 'EU law' prior to the Lisbon Treaty?

KEY FACTS

The Community	
Set out in EC Treaty as amended:	
• Part 1: Community principles	economic, social and political tasks to 'create a common market'. sets out activities to engage in to achieve objectives.
• Part 2: Citizenship of the Union	Guaranteed by TEU – but before Lisbon Treaty only to do with Union, not Community.
• Part 3: Community policies	'Four Freedoms' – together with competition policy etc plus expanded policies from the TEU.
• Part 4: Association with overseas countries	Through Council.
• Part 5: Rules governing the institutions • Part 6: General and Final Provisions	Sets out powers and responsibilities, eg liability of institutions Art 240, general ability to legislate to achieve Community objectives (Art 217).
The Union	
Six major purposes	• Extend scope of the Community. • Create Union with new structure, existing legal order plus common foreign and defence policy, common justice system. • Redistribute power of institutions. • Create concept of citizenship. • To introduce monetary union. • Community Charter of Fundamental Social Rights.

Three-pillar structure	• Pillar 1 – existing Community with legal order (now merged by the Lisbon Treaty). • Pillar 2 – co-operation on foreign policy and security. • Pillar 3 – co-operation on justice and police.
Institutions	Same as EC but with some additions – European Council more important.

SUMMARY

- Between the original Treaties and the TEU there was a European Community based on a legal order for the achievement of a single market.
- The Community represents the original legal order from the original three Treaties including the EC Treaty.
- Following the TEU, which created the European Union, there was a complex three pillar structure to the Union with the Community being based on a legal order but the other pillars based only on co-operation.
- The Treaty on European Union in 1992 also created the concept of European Union citizenship.
- Following the Lisbon Treaty these pillars have been merged, although there are still special procedures in place for the second and third pillars.

Further reading

Articles

Dougan, M 'The Treaty of Lisbon:Winning minds not hearts' (2008) 45 CML Rev 617.

Yaataganas, X, 'The Treaty of Nice: The Sharing of Power and the Institutional Balance in the European Union – A Continental Perspective' (2001) ELJ 242.

Books

Douglas-Scott, S, *Constitutional Law of the European Union* (Longman, 2002), Chapter 1.

Ward, I, *A Critical Introduction to European Law* (Butterworths, 1996), Chapter 1.

Websites

More information on the European Union can be obtained on the website http://europa.eu

3

The political and legal institutions of the European Union

AIMS AND OBJECTIVES

After reading this chapter you should be able to:

- Understand the origins and development of the different institutions
- Understand the composition and role of the Council of Ministers
- Understand the function of the European Council
- Understand the composition and role of the European Commission
- Understand the composition and role of the European Parliament
- Understand the role and composition of the Court of Justice and of the General Court
- Understand the rationale for and character of the other major institutions
- Evaluate the effectiveness of each institution
- Analyse the interrelationship between the institutions
- Evaluate the democratic nature and accountability of the institutions

3.1 The origins and development of the institutions

Both the original concept and indeed the major character of the key institutions of the EU actually came about in the ECSC Treaty. The framers of the Treaty realised that in order to have the sort of Community envisaged by the founders such as Jean Monnet, which could work effectively and prevent outbreak of another European war, it was vital to have both a legal order and a legislative system that could work independently of the Member States.

The next realisation was that this in itself would require the creation of institutions that were demonstrably supranational, bodies that could work independently of the Member States for the achievement of the aims of the Treaty.

In this way the ECSC Treaty introduced the essential concept of 'community', as we know it now. The European Coal and Steel Community was created with a number of significant features in mind:

- that the Community should have a distinct legal personality
- that it should work through and be represented by entirely autonomous institutions
- that Member States which became signatories to the Treaty should agree to cede (or more precisely pool) certain aspects of **their** national sovereignty in order to achieve defined objectives identified in the Treaty.

The institutions of the new 'Community' were created on this basis. The first of these institutions was originally known as the 'High Authority'. This body was to effectively control the production of coal and steel and was given power by the Treaty to make legally binding decisions as well as recommendations.

This body was supplemented by the creation of a 'Common Assembly'. This was a representative assembly to be made up of members from the various signatory states. It would have only very limited supervisory powers.

To these bodies was added a 'Special Council of Ministers' of the Member States. The Council's powers were partly legislative and partly consultative.

The final body devised in the Treaty was a 'Court of Justice'. The straightforward role of the court was laid out in Art 31 of the Treaty, 'to ensure that in the interpretation and application of this Treaty … the law is observed'.

When both the EEC Treaty and the EURATOM Treaty were created they followed exactly the same pattern, establishing 'Communities' with four key institutions, all autonomous, and all able to exercise powers stipulated in the Treaties creating them.

In these two Treaties, bodies called 'Commissions' in fact replaced the 'High Authority' of the ECSC. These Commissions initially had more limited powers and ranked behind both the Assembly and the Council.

At the same time that these two later Treaties were signed, a Convention created a single Assembly and a single Court of Justice that would represent all three Communities rather than having separate institutions for each.

Much later, in the Brussels Treaty 1967 (referred to as the Merger Treaty), a single Council was introduced for all three Communities. Also in the same Treaty the High Authority of the ECSC and the two Commissions of the other two Communities were merged into a single Commission. The Communities were nevertheless kept separate and the powers exercised by the individual institutions would be by reference to the specific Treaty.

The institutional structure of the EU is in fact quite unique. For instance it is not like the governing structure of any international organisation since the institutions are able to exercise sovereign powers that are in effect transferred to them by the Member States on joining.

Neither is it like any normal parliamentary democracy. There is of course no clear separation of powers between the executive and legislative functions as there would be in the constitutions of the Member States. However, there is a separation of interests.

There are complex legislative processes with both the Commission and the Council being potential sources of interpretation for legislation and the possibility of amendment or consultation by Parliament before legislation is in fact passed or created by the Council. Indeed there are even other bodies before which draft legislation might be presented before it is actually passed by the Council.

The nature of the different institutions and the various powers or responsibilities given to them means that the Commission is in fact a sort of executive but one without real executive powers. The Court of Justice is not a court of the type that we are familiar with but exercises a supervisory function and ensures that the division of power between the other institutions and between the EU and the Member States is maintained and preserved.

In keeping with the wishes of the founders of the Treaties the institutions all have broad autonomy and also their own rules of procedure. However, whatever the power of the individual bodies the overriding ruler of the EU is in fact the Treaties themselves. Everything done by the institutions must be for the furtherance of the objectives set in the Treaties.

These four basic institutions are still the main ones but they have also been added to over the years through provisions in the original Treaties or in the different subsequent Treaties:

- Article 4 of the EC Treaty allowed for the setting up of both an Economic and Social Committee and a Court of Auditors (to audit the accounts of the institutions). These two bodies have been created and the latter was made an independent body as the result of the TEU.

- Article 4 also allowed for the creation of COREPER, the Committee of Permanent Representatives. This is a vital part of the legislative process.
- The SEA 1986 then also established the Court of First Instance, a vital addition to ease the burden on the ECJ.
- A Committee of the Regions was also added by the TEU 1992.
- The TEU also provided for a European Investment Bank as well as a European Central Bank.

Besides new institutions being added to the original four, the role of the original institutions has also changed over the years. The new institutions have created extra complexity in the overall administration but have not necessarily improved it.

The balance of power between the Council and the Commission has shifted in a way that was never envisaged in the Treaties. As a result, intergovernmental decision-making has actually taken precedence over supranational authority. In fact, the power of the Council has increased because of the evolution of the European Council, the importance of the presidency and the co-operation procedure. Besides this the work of COREPER in many ways supports the individual states.

The role of Parliament has also increased. It now has a much greater and more significant role in legislation. It also has in effect control over a significant part of the budget and in its supervisory capacity was able to react dramatically in forcing the resignation of the Commission in 1999.

Article 7(1) of the EC Treaty originally identified that each institution is bound to act within the limits of the powers granted to it in the Treaty and the ECJ has been active in ensuring that this is the case. Nevertheless, there is seen to be a 'democratic deficit' in the relationship between the different institutions and it is unlikely that the developments that have occurred have really altered this.

> '... the Commission remains a fundamentally undemocratic institution, whilst the increasingly democratic Parliament remains unacceptably ineffective. The intergovernmental Council remains, after Maastricht as before, the most powerful institution, and whilst it does so, the Community will, in the last resource, remain in the service of the nation states'.
>
> I Ward, *A Critical Introduction to European Law* (Butterworths, 1996), p 44

3.2 The Council and the European Council

3.2.1 The Council

The Council is governed by Arts 237–243 TFEU and Art 16 TEU. While the Treaty itself merely refers to it as 'Council' it was traditionally referred to as the 'Council of Ministers'. However, following the TEU the Council chose to change its name to the 'Council of the European Union'. The Lisbon Treaty also refers to 'Council'.

Composition

The Council in terms of its membership is in fact a fluid concept with what amounts to a floating membership. In this sense it is unlike other bodies with similar functions.

According to Art 16(6) TEU: 'The Council shall consist of an authorised representative of each Member State at ministerial level, authorised to commit the government of that State', although the original intention was that the Council should in effect be a college of delegates with each state appointing a Minister for the specific purpose.

The consequence of the definition is that the specific identity of a Minister attending a meeting of the Council depends entirely on the subject of discussion at the meeting. If the meeting concerns agriculture it will be the Agriculture Minister. If it concerns transport it will be the Transport Minister, and so on. The important point is that each Minister has the power to commit the whole government of the Member State but is then accountable to his national Parliament which is said to ensure democratic legitimacy. The composition of the Council would also have been changed significantly under the Constitutional Treaty.

The role of Council

Article 16(1) TEU identifies the role of Council in the following way: 'Council shall, jointly with the European Parliament, exercise legislative and budgetary functions. It shall carry out policy-making and co-ordinating functions as laid down in the Treaties.' In fact, Council actually has six key responsibilities:

- Legislation – it is often said that 'the Commission proposes and Council disposes'. Council, through the different legislative procedures, acts on proposals from the Commission and with the advice of Parliament passes EU law. In this respect Council is the key decision-maker within the EU.
- Co-ordinating economic policy within the Union – the EU is an economic union and the Common Market is a significant part of that.
- Forming international agreements on behalf of the Member States – possibly on trade, technology, development etc.
- Approving the EU budget – the budget is in two parts: compulsory (for instance agricultural) and non-compulsory (which deals with the upkeep of the institutions). Both Council and Parliament must agree on the budget.
- Developing common foreign and security policies – this is only based on co-operation as Member States retain their own independent control over, eg defence. But there is much to be gained by working together and there is for instance an EU 'Rapid Reaction Force' of military personnel.
- Co-ordinating co-operation of justice systems of the Member States – different Member States have different legal systems but the EU can usefully work in co-operation on areas such as drug-trafficking, international fraud and terrorism.

The presidency

Prior to the Lisbon Treaty the Council had a rotating presidency. This was for six-month periods and each period was headed by a representative of a different Member State. This practice has now ceased.

Instead there is now what is known as 'Team Presidencies'. Because the Council meets with a different make up according to the area covered, this allows each configuration to be headed by a representative of each Member State on rotation.

As with the former system there are advantages to being President since the President sets the agenda.

Voting

Council is the major legislative organ, although there are some limited exceptions to this. It does consult both Parliament and the Economic and Social Committee but nevertheless it makes the final decision on any legislation. On this basis the voting system in Council is also very important.

Voting procedure is identified in Art 205 and it is of two main types:

- **Unanimous**: This is required for a number of areas, notably common foreign and security policy, taxation, and asylum and immigration. Since the 'Luxembourg Accords' it was always available if vital national interests were at stake. The consequence of a unanimous vote is that Member States in effect have a veto on issues. With enlargement it would seriously damage the development of the EU if too many issues required unanimous voting. As a result the Treaty of Nice reduced quite drastically the number of areas requiring unanimity. In any case the Treaties envisaged that all voting after the transitional period would be by qualified majority.
- **Qualified Majority Voting**: Since the 1960s, when numerous vetoes by France caused stagnation, this has been the most common method of voting. Under the old system of 87 votes a minimum of 62 votes was needed to carry a measure. The process was

obviously also designed to prevent large states from abusing their power at the expense of the smaller ones. Since 1995, therefore, 26 votes represented a blocking minority, well within the capability of smaller states joining together.

All decisions are voted on. Because of the diversity of the countries that are members of the EU voting is inevitably weighted. Countries are given more votes according to the size of their populations and their economic influence. However, the weighting is also artificial in these terms to favour the smaller countries.

Before 1st May 2004 there were only 15 Member States and the voting system was limited to 87 votes as follows.

Enlargement in 2004 increased membership of the EU by a further 10 countries. The weighting of votes inevitably had to change to accommodate the new members. There was a new system of weighting from 1st November 2004, with the total number of votes 321, broken down as follows:

Germany, France, Italy, UK	29 votes each
Spain, Poland	27 votes each
Netherlands	13 votes
Belgium, Czech Republic, Greece, Hungary, Portugal	12 votes each
Austria, Sweden	10 votes each
Denmark, Ireland, Lithuania, Slovakia, Finland	7 votes each
Cyprus, Estonia, Latvia, Luxembourg, Slovenia	4 votes each
Malta	3 votes

From 1st November 2004 a Qualified Majority Vote occurs in the following circumstances:

- a majority of Member States (in some cases a two-thirds majority) approve the measure and
- a minimum of 232 votes is cast in favour of the measure – this represents 72.3 per cent of the votes available (and is roughly the same as the previous 62 votes from 87).

In addition, under the new system Member States are able to ask for confirmation that the vote represents at least 62 per cent of the total population of the EU. If not, then the measure may not be adopted.

As from 1st January 2007, reflecting the membership of Romania and Bulgaria, the allocation of votes under the procedure is now as follows:

Germany, France, Italy, UK	29 votes each
Spain, Poland	27 votes each
Romania	14 votes
Netherlands	13 votes
Belgium, Czech Republic, Greece, Hungary, Portugal	12 votes each
Austria, Sweden, Bulgaria	10 votes each
Denmark, Ireland, Lithuania, Slovakia, Finland	7 votes each
Cyprus, Estonia, Latvia, Luxembourg, Slovenia	4 votes each
Malta	3 votes

After 2014 the means of identifying the votes available to each Member State is to change. After that time a double majority system is to be introduced based on the number of states and population.

3.2.2 The European Council

The European Council is not a creation of the Treaties. It was devised and agreed on by a meeting of heads of state in 1974 and was formally put in place in the Single European Act in 1986. Following the Lisbon Treaty it is now an established institution of the EU governed by Arts 235–36 TFEU and Art 15 TEU.

Its role is to 'provide the Union with the necessary impetus for development [and to] define the general political guidelines'.

It involves twice-yearly meetings of the heads of state of the Member States together with their Foreign Ministers. These are usually referred to as 'summits'. These involve general policy-making and also the two pillars that do not have the force of Community law: common foreign and security policy, and police and judicial co-operation in criminal matters.

One other useful aspect of these meetings is that they provide the means of assuring approval of measures proposed by the Commission. If the European Council has accepted proposals then it is unlikely that they would be rejected by vote in the Council of Ministers. This helps to streamline the process of legislation.

Presidency of the European Council used to rotate with the presidency of Council between Member States. The Lisbon Treaty created a new system. The President is elected by a qualified majority of the members for a period of two and a half years. This term of office can be extended once. The President represents the EU in common foreign and security policies, and also acts as chair.

3.3 The European Commission

The Commission is governed by Arts 244–250 TFEU. Of all the EU institutions it probably has the clearest claim to being a supranational body of the type envisaged by the founders of the Treaties.

The Commission actually refers to two groups of people. It refers to the Commissioners themselves, those representatives appointed from Member States who run the various departments. It also of course refers to the whole staff of the Commission, administrative officials, translators, secretaries and other staff of which there are about 24,000.

The Commission essentially acts as an executive arm of the EU. It is sometimes compared to a civil service but in fact it has much broader powers and roles than any civil service.

Composition and appointment

Prior to enlargement the Commission comprised 20 Commissioners. According to Art 213 there should be at least one from each Member State but not more than two. In practice, then, traditionally the larger states – France, Germany, Italy, the UK, and Spain – had two Commissioners while the other states had one each.

Because of impending enlargement the Treaty of Nice provided in an amended Art 213(1) that from 1st January 2005 the Commission should include one national of each Member State. This means that the larger states will lose their extra Commissioner and this is to prevent the Commission from becoming too large and unmanageable with enlargement. The amended Article also stipulates that once there are 27 Member States there will be fewer Commissioners than Member States so that the Council will introduce a rotation system. However, the Accession Treaty for the entry of Romania and Bulgaria provided for both to gain a Commissioner, so the number is now 27. However, under the Reform Treaty, if ratified, from 2014 the number of Commissioners will reduce to a number equivalent to two thirds of the number of Member States, and these will be selected on a strict rotational basis. A fixed-term presidency would also be introduced.

The Draft Constitution proposed that the composition should be modified, with a President, the Minister of Foreign Affairs (who would have the title of Vice-President) and 13 Commissioners. These would be selected on the basis of an equal rota system between the Member States. Besides these, the President would have the power to appoint additional 'Commissioners' from all other Member States, who would have no voting rights. However, because of the first Irish referendum on ratification of the Lisbon Treaty, the European Council has agreed to keep to the current system of one member for each Member State.

A new Commission is appointed every five years. Commissioners are chosen on grounds of general competence, from persons 'whose independence is beyond doubt'. In practice they are nominated by their Member States but the process of approval and appointment involves the approval of Parliament too.

Commissioners, although they are nominated by their Member States, are required by Art 213 to take an oath to be independent and neither to seek nor to take instructions from their Member State. The Member State also undertakes not to influence the Commissioners. Each Commissioner is appointed for a five-year term and is appointed a Directorate General with specific responsibilities, for example for employment or transport or the Internal Market.

The President

The Commission is headed by a President. The President is nominated by the governments of the Member States but must be approved as part of the whole Commission by Parliament.

According to Art 250 TFEU, 'The Commission shall work under the political guidance of its President'. The President has the authority to decide on the internal organisation of the Commission and the President clearly has the authority within this to allocate responsibilities among the Commissioners.

The role of the Commission

The Commission is collegiate in character and it tends to act on the basis of simple majority votes.

Its key responsibilities are:

- **To initiate legislation**: The Commission proposes legislation and can draft proposals on anything covered by the Treaties which it presents to Parliament and the Council. In doing so it takes advice from the Economic and Social Committee and the Committee of the Regions. So that it does not interfere in issues that can be better dealt with by the Member States themselves, the Commission also operates according to the 'subsidiarity' principle.
- **To enforce the law**: The Commission has often been referred to as the 'watchdog' or 'guardian' of the Treaties. Article 10 demands that all Member States are obliged to achieve the objectives of the Treaties. The Commission must then ensure that all Member States are applying EC law properly. It can then deal with breaches of EC law by Member States through Art 226 proceedings. Initially the Commission would use the 'infringement procedure' but if a Member State fails to respond then it can take the matter to the ECJ.
- **To implement policy and the EU budget**: The Commission has executive functions. As a result, it is responsible for managing policy. For instance, traditionally it had a key role in EU competition law. It is also responsible for the compulsory budget. Even though it is actually national and local authorities that usually spend the money the Commission still has supervisory responsibility. In particular, the Commission would be responsible for the European Social Fund and the Regional Development Fund.
- **To represent the EU internationally**: The Commission speaks for all the Member States in international meetings such as in the World Trade Organisation or the United

Nations. It also negotiates international agreements for the EU, an example being the Cotonou Agreement which is a trade agreement between the EU and certain developing nations in Africa and the Caribbean.

Through a process known as **comity** the Council can delegate power to the Commission for it to produce detailed regulations following the passing of a framework regulation by the Council.

It must be remembered, though, that the Commission is also accountable to Parliament in certain ways. Parliament is able to pass a motion of censure on the Commission under Art 201, causing the Commission to resign. This in fact happened in 1999 following a lengthy inquiry into fraud.

3.4 The European Parliament

In the original EC Treaty Parliament was identified as the Assembly and its role was to 'exercise the advisory and supervisory powers' conferred upon it. It was not a democratically elected body and it was made up of appointed nominees from the Member State governments. The limited powers of the Assembly was another reason for the complaint of a democratic deficit since it had no legislative power and could only act in a consultative capacity.

Since 1979, however, it has been an elected body with elections every five years using proportional representation. Parliament is governed by Arts 123–234 TFEU.

Composition

Prior to enlargement the total membership of Parliament was 626 MEPs. Membership in fact depends on the size and importance of the particular Member State. The Treaty of Amsterdam amended Art 189 to provide a maximum number of 700 MEPs. Because of impending enlargement Art 189 was subsequently amended also in the Treaty of Nice to provide for a maximum number of 732 MEPs.

The number of seats in the European Parliament for the 2009–14 term is 736. The allocation of MEPs by country from the start of the parliamentary term from 2009–2014 will be as follows:

Member State	Number of MEPs each
Germany	99
France, Italy, UK	72
Poland, Spain	50
Romania	33
Netherlands	25
Belgium, Greece, Portugal, Czech Republic, Hungary	22
Sweden	18
Austria, Bulgaria	17
Denmark, Finland, Slovakia	13
Ireland, Lithuania	12
Latvia	8
Slovenia	7
Cyprus, Estonia, Luxembourg	6
Malta	5

MEPs are elected for a period of five years. They in fact sit in Parliament according to loose political groupings including representatives from a number of Member States rather than according to any national interest. In this respect there is no mandatory voting for Member State interests, as MEPs are representatives and not delegates.

Parliament sits for one week in each month except August, although it can also sit at other times when certain items require discussion. Voting is on a simple majority basis. There are also a number of specialist parliamentary committees. Parliament also elects its own President and various officials.

The role of Parliament

Parliament currently enjoys three main powers:

- It has a role in **legislation**. In the co-decision procedure, introduced by the TEU, and which is now probably the most common method for introducing legislation, Parliament has an important role and can make amendments and in some cases exercise a veto. Under the co-operation procedure, introduced in the SEA, it also has a consultative role. It is also able to examine the annual work programme of the Commission.
- It has a **supervisory** role over other EU institutions. This is particularly the case with the Commission. Parliament must approve each new Commission. It can also pass a motion of censure on the Commission. The effect of such a censure was seen in 1999 when it led to the resignation of the entire Commission. It is also able to send questions to the Council and also can express its views to each meeting of the European Council. The supervisory power of Parliament over the Commission has also been extended. Article 17(7) TEU requires that the commissioners, including the President and the High Representative of the Union for Foreign Affairs and Security Policy, are subject to the consent of Parliament subject to taking up office.
- It has powers over the **budget**. Parliament is required to approve each annual budget. In the case of a failure to accept the budget the effect is dramatic since this includes the day-to-day payment of all officials in the institutions. The Treaty of Lisbon extended the power of Parliament over the budget. Now under Art 314(4) TFEU it has the power to amend any part of the budget, whether the compulsory or the non-compulsory.

There is still felt to be a democratic deficit where Parliament is concerned. There is some discontent that it is unable to initiate legislation itself. Also, the censure facility only covers the whole Commission and some feel there should be the power to censure and remove individual Commissioners. It is also felt by some that the Council should be more accountable to Parliament. The main suggestion in the EU Constitution affecting Parliament is for an extension of the co-decision procedure in legislating.

3.5 Court of Justice of the European Union (and the General Court)

3.5.1 The European Court of Justice

The Court of Justice is not like any court in the English legal system. In fact, it is a court with few meaningful comparisons. As can be seen in both Chapter 8 and Chapter 9, the court has played an absolutely vital role in the development of EC law.

The rules governing the Court of Justice are found in Arts 251–281 TFEU and by the Statute of the Court of Justice, but also in the Protocol on the Statute of the Court of Justice of the European Community. The latter is added to the Treaty in effect as an annex and contains all the procedural rules of the court. The procedures must be voted on by Council but since the Treaty of Nice this is done with a Qualified Majority Vote rather than requiring a unanimous vote as was the case before. The court and the CFI made representations at the Nice summit that they should be able to determine and adapt the procedure themselves but this has not been accepted.

The composition of the court

The ECJ is composed of *juges rapporteurs* (the judges) who are assisted by *Advocates-General*. Article 253 identifies the requirements for appointment of both:

ARTICLE

> '[they] shall be chosen from persons whose independence is beyond doubt and who possess the qualifications required for appointment to the highest judicial offices in their respective countries or who are jurisconsults of recognised competence'.

As a result of this the judges are chosen from high-level judges from the Member States or highly competent lawyers who are independent beyond doubt so that they can be relied upon to show impartiality. Indeed, they must all swear an oath of impartiality.

In terms of numbers, before enlargement Art 19 TEU provided that 'The ECJ shall consist of 15 judges'. This did in fact reflect the number of Member States and a judge for each one. The Treaty of Nice amends Art 221 to provide that the court will consist of 'one judge per Member State'. Following the accession of Romania and Bulgaria this then stands at 27.

Both the judges of the ECJ and the Advocates-General are appointed by joint agreement of the governments of the Member States.

Article 19 TEU, stipulates that there shall be one judge appointed from each Member State. The Treaty also provides for the appointment of eight Advocates-General to assist the court. Both judges and Advocates-General serve for a six-year term. There is a staggered re-appointment system and it is possible to be re-appointed for a further one or two periods of three years. Removal of a judge is possible only if all colleagues agree that the judge in question is unfit to serve.

Under Art 254 TFEU, the judges appoint a President from among themselves. The President serves for a three-year period. The President generally directs the business of the court, appoints a specific *juge rapporteur* to manage a specific case, and tends also to deal with all interlocutory matters.

The role of the court

By Art 13(2) TEU the Court of Justice and the General Court can only act in areas where jurisdiction has been specifically given to them in the Treaties.

There are three central objectives in the work of the court:

- to ensure that in application and interpretation the law is observed
- to provide a forum for resolving disputes between institutions, Member States and individuals
- to protect individual rights.

The court hears five main types of action:

- Art 267 references from Member States for a preliminary ruling on an interpretation of EU law (known also as indirect actions) (see Chapter 7)
- Art 258 actions against Member States for failing to implement Treaty obligations (a direct action known also as infringement proceedings)
- Art 263 actions against an institution for abuse of power
- Art 265 actions against an institution for a failure to act
- Art 340 actions for damages against an institution that has been responsible for loss to the individual (for example where the Commission has failed to address a decision to a body engaging in anti-competitive practices and an individual suffers loss as a result).

(See Chapter 6 for the last four.)

Procedure

Traditionally, most issues involving Member States or an institution were heard by a full court. There were some straightforward issues where it was possible for a bench of three or five judges to reach a decision. This was appropriate where the court was limited in size to 15 judges. Obviously, enlargement means that a plenary session of the court could involve a very large number of judges. Therefore, for the sake of efficiency, the Treaty of Nice allows the court to sit as a 'Grand Chamber' of fewer judges instead of always having to meet in plenary session. In any case, Art 17 of the Statute of the Court of Justice provides that a decision of the court is valid only if the court is comprised of an uneven number of judges.

Decisions of the court are thus based on a majority. Procedure is essentially inquisitorial. There is no provision for individual judges to deliver dissenting judgments.

Cases are submitted through the 'registry' and the President of the court assigns the case to a specific judge to manage. In the first stage all parties make written submissions on which the judge writes a report and then passes everything on to an Advocate-General assigned to the case. The Advocate-General then produces a reasoned opinion for the court. This does not have to be followed by the court but it may be. Following the introduction of the reasoned opinion the judge prepares a draft ruling which is passed to the other members of the court.

A public hearing of the action is held before the whole court in plenary session (or post-enlargement a grand chamber of the court) or, depending on the type and complexity of the issue, a chamber of three or five judges. All parties can put their case and the court can ask questions.

3.5.2 The General Court

Because of the excess workload of the Court of Justice and the long delays that resulted from this, a Court of First Instance (CFI) was created in the SEA. This is now the General Court. The court is governed by Art 256 TFEU which also identifies the types of case that could be heard by the court.

The jurisdiction of the General Court when it was the CFI was limited to actions including staff cases and some actions under competition law.

An amendment in the TEU added another category:

- actions by natural or legal persons under either Art 230 or Art 232 (now Arts 263 and 265 TFEU), including anti-dumping cases.

Originally the court was specifically excluded from hearing Art 267 references. Following the Treaty of Nice, the court can hear references for preliminary rulings on specific areas. There are as yet no specific areas identified in the Treaty.

The Treaty of Nice expanded the jurisdiction of the CFI, now the General Court, so that it can hear all actions under Arts 263, 265, 268, 270, and 272 that are not already attached to a 'judicial panel' or those that are required by the Statute of the Court of Justice to be heard in the ECJ. Judicial panels annexed to the General Court (formerly the CCFI) were 'another creation of the Treaty of Nice. The Council may set up such panels to hear specific types of action in specific areas to deal with issues speedily.

The regulations and requirements for the General Court are similar to those for the ECJ. Membership of the court again is based on a representative from each Member State, with similar qualifications needed. In this case, while independence again is an absolute requirement, members of the court must merely 'possess the ability required for appointment to judicial office'.

In diagram form, the courts can be represented as shown in Figure 3.5.2.

Member State governments appoint:

Juges rapporteurs (one for each Member State) together with eight Advocates-General

Both sit for a six-year (renewable) period

Judges must hold high judicial office and be independent and act impartially.

They sit in:

The European Court of Justice –

Different types of actions are heard:

Against Member States:

Enforcement proceedings for a failure to honour Treaty obligations (Art 258).

Against EU institutions:

- For annulment of acts beyond the capacity of the institution (Art 263).
- For failing to act (Art 265).
- For a claim of damages where the institution has caused claimant loss (Art 340).

References from Member States:

For preliminary rulings on the meaning of EU law provisions (Art 267).

General Court (one Judge from each Member State) hears different actions:

- direct actions by natural and legal persons (not anti-dumping)
- staff cases
- now jurisdiction is expanded after Treaty of Nice

Figure 3.5.2 The work of the ECJ and the General Court

ACTIVITY

Quick quiz

In each of the situations below, identify which institution or institutions is or are likely to be mainly involved (your answer should only refer to the main institutions):

1. Antoinette, a French national and a nurse, has complained that she is being discriminated against because her employer pays her less than is paid to a male hospital administrator, even though Antoinette argues that her work is of equal value to the employer. The French court has identified that an interpretation of EU law would be decisive.
2. Research by various bodies has indicated that a regulation should be introduced on levels of a particular chemical in certain foodstuffs because the chemical is potentially harmful to children.
3. The Commission has been exposed for financial irregularities in relation to certain aspects of the budget.
4. Various Member States wish there to be a meeting to determine a combined foreign and security policy in the light of various civil disturbances in parts of the old Soviet Union which are close to the eastern borders of the EU.

ACTIVITY

Self-assessment questions

1. What was the significance of the 'High Authority' in the ECSC?
2. How does it compare with the modern EU institutions?
3. What are the four main institutions of the EU?
4. Which is the main legislator of the EU?
5. What powers, if any, does Parliament have over the Commission?
6. How did the TEU alter the role of Parliament?
7. How has the Council managed to extend its influence?
8. In what ways is this damaging to the original objectives of the Treaties?
9. What are the main functions of the Commission?
10. In what ways is the Court of Justice different from any English court?
11. What are the major functions of the court?
12. What are the functions of the General Court?
13. How did the role of the General Court develop after the Treaty of Nice?
14. How important is the Commission in achieving the objectives of the Treaties?
15. Why is there a weighted voting system in the Council?
16. What are the major consequences of the Qualified Majority Voting system?
17. Why do different Member States have different numbers of MEPs?
18. To what extent is the weighting fair?
19. Can small States ever have an influence on policy-making in the EU?
20. What advantage is the use of Advocates-General to the ECJ?
21. What were the major changes to the institutions made by the Treaty of Nice in anticipation of enlargement?
22. What are the major institutional reforms made by the Lisbon Treaty?

ACTIVITY

Essay-writing skills

Read the extract below and give brief answers to the questions that follow it.

'It is suggested that Maastricht, even if it does not effect it, symbolises the respectability of supranationalism as a political idea. The enhancement of the power of the Commission, particularly in A171.2, where it is empowered to enforce ECJ decisions, is at least a gesture of significance … However, the Commission remains a fundamentally undemocratic institution, whilst the increasingly democratic Parliament remains unacceptably ineffective. The intergovernmental Council remains, after Maastricht as before, the most powerful institution, and whilst it does so, the Community will, in the last resource, remain in the service of the nation states. In conclusion, it might be suggested that Maastricht represents a spiritual victory for supranationalism. Ultimately, however, integration still remains subject to intergovernmental control. The Community remains, after the SEA and Maastricht, a sui generis constitutional order, beyond sovereignty but not federal, characterised by a "pooling of sovereignty." '

Adapted from I Ward, *A Critical Introduction to European Law* (Butterworths, 1996), p 44

1. In what ways is the Commission a 'fundamentally undemocratic institution'?
2. To what extent is Parliament 'increasingly democratic but unacceptably ineffective'?
3. What justifications are there for saying that Council is 'the most powerful institution'?

3.6 The other major institutions

3.6.1 The Committee of Permanent Representatives (COREPER)

COREPER is the Committee of Permanent Representatives. The name is an acronym from the French way of referring to the committee. The committee was not a product of the original Treaties but was created by Art 4 of the Merger Treaty in 1965 and now under Art 240 TFEU forms part of the decision-making procedure.

COREPER is a permanent body of representatives from all of the Member States. It was felt to be necessary because of the fluid Membership of Council as a means of informing Ministers from the Member States and streamlining the process of legislation.

In this way individual representatives prepare items of discussion at Council meetings and examine the Commission's legislative proposals for the individual Ministers. Generally, if a proposal can be agreed upon by COREPER before the Council meeting then it will be accepted without need for lengthy discussion.

3.6.2 The Court of Auditors

Again, this body is not a product of the original Treaties but was created by a Secondary Budget Treaty in 1975 and inserted into the Treaty and was eventually made a full institution in the TEU.

The basic role of the court is to control and supervise the Community budget. It examines the accounts of all revenue and expenditure and in effect checks that the EU budget is correctly implemented by those institutions that are responsible for it. In this way it can investigate the paperwork of any body handling EU funds and can carry out spot checks if appropriate. It also prepares an annual report for Parliament and the Council. It will in any case produce an 'opinion' before any financial measure is adopted. However, it does not have any legal powers of its own but passes information on to the other bodies for them to deal with.

It has qualified members from each Member State who are independent and who are chosen for these qualities.

3.6.3 The Economic and Social Committee

The Economic and Social Committee was established in Art 257 of the EC Treaty and Art 165 of the EURATOM Treaty. It now falls under Art 300 TFEU.

Its purpose is clearly to give advice to either the Council or the Commission on social and economic matters. Advice is given in the form of an opinion. The committee is not officially recognised as one of the institutions so there is no overall obligation to consult it. These institutions do consult the committee then whenever there is a specific obligation in the Treaty. However, where the Council or the Commission fails to consult on a matter where consultation is called for it is possible for the ECJ to annul the measure in question so the committee does actually have some influence. It can in any case deliver an opinion even where it has not been called for.

Article 301 TFEU identifies that after enlargement the committee shall not exceed 350 in number. Council appoints the members of the committee for a period of five years, although this is renewable. Representation on the committee is based on the size of the Member State. After enlargement it is as follows:

Member State	Members
Germany, France, Italy, UK	24 each
Poland, Spain	21 each
Romania	15
Austria, Belgium, Bulgaria, Czech Republic, Greece, Hungary, Netherlands, Portugal, Sweden	12 each
Denmark, Finland, Ireland, Lithuania, Slovakia	9 each
Estonia, Latvia, Slovenia	7 each
Cyprus, Luxembourg	6 each
Malta	5

Membership is based on representation of various social or economic activities so it includes various interest groups such as farmers, carriers, dealers and craftsmen of different types.

3.6.4 The Committee of the Regions

The Committee of the Regions is also not recognised as one of the institutions and was not a product of the original Treaties. The committee was created in 1994 after the Treaty of Lisbon under Arts 305–307 TFEU.

It is essentially an advisory body to represent local and regional interests. It will be consulted within the legislative process on matters of regional and local concern such as education, public health, culture and other matters of social concern.

By Art 300 its membership must come from elected members of local and regional bodies (although not national government).

It has the same ceiling on numbers as the Social and Economic Committee and allocation of representation from each Member State is on the same basis.

3.6.5 The European Central Bank

The European Central Bank (ECB) was a creation of the TEU in which provision was made in the Protocol (and now under Arts 282–284 TFEU) to have a Central Bank to act for the EU.

The purpose of setting up such a body is clear. It is an essential element of the policy of European monetary union (EMU) and the move to a single currency.

The bank has been in place since 1st January 1999 and has responsibility for monetary policy in the EU. Its primary aim is to maintain price stability. It is the only body allowed to issue euro banknotes.

3.6.6 The European Investment Bank

The Investment Bank was set up by Art 7 of the EC Treaty. The bank's basic mission is to invest in projects that promote the objectives of the EU. It is not financed by the EU budget but by borrowing in the financial markets and also from the Member States.

The bank only invests in projects according to strict criteria:

- the project must help achieve EU objectives, eg making small businesses more competitive
- the project must help mainly disadvantaged regions
- the project must help to attract other sources of funding.

3.6.7 The European Ombudsman

The position of Ombudsman was created in the TEU. The European Ombudsman operates in the same way as all Ombudsmen and is an intermediary between European citizens and EU institutions. The Ombudsman is elected by the European Parliament for a period of five years.

The Ombudsman acts independently and listens to complaints from EU citizens and investigates examples of maladministration. In an EU context 'maladministration' can concern:

- unfairness
- discrimination
- abuse of power
- lack of information or refusal to give information
- unnecessary delay in making decisions
- using incorrect procedures.

The Ombudsman can refer matters to the other institutions to take appropriate action but will not investigate a complaint that has been the subject of a court case.

ACTIVITY

Self-assessment questions

1. Which of the other institutions have been created after the original Treaties?
2. What is the major role of the Economic and Social Committee?
3. Why are there different weightings between the different Member States for membership of the committee?
4. Why was the creation of COREPER necessary or desirable?
5. What was the prime purpose of creating a European Central Bank?
6. What is the major function of the European Investment Bank?
7. What is the role of the Court of Auditors?
8. How does a European Ombudsman help citizens of the Union?

SAMPLE ESSAY QUESTION

'The relationship between the institutions is important because it is the different powers ascribed to the institutions and the way they have to work together that provides the "checks and balances" within the Union legal order.' [Josephine Steiner and Lorna Woods, *EU Law*, 10th edition, 2009, OUP, p 25]

Discuss the role and composition of the political institutions of the EU in the light of the above statement.

Explain that there are 3 main political institutions:
- Council, the Commission and Parliament.

Explain the basic role of each:

- Council – main law maker; composed of ministers from each MS; fluid membership based on subject of legislation; but also co-ordinates economic policy and reaches international agreements; votes with a 'qualified majority' voting system
- Commission – main proposer and drafter of legislation; membership is 1 for each MS, Commissioners also have individual areas of responsibility; also acts as 'watchdog' of Treaties and has *locus standi* in court actions against institutions and against MSs; act independently of MSs
- Parliament – elected body, number of MEPs per MS based on importance of MS; originally no legislative power; but now is consulted on legislation and has power to make amendments.

Discuss the relationship between the different institutions:

- the original undemocratic nature of the institutions and the existence of a so-called 'democratic deficit'
- Council was always subject to national self interest by member states – hence Luxembourg Accords – now subject mostly to qualified majority voting – still the main law making body and since co-decision it must work more closely with the other bodies
- Commission oath bound to EU but drafting legislation has to work more cooperatively because of the co-decision process
- Parliament until Nice lacked power or real impact on the legislative process, but after 1979 became a democratically elected body – and since the Treaty of Nice has a much greater influence through the co-decision procedure – and has other checks on the power of the Commission, eg 1999.

Discuss the involvement of other institutions:

- after Treaty of Lisbon, consideration also should be given to policy making powers of the European Council
- Social and Economic Committee and the Committee of the Regions are also involved in either policy making or legislation
- ECJ in achieving the objectives of the Treaty and ensuring that the Treaty is observed is probably the most effective check.

KEY FACTS

The Council of Ministers	
Role	Main legislator of the EU. Represents Member States' interests. Co-ordinates economic policy. Concludes international agreements. Approves EU budget. Develops co-operation between Member States on justice and foreign policy.
Membership	One Minister for each Member State.
Presidency	Team presidencies.
Voting	Changes to Treaties by unanimous vote – on most things now by 'Qualified Majority' (different votes for size and importance of State).
The European Council	
Role	In Art 4 of the TEU – impetus for development and policy-making. Deals with policy.
Meetings	Twice-yearly summits of Heads of State and Foreign Ministers.
Presidency	Appointed by European Council to serve a two and a half year term which is renewable once.
The Commission	
Role	Proposes and prepares draft legislation. Manages budget. Acts as 'watchdog' of the Treaties – enforcing EC law.
Membership	One Commissioner from each Member State for period of five years – have responsibility for heading different departments.
The Court of Justice	
Role	Ensures that law from Treaties is observed – five main actions: • Art 258 infringement proceedings against Member States • Art 263 against institutions for exceeding powers • Art 265 against institutions for failure to act • Art 340 by natural/legal persons for damage caused by institution • Art 267 references from Member State courts for interpretations of EU law.
Membership	One *juge-rapporteur* for each Member State plus eight Advocates-General. Appointed for six-year period.
The General Court	
Role	Eases workload of ECJ – hears specific types of action, eg staff cases, competition law, but now Arts 263 and 265 etc as directed.
Membership	Similar to ECJ.
The other institutions	
COREPER	Permanent staff to support individual Ministers prior to meetings of Council.

The Court of Auditors	Checks that EU funds are properly used – has member from each State.
The Economic and Social Committee	Membership on basis of size of country – is consulted by Commission and Council prior to some legislation on social or economic policy – can give opinions on own initiative or where asked for.
The Committee of the Regions	Membership as for Social and Economic Committee but represents local or regional government – consulted on local or regional issues.
European Central Bank	An independent body to oversee European Monetary Union (EMU) – controls money supply and monitors pricing trends.
European Investment Bank	Invests in projects that support small businesses.
European Ombudsman	Investigates complaints of maladministration.

SUMMARY

- There are four main EU institutions.
- Council is the major legislator – using proposals from the Commission and with input from Parliament.
- The Commission prepares draft legislation, is the major administrator, and is also 'the watchdog of the Treaties'.
- Parliament – is the only elected body and has powers to make amendments to legislation as well as having some control over the budget.
- The Court of Justice, which provides preliminary rulings on interpretation, hears actions against Member States for breaches of EU law, hears judicial review for abuses by the institutions and for their failure to act, and actions for damages by citizens.
- There are also other institutions including CORPER, the Economic and Social Committee, the Committee of the Regions, the Court of Auditors and the European Central Bank – and the Court of Justice is also supported by the General Court.

Further reading

Articles

Bradley, K, 'Institutional design in the Treaty of Nice' (2001) 38 CMLR 1095.

Books

Douglas-Scott, S, *Constitutional Law of the European Union* (Longman, 2002), Chapters 2 and 5.

Tillotson, J and Foster, N, *Text, Cases and Materials on European Union Law* (4th edn, Cavendish Publishing, 2003), Chapters 4 and 7.

Ward, I, *A Critical Introduction to European Law* (Butterworths, 1996), Chapter 1.

4

The sources of EU law

AIMS AND OBJECTIVES

After reading this chapter you should be able to:

- Understand that EU law derives from a number of different sources
- Understand the binding character of the primary source, the Treaties
- Understand the binding character of the secondary sources, EU legislation in the form of regulations, directives and decisions, and the persuasive effect of recommendations, opinions and 'soft law'
- Understand the nature of the tertiary sources, case law of the European Court of Justice (binding), the general principles (part of the interpretation process of ECJ) and other acts, eg international treaties entered into by the EU
- Analyse the interrelationship of the different sources
- Evaluate the binding or persuasive nature of each source
- Evaluate the effect of different sources on national law
- Just as with English law, where the law is found in a number of different sources, so also EU law is made up of a number of different sources. The major sources of law can be very easily identified from the following table:

<table>
<tr><td rowspan="2">Primary sources</td><td colspan="2">The Treaties:
ECSC; EURATOM; EC; SEA; TEU; ToA; ToN; ToL – divide into:</td></tr>
<tr><td>Procedural Treaty Articles:
eg Art 288 after Lisbon Treaty which identifies the legislation; or Art 258 an action against a Member State.</td><td>Substantive Treaty Articles:
eg Art 157 TFEU ensuring equal pay for men and women; or Art 45 TFEU the free movement of workers.</td></tr>
<tr><td rowspan="4">Secondary sources</td><td colspan="2">Legislation: Identified in Art 288 TFEU and including:</td></tr>
<tr><td>Regulations</td><td>Automatically become law in Member States. They are generally applicable, binding in their entirety, and directly applicable.</td></tr>
<tr><td>Directives</td><td>Binding as to the effect to be achieved. Member States have an implementing period within which they must be incorporated into national law by their chosen means.</td></tr>
<tr><td>Decisions</td><td>Addressed to a specific party, whether a company, individual or Member State. They are then binding in their entirety on the party to whom they are addressed.</td></tr>
</table>

<table>
<tr><td></td><td>Recommendations</td><td>Have no legal force but are persuasive.</td></tr>
<tr><td></td><td>Opinions</td><td>Have no legal force but are persuasive.</td></tr>
<tr><td></td><td>'Soft law'</td><td>eg Commission guidelines or notices – no legal force but a good way of influencing policy.</td></tr>
<tr><td rowspan="4">Tertiary sources</td><td colspan="2">Case law of European Court of Justice – vital because of:</td></tr>
<tr><td>The power to ensure observance of Treaty objectives through Art 267 TFEU references.</td><td>The judicial creativity of the ECJ in comparison with the relative inertia of the legislative bodies.</td></tr>
<tr><td colspan="2">General principles: Proportionality; equality; legal certainty; natural justice; protection of fundamental human rights; subsidiarity.</td></tr>
<tr><td colspan="2">Acts adopted by representatives of Member State governments meeting in Council.
National law of Member States.
International Treaties negotiated by the EU.</td></tr>
</table>

4.1 Primary sources – the Treaties

4.1.1 The importance of the Treaties

The Treaties are the most significant source of EU law and are the primary source of law. The original founding Treaties – the ECSC, the EURATOM Treaty and the EC Treaty (now TFEU) – are all primary law and all subsequent law must fulfil the objectives of those founding Treaties.

As the Community expanded and the Union was created, a number of related Treaties have been introduced. These all have the force of Community law and create enforceable rights and obligations. They include:

- the various Accession Treaties expanding the original Community territorially
- the Merger Treaties 1965
- the Single European Act 1986 (which put in place the processes to eventually achieve the Common Market)
- the Treaty on European Union 1992 (which created the Union and its three-pillar structure)
- the Amsterdam Treaty 1997 (which rationalised the existing structure and re-numbered the original EC Treaty)
- the Treaty of Nice 2000 (which focused on institutional reform)
- the Treaty of Lisbon, which was introduced in place of the rejected Constitutional Treaty (has introduced further institutional reform as well as amending both the TEU and the EC Treaty and renaming the latter as the Treaty on the Functioning of the European Union (TFEU)).

4.1.2 The Treaty for the Functioning of the European Union (incorporating the EC Treaty and the TEU)

The EC Treaty is clearly the most important Treaty in terms of establishing the legal order of the Community. It is divided into various key components. It begins with a preamble, one of the major functions of which is for interpretation of what follows.

It is then split into six parts:

- **Part One (Arts 1–17)** is the 'Principles' (the basic ground rules of the Community and the key objectives)

- **Part Two (Arts 18–25)** concerns 'Citizenship of the Union'
- **Part Three** contains the 'Policies' – this itself is broken down into a series of 'Titles'. These include:
  - Title I – The internal market,
  - Title II – free movement of goods
  - Title III – agriculture and fisheries
  - Title IV – free movement of persons, services and capital
  - Tile IV – visas, asylum, immigration
  - Title V – area of freedom, security and justice
  - Title VI – Transport
  - Title VII – common rules on competition, taxation and approximation of laws
  - Title VIII – economic and monetary policy
  - Title IX – employment
  - Title X – social policy
  - Title XI – the European Social Fund
  - Title XII – education, vocational training, youth and sport
  - Title XIII – culture
  - Title XIV – public health
  - Title XV – consumer protection
  - Title XVI – trans-European networks
  - Title XVII – industry
  - Title XVIII – economic, social and territorial cohesion
  - Title XIX – research and technological development and space
  - Title XX – environment
  - Title XXI – energy
  - Title XXII – tourism
  - Title XXIII – civil protection
  - Title XXIV – administrative co-operation.
- **Part Four (Arts 198–204)** concerns association of overseas countries and territories
- **Part Five (Arts 205–226)** – external action by the Union
- **Part Six (Arts 223–358)** institutional and financial provisions.

The importance of the Treaty can be seen just by listing its contents in this way. The Treaty includes, as is evident from Part Three, the major areas of substantive law which are then enforceable through the means identified in Chapter 9. It also contains in Part Six the powers and jurisdiction of the various institutions. In this way the Treaty has a constitutional significance.

The Treaty repeats the institutional reforms of the Constitutional Treaty so that a new institutional framework is created including the European Council and renaming the Council of Ministers and the European Commission as the Council and the Commission respectively.

ACTIVITY

Self-assessment questions

1. What are the key Treaties in the development of the European Community and the European Union?
2. Why are the Treaties referred to as 'primary law'?
3. What was the importance of the Single European Act?
4. In what ways did the Treaty of Amsterdam develop the Treaties?

4.2 Secondary sources – legislation under Art 288

4.2.1 Introduction

'Secondary legislation' is merely a collective term that is used to describe all of the various types of law that the institutions can make. The legislation is clearly of major importance since it is the way that EU law is expanded and developed out of the broad principles contained in the Treaties themselves. Nevertheless, it is also important to remember that legislation is still subordinate to the primary law in the Treaties and must only be used for the furtherance of the objectives of the Treaties. As a result, the legislation cannot amend, repeal or alter the scope of the Treaties.

In this way the institutions may only act in legislation:

- in order to carry out the tasks assigned to them by the Treaties
- in strict accordance with the provisions of the Treaties for the fulfillment of the objectives of the Treaties
- and only within the strict limits of the powers that are actually conferred upon them in the Treaties, and specifically those identified in Art 288 of the EC Treaty.

It is the TFEU through Art 288 that defines the role of the institutions in producing legislation:

ARTICLE

'To exercise the Union's competences, the institutions shall adopt regulations, directives, decisions, recommendations and opinions.'As well as defining the power of the institutions to introduce legislation, Art 288 also defines the different forms of secondary legislation. As can be seen from the wording of Art 288, it is their scope and effect which distinguish them from each other.

4.2.2 The different types of secondary legislation

Binding secondary legislation

Regulations

Regulations are defined in paragraph 2 of Art 288:

ARTICLE

'A regulation shall have general application. It shall be binding in its entirety and directly applicable in all Member States.'

The terminology used in the Article obviously needs to be understood in order to appreciate the scope and effect of a Regulation:

- 'General application' (otherwise referred to as 'general applicability') simply means that the measure applies generally to all Member States.
- 'Binding in its entirety' means that the Member States have no choice whether to give effect to the measure. They are bound by the regulation in its entirety.
- 'Directly applicable' (again commonly referred to as 'direct applicability') means that the measure automatically becomes law in each Member State on the date specified. The consequence of this is that there is no requirement for the State to implement the measure. (See section 9.1.)

It would be easy from the description given to compare regulations with Acts of Parliament in the UK. They automatically become law on the date specified and are absolutely binding.

Obviously, they also operate in this sense slightly differently to the Treaties themselves. Having a dualist constitution, the UK only became bound by the Treaties once they had been ratified and incorporated into UK law in the European Communities Act 1972. Once the UK had signed the Treaties and incorporated them into English law there is no similar requirement for the introduction of Regulations into English law. They are binding once introduced.

Regulations are also obviously capable of creating rights and obligations which are then directly enforceable in the national courts through the principle of direct effect (see Chapter 9): *Leonesio v Ministero dell'Agricoltora & delle Foreste* (Case 93/71) [1972] ECR 287.

Directives

Directives are defined in paragraph 3 of Art 288:

ARTICLE

> 'A directive shall be binding, as to the result to be achieved, upon each Member State to which it is addressed, but shall leave to the national authorities the choice of form and methods.'

Again, the wording in Art 288 indicates the scope and effect of Directives, although in this case there are more significant problems in terms of their possible effects as legislative measures.

The two key aspects to the paragraph are:

- 'binding as to the object to be achieved' and
- 'shall leave to the national authorities the choice of form and methods'.

The wording here is clearly significant. It indicates that Directives are quite unlike Regulations which are directly applicable and demand absolute uniformity. Instead, Directives are not directly applicable but are used to ensure that Member States adapt their own laws for the application of common standards. They are about the harmonisation of Member State law on specific issues.

As such, they leave an element of discretion to the Member States and allow the Member States to select what is for them the most appropriate method of implementation. However, they are bound to do so within a set deadline.

Because they are harmonising measures they are mainly used in those areas where the diversity of national laws could prevent the proper establishment or even the effective functioning of the Single Market. A classic example of this harmonising process can be found in the so-called 'sectoral Directives' introduced for the recognition of different professional and vocational qualifications under Art 49 for the furtherance of freedom of establishment. This also applies to the more generalised Directives 89/48 and 92/51 and the 'Slim Directive' 2001/19 (see Chapter 13).

In contrast, then, whereas a Regulation is applicable to all Member States as well as individual citizens alike, a Directive is really only intended to create legal obligations on the Member States. In this way directives were not originally seen as being intended to create rights that could be directly enforced by individuals. Nevertheless, to avoid the possibility of EU law being ignored by the Member States the ECJ has created the means to ensure that they can be enforced. This has been controversial and a more detailed explanation is given in Chapter 9, but the main ways are:

- **Vertical direct effect:** This is a process by which individuals may enforce an unimplemented Directive, provided that the date for implementation has passed (*Pubblico Ministero v Ratti* (Case 148/78) [1979] ECR 1629 and the claim is against either the state (*Marshall v Southampton and South West AHA (No 1)* (Case 152/84) [1986] QB 401 or an 'emanation of the state' (*Foster v British Gas plc* (Case C–188/89)) [1991] 1 QB 405.

- **Indirect effect:** This is the principle developed in *Von Colson v Land Nordhein–Westfalen* (Case (14/83) [1984] ECR 1891 and *Marleasing SA v La Commercial Internacional de Alimentacion SA* (Case C–106/89) [1990] ECR I–4135. The ECJ has held that, because Art 10 (now Art 4(3) TFEU) of the EC Treaty demands that Member States fulfil all Treaty obligations, national courts should interpret national law so as to give effect to the Directive whether it is ineffectively implemented or not implemented at all.
- **State liability:** This principle, stemming from the case of *Francovich v Italy* (Case C–6,9/90) [1991] ECR I–5357 holds that while there can be no horizontal direct effect based on a Directive as between ordinary individuals, an individual who has suffered loss as a result of the Member State's failure to implement a Directive may claim damages from the state.

Decisions

Decisions are defined in paragraph 4 of Art 288:

ARTICLE

> 'A decision shall be binding in its entirety. A decision which specifies those to whom it is addressed shall be binding only on them.'

The two key elements of the definition are:

- 'binding in its entirety'
- 'upon those to whom it is addressed'.

In terms of scope and effect, obviously the first point about a decision is its effect. A decision is immediately and totally binding on the party to whom it is addressed. As a result of this it is equally clear that a decision is capable of creating obligations that are then enforceable by third parties. For instance, see *Grad v Finanzamt Traustein* (Case 9/70) [1970] ECR 825.

The next point to make is that a decision is clearly not generally applicable as it may be addressed to a limited range of parties and not to the Community generally.

What is also clear is that decisions are the least easy form of legislation to define. They could be legally binding measures created according to a specific legal form. However, they could also be non-binding, informal acts which lay down guidelines. A common context for the use of decisions has been in EC competition law. (See Chapter 15.)

Non-legally binding secondary legislation: recommendations and opinions

Article 288 also gives the Commission the power to 'formulate recommendations' and also to 'deliver opinions'. The Article also identifies these as having no binding force.

As law, then, such measures can be seen as ineffective. Nevertheless, they are a useful means of clarifying issues in a less formal way than by introducing binding legislation.

While the measures are not enforceable as law, it is possible for them to have a persuasive effect on the Court of Justice in its decision-making. In fact, in *Grimaldi v Fonds des Maladies Professionelles* (Case 322/88) [1989] ECR 4407 the ECJ considered that national courts were bound to take recommendations and opinions into account in deciding cases. However, it is unlikely that this would be followed in practice.

	General applicability	**Direct applicability**	**Direct effect** (see Chapter 9)
Treaty Articles	These apply generally throughout the whole Community (so are generally applicable)	Once Treaty is incorporated there is no need for further enactment of Articles	Will have if they conform to the *Van Gend* (1963) criteria
Regulations	These apply generally throughout the whole Community (so are generally applicable)	These require no further implementation (so are directly applicable)	Will have if they conform to the *Van Gend* (1963) criteria
Directives	Usually addressed to all Member States (in which case are generally applicable)	These are an order for Member States to comply (so need implementation and are not directly applicable)	Vertical direct effect only (if unimplemented/ incorrectly implemented and past implementation date)
Decisions	Addressed to particular individuals (so are not generally applicable)	These are an order that must be complied with by the addressee	May confer rights on other individuals affected by them – so can be directly effective

ACTIVITY

Self-assessment questions

1. What are the three main secondary sources of law?
2. What is the significance of Art 288 TFEU?
3. What does the term 'direct applicability' mean?
4. In what ways does a Directive differ from a Regulation?
5. On whom would a Decision be binding? How wide could this definition be?
6. What is the legal effect of a recommendation?

4.3 Tertiary sources

4.3.1 The case law of the ECJ

The ECJ has played a vital role in the development of EU law. The Art 267 procedure is the major means by which the application of EU law in the Member States is tested (see Chapter 7). References from national courts under this procedure lead to binding interpretations of Treaty provisions and legislation.

The importance of the court in illuminating principles of EU law is obvious since the Treaties are framed in broad terms and cover broad principles. To a degree, the same point can be made, of the secondary legislation. The ECJ adds detail and context to these broad principles and provides more precise principles for the national courts in the Member States to follow.

The ECJ is unlike any court that we are familiar with in the UK. In character it is based on the continental 'civil' or 'Roman' law systems. As such, there is no strict system of binding precedent as exists in English law and, in theory, the court is not bound by its past decisions, as an English court would be.

In this way the court could be said in the strictest sense to have moral rather than legal authority and in a technical sense the court's decisions could be argued not to be a formal source of law. Nevertheless, a number of points could be made:

- firstly, it is true that the courts will not depart from its past decisions without good reason

- secondly, in its reasoning and in its judgments the courts as well as the General Court have shown a remarkable consistency over the years
- in any case the rules in *CILFIT v Ministry of Health* (Case 283/81) [1982] ECR 3415 on application of the preliminary reference procedure under Art 267 in essence prevents repetitious references by Member States trying to gain different rulings on the same principle of law
- finally, the court in any case has proved to be very 'legislatively active' in its eagerness to achieve the '*effet utile*' (effectiveness) in ensuring the attainment of the objectives of the Treaties.

In this sense the case law of the ECJ is in fact a major source of EU law and has been a key element in the development of EU law in two ways:

- it has defined the principles that apply in all of the main areas of substantive law, eg the 'Four Freedoms', discrimination law, competition law etc (see Chapters 10–19)
- it has ensured that the objectives of the Treaties are achieved in the Member States by developing the principles of supremacy and direct effect (see Chapters 8 and 9).

4.3.2 General principles of law

There was nothing in the original Treaties that directed the ECJ to apply general principles of law in deciding cases. Article 6(1) of the TEU, as amended by the Treaty of Amsterdam, does identify that the Union is founded on principles of liberty, democracy and the rule of law as well as respect for human rights and fundamental freedoms, and also principles that are common to the Member States.

However, the court has developed a number of unwritten principles that it will use when it interprets the Treaties and the secondary legislation. In doing so the court relied on the authority of Art 220 which obliges it to interpret provisions so as to ensure that the law is observed by the Member States. In this way the general principles of law have been recognised as binding on the institutions, the Member States, and indeed on individual citizens.

Subjecting interpretation of the law to general principles is not a novel idea. In fact, the practice is a familiar one in those states that have a 'civil' or 'Roman' law tradition. The general principles of law are in essence a statement of essential values and basic standards which are broad enough to be generally acceptable as principle. The process itself is not particularly controversial. It is the application of the general principles in specific situations that has been felt to be so at times.

Because a lot of EU law is essentially administrative, certain of the principles have derived quite naturally from the administrative law of both France and Germany. Nevertheless, some of the principles have their origins in UK law.

The main ones are:

- proportionality
- equality
- legal certainty
- natural justice
- the protection of fundamental human rights
- subsidiarity.

Proportionality

Proportionality is a concept that comes from German administrative law and is known as '*verhaltnismassigkeit*'. The basic principle is that any measure or any action taken must be proportionate to the actual end to be achieved. A simpler explanation would be to say that nothing should be done that is more than is necessary to achieve the end.

The idea of applying the principle of proportionality in EC law first came about in the *Internationale Handelsgesselschaft* case (*Internationale Handelsgesselschaft GmbH v*

Einfuhr und Vorratsstelle fur Getreide und Futtermittel (Case 11/70) [1970] ECR 1125). Here, the ECJ adopted the principle in the following terms:

JUDGMENT

'No burdens should be placed on the citizens except to the extent that it is necessary to achieve the purpose.'

The TEU also inserted this principle into the EC Treaty. The court will apply the principle in relation to legislation, for instance by determining whether the legislation goes beyond what is necessary to achieve the actual purpose in the Treaty provision behind the legislation.

CASE EXAMPLE

R v Intervention Board, ex p Man (Sugar) Ltd (Case 181/84)

Here, a sugar trader did not apply for export licences within the specified time. The bank where securities had to be lodged acted in accordance with Regulation 1880/83 and forfeited the securities, amounting to a loss of £1,670 to the trader. The ECJ, in a preliminary reference, accepted that this total forfeiture provided for by the Regulation was disproportionate to the actual offence committed by the trader when the licensing requirement under the Regulation was only intended to ensure sound management of the market. The court felt that the forfeiture procedure under the Regulation was therefore invalid.

The court also applies the principle when reviewing acts of the institutions, again, for example, in determining whether the action imposes too great a burden for the actual breach of EU law. An obvious context for this is the fines imposed for breaches of Arts 101 and 102 (see Chapter 16).

Another way in which the court has exercised the principle is in reviewing the actions of Member States when claming derogations under the various freedoms, particularly those in Art 36 in relation to the free movement of goods (see Chapter 14) and under Art 45(3) and Directive 2004/38 in relation to the free movement of workers (see Chapter 12).

CASE EXAMPLE

Italy v Watson and Belmann (Case 118/75) [1976] ECR 1185

A young English woman had settled in Italy with her Italian boyfriend but without obtaining the necessary work permit. When they split and the boyfriend reported her to Italian immigration authorities the penalty under Italian law was deportation. The ECJ held that this action was disproportionate to the required objective.

Equality

The concept of equal treatment or non-discrimination is not just a general principle; it is also one of the founding principles of the TEU itself. The original TEU included three specific prohibitions against discrimination:

- Art 18 prohibits any discrimination based on nationality (this is a base Article that also operates behind the various Treaty Articles creating the Common Market through the 'Four Freedoms')
- Art 157 demands that men and women shall receive equal pay for equal work (and has subsequently been extended to cover all discrimination between the sexes as well as other areas such as race and religion)
- Art 40 prohibits discrimination between producers and consumers in relation to the Common Agricultural Policy (CAP).

Besides this, the principle of equality was extended in the Treaty of Amsterdam, so the Treaty now includes a general aim of 'equality between men and women'. This is a major development since it is not restricted to work as it previously was. An even more impressive development gives the Council the power to legislate on discrimination in a much more general sense. Article 18 now allows the Council the power to take action to remove discrimination based on 'sex, race or ethnic origin, religion and belief, disability, age, and sexual orientation'. In fact, even before this the Commission was active in tackling discrimination and promoting equality. While English law included no specific provisions for tackling sexual harassment (so that women claiming had to use the residual category of 'subjecting to any other detriment' under s 6(2)(b) of the Sex Discrimination Act 1975) a Commission Code of Practice had defined 'sexual harassment' as any 'unwanted conduct of a sexual nature, or other conduct based on sex affecting the dignity of women and men at work'.

The ECJ has also been proactive in combating discrimination and advancing equality. In implementing the principle in Art 141 the court has identified in *Bilka-Kaufhaus GmbH v Weber von Hartz* (Case 170/84) [1986] ECR 1607 that unequal pay can only be accepted if it is based on objective justification. In defining 'objective justification' the court also relied on the principle of proportionality (see above). The idea of objective justification itself has subsequently been extended to apply to any inequality in *Graff v Hauptzollamt Kohn-Rheinau* (Case C–351/92) [1994] ECR I–3361.

Similarly, while English courts have accepted the legitimacy of discrimination against both transsexuals and gay people, the ECJ has been more prepared to apply the principle of equality in such cases. In *P v S and Cornwall County Council* (Case C–13/94) [1996] All ER (EC) 397 the court applied the principle of equality to the dismissal of a transsexual. While in *Grant v South West Trains Ltd* (Case C–249/96) [1998] All ER (EC) 193 the court did not feel bound to apply the principle to same-sex couples, who it felt were not in an 'equal situation' to heterosexual couples, the development in Art 13 is likely to see a change on this position.

The court has in any case already taken the principle of equality to extend to discrimination on religious grounds in *Prais v The Council* (Case 130/75) [1976] ECR 1589 (see further discussions in Chapters 17 and 18).

Legal certainty

This is not a novel concept and it is one that is familiar to most legal systems. The basic principle is that the law in its application must be both certain and predictable. This was identified at a very early stage in *Da Costa en Schaake NV v Nederlandse Belastingadministratie* (Cases 28 to 30/62) [1963] ECR 61. The court has subsequently stated in *Officer van Justitie v Kolpinghuis Nijmegen BV* (Case 80/86) [1987] ECR 3969 that it is the duty of national courts to interpret EU law in such a manner that is 'limited by the general principles of law' and also that in particular national courts should observe 'the principles of legal certainty and non-retroactivity'.

There are a number of potential consequences of applying the principle. One obvious consequence is that there should be no retroactive laws. This indeed was at least partly the case for refusing to say that Art 157 was retrospectively directly effective in *Defrenne v SABENA (No 2)* (Case 43/75) [1981] All ER 122. Of course, the judgment was affected by the objections by both the UK and Irish Governments and the ECJ did accept that this principle would only apply in exceptional cases where extreme difficulties would otherwise occur.

Legal certainty is also the basis of application of measures such as the Acquired Rights Directive 77/187. This in itself is demonstration of the fact that there is respect for acquired rights that cannot later be withdrawn. This in effect feeds into another aspect of the principle, that there should be protection of legitimate expectations. In simple terms it means that 'assurances relied on in good faith should be honoured'.

CASE EXAMPLE

Mulder v Minister of Agriculture and Fisheries (Case 120/86) [1988] ECR 2321

Here, a dairy farmer entered into an agreement not to supply milk for a period of five years in return for a payment. A regulation on milk quotas was then introduced during the period while this agreement was still in force. There was no provision within the quota system for farmers who had been party to the agreement, the effect of which was that the farmer would be prevented from supplying milk once the agreement was ended. The ECJ held that, on the basis of legitimate expectation, the farmer must be entitled to resume production and supply at the end of the agreement.

However, it must also be remembered that the institutions are still bound to act in furtherance of the objectives of the Treaties and the principle cannot be employed to frustrate that end.

CASE EXAMPLE

R v Ministry of Agriculture, Fisheries and Food, ex p Hamble (Offshore) Fisheries Ltd [1995] 2 All ER 714

The Ministry introduced a more stringent system for the granting of fishing licences in order to protect overworked fish stocks in UK waters. In the event, the Court of First Instance held that there was no infringement of the legitimate expectations of the holders of fishing licences since such arrangements must be allowed to cater for changes in circumstances.

JUDGMENT

'The principles of legal certainty and the protection of legitimate expectation are fundamental to European Community (now Union) law. Yet these principles are merely general maxims derived from the notion that the Community (now Union) is based on the rule of law and can be applied to individual cases only if expressed in enforceable rules … other principles … run counter to legal certainty and … the right balance will need to be struck.'

Natural justice

This is another concept that will be familiar to students of English constitutional law. In fact, the ECJ has on occasions referred to it simply as 'fairness'.

Within English law there are two distinct strands to the principle:

- the right to a fair and unbiased hearing and
- the right to be heard before the making of a potentially adverse decision is made.

A third aspect that is explicit in many areas of EU law is:

- the right to a reasoned decision.

The ECJ first addressed the right to a hearing at quite an early stage:

CASE EXAMPLE

Transocean Marine Paint Association v The Commission (Case 17/74) [1974] ECR 1063

Here, in a case involving an alleged breach of Art 81 (now Art 101), the Commission addressed a decision to the applicants but failed to make known a specific condition which was later applied against them. The ECJ accepted the applicants' argument that this aspect of the decision should be annulled. As the court identified, the applicants would be adversely affected by the condition but had never had the opportunity of a hearing to challenge it.

EU law in any case includes many express provisions that guarantee the principle. If Member States choose to claim the derogations under Directive 64/221 (now in Directive 2004/38) as applied to Arts 45, 49 or 56 then they must provide both a proper hearing and a right to appeal. Indeed, this is also the case when Member States make decisions on recognition of qualifications for establishment under Art 43 or provision of services under Art 49: Directives 89/48, 92/51 and the overarching 'Slim Directive' 2001/19 (now incorporated in the Qualifications directive 2005/36) (see Chapters 12 and 13). The ECJ has also enforced the principle in the case law on those areas.

Those Directives also guarantee the right to a reasoned decision. The ECJ has also upheld this right in the case law.

CASE EXAMPLE

Union Nationale des Entraineurs et Cadres Techniques Professionels du Football (UNECTEF) v Heylens (Case 222/86) [1987] ECR 4097

A Belgian football trainer with a Belgian diploma was refused the right to practise his trade in France but no hearing was held and no reason given for the decision. The ECJ held that this was a breach of process.

JUDGMENT

The court stated that: '[in] a question of securing the effective protection of a fundamental right conferred by the Treaty on Community (now EU) workers [they] must be able to defend that right under the best possible conditions and have the possibility of deciding, with a full knowledge of the relevant facts, whether there is any point in applying to the courts.'

The protection of fundamental human rights

There was no mention of human rights in the original EC Treaty. This is actually not all that surprising since the major concern of the Treaty was the creation of the Common Market, so it was essentially economic in its direction.

The first statement of the ECJ on the matter came in *Stauder v City of Ulm* (Case 29/69) [1969] ECR 419. Here, the court did little more than to confirm that there was nothing in the provision that was being challenged that was 'capable of prejudicing the fundamental human rights enshrined in the general principles of Community law and protected by the court'.

In *Internationale Handelsgesellschaft* (1970) the court was more explicit and more expansive in its statement:

JUDGMENT

'respect for fundamental human rights forms an integral part of general principles of law protected by the Court of Justice. The protection of such rights, while inspired by the constitutional traditions common to the member states, must be ensured within the framework of the structure and objectives of the European Community (now EU)'.

Now Art 11, guarantees human rights:

ARTICLE

'Art 11(1) The Union is founded on the principles of liberty, democracy, respect for human rights and fundamental freedoms, and the rule of law, principles which are common to the member states.

(2) The Union shall respect fundamental rights as guaranteed by the European Convention for the Protection of Human Rights and Fundamental Freedoms signed in Rome on 4 November 1950 and as they result from the constitutional traditions common to the member states, as general principles of Community law.'

Article 11(2) means that the ECJ is able to apply the principles found in the Convention provided that the issue in question is a matter that is within the competence of the Community to deal with. The consequence is that the court can rule that a national measure that breaches the Convention is in breach of EU law too. Besides this, the Council has been given the power to suspend the voting rights of any Member State that is found to be in breach of the principle.

Decisions of the ECJ have taken into account many of the Articles of the European Convention of Human Rights. A classic example concerns Arts 6 and 13 of the Convention, concerning the right to a fair trial and the right to an effective remedy respectively.

CASE EXAMPLE

Johnston v Chief Constable of the Royal Ulster Constabulary (RUC) (Case 222/84) [1987] QB 129

Here, a female officer claimed that the RUC policy of not issuing firearms to female officers was in breach of Directive 76/207 '(now contained in the Recast Directive) and that the effect of the policy was that it acted as a bar to the promotion of female officers. The RUC claimed that the policy was justified on grounds of public safety and national security and was in any case authorised by a statutory instrument. The Secretary of State for Northern Ireland issued Mrs Johnston with a certificate confirming the point conclusively. The ECJ held that the certificate in effect deprived the applicant of a judicial hearing or remedy and so would be in breach of EC (now EU) law.

The meeting of the European Council at Cologne in 1999 decided that a Charter of Fundamental Rights for the EU should be drawn up in order to provide a more visible means of protection of the citizens of the Union. A Draft Charter has subsequently been produced which was signed by all of the then 15 Member States at Nice in 2000. This is based on six fundamental values: dignity, freedom, equality, solidarity, citizenship and justice. The Charter contains a number of express rights including quite diverse ones such as freedom of scientific research and the right to good administration. Most rights cover all citizens of the Union although some are specifically directed at particular groups such as children. The Commission has called for the Charter to be incorporated into the Treaties to gain the force of law, although the UK has been consistently against this.

Subsidiarity

Subsidiarity is also not a new concept. In fact, there were references to the principle in the founding Treaties which identified that decisions should be taken as closely as possible to the citizens that are affected by them.

However, at the insistence of the UK the principle was also incorporated into the EC Treaty by the TEU. Article 5 provided that:

ARTICLE

'Art 5 In areas which do not fall within its exclusive competence, the community shall take action, in accordance with the principle of subsidiarity, only if and in so far as the objectives of the proposed action cannot be sufficiently achieved by the Member States and can therefore, by reason of the scale or effects of the proposed action, be better achieved by the community.'

In simple terms, then, the principle is that the institutions of the Union should only act to introduce measures where it is more appropriate than for the Member States to act individually. The result is in effect a two-part test:

- it must be determined that the measure is one which is within the competence of EU law to deal with and

- introduction of EU measures can only then be justified if this serves an end which:
  - cannot be achieved satisfactorily at national level and
  - can be achieved in a more satisfactory way by the EU.

4.3.3 Other tertiary sources

There are certain other tertiary sources of less certain legality. These are of three main types:

- **Acts adopted by representatives of Member State governments meeting in Council.** (The Council is part of the legislative process under Art 288. However, meetings of representatives of the Member States in the Council are also used to decide on various joint action. This is a quick and easy method of making decisions that fall outside the competence of the EU. While resolutions coming out of such meetings do not have the full force of law, the ECJ will consider them. An example is *Commission v Council (Re ERTA)* (Case 22/70) [1971] ECR 263 on the legality of an agreement to co-ordinate approaches in negotiation towards a European Road Transport Agreement)
- **National law of Member States** (National law is not formally recognised as being part of EU law. There are, however, two instances when it will be taken into account: firstly, where Community law actually makes reference to national law, as, for example, in determining the legal status of individuals, ie capacity; secondly, where national law has developed EU law and the ECJ looks to that law for guidance when there is a gap in the law)
- **International Treaties negotiated by the EU** (This refers to multinational Treaties to which the EU is a party. An example would be the General Agreement on Tariffs and Trade (GATT). In *International Fruit Co NV v Produktschap voor Groenten en Fruit* (Cases 21 & 22/72) [1972] ECR 1219 the ECJ held that GATT could be referred to when determining what practices breach Community (now EU) commercial policy).

ACTIVITY

Self-assessment questions

1. In what ways has the case law of the ECJ been an important source of law?
2. In what ways do the judges of the ECJ apply the 'general principles of law'?
3. What does the term 'proportionality' mean and what is its practical effect?
4. What are the differences between 'legal certainty' and 'natural justice'?
5. In what ways is it true to say that the principle of 'human rights' has developed in significance?
6. How does the principle of 'subsidiarity' affect the supranational character of the EU?

SAMPLE ESSAY QUESTION

'Discuss the relative importance of the different sources of law of the European Union to the development of EU law.'

Explain that there are different sources:
- Primary – the Treaties (particularly TFEU)
- Secondary – the legislation – regulations, directives and decisions (and also recommendations and opinions)
- Tertiary – the ECJ case law and the general principles of law.

Explain the character of the different legislation under Art 288:
- Regulations – generally applicable, binding in their entirety, and directly applicable
- Directives – binding as to the effect to be achieved – so subject to implementation by MSs within time limit
- decisions – binding in their entirety on the party to whom they are addressed
- recommendations/opinions – persuasive only.

Explain the character of the tertiary sources:
- case law of the ECJ – all MSs are bound by the rulings of the court which then becomes binding on national law
- general principles of law underpins judgment, eg proportionality.

Discuss the significance of the Treaties:
- these regulate the Union but also contain much substantive law:
- MSs have signed accession treaty and so accept all of the objectives of the Treaty and all subsequent legislation which becomes part of the law of each MS
- treaties provide only a framework and broad objectives – so the interpretation given by ECJ allows EU law to be applied harmoniously.

Discuss the significance of the secondary sources:

- all other sources of law are invalid unless they achieve the objectives of the Treaty
- the binding nature and general applicability of regulations means they present no problem
- the binding nature of decisions – but also the narrow focus
- the key purpose of directives is harmonisation – but they are conditional and may be implemented in different ways – so problems of enforceability
- other secondary legislation is non-binding.

Discuss the significance of tertiary sources:

- ECJ has been proactive in the creation of supremacy, direct effect, etc – so the development of the legal order has really depended on the judges
- unique nature and effectiveness of the general principles of law.

KEY FACTS

Primary sources	
The Treaties	• ECSC (1951), EURATOM (1957), EC Treaty (1957) – created the Community – based on legal order. • Merger Treaty (1965) – merged communities and institutions. • Single European Act (SEA) (1986) – put in place the Common Market. • Treaty on European Union (TEU) (1992) – created the Union and some new institutions. • Treaty of Amsterdam (1997) – re-numbered the Articles of the EC Treaty – some institutional reform. • Treaty of Nice (2000) – institutional reform in preparation for enlargement. NB: The EC Treaty, as amended, identifies the aims, tasks, and activities of the Community (and the Union).
Secondary sources	
Defined in Art 288	
Regulations	• Binding in their entirety. • Generally applicable. • Directly applicable. • Directly effective if satisfy *Van Gend en Loos* (1963) criteria (*Leonesio v Ministero dell'Agricoltora & delle Foreste* (1972)).
Directives	• Binding as to the result to be achieved. • But method of implementation left to Member State. • Cannot be 'horizontally' directly effective because dependent (*Marshall v Southampton AHA (No 1)* (1986)).

	• But can be 'vertically' directly effective if time for implementation passed (*Pubblico Ministero v Ratti* (1979)) and if against State or emanation of the State (*Foster v British Gas plc* (1991)).
Decisions	• Binding in their entirety on party to whom addressed. • Can be directly effective if satisfy *Van Gend en Loos* (1963) criteria (*Grad v Finanzamt Traustein* (1970))
Recommendations and opinions	• 'Soft law' – not binding. • But can be persuasive (*Grimaldi v Fonds des Maladies Professionelles* (1989))
Tertiary sources	
Case law of ECJ	Instrumental in developing, eg supremacy, direct effect etc.
General principles of law:	
Proportionality	No measure should place a burden on a citizen beyond what is necessary to achieve the purpose (*Internationale Handelsgesselschaft* (1970))
Equality	Evidence in Art 18 no discrimination on nationality, Art 157 equality between men and women
Legal certainty	The law must be both certain and predictable (*Da Costa en Schaake v Nederlandse Belastingadministratie* (1963))
Natural justice	The right to an unbiased hearing, the right to be heard, the right to a reasoned decision (*UNECTEF v Heylens* (1987))
Human rights	Now in Art 6 – The Union is founded on the principles of liberty, democracy, respect for human rights and fundamental freedoms, and the rule of law.
Subsidiarity	Now in Art 5 – EU should only act if result cannot be achieved satisfactorily at national level; and can be achieved in a more satisfactory way by the Community.
Other sources	• Acts of Member States in Council. • National law. • International Treaties negotiated by EC.

SUMMARY

- The sources of EU law are of three types: primary, secondary and tertiary.
- Primary sources are the Treaties themselves, and as well as outlining the objectives and indicating the roles of the institutions and processes these also contain much substantive law.
- Secondary sources are the legislation from Art 288 TFEU – the main three types are regulations, directives and decisions.
- The main tertiary sources are the case law of the Court of Justice and the general principles of law – many of the major principles of EU Law, eg supremacy – have developed from the case law.

Further reading

Articles

Meyring, B, 'Intergovernmentalism and Supranationality: Two Stereotypes for a Complex Reality' (1997) 22 ELR 221.

Wouters, J, 'Institutional and Constitutional Challenges for the European Union: Some Reflections in the Light of the Treaty of Nice' (2001) 26 ELR 342.

Books

Ward, I, *A Critical Introduction to European Law* (Butterworths, 1996), Chapter 1.

5

The legislative process

AIMS AND OBJECTIVES

After reading this chapter you should be able to:
- Understand the different legislative processes
- Understand the role of the institutions in the different legislative processes
- Understand the context in which the different legislative processes operate
- Analyse the reasons for the development of different processes
- Evaluate the democratic effectiveness of the processes

5.1 The role of the institutions

The process of legislating within EU law appears to be quite complex. One of the reasons for this is that all rules and procedures for legislating are laid down in the Treaties at different points. Every EU law is based on a specific Treaty Article, in this case referred to as the 'legal basis' of the legislation. The second reason is that there are different processes of legislating and the appropriate process depends on the particular area of the Treaty objectives that requires legislating.

The process of legislating has been modified very significantly since the original Treaties, as the result of the different subsequent Treaties. The introduction of new legislative procedures arose from the criticism of the early legislative process that there was a so-called 'democratic deficit', in other words that those institutions that existed on the basis of appointment rather than election controlled the processes. This democratic deficit was considered to be particularly true of the role of Parliament which originally had little effect on the legislative process other than to suggest amendments. The Lisbon Treaty has modified and simplified the legislative process and now most legislation is created under the co-decision procedure.

The three institutions mainly involved in the legislative process are:
- The **Commission** (the body mainly responsible for 'proposing' legislation and producing draft legislation; in short it is for the Commission to initiate legislation except where the Treaties provide otherwise).
- Parliament (which either has a consultative role or in certain instances can propose amendments).
- **Council** (the body that in effect is responsible for passing new legislation).

Other institutions also have a role in terms of receiving draft proposals for legislation and providing consultation, particularly the Economic and Social Committee and the Committee of the Regions. COREPER, of course, has a role to play in supporting Council through all legislation.

Prior to the Treaty of Lisbon there were basically four types of legislative procedure that were now possible within the Community legal order. However, it is also true that there are limited circumstances where the Commission is authorised to legislate on its own and there are other instances where the Council and Commission can act without consulting Parliament, although in practice they still do.

The four main processes were:

- the proposal (or consultation) procedure
- the co-operation procedure (this has now been discontinued)
- the co-decision procedure (this is now the main legislative process now known as the ordinary legislative procedure under Art 294 TFEU)
- the process of assent.

The proposal procedure was in fact the original legislative procedure which was used prior to the SEA.

Because of the criticism that there was insufficient accountability, the so-called 'democratic deficit', a new procedure was introduced in the SEA to give Parliament a greater and more meaningful role. This was the **'co-operation procedure'**. It was introduced to provide a relatively straightforward means of involving the European Parliament, which would have two readings of the draft proposals. It was also based entirely on Qualified Majority Voting by Council. Its main context was for Internal Market measures. Although it was introduced to reduce the democratic deficit and did indeed succeed in giving Parliament a greater level of involvement, the procedure was still criticised:

QUOTATION

> 'Although it increased the involvement of the Parliament, the cooperation procedure was criticised for having the following weaknesses: that the Council of Ministers could still overrule the Parliament in any case and that the Parliament had been given a dubious benefit in the power to hinder EC legislation (as the Parliament prefers to be seen as a positive force in the legislative process). In fact by 1997, only 21 per cent of Parliament's amendments had been accepted by the Council at the second reading. However [it] did instil changes in inter-institutional relationships … greater dialogue between Council and Parliament [and] between the Parliament and the Commission, which introduced considerable internal reforms to accommodate the … procedure.'
>
> S Douglas-Scott, *Constitutional Law of the European Union* (Longman, 2002), p 119

The TEU then introduced the predominant process nowadays: the **'co-decision procedure'** (now the ordinary legislative procedure under Art 294 TFEU). A complex process originally, it has subsequently been somewhat modified by the Treaty of Amsterdam for the sake of simplification. Use of the procedure has been expanded by the Treaty of Nice and by the Treaty of Lisbon.

Finally, the **'assent procedure'** was in some ways similar to the co-decision procedure. It was first introduced in the SEA and then extended by the TEU.

The most significant difference between the different procedures was the involvement of Parliament. Under the consultation procedure, for instance, Parliament only gave its opinion on draft legislation. By contrast, in the co-decision procedure (now the ordinary legislative procedure) Parliament in effect shares power with the Council and has much more influence over legislation.

Following the Treaty of Lisbon coming into force, the ordinary legislative procedure (formerly the co-decision procedure) is the major process for legislating. It involves an active role by all three institutions, including Parliament.

As a result of the Treaty of Lisbon, Art 5(1) TEU requires for a process of conferral to limit the competences of the EU to legislate in particular areas. Where the EU institutions are not granted competence in the Treaties then there may be shared competence with the Member States, or the EU may act to support, co-ordinate or supplement the actions of Member States.

Areas where the EU institutions have exclusive competence are: the customs union, competition rules, monetary policy for member states in the euro zone, marine biology and fisheries policy and international agreements.

5.2 The ordinary legislative procedure (formerly the co-decision procedure)

The TEU introduced the process known as the 'co-decision procedure'. The aim was to give far greater power to Parliament by allowing it not only to suggest significant amendments but also ultimately to have some right of veto on draft legislation. In this respect it can be said that Council and Parliament share legislative power. The process was amended and simplified by the Treaty of Amsterdam and to a lesser extent by the Treaty of Nice. Following the Treaty of Lisbon this is now the ordinary legislative procedure used for most legislation.

Parliament gains more power because after it proposes amendments Council must then consider them before it acts and if Parliament rejects the proposals then the act is not adopted. Both Council and Parliament have two readings of the proposal and if they cannot agree then the measure is put before a 'conciliation committee' which is made up of members from both institutions in equal numbers. Both bodies then hold a third reading so that they may finally adopt the proposal as law.

After the first consultation of Parliament Council may adopt the proposal by Qualified Majority Vote if either:

- it agrees with all of Parliament's amendments or
- Parliament has not made any amendments.

If this is not the case then Council adopts a 'common position' by Qualified Majority Vote which is then communicated to Parliament. Within three months if Parliament either approves the common position or does nothing then Council can adopt the common position.

Parliament can, however, within this three-month period:

- reject the common position by absolute majority of MEPs – in which case this acts like a veto and the measure cannot be adopted or
- propose new amendments by an absolute majority.

If new amendments are introduced these are forwarded to the Commission which itself has three choices:

- it can accept them all or
- it can reject them all or
- it can selectively accept some and reject others.

On receiving Parliament's amendments Council also has choices:

- it can approve them all and adopt the amended measure by Qualified Majority Vote or
- it can fail to adopt the proposal and convene a 'Conciliation Committee'.

Within six weeks the committee then has two choices:

- it can approve a new joint proposal decided upon by the committee which can then be adopted by Parliament by absolute majority and Council by qualified majority or
- it can fail to find any possible compromise, in which case the measure is not adopted.

The procedure can be explained in diagram form as in Figure 5.2.

The development of the procedure through both the Treaty of Amsterdam and the Treaty of Nice means that the procedure is now used for most areas of legislation. These now include:

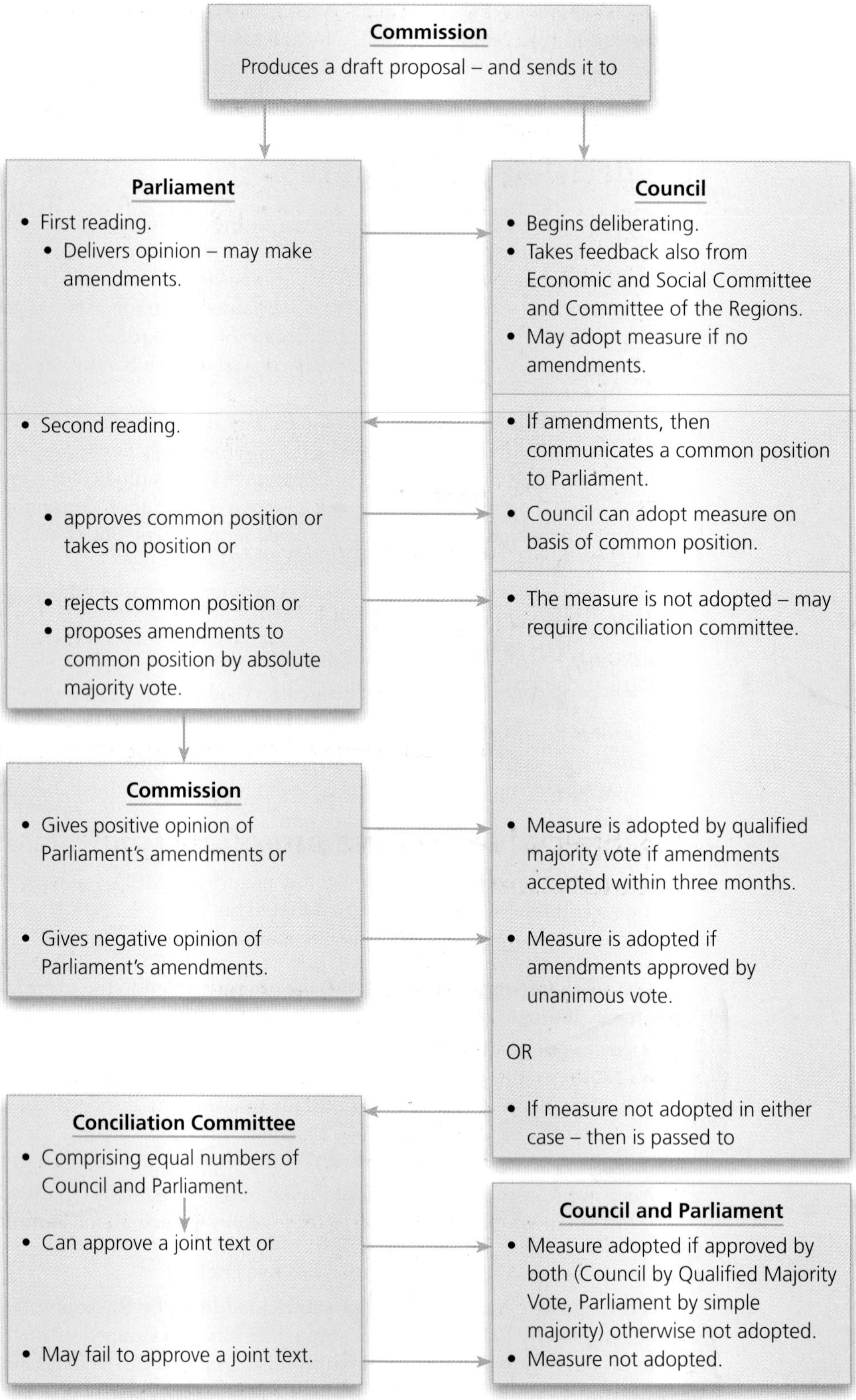

Figure 5.2 The different stages in the ordinary legislative procedure (formerly the co-decision procedure)

- non-discrimination on the basis of nationality
- the right to move and to reside
- the free movement of workers and social security for migrant workers
- the right of establishment
- transport
- employment
- Customs co-operation
- the fight against social exclusion
- equal opportunities and equal treatment
- implementing decisions involving the European Social Fund or the Regional Development Fund
- education and vocational training
- culture
- health
- consumer protection
- trans-European networks
- research
- the environment
- transparency
- the prevention of fraud
- statistics
- the setting up of a data protection advisory body.

> 'Initial reactions were … critical. "the effective balance of power indisputably weighted toward the Council". However, following Amsterdam, the legislative balance seems to have shifted in Parliament's favour. Parliament may reject outright the Council's common position at the second reading, thus effectively having the final say in adoption of legislation … Parliament at last has some real power.'
>
> S Douglas-Scott, *Constitutional Law of the European Union* (Longman, 2002), p 120

5.3 Special legislative procedure (previously consultation)

This was the original process used for all legislation. Following the Treaty of Nice, it was still the basis for the adoption of certain general EC (now EU) instruments or policy areas. Examples are in Art 64(3) TFEU and Art 86(1) TFEU.

This procedure most accurately represents the notion that it is the Commission that 'proposes' and the Council that 'disposes'.

Nevertheless, the process still depends also on some consultation with Parliament as well as with the Economic and Social Committee or the Committee of the Regions, and discussions in COREPER. Failure genuinely to consult may amount to a breach of an essential procedural requirement. On this basis it may result in the measure being declared void.

The importance of consultation was recognised by the ECJ in *Roquette Frères SA v Council* (Case 138/79) [1980] ECR 3333.

JUDGMENT

> 'consultation … represents an essential factor in the institutional balance intended by the Treaty. Although limited, it reflects … the fundamental principle that the peoples should take part in the exercise of power through the intermediary of a representative assembly. Due consultation of Parliament in the cases provided for by the Treaty therefore constitutes an essential formality disregard of which means that the measure concerned is void.'

The process involves the Commission sending its proposal to both Council and Parliament, as well as one of the committees if appropriate. The measure cannot then become law until Parliament has delivered its opinion. Even so, Council has the final say.

QUOTATION

> 'this … is undermined somewhat by the fact that there is no requirement that Council actually take account of the Parliament's opinion, nor indeed, give any reason for rejecting it. Thus in the context of the Consultation procedure, the Parliament may not force its opinion on the Council as a lower house could in most … systems.'
>
> S Douglas-Scott, *Constitutional Law of the European Union* (Longman, 2002), p 118

So this was one more justification that there was a democratic deficit in the administration and law-making of the EC.

The process can be explained in diagram form, as shown in Figure 5.3.

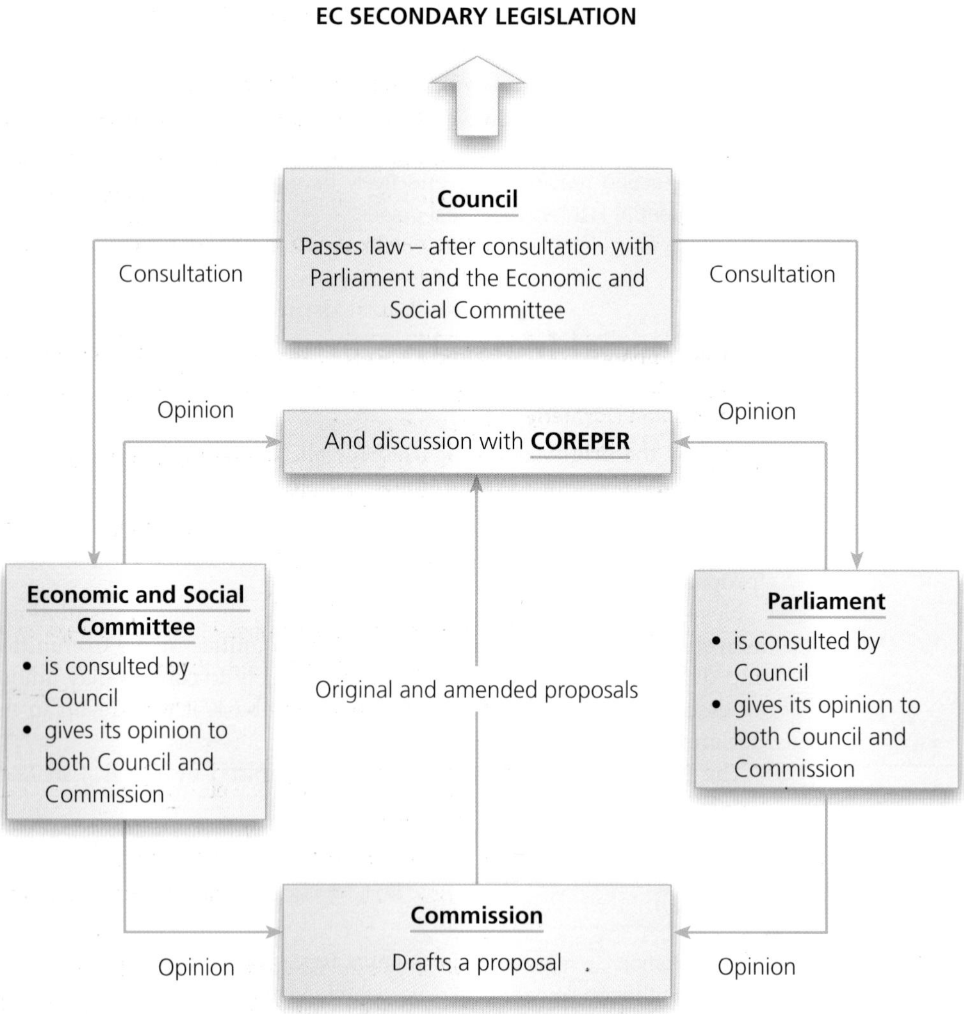

Figure 5.3 The different stages in the proposal (consultation) procedure

ACTIVITY

Self-assessment questions

1. What institutions have a role to play in the legislative process?
2. In what way is COREPER important to the legislative process?
3. Why was the co-decision procedure introduced?
4. In what ways is Parliament's role different under the co-decision procedure?
5. How is a 'conciliation committee' comprised and what does it do?
6. What is the effect on the Commission of the changes in the legislative process?
7. What has been the effect on (i) unanimous voting and (ii) Qualified Majority Voting in Council of the changes to the legislative procedure?

KEY FACTS

The role of the institutions	Three main institutions involved: • Commission – drafts new legislation (proposes) • Parliament – has consultative role or can make amendments and sometimes veto, depending on process • Council – votes on legislation. Three others involved in process: • COREPER – permanent body supporting Council Ministers • Social and Economic Committee – consultative role • Committee of the Regions – consultative role.
The co-operation	Introduced by SEA to give Parliament more involvement, but its use was limited after ToA. Now only used for EMU.
The ordinary legislative procedure (formerly the co-decision procedure	Introduced by TEU and simplified by Treaty of Amsterdam and Treaty of Nice retained after Treaty of Lisbon and now the main legislative procedure. Involves two readings by both Parliament and Council – and possibly a 'conciliation committee': • draft legislation sent by Commission to Council and Parliament which sends an 'opinion' • Parliament may suggest amendments • Council can adopt proposal by qualified majority if either: • agrees with all of Parliament's amendments or • Parliament has made no amendments or:

	• Council adopts 'common position' by qualified majority and sends to Parliament
	• within three months Parliament can approve common position or
	• if does nothing then Council can adopt the common position
	or:
	• within three-month period Parliament can:
	  • reject common position by absolute majority of MEPs – acts like veto and measure cannot be adopted or
	  • propose new amendments by an absolute majority

	• if amendments introduced, then are sent to Commission which can:
	  • accept them all or
	  • reject them all or
	  • selectively accept some and reject others
	• Council can then either:
	  • approve them all and adopt by qualified majority or
	  • fail to adopt and convene a 'Conciliation Committee'.
	• within six weeks, committee has two choices:
	  • can approve new joint proposal decided upon by committee which can then be adopted by Parliament by absolute majority and Council by qualified majority or
	  • can fail to find any compromise, then measure is not adopted.
	Procedure is now used for most areas.

SUMMARY

- Originally most legislation was introduced through the proposal procedure which had a very limited role for Parliament.
- Complaints of a 'democratic deficit' led to the introduction of the co-operation procedure, which involved greater consultation of Parliament but still little power to influence legislation.
- Following the ToA, and with modification by ToN, the co-decision procedure was introduced – this is now known as the ordinary legislative procedure, it is used for most legislation and gives Parliament greater powers to make amendments and influence their outcome.

Further reading

Articles

Dashwood, A, 'The Constitution of the European Union after Nice: law-making procedures' (2001) 26 ELR 215.

Books

Douglas-Scott, S, *Constitutional Law of the European Union* (Longman, 2002), Chapter 3.

Fairhurst, J, *Law of the European Union* (8th edn, Pearson 2010), Chapter 4.

Steiner, J and Woods, L, *Textbook on EC Law* (8th edn, Oxford University Press, 2003), Chapter 3.

6

Enforcement of EU law (through 'direct' and 'indirect' actions)

AIMS AND OBJECTIVES

After reading this chapter you should be able to:

- Understand the nature and purpose of enforcement actions
- Understand the procedure for indirect actions against Member States for breaches of EU obligations
- Understand which breaches give rise to an action and the defences that can be raised by a Member State
- Understand the processes for direct actions against EU institutions for exceeding their powers, for a failure to act, and actions for damages
- Understand the significance of locus standi
- Understand the grounds for review of acts of EU institutions
- Understand the rules relating to claims for damages
- Evaluate the effectiveness of enforcement procedures

6.1 The nature and purpose of enforcement

'Enforcement' in simple terms refers to the actions created in the EC Treaty (now TFEU) for the purpose of ensuring that both the Member States and the institutions of the EU comply with their relative obligations within the Treaties.

The Treaties and their secondary legislation clearly create many and various substantive rights and obligations by which all parties to the Treaties are bound. These substantive rights and obligations granted under Treaties would, nevertheless, be left completely ineffective if they were left merely to the co-operation of Member States without the means of enforcing them.

Similarly, it would also be possible that the individual rights might be abused by the institutions of the EU themselves.

For these reasons the framers of the EC Treaty were wise enough to include a variety of enforcement proceedings, and the methods for reviewing the actions of both the institutions and the Member States. These were then placed under the scrutiny of the ECJ, with individuals able to gain remedies following actions in their favour.

These procedures are generally referred to as the 'direct actions'. They supplement the 'indirect actions' of the Art 267 reference procedure (considered in Chapter 7).

The measures are broadly based in that they allow a wide range of applicants to take the initiative in setting an action in motion and bringing proceedings. So this might include, eg, other institutions of the EU, as well as private citizens in certain circumstances.

There are essentially four types of action to be considered here:

- actions under Art 258 (formerly Art 226) – against Member States – for a failure to honour their Treaty obligations (and generally known as 'infringement proceedings')
- actions under Art 263 (formerly Art 230) – against institutions of the EU – for acting in excess of their actual powers – since the powers of the various institutions are defined in the Treaties, and since, in legislating, the institutions are only capable of acting for furtherance of the actual objectives of the Treaties
- actions under Art 265 (formerly Art 232) – again against the institutions of the EU – in this case for a failure to act when they are required to act
- actions under Art 340 (formerly Art 288) – once again this is an action against the institutions – this action, though, is an action for damages, compensating a citizen for loss caused by one of the institutions, so it is inevitably linked with grievances pursued under the previous two.

6.2 Indirect actions – Art 258 infringement proceedings against Member States

6.2.1 Actions against Member States under Arts 258 and 259

It is in the very nature of EU law that it depends on a partnership between the Member States and the institutions. This can be seen, for instance, in the implementation of Directives where the legislation is created under the various processes (see Chapter 5 and also section 4.2.2) but in the form of a written obligation containing various objectives that the Member States must incorporate into their national law but in a manner of their choosing and within an implementation period set by the Council.

While this partnership exists, it is not uncommon for Member States to show carelessness in implementing them (eg this was the case in the deficiencies in UK sex discrimination law in relation to the issue of different retirement ages for men and women based on state pension ages highlighted in the case of *Marshall v Southampton and South West AHA* (Case 152/84) [1986] QB 401). It is even possible that Member States may show real reluctance in fulfilling their obligations. (An obvious example of this is the arguments presented by the Tory Government before 1997 in refusing to implement the Working Time Directive, despite its argument of an opt-out applying to the provision having been rejected out of hand by the ECJ.)

It is because of these possibilities that the Treaty sensibly provided the means of calling Member States to account for their failures to honour Treaty and legislative obligations. The process can be initiated in one of two ways:

- in most cases the process would normally be invoked by the Commission under Art 258
- however, it is also possible for proceedings to be initiated by other Member States under Art 259.

6.2.2 Actions by the Commission under Art 258

The Commission has always been described as the 'watchdog of the Treaties' and so it was empowered by Art 258 to act in such manner monitoring the behaviour of Member States and, if necessary, enforcing compliance with Treaty and other obligations. It therefore has *locus standi* in Art 258 actions.

Article 258 itself provides the following:

ARTICLE

> 'Art 258 … if the Commission considers that a member state has failed to fulfil an obligation under the Treaty it shall deliver a reasoned opinion on the matter after giving the state concerned the opportunity to submit its observations. If the state concerned does not comply with the opinion within the period laid down by the Commission, the latter may bring the matter before the Court of Justice of the European Union.'

As a result, it is possible to identify three clear purposes of the Art 258 action:

- to ensure that Member States comply with their Treaty obligations
- to provide a procedure for resolution of disputes between the Commission and Member States (it must be noted in this respect that four-fifths of disputes are actually settled within the preliminary stages)
- where proceedings do nevertheless end up in the ECJ, the action also provides a means of clarifying the law for all Member States to follow in the future.

There are in fact three formal stages in the procedure. However, these are usually preceded by an informal stage.

The informal stage

Mediation

Once the possibility of non-compliance has been notified, the Commission at first engages in informal discussions with the Member State. The Commission identifies the nature of the breach by the Member State and will prescribe a time limit within which it expects the Member State to comply. Usually the Member State is prepared to remedy its mistake at this point, as a result of which the action is generally then suspended.

Formal stages

Formal notice of default

It may be that the Commission is dissatisfied with the response of the Member State. If this is the case then the Commission issues a notice inviting the Member State to submit its own observations on the alleged non-compliance.

It is this stage that in effect defines exactly what the failure by the Member State is and therefore also the terms of reference of the action. These are then fixed and the Commission cannot afterwards extend the scope of the action.

CASE EXAMPLE

> *Commission v Italy (Re Payment of Export Rebates)* (Case 31/69) [1970] ECR 25
>
> Here, Italy was alleged to be in breach of its Community obligations by failing to pay certain rebates to farmers, in line with Community policy. The Italian Government then rectified the breach and to a certain extent paid rebates in respect of breaches falling before 1967. It did not, however, pay for certain rebates occurring after that time. Since the Commission's notice of default had not included those breaches either, the ECJ was unable to refer to them or give judgment.

Reasoned opinion

If the notice of default fails to force the Member State into remedial action and it has still not complied with its obligations then the Commission issues a reasoned opinion.

This formal document sets out all the reasons why the Commission considers that the Member State is in default. The reasoned opinion also sets a time limit within which the Commission expects the Member State to act.

Nevertheless, the reasoned opinion is not a binding act in its own right, as a result of which action in the Court of Justice may still be necessary.

CASE EXAMPLE

Alfons Lütticke GmbH v Hauptzollamt Sarrelouis (Case 57/65) [1966] ECR 205

Here, Lütticke was unable to ask the Commission to bring an action under Art 226 [now Art 258 TFEU]. His complaint concerned a tax on powdered milk by Germany. However, the German Government had already withdrawn the tax to comply with the Commission and Lütticke was unable to use either Art 230 or Art 232 [now Arts 263 and 265] in respect of losses that had been suffered before the proceedings.

Court proceedings in the ECJ

Court proceedings depend on the action taken by the Member State following the earlier proceedings. If the Member State still fails to comply even after the other stages then the Commission will bring an action in the ECJ.

Nevertheless, it is still possible for the action to be settled even without a decision of the Court. Interim relief under Art 243 is an example of this. In fact, something in the region of 44 per cent of cases are settled at this point without further court action.

There are, of course, many defences that Member States have attempted to use, but most have failed:

- Member States have tried to claim that internal difficulties have genuinely prevented them from meeting their obligations:

CASE EXAMPLE

Commission v Belgium (Case 77/69) [1970] ECR 237

Here, Belgium was in breach of Art 90 [now Art 110 TFEU] for a discriminatory tax on wood. The Belgian Government argued that an amendment was actually put before its Parliament but never gained force because Parliament was dissolved in the meantime. It argued that it was thus prevented from legislating and that the breach was, therefore, beyond its control. The ECJ would not accept this reasoning.

JUDGMENT

The court identified that 'liability under [Art 258] arises whatever the agency of the State whose action or inaction is the cause of the failure to fulfil its obligations'.

- reciprocity has also been argued – that national compliance is dependent on compliance by the other Member States:

CASE EXAMPLE

Commission v France (Re restrictions on lamb imports) (Case 232/78) [1979] ECR 2729

Here, the French Government tried to argue that its ban on British lamb could be justified on the ground that it was not the only state in breach. The argument had no substance in law and failed.

- Member States have also argued the application of *force majeure* – that they are excused from acting when the circumstances are beyond the control of the national authorities:

CASE EXAMPLE

Commission v Italy (Case 101/84) [1985] ECR 2629

Here, it was held that the concept of force majeure could not be used as a defence where the Italian state had failed to provide statistical data as required, with the excuse that the database had been destroyed in a bomb attack. This was rejected because the data could easily have been replaced by the time the action took place.

- failing to act because of internal political difficulties such as objections by trade unions has also been rejected as a defence:

CASE EXAMPLE

Commission v UK (Case 128/78) [1978] ECR 419

Here, there was much controversy surrounding the proposed introduction of tachographs to which many hauliers were objecting. This was not accepted by the ECJ as sufficient justification for avoiding obligations under EC [now EU] law.

- Member States have also tried to justify breaches of EU law on ethical grounds:

CASE EXAMPLE

Commission v Poland C-165/08 [2009] ECR I–6843

Poland tried to argue that its law prohibiting the growing of genetically modified foods was justified on ethical and religious grounds, despite the law being inconsistent with an EU directive, and that the government was bound to respect the wishes of the Catholic majority. The Court of Justice held that Poland had breached its obligation, which could not be justified on populist grounds, although it made no decision on whether ethical or religious grounds are a justification.

Enforcement

Before the signing of the Maastricht Treaty (TEU) decisions made by the ECJ lacked the possibility of actual enforcement. Because of this, repeated failure by a Member State to comply would simply lead to further Art 258 proceedings.

Following the TEU it was possible under Art 258 for a financial penalty to be imposed on the Member State. An example of this is in *Commission v Greece* (Case C–387/97) [2000] ECR I–5047 which concerned the dumping of toxic waste. The Court of Justice applied a penalty, taking into account guidelines issued by the Commission. The penalty is based on a basic sum for every day of the breach, multiplied by other significant factors such as the seriousness and length of the breach, and also takes into account the ability of the Member State to pay. The Lisbon Treaty has made procedural improvements to the enforcement procedure through Art 260 TFEU. Now, where a directive has not been implemented, the ECJ can apply a penalty against a Member State at the same time that it gives its ruling. Also, in the case of other breaches, it does not have to provide a reasoned opinion.

6.2.3 Actions by other Member States under Art 259

It was always intended in the Treaty that the Commission should be the prime body in enforcing EC law against Member States that were failing to comply with their obligations. For this reason also, while it is possible for other Member States to bring action, it was always intended to be an exceptional procedure rather than the norm. This is reflected in the wording of the Article:

ARTICLE

'Art 259 A Member State which considers that another Member State has failed to fulfil an obligation under this Treaty may bring the matter before the Court of Justice.
Before a Member State brings an action against another Member State for an alleged infringement of an obligation under this Treaty, it shall bring the matter before the Commission.'

However, the ability of other Member States to use the procedure is nevertheless a very useful safeguard against possible errors of judgement by the Commission.

It involves similar processes to those that we have looked at above. However, the Article clearly demands that the Member State must inevitably work closely with the Commission in the preliminary stages.

To date, only one such case has been brought:

CASE EXAMPLE

France v UK (Case 141/78) [1979] ECR 2923

Here, France, using the procedure, was able to show that the United Kingdom's rules on the mesh size of fishing nets was in fact a unilateral action, contrary to EU law and thus in breach of its obligations.

Nevertheless, the possibility of such action can be useful in focusing the attention of the Commission on the issue. This was the case when the EU lifted its ban on British beef but both the French and German Governments declined to do so.

ACTIVITY

Self-assessment questions

1. Which institution would normally take action against a Member State under Art 258?
2. What are the stages in an action under Art 258? Why would the action proceed to a hearing in the ECJ?
3. For what reasons can Member States take a similar action under Art 259?
4. How successful have Member States been in trying to raise a defence to Art 258 proceedings?

6.3 Direct actions against Community institutions

6.3.1 Article 263 TFEU actions against EU institutions for exceeding powers

The action for annulment of a Community instrument under Art 263

Article 263 provides one of the few circumstances in which ordinary individuals are able to bring an action in the ECJ. While such an action is possible, it is nevertheless true that the ability of citizens to do so is much more restricted than it is for the institutions.

The procedure is a very specific one and it has two major functions:

- it provides a means of questioning and indeed controlling the legality of binding acts of Community institutions
- it offers a form of legal protection to those who are subject to the instruments of the Community and who are adversely affected by instruments that are in fact illegal.

There are three key aspects to Art 263 actions that must be considered:

- the identity of those who may bring an action, in other words the *locus standi* of individuals

- the type of actions by the institutions that are capable of being reviewed under the procedure and the grounds on which an action may be brought
- the actual procedure itself.

Locus standi (the right to sue)

Article 263 is quite explicit on those who have *locus standi*. There are three significant groups enjoying slightly different *locus standi*:

- The **Member States**, the **Commission** and the **Council** are all named as possible parties to an action. In this respect they are all classed as 'privileged claimants' and possess virtually unlimited rights of challenge against any act of any of the institutions. The exception to this is recommendations and opinions. The necessary requirement for being a privileged claimant is that the body is bound by the measure in question. This will be determined by the ECJ on studying the context and legal effect.
- **Parliament** and the **European Central Bank** are also privileged claimants. However, they have more limited powers of challenge. Traditionally, it was held that they could only use the procedure if it was 'for the purpose of protecting their prerogatives'. An example of this is *Parliament v Council (Chernobyl)* (Case 70/88) [1991] ECR I–4529. The Treaty of Nice, however, has identified Parliament as having full status as a privileged claimant.
- **Natural** and **legal persons** are also identified in Art 263 as having *locus standi*. Their rights of challenge before the Treaty of Lisbon were limited to '… a Decision addressed to that person, or a decision which, although in the form of a Regulation or a Decision addressed to another person, is of direct and individual concern to the individual …'. Article 263 TFEU extends the challenges available to individuals to also include a regulatory act which is of direct concern to them and does not entail implementing measures. In this case the individual only needs to show direct concern and not individual concern also. All challenges by natural and legal persons are now brought in the General Court. There is the possibility of an appeal to the ECJ but on a point of law only.

Looking at the requirements above, it is clear that, apart from in the case of decisions addressed to an individual, three key issues need to be considered in establishing whether or not there is *locus standi*:

- what amounts to 'individual concern'
- what amounts to 'direct concern'
- the circumstances in which a Regulation may be of individual or direct concern.

Individual concern

In order for a private applicant to make a claim, 'individual concern' must mean that the decision or Regulation must affect the applicant. How an applicant could claim to be affected by the measure was explained in *Plaumann v Commission* (Case 25/62) [1963] ECR 95.

CASE EXAMPLE

Plaumann v Commission (Case 25/62) [1963] ECR 95

Plaumann was one of 30 German importers who were all complaining about a Commission refusal to suspend certain Customs duties on mandarin oranges and tangerines. The thing that defeated their argument was that any individual in Germany might have imported the fruit, so it was impossible to show 'individual concern'.

JUDGMENT

It would be '... by reason of certain attributes which are peculiar to them or by reason of circumstances in which they are differentiated from all other persons and by virtue of these factors distinguishes them individually just as in the case of the person addressed'.

However, this basic test has subsequently been modified so that now it must be possible to determine the number and the identity of those persons affected at the time that the measure complained about was adopted.

CASE EXAMPLE

Toëpfer v Commission (Cases 106 and 107/63) [1965] ECR 405

Here, Toepfer challenged a protectionist German measure which had the effect of preventing Toepfer from obtaining a licence to import maize. The Commission then accepted the legitimacy of the measure and Toepfer challenged this decision. It was accepted that there was individual concern and that Toepfer had locus standi because it was possible to identify precisely all of the people applying for a licence before the decision.

This has also been modified further by the ECJ which, in *International Fruit Co v Commission* (Cases 41 to 44/70) [1971] ECR 411, has stated that there will be individual concern and therefore *locus standi* is possible if there is a 'closed group' of people affected by the decision. In the case there was such a 'closed group' because the decision only applied to a limited number of importers who had been granted licences before a specific date.

However, the ECJ has not always shown consistent application of the criteria that it has set:

CASE EXAMPLE

Piraiki-Patraiki v Commission (Case 11/82) [1985] ECR 207

In this case Greek exporters challenged a decision which allowed a French quota system to be imposed on imports of Greek yarn. The ECJ acknowledged that the exporters had locus standi because they had been contracted during the period in which the quota was in place. This appears to fit the *Plaumann* reasoning but not that in the International Fruit case since the exporters could not fit into the category of a closed group.

Nevertheless, the definition of individual concern in *Plaumann* (1963) is restrictive and makes it difficult for individuals to protect themselves against breaches of their rights resulting from Community legislation. The test has been consistently criticised. The definition has recently been reviewed and a more liberal approach suggested. However, the ECJ has ultimately confirmed *Plaumann* as the appropriate test.

In *Union de Pequenos Agricultores (UPA) v Council* (Case C–50/00) [2003] QB 893 UPA, a trade association, had unsuccessfully challenged a Regulation in the CFI (now the General Court), being unable to show individual concern. The CFI (now the General Court) had also pointed out that UPA could instead have brought an action in the national courts and then asked for an Art 267 reference to be made. When the case came before the ECJ the Advocate-General identified that a challenge under Art 263 was a more appropriate procedure and recognised that there were inherent difficulties in trying to take the course of action suggested by the CFI (now the General Court). Firstly, a national court would not have the power to annul the measure and so could only consider whether there was sufficient doubt as to its legality to justify a reference being made. Secondly, certain measures could not give rise to an action in a national court and so would be beyond any challenge by the individual. He also felt that the definition of 'individual concern' was too restrictive and that there was no reason why an individual should have to show a difference from other individuals affected by the measure. He preferred a test based on an individual having suffered a substantial adverse affect because of his particular circumstances.

Between the Advocate-General's opinion and the ruling in the ECJ the CFI in another case, *Jego-Quere et Cie v Commission* (Case T–177/01) [2003] QB 854, suggested a different test for individual concern based on the Advocate-General's opinion in *UPA*. Individual concern would be shown if the measure: 'affects his legal position in a manner which is both definite and immediate, by restricting his rights or imposing obligations on him'.

The ECJ in *UPA*, however, confirmed the *Plaumann* (1963) test on individual concern so that there is unlikely to be change without amendment to the Treaty.

Direct concern

'Direct concern' has a somewhat different meaning, and once again has been subject to some inconsistent interpretation by the ECJ.

It does not only refer to the causal connection between the decision and any loss suffered but has also been said to refer to the 'immediate, automatic and inevitable disadvantageous legal effects' without need for further intervention.

CASE EXAMPLE

Alcan Aluminium Raeren v Commission (Case 69/69) [1970] ECR 385

Here, several aluminium refining companies applied for annulment of a refusal by the Commission to meet a request by Belgium and Luxembourg on additional tariffs for imports of aluminium. There was no direct concern because the decision in effect conferred no rights and the Member States were in fact given discretion to act.

However, this somewhat strict approach was later relaxed in *Bock v Commission* (Case 62/70) *(The Chinese Mushrooms Case)* [1971] ECR 897 where the applicant who had applied for a licence to import Chinese mushrooms was granted *locus standi* because only he had been affected.

When a Regulation is of individual or direct concern

Because of their nature genuine Regulations can never be capable of challenge by an individual applicant. This was stated clearly in *Calpak SpA v Commission* (Case 789/79) [1980] ECR 1949.

Because of this it is vital to determine whether or not a particular Regulation conforms to the standard definition, otherwise there can be no *locus standi* in any application challenging it. In *Confederation Nationale des Producteurs de Fruits et Legumes v Council* (Cases 16 and 17/62) [1962] ECR 901 Advocate-General Lagrange identified that:

JUDGMENT

'What distinguishes a Regulation is not the greater or lesser extent of its application, material or territorial, but the fact that its provisions apply impersonally in objective situations …'.

In this way a Regulation can only be challenged when it is not a provision having general application within the meaning given in Art 288 but is rather '… a bundle of individual Decisions taken by the Commission, each of which, although taken in the form of a Regulation, affected the legal position of the applicant …' *International Fruit Co v Commission* (1971).

The substantive grounds for review

Once admissibility of an application has been established then it is for the applicant to show that the challenge to the decision concerns one of four specific grounds identified in the Article:

- lack of competence
- infringement of an essential procedural requirement

- infringement of the Treaties or of any rule that relates to the application of the provision of the Treaties
- misuse of power.

Lack of competence

This ground for complaint has no real comparison in English administrative law. However, Lasok and Bridges have suggested that it is 'broadly comparable' with the ultra vires doctrine with which we are all familiar.

In simple terms it is possible to identify lack of competence when a EU institution appears to exercise a power that is not in fact conferred upon it by EU law; or where it appears to exercise a non-existent power; or where it in fact encroaches on the power given to another institution.

The ECJ has defined the ground in the case law but it will rarely accept a challenge by one institution against another because, firstly, the powers of the different institutions are clearly laid out in the EU Treaty and, secondly, because it will in any case usually interpret these powers broadly.

CASE EXAMPLE

Commission v Council (Re European Road Transport Agreement) (Case 22/70) (The ERTA case) [1971] ECR 263

Here, the ECJ rejected a claim by the Commission that the Council lacked the power to take part in the shaping of the agreement in question despite the fact that the Commission is the body that negotiates international agreements while it is the Council's role to conclude them.

In this way it is more likely for the ground to be used in respect of powers that are not possessed at all by the institution challenged in the application.

CASE EXAMPLE

Ford (Europe) v Commission (Cases 228 and 229/82) [1984] ECR 1129

Here, the Commission had delivered an interim decision on a ban by Ford on the sale of right-hand drive Ford vehicles to dealers in Germany. A challenge was possible because the Commission had no power to make interim decisions.

Most commonly, the ground will be accepted in the case of an improper delegation of power. This was the case in *Meroni v High Authority* (Case 9/56) [1956–58] ECR 133 where the Commission (High Authority) had delegated powers to make a decision to another body that did not in fact have any authority to make decisions. The action of the Commission in this instance was invalid.

Infringement of an essential procedural requirement

EC law puts in place a number of procedural mechanisms in order to act as safeguards in protection of natural justice. Such essential procedural requirements fall into distinct categories:

- Firstly, there are procedural requirements in relation to the preparation of the measure, for instance the requirement of prior consultation. For example, in *Roquette Frères v Council* (Case 138/79) [1980] ECR 3333 the Council had failed to consult Parliament, as required, on agricultural budgeting measures and so the measure was invalid.
- Also, there are requirements in respect of the form by which the measure is created. An example of this would be the requirement to give reasons so that any party affected by the measure can understand how the institution has applied the law. Such an infringement occurred in *Germany v Commission* (Case 24/62) [1963] ECR 63 where a decision addressed to Germany concerning wine imports provided no reasons and so was invalid.

Infringement of the Treaties or of any rule relating to their application

This ground is easily explained. It clearly allows the ECJ to review how the acts of the institution in question conform with EU law. The law in this instance includes the general principles of law so that any kind of violation of EU law of whatever type may be declared invalid under this ground.

CASE EXAMPLE

Transocean Marine Paint Association v Commission (Case 17/74) [1975] 2 CMLR D75

Here, the association had been in receipt of an exemption from Art 81 (now Art 101 TFEU) for 10 years. The Commission then unilaterally reviewed the exemption and imposed entirely new conditions. This was a general breach of the right to be heard, and thus a breach also of the general principle of legal certainty and was thus invalid.

Misuse of powers

This ground quite simply refers to the situation where an institution is using a power that it does in fact possess but for an objective that is contrary to those for which the power was given. It might therefore include any illegitimate use of a power.

CASE EXAMPLE

Bock v Commission (Case 62/70) [1971] ECR 897 (The Chinese Mushrooms case)

Here, although the case was actually decided on the issue of proportionality, the question of misuse of power was also considered and it was found that there was evidence of collaboration between the Commission and the German Government in the issuing of a decision.

The procedure

The most important procedural requirement in making an application is the existence of a strict time limit for bringing an action. The time limit is within two months of the date on which the measure was published, or from the date on which the applicant was notified of the decision, or on which it came to the applicant's attention.

The consequences of an application being successful is that the instrument is declared void by the ECJ. The effect of this is that the measure is treated as though it never in fact existed.

6.3.2 Article 265 actions against institutions for a failure to act

Article 265 gives both the Member States and the Community institutions the right to call to account any of the Council, the Commission, Parliament, and the European Central Bank for failing to take action when they would be required to. This is an obviously necessary addition to the annulment proceedings in Art 263. Just as there are times when the institutions go beyond the powers given to them by the Treaties, then there is also the possibility that in situations where one of the institutions would be bound to act according to the law, it fails to act. A classic example is where the Commission fails to issue a decision following a breach of competition law under Art 101 or Art 102. In such situations the Treaty has provided a form of redress to the injured party through the Art 265 action. Applicants are required to satisfy a test for admissibility and also to show that there are suitable grounds for the review.

Admissibility

There is no set time limit for a claim under Art 265 but in order for the Court to accept that there is an admissible claim it will first see whether three conditions are met:

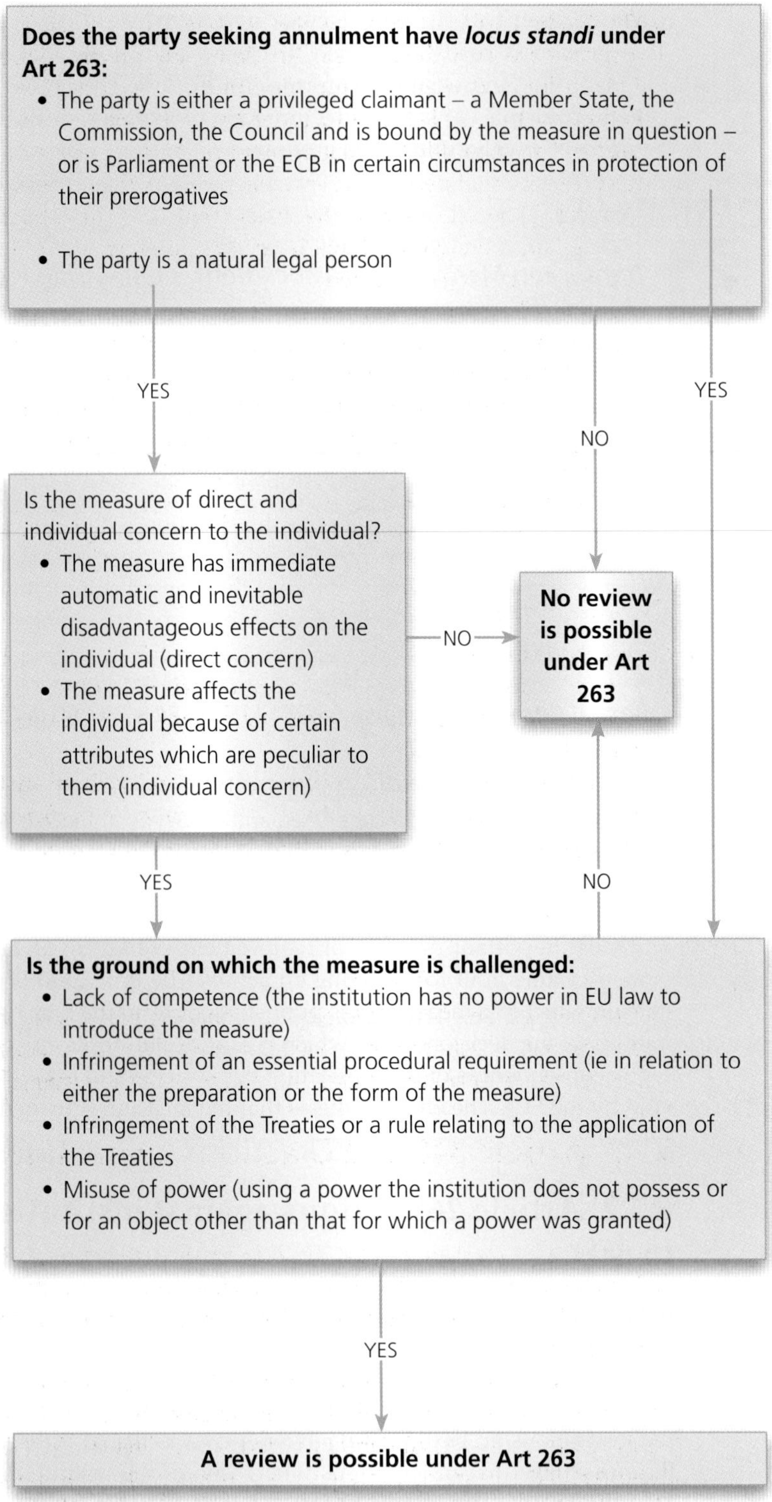

Figure 6.3.2 Diagram illustrating the requirements for an action for annulment under Art 230

1. Firstly, the applicant must be able to show *locus standi*. The 'privileged claimants' in this case are described in the Article as 'the member states and other institutions'. This includes Parliament since *Parliament v Council* (Case 377/87) [1988] ECR 4051. Following the TEU it also includes the European Central Bank. 'Natural and legal persons' are also able to bring an action against a Community institution which failed to address to that person any instrument other than a recommendation or an opinion. Inevitably, this means that the instrument must be a binding act. It also obviously means that there would have been a requirement to address the instrument to the applicant had it been enacted.
2. Secondly, there must be what is referred to as an 'Indictable Institution'. The institutions covered by the Article are the Council, the Commission, Parliament and the Central Bank. For the claim to be admissible there must have been a failure to act by that institution in circumstances where it was in fact legally required to act.
3. Thirdly, there must have been a prior approach to the institution. Before the ECJ will consider an application it must be satisfied that the applicant has already approached the institution seeking redress. This approach must be explicit in its terms and refer to the possibility of a challenge under Art 265 if no reply is received within two months.

Grounds for review

The grounds under which the ECJ will undertake a review are where the applicant is able to show that they were entitled to a decision and none was actually addressed to them. An alternative ground is where an action has not been taken which is of direct and individual concern to them.

In fact, few cases are found to be admissible and so there are few guidelines. Generally, if there is a result to be achieved and an obligation is sufficiently well defined then any attempt to disregard it will fall within the scope of Art 265.

CASE EXAMPLE

Parliament v Council (Case 13/83) [1987] ECR 1513

Here, there was an alleged failure by the Council to ensure freedom to provide international transport and to establish the conditions in which non-resident transporters were able to operate in another Member State. This was accepted as a ground for review.

6.3.3 Article 340 TFEU actions against institutions for damages

Article 340 in para 2 states that 'In the case of non-contractual liability the Community shall, in accordance with the general principles common to the laws of the member states, make good any damage caused by the institutions or by its servants in the performance of their duties.'

It is possible, then, to see the similarity between the Art 340 action and a form of general tort action. However, it should be remembered that five of the original six members of the EC had forms of civil liability based on the French Civil Code. As a result, liability under Art 340 is more accurately seen as based on this form of liability.

The Treaty in any case provides that the ECJ should hear all actions under Art 340. There are two significant issues to consider:

- the requirements for admissibility of claims and
- the conditions for liability.

Admissibility

Locus standi in such claims is necessarily almost unrestricted. As a result, any natural or legal person is capable of bringing an action. The key requirement for admissibility is that the individual making the claim can make out a *prima facie* case that he has personally suffered damage resulting from an act or omission of an institution or of its servant. In this way the action could not, for instance, be brought by a trade union on behalf of a member or members.

The ECJ has ruled in *Werhahn Hansamuhle v Council* (Cases 63 to 69/72) [1973] ECR 1229 that the claim must be alleged specifically against an institution or its servant. Therefore a claim could not be made against the Community as a whole.

The appropriate time limit on claiming is five years from the date of the event that it is alleged caused the damage and gave rise to the action.

Conditions for liability

There are three elements that must be satisfied for a successful claim to be made:

Firstly, the occurrence of **damage** suffered by the applicant:

- This might include any physical damage as well as economic loss, including both actual damage and loss of earnings. The general qualification is that the damage is certain, provable and quantifiable.
- Future loss is also recoverable but only in limited circumstances. In *Kampffmeyer et al v Commission* (Cases 5, 7 and 13 to 24/66) [1967] ECR 245 a claim for a future loss was accepted where the cancellation of contracts had already occurred by the time of the creation of the wrongful measure.
- Even highly speculative and non-material loss has been accepted in some circumstances:

CASE EXAMPLE

Adams v Commission (Case 145/83) [1986] QB 138

Adams worked for Hoffman LaRoche, the pharmaceutical company, and he discovered that the company was in breach of EC [now EU] competition law, as a result of which he informed the Commission, for which there was legitimate provision within the law. Nevertheless, he was then arrested for industrial espionage and his wife hanged herself. This was accepted as recoverable damage giving rise to liability.

Secondly, the presence of **fault** on the part of the institution complained about:

- it is sufficient in this sense to show that the applicant was owed a duty which was then breached by the institution, as was the case in *Adams v Commission* (1986)
- however, the ECJ may be less likely to conclude that there is fault where the institution was involved in making policy decisions and made errors of judgement leading on to the damage suffered.

CASE EXAMPLE

Zuckerfabrik Schoppenstedt v Council (Case 5/71) [1971] ECR 975

Here, a Regulation laid down measures to offset the differences between national sugar prices and Community [now EU] reference prices that were applicable from a particular date. The applicant complained that the criteria were in fact erroneous and had caused him loss, but failed in his complaint. The ECJ laid down some criteria for determining fault, known as the 'Schoppenstedt formula':

(i) there must be a legislative measure which involves choices of economic policy and
(ii) this must involve a breach of a superior rule of law
(iii) which is sufficiently serious and
(iv) the superior rule is of a type which was for the protection of individuals.

Only if all parts are satisfied will fault be shown.

Thirdly, it must be possible to show a **causal connection** between the measure complained of and the damage suffered:

- on this basis the mere existence of damage by itself is insufficient to give rise to an action for damages under Art 340
- proof of damage alone is insufficient for liability without proof also that the act of the institution challenged directly caused the damage
- in this way remoteness of damage is clearly an important factor to be taken into account:

CASE EXAMPLE

Pool v Council (Case 49/79) [1981] ECR 569

An English cattle farmer claimed that the conversion rates for sterling (UK currency) in the agricultural sector, known as 'green rates', had caused him loss. The ECJ rejected his claim since it was too speculative.

ACTIVITY

Exercise

Identify and explain which type of enforcement action might be brought in the following situations:

a) A large French wine-producing company, Vin Francais, has been found to have infringed Art 102 by refusing discounts that it normally gives to all retailers of its wines unless these traders cease to order wine from a small English company, Anglovin. Twelve months have now passed and the Commission has not addressed a Decision to Vin Francais.

b) As a result of the Commission not issuing a Decision, many European wine retailers have ceased buying products from Anglovin in order to retain the discounts from Vin Francais. Anglovin has lost a significant amount of its trade and is now facing liquidation.

c) A Council Regulation has been issued requiring a measured reduction of the overall production of wine in the EU based on percentage reductions in all wine-producing Member States. The Commission has subsequently addressed a Decision to the UK Government demanding a total halt to wine production in the UK.

ACTIVITY

Self-assessment questions

1. In an action to annul a measure under Art 263, against which institutions are actions usually brought?
2. In an Art 263 action, which bodies are privileged applicants?
3. When can a natural or legal person take action under Art 263?
4. How is the phrase 'direct concern' defined?
5. What is the meaning of the phrase 'individual concern'?
6. When can a Regulation be subject to review under Art 263?
7. What are the grounds for review under Art 263?
8. How broadly has the term 'misuse of powers' been defined?
9. What is the basic difference between an action under Art 263 and an action under Art 265?
10. What are the requirements for admissibility for an action under Art 265?
11. What is the usual context for an action under Art 265?
12. What does the case of *Werhahn Hansamuhle v Council* state about who an action can be brought against under Art 340?
13. What are the three conditions that must be proved for there to be liability under Art 340?
14. What guidelines were issued in the case of *Zuckerfabrik Schoppenstedt v Council*?

KEY FACTS

Infringement proceedings against Member States under Arts 258 and 259	

• Usually brought by the Commission as 'watchdog' of Treaties.
• Three clear purposes:
  • ensure Member States comply with Treaties
  • provide a procedure for dispute resolution
  • provide means of clarifying law
• starts with mediation – then three formal stages:	

• notice of default	*Commission v Italy (Re Payment of Export Rebates)* (1970)
• reasoned opinion	
• proceedings in ECJ	*Alfons Lütticke* (1966)
• penalties possible in Art 260	*Commission v Belgium* (1970)
• an action by another state possible under Art 259	*France v UK* (1979)

Actions against institutions for an abuse of power under Art 263	

• Two major functions:
  • provides a way of controlling legality of binding acts
  • gives legal protection to those subject to Community instruments adversely affected by illegal ones.	

• Commission, Council and Member States are privileged claimants.	*Parliament v Council (Chernobyl)* 70/88 (1991)
• Natural and legal persons gain *locus standi* for a decision addressed to them or a Regulation or a Decision addressed to another person of direct and individual concern to them.	
• 'Individual concern' means decision affects them because of attributes.	*Plaumann v Commission* (1963)
• 'Direct concern' means 'immediate, automatic and inevitable disadvantageous legal effects'.	*Alcan Aluminium Raeren et al v Commission* (1970)
• A Regulation may be challenged if has no general application but is a 'bundle of individual Decisions'.	*International Fruit Co v Commission* (1971)
• Grounds for review include:	
• lack of competence	*Ford (Europe) v Commission* (1984)
• Infringement of an essential procedural requirement	*Roquette Frères v Council* (1980)
• infringement of Treaties or procedural rules	*Transocean Marine Paint Association v Commission* (1975)
• misuse of powers.	*Bock v Commission* (1971)

Actions against institutions for a failure to act under Art 265	
• Can challenge Commission, Council, Parliament and European Central Bank. • Privileged claimants are Member States and institutions. • Natural and legal persons must show institution failed to address to them any instrument other than an opinion or recommendation.	

• Grounds for review are where applicant can show he was entitled to a Decision and none was addressed to him, or an action has not been taken which is of direct and individual concern to him.	*Parliament v Council* (1987)
Actions for damages against institutions under Art 288	
• 'To make good any damage caused by institutions'.	
• Almost unrestricted *locus standi*.	
• Defendant must be an institution or its servant, not Community as a whole.	*Werhahn Hansamuhle v Council* (1973)
• Conditions for liability are:	
• damage suffered by claimant	*Adams v Commission* (1986)
• fault of institution	*Zuckerfabrik Schoppenstedt v Council* (1971)
• causal connection.	*Pool v Council* (1981)

SAMPLE ESSAY QUESTION

'Discuss the scope of the infringement procedures and judicial review of the EU.'

Explain EU infringement procedures:
- usually brought by Commission against Member States for breaches of EU law
- starts with mediation – then formal stages, notice of default, proceedings in ECJ
- and penalties possible under Art 260
- and action by another state possible.

Discuss the purpose and scope of the procedure:
- 3 main purposes -- ensures Member States comply with Treaties, provides procedure for dispute resolution, and means of clarifying law
- fact of penalties and possible action by other Member States gives broad scope.

Explain action for abuse of power:
- privileged claimants are Council, Commission and Member States – but individuals also, although must generally show direct concern
- grounds for review include: lack of competence, infringement of an essential procedural requirement, infringement of Treaties or procedural rules, misuse of powers.

Discuss the purpose and scope of the procedure:
- provides a way of controlling legality of binding acts
- gives legal protection to those subject to EU instruments adversely affected by illegal ones.

Explain actions for a failure to act:
- can challenge Commission, Council, Parliament, European Central Bank
- privileged claimants are Member States & institutions – individuals must show institution failed to address to them any instrument other than an opinion or recommendation.

Discuss the purpose and scope of the procedure:
- grounds for review are where applicant can show he was entitled to a decision and none was addressed to him, or an action has not been taken which is of direct and individual concern to him
- So provides protection against failures to act.

Explain action for damages:
conditions for liability are:
- damage suffered by claimant
- fault of institution
- causal connection.

Discuss the purpose and scope of the procedure:
- aimed at making good any damage caused by institutions
- almost unrestricted *locus standi* – so wide scope
- must involve an institution or its servant, not EU as a whole – so some restriction there.

SUMMARY

- Other than references for preliminary rulings there are four types of action in the Court of Justice – infringement proceedings under Art 258, judicial review of acts by EU institutions under Art 263, and for a failure to act under Art 265, and damages claims under Art 340.
- Infringement proceedings are against Member States for breaches of EU law and penalties are possible.
- Judicial review of abuse of powers by EU institutions have two major functions: to ensure the legality of binding acts, and to give legal protection to those subject to EU instruments who are adversely affected by illegal ones.

- Actions against EU institutions for a failure to act allow privileged claimants and natural and legal persons to claim where the institution has failed to act, for instance where a decision should have been issued.
- Claims for damages against EU institutions allow for making good any damage caused by those institutions.

Further reading

Books

Douglas-Scott, S, *Constitutional Law of the European Union* (Longman, 2002), Chapters 10, 11 and 12.

Fairhurst, J, *Law of the European Union* (8th edn, Pearson 2010), Chapter 4.

7

Article 267 TFEU and the preliminary reference procedure

AIMS AND OBJECTIVES

After reading this chapter you should be able to:

- Understand the purpose of the preliminary rulings procedure
- Understand the meaning of the phrase 'court or tribunal'
- Understand the difference between those courts and tribunals which 'may' seek a preliminary ruling and those that 'shall' do so
- Understand the circumstances in which national courts may refrain from seeking rulings, in particular the '*acte clair*' doctrine
- Understand why reform of the preliminary rulings procedure is regarded as important
- Analyse critically the various reform proposals that have been made

ARTICLE

'Art 267 The Court of Justice of the European Union shall have jurisdiction to give preliminary rulings concerning:

(a) the interpretation of the Treaties;

(b) the validity and interpretation of acts of the institutions, bodies, offices or agencies of the Union;

Where such a question is raised before any court or tribunal of a Member State, that court or tribunal may, if it considers that a decision on the question is necessary to enable it to give judgment, request the Court of Justice to give a ruling thereon.

Where any such question is raised in a case pending before a court or tribunal of a Member State against whose decisions there is no judicial remedy under national law, that court or tribunal shall bring the matter before the Court.

If such a question is raised in a case pending before a court or tribunal of a Member State with regard to a person in custody, the Court of Justice of the European Union shall act with the minimum of delay.'

7.1 The relation with Member States

The Art 267 procedure allows any national court or tribunal in any of the Member States to request that the ECJ interpret provisions of EU law. It is crucial to remember that the

ECJ simply **interprets** EU law: the national court then has the task of **applying** that law, as interpreted. As Lord Denning explained in the Court of Appeal in *Bulmer v Bollinger* [1974] Ch 401:

JUDGMENT

'It is important to distinguish between the task of interpreting the Treaty – to see what it means – and the task of *applying* it – to apply its provisions to the case in hand. [First], the task of applying the Treaty. On this matter in our courts the English judges have the final word. They are the only judges who are empowered to decide the case itself. They have to find the facts, to state the issues, to give judgment for one side or the other, and to see that the judgement is enforced. Before the English judge can apply the Treaty, they have to see what it means and what is its effect. In the task of *interpreting* the Treaty, the English judges are no longer the final authority … They are no longer in a position to give rulings which are of binding force. The supreme tribunal for *interpreting* the Treaty is the European Court of Justice.'

It is crucial to appreciate that Art 267 is **not** an appeal procedure. It is triggered by national courts or tribunals during the course of litigation itself. This is why it is known as the 'preliminary reference' procedure, and the Court's judgments are known as 'preliminary rulings'. The rulings are designed to assist the national court or tribunal to reach a final ruling.

There is, therefore, a shared jurisdiction between the national courts and the ECJ. The national courts decide questions of fact and national law; it is also the national courts who apply national and EU law. The ECJ determines abstract questions of the interpretation of EU legislation only (and deals with issues involving the validity of EU secondary legislation). In the first ever preliminary reference case, *De Geus v Robert Bosch* (Case 13/61) *[1962] ECR 45*, Advocate-General Lagrange said that the 'provisions of [Art 267] must lead to a real and fruitful collaboration between the municipal courts and the Court of Justice with mutual respect for their respective jurisdiction'.

Much more recently, in *Gintec* (Case C–374/05) [2007] ECR I-9517, Advocate-General Ruiz-Jarabo Colomer offered the following culinary metaphor as a means of explaining the operation of the preliminary rulings procedure:

JUDGMENT

'The various ingredients which go into the recipe for a preliminary ruling are clearly enough set out in the European Union cookbook, but theory comes up against the varying circumstances which apply each time the dish is prepared, as the chosen heat source, the pans, the condition and origin of the ingredients and even the state of mind of whoever is cooking are always different … While the national courts take primary responsibility for the dish, the Court of Justice merely provides them with the all-important [Union] seasoning, without interfering in matters which do not concern it. Nevertheless, the European and national elements frequently become mixed up and, to allow them to perform their functions, each must absorb and refine the flavours of the other … It falls to the Court of Justice, like a reliable kitchen hand who is unable to create a whole meal but acts as the chef's adviser, to provide the [national court] with some guidelines … by offering it a valuable tool for resolving the dispute.'

7.2 The character of the reference procedure

7.2.1 References seeking interpretation of EU law

If a dispute as to the proper interpretation of a provision of EU legislation arises during a legal dispute before a court or tribunal in one of the Member States, a request may be made for a ruling on the interpretation of the disputed provision. The national court or tribunal suspends the case until the ECJ gives its ruling. When the ECJ has made its decision, the national court or tribunal then continues from where it left off, applying the EU law as interpreted by the ECJ.

This is supposed to achieve uniformity or consistency of interpretation of all EU law, because once the ECJ has made its preliminary ruling, this establishes a precedent for all the courts and tribunals in the Member States to follow in future cases. Having one court to interpret all EU law means that the same meaning is given throughout the Union; if it was left to national courts they might all come up with different interpretations. This would be likely given that the EU presently has 23 official languages. The Treaties are reproduced in all of them. Given that translation is not a precise science, there are bound to be differences between all the different versions; but using the ECJ helps keep the differences to a minimum. If the preliminary reference procedure did not exist, courts and tribunals in the Member States would have to make their own interpretations of EU law. This would create a very real risk of divergent meanings being given to the same provisions of EU law in different Member States and, if that happened, the whole fabric of EU law could begin to unravel.

The Court can give interpretations of provisions in both of the Treaties, and 'acts of the institutions, bodies, offices or agencies of the Union' – which basically means all secondary EU legislation (primarily Regulations and Directives). It can also rule on the interpretation of international treaties entered into by those institutions (*Hageman* (Case 181/73) [1974] ECR 449). An 'act' need not be directly effective in order to be capable of interpretation (*Mazzalai* (Case 111/75) [1976] ECR 657).

The EU's approach to interpretation

Any court in the world has a choice as to its approach to interpretation, and the ECJ is no exception. There are three main methods:

1. **Literal**: The ordinary dictionary meaning. Popular with English courts, but not with the ECJ. The mutli-lingualism situation makes this method impracticable.
2. **Contextual**: Look to EU law as a whole, not just the particular piece of legislation.
3. **Purposive**: Interpret the legislation in the way which most furthers the purposes of the Union. EU legislation (whether primary or secondary) lends itself to this approach because of the presence of a 'preamble' setting out the aims and objectives of the legislation.

Generally, the ECJ takes a 'teleological' approach, which may be described as a combination of the second and third approaches. The position is summed up in the following extract from *Re Adidas AG* (Case C–223/98) [1999] ECR I–7081:

JUDGMENT

> 'In interpreting a provision of [EU] law it is necessary to consider not only its wording but also the context in which it occurs and the objects of the rules of which it is part … where a provision of [EU] law is open to several interpretations, only one of which can ensure that the provision retains its effectiveness, preference must be given to that interpretation.'

Using the teleological approach allows the ECJ to update the law and meet new social and political developments.

Language differences

The Court has frequently dealt with the issue of linguistic divergences in EU legislation. For example, it held in *Stauder v Ulm* (Case 29/69) [1969] ECR 419, that:

JUDGMENT

> 'The necessity for uniform application and accordingly for uniform interpretation makes it impossible to consider one version of … text in isolation but requires that it be interpreted on the basis of both the real intention of its author and the aim he seeks to achieve, in the light in particular of the versions in all [the] languages.'

The role of the ECJ in the preliminary reference procedure

The ECJ is supposed to be 'reactive', that is, it responds to questions submitted to it by the national courts. Occasionally, the ECJ will take a more 'proactive' approach and re-formulate a question so that the answer it gives is more useful to the national court. Even more rarely, the ECJ will answer a question that was **not actually asked**, if the Court thinks that this will assist the national court in giving judgment. A good example of this is *Marks & Spencer v Customs and Excise Commissioners* (Case C–62/00) [2003] QB 866. The Court of Appeal had asked a question of the ECJ relating to Directive 77/388. The ECJ noted that the question was based on a mistaken premise regarding direct effect and, having put the Court of Appeal straight on that point, concluded that it (the ECJ) therefore needed to re-phrase the question (otherwise the answer would not make sense). The Court stated:

JUDGMENT

> 'In the procedure laid down by [Art 267] for co-operation between national courts and the [ECJ], it is for the latter to provide the referring court with an answer which will be of use to it and enable it to determine the case before it. To that end, the Court may have to reformulate the question referred to it.'

The ECJ is not allowed to consider the validity of national law. If it is asked to do so, it may re-formulate the question and return an abstract answer on the point of [EU] law involved (*Costa v ENEL* (Case 6/64) [1964] ECR 1141) or simply refuse to answer the question asked (see *Foglia v Novello* (Case 104/79) [1981] ECR 745; *Bacardi-Martini v Newcastle United* (Case C–318/00) [2003] ECR I–905). Nor is the Court supposed to consider how EU legislation should be applied by the national courts; however, it has done this in the past by giving 'practical' rulings (*Stoke-on-Trent City Council v B&Q* (Case C–169/91) [1993] 2 WLR 730). This is unsurprising, given that the line between interpretation and application is likely to be very fine.

The role of the national courts

The national courts, having requested a preliminary ruling, are then expected to apply it to the facts of the case and give judgment. However, legal history was made in 2003 in *Arsenal FC v Reed* (Case C–206/01) [2003] Ch 454, when Laddie J in the English High Court refused to apply a preliminary ruling of the ECJ that he himself had requested. Arsenal Football Club had accused Matthew Reed of infringing its trademarks by selling unofficial merchandise such as scarves and shirts bearing Arsenal's logos (a shield and a cannon) outside the club's ground, Highbury Stadium in north London. During the course of the subsequent trademark infringement action, Laddie J had requested a preliminary ruling on the interpretation of certain provisions in Directive 89/104. However, when the ruling was delivered, Laddie J decided that the ECJ had overstepped its interpretative jurisdiction and had made certain findings of fact (with which he disagreed) regarding the question of whether or not Arsenal supporters were likely to confuse Arsenal's official merchandise with Reed's unofficial merchandise. Strictly speaking, the ECJ is only supposed to make rulings on the interpretation of points of EU legislation and, thus, if Laddie J was correct then he was perfectly entitled to reach this conclusion. Nevertheless, it was a controversial decision. However, a potential crisis in the relationship between the ECJ and the High Court was averted. Having lost the case in the High Court, Arsenal FC appealed to the Court of Appeal which found, reversing Laddie J's decision, that the ECJ had not overstepped its jurisdiction. The Court of Appeal therefore applied the preliminary ruling in full and gave judgment to Arsenal.

7.2.2 References challenging validity of EU law

Special considerations apply where the question is the **validity** of EU law rather than **interpretation**. Firstly, the ECJ may not rule on the validity of the Treaties. It is therefore only secondary EU legislation that can be challenged on validity grounds. Secondly, whereas a national court may declare EU law **valid** and not refer, it may not declare EU law **invalid** (*Firma Foto-Frost v Hauptzollamt Lübeck-Ost* (Case 314/85) [1987] ECR 4199). The ECJ has exclusive authority in this situation. Where a national court suspects that a provision of EU secondary legislation may be invalid, therefore, a reference **must** be made. A good example is *R (on the application of British American Tobacco) v Secretary of State for Health* (Case C–491/01) [2002] ECR I–11453.

CASE EXAMPLE

R (on the application of British American Tobacco) v Secretary of State for Health (Case C–491/01) [2002] ECR I–11453

Directive 2001/37 had been adopted by the Council on the basis of Art 114 (measures to ensure the functioning of the Internal Market) and Art 207 (Common Commercial Policy). According to Art 1 of the Directive, its aim was to 'approximate the laws, regulations and administrative provisions of the Member States concerning the maximum tar, nicotine and carbon monoxide yields of cigarettes and the warnings regarding health and other information to appear on unit packets of tobacco products, together with certain measures concerning the ingredients and the descriptions of tobacco products, taking as a basis a high level of health protection'. In September 2001, British American Tobacco and Imperial Tobacco sought permission from the High Court in London to apply for judicial review of 'the intention and/or obligation' of the UK Government to transpose the Directive into national law. The application was based on several grounds, including inappropriate legislative base. The case was referred to the ECJ for a ruling, and in due course the Court held that the Directive was valid; Art 114 was the correct legislative base. Article 207 should not have been used in addition but this was a purely formal defect and did not affect the validity of the Directive.

7.2.3 'Docket control': Inadmissible references

The ECJ rarely refuses a request for a preliminary ruling. Provided that the question referred to the ECJ is one of interpretation, the ECJ is bound in principle to respond. However, there are three situations when requests for preliminary rulings have been declared inadmissible.

Contrived dispute

In *Leur-Bloem* (Case C–28/95) [1998] QB 182, the ECJ stated:

JUDGMENT

'A reference by a national court can be rejected only if it appears that the procedure laid down by [Art 267] has been misused and a ruling from the Court elicited by means of a contrived dispute, or it is obvious that [Union] law cannot apply, either directly or indirectly, to the circumstances of the case referred to the Court.'

This situation arose in *Foglia v Novello (No 2)* (Case 244/80) [1981] ECR 3045:

CASE EXAMPLE

Foglia v Novello (No 2) (Case 244/80) [1981] ECR 3045

Ms Novello, a French national, ordered a number of cases of an Italian liqueur wine from Foglia, an Italian wine merchant. The sales contract specified that Novello should not be liable for any charges imposed by either the Italian or French authorities contrary to [Union] law. The French Customs authorities imposed an allegedly unlawful tax on the wine when it entered France. Foglia paid this and then instituted proceedings against Ms Novello to recover the cost from her. In the Italian court, the judge requested a ruling regarding the interpretation of Art110 (the prohibition of discriminatory internal taxation – see Chapter 15). However, the ECJ refused to answer the question, saying the proceedings had been created by the parties to test the validity of the French tax rules, and were 'artificial'.

This decision has been criticised, but is understandable: there was no real issue of EU law for the ECJ to determine. In *Meilicke v Meyer* (Case C–89/91) [1992] ECR I–4871, the ECJ, following *Foglia v Novello* (1981), refused to consider a series of questions referred to it from the Hanover Regional Court, as they all related to Professor Meilike's theories regarding EU company law and there was no genuine dispute between the parties. The Court announced that the purpose of Art 267 was to contribute to the administration of justice in the Member States, not to deliver advisory opinions on general or hypothetical questions.

In a number of subsequent cases the ECJ has accepted that the dispute was genuine, despite suggestions to the contrary by an interested observer. For example, in *Idéal Tourisme* (Case C–36/99) [2000] ECR I–6049 the ECJ rejected a suggestion by the Belgian Government that a dispute over VAT (between a Belgian company and the Belgian tax authorities) was contrived, holding that:

JUDGMENT

'The documents in the case contain nothing to show that the parties to the main proceedings manifestly colluded to obtain a ruling from the Court by means of an artificial dispute, as was the case in *Foglia v Novello*. On the contrary, it is plain that the parties disagree on a number of important points, and it is clear from the documents that Idéal Tourisme did not come to an agreement with the Belgian State to refer hypothetical questions to the Court for a preliminary ruling.'

In *Bacardi-Martini v Newcastle United FC* (2003), the ECJ refused to respond to a request from the English High Court on facts not dissimilar to those in *Foglia v Novello* (1981).

CASE EXAMPLE

Bacardi-Martini v Newcastle United FC (Case C–318/00) [2003] ECR I–905

A contract had been signed between Bacardi and NUFC to advertise the former's products on advertising hoardings at the latter's ground during a UEFA Cup match involving NUFC and a French club, Metz, in December 1996. However, NUFC pulled out of the deal when it discovered that the game was to be televised live on French television via satellite – because French law prohibits the TV advertising of alcohol. Bacardi brought an action against NUFC and the case was heard in the High Court, which requested a ruling on the interpretation of Art 56 (the free movement of services). The ECJ refused to deal with the reference, stating that it had to apply 'special vigilance' when a reference request came in from a court in one Member State seeking to question the compatibility of legislation in another Member State with EU law.

Irrelevance

Where the request relates to provisions of EU law that are incidental to the actual dispute, the request may be refused by the ECJ. According to the ECJ in *BP Supergas v Greece* (Case C–62/93) [1995] ECR I–9883, a request will be refused if it is 'quite obvious' that the question bears 'no relation' to the actual subject-matter of the litigation.

Insufficient information of factual/legal background

In *Telemasicabruzzo* (Cases C–320 to 322/90) [1993] ECR I–393, the ECJ rejected a reference that had insufficient information about the factual background or the legal dispute between the parties. This was confirmed in *La Pyramide* (Case C–378/93) [1994] ECR I–3999, the ECJ stating that this would be the case especially where the factual situation was complex.

KEY FACTS

The character of the reference procedure	
The procedure allows national courts and tribunals to seek rulings on the interpretation of EU legislation	Article 267 TFEU
Seeks to ensure that words or phrases in EU legislation are given the same, uniform interpretation throughout the EU, helping to ensure that EU law is applied consistently	*Stauder v Ulm* (1969)
The procedure can also be used to challenge the validity of EU secondary legislation, as only the ECJ has authority to declare EU legislation invalid	*Firma Foto-Frost* (1987)
In interpretation cases, the ECJ usually takes a 'teleological' approach, looking to interpret EU legislation in such a way as to promote the underlying purpose of the legislation, and taking into account the context	*Re Adidas* (1999)
References will be declared inadmissible if the procedure has been abused (contrived dispute), or if the question is irrelevant, or if insufficient factual/legal background information is provided	*Foglia v Novello* (1981); *BP Supergas v Greece* (1995); *Telemasicabruzzo* (1993)

7.3 The meaning of 'court or tribunal'

There are limitations on who can request a ruling. Only a 'court or tribunal' may do so. The phrase 'court or tribunal' has been interpreted very widely. (Article 267 has itself been interpreted by the ECJ, after national courts referred questions to it, under the Art 267 procedure!) It is certainly not required that a forum have the name 'court' or 'tribunal'.

7.3.1 The *Dorsch Consult factors*

According to the ECJ in *Dorsch Consult* (Case C–54/96) [1997] ECR I–4961:

JUDGMENT

> 'In order to determine whether a body making a reference is a "court or tribunal" ... which is a question governed by [Union] law alone, the Court takes into account a number of factors, such as whether the body is established by law, whether it is permanent, whether its jurisdiction is compulsory, whether its procedure is inter partes, whether it applies rules of law and whether it is independent.'

This is a very important case, as it establishes what might be described as a 'functional' test for establishing which bodies may invoke the Art 267 procedure. The practical result is that more bodies can seek preliminary rulings than would have been the case had the ECJ adopted a 'literal' approach, that is, only answering requests from bodies actually called 'court' or 'tribunal'. The advantages of this 'functional' approach are:

- Many bodies which do not have the name 'court' or 'tribunal' nevertheless carry out judicial functions, that is, they are deciding disputes between parties. The functional approach helps to ensure that these bodies do not have to decide on the interpretation of EU legislation themselves, which in turn means that the legislation is more likely to be applied accurately in order to resolve the disputes.
- The functional approach means more bodies can request rulings on different provisions of EU law, which allows the ECJ to give definitive rulings on ambiguous provisions of EU legislation which may not have otherwise reached the ECJ at all.
- The functional approach reduces the need for expensive and time-consuming appeals in the national legal systems. Often, appeals are available against decisions made by various bodies to 'courts'. Without a functional approach, these appeals might be triggered in order to get a case into a 'court' in order for a request for a preliminary ruling to be made. With a functional approach, any body performing a judicial function can seek a ruling itself.

A good example of the 'functional' approach is *Broekmeulen* (Case 246/80) [1981] ECR 2311. Dr Broekmeulen's registration as a GP had been refused. His appeal, to the Appeals Committee of the Royal Netherlands Society for the Protection of Medicine, was based on EU law. References were made to the ECJ, one of which asked whether or not the Appeals Committee was a 'court or tribunal'. The ECJ held that:

JUDGMENT

> 'In the practical absence of an effective means of redress before the ordinary courts, in a matter concerning the application of [Union] law, the Appeals Committee, which performs its duties with the approval of the public authorities and operates with their assistance, and whose decisions are accepted following contentious proceedings and are in fact recognised as final, must be deemed to be a court or tribunal for the purpose of [Art 267].'

The wide scope of 'court or tribunal' can be seen in the following cases:

- *Royal Copenhagen* (Case C–400/93) [1995] ECR I–1275 – administration board in Copenhagen, Denmark
- *O'Flynn v Adjudication Officer* (Case C–237/94) [1996] ECR I–2617 – Social Security Commissioner, UK
- *Gebhard* (Case C–55/94) [1995] ECR I–4165 – Milan Bar Council
- *El-Yassini* (Case C–416/96) [1999] ECR I–1209 – immigration adjudicator, UK
- *Abrahamsson and Andersson* (Case C–407/98) [2000] ECR I–5539 – Universities Appeals Board, Sweden
- *Cadbury Schweppes* (Case C–196/04) [2006] ECR I–7995 – Special Commissioners of Income Tax, UK
- *Jia* (Case C–1/05) [2007] ECR I–1 – Alien Appeals Board, Sweden

In *El-Yassini* (1999), the ECJ gave very careful consideration to the question of whether or not an immigration adjudicator in the UK qualified as a 'court or tribunal'. In the end it decided that an adjudicator did qualify. Read this quote from the judgment and note how many of the *Dorsch Consult* (1997) factors are satisfied:

JUDGMENT

'It should be first noted that the office of Immigration Adjudicator was established by the Immigration Act 1971. That statute confers on the Immigration Adjudicator jurisdiction to hear and determine disputes concerning the rights of foreigners to enter and remain on the territory of the UK. Further, Immigration Adjudicators constitute a permanent organ. Their determinations are to be made in accordance with the law, pursuant to the 1971 Act and in compliance with the rules of procedure. That procedure is inter partes in nature. Immigration Adjudicators are required to give reasons for their determinations, which are binding and may, in certain circumstances, be appealed against to the Immigration Appeal Tribunal. Lastly, Immigration Adjudicators are appointed by the Lord Chancellor for a renewable ten-year or one-year term, depending on whether they sit on a full-time or part-time basis. During their period of office, they enjoy the same guarantees of independence as judges. It follows that the Immigration Adjudicator must be regarded as a court or tribunal within the meaning of [Art 267].'

Conversely, in *Nordsee* (Case 102/81) [1982] ECR 1095, an independent arbitrator was held not to be a court. This was because the arbitrator lacked compulsory jurisdiction. A similar decision was reached in *Denuit & Cordenier* (Case C–125/04) [2005] ECR I–923, where the Court stated:

JUDGMENT

'An arbitration tribunal is not a "court or tribunal of a Member State" within the meaning of [Art 267] where the parties are under no obligation, in law or in fact, to refer their disputes to arbitration and the public authorities of the Member State concerned are not involved in the decision to opt for arbitration nor required to intervene of their own accord in the proceedings before the arbitrator.'

In *Procura Della Republica v X* (Case C–74/95) [1996] ECR I–6609, the ECJ held that questions referred to it by the Italian Public Prosecutor were inadmissible, as he did not constitute a 'court or tribunal'. And in *Victoria Film A/S* (Case C–134/97) [1998] ECR I–7023 a reference from a body within the Swedish tax administration was held inadmissible (it did not carry out a judicial function). Rather, the body carried out a purely administrative function. If anything, the body tried to prevent disputes arising in the first place, as opposed to resolving disputes which had already arisen.

Even a court may not be a 'court' if it is carrying out an administrative (as opposed to judicial) function. In *Salzmann* (Case C–78/99) [2001] ECR I–4421, the ECJ held that the District Court, Bregenz, Austria was not a 'court' when it was acting as a land registry. Similarly, in *Lutz & Others* (Case C–182/00) [2002] ECR I–547, the Regional Court, Wels, Austria was not a 'court' when acting as a companies registry. The ECJ held that:

JUDGMENT

'A national court may refer a question to the [ECJ] only if there is a case pending before it and if it is called upon to give judgment in proceedings intended to lead to a decision of a judicial nature ... when it makes an administrative decision without being required to resolve a legal dispute, the referring body, even if it satisfies the other conditions [identified in Dorsch Consult (1997)], cannot be regarded as exercising a judicial function.'

The wide scope given to the words 'court or tribunal' has allowed for a much greater number of bodies to invoke the preliminary rulings procedure. This has obvious benefits: it means that those bodies are able to apply EU legislation after it has been interpreted by the ECJ, rather than having to try to interpret the law themselves; it allows the ECJ to clarify the law on legislative provisions which may otherwise not have reached the Court; it may even reduce the number of appeals at national level. However, there has been persistent criticism of the Court's policy – from one of the Court's own advisors. In several opinions – starting with *De Coster* (Case C-17/00) [2001] ECR I-9445, repeated in *Österreichischer Rundfunk* (Case C-195/06) [2003] ECR I-4989, and most recently in *Umweltanwalt von Kärnten* (Case C-205/08) [2010] 2 CMLR 19 – Advocate-General Ruiz-Jarabo Colomer has complained that the ECJ's interpretation of 'court or tribunal' is 'too flexible', opening up the preliminary rulings procedure to what he calls 'quasi-judicial bodies', by which he means administrative bodies outside of the 'ordinary judicial structure'. He has invited the Court to 'lay down a stricter and more consistent body of rules' on admissibility, and to re-define the concept of 'court or tribunal', to mean only to 'bodies forming part of the judicial power of every State' with only occasional exceptions. However, the Court has (so far) ignored the Advocate-General's advice.

7.3.2 'Independence'

This criterion has generated some important case law. In England, a number of tribunals are closely connected with government departments whose decisions they are called upon to examine. Does this satisfy the criterion of independence? This issue arose in a case involving the Austrian legal system. In *Köllensperger & Atswanger* (Case C–103/97) [1999] ECR I–551, a reference had been made by the Procurement Office of the *Land* of Tyrol, Austria. Its members were appointed by the Tyrol Government, and could be removed 'if the conditions for appointment are no longer met or if circumstances occur which prevent proper exercise of the office and are likely to do so for a long time'. According to the ECJ, this 'appears *prima facie* too vague to guarantee against undue intervention or pressure on the part of the executive'. However, the Court found that there were guarantees of independence in other provisions of Austrian law, including a provision expressly prohibiting the giving of instructions to members of the Procurement Office in the performance of their duties.

Two other cases illustrate the problem of ensuring 'independence'. In the first case, *Gabalfrisa & Others* (2000), the request was declared admissible, but in the second case, *Schmid* (2002), the Court declared that the ruling was inadmissible.

CASE EXAMPLE

Gabalfrisa & Others (Cases C–110 to 147/98) [2000] ECR I–1577

This case involved several references from the Regional Economic/Administrative Court (EAC) in Catalonia, Spain. There was a question regarding the independence of this court from the tax authorities whose decisions it reviewed. In the end, the Court stated that it was satisfied that Spanish law 'ensures a separation of functions between, on the one hand, the departments of the tax authority responsible for management, clearance and recovery and, on the other hand, the [EAC] which rule on complaints lodged against the decisions of those departments without receiving any instruction from the tax authority'.

CASE EXAMPLE

Schmid (Case C–516/99) [2002] ECR I–4573

This case involved a reference from the Appeal Chamber of the Regional Finance Authority of Vienna. The ECJ declared the reference inadmissible: the Appeal Chamber lacked independence. The problem was that the Appeal Chamber had five members, two of whom were also members of the regional tax authority whose decisions the Chamber was intended to examine. (Indeed, the President of the regional tax authority was automatically also the President of the Appeal Chamber.)

In *Schmid*, the ECJ held that a body cannot be regarded as an independent 'court or tribunal' for the purposes of Art 267 where it has 'an organisational and functional link' with a government department whose decisions it is called upon to review.

In *Wilson* (Case C–506/04) [2006] ECR I–8613, the Court offered extensive guidance on the 'concept of independence', as follows:

JUDGMENT

'The concept of independence, which is inherent in the task of adjudication, involves primarily an authority acting as a third party in relation to the authority which adopted the contested decision. The concept has two other aspects. The first aspect, which is external, presumes that the body is protected against external intervention or pressure liable to jeopardise the independent judgment of its members as regards proceedings before them. That essential freedom from such external factors requires certain guarantees sufficient to protect the person of those who have the task of adjudicating in a dispute, such as guarantees against removal from office. The second aspect, which is internal, is linked to impartiality and seeks to ensure a level playing field for the parties to the proceedings and their respective interests with regard to the subject-matter of those proceedings. That aspect requires objectivity and the absence of any interest in the outcome of the proceedings apart from the strict application of the rule of law. Those guarantees of independence and impartiality require rules, particularly as regards the composition of the body and the appointment, length of service and the grounds for abstention, rejection and dismissal of its members, in order to dismiss any reasonable doubt in the minds of individuals as to the imperviousness of that body to external factors and its neutrality with respect to the interests before it.'

KEY FACTS

The Court can only accept requests from a national 'court or tribunal'... but this means any body carrying out a judicial function	*Broekmeulen* (1981), *Dorsch Consult* (1997), *El-Yassini* (1999)
Arbitrators, prosecutors and administrative bodies are not 'courts or tribunals'	*Nordsee* (1982), *Procura Della Republica v X* (1996), *Victoria Film* (1998), *Salzmann* (2001)
The body requesting a ruling must be independent. It must have no 'organisational or functional link' with any government department.	*Schmid* (2002)
The body must be protected from external intervention or pressure and it must be impartial	*Wilson* (2006)

7.4 The discretionary reference procedure

The decision on when to refer questions, and on what issues, is left entirely up to the national courts (*Pigs Marketing Board v Redmond* (Case 83/78) [1978] ECR 2347). It is normal, but not essential, that one or more of the parties will have attempted to rely upon some provision of EU legislation during the case. However, the national court may issue a reference of its own volition if it deems it necessary to reach a decision (*Verholen* (Cases C–87 to 89/90) [1991] ECR I–3757). It is essential that the request for a ruling be made while the case is still proceeding in the national court. After that point it is too late, because the ECJ decision would no longer be 'necessary' to enable the national court to give judgment (*Pardini* (Case 338/85) [1988] ECR 2041).

For those national courts or tribunals falling within the second paragraph of Art 267 (and this is the vast majority of them), there is a discretion whether or not to refer the case to the ECJ (note the word 'may'). This discretion cannot be removed by national rules as to precedent (*Rheinmuhlen-Dusseldorf* (Case 166/73) [1974] ECR 33). A lower court may refer a matter to the ECJ despite a superior court's ruling to the contrary.

The fact that the ECJ has already decided a particular matter should not of itself prevent a further reference. In *Da Costa en Schaake* (Cases 28 to 30/62) [1963] ECR 61, the ECJ declared it had the right to depart from previous decisions.

In the Court of Appeal case of *Bulmer v Bollinger* (1974), Lord Denning MR noted that national courts need only seek a ruling when it was 'necessary' to enable them to give judgment. He continued:

JUDGMENT

> 'It is to be noticed ... that the word is "necessary". This is much stronger than "desirable" or "convenient". There are some cases where the point, if decided one way, would shorten the trial greatly. But, if decided the other way, it would mean that the trial would go to its full length. In such a case it might be "desirable" or "convenient" to take it as a preliminary point ... But it would not be "necessary" at that stage. When the facts were investigated, it might turn out to have been quite unnecessary. The case would be determined on another ground altogether. As a rule you cannot tell whether it is necessary to decide a point until all the facts are ascertained. So, in general, it is best to decide the facts first.'

He went on to list various factors that should be considered by national judges in deciding whether or not to invoke the procedure:

- time
- cost
- the workload of the ECJ
- the wishes of the parties.

The words of the Master of the Rolls (as Lord Denning was at the time) are obviously important, but remember that the above guidance does not necessarily reflect the view of the ECJ. Nevertheless, time is obviously particularly relevant in criminal cases, where a defendant may have to wait on remand while the ECJ is considering its ruling. This issue has recently been addressed: the fourth paragraph of Art 267, requiring the ECJ to act 'with the minimum of delay' in cases involving 'a person in custody', was added by the Lisbon Treaty.

7.5 The mandatory reference procedure

7.5.1 Introduction

Under the second paragraph of Art 267, the court or tribunal '**may**' make a request; under the third paragraph of Art 267, courts or tribunals, against whose decisions there is no judicial remedy under national law, '**shall**' refer. So, only for certain courts or tribunals is it mandatory to refer. The question is: which courts are they? In *Costa v ENEL* (Case 6/64) [1964] ECR 1141, a request had come from an Italian magistrates' court. There was no appeal from the magistrates' decision, because of the small amount of money involved. The ECJ stated (emphasis added): 'By the terms of this Article ... national courts against whose decision, **as in the present case**, there is no judicial remedy, **must** refer the matter to the Court of Justice.'

Although slightly ambiguous, this has been taken to imply that certain courts (such as the English Court of Appeal), although generally subject to the second paragraph, could find themselves subject to the third paragraph if no appeal was available in a particular case. Initially, the view of the Court of Appeal itself was that it was never subject to the third paragraph. In *Bulmer v Bollinger* (1974), Lord Denning MR said that 'short of the House of Lords, no other English court is bound to refer a question' to the ECJ. However, in *Chiron Corporation v Murex Diagnostics (No 8)* [1995] All ER (EC) 88, Balcombe LJ pointed out that:

JUDGMENT

'[Article 267] refers to "a court ... against whose decisions there is no judicial remedy under national law". For convenience, I will refer to such a court as the court of last resort ... Where there is no right even to apply to the House of Lords for leave to appeal from a decision of the Court of Appeal – e.g. on a refusal by the Court of Appeal for leave to appeal against the decision of the court below, or a refusal by the Court of Appeal, on a renewed application, to grant leave to apply for judicial review – then the Court of Appeal will be the court of last resort. So Lord Denning MR stated the matter too widely [in *Bulmer v Bollinger*].'

Note: the House of Lords has now been replaced by the Supreme Court of the United Kingdom as the UK's 'court of last resort'. This issue has been examined by the ECJ, albeit in the context of the Swedish judicial system.

CASE EXAMPLE

Lyckeskog (Case C–99/00) [2003] 1 WLR 9

The ECJ was asked whether a rule of Swedish procedural law, which required a 'declaration of admissibility' to be obtained before a case could be appealed from the Court of Appeal to the Supreme Court, meant that the former court was, in effect, a 'court of last resort' (to borrow Balcombe LJ's expression). According to its own Code of Procedure, the Supreme Court may declare an appeal admissible only if:

- it is important for guidance in the application of the law that the appeal be examined by the Supreme Court or
- there are special grounds for examination of the appeal, such as the existence of grounds of review on a point of law, formal defect, or where the outcome of the case before the Court of Appeal is manifestly attributable to negligence or serious error.

The ECJ held that these procedural rules did not convert the Swedish Court of Appeal into a court of last resort:

JUDGMENT

'Decisions of a national appellate court which can be challenged by the parties before a supreme court are not decisions of a "court or tribunal of a Member State against whose decisions there is no judicial remedy under national law" within the meaning of [Art 267]. The fact that examination of the merits of such appeals is subject to a prior declaration of admissibility by the supreme court does not have the effect of depriving the parties of a judicial remedy.'

The decision in *Lyckeskog* was followed and applied in *Cartesio* (Case C-210/06) [2008] ECR I-9641. That case raised the question whether the Regional Court of Appeal in Hungary was subject to the third paragraph of Art 267, given that its decisions were final, subject to an 'extraordinary' appeal to the Hungarian Supreme Court. The ECJ ruled that, because appeals were available, albeit only in limited circumstances, the Regional Court of Appeal was not subject to the mandatory reference procedure.

7.5.2 Mandatory references and hypothetical questions

Although national supreme courts are obliged to make references to the ECJ when a question is raised before them, that does not mean they have to seek rulings if the question raised is actually irrelevant to the case. However interesting the question may be, if it is not essential to the outcome of the case it is hypothetical. In *CILFIT* (Case 283/81) [1982] ECR 3415, the ECJ held that:

JUDGMENT

'National courts or tribunals are not obliged to refer to the Court of Justice a question concerning the interpretation of [Union] law raised before them if that question is not relevant, that is to say, if the answer to that question, regardless of what it may be, can in no way affect the outcome of the case.'

7.5.3 Mandatory references and previous rulings

Does a national court of last resort have to make a preliminary reference even if the point has already been decided? If so, that would generate a large number of 'repeat' references, which would be very inefficient. Hence, the ECJ has decided that national courts of last resort do not have to make references in such cases. In *Da Costa* (1963), the ECJ stated:

JUDGMENT

'The authority of an interpretation ... already given by the Court may deprive the obligation [under the third paragraph of Art 267] of its purpose and thus empty it of its substance. Such is the case especially when the question is materially identical with a question which has already been the subject of a preliminary ruling in a similar case.'

This was subsequently endorsed by the ECJ in *CILFIT* (1982). The ECJ referred to *Da Costa* and added that 'the same effect ... may be produced ... even though the questions at issue are not strictly identical'. And in *Bulmer v Bollinger* (1974), Lord Denning said that 'In some cases ... it may be found that the same point ... has already been decided by the [ECJ] in a previous case. In that event it is not necessary for the English court to decide it. It can follow the previous decision without troubling the [ECJ]'.

7.5.4 Mandatory references and *acte clair*

According to the ECJ in *CILFIT* (1982), 'the correct application of [Union] law may be so obvious as to leave no scope for any reasonable doubt as to the manner in which the question raised is to be resolved'. This would entitle a national 'court of last resort' to decide not to invoke the Art 267 procedure. A decision not to request a ruling because the provision is 'so obvious as to leave no scope for reasonable doubt' is an example of *acte clair* (literally, 'clear act'), a doctrine developed from French law. However, in *CILFIT* (1982), the ECJ gave very clear instructions that *acte clair* must be used with caution:

JUDGMENT

'Before it comes to the conclusion that such is the case, the national court or tribunal must be convinced that the matter is equally obvious to the courts of the other Member States and to the Court of Justice. Only if those conditions are satisfied may the national court or tribunal refrain from submitting the question to the Court of Justice and take upon itself the responsibility for resolving it.'

The Court went on to list those conditions in the next paragraph:

JUDGMENT

> 'To begin with, it must be borne in mind that [Union] legislation is drafted in several languages and that different language versions are equally authentic. An interpretation of a provision of [Union] law thus involves a comparison of the different language versions. It must also be borne in mind, even when the different language versions are entirely in accord with one another, that [Union] law uses terminology which is peculiar to it. Furthermore, it must be emphasised that legal concepts do not necessarily have the same meaning in [Union] law and in the law of the various Member States. Finally, every provision of [Union] law must be placed in its context and interpreted in the light of the provisions of [Union] law as a whole, regard being had to the objectives thereof and to the state of its evolution at the date on which the provision in question is to be applied.'

The instruction not to abuse *acte clair* was subsequently emphasised in *Intermodal Transports* (Case C-495/03) [2005] ECR I-8151, where the Court stated that the national court or tribunal must 'in particular' be convinced that the other Member States' national courts and the ECJ itself would find the matter 'equally obvious'.

7.5.5 *Acte clair* and the courts in the UK

In *Bulmer v Bollinger* (1974), Lord Denning MR in the Court of Appeal enthusiastically endorsed *acte clair*: 'the English court may consider the point is reasonably clear and free from doubt. In that event there is no need to interpret the Treaty but only to apply it, and that is the task of the English court.' Similarly, Lord Diplock in *Garland v BREL* [1979] 1 WLR 754 in the House of Lords said that where there was a 'considerable and consistent line of case law' such that the answer was 'obvious and inevitable' then a reference would not be required. In *Commissioners of Customs & Excise Commissioners v Samex* [1983] 1 All ER 1042, however, Lord Bingham MR in the Court of Appeal said that national courts should be mindful of the differences between national and EU legislation, of the pitfalls if they got it wrong, and of the overriding need for uniform interpretation throughout the EU. Lord Bingham MR stated:

JUDGMENT

> 'We understand the correct approach in principle of a national court (other than a final court of appeal) to be quite clear; if the facts have been found and the [Union] law issue is critical to the court's final decision, the appropriate course is ordinarily to refer the issue to the ECJ unless the national court can with complete confidence resolve the issue itself ... In considering [this], the national court must be mindful of the difference between national and [EU] legislation, of the pitfalls which face a national court when venturing into an unfamiliar field, of the need for uniform interpretation throughout the [Union] and of the great advantages enjoyed by the ECJ in construing [EU legislation].'

The *acte clair* doctrine is extremely important in cutting out unnecessary, time-consuming requests. However, it can be abused, as happened in *R v Chief Constable of Sussex, ex parte International Trader's Ferry Ltd* [1998] 3 WLR 1260, where the House of Lords declined to seek rulings on the interpretation of the word 'measures' in Art 35 and the phrase 'public policy' in Art 36 (see Chapter 14 for discussion of these issues). Academic reaction to the ITF case was hostile:

> '*ITF* is far from an exemplary illustration of the courts discharging their duty to apply [Union] law. Although it is probable that the end result is the correct one, it is impossible to be certain. At least three moot points lie buried in the case. Therefore, despite the palpable reluctance of the House of Lords to make use of the preliminary [rulings] procedure in order

to seek clarification from the Court of Justice, there is a persuasive argument that a reference should have been made.'

E Baker, 'Policing, Protest and Free Trade' [2000] Crim LR 95

Erika Szyszczak, in 'Fundamental Values in the House of Lords' (2000) 25 ELR 443 made the same point, observing that it was 'surprising that the House of Lords did not make an [Article 267] reference'.

A more recent example of the UK Supreme Court displaying 'palpable reluctance' when it comes to invoking the preliminary rulings procedure – despite its obligation to do so in the third paragraph of Art 267 – is the case of *Abbey National plc v OFT* [2009] UKSC 6; [2009] 3 WLR 1215. Although all five judges decided that the case should not be referred to the ECJ, only one – Lord Mance – actually paid any attention to the *CILFIT* conditions. He decided that the possibility of the disputed provision having a different meaning in other versions of the legislation was 'very limited' and that the likelihood of the ECJ or the other Member States' courts coming up with a different interpretation to that of the Supreme Court was 'remote'. In contrast, Lord Walker simply stated that 'we should treat the matter as *acte clair*'. Meanwhile, Lord Phillips said that the matter was not *acte clair*, but should not be referred anyway because 'it would not be appropriate'.

7.5.6 Academic reaction to *acte clair*

Academic reaction to the doctrine of *acte clair* itself has been mixed. The consensus seems to be that the ECJ in *CILFIT* (1982) was right to endorse *acte clair*. However, opinion is divided about the criteria to be satisfied by national courts before invoking the doctrine.

> 'The effect of the *CILFIT* decision ... would be to enable national judges to justify any reluctance they might feel to ask for a preliminary ruling ... Of the factors to be borne in mind by national courts before they concluded that the meaning of a provision of [Union] law was clear, only the requirement that the different language versions be compared ... had any teeth ... In short, the overall effect of *CILFIT* would be to encourage national courts to decide points of [Union] law for themselves.'

A Arnull, 'The Use & Abuse of Article 177 EEC' (1989) 52 MLR 622

On the other hand, Professor Rasmussen is perhaps the most highly critical commentator of *CILFIT* (1982). While he endorses the ECJ's decision to allow national courts of last resort to decide questions of EU law for themselves, he believes that the *CILFIT* (1982) criteria are so stringent that, taken as a whole, the judgment achieves the opposite of what the Court said it intended to do. Writing in 1984, he said:

> 'The author believes that ... *CILFIT* means something very different from what it *prima facie* establishes ... The real strategy is different from the apparent strategy. The real strategy of *CILFIT* is not to incorporate an *acte clair* concept into [Union] law. It is to call the national judiciaries to circumspection when they are faced with problems of interpretation and application of [Union] law.'

H Rasmussen, 'The European Court's *Acte Clair* Strategy in *CILFIT*' (1984) 9 ELR 242

He repeated his criticism in 2000, calling for the ECJ to rewrite the *CILFIT* (1982) judgment to make *acte clair* more easily available:

> 'The Court of Justice's present predicaments are self-inflicted ... I refer to the submission straightjacket designed by the Court in *CILFIT*. This judgment has functioned as a magnet, drawing numerous, and often less-than-necessary, cases up to the Court. The ECJ ought ... to rewrite *CILFIT*'s submission criteria, thereby watering down some of the stringency of the conditions to which it subjects national courts' duty to make use of [Art 267].'

H Rasmussen, 'Remedying the Crumbling EC Judicial System' (2000) 37 CMLR 1071

KEY FACTS

Discretionary and mandatory referral	
Most national courts and tribunals have a discretion whether to invoke the procedure	Article 267, paragraph 2
National courts and tribunals against whose decisions there is no judicial remedy under national law 'shall' invoke the procedure. This means it is mandatory for them to refer cases to the ECJ (subject to certain exceptions)	Article 267, paragraph 3
There is no obligation to refer hypothetical or irrelevant questions	*CILFIT* (1982)
There is no obligation to refer questions which have already been answered by the ECJ in a previous ruling	*Da Costa* (1963)
There is no obligation to refer questions where the answer is 'obvious'. This is '*acte clair*'. However, national courts must be convinced that other Member States' courts and the ECJ would find the answer 'equally obvious'	*CILFIT* (1982), *Intermodal Transports* (2005)

7.6 Reform of the preliminary reference procedure

The ECJ is faced with a very large backlog of cases, such that the average waiting time (from a national court or tribunal requesting a preliminary ruling until the ruling itself) is approximately 20 months. In some cases four years have elapsed between the question being asked and its answer. If the delay is not reduced, national judges may be inhibited from asking questions, instead attempting to answer the questions themselves, which threatens both individual rights (if the judges get the answer wrong) and the 'co-operation' between the various courts.

One thing about which there is academic agreement is that the preliminary reference procedure is in urgent need of reform. According to Professor Rasmussen ('Remedying the Crumbling EC Judicial System' (2000) 37 CMLR 1071): 'It is a generally shared view today that the case for a comprehensive and profound judicial reform has become compelling.' Johnston ('Judicial Reform and the Treaty of Nice' (2001) 38 CMLR 499) agrees that 'Clearly, there is a serious workload problem for the Court, due to a number of factors. It is particularly serious in the context of references for a preliminary ruling.'

The delay has been caused by, among other things:

- The expansion of the EU (from 6 in 1958 to 9 in 1973, to 10 in 1981 and 12 in 1986, to 15 in 1995 to 25 in 2004 and to 27 Member States in 2007), allowing more courts and tribunals to refer questions.
- The associated growth in the number of official EU languages (from 4 in 1958 to 6 in 1973, to 7 in 1981, 9 in 1986, 11 in 1995 and now 23). This imposes massive burdens on the ECJ in terms of the translation of judgments.
- The width of the ECJ's own definition of 'court or tribunal' in cases such as *Dorsch Consult*.
- The ever-increasing scope and volume of EU secondary legislation. For example, during 2003 two new discrimination Directives (Directive 2000/43, the 'Race Directive', and Directive 2000/78, the 'General Framework Directive') entered into force. Both are 'ripe' for preliminary rulings over the next few years, in that they contain ambiguous words and concepts. These Directives will be examined in detail in Chapter 18.

- The ECJ's development of concepts such as fundamental rights and State liability, and the reliance placed on the Charter of Fundamental Rights (2000), all of which have triggered waves of new requests for preliminary rulings.

Against this, the ECJ's own tentative steps to reduce its workload through *acte clair* in *CILFIT* in 1982 has had negligible impact. All of this has led to a net increase in the number of preliminary references which the Court has to deal with, as the table shows:

Year	Number of preliminary references
1961	1
1971	37
1981	108
1991	186
2001	237

7.6.1 Conferral of jurisdiction on the General Court

In the future, some preliminary rulings will be transferred to the General Court, albeit in 'specific areas' and with the possibility of reference to/review by the ECJ. The procedure is set out in Art 256(3).

ARTICLE

'Art 256(3) The General Court shall have jurisdiction to hear and determine questions referred for a preliminary ruling under Article 267, in specific areas laid down by the Statute.

Where the General Court considers that the case requires a decision of principle likely to affect the unity or consistency of Union law, it may refer the case to the Court of Justice for a ruling.

Decisions given by the General Court on questions referred for a preliminary ruling may exceptionally be subject to review by the Court of Justice, under the conditions and within the limits laid down by the Statute, where there is a serious risk of the unity or consistency of Union law being affected.'

Although the General Court has been in operation since 1989, it has never actually handled preliminary rulings. When the General Court was created it had no jurisdiction in this area. That changed when Art 256(3) was inserted into what was then the EC Treaty in 2003. However, the procedure has not yet been brought into operation, the main stumbling block being the lack of any decision on what the 'specific areas' should be. Numerous suggestions have been made (see in particular P Dyrberg, 'What Should the Court of Justice be Doing?' (2001) 26 EL Rev 291) but, as yet, none of the suggestions has been adopted.

Assuming that the General Court is allowed to start hearing preliminary rulings at some point, there are likely to be teething problems until the new procedure is fully developed. For example:

- The General Court 'may' refer cases onto the ECJ when a 'decision of principle' is involved – but what does that mean?
- Although the ECJ is only to review General Court rulings 'exceptionally', this nevertheless undermines the authority of all those rulings. Can any national court apply any General Court ruling whilst a possible review is still pending? Should the ECJ be given a time limit by which it must decide whether it is to invoke its review power?

Academic reaction to the conferral of preliminary ruling jurisdiction on the General Court has been mixed, although mostly positive. Tridimas described the procedure as setting an 'acceptable balance between competing demands' – the need for consistent interpretation of EU legislation on one hand, and the need for a reduction in the waiting time on the other. He described the idea of the ECJ and General Court sharing jurisdiction over preliminary rulings as 'preferable over alternative reforms' (T Tridimas, 'Knocking on Heaven's Door: Fragmentation, Efficiency and Defiance in the Preliminary Reference Procedure' (2003) 450 CML Rev 9). Another commentator described the new procedure as 'very important', adding 'the sooner this possibility is exercised the better' (B Vesterdorf, 'The Community Court System Ten Years from Now and Beyond: Challenges and Possibilities' (2003) 28 EL Rev 303). However, Heffernan was less enthusiastic, suggesting that 'there is every reason to believe that [the General Court's] contribution will be limited' (L Heffernan, 'The Community Courts post-Nice': a European *Certiorari* Revisited' (2003) 52 ICLQ 907).

7.6.2 The urgent preliminary ruling procedure

In March 2008, a new urgent preliminary rulings procedure was adopted, to be used in exceptional cases. The Court of Justice explained the thinking behind the new procedure as follows:

> This procedure is applicable as from 1st March 2008 and should enable the Court to deal far more quickly with the most sensitive issues relating to the area of freedom, security and justice, such as those which may arise, for example, in certain situations where a person is deprived of his liberty and the answer to the question raised is decisive as to the assessment of the legal situation of the person detained or deprived of his liberty; or, in proceedings concerning parental authority or custody of children, where the jurisdiction under [Union] law of the court hearing the case depends on the answer to the question referred for a preliminary ruling.

The new procedure cuts the waiting time by:

- restricting the number of parties entitled to submit written observations
- referring all cases involving the area of freedom, security and justice to a special chamber of five judges who will decide whether to apply the new procedure and, if they decide to do so, to give their ruling shortly afterwards
- using only electronic communication.

The new procedure was used for the first time in *Rinau* (case C-195/08 PPU) [2008] ECR I-5271; [2009] 2 WLR 972. On 30th April 2008, a preliminary ruling was requested by the Supreme Court of Lithuania in a case involving child custody. Luisa Rinau's parents were divorced and she lived with her mother in Lithuania, but her father, who lived in Germany, was seeking custody. The ECJ applied the new procedure and the ruling was delivered on 11th July, a little over ten weeks later. The Court explained that the urgency was justified by the need to protect Luisa from harm, the need to avoid damaging her relationship with her father, and the need to ensure a 'fair balance' between Luisa's interests and those of her parents.

An even faster turnaround was achieved in *Santesteban Goicoechea* (case C-296/08 PPU) [2008] ECR I-6307. Here, the Court of Appeal in Montpellier, France, requested a preliminary ruling in a case involving the possible extradition of a Spanish national from France to face criminal charges in Spain. The ruling was requested on 3rd July 2008 and the ECJ ruling was given on 12th August, less than six weeks later. Here, the urgency was justified because the individual concerned was being held in detention in France following the completion of a prison sentence there pending his possible extradition to Spain.

Academic reaction to the new procedure has been positive, but Koutrakos ('Speeding up the Preliminary Reference Procedure – Fast but not too Fast' (2008) 33 EL Rev 617) has pointed out that 'there is a balance which must be struck' between delivering judgments as quickly as possible (on the one hand) and providing sufficient time for the ECJ's judges 'to reflect on the questions put before them, assess the arguments ... and consider the wider ramifications of their conclusions' (on the other). He notes that taking time to deliver a judgment is not a 'luxury' but 'an essential prerequisite for the proper administration of justice'.

7.6.3 Other reform proposals

Numerous proposals for reform of the preliminary rulings procedure have been advanced over the years. These proposals fall into two distinct groups:

1. those proposals which seek to reduce the volume of requests coming into the ECJ and
2. those that seek to boost or streamline the European Union's judicial capacity for dealing with these cases.

(The conferral of jurisdiction on the General Court, noted above, falls into the latter group.) Group 1 proposals include:

- Restricting the range of national courts or tribunals with the discretion to seek rulings. This could entail removing the right of 'first instance' national courts and tribunals (such as magistrates' and county courts plus most tribunals in England) from seeking rulings. This would probably have little practical impact as 'first instance' courts tend not to seek many references anyway.
- Removing the right of 'first tier' appeal courts and tribunals (such as the High Court and the Employment Appeal Tribunal (EAT)) from seeking rulings. This would probably have a significant impact in terms of cutting down requests. Statistics indicate that a large proportion of the preliminary rulings requested by British courts come from the High Court and the EAT. If these bodies lost the right to seek rulings, they would have to interpret EU legislation themselves (with the risk of divergent rulings being made).
- Tightening up the *Dorsch Consult* (1997) criteria, thereby cutting out requests from bodies such as 'appeal boards' and 'adjudicators'.
- Abolishing mandatory referral for national courts of last resort. Arguably, this has already been achieved through the doctrine of *acte clair.;*
- Re-wording Art 267 to require national judges to consider the importance, difficulty and/or novelty of the ruling requested.

Group 2 proposals include:

- Allowing the ECJ to filter questions. Most national courts of last resort can filter out cases deemed to be insufficiently important or novel. There are grounds for saying that the ECJ should be given the same power.
- Setting up regionalised courts with EU legal specialism, with the ECJ re-styled as a 'European High Court of Justice' overseeing the new regionalised courts. This is not dissimilar to the organisation of federal courts in the United States, with the Supreme Court in Washington DC at the apex, overseeing the decisions of the various federal 'circuit' courts, which in turn oversee the federal courts in the states within each 'circuit'.

The latter suggestion was first proposed by the academics Jacque and Weiler

> 'At the apex of the system will remain the [ECJ], renamed perhaps as the European High Court of Justice. We propose the creation of four new Community Regional Courts which will have jurisdiction to receive preliminary references from, and issue preliminary rulings to, national courts within each region. Upon the decision or preliminary ruling of the Regional Court being issued, a party to the proceedings and the Commission, Council, Parliament or Member States as interveners, may appeal to the European High Court of Justice.'
>
> J P Jacque and J Weiler, *'On the Road to European Union – A New Judicial Architecture'* (1990) 27 CMLR 185

All of these proposals would reduce the workload of the ECJ and hence reduce the time delay, but at what cost?

- Restricting national courts' ability to seek rulings will probably lead to more appeals in the national courts as disappointed litigants try to get a case into a national court which has retained the power to request rulings.
- Filtration may undermine the 'co-operation' that exists between the ECJ and the Member States' courts and tribunals. This may deter national courts from seeking rulings in cases where, now, they would seek such a ruling, possibly leading to inconsistency of interpretation in different Member States and stifling the development of EU legal principles (key doctrines such as direct effect, indirect effect, state liability and fundamental rights were all developed during preliminary ruling cases).
- Regionalisation threatens uniformity, and setting up several new courts will incur considerable cost in terms of infrastructure, staffing, communications and IT. There may also be squabbles as to the location of any new regional courts.

KEY FACTS

Reform of the preliminary rulings procedure	
The General Court has jurisdiction to give preliminary rulings in 'specific areas', subject to referral to/review by the ECJ. But no 'specific areas' have been identified	Article 256(3) TFEU
An urgent procedure was introduced in 2008, to deal with child custody disputes and cases where a person's liberty is at stake	*Rinau* (2008), *Santesteban Goicoechea* (2008)
Other reform proposals have been made, including restricting the range or ability of national courts and tribunals to seek rulings, re-defining the phrase 'court or tribunal', or abolishing mandatory referrals	
Other proposals include allowing the ECJ to filter questions, or setting up specialised, regionalised courts	

SAMPLE ESSAY QUESTION

The biggest problem facing the Court of Justice of the European Union is the unacceptable delays resulting from its preliminary rulings caseload. This problem does not just affect the parties to the individual cases, but threatens the future development of the EU itself. There are several causes of the problem, not least of which is the Court's own 'functional' test for deciding whether or not a body may request a ruling. However, there are also several possible solutions to the problem. Discuss.

Outline the purpose and operation of the preliminary rulings procedure:

- Allows ECJ to give definitive interpretations of EU law, ensuring consistency throughout the EU (*Stauder v Ulm*)
- National courts and tribunals may, at their discretion, request rulings; national 'courts of last resort' are obliged to do so, unless the point of law has already been decided by the ECJ in a previous case (*Da Costa*), is irrelevant to the dispute or is *'acte clair'*, meaning that the answer is obvious (*CILFIT*)
- Once the ECJ gives its ruling, it must then be applied in all cases
- There is an urgent procedure for cases raising sensitive issues relating to the area of freedom, security and justice, such as child custody disputes (*Inga Rinau*).

Explain the 'functional' test for deciding whether a body is a 'court or tribunal':

- The name of a body is immaterial; the key question is whether a body performs a judicial function
- Factors to determine this question include whether the body: is established by law, is independent, is permanent, has compulsory jurisdiction, has an *inter partes* procedure, and applies rules of law (*Dorsch Consult*)
- Give some examples of cases where requests were denied, e.g. *Nordsee, Victoria Film*
- Independence is crucial (*Schmid*).

Discuss implications of the delays in the procedure:

- The dispute in the national court is prolonged
- National courts and tribunals may be discouraged from seeking rulings, and may decide to interpret EU legislation themselves. This could lead to EU law fragmenting (with different meanings in different Member States)
- The preliminary rulings procedure has allowed the ECJ to develop several key principles of EU law, such as direct effect, supremacy, and state liability. The ECJ relies on new cases to continue to develop EU law.

Discuss potential solutions:

- The Nice Treaty conferred jurisdiction on the General Court, but only in 'specific areas', as yet undecided, subject to referral to/review by the ECJ
- Redefine 'courts or tribunals'
- Restrict the national courts with access to the ECJ
- Abolish mandatory referral for national supreme courts
- Introduce a system of case filtering
- 'Decentralisation' – the creation of new EU courts with the ECJ re-styled as a European High Court of Justice to hear appeals
- All reform options must be carefully considered. The key point is that the procedure must continue to ensure consistency of EU legislation.

SUMMARY

- Article 267 TFEU allows any 'court or tribunal' of a Member State to request the Court of Justice to interpret provisions of EU legislation. The national court or tribunal then has the task of applying that law, as interpreted. Having one court to interpret all EU legislation ensures uniform application (*Stauder v Ulm*).
- The Court usually adopts a 'purposive' approach to interpretation, seeking to interpret ambiguous EU law in a way which most promotes the purpose behind the legislation (*Adidas*).
- Only a 'court or tribunal' may request a ruling, but this means that the body must be carrying out a judicial function, taking into account various factors such as permanence, an inter partes procedure, compulsory jurisdiction (*Dorsch Consult*). Independence is crucial (*Schmid*).
- Arbitrators, public prosecutors and administrative bodies are not a 'court or tribunal' (*Nordsee, Victoria Film*). Even a court may not be a 'court' if it is carrying out an administrative function (*Salzmann, Lutz*).
- Under Article 267 (2), any court or tribunal 'may' request a ruling. Under Article 267 (3), 'courts of last resort' must do so where a point of EU law is involved, subject to three exceptions: previous rulings (*Da Costa*), irrelevance (*CILFIT*), and '*acte clair*', i.e. the national court is convinced that the answer to the question is obvious (*CILFIT*). *Acte clair* must be used with caution. In particular, the national court must be convinced that the matter is equally obvious to the courts of the other Member States and to the Court of Justice (*Intermodal Transports*).
- The ECJ is bound in principle to respond to a request for a ruling, subject to requests declared to be inadmissible: contrived disputes (*Foglia v Novello*); irrelevance; lack of background factual and/or legal information.
- Under the urgent procedure, certain cases may be dealt with very quickly. Typical cases involve child custody (*Inga Rinau*) or where a person is in custody (*Santesteban Goicoechea*).
- The ECJ is faced with a very large backlog of cases; the <u>average</u> waiting time (from a national court requesting a ruling until the ruling itself) is around 19 months. If the delay is not reduced further, national judges may be inhibited from asking questions, instead attempting to answer the questions themselves, which threatens the whole point of the procedure and the 'co-operation' between the ECJ and the national courts.

- The delay has been caused by, inter alia, the expansion of the EU (from 6 to 27 Member States), allowing more courts and tribunals to refer questions; the associated growth in the number of official EU languages; the width of the ECJ's own functional definition of 'court or tribunal'; the ever-increasing scope and volume of EU secondary legislation.
- One solution is to confer jurisdiction on the General Court in 'specific areas' (Article 256 (3) TFEU). As yet, no 'specific areas' have been decided. Under this procedure, there will be the possibility of cases involving 'decisions of principle' being referred on to/reviewed by the ECJ.
- Other proposals for reform include: appointing more judges; restricting the range of national courts and tribunals with the discretion to seek rulings; abolishing mandatory referral for 'courts of last resort'; filtering questions; setting up regional courts with EU legal specialism (decentralisation). All of these proposals would reduce the workload of the ECJ and hence reduce the time-delay, but there are risks, especially to consistency.

Further reading

Articles

Anagnostaras, G, 'Preliminary problems and Jurisdiction Uncertainties: the Admissibility of Questions referred by Bodies Performing Quasi-judicial Functions' (2005) 30 EL Rev 878.

Arnull, A, 'Judicial Architecture or Judicial Folly? The Challenge Facing the European Union' (1999) 24 ELR 516.

Barnard, C, 'The PPU: Is it Worth the Candle? An Early Assessment' (2009) 34 EL Rev 281.

Jacque, J P and Weiler, J, 'On the Road to European Union – A New Judicial Architecture' (1990) 27 CMLR 185.

Johnston, A, 'Judicial Reform and the Treaty of Nice' (2001) 38 CMLR 499.

Komarek, J, 'In the Court(s) We Trust? On the need for Hierarchy and Differentiation in the Preliminary Ruling Procedure' (2007) 32 EL Rev 467.

Rasmussen, H, 'Remedying the Crumbling EC Judicial System' (2000) 37 CMLR 1071.

Vesterdorf, B, 'The Community Court System Ten Years from now and Beyond: Challenges and Possibilities' (2003) 28 ELR 303.

8

The relationship between EU law and national law – supremacy

AIMS AND OBJECTIVES

After reading this chapter you should be able to:

- Understand the meaning of supranationalism and the reasons for it
- Understand the meaning of supremacy and its link with supranationalism and why it was created by the ECJ
- Understand how supremacy was developed and how it is defined
- Understand the attitudes of the UK and other Member States to supremacy
- Analyse the effects and consequences of supremacy for Member States and for the EU

8.1 The origins of supremacy and the link with supranationalism

8.1.1 The basic meaning of 'supremacy'

'Supremacy' in simple terms means no more than that, in areas where EU law is relevant to a case before a national court, EU law prevails over national law. This mirrors in some senses the way that we are told in English law that parliamentary law, in the form of Acts of Parliament, prevails over all other forms of English law. The practical consequence, then, of this supremacy is that wherever there is a conflict between the national law of a Member State and EU law itself it is EU law that must be applied.

Supremacy is merely one of the key doctrines created by the European Court of Justice that ensure the enforceability of the legal order. The others are:

- direct effect
- indirect effect and
- state liability.

These are all discussed in the next chapter, Chapter 9.

It would be fair to describe all of these as fundamental principles without which EU law could not have developed. So the European Court of Justice has been active in ensuring the success of the EU and its gradual evolution.

Supremacy has probably become one of the most entrenched of all principles associated with EU law. Nevertheless, despite the inevitable political tensions between Member States and the EU institutions and some testing times between the European Court of Justice and the national courts, it is possibly also fair to say that it has ultimately proved to be one of the least controversial aspects.

8.1.2 The reasons for a doctrine of supremacy

While there is no actual mention of the principle within the Treaties, it is simple to see why the European Court of Justice created and then developed the principle of supremacy (or 'primacy of EU law', as it is sometimes known):

- The fundamental objective of creating a single Internal Market demands that there should be harmonisation between Member States, which in itself then depends on a uniform application of EU law within the Member States.
- The whole structure of the Community was founded on the idea of supranationalism. Without supremacy of EU law the institutions would be deprived of supranational effect and uniformity might instead be sacrificed to national self-interest.

In this way the real justifications for the existence of a doctrine of supremacy are two-fold:

- Firstly, it prevents any possibility of a questioning of the validity of EU law within the Member States themselves.
- Secondly, it fulfils what is sometimes referred to as the 'doctrine of pre-emption', and it does so in two ways:
  - the fact that EU law is supreme means that the national courts in Member States are prevented from producing alternative interpretations of EU law
  - the existence of such a doctrine also means that the legislative bodies of the individual Member States are prevented from enacting legislation that would conflict with EU law.

However, as has already been noted, there is nothing in the Treaties that specifically states that EU law, in whatever form, takes precedence over national law. The closest the Treaties come is in the so-called 'duty of loyalty' contained in Art 10, EC Treaty which can be paraphrased in the following terms:

ARTICLE

'Art 10 Member States shall take all appropriate measures ... to ensure fulfillment of the obligations arising out of this Treaty or resulting from any actions taken by the institutions ... They shall abstain from any measure which could jeopardise the attainment of the objectives of the Treaty ...'

Article 10 is now repealed and amended by the Lisbon Treaty.

The European Court of Justice, then, has been proactive and instrumental in ensuring that the objectives of the Treaties are achieved in the Member States, and in doing so supremacy has been a powerful tool in its hands.

Quite simply, the full economic integration necessary for the achievement of a Single Market would have proved impossible if it had been possible for Member States to ignore or even deliberately defy the supranational powers of the institutions of the EU.

Taking a long-term view, probably the most logical basis for supremacy is that without it a full integration, including the political integration required for a federalist system, would also prove impossible.

The abandoned Constitutional Treaty would have included a statement on supremacy of EU law. Declaration 17 of the Treaty of Lisbon identifies merely that '... in accordance with well settled case law of the Court of Justice of the European Union, the Treaties and the law adopted by the Union on the basis of the Treaties have primacy over the law of Member States, under the conditions laid down by the said case law.'

8.2 The development of a doctrine of supremacy

8.2.1 The early definitions of 'supremacy'

The earliest indication of a concept of supremacy comes from the judgment of the ECJ in the case of *Van Gend en Loos v Nederlandse Administratie der Belastingen* (Case 26/62) [1963] ECR 1; [1963] CMLR 105. (The case principally concerns the issue of direct effect and is therefore more fully discussed in Chapter 9.) The case involved an introduction of a Dutch law which was contrary to obligations imposed on Member States in an EC Treaty Article. Because the Article implicitly conferred rights on individuals and the litigant suffered financial loss as a result of the Dutch law, an Art 234 (Art 267 TFEU following the Lisbon Treaty) reference posed the question for the ECJ of whether or not the Treaty created rights on behalf of individuals that national courts must then protect.

In the reasoned opinion the Advocate-General declared that this was not the case and that the appropriate means of resolution in such circumstances was in an action against the Member State under Art 226 (Art 258 TFEU following the Lisbon Treaty). The judges in the ECJ disagreed and in their judgment identified that:

JUDGMENT

'The Community constitutes a new legal order in international law for whose benefits the states have limited their sovereign rights, albeit within limited fields …'.

This is not a complete definition of 'supremacy'. Nevertheless, the ECJ avoided the problems that would go with classing EU law as international law, to which different Member States, because of their different constitutions, would adopt completely different approaches. What the ECJ identified in the case was that the EU must be viewed as a different and unique legal order distinct from either national law or international law. The key point, of course, was the clear statement that by accepting entry into the Community the Member States were limiting their otherwise sovereign rights to legislate contrary to the requirements of EU law in those areas affected by EC law.

The ECJ had to wait only two years to produce a more complete definition and more extensive explanation. This came in another Art 234 reference (Art 267 TFEU following the Lisbon Treaty) this time from an Italian court. Again, it involved legislation that was passed after accession to the Treaties that was inconsistent with provisions of EU law.

CASE EXAMPLE

Costa v ENEL (Case 6/64) [1964] ECR 585; [1964] CMLR 425

ENEL (more formally known as Ente Nazionale per l'Energia Elettrica) was a state electric company under which the Italian Government had nationalised (put under state ownership) both the production and distribution of electricity. Costa was a lawyer who had owned shares in one of the pre-nationalised electric companies. He had argued in his local court that the law nationalising the industry was unlawful because it contravened EC monopoly laws. The court used the Art 234 [now Art 267 TFEU] procedure to refer several questions to the ECJ. The Italian Government, following a judgment of the Italian constitutional court between the parties, argued that the proceedings themselves were flawed since the Italian court should have followed the law nationalising the industry, which came later than the law ratifying the EC Treaty. The ECJ repeated the line that it had taken in *Van Gend en Loos* (1963) but expanded on it:

JUDGMENT

'By contrast with ordinary international treaties, the EC Treaty has created its own legal system which on entry into force of the Treaty became an integral part of the legal systems of the member states and which their courts are bound to apply. By creating a Community of limited duration having … powers stemming from a limitation of the sovereignty, or a transfer of powers from the states to the community, the member states have limited their sovereign rights, albeit within limited fields, and have thus created a body of law which binds both their nationals and themselves.'

The court also continued by identifying the clear consequence of the transfer of powers:

JUDGMENT

'The transfer, by member states from their national orders in favour of the Community order of its rights and obligations arising from the Treaty, carries with it a clear limitation of their sovereign right upon which a subsequent unilateral law, incompatible with the aims of the community cannot prevail.'

In reaching its decision the court identified that supremacy was confirmed by the wording of Art 288 which refers to the concept of direct applicability (see section 4.2) and also the binding nature of Community legislation. In its conclusion it explains fully its reasoning:

JUDGMENT

'It follows from all these observations that the law stemming from the Treaty, an independent source of law, could not, because of its special and original nature, be overridden by domestic legal provisions, however framed, without being deprived of its character as Community law and without the legal basis of the Community itself being called into question.'

Three clear propositions emerge from the statements in these two cases:

- the Member States, by joining the EU, had given up certain of their sovereign powers to make law on certain issues
- both the Member States themselves as well as their citizens are bound by EU law
- the Member States, as a result, cannot unilaterally introduce new national laws that would then contradict EU law.

8.2.2 The wider application of the doctrine of supremacy

The ECJ has had the opportunity to re-state the principle on a number of occasions. On one occasion it was able to expand by explaining that EU law cannot be invalidated by any measure of national law, from whatever source.

CASE EXAMPLE

International Handelsgesellschaft GmbH v EVGF (Case 11/70) [1970] ECR 1125; [1972] CMLR 255

Here, an applicant in a German court was challenging the legitimacy of a Regulation. The regulation required the introduction of export licences in respect of certain agricultural products falling under the Common Agricultural Policy (CAP). One further requirement was for payment of deposits which would be forfeited in the event that there was no export of the products during the period of the licence, as a result of which the individual in the case had lost a deposit. The German court accepted his argument that the measure was unconstitutional under the German Constitution because it infringed basic guaranteed rights to run a business freely and to be free of compulsory payment without proof of fault. Nevertheless, the German court felt that it was necessary to make an Art 234 reference asking the question of whether or not national constitutional law took precedence over EC law. The ECJ responded that:

JUDGMENT

'Recourse to the legal rules or concepts of national law in order to judge the validity of measures adopted by the Institutions … would have an adverse effect on the uniformity and efficacy of EC law. The validity of such measures can only be judged in the light of Community law. … The validity of a Community measure or its effect within a member state cannot be affected by allegations that it runs counter to either fundamental rights, as formulated by the constitution of the state or the principles of a national constitutional structure.'

The message from the ECJ was very clear: in determining any 'pecking order' of laws, EU law takes precedence over even the constitutions of the Member States.

In further re-stating the principle of supremacy the ECJ has subsequently made it abundantly clear that, in the event of any conflict or inconsistency between national law and EU law, the domestic court has an absolute requirement to give effect to EU law over any conflicting law, whatever the date of passing of that law.

CASE EXAMPLE

Simmenthal SpA v Amministrazione delle Finanze dello Stato (Case 70/77) [1978] ECR 1453; [1978] 3 CMLR 670

Simmenthal imported beef into Italy from France. Under an Italian law introduced in 1970, he was bound to pay for an inspection of the goods at the frontier. However, this national law was inconsistent not only with the requirements of Art 28 [now Art 34 TFEU] but also with EC Regulations introduced in 1964 and in 1968. The Italian court made a reference to the ECJ on the question of whether it must follow the EC law or should wait for the provision of Italian law to be annulled by the Italian constitutional court according to the usual state procedure.

The ECJ in its response made the following observations:

JUDGMENT

'… in accordance with the principles of precedence of Community law, the relationship between the provisions of the Treaty and directly applicable measures of the institutions on the one hand and the national law of the member states on the other is such that those provisions and measures not only by their entry into force render automatically inapplicable any conflicting provision of current national law but, insofar as they are an integral part, and take precedence in, the legal order applicable in the territory of each of the member states, also preclude the valid adoption of new national legislative measures to the extent that they would be incompatible with Community provisions …'.

In its conclusions the ECJ again clearly stated the consequences for Member State courts:

JUDGMENT

'… it follows that every national court must, in a case within its jurisdiction, apply Community law in its entirety and protect rights which the latter confers on individuals and must accordingly set aside any provision of national law which may conflict with it, whether prior or subsequent to the Community rule'.

Over time, EU law has been held to be supreme over conflicting national law in many cases. What the cases clearly identify is that supremacy applies whatever the particular type of EU law. We have already seen the applicability of the doctrine in relation to Treaty Articles and also Regulations. EU law has also been held to be supreme in the case of:

- **Directives** – *Becker v Finanzamt Munster-Innenstadt* (Case 8/81) [1982] ECR 53, [1982] 1 CMLR 499 (where the applicant was then permitted to enforce a VAT Directive against the German tax authorities)
- **Decisions** – *Salumifico di Cornuda* (Case 130/78) [1979] ECR 867
- **general principles of law** – *Wachauf v Germany* (Case 5/88) [1989] ECR 2609
- **international agreements made between EU and non-EU states** – *Nederlandse Spoorwegen* (Case 38/75) [1975] ECR 1439

The doctrine of supremacy also will apply not merely where there is national law that directly conflicts with a provision of EU law. The doctrine will apply also in circumstances where a contradictory provision in national law, while not directly conflicting, nevertheless by its existence encroaches on the field of Community legislative powers.

CASE EXAMPLE

Commission v France (Re French Merchant Seamen) (Case 167/73) [1974] ECR 359; [1974] CMLR 216

The case here concerned a French statutory provision requiring that a certain percentage of crew on French registered merchant ships had to be French nationals. The provision had inevitably come into conflict with the rules on free movement of workers under Art 45. The Commission brought an action under Art 226 [now Art 258 TFEU], seeking to declare the French law contrary to the objectives of the Treaty and thus unlawful. The French argued in their defence that they were not acting in breach of their EC obligations since they no longer actually operated the law and that there was nothing in the Treaty requiring that Member States must specifically repeal outdated incompatible law. Nevertheless, the ECJ held that the continued existence of conflicting national law in itself created an ambiguity that was unsustainable and unacceptable in the pursuit of harmony.

8.2.3 The extreme consequences of a doctrine of supremacy

The ECJ has had many opportunities to state and re-state the rule. This occurred not just in the early years of the Treaties but has surfaced in recent times too.

Possibly the most far-reaching application of the rule has come in a case involving the UK. The case is dramatic because in the most positive terms it conflicts with the notion of parliamentary supremacy within the English Constitution and directs English judges to exercise a power that would have formerly been considered to be beyond them: to suspend operation of and in effect declare invalid provisions of an Act of Parliament.

CASE EXAMPLE

R v Secretary of State for Transport, ex parte Factortame Ltd (Case C–213/89) [1990] ECR 1–2433; [1990] 3 CMLR 375

The case involved companies registered in the UK but where the majority ownership was in the hands of Spanish nationals. The companies had in fact been registered in the UK, with the specific object of purchasing trawlers registered in the UK. Provisions of the Merchant Shipping Act 1988 and the Merchant Shipping (Registration of Fishing Vessels) Regulations

1988 had inserted a nationality requirement so that for registration of the vessel more than a certain percentage of ownership had to be in the hands of UK nationals. The applicants argued before the English court that these requirements violated the 'non-discrimination on nationality' rule in Art 12 [now Art 18 TFEU] and as a result of their operation that they were denied rights to fish that would otherwise have been guaranteed by EC law [now EU]. The House of Lords was confronted with the difficult question of an Act of Parliament enacted after accession to the Treaties in 1972 which specifically contradicted EC [now EU] law. As the applicants had also sought an injunction if the court was to grant this, it would have the effect of suspending operation of an Act of Parliament until the inconsistency issue could be settled on reference to the ECJ. The Divisional Court decided that a reference should be made under Art 234 [now Art 267 TFEU] and had granted the injunction. As a result, it had ordered that the Secretary of State should be prevented from applying the parts of the Act in question until a preliminary ruling had been given under the reference. The Secretary of State appealed and the Court of Appeal granted the appeal and set aside the order of the Divisional Court. Appeal was then made to the House of Lords. Their Lordships were faced with a difficult situation. As they identified in the judgment, there was no rule in English constitutional law that would allow the type of interim relief granted by the Divisional Court; neither could it see that there existed such an overriding principle in EC (now EU) law allowing a national court to suspend operation of a national law. As a result, it made a reference to the ECJ, posing the question whether, in order to protect EC (now EU) rights, a national court must grant the interim suspension of an Act of Parliament.

The ECJ restated the relationship between national law and Community (now EU) law:

JUDGMENT

'In accordance with the case law of the court, it is for the national courts in application of the principle of co-operation laid down in Article 10 [now repealed] … to ensure the legal protection which persons derive from the direct effect of provisions of EC law … any provision of a national legal system and any legislative, administrative, or judicial practice which might impair the effectiveness of Community law by withholding from the national court having jurisdiction to apply such law the power to do everything necessary at the moment of its application to set aside national legislative provisions which might prevent, even temporarily, Community rules from having full force and effect are incompatible with those requirements which are the very essence of EC law.'

In its conclusions the ECJ was clear on the course of action to be taken by the national court and the effect of supremacy on the situation:

JUDGMENT

'… the full effectiveness of Community law would be just as much impaired if a rule of national law could prevent a court seized of a dispute governed by Community law from granting interim relief in order to ensure the full effectiveness of the judgment to be given on the existence of the rights claimed under Community law. It therefore follows that a court which in those circumstances would grant interim relief, if it were not for a rule of national law, is obliged to set aside that law.'

Factortame (1990) then represents a major statement of supremacy by the ECJ over national courts and of EU law over national law and demonstrates the supranational power of the institutions of the EU.

The Treaty creates 'a new legal order' under which Member States have 'limited their sovereign rights, albeit within limited fields' *Van Gend en Loos v The Netherlands*

The Treaty carries with it a clear limitation of (Member States') sovereign right upon which a subsequent unilateral law, incompatible with the aims of the Community cannot prevail. *Costa v ENEL*

The validity of a Community measure or its effect within a Member State cannot be affected by allegations that it runs counter to either fundamental rights, as formulated by the constitution of the state or the principles of a national constitutional structure. *International Handellsgesellshaft case*

Every national court must, in a case within its jurisdiction, apply Community law in its entirety ... and must accordingly set aside any provision of national law which may conflict with it, whether prior or subsequent to the Community rule. *Simmenthal*

It is for national courts ... to set aside national legislative provisions which might prevent even temporarily, Community rules from having full force and effect. *Factortame*

Figure 8.2.3 Diagram illustrating the development of a definition of supremacy of EU law

ACTIVITY

Self-assessment questions

1. Why is a doctrine of supremacy of EU law necessary?
2. What precisely is the 'doctrine of pre-emption' and how does it affect the Member States?
3. What was the relationship between the former Art 10 of the EC Treaty and the concept of supremacy of EU law?
4. In *Van Gend en Loos* (1963) the ECJ identified that 'the Community constitutes a new legal order in international law'. What exactly does this mean?
5. What is the significance of the definition of supremacy given by the ECJ in *Costa v ENEL* (1964)?
6. What effect does the doctrine of supremacy of EU law have upon the sovereignty of the Member States?
7. To what extent is supremacy the sole creation of the ECJ and to what extent does it actually derive from the obligations in the Treaty?
8. How broadly have the effects of supremacy been interpreted by the ECJ?
9. Why is *Factortame* (1990) such an important case?

8.3 Supremacy and the UK

In *Factortame* (1990) the English judges recognised the supremacy of EU law and applied the clear direction given in the reference by granting the interim relief that had been applied for.

Nevertheless, English judges have not always reacted in this manner and there has inevitably been much discussion on the key provisions of the European Communities Act 1972 and the extent to which the Treaties are entrenched in English law.

8.3.1 UK membership of the European Union

Having signed the Treaty of Accession, the UK ratified its membership of the EC and incorporated EC law into English law with the passing of the European Communities Act 1972.

Initially, the key provision accomplishing this incorporation was s 2(1):

SECTION

'All such rights, powers, liabilities, obligations and restrictions from time to time created or arising by or under the Treaties, as in accordance with the Treaties, are without further enactment to be given legal effect or used in the UK and shall be recognised and available in law, and be enforced, allowed and followed accordingly, and the expression "enforceable Community right" and similar expressions shall be read as referring to one to which the subsection applies.'

This would appear to be a simple enough statement of intent: all existing EC law would automatically be incorporated into English law, and all future legislative provisions of the Community would become law and be recognised as enforceable.

In any case, the section seems to have been further reinforced by s 2(4), which states that:

SECTION

'… any enactment passed or to be passed, other than one contained in this part of the Act, shall be construed and have effect subject to the foregoing provision of this section …'.

Following the enactment of the Act the existence of previous English law that might conflict with EU objectives would appear to present no real problem. On achieving membership the Act ensured that EU law would in any case prevail over any inconsistent national law. Besides this, by virtue of the doctrine of implied repeal, the very fact that the Act itself came after this law meant that, even without repealing statutes, the EU law would prevail.

The major problem, then, concerns English law made after the passing of the Act which is inconsistent with provisions of EU law. The problem seems to hinge on the extent to which the above sections are in fact entrenched or whether they are merely aids to construction.

8.3.2 The attitude of English judges

Certainly, membership has meant that EU law has affected the interpretation of statutes by judges. Judges are now more likely to use a purposive approach and possibly EU law has introduced another rule of interpretation in its own right. Different judges at different times have in any case taken a different line.

In *Garland v British Rail Engineering Ltd (BREL)* [1982] 2 All ER 402, HL the House of Lords considered an exemption in respect of death and retirement in the Equal Pay Act 1970 and its compatibility with EC (now EU) law. The House held that the provision must be construed in order to conform with EC (now EU) law. The Law Lords took s 2 of the European Communities Act 1972 as creating a rule of construction and Lord Diplock identified that the English courts were used to interpreting national law in this way.

A similar approach was taken in both *Pickstone v Freemans plc* [1988] 2 All ER 803 and *Litster v Forth Dry Dock and Engineering Co* [1989] 1 All ER 1134. In both cases the court felt that UK law had to be construed in a manner that was consistent with EC (now EU) law. In the latter case the House of Lords observed that when applying EC (now EU) law a purposive approach to interpretation must be taken.

However, courts have not always accepted this approach. In *Duke v GEC Reliance* [1988] 2 WLR 359 the House of Lords decided that it was not bound to interpret the Sex Discrimination Act 1975 so that it gave full effect to Directive 76/207 (the Equal Treatment Directive).

Lord Templeman concluded that the effect of s 2(4) of the 1972 Act is not to allow the court to 'distort a statute to enforce a directive which has no direct effect between individuals'.

The House also refused to allow a reference on the issue despite the ruling in *Marshall*.

Obviously, the doctrine of supremacy of EC (now EU) law creates fewer problems in relation to national law that pre-dates entry into the EC (now EU). Parliament in the 1972 Act accepted that all existing EC (now EU) law should be incorporated into English law. In this way it is national law and also EC (now EU) law coming after the Act that is the cause of difficulties for the judges. Judges have tried hard to ensure that EU law is observed and that national law is interpreted so that it can be seen as harmonious with EU law. Nevertheless, it is not just a question of interpretation: English judges are called on to **enforce** rights granted under EU law, but they also feel the need to reconcile this with parliamentary supremacy by which they still feel bound.

Lord Denning, at an early point in the UK's membership, identified the impact of membership on English law in quite poetic but nevertheless quite abrupt terms, in the case of *Bulmer v Bollinger* [1974] Ch 401, CA:

JUDGMENT

'The Treaty is like an incoming tide. It flows into the estuaries and up the rivers. It cannot be held back.'

The major problems will occur when Parliament appears to act inconsistently with the objectives of the Treaties or their subsidiary legislation and in the early years it was this that caused much debate among English judges. As we have seen, they would try to interpret national law, as far as possible, to be in harmony with EU law. The more dramatic problem comes if it can be seen that Parliament appears to be legislating deliberately contrary to the requirements of EU law. In *Felixstowe Dock and Railway Co v British Transport and Docks Board* [1976] 2 CMLR 655 Lord Denning again commented on the difficulties that this presented for English judges in the context of parliamentary supremacy. He concluded that all the judge could do was to follow the provision in the Act.

He later reaffirmed this in *Macarthys v Smith* [1979] WLR 1189 where he observed:

JUDGMENT

'... if the time should ever come when our Parliament deliberately passes an Act with the intention of repudiating the Treaty or any provisions in it, or intentionally of acting inconsistently with it, and says so in express terms, then I should have thought that it would be the duty of our courts to follow the statute of our Parliament'.

The view was expressed at a point when membership was fairly recent and when judges had spent their careers as lawyers in a common law tradition, with parliamentary supremacy as an absolute rule. It is not surprising at this stage that judges would reject the suggestion that the provisions of the European Communities Act 1972 were entrenched against either express or implied repeal by later Acts of Parliament.

Nevertheless, a greater acceptance of the consequences of membership has developed over time. The statements of judges in more recent cases demonstrate this. In the case of *Stoke-on-Trent City Council v B & Q plc* [1990] 3 CMLR 897 the issue involved was the compatibility of the then UK Sunday trading laws and Art 34 which guarantees free movement of goods. Hoffmann J, as he then was, commented on the effects of EU law on UK legislation:

JUDGMENT

'The EC Treaty is the supreme law of the UK taking precedence over Acts of Parliament. Entry into the EC meant Parliament surrendered its sovereign right to legislate contrary to the provisions of the Treaty on matters of social and economic policy which the Treaty regulated. Entry into the EC and its attendant partial surrender of sovereignty was more than compensated for by the advantages of membership'.

The current attitude of the English courts is that demonstrated by Lord Bridge in *Factortame* (1990):

JUDGMENT

'If the supremacy within the EC of Community law over national law was not always inherent in the EC Treaty, it was certainly well established in the jurisprudence of the Court of Justice long before the United Kingdom joined the Community. Thus, whatever limitation of its sovereignty Parliament accepted when it enacted the European Communities Act 1972 was entirely voluntary. Under the terms of the Act of 1972 it has always been clear that it is the duty of a United Kingdom court, when delivering final judgment, to override any rule of national law found to be in conflict with any directly enforceable rule of Community law'.

Lord Bridge's choice of the word 'voluntary' is clearly very important. It allowed the judges to ensure observance of Treaty objectives while also maintaining the principle of parliamentary supremacy. All EU law will be followed in preference to inconsistent national law, either by harmonious interpretation or simply by declaring EU law superior, because that is what Parliament volunteered for on membership. The clear inference is that when Parliament's voluntary participation in the EU ceases then parliamentary supremacy would be observed.

8.4 Supremacy and other Member States

The UK is not on its own in experiencing constitutional problems with the supremacy of EU law over national law. The extent of the problem depends on the character of the particular constitution in question. In the BENELUX countries, for instance, the problems are limited and those Member States are able to accept supremacy with little difficulty because of the general effect of international Treaties in their constitutions. In France, Germany and Italy, on the other hand, there are issues that have been the subject of concern for national courts.

8.4.1 Belgium and supremacy of EU law

The Belgian Constitution operates according to a 'monist' system, in contrast to the dualist constitution of the UK. In simple terms, a monist constitution operates so that international Treaties automatically become part of the national legal order on signing of the Treaty. In contrast, a dualist approach requires that, besides becoming a signatory to a Treaty, the state in question is required to ratify and incorporate the provisions into its national law by further legislation. This was the reason the UK passed the European Communities Act 1972.

In Belgium, then, the Treaties automatically became incorporated in national law once entry into the EC was achieved by signing the Treaty of Accession.

The issue of supremacy was in any case settled in subsequent case law:

CASE EXAMPLE

Ministère des Affaires Economiques v SA Fromagerie Franco–Suisse ('Le Ski') [1972] CMLR 330

Article 25 (at that time Art 12, now Art 18 TFEU) required the gradual removal of Customs duties during the transitional period. This was the same issue that was under discussion in the leading case of Van Gend en Loos, as we have already seen. The Belgian Government had removed certain import duties on dairy products, but had also passed later law preventing the return of money already paid in duties. The Customs duties had been identified as unlawful in Art 226 (now Art 258 TFEU) proceedings before the ECJ. The court identified that the normal rule, that a later legislative provision repealed an earlier one, could not apply here. The second Belgian law was unlawful in the context of Art 12 (now Art 18 TFEU), and the consequence is that the supremacy of EU law was firmly established.

8.4.2 France and supremacy of EU law

In France the judiciary has been divided in its attitude towards the supremacy of EU law over national law. This division initially manifested itself between the appeal courts, which had no problem in accepting supremacy, and the administrative court, the Conseil d'Etat, which originally did not.

At quite an early stage, the appeal court in *Von Kempis v Geldof (Cour de Cassation)* [1976] 2 CMLR 462 accepted both the reasoning and the case law of the ECJ in declaring that EU law takes precedence over French legislation.

However, in *Minister for the Interior v Cohn-Bendit (Conseil d'Etat)* [1980] 1 CMLR 543, on Directives issued under Art 39 (now Art 45 TFEU), the French constitutional court stated that a Directive could not be used as a means of challenging internal administrative law.

However, the Conseil d'Etat has subsequently been more prepared to accept supremacy.

8.4.3 Italy and supremacy of EU law

The Italian constitutional court initially took quite a hard line, as has been seen earlier in *Costa v ENEL* (1964). At this point the view clearly expressed was that Italian legislation coming after the Treaty must be followed and this was the argument presented in the reference at that time.

However, the court then moved sharply away from that position, accepting the supremacy of EC (now EU) law:

CASE EXAMPLE

Frontini [1974] 3 CMLR 381

Here, a cheese importer was challenging the legitimacy of levies imposed as a result of EC (now EU) law in that, under the Italian Constitution, taxes could only be imposed by Italian statutory provision. The Italian constitutional court was clear that EC (now EU) law was both separate and superior and that Italian constitutional law does not apply to issues subject to EC (now EU) law. In reaching its decision the court based its judgment almost entirely on the reasoning of the ECJ. It held that there could be no further questioning of the validity of the incorporation of Art 249 (now Art 288 TFEU) into Italian law.

Since that time Italy has been firm in its observance of the principle of supremacy. It has tended to operate towards a constructionist approach: that construction of Italian law must be consistent with the demands of EU law.

8.4.4 Germany and supremacy of EU law

Initially, Germany was unwilling to accept supremacy as an absolute principle because of the potential conflict with the protections of human rights contained in the German Constitution. This position was clearly demonstrated in the position taken by the German court in *International Handelsgesellschaft GmbH v EVGF* (1970) discussed in section 8.2.2.

It was also discussed at length in *Wunsche Handelsgesellschaft* [1987] 3 CMLR 225. Here, the German constitutional court reversed its position in the former case and accepted the principle of supremacy provided that the EU law could guarantee the protection of human rights.

In a different context, in *Kloppenberg* [1988] 3 CMLR 1, where the tax courts had originally held against the direct effect of a Directive on VAT, the constitutional court reversed this and upheld the supremacy of EU law in clear terms.

There is, then, some discrepancy between the attitude of different courts to supremacy. This debate has continued. In *Brunner v The European Treaty* [1994] 1 CMLR 57 the applicant had challenged the constitutional legitimacy of Germany's signing of the Treaty on European Union. The German constitutional court disagreed and upheld the validity of German membership of the new Treaty. Nevertheless, the judges passed significant comment on the relationship between the German state and the EU:

JUDGMENT

'[the TEU] can only have binding effects … by virtue of the German instruction that its law be applied. Germany is one of the "Masters of the Treaties" which have established their adherence to the Union Treaty. … but could ultimately revoke that adherence by a contrary act. The validity and application of European law in Germany depends on the application-of-law instruction of the Accession Act. Germany thus preserves the quality of a sovereign state in its own right'.

ACTIVITY

Self-assessment questions

1. In what ways does the European Communities Act 1972 actually define the relationship between the UK and the EU?
2. What is the importance of s 2(4) of the European Communities Act 1972?
3. To what extent have the English courts willingly accepted a doctrine of supremacy of EU law?
4. Is the reaction of English courts significantly different to those in other Member States?
5. How important are national constitutions to the reactions of different Member States to the issue of supremacy?
6. Why is *International Handelsgesellschaft* (1970) particularly significant to the development of a doctrine of supremacy of EU law?

KEY FACTS

The meaning of and need for supremacy	**Treaty provision/case**

Supremacy simply means that in any conflict between national law and EU law EU law prevails.
Supremacy is necessary because full economic integration would be impossible if the institutions were denied supranational status.
There are two main justifications:
• it prevents Member States from questioning the validity of EU law
• the doctrine of pre-emption:
  • prevents Member State courts from giving judgments inconsistent with EU law
  • prevents Member State governments from legislating contrary to EU law	

The definition and application of supremacy	**Treaty provision/case**
EU law first identified as creating a 'new legal order' under which Member States have partially surrendered sovereignty.	*Van Gend en Loos* (1963)
Definition and consequences expanded so that EU law 'cannot be overridden by domestic legal provisions, however framed'.	*Costa v ENEL* (1964)
EU law prevails over all inconsistent national law whether coming before or after the Treaty.	*Simmenthal* (1978)
EU law prevails even over a national constitutional provision.	*International Handelsgesellschaft* (1970)
And allows judges to suspend operation of a national legislative provision.	*Factortame* (1990)
The UK and supremacy	**Treaty provision/case**
UK approach originally one of construction.	*Garland v BREL* (1982)
And would not apply a Directive that would not be enforceable between individuals.	*Duke v GEC Reliance* (1988)
Judges were clear that if Parliament deliberately passed conflicting law they would have to give effect to parliamentary supremacy.	*Macarthys v Smith* (1979)
But now are prepared to accept supremacy because limiting of sovereignty was a voluntary concession in European Communities Act 1972.	*Factortame* (1990)

Other Member States and supremacy	Treaty provision/case
Belgium – accepts because it is a monist constitution.	*Le Ski* (1972)
France – appeal courts accepted but more reluctance from Conseil d'Etat.	*Von Kempis* (1976) *Cohn-Bendit* (1980)
Italy – originally more inclined to follow Italian Constitution but later accepted the principle.	*Costa v ENEL* (1964) *Frontini* (1974)
Germany – at first was prone to follow constitution because of human rights but later accepted supremacy if human rights upheld although still prone to insist that sovereignty survives.	*International Handelsgesellschaft* (1970) *Wunsche Handelsgesellschaft* (1987) *Brunner* (1994)

SAMPLE ESSAY QUESTION

'Discuss the argument that "Despite there being no mention of supremacy in the Treaty, even in the UK the doctrine of supremacy of EU Law has proved an uncontroversial creation of the European Court of Justice".'

Explain the basis of supremacy from ECJ case law:

- a new legal order … for whose benefits the states have limited their sovereign rights *Van Gend en Loos*
- 'The Treaty has created its own legal system which on entry into force … became an integral part of the legal systems of the Member States and which their courts are bound to apply … The transfer … carries with it a clear limitation of their sovereign right upon which a subsequent unilateral law, incompatible with the aims of the Community cannot prevail …' *Costa v ENEL.*

Explain the basis for the doctrine:

- under the Treaty – MSs should do everything in their power to achieve the objectives of the Treaty and refrain from doing anything that would prevent achieving those objectives
- the supranational character of the EU institutions including the ECJ.

Discuss the justifications for the doctrine:

- the absence of a specific reference to supremacy in the Treaty
- the fact that the supranational character of the institutions and the law would be impaired without a doctrine of supremacy
- the objectives of the EU might be compromised.

Discuss the position in the UK and whether the doctrine is 'uncontroversial':

- supremacy of EU Law conflicts with this parliamentary supremacy
- s2(1) 1972 Act gives force to EU law
- supremacy appears to be guaranteed by s2(4) 'any enactment passed or to be passed ... shall be construed and have effect subject to the foregoing provision of this section ...'
- the original view of judges was that ultimately the UK Parliament was supreme – Lord Denning in *Macarthys v Smith*
- But that now HL in *Factortame* has accepted: 'whatever limitations of its sovereignty Parliament accepted when it enacted the EC Act 1972 was entirely voluntary. Under the terms of the 1972 Act it has always been clear that it is the duty of a UK court ... to override any rule of national law found to be in conflict with any directly enforceable rule of Community law'.

SUMMARY

- There is no mention of supremacy in the Treaties – however supranationalism would be impossible without some recognition of supremacy of EU Law and institutions.
- It is the creation of the Court of Justice that, in a very early statement, identified that states have given up certain of their sovereignty to a new legal order.
- The clearest definition is that it involves a limitation of sovereign rights upon which subsequent unilateral law, incompatible with the aims of the EU, cannot prevail – so where there is any inconsistency between national law and EU Law it is the latter that takes precedence.
- Ultimately a national court can do everything necessary to set aside national legislative provisions which might prevent EU rules from having full force and effect.

Further reading

Books

Douglas-Scott, S, *Constitutional Law of the European Union* (Longman, 2002), Chapter 7.

Steiner, J and Woods, L, *Textbook on EC Law* (8th edn, Oxford University Press, 2003), Chapter 4.

Weatherill, S, *Cases and Materials on EC Law* (5th edn, Oxford University Press, 2003), Chapter 2.

9

The relationship between EU law and national law – direct effect

AIMS AND OBJECTIVES

After reading this chapter you should be able to:

- Understand the concept of direct effect and why it was developed by the ECJ
- Understand the criteria for achieving direct effect
- Differentiate between horizontal direct effect and vertical direct effect
- Understand the application of direct effect to Treaty Articles, regulations and decisions
- Understand the difficulty of applying direct effect to directives
- Understand how the ECJ has got round the problem using vertical direct effect and how it has expanded the meaning of the state to include emanations of the state
- Understand the concept of indirect effect
- Evaluate the difficulties of applying indirect effect
- Understand the concept of state liability
- Understand the conditions for state liability to apply
- Understand the principle of incidental horizontal direct effect
- Analyse the effectiveness of the processes

9.1 Introduction

If supremacy defines the relationship between the Member States and the EU, then direct effect defines the relationship between the citizens of the various Member States and the EU in the form of its laws. Direct effect is therefore another major element in ensuring that EU law is applied harmoniously throughout the Member States.

Supremacy gives practical effect to the concept of supranationalism by ensuring that the Member States cannot put national self-interest before the law of the EU. Direct effect again demonstrates the supranational nature of EU law by ensuring that citizens are able to enforce it in the Member States' courts.

Direct effect was not created in the Treaties and so neither is it defined in them. It is entirely a creation of the European Court of Justice. It does in some ways relate to, and therefore must be distinguished from, other concepts that are identified in the Treaties. Article 288, in establishing and defining the various types of legislation, for instance refers to:

General applicability

This merely refers to the fact that the measure in question applies universally throughout every Member State of the EU. In this way a Regulation is described as being generally applicable, whereas a Decision could never be generally applicable because it is addressed to a specific party.

Direct applicability

Direct applicability refers to the legal standing of the measure. A measure that is directly applicable automatically becomes law in the Member States once issued by the Council. Once again, a Regulation is described as directly applicable. The Regulation automatically becomes law in the Member States and there is no requirement for implementing legislation by the Member States. What may be appropriate is for them to produce law which repeals what would otherwise be inconsistent national legislation. However, even without this the EU measure has effect and, because of the doctrine of supremacy, must be applied in preference to the national law. A Directive, on the other hand, requires implementation by Member States within a set period and cannot, therefore, be directly applicable.

Direct effect, on the other hand, refers to the actual enforceability of EU law, of whatever type, in the national courts of Member States. Where the law creates actual rights and obligations then the concept can be applied to Treaty Articles, and to Regulations, and even to Decisions. However, the concept is much more problematic when it is applied to Directives.

Inevitably, this means that there are significant distinctions between direct applicability and direct effect:

- A measure may be directly applicable without necessarily creating rights that are enforceable. This would be the case with a procedural Regulation. Therefore the fact that a measure is directly applicable does not ensure that it will also have direct effect.
- It is possible that a measure can create rights and therefore be directly effective although not being directly applicable. This is the case with Directives, but only in limited circumstances.
- However, it is also of course possible that a measure could be both directly applicable and directly effective.

There is no doubt that direct effect is one of the most important of the creations of the ECJ. It has been instrumental in ensuring that the broad objectives of the Treaties have been observed by the Member States and incorporated into national law.

Various academics have commented on the significance of the concept:

> [Direct effect is] '... the first step in the judicial contribution to federalism ...'.
>
> P Craig, 'Once upon a time in the west: direct effect and the federalisation of EC law' 1992 OJLS 453

> '... a second principle of western jurisprudence to run alongside supremacy; namely the rule of law ...'.
>
> I Ward, 'A Critical Introduction to European Law' (Butterworths, 1996), p 57

> '[The most powerful justification for the creation of the concept is that it] ... enhances the effectiveness or *effet utile* of binding norms of Community law ...'.
>
> J Shaw, *European Community Law* (Macmillan Professional Masters, 1993), p 151

As with supremacy, one of the most interesting aspects of the area is that it is entirely the creation of the ECJ. It is difficult to imagine where the EU would have stood today without the ECJ taking such an uncompromising stance in creating through supremacy and direct effect the means by which the broad objectives of the Treaties can become established in national law. Inevitably, the uncompromising nature of the court has resulted in conflict with Member States. This in turn has led to even more uncompromising behaviour by the ECJ in developing the principles of indirect effect and state liability.

Nevertheless, the ECJ has still been dependent on the national courts to develop the principle. F Mancini identifies the significance of this:

'The national courts … by referring to Luxembourg sensitive questions of interpretation of Community law … have been indirectly responsible for the boldest judgments the Court has made. Moreover, by adhering to these judgments in deciding the cases before them, and therefore by lending them the credibility which national judges usually enjoy in their own countries, they have rendered the case-law of the Court both effective and respected throughout the Community.'

F Mancini, 'The making of a constitution for Europe' (1989) 26 CMLR 595

9.2 The concept of direct effect

9.2.1 The origins of direct effect

Direct effect, as a concept, is not mentioned anywhere in the Treaties. It is entirely the creation of the ECJ. In fact, the ECJ had the opportunity to consider the enforceability of EU law first in the same case in which it also effectively developed the doctrine of supremacy.

Inevitably, the two concepts go hand in hand and are essential for the ultimate success of the Treaties and the principle of supranationalism on which the Common Market is based.

Direct effect was relevant to the case because there was a conflict between what fell within national law and how it conflicted with EU law. The citizen would have had no protection if he had been unable to rely on EU law in the case.

CASE EXAMPLE

Van Gend en Loos v Nederlandse Administratie der Belastingen (Case 26/62) [1963] ECR 1

In Van Gend en Loos, as we have already seen in Chapter 8, the Dutch Government had re-classified certain import duties and this re-classification had meant an increase in duty on a chemical product imported from Germany, and which therefore caused increased cost to a Dutch bulb grower. Van Gend was objecting to paying the increase and argued that the re-classification in fact contravened the then Art 12 (now Art 30 TFEU following Treaty of Lisbon) of the EC Treaty. The Dutch court made an Art 267 reference seeking a correct interpretation of the requirements of Art 12 (Art 25 now Art 30 TFEU following Treaty of Lisbon), which was then what was known as a 'standstill' Article requiring that there should be no increases on existing duties and no introduction of new duties during the transitional period. The Dutch court, since it was taking a dualist view of the Treaties and challenging the right of a citizen to invoke rights granted under the Treaties, also posed the question in the reference as to whether Art 12 (Art 25 now Art 30 TFEU following Treaty of Lisbon) was capable of creating rights in favour of individuals which a national court was then bound to protect.

The Advocate-General initially prepared a reasoned decision which took a purely literalist interpretation of the Article and suggested as a result that, since the Article contained no explicit mention of individual rights, it could not be construed as granting individual rights. He was also of the opinion that, if the re-classification of the duty was indeed contrary to EC law, then the appropriate action should be by the Commission against the Dutch State in Art 258 proceedings.

The *juges* in the ECJ, however, preferred a teleological (purposive) interpretation of the Article. It held that, since the Treaty was clearly intended to affect individuals, even though it made no specific mention of rights, it must clearly be capable of creating rights that would be enforceable by individuals in national courts.

JUDGMENT

'Independently of the legislation of the member states Community law … not only imposes obligations on individuals but is also intended to confer upon them rights which become part of their legal heritage. These rights are granted not only where they are expressly granted by the Treaty, but also by reason of obligations which the Treaty imposes in a clearly defined way upon individuals as well as upon member states and the institutions of the Community …'.

The ECJ pointed out then that, since the Treaty was clearly intended to affect individuals as well as Member States, it must also be capable of creating rights that would also be enforceable by individuals within the national courts.

In this way the court concluded that since Art 12 (Art 25 now Art 30 TFEU)

JUDGMENT

'… contains a clear and unconditional prohibition … it [is] ideally adapted to produce direct effects between member states and their subjects …'.

The court was also conscious of the limited value of the course of action that had been proposed by the Advocate-General, an action against the Dutch State under Art 258. The court explored this possibility and gave its reasons against it.

JUDGMENT

'The implementation of Article 12 (now Art 18 TFEU) does not require any legislative intervention on the part of the states. The fact that under this Article it is the Member States who are made the subject of the negative obligation does not imply that their nationals cannot benefit from this obligation … The argument based on Articles 169 and 170 (now Arts 258 and 259 TFEU) … is misconceived. The fact that the Article enables the Commission and the Member States to bring before the Court a State which has not fulfilled its obligations does not mean that individuals cannot plead these obligations … A restriction of the guarantees against infringement of Article 12 (now Art 18 TFEU) by Member States to the procedures under Articles 169 and 170 (now Arts 258 and 259 TFEU) would remove all direct legal protection of the individual rights of their nationals. There is the risk that recourse to the procedure under these Articles would be ineffective if it were to occur after the implementation of a national decision taken contrary to the provisions of the Treaty.'

The original method used to ensure that EU law was in fact enforced in Member States was by an action against the state through the enforcement proceedings in Arts 258 and 259 TFEU. As seen in the passage above, the ECJ established the concept of direct effect because it was a more effective means of ensuring that citizens of Member States could enforce the rights given to them by the Treaties than the traditional means.

9.2.2 The criteria for direct effect

Of course, the effect of *Van Gend en Loos* (1963) was initially quite limited in that direct effect only had to be applied to what are often referred to as 'standstill' Articles, or in other words prohibitive Treaty Articles. Of course, the action was in any case against the state itself.

The ECJ was able to develop the doctrine in *Van Gend* (1963) because the Article in question involved an obligation on the part of the Member States not to increase existing Customs duties or indeed create new ones. In this way the ECJ could quite easily justify enforcement of the provision because it was, as the court described it, 'clear, precise and unconditional' and did not depend on any further action being taken for its implementation, either by the Community institutions or by the Member States themselves.

However, the original limitations in *Van Gend* (1963) soon disappeared in later judgments, with the ECJ extending the scope of direct effect. In this way not only could a wider range of EU law be enforced but also measures could be directly effective against other individuals as well as against the state.

Later judgments did confirm the criteria for establishing direct effect developed by the Court in *Van Gend* (1963), for instance that in *Reyners v Belgian State* (Case 2/74) [1974] ECR 631. The criteria for direct effect are nevertheless most commonly referred to as the '*Van Gend en Loos* criteria':

- The provision must be **sufficiently clear and precisely stated** – the ECJ in *Defrenne v SABENA* (Case 43/75) [1976] ECR 455 was satisfied that the principle that 'men and women shall receive equal pay for equal work' was sufficiently precise to create direct effect even though the exact meaning of 'equal pay' and 'equal work' would inevitably require further definition by the courts.
- The provision must be **unconditional or 'non-dependent'** – in the sense that it should not depend on the intervention of another body nor require further legislative action either by the Community institutions or by Member States.

Added to this, of course, for individuals to gain enforceable rights from the provision:

- There must in fact be an identifiable right granted by the Treaty or legislative provision and on which the citizen can then rely.

Not all provisions do conform to the criteria, even though they may appear to be worded in unconditional terms. In *Casati* (Case 203/80) [1981] ECR 2595 the ECJ was concerned with whether the provision under the old Art 71 (now repealed) that 'member states shall endeavour to avoid introducing … new exchange restrictions' was directly effective. The court held that the words 'shall endeavour' were in fact insufficient to create unconditional obligations and that therefore the provision could not be directly effective.

9.2.3 Vertical direct effect and horizontal direct effect

Because the action was against the state, the case of *Van Gend en Loos* (1963) did not deal with the issue of whether or not a citizen could rely on the principle of direct effect to enforce a provision against another citizen as the case had confirmed they could against the state.

This was one of the questions for the court in *Defrenne v SABENA* (1976), which involved a claim for equal pay made against an employer under Art 157 (see Chapter 18). The ECJ rejected the argument that direct effect was a means only of enforcing substantive EU laws against the Member States. The court identified that there were two types of direct effect: **vertical** direct effect and **horizontal** direct effect. This was necessary because otherwise citizens would be denied effective remedies where they were granted rights under EU law.

JUDGMENT

'the reference to "Member States" in [Art 141] (now Art 157) cannot be interpreted as excluding the intervention of the courts in the direct application of the Treaty … Since [Art 141] (now Art 157) is mandatory in nature, the prohibition on discrimination between men and women applies not only to the action of public authorities, but also extends to all agreements which are intended to regulate paid labour collectively, as well as to contracts between individuals'.

The court, in essence, then, also clarified the distinctions between the two:

Vertical direct effect in one sense concerns the relationship between EU law and national law:

- measures of EU law creates obligations on the state to ensure their observance
- a failure on the part of Member States to honour Treaty obligations would usually give rise to an action against the state under Art 258 TFEU
- but vertical direct effect means that the process is not necessary since an individual can rely on the measures in an action against the state (as was the case in the original *Van Gend en Loos* case and in both *Van Duyn v Home Office* (Case 41/74) [1974] ECR 1337 and *Pubblico Ministero v Ratti* (Case 148/78) [1979] ECR 1629 which were both fought against government departments)
- indeed the principle has been extended to cover other 'public bodies' other than the state itself, and these are known as 'emanations of the state'.

Horizontal direct effect, on the other hand, is concerned instead with the relationship between individuals and other individuals:

- this could include any private body including companies
- where a measure is horizontally directly effective it creates rights between citizens and is therefore enforceable by them in national courts
- inevitably, because of the nature of a Directive, the ECJ has stated that Directives do not have horizontal direct effect (which is why the ECJ has been so active in ensuring that citizens will not lose out merely because the provision in question is a Directive).

As a result, the distinction between the two can be critical in determining whether or not a citizen is able to enforce the law and has an action where there is a breach of EU law.

ACTIVITY

Self-assessment questions

1. What is the difference between general applicability and direct applicability?
2. What is the difference between direct applicability and direct effect?
3. What is the relationship between supremacy and direct effect?
4. What are the *Van Gend en Loos* (1963) criteria and why did the ECJ create them?
5. How did the ECJ in the case justify ignoring the normal method of dealing with the problem?
6. What is the major difference between vertical direct effect and horizontal direct effect?

The relationship between horizontal direct effect and vertical direct effect can be shown in diagram form as in Figure 9.3.

9.3 The application of direct effect

The Court of Justice has developed the principle of direct effect so that it applies generally to most types of EU law, both primary and secondary. It has generally followed its own criteria in *Van Gend en Loos* (1963). However, the test from the case was originally strictly applied but the ECJ has also gradually taken a more relaxed approach to ensure that citizens can take advantage of the rights given to them in the Treaties.

There are a number of consequences of this relaxation:

- the court has in effect assumed responsibility for ensuring the effective integration of EU law
- provided that the criteria are generally met, then direct effect of a substantive measure is almost assumed
- the direct effect of a provision is only likely to be denied when there would be serious political or social consequences
- as a result, direct effect has become essentially a question of policy for the ECJ.

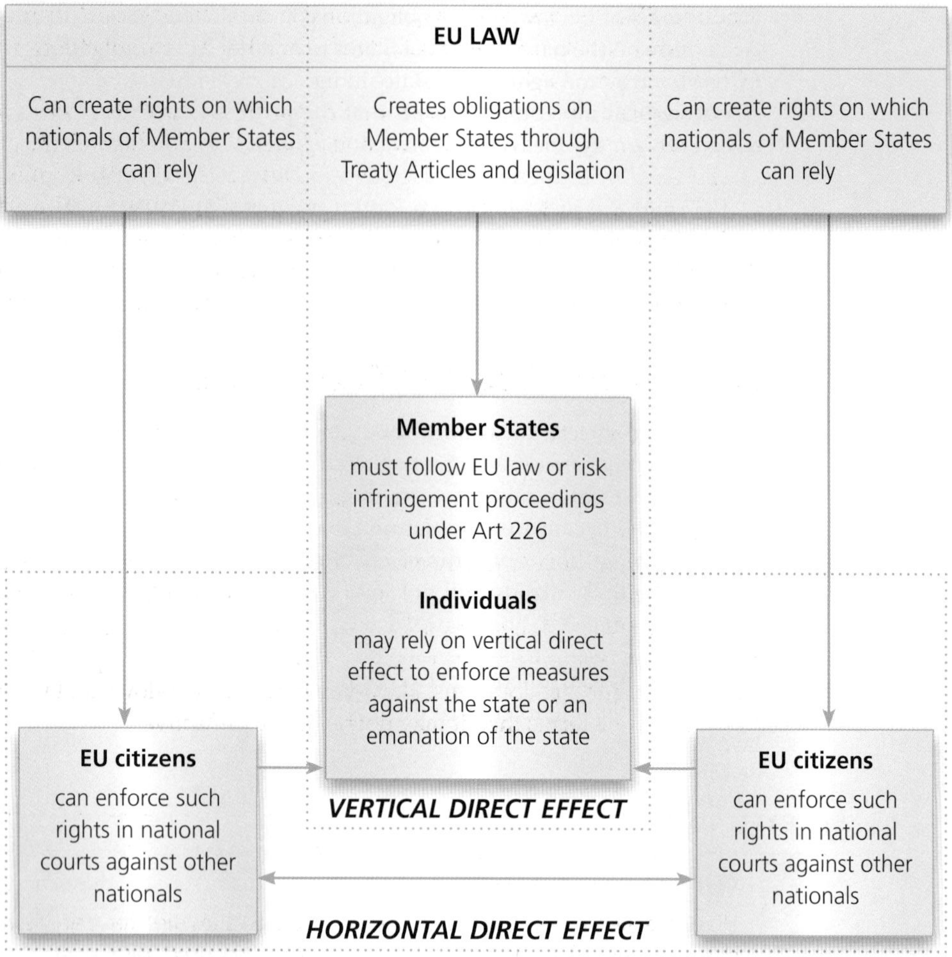

Figure 9.3 The relationship between vertical direct effect and horizontal direct effect

9.3.1 Direct effect and Treaty Articles

The concept of direct effect was first accepted in *Van Gend en Loos* (1963) and this case of course involved a Treaty Article, Art 12 (now Art 25).

This was a so-called 'standstill' Article. The principle of direct effect was also applied in respect of Treaty Articles imposing a duty on Member States to act, which would have been the case with removal of features from their national laws during the transitional period that would be detrimental to the attainment of the Common Market.

The principle, however, has been extended to cover all of the main substantive Treaty Articles. So, for example, it has been applied to both Art 34 and Art 35 on the free movement of goods in *Dansk Supermarked A/S v A/S Imerco* (Case 58/80) [1981] ECR 181 (see Chapter 14).

It has also been applied to the free movement of workers under Art 45 in *Van Duyn v Home Office* (1974) (see Chapter 12) as well as to rights of establishment under Art 49 in *Reyners v Belgium* (1974), and the freedom to provide services under Art 56 in *Van Binsbergen v Bestuur van de Bedrijfsvereniging voor de Metaalnijverheid* (Case 33/74) [1974] ECR 1299 (see Chapter 13). Both Art 49 and Art 56 envisage the introduction of Directives for the harmonisation of qualifications throughout the EU. The argument that this made the Articles conditional and dependent and that they could not as a result be directly effective was expressly rejected in the *Reyners* (1974) case.

Besides this, the principle has also ensured enforceability of EU competition law under Art 101 and Art 102 in *Brasserie de Haecht SA v Wilkin-Janssen (No 2)* (Case 48/72) [1973] ECR 77 (see Chapter 16).

We have also seen already that the principle of equal pay for equal work in Art 157 was declared directly effective in *Defrenne v SABENA* (1976). The court did, however, take the unique step of declaring the Article only prospectively directly effective.

The role of the ECJ in declaring the major EU policies directly effective has clearly been critical in defining those Treaty provisions as well as in ensuring that citizens can rely on them. One further point to add, which is of course apparent from the cases above, is that a Treaty Article will be both vertically and horizontally directly effective.

9.3.2 Direct effect and Regulations

The definition of 'Regulations' under Art 288 means that they are both of 'general application' and 'directly applicable'. The consequence of this is that they may also create obligations without need for further enactment by either the institutions or the Member States.

It therefore follows that they are also capable of direct effect provided that they satisfy the *Van Gend en Loos* (1963) criteria. Because a Regulation is directly applicable it can never be construed as conditional. On this basis, provided also that it contains a recognisable right, the only real test for the ECJ is whether or not the provision is stated in sufficiently clear and precise terms. However, it naturally follows that where a Regulation is too vague in its terms then it may not be directly effective.

CASE EXAMPLE

Leonesio v Ministero dell'Agricoltora & delle Foreste (Case 93/71) [1972] ECR 287 (The widow Leonesio)

Here, the Regulation concerned the provision of subsidies for dairy farmers prepared to slaughter their dairy herds. The provision was introduced with a view to easing the 'milk lake' (over-production of milk within the Community). The applicant here had killed her cows as directed by the Regulation but was being refused the subsidies by the Italian state. On a reference under Art 267 the ECJ held that the Regulation did indeed conform to the Van Gend en Loos (1963) criteria, was very precisely stated and in no way ambiguous, as a result of which it was also directly effective and enforceable.

Again, where the ECJ accepts the direct effect of a Regulation then direct effect is both vertical and horizontal.

9.3.3 Direct effect and Decisions

As we have seen, a 'Decision' is defined in Art 288 as being 'binding in its entirety on the party to whom it is addressed'

Since Decisions generally are addressed to parties who are in breach of EU obligations there is a clear need for the citizens who suffer as a result of those breaches to be able to rely on the decisions. The ECJ has itself accepted that.

CASE EXAMPLE

Grad v Finanzamt Traustein (Case 9/70) [1970] ECR 825

This case involved a challenge by a German company to a tax imposed upon it. The company argued that the tax was in contravention of a Directive that required amendment to national VAT laws and in effect also of a decision which gave a time limit for doing so. The question for the ECJ, therefore, was whether the company was entitled to rely on the decision.

The ECJ concluded that it could and identified that it would be:

JUDGMENT

> 'incompatible with the binding nature of decisions ... to exclude the possibility that persons affected may invoke the obligation imposed by a decision ... the effectiveness of such a measure would be weakened if ... nationals ... could not ... invoke it ... and the national courts could not take it into consideration.'

Of course, once again, all of the criteria for direct effect would need to be present. The fact that decisions are binding only on the party to whom the decision is addressed means that there is not the same problem of lack of direct applicability that occurs with Directives. Nevertheless some of the problems that occur with Directives in relation to private parties could occur where that party is not the one to whom the decision is addressed.

9.4 The problem of enforceability of Directives

9.4.1 Direct effect and Directives

Again, the character of a Directive is defined in Art 288. Under the Article, Directives are said to be 'binding as to the result to be achieved' but 'leave to the national authorities the choice of form and method'. This means that Directives have distinct objectives but in effect create obligations on Member States to pass national laws within a set time to achieve those objectives.

In this way Directives cannot in themselves automatically create substantive rights that citizens are then able to enforce.

- Firstly, they are not directly applicable. They do not automatically become laws in the Member States. On the contrary, the Member States are allowed to achieve the objects contained in the Directives in whatever way they choose.
- Secondly, because they fail one part of the test in *Van Gend en Loos* (1963). They are conditional; they are not non-dependent; and they are entirely dependent on implementation by the Member States.

The problem first came to the attention of the ECJ in a situation where it was not so vital in one sense because it was in effect the Member State that was trying to plead that the Directive was enforceable. The important point for the citizen involved was whether the procedural safeguards contained in the Directive bound the Member State.

CASE EXAMPLE

Van Duyn v Home Office (Case 41/74) [1974] ECR 1337

Here, the issue was whether the UK could make use of the derogations from free movement of workers under both Art 45 and more precisely in Directive 64/221 (now under Directive 2004/38) (see Chapter 12). The ECJ considered the problem of the direct effect of Directives and reached an important conclusion, identifying that

JUDGMENT

> 'it would be incompatible with the binding effect attributed to a Directive by [Art 249] to exclude, in principle, the possibility that the obligation which it imposes may be invoked by those concerned ...'.

The ECJ was thus prepared to overlook the potential limitation involved in the definition of 'Directives' given by Art 288 again to ensure the *effet utile* (usefulness) of the measure. The court foresaw that this type of legislation could be made ineffective without allowing direct effect. Another way of looking at it is to say that there would be no purpose to this type of legislation if Member States were allowed to plead their own failure to implement as the reason for the right not being enforced.

As the court also observed in *Van Duyn* (1974):

JUDGMENT

'where the Community authorities have, by directive, imposed on Member States the obligation to pursue a particular course of conduct, the useful effect of such an act would be weakened if individuals were prevented from relying on it before their national courts and if the latter were prevented from taking it into consideration …'.

On this basis, while the court gave little other reasoning it identified that a Directive can indeed be enforced by the means of direct effect provided that the remaining criteria from *Van Gend en Loos* (1963) are met.

Nevertheless, it must be remembered that, because Directives include objectives that are left for Member States to enact in their own chosen method, if the Member States carry out their obligations the rights identifiable in the Directives would not be enforceable through EU law but rather through the national law as enacted. For this reason, Directives are only a problem where they are unimplemented or improperly implemented.

Of course, there is nothing to stop the ECJ or the national courts from referring to the Directive after its implementation into national law in order to ensure that its objectives have indeed been achieved. This was confirmed in the case of *Verbond van Nederlands Ondernemingen v Inspecteur der Invoerrechten en Accijzen* (Case 51/76) [1977] ECR 113.

However, it is equally true that during the implementation period the rights contained in the Directive are not enforceable by any means. This would clearly be unfair since the Member States have been given a time limit within which to comply. For this reason the Court of Justice added an extra criterion to the *Van Gend en Loos* (1963) test in respect of Directives. In *Pubblico Ministero v Ratti* (1979) the ECJ stated that direct effect of a Directive is not in question until such time as the implementation period has expired.

Another significant point is that a Directive can only ever be vertically directly effective. It could never be horizontally directly effective. This means that an unimplemented or improperly implemented Directive can only be relied upon and enforced against the state which, according to the reasoning in *Van Duyn* (1974), the member state is prevented from its own failure to implement to avoid the obligation owed under the Directive.

CASE EXAMPLE

Marshall v Southampton and South West Hampshire AHA (No 1) (Case 152/84) [1986] QB 401

A reference was made under Art 267 on the issue of whether different retirement ages for men and women in the UK amounted to discrimination under Directive 76/207 (now the Recast Directive), the 'Equal Access Directive' (see Chapter 18). The ECJ confirmed that it was. It also identified that the applicant was able to use the Directive against her employer but only because her employer was in fact the Health Service, an organ of the state.

The ECJ also made it plain that a Directive could be only vertically directly effective, stating:

JUDGMENT

'according to [Art 288] … the binding nature of a directive … exists only in relation to "each Member State to which it is addressed". It follows that a directive may not of itself impose obligations on an individual and that a provision of a directive may not be relied upon as such against such a person.'

The ECJ subsequently identified that the national courts should decide against what bodies a Directive could be enforced using vertical direct effect. It has explained also that vertical direct effect may affect not only the state itself but also bodies that could be described as an 'emanation of the state' (or 'arm of the state'). The court also has devised the test of which bodies can be classed as emanations of the state.

CASE EXAMPLE

Foster v British Gas plc (Case C–188/89) [1990] ECR I–3313

The applicant was making the same basic claim as that in the Marshall (1986) case, that British Gas was in breach of Directive 76/207 (now the Recast Directive) by compelling her to retire at 60 when male employees retired at 65 (a legitimate difference under s 6(4) of the Sex Discrimination Act 1975 – but later repealed in the Sex Discrimination Act 1986). At the time of her complaint British Gas was not a private company but was still owned by the state. The House of Lords, in a reference to the ECJ under Art 267, posed the question of whether British Gas was a body against which the Directive could be enforced. The ECJ developed a test for determining whether a body could be classed as an emanation of the state. The Court declared (in paragraph 18) that a Directive could be relied on against any organisation or body which:

> was 'subject to the authority or control' of the State, or had 'special powers' that would not be available to a private body.

In paragraph 20, the Court then ruled on whether British Gas at the material time (before it was privatised) was such a body. The Court noted it was definitely an 'emanation of the state' because it provided a public service, was under the control of the state and was able to exercise special powers. However, when the case returned to the House of Lords, the Law Lords adopted paragraph 20 as the test for determining an 'emanation of the state', rather than paragraph 18. According to this test, a body must satisfy three criteria. It must:

- be one that provides a public service, and
- be under the control of the state, and
- be able to exercise special powers that would not be available to a private body.

It is obvious that the paragraph 20 test is much more difficult to satisfy than the paragraph 18 test. Nevertheless, a number of subsequent British cases have considered and applied the three-part paragraph 20 test. In *Doughty v Rolls Royce plc* [1992] 1 CMLR 1045 a publicly owned manufacturing company was held not to be an emanation of the state since it failed the first and third criteria. On the other hand, in *Griffin v South West Water* [1995] IRLR 15 the national court considered that a privatised water company was an emanation of the state. While the body itself was not as such under the control of the state, certain of the services it operated were.

There is inconsistent application of the principles regarding when a body can be classed as an emanation of the state. Nevertheless, there have been quite liberal interpretations by the ECJ, so that a private company has been held to be an emanation of the state where it is carrying out a public duty.

CASE EXAMPLE

Rieser Internationale Transporte GmbH v Autobahnen-und-Schnellstrasse Finanzierungs AG (Asfinag) C–157/02

An Austrian company, Asfinag, was involved in the construction of motorways in Austria. Besides this it was involved in and had certain involvement in respect of planning, maintaining and financing motorways. More importantly it was able to levy tolls on users. It was shown in the case that the Austrian state was the sole shareholder in the company, had the right to check everything done by the company, and could impose rules regarding construction, safety and the organisation of traffic. Besides this Asfinag was required to submit detailed plans to the Austrian state each year as well as having to provide details of estimated costs for the year. As a result, for the purposes of enforcing the provisions of a directive, the ECJ held that Asfinag was engaged in a public service, was under the control of the state, and also had special powers beyond those normally enjoyed by private companies and so was an emanation of the state, and therefore subject to vertical direct effect of the directive.

The fact that Directives can be only vertically directly effective inevitably creates major anomalies and injustices where an applicant's case is against another individual or a private body. This can be seen in the contrasting decisions above and also in *Duke v GEC Reliance* [1988] 2 WLR 359. The case involved the identical point to that in *Marshall* (1986), but the employer was not the state but a private company. The House of Lords held that it was not bound to apply Directive 76/207 (now the Recast Directive) because the Directive could not be effective horizontally. Even though the UK was at fault for failing to implement the Directive fully, the availability of a remedy then was entirely dependent on the identity of the employer.

Clearly, the process of ensuring vertical effect of Directives in actions against the State or an emanation of the State was one way of getting round the defects in the definition of 'Directives' in Art 288. Nevertheless, the absence of horizontal effect still meant that there were problems in enforcing rights granted by Directives.

> 'In *Marshall* the Court held that an individual may rely upon a directive against the State, regardless of whether the State is acting as a public authority or employer. The consequence of this ruling is that, for example, a private employee may not rely on a directive but a state employee may. The ruling has been attacked as provoking unjust and anomalous situations, particularly in the field of labour law, where the scope of the Equal Treatment Directive has been reduced. The decision also led to the necessity for an impossibly rigorous definition of the state which proved very difficult to apply in case law.'
>
> S Douglas-Scott, *Constitutional Law of the European Union* (Longman, 2002), p 296

The means for determining the direct effect of a Directive can be represented in diagram form as shown in Figure 9.4.2.

9.4.2 Indirect effect

Making use of vertical direct effect was one way in which the ECJ was able to ensure that rights gained through a Directive could be enforced but of course it had severe limitations. Another way round the problem was the introduction of the process of sympathetic interpretation (or indirect effect).

The ECJ identified that since Member States had an obligation at that time under Art 10 to 'take all appropriate measures ... to ensure fulfilment of the obligations arising out of this Treaty' then the national courts also had a duty to interpret national law so that it would give full effect to EU law (irrespective of whether or not it is directly effective).

This is the principle of indirect effect, known also as the *Von Colson* principle, and it applies to EU law in general, not only to Directives, but it can obviously be useful in avoiding the problem of the lack of horizontal effect of Directives. The ECJ explained the principle in two cases that were referred to the court by the German Labour Court:

CASE EXAMPLE

Von Colson and Kamann v Land Nordrhein-Westfalen (Case 14/83) [1984] ECR 1891; Harz v Deutsche Tradax GmbH (Case 79/83) [1984] ECR 1921

The cases both involved improper implementation of Directive 76/207 by the German Government. The failure by Germany was one that was also highlighted in the second of the Marshall cases (Marshall v Southampton and South West Hampshire AHA (No 2) (Case C–271/91) [1993] ECR 586 on the provision of inadequate compensation in contrast with the full compensation required by the Directive.

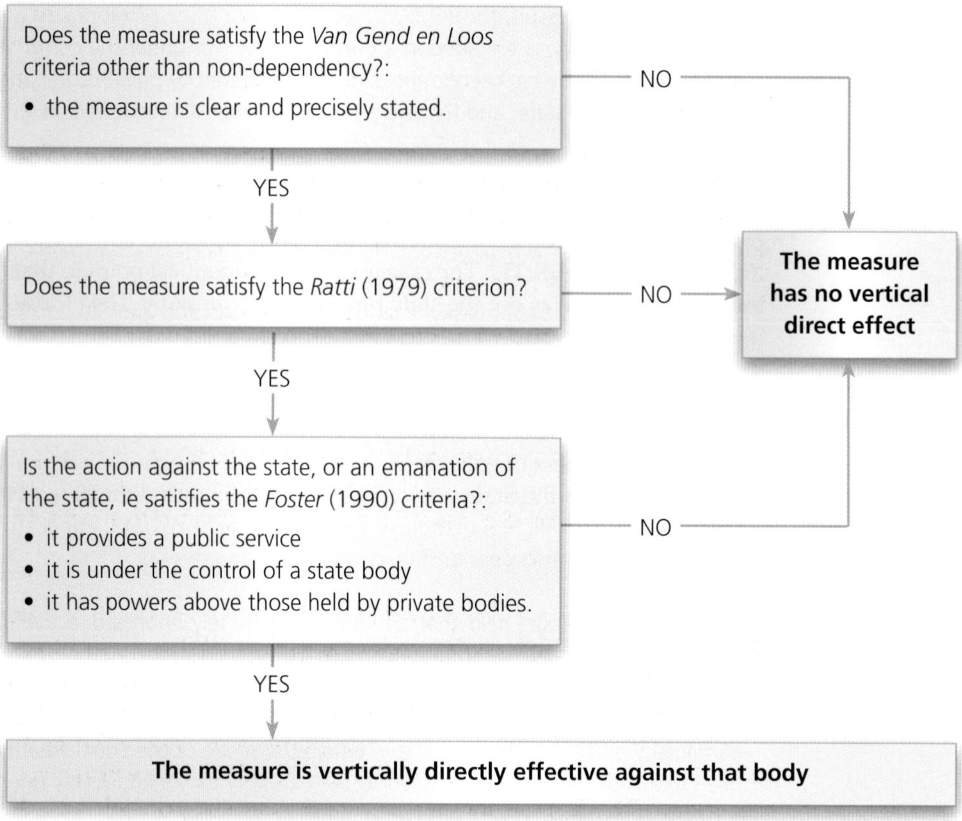

Figure 9.4.2 The requirements to prove vertical direct effect of a Directive

Von Colson applied to work for a state body, the prison service, while Harz applied to work for a private company. The ECJ identified that the failure to provide compensation did amount to improper or incomplete implementation. Even so, while a remedy would have been available to Von Colson through vertical direct effect, Harz would have been denied a remedy because of the anomaly resulting from lack of horizontal effect. The ECJ took a different and at the time a very novel approach by using the obligation in Art 10 [now repealed] of the EC Treaty to introduce the principle of indirect effect. The German court was bound to give full effect to the Directive and so must order full compensation in both cases.

JUDGMENT

'Since the duty under [Art 10] to ensure fulfillment of [an] obligation was binding on all national courts … it follows that … courts are required to interpret their national law in the light of the wording and purpose of the Directive …'.

The ECJ in *Von Colson* (1984) in this way ignored the problem of horizontal and vertical effect, and in fact ignored direct effect in general so it was a means of overcoming the problems seen above in section 9.4.1. Nevertheless, the judgment did leave ambiguous the question of to which national law the process of indirect effect could actually apply. This then allowed the House of Lords to refuse to apply the principle in *Duke* (1988) even though it would have been a means of providing a remedy for the applicant.

Another limitation in the case itself was that it also left ambiguous or unexplained just how far national courts should go in order to ensure conformity of their own national law and EU law. However, subsequent development or clarification of the principle may have overcome these problems.

CASE EXAMPLE

Marleasing SA v La Commercial Internacional de Alimentacion (Case C–106/89) [1990] ECR I–4135

Whereas Von Colson involved an improperly implemented Directive, this case concerned a Directive that had not been implemented at all. On a reference from the Spanish court the question for the ECJ was whether the applicant could rely on the rules on the constitution of companies in Directive 68/151, the Directive on company law harmonisation. Spain had not implemented the Directive and Spanish law conflicted with its provisions. The ECJ applied the principles of indirect effect and expanded on the definition given in Von Colson.

JUDGMENT

'... in applying national law, whether the provisions concerned pre-date or post-date the directive, the national court asked to interpret national law is bound to do so in every way possible in the light of the text and the aims of the directive to achieve the results envisaged by it'.

The scope of indirect effect provided for by *Marleasing* (1990) is potentially very wide, then, and it has the effect of introducing horizontal direct effect but by indirect means, hence the title given to the process. However, there does seem to be a significant difference between the *Von Colson* (1984) approach, which is to do 'everything possible' to achieve conformity, and the original approach in *Simmenthal SpA v Amministrazione delle Finanze dello Stato* (Case 70/77) [1978] ECR 1453, which was to do 'everything necessary'. The ECJ has more recently held that the principle of indirect effect extends beyond directives and can apply also to a framework decision. *Pupino* C–105/03 [2005] 2 CMLR 63.

The ECJ does seem to have linked the concepts of direct effect and indirect effect as different ways of dealing with the same problem. In *Johnston v Chief Constable of the RUC* (Case 222/84) [1986] ECR 1651 the court suggested that it was the duty of national courts to interpret national law in conformity with EU law (indirect effect) and only if this was not possible to then enforce EU law in preference to inconsistent national law (direct effect).

There are limitations to the process. In *Arcaro* (Case C–168/95) [1996] ECR I–4705 the ECJ held that the provisions of an unimplemented Directive cannot be imposed on an individual where to do so would lead to criminal liability. The most important limitation, of course, is that the process is entirely dependent on the willingness of the national courts to use it. As has been seen in *Duke* (1988), the national courts are not always so willing so that there is the possibility of lack of uniformity throughout the EU. Inconsistency indeed has been shown. The House of Lords in *Litster v Forth Dry Dock and Engineering Co* [1989] 1 All ER 1134 had to consider the incompatibility of the then English TUPE law and provisions of the Acquired Rights Directive 77/187. The court, taking a different approach to that in *Duke* (1988), felt bound to interpret the English Regulations in a way that would give full effect to the Directive.

> 'the indirect application of EC directives by national courts cannot be guaranteed. This reluctance on the part of the national courts to comply with the *Von Colson* principle, particularly as applied in Marleasing, is hardly surprising. It may be argued that in extending the principle of indirect effect in this way the ECJ is attempting to give horizontal effect to directives by the back door, and impose obligations, addressed to Member States, on private parties, contrary to their understanding of domestic law. Where such is the case, as the House of Lords remarked in *Duke* ... this could be most unfair'.
>
> J Steiner, *Textbook on EC Law* (8th edn, Oxford University Press, 2003), p 109

9.4.3 State liability for breach of EU law obligations

As we have seen, both vertical direct effect and the process of indirect effect have limitations and there are still situations where a party could be without a remedy because of the failure of a Member State to implement a Directive or because of improper implementation.

The ECJ devised a third way of avoiding the problems of direct effect and Directives. This is state liability. In simple terms, if the reason that a citizen lacks a remedy and suffers loss or damage is the failure of a Member State to implement EU law then that Member State should be made liable for the damage suffered.

CASE EXAMPLE

Francovich and Bonifaci v Republic of Italy (Cases C–6 and 9/90) [1991] ECR I–5357

Italy had failed to set up a scheme to provide a minimum compensation for workers on the insolvency of their employers in breach of a set requirement under Directive 80/987. As a result, the claimants, who had been made unemployed, were unable to recover wages due to them. The ECJ found that Italy was in breach of its obligations and was liable to compensate the workers for the loss resulting from that breach.

The ECJ identified that:

JUDGMENT

'… the full effectiveness of Community rules would be impaired and the rights they recognise would be undermined if individuals were unable to recover damages where their rights were infringed by a breach of EC law attributable to a member state …'.

On this basis *Francovich* (1991) introduced the principle that citizens should be able to sue the state for non-implementation of a Directive. The court did state that liability was not unlimited so that three conditions must be met for liability:

- the Directive must confer rights on individuals
- the contents of those rights must be identifiable in the wording of the measure
- there must be a causal link between the damage suffered and the failure to implement the Directive.

The ECJ left the matter of determining the extent of liability to the national courts. A number of other questions remained unanswered. However, the principle has subsequently been expanded and re-defined.

CASE EXAMPLE

Brasserie du Pêcheur SA v Federal Republic of Germany; R v Secretary of State for Transport, ex p Factortame Ltd (Cases C–46 and C–48/93) [1996] ECR I–1029

The first of these two cases involved a German beer purity law that was found to be in breach of Art 34 that provides for the removal of all quantitative restrictions on imports or exports or measures having an equivalent effect (See Chapter 14). The second involved quotas under the Merchant Shipping Act 1988 in breach of Art 49 on rights of establishment (see Chapter 13), and a breach of a previous ruling of the ECJ. Both cases involved breaches of Treaty Articles and the reference was for clarification of the conditions for and the scope of state liability. The ECJ held that it was irrelevant that the breaches involved directly effective Treaty Articles and that it was also irrelevant what organ of the Member State was in fact responsible for the breach.

The court also re-defined the conditions from *Francovich* (1991), ignoring the original second condition and replacing it with a new one. The new conditions the court decided were:

- the rule of Union law infringed must be intended to confer rights on individuals
- the breach must be sufficiently serious to justify imposing state liability
- there must be a direct causal link between the breach of the obligation imposed on the state and the damage actually suffered by the applicant.

As a result of the case, the definition of 'state' has clearly widened to include acts and omissions of any organ of the state. Also, the scope of liability has been extended beyond Directives to include any breach of Union law, regardless of whether or not it has direct effect.

Directives clearly give Member States a wide discretion on how to act. This was the next point for the ECJ to consider since where a discretion exists the Member State might be excused for acting differently to the requirements of the Directive if it was not phrased in sufficiently precise terms.

CASE EXAMPLE

R v HM Treasury, ex p British Telecommunications plc (Case C–392/93 [1996] ECR I–1631

Here, BT alleged that the UK Government had incorrectly implemented a Directive on public procurement in water, transport, energy and telecommunications, as a result of which BT, suffered loss. The ECJ accepted that the Directive was imprecisely worded so that the meaning given to it by the UK Government was indeed possible. In fact, the court also accepted that it was an interpretation of the Directive that was shared by other Member States. Besides this, there was no ECJ case law on the Directive that might direct the Member State. On this basis the Court of Justice decided that the breach could not be classed as 'sufficiently serious' as required by the Brasserie du Pêcheur (1996) test.

Inevitably, then, what will amount to a sufficiently serious breach to warrant state liability may vary with the nature of the act and indeed the amount of discretion available to the Member State. It is possible in this way that even a mere infringement of EU law by a Member State could be classed as sufficiently serious.

CASE EXAMPLE

R v Ministry of Agriculture, Fisheries and Food, ex p Hedley Lomas (Ireland) Ltd (Case C–5/94) [1996] ECR I–2553

Here, the act involved was one of government rather than legislation introducing an EU measure in an improper manner. The Ministry had refused to grant licences for export of live cattle to Spain. The Ministry's justification for doing so was that Spain, in allowing export of animals before slaughter, was failing to comply with Directive 74/577. The ECJ held that the refusal by the Ministry was a clear breach of Art 35 and that there was no justifiable exemption available under Art 36 (see Chapter 14). It also accepted that state liability was appropriate in the case.

In applying the test for state liability, the court stated that:

JUDGMENT

'where, at the time when it committed the infringement, the Member State in question was not called upon to make any legislative choices and had only considerably reduced, or even no, discretion, the mere infringement of Community law may be sufficient to establish the existence of a sufficiently serious breach'.

The court has also established, then, that there are situations where the seriousness of the breach is obvious. In such circumstances the imposition of state liability is almost a form of strict liability. The failure to implement a Directive is a classic example.

CASE EXAMPLE

Dillenkofer and others v Federal Republic of Germany (Cases C–178, 179, 188, 189 and 190/94) [1996] ECR I–4845

This involved a failure by Germany to implement the Package Holidays Directive 90/314. The ECJ held that a failure to implement a Directive by the due date was in itself a sufficiently serious breach to justify state liability.

The *Francovich* (1991) principle is the most far-reaching means by which the ECJ has attempted to deal with the problem of ensuring the enforceability of Directives. As such, it has many implications. The principles do have to be applied within the legal systems in each Member State, as a result of which there is an issue over the compatibility with national rules on non-implementation. However, the need to show direct effect is less pressing as well as the rather strained construction of national law through the process of indirect effect.

What state liability has achieved is that it focuses instead on the duty of the Member State to implement EU law while in effect attaching rigorous sanctions for failure to implement. In consequence, it does ultimately have the effect of removing any advantage that might be gained by non-implementation.

It has also been shown that state liability can extend to all branches of government including the judiciary of a Member State.

CASE EXAMPLE

Gerhard Kobler v Republic of Austria C–224/01

Kobler, a German national working in Austria, had complained in the Austrian court that he had been denied additional pay due to professors after 15 years' service. Kobler had 10 years' service in Austria but would have qualified if his service in other Member States had been taken into account. The Austrian Supreme Administrative Court initially made a reference to the European Court of Justice, but withdrew it and in effect decided the point of EU law itself declaring it to be clear and therefore not requiring a reference. Kobler sought damages from the Austrian state. The ECJ held that EU law on that point was not clear and, since the Austrian court was a court of final resort, a reference should have been made. It also identified that state liability could be applied where a national court made an incorrect judgment on EU law and where the breach was sufficiently serious. In the event the ECJ did not consider that the breach was sufficiently serious in this instance.

In *Tragghetti del Mediterraneo SpA v Italy* C–173/03, a competition case under Article 102, the ECJ held that intentional fault and serious misconduct on the part of a national court cannot be used as the sole means of determining that there has been a sufficiently serious breach of EU law if this would have the effect of excluding the state from liability and denying the citizen a remedy.

The case law on state liability has thus developed to the point of ensuring that there is a uniform application of the principle throughout all Member States.

The means for determining whether an individual can make a claim under the *Francovich/Brasserie du Pêcheur* (1996) principle can be represented in diagram form as shown in Figure 9.4.3.

A recent case has posed the question of whether there is also a horizontal version of the (1991) *Francovich* principle.

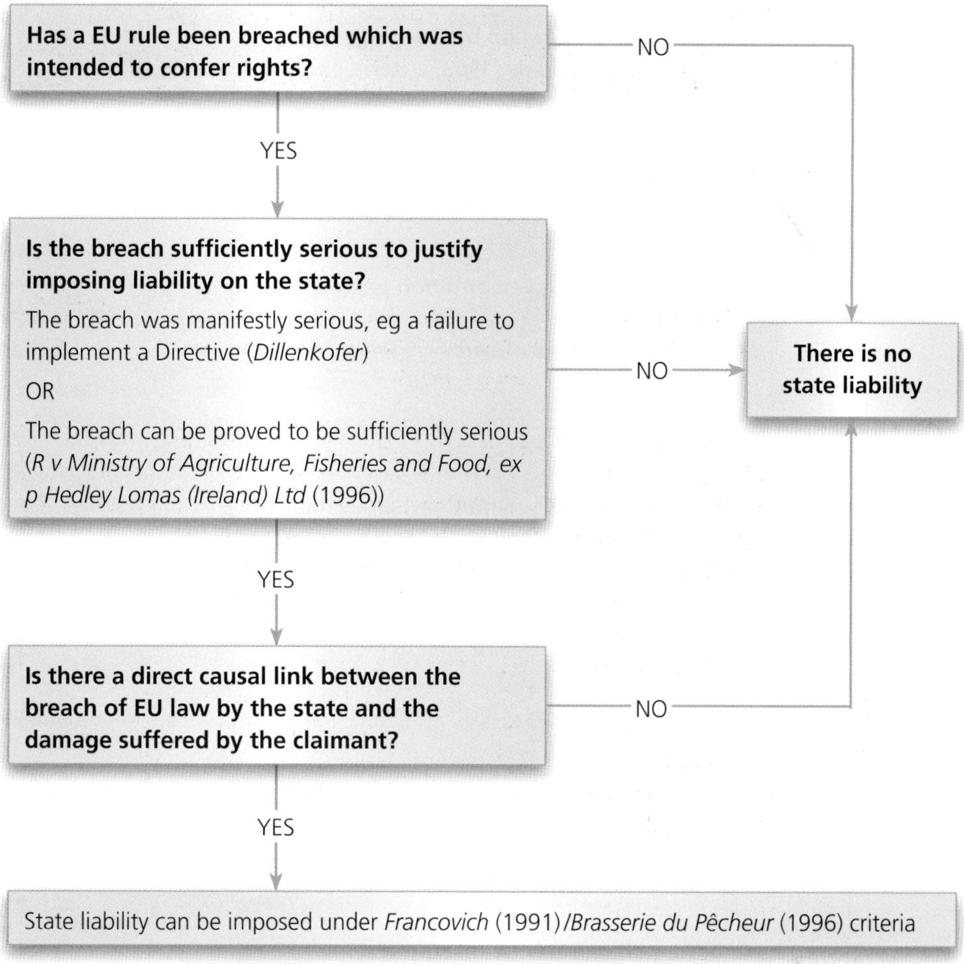

Figure 9.4.3 The criteria to establish state liability under *Brasserie du Pêcheur* (1996)

CASE EXAMPLE

Courage Ltd v Crehan (Case C–453/99) [2001] ECR I–6297

Here, Crehan was in a tying arrangement under which he had to buy all his beer supplies from Courage which was suing for £15,000 for unpaid beer. Crehan counter-claimed for money already paid under the contract, on the basis that the contract was in fact contrary to Art 101. Since English law meant that a party could not rely on his wrongdoing to found a claim, neither party could rely on the contract to claim against the other. The ECJ held that the English rules would render Art 101 ineffective and so allowed an action by Crehan against Courage. In fact, the case concerned restitution rather than damages but some commentators have suggested that the judgment is allowing what amounts to state liability but against a private party.

It is possible to illustrate how the problem of enforceability of Directives might be resolved using all three approaches above in diagram form as shown in Figure 9.4.4.

9.4.4 'Incidental' horizontal effect

In *Faccini Dori v Recreb Srl* (Case C–91/92) [1994] ECR I–3325 Advocate-General Lenz argued that Directives should be capable of horizontal direct effect because of changes in

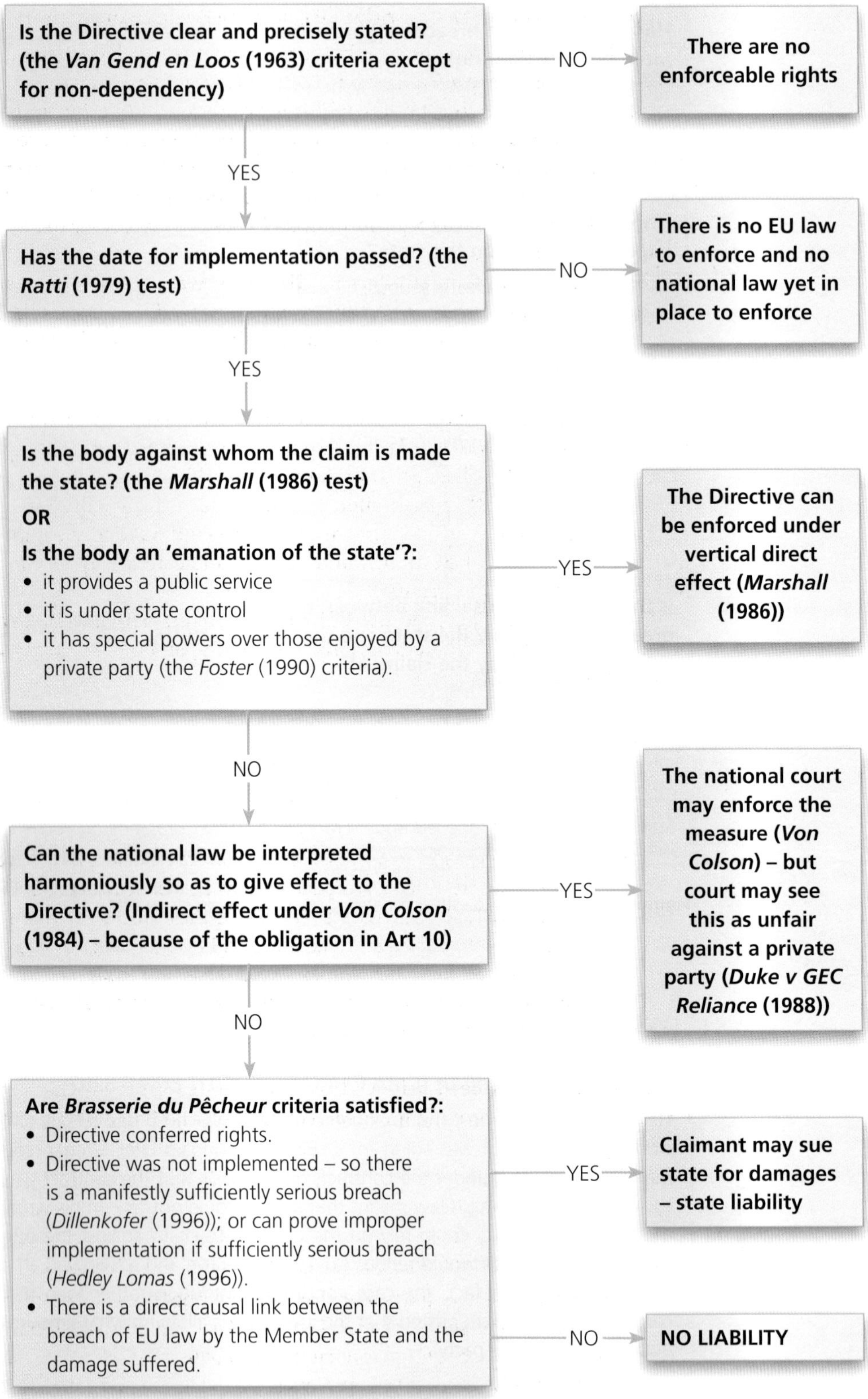

Figure 9.4.4 The possible means of enforcing rights contained in Directives

the TEU and also because the fact that they were not meant that individuals were being denied rights that they otherwise might claim legitimately through EU law. However, the ECJ did not follow his argument but instead applied *Marshall* (1986) criteria in the case.

Three arguments were originally used to deny the horizontal effect of Directives:

- The **lack of legal certainty** – however, now that all Directives are published, the argument cannot apply and it is in fact the lack of horizontal effect and now the main uncertainties are what bodies will be considered public for vertical effect and the circumstances in which national courts will be prepared to impose indirect effect.
- The **estoppel argument**, that since individuals had no control over the implementation of Directives they were not at fault and should not be fixed with fault – however, the widening of the concept of the state in *Foster* in effect means that that is precisely what is happening.
- That to allow horizontal effect to Directives was to **blur the distinction** between Regulations and Directives – this again is not really an argument since, if Member States implemented Directives as national law, there would effectively be no distinction anyway.

One interesting off-shoot of the problems associated with direct effect of Directives has arisen in situations where individuals have tried to exploit the principle of direct effect to establish the illegal nature of the national law rather than to try to enforce any EU rights. The way that such situations have been dealt with has become known as 'incidental' horizontal effect. Some recent cases stand out and they appear to go against the eventual stance taken in *Dori* and seem to indicate a way in which Directives can indeed be horizontally effective.

The first allowed a party to use a Directive in effect horizontally in a defence against another private party where that party was relying on national law which had not fully followed the Directive.

CASE EXAMPLE

CIA Security International SA v Signalson and Securitel (Case C–194/94) [1996] ECR I–2201

Signalson brought an action against CIA for a breach of Belgian law on unfair trading in the marketing of security products. CIA argued that the Belgian regulations could not be applied because Directive 83/189 required that Member States should obtain clearance from the Commission before introducing such measures and Belgium had not notified the Commission. The ECJ accepted the argument, as a result of which Signalson's action failed. There was no EC [now EU] right being relied on: the Directive was merely being used to disapply national law, hence 'incidental' horizontal effect.

A similar result has been achieved in a contractual dispute where the Directive was merely incidental to proving the breach of contract and had nothing to do with enforcing an EU right.

CASE EXAMPLE

Unilever Italia SpA v Central Food SpA (Case C–443/98) [2000] ECR I–7535

Here, the conflict was over the relevance of different labelling requirements and the question of which requirements should be complied with. Again, Directive 83/189 was involved since Italy had introduced labelling requirements for geographical origin on olive oil. Under the Directive Italy should have notified the Commission of its intention to regulate. The Commission intended to regulate itself Community-wide and so under the Directive Italy should not have introduced the regulation but had done so. Central Food was supplied by Unilever without the labelling required under the Italian regulation and was refusing to pay because the labelling did not conform with Italian law. Unilever argued that the Italian law could not apply since it was in effect in breach of the Directive. The ECJ held that the Italian law could not apply and that this did not conflict with the rules on horizontal direct effect of Directives since the Directive in this case did not involve rights on which individuals might rely.

ACTIVITY

Applying the law

Study the scenarios below and consider how, if at all, the principles of:

- direct effect
- indirect effect and
- state liability

could be applied in the light of the **fictitious** Council Directives.

The Council passed two Directives concerning air levels of two different chemicals, Directive 99/4004 [fictitious] on the chemical CCO1, and Directive 99/5200 [fictitious] on the chemical OTT66, both of which are common in the production of paint. The two Directives were passed after scientific research demonstrated that both chemicals are dangerous if certain levels of the chemicals in the air are exceeded, and also that they are likely to cause respiratory illnesses. Both Directives had an implementation date of 31st August 2004 and set maximum levels of the chemical in the air. An additional requirement of each Directive was compulsory testing for the chemical and allied industries.

1. The UK Government has not yet implemented Directive 99/4004. A paint manufacturer, Coverall, uses CCO1 extensively in its paint production. Residents living near to the factory have commissioned a survey of the air around the plant which has revealed levels of CCO1 in the air that are well beyond those identified in the Directive. Several local residents have recently developed asthmatic complaints.

   Suggest whether the residents can rely on Directive 99/4004 against either Coverall or the UK Government.

2. The UK did implement Directive 99/5200 within the time limit but in its legislation did not provide for compulsory testing as required in the Directive. Lawyers representing the residents above believe the lack of testing has allowed Coverall to adopt dangerous practices and that these have led to leaks of OTT66 into the atmosphere, causing higher levels of the chemical than if proper scrutiny had occurred.

   Advise the lawyers as to whether the residents are able to use Directive 99/5200 in a claim against the UK Government.

ACTIVITY

Self-assessment questions

1. What were the original problems of allowing direct effect of Directives?
2. Why did the ECJ feel in *Van Duyn* (1974) that Directives should be enforceable through direct effect?
3. How did the ECJ overcome this problem?
4. What are the major effects of the decision in *Marshall (No 1)* (1986)?
5. What impact does the test in *Foster v British Gas* (1990) have on the principle of direct effect?
6. What shortcomings are there in using vertical direct effect as a means of enforcing Directives?
7. How does the principle in *Von Colson* (1984) assist individuals to enforce rights that are granted them by EU law?
8. How effective is the *Von Colson* (1984) principle?
9. In what ways does the case of *Marleasing* (1990) extend the principle in *Von Colson* (1984)?
10. How does the principle in *Francovich* (1991) add to the rules on direct effect?
11. In what significant way does the test in *Brasserie du Pêcheur* (1996) add to or alter the *Francovich* (1991) test?
12. How did the cases of *Dillenkofer* (1996) and *Hedley Lomas* (1996) develop the test further?

KEY FACTS

Direct applicability	
Direct applicability: • the measure becomes part of national law without need for further enactment • it applies to Regulations but not to Directives because Directives require implementation by Member States.	
Direct effect	
• Accepted that certain measures should be enforceable by citizens of Member States – if they were clear, precise and unconditional, and conferred rights on individuals.	*Van Gend en Loos v Nederlands Administratie der Belastingen* (1963)
• Not all provisions do conform to the criteria.	*Casati* (1981)
• This is straightforward in the case of substantive Treaty Articles.	*Reyners v Belgium* (1974)
• And in the case of Regulations.	*Leonesio v Ministero dell'Agricoltora & delle Foreste* (1972)
• And even in the case of Decisions.	*Grad v Finanzamt Traustein* (1970)
• But not for Directives which are not a complete legal instrument.	
• Direct effect can be vertical (against the state) or horizontal (against another citizen).	*Defrenne v SABENA* (1976)
Direct effect of Directives	
• Recognised that it would be incompatible with the binding nature of a Directive in Art 288 if they could not be enforced.	*Van Duyn v Home Office* (1974)
• So can be directly effective if date for implementation passed.	*Pubblico Ministero v Ratti* (1979)
• But only 'vertically' against the state itself.	*Marshall v Southampton and SW Hants AHA (No 1)* (1986)
• Or an 'emanation of the state' – must provide public service, be under control of state, have powers over and above those of private bodies.	*Foster v British Gas plc* (1990)
• Creates unfair anomalies when claim is against private party.	*Duke v GEC Reliance* (1988)
Indirect effect	
• Since Member States have obligation formerly under Art 10 to give full effect to EU law then national court should interpret improperly implemented Directive to give effect to its objectives.	*Von Colson and Kamann v Land Nordrhein-Westfalen* (1984); *Harz v Deutsche Tradax* (1984)
• Applies whether national law concerned pre-dates or post-dates the Directive.	*Marleasing SA v La Commercial Internacional de Alimentacion* (1990)
• But inconsistent approach taken by national courts – so unpredictable.	Compare *Litster v Forth Dock & Engineering* (1989) with *Duke* (1988)
State liability	
• Possibility of state liability where: Directive confers rights on individuals; those rights are identifiable in wording; causal link between damage suffered and failure to implement Directive.	*Francovich and Bonifaci v Republic of Italy* (1991)

• Criteria now modified and apply to all EU measures if: rule of Union law infringed intended to confer rights; breach is sufficiently serious; direct causal link between breach by state and damage suffered by applicant.	*Brasserie du Pêcheur v Germany* (1996); *R v Secretary of State for Transport, ex p Factortame* (1990)
• Failure to implement Directive is manifestly sufficiently serious breach.	*Dillenkofer and others v Germany* (1996)
• Otherwise, must prove breach of EU law is sufficiently serious to justify state liability.	*R v Ministry of Agriculture, Fisheries and Food, ex p Hedley Lomas* (1996)

SAMPLE ESSAY QUESTION

'Discuss the ways in which the European Court of Justice has been instrumental in ensuring that EU citizens have been able to enforce rights given to them by directives.'

Define directives:
- binding as to the result to be achieved – so left to Member States to implement in their own way within a defined period
- so not automatically incorporated into national law or directly enforceable.

Define direct effect:
- the criteria from *Van Gend en Loos*
- the measure must be clear, precise and unconditional.

Discuss the problem of enforcing directives:
- that they are not unconditional
- but ECJ in *Van Duyn* recognised that it would be incompatible with the binding nature of Art 288 if they were unenforceable.

Discuss how direct effect can apply to directives:
- date for implementation must have passed before they are enforceable
- the principle in *Marshall* that Directives can never be horizontally directly effective (against other citizens) but can be vertically directly effective (against the state).

Discuss the problems this created and how the ECJ overcame them:

- no horizontal direct effect – so not enforceable against a private body
- ECJ extended vertical effect to emanations of the state where *Foster* test applied
- indirect effect – sympathetic interpretation where there was partial implementation
- if no remedy then state liability if test in *Factortame (No 2)/Brasserie du Pecheur* satisfied.

SUMMARY

- Direct effect, indirect effect and state liability are all devices created by the Court of Justice to ensure effective enforcement of the Treaties.
- Direct effect means the measure can be enforced and the Court of Justice has established a test of direct effect – the measure is clear, precise and unconditional.
- Direct effect can be both horizontal, the measure is enforceable against other citizens of the EU, or vertical, the measure is enforceable against the state or an emanation of the state.
- A problem arises in the case of unimplemented directives because directives are conditional on implementation by Member States – so the Court of Justice also created indirect effect, a means by which the national court can use the basic obligation of Member States to uphold EU law to sympathetically interpret the defective national law to incorporate the EU measure.
- An aggrieved citizen can recover compensation under state liability if the EU measure was clear and precise in creating a right, was a manifestly sufficiently serious a breach of EU law to warrant imposing liability on the state, and there was a direct causal link between the breach and the damage suffered.

Further reading

Articles

Craig, P, 'Once upon a time in the west: direct effect and the federalisation of EC law' 1992 OJLS 453.

Mancini, F, 'The making of a constitution for Europe' (1989) 26 CMLR 595.

Prechal, S, 'Does direct effect matter?' (2000) 37 CMLR 1047.

Books

Douglas-Scott, S, *Constitutional Law of the European Union* (Longman, 2002), Chapter 8.

Shaw, J, *European Community Law* (Macmillan Professional Masters, 1993), Chapter 8.

Steiner, J and Woods, L, *Textbook on EC Law* (8th edn, Oxford University Press, 2003), Chapter 5.

Ward, I, *A Critical Introduction to European Law* (Butterworths, 1996), Chapter 2.

10

The internal market

AIMS AND OBJECTIVES

After reading this chapter you should be able to:

- Understand the aims of the Internal Market
- Understand the law relating to the free movement of capital
- Understand differences between 'capital', 'goods' and 'services'

10.1 The aims of the Internal Market

The Internal Market principle is located in Art 26(2) TFEU. It states:

ARTICLE

'Art 26(2) The internal market shall comprise an area without internal frontiers in which the free movement of goods, persons, services, and capital is ensured in accordance with the provisions of the Treaties.'

Following the EU's enlargements in May 2004 and January 2007, the Internal Market is now – in population terms at least – the world's largest single trading bloc (overtaking NAFTA (the North American Free Trade Association), comprising the USA, Canada and Mexico). Moreover, the Internal Market is much more than a free trade area (which characteristically only seeks to remove trade barriers between its Member States). There is also a common policy on the imposition of Customs duties both internally and externally (known as a Customs union), and a whole series of rules promoting the free movement of persons, services and capital as well as goods. NAFTA is essentially a free trade area, as is EFTA (the European Free Trade Association) which the UK helped form in the late 1950s as a 'rival' organisation to what was then the EEC. EFTA still exists, although the only surviving members are Iceland, Norway and Liechtenstein (all of whom are members of the European Economic Area (EEA)) and Switzerland. The purpose of the EEA was to allow those European states who were not committed to full EU membership to obtain some of the benefits of the Internal Market.

The Internal Market is the cornerstone of the EU. Free movement in EU law has several mechanisms and produces numerous advantages:

- Removal of trade barriers ensures that manufacturers and producers will have easier access to more consumers.
- As a corollary, those consumers will have access to more, and better, goods.
- Economies of scale and increased competition from manufacturers and producers in other countries will also drive down the prices of goods.

- The abolition of Customs charges and other tariffs will stop individual states from protecting inefficient domestic manufacturers and producers.
- Removal of obstacles to personal movement helps workers (and potential workers) to move from areas of high unemployment and/or areas of low wages to areas of high employment and/or better wages in different countries. Mutual recognition of vocational qualifications and practical experience obtained in different countries facilitates the movement of workers and self-employed people.
- The abolition of discrimination based on nationality (except where absolutely necessary) ensures employers taking on those foreign workers cannot exploit them *vis-à-vis* domestic workers, further encouraging free movement.

10.2 The 'Four Freedoms'

The 'Four Freedoms' are:

1. the free movement of persons
2. the free movement of services
3. the free movement of goods and
4. the free movement of capital.

The first three of these will be explored in detail in Chapters 11 and 12 (persons), 13 (services), 14 and 15 (goods). This chapter will look at some of the issues that have arisen that are common to all Four Freedoms, and those issues which involve the relationship between one or more of them. The fourth freedom, capital, will also be discussed briefly.

10.2.1 Common features

The free movements of persons, services, goods and capital all involve essentially the same basic principle: the removal of all barriers to movement imposed by national legislation, regulation or administration except those which are objectively necessary in order to protect some essential national interest. In other words, there is not 'absolute' free movement. Member States of the EU are entitled to retain in force, or even introduce new, barriers to free movement. However, they must be able to justify those barriers, either by invoking specific derogations contained in the TFEU or by invoking derogations authorised by the ECJ.

The TFEU allows Member States to derogate from the free movement of persons, services, goods and capital on the grounds of public policy and public security. These are the only derogations common to all Four Freedoms. There are other derogations which are specific to one or more of the free movements. Derogations on grounds of 'public health' are available for the freedoms of persons and services, while Art 36 allows Member States to derogate from the free movement of goods on the ground of 'human health protection'. Article 36 also allows Member States to derogate from the free movement of goods on grounds of 'public morality', 'the protection of national treasures possessing artistic, historic or archaeological value' and 'the protection of industrial or commercial property'. None of these derogations applies to the other freedoms.

In addition to the specific Treaty derogations, the ECJ has introduced and developed a doctrine under which some restrictions on the freedoms imposed by national legislation, regulation or administration can be justified on any other grounds (sometimes referred to as a 'rule of reason'). However, four criteria have to be satisfied. In *Gebhard* (Case C–55/94) [1995] ECR I–4165, the ECJ stated that, in order for a national rule which restricts any of the freedoms to be justified, it must:

i) be non-discriminatory
ii) be justified by imperative requirements in the general interest
iii) be suitable for the attainment of the objective which it pursues
iv) not go beyond what is necessary in order to attain its objective (the 'proportionality' doctrine).

The application of these principles to specific cases will be dealt with in the respective chapters (and later in this chapter). However, it should be noted that the ECJ's application of a uniform, four-part test to the three freedoms of movement for persons, services and goods has attracted academic criticism. Luigi Daniele has argued that there is a lack of common ground between the movement of persons and the movement of services. The former involves the physical movement of a person to another EU Member State on a more or less permanent basis; the latter requires only that a service is provided by a person established in one Member State and received by a person from another Member State. There is no requirement of physical movement at all. Daniele suggests that applying the same rules to fundamentally different situations can create more problems than it solves. He concludes by suggesting that:

> 'The global approach to the free movement of persons risks bringing the Court unduly to put on the same footing rather different situations. More care should be taken in future when transposing the results achieved by case law in one field to another ... The Court should refrain from relying too much on the so-called "rules of reason". The uncertainty of the criteria on which such rules are based often forces the Court to follow a case-by-case approach. It is therefore extremely hard for the interpreter to predict how the Court will decide a given case. This might also cause an undesirable flow of mostly ill-founded cases. Before the situation gets out of hand, a re-consideration would be welcomed.'
>
> L Daniele, 'Non-Discriminatory Restrictions to the Free Movement of Persons' (1997) 22 ELR 191

As of 2011, however, the ECJ shows no sign of abandoning its 'globalisation' policy of applying the same 'rules of reason' to the free movements of persons, services and goods. Nor has it shown any intention of tightening up the criteria on which its 'rules' are based.

10.2.2 The free movement of capital

Space precludes a detailed analysis of the free movement of capital provisions. The key provisions are found in Arts 63–66 TFEU. Article 63(1) provides that 'within the framework of the provisions set out in this chapter, all restrictions on the movement of capital between Member States and between Member States and third countries shall be prohibited'.

The original Treaty provisions on the free movement of capital were far less sweeping, however, and liberalisation of capital movements has been a slower process than that of the other freedoms. In *Casati* (Case 203/80) [1981] ECR 2595, for example, the ECJ stated that complete freedom of movement of capital could undermine the economic policy of one of the Member States or create an imbalance in its balance of payments. According to the ECJ in *Bordessa and Others* (Cases C–358 and 416/93) [1995] ECR I–361, full liberalisation of capital movements did not occur until the Council adopted Directive 88/361.

'Capital'

The TFEU does not define 'capital', although a non-exhaustive list of capital movements can be found in the Annex of Directive 88/361. The following have been held to fall within the provisions on capital movements:

- **Shares**. In *Commission v Portugal* (Case C–367/98) [2002] ECR I–4731, where Portuguese rules precluded investors from other EU Member States from acquiring more than a fixed number of shares in Portuguese companies, the ECJ held that the rules constituted a restriction on capital movements. The ECJ extended this concept in *Commission v UK* (Case C–98/01) [2003] ECR I–4641, by holding that national rules which restricted share ownership without distinction (ie the restriction applied to British nationals as well as foreign investors) were capable of restricting capital movements contrary to EU law.
- **Loans**. In *Sandoz* (Case C–439/97) [1999] ECR I–7041, the ECJ held that provisions of Austrian law which imposed stamp duty, a type of tax, on all loans taken out by

Austrian residents, even if the lender was based in another EU Member State, breached EU law on capital movements. The Court ruled that this law would deter Austrian residents from seeking to obtain loans from lenders based in other EU Member States, some of which did not charge stamp duty. Another case in which national provisions which restricted nationals from obtaining loans from foreign providers was *Commission v Belgium* (Case C–478/98) [2000] ECR I–7587, where the Court stated that 'measures taken by a Member State which are liable to dissuade its residents from obtaining loans or making investments in other Member States constitute restrictions on the free movement of capital'.

- **Mortgages**. In *Trummer and Meyer* (Case C–222/97) [1999] ECR I–1661, the ECJ held that provisions of Austrian legislation which prohibited the registration of mortgages in the currency of another Member State breached EU law on capital movements.
- **Acquisition of real property, ie land**. For example, in *Konle* (Case C–302/97) [1999] ECR I–3099, where Austrian legislation forcing all foreign nationals purchasing property in certain tourist-friendly regions of Austria to obtain authorisation first, the ECJ held that a breach of EU rules on capital movements had occurred. The same result was reached in *Albore* (Case C–423/98) [2000] ECR I–5965, involving Italian legislation which required foreign nationals to obtain authorisation prior to acquiring property in areas of military importance, and in *Ospelt* (Case C–452/01) [2003] ECR I–9743, involving Austrian legislation requiring prior authorisation to be obtained before purchasing agricultural land.
- **Inheritances**. An inheritance, whether of money, personal property or 'immovable property' (land and buildings), is a movement of capital – provided there is some cross-border element. Recent examples include *Eckelkamp & Others* (Case C-11/07) [2008] ECR I-6845, involving German and Dutch residents who inherited immovable property in Belgium following their mother's death; *Arens-Sikken* (Case C-43/07) [2008] ECR I-6887, involving an Italian resident who inherited a share of immovable property in the Netherlands following the death of her husband; and *Block* (Case C-67/08) [2009] ECR I-883, involving a German resident who inherited money invested in Spain. *Jäger* (Case C-256/06) [2008] ECR I-123 was slightly different, in that it involved a French resident inheriting an estate comprising agricultural land and forest in France following the death of his mother. However, the Court found a cross-border element: the mother was living in Germany at the time of her death.
- **Gifts**. In *Persche* (Case C-318/07) [2009] ECR I-359, the ECJ held that provisions of German legislation allowing taxpayers to deduct from their income the cost of gifts to charitable, benevolent or church organisations, but only if the recipient of the gift was a body established in Germany, breached EU law on capital movements. Gifts were a form of capital whether the gift involved money or some item of property.

Derogations

Article 65 specifies certain derogations from the free movement of capital provisions. It states, *inter alia*, that Member States are entitled 'to take all requisite measures to prevent infringements of national law and regulations, in particular in the field of taxation and the prudential supervision of financial institutions, or to lay down procedures for the declaration of capital movements for purposes of administrative or statistical information, or to take measures which are justified on grounds of public policy or public security'.

Considering this provision in *Association Eglise de Scientologie de Paris* (Case C–54/99) [2000] ECR I–1335, the Court stated that these derogations had to be interpreted strictly, could not be used to serve purely economic ends and were subject to the 'proportionality' doctrine. The derogation was successfully relied upon in *Sandoz* (1999) (noted above). The ECJ accepted the argument of the Austrian Government that the requirement to pay stamp duty on all loans was designed to prevent 'taxable persons from evading the requirements of domestic tax legislation through the exercise of freedom of movement of capital'. However, the derogation was unsuccessfully raised in *Commission v Belgium*

(2000), the Court holding that Belgian rules preventing all Belgian residents from obtaining loans abroad was an excessive and disproportionate restriction on the free movement of capital.

In addition, the four-part test set out in *Gebhard* (1995) has been held to apply to capital movements. The Austrian legislation in *Konle* (1999) was found to be justifiable (after certain modifications to remove the discriminatory aspects) because it helped the authorities to ensure that large numbers of properties in tourist-friendly areas were not being bought as second or 'holiday' homes, whether by foreign nationals or by Austrian nationals looking to escape from the cities and suburbia. This in turn helped to ensure that those areas retained a 'permanent population and an economic activity independent of the tourist sector' (in other words, it ensured that those areas did not turn into 'ghost towns' when there were no tourists).

The Austrian rules in *Ospelt* (2003) were also held to be justifiable, on the grounds that they helped to preserve 'agricultural communities, maintaining a distribution of land ownership which allows the development of viable farms and sympathetic management of green spaces and the countryside as well as encouraging a reasonable use of the available land by resisting pressure on land and preventing natural disasters'.

However, in both cases the Court found that the requirement of authorisation went beyond what was necessary to achieve its objective. The Court thought that there were other mechanisms available to the national authorities to ensure compliance with planning legislation in tourist-friendly and/or agricultural areas, which would achieve the same objective as authorisation but impose less of an obstacle to capital movements in doing so.

Economic and Monetary Union

Economic and Monetary Union (EMU) dates back to 1969, when the six Heads of State of the EEC agreed a plan, which would have achieved such a union by 1980, although the plan did not work. Nevertheless, by the late 1980s some progress had been made with the establishment of the Exchange Rate Mechanism (ERM), which replaced the normal fixed rate of exchange between different currencies with a floating rate for those states in the ERM. The system was relatively stable and successful until 'Black Wednesday' in October 1992 when the UK (and Italy) was forced to withdraw at the cost of billions of pounds to the British Treasury. However, this disaster prompted the Member States to concentrate on taking EMU to the next level: a single currency. First, the various advantages and disadvantages had to be examined.

Advantages and disadvantages of a single (European) currency

- **Advantages**: 'transaction costs' incurred in the form of commission as one currency is exchanged for another disappear; greater transparency in terms of price comparison between the same or similar goods on sale in different countries; elimination of exchange rate fluctuations should improve confidence for producers and retailers when setting prices.
- **Disadvantages**: Member States are often at different points in the economic cycle (ie some have growing economies and some have shrinking economies, with differing levels of inflation) but a single currency prevents them from responding individually to these issues, eg by unilaterally raising or lowering interest rates.

After weighing up these advantages and disadvantages, most of the EU's Member States decided to forge ahead. Over the 1990s, these States began to co-ordinate their economic policies and forge closer co-operation between their central banks. A body called the European Monetary Institute (EMI) was established to help. The Treaty on European Union established a set of 'convergence criteria' which would be used to determine which states would be eligible to join the single currency. These included:

- a high degree of price stability, ie a rate of inflation close to the three best-performing Member States
- sustainability of government deficit at not more than 3 per cent of gross domestic product (GDP) and government debt at not more than 60 per cent of GDP
- the observance of the fluctuation margins permitted by the ERM for at least two years.

The criterion concerning government deficit and debt did not just apply at the point of Member States joining the single currency – it continues to apply afterwards. In 1997, the Member States agreed, in the Stability and Growth Pact (SGP), to maintain 'budget discipline', ie to respect the requirement to keep government deficit at or below 3 per cent of GDP and, if necessary, take immediate corrective action (subject to economic sanctions for failure to do so).

Eleven Member States (Austria, Belgium, Finland, France, Germany, Ireland, Italy, Luxembourg, the Netherlands, Portugal and Spain) satisfied these convergence criteria and in January 1999 the European Currency Unit (ECU, subsequently renamed the euro) came into operation in these States for electronic payments. At the same time, the EMI became the European Central Bank (ECB). The ECB, which is based in Frankfurt in Germany, has several tasks including defining and implementing monetary policy and issuing euro banknotes (individual states issue euro coins).

National currencies continued to be used for all other transactions. Greece was deemed to have satisfied the criteria in 2001, and the so-called 'euro zone' grew to 12 members. On New Year's Day 2002, however, euro notes and coins came into operation and, two months later, national currencies of the 12 participating states were finally withdrawn. Thus, the Austrian schilling, Belgian and French francs, Dutch guilder, German mark, Greek drachma, Irish punt, Italian lira, Portuguese escudo and Spanish peseta all ceased – overnight – to be legal tender. Slovenia became the thirteenth Member State to join the 'euro zone' in January 2007, followed by Cyprus and Malta in January 2008, Slovakia in January 2009 and Estonia in January 2011. At the time of writing there are therefore 17 Member States in the 'euro zone', representing over 328 million people. Denmark, Sweden and the UK remain outside the euro zone – for the time being – although they have the option of joining in the future (subject to satisfying the 'convergence criteria').

10.2.3 The relationship between 'services' and 'goods'

No definition of 'goods' is provided in the TFEU, or in any provisions of secondary legislation. The task has been left to the ECJ. In *Commission v Italy* (Case 7/68) [1968] ECR 617, the ECJ defined 'goods' very widely:

JUDGMENT

> 'By "goods" … there must be understood products which can be valued in money, and which are capable, as such, of forming the subject of commercial transactions.'

There is a definition of 'services' in the TFEU, although it is a far from comprehensive definition. Article 57 states that the word includes 'activities of an industrial character', 'activities of a commercial character', 'activities of craftsmen' and 'activities of the professions'.

In a number of cases the ECJ has had to decide which of the freedoms of 'services' or 'goods' applies to the facts. *Customs and Excise Commissioners v Schindler* (Case C–275/92) [1994] ECR I–1039 is illustrative of the problem facing the ECJ when it is not immediately obvious whether the free movement of goods provisions should apply or whether those on services are more appropriate.

CASE EXAMPLE

Customs and Excise Commissioners v Schindler (Case C–275/92) [1994] ECR I–1039

Gerhart and Jörg Schindler posted envelopes from the Netherlands to various addresses the UK. Each contained invitations to participate in the German national lottery, an application form and a pre-paid envelope. Customs in Dover confiscated the envelopes on the ground that they were in breach of UK law, the Lotteries and Amusement Act 1976, which provided that anyone who, in connection with any lottery, brought into the UK for the purposes of sale or distribution any ticket to participate in, or advertisement of, a national lottery, would be guilty of an offence. The Schindlers contested the compatibility of the 1976 Act with EU law. The first question for the ECJ was whether Art 34 (free movement of goods) or Art 56 (free movement of services) applied. In the event, the ECJ decided that the case fell within the scope of Art 56, because the UK legislation primarily restricted a service (the promotion of a lottery) rather than goods (the envelopes and their contents). The restriction on the movement of goods was an indirect consequence of the restriction on the service.

CASE EXAMPLE

Commission v Italy (Case C–158/94) [1997] ECR I–5789

One question for the ECJ was whether electricity could be regarded as 'goods'. The Italian Government argued that electricity bore much greater similarity to the category of 'services' than to that of 'goods'. It was argued that electricity is 'an incorporeal substance' which cannot be stored and 'has no economic existence as such', in that it is never useful in itself but only by reason of its possible applications. Moreover, imports and exports of electricity were 'merely aspects of the management of the electricity network' which, by their nature, fell within the category of 'services'. However, the ECJ rejected the argument, citing Almelo and Others (Case C–393/92) [1994] ECR I–1477 in which it was accepted that EU law, and indeed the national laws of the Member States, regarded electricity as constituting 'goods'.

Conversely, in *Jägerskiöld v Gustafsson* (Case C–97/98) [1999] ECR I–7319, the ECJ held that the provisions on services, and not those on goods, applied in a case concerning disputed fishing permits. Although the permits had a tangible existence, and could be regarded as a product with a monetary value, the ECJ decided that this was ancillary to the service which the permit allowed its holder to carry out.

10.2.4 The relationship between 'capital' and 'goods'

Current legal tender in the form of banknotes and coins is subject to the provisions on the free movement of capital rather than the provisions on the free movement of goods (*Bordessa* (1995)). By way of contrast, old coins that are no longer legal tender have been held to fall within the provisions on the free movement of goods (*R v Thompson and Others* (Case 7/78) [1979] ECR 2247, which is examined in Chapter 14).

CASE EXAMPLE

Bordessa and Others (Cases C–358 and 416/93) [1995] ECR I–361

Aldo Bordessa (an Italian living in Spain) was stopped at Gerona on the Spanish/French border, driving through the 'nothing to declare' channel with 50 million Spanish pesetas stuffed in various hiding places in his car. Meanwhile, Vicente Marí Mellado and Concepción Barbero Maestre, a Spanish couple, were arrested at the same Customs point, heading for France with 38 million pesetas in their possession. All three were prosecuted for breaching Spanish legislation which required authorisation for the export of notes in excess of five million pesetas per person per journey. The three defendants contended that the Spanish legislation was in breach of EU rules on the free movement of goods. However, the ECJ disagreed, distinguishing its earlier judgment in R v Thompson (1979), and held that that the exportation of current bank notes was not governed by the provisions on the free movement of goods but those concerning the free movement of capital. Applying these rules, the Court found that, although Member States were entitled to monitor exports of their own currencies, the prior authorisation requirement imposed a disproportionate restriction on legitimate capital movements. The Court stated that a prior declaration requirement would achieve the same objective while imposing less of an obstacle to capital movements.

In *Persche* (2009), discussed above, a German taxpayer had donated over €18,000 worth of bed linen, towels, zimmer frames and toy cars (all 'everyday consumer goods') to a charitable organisation in Portugal. Under German legislation, he was unable to deduct this expense from his taxable income because the organisation was based in another Member State, whereas he would have been able to do so had the organisation been based in Germany. When he challenged this, the ECJ held that Art 63 applied (and had been breached). The Court rejected a suggestion that the rules on the free movement of goods should have been applied instead. The Court noted that the German legislation applied to all gifts, whether of money or consumer goods (and in the case of the latter, regardless of where the goods were purchased).

KEY FACTS

The Internal Market	
• The Internal Market is established by Art 26 TFEU. The Internal Market is 'an area without internal frontiers in which the free movement of goods, persons, services, and capital is ensured'.	Article 26 TFEU
• 'Goods' is not defined in the Treaty but has been defined by the ECJ as covering all 'products which can be valued in money'.	*Commission v Italy* (1968)
• 'Services' is not defined in the Treaty although Art 57 states that it includes 'activities of an industrial character', 'activities of a commercial character', 'activities of craftsmen' and 'activities of the professions'.	Article 57 TFEU
• In the event of a dispute as to whether the provisions on 'goods' or 'services' or 'capital' apply then a court may need to decide.	*Schindler* (1994); *Bordessa* (1995); *Persche* (2009)
• 'Capital' is not defined in the Treaty but has been held to include shares, loans and mortgages.	
• The Treaty does not guarantee absolute free movement of goods, persons, services, and capital. The Treaty itself contains specific limitations or derogations (such as public policy and public health) which Member States may invoke to justify the imposition of barriers to free movement. However, these derogations are strictly interpreted by the ECJ.	TFEU; Directive 2004/38
• The ECJ has established a principle that national laws and policies are capable of restricting free movement even if they are non-discriminatory. Examples include packaging requirements for goods and residence requirements for persons.	

• However, these rules can be justified provided four conditions are satisfied. They must (i) be non-discriminatory; (ii) be justified by imperative requirements in the general interest; (iii) be suitable for the attainment of the objective which it pursues; (iv) not go beyond what is necessary in order to attain its objective (the proportionality doctrine).	*Gebhard* (1995)
• Economic and Monetary Union (EMU) describes the system of financial convergence between the Member States dating back to the late 1960s. It includes the Exchange Rate Mechanism (ERM) and the single European currency, the euro. The 'euro' was adopted as a single currency in 12 Member States (the euro zone) in 2002. There are presently 17 countries in the euro zone.	

SUMMARY

- The internal market is an area without internal frontiers in which the free movement of goods, persons, services, and capital is ensured (Art 26 TFEU).
- There is potential difficulty in distinguishing the free movement of goods from the free movement of services, but it is important to decide which one applies in any given case because different Treaty provisions will then operate. 'Goods' are defined as 'products which can be valued in money, and which are capable, as such, of forming the subject of commercial transactions' (*Commission v Italy*) whereas 'services' are defined as simply including 'activities of an industrial character', 'activities of a commercial character', 'activities of craftsmen' and 'activities of the professions' (Art 57 TFEU).
- A similar problem arises when distinguishing the free movement of goods from the free movement of capital. In *Bordessa*, the ECJ decided that current legal tender in the form of banknotes and coins is subject to the provisions on the free movement of capital rather than the provisions on the free movement of goods. In contrast, old coins that are no longer legal tender fall within the provisions on the free movement of goods (*R v Thompson and Others*).
- The free movements are not 'absolute' freedoms. The Member States are allowed to derogate, using justifications found in the TFEU. All four freedoms are subject to derogations on grounds of public policy and public security. Public health can be used to derogate from the freedoms of goods, persons and services.
- In addition, the ECJ has introduced a policy, common to all of the freedoms, of allowing Member States to justify national legislation which hinders one or more of the freedoms. The legislation must pass four tests (*Gebhard*): it must (i) be non-discriminatory; (ii) be justified by imperative requirements in the general interest; (iii) be suitable for the attainment of the objective which it pursues; and (iv) not go beyond what is necessary in order to attain its objective (the 'proportionality' doctrine).
- The free movement of capital provisions are found in Arts 63–66 TFEU.
- 'Capital' includes shares, gifts, inheritances, loans, mortgages, and the acquisition of real property.
- Derogations are available to the Member States (Art 65)
- The idea of Economic and Monetary Union dates back to the late 1960s and came to fruition in the early 21st century with the introduction of the single European currency, the Euro, in January 2002. The 'Eurozone' now comprises seventeen Member States.

Further reading

Articles

Barnard, C, 'Fitting the Remaining Pieces into the Goods and Persons Jigsaw?' (2001) 26 ELR 35.

Daniele, L, 'Non-Discriminatory Restrictions to the Free Movement of Persons' (1997) 22 ELR 191.

Dunnett, D, 'Some Legal Principles Applicable to the Transition to the Single Currency' (1996) 33 CMLR 1133.

Flynn, L, 'Coming of Age: The Free Movement of Capital Case Law 1993–2002' (2002) 39 CMLR 773.

Greaves, R, 'Advertising Restrictions and the Free Movement of Goods and Services' (1998) 23 ELR 305.

Mortelmans, K, 'The Common Market, the Internal Market and the Single Market – What's in a Market?' (1998) 35 CMLR 101.

Nic Shuibhne, N, 'Margins of Appreciation: National Values, Fundamental Rights and EC Free Movement Law' (2009) 34 EL Rev 230.

Oliver, P and Roth, W-H, 'The Internal Market and the Four Freedoms' (2004) 41 CMLR 407.

Prechal, S & De Vries, S, 'Seamless Web of Judicial Protection in the Internal Market?' (2009) 34 EL Rev 5.

11

Citizenship of the Union

AIMS AND OBJECTIVES

After reading this chapter you should be able to:

- Understand the meaning and scope of the law on EU Citizenship, in particular Articles 20 and 21 TFEU and Directive 2004/38
- Understand the meaning and scope of a Citizen's 'family members'
- Analyse critically the law relating to EU Citizenship
- Apply the law to factual situations involving EU Citizenship

11.1 Introduction

The original EC Treaty signed in 1957 made no reference to any form of European 'citizenship'. At that time, people were regarded as being citizens of their own Member States, and nothing more. That was to change when the Treaty on European Union came into force in November 1993, and several new provisions were inserted into the EC Treaty. These provisions now form Part Two of the TFEU, Arts 18–25. Article 20 provides (in part) as follows:

ARTICLE

'Art 20(1) Citizenship of the Union is hereby established. Every person holding the nationality of a Member State shall be a citizen of the Union. Citizenship of the Union shall be additional to and not replace national citizenship.

(2) Citizens of the Union shall enjoy the rights and be subject to the duties provided for in the Treaties…'

11.2 Nationality requirements: Art 20 TFEU

Thus, according to Art 20, in order to be a 'Citizen of the Union', it is first necessary to hold 'the nationality of a Member State'. Nationality is conferred purely by way of the national law of the State concerned. In *Micheletti* (C–369/90) [1992] ECR I–4239, the ECJ stated that 'it is for each Member State, having due regard to [Union] law, to lay down the conditions for the acquisition and loss of nationality'. However, 'nationality' is wide enough to include dual nationals. This is most obviously the case with people holding the nationality of two Member States (for example, *Garcia Avello v Belgium* (Case C–148/02) [2003] ECR I–11613, involving dual Belgian–Spanish nationality). However, it is enough if a person holds the nationality of one of the Member States and that of a non-Member State, as *Micheletti* (1992) illustrates:

CASE EXAMPLE

Micheletti (Case C–369/90) [1992] ECR I–4239

Mario Micheletti, born in Argentina to Italian parents, had dual Italian–Argentinean nationality. He wished to set up as a dentist in Spain, but was rejected by the Spanish authorities, as Spanish law deemed him to have the nationality of his country of birth, Argentina. He challenged this, claiming to be entitled to invoke EU law (specifically Art 49, the freedom of establishment) because, under Italian law, the fact that he was born of Italian parents conferred on him Italian nationality – regardless of where in the world he was born. The ECJ held that he was both Italian and Argentinean, and that was enough for the purposes of Art 49.

Although *Micheletti* pre-dates the introduction of the citizenship provisions, the case is still good authority for the proposition that holders of dual nationality (only one of the nationalities being in the EU) is sufficient for Art 20 to apply, and hence Art 21 also. This was confirmed in *Collins v Secretary of State for Work and Pensions* (Case C–138/02) [2004] 3 WLR 1236, where the ECJ held that a dual Irish–American national could rely upon EU law (specifically Art 45 TFEU, the free movement of workers).

11.3 Citizens' rights of free movement and residence: Art 21(1) TFEU

ARTICLE

'Art 21(1) Every citizen of the Union shall have the right to move and reside freely within the territory of the Member States, subject to the limitations and conditions laid down in the Treaties and by the measures adopted to give them effect.'

In *Kaur* (Case C–192/99) [2001] ECR I–1237 the ECJ confirmed that it was for each State to determine which persons are entitled to nationality of that State and, in turn, whether such nationality actually entitled the holder of it to entry into and residence within the State in question.

CASE EXAMPLE

Kaur (Case C–192/99) [2001] ECR I–1237

Manjit Kaur was born in Kenya in 1949 to a family of Asian origin, but became a citizen of the UK under the terms of the British Nationality Act 1948. However, she did not come within any of the categories of citizens of the UK recognised under the Immigration Act 1971 as having a right of residence in the UK. Subsequently, the British Nationality Act 1981 conferred on her the status of a 'British Overseas Citizen'. As such, she had, in the absence of special authorisation, no right under UK law to enter or remain in the UK. In 1996 she was in the UK (not for the first time) and applied for leave to remain and obtain gainful employment. However, the Home Secretary refused. She sought judicial review of this refusal, relying in part on the provisions in Arts 20 and 21. The High Court referred the case to the ECJ, which rejected her argument.

This decision must be correct. If Ms Kaur was regarded as a 'Citizen of the Union' purely because of her status as a 'British Overseas Citizen' then she would have rights to move around the EU and reside in any State of her choosing – except the UK, where British law did not confer on her a right of residence. Such an outcome would be deeply illogical. It must be the case that, before Art 21 can be invoked, the claimant must first have a right of residence in one of the Member States under its national law.

The 'direct effect' question: can Art 21(1) be relied upon in national courts?

In *Baumbast v Secretary of State for the Home Dept* (Case C–413/99) [2002] ECR I–7091, the ECJ held that Art 21(1) could be relied upon by EU citizens, to claim a right of residence in other EU Member States. Although Art 21(1) was subject to certain limitations and conditions, this did not deprive it of direct effect. The ECJ held that the competent authorities of the Member State and, where necessary, national courts, must ensure that those limitations and conditions were applied in compliance with the general principles of EU law and, in particular, the principle of proportionality.

CASE EXAMPLE

Baumbast v Secretary of State for the Home Dept (Case C–413/99) [2002] ECR I–7091

In 1990, the Baumbast family arrived in the UK. The father, a German national, was employed in the UK. He resided with his wife (who was Colombian) and their two school-age daughters, the younger one of whom, Idanella, had dual German–Colombian nationality. The elder daughter, being Mrs Baumbast's daughter from a previous relationship, held only Colombian nationality. Over the next three years, Mr Baumbast was economically active either as a worker or in a self-employed capacity in the UK. In 1993, however, economic circumstances forced him to take work outside of the EU (first in China and then in Lesotho in southern Africa). In 1995, Mrs Baumbast applied for indefinite leave to remain in the UK for herself and her daughters. This was refused and she appealed. The ECJ held that Art 21(1) was directly effective and Mrs Baumbast therefore had the right to residence in the UK despite the fact that her husband was no longer working or self-employed in the UK. (Strictly speaking, Idanella would be classed as the 'Citizen of the Union', being the only member of the family other than Mr Baumbast holding the nationality of a Member State, with her mother claiming a right of residence as her primary carer. This aspect of the case is examined below (see section 11.5.3.)

Who is entitled to rely upon Article 21(1)?

The case of *Baumbast* (2002) therefore establishes that Art 21(1) is directly effective, and confers on anyone holding the nationality of a Member State a legally enforceable right of movement to, and residence in, any other EU Member State. That on its own is an important decision, as it apparently obviates the need for persons to establish some form of economic activity (whether as worker, work-seeker, self-employed person, service provider or service recipient) in order to claim residence rights under EU law. Over the years, the ECJ has allowed Art 21(1) to be relied upon by a variety of people who, prior to the introduction of Citizenship rights, may have struggled to build a case using the more traditional free movement provisions (Arts 45, 49 and 56 – workers, the self-employed and service-providers). The cases to date can be grouped into the following categories:

- the unemployed – *Martínez Sala* (Case C–85/96) [1998] ECR I–2691; *Collins* (Case C–138/02) [2004] ECR I–2703; *De Cuyper* (Case C–406/04) [2006] ECR I–6947
- students – *Grzelczyk* (Case C–184/99) [2001] ECR I–6193; *D'Hoop* (Case C–224/98) [2002] ECR I–6191; *Bidar* (Case C–209/03) [2005] ECR I–2119; *Morgan & Bucher* (Cases C–11 & 12/06) [2007] ECR I–9161; Case C-158/07 Förster [2008] ECR I-8507
- children – *Zhu & Chen* (Case C–200/02) [2004] ECR I–9925; *Schwarz* (Case C–76/05) [2007] ECR I-6849
- the retired – *Pusa* (Case C–224/02) [2004] ECR I–5763; *Turpeinen* (Case C–520/04) [2006] ECR I–10685; *Zablocka-Weyhermüller* (Case C–221/07) [2008] ECR I-9029; *Rüffler* (Case C-544/07) [2009] 3 CMLR 20
- those incapable of working for health reasons – *Tas-Hagen* (Case C–192/05) [2006] ECR I–10451; *Nerkowska* (Case C–499/06) [2008] ECR I-3993.

The crucial threshold that has to be crossed in all Citizenship cases is that 'beneficiaries of the right of residence must not become an unreasonable burden on the public finances of the host Member State' (*Grzelczyk* (2001)). That criterion itself begs the (as yet unanswered) question – what exactly is an 'unreasonable burden'? In several of the Art 21 cases, EU Citizens have been held to be entitled to claim social security or other financial benefits such as:

- a child-raising allowance – *Martínez Sala* (1998)
- a 'minimum subsistence allowance' – *Grzelczyk* (2001)
- a 'tideover allowance' – *D'Hoop* (2002)
- a student loan – *Bidar* (2005)
- a student grant – *Förster* (2008).

So, it is clear that, just because the EU Citizen is in need of financial help from the State, this does not make him or her an 'unreasonable burden'.

The right of Citizens to invoke Art 18 TFEU to challenge discrimination based on nationality

A right of residence alone is potentially of little assistance unless it is accompanied by a right not to be discriminated against. Article 21(1) itself says nothing about such a right, but the ECJ has allowed Citizens to invoke Art 18 TFEU in order to challenge discrimination based on nationality. Article 18 states that:

ARTICLE

Art 18 Within the scope of application of the Treaties, and without prejudice to any special provisions contained therein, any discrimination on grounds of nationality shall be prohibited.'

The earliest case was *Martínez Sala* (1998).

CASE EXAMPLE

Martínez Sala (Case C–85/96) [1998] ECR I–2691

María Martínez Sala, a Spanish national, had lived in Germany since 1968 and had worked there intermittently from 1976 until 1986 and again for a short time in 1989. Since then she had not worked and was in receipt of social security. When, after her daughter was born in 1993, she applied for a child-rearing benefit, this was refused, essentially on grounds of nationality. She contested this refusal. The ECJ ruled that, as a Spanish national, and therefore EU Citizen, lawfully resident in Germany, María could invoke Art 18 in conjunction with Art 21(1) in order to challenge discrimination on grounds of nationality.

The Court stated that:

JUDGMENT

'[Article 21(1)] attaches to the status of Citizen of the Union the rights and duties laid down by the Treaty, including the right, laid down in [Article18], not to suffer discrimination on grounds of nationality within the scope of application ratione materiae of the Treaty. A citizen of the European Union … lawfully resident in the territory of the host Member State, can rely on [Article 18] in all situations which fall within the scope ratione materiae of [Union] law.'

Martínez Sala was applied in *Grzelczyk* (2001), a case involving a French national in his final year as a student at a university in Belgium. He submitted a claim for financial assistance from the Belgian social service, known as the *minimex*, to allow him to concentrate on his dissertation rather than having to take part-time jobs. However, this was turned down, on the basis that he was neither a Belgian national nor a migrant worker, as required by Belgian legislation. The ECJ, however, held that, as a French national lawfully resident in Belgium, he was protected by Art 21(1) and allowed to invoke Art 18 to claim the *minimex*. The Court stated:

JUDGMENT

'Union citizenship is destined to be the fundamental status of nationals of the Member States, enabling those who find themselves in the same situation to enjoy the same treatment in law irrespective of their nationality, subject to such exceptions as are expressly provided for.'

Other cases involving students invoking the combined effect of Art 21(1) (residence) and Art 18 (non-discrimination) include *D'Hoop* (2002), considered below, and *Bidar* (2005).

CASE EXAMPLE

Bidar (Case C–209/03) [2005] ECR I–2119

Dany Bidar, a French national, had enrolled to study economics at University College London (UCL). He submitted an application for a student loan, but this was turned down on the ground that, under UK legislation, applicants had to have been 'ordinarily resident' in the UK for at least three years prior to submitting the application. Although Bidar had been resident in the UK for three years he had spent this time in full-time education and the UK legislation excluded time spent 'wholly or mainly for the purpose of receiving full-time education'. Bidar challenged this, alleging that it was (indirectly) discriminatory against someone like him, who had come to live in the UK for the purposes of full-time education. The ECJ held that (1) the British rules were indirectly discriminatory, and (2) Bidar, as a French national lawfully resident in the UK, had the right to challenge these rules using a combination of Arts 18 and 21(1). The Court stated emphatically that Article 18 'must be read in conjunction with the provisions of the Treaty on citizenship of the Union'.

The right of Citizens to invoke Art 21(1) to challenge national legislation which places them 'at a disadvantage'

In a number of cases the ECJ has upheld claims brought by EU Citizens challenging national legislation based purely on Art 21(1), on the basis that the legislation had placed them 'at a disadvantage' because they had 'exercised their freedom to move and to reside in another Member State'. Examples include *Pusa* (2004), *Turpeinen* (2006), *De Cuyper* (2006), *Tas-Hagen* (2006) and *Morgan & Bucher* (2007).There is no requirement in such cases to establish that the legislation in question was either directly or even indirectly discriminatory (although if it was, then Art 18 could be invoked as well).

A recent case on students, *Morgan & Bucher* (2007), illustrates this point. The case involved two German students at educational establishments in other Member States. Rhiannon Morgan was studying applied genetics at the University of the West of England in Bristol, while Iris Bucher was a student of ergotherapy at the Hogeschool Zuyd in Heerlen, in the Netherlands. Both women applied for a training grant from the authorities in Germany, but in each case it was turned down on the basis that, although funding was available for study abroad, this was only the case where students were continuing studies that had been commenced in Germany. Both women appealed, and the ECJ agreed that in each case the women, being German nationals lawfully resident in the UK and the Netherlands, respectively, could invoke Art 21(1). The Court ruled that the restriction of funding for overseas students was simply a breach of Art 21(1) itself. The Court stated that:

JUDGMENT

'National legislation which places certain nationals of the Member State concerned at a disadvantage simply because they have exercised their freedom to move and to reside in another Member State constitutes a restriction on the freedoms conferred by Art 21(1) on every citizen of the Union. Indeed, the opportunities offered by the Treaty in relation to freedom of movement for citizens of the Union cannot be fully effective if a national of a Member State can be deterred from availing himself of them by obstacles placed in the way of his stay in another Member State by legislation of his State of origin penalising the mere fact that he has used those opportunities. That consideration is particularly important in the field of education in view of the aims of … encouraging mobility of students and teachers.'

This development can also be seen in *Pusa* (2004) and *Turpeinen* (2006), both involving retired Finnish nationals who went to live in Spain (presumably to take advantage of the more clement weather in Iberia compared to Scandinavia). The situation where retired persons seek to invoke Citizenship rights can only increase in significance in the future, given improving health and living conditions, so these cases are clearly very significant. Both Heikki Pusa and Pirkko Turpeinen had encountered problems after having moved to Spain. Essentially the disputes involved their Finnish retirement pensions being subjected to greater tax liability, as a result of their move to Spain, than would have been the case had they remained in Finland. In each case the ECJ held that Art 21(1) was available, in principle at least, to challenge any disadvantage incurred as a result of exercising their freedom of movement rights. In *Pusa*, the Court stated that:

JUDGMENT

'National legislation which places at a disadvantage certain of its nationals simply because they have exercised their freedom to move and to reside in another Member State would give rise to inequality of treatment, contrary to the principles which underpin the status of citizen of the Union, that is, the guarantee of the same treatment in law in the exercise of the citizen's freedom to move.'

The judgment in *Turpeinen* was worded almost identically. Another, similar, category of person seeking to invoke Citizenship rights under Art 21(1) is those who have been forced to give up working because of health reasons. The leading case to date is *Tas-Hagen* (2006).

CASE EXAMPLE

Tas-Hagen (Case C–192/05) [2006] ECR I–10451

The case involved two Dutch nationals who had submitted claims for civilian war benefit, which was payable to any Dutch national who had suffered physical and/or mental injury during the Netherlands' involvement in World War II. The problem for the two claimants was that, although they had suffered such injuries, the Dutch benefit eligibility rules required claimants to be resident in the Netherlands at the date the claim was submitted. However, by the time both Mr Tas and Mrs Tas-Hagen submitted their claims, in 1999, they were both living in Spain, having moved there after being forced to give up work for health reasons in 1983 and 1987 respectively. Their claims were, therefore, rejected. When the two claimants challenged the rejections, the ECJ held that Art 21(1) had been, in principle at least, infringed. The Dutch benefit eligibility rules made it more difficult for claimants who had exercised free movement rights to claim benefits than those who had stayed in the Netherlands.

Therefore, *Tas-Hagen* decides that a restriction on the availability of civilian war benefit can be challenged using Art 21(1). Now, civilian war benefit is not something that falls within the scope of EU law generally (compare the case of *Baldinger* (Case C–386/02)

[2004] ECR I–8411, discussed in Chapter 12, where war compensation was held not to fall within the scope of Regulation 1612/68). However, that appears to have no importance where an Art 21(1) claim is involved. Yuri Borgmann-Prebil ('The Rule of Reason in European Citizenship' (2008) 14 ELJ 328) argues this point as follows (emphasis added):

QUOTATION

'The question is whether a citizen of the EU can invoke and rely on [Art 21(1)] in all situations in which he exercises his free movement right, or whether it is a pre-requisite that, in addition to the mere exercise of the free movement right, the situation must concern a substantive area of law that is covered by [Union] law. If the latter were true, the material scope of the [Article] would be delimited by other provisions of [EU] law. If the former were correct, [Art 21(1)] itself would expand the material scope of the Treaty … According to one view … reliance on [Art 21(1)] requires that the factual situation falls within the ambit of *other* provisions of [EU] law. The opposite view is epitomised by the Court's jurisprudence ever since Grzelczyk, where the Court held that a situation falls within the material scope *whenever a citizen exercises his free movement rights* … It is submitted that, while the fact that a situation is covered by other provisions of [Union] law may help to clarify that the activity falls within the scope of [Union] law, this does not constitute a necessary pre-condition … citizens of the EU can even rely on the fundamental freedom enshrined in [Art21(1)] in situations that are not specifically covered by [EU] law.'

Citizenship rights can be invoked in the Citizen's 'home' State

In *D'Hoop v Office National de l'Emploi* (Case C–224/98) [2002] ECR I–6191 the ECJ decided that Art 21(1) could be relied upon **in the Citizen's home State**, provided that she had gone to another EU Member State in order to exercise her free movement rights before returning.

CASE EXAMPLE

D'Hoop v Office National de l'Emploi (Case C–224/98) [2002] ECR I–6191

Marie-Nathalie D'Hoop, a Belgian national, had undertaken her secondary school education in France (1985–91) before studying for a degree in Belgium (1991–95). On graduating, she applied for a 'tideover allowance', a social security benefit paid to recent graduates who had undertaken their schooling in Belgium. As Ms D'Hoop had spent some years as a student in France, this was refused. She challenged this, alleging discrimination contrary to Art 18 and relying on her status as a 'Citizen of the Union' under Art 21(1). The ECJ, following *Grzelczyk*, held that she was entitled to the allowance.

Children's rights to invoke Art 21(1)

In *Zhu & Chen v Secretary of State for the Home Dept* (Case C–200/02) [2004] 3 WLR 1453, the question arose as to (1) whether an infant child could rely upon her status as a 'Citizen of the Union' in order to claim a right of residence in another EU Member State and, if so, (2) whether her mother, as 'primary carer', was entitled to residence with her. The ECJ answered both questions in the affirmative.

CASE EXAMPLE

Zhu and Chen v Secretary of State for the Home Dept (Case C–200/02) [2004] 3 WLR 1453

Man Lavette Chen and her husband, both Chinese nationals, already had one child, a son, born in 1998. The couple wished to have another child but, because of strict Chinese laws on the number of children allowed per couple, desired that it should be born outside of China. When she was six months pregnant, Chen travelled to the UK and, three months later, gave birth to a daughter, named Catherine Zhu, in Belfast in Northern Ireland. Under Irish law, any child born on the island of 'Ireland' (whether the Republic or Northern Ireland) acquired Irish nationality and, thus, Catherine became an Irish citizen. Chen took her daughter to live in Cardiff in Wales. Subsequently, a question arose as to their entitlement to residence in the UK. The ECJ held that, as an Irish national and therefore 'Citizen of the Union', Catherine was entitled to reside in the UK. As her mother and 'primary carer', Chen was allowed to live in the UK with her. No time limit was placed on the right of residence of either Catherine or her mother. (The meaning and scope of the 'primary carer' doctrine is examined below – see section 11.5.3.)

The Court stated:

JUDGMENT

'A young child can take advantage of the rights of free movement and residence guaranteed by [EU] law. The capacity of a national of a Member State to be the holder of rights guaranteed by the Treaty … cannot be made conditional upon the attainment by the person concerned of the age prescribed for the acquisition of legal capacity to exercise those rights personally … A refusal to allow the parent, whether a national of a Member State or a national of a non-member country, who is the carer of a child … to reside with that child in the host Member State would deprive the child's right of residence of any useful effect. It is clear that enjoyment by a young child of a right of residence necessarily implies that the child is entitled to be accompanied by … his or her primary carer and accordingly that the carer must be in a position to reside with the child in the host Member State for the duration of such residence.'

Another case in which children were held to be entitled to invoke Art 21(1) is *Schwarz* (Case C–76/05) [2007] ECR I-6849. The Schwarz family lived in Germany. In 1998, Herbert Schwarz and his wife Marga decided to send two of their three teenage children to the Cademuir International School in Scotland which specialised in exceptionally gifted children. Under German law, however, this meant that they could not claim tax relief on school fees (around 10,000 DM per year) which would have been available had the children been schooled privately in Germany. They challenged this decision, invoking Art 56 (the freedom to receive services) or, alternatively, Art 21(1). The ECJ decided that the case would fall within Art 56 if the Cademuir School was 'essentially financed by private funds', this being a question of fact for the national court. If not, then Art 21(1) would apply. The Schwarz children had exercised their free movement rights, notwithstanding their youth (following *Zhu & Chen*). In either case, there was a breach, because there was no justification for the discrimination between schooling in Germany and schooling abroad for the purposes of conferring tax relief on school fees. On the ability of children to invoke Art 1(1), the Court stated:

JUDGMENT

'The Schwarz children, by attending an educational establishment situated in another Member State, used their right of free movement. As is shown by the judgment in Zhu and Chen, even a young child may make use of the rights of free movement and residence guaranteed by [Union] law.'

NB The German deutschmark ceased to be legal tender when the single European currency was introduced in 2002.

Justification for restrictions on Citizens' rights

In many of the cases discussed above, the ECJ ruled that EU Citizens could invoke Art 21(1) (either on its own or in conjunction with Art 18) in order to challenge national legislation which is either discriminatory or places the Citizen 'at a disadvantage' as a result of his or her exercising their free movement rights. However, in most of those cases, that was not the end of the story. The Court is prepared to listen to arguments that national legislation imposing restrictions on a Citizen's free movement rights constituting a *prima facie* breach of Art 21(1) can be justified by referring to 'objective considerations of public interest'. For example, in *Tas-Hagen* (2006), discussed above, the Court stated that:

JUDGMENT

'Such a restriction can be justified [but] only if it is based on objective considerations of public interest independent of the nationality of the persons concerned and is proportionate to the legitimate objective of the national provisions... a measure is proportionate when, while appropriate for securing the attainment of the objective pursued, it does not go beyond what is necessary in order to attain it.'

It is essential to note the four elements of this extract from the Tas-Hagen *judgment. In order for a restriction on a Citizen's rights to be justified it must be:*

- 'based on objective considerations of public interest' – the cases of *D'Hoop* (2002), *Bidar* (2005) and *Tas-Hagen* itself, discussed below, provide examples of such 'objective considerations'
- 'independent of the nationality of the persons concerned' – the national legislation must either be non-discriminatory or, at the most, 'indirectly' discriminatory. This typically means legislation that, at first sight, appears not to discriminate but in practice has that effect. The most common example is a residency requirement. The cases of *Bidar* and *Tas-Hagen* both illustrate this situation. See also section 12.4.2 in the next chapter for more examples of 'indirect' discrimination
- 'appropriate' – the restriction must be capable of achieving the desired objective
- 'proportionate' – the restriction must be absolutely necessary. In other words, it should impose the minimum restriction needed in order to achieve the desired objective, and not go any further than that.

D'Hoop (2002), discussed above, illustrates these points. First, the Court accepted that it was 'legitimate for the national legislature to wish to ensure that there is a real link between the applicant for that allowance and the geographic employment market concerned'. In other words, the requirement that claimants had undertaken their schooling in Belgium was potentially justifiable in order to establish a 'real link'. Second, the legislation did not expressly refer to nationality. However, the Belgian legislation failed the appropriateness test. The schooling requirement was not capable of establishing the 'real link', being 'too general and exclusive in nature'.

Bidar (2005) further illustrates this point. In that case the ECJ accepted, in principle, that the British legislation imposing a residency requirement on applicants for a student loan was *prima facie* justifiable. The Court held that it was 'legitimate' for the UK to seek to ensure 'that an applicant for assistance has demonstrated a certain degree of integration into the society of that State [which] may be regarded as established by a finding that the student in question had resided in the host Member State for a certain length of time'. However, the British legislation also failed the appropriateness test. The Court stated:

JUDGMENT

'It is common ground that the rules at issue in the main proceedings preclude any possibility of a national of another Member State obtaining settled status as a student. They thus make it impossible for such a national, whatever his actual degree of integration into the society of the host Member State, to satisfy that condition … Such treatment cannot be regarded as justified by the legitimate objective which those rules seek to secure.'

Tas-Hagen (2006), discussed above, provides another example. The Dutch Government argued that the requirement in Dutch law that claimants for civilian war benefit had to be resident in the Netherlands when the claim was made reflected the 'legislature's wish to limit the obligation of solidarity with civilian war victims to those who had links with the population of the Netherlands during and after the war'. Although the ECJ was prepared to accept 'the obligation of solidarity' as an 'objective consideration of public interest', the ECJ held that the residency criterion was not an appropriate means of establishing 'solidarity'. The Court stated that 'a residence criterion … based solely on the date on which the application for the benefit is submitted, is not a satisfactory indicator of the degree of attachment of the applicant to the society which is thereby demonstrating its solidarity with him'.

One case where all four elements were satisfied, including both the appropriateness and proportionality tests, is *Förster* (2008).

CASE EXAMPLE

Förster (Case C-158/07) [2008] ECR I-8507

Jacqueline Förster, a German national, enrolled on a course in educational theory at the College of Amsterdam in the Netherlands. She was initially awarded a student grant, but was subsequently ordered to repay some of the money because, under Dutch law, maintenance grants were only available to students who had been continuously resident in the Netherlands for five years. She challenged the lawfulness of this. The ECJ held that the residency period constituted indirect discrimination but also held that not only was it legitimate in principle (on exactly the same grounds as those identified in *Bidar*, ie the need to demonstrate a 'certain degree of integration' into the society of the host State), but that it also satisfied the appropriateness and proportionality tests. The Court stated:

JUDGMENT

'A condition of five years' uninterrupted residence is appropriate for the purpose of guaranteeing that the applicant for the maintenance grant at issue is integrated into the society of the host Member State… A condition of five years' continuous residence cannot be held to be excessive.'

There has been criticism of the justifications in some of the cases involving Art 21(1). Samantha Besson and André Utzinger ('Future Challenges of European Citizenship – Facing a Wide-Open Pandora's Box' (2007) 13 ELJ 573) criticise 'the elaboration of overbroad justifications' in some of the Art 21(1) cases, which they argue are 'quite vague and leave it to national authorities and courts to determine where to draw the line; this is quite paradoxical given the traditionally strict limitations placed by [EU] law on national restrictions to [EU] rights and principles'. *Bidar* itself provides a perfect illustration of their point – the justification accepted by the ECJ was 'a certain degree of integration', which does appear to be 'quite vague'.

KEY FACTS

Citizenship of the Union	
'Citizenship of the Union' was introduced in November 1993 when the Treaty on European Union came into force	
Anyone holding the nationality of one of the EU's Member States is a Citizen of the Union	Article 20 TFEU

This includes dual nationals	*Micheletti* (1992), *Garcia-Avello* (2003)
Citizens of the Union have the right 'to move and reside freely within the territory of the Member States'. This is not just a political statement but is a legally enforceable right	Article 21(1) TFEU *Baumbast & R* (2002)
Citizenship rights can be invoked by people who are not economically active. Thus the unemployed, students, children and retired people have all been held to have enforceable rights using Art 21(1) TFEU	*Martinez Sala* (1998), *Grzelczyk* (2001), *Zhu & Chen* (2004), *Pusa* (2004)
Article 21(1) TFEU, when combined with Art 18 TFEU, can be used to challenge discrimination based on nationality	*Martinez Sala* (1998), *Bidar* (2005),
Article 21(1) TFEU can also be used to challenge any national legislation which places a Citizen 'at a disadvantage' because they invoked their free movement rights	*Pusa* (2004), *Tas-Hagen* (2006), *Morgan & Bucher* (2007).
Restrictions on Citizens' free movement rights are justifiable, if based on objective considerations of public interest, are independent of the nationality of the persons concerned, and capable of achieving the desired objective and which are proportionate (ie they go no further than necessary)	*D'Hoop* (2002), *Bidar* (2005), *Tas-Hagen* (2006), *Förster* (2008)

11.4 Citizens' rights of exit, entry and residence: Directive 2004/38

The rights of a Citizen to leave the territory of his or her 'home' State, to enter the territory of the 'host' State, to bring their family with them and to set up home there, and even to retire there after their working life is over, are all covered by Directive 2004/38. This repealed pre-existing legislation, Directive 68/360, although some of the case law on that directive is potentially of relevance today. Indeed, some of that case law has been incorporated into the new directive. This section will provide an overview of the main provisions of the new directive.

11.4.1 Rights of exit: Art 4

Article 4 deals with the right of a Citizen to leave their 'home' State in order to work in another State (the 'host' State). Article 4(1)–(3) provides as follows:

ARTICLE

'Art 4(1) … all Union citizens with a valid identity card or passport and their family members who are not nationals of a Member State and who hold a valid passport shall have the right to leave the territory of a Member State to travel to another Member State.

(2) No exit visa or equivalent formality may be imposed on the persons to whom paragraph 1 applies.

(3) Member States shall, acting in accordance with their laws, issue to their own nationals, and renew, an identity card or passport stating their nationality.'

Note: the meaning and scope of a Citizen's 'family members' will be discussed in the next section of this chapter (11.5, below).

11.4.2 Rights of entry: Art 5

Article 5 deals with the right of a Citizen to enter the 'host' State in order to take up residence there. Article 5(1) provides that Member States must grant to all Union citizens the right to enter their territory with a valid ID card or passport. The 'host' State must also grant family members who are non-EU nationals the right to enter their territory with a valid passport. Host Member States cannot require an entry visa from Union citizens, but Art 5(2) states that they may do so for non-EU nationals, in certain circumstances. However, Art 5(4) provides that:

ARTICLE

> 'Art 5(4) Where a Union citizen, or a family member who is not a national of a Member State, does not have the necessary travel documents or, if required, the necessary visas, the Member State concerned shall, before turning them back, give such persons every reasonable opportunity to obtain the necessary documents or have them brought to them within a reasonable period of time or to corroborate or prove by other means that they are covered by the right of free movement and residence.'

Finally, Art 5(5) provides that the host Member State may require the person concerned to report his or her presence within its territory within a 'reasonable and non-discriminatory period of time'. Failure to comply with this requirement may make the person concerned 'liable to proportionate and non-discriminatory sanctions'.

11.4.3 Rights of residence for up to three months: Art 6

Article 6(1) provides that Union citizens shall have the right of residence in the 'host' State for a period of up to three months without any 'conditions' or 'formalities' other than the requirement to hold a valid ID card or passport. Article 6(2) applies the provisions of Art 6(1) to non-EU family members who are 'accompanying or joining' the Union citizen, provided that they are in possession of a valid passport.

11.4.4 Rights of residence for more than three months: Art 7

Article 7(1) provides that Union citizens have a right of residence for more than three months in the 'host' State if they:

a) are workers or self-employed
b) have 'sufficient resources' for themselves and their family members not to become a 'burden' on the social assistance system of the 'host' State during their period of residence and have 'comprehensive sickness insurance cover'
c) are students, have 'comprehensive sickness insurance cover', and 'assure the relevant national authority' that they have 'sufficient resources'.

Article 7(1)(d) adds that the right of residence is also conferred on 'family members accompanying or joining a Union citizen who satisfies the conditions referred to in points (a), (b) or (c)'. Article 7(2) confirms that this right extends to non-EU family members. Article 7(3) provides that the right conferred by Art 7(1)(a) is not lost by a worker if he or she:

- is temporarily unable to work as the result of an 'illness or accident'
- is in 'duly recorded involuntary unemployment'. If the period of work prior to that point was less than a year, then the 'worker' status is only retained for six months
- embarks on 'vocational training'. Unless he or she is involuntarily unemployed, the retention of the status of worker shall require the training to be related to the previous employment.

Note: the meaning of the word 'worker' and the additional rights enjoyed by workers and their family members will be examined in more detail in Chapter 12; the rights enjoyed by those in self-employment will be examined in more detail in Chapter 13.

11.4.5 Registration: Arts 8–11

Article 8(1) provides that, for periods of residence longer than three months, the 'host' State may require Citizens to register with the relevant authorities. Failure to do so 'may render the person concerned liable to proportionate and non-discriminatory sanctions' (Art 8(2)). This point was originally established by the ECJ in a case on Directive 68/360, *Royer* (Case 48/75) [1976] ECR 497, in which the Court ruled that it would be disproportionate to expel or imprison a migrant worker for failing to register.

Once registered, the host State must then immediately issue to the Citizen a '**registration certificate**'. In order to register, Art 8(3) provides that the Citizen needs to produce certain documents, depending on the capacity in which he or she is seeking to register. In all cases, a valid ID card or passport is required, plus:

- confirmation of engagement from the employer or a certificate of employment, or proof that they are self-employed persons (for those under Art 7(1)(a)); or
- proof that they satisfy the relevant conditions laid down in Art 7(1)(b); or
- proof of enrolment at an accredited establishment, proof of comprehensive sickness insurance cover, and the declaration about 'sufficient resources' (for those under Art 7(1)(c)).

Article 8(5) deals with the right of family members (who are also EU nationals) to claim registration certificates. As with the Citizen, a valid ID card or passport is required, plus certain additional documents proving the family member's relationship with the Citizen (eg as spouse, partner, dependant, etc). Non-EU nationals cannot claim such certificates. Instead, Art 9(1) states that non-EU family members are to be issued with a '**registration card**'. As above, failure to comply with the requirement to apply for a registration card may make the person concerned liable to 'proportionate and non-discriminatory sanctions' (Art 9(3)). Article 10 sets out the documents to be provided by the non-EU family member (these are essentially the same as those set out in Art 8(5)). Registration cards 'shall be valid for five years from the date of issue or for the envisaged period of residence of the Union citizen, if this period is less than five years' (Art 11(1)).

11.4.6 Effect of death or departure of the Citizen: Art 12

If the Citizen dies, or departs the 'host' State, then his or her family members (who are also EU nationals) do not lose their right of residence in that State (Art 12(1)). The situation for non-EU family members is slightly more complicated. Article 12(2) provides that the death of the Citizen shall not entail loss of the right of residence of his or her non-EU family members, provided that they have been residing in the host Member State as family members for at least one year before the Citizen's death. Article 12(3) adds that neither the death of the Citizen, nor their departure from the host Member State, shall entail loss of the right of residence of either his or her children, or of the parent who has actual custody of the children, irrespective of nationality, if the children reside in the host Member State and are enrolled at an educational establishment, for the purpose of studying there, until the completion of their studies. Article 12(3) gives effect to the ECJ's decision in *Baumbast v Home Secretary* (Case C–413/99) [2002] ECR I–7091, which was discussed above.

11.4.7 Effect of divorce, annulment of marriage or termination of registered partnership: Art 13

Article 13 deals with the entitlement of former husbands, wives and partners to remain in the host State after divorce, marriage annulment or the termination of a registered partnership. Article 13 is discussed below (see section 11.5).

11.4.8 Retention of residence rights: Art 14

Article 14 deals with retention of residence rights. It states:

ARTICLE

'Art 14(1) Union citizens and their family members shall have the right of residence provided for in Article 6, as long as they do not become an unreasonable burden on the social assistance system of the host Member State.

(2) Union citizens and their family members shall have the right of residence provided for in Articles 7, 12 and 13 as long as they meet the conditions set out therein ...

(3) An expulsion measure shall not be the automatic consequence of a Union citizen's or his or her family member's recourse to the social assistance system of the host Member State.

(4) By way of derogation from paragraphs 1 and 2 ... an expulsion measure may in no case be adopted against Union citizens or their family members if:

(a) the Union citizens are workers or self-employed persons, or

(b) the Union citizens entered the territory of the host Member State in order to seek employment. In this case, the Union citizens and their family members may not be expelled for as long as the Union citizens can provide evidence that they are continuing to seek employment and that they have a genuine chance of being engaged.'

Article 14(4)(b) is designed to implement the ECJ decision in *Antonissen* (Case C–292/89) [1991] ECR I–745 (subsequently confirmed in *Collins* (Case C–138/02) [2004] ECR I–2703), which are discussed in more detail in Chapter 12.

11.4.9 Right of permanent residence: Arts 16–21

Articles 16–18 of Directive 2004/38 deal with the acquisition of a permanent right of residence. Article 16 sets out the conditions under which Citizens and their family members can acquire a right of permanent residence in the 'host' State. According to Art 16(1), this right is conferred on all Citizens who 'have resided legally for a continuous period of five years' in the host State. Article 16(2) provides for non-EU family members. They may also acquire a right of permanent residence provided they have 'legally resided with the Citizen in the host Member State for a continuous period of five years'. Thus both Art 16(1) and (2) require 'continuous' residence. This point is amplified in Art 16(3):

ARTICLE

'Art 16(3) Continuity of residence shall not be affected by temporary absences not exceeding a total of six months a year, or by absences of a longer duration for compulsory military service, or by one absence of a maximum of 12 consecutive months for important reasons such as pregnancy and childbirth, serious illness, study or vocational training, or a posting in another Member State or a third country.'

Article 16(4) states that, once acquired, the right of permanent residence is lost only through absence from the 'host' State for a period exceeding two consecutive years.

Article 17 deals with certain exemptions from the normal five-year qualification period. Article 17(1) states that the right of permanent residence in the 'host' State may be acquired before completion of the continuous five-year residence period laid down in Art 16 by workers or self-employed persons who:

a) At the time they stop working, have reached the age laid down by the law of that Member State for entitlement to an old age pension or workers who cease paid employment to take early retirement, provided that they have been working in that

Member State for at least the preceding 12 months and have resided there continuously for more than three years.

b) Have resided continuously in the host Member State for more than two years and stop working there as a result of permanent incapacity to work. If such incapacity is the result of an accident at work or an occupational disease entitling the person concerned to a benefit payable in full or in part by an institution in the host Member State, no condition shall be imposed as to length of residence.

c) After three years of continuous employment and residence in the host Member State, work in an employed or self-employed capacity in another Member State, while retaining their place of residence in the host Member State, to which they return, as a rule, each day or at least once a week.

The remainder of Art 17 deals with family members. Article 17(2) states that the conditions as to length of residence and employment laid down in Art 17(1)(a), and the condition as to length of residence laid down in Art 17(1)(b), shall not apply if the worker's or the self-employed person's spouse or partner is a national of the 'host' State or lost such nationality on marriage to that worker or self-employed person. Otherwise, Art 17(3) or (4) apply. These provisions are as follows:

ARTICLE

'Art 17(3) Irrespective of nationality, the family members of a worker or a self-employed person who are residing with him in the territory of the host Member State shall have the right of permanent residence in that Member State, if the worker or self-employed person has acquired himself the right of permanent residence in that Member State on the basis of paragraph 1.

(4) If, however, the worker or self-employed person dies while still working but before acquiring permanent residence status in the host Member State on the basis of paragraph 1, his family members who are residing with him in the host Member State shall acquire the right of permanent residence there, on condition that:

(a) the worker or self-employed person had, at the time of death, resided continuously on the territory of that Member State for two years; or

(b) the death resulted from an accident at work or an occupational disease; or

(c) the surviving spouse lost the nationality of that Member State following marriage to the worker or self-employed person.'

Article 17(4)(a) is slightly ambiguous – does the two-year residency have to have occurred at any time in the Citizen's past, or does it have to immediately precede their death? The ECJ considered the meaning of the phrase 'resided continuously' in *Givane* (Case C–257/00) [2003] ECR I–345. The Court stated that the provision was 'intended to establish a significant connection between, on the one hand, [a] Member State and, on the other hand, [a Citizen] and his family, and to ensure a certain level of their integration in the society of that State'. It therefore ruled that the residence period had to occur immediately prior to the Citizen's death.

CASE EXAMPLE

Givane (Case C–257/00) [2003] ECR I–345

Rama Givane, a Portuguese national, had lived and worked in the UK for three years (between 1992 and 1995) before leaving for India for 10 months. He returned to the UK in February 1996, this time accompanied by his wife Nani and their three children, all of whom were Indian nationals. Rama died in November 1997, some 21 months after his returning to the UK. His relatives argued that he had 'resided continuously' in the UK for at least two years (between 1992 and 1995); the UK Home Office argued that the residence had to be immediately preceding the death. The ECJ agreed with the Home Office.

Article 18 states that the non-EU family members of a Citizen may acquire a right of permanent residence in the 'host' State after residing there legally for five consecutive years. Article 19 provides that Member States are to issue to Citizens who comply with the above provisions a 'document certifying permanent residence'. Similarly, non-EU family members who comply with the above provisions are to be issued with 'a permanent residence card' (Art 20(1)). Article 21 states that 'Continuity of residence is broken by any expulsion decision duly enforced against the person concerned' (see section 11.7 below for discussion of the situations in which Member States can expel other States' nationals).

11.4.10 Territorial restrictions: Art 22

Art 22 states that:

ARTICLE

'Art 22 The right of residence and the right of permanent residence shall cover the whole territory of the host Member State. Member States may impose territorial restrictions on the right of residence and the right of permanent residence only where the same restrictions apply to their own nationals.'

11.4.11 Equal treatment: Art 24

Article 24 provides for a general principle of 'equal treatment' for all Citizens (including family members) with the nationals of the 'host' State 'within the scope of the Treaty'. This new provision is probably not as far-reaching as it might at first appear, given the flexibility of interpretation that the ECJ has adopted in cases going back over 30 years involving Art 7(2) of Regulation 1612/68 (see Chapter 12). The 'equal treatment' right is extended to non-EU family members.

KEY FACTS

Citizens' rights under Directive 2004/38	
Citizens have a right to exit a Member State with an ID card or passport	Article 4
Citizens have a right to enter a Member State with an ID card or passport	Article 5
Citizens have an unconditional right of residence in a Member State for 3 months	Article 6
Citizens have an right of residence in a Member State for more than 3 months if working, self-employed, studying, or if they are financially self-sufficient	Article 7
Citizens may acquire a right of permanent residence in a Member State after 5 years' continuous residency, or earlier than that in certain circumstances	Articles 16 and 17
Citizens have a right to equal treatment with the nationals of the 'host' State	Article 24

11.5 The rights of a Citizen's family members and Directive 2004/38

11.5.1 The scope of the Citizen's family: Art 2

Directive 2004/38 extends the scope of the free movement provisions to a Citizen's 'family members'. This is designed to further promote the free movement of Citizens: there would clearly be a massive disincentive – financial as well as emotional – if Citizens were not permitted by EU law to be accompanied by their families when working or studying abroad. Article 2(2) of the directive defines the Citizen's 'family members' as follows:

ARTICLE

'Art 2(2) 'Family member' means:
(a) the spouse;
(b) the partner with whom the Union citizen has contracted a registered partnership, on the basis of the legislation of a Member State, if the legislation of the host Member State treats registered partnerships as equivalent to marriage and in accordance with the conditions laid down in the relevant legislation of the host Member State;
(c) the direct descendants who are under the age of 21 or are dependants and those of the spouse or partner as defined in point (b);
(d) the dependent direct relatives in the ascending line and those of the spouse or partner as defined in point (b).'

The directive was adopted by the Council in April 2004 and its implementation date was 30th April 2006. However, it is very important to appreciate that this was not the first legislative definition of family members. The directive repealed Art 10 of Regulation 1612/68, which contained the original definition of 'family members', and which was narrower than that set out above. In particular, while Art 10 referred to 'spouse' and 'descendants' there was no provision for 'partners' nor for 'relatives in the ascending line'. However, where there is overlap between the two pieces of legislation, then any case law on the earlier Regulation continues to be relevant.

'Spouse'

The ECJ has held that 'spouse' means only marital relationships. In *Netherlands v Reed* (Case 59/85) [1986] ECR 1283 the ECJ stated:

JUDGMENT

'In the absence of any indication of a general social development which would justify a broad construction, and in the absence of any indication to the contrary in the Legislation, it must be held that the term "spouse" refers to a marital relationship only.'

This decision has attracted criticism (Clare McGlynn, 'Families and the European Union Charter of Fundamental Rights' (2001) 26 ELR 582) on the basis that it reinforces stereotypical assumptions about marriage. Separated, but not yet divorced, couples are still treated as spouses. In *Diatta v Land Berlin* (Case 267/83) [1985] ECR 567 the ECJ stated that 'the marital relationship cannot be regarded as dissolved so long as it has not been terminated by the competent authority. It is not dissolved merely because the spouses live separately, even where they intend to divorce at a later date'. This is so even if they live apart. The ECJ has held that it is not necessary for spouses to cohabit (*Diatta* (1985)): 'It is not for the immigration authorities to decide whether a reconciliation is possible. Moreover, if co-habitation of the spouses were a mandatory condition, the [Citizen] could at any time cause the expulsion of his spouse by depriving her of a roof.'

CASE EXAMPLE

Diatta v Land Berlin (Case 267/83) [1985] ECR 567

Aissatou Diatta, a Senegalese woman, married a Frenchman in 1977 and in 1978 they set up home together in Germany where he had been working for several years. From August 1978, however, they began living apart. Now separated from her husband and living in rented accommodation in Germany, Mrs Diatta intended to get a divorce as soon as possible.

However, she was working in her own right and intended to stay in Germany. When her residence permit expired, in 1980, she applied for a renewal but this was refused on the ground that she was no longer a member of her husband's family. She challenged this and the ECJ held that, while separated but not yet divorced, she had not yet lost her right of residence.

Location and timing of the marriage

The ECJ has held that it is immaterial where the marriage between Citizen and spouse took place. In *Metock & Others* (case C-127/08) [2008] ECR I-6241, the ECJ pointed out that there were no provisions in Directive 2004/38 stipulating 'any requirements as to the place where the marriage of the Union citizen and the national of a non-member country is solemnised'. Moreover, it followed from that conclusion that there were no requirements that the marriage had to have taken place prior to the spouse entering the host Member State. This was despite the fact that Directive 2004/38, Art 3(1) states that 'This Directive shall apply to all Union citizens who move to or reside in a Member State other than that of which they are a national, and to their family members as defined in Article 2(2) who *accompany* or *join* them' (emphasis added). In the *Metock* case itself, a number of non-EU nationals had entered Ireland, the host State (as asylum seekers) and each had subsequently met and then married a Citizen of the Union who had arrived in that State after the asylum seeker. When the Irish government decided to commence deportation proceedings against the asylum seekers (who by this stage had had their asylum applications rejected), the ECJ ruled that the order in which the Citizen and his or her spouse arrived in the host State was immaterial; what mattered was that the marriage was recognised as genuine.

The Court stated (emphasis added):

JUDGMENT

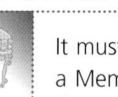

It must be determined whether, where the national of a non-member country has entered a Member State before becoming a family member of a Union citizen who resides in that Member State, he accompanies or joins that Union citizen within the meaning of Article 3(1). It makes *no difference* whether nationals of non-member countries who are family members of a Union citizen have entered the host Member State *before* or *after* becoming family members of that Union citizen, since the refusal of the host Member State to grant them a right of residence is equally liable to discourage that Union citizen from continuing to reside in that Member State.

The rule that 'spouse' means only marital relationships does not, however, mean that partners in other relationships do not have any rights (*Reed* (1986) – see below). The question whether a **divorced** spouse remained entitled to residence in another EU Member State under EU law was left undecided in *Diatta* (1985), but in *Baumbast and R v Secretary of State for the Home Department* (Case C–413/99) [2002] ECR I–7091 the ECJ made it clear that a divorcee cannot be regarded as a 'spouse'.

Implications of divorce/marriage annulment/termination of registered partnership

Although a divorce terminates the ex-wife or ex-husband's entitlement to residence as a 'spouse', that does not mean that they are no longer protected by EU law. Likewise with the situation of a former registered partner. Article 13 of Directive 2004/38 deals with these situations. Article 13(1) states that if an ex-wife, ex-husband or ex-partner are themselves an EU citizen then they can remain in the 'host' State, based on their own personal free movement entitlements. Article 13(2) deals with the more problematical situation where the ex-wife, ex-husband or ex-partner is a non-EU citizen (as would have been the case if the Senegalese wife in *Diatta* had actually divorced her husband).

ARTICLE

'Art 13(2) … divorce, annulment of marriage or termination of the 'registered partnership' … shall not entail loss of the right of residence of a Union citizen's family members who are not nationals of a Member State where:

(a) prior to initiation of the divorce or annulment proceedings or termination of the registered partnership … the marriage or registered partnership has lasted at least three years, including one year in the host Member State; or

(b) by agreement between the spouses or the partners … or by court order, the spouse or partner who is not a national of a Member State has custody of the Union citizen's children; or

(c) this is warranted by particularly difficult circumstances, such as having been a victim of domestic violence while the marriage or registered partnership was subsisting; or

(d) by agreement between the spouses or partners … or by court order, the spouse or partner who is not a national of a Member State has the right of access to a minor child, provided that the court has ruled that such access must be in the host Member State, and for as long as is required.'

Article 13(2) has yet to be tested by litigation but, generally speaking, it seems a relatively straightforward piece of legislation. However, the scope of Art 13(2)(c), especially the phrases 'particularly difficult circumstances' and 'victim of domestic violence' are somewhat ambiguous and might attract preliminary ruling requests in the future.

'Marriages of convenience'

Although the ECJ has held that 'spouse' means 'part of a married couple' only, it subsequently had to qualify that statement by pointing out that 'marriages of convenience' will be regarded as an abuse of this situation. This point was made in *Akrich* (Case C–109/01) [2003] ECR I–9607, the facts of which will be examined in chapter 12. The Court held that there would be an abuse of EU law if spousal rights to residence had been invoked in the context of 'marriages of convenience', entered into in order to 'circumvent the national immigration provisions'.

'Registered partners'

Some care is required here. Directive 2004/38 does not confer 'family member' status on 'partners' in the loose sense of a boyfriend or girlfriend (irrespective of the gender of the Citizen). Article 2(2)(b) of the new directive only confers 'family member' status on 'partners':

- who have 'contracted a registered partnership, on the basis of the legislation of a Member State' and
- where 'the legislation of the host Member State treats registered partnerships as equivalent to marriage'.

The reference to 'the legislation of a Member State' means that a partnership registered in, say, Brazil or China would not count. For UK nationals seeking to invoke Art 2(2)(b) to confer 'family member' status on a partner, the only relevant legislation is the Civil Partnership Act 2004. Section 1 of the Act defines a 'civil partnership' as 'a relationship between two people of the same sex ('civil partners') … which is formed when they register as civil partners of each other'. In other words, heterosexual couples cannot enter into registered partnerships under UK law. Even for registered partners, the host Member State must have legislation which 'treats registered partnerships as equivalent to marriage'. Not all Member States have such legislation.

However, unregistered partners – whatever their sexual orientation – may invoke Art 3(2)(b) instead. This refers to a 'partner with whom the Union citizen has a durable relationship' – clearly, a much wider concept. This will be examined in more detail below.

'Descendants'

Article 2(2)(c) confers 'family member' status on any 'direct descendants' of the Citizen, or of the Citizen's spouse or partner, provided that they are under 21 years of age or 'dependent'. As well as blood-relative children, this provision is designed to ensure that the Citizen's step-children are included in the family. The previous legislation, Art 10 of Regulation 1612/68, defined the 'family' in terms of a worker, his spouse and 'their descendants'. This was more ambiguous about the position of step-children, and the ECJ was called upon to decide the point in *Baumbast v Secretary of State for the Home Department* (Case C–413/99) [2002] ECR I–7091, the facts of which were given above. The question was whether a Citizen's step-daughter (specifically, his wife's daughter from a previous relationship) could be classed as one of 'their descendants'. The Court – adopting a purposive rather than a literal interpretation of the legislation – held that she could.

Although the position of a Citizen's step-children is now clear, the position regarding adopted children has never been resolved through litigation and the new directive does not refer to them specifically. It is therefore a moot point as to whether an adopted child could be categorised as a 'descendant'.

'Dependants'

The test of dependency is a question of fact, that is: does the Citizen provide financial support? It does not depend upon any objective criteria indicating the need for support. In *Lebon* (1987), a case on Art 10 of Regulation 1612/68 involving a worker's adult daughter, the ECJ held that:

JUDGMENT

'The status of dependent member of a worker's family is the result of a factual situation. The person having that status is a member of the family who is supported by the worker and there is no need to determine the reasons for recourse to the worker's support or to raise the question whether the person concerned is able to support himself by taking up paid employment.'

There is therefore no requirement that the Citizen be under a legal obligation to provide support to his or her descendants. In *Lebon* (1987), the ECJ also ruled that a member of the Citizen's family does not cease to be dependent simply because they make a claim for a social welfare benefit. If it were otherwise, no member of a Citizen's family (apart from the spouse or registered partner and any children under 21) could ever make such a claim without taking themselves outside the scope of the family.

CASE EXAMPLE

Lebon (Case 316/85) [1987] ECR 2811

Marie-Christine Lebon had been born to French parents working in Belgium. She had lived there ever since, apart from two years when she returned to France. On her return to Belgium she was initially granted income support but shortly afterwards this was withdrawn on the basis that she was not seeking work. By this time she was 24 years old. She claimed to be a 'dependant' and thus entitled to the benefit. The ECJ held that the test for dependency was purely a question of fact.

'Ascendants'

Article 2(2)(d) confers 'family member' status on 'dependent direct relatives in the ascending line', whether that be the 'line' of the Citizen or their spouse or partner (as the case may be). This provision is designed to allow Citizen's parents and grandparents, and in-laws, to claim 'family member' status. However, in a similar way to the situation of descendants who are aged 21 or over, 'family member' status is not automatic – the ascendant relative must be 'dependent'. The situation is demonstrated by the case of *Jia* (Case C–1/05) [2007] ECR I–1.

CASE EXAMPLE

Jia (Case C–1/05) [2007] ECR I–1

Svanja Schallehn, a German national, had been living and working in Sweden since 1995. Her husband, Shenzhi Li, a Chinese national, was living with her. In May 2003, Li's mother, Yunying Jia, was granted a 90-day single entry visitors visa by the Swedish Embassy in Beijing to visit her son and daughter-in-law in Sweden, and she duly arrived 10 days later. Two months after that, she made an application for residence in Sweden as the ascendant relative of an EU Citizen's spouse. In order to establish dependency she produced a certificate from her former employer, China Forestry Publishing House, stating that she was financially dependent on her son and daughter-in-law. The Swedish authorities refused and she appealed to the Aliens Appeal Board, which requested a preliminary ruling seeking clarification of Jia's rights of residence. The ECJ decided that she was entitled to reside in Sweden.

One issue in particular was the appropriate test to be used to establish 'dependency'. On this point, the ECJ stated that:

JUDGMENT

'In order to determine whether the relatives in the ascending line of the spouse of a [Union] national are dependent on the latter, the host Member State must assess whether, having regard to their financial and social conditions, they are not in a position to support themselves. The need for material support must exist in the State of origin of those relatives or the State whence they came at the time when they apply to join the [Union] national.'

'Irrespective of their nationality'

Under Directive 2004/38, the family members may be of any nationality. Among many cases demonstrating this point are *Diatta* (1985), where the spouse was from Senegal; *Baumbast* (2002), where the spouse and one child were Colombian nationals; *Givane* (2003), where the spouse and children were from India; *Akrich* (2003), where the spouse was from Morocco; and *Jia* (2007) where the spouse and ascendant relatives were from China. In *Baumbast* the ECJ confirmed that:

JUDGMENT

'As to the fact that the children are not themselves citizens of the Union ... suffice it to state that the descendants of a [Union Citizen] who are under the age of 21 or are dependants, *irrespective of their nationality*, are to be regarded as members of his family and have the right to install themselves with that [Citizen].'

No requirement that family members have lived in the Citizen's home State

In *Akrich* (2003), the ECJ had appeared to suggest that, in order to qualify for residence rights as a 'family member' – in that case, as a spouse – it was necessary that the person had been lawfully resident in the Citizen's home State. However, in *Jia* (2007), the ECJ stated that there was no such general requirement:

JUDGMENT

'[EU] law does not require Member States to make the grant of a residence permit to nationals of a non-Member State, who are members of the family of a [Union Citizen] who has exercised his or her right of free movement, subject to the condition that those family members have previously been residing lawfully in another Member State.'

Hence, there was no legal obstacle to Mrs Jia, a Chinese national, taking up residence in Sweden as an ascendant relative of her son and daughter-in-law, despite the fact that she (Mrs Jia) had never set foot in Germany, her daughter-in-law's home State.

Situation when the Citizen returns 'home'

Consider this question: what would happen if, in the *Jia* case, the German daughter-in-law were to return to Germany, her 'home' State? Would her Chinese husband and mother-in-law be entitled to come to live in Germany with her? This question was raised in *Eind* (Case C–291/05) [2007] ECR I-10719, the Court answering 'yes'.

CASE EXAMPLE

Eind (Case C–291/05) (2007)

Runaldo Eind, a Dutch national, came to the UK to work. Shortly afterwards, he was joined by his 11-year-old daughter Rachel. Prior to that point she had been living in Surinam and held Surinamese nationality. Subsequently, Runaldo returned to the Netherlands, accompanied by Rachel, but, the Dutch authorities refused to recognise her claim for residency. The ECJ, however, held that Runaldo, as a Dutch national who had exercised his free movement rights by living and working in the UK before returning to the Netherlands, was entitled on his return to be accompanied by any relatives, irrespective of their nationality, falling within the definition of 'family'. Neither the fact that Mr Eind was now economically inactive (he was not working in the Netherlands because of ill health) nor the fact that Rachel had no pre-existing entitlement to residency in the Netherlands, had any relevance.

11.5.2 Other family members: Art 3

Article 3 of Directive 2004/38 refers to some more categories of family members. Article 3(2) states that Member States are to 'facilitate entry and residence for the following persons':

a) other family members, irrespective of their nationality, not falling under the definition in Article 2(2) who, in the country from which they have come, are dependants or members of the household of the Union citizen having the primary right of residence, or where serious health grounds strictly require the personal care of the family member by the Union citizen;
b) the partner with whom the Union citizen has a durable relationship, duly attested.

As yet, there is no case law guidance on any of these provisions. Litigation is inevitable, therefore, to establish what exactly is meant by:

- 'serious health grounds';
- 'personal care';
- 'durable relationship'.

There are several ambiguous concepts in Art 3(2). For example, what is meant by a 'durable' relationship? Is it purely a question of longevity, in which case, how long – two years? One year? Six months? Two months? Would a holiday romance count? If there's more to durability than longevity, what else should be required – that the couple had moved in together? What other criteria could be used to establish such a relationship? What if the couple had never actually met face-to-face but had perhaps come into contact with each other via a social networking site on the Internet and had corresponded regularly ever since?

11.5.3 The concept of 'primary carer'

In addition to the above legislative definitions, the ECJ has added a further category of family member: the 'primary carer'. In *Baumbast and R v Home Secretary* (2002) the

ECJ invented this concept as a means of conferring a continued right of residence on two mothers who would otherwise have faced deportation from the UK (and possible separation from their children):

- *Baumbast*: Mrs Baumbast, a Colombian national, faced being deported because her German husband had left the UK to work, initially in China and subsequently in Lesotho in southern Africa. She was therefore no longer the spouse of an EU Citizen **in the UK.**
- *R*: Mrs R, an American national, faced deportation following her divorce from her French husband because she was no longer the **spouse** of an EU Citizen.

However, the ECJ held that both women retained rights of residence as 'primary carer' of their children, who were still being educated in British schools. The 'primary carer' doctrine is actually based on Art 12 of Regulation 1612/68, which confers on all children of Union Citizens who have worked in another Member State the right to be educated in that State. Article 12 is examined in more detail in Chapter 12. In *Baumbast and R*, the Court stated:

JUDGMENT

'The right conferred by Article 12 of Regulation 1612/68 ... necessarily implies that that child has the right to be accompanied by the person who is his primary carer and, accordingly, that that person is able to reside with him in that Member State during his studies.'

The judgment in *Baumbast and R* did leave some questions unanswered. In particular, for how long does 'primary carer' status continue? That question has now been answered by the ECJ in *Teixeira* (Case C-480/08) [2010] 2 CMLR 50. The ECJ held that 'in principle' children who have reached adulthood are assumed not to require parental care, but that it was possible for the 'primary carer' to be needed beyond that age to help their son or daughter complete their education.

CASE EXAMPLE

Teixeira (Case C-480/08) [2010] 2 CMLR 50

Maria Teixeira, a Portuguese national, had come to live in London with her husband in 1989, and their daughter Patricia had been born in 1991. Subsequently, the couple divorced and, although Patricia initially lived with her father, she subsequently went to live with her mother. However, Maria did not satisfy any of the conditions for residence in the UK under Art 7 of Directive 2004/38, so the question arose whether she was entitled to exercise a continued residence in the UK based on her being a 'primary carer'. The answer to that question was complicated by the fact that, by this time, Patricia had celebrated her 18th birthday. The Court ruled that it was possible for someone in Patricia's situation to need continued parental care in order to complete their education.

The Court stated:

JUDGMENT

'Although children who have reached the age of majority are in principle assumed to be capable of meeting their own needs, the right of residence of a parent who cares for a child exercising the right to education in the host Member State may nevertheless extend beyond that age, if the child continues to need the presence and the care of that parent in order to be able to pursue and complete his or her education. It is for the referring court to assess whether that is actually the case.'

The 'primary carer' therefore enjoys a right of residence as long as they have a child in education who needs parental support. There are no other conditions or restrictions on the primary carer's rights of residence, a point that was made very clearly in *Ibrahim* (Case C-310/08) [2010] 2 CMLR 51, decided on the same day as *Teixeria*.

CASE EXAMPLE

Ibrahim (Case C-310/08) [2010] 2 CMLR 51

Nimco Ibrahim, a Somali national, had come to live in the UK with her husband Yusuf, a Danish national, and their children, all of whom were Danish nationals. Yusuf worked for around 8 months. Subsequently, he left the UK but Nimco remained in London. According to the ECJ, 'she was never self-sufficient. She does not work and depends entirely on social assistance to cover her living expenses and housing costs. She does not have comprehensive sickness insurance cover and relies on the National Health Service'. In other words, she did not satisfy any of the conditions for residence in Art 7 of Directive 2004/38. Nimco's right to continued residence in the UK therefore depended entirely on her being the primary carer of her children. The Court nevertheless held that primary carer status on its own was sufficient as the basis for residency.

The Court stated:

JUDGMENT

'The children of a national of a Member State who works or has worked in the host Member State and the parent who is their primary carer can claim a right of residence in the latter State on the sole basis of Article 12 of Regulation 1612/68, without being required to satisfy the conditions laid down in Directive 2004/38 [and] without such a right being conditional on their having sufficient resources and comprehensive sickness insurance cover in that State.'

11.5.4 Rights to employment: Art 23

Article 23 of Directive 2004/38 confers the right to work on the Citizen's family members. It states:

ARTICLE

'Art 23 Irrespective of nationality, the family members of a Union citizen who have the right of residence or the right of permanent residence in a Member State shall be entitled to take up employment or self-employment there.'

It is particularly important to bear in mind that this right is conferred on all family members, 'irrespective of nationality', so that even non-EU nationals can work legally in the EU. Article 23 replaces Art 11 of Regulation 1612/68, which has now been repealed. However, the two leading cases on Art 11 are, it is submitted, relevant as a guide to the interpretation of Art 23. Both of the cases involve family members – spouses – who were non-EU nationals.

Article 11 was applied in *Gül* (Case 131/85) [1986] ECR 1573, involving a Cypriot national, a doctor, who had been refused the right to work in Germany, despite being the spouse of a UK national who was employed there. The ECJ held that such a refusal was in breach of Regulation 1612/68, and emphasised that the authorities of the host State were obliged to 'treat the spouse in a non-discriminatory fashion' in so far as access to employment was concerned.

CASE EXAMPLE

Gül (Case 131/85) [1986] ECR 1573

Dr Emir Gül, a Cypriot national, was married to an English woman working as a hairdresser in Germany. He had qualifications in medicine from Istanbul University in Turkey. He had worked as an anaesthetist in Germany on a temporary basis for some time, where he gained specialist qualifications. When he applied for permission to practise in Germany permanently, however, this was refused on the ground of his nationality. The ECJ held that Dr Gül was entitled to practise in Germany, provided only that his qualifications were recognised in German law.

It should be noted that Cyprus became a Member State of the EU in May 2004, which would have entitled Dr Gül to rely upon EU law in his own right. Nevertheless, the principle of law established remains applicable to other non-EU family members.

In *Mattern & Cikotic* (Case C–10/05) [2006] ECR I-3145, the ECJ was again asked to rule on Art 11 of Regulation 1612/68. The case involved a Luxembourg national, Cynthia Mattern, who was married to a 'Yugoslav' national, Hajrudin Cikotic. Ms Mattern had obtained work in Belgium, so clearly Mr Cikotic would have been entitled to work there, applying the precedent from *Gül*. However, the issue was whether he was entitled to work in a different state – specifically, Ms Mattern's home State of Luxembourg (the couple lived near the border between those two countries). The ECJ refused, stating that:

JUDGMENT

'[EU law] does not confer on a national of a third country the right to take up an activity as an employed person in a Member State other than the one in which his spouse, a [Union] national, pursues or has pursued an activity as an employed person in exercise of her right to free movement.'

KEY FACTS

Citizens' family members and their rights under Directive 2004/38	
Citizens are entitled to be accompanied by their family members, irrespective of their nationality	Article 3(1)
Family members include the spouse, registered partner, direct descendants (who are under 21 or dependent) and dependent relatives in the ascending line	Article 2(2)
'Spouse' means a marital relationship. Separation does not terminate the spousal status	*Diatta* (1985), *Reed* (1986)
There are no requirements as to when or where the marriage took place	*Metock and others* (2008)
But the marriage must be genuine. 'Marriages of convenience' do not count	*Akrich* (2003)
Descendants includes step-children. Where dependency has to be established, this is a question of fact	*Lebon* (1987), *Baumbast and R* (2002)
Relatives in the ascending line includes parents and grandparents. Dependency has to be shown	*Jia* (2007)
Family members may acquire the right of permanent residence in the Member State	Article 17
Family Members have the right to work, or self-employment, without discrimination, in the same State as the Citizen	Article 23; *Gül* (1986); *Mattern & Cikotic* (2006)

Family members have the right to equal treatment with nationals of the host State	Article 24
Other family members have a right of entry and residence. This includes partners in a 'durable relationship'	Article 3(2)
The ECJ has invented a further category: the primary carer	*Baumbast and R* (2002)
This is based on Art 12 of Regulation 1612/68 (children's rights to education) and, in principle, ends when the child reaches the age of majority – although it may be extended	*Teixeira* (2010)
The primary carer enjoys a right of residence based purely on Art 12. None of the conditions in Directive 2004/38 apply	*Ibrahim* (2010

11.6 Limitations on free movement – the derogations in Directive 2004/38

The right of free movement for Citizens and their family members is not an 'absolute' right. Specifically, the right is subject to 'limitations justified on grounds of public policy, public security or public health'. Further guidance is given in Art 27 of Directive 2004/38.

ARTICLE

'Art 27(1) … Member States may restrict the freedom of movement and residence of Union citizens and their family members, irrespective of nationality, on grounds of public policy, public security or public health. These grounds shall not be invoked to serve economic ends.

(2) Measures taken on grounds of public policy or public security shall comply with the principle of proportionality and shall be based exclusively on the personal conduct of the individual concerned. Previous criminal convictions shall not in themselves constitute grounds for taking such measures. The personal conduct of the individual concerned must represent a genuine, present and sufficiently serious threat affecting one of the fundamental interests of society. Justifications that are isolated from the particulars of the case or that rely on considerations of general prevention shall not be accepted …'

This provision largely replaces Arts 1–3 of Directive 64/221, which only dealt with workers and their family members, and which has now been repealed. However, many of the cases decided by the ECJ under the old directive have continuing relevance today, given that both directives use very similar – in some cases, identical – terms. Indeed, some of the jurisprudence of the ECJ has been adopted into the new directive. Compare, for example, Art 27(2), above, with the quote from the case of *R v Bouchereau* (1978), below.

11.6.1 Scope of the derogations

The ECJ had handed down a number of important judgments on the scope of Directive 64/221. Although that legislation has now been repealed, many of those judgments are still relevant as a guide to the scope of the derogations under Directive 2004/38.

Directive 2004/38 only applies to restrictions placed on the movement of 'Union citizens and their family members'

This point is made explicitly in Art 27(1), but had already been stated by the ECJ in *Commission v Spain* (Case C–503/03), a case involving Directive 64/221. The ECJ stated that EU law: 'enables Member States to prohibit nationals of other Member States or their spouses who are nationals of third countries from entering their territory on grounds of "public policy" or "public security". The [Union's] legislature has nevertheless made reliance by the Member States on such grounds subject to strict limits.'

Implicit in this judgment is a principle that Directive 2004/38 does not apply to any case only involving a non-EU national (or, as the Court describes them, 'nationals of third countries'). This can be seen in the decision in *Dem'Yanenko* (Case C–45/03) (2005), unreported, where the ECJ declined jurisdiction in a case involving the deportation of a Ukrainian national from Italy.

EU nationals do not need to have been lawfully resident in another Member State in order to be protected

This point was made in another case involving Directive 64/221, *Commission v Netherlands* (Case C–50/06) [2006] ECR I–1097, where the ECJ stated that:

JUDGMENT

'The safeguards provided by Directive 64/221 call for a broad interpretation as regards the persons to whom they apply. Member States must take all steps to ensure that the safeguard of the provisions of the directive is available to any national of another Member State who is subject to a decision ordering expulsion. To exclude from the benefit of those substantive and procedural safeguards citizens of the Union who are not lawfully resident on the territory of the host Member State would deprive those safeguards of their essential effectiveness.'

The fact that Member States cannot deport their own nationals does not prevent them from deporting other States' nationals

This point was emphasised in *Pereira Roque* (Case C–171/96) [1998] ECR I–4607, where the ECJ stated that (emphasis added):

JUDGMENT

'[EU law] permits Member States to adopt, with respect to the nationals of other Member States and on the grounds specified in that provision … measures which they ***cannot*** apply to their own nationals, inasmuch as they have no authority to expel the latter from the national territory or deny them access thereto. That difference of treatment between a State's own nationals and those of other States derives from a principle of international law which precludes a State from denying its own nationals the right to enter its territory and reside there, and which the [TFEU] cannot be assumed to disregard in the context of relations between Member States.'

11.6.2 'Public policy'

The situations when 'public policy' measures may be invoked are not necessarily concerned with criminal activities (see *Van Duyn v Home Office* (Case 41/74) [1974] ECR 1337 – permission to enter the UK refused to a member of the Church of Scientology). The ECJ has given guidance on what sort of behaviour will justify public policy measures. In *R v Bouchereau* (Case 30/77) [1978] ECR 1999, the ECJ held that:

JUDGMENT

'Recourse by a national authority to the concept of public policy presupposes, in any event, the existence, in addition to the perturbation of the social order which any infringement of the law involves, of a genuine and sufficiently serious threat to the requirements of public policy affecting one of the fundamental interests of society.'

In *Adoui and Cornuaille* (1982) the ECJ noted that prostitution could amount to a threat to public policy. In *Calfa* (Case C–348/96) [1999] ECR I–11, confirmed in *Orfanopoulos and Oliveri* (Case C–482/01) [2004] ECR I–5257, the ECJ stated that 'the use of drugs constitutes a danger for society such as to justify special measures against foreign nationals who contravene its laws on drugs, in order to maintain public order'. There is no requirement that the activity be criminal according to the law of the Member State (*Van Duyn* (1974)). However, it is important that the Member State concerned is regulating the conduct of which the Citizen is accused among its own nationals. This point was made in *Adoui and Cornuaille* (1982).

CASE EXAMPLE

Adoui and Cornuaille v Belgium (Case 115/81) [1982] ECR 1665

Rezguia Adoui and Dominique Cornuaille, both young French women, were employed as waitresses in a bar in Liège in Belgium, which was considered 'suspect from the point of view of morals'. They were prostitutes. The Belgian authorities refused to grant them residence permits. The particular conduct that the authorities were complaining about was that the two women were sitting semi-naked in windows. Such behaviour was subject to, at most, minor penalties in some, but not all, Belgian municipalities. In Liège minor penalties were imposed. The women challenged the refusal of the permits. The ECJ held that public policy measures could only be invoked in situations when the Member State concerned took 'repressive measures' or other 'genuine and effective measures' against its own nationals. The Court left it to the Belgian court to decide whether the test had been satisfied.

The Court stated that:

JUDGMENT

'Conduct may not be considered as being of a sufficiently serious nature to justify restrictions on the admission to or residence within the territory of a Member State of a national of another Member State in a case where the former Member State does not adopt, with respect to the same conduct on the part of its own nationals repressive measures or other genuine and effective measures intended to combat such conduct.'

This point was reiterated in *Jany and Others* (Case C–268/99) [2001] ECR I–8615, involving six women who were refused residence permits despite working as self-employed prostitutes in Amsterdam. The ECJ stated that EU law did not 'impose on Member States a uniform scale of values as regards the assessment of conduct which may be considered to be contrary to public policy', before repeating its judgment in *Adoui* (1982). In *Oteiza Olazabal* (Case C–100/01) [2002] ECR I–10981, the ECJ made a subtle change to *Adoui*. In the earlier case, the ECJ refers to 'repressive measures' while in *Oteiza Olazabal* the ECJ uses the phrase 'punitive measures'. It may be that the ECJ did not intend any substantive change in the law. Nevertheless, the words 'repressive' and 'punitive' are not synonymous, and it is submitted that, following *Oteiza Olazabal*, the Member States' discretion has been narrowed even further.

In *Oteiza Olazabal*, the ECJ authorised the imposition of 'public policy' measures involving an EU Citizen's residence rights in specific areas of another Member State. The ECJ stated:

JUDGMENT

'In situations where nationals of other Member States are liable to banishment or prohibition of residence, they are also capable of being subject to less severe measures consisting of partial restrictions on their right of residence, justified on grounds of public policy, without it being necessary that identical measures be capable of being applied by the Member State in question to its own nationals.'

It seems that the ECJ reached its decision because otherwise the complainant (a Spanish national convicted of terrorism offences in France) would have to be deported from France. This would not be in keeping with the fundamental requirement of proportionality.

In *Rutili* (Case 36/75) [1975] ECR 1219, the ECJ explained that the 'genuine and serious threat' test was designed to ensure compliance with Arts 8–11 of the European Convention on Human Rights (ECHR), that restrictions were available in the interests of national security or public safety only when **necessary** for the protection of those interests in a democratic society. The English Court of Appeal in *B v Home Secretary* [2000] HRLR 439 quashed a deportation order against an Italian national who had lived in the UK for about 35 years since the age of seven when his parents had moved there. Although he had committed sex offences, the court held that his links with the UK were much stronger than with Italy – he had been to Italy twice in the preceding 20 years. It would therefore be disproportionate to deport him, bearing in mind that it would remove him from all family links. This allowed the court to refer to Art 8 of the ECHR.

11.6.3 'Public security'

This is reserved for serious crimes and subversive, anti-State activities, eg terrorism and espionage. Public security was specifically referred to in *Oteiza Olazabal* (2002), involving a member of ETA (*Euskadi Ta Askatasuna* (Basque Homeland and Freedom)). Formed in 1959, the organisation seeks autonomy for the Basque area of north-western Spain. The ECJ stated:

JUDGMENT

'The defendant in the main proceedings … has been sentenced in France to 18 months' imprisonment and a four-year ban on residence for conspiracy to disturb public order by intimidation or terror … he formed part of an armed and organised group whose activity constitutes a threat to public order in French territory. Prevention of such activity may, moreover, be regarded as falling within the maintenance of public security.'

Any conduct that is contrary to public security must also be contrary to public policy although the converse is not true. Hence the ECJ has dealt with all the cases referred to it on public policy grounds without reference to public security.

11.6.4 'Public health'

Article 29 of Directive 2004/38 provides as follows:

ARTICLE

'Art 29(1) The only diseases justifying measures restricting freedom of movement shall be the diseases with epidemic potential as defined by the relevant instruments of the World Health Organisation and other infectious diseases or contagious parasitic diseases if they are the subject of protection provisions applying to nationals of the host Member State.

(2) Diseases occurring after a three-month period from the date of arrival shall not constitute grounds for expulsion from the territory.

(3) Where there are serious indications that it is necessary, Member States may, within three months of the date of arrival, require persons entitled to the right of residence to undergo, free of charge, a medical examination to certify that they are not suffering from any of the conditions referred to in paragraph 1. Such medical examinations may not be required as a matter of routine.'

The above provision replaces Art 4 of Directive 64/221, which has now been repealed. There is no ECJ case law under either directive to provide any guidance on phrases such as 'diseases with epidemic potential', or 'other infectious diseases or contagious parasitic diseases'.

11.6.5 'Proportionality'

Article 27(2) states that 'Measures taken on grounds of public policy or public security shall comply with the principle of proportionality'. An example of this can be seen in the case of *Oulane* (Case C–215/03) [2005] ECR I–1215, where a French national had been arrested behaving suspiciously at Rotterdam railway station in the Netherlands, in an area closed off to the public. He was unable to produce any ID, nor could he give a residence address and had no luggage. He was detained and, a week later, he was deported. Subsequently he brought a legal challenge to the deportation. The ECJ decided that deportation in such circumstances would be disproportionate. The Court stated:

JUDGMENT

'Detention and deportation based solely on the failure of the person concerned to comply with legal formalities concerning the monitoring of aliens impair the very substance of the right of residence directly conferred by [Union] law and are manifestly disproportionate to the seriousness of the infringement.'

11.6.6 'Personal conduct'

Article 27(2) of the Directive states that 'measures taken on grounds of public policy or public security shall be based exclusively on the personal conduct of the individual concerned'. Applying this, the ECJ has held that Member States may not justify deportation of an individual on the ground that it will serve as an example to others. In *Bonsignore* (Case 67/74) [1975] ECR 297, the ECJ emphasised how public policy and/or public security measures 'cannot be justified on grounds extraneous to the individual'. In the same case the ECJ held that 'The concept of "personal conduct" expresses the requirement that a deportation order may only be made for breaches of the peace and public security which might be committed by the individual affected'. In *Calfa* (1999), the complainant faced automatic deportation from Greece, having committed a relatively minor drugs offence. The ECJ held that deportation was not permissible without taking account of the individual's personal conduct.

CASE EXAMPLE

Calfa (Case C–348/96) [1999] ECR I–11

Donatella Calfa, an Italian national, was convicted of the possession and use of prohibited drugs while on holiday in Greece. The Greek court sentenced her to three months' imprisonment and expelled her for life from Greece, as required by Greek law. The law in question provided for **automatic** expulsion for life **unless** there were compelling reasons, in particular family reasons, that would justify the person's continued residence in Greece. The expulsion could be revoked only by and at the discretion of the Minister for Justice. Miss Calfa appealed against the expulsion, arguing that Greece was not empowered to expel a national of another Member State for life if a comparable measure could not be taken against a Greek citizen. The ECJ held that automatic expulsion was contrary to the 'personal conduct' requirement. The Court noted that expulsion for life 'automatically' followed a criminal conviction, without any account being taken of the 'personal conduct' of the offender or of the danger that that person represented.

The Court stated:

JUDGMENT

'The existence of a previous criminal conviction can … only be taken into account in so far as the circumstances which gave rise to that conviction are evidence of personal conduct constituting a present threat to the requirements of public policy … an expulsion order could be made against [an EU Citizen] only if, **besides her having committed an offence under [national] laws**, her personal conduct created a genuine and sufficiently serious threat affecting one of the fundamental interests of society.'

This seems correct. After all, there is a huge difference between, on one hand, someone who is caught with a substantial amount of a highly dangerous drug such as heroin which they clearly intend to sell and, on the other hand, someone who has only a small amount of a recreational drug for her own personal use. Yet, under Greek law, all drug offenders were subject to the same blanket rule: automatic life-time expulsion.

A similar provision of national legislation was examined by the ECJ in *Oliveri* (2004). The case concerned the *Ausländergesetz* (German law on aliens), which provided for mandatory deportation for foreign nationals in certain circumstances, one being where a foreign national committed a drugs offence or a public order offence and was sentenced to a term of imprisonment (para 47). The ECJ stated that such mandatory deportation would be incompatible with the Directive.

The Court also held that a practice adopted in Germany, whereby courts were prohibited, when reviewing the legality of national authorities' deportation orders, from taking into account any subsequent factual developments, constituted a breach of the personal conduct criterion.

CASE EXAMPLE

Oliveri (Case C–493/01) [2004] ECR I–5257

Raffaele Oliveri, an Italian national, was born in Germany in 1977 and had lived there ever since. He became a drug addict and committed several offences of theft and one offence of dealing illegally in drugs, for which he received a prison sentence. As a result of his drug-taking, he developed HIV in 1998 which subsequently became full-blown AIDS in 2001. He had been sentenced to prison in April 2000 and, in August 2000, the German authorities issued a deportation order against him. The decision was based on his lengthy criminal record for drugs offences, but his deportation order was mandatory under para 47 of the *Ausländergesetz*. In September 2000, Oliveri challenged this, claiming that he had 'gained maturity' while in prison, such that there was no risk of re-offending following his eventual release. In addition, the prison hospital service indicated that Oliveri was seriously ill and 'likely soon to die of his illness'. The ECJ upheld his challenge.

The Court stated:

JUDGMENT

'In practice, circumstances may arise between the date of the expulsion order and that of its review by the competent court which point to the cessation or the substantial diminution of the threat which the conduct of the person ordered to be expelled constitutes … That is especially so if a lengthy period has elapsed between the date of the decision to expel the person concerned and that of the review of that decision by the competent court.'

The Court dealt with a similar issue in *Orfanopoulos* (2004). This case involved another provision of the *Ausländergesetz*, under which certain foreign nationals have 'special protection', including those living in a family relationship with a German national (para 48). This protection means that deportation is only available on 'serious' grounds of public security and policy. When a foreign national entitled to special protection commits an offence that would normally lead to mandatory deportation, such as those in para 47, he can still be deported – not automatically, but 'as a general rule'. In effect, there is a presumption in favour of deportation. The Court held that the presumption in para 48 also breached the personal conduct requirement of the directive. The Court held that it was essential in **every** case to take into account a number of factors:

- the nature and seriousness of the offences committed
- the length of residence in the host Member State
- the period which has elapsed since the commission of the offence
- the family circumstances of the person concerned
- the seriousness of the difficulties which the spouse and any of their children risk facing in the country of origin of the person concerned.

CASE EXAMPLE

Orfanopoulos (Case C–482/01) [2004] ECR I–5257

Georgios Orfanopoulos, a Greek national, had gone to live in Germany in 1972, when aged 13. In 1981, he married a German national, and they went on to have three daughters. Georgios was occasionally in employment but these jobs were interrupted by long periods of unemployment. He became a drug addict, and was convicted nine times for drug-related offences and crimes of violence. He was sentenced to six months' imprisonment in 1999 and in January 2000 he was hospitalised for detoxification. By September 2000 he was back in prison. Eventually, in February 2001, the German authorities ordered his expulsion, to take effect on his release from prison. The decision was based in part on the length and seriousness of his criminal record and partly on the risk of re-offending (because of his drug dependency). As he was married to a German national, his deportation order was based on para 48 of the *Ausländergesetz*, in that he posed a serious threat to German public policy. He challenged this outcome, and the ECJ held that para 48 breached both Art 8 of the ECHR (protection of family life) and the Directive (personal conduct requirement).

The Court stated:

JUDGMENT

'The importance of ensuring the protection of the family life of [Union Citizens] in order to eliminate obstacles to the exercise of the fundamental freedoms guaranteed by the Treaty has been recognised under [EU] law. It is clear that the removal of a person from the country where close members of his family are living may amount to an infringement of the right to respect for family life as guaranteed by Article 8 of the ECHR, which is among the fundamental rights which are protected in [EU] law.'

Membership of organisations and the 'personal conduct' rule

According to *Van Duyn* (1974), membership of an organisation may constitute 'personal conduct'. Thus, members of organisations known to pose a threat to public policy or security (most obviously terrorist groups) can be made subject to deportation orders or refusals of entry purely on the basis of their membership. However, the ECJ distinguished between past and present membership.

CASE EXAMPLE

Van Duyn v Home Office (Case 41/74) [1974] ECR 1337

Yvonne Van Duyn, a Dutch national and member of the Church of Scientology, was offered a position as secretary in the UK's branch of the church, the Hubbard College of Scientology in East Grinstead. On arriving at Gatwick Airport she presented her offer of employment to immigration officials, but was refused entry, on the ground that the Home Office had declared undesirable any person entering the country to work for the Church. However, the Church itself was not banned under UK law, and no restrictions were placed on UK nationals becoming employees of the Church. Miss Van Duyn therefore sought a declaration from the High Court that this refusal infringed her right to free movement, in particular the 'personal conduct' criterion. The ECJ held that it was possible for an individual, by reason of their **present** membership of an organisation to be engaging in 'personal conduct'.

The Court stated:

JUDGMENT

'Although a person's *past* association cannot, in general, justify a decision refusing him the right to move freely within the [EU] … *present* association, *which reflects participation in the activities of the body or the organisation as well as identification with its aims or designs*, may be considered a voluntary act of the person concerned and, consequently, as part of his personal conduct.'

This decision is highly significant, as it allows Member States to expel EU nationals who are known to be a present member of a terrorist organisation, without having to prove that the individual has committed any specific offence. For example, in *R v Secretary of State for the Home Dept, ex p Gallagher* (Case C–175/94) [1995] ECR I–4253, the UK authorities expelled a known IRA member. Although there was evidence that he had committed a firearms offence, under the *Van Duyn* (1974) ruling this would not have been necessary. Establishing his membership of the IRA alone would have sufficed. Another case example is *Oteiza Olazabal* (2002), discussed above. Again, he had been convicted by a French court of a terrorist offence but, under *Van Duyn* (1974), restrictions could have been placed on his free movement simply by establishing his membership of the terrorist group ETA.

11.6.7 Excluded situations

Directive 2004/38 provides that measures taken on the grounds of public policy, security or health will **not** be justified in two situations.

'Economic ends': Art 27(1)

This would mean, for example, that a Member State could not deny entry to an EU Citizen from another State on the ground that there was high unemployment in the State.

'Previous criminal convictions': Art 27(2)

Previous criminal convictions shall not 'in themselves' constitute grounds for the taking of such measures. So what significance do they have? In *R v Bouchereau* (1978) the ECJ emphasised that the individual had to represent a 'present' threat.

CASE EXAMPLE

R v Bouchereau (Case 30/77) [1978] ECR 1999

Pierre Bouchereau, a French national working in the UK, was convicted of possession of a small quantity of cannabis and amphetamine in January 1976. He was given a 12-month suspended sentence. In June 1976, Pierre was back before the courts, this time pleading guilty to a charge of possession of a small amount of LSD and amphetamine. The stipendiary magistrate contemplated a recommendation for deportation. However, he sought guidance from the ECJ, which held that deportation was permissible only when the individual posed a 'genuine and serious threat' to society. Having received this guidance, the magistrate decided that Pierre did not constitute such a threat and fined him £35 instead.

The Court offered the following guidance:

JUDGMENT

'The existence of a *previous* criminal conviction can … only be taken into account in so far as the circumstances which gave rise to that conviction are evidence of personal conduct constituting a *present* threat to the requirements of public policy. Although, in general, a finding that such a threat exists implies the existence in the individual concerned of a propensity to act in the same way in the future, it is possible that past conduct alone may constitute such a threat to the requirements of public policy.'

This distinction between a 'previous conviction' and a 'present threat' was utilised by the English Immigration Appeal Tribunal in the following cases:

- *Monteil v Secretary of State for the Home Dept* [1984] 1 CMLR 264 – a deportation order issued against M, a French national working in the UK, was quashed, despite a string of criminal convictions. The tribunal found that there was evidence that M was a reformed character, having undertaken treatment for alcoholism while in prison.
- *Proll v Secretary of State for the Home Dept* [1985] Imm AR 118 – an immigration officer's decision to deny entry into the UK to P, a German national, was quashed, despite the fact that she was a former member of the Baader–Meinhof terrorist organisation and had served a year in prison for armed robbery. The tribunal found that there was evidence that she had reformed after her time in prison; she had also matured over the years since her time in the terrorist organisation.

The decision in *R v Bouchereau* (1978) suggested that a single conviction of a serious offence could be enough to justify deportation. This was confirmed by the English High Court in *R v Secretary of State for the Home Dept, ex p Marchon* [1993] 2 CMLR 132, involving the smuggling of a large quantity of illegal drugs.

11.6.8 Procedural safeguards

The need to examine the individual's circumstances: Art 28(1)

Article 28(1) of Directive 2004/38 provides as follows:

ARTICLE

'Art 28(1) Before taking an expulsion decision … the host Member State shall take account of considerations such as how long the individual concerned has resided on its territory, his/her age, state of health, family and economic situation, social and cultural integration into the host Member State and the extent of his/her links with the country of origin.'

Although there is no case law guidance on this provision as yet, it seems to be consistent with existing ECJ case law on Directive 64/221, in particular *Orfanopoulos* (2004), discussed above. The English Court of Appeal has also offered some guidance on this issue, specifically on the question as to who, exactly, should actually undertake the task of taking into account the various 'considerations'. *R v Carmona* [2006] EWCA Crim 508; [2006] 1 WLR 2264 involved a Portuguese national living in the UK with his wife and family who had been convicted of a number of criminal offences. The trial judge had then recommended deportation on completion of his prison sentence. On appeal against that, Burnton J stated:

JUDGMENT

'Where the court imposes a substantial custodial sentence, if the sentencing court is to consider the effect of deportation on the offender's family, it must necessarily gaze into the future. The court would have to consider the effect on third parties and on the offender of his deportation on the expiry of the sentence. However, circumstances may have changed very considerably at the end of his sentence. Conditions in the country to which he is to be deported may have changed dramatically … His domestic situation may have changed: his partner may not have stood by him, or his marriage may not have survived his imprisonment. The future is necessarily unknown. It is far better for issues as to the effect of deportation on the offender and his family to be addressed, by the Home Secretary or by the [Asylum & Immigration Tribunal], close to the time of the proposed deportation rather than at the time of sentence.'

Special protection for those with a right of permanent residence: Art 28(2)

Article 28(2) applies to anyone with a right of permanent residence, meaning those who have been resident for at least five years in the host State. It states:

ARTICLE

'Art 28(2) The host Member State may not take an expulsion decision against Union citizens or their family members, irrespective of nationality, who have the right of permanent residence on its territory, except on serious grounds of public policy or public security.'

As Directive 2004/38 introduced the concept of permanent residence, there was no forerunner of this provision under Directive 64/221 and hence no case law either to provide guidance. It is therefore presently a matter of speculation as to what exactly is meant by 'serious' grounds of policy or security and what, if anything, this adds to the general tests under Art 27 for a public policy or security measure to be justified.

Extra protection for those with ten years' residence and minors: Art 28(3)

Article 28(3) applies to those with at least ten years' residence in the host State, and to minors.

ARTICLE

'Art 28(3) An expulsion decision may not be taken against Union citizens, except if the decision is based on imperative grounds of public security, as defined by Member States, if they:

(a) have resided in the host Member State for the previous 10 years; or

(b) are a minor, except if the expulsion is necessary for the best interests of the child.'

Article 28(3)(a) (or, rather, the UK legislation implementing Directive 2004/38) was considered by the UK's Asylum & Immigration Tribunal (AIT) in the case of *Chindamo v Home Secretary* (2007) NLJ 1442. This is the case of convicted murderer Learco Chindamo, an Italian national who, in 1995, stabbed to death his school headmaster, Philip Lawrence. Chindamo, who came to live in the UK when he was aged six and has lived here ever since, was aged 15 at the time of the stabbing. He was convicted of murder in 1996 and the trial judge recommended that he serve a minimum of 12 years in prison before being considered for parole. In the summer of 2007, the Home Secretary made a decision that Chindamo be deported on his release. That decision was appealed against, and the AIT decided that, although Chindamo had now been living in the UK for over 20 years, because 12 of those years were or would have been spent in prison by the time of his release, he fell outside of the provisions of Art 28(3)(a). Nevertheless, the AIT decided that he could not be deported on the basis that he did not pose a present threat to public policy.

Article 28(3)(b) applies to cases involving children, ruling out deportation except where it would be in their 'best interests'. This is an intriguing concept and it will be interesting to see what guidance the ECJ offers as to when it will be in a child's 'best interests' to be deported.

Giving reasons: Art 30

Article 30(1) states that 'the persons concerned shall be notified in writing of any decision taken under Article 27(1), in such a way that they are able to comprehend its content and the implications for them'.

The person concerned should be informed of the grounds of public policy, public security or public health upon which the decision taken in his case is based, unless this is contrary to the interests of the security of the State involved. In *R v Secretary of State for the Home Dept, ex p Dannenberg* [1984] QB 766 a recommendation for deportation made by Mid-Sussex Magistrates' Court was quashed by the English Court of Appeal on the basis that the magistrates had failed to give reasons. The authorities must give the person a precise and comprehensive statement of the reasons for its decision (*Rutili* (1975)). Without adequate reasons, the person cannot prepare a full defence.

Appeals and reviews: Art 31

Article 31 provides for appeals against, and reviews of, measures taken by Member States to restrict the free movement of other States' nationals. Article 31(1) provides that:

ARTICLE

> 'Art 31(1) The persons concerned shall have access to judicial and, where appropriate, administrative redress procedures in the host Member State to appeal against or seek review of any decision taken against them on the grounds of public policy, public security or public health.'

This replaces Art 8 of Directive 64/221, which has been repealed, although some of the case law on that provision is of continuing relevance, for example *Royer* (1976) and *Pecastaing* (1981).

In *Royer*, the ECJ was asked whether a deportation order could be executed immediately, or whether such an order became effective only after all national judicial remedies had been exhausted. The ECJ stated:

JUDGMENT

> 'All steps must be taken by the Member States to ensure that the safeguard of the right of appeal is *in fact* available to anyone against whom a restrictive measure of this kind has been adopted. However, this guarantee would become illusory if the Member States could, by the immediate execution of a decision ordering expulsion, deprive the person concerned of the opportunity of *effectively* making use of the remedies which he is guaranteed by legislation.'

In *Pecastaing* (Case 98/79) [1981] ECR 691, the ECJ stated that 'A Member State cannot … render the right of appeal for persons covered by the directive conditional on *particular requirements as to form or procedure* which are less favourable than those pertaining to remedies available to nationals in respect of acts of the administration'.

Duration of exclusion orders: Art 32

Article 32 deals with the duration of any exclusion order made by a Member State. Art 32(1) provides:

ARTICLE

'Art 32(1) Persons excluded on grounds of public policy or public security may submit an application for lifting of the exclusion order after a reasonable period, depending on the circumstances, and in any event after three years from enforcement of the final exclusion order which has been validly adopted in accordance with [Union] law, by putting forward arguments to establish that there has been a material change in the circumstances which justified the decision ordering their exclusion.'

Expulsion as a penalty or legal consequence: Art 33

Article 33(1) provides that Member States may not make expulsion an automatic consequence of a person from another Member State committing a criminal offence in their territory. This is consistent with pre-existing ECJ case law on the 'personal conduct' criterion, examined above, in particular *Calfa* (1999) and *Orfanopoulos & Oliveri* (2004). In that sense Art 33(1) simply confirms existing law and practice. Art 33(2), however, is new. It provides that:

ARTICLE

'Art 33(2) If an expulsion order, as provided for in paragraph 1, is enforced more than two years after it was issued, the Member State shall check that the individual concerned is currently and genuinely a threat to public policy or public security and shall assess whether there has been any material change in the circumstances since the expulsion order was issued.'

The separation in time between a deportation order being made and its enforcement, as contemplated by Art 33(2), is likely to occur if an order is made when a convicted criminal is serving a prison sentence, with the order to take effect on release. This situation can be illustrated using the facts of *R v Secretary of State for the Home Department, ex p Santillo* (Case 131/79) [1980] ECR 1585. This case actually involved a different issue – the question for the ECJ was whether a trial judge's recommendation to deport could be regarded as valid some four and a half years later (the ECJ ruled that this was a matter for national courts to decide). Were the facts of this case to recur now, then there would be no need to have recourse to Art 33(2) as the date when the Home Secretary's deportation order was made (September 1978) was only seven months before the date when the order was enforced (April 1979).

CASE EXAMPLE

R v Secretary of State for the Home Dept, ex p Santillo (Case 131/79) [1980] ECR 1585

Mario Santillo, an Italian, was living in the UK. In December 1973, after a Crown Court trial, he was convicted of the rape and indecent assault of two prostitutes. In January 1974 he was sentenced to eight years' imprisonment, with a recommendation from the trial judge that it be followed by deportation. Four and a half years later, in September 1978, the Home Secretary made an order for his deportation as soon as his sentence was completed. Santillo completed his sentence in April 1979 after remission for good behaviour. He was due to be released but was retained in detention pending deportation. He sought judicial review to quash the deportation order, on the basis that four and a half years had passed between the 'recommendation' and the deportation order. The High Court referred the case to the ECJ, which held that a lapse in time between the judicial recommendation of deportation, and the deportation order itself, was 'liable to deprive the recommendation of its function'. Whether or not it did so was a question of fact for the national court to decide. Applying this to the facts, the High Court decided that the trial judge's recommendation **was** still valid, there being no evidence that the position had changed in the intervening four and a half years.

11.6.9 Application to Member States' own nationals

All of the above cases in this section involve restrictions imposed by Member States on other States' nationals. One question which had not, until very recently, been addressed by the ECJ is whether a Member State can impose a restriction on one of its own nationals. However, the Court was given the opportunity to do so in *Jipa* (Case C–33/07) [2008] ECR I-5157.

CASE EXAMPLE

Jipa (Case C–33/07) [2008] ECR I-5157

In September 2006, Gheorghe Jipa, a Romanian national, left Romania to go to Belgium. However, he was repatriated to Romania on account of 'illegal residence' by the Belgian authorities two months later, pursuant to a 'Re-admission Agreement' concluded between Romania and the Benelux countries. This triggered a provision of Romanian law, which provides that restrictions may be imposed on the free movement rights of Romanian citizens, for up to three years, under certain conditions. One such condition involved the citizen being repatriated by a State under a readmission agreement concluded between Romania and that State. Subsequently, in January 2007, the Romanian Government sought to impose a restriction on Jipa's movement. He challenged this, and the case was referred to the ECJ. There, it was held that Directive 2004/38 applied to such a situation (especially given the 'right of exit' in Art 4) and would have to be justified using the criteria in Art 27, as described above.

The Court stated:

JUDGMENT

'The fact that a citizen of the Union has been subject to a measure repatriating him from the territory of another Member State, where he was residing illegally, may be taken into account by his Member State of origin for the purpose of restricting that citizen's right of free movement only to the extent that his personal conduct constitutes a genuine, present and sufficiently serious threat to one of the fundamental interests of society.'

The English Court of Appeal has also addressed this point, in the context of football banning orders, in *Gough and Others* [2001] 4 All ER 289. These are orders which may be imposed under the UK's Football Spectators Act 1989 (as amended by the Football (Disorder) Act 2000) on English football hooligans in order to prevent them travelling to watch matches in Europe involving the England national side or English clubs. When banning orders were imposed on four individuals, they challenged the legality of the orders under EU law and the European Convention on Human Rights. Laws LJ dismissed the challenges, holding that: 'in a proper case a Member State may be justified on public policy grounds in preventing a citizen of the Union from leaving its shores'.

KEY FACTS

Limitations on Citizens' rights of free movement and residence under Directive 2004/38	
Member States may limit the free movement and residence of EU Citizens and their family members on grounds of public policy, security or health	Article 27(1)
Any 'measures' must be based exclusively on the personal conduct of the individual. Present membership of an organisation amounts to 'personal conduct'	Article 27(2); *Bonsignore* (1975); *Calfa* (1999); *Van Duyn* (1974)

Any 'measures' must comply with the principle of proportionality	Article 27(2); *Oulane* (2005)
Previous criminal convictions do not, in themselves, constitute grounds for taking measures. But they may be relevant if they provide evidence of a present threat	Article 27(2); *R v Bouchereau* (1977)
Member States may take measures (such as deportation) against Citizens from other States which they cannot take against their own nationals	*Pereira Roque* (1998)
Measures will only be permitted if the Member State imposes genuine and effective measures against its own nationals for the same conduct	*Adoui and Cornuaille* (1982); *Jany and others* (2001)
The person must pose a genuine, present and sufficiently serious threat to society	Article 27(3); *R v Bouchereau* (1977)
Measures must not be 'based on considerations of general prevention'	Article 27(3); *Orfanopoulos and Oliveri* (2004)
Before taking an expulsion decision, Member States must take into consideration factors such as the Citizen's age, health, family and economic situation, etc.	Article 28(1)
This is to ensure compliance with the right of all Citizens to respect for their private and family life	Article 8 ECHR; *Rutili* (1975); *Orfanopoulos and Oliveri* (2004)
An expulsion decision may only be taken against Citizens with the right of permanent residence on 'serious' grounds of policy or security	Article 28(2)
An expulsion decision may only be taken against Citizens with 10 years' residency, or minors, on 'imperative' grounds of public security	Article 28(3)
Public health refers only to diseases with epidemic potential, infectious diseases and contagious parasitic diseases	Article 29
Persons must be notified in writing of any decisions taken under the directive	Article 30
Persons have the right to appeal against and/or seek judicial review of any decision taken under the directive. These remedies must be made available in fact	Article 31; *Royer* (1976); *Pecastaing* (1981)
Expulsion from a Member State may not follow automatically from a criminal conviction	Article 33(1); *Calfa* (1999); *Orfanopoulos and Oliveri* (2004)
Expulsion orders enforced more than 2 years after issue must be checked to ensure the person is still a present threat	Article 33(2)
Member States may impose restrictions on the free movement of their own nationals, subject to the provisions of the Directive	*Jipa* (2008)

11.7 Citizens' political rights: Arts 22–25 TFEU

Article 22(1) TFEU states that every Citizen of the Union, if residing in an EU Member State of which he or she is not a national, has the right to both vote in, and even to stand as a candidate at, 'municipal elections' of the host State 'under the same conditions as nationals of that State'. This would mean, for example, that any French or German national living in the UK would be entitled to vote in any UK municipal elections provided that they were at least 18 years of age (the minimum British voting age). They could also stand for election if they were at least 18 years of age (the minimum age for

British candidates) and, if elected, could then serve provided they were not disqualified (UK law disqualifies certain people from holding political office, such as some convicted criminals, undischarged bankrupts and the mentally disordered).

Article 22(2) adds that 'every citizen of the Union residing in a Member State of which he is not a national shall have the right to vote and to stand as a candidate in elections to the European Parliament in the Member State in which he resides, under the same conditions as nationals of that State'. Article 22(2) was examined by the ECJ in *Eman & Sevinger* (Case C–300/04) [2006] ECR I–8055. The case involved two Dutch nationals who were resident in Aruba, a Caribbean island some 15 miles off the coast of Venezuela. Aruba is classed as an overseas territory of the Netherlands. However, the Dutch authorities had refused to register them for the European Parliament elections in 2004 because of provisions in Dutch law which conferred the voting franchise on all Dutch nationals resident in the Netherlands (but excluding the Dutch Antilles and Aruba), plus other Member States' nationals resident in the Netherlands. The complainants contested that this was a breach of their rights under Art 22(2).

However, the ECJ rejected their claim on this basis. Although the Court accepted that EU Citizens resident in one of the 'overseas countries and territories' (OCTs) could rely on EU law, it held that Art 22(2) did not apply to 'a citizen of the Union residing in an OCT who wishes to exercise his right to vote in the Member State of which he is a national'. The Court stated that, as a general principle, there was nothing in the present state of EU law which prevented Member States from insisting on residency as a criterion in conferring the franchise on voters and also for establishing the right to stand for election. Here the Court noted that the European Court of Human Rights had earlier held, in *Melnychenkov v Ukraine* (2004), that the obligation to be resident within national territory in order to be able to vote is a requirement which is not, in itself, unreasonable or arbitrary and which can be justified on several grounds. The ECJ concluded that 'the criterion linked to residence does not appear, in principle, to be inappropriate to determine who has the right to vote and to stand as a candidate in elections to the European Parliament'.

Article 23 TFEU confers certain diplomatic rights on Citizens of the Union. Specifically, Citizens have the right to protection by the diplomatic or consular authorities of other Member States if they are in a non-EU country and there is no diplomatic or consular office from that person's own state. For example, a Latvian national – and hence also a Citizen of the Union – would be able to rely upon protection from a British embassy in any country in the world if there happened to be no Latvian diplomatic presence in that country.

Finally, Art 24 TFEU allows Citizens of the Union to:

- petition the European Parliament
- apply to the Ombudsman established under Art 228 TFEU and
- write to 'any of the institutions' (namely the European Parliament, the European Commission, the Council, the European Council, the ECJ, the European Central Bank and the Court of Auditors) in any of the 'authentic' languages mentioned in Art 55(1) TEU and to receive a reply in the same language.

KEY FACTS

Citizens' political rights	
Citizens of the Union have the right to vote and stand for election in EU Member States other than their home State	Article 22(1) TFEU
Citizens of the Union have diplomatic protection	Article 23 TFEU
Citizens of the Union have the right to write to any of the EU's institutions (in particular the European Parliament) in any of the EU's authentic languages and to receive a reply in the same language	Article 24 TFEU

SAMPLE ESSAY QUESTION

Essay 1: The rights enjoyed by Citizens of the Union and their family members under Articles 18 and 21(1) TFEU, and Directive 2004/38, are extensive - but not unconditional. Critically consider the extent to which Member States can legitimately restrict those rights (other than on grounds of public policy, security or health).

Explain the concept of Citizenship:

- All nationals of the EU's Member States are automatically EU Citizens (Article 20 TFEU)
- This includes dual nationals (*Micheletti*)
- EU Citizenship complements but does not replace nationality
- There is no minimum age limit, ie children can invoke Citizenship rights (*Zhu & Chen*)
- There is no requirement of economic activity (*Martinez Sala*).

Explain the scope of the Citizen's 'family members':

- Identify family members as defined in Directive 2004/38, Article 2(2):
  - Spouse – discuss the case law, eg *Reed, Diatta, Akrich, Metock*
  - Registered partners
  - Descendants under 21 or dependent
  - Dependent relatives in the ascending line
- Consider meaning of 'dependency' – *Lebon, Jia*
- Note that the nationality of each family member is irrelevant
- Note that other relatives, and partners in a durable relationship, may be entitled to join the Citizen, but are not classed as 'family members' (Article 3(2)).

Explain the rights enjoyed by Citizens and their family members:

- The right not to be discriminated against on grounds of nationality (Art 18 TFEU; Directive 2004/38, Art 24)
- The right to free movement and residence in any Member State (Art 21 (1) TFEU). Elaborate on the free movement rights by reference to Directive 2004/38, Arts 4, 5, 6 and 7
- A right of permanent residence after 5 years' continuous residence (Directive 2004/38, Arts 16 and 17)
- Family members – regardless of nationality – have the right to accompany or join the Citizen in the host State, to take up employment or self-employment (Directive 2004/38, Art 23) and to equal treatment *vis-à-vis* host State nationals (Directive 2004/38, Art 24).

Discuss limitations on Citizens' rights

- Citizens seeking residence rights for longer than three months need to be in work, self-employment, in education or have independent financial resources (Directive 2004/38, Art 7)
- Consider why this is
- Member States are entitled to restrict Citizens' access to social benefits, typically by imposing a minimum residence period
- This is justifiable if it aims to ensure that benefit claimants have established a sufficient 'link' with the society of the host State (*Bidar*, *Förster*), subject to proportionality
- Again consider why this is, perhaps to discourage benefit 'tourism'?

Essay 2: Critically consider the extent to which Member States may restrict the free movement of persons (including their own nationals) under EU law on grounds of public policy, public security or public health.

Explain general principles:

- Citizens and their family members' free movement rights can be restricted on grounds of 'public policy', 'public security', or 'public health' (Directive 2004/38, Art 27)
- These grounds must not be used to achieve 'economic ends' (Art 27)
- Policy or security measures must comply with the principle of proportionality (*Oulane*)
- 'Measures' can include: refusal of entry, refusal of exit, expulsion, territorial restrictions
- Must be notification in writing (Art 30)
- Must be able to appeal against, or seek review of, restrictions on movement (Art 31).

Explain the 'personal conduct' requirement

- Policy or security measures must be based 'exclusively' on the individual's 'personal conduct', not on 'considerations of general prevention' (Art 27). Discuss case law, eg *Bonsignore, Calfa, Orfanopoulos & Oliveri*
- Consider the ruling in *Van Duyn* that membership of an organisation may constitute 'personal conduct'.

Explain the scope of the 'public policy' and 'public health' requirements:

- 'Public policy' implies the existence of a genuine and serious threat to the requirements of public policy affecting one of the fundamental interests of society (Art 27)
- Note that Member States must adopt effective measures in order to repress the same conduct on the part of their own nationals (*Adoui & Cornuaille, Jany*)
- Consider the significance of previous criminal convictions – need for evidence of a 'propensity' to re-offend (*R v Bouchereau*)
- Examine the 'public health' derogation – consider meaning of diseases with 'epidemic potential', 'infectious diseases or contagious parasitic diseases'.

Explain the powers of Member States to take expulsion decisions:

- States must take into account various factors, eg how long the individual has resided on its territory, his/her age, state of health, family and economic situation, etc (Art 28 (1))
- Consider meaning of 'serious' grounds of policy or security, required for expulsion of those with permanent residency (Art 28 (2))
- Consider meaning of 'imperative' public security grounds, required for expulsion of those with 10 years' residency, or minors (unless in the child's best interests) (Art 28 (3))
- When will expulsion be in a child's 'best interests'?

Critical considerations:

- Member States cannot refuse entry to, or expel from, national territory their own nationals (*Pereira Roque*), so there is a degree of discrimination inherent in this area of EU law
- The principles found in *Adoui & Cornuaille, Jany* minimise this discrimination
- Also, refusal of exit means that States can restrict the movement of their own nationals (*Jipa*)
- Directive 2004/38, Art 28 (1) acknowledges the problem that deportation of an EU Citizen could involve separation from his/her family, bringing EU law into conflict with the right to family life (European Convention of Human Rights, Art 8)
- Decision in *Van Duyn* helps national authorities to restrict the movement of members of criminal gangs/ terrorist groups, but arguably strains the meaning of 'personal conduct'.

SUMMARY

- Art 20 TFEU establishes 'Citizenship of the Union' for every person holding the nationality of a Member State, including dual nationals (*Micheletti, Collins*). The acquisition of nationality is a matter of national law (*Micheletti, Zhu & Chen*).
- The Citizen need not be economically active. Citizenship rights may be invoked by: the unemployed (*Martínez Sala*); students (*Grzelczyk, D'Hoop, Bidar, Förster*); the retired (*Pusa*); those incapable of working for health reasons (*Tas-Hagen*).
- The age of the Citizen is immaterial. Children can invoke Citizenship status (*Zhu & Chen*).
- Citizens have 'the right to move and reside freely within the territory of the Member States' (Art 21 TFEU), which is directly effective (*Baumbast & R*). Citizens may invoke Art 21 TFEU, in combination with Art 18 TFEU, in order to challenge national legislation which discriminates (directly or indirectly) against nationals of other Member States.
- Citizens may also invoke Art 21 TFEU in order to challenge any national legislation which places them at a 'disadvantage' following the exercise of free movement rights (*Pusa, Tas-Hagen*).
- Citizens must not become 'an unreasonable burden' on the host State (*Grzelczyk*). But this does not mean that Citizens cannot claim financial benefits (*Martínez Sala, D'Hoop, Grzelczyk, Collins, Bidar*). The key word is 'unreasonable'.
- Certain restrictions on Citizens' rights are justifiable if based on 'objective considerations of public interest', do not directly discriminate on grounds of nationality, are suitable and proportionate. One 'objective consideration' is the need to ensure that there is a 'real link' between the claimant and the State (*D'Hoop*).
- Citizens have a range of political rights, e.g. to participate in elections (Art 22 TFEU).
- Under Directive 2004/38, Citizens have a right of 'exit' from their home State (Art 4); a right of 'entry' into the host State (Art 5); a right of residence in the host State for up to 3 months without any conditions or formalities (Art 6). For longer residence periods, the Citizen should either be working, self-employed, financially independent or a student (Art 7).
- Citizens may acquire a right to remain permanently in the host State after 5 years' continuous residence (Art 16). A right of permanent residence may also be acquired on reaching retirement age (after 3 years' residence), or if forced to retire from work as a result of permanent incapacity (Art 17).
- Citizens are entitled to equal treatment with the nationals of that Member State 'within the scope of the Treaty' (Art 24).
- Directive 2004/38 confers rights on a Citizen's 'family members', 'irrespective of their nationality':
  - 'Spouse' refers to genuine marital relationships only (*Reed, Akrich*). It is immaterial where or when the marriage was solemnised (*Metock & Others*). Marital status continues after separation (*Diatta*). The spouse is not obliged to remain in the same accommodation as the Citizen (*Diatta*). Divorce terminates the spouse's status (*Baumbast & R*) but under Directive 2004/38, Art 13, ex-spouses retain residence rights in some situations.
  - 'Registered partners', but only if the legislation of the host Member State treats registered partnerships as equivalent to marriage.
  - 'Descendants' of the Citizen/spouse/partner, if under 21 or 'dependent'. 'Dependence' is a factual issue (*Lebon*).
  - 'Dependent relatives in the ascending line' of the Citizen/spouse/partner. The 'need for material support must exist in the State of origin' (*Jia*).
- Directive 2004/38, Art 3, confers rights of entry and residence on 'other family members', irrespective of their nationality, if 'dependants' or 'members of the household' of the Citizen, or where 'serious health grounds strictly require...

personal care', and on 'the partner with whom the Union citizen has a durable relationship, duly attested'.

- Family members have rights to take up 'employment or self-employment' (Directive 2004/38, Art 23), but only in the same Member State as the Citizen (*Gül, Mattern & Cikotic*), and to 'enjoy equal treatment' with nationals of the host State (Directive 2004/38, Art 24).
- Under Directive 2004/38, Member States may impose 'measures' which restrict free movement on grounds of public policy, public security or public health, such as refusal of entry (*Van Duyn*); refusal of exit (*Jipa*); expulsion (*R v Bouchereau*); territorial restrictions (*Rutili*).
- Although Member States cannot refuse entry to/expel from national territory their own nationals, they are not prevented from refusing entry to/expelling other States' nationals (*Pereira Roque*).
- The concept of 'public policy' must 'be interpreted strictly, so that its scope cannot be determined unilaterally by each Member State' (*Rutili*). 'Public policy' measures require a 'genuine, present and sufficiently serious threat affecting one of the fundamental interests of society' (Directive 2004/38, Art 27(2)). States must be prepared to impose 'repressive' measures on their own nationals before invoking 'public policy' measures (*Adoui & Cornuaille, Jany*).
- Public security implies involvement in espionage, organised crime, or terrorism (*Oteiza Olazabal*).
- Public policy or security measures must be based 'exclusively' on the individual's 'personal conduct', and not on considerations of general prevention (Directive 2004/38, Art 27(2); *Bonsignore, Calfa, Orfanopoulos & Oliveri*). But present membership of an organisation may constitute 'personal conduct' (*Van Duyn*).
- Previous criminal convictions must not 'in themselves' constitute grounds for the taking of measures (Art 27(2)), but may do so if they provide evidence of a 'present threat' (*R v Bouchereau*).
- Measures taken on grounds of public policy or security must comply with the principle of 'proportionality' (Art 27(2); *Oulane*).
- Before seeking expulsion, Member States must take into account how long the individual concerned has resided on its territory; his/her age; state of health; family and economic situation; social and cultural integration into the host Member State; the extent of his/her links with the country of origin (Directive 2004/38, Art 28(1)).
- For individuals with a permanent right of residence, expulsion is only possible on 'serious' grounds of public policy or security (Art 28(2)). Minors, or someone with 10 years' residence, may only be expelled 'on imperative grounds of public security' (Art 28(3)).
- States may take public health measures against those suffering from 'diseases with epidemic potential' as well as 'infectious diseases or contagious parasitic diseases' (Directive 2004/38, Art 29).
- All decisions require notification 'in writing' (Directive 2004/38, Art 30(1)). The individual must be able to appeal and/or seek judicial review of any decision taken against them (Art 31(1)). Persons excluded on public policy or security grounds may apply to have it lifted after three years (Art 32).

Further reading

Articles

Currie, S, 'Accelerated Justice or a Step too Far? Residence Rights of non-EU Family Members and the Court's Ruling In *Metock* (2009) 34 EL Rev 310.

Dautricourt, C & Thomas, S, 'Reverse Discrimination and Free Movement of Persons Under Community Law: All For Ulysses, Nothing For Penelope' (2009) 34 EL Rev 433.

Epiney, A, 'The Scope of Article 12 EC: Some Remarks on the Influence of European Citizenship' (2007) 13 ELJ 611.

Jacobs, F, 'Citizenship of the European Union – A Legal Analysis' (2007) 13 ELJ 591.
Mather, J, 'The Court of Justice and the Union Citizen' (2005) 11 ELJ 722.
O'Brien, C, 'Real Links, Abstract Rights and False Alarms: The Relationship between the ECJ's "Real Link" Case Law and National Solidarity' (2008) 33 EL Rev 643.
Somek, A, 'Solidarity Decomposed: Being and Time in European Citizenship' (2007) 32 EL Rev 787.
Spaventa, E, 'Seeing the Wood Despite the Trees? On the Scope of Union Citizenship and its Constitutional Effects' (2008) 45 CML Rev 13.

12

The free movement of workers

AIMS AND OBJECTIVES

After reading this chapter you should be able to:

- Understand the law relating to the free movement of workers, in particular Article 45 TFEU and Regulation 1612/68
- Understand the meaning and scope of the concept of 'worker'
- Understand the circumstances in which the free movement of workers may be restricted
- Analyse critically the law relating to the free movement of workers
- Apply the law to factual situations involving the free movement of workers in the EU

ARTICLE

'Art 45(1) Freedom of movement for workers shall be secured within the Union.

(2) Such freedom of movement shall entail the abolition of any discrimination based on nationality between workers of the Member States as regards employment, remuneration and other conditions of work and employment.

(3) It shall entail the right, subject to limitations justified on grounds of public policy, public security or public health:

(a) to accept offers of employment actually made;

(b) to move freely within the territory of Member States for this purpose;

(c) to stay in a Member State for the purpose of employment in accordance with the provisions governing the employment of nationals of that State laid down by law, regulation or administrative action;

(d) to remain in the territory of a Member State after having been employed in that State, subject to [Directive 2004/38].

(4) The provisions of this Article shall not apply to employment in the public service.'

12.1 The objectives of Art 45 TFEU

The objectives of Art 45 are, broadly speaking, two-fold:

To allow for workers to move from one EU Member State to another for the purposes of employment

This benefits both individual workers and their employers. Individual workers benefit because they can move from areas of high unemployment and/or low wages to areas of low unemployment and/or higher wages. This is true whether the workers are skilled or not, and whether they possess professional qualifications or not. Readers of this book who are familiar with the TV programme *Auf Wiedersehen, Pet* will recall how the plot of the original series involved British manual workers (bricklayers, plasterers etc) moving from the UK (where their skills were not in high demand) to Germany, where their skills were put to good use working on building sites.

A real-life example of people exploiting EU rules on the free movement of workers is provided by the huge numbers of professional footballers from across the EU who have come to play in the English Premiership and Championship, particularly since the *Bosman* ruling of December 1995, which applied Art 45 to professional sport. The wages on offer at Premiership clubs – generated by large attendances at bigger capacity grounds, by TV and satellite broadcasting revenue and by highly lucrative sponsorship deals – dwarf those on offer in most other European leagues (the obvious exceptions being Italy and Spain). This explains why so many top French players, in particular, have come to England in recent years; it also explains who so few English players have moved in the opposite direction. Again, the exception is Spain, specifically Real Madrid, who signed England captain David Beckham from Manchester United in 2003, Michael Owen from Liverpool and Jonathan Woodgate from Newcastle United in 2004. All of these players were 'workers' who invoked rights under Art 45 to go from the UK to play – or, rather, work – in Spain.

Employers also benefit because they have a greater choice of potential workers to choose from. This may mean they can employ workers with better qualifications or greater experience than they otherwise would be able to if restricted to workers from the same Member State. Workers from states where there are relatively low average wages may be prepared to move to other states to take on unskilled work, or work anti-social hours (which national workers may be unwilling to do) and still receive better salaries than they would had they stayed at home. An influx of foreign workers can also help resolve 'skills shortages'. At the time of the EU's expansion in May 2004 it was widely reported in the British media that highly skilled engineers and scientists from central and eastern Europe (Poland in particular) were planning on coming to the UK to work. This benefits the individual workers (average wages in the UK being much higher than those in Poland), and their employers, who were struggling to find suitably qualified British engineers and scientists.

To prohibit discrimination on grounds of nationality against workers who have moved

Article 45(2) prohibits Member States, through legislation, and employers, through their terms and conditions of employment, from discriminating against workers who have moved under Art 45(1). After all, there would be a massive disincentive to move if employers were free openly to discriminate against migrant workers. The dual objectives of Art 45 were neatly summarised by the ECJ in the case of *Lyyski* (Case C–40/05) [2007] ECR I–99, when the ECJ stated that:

JUDGMENT

> 'The Treaty provisions relating to freedom of movement for persons are intended to facilitate the pursuit by [Union Citizens] of occupational activities of all kinds throughout the [Union], and preclude measures which might place [Union Citizens] at a disadvantage when they wish to pursue an economic activity in the territory of another Member State.'

12.2 The scope of Art 45

Article 45(1) provides that 'Freedom of movement for workers shall be secured within the Union'. This means that workers are (subject to very narrowly defined derogations) free to move from one Member State to another without restriction. The ECJ offered some guidance on this in *Graf* (Case C–190/98) [2000] ECR I–493:

CASE EXAMPLE

Graf (Case C–190/98) [2000] ECR I–493

Under Austrian law, workers who had worked a minimum three years with the same employer were entitled to a termination payment. However, that payment was forfeited if the employee resigned, left prematurely for no important reason or bore responsibility for his premature dismissal. Volker Graf had worked for the same Austrian company for three and a half years when he resigned in order to go to work for a German company. His employers refused to pay up. When he challenged this, arguing Art 45, they responded that the refusal to pay him did not constitute a restriction on his mobility. The ECJ agreed: the Austrian legislation imposed no obstacle to the free movement of workers.

The Court stated:

JUDGMENT

'Provisions which, even if they are applicable without distinction, preclude or deter a national of a Member State from leaving his country of origin in order to exercise his right to freedom of movement therefore constitute an obstacle to that freedom. However, in order to be capable of constituting such an obstacle, *they must affect access of workers to the labour market*.'

Article 45(2) states that, having moved, workers are entitled not to be discriminated against in terms of nationality. This provision is directly effective and can be enforced in national courts in order to challenge discriminatory national legislation, or to challenge discriminatory employment practices. Article 45(2) even applies to private employers, as *Angonese* (Case C–281/98) [2000] ECR I–4139 demonstrates:

CASE EXAMPLE

Angonese (Case C–281/98) [2000] ECR I–4139

Roman Angonese, an Italian national, spoke fluent German as well as Italian. He also spoke English, Polish and Slovene. In July 1997 he applied for a job with a bank in the northern Italian city of Bolzano. One of the conditions of entry was possession of a special certificate issued in Bolzano which confirmed bilingualism in German and Italian. Angonese, who had studied languages and translation for a number of years at the University of Vienna, asked for his degree certificate to be accepted instead of the Bolzano bilingualism certificate. The bank refused. Angonese challenged this, relying upon Art 45(2). The ECJ agreed that the bank's insistence on accepting only the certificate issued in Bolzano constituted a form of discrimination based on nationality and was therefore prohibited by Art 45(2).

The ECJ has held that Art 45(2) can also be invoked by employers. In *Innovative Technology Center* (Case C–208/05) [2007] ECR I–181, the Court decided that the right of workers to be engaged and employed without discrimination necessarily entailed, as a corollary, an employer's entitlement to engage them without discrimination. That right also entailed, as a further corollary, the right of intermediaries, such as recruitment agencies, to assist work-seekers in finding employment. Hence, provisions of German law, under which the Federal Employment Agency was obliged to pay recruitment agencies for finding work for unemployed people – but only if the employment was based in Germany – constituted a *prima facie* infringement of Art 45(2).

Article 45(2) applies throughout the territories of the Member States and even extends beyond the EU itself, to workers who, although situated outside the geographical scope of the EU, have an employment relationship with their employer which is founded within one of the Member States or where the relationship retained a 'sufficiently close link' with the EU. In *SARL Prodest* (Case 237/83) [1984] ECR 3153 the ECJ ruled that:

JUDGMENT

'The principle of non-discrimination applies to the case of a national of a Member State who is employed by an undertaking of another Member State even during a period in which the employee temporarily works outside the territory of the [EU].'

KEY FACTS

The Scope of Art 45

Workers are entitled to 'free movement' in the EU	Article 45(1) TFEU
Any provisions of national legislation which 'preclude or deter' a worker from exercising their free movement rights are prohibited	*Graf* (2000)
Workers are entitled not to be discriminated against on grounds of nationality	Article 45(2) TFEU
The entitlement to non-discrimination can be enforced against employers in order to challenge discriminatory provisions in employment contracts	*Angonese* (2000)
The non-discrimination provision can also be invoked by employers	*Innovative Technology Center* (2007)

12.3 The definition of 'worker'

The definition of 'worker' has the same meaning in all EU Member States because, otherwise, Member States could define 'worker' in such a way as to prevent the access of migrant workers (*Levin* (Case 53/81) [1982] ECR 1035). However, the word is not defined in any EU legislation. The ECJ has therefore been called upon in several cases to explain the meaning and scope of the 'worker' concept. In *Lawrie-Blum* (Case 66/85) [1986] ECR 2121, the ECJ noted that the free movement of workers was a fundamental principle, and it therefore had to be defined widely. It then stated:

JUDGMENT

'Objectively defined, a "worker" is a person who is obliged to provide services to another in return for monetary reward and who is subject to the direction or control of the other person as regards the way in which the work is done … The essential feature of an employment relationship is that for a certain period of time a person performs services for and under the direction of another in return for which he receives remuneration.'

The employer need not necessarily be a company of any particular nationality. EU nationals employed by international organisations based in another EU Member State are entitled to the protection afforded by Art 45:

- *Echternach* (Case 389/87) [1989] ECR 723 – German national employed by the European Space Agency in Belgium
- *Schmid* (Case C–310/91) [1993] ECR I–3011 – German national employed by Eurocontrol (the European Organisation for the Safety of Air Navigation) in Belgium
- *Ferlini* (Case C–411/98) [2000] ECR I–8081 – Italian national employed at the European Commission in Luxembourg

- *My* (Case C–293/03) [2004] ECR I–12013 – Italian national employed at the Council of the European Union in Brussels, Belgium
- *Öberg* (Case C–185/04) [2006] ECR I–1453 – Swedish national employed at the European Court of Justice in Luxembourg
- *Rockler* (Case C–137/04) [2006] ECR I–1441 – Swedish national employed at the European Commission in Brussels, Belgium
- *Alevizos* (Case C–392/05) [2007] ECR I–3505 – Greek national and member of the Greek Air Force, seconded to the North Atlantic Treaty Organisation (NATO) in Italy.

12.3.1 Part-time and low-paid employees

The ECJ has been very flexible here. Some activity of an economic nature, even if it is poorly paid, qualifies an individual as a 'worker'. On the question of whether part-time workers are covered, the ECJ has stated (*Levin* (1982):

JUDGMENT

'Whilst part-time employment is not excluded from the field of application of the rules on freedom of movement for workers, those rules cover only the pursuit of effective and genuine activities, to the exclusion of activities on such a small scale as to be regarded as marginal and ancillary.'

The ECJ had consistently refused to lay down a rule setting any sort of **quantitative threshold** of work, either in terms of the number of hours per week or in terms of a minimum salary. Rather, what matters to the ECJ is that a basic **qualitative threshold** of work has been met.

CASE EXAMPLE

Levin (Case 53/81) [1982] ECR 1035

Mrs Levin, a British national, had gone to the Netherlands with her South African husband. It seems that the couple were financially independent and simply wanted to live there. The authorities were reluctant to allow this, so Mrs Levin took work as a chambermaid in a Dutch hotel, working 20 hours a week for which she was paid the equivalent of £25. However, this meant that her wages were below the Dutch minimum wage and so the authorities refused to regard her as a 'worker' for the purposes of EU law. When Mrs Levin challenged this, the ECJ held that whether or not a person was a 'worker' was not a question of how much money they earned but whether or not it was 'genuine'. The ECJ also rejected the argument that Mrs Levin was not a 'worker' because she had taken the chambermaid job simply to qualify for 'worker' status. The Court held that motivation was immaterial: the fact of employment is what mattered.

The fact that a worker has to supplement his income in order to subsist is also irrelevant – thereby narrowing what the ECJ suggested in *Levin* (1982): that employment must be 'effective'. This principle is clearly illustrated in *Kempf* (Case 139/85) [1986] ECR 1741.

CASE EXAMPLE

Kempf (Case 139/85) [1986] ECR 1741

Kempf, a German national, was working as a music teacher in the Netherlands. However, he was only working for 12 hours a week. His income was not enough to live on, so he claimed Dutch supplementary benefit (sickness benefit as well as more general income support). In 1981 he applied for a Dutch residence permit. This was refused on the ground that his income was insufficient to support himself. Kempf challenged this. The ECJ held that the fact that Kempf claimed financial assistance in order to supplement the income he received from teaching activities did not exclude him from the provisions of Art 45.

The Court stated:

JUDGMENT

'A person in effective and genuine part-time employment cannot be excluded from [Art 45] merely because the remuneration he derives from it is below the level of the minimum means of subsistence and he seeks to supplement it by other lawful means of subsistence. In that regard it is irrelevant whether those supplementary means of subsistence are derived from property or from the employment of a member of his family … or whether, as in this instance, they are obtained from financial assistance drawn from the public funds of the member state in which he resides, provided that the effective and genuine nature of his work is established.'

Although the ECJ has been generous with its definition of 'worker', the principle will not be taken to extremes. Where a person's activities can be described as 'marginal and ancillary', they will not be classed as a 'worker'. The ECJ has subsequently stated that the duration of the activity performed is relevant in determining whether activities amount to genuine employment or are simply marginal and ancillary (*Raulin* (Case C–357/89) [1992] ECR I–1027).

In *Ninni-Orasche* (Case C–413/01) [2003] ECR I–13187, the ECJ explicitly refused to hold that the fact that an Italian national had been employed for two and a half months over a period of three years in Austria automatically excluded her from the scope of Art 45. Ultimately, whether or not she was a 'worker' was a question of fact for the national court, applying the 'effective and genuine activities' test. The ECJ stated:

JUDGMENT

'The fact that a national of a Member State has worked for a temporary period of 2½ months in the territory of another Member State, of which he is not a national, can confer on him the status of a worker within the meaning of [Art 45] provided that the activity performed as an employed person is not purely marginal and ancillary.'

Two cases have raised questions regarding whether or not work was 'genuine'. In *Bettray* (Case 344/87) [1989] ECR 1621, involving a German national who was living in the Netherlands, the ECJ held that activities described as 'social employment' which were carried out as part of a State-sponsored drug rehabilitation programme, did not constitute genuine employment. However, in *Trojani* (Case C–456/02) [2004] ECR I–7573, the ECJ took a more generous view with what was described as 'a personal socio-occupational reintegration programme'. Although the ECJ distinguished *Bettray* (1989), it conceded that the ultimate decision whether or not a person qualified as a worker was a question for the national court.

CASE EXAMPLE

Trojani (Case C–456/02) [2004] ECR I-7573

Michel Trojani, a French national, had gone to live in Belgium in 2000. He lived for a time on a campsite and later stayed in a youth hostel. By early 2002 he was living in a Salvation Army hostel, and in return for board and lodging and 'some pocket money' he did 'various jobs for about 30 hours per week as part of a personal socio-occupational reintegration programme'. The ECJ held that this was, in principle, capable of being regarded as falling within the scope of Art 45, although ultimately it was a question for the national court.

The Court stated:

JUDGMENT

'Neither the *sui generis* nature of the employment relationship under national law, nor the level of productivity of the person concerned, the origin of the funds from which the remuneration is paid or the limited amount of the remuneration can have any consequence in regard to whether or not the person is a "worker" for the purposes of [EU] law ... The national court must ascertain whether the services actually performed are capable of being regarded as forming part of the normal labour market.'

12.3.2 Trainees

Students undertaking vocational training are 'workers'. In *Lawrie-Blum* (1986), involving a British woman who had applied to become a trainee teacher in Germany, the ECJ held:

JUDGMENT

'The fact that teachers' preparatory service, like apprenticeships in other occupations, may be regarded as practical preparation directly related to the actual pursuit of the occupation in point is not a bar to the application of [Art 45] if the service is performed under the conditions of an activity as an employed person ... the fact that trainee teachers give lessons for only a few hours a week and are paid remuneration below the starting salary of a qualified teacher does not prevent them from being regarded as workers.'

Lawrie-Blum (1986) was followed in *Bernini* (Case C–3/90) [1992] ECR I–1071, involving an Italian woman working as a trainee in a furniture factory in the Netherlands.

More recently, in *Kranemann* (Case C–109/04) [2005] ECR I–2421, the ECJ was asked whether a trainee lawyer qualified as a 'worker'. The case involved a German national who had completed his legal education in Germany and was spending part of his legal training with a law firm in London. The ECJ had no doubt that the trainee was a 'worker':

JUDGMENT

'As regards the activities carried out by trainee lawyers ... such trainees are required to apply in practice the legal knowledge acquired during their course of study and thus make a contribution, under the guidance of the employer providing them with training, to that employer's activities and trainees receive payment in the form of a maintenance allowance for the duration of their training ... Such an employment relationship cannot fall outside the scope of [Article 45] merely because the allowance paid to trainees constitutes only assistance allowing them to meet their minimum needs ... Given that trainee lawyers carry out genuine and effective activity as an employed person they must be considered to be workers within the meaning of [Article 45].'

12.3.3 Work-seekers

Could Art 45 be interpreted so as to give work-seekers protection? A literal reading of Art 45(3) would seem to indicate not, as it states that the freedom of movement for workers includes the right 'to accept offers of employment actually made'. However, the ECJ very rarely adopts a literal reading of EU legislation, preferring to take a purposive approach (favouring any interpretation which promotes free movement over one which inhibits it). Hence, in *Antonissen* (Case C–292/89) [1991] ECR I–745, the ECJ held that work-seekers did have certain rights:

JUDGMENT

'[Article 45(3)] must be interpreted as enumerating, in a non-exhaustive way, certain rights benefiting nationals of Member States in the context of the free movement of workers … that freedom also entails the right for nationals of Member States to move freely within the territory of the other Member States and to stay there for the purposes of seeking employment.'

The ECJ added that migrant nationals seeking employment in other EU Member States had to be able to 'appraise themselves … of offers of employment' and to take the 'necessary steps in order to be engaged'. Work-seekers could not, therefore, be deported as long as they could provide evidence that they were (a) continuing to seek employment and (b) had genuine chances of becoming employed.

CASE EXAMPLE

Antonissen (Case C–292/89) [1991] ECR I–745

Gustaff Antonissen, a Belgian national, challenged a deportation order that had been made against him following his conviction at Liverpool Crown Court for possession of cocaine. He had been looking for work in the UK for over two years, without success. Under UK law, deportation of unemployed people was permitted after six months. The Immigration Appeal Tribunal referred to the ECJ the question of the compatibility of this rule with EU law on the free movement of workers. The Court held that work-seekers were protected by EU law, but not indefinitely. The ECJ added that the six-month limit was not insufficient to enable work-seekers to appraise themselves of the work situation and, therefore, did 'not jeopardise the effectiveness of the principles of free movement'. However, that time limit could be extended if the person concerned was still actively work-seeking.

Work-seekers and social benefits

In *Lebon* (Case 316/85) [1987] ECR 2811, the ECJ held that persons seeking work have no right to 'social and tax advantages' under Art 7(2) of Regulation 1612/68. That ruling has now been overturned by the ECJ in *Collins* (Case C–138/02) [2004] ECR I–2703. The ECJ held that the introduction of the concept of 'Citizenship' in 1993 meant that the ruling in *Lebon* (1987) could no longer be relied upon. The Court held that a work-seeker could therefore claim entitlement to certain social benefits, such as job-seeker's allowance. That does not guarantee they will receive those benefits, however. In *Collins*, the issue was whether a particular benefit for unemployed people in the UK could be made subject to a requirement of 'habitual residence'. The ECJ held that this requirement was potentially indirectly discriminatory against foreign nationals, on the basis that UK nationals would be more likely to satisfy it, but it was nevertheless justifiable. The Court stated that it 'may be regarded as legitimate for a Member State to grant such an allowance only after it has been possible to establish that a genuine link exists between the person seeking work and the employment market of that State'.

However, the 'habitual residence' test was subject to the 'proportionality' principle. The ECJ held that its application by the national authorities 'must rest on clear criteria known in advance and provision must be made for the possibility of a means of redress of a judicial nature'. Finally, any period of residence laid down in the national rules 'must not exceed what is necessary in order for the national authorities to be able to satisfy themselves that the person concerned is genuinely seeking work in the employment market of the host Member State'.

CASE EXAMPLE

Collins (Case C–138/02) [2004] ECR I–2703

Brian Collins, of dual US–Irish nationality, arrived in the UK in May 1998 to look for work. In June, he applied for job-seeker's allowance, a benefit under the Jobseekers Act 1995. In July, his application was refused on the ground that he was not 'habitually resident' in the UK as required by the Jobseekers' Allowance Regulations 1996. Although EU nationals who were 'workers' or who had a right of residence under Directive 68/360 (see below) were exempted from that requirement, neither exemption applied to Collins. He challenged this. The ECJ held that, although Collins was a work-seeker, following *Antonissen* (1991), he was protected from all discrimination based on nationality within the scope of EU law by Art 18 TFEU. The limitation on entitlement to 'social and tax advantages' imposed by *Lebon* (1987) was no longer permissible following the introduction of EU citizenship provisions in 1993. The requirement of 'habitual residence' constituted 'indirect' discrimination, although it was objectively justifiable.

12.3.4 The previously employed

The ECJ has held that persons who have lost their job but are capable of taking another are still within the definition of 'worker'. In *Leclere and Deaconescu* (Case C–43/99) [2001] ECR I–4265 the ECJ stated:

JUDGMENT

'Once the employment relationship has ended, the person concerned as a rule loses his status of worker, although that status may produce certain effects after the relationship has ended, and a person who is genuinely seeking work must also be classified as a worker.'

This is a remarkable statement – a person who is seeking work is, clearly, not actually working. However, the Court says that such a person is nevertheless to be 'classified' as a worker. It appears that this statement only applies to those persons who have at one time been workers for the purposes of Art 45. Those people who have never worked – such as the claimants in *Antonissen* (1991) and *Collins* (2004) – remain in the pure 'work-seekers' category.

12.3.5 Frontier workers

It is obvious from an examination of all of the cases above that Art 45 applies when a person moves from his or her 'home' State to work (or at least look for work) in another Member State. However, Art 45 also applies to the situation where a person lives in their 'home' State but works in a neighbouring State, effectively commuting to work across a national border. An example is provided by *Geven* (Case C–213/05) [2007] ECR I–6347, in which a Dutch national, although living in her 'home' State of the Netherlands, commuted to work in Germany. Such a person is known as a 'frontier worker'.

Subsequently, the ECJ was asked whether Art 45 applies in a less obvious 'frontier' situation, namely when a person has found employment in his or her 'home' State, but then moves their residence to another State, and commutes from there to their 'home' State to work. The cases are:

- *Hartmann* (Case C–212/05) [2007] ECR I–6303 – a German national, employed by the Post Office in Germany, moved to Austria to live but continued working in Germany.
- *Hendrix* (Case C–287/05) [2007] ECR I–6909 – a Dutch national, employed at a DIY store in the Netherlands, moved to Belgium to live but continued working in the Netherlands.

In both cases, the ECJ confirmed that Art 45 applied on these facts. In *Hartmann*, confirmed in *Hendrix*, the Court stated that:

JUDGMENT

'A national of a Member State who, while maintaining his employment in that State, has transferred his residence to another Member State and has since then carried on his occupation as a frontier worker can claim the status of migrant worker.'

The case of *Hartmann* will be examined in more detail below, in the section dealing with 'social and tax advantages'.

KEY FACTS

The definition of 'worker'

The word 'worker' has an EU-wide definition. It requires the provision of services, under the direction or control of another person, in return for remuneration	*Lawrie-Blum* (1986)
Part-time and low-paid employees are 'workers' provided they pursue 'effective and genuine activities'	*Levin* (1982), *Kempf* (1986), *Ninni-Orasche* (2003), *Trojani* (2004)
Trainees are 'workers'	*Lawrie-Blum, Bernini* (1992), *Kranemann* (2005)
Work-seekers are also entitled to protection under Art 45, provided they are actively seeking work and have genuine chances of finding work	*Antonissen* (1991), *Collins* (2004)
Former workers who are seeking re-employment must be 'classified' as a worker	*Leclere & Deaconescu* (2001)
Frontier workers who live in one State and commute to work in another are also regarded as 'workers' under Art 45	*Geven* (2007), *Hartmann* (2007), *Hendrix* (2007)

12.4 Equality in social and welfare provisions and Regulation 1612/68

Regulation 1612/68 was passed in order to implement Art 45(2) and (3). The preamble to the Regulation states that the purpose of the free movement provisions, as well as rights of entry and residence, is to abolish 'discrimination based on nationality … as regards employment, remuneration and other conditions of work and employment'. It also requires equality of treatment in 'all matters relating to the actual pursuit of activities as employed persons', and that 'obstacles to the mobility of workers shall be eliminated'.

12.4.1 Eligibility for employment: Arts 3 and 4

ARTICLE

'Art 3(1) Under this Regulation, provisions laid down by law, regulation or administrative action or administrative practices of a Member State shall not apply:

- where they limit application for and offers of employment, or the right of foreign nationals to take up and pursue employment or subject these to conditions not applicable in respect of their own nationals; or

- where, though applicable irrespective of nationality, their exclusive or principal aim or effect is to keep nationals of other Member States away from the employment offered.

This provision shall not apply to conditions relating to linguistic knowledge required by reason of the nature of the post to be filled.'

Linguistic knowledge

The proviso to Art 3(1) was invoked in the context of school teachers in *Groener v Minister for Education* (Case 379/87) [1989] ECR 3967:

CASE EXAMPLE

Groener v Minister for Education (Case 379/87) [1989] ECR 3967

Anita Groener, a Dutch national, applied for a job teaching art at the College of Marketing and Design in Dublin. Even though the classes were to be taught in English, Irish law requires all teachers to have a certificate of proficiency in Irish which, under the Irish Constitution, is the national and first official language of Ireland. Miss Groener failed a proficiency test in Irish and was thus denied the job. She appealed and the case was referred to the ECJ. The Court held that the Irish law was justified under Art 3(1). Language was an important aspect of any country's culture and identity, although this was only the case provided that it was not being used as a means of discriminating against non-Irish nationals.

The Court stated:

JUDGMENT

'Teachers have an essential role to play, not only through the teaching which they provide but also by their participation in the daily life of the school and the privileged relationship which they have with their pupils. In those circumstances, it is not unreasonable to require them to have some knowledge of the first national language.'

ARTICLE

'Art 4(1) Provisions laid down by law, regulation or administrative action of the Member States which restrict by number or percentage the employment of foreign nationals in any undertaking, branch of activity or region, or at a national level, shall not apply to nationals of the other Member States.'

Article 4(1) was infringed in *Commission v France* (Case 167/73) [1974] ECR 359, where French legislation, the *Code du Travail Maritime 1926*, imposed a ratio of 3:1 in favour of Frenchmen for the crew of French merchant ships. It was also used in *Bosman* (Case C–415/93) [1995] ECR I–4921, to challenge what was known as the '3+2' rule. This case is examined in the section on sport, below.

12.4.2 Article 7(1) – prohibition of discrimination in employment

ARTICLE

'Art 7(1) A worker who is a national of a Member State may not, in the territory of another Member State, be treated differently from national workers by reason of his nationality in respect of any conditions of employment and work, in particular as regards remuneration, dismissal, and should he become unemployed, reinstatement or re-employment.'

Discrimination comes in two forms: direct and indirect. Both are prohibited, although either form of discrimination could be exempted in two circumstances:

- by Art 45(3), which deals with derogations justified on grounds of 'public policy, public security or public health' (discussed in the previous chapter)
- by Art 45(4), which deals with employment in the 'public service'(discussed below).

Apart from that, however, direct discrimination cannot be justified. Indirect discrimination could be justified on the basis that it was necessary to satisfy some overriding national interest (this is discussed below – see section 12.7).

Direct discrimination

National legislation which, on its face, discriminates against workers because of their nationality, is clearly contrary to Art 45(2). For example, in order to join the British Army (combat units), applicants will be eligible only if they are a British citizen, an Irish citizen or a citizen of an independent Commonwealth country. These nationality criteria clearly directly discriminate against nationals of the 25 EU Member States other than the UK and Ireland and hence are a *prima facie* breach of Art 45(2). However, they would be exempted under Art 45(4).

Indirect discrimination

National rules which are not directly discriminatory (in that they appear on their face to apply regardless of nationality) may nevertheless be in breach of Art 45(2), if the effect of those rules is to discriminate either in favour of that state's nationals or against nationals of other states. *O'Flynn v Adjudication Officer* (Case C–237/94) [1996] ECR I–2617 provides an example.

CASE EXAMPLE

O'Flynn v Adjudication Officer (Case C–237/94) [1996] ECR I–2617

UK social security legislation provided for a benefit to cover the cost of burial or cremation of deceased persons incurred by the person taking responsibility for the arrangements – but only if the burial had taken place in the UK. O'Flynn, an Irish national working in the UK, was denied this benefit which he claimed for the cost of his father's burial because that was to take place in Ireland. The ECJ found that a greater proportion of UK nationals than nationals of other EU Member States would satisfy the burial requirement and thus it was indirectly discriminatory.

In *O'Flynn*, the ECJ explained the sort of national rules which may be found to be indirectly discriminatory:

JUDGMENT

'Conditions imposed by national law must be regarded as indirectly discriminatory where, although applicable irrespective of nationality, they affect essentially migrant workers or the great majority of those affected are migrant workers, where they are indistinctly applicable but can more easily be satisfied by national workers than by migrant workers, or where there is a risk that they may operate to the particular detriment of migrant workers ... It is not necessary in this respect to find that the provision in question does in practice affect a substantially higher proportion of migrant workers. It is sufficient that it is liable to have such an effect.'

Indirect discrimination was found in the following cases:

- *Sotgiu v Deutsche Bundespost* (Case 152/73) [1974] ECR 153 – the German Post Office paid a separation allowance to all employees forced by work to live away from their families. 10 DM per day was paid to workers whose family home was in Germany; 7.5

DM per day was paid to all other employees. The ECJ found that German nationals were far more likely to qualify for the higher allowance than migrant workers.

- *Alluè & Coonan* (Case 33/88) [1989] ECR 1591 – Italian legislation provided that foreign-language assistants could only be employed on year-long contracts. No such limits were imposed on other university workers. Evidence showed that 75 per cent of foreign-language assistants in Italian universities were from outside Italy.
- *Scholz* (Case C–419/92) [1994] ECR I–505 – the recruitment procedure adopted by the University of Cagliari in Italy took account of each candidate's previous public-sector employment – but only if it had been in Italy. The ECJ found that most Italians would satisfy this criterion but only a minority of migrant workers.
- *Schöning-Kougebetopoulou* (Case C–15/96) [1998] ECR I–47 – German legislation conferred automatic promotion on public-sector workers (such as health care workers) after eight years' employment – but only if that employment had been in Germany. The ECJ found that most Germans would satisfy this criterion but only a minority of migrant workers.
- *Köbler v Austria* (Case C–224/01) [2003] ECR I–10239 – Austrian legislation conferred a special length-of-service increment on professors who had completed 15 years' service in Austrian universities. The ECJ found that most Austrian professors would satisfy this criterion but only a minority of professors from other Member States.

Note: The German deutschmark (DM) ceased to be legal tender when the single European currency was introduced in 2002.

12.4.3 Article 7(2) – 'social and tax advantages'

Article 7(2) provides that the worker 'shall enjoy the same social and tax advantages as national workers'. Article 7(2) has been defined very widely, as the case of *Fiorini v SNCF* (Case 32/75) [1975] ECR 1085 demonstrates.

CASE EXAMPLE

Fiorini v SNCF (Case 32/75) [1975] ECR 1085

Anita Fiorini was the widow of an Italian national, Euginio Fiorini, who had worked in France since 1962 but had been killed in an industrial accident in 1968. Anita, who decided to stay in France with her four children, had never been employed. She claimed entitlement to reduced rail travel, which was granted to large families in France. Initially, her claim was refused by the French authorities, who restricted Art 7(2) to advantages granted to citizens within the ambit of work as employed persons. Mrs Fiorini appealed and the case was referred to the ECJ, which held that Art 7(2) covered **all** social and tax advantages, whether or not attached to contracts of employment. These rights continued even after the worker's death and so Mrs Fiorini was entitled to the rail travel reduction.

The Court stated:

JUDGMENT

'The reference to "social advantages" in Article 7(2) cannot be interpreted restrictively. It therefore follows that, in view of the equality of treatment which the provision seeks to achieve, the substantive area of application must be delineated so as to include *all* social and tax advantages, whether or not attached to the contract of employment.'

In *Even* (Case 207/78) [1979] ECR 2019 the ECJ defined 'social advantages' as follows:

JUDGMENT

'Those which, whether or not linked to a contract of employment, are generally granted to national workers primarily because of their objective status as workers, or by virtue of the mere fact of their residence on national territory and the extension of which to workers who are nationals of other member countries therefore seems suitable to facilitate their mobility within the [Union].'

This definition has been employed in many subsequent cases, mostly involving entitlement to state benefits. However, such is the width of the interpretation given to Art 7(2) that it has extended into a number of unexpected areas:

- the right to have a trial conducted in a particular language (*Mutsch* (Case 137/84) [1985] ECR 2681)
- the right to reside with an unmarried companion (*Reed* (Case 59/85) [1986] ECR 1283)
- the right to funding and maintenance to pursue full-time education (*Lair* (Case 39/86) [1988] ECR 3161).

Funding and maintenance for education

Lair established the proposition that Art 7(2) could be relied upon by a migrant worker to claim funding and maintenance to pursue full-time education. The rule established in *Lair* is controversial, as it generally entails the worker giving up their status as worker in order to pursue the course of full-time education. Hence, the ECJ has imposed limitations.

CASE EXAMPLE

Lair (Case 39/86) [1988] ECR 3161

Sylvie Lair, a French national, had spent over five years in Germany, working intermittently, with spells of involuntary unemployment, before securing a place at Hanover University to study languages and literature. She claimed a maintenance grant. This was rejected on the basis that she had not been employed in Germany for at least five years prior to enrolment, a condition applicable only to foreigners. Sylvie challenged this refusal. The ECJ held that, provided she was a 'worker', she was entitled to a grant by virtue of Art 7(2). Germany's five-year employment requirement for foreigners was clearly discriminatory and contrary to Art 7(2). Applying this, Sylvie was therefore entitled to a grant provided that she could show that her course was connected in some way to her previous employment.

The Court stated:

JUDGMENT

'Migrant workers are guaranteed certain rights linked to the status of "worker" even when they are no longer in an employment relationship. In the field of grants for university education, such a link between the status of "worker" and a grant awarded for maintenance and training with a view to the pursuit of university studies does, however, presuppose some continuity between the previous occupational activity and the course of study; there must be a relationship between the purpose of the studies and the previous occupational activity. Such continuity may not, however, be required where a migrant has involuntarily become unemployed and is obliged by conditions on the job market to undertake occupational retraining in another field of activity.'

Thus, in order for a migrant worker to be entitled for funding and/or maintenance grants to pursue education, there must be 'some continuity' unless the worker became 'involuntarily' unemployed.

Continuity

In the following cases the element of continuity was satisfied:

- *Matteucci* (Case 235/87) [1988] ECR 5589 – period of employment as a teacher of eurythmics; followed by a singing and voice-training course.
- *Bernini* (1992) – period of employment in design and planning department of a furniture factory; followed by architectural studies degree.

In *Lair*, the ECJ referred to 'the previous occupational activity', ie the singular, suggesting that the migrant worker's most recent employment had to be connected to the course of study. However, the ECJ has relaxed this requirement. In *Raulin* (Case C–357/89) [1992] ECR I–1027, the ECJ stated that it was 'for the national court to assess whether *all the occupational activities* previously exercised in the host Member State, regardless of whether or not they were interrupted by periods of training or retraining, bear a relationship to the studies in question'.

Involuntary unemployment

This point was addressed by the ECJ in *Ninni-Orasche* (2004), where an Italian worker had applied for a maintenance grant for a higher education course in languages at an Austrian university after losing her job as a waitress. There was clearly no 'continuity', so her claim depended entirely on her being 'involuntarily' unemployed. Her waitressing job had been on a fixed-term basis, and she had known this from the outset. It was argued that, because she knew before she took the job that she would subsequently lose it, her unemployment was in a sense chosen and thus 'voluntary'. The ECJ rejected this:

JUDGMENT

> 'While a contract of employment is generally the result of negotiations, it is nonetheless true that cases in which the worker has no influence over the term and type of contract of employment which he may conclude with an employer are not unusual … in some occupations it is common practice to conclude fixed-term contracts of employment and there are various reasons for this such as the seasonal nature of the work, the fact that the relevant market is sensitive to economic fluctuations or the possible inflexibility of national employment law.'

Studying abroad

Assuming that the above conditions are satisfied, however, there are no other restrictions. Article 7(2) may even be relied upon to claim funding for migrant workers to study abroad. This point was made in *Matteucci* (1988), where the ECJ stated:

JUDGMENT

> 'Article 7(2) lays down a general rule which imposes responsibility in the social sphere on each Member State with regard to every worker who is a national of another Member State and established in its territory as far as equality of treatment with national workers is concerned. Consequently, where a Member State gives its national workers the opportunity of pursuing training provided in another Member State, that opportunity must be extended to [Union] workers established in its territory.'

This principle applies even if it means the migrant worker returning to their home State! This point was established in *Di Leo* (1990), involving Art 12 of Regulation 1612/68. The daughter of an Italian national working in Germany wanted to study medicine at the University of Sienna in Italy. German legislation made provision for grants for Germans who wished to study abroad. This was extended to the children of non-Germans working in Germany, provided that the child did not return to their home State. The ECJ held that this proviso was contrary to Art 12. *Di Leo* (1990) was then applied to Art 7(2) in *Bernini* (1992):

CASE EXAMPLE

Bernini (Case C–3/90) [1992] ECR I–1071

Mrs Bernini, an Italian national who had lived in the Netherlands since she was aged two, spent 10 weeks as a salaried trainee in the design and planning department of a furniture factory in Haarlem, in the Netherlands. She then began a course of architectural studies at the University of Naples in Italy. She applied to the Dutch Education Ministry for funding but this was rejected on various grounds. She claimed to be a 'worker' and therefore entitled to the funding under Art 7(2) of Regulation 1612/68. The ECJ held that, if she was a worker (that being a question for the national court), then the question of whether she was entitled to funding required proof that a link existed between her work and her proposed course, following *Lair* (1988). However, the fact that the course was to be studied abroad was irrelevant, following *Matteucci* (1988), as was the fact that she was to be studying in her home State, following *Di Leo* (1990). It all depended simply on whether Dutch nationals would be entitled to funding from the Dutch authorities to study in Italy.

The Court stated:

JUDGMENT

'Once a Member State offers to its national workers grants to pursue studies in another Member State, that opportunity must be extended to [Union] workers established within its territory ... the fact that the studies are pursued in the State of which the person concerned is a national is without significance in this connection.'

Summary of the 'funding and maintenance' cases

Case	Home State	Host State	Course
Lair (1988)	France	Germany	Languages and literature; University of Hanover, Germany
Matteucci (1988)	Italy	Belgium	Singing and voice-training course in Germany
Raulin (1992)	France	Netherlands	Visual arts course at the Gerrit Rietveld Academy, Amsterdam
Bernini (1992)	Italy	Netherlands	Architectural studies at the University of Naples, Italy
Meeusen (Case C–337/97) [1999] ECR I–3289	Belgium	Netherlands	Chemistry at the Provincial Higher Technical Institute for Chemistry in Antwerp, Belgium
Ninni-Orasche (2004)	Italy	Austria	Languages and literature, specialising in Italian and French; University of Klagenfurt, Austria

This case law is still relevant today, despite the rapidly expanding jurisprudence on students' rights as Citizens to claim funding for education (discussed in Chapter 11). This is because of Art 24(2) of Directive 2004/38, which provides as follows:

ARTICLE

[The] host Member State shall not be obliged... prior to acquisition of the right of permanent residence, to grant maintenance aid for studies, including vocational training, consisting in student grants or student loans to persons other than workers, self-employed persons, persons who retain such status and members of their families.

You may also recall from reading Chapter 11 that 'the right of permanent residence' is only conferred on those who have resided continuously in the host State for five years (Art 16, Directive 2004/38). In *Förster* (Case C-158/07) [2008] ECR I-8507 (discussed in Chapter 11), Art 24(2) was explicitly referred to by the ECJ to support its conclusion that the five-year continuous residency period imposed under Dutch law for students to become eligible for a maintenance grant was legitimate and proportionate.

The decision of the ECJ in *Förster* is criticised here for failing to acknowledge that the principles in *Lair, Matteucci* and *Bernini* applied to Ms Förster. She had actually worked in the Netherlands as a primary school teacher (and later in a 'special school providing secondary education to pupils with behavioural and/or psychiatric problems') before embarking on her degree course in educational theory. It is fairly clear that there was a very close connection between her work and her course of study, bringing her situation into line with cases such as *Lair*. Ms Förster should therefore have been able to rely upon Art 7(2) of Regulation 1612/68 in order to claim her full grant. This argument was actually put to the Court by the European Commission and A-G Mazák, but the Court completely ignored it.

Unsuccessful claims

Unsuccessful claims based on Art 7(2) are rare. In *Leclere* and *Deaconescu* (2001), the ECJ held that Art 7(2) could not be invoked to challenge the refusal of a benefit where the claimant was no longer working or even resident in the country in which they had been employed. More recently, in *Baldinger* (Case C–386/02) [2004] ECR I–8411, the ECJ dismissed a claim based on Art 7(2) for entitlement to war compensation. This was a benefit introduced in 2000 and payable to Austrian nationals who had been taken as prisoners of war during or immediately after the Second World War. The ECJ held that this benefit could not be classed as a 'social and tax advantage':

JUDGMENT

'An allowance such as [war compensation], apart from not being linked to the status of worker, is provided … in testimony of national gratitude. It is thus paid as a *quid pro quo* for the service they rendered to their country.'

Family members' entitlement to Art 7(2) protection

This entitlement to 'social and tax advantages' is afforded to workers' families too. The ECJ has pointed out that to allow Member States to discriminate against migrant workers' families in this respect could inhibit the free movement of those workers. In the earliest case on this point, *Fiorini v SNCF* (1975), the ECJ allowed the Italian widow of an Italian worker in France to claim reduced rail travel, but on the basis that he would have been entitled to it had he been alive. Subsequently, in *Inzirillo* (Case 63/76) [1976] ECR 2057 and *Castelli* (Case 261/83) [1984] ECR 3199 the ECJ held that migrant workers could make claims for benefits on behalf of their families. Finally, in *Bernini* (1992), the ECJ went further and held that the family members themselves could make a claim under Art 7(2). The ECJ held:

JUDGMENT

'The dependent members of the family are the indirect beneficiaries of the equal treatment accorded to the migrant worker. Consequently, where the grant of financing to a child of a migrant worker constitutes a social advantage for the migrant worker, the child may itself rely on Article 7(2) in order to obtain that financing if under national law it is granted directly to the student.'

This was confirmed in *Meeusen* (1999). The nationality of the worker's family member is irrelevant (*Deak* (Case 94/84) [1985] ECR 1873).

Summary of cases involving Art 7(2) and family members

Case	Home State	Host State	Family member(s)
Fiorini (1975)	Italy	France	Wife and children
Inzirillo (1976)	Italy	Belgium	Son
Castelli (1984)	Italy	Belgium	Mother
Deak (1985)	Italy	Belgium	Son
Bernini (1992)	Italy	Netherlands	Daughter
Schmid (1993)	Germany	Belgium	Daughter
Meeusen (1999)	Belgium	Netherlands	Daughter

The ECJ's flexible approach as to whether it is the worker or a family member who claims the 'social advantage' can be seen in *Hartmann* (Case C–212/05) [2007] ECR I–6303, a case involving a claim for child-raising allowance, a benefit payable under German social security legislation. The Court confirmed that this constituted a 'social advantage' and, moreover, that it was immaterial which parent claimed the allowance. The Court stated that (emphasis added):

JUDGMENT

'A benefit such as child-raising allowance, which enables one of the parents to devote himself or herself to the raising of a young child, by meeting family expenses, benefits the family as a whole, *whichever parent it is who claims the allowance*. The grant of such an allowance to a worker's spouse is capable of reducing that worker's obligation to contribute to family expenses.'

12.4.4 Article 12: Access for worker's children to education

ARTICLE

'Art 12 The children of a national of a Member State who is or has been employed in the territory of another Member State shall be admitted to that State's general educational, apprenticeship and vocational training courses under the same conditions as the nationals of that State, if such children are residing in its territory.

Member States shall encourage all efforts to enable such children to attend these courses under the best possible conditions.'

Article 12 has been extended beyond conditions of entry to 'general measures to facilitate attendance', including funding in the shape of grants and loans to undertake such courses. In *Casagrande* (Case 9/74) [1974] ECR 773, the ECJ stated:

JUDGMENT

'It follows from the provision in the second paragraph of Article 12 … that the article is intended to encourage special efforts, to ensure that the children may take advantage on an equal footing of the education and training facilities available. It must be concluded that in providing that the children in question shall be admitted to educational courses "under the same conditions as the nationals" of the host State, Article 12 refers not only to rules relating to admission, but also to general measures intended to facilitate educational attendance.'

Age limits

For the purposes of Art 12, there is no age restriction as far as the child is concerned. This point was made in *Gaal* (Case C–7/94) [1995] ECR I–1031, where the 'child' in question was a 22-year-old biology student.

CASE EXAMPLE

Gaal (Case C–7/94) [1995] ECR I–1031

Lubor Gaal was born in Belgium in 1967 but from the age of two was brought up in Germany. He subsequently began a biology degree at a German university. In 1989, when aged 22, he applied for funds to study biology for a year at a British university. His father had died in 1987 and he was not financially dependent on his mother. The authorities in Germany refused his application, as he was over 21 and was not financially dependent on either parent. The ECJ held that the definition of 'child' for the purposes of Art 12 was not subject to any conditions (in terms of age). Gaal could therefore rely upon Art 12 to challenge the refusal to award funding.

The Court stated:

JUDGMENT

'Article 12 … encompasses financial assistance for those students who are already at an advanced stage in their education, even if they are already 21 years of age or older and are no longer dependants of their parents. Accordingly, to make the application of Article 12 subject to an age-limit or to the status of dependent child would conflict not only with the letter of that provision, but also with its spirit.'

Article 12 may, therefore, encompass children aged over 21 and no longer dependent. Otherwise, students would be rendered ineligible for State financial assistance as soon as they reached 21 and were financially independent of their parents.

Death, retirement, etc of the 'worker'

In order for Art 12 to apply, it is essential that one of the child's parents is, **or has been**, working in the State providing the education (*Brown v Secretary of State for Scotland* (Case 197/86) [1988] ECR 3205; *Humbel* (Case 263/86) [1988] ECR 5365). However, because Art 12 refers to the children of a worker who is 'or has been' employed, provided that the working parent did work in the State at some point, it is immaterial that he has since retired, died or moved on to work in another country, as these cases illustrate:

- *Michel S* (Case 76/72) [1973] ECR 457 – Italian national worked in Belgium until his death. Son entitled to continue to rely on Art 12.
- *Casagrande* (1974) – Italian national worked in Germany until his death. Son entitled to continue to rely on Art 12.
- *Gaal* (1995) – Belgian national worked in Germany until his death. Son entitled to continue to rely on Art 12.
- *Baumbast* (2002) – German national worked in the UK until economic circumstances forced him to leave the UK and work in China and Lesotho in southern Africa. Daughter and step-daughter entitled to continue to rely on Art 12.
- *Ibrahim* (Case C-310/08) (2010) – Danish national worked in the UK, followed by a period of unemployment, and then left the country. Children entitled to continue to rely on Art 12.

A similar situation exists if the child's parents divorce and the child lives with the non-working parent (*R v Home Secretary* (Case C–413/99) [2002] ECR I–7091); *Teixeira* (Case C-480/08) (2010)). What happens if the worker leaves the host State and the child accompanies him but **then** decides to return in order to complete their education? The

ECJ has held that in such circumstances the child may be covered by Art 12, in the interests of education continuity. This occurred in *Moritz* (Case 389/87) [1989] ECR 723, where M, a German national, had gone to live with his father in the Netherlands when the latter worked there. Subsequently the father returned to Germany and the son again accompanied him. However, the son later applied to return to the Netherlands to complete his education. The ECJ held that M had not forfeited his rights to complete his education in the Netherlands.

Right to education abroad

Article 12 is available to secure funding even if the course is abroad, **provided** that such right is available to nationals of the host State. In *Di Leo v Land Berlin* (Case C–308/89) [1990] ECR I–4185, the ECJ stated:

JUDGMENT

> 'Article 12 … lays down … a general rule which, in matters of education, requires every Member State to ensure equal treatment between its own nationals and the children of workers who are nationals of another Member State established within its territory. Accordingly, where a Member State gives its nationals the opportunity to obtain a grant in respect of education or training provided abroad, the child of a [Union] worker must enjoy the same advantage if he decides to pursue his studies outside the host State. That interpretation cannot be invalidated by the fact that a person seeking education or training decides to follow a course in the Member State of which he is a national.'

'Vocational training'

In *Gravier v Liège* (Case 293/83) [1985] ECR 593, the ECJ was asked to define 'vocational training' and duly provided a very generous interpretation of the phrase.

CASE EXAMPLE

> *Gravier v Liège* (Case 293/83) [1985] ECR 593
>
> Françoise Gravier, a French national, was studying a four-year course in strip-cartoon art at the Académie Royale des Beaux-Arts in Liège in Belgium. She refused to pay the *minerval* (supplementary fees imposed on foreign students in Belgian universities). Her enrolment was cancelled. She brought an action against the city authorities, claiming discrimination on grounds of nationality, contrary to Art 18 TFEU. The question was whether her programme of study fell within the scope of EU law, which it would if it could be described as 'vocational training'. The ECJ defined 'vocational training' in such a way as to include most university courses, bringing them within the scope of Art 18.

The Court stated:

JUDGMENT

> 'Any form of education which prepares for a qualification for a particular profession, trade or employment or which provides the necessary skills for such profession, trade or employment is vocational training, whatever the age and the level of training of the pupils or students, and even if the training programme includes an element of general education.'

In *Blaizot v University of Liège* (Case 24/86) [1988] ECR 379, the ECJ went further and held that university education could constitute 'vocational training' 'where the student needs the knowledge so acquired for the pursuit of a profession, trade or employment, even if no legislative or administrative provisions make the acquisition of such knowledge a prerequisite for that purpose'.

CASE EXAMPLE

Blaizot v University of Liège (Case 24/86) [1988] ECR 379

Vincent Blaizot, a French national, was studying veterinary medicine at the University of Liège in Belgium. He wished to recover the *minerval* he had been required to pay prior to the *Gravier* decision. The question for the ECJ was whether university courses constituted 'vocational training' so as to be subject to Art 18 TFEU. The university, supported by the Belgian Government, argued that as university courses were essentially academic they were not vocational. Blaizot, supported by the Commission, argued the opposite. The ECJ agreed with Blaizot.

KEY FACTS

Workers' rights under Regulation 1612/68

Member States must not limit employment opportunities for 'foreign nationals'	Article 3
Member States may demand 'linguistic knowledge' where the 'nature of the post' requires it	Article 3; *Groener* (1989)
Member States must not restrict the employment of 'foreign nationals' by reference to a number or percentage	Article 4; *Commission v France* (1974); *Bosman* (1995)
Discrimination on grounds of nationality in the context of employment is prohibited. Both direct and indirect discrimination is prohibited	Article 7(1)
Workers are entitled to the same 'social and tax advantages' as national workers. This provision has been defined very widely. In particular, no link is required with the worker's actual employment	Article 7(2); *Fiorini v SNCF* (1975); *Even* (1979)
Article 7(2) includes the right to claim funding and grants for full-time education, provided there is 'some continuity' between the work and education, or the worker became involuntarily unemployed	*Lair* (1988); *Matteucci* (1988), *Bernini* (1992), *Ninni-Orasche* (2004)
Worker's family members can rely on Art 7(2) to claim 'social and tax advantages'	*Fiorini v SNCF, Bernini, Hartmann* (2007)
Worker's children are entitled to be educated under the same conditions as nationals	Article 12
Article 12 extends to funding for education	*Casagrande* (1974), *Gaal* (1995)
Article 12 is not subject to a maximum age limit. It therefore applies to university education	*Di Leo* (1990), *Gaal*
Article 12 can be used to pursue education in another Member State	*Di Leo, Gaal*
The child's right to education continues even if the worker is no longer working (because of death or retirement) or no longer resident in the State	*Michel S* (1973), *Casagrande, Gaal, Baumbast and R* (2002), *Ibrahim* (2010), *Teixeira* (2010)
The 'primary carer' doctrine, which is based on Art 12, allows the 'primary carer' of a child to residence rights until the child reaches the age of majority or even beyond that if continued support is needed to complete education	*Baumbast and R, Ibrahim, Teixeira*

12.5 Purely internal situations

If all the facts of a particular case occur within the territory of a single EU Member State, then EU law has no role to play. This point was first made in the context of Art 45, although it has since been confirmed and applied to Art 49 (freedom of establishment) and Art 56 (freedom to provide services) as well (these freedoms are discussed in the next chapter).

12.5.1 Workers and the 'purely internal' rule

CASE EXAMPLE

R v Saunders (Case 175/78) [1979] ECR 1129

Vera Saunders, from Northern Ireland, pleaded guilty to theft at Bristol Crown Court and was bound over on condition that she returned to Northern Ireland and did not return to England or Wales for three years. However, within six months she was arrested in Wales. When charged with breaching the terms of her binding over, she alleged a breach of Art 45. However, the ECJ pointed out that there was no cross-border movement and hence Art 45 did not apply.

This principle was applied in the following cases:

- *Iorio* (Case 298/84) [1986] ECR 247 – Paolo Iorio, an Italian national, was fined for not having the proper ticket on the Rome–Palermo train. He appealed, claiming that the Italian legislation imposing the fine infringed Art 45 on the basis that it inhibited free movement, but he was unsuccessful. There was no cross-border element to the case.
- *Steen* (Case C–332/90) [1992] ECR I–341 – Volker Steen, a German national, had worked for the German Post Office for 12 years. In 1985, he applied for a promotion, but withdrew from it when he discovered that this would mean classifying him as a 'civil servant'. He complained that this classification constituted a breach of Art 45, because under German law only German nationals could be appointed as civil servants. The ECJ again held that Art 45 did not apply.

12.5.2 Workers' family and the 'purely internal' rule

As with the worker, if the family member has not sought to exercise their free movement rights, EU law has no role to play. This principle has been seen in several cases:

- *Morson and Jhanhan* (Case 35/82) [1982] ECR 3723 – Surinamese nationals and parents of Dutch nationals in the Netherlands could not rely upon EU law because there was only one Member State involved.
- *Dzodzi v Belgium* (Case 297/88) [1990] ECR I–3763 – Togolese national married to Belgian national working in Belgium could not enforce EU law (only one Member State involved).
- *Uecker and Jacquet* (Cases C–64 and 65/96) [1997] ECR I–3171 – Norwegian and Russian nationals married to German nationals working in Germany could not enforce EU law (only one Member State involved).
- *Mayeur* (Case C–229/07) [2008] ECR I-8 – Peruvian national married to French national working in France could not enforce EU law (only one Member State involved).

In *Carpenter* (Case C–60/00) [2002] ECR I–6279, however, the ECJ ruled that EU law applied to the case of a Filipino woman married to a UK national and living and working in the UK. Although this case looks superficially identical to the cases of *Dzodzi, Uecker* and *Jacquet* above, the ECJ distinguished them. The reason was that, although the UK national lived and worked in the UK, his business involved providing services to customers in other EU Member States. The ECJ therefore held that a cross-border element had been satisfied and hence his wife could invoke EU law.

CASE EXAMPLE

Carpenter v Secretary of State for the Home Dept (Case C–60/00) [2002] ECR I–6279

Peter Carpenter was a self-employed UK national who provided services to customers based in other EU Member States. Specifically, he sold advertising space in various British medical and scientific journals. In 1996 he married Mary, a Philippines national. Shortly afterwards, she applied for leave to remain in the UK, but this was refused and a deportation order was made against her. (She had entered the UK in 1994 and stayed on in breach of her visitor status.) Mary sought to rely upon Art 56 (the freedom to provide and receive services – see Chapter 13), on the basis that if she were to be deported it would detrimentally affect Peter's ability to run his business and thus his freedom to provide services. In particular, she helped to look after his children from his first marriage. The question was whether the case raised any cross-border element sufficient to bring EU law into play. The ECJ held that there was, and went on to hold that Mary was entitled to rely upon EU law to remain in the UK.

12.5.3 Exceptions to the 'purely internal' rule

The 'purely internal' rule does not apply to 'returnees', that is, persons who have left their home State to exercise free movement rights (whether under Art 45, Art 49 or Art 56, or some other provision) and have then returned to their home State. Such persons may invoke EU law (*Singh* (Case C–370/90) [1992] ECR I–4265). Perhaps the most frequently occurring situation where EU law may be brought into play, despite a *prima facie* 'purely internal' situation, is if the person involved had exercised freedom of movement rights previously in order to obtain a qualification abroad before returning to work in their home State. In *Kraus* (Case C–19/92) [1993] ECR I–1663 the Court stated that:

JUDGMENT

'If a national of a Member State, owing to the fact that he has lawfully resided on the territory of another Member State and has acquired a professional qualification there, finds himself with regard to his state of origin in a situation which may be assimilated to that of a migrant worker, he must also be entitled to enjoy the rights and freedoms guaranteed by the Treaty.'

This exception to the 'purely internal' rule can be seen in the following cases:

- *Knoors* (Case 115/78) [1979] ECR 399 – Dutch national permitted to rely on qualification obtained in Belgium while employed in the Netherlands.
- *Bouchoucha* (Case C–61/89) [1990] ECR I–3551 – French national permitted to rely on qualification obtained in the UK while employed in France.
- *Kraus* (1993) – German national permitted to rely on qualification obtained in the UK while employed in Germany.
- *Fernández de Bobadilla* (Case C–234/97) [1999] ECR I–4773 – Spanish national permitted to rely on qualification obtained in the UK while employed in Spain.
- *Dreessen* (Case C–31/00) [2002] ECR I–663 – Belgian national studied civil engineering in Germany (at Aachen State Civil Engineering College) before returning to Belgium.

12.5.4 Circumventing the 'purely internal' rule

Given that some cross-border element is essential, is there anything to stop a UK national from going to work in Ireland for six months and then returning to the UK in order to then make a claim based on EU law? This was the situation in *Akrich* (2003). The Court held that the motives of any EU citizen intending to work in another EU Member State were irrelevant in assessing the legal situation of the couple at the time of their return to the 'home' Member State. Such conduct cannot constitute an abuse even if the spouse did not have a right to remain in the 'home' Member State at the time when the couple installed themselves in the other Member State. There would be an abuse of EU law only if the couple's marriage had been one of 'convenience', that is, if it had been entered into for cynical reasons of acquiring marital status only, as opposed to genuine feelings of love.

CASE EXAMPLE

Akrich (Case C–109/01) [2003] ECR I–9607

Hacene Akrich, a Moroccan national, married Halina Jazdzewska, a British national, in June 1996. In June 1997, Halina moved to Ireland, where she found work in a bank, before returning to the UK approximately six months afterwards. In February 1998, Hacene applied for leave to enter the UK as the spouse of a migrant worker. In September 1998 the Home Secretary refused him clearance to enter the UK. The Home Secretary took the view that Halina's move to Ireland was a temporary move designed to circumvent UK immigration law by artificially bringing EU law into play. Hacene appealed and, in October 2000, the case was referred to the ECJ, which held that Art 45 could be applied to these facts.

Directive 2004/38 now provides explicitly for situations in which free movement rights are 'abused', such as the alleged marriage of convenience in *Akrich*. Article 35 provides that:

ARTICLE

'Art 35 Member States may adopt the necessary measures to refuse, terminate or withdraw any right conferred by this Directive in the case of abuse of rights or fraud, such as marriages of convenience. Any such measure shall be proportionate and subject to the procedural safeguards provided for in Articles 30 and 31.'

ACTIVITY

Applying the law

If these was no abuse of Art 45 in *Akrich* (2003), would there have been an abuse if Halina had moved to Ireland for three months, or three weeks? *Carpenter* (2002) establishes that any cross-border economic activity suffices to bring EU law into play (albeit not necessarily Art 45). If a British national goes on holiday to Spain for a fortnight before returning to the UK, has he established a cross-border economic activity sufficient to allow *Carpenter* or *Akrich* to be relied upon? Would a long weekend in Rome be enough? What about a day trip to Calais?

KEY FACTS

The 'purely internal' rule

As a general rule, EU law does not apply if the worker is employed in their home State	*Saunders* (1978), *Iorio* (1986), *Steen* (1992)
Worker's family members are not protected by EU law if the worker has never exercised free movement rights	*Morson & Jhanjan* (1982), *Dzodzi* (1990), *Uecker & Jacquet* (1997)
The 'purely internal' rule does not apply in cases where there is some cross-border element	*Carpenter* (2002)

The 'purely internal' rule does not apply where a person has exercised free movement rights, typically by working or studying abroad and then returning 'home'	*Knoors* (1979), *Singh* (1992), *Kraus* (1993), *D'Hoop* (2002)
Working abroad for a few months before returning 'home' does not constitute an abuse of the 'purely internal' rule	*Akrich* (2003)

12.6 The public service exemption and Art 45(4) TFEU

Member States are permitted to exclude foreign nationals from working in the 'public service' by virtue of Art 45(4). Member States could potentially exploit this derogation in order to limit the freedom of migrant workers to take up work in that State. It has therefore been restrictively interpreted by the ECJ. First, it only applies to **access to** employment, not **conditions of** employment after access has been granted (*Sotgiu v Deutsche Bundespost* (Case 152/73) [1974] ECR 153).

More significantly, the ECJ has held that Art 45(4) does not apply to **all** employment in the public service, only 'certain activities' involving the exercise of official authority (*Sotgiu*). In *Commission v Belgium* (Case 149/79) [1980] ECR 3881, the ECJ laid down the following test in determining whether a worker is employed in the 'public service':

JUDGMENT

'Classification depends on whether or not the posts in question are typical of the specific activities of the public service in so far as the exercise of powers conferred by public law and responsibility for safeguarding the general interests of the State are vested in it.'

Further guidance was given in *Lawrie-Blum* (1986), where the ECJ held that the derogation only applied to those posts which required 'a special relationship of allegiance to the State on the part of persons occupying them and reciprocity of rights and duties which form the foundation of the bond of nationality'.

CASE EXAMPLE

Lawrie-Blum (Case 66/85) [1986] ECR 2121

Deborah Lawrie-Blum, a British national, was refused entry to a teacher training course in Germany, purely on national grounds. There were two questions for the ECJ:

1. Was she a worker, given her trainee status?
2. Did the 'public service' derogation apply to teaching?

The ECJ held:

1. that she was a worker, because trainee teachers received a salary and would be required to teach up to 11 hours of classes per week and
2. that teaching was not a 'public service' occupation, because teachers did not owe 'a special relationship of allegiance to the State'.

These principles can be seen in the following cases, where the jobs in question were all held **not** to be in the 'public service':

- *Commission v France* (Case 307/84) [1986] ECR 1725 – nurses
- *Lawrie-Blum* (1986) – school teachers
- *Alluè & Coonan* (Case 33/88) [1989] ECR 1591 – university teachers
- *Schöning-Kougebetopoulou* (Case C–15/96) [1998] ECR I–47 – *doctors.*

Commission v Luxembourg (Case C–473/93) [1996] ECR I–3207, *Commission v Belgium* (Case C–173/94) [1996] ECR I–3265 and *Commission v Greece* (Case C–290/94) [1996] ECR

I–3285 all involved attempts to exclude a wide range of activities from non-nationals. In the latter case, the ECJ held that Art 45(4) did not apply, because the lists were too general. *Colegio de Oficiales de la Marina Mercante Española* (Case C–405/01) [2003] ECR I–10391 introduced further limitations on the scope of the Art 45(4) derogation.

CASE EXAMPLE

Colegio de Oficiales de la Marina Mercante Española (Case C–405/01) [2003] ECR I–10391

The case involved the post of ship's master. Under Spanish law, such posts were reserved to Spanish nationals. It was argued that the Art 45(4) derogation applied, because ship's masters had a range of public order powers while on board, which they could exercise in emergencies. The ECJ held that Art 45(4) potentially applied because ship's masters' powers to enforce public safety did 'constitute participation in the exercise of rights under powers conferred by public law for the purposes of safeguarding the general interests of the flag State'. The fact that, at any given time, masters may be employed by private individuals or companies did not affect this conclusion because they continued to act as representatives of public authority. However, it was 'necessary that such rights are in fact exercised on a regular basis by those holders and do not represent a very minor part of their activities'.

The ECJ stated that:

JUDGMENT

'The scope of [Art 45(4)] must be limited to what is strictly necessary for safeguarding the general interests of the Member State concerned, which cannot be imperilled if rights under powers conferred by public law are exercised only sporadically, even exceptionally, by nationals of other Member States.'

See also, to the same effect *Anker and Others* (Case C–47/02) [2003] ECR I–10447, involving provisions of German legislation restricting the post of ship's master to German nationals.

In *Alevizos* (Case C–392/05) [2007] ECR I–3505, the ECJ considered that a Greek national and member of the Greek Air Force might be classed as working in the public service:

JUDGMENT

'The position occupied by Mr Alevizos in the Greek Air Force … might fall within the concept of "employment in the public service" within the meaning of Article 45(4) in so far as it involves direct or indirect participation in the exercise of powers conferred by public law and duties designed to safeguard the general interests of the State or of other public authorities.'

KEY FACTS

The public service derogation

Member States are permitted to exclude foreign nationals from their 'public service'	Article 45(4) TFEU
Art 45(4) applies only to access to employment, not conditions of employment (eg salary, promotion)	*Sotgiu* (1974)
'Public service' is narrowly defined, requiring the 'exercise of powers conferred by public law and responsibility for safeguarding the general interests of the State'; a 'special relationship of allegiance' to the state	*Commission v Belgium* (1980); *Lawrie-Blum* (1986);

It does not apply if public law powers are exercised only 'sporadically' or 'exceptionally'	*Colegio de Oficiales de la Marina Mercante Española* (2003)
It does not apply to civil servants, teachers, doctors, nurses, etc	*Lawrie-Blum, Commission v France* (1986); *Schöning-Kougebetopoulou* (1998)

12.7 Justification for non-discriminatory rules

In addition to the specific Art 45 derogations, the ECJ has created a parallel set of derogations which may be pleaded by Member States to justify restrictions on the free movement of workers. The ECJ has authorised Member States to impose restrictions on the free movement of workers, provided that the national rule in question satisfies four criteria:

i) it is non-discriminatory
ii) it is justified by imperative requirements in the general interest
iii) it is suitable for the attainment of the objective it pursues
iv) it does not go beyond what is necessary in order to attain its objective (the 'proportionality' doctrine).

Two of the leading cases in this area are dealt with in the next section as they involve national rules curtailing free movement in the interests of sport (see *Bosman* (1995) and *Lehtonen* (2000)). Other cases where the ECJ has considered the application of the four-part test include *Alluè and Coonan* (1989) and *Clean Car Autoservice* (Case C–350/96) [1998] ECR I–2521. The former case involved a challenge to a provision of Italian legislation, which provided that foreign-language teaching assistants in Italian universities could only be employed on year-long contracts, and for a maximum of six years. It was argued by Ms Alluè (who was Spanish) and Ms Coonan (a British national), both of whom worked as foreign-language teaching assistants at the University of Venice, that this breached Art 45 as it restricted their freedom to work in Italy for as long as they wished. The Italian Government sought to justify the restriction, and the ECJ applied the four-part test:

i) Was the rule non-discriminatory? The rule applied to all foreign-language teaching assistants, including those of Italian nationality.
ii) Was it justified by imperative requirements in the general interest? The Italian Government suggested that the rule was necessary in order to ensure that foreign-language teaching assistants retained sufficient familiarity with the language that they taught.
iii) Was it suitable for the attainment of the objective which it pursues? The ECJ thought not. The Court said that the danger of foreign-language teaching assistants losing contact with their mother tongue was 'slight, in the light of the increase in cultural exchanges and improved communications'.
iv) Did it not go beyond what is necessary in order to attain its objective (the 'proportionality' doctrine)? Again, the Court thought not. It was 'open to the universities in any event to check the level of assistants' knowledge'.

In *Clean Car Autoservice* (1998), a challenge was brought to a provision of Austrian legislation which required companies to appoint a manager who was resident in Austria. CCA, an Austrian company, appointed a manager, a German national, who was resident in Berlin. Vienna City Council refused to register the company until he acquired a residence in Austria. CCA challenged this and the ECJ applied the four-part test:

i) Was the rule non-discriminatory? The rule applied to all companies operating in Austria, regardless of the nationality of their managers.
ii) Was it justified by imperative requirements in the general interest? The Austrian Government argued that it could be justified on two grounds. First, to ensure that the person appointed would be in a position to act effectively as manager. Second, to

ensure that he could be served with notice of any fines which may be imposed upon him, and also to ensure that any fines imposed could be enforced.

iii) Was it suitable for the attainment of the objective it pursued? The ECJ decided that the residence requirement did not serve its objective. As far as the effective management point was concerned, a person could reside in the same State but be **further** from the place of business than someone living just over the border in a different State.

iv) Did it not go beyond what is necessary in order to attain its objective (the 'proportionality' doctrine)? The ECJ held that the rule was disproportionate as other means, less restrictive of the freedom of movement of workers, were available. Regarding the argument about the imposition of fines, the Court held that fines could be served at the company's registered office instead.

12.8 Free movement of workers and professional sport

12.8.1 Introduction

EU law does apply to sport, but it is important to bear in mind the following basic propositions:

- Art 45, on the free movement of workers, applies to team sports such as football, rugby, basketball and hockey. Individual sportsmen and women, such as golfers and tennis players, are not protected by Art 45 because they are not employed by anyone. However, they are entitled to invoke Art 56, on the freedom to provide services. For an example, see *Deliège* (Cases C–51/96 and C–191/97) [2000] ECR I–2549, discussed in the next chapter, at section 13.3.3).
- EU law only applies to any type of sport if there is some economic activity. In other words, it applies to professional or semi-professional sport, but not to purely amateur sporting activities.
- EU law does not apply to 'questions of purely sporting interest', such as the number of players on a team or the actual rules of the sport itself, whether in a professional, semi-professional or amateur contest.

The first ECJ case to examine the compatibility of national laws regulating sporting activity with EU law, specifically the free movement provisions, occurred in *Walrave and Koch* (Case 36/74) [1974] ECR 1405. The ECJ ruled that the rule of non-discrimination on grounds of nationality found in Arts 18, 45 and 56 TFEU did **not** affect the composition of sports teams, in particular national teams, the formation of which was 'a question of purely sporting interest and as such has nothing to do with economic activity'. However, this clearly left open the possibility of invoking EU law to challenge other sporting rules which did have something 'to do with economic activity'.

CASE EXAMPLE

Walrave and Koch (Case 36/74) [1974] ECR 1405

Bruno Walrave and Longinus Koch, Dutch nationals, were motorcycle pacemakers. This entailed them riding ahead of cyclists in medium-distance cycle races, for which they received payment. In 1973, the Association Union Cycliste International (AUCI) issued a rule that pacemakers in the World Championships, which the AUCI organised, had to be of the same nationality as the cyclist. W and K challenged this rule on the basis that it interfered with their freedom to provide services under Art 56. The ECJ decided that both Arts 18 and 56 were directly effective and could, in principle, be used to challenge discriminatory treatment in the sporting context, provided that there was some economic activity involved. On the facts, however, this case involved 'a question of purely sporting interest' and EU law did not apply.

The next development was *Donà v Mantero* (Case 13/76) [1976] ECR 1333, which involved a challenge to rules of the Italian football federation, under which only Italian nationals could play in federation games. Here the ECJ ruled that Arts 18, 45 and 56 TFEU (as the case may be) could be invoked to challenge national sporting rules in the context of professional or semi-professional sport.

12.8.2 Using EU law to challenge transfer restrictions

The leading case here is the famous 'Bosman ruling', *Bosman v Royal Belgian Football Association and Union des Associations Européennes de Football (UEFA)* (1995). In this case the ECJ held that the 'transfer fee' system used in professional football whenever one player (if he was out of contract) moved to another club imposed an obstacle to the free movement of workers and was prohibited by Art 45(1). The expression 'Bosman free' to describe the free transfer of an out-of-contract football player from one club to another has now entered the vocabulary of professional football. The ECJ rejected a number of arguments advanced by the defendants to justify retention of the transfer fee system.

CASE EXAMPLE

Bosman v Royal Belgian Football Association and UEFA (Case C–415/93 [1995] ECR I–4921

Jean-Marc Bosman was a midfield football player with Liège FC in Belgium whose employment contract had expired in June 1990. He found a new football club willing to give him a new contract, Dunkerque FC in France. However, under rules adopted by all of the national football associations operating under the umbrella of the UEFA organisation, Liège retained Bosman's playing registration and would only release it to Dunkerque (or indeed anyone else) if the latter paid a 'transfer fee', set by Liège at 11.7 million Belgian francs. The transfer collapsed as a result, prompting Bosman to launch a challenge to the 'transfer fee' system which culminated, in December 1995, in a historic victory for Bosman.

Note: The Belgian franc ceased to be legal tender when the single European currency was introduced in 2002.

It is also important to note that the *Bosman* ruling meant the abolition of transfer fees for **out-of-contract** football players only. One of the first players to benefit from this ruling was Steve McManaman, who transferred from Liverpool FC to Real Madrid in the summer of 1999 on a 'Bosman free' transfer. Players who are transferred while **still under contract** are potentially subject to a transfer fee – the fee operates as compensation to the 'selling' club for the loss of the player. In some cases these transfer fees can be very large indeed. Recent examples from the summer of 2009 include the transfers of the Portuguese winger Cristiano Ronaldo from Manchester United to Real Madrid for £80 million and Swedish striker Zlatan Ibrahimovic from Internazionale in Italy to Barcelona for just under £61 million. Both players were under contract to the 'selling' club at the dates of their moves to Spain and hence a fee was payable.

Bosman was followed, but distinguished, in an ECJ case involving the compatibility of 'transfer deadlines' with EU law. While in *Bosman* the ECJ had held that transfer fees for out-of-contract players imposed an unjustifiable restriction on the free movement of workers, in *Lehtonen* (2000), the ECJ held that 'transfer deadlines' imposed a justifiable restriction.

CASE EXAMPLE

Lehtonen (Case C–176/96) [2000] ECR I–2681

In March 1996, towards the end of the 1995–96 basketball season, Jyri Lehtonen, a Finnish national, transferred from a team in Finland to Castors, in Belgium, who intended to play him during the final stages of the Belgian championships. However, rule 3(c) of the International Basketball Federation (FIBA) provided that European clubs were not allowed, after a deadline of 28th February, to include in their teams players who had already played in another European country during that season. Consequently, FIBA refused to issue a licence for Lehtonen to play in Belgium that season and warned Castors that the club might be penalised if it played him. However, Castors did play him in a match the next day, which they won, only to have the game awarded to their opponents by a score of 20–0. As the club ran the risk of being penalised again or even relegated if he played, Lehtonen was dropped for the remainder of the 1995–96 season. A few days later, Castors and Lehtonen brought proceedings challenging the FIBA rules. The case was referred to the ECJ, which held firstly that r 3(c) did restrict the free movement of basketball players but secondly that it was justified. In particular, it prevented bigger clubs from 'distorting' the run-in to the league championship by trying to buy the best players from rival clubs.

Following *Bosman* and the abolition of transfer fees for out-of-contract players, UEFA introduced a new system of 'transfer windows' to try to regulate the movement of professional footballers. Under this system, players are only free to move from one club to another during the 'close season', which in Europe is June to August, and for one month mid-season (January). Although transfer windows clearly do restrict 'free' movement, they are probably justifiable by applying the precedent in *Lehtonen* (2000).

The ECJ has recently given judgment in another case involving football which raised similar issues to those in *Bosman*. In *Olympique Lyonnais* (Case C-325/08) [2010] 3 CMLR 14, the issue was whether provisions of French law, requiring young footballers to pay damages to the club which had trained them in the event that the player did not subsequently sign professionally for that club, were compatible with Art 45. The ECJ held not.

CASE EXAMPLE

Olympique Lyonnais (Case C-325/08) [2010] 3 CMLR 14

Olivier Bernard spent his early playing career at Olympique Lyonnais, a football club in central France. However, he rejected the opportunity to sign a professional contract with Lyon, although one was offered, preferring to join Newcastle United in the English Premiership instead. This triggered a provision of French law, according to which he was liable to pay damages to Lyon. He refused, contending that the French rules infringed his rights as a worker under Art 45. The case reached the ECJ which held that the French rules were potentially justifiable. The Court accepted that the objective of 'encouraging the recruitment and training of young players' must be accepted as legitimate. Moreover, 'the prospect of receiving training fees is likely to encourage football clubs to seek new talent and train young players'. However, in this case, the French rules provided for the payment of damages, not compensation for training. This went beyond what was permitted, and therefore constituted an unjustified breach of Art 45.

12.8.3 Using EU law to challenge other sporting rules

Bosman also involved a challenge to a rule devised by UEFA, known as the '3+2' rule. The rule, which was enforced by all national football associations in Europe, applied to football clubs competing in certain competitions (national championships or UEFA-organised competitions – the UEFA Cup (now the Europa League), the Champions' Cup (now the Champions' League) and the European Cup Winners' Cup (now defunct)). It meant that they could only field three non-nationals plus two 'affiliated' players (meaning those players who had played in the country for an uninterrupted period of five years). The ECJ held that the rule constituted a breach of Art 4 of Regulation 1612/68, which prohibits the imposition of 'quotas' on the employment of foreign nationals. The net result is that the '3+2' rule was disapplied as far as it concerned EU nationals, although it could still be applied to non-EU nationals. UEFA suggested several justifications for the rule, all of which were rejected. One such argument was that the rule helped to maintain a connection between clubs and local players. This was rejected, the ECJ pointing out that there was no requirement that clubs had to employ local players. Even before *Bosman* (1995), many clubs fielded players born hundreds of miles away.

The implications of this aspect of the *Bosman* ruling have been enormous, especially in the English Premiership. The amount of extra revenue that has been generated in this country through the upsurge in the game's popularity since the Premiership's introduction, higher ticket prices linked to better facilities and all-seater stadia, bigger ground capacities and Sky sponsorship, has allowed English clubs to attract large numbers of foreign nationals. Chelsea made football history in 1999 when it fielded a team containing no English players. It is quite common now for some Premiership games, say Arsenal v Liverpool, to involve mostly players from EU Member States (particularly France, Germany and Spain) and perhaps only two or three British players. This would have been unthinkable before *Bosman*.

This aspect of *Bosman* was followed in the context of another sport, handball, which is very popular in Germany, in *Kolpak* (2003). This case involved a Slovakian national playing in Germany who found his opportunities limited by a rule allowing clubs to field only two foreigners. It was argued that the rule was justified on the ground that it was intended 'to safeguard training organised for the benefit of young players of German nationality and to promote the German national team'. This was rejected. The rule did not benefit young German players because, following *Bosman*, it had already been repealed in the context of the other EU Member States and the signatories of the European Economic Area Treaty (Iceland, Liechtenstein and Norway). The ECJ held that it could not be applied to those states with which the EU had signed Association Agreements, including Slovakia, either.

CASE EXAMPLE

Kolpak (Case C–438/00) [2003] ECR I–4135

In March 1997, Maros Kolpak, a Slovakian handball player, signed for the German club TSV Östringen. The German Handball Association (DHB) issued him with a player's permit marked 'A' for '*Auslander*' (foreigner). Under DHB rules only two squad places were available to foreigners. Kolpak challenged this, claiming that it limited his playing opportunities and was contrary to the prohibition of discrimination against foreign nationals. The ECJ held that the rules were discriminatory and could not be justified on 'purely sporting grounds'. In future, clubs were free to field an unlimited number of nationals of other EU Member States, nationals of EEA states, and nationals of EU Association states.

A similar outcome to *Kolpak* was seen in *Simutenkov* (Case C–265/03) [2005] ECR I–2579, a case involving the EU/Russia Partnership Agreement. Igor Simutenkov, a Russian national, was playing in the Spanish football league with Tenerife. He was issued with a player's licence identifying him simply as a non-EU player. This meant that he could be excluded from certain games where only a limited number of non-EU players could be fielded. He contested this and the ECJ held that discrimination against Russian nationals was prohibited by the partnership agreement between the EU and Russia. The same result occurred in *Kahveci* (Case C-152/08) [2008] ECR I-6291, involving a Turkish national playing in the Spanish football league. He successfully invoked the Association Agreement between the EU and Turkey to challenge playing restrictions imposed on him.

KEY FACTS

The application of Art 45 to sport

Sport is subject to EU law only when there is some 'economic activity' That means professional or semi-professional sports only	*Walrave & Koch* (1974), *Donà v Mantero* (1976)
Sportsmen and women who play team sports such as football, basketball and handball are 'workers' and are protected by Art 45	*Donà v Mantero, Bosman* (1995), *Lehtonen* (2000), *Kolpak* (2003)
Sportsmen and women who play individual sports are protected by Art 56 (the freedom to provide services)	*Deliège* (2000)
Transfer fees for out-of-contract sportsmen and women are in breach of Art 45(1) TFEU. Transfer fees for players under contract are permitted	*Bosman*
Transfer deadlines are a justifiable restriction on the free movement of workers	*Lehtonen*
Payments in the form of compensation for the training of young players are a justifiable restriction on the free movement of workers	*Olympique Lyonnais* (2010)
'Quotas' restricting the number of foreign players who can be employed by a club or fielded in a game are prohibited	Article 45(2) TFEU; Article 4, Regulation 1612/68; *Bosman*
This prohibition extends to players from EU Association countries such as Russia and Turkey	*Kolpak, Simutenkov* (2005), *Kahveci* (2008)

ACTIVITY

Applying the Law

1. Franco, an experienced heart surgeon, from Italy, was recently offered a professorial position at a teaching hospital in Nice, France, regarded as one of the best in Europe. He immediately accepted the offer and handed in his notice to his previous employer, a health authority in Rome in Italy. He also sold his house in Rome and most of his furniture, intending to make a fresh start in the south of France.

   Last month Franco flew to Nice, accompanied by his wife, Gisele, who is from Albania, their nine-year-old daughter Heidi, and Julio, Franco's son from a previous relationship. Julio is 23 years old but has a mental age of 10, the result of a brain tumour when he was a child. Soon afterwards, Franco started work and Heidi was enrolled at school.

   However, a few days after starting work, Franco arrived at his office to be told that his post was being re-advertised. He was told that new French legislation had just come into force, stating that all senior teaching posts in France had to be held by French nationals. Franco has decided to stay in Nice to fight this decision, which he regards as blatantly wrong.

   Julio loves gardens and would like to be a gardener. Franco, therefore, had arranged for Julio to be enrolled on a training course for adults with educational difficulties, run by Nice University. The course offers tuition in a variety of skills including cooking and gardening. However, when Franco applied (on Julio's behalf) for a special grant from the French Government, available for victims of brain injuries to commence education, he was told that the grants are only available to French nationals.

   The strain of the move to Nice, followed by the sudden withdrawal of Franco's job, proved too much for Gisele, who has decided to seek a divorce. She has already moved out of the apartment and is renting a flat. Ideally, she would like to stay in France and get a job and a place for herself and Heidi to live, rather than return to Albania or Italy.

Is the migrant an EU citizen
NO
There are no automatic rights of entry
YES
Automatic right to enter for 3 months – can stay longer if not an unreasonable burden on the host state
Is the migrant a worker?
• Performs work for another for remuneration for a certain period of time Lawrie-Blum
• Has offer of work Van Duyn v Home Office
• Has lost job but is capable of finding other work Leclere and Deaconescu
• the worker engaged in genuine economic activity Kempf
• Is actively seeking work Antonissen
NO
e.g. The migrant is not involved in genuine economic activity Bettray
There are no Art 45 rights
YES
Can anyone accompany the worker?
Family members
By Directive 2004/38 these are:
• A spouse (even if not of EU nationality) (even if separated Diatta) – (but generally not a cohabitee unless social advantage can be claimed Reed)
• A dependent relative under 21
• An ascendant dependant
• Any other dependent family member
• A partner in a civil partnership arrangement
• A partner in a durable relationship
• Also those who have their own Art 45 rights
Can the Member State refuse entry?
By Art 39(3) and Dir 2004/38 – yes on grounds of:
• Public policy/public security
• but only based on the personal conduct of the worker Van Duyn
• and policy may vary from state to state
• and past convictions on their own are insufficient grounds Bonsignore
• There must be a current and sufficient threat to the interests of the state Bouchereau
• And equal treatment is required Adoui & Cornaille
• And must represent an imperative threat to the state
• Public health
• Follows a proscribed list of contagious diseases
What are the worker's rights?
• By Dir 2004/38 —to enter and seek work/take up offers of work and to reside on production of a valid Passport/ID
• Not to be reused entry Pieck or be treated disproportionately, ie deported Watson & Belmann for breach of formalities
• By Reg 1612/68 to equal eligibility to employment Groener
• By 1612/68 to equality in conditions in employment Sotgiu
• By 1612/68 to enjoy the same social and tax advantages as host workers and their families
• By 1612/68 workers' children have same educational rights as children of host state workers
• to remain after employment – and permanent residence after 5 years continuous residence
Are there any occupations from which the migrant worker is excluded?
Yes – the public service exemption under Art 45(4)
• Must involve something to do with allegiance to the state – involving the administration of the security of the state Commission v Belgium
• So there is an institutional or functional test Commission v France

Figure 12.8.3 Flow chart illustrating the free movement of workers under Art 45 and associated secondary legislation

Advise:

(a) Franco as to his rights under EU law to challenge the Mayor's decision regarding the professorial position

(b) Gisele as to her rights to stay in France, to get accommodation there and to get a job, both in the immediate future and in the event of a divorce

(c) Julio as to his rights to the government grant.

Note: to answer this question you will also need to refer back to Chapter 11.

SAMPLE ESSAY QUESTION

Cases involving Article 45 TFEU and/or Regulation 1612/68 reveal that the ECJ is prepared to adopt a very wide interpretation of most concepts, such as the words 'worker', but also a very narrow interpretation of certain concepts, such as the phrase 'public service'. However, this apparent contradiction is actually perfectly coherent – the ECJ is seeking to promote as much freedom for workers as possible. Discuss.

Examine case law on meaning of 'worker':

- Cases such as *Lawrie-Blum* and *Trojani* show that the ECJ is very generous with its definition
- There is no minimum wage or minimum hourly rate threshold
- Case law has focussed on the quality of the work – 'effective and genuine' activities – rather than the quantity of work
- Part-time and/or low-paid workers are covered (*Levin, Kempf, Ninni-Orasche*)
- Frontier workers are also covered (*Geven, Hartmann, Hendrix*)
- Trainees are workers (*Lawrie-Blum, Bernini*)
- The previously employed are also classed as workers (*Leclere and Deaconescu*)
- Even the unemployed have rights – despite not being in 'work' (*Antonissen*)
- But note that there are some limits (*Bettray*).

Examine case law on meaning 'social and tax advantages':

- In *Even* the ECJ refused to limit Regulation 1612/68, Art 7(2), to employment-related benefits and expanded the provision to include all benefits available to nationals
- Give examples form the case law, eg *Fiorini v SNCF, Mutsch, Reed, Lair, O'Flynn*
- Discuss how worker's family members may invoke Art 7(2) – *Fiorini v SNCF, Bernini, Meeusen*, even if they are not themselves EU citizens (*Deak*)
- Note that there are some limits (*Leclere and Deaconescu, Baldinger*).

Examine case law on meaning and scope of children's education:

- Despite referring only to 'access' to education, Regulation 1612/68, Art 12, has been defined very widely, to include funding for education up to and including University education (*Casagrande, Di Leo, Gaal*)
- The 'child' of a worker can be an adult (*Di Leo, Gaal*)
- Art 12 can even be used to claim funding for education in another Member State (*Echternach & Moritz, Di Leo, Gaal*)
- Art 12 continues to apply even after the death/retirement/departure of the worker (*Michel S, Casagrande, Gaal, Baumbast, Ibrahim*)
- Art 12 has also inspired the 'primary carer' doctrine (*Baumbast, Ibrahim, Teixeira*).

Examine case law on meaning and scope of the 'public service' derogation:

- Art 45 (4) TFEU only applies to access, not conditions in, employment (*Sotgiu*)
- Explain characteristics of 'Public service' employment – 'exercise of powers conferred by public law', 'responsibility for safeguarding the general interests of the State', 'a special relationship of allegiance to the State' (*Commission v Belgium*; *Lawrie-Blum*)
- Article 45 (4) does not apply to posts where public law powers are 'exercised only sporadically, even exceptionally' (*Colegio de Oficiales*)
- Give examples of when Art 45 (4) does apply, eg *Alevizos*.

SUMMARY

- The free movement of workers is provided for by Art 45 (1) TFEU. National rules which preclude or deter nationals of one State going to work in another are prohibited (*Graf*).
- Art 45 (2) TFEU prohibits discrimination in employment based on nationality. It can be invoked by workers to challenge discrimination in national legislation or in the policies of individual employers (*Angonese*). Art 45 (2) can also be invoked by employers (*Innovative Technology Center*). The prohibition of discrimination is emphasised by Regulation 1612/68, Art 7(1).
- Discrimination can be direct or indirect. Direct discrimination occurs when a rule of national legislation or practice clearly applies different rules depending on nationality (*Wood*). Indirect discrimination occurs when a national rule is superficially neutral, but in practice is easier for nationals to satisfy and/or harder for non-nationals to satisfy (*Sotgiu, Allué & Coonan, Scholz, Schöning-Kougebetopoulou, Köbler v Austria*).

- Direct discrimination can only be justified using the TFEU (i.e. on grounds of public policy, security and health, under Art 45 (3) (see Chapter 11), or using the public service derogation in Art 45 (4) (see below)). Indirect discrimination is justifiable if it pursues a legitimate objective; is capable of achieving that objective; and satisfies proportionality, i.e. it does not go beyond what is necessary to achieve that objective (*Allué & Coonan, Clean Car Autoservice, Lehtonen*).
- The word 'worker' is not defined in any EU legislation. In *Lawrie-Blum*, the ECJ established the conditions for a 'worker': provision of services; for another person; in return for monetary reward. Subsequent cases have emphasised the need for 'remuneration' (*Trojani*).
- Part-time and/or low-paid workers qualify for Art 45 protection regardless of the level of remuneration. The minimum threshold is the provision of 'effective and genuine' activities (*Levin, Kempf, Kranemann*).
- The following are also classed as workers: trainees (*Lawrie-Blum, Bernini*); frontier workers (*Hartmann, Geven, Hendrix*); the previously employed (*Leclere and Deaconescu*)
- People genuinely seeking work who can provide evidence to that effect are entitled to remain in the 'host' Member State indefinitely (*Antonissen, Collins*).
- Workers and their family members (see Chapter 11) are provided with further rights under Regulation 1612/68. Under Art 3, Member States may not make eligibility for employment more difficult for foreign nationals. However, it is permissible, if the 'nature of the post' requires it, that workers have certain linguistic knowledge. This applies to teaching (*Groener*) and banking (*Angonese*).
- Under Art 4, Member States may not discriminate against other EU nationals by imposing 'quotas' on the number of foreign workers (*Commission v France (Merchant Seamen), Bosman*).
- Art 7(2) extends the anti-discrimination principle to 'social and tax advantages'. 'Social advantages' is not restricted to work-related benefits. It covers benefits which are 'generally granted to national workers primarily because of their objective status as workers or by virtue of the mere fact of their residence on the national territory' (*Even*). Examples include rail travel packages (*Fiorini v SNCF*); the right to have a partner (*Reed*); the right to funding for full-time education (*Lair, Bernini, Ninni-Orasche*).
- Worker's family members can invoke Art 7(2), regardless of their nationality (*Fiorini v SNCF, Deak, Bernini, Hartmann*).
- However, Art 7(2) is not without some limits (*Leclere and Deaconescu; Baldinger*).
- Under Art 12, worker's children have the 'right of access to general educational, apprenticeship and vocational training courses under the same conditions as the nationals of that State'. This extends to funding for education (*Casagrande; Di Leo*).
- There is no age restriction; a 'child' can be an adult (*Di Leo; Gaal*).
- Art 12 extends to 'all forms of education, whether vocational or general, including University courses' (*Echternach & Moritz, Di Leo, Gaal*).
- Art 12 includes a right for a child's 'primary carer' to reside in the Member State with the child, irrespective of the carer's nationality (*Baumbast & R*). The primary carer acquires a right of residence 'on the sole basis' of Art 12; the residency conditions in Directive 2004/38 do not apply (*Ibrahim*). In principle, the primary carer's right of residence ends when the child reaches the age of majority, but it may continue if necessary to enable the child to complete their education (*Teixeira*).
- Purely internal situations are not covered by Art 45 (*R v Saunders*).
- Even where family members are involved, if the worker has not exercised free movement rights, Art 45 does not apply (*Morson & Jhanhan*).
- The purely internal rule does not apply to 'returnees' – workers who have exercised their right to move to another State, before returning home (*Kraus*). Working abroad for a few months before returning home is enough to bring Art 45 into operation (*Akrich*).

- Employment in the 'public service' is exempted from the freedom to work provisions by Art 45 (4). This allows Member States to restrict access to public service employment; it does not justify discrimination against non-nationals in conditions of employment (*Sotgiu*).
- 'Public service' employment involves 'the exercise of powers conferred by public law and responsibility for safeguarding the general interests of the state' (*Commission v Belgium*) and 'a special relationship of allegiance to the state' (*Lawrie-Blum*). It does not apply if public law powers are 'exercised only sporadically, even exceptionally' (*Colegio de Oficiales de la Marina Mercante Española*).
- The following are not employed in the 'public service': doctors (*Schöning-Kougebetopoulou*); nurses (*Commission v France (Nurses)*); teachers (*Lawrie-Blum; Bleis*); university lecturers (*Allué & Coonan*); utilities company workers (*Commission v Belgium*); telecommunications workers (*Commission v Greece*); private security firm employees (*Commission v Spain*).
- Art 45 (4) has been held to be applicable to the captains of merchant ships (*Colegio*) and to air force pilots (*Alevizos*). Other occupations where Art 45 (4) may apply include national security services, the higher levels of the civil service, and the police force.
- Art 45 applies to sport to the extent that sport is an economic activity (*Walrave and Koch, Donà v Mantero*). Art 45 applies to professional and semi-professional team sports.
- Art 45 was successfully used to challenge transfer restrictions for out-of-contract footballers and for nationality quotas in football (*Bosman*) and the requirement that young players pay damages to their first club if they chose not to sign professionally for them (*Olympique Lyonnais*). But transfer deadlines used in basketball were held to be justifiable (*Lehtonen*).
- Sportsmen and women who play individual sports are not 'workers' but are protected by Art 56, the freedom to provide services (*Deliège*)

Further reading

Articles

Currie, S, '"Free" Movers? The Post-Accession Experience of Accession – 8 Migrant Workers in the UK' (2006) 31 EL Rev 207.

Golynker, O, 'Jobseekers' Rights in the European Union' (2005) 30 EL Rev 111.

O'Brien, C, Case note on *Hartmann* (2008) 45 CML Rev 499.

Van den Bogaert, S, '… And Another Uppercut from the ECJ to Nationality Requirements in Sports Regulations (*Kolpak*)' (2004) 29 EL Rev 267; 'Sport and the EC Treaty: A Tale of Uneasy Bedfellows' (2006) 31 EL Rev 821.

Weatherill, S, 'Fair Play Please!: Recent Developments in the Application of EC Law to Sport' (2003) 40 CMLR 51.

13 Freedom of establishment and the freedom to provide and receive services under articles 49 and 56 TFEU

AIMS AND OBJECTIVES

After reading this chapter you should be able to:

- Understand the law relating to the freedom of establishment, in particular Article 49
- Understand law relating to the provision of services, in particular Article 56
- Understand the law relating to the mutual recognition of qualifications, in particular Directive 2005/36
- Understand the circumstances in which the freedom of establishment and the provision of services may be restricted
- Analyse critically the law relating to the freedom of establishment and the provision of services
- Apply the law to factual situations involving the freedom of establishment and the provision of services in the EU

Article 49 provides for the freedom of establishment; Art 56 provides the freedom to provide (or receive) services. Both provisions are directly effective – *Reyners v Belgium* (Case 2/74) [1974] ECR 631 (Article 49) and *Van Binsbergen* (Case 33/74) [1974] ECR 1299 (Article 56).

- A right of **establishment** is the right to install one's self in another Member State, permanently or semi-permanently, on a self-employed basis, for the purpose of performing a particular activity there. It also gives companies the right to set up a branch or a subsidiary in another Member State.
- The right to provide **services** allows an individual, established in one Member State, to provide their services in another Member State, on a temporary or spasmodic basis. It also allows a company, established in one Member State, to provide their services to anyone in another Member State. If necessary, it allows them to visit the other Member State, on a temporary or spasmodic basis, in order to do so.

13.1 Freedom of establishment and Art 49 TFEU

ARTICLE

'Art 49 Within the framework of the provisions set out below, restrictions on the freedom of establishment of nationals of a Member State in the territory of another Member State shall be prohibited. Such prohibition shall also apply to restrictions of the setting up of agencies, branches or subsidiaries by nationals of any Member State established in the territory of any Member State.

Freedom of establishment shall include the right to take up and pursue activities as self-employed persons and to set up and manage undertakings, in particular companies or firms ... under the conditions laid down for its own nationals by the laws of the country where such establishment is effected ...'.

Article 49 refers to the taking up as well as the pursuit of professional activities for individual, self-employed persons. For companies, the freedom of establishment **includes** the right to set up and manage 'undertakings', in particular companies and firms; and the setting up of agencies, branches or subsidiaries; under the same conditions laid down for nationals of the State where establishment is effected. This list is non-exhaustive, and has been expanded on. In *Commission v Germany (Insurance Services)* (Case 205/84) [1986] ECR 3755, the ECJ suggested that 'establishment' could also include the presence in a State of an office managed by a company's own staff, or a person who is independent but authorised to act on a permanent basis for the company.

It is possible to be established in two Member States at the same time. *Paris Bar Council v Klopp* (Case 107/83) [1984] ECR 2971 and *Gebhard v Milan Bar Council* (Case C–55/94) [1995] ECR I–4165 are two similar cases in which qualified German lawyers (already established in Germany) wished to set up second sets in France and Italy respectively. They were challenged by the Paris and Milan Bar Councils but successfully invoked Art 49 to overcome any objections that they could not operate from more than one set simultaneously. These cases will be discussed in more detail in section 13.9, below.

13.1.1 The scope of Art 49 TFEU

Article 49 abolishes restrictions on the freedom of nationals (whether individuals or companies) to establish themselves in another Member State. The ECJ has stated that, for persons, Art 49 relates not only to the taking up of an activity as a self-employed person, but also to the pursuit of that activity, in the widest sense. The most obvious situation where Art 49 will apply is to prohibit national laws which clearly discriminate against nationals from other Member States seeking to establish themselves, perhaps by imposing extra conditions on them or by denying them rights available to nationals. This discrimination could be:

- **Direct**. For example *Steinhauser v City of Biarritz* (Case 197/84) [1985] ECR 1819 – French law gave specific advantages to French nationals working as self-employed artists. This was successfully challenged by a German national who had travelled to Biarritz in south-west France to ply his trade as a landscape artist. See also *Thijssen* (Case C–42/92) [1993] ECR I–4047 – Belgian rules restricted the post of Insurance Commissioner to Belgian nationals.
- **Indirect**. For example *Stöber and Pereira* (Cases C–4 and 5/95) [1997] ECR I–511 – German law provided child benefits to self-employed nationals only if their children were habitually resident in Germany. This was held to discriminate indirectly against foreign nationals who had come to Germany to set up a business but whose family had decided to remain at 'home'.

However, Art 49 is not limited to prohibiting cases of nationality discrimination. Article 49 states that 'restrictions on the freedom of establishment of nationals of a Member State in the territory of another Member State shall be prohibited'. Thus, **any** restriction imposed by one Member State on the freedom of establishment – even if it applies equally to that State's own nationals – is potentially prohibited by Art 49. This point was first made by the ECJ in *Klopp* (1984). It has been confirmed in several cases since, including *Gebhard* (1995). However, the ECJ has also acknowledged in such cases that **non-discriminatory** national rules may be justified (see below).

In *International Transport Workers' Federation & Finnish Seamen's Union v Viking Line* (Case C–438/05)[2007] ECR I-10779, the *Viking Line* case, the ECJ was asked whether Art 49 could be invoked to challenge threatened strike action by a trade union (in other words, whether Art 49 had 'horizontal' direct effect). The Court held that it did:

JUDGMENT

'In principle, collective action initiated by a trade union or a group of trade unions against an undertaking in order to induce that undertaking to enter into a collective agreement, the terms of which are liable to deter it from exercising freedom of establishment, is not excluded from the scope of [Article 49].'

13.1.2 Rights of entry and residence and Directive 2004/38

Self-employed persons have the same rights as all Citizens to enter another Member State and to live there, to be accompanied by their family members, and even to retire in that State after their working life is over. The detailed rules are set out in Directive 2004/38, which was discussed in Chapter 11.

KEY FACTS

Freedom of establishment	
Freedom of establishment allows self-employed persons to go to another EU Member State and set up in business there. Also allows companies based in one EU Member State to establish a subsidiary or branch in another state	Article 49 TFEU
It is possible to be established in more than one state simultaneously	*Klopp* (1984); *Gebhard* (1995)
Article 49 prohibits discrimination (whether direct or indirect) based on nationality and any other 'restrictions' on the freedom of establishment	*Steinhauser* (1985), *Stöber and Pereira* (1997)
Article 49 is directly effective, vertically and horizontally	*Reyners* (1974); *Viking Line* (2007)

13.2 The problem of qualifications

13.2.1 The law prior to 2007

Although Art 49 removes restrictions on the freedom of EU nationals to establish themselves in another EU Member State, it says nothing about the various conditions which may be laid down in other States by legislation or by rules of trade or professional bodies relating to the education and/or training required to practise. These may vary widely from State to State and, left to their own devices, Member States may have been slow to recognise other states' qualifications. There was thus a major barrier to the free movement of the self-employed, as well as employees whose trade is subject to national regulation.

To tackle this, the EU's legislative bodies were empowered to 'issue directives for the mutual recognition of diplomas, certificates and other evidence of formal qualifications' (Art 53). During the 1970s and early 1980s many Directives were passed, largely in the health services field. But progress was slow, especially in heavily regulated areas like architecture (Directive 85/433 was **17 years** in the making). Because harmonising by profession was proving slow, it was decided in 1984 to abandon the 'sectoral' approach, and instead adopt a general approach. This was not based on harmonisation of individual professions, but the mutual recognition of qualifications in all areas where a higher education diploma was required. The underlying rationale was that a professional person, fully qualified in one Member State, was likely to have much the same skill, knowledge and competence as that required of a counterpart in another Member State.

The result was Directive 89/48, often referred to as the Mutual Recognition Directive. Directive 89/48 essentially created a presumption that those in possession of higher-education qualifications (referred to in the directive as 'diplomas') which entitled them to practise a 'regulated profession' in one Member State were entitled to practise that profession in any other Member State, subject to certain limited derogations. Directive 89/48 was subsequently complemented by a second Mutual Recognition Directive, Directive 92/51, which applied the same principles to all post-secondary qualifications. Neither of these directives applied to professions where specific harmonising directives applied. Finally, Directive 99/42 covered the recognition of qualifications in various commercial and industrial sectors such as agriculture, carpentry, the hotel and restaurant sector, and textiles. Until 2007, therefore, there were three separate regimes:

- Professions where specific harmonising directives existed. This covered the professions of general practitioner (GP), dentist, nurse, veterinary surgeon, midwife, pharmacist, and architect.
- All other professions, such as accountants, lawyers and bankers, where one of the Mutual Recognition Directives applied.
- Those commercial and industrial sectors where Directive 99/42 applied.

13.2.2 The new Qualifications Directive 2005/36

Those three separate regimes have now been consolidated by Directive 2005/36 (the Qualifications Directive). All the pre-existing legislation on qualifications, including the two Mutual Recognition Directives and Directive 99/42, was repealed, although some of the case law decided under these directives may still be of relevance today. The general purpose of Directive 2005/36 is set out in Art 1, which states:

ARTICLE

'Art 1 This Directive establishes rules according to which a Member State which makes access to or pursuit of a regulated profession in its territory contingent upon possession of specific professional qualifications (referred to hereinafter as the host Member State) shall recognise professional qualifications obtained in one or more other Member States (referred to hereinafter as the home Member State) and which allow the holder of the said qualifications to pursue the same profession there, for access to and pursuit of that profession.'

Article 2 sets out the scope of the Directive as follows:

ARTICLE

'Art 2(1) This Directive shall apply to all nationals of a Member State wishing to pursue a regulated profession in a Member State, including those belonging to the liberal professions, other than that in which they obtained their professional qualifications, on either a self-employed or employed basis.

(2) Each Member State may permit Member State nationals in possession of evidence of professional qualifications not obtained in a Member State to pursue a regulated profession … on its territory in accordance with its rules.'

A 'regulated profession'

A 'regulated profession' is defined in Art 3(1)(a) as a 'professional activity or group of professional activities, access to which, the pursuit of which, or one of the modes of pursuit of which is subject, directly or indirectly, by virtue of legislative, regulatory or administrative provisions to the possession of specific professional qualifications; in particular, the use of a professional title limited by legislative, regulatory or administrative provisions to holders of a given professional qualification shall constitute a mode of pursuit.'

It follows, therefore, that it is possible that a 'profession' may be regulated in some Member States but not necessarily all of them. It depends on whether access to the 'profession' is subject in any given State to the possession of qualifications. In *Aranitis* (Case C–164/94) [1996] ECR I–135, a case on Directive 89/48, for example, the applicant had higher-education qualifications in geology awarded in Greece. However, when he purported to rely upon these in Germany he was told that the 'profession' of geology was unregulated in Germany and hence the directive did not apply. This was confirmed in the following cases:

- *Fernández de Bobadilla* (Case C–234/97) [1999] ECR I–4773, another case on Directive 89/48, involving the question whether the 'profession' of art restorer was regulated in Spain (the ECJ held that this was a matter for the national court to decide).
- *Gräbner* (Case C–294/00) [2002] ECR I–6515, a case on Directive 92/51, involving the question whether the 'profession' of 'health practitioner' was regulated in Austria (the ECJ answered this question in the negative).

In *Burbaud* (Case C–285/01) [2003] ECR I–8219, another case on Directive 89/48, the ECJ held that, just because an activity was carried out in the public sector, it could still be regarded as a 'regulated profession'. The case involved a Portuguese national who wished to rely upon her hospital administrator's qualification awarded by the University of Lisbon in order to secure a managerial position within the French national health service. The French authorities refused, insisting upon possession of specific French qualifications. The Court, however, rejected the French Government's arguments and held that the definition of 'regulated profession' was a matter of EU law – indeed, it had to be, otherwise national legislatures could arbitrarily and unilaterally determine what was within the scope of the EU legislation on qualifications.

Article 3(2) of the Qualifications Directive adds that a profession practised by the members of an association or organisation listed in Annex I shall be treated as a 'regulated profession'. This includes, in the UK, bodies as diverse as the British Computer Society, the Institute of Chartered Accountants, the Royal Institution of Chartered Surveyors, the Royal Aeronautical Society and the Engineering Council.

Article 4 elaborates on the 'effect' of the Qualifications Directive:

ARTICLE

'Art 4(1) The recognition of professional qualifications by the host Member State allows the beneficiary to gain access in that Member State to the same profession as that for which he is qualified in the home Member State and to pursue it in the host Member State under the same conditions as its nationals.

(2) For the purposes of this Directive, the profession which the applicant wishes to pursue in the host Member State is the same as that for which he is qualified in his home Member State if the activities covered are comparable.'

Directive 2005/36 then divides into two broad areas:

- The free provision of services (Title II; Arts 5–9).
- Freedom of establishment (Title III; Arts 10–52).

The Qualifications Directive is a lengthy, detailed and technical piece of legislation and the following is necessarily only an overview of the main provisions.

The free provision of services

The main substantive provision here is Art 5, which states:

ARTICLE

'Art 5(1) ... Member States shall not restrict, for any reason relating to professional qualifications, the free provision of services in another Member State:

(a) if the service provider is legally established in a Member State for the purpose of pursuing the same profession there (hereinafter referred to as the Member State of establishment), and

(b) where the service provider moves, if he has pursued that profession in the Member State of establishment for at least two years during the 10 years preceding the provision of services when the profession is not regulated in that Member State. The condition requiring two years' pursuit shall not apply when either the profession or the education and training leading to the profession is regulated.

(2) The provisions of this title shall only apply where the service provider moves to the territory of the host Member State to pursue, on a temporary and occasional basis, the profession referred to in paragraph 1. The temporary and occasional nature of the provision of services shall be assessed case by case, in particular in relation to its duration, its frequency, its regularity and its continuity.

(3) Where a service provider moves, he shall be subject to professional rules of a professional, statutory or administrative nature which are directly linked to professional qualifications, such as the definition of the profession, the use of titles and serious professional malpractice which is directly and specifically linked to consumer protection and safety, as well as disciplinary provisions which are applicable in the host Member State to professionals who pursue the same profession in that Member State.'

Article 6 adds that Member States may exempt service providers from the requirements which it places on professionals established in its territory relating to authorisation by, registration with or membership of a professional organisation or body. Article 7 allows Member States to require that, where a service provider first moves from one State to another in order to provide services, he or she informs the competent authority of the host State, in writing, in advance of doing so. Article 8 provides that the competent authorities of the host State may ask the competent authorities of the service provider's State of establishment to provide any information relevant to:

- the legality of that establishment
- the service provider's 'good conduct' and
- the absence of any disciplinary or criminal sanctions of a professional nature.

Under Art 9, the competent authorities of the host State may also require the service provider to provide the service recipient with various information, such as:

- the name and address of the competent supervisory authority (if any) in the State of establishment
- the service provider's professional title or formal qualification and the State in which it was awarded
- details of any insurance cover or other means of professional liability protection.

Freedom of establishment

The Title on establishment further subdivides into three Chapters:

- General system for the recognition of evidence of training (Chapter 1; Arts 10–15).
- Recognition of professional experience (Chapter 2; Arts 16–20).
- Recognition on the basis of co-ordination of minimum training conditions (Chapter 3; Arts 21–52)

General system for the recognition of evidence of training (Chapter 1)

This Chapter applies to all 'regulated professions' not covered by Chapters 2 and 3 (Art 10). It is this Chapter which replaces the Mutual Recognition Directives. It divides professional competence into five levels:

- Level 1 – an '**attestation of competence**' issued by a competent authority in the home State on the basis of a training course not forming part of a certificate or diploma, or three years' full-time professional experience, or general primary or secondary education, attesting that the holder has acquired 'general knowledge' (Art 11(a)).
- Level 2 – a '**certificate**' attesting to successful completion of a secondary course which is either 'general' or 'technical or professional' in character, and which in either case is supplemented by a course of study or professional training (Art 11(b)).
- Level 3 – a '**diploma**' certifying either (i) successful completion of training at post-secondary level of at least one year's duration (full-time) or the equivalent part-time duration, or (ii) training with a 'special structure' which provides a comparable professional standard and which prepares the trainee for a 'comparable level of responsibilities and functions' (Art 11(c)).
- Level 4 – a '**diploma**' certifying successful completion of training at post-secondary level of at least three and not more than four years' duration (full-time), or the equivalent part-time duration, at a university or equivalent establishment, plus any additional professional training which may be required (Art 11(d)).
- Level 5 – a '**diploma**' certifying successful completion of a post-secondary course of at least four years' duration (full-time), or the equivalent part-time duration, at a university or equivalent establishment, plus successful completion of any additional professional training required (Art 11(e)).

Conditions for recognition: Art 13

Article 13 is the main substantive provision of Chapter 2. It provides that:

ARTICLE

'Art 13(1) If access to or pursuit of a regulated profession in a host Member State is contingent upon possession of specific professional qualifications, the competent authority of that Member State shall permit access to and pursuit of that profession, under the same conditions as apply to its nationals, to applicants possessing the attestation of competence or evidence of formal qualifications required by another Member State in order to gain access to and pursue that profession on its territory. Attestations of competence or evidence of formal qualifications shall satisfy the following conditions:

(a) they shall have been issued by a competent authority in a Member State, designated in accordance with the legislative, regulatory or administrative provisions of that Member State;

(b) they shall attest a level of professional qualification at least equivalent to the level immediately prior to that which is required in the host Member State, as described in Article 11.

(2) Access to and pursuit of the profession, as described in paragraph 1, shall also be granted to applicants who have pursued the profession referred to in that paragraph on a full-time basis for two years during the previous 10 years in another Member State which does not regulate that profession, providing they possess one or more attestations of competence or documents providing evidence of formal qualifications. Attestations of competence and evidence of formal qualifications shall satisfy the following conditions:

(a) they shall have been issued by a competent authority in a Member State, designated in accordance with the legislative, regulatory or administrative provisions of that Member State;

(b) they shall attest a level of professional qualification at least equivalent to the level immediately prior to that required in the host Member State, as described in Article 11;

(c) they shall attest that the holder has been prepared for the pursuit of the profession in question.'

Trevor Tayleur (Qualified Approval (2007) NLJ 1494) provides some useful examples of how the new provisions in the Qualification Directive might operate in practice. He writes:

> 'Under the new system the first step is to find out how the professional qualification is obtained in the Member States concerned. For example, imagine that Germany requires five years' study at university for a given profession, while the UK merely requires three years. The German qualification will be at level 5, and the British at level 4. Germany cannot reject the British qualification, as the Qualifications Directive requires Member States to accept qualifications obtained in other Member States at least equivalent to the level immediately below that which is required in the host State. Thus, Germany must accept a level 4 qualification, though may impose compensation measures. Imagine that in Hungary, members of that same profession only had to go to university for two years; that would be a level 3 qualification. The UK must accept it, subject to compensation measures, as the UK qualification is at level 4. However, Germany would not have to, as its qualification is at level 5 and level 3 is too far below that level.'

'Compensation measures': Art 14

Article 14 provides for 'compensation measures'. It states that:

ARTICLE

'Art 14(1) Article 13 does not preclude the host Member State from requiring the applicant to complete an adaptation period of up to three years or to take an aptitude test if:

- (a) the duration of the training of which he provides evidence under the terms of Article 13, paragraph 1 or 2, is at least one year shorter than that required by the host Member State;
- (b) the training he has received covers substantially different matters than those covered by the evidence of formal qualifications required in the host Member State;
- (c) the regulated profession in the host Member State comprises one or more regulated professional activities which do not exist in the corresponding profession in the applicant's home Member State within the meaning of Article 4(2), and that difference consists in specific training which is required in the host Member State and which covers substantially different matters from those covered by the applicant's attestation of competence or evidence of formal qualifications.

(2) If the host Member State makes use of the option provided for in paragraph 1, it must offer the applicant the choice between an adaptation period and an aptitude test ...

(3) By way of derogation from the principle of the right of the applicant to choose, as laid down in paragraph 2, for professions whose pursuit requires precise knowledge of national law and in respect of which the provision of advice and/or assistance concerning national law is an essential and constant aspect of the professional activity, the host Member State may stipulate either an adaptation period or an aptitude test.

(4) ... "substantially different matters" means matters of which knowledge is essential for pursuing the profession and with regard to which the training received by the migrant shows important differences in terms of duration or content from the training required by the host Member State.

(5) Paragraph 1 shall be applied with due regard to the principle of proportionality. In particular, if the host Member State intends to require the applicant to complete an adaptation period or take an aptitude test, it must first ascertain whether the knowledge acquired by the applicant in the course of his professional experience in a Member State or in a third country, is of a nature to cover, in full or in part, the substantial difference referred to in paragraph 4.'

In *Beuttenmüller* (Case C–102/02) [2004] ECR I–5405, a case under Directive 89/48, the ECJ discussed the role of the 'compensation measures' under that directive (which are essentially the same as those set out above). The Court stated that:

JUDGMENT

'The system of mutual recognition of diplomas ... does not imply that diplomas awarded by the other Member States certify that the education and training are similar or comparable to that required in the host Member State ... A diploma is not recognised on the basis of the intrinsic value of the education and training to which it attests, but because it gives the right to take up a regulated profession in the Member State where it was awarded or recognised ... Differences in the organisation or content of education and training acquired in the Member State of origin by comparison with that provided in the host Member State are not sufficient to justify a refusal to recognise the professional qualification concerned. At most, where those differences are 'substantial', they may justify the host Member State's requiring that the applicant satisfy one or other of the "compensatory measures".'

In *Colegio de Ingenieros de Caminos, Canales y Puertos* (Case C–330/03) [2006] ECR I–801, another case under Directive 89/48, the ECJ again examined the role of the 'compensation measures'. The Court concluded that, just because a host Member State was *entitled* to require an applicant from another State to satisfy one of the measures before being allowed to practise a profession in the host State, it did not follow that it was *obliged* to do so. Instead, the Court created the possibility of 'partial recognition' of an applicant's qualifications, allowing him or her to practise in the areas in which they were actually qualified.

CASE EXAMPLE

Colegio de Ingenieros de Caminos, Canales y Puertos (Case C–330/03) [2006] ECR I–801

In June 1996, Mr Imo, an Italian national with an Italian civil engineering diploma (specialising in hydraulics) applied for permission to practise as a civil engineer in Spain. His application was approved by the Spanish Ministry of Development, but the Institution of Civil Engineers in Spain (the Colegio) challenged this, on the basis that the Italian diploma was very different to the Spanish diploma. Under Spanish legislation, the profession of civil engineer covers a very broad range of activities, including the design and construction of hydraulic installations; land, sea and inland waterway transport infrastructures; conservation of beaches; and town and country planning. The Spanish diploma is awarded after six years of specific post-secondary education and training. Mr Imo's Italian diploma, on the other hand, only covered certain aspects of the Spanish diploma (namely, hydraulics). The ECJ decided that Mr Imo should be allowed 'the possibility of partial taking-up' of the profession in Spain.

The Court stated that:

JUDGMENT

'The scope of [the 'compensation measures'] ... must be restricted to those cases where they are proportionate to the objective pursued. In other words, although [compensation] measures are expressly authorised, they may, in certain cases, be a highly dissuasive factor for a national of a Member State exercising his rights under the Directive. An 'adaptation period' and an 'aptitude test' both call for considerable time and effort on the part of the party concerned. A non-application of those measures might be significant, and even decisive, for a national of one Member State wishing to take up a regulated profession in another Member State. In [certain] cases ... partial taking-up of the profession in question, granted at the request of the party concerned, dispensing that party from having to comply with the compensatory measures and allowing him to take up immediately professional activities for which he is already qualified, would be in keeping with the objectives pursued by the Directive. It therefore follows that the Directive [does] not preclude the possibility of partial taking-up of a "regulated profession".'

Generally speaking, where one of the 'compensation measures' is required, then the individual applicant can choose either to undergo an 'adaptation period' or take an 'aptitude test' (full definitions of these expressions are given below). By way of derogation from this, Art 14(3) provides that host States can specify one or the other for those professions requiring 'precise knowledge of national law'. This most obviously includes judges and lawyers – but does it extend to other professions as well? In *Price* (Case C–149/05) [2006] ECR I–7691, a case under Directive 89/48 involving an auctioneer, the ECJ considered what was meant by the phrase 'precise knowledge of national law'. The Court stated:

JUDGMENT

> 'The application of that requirement cannot lead to the result that only "traditional" legal professions, such as that of judge, notary or lawyer, fall within the scope of [what is now Art 14(3)] ... It is not necessary for the advice and/or assistance provided to clients to concern all national law. It is sufficient that it concerns a specialised area. In order to determine the extent to which the provision of advice and/or assistance on national law is an "essential and constant" element of the activity concerned, it is necessary to refer in particular to normal practice of the relevant profession. It is for the national court to decide that issue.'

More recently, in *Van Leuken* (Case C–197/06) [2008] ECR I-2627, another case under Directive 89/48, the ECJ held that the 'profession' of estate agent in Belgium was not one 'whose practice requires precise knowledge of national law'. The Court pointed out that 'it is sufficient to be the holder of a Belgian diploma in civil, agricultural, technical or industrial engineering in order to become a member of the profession of estate agent in Belgium and the education and training leading to those diplomas does not include significant legal training'. This meant that the Belgian authorities could not demand that Willem Van Leuken – a Dutch estate agent based in the Netherlands whose activities included selling property in Belgium to Dutch clients – undertake an aptitude test in Belgian property law.

'Adaptation period': Art 3(1)(g)

An 'adaptation period' is defined in Art 3(1)(g) of the Qualifications Directive as 'the pursuit of a regulated profession in the host Member State under the responsibility of a qualified member of that profession, such period of supervised practice possibly being accompanied by further training. This period of supervised practice shall be the subject of an assessment. The detailed rules governing the adaptation period and its assessment as well as the status of a migrant under supervision shall be laid down by the competent authority in the host Member State'.

'Aptitude test': Art 3(1)(h)

An 'aptitude test' is defined in Art 3(1)(h) of the Qualifications Directive as a 'test limited to the professional knowledge of the applicant, made by the competent authorities of the host Member State with the aim of assessing the ability of the applicant to pursue a regulated profession in that Member State. In order to permit this test to be carried out, the competent authorities shall draw up a list of subjects which, on the basis of a comparison of the education and training required in the Member State and that received by the applicant, are not covered by the diploma or other evidence of formal qualifications possessed by the applicant.' Article 3(1)(h) goes on to provide that the test must 'take account of the fact that the applicant is a qualified professional in the home Member State or the Member State from which he comes. It shall cover subjects to be selected from those on the list, knowledge of which is essential in order to be able to pursue the profession in the host Member State. The test may also include knowledge of the professional rules applicable to the activities in question in the host Member State.'

'Common platforms': Art 15

Article 15 introduces a new concept into the mutual recognition of qualifications area: 'common platforms'. These are defined as 'a set of criteria of professional qualifications which are suitable for compensating for substantial differences which have been identified between the training requirements existing in the various Member States for a given profession' (Art 15(1)). The 'substantial differences' are to be identified by comparing the 'duration and contents of the training in at least two thirds of the Member States, including all Member States which regulate this profession'. The Member States or 'professional associations or organisations which are representative at national and European level' may submit 'common platforms' for consideration by the European Commission for possible adoption (Art 15(2)). If, when such platforms are adopted in the future, host States must then waive the application of the compensation measures under Art 14 in the case of any applicant whose professional qualifications satisfy the criteria in the platform (Art 15(3)).

Recognition of professional experience (Chapter 2)

This Chapter deals with those commercial and industrial sectors where previously Directive 99/42 applied. Article 16 now provides that if, in a Member State, access to or pursuit of one of the activities listed in Annex IV of the Qualifications Directive is contingent upon possession of 'general, commercial or professional knowledge and aptitudes', that State must recognise previous pursuit of the activity in another State as sufficient proof of such knowledge and aptitudes. The list of 'activities' in Annex IV is very lengthy but, by way of example, it includes agriculture, carpentry, construction, footwear and clothing manufacturers, and the beverage, chemicals and petroleum industries. Articles 17–19 stipulate various minimum time periods over which the activities must have been pursued in the home State.

Recognition on the basis of co-ordination of minimum training conditions (Chapter 3)

This Chapter deals with those professions which previously had their own directive. They now have their own provisions in the Qualifications Directive (GPs are covered by Arts 24–30; nurses by Arts 31–33; dentists by Arts 34–37; vets by Arts 38 and 39; midwives by Arts 40–43; pharmacists by Arts 44 and 45; and architects by Arts 46–49), but the essential principles are the same for each of these areas. The Qualifications Directive:

- co-ordinates across all States the training required in order for qualification (as a nurse, dentist, architect, etc); and
- provides that, once a professional in one of these areas is qualified to practise in one Member State then they are automatically entitled to practise in any other State.

13.2.3 Obligation to assess equivalence

Prior to Directive 89/48, many cases arose involving professions where no separate harmonising Directive existed. The ECJ has developed a line of case law according to which it is unlawful discrimination, and a breach of Arts 49 or 56 TFEU, to refuse permission to practise to a person whose qualifications in one State have been recognised, by the competent authorities, as equivalent to those awarded in the State in which he seeks to practise. Examples of this approach are *Thieffry* (Case 71/76) [1977] ECR 765 and *Patrick v Minister of Cultural Affairs* (Case 11/77) [1977] ECR 1199.

CASE EXAMPLE

Thieffry (Case 71/76) [1977] ECR 765

Jean Thieffry was a Belgian national with a doctorate in law from Louvain University, in Belgium, which had been recognised by the University of Paris as equivalent to a French law degree. He then undertook professional examinations and was awarded the *certificat d'aptitude a la profession d'avocat*. However, the Paris Bar Council refused to recognise his doctorate when he applied to undertake admission to the French bar. The ECJ held that this was a breach of Art 49.

CASE EXAMPLE

Patrick v Minister of Cultural Affairs (Case 11/77) [1977] ECR 1199

Richard Patrick was a qualified English architect who wished to practise in France. At the time (1973) there was no harmonising Directive on architectural qualifications. His qualifications had, however, been recognised as equivalent to the corresponding French qualifications under a Ministerial Decree of 1964. However, the French Minister of Cultural Affairs refused him permission – purely on nationality grounds. The ECJ held that this refusal was a breach of Art 49.

The ECJ then developed this rule to impose an obligation on the authorities of the host State to compare the candidate's qualifications with those awarded in the host State in order to establish whether or not they were equivalent (*UNECTEF v Heylens* (Case 222/86) [1987] ECR 4097). The person concerned must be given reasons why their qualifications are not deemed to be equivalent, and the decision must be subject to judicial review. The leading case in this area is *Vlassopoulou* (Case C–340/89) [1991] ECR I–2357.

CASE EXAMPLE

Vlassopoulou (Case C–340/89) [1991] ECR I–2357

Irène Vlassopoulou, a Greek national, was qualified as a lawyer in Greece. In 1983 she began work in a law office in Germany. In 1984 she was authorised by the German authorities to advise on Greek and EU law. In 1988 she applied to join the German Bar, but this time the German authorities refused her permission on the basis of a lack of qualifications. Conditions for entry to the German Bar included studying at a German university. The ECJ held that the German authorities were obliged to assess the level of equivalence between her Greek qualifications and those available under German study.

The ECJ held that the competent authorities are obliged to make:

JUDGMENT

'A comparison between the specialised knowledge and abilities certified by [the individual's qualifications] and the knowledge and qualifications required by the national rules. That examination procedure must enable the authorities of the host State to assure themselves, on an objective basis, that the foreign diploma certifies that its holder has knowledge and qualifications which are, if not identical, at least equivalent to those required by the national diploma. That assessment of the equivalence of the foreign diploma must be carried out exclusively in the light of the level of knowledge and qualifications which its holder can be assumed to possess in the light of that diploma, having regard to the nature and duration of the studies and practical training to which the diploma relates. In the course of that examination, a Member State may, however, take into consideration objective differences relating to both the legal framework of the profession in question in the Member State of origin and to its field of activity. In the case of the profession of lawyer, a Member State may therefore carry out a comparative examination of diplomas, taking account of the differences identified between the national legal systems concerned.'

The ECJ laid down some guidelines as to what Member States' authorities should do after the assessment was completed. It distinguished between three situations: full, partial and no equivalence:

- **Full equivalence**: the Member State had to accept the candidate's qualification.

- **Partial equivalence**: the candidate might be required to show that he had acquired the knowledge and qualifications lacking. Any examination of documents made in order to discover which was the case had to be done in such a way as to ensure that the person's EU legal rights were protected. Any decision taken after the examination had to be capable of judicial review. The candidate had to be able to ascertain the reasons for any adverse decision, and also told of the remedies available against such a decision.
- **No equivalence**: the Member State was under no obligation to allow the candidate to practise.

These tests have since been applied in several cases (*Borrell and Others* (Case C–104/91) [1992] ECR I–3003; *De Bobadilla* (1999); *Dreessen* (Case C–31/00) [2002] ECR I–663). In *Dreessen* (2002), the ECJ summarised the position as follows:

JUDGMENT

'The authorities of a Member State to which an application has been made by [an EU Citizen] for authorisation to practise a profession, access to which depends, under national legislation, on the possession of a diploma or professional qualification or on periods of practical experience, are required to take into consideration all of the diplomas, certificates and other evidence of formal qualifications of the person concerned and his relevant experience, by comparing the specialised knowledge and abilities so certified and that experience with the knowledge and qualifications required by the national legislation.'

The cases can be summarised as follows:

Case	Year	Candidate's nationality	Candidate's qualifications	Awarding State	Host State
Heylens	1987	Belgium	coaching	Belgium	France
Vlassopoulou	1991	Greece	law	Greece	Germany
Aguirre Borrell and Others	1992	UK	estate management	UK	Spain
Fernández De Bobadilla	1999	Spain	art restoration	UK	Spain
Dreessen	2002	Belgium	civil engineering	Germany	Belgium
Morgenbesser	2004	France	law	France	Italy

In *Morgenbesser* (Case C–313/01) [2003] ECR I–13467, Christine Morgenbesser, a French national, had studied law in France and obtained her diploma of *maîtrise en droit* in 1996, signifying completion of the academic stage of legal education. She did not, however, go on to study for her *certificate d'aptitude à la profession d'avocat* which would have allowed her to practise as a lawyer in France. Instead, she spent several months working in a law firm in Paris. Then, in 1998, she joined a firm of lawyers (*avvocati*) in Genoa, Italy. In 1999, she applied for enrolment in the register of '*praticanti*' – lawyers who have the academic qualifications but not the practical training. However, her application was refused by both the Genoa Bar Council and the National Bar Council on the basis that Italian legislation required that *praticanti* held a diploma awarded or confirmed by an Italian University. She challenged this.

The ECJ rejected her claim to rely upon Directive 89/48, on the basis that she did not have a 'diploma' as defined in that legislation. However, the Court went on to hold that, under Art 49, the Italian authorities were nevertheless obliged to undertake an examination of her French qualifications (namely, her *maîtrise en droit*) plus whatever practical experience she had acquired, and to assess that for equivalence to the Italian qualifications. She would then be in a position, if she wished, to undertake whatever additional education and/or practical training was required in order to become fully qualified as an *avvocato* in Italy. The Court relied on several of the cases described above, including *Thieffry, Heylens, Vlassopoulou* and *Fernández de Bobadilla.*

Obviously, *Morgenbesser* and all of the cases relied upon in that case pre-date the new Qualifications Directive but the principles established in those cases continue to be relevant today. If, for whatever reason, the Qualifications Directive does not apply, then the above principles will need to be invoked. There are at least two situations where this is possible:

- where an individual does not have a 'diploma'
- where a profession is unregulated in the 'host' State.

13.2.4 Qualifications obtained outside the EU

In *Tawil-Albertini* (Case C–154/93) [1994] ECR I–451, where the candidate, a French national, had a qualification in dentistry awarded in Lebanon and wanted to practise in France, the ECJ held that the Member States were **not** obliged to recognise qualifications obtained in a country outside the EU. This was the case even if one Member State recognises the non-EU qualification as equivalent to its own: this does not bind the other Member States. Thus, the fact that the Belgian authorities were prepared to recognise the candidate's Lebanese qualification did not oblige the authorities in France to recognise it.

However, if one Member State does recognise non-EU qualifications, and allows the person to practise there, then the other Member States are required to recognise **that practical experience**. This was decided in *Haim* (Case C–319/92) [1994] ECR I–425, where an Italian national acquired a Turkish diploma in dentistry before practising in Belgium, where his diploma was recognised, and then sought to rely upon his diploma in Germany, where it was not recognised. The ECJ held that the German authorities had to take into account Haim's professional experience acquired in Belgium. This point was confirmed in *Hocsman* (Case C–238/98) [2000] ECR I–6623. Moreover, in *Hocsman* the ECJ seemed to say that the authorities would be obliged to recognise all qualifications awarded 'abroad'. This would amount to an overruling of *Tawil-Albertini* (1994), although the ECJ did not make this explicit.

CASE EXAMPLE

Hocsman (Case C–238/98) [2000] ECR I–6623

Hugo Fernando Hocsman, a Spanish national, obtained qualifications in medicine in 1976 from the University of Buenos Aires in Argentina. He was then authorised to practise in Spain, which recognised his Argentinean qualifications as equivalent to the Spanish. He went on to obtain a diploma in urology in 1982 from the University of Barcelona. However, when he attempted to obtain authorisation to practise in France in 1997, the French authorities refused to recognise his qualifications. The French authorities argued that Hocsman could not rely upon Art 49 but the ECJ disagreed, and held that Hocsman could rely on Art 49 and oblige the French authorities to examine both his Argentinean qualifications and his experience in Spain for equivalence with the French qualification requirements.

The ECJ held that:

JUDGMENT

'The authorities of a Member State to whom an application has been made by [an EU] national for authorisation to practise a profession access to which depends, under national law, on the possession of a diploma or professional qualification, or on periods of practical experience, must take into consideration *all the diplomas, certificates and other evidence of formal qualifications* of the person concerned and his relevant experience, by comparing the specialised knowledge and abilities so certified and that experience with the knowledge and qualifications required by the national rules. If that comparative examination of diplomas and professional experience results in the finding that the *knowledge and qualifications certified by the diploma awarded abroad* correspond to those required by the national provisions, the competent authorities of the host Member State must recognise that diploma.'

Summary of cases involving the recognition of non-EU qualifications:

Case	**Year**	**Nationality of complainant**	**Non-EU State and qualification obtained**	**Member State where qualification recognised**	**Member State refusing to recognise qualification**
Tawil-Albertini	1994	French	Lebanon – dentistry	Belgium	France
Haim	1994	Italian	Turkey – dentistry	Belgium	Germany
Hocsman	2000	Spanish	Argentina – medicine	Spain	France

These case law developments have now been recognised in legislation. Article 3(3) of the Qualifications Directive provides that:

ARTICLE

'Art 3(3) Evidence of formal qualifications issued by a third country shall be regarded as evidence of formal qualifications if the holder has three years' professional experience in the profession concerned on the territory of the Member State which recognised that evidence of formal qualifications in accordance with Article 2(2), certified by that Member State.'

KEY FACTS

The problem of qualifications	
Persons in possession of professional qualifications obtained in one Member State may, subject to certain conditions, practise that profession in other Member States	Directive 2005/36
Compensation measures in the form of adaptation periods of aptitude tests may apply if there are differences in the duration of training or the matters covered during training	Directive 2005/36
If for any reason Directive 2005/36 does not apply, professionals can fall back on Art 49 TFEU, which requires the host state's authorities to undertake a comparison of qualifications and/or professional experience and recognise that if fully or even partially equivalent	*Thieffry* (1977), *Patrick* (1977), *Vlassopoulou* (1991), *Morgenbesser* (2003)
Qualifications obtained outside of the EU must be recognised by all Member States, at least where one State has recognised them and allowed the holder to practise for three years	*Directive* 2005/36, *Haim* (1994), *Hocsman* (2000)

13.3 The freedom to provide services under Art 56 TFEU

Article 56 provides that 'restrictions on freedom to provide services ... shall be prohibited in respect of nationals of Member States who are established in a [Member State] other than that of the person for whom the services are provided'.

13.3.1 'Services'

This is defined in Art 57.

ARTICLE

> 'Art 57 Services shall be considered to be "services" within the meaning of the Treaties where they are normally provided for remuneration, insofar as they are not governed by the provisions relating to freedom of movement for goods, capital and persons.
>
> "Services" shall in particular include:
>
> (a) activities of an industrial character;
> (b) activities of a commercial character;
> (c) activities of craftsmen;
> (d) activities of the professions.
>
> Without prejudice to the provisions ... relating to the right of establishment, the person providing a service may, in order to do so, temporarily pursue his activity in the State where the service is provided, under the same conditions as are imposed by that State on its own nationals.'

Article 56 therefore has a very wide scope. It covers all commercial activities, financial and legal advice, medical treatment, even holidays. *SPUC v Grogan* (Case C–159/90) [1991] ECR I–4685 established that abortions provided by private clinics amounted to 'services' for the purpose of Art 56. In *Jany and Others* (Case C–268/99) [2001] ECR I–8615 the ECJ held that Art 56 could apply to prostitution!

13.3.2 'Freedom to provide services'

Article 56 prohibits national laws which discriminate against service providers from other Member States. This discrimination may be direct or indirect. In fact, most of the cases involve indirect discrimination. For example, in *Van Binsbergen* (Case 33/74) [1974] ECR 1299, Dutch rules required lawyers to be habitually resident in the Netherlands. This was held to discriminate indirectly against foreign nationals who were less likely to be living in the Netherlands. The ECJ stated:

JUDGMENT

> 'A requirement that the person providing the service must be habitually resident within the territory of the State where the service is to be provided may, according to the circumstances, have the result of depriving [Art 56] of all useful effect.'

A similar case of indirect discrimination is *Coenen* (Case 39/75) [1976] ECR 1547 – Dutch rules required insurance brokers to be habitually resident in the Netherlands. A more recent example is *Bickel and Franz* (Case C–274/96) [1998] ECR I–7637.

CASE EXAMPLE

Bickel and Franz (Case C–274/96) [1998] ECR I–7637

Italian law giving people resident in the northern Italian region of Bolzano the right to choose whether to have criminal proceedings against them conducted in either Italian or German was held to discriminate indirectly against foreign nationals. Bickel was an Austrian national visiting Bolzano on business; Franz was a German national who had gone there on holiday. Both were prosecuted for relatively minor offences (drink-driving; possession of an unlawful weapon) and asked to have the trial conducted in German; this was refused. They successfully argued that this refusal infringed Art 56.

Article 56 may even be invoked to challenge all national legislation which is not discriminatory at all (directly or indirectly), provided that it has the potential to inhibit the freedom to provide services. This was clearly acknowledged in *Säger v Dennemeyer & Co.* (Case C–76/90) [1991] ECR I–4221, where the ECJ stated that:

JUDGMENT

'[Article 56] requires not only the elimination of all discrimination against a person providing services on the ground of his nationality but also the abolition of any restriction, *even if applied without distinction to national providers of services and to those of other Member States*, when it is liable to prohibit or otherwise impede the activities of a provider of services established in another Member State where he lawfully provides similar services.'

In *Scorpio Konzertproduktionen* (Case C–290/04) [2006] ECR I–9461, the ECJ offered the following guidance on when Art 56 applies:

JUDGMENT

'The provisions governing the freedom to provide services apply if the following conditions are satisfied:

– the service must be provided within the [Union];

– the provider of services must be a national of a Member State and established in a State of the [Union].

It follows that the [TFEU] does not extend the benefit of those provisions to providers of services who are nationals of non-member countries, even if they are established within the [Union] and an [intra-Union] provision of services is concerned.'

The Services Directive 2006/123

Reference must be made here to the recently adopted Services Directive (Directive 2006/123). The key points are that:

- The directive apples to services supplied by providers established in a Member State (Art 2(1)).
- A number of services are excluded, including 'non-economic services of general interest', financial services, electronic communications services, transport, temporary work agencies, healthcare, gambling, audiovisual, private security and social services (Art 2(2)).
- Otherwise, the directive applies to 'any self-employed economic activity, normally provided for remuneration' (Art 4(1)).
- The directive provides that cross-border service providers must be free to do so, except where it is justifiable to restrict that freedom 'for reasons of public policy, public security, public health or the protection of the environment' (Art 16). These

derogations must 'respect the principles' of 'non-discrimination: the requirement may be neither directly nor indirectly discriminatory with regard to nationality or, in the case of legal persons, with regard to the Member State in which they are established' and 'proportionality: the requirement must be suitable for attaining the objective pursued, and must not go beyond what is necessary to attain that objective' (Art 16).

At one point during the proposal stage, the directive would have introduced a so-called 'country of origin' principle, requiring host States to allow service providers to operate in their territory regulated by the laws and regulations of the provider's home State. This was a radical (and highly contentious) proposal which did not make the final directive. Instead, Art 16 overlaps with and essentially confirms existing ECJ case law on Art 56 TFEU. It is therefore debatable what practical impact, if any, the Services Directive will have. The omens are not good: Craig & De Búrca, *EU Law* 4th edition (Oxford), 2007, page 845, for example, describe the directive as 'patchy, complicated, and legally rather unsatisfactory'.

13.3.3 'Remuneration'

Article 56 applies whenever a cross-border service is provided in return for remuneration. In the vast majority of cases this proposition will be straightforward, but in certain circumstances it has prompted questions that needed to be resolved by the ECJ. For example, in *Bond van Adverteerders* (Case 352/85) [1988] ECR 2085, subsequently confirmed in *Deliège* (Cases C–51/96 and C–191/97) [2000] ECR I–2549, the ECJ held that it is not essential that the person who receives the services be the person who provides the remuneration.

CASE EXAMPLE

Deliège (Cases C–51/96 and C–191/97) [2000] ECR I–2549

Christelle Deliège, a Belgian national, had been competing in national and international judo tournaments since 1987. She complained that the Belgian judo federation was unlawfully frustrating her career by not selecting her for a number of important international competitions. Matters came to a head when she was not picked for a tournament in Paris in February 1996. She brought a claim alleging breach of Art 56. The question was: as an amateur *judoka*, could she rely upon Art 56? The ECJ held that sporting activities did fall within the scope of EU law, but only to the extent that they constituted an economic activity. However, a high-ranking athlete capable of participating in international tournaments was capable of attracting sponsorship; the presence of international standard athletes would attract the paying public, TV companies and advertisers. Thus, an athlete's participation in a tournament could be regarded as the provision of services for 'remuneration', as required by Art 57, even if the services were provided for someone other than the person(s) providing the remuneration.

Two areas of cross-border provision of services have generated controversy, because of the question of remuneration.

Educational services

In *Humbel* (Case 263/86) [1988] ECR 5365 the ECJ made it very clear that while privately funded education is covered by Art 56, State-funded education is not. *Humbel* (1988) has been followed ever since. In *Wirth* (Case C–109/92) [1993] ECR I–6447, the ECJ held that courses 'given in an establishment of higher education which is financed essentially out of public funds' do not constitute 'services', while in *Schwarz* (Case C–76/05) [2007] ECR I-6849, the Court stated:

JUDGMENT

'Article 56 is applicable where taxpayers of a given Member State send their children to a private school established in another Member State which may be regarded as providing services for remuneration, that is to say which is essentially financed by private funds.'

Medical treatment

Luisi and Carbone (Cases 286/82 and 26/83) [1984] ECR 377 established that privately funded medical treatment is covered by Art 56. This was confirmed in *Kohll* (Case C–158/96) [1998] ECR I–1931 – the mere fact that the cost of the treatment would be reimbursed by the State did not affect this decision. The cases of *Vanbraekel* (Case C–368/98) [2001] ECR I–5363 and *Geraets-Smits and Peerbooms* (Case C–157/99) [2001] ECR I–5473 have rather blurred the distinction between private and state-funded medical treatment. The ECJ held that, because the medical treatment was paid for (at least initially) by the patients, the treatment therefore amounted to a service provided for remuneration, and hence Art 56 applied. The fact that the costs could potentially be reimbursed by the social security authorities in the patients' home State did not prevent Art 56 from applying. However, the ECJ then went on to hold that various derogations might be applied in order to take such medical treatment cases out of the scope of Art 56 after all (the public health derogation under Art 52 or 'maintaining the financial balance of a State's social security system' under the rule of reason – see below, sections 13.7 and 13.8, respectively).

The principle that private medical treatment is a 'service' and therefore subject to Art 56 was confirmed in *Watts v Bedford Primary Care Trust* (Case C–372/04) [2006] ECR I–4325. The case involved Mrs Yvonne Watts, a British woman who underwent a hip replacement operation at a private hospital in France, because she would have had to wait for a year to have the operation in the UK. Regarding the question whether Art 56 applied on these facts, the ECJ stated that:

JUDGMENT

'Article 56 applies where a patient such as Mrs Watts receives medical services in a hospital environment for consideration in a Member State other than her State of residence … It must therefore be found that a situation such as that which gave rise to the dispute in the main proceedings, in which a person whose state of health necessitates hospital treatment goes to another Member State and there receives the treatment in question for consideration, falls within the scope of the Treaty provisions on the freedom to provide services.'

13.3.4 What if the 'service' is illegal?

This issue arises because a service may be permitted in one Member State but prohibited (or at least restricted) in another. Article 56 applies provided that the service is lawful in **some**, but not necessarily **all**, Member States. The best example is perhaps an English case that did not even reach the ECJ. *R v Human Fertilisation and Embryology Authority, ex p Blood* [1997] 2 CMLR 591 involved the famous case of Diane Blood. Her husband, Stephen, suddenly contracted meningitis and lapsed into a coma (from which he never recovered). The couple were childless but they had both wanted children. Mrs Blood therefore applied to the High Court for permission to use Stephen's sperm for artificial insemination. However, the court refused because UK legislation, the Human Fertilisation and Embryology Act 1990, requires the written consent of the man concerned, and Stephen had not given this consent. Mrs Blood appealed and the Court of Appeal held that she had a right under Art 56 to take Stephen's sperm for insemination treatment in Belgium, where written consent was not required. Treatment was duly carried out, successfully, in 1998 and Mrs Blood had her first child in 1999.

Society for the Protection of Unborn Children (SPUC) v Grogan (1991) raised the question of whether Art 56 could be relied upon by students in one Member State (Ireland) to disseminate information about abortion clinics in another Member State (the UK), given that, at the time, abortion was absolutely prohibited in Ireland.

CASE EXAMPLE

SPUC v Grogan (Case C–159/90) [1991] ECR I–4685

Article 40 of the Irish Constitution contained the following provision: 'The State acknowledges the right to life of the unborn and, with due regard to the equal right to life of the mother, guarantees in its laws to respect, and, as far as practicable, by its laws to defend and vindicate that right.' Abortion was specifically prohibited by the Health (Family Planning) Act 1979. This meant that Irish women wanting an abortion were forced to travel to the UK, where abortions are lawful (subject to the conditions in the Abortion Act 1967 being satisfied). Stephen Grogan, a university student in Dublin, published information on how and where female students could get abortions in London and other British cities. The SPUC went to the Irish High Court to secure an injunction to prevent further publication, successfully arguing that abortion was unlawful in Ireland. Grogan challenged the injunction on the basis that Art 40 of the Irish Constitution was a breach of Art 56, in that it imposed a limitation on his freedom to provide information about the services of abortion clinics in the UK. The SPUC argued Art 52 (the public policy derogation) but, in the end, the ECJ avoided the issue by holding that there was too tenuous a connection between the providers of the service (the abortion clinics in the UK), and the students distributing information about it, for an injunction to be regarded as a restriction on the freedom to provide services. There was therefore no breach of Art 56, so it was unnecessary to consider whether Art 52 would apply.

Recently there have been several ECJ cases examining the compatibility of national legislation regulating gambling with Art 56. These cases, including *Schindler* (Case C–275/92) [1994] ECR I–1039 (restriction of gambling in the UK), *Läärä* (Case C–124/97) [1999] ECR I–6067 (restrictions in Finland), *Zenatti* (Case C–67/98) [1999] ECR I–7289 and *Gambelli and Others* (Case C–243/01) [2003] ECR I–13031 (restrictions in Italy), *ANOMAR and Others* (Case C–6/01) [2003] ECR I–8621 (restrictions in Portugal), will be discussed below (in section 13.8).

13.3.5 The scope of 'cross border' services

Although the provider of services will typically travel to another State to do so, it is not necessary. Article 56 also applies where the service **recipient** travels to a State other than their own in order to receive a service – most obviously, tourists and those seeking specialist medical treatment (see section 13.5, below). Indeed, it is not actually necessary for **either** the service provider **or** the recipient to leave their own State. Provided that they are established in different States, and the service is provided by one and received by the other, then Art 56 will apply. This allows service providers to challenge measures adopted by their own State where those measures prohibit or restrict their freedom to provide services to nationals established in other Member States. This is increasingly likely to become the case where instantaneous telecommunication systems – most obviously the Internet – are relied upon. In *Alpine Investments* (Case C–384/93) [1995] ECR I–1141, the ECJ stated that Art 56 'covers services which the provider offers by telephone to potential recipients established in other Member States and provides without moving from the Member State in which he is established'. In *Carpenter* (Case C–60/00) [2002] ECR I–6279, the facts of which were given in the previous chapter (see section 12.5.2), the ECJ confirmed *Alpine Investments* (1995) and stated:

JUDGMENT

'Services come within the meaning of "services" in [Art 56] both in so far as the provider travels for that purpose to the Member State of the recipient and in so far as he provides cross-border services without leaving the Member State in which he is established.'

KEY FACTS

The freedom to provide services	
The freedom to provide services allows a service provider, based in one Member State, to provide a service to any person based in another State	Article 56 TFEU
The service provider must be a national of a Member State and the service must be provided within the EU	*Scorpio Konzertproduktionen* (2006)
Article 56 prohibits discrimination (whether direct or indirect) based on nationality and any other 'restrictions' on the freedom to provide services	*Van Binsbergen* (1974), *Säger v Dennemeyer & Co.* (1991)
Article 56 applies when there is a cross-border service, even if neither service provider nor recipient moves. This is increasingly noticeable in cases involving services provided electronically, such as financial services and gambling services	*Alpine Investments* (1995), *Carpenter* (2002)
Article 56 is directly effective	*Van Binsbergen*
'Services' are defined very widely, including commercial and professional activities	Article 57 TFEU
Services must be 'normally' provided for 'remuneration', ie paid for, although there is no requirement that the service recipient provides it	Article 57; *Deliège* (2000)
Education and medical treatment are 'services', but only if provided for 'remuneration'	*Humbel* (1988), *Wirth* (1993), *Kohll* (1998), *Watts* (2006)
Article 56 applies even though a service may be prohibited in some Member States – such as abortions or gambling	*SPUC v Grogan* (1991); *Schindler* (1994)

13.4 Distinguishing establishment and services

The difference between the two is a matter of degree – whether someone is simply providing services, or is actually established, in a Member State other than their own may simply depend on how lengthy is their stay in that other State. It is sometimes difficult to differentiate between established persons and service providers. Occasionally, the ECJ may need to decide. The leading case is *Gebhard* (1995), where the ECJ stated:

JUDGMENT

'The chapter on the right of establishment [and] the chapter on services [are] mutually exclusive ... The provisions of the chapter on services are subordinate to those of the chapter on the right of establishment ... The concept of establishment is a very broad one, allowing [an EU] national to participate, on a stable and continuous basis, in the economic life of a Member State other than his State of origin and to profit therefrom, so contributing to economic and social interpenetration within the [Union] in the sphere of activities as self-employed persons. In contrast, where the provider of services moves to another Member

State, the provisions of the chapter on services envisage that he is to pursue his activity there on a temporary basis … The temporary nature of the activities in question has to be determined in the light, not only of the duration of the provision of the service, but also of its regularity, periodicity or continuity.'

In *Schnitzer* (Case C–215/01) [2003] ECR I–14847, the ECJ offered further guidance on the difference between establishment and the provision of services. The Court stated that Art 56 may cover services 'varying widely in nature', including services which are provided 'over an extended period, even over several years, where, for example, the services in question are supplied in connection with the construction of a large building'. The Court then stated:

JUDGMENT

'No provision of the Treaty affords a means of determining, in an abstract manner, the duration or frequency beyond which the supply of a service or of a certain type of service in another Member State can no longer be regarded as the provision of "services". It follows that the mere fact that a business established in one Member State supplies identical or similar services with a greater or lesser degree of frequency or regularity in a second Member State, without having an infrastructure there enabling it to pursue a professional activity there on a stable and continuous basis and, from the infrastructure, to hold itself out to, amongst others, nationals of the second Member State, is not sufficient for it to be regarded as established in the second Member State.'

The ECJ has held that, where an enterprise is situated in one Member State, but its activities are directed **entirely** or **mainly** towards another Member State (often in order to avoid more stringent rules and regulations applying in the latter State), then the enterprise will be deemed to be established in the latter State and not simply providing services there (*TV 10* (Case C–23/93) ECR I–4795).

13.5 The freedom to receive services

Although Art 56 refers to the right to provide services, it has been extended to the right to receive them too. The first case was *Luisi and Carbone* (1984).

CASE EXAMPLE

Luisi and Carbone (Cases 286/82 and 26/83) [1984] ECR 377

Two Italian nationals, Graziani Luisi and Giuseppe Carbone, were prosecuted under Italian law for taking excess foreign currency out of the country. Luisi had withdrawn a considerable sum in US dollars, French and Swiss francs and Deutschmarks from various Italian banks and taken this to Germany and France for a combination of tourism and medical purposes. Carbone had taken a sizeable amount of US dollars, Swiss francs and Deutschmarks to Germany on a three-month holiday. Each was convicted and fined the difference between the amount they had taken and the amount they were permitted to take. They appealed against their fines. The Italian court referred the matter to the ECJ, which held that the Italian rules constituted a breach of Art 56.

The Court stated:

JUDGMENT

'The freedom to provide services includes the freedom, for the recipient of services, to go to another Member State in order to receive a service there, without being obstructed by restriction … and that tourists, persons receiving medical treatment and persons travelling for the purposes of education or business are to be regarded as recipients of services.'

Note: the French franc and the German deutschmark ceased to be legal tender when the single European currency was introduced in 2002.

This ruling has since been followed in several cases:

- **tourists** – *Cowan* (Case 186/87) [1989] ECR 195; *Bickel and Franz* (1998); *Calfa* (Case C–348/96) [1999] ECR I–11
- **persons receiving private education** (see above)
- **persons receiving medical treatment** (see above).

CASE EXAMPLE

Cowan v Trésor Public (Case 186/87) [1989] ECR 195

Ian Cowan, an Englishman on holiday in France, was violently assaulted outside a Métro station in Paris. He applied for compensation to the *Commission d'Indemnisation des Victims d'Infraction*. Under French law, compensation was payable from public funds only to French nationals and holders of French residence permits. Cowan argued that this discrimination was contrary to Art 56 in that it obstructed his freedom to move to France for the purpose of receiving services (ie tourism). The ECJ upheld Cowan's claim.

A variation on this theme occurred in *De Coster* (Case C–17/00) [2001] ECR I–9445, which involved the imposition of a satellite dish tax by a local authority in Belgium. One of the residents challenged this, alleging that it restricted his freedom to receive services (in the form of satellite television broadcasts) from other Member States. The ECJ agreed (although it found the tax was at least potentially justifiable because it helped to control the proliferation of satellite dishes, which was beneficial to the environment).

13.6 The 'official authority' derogation in Art 51 TFEU

Article 51 provides that 'activities … that are connected, even occasionally, with the exercise of official authority' are **not** covered by the Treaty rules on establishment and services. The derogation has, however, been given a very narrow scope. The ECJ has pointed out that Art 51 applies only to **activities** connected with the exercise of official authority; not professions or occupations **as a whole**. In *Reyners v Belgium* (Case 2/74) [1974] ECR 631, involving Belgian law restricting the profession of *avocat* (similar to barrister) to Belgian nationals, the ECJ stated:

JUDGMENT

'Professional activities involving contacts, even regular and organic, with the courts, including even compulsory co-operation in their functioning, do not constitute, as such, connection with the exercise of official authority. The most typical activities of the profession of *avocat*, in particular, such as consultation and legal assistance and also representation and the defence of parties in court, even where the intervention or assistance of the *avocat* is compulsory or is a legal monopoly, cannot be considered as connected with the exercise of official authority.'

13.7 Derogation on grounds of public policy, public security or public health in Art 52 TFEU

The 'public policy' derogation is rarely invoked, although *Calfa* (1999), discussed in Chapter 11, involved the application of the public policy derogation to an Italian national convicted of possessing drugs while on holiday in Greece, that is, she was exercising her rights to receive services under Art 56. A more recent case is *Omega* (Case C–36/02) [2004] ECR I–9609, which involved the question of whether or not the protection of human dignity, as provided for in the German Constitution, could be invoked to derogate from the freedom to provide services. The ECJ held that it could.

CASE EXAMPLE

Omega (Case C–36/02) [2004] ECR I–9609

Omega, a German company, operated a 'laserdrome' centre in the German city of Bonn. This allowed paying customers to play 'laser quest' games whereby they would attempt to shoot each other using sub-machine gun-type laser guns aimed at sensor tags which attached to the jackets of the players. Omega used equipment supplied by a British company, Pulsar Advanced Games Systems Ltd. However, the local police objected and issued an order forbidding Omega from operating 'laser quest' games. According to the order, the 'acts of simulated homicide and the trivialization of violence thereby engendered were contrary to fundamental values prevailing in public opinion'. This contravened the provision in German constitutional law of respect for human dignity. Omega challenged this, alleging a breach of Art 56, in that the order would prevent Pulsar in the UK from supplying their services to Omega in Germany. The case was referred to the ECJ, which held that the order *prima facie* infringed Art 56. However, it was justifiable under Art 52.

The Court stated:

JUDGMENT

'The [Union] legal order undeniably strives to ensure respect for human dignity as a general principle of law. There can therefore be no doubt that the objective of protecting human dignity is compatible with [Union] law ... Since both the [Union] and its Member States are required to respect fundamental rights, the protection of those rights is a legitimate interest which, in principle, justifies a restriction of the obligations imposed by [Union] law, even under a fundamental freedom guaranteed by the Treaty such as the freedom to provide services.'

In *Watts v Bedford Primary Care Trust* (2006), the ECJ confirmed principles established in earlier case law that private medical treatment constituted a 'service' within the scope of Art 56. The Court also confirmed earlier case law in which it had been established that Member States are, in certain circumstances, entitled to restrict access to medical services on public health grounds under Art 52. Specifically, the Court ruled that:

- The 'objective of maintaining a balanced medical and hospital service open to all' falls within Art 52 'insofar as it contributes to the attainment of a high level of health protection'.
- Article 52 permits Member States to restrict the freedom to provide medical and hospital services 'insofar as the maintenance of treatment capacity or medical competence on national territory is essential for the public health, and even the survival, of the population'.

Those considerations might justify Member States placing limitations on the freedom of access to medical services. The Court elaborated as follows:

JUDGMENT

'It is well known that the number of hospitals, their geographical distribution, the way in which they are organised and the facilities with which they are provided, and even the nature of the medical services which they are able to offer, are all matters for which planning, generally designed to satisfy various needs, must be possible. For one thing, such planning seeks to ensure that there is sufficient and permanent access to a balanced range of high-quality hospital treatment in the State concerned. For another thing, it assists in meeting a desire to control costs and to prevent, as far as possible, any wastage of financial, technical and human resources. Such wastage would be all the more damaging because it is generally recognised that the hospital care sector generates considerable costs and must satisfy increasing needs, while the financial resources which may be made available for healthcare are not unlimited, whatever the mode of funding applied.'

KEY FACTS

Derogations under Arts 51 and 52	
Member States may exclude non-nationals from practising activities connected with the 'exercise of official authority'	Article 51 TFEU
This is interpreted very narrowly. It only applies to specific activities, not whole professions	*Reyners* (1974)
Member States may restrict the freedoms of establishment and services on grounds of public policy, security and health	Article 52 TFEU
The Public health derogation allows Member States to impose restrictions on people seeking private medical treatment in order to maintain both 'a balanced medical and hospital service' and 'treatment capacity or medical competence'	*Kohll* (1998), *Watts* (2006)

13.8 Justification for non-discriminatory rules

In addition to the specific Treaty derogations, the ECJ has created a parallel set of derogations which may be pleaded by Member States to justify restrictions on establishment or the provision of services.

In *Van Binsbergen* (1974), the ECJ was asked whether a Dutch rule requiring lawyers to be habitually resident in the Netherlands before they could exercise rights of audience before Dutch courts and tribunals was compatible with Art 56. The ECJ stated:

JUDGMENT

'A requirement that the person providing the service must be habitually resident within the territory of the State where the service is to be provided may, according to the circumstances, have the result of depriving [Art 56] of all useful effect. However, taking into account the particular nature of the services to be provided, specific requirements imposed on the person providing the service cannot be considered incompatible with the Treaty where they have as their purpose the application of professional rules justified by the general good – in particular rules relating to organisation, qualification, professional ethics, supervision and liability.'

In *Säger v Dennemeyer & Co* (1991), the ECJ stated that:

JUDGMENT

'The freedom to provide services may be limited only by rules which are justified by imperative reasons relating to the public interest and which apply to all persons and undertakings pursuing an activity in the State of destination in so far as that interest is not protected by rules to which the person providing the service is subject in the State in which he is established. In particular, these requirements must be objectively necessary in order to ensure compliance with professional rules and must not exceed what is necessary to attain those objectives.'

The ECJ confirmed the applicability of these criteria in *Gebhard* (1995) (an Art 49 case). Thus, for a national rule which restricts either the freedom of establishment or the freedom to provide services to be compatible with Art 49 or Art 56, a four-part test has to be satisfied:

i) the rule must be non-discriminatory
ii) it must be justified by imperative requirements in the general interest

iii) it must be suitable for the attainment of the objective it pursues
iv) it must not go beyond what is necessary in order to attain its objective (the 'proportionality' doctrine).

Commission v France (Tourist Guides) (Case C–154/89) [1999] ECR I–659 provides a good example of these conditions being applied. French legislation required all tourist guides accompanying groups of tourists to take an exam in order to become licensed. The Commission alleged that this was in breach of Art 56. France argued that it was necessary to ensure that guides gave tourists correct artistic and cultural information. The ECJ held that the French legislation was a *prima facie* infringement of Art 56, because it prevented self-employed tour guides from offering their services to tourists; it also prevented tourists from taking part in such organised tours from availing themselves at will of the services in question. However, the Court held that the licence requirement was justifiable, in principle.

i) It was non-discriminatory, as it applied to French nationals hoping to work as tourist guides as well as to other nationals.
ii) It was at least justifiable, as it sought to 'ensure the protection of general interests relating to the proper appreciation of places and things of interest and the widest possible dissemination of knowledge of the artistic and cultural heritage of the country'.
iii) It was capable of achieving this objective.
iv) The final question was whether the licence requirement was actually necessary. Here, the Court held that it went too far, at least as far as general tourist information was concerned. Forcing tourist companies to employ only licensed guides would inevitably lead some tour operators to have recourse to local guides instead of their own staff. That, in turn, could leave tourists with a guide unfamiliar with their language, their interests and their specific expectations. Moreover, the fierce competition under which tour companies operated meant that they were obliged voluntarily to exercise control over the tour guides they employed.

In *Alpine Investments* (1995), the ECJ held that the restriction under Dutch law of 'cold-calling' practices in the financial services sector was a *prima facie* infringement of Art 56. However, it was justifiable in the interests of consumer protection and the protection of the reputation of that service industry. The ECJ concluded with the wry observation that since 'the commodities futures market is highly speculative and barely comprehensible for non-expert investors, it was necessary to protect them from the most aggressive selling techniques'. The ECJ was also prepared to hold that the Dutch rules were not disproportionate:

- the legislation prohibited cold-calling **only**, ie it did not prohibit other forms of approaching potential clients
- there was no prohibition on contacting existing clients by telephone
- the legislation only prohibited cold-calling **in the commodities futures market**; ie brokering in other markets was not subject to the same rules.

Alpine had argued that simply requiring unsolicited telephone calls to be tape-recorded would suffice to protect customers as effectively. Moreover, in the UK, the Securities and Futures Authority had adopted similar rules. However, the ECJ was not persuaded, commenting that the fact that one Member State imposes less strict rules than another does not mean that the latter State's rules are disproportionate and hence incompatible with EU law.

In *Viking Line* (Case C–438/05) [2007] ECR I-10779, the ECJ recognised that the protection of workers was a legitimate interest capable of overriding the freedom of establishment.

CASE EXAMPLE

International Transport Workers' Federation & Finnish Seamen's Union v Viking Line (Case C–438/05) [2007] ECR I-10779

Viking Line, a Finnish ferry company, owned seven vessels which it used to sail the Baltic Sea route between Helsinki in Finland and Tallinn in Estonia. These ships were registered in Finland, which meant that the crew were protected by Finnish law and entitled to wages comparable to those payable in Finland generally. Viking Line was, however, operating at a loss as it was competing with Estonian ferry companies whose crew wages and hence operating costs were much lower. Consequently, Viking Line gave notice that it intended to re-flag one its ships, the *Rosella*, under the Estonian flag. The crew were all members of the Finnish Seamen's Union (the FSU) (which was affiliated to the International Transport Workers' Federation (the ITF)). The ITF had a 'flag of convenience' policy, which meant that it opposed ship-owners flagging their ships under the flag of a country with which it had no connection, in order to exploit lower wages and/or weaker worker protection in that country. Consequently, the FSU and ITF threatened strike action against Viking Line. Eventually, Viking Line brought an action, alleging that the threatened strike was contrary to Art 49. The ECJ ruled that (1) the threatened strike was a *prima facie* breach of Art 49 but (2) the breach was – in principle, at least – justified on the basis of worker protection.

More recently, the Court acknowledged that environmental protection (long recognised as capable of justifying restrictions on the free movement of goods – see Chapter 14) was also capable of justifying restrictions on the freedom to provide services.

CASE EXAMPLE

Regione Sardegna (Case C-169/08) [2010] 2 CMLR 8

Legislation in the Mediterranean island of Sardinia (which is part of France) imposed a 'stopover tax' on recreational boats and tourist aircraft stopping at the island. The tax was designed to achieve two objectives: (1) 'discourage squandering of the environmental and coastal landscape heritage' and (2) finance measures to restore coastal areas. The ECJ held that the legislation was capable of restricting the freedom to provide and receive services (tourism firms being less likely to call at Sardinian ports or land at Sardinian airports because of the tax) and so amounted to a prima facie breach of Art 56. The restriction was potentially justifiable on environmental protection grounds by leading to a reduction in pollution. However, it was not justified, because the tax exempted tourism firms domiciled in Sardinia itself. The Court ruled that that 'national legislation is appropriate to ensuring attainment of the objective pursued only if it genuinely reflects a concern to attain it in a consistent and systematic manner'.

'Overriding reasons relating to the public interest': summary

The case law reveals that a number of different 'overriding interests' have been accepted by the ECJ. They include (bear in mind that this is not a comprehensive list – indeed, new interests may be added to the list at any time):

- Consumer protection – *Alpine Investments* (1995).
- The 'sound administration of justice' – *Wouters and Others* (Case C–309/99) [2002] ECR I–1577.
- The need to 'ensure high standards of university education' – *Neri v European School of Economics* (Case C–153/02) [2003] ECR I–13555.
- The 'protection of workers' – *Viking Line* (2007).
- The 'promotion of research and development' – *Jundt* (Case C–281/06) [2007] ECR I-12231.
- Environmental protection – *Regione Sardegna* (2009).

A non-exhaustive list of 'overriding reasons relating to the public interest' is also provided in Art 4(8) of the Services Directive 2006/123, all of which are based on cases decided by the ECJ. In that sense the directive does not add anything new to this area of law.

Regulation of gambling

Several cases have addressed the question of whether Member States can regulate gambling services. In *Schindler* (1994), the ECJ observed that UK anti-lottery legislation (prior to its abolition by the National Lotteries Act 1993), was capable of infringing Art 56. However, it was justifiable because it pursued the following objectives:

- to prevent crime and to ensure that gamblers would be treated honestly
- to avoid stimulating demand in the gambling sector which has damaging social consequences when taken to excess and
- to ensure that lotteries could not be operated for personal or commercial profit but solely for charitable, sporting or cultural purposes.

The ECJ concluded that the UK legislation was more concerned with 'the protection of the recipients of services and, more generally, of consumers' and was, therefore, justified. The ECJ was also prepared to accept the 'maintenance of order in society' as an alternative public interest reason. The ECJ observed that it was 'not possible to disregard the moral, religious or cultural aspects of lotteries, like other types of gambling'. After observing that 'lotteries involve a high risk of crime or fraud … particularly when they are operated on a large scale' it then declared, slightly pompously, that 'they are an incitement to spend which may have damaging individual and social consequences'. Consequently, the legislation did not infringe Art 56 'in view of the concerns of social policy and of the prevention of fraud which justify it'. Somewhat paradoxically, the ECJ concluded by extolling the virtues of national lotteries, pointing out how they 'may make a significant contribution to the financing of benevolent or public interest activities such as social works, charitable works, sport or culture'.

Similar outcomes were reached in *Läärä* (1999), concerning Finnish legislation restricting the availability of gaming licences, and in *Zenatti* (1999), concerning Italian law regulating gambling. In the latter case, the ECJ held that the Italian law (*prima facie* contrary to Art 56 but justifiable) sought to:

- prevent gambling from being a source of private profit
- avoid risks of crime and fraud and the damaging individual and social consequences of the incitement to spend which it represents and
- allow gambling only to the extent to which it may be socially useful as being conducive to the proper conduct of competitive sports.

In *ANOMAR and Others* (2003), Portuguese legislation restricted the running of games of chance to casinos within gaming zones created by decree. The *Associação National de Operadores de Máquinas Recreativas* (ANOMAR), an association of gaming machine operators in Portugal, challenged this as restricting the freedom to provide services (ie gambling services to foreign tourists and business people). The ECJ held that the Portuguese legislation was capable of restricting the freedom to provide services, as it prevented operators from providing gambling opportunities outside the gaming zones. However, it was justified. The ECJ referred to the familiar objectives of consumer protection and maintaining order in society.

However, the ECJ refused to apply the usual justifications in *Gambelli and Others* (2003), which involved Italian rules restricting the provision of Internet gambling services to state-run or state-licensed organisations. The ECJ stated:

JUDGMENT

'In so far as the authorities of a Member State incite and encourage consumers to participate in lotteries, games of chance and betting to the financial benefit of the public purse, the authorities of that State cannot invoke public order concerns relating to the need to reduce opportunities for betting in order to justify measures such as those at issue in the main proceedings.'

Gallo & Damonte (Case C–191/06) [2007] ECR I–30 involved Italian legislation which prohibited the collecting, taking, booking and forwarding of bets, in particular bets on sporting events, without a licence or a police authorisation. The ECJ held that this was *prime facie* prohibited by Arts 49 and 56 but was justifiable on the basis that it sought to prevent the exploitation of activities in the gambling sector for criminal or fraudulent purposes.

A similar outcome to that in *ANOMAR* occurred in *Liga Portuguese de Futebol Profissional* (Case C-42/07) [2010] 1 CMLR 1, also known as the Santa Casa case. Portuguese legislation conferred an exclusive right on an organisation called Santa Casa to operate lotteries and all forms of sports betting (including online gambling) throughout Portugal. The Court held that, although clearly capable of restricting both the freedom of rival companies based in other Member States to provide gambling services, and the freedom of Portuguese consumers to receive those services, the Portuguese legislation was justified. In giving judgment, the ECJ focused on crime prevention, stating that:

JUDGMENT

'The fight against crime may constitute an overriding reason in the public interest that is capable of justifying restrictions in respect of operators authorised to offer services in the games-of-chance sector. Games of chance involve a high risk of crime or fraud, given the scale of the earnings and the potential winnings on offer to gamblers ... Limited authorisation of games on an exclusive basis has the advantage of confining the operation of gambling within controlled channels and of preventing the risk of fraud or crime in the context of such operation.'

KEY FACTS

Justification for non-discriminatory rules	
Non-discriminatory restrictions on the freedoms of establishment or services may be justified by reference to 'imperative reasons relating to the public interest'	*Säger v Dennemeyer & Co.* (1991); *Gebhard* (1995)
The restrictions must be both suitable for attaining the desired objective and proportionate	
Examples of imperative reasons include consumer protection, the sound administration of justice, the protection of workers	*Van Binsbergen* (1974), *Wouters and Others* (2002), *Viking Line* (2007)
Member States may restrict gambling services in order to protect consumers from the dangers of addiction, and to prevent crime and fraud	*Schindler* (1994), *Läärä* (1999), *Zenatti* (1999), *ANOMAR and Others* (2003), *Santa Casa* (2010)

13.9 The free movement of lawyers

Lawyers are called a variety of names in the EU, as the following list illustrates:

- *abogado* (used in Spain)
- *advocaat* (used in the Netherlands and parts of Belgium)
- *advocat* or *Advokat* (used in Denmark, Finland, Slovakia and Sweden)
- *advogado* (used in Portugal)
- *advokáat* (used in the Czech Republic)
- *advokāts* (used in Lithuania)
- *adwocat* (used in Poland)
- *avocat* (used in France, Luxembourg and parts of Belgium)
- *avukat* (used in Malta)
- *avvocato* (used in Italy)

- *barrister/solicitor* (used in Ireland and the UK)
- *dikigoros* (used in Cyprus and Greece)
- *odvetnik/odvetnica* (used in Slovenia)
- *rechtsanwalt* (used in Austria, Germany and parts of Belgium)
- *ügyvéd* (used in Hungary)
- *vandeadvokaat* (used in Estonia)
- *zvērināts* (used in Latvia).

13.9.1 Freedom of establishment under Art 49 TFEU

Many lawyers, particularly barristers, are self-employed. This means that there have been several cases involving the free movement of lawyers under Art 49. In *Paris Bar Council v Klopp* (1984), the ECJ was asked to rule on the compatibility of a rule of French law that said that lawyers could have only one place of establishment at a time. This was allegedly designed to ensure that lawyers 'should practise in such a way as to maintain sufficient contact with their clients and the judicial authorities and abide by the rules of the profession'. The ECJ held that this rule imposed an unjustifiable restriction on the freedom of lawyers to establish themselves in other EU Member States.

CASE EXAMPLE

Paris Bar Council v Klopp (Case 107/83) [1984] ECR 2971

Onno Klopp was a German national, a qualified *rechtsanwalt* and a member of the Düsseldorf Bar. In 1981 he applied to be registered as an *avocat* at the Paris Bar. He planned to set up chambers there, as well as retaining his chambers in Germany. However, he was refused permission by the Paris Bar Council, whose rules required *avocats* to establish chambers in one place only. The ECJ held that this rule breached Art 49. The Court stated that although Art 49 allowed Member States some flexibility to organise rules on professionals, that did not allow them to force lawyers to have only one place of establishment at a time.

The Court stated:

JUDGMENT

'In the absence of specific [EU] rules in the matter each Member State is free to regulate the exercise of the legal profession in its territory. Nevertheless that rule does not mean that the legislation of a Member State may require a lawyer to have only one establishment throughout the [Union]. Such a restrictive interpretation would mean that a lawyer once established in a particular Member State would be able to enjoy the freedom of the Treaty to establish himself in another Member State only at the price of abandoning the establishment he already had.'

However, national legal authorities may be able to justify other restrictions, such as supervision and compliance with professional rules. *Gullung v Colmar and Saverne Bar Council* (Case 292/86) [1988] ECR 111, involved a German lawyer who had been refused permission to practise in France after contravening French regulations relating to the professional ethics of those in the legal professions. The Court stated:

JUDGMENT

'Members of the legal profession, when providing services, are required to comply with the rules relating to professional ethics in force in the host Member State … the requirement that lawyers be registered at a Bar laid down by certain Member States must be regarded as lawful in relation to [EU law] provided, however, that such registration is open to nationals of all Member States without discrimination. The requirement seeks to ensure the observance of moral and ethical principles and the disciplinary control of the activity of lawyers and thus pursues an objective worthy of protection.'

In what is now the leading case, *Gebhard v Milan Bar Council* (1995), the ECJ confirmed *Gullung*. The ECJ acknowledged that national professional regulatory bodies (such as the Solicitors Regulation Authority and the Bar Standards Board in England and Wales) have rules governing issues such as client care, confidentiality and professional ethics which are capable of imposing restrictions on the free movement of lawyers. Nevertheless, these rules are designed to protect clients and the reputation of the profession as a whole and, therefore, are justifiable.

CASE EXAMPLE

Gebhard v Milan Bar Council (Case C–55/94) [1995] ECR I–4165

Reinhard Gebhard was a German national, a qualified *rechtsanwalt* and a member of the Stuttgart Bar. Since 1978 he had resided in Milan. Initially he operated as an associate with a set of chambers in Milan, advising clients on aspects of German law. However, in 1989, he opened his own chambers there and began to use the title '*avvocato*' on the letterhead of his notepaper. Several Italian practitioners complained about this as the title is reserved for lawyers possessing Italian legal and professional qualifications. The Milan Bar Council banned him from using the title. In subsequent disciplinary proceedings, the Council held that he had also infringed Italian law which allowed professional activities to be carried out on a **temporary** basis by lawyers qualified in other Member States, but prohibited 'the establishment [in Italy] either of chambers or of a principal or branch office'. Gebhard was suspended for six months. On appeal, before the National Council of the Bar, Gebhard argued that Directive 77/249 (see below) entitled him to pursue his professional activities from his own chambers in Milan. The ECJ decided that, because of the amount of time he spent in Milan, he had gone beyond merely providing services and had become established there. This meant that Directive 77/249 did not apply. Nevertheless, he was entitled to rely on Art 49. However, although the Italian rules did, *prima facie*, infringe his freedom of establishment, they were justifiable in that they sought to protect clients from unscrupulous people adopting professional titles and passing themselves off as qualified lawyers.

The Court stated:

JUDGMENT

'The taking-up and pursuit of certain self-employed activities may be conditional on complying with certain provisions laid down by law, regulation or administrative action justified by the general good, such as rules relating to organization, qualifications, professional ethics, supervision and liability. Such provisions may stipulate in particular that pursuit of a particular activity is restricted to holders of a diploma, certificate or other evidence of formal qualifications, to persons belonging to a professional body or to persons subject to particular rules or supervision, as the case may be. They may also lay down the conditions for the use of professional titles.'

13.9.2 The Lawyers' Establishment Directive 98/5

Directive 98/5 confers rights on lawyers qualified in one Member State (the home State) to practise in another Member State (the host State), although they must be clearly 'badged' as a sign to potential clients that the migrant lawyer is qualified in another State's law.

Practice under the 'home country professional title'

According to Art 2, migrant lawyers are entitled to practise various activities which are listed in Art 5, but only using their original title, in the host State's language. According to Art 4, this title 'must be expressed in the official language ... of his home Member State, in an intelligible manner and in such a way as to avoid confusion with the professional title of the host Member State.' Under Art 3, migrant lawyers are required to 'register with the competent authority' in the host Member State. The areas of activity in Art 5(1) include advice on:

- the law of the home Member State
- EU law
- international law and
- the law of the host Member State.

Rules of professional conduct

When practising in the host State, even under his home State's professional title, the migrant lawyer will be expected to abide by 'the local codes of conduct in respect of all activities he pursues in its territory' (Art 6). This will extend to, for example, rules on advertising.

Disciplinary proceedings

The migrant lawyer will be subject to all the local disciplinary rules (Art 7(1)). Provision is made for his home State's professional body to be fully informed of any disciplinary action, including 'all the relevant details', ie the evidence on which it is based, before any action is taken (Art 7(2)). A duty of co-operation is imposed on the host State's disciplinary body, while the home State's body has a right to 'make submissions to the bodies responsible for hearing any appeal' (Art 7(3)).

The registration requirement in Art 3, as well as the professional conduct and disciplinary proceedings requirements in Arts 6 and 7, of Directive 98/5 were all examined in *Wilson* (Case C–506/04) [2006] ECR I–8613, involving a British barrister, Graham Wilson, who wished to register in Luxembourg. The Court held that Art 3 did not allow the registration of a lawyer in a Member State to be made conditional on them being proficient in the language(s) of that State. The Court stated that 'presentation ... of a certificate attesting to registration with the competent authority of the home State is the only condition to which registration of the person concerned in the host Member State may be subject'. However, the Court noted that, under Art 6, a lawyer must comply with the rules of professional conduct applicable in the host State. One of those rules is an obligation not to handle matters which a lawyer knows, or ought to know, they are not competent to handle, for example, because they lack linguistic knowledge. The Court held that communication with clients, with the national authorities and/or with the professional bodies of the host State may all require a lawyer to have sufficient linguistic knowledge, or at least recourse to assistance where that knowledge is insufficient. Acting without such knowledge may amount to a breach of Art 6 of the directive leading to possible disciplinary action under Art 7. Nevertheless, the Court concluded, the linguistic knowledge requirement did not justify the national authorities demanding an examination of the lawyer's proficiency in the language(s) of the host Member State *prior to* registration.

13.9.3 The Lawyers' Services Directive 77/249

Directive 77/249 harmonises the rules under which lawyers established in one Member State may provide their services in the territory of another State. Article 2 provides that 'Each Member State shall recognise as a lawyer for the purpose of pursuing the activities specified in Article 1(1) any person listed in Article 1(2)'. This is the same list as found in Directive 98/5. Article 1(1) simply states that 'This directive shall apply, within the limits and under the conditions laid down herein, to the activities of lawyers pursued by way of provisions of services'.

KEY FACTS

The free movement of lawyers	
Self-employed lawyers are entitled to establish themselves in another Member State	Article 49 TFEU; Directive 98/5
Lawyers can establish themselves in more than one State simultaneously	*Klopp* (1984), *Gebhard* (1995)
Member States may restrict lawyers's freedom of establishment where necessary in order to ensure compliance with professional rules on conduct, ethics, liability, and consumer protection	*Directive* 98/5; *Gullung* (1988), *Gebhard*; *Wilson* (2006)
Self-employed lawyers are also entitled to provide legal services in another Member State	Article 56 TFEU; Directive 77/249

ACTIVITY

Applying the law

(a) Connie has been running a successful nursery and nanny agency in London for over 10 years. In the past year Connie has identified a niche in the market for high-quality, stimulating pre-school education and care, particularly in demand from professional parents. Her business has gone from strength to strength and she is now ready to expand it. Following extensive market research, Connie has decided to establish a new nanny agency in Bonn. Initially, she intends to set up an office in Bonn, recruit suitably qualified nannies and place them with families.

Advise Connie whether she has any rights under EU law to carry out her plans.

(b) The German Small Business Association provides free advice and consultancy to new small businesses. Connie has approached the Association for advice but has been told that she is not eligible to receive this service because she is not a German national.

Advise Connie.

SAMPLE ESSAY QUESTION

Article 56 TFEU provides for the freedom to provide services, while Article 57 TFEU defines 'services'. These Articles give this freedom a very wide scope, and the case law of the European Court of Justice has expanded it even further. As a result, there are virtually no limits on this freedom. Discuss.

Explain the meaning and scope of the 'free movement' of services:

- Art 56 TFEU applies to any cross-border service provision (*Scorpio Konzertproduktionen*)
- Art 56 applies to any national legislation which hinders the movement of services, whether or not discriminatory (*Säger v Dennemeyer*)
- Art 56 may be invoked by the service provider to challenge legislation in their 'home' state (*Alpine Investments*; *Carpenter*)
- Services must 'normally' be provided for 'remuneration', which is interpreted widely (*Bond van Adverteerders; Deliège*)
- Rights have been conferred on service recipients through case law. Give examples from the case law, eg *Luisi & Carbone, Kohll, Watts, Schwarz*. This case law has significantly expanded the scope of Art 56.

Explain the meaning and scope of 'services':

- Art 57 TFEU defines services provided by, inter alia, craftsmen and professionals, including legal services (*Reyners, Van Binsbergen, Säger v Dennemeyer*)
- Case law has expanded the scope of Art 57 by including less obvious 'services' such as prostitution (*Jany & Others*), abortion (*SPUC v Grogan*) and sport (*Deliège*)
- Discuss the fact that just because a service is restricted or even prohibited in some Member States does not prevent Art 56 from applying, e.g. abortion, online gambling, artificial insemination (*Blood*).

Explain that there are limits on the scope of the freedom:

- There must be a cross-border element (*Scorpio Konzertproduktionen*)
- There must be 'remuneration' – so publicly funded services are not covered (*Humbel*)
- Art 51 TFEU exempts 'official authority' activities – although this has been interpreted narrowly (*Reyners*)
- Art 52 TFEU allows for derogations on policy, security and health grounds. 'Public policy' has also been interpreted narrowly (*Calfa*). Discuss the case law on 'public health' and attempts by Member States to avoid paying for private medical treatment obtained in other States (*Kohll, Vanbraekel, Geraets-Smits and Peerbooms, Watts, Inistan*, etc)
- Examine the case law on 'imperative requirements' which may justify restrictions (*Van Binsbergern, Säger v Dennemeyer, Schindler*). Give example, eg the protection of consumers, workers, cultural heritage, the environment, human dignity; the fight against crime and prevention of fraud
- Conclude that, although Art 56 is defined widely, there are some limitations.

SUMMARY

- Art 49 TFEU covers the freedom of establishment; Art 56 TFEU covers the freedom to provide services. Both are directly effective: *Reyners* (Art 49) and *Van Binsbergen* (Art 56)
- **Establishment** is the right to install oneself in another Member State, permanently or semi-permanently, on a self-employed basis, for the purpose of performing a particular activity there. It also gives companies the right to set up a branch or a subsidiary, in another Member State.
- **Provision of services** allows an individual, established in one Member State, to provide their services in another Member State, on a temporary or intermittent basis. It also allows a company, established in one Member State, to provide their services to anyone in another Member State. If necessary, it allows them to visit the other Member State, on a temporary or intermittent basis, in order to do so.
- Art 49 refers to the taking-up as well as the pursuit of professional activities for individual, self-employed persons. For companies, the freedom of establishment includes the right to set up and manage 'undertakings'. In both cases, establishment is under the same conditions laid down for nationals of the State where establishment is effected (*Steinhauser*).
- It is possible to be established in two Member States at the same time (*Klopp, Gebhard*).
- Art 49 can be invoked vertically (*Reyners*) and horizontally (*Viking Line*).
- Directive 2005/36 consolidates the rules for the mutual recognition of qualifications required in order to pursue a 'regulated profession' in another Member State.
- A profession is 'regulated' if access to it depends on the possession of qualifications (*Aranitis*).

- Once qualifications have been recognised, the holder of them can pursue a profession in the host Member State under the same conditions as its nationals.
- Member States are allowed to impose 'compensation measures' on holders of qualifications obtained in other States in certain situations, e.g. if the duration of training is at least one year shorter than in the host State, or if training covers 'substantially different matters'.
- Where that happens, States may require the completion of an 'adaptation period' or the passing of 'aptitude test'. Usually, the candidate can choose which, except for professions 'whose pursuit requires precise knowledge of national law', in which case the State can specify. This exception does not just apply to 'traditional' legal professions (*Price*). Alternatively, States can offer 'partial recognition' of a candidate's qualifications (*Colegio de Ingenieros*).
- Where Directive 2005/36 does not apply, States are obliged to undertake an assessment of a candidate's qualifications to establish the extent of equivalence, which may be full, partial, or not equivalent (*Thieffry, Patrick, Vlassopoulou, Morgenbesser*).
- Where qualifications obtained outside of the EU have been accepted by one Member State as equivalent to their qualifications and the candidate has practised there, other States must recognise that practical experience (*Haim, Hocsmann*).
- Art 56 TFEU provides that 'restrictions on freedom to provide services… shall be prohibited'. It is crucial that there is a cross-border element. Art 56 EC applies if two conditions are satisfied: (1) the service must be provided within the EU; (2) the provider of services must be a national of a Member State and established in a State of the EU other than that of the service recipient (*Scorpio Konzertproduktionen*).
- Art 56 may be invoked by service providers to challenge all national legislation, whether discriminatory or not, if it inhibits the freedom to provide services (*Säger v Dennemeyer & Co*).
- Art 56 may be used by service providers to challenge legislation in their state of establishment (*Alpine Investments, Carpenter*).
- Art 56 may be invoked by the recipients of services, eg tourists (*Luisi & Carbone, Calfa*); persons receiving private education (*Humbel; Schwarz*); persons receiving medical treatment (*Kohll, Watts*).
- 'Services' has a very wide scope, including: TV broadcasting (*Bond van Adverteerders*); gambling (*Schindler*); abortions (*SPUC v Grogan*); prostitution (*Jany and Others*); sporting activities (*Deliège*).
- The service must normally be provided for 'remuneration' (Art 57 TFEU). Thus, while private education is included, public education is not (*Humbel, Schwarz*). It is not essential that the service recipient be the person who provides the remuneration (*Bond van Adverteerders, Deliège*).
- Establishment and services are mutually exclusive; the freedom to provide services is subordinate to the freedom of establishment; the concept of establishment assumes the person/company in question is in another Member State 'on a stable and continuous basis', whereas the provisions on services 'envisage that he is to pursue his activity there on a temporary basis' (*Gebhard*).
- Ultimately, whether Art 49 or 56 applies is 'determined in the light, not only of the duration of the provision of the service, but also of its regularity, periodicity or continuity' (*Gebhard*).
- 'Activities… that are connected, even occasionally, with the exercise of official authority' are *not* covered by the Treaty (Art 51 TFEU). This only applies only to official authority *activities*; not professions or occupations *as a whole* (*Reyners*).
- Member States may derogate from the freedoms on grounds of public policy, security or health (Art 52 TFEU). For further explanation, see Chapter 11.
- Art 52 allows Member States, in principle, to restrict access to medical services on public health grounds. This is justifiable because it 'seeks to ensure that there is sufficient and permanent access to a balanced range of high-quality hospital treatment in the State concerned' (*Kohll, Watts*).

- National legislation restricting either of the freedoms is justifiable if it is non-discriminatory; pursues a legitimate objective; is capable of achieving that objective; and satisfies proportionality, i.e. it does not go beyond what is necessary to achieve that objective (*Van Binsbergern, Gebhard*).
- Examples of legitimate objectives include 'the proper appreciation of places and things of historical interest; dissemination of knowledge of national artistic and cultural heritage' (*Commission v France (Tourist Guides)*); consumer protection (*Alpine Investments, Schindler*); the protection of workers (*Viking Line*); protection of the environment (*Regione Sardegna*); the prevention of crime (*Zenatti, Gallo & Damonte, Santa Casa*).
- In addition, Art 16 of Directive 2006/123 (the Services Directive), states that Member States must not make access to or exercise of a service activity in their territory subject to compliance with any requirements which do not respect the principles of non-discrimination; necessity (the requirement must be justified for reasons of public policy, public security, public health or the protection of the environment); and proportionality (the requirement must be suitable for attaining the objective pursued, and must not go beyond what is necessary to attain that objective).
- Lawyers seeking establishment in another Member State may rely on Directive 98/5, while lawyers providing services may rely on Directive 77/249, in addition to the rights provided by Arts 49 and 56.

Further reading

Articles

Barnard, C, 'Unravelling the Services Directive' (2008) 45 CML Rev 323.

Bulterman, M & Kranenborg, H, 'What if Rules on Free Movement and Human Rights Collide? About Laser Games and Human Dignity: The *Omega* Case' (2006) 31 EL Rev 93.

Davies, G, 'The Services Directive: Extending the Country of Origin Principle, and Reforming Public Administration' (2007) 32 EL Rev 232.

Dawes, A & Struckmann, K, 'Rien ne va plus? Mutual recognition and the free movement of services in the gambling sector after the Santa Casa judgment' (2010) 35 EL Rev 236.

Hatzopoulos, V, 'Killing national health and insurance systems but healing patients? The European market for health care services after the judgments of the ECJ in *Vanbraekel* and *Peerbooms*' (2002) 39 CMLR 683.

Kaczorowska, A, 'A Review of the Creation by the European Court of Justice of the Right to Effective and Speedy Medical Treatment and its Outcomes' (2006) 12 ELJ 345.

Littler, A, 'Regulatory Perspectives on the Future of Interactive Gambling in the Internal Market' (2008) 33 EL Rev 211.

14

The free movement of goods and articles 34 and 35 TFEU

AIMS AND OBJECTIVES

After reading this chapter you should be able to:

- Understand the law relating to the prohibition of 'quantitative restrictions' and measures of 'equivalent effect' on imports and exports in Articles 34 and 35 TFEU
- Understand the meaning and scope of the *Dassonville* judgment
- Understand the meaning and scope of the *Keck & Mithouard* judgment
- Understand the derogations available to Member States under Article 36
- Understand the principles established in *Cassis de Dijon*, and their application
- Analyse critically the law relating to the free movement of goods
- Apply the law to factual situations involving the free movement of goods in the EU

14.1 The removal of non-fiscal barriers to trade

In Chapter 15 we will examine how EU law has sought to prevent Member States from imposing fiscal barriers (in the forms of Customs charges and discriminatory taxation) to the free movement of goods. In this chapter, we will examine how EU law prevents Member States from imposing non-fiscal barriers. There is a potentially infinite variety of such barriers, from measures such as hygiene inspections at border crossing points to technical legislation prescribing the permitted amount of salt in bakery products or the shape of margarine tubs. National legislation making it a criminal offence to import pornographic videos or banning the advertising of junk food could all have the effect of imposing trade barriers.

14.2 Prohibition of quantitative restrictions on imports – Art 34 and exports – Art 35 and all measures having equivalent effect

14.2.1 Introduction

ARTICLE

'Art 34 Quantitative restrictions on imports and all measures having equivalent effect shall be prohibited between Member States.'

ARTICLE

'Art 35 Quantitative restrictions on exports, and all measures having equivalent effect, shall be prohibited between Member States.'

Article 34 prohibits quantitative restrictions, and all measures having equivalent effect, on imports; Art 35 does the same for exports. A measure which infringes Arts 34 or 35 is *prima facie* contrary to EU law; however, Art 36 provides that Arts 34 or 35 will not apply to certain restrictions, justifiable on various grounds, which are not disproportionate (Art 36 is discussed in section 14.5; proportionality is discussed in section 14.7). In addition to this, the ECJ has developed its own line of case law, allowing justifications on other grounds, again provided that they are not disproportionate (see *Cassis de Dijon* (Case 120/78) [1979] ECR 649, discussed in section 14.6).

14.2.2 Direct effect of Arts 34 and 35

In *Ianelli & Volpi SpA v Meroni* (Case 74/76) [1977] ECR 595, the ECJ announced that:

JUDGMENT

'The prohibition of quantitative restrictions and measures having equivalent effect laid down in [Art 34] is mandatory and explicit and its implementation does not require any subsequent intervention of the Member States or [Union] institutions. The prohibition therefore has direct effect and creates individual rights which national courts must protect.'

14.2.3 Scope of Arts 34 and 35

Articles 34 and 35 are addressed to the Member States and therefore apply only to acts or omissions on behalf of the Member States. This essentially means the legislative and executive arms of each State's government although it extends beyond that. In *Aragonesa and Publivia* (Cases C–1 and 176/90) [1991] ECR I–4151, which concerned provisions of Catalan law, the ECJ stated that Art 34 'may apply to measures adopted by all the authorities of the Member States, be they the central authorities, the authorities of a federal State, or other territorial authorities'. Apart from central and local government, the actions of the following have been held capable of infringing Arts 34 and 35:

- semi-public bodies such as quangos (eg *Apple and Pear Development Council v K J Lewis Ltd*) (Case 222/82) [1983] ECR 4083
- nationalised industries such as the Post Office (*Commission v France* (Case 21/84) [1985] ECR 1355)
- regulatory agencies and professional bodies established under statutory authority (*R v Pharmaceutical Society of GB, ex parte Association of Pharmaceutical Importers* (Cases 266 and 267/87) [1989] ECR 1295)
- the police force (*R v Chief Constable of Sussex, ex parte ITF Ltd* [1998] 3 WLR 1260, HL)
- even the EU's own institutions are bound to comply with the provisions of Arts 34 and 35 (*Denkavit* (Case 15/83) [1984] ECR 2171).

The word 'goods' does not appear in either Art 34 or Art 35. The word does appear in Art 36, however, which refers to 'prohibitions or restrictions on imports, exports or goods in transit'. It also appears in Art 26(2) and Art 28(1) TFEU, and it has been defined – very widely – by the ECJ (refer to Chapter 10, section 10.2.3). In practice, all products (whether manufactured or not) taken across an internal border of the EU for the purpose of commercial transactions are subject to the free movement of goods provisions – even waste (*Commission v Belgium* (Case C–2/90) [1992] ECR I–4431; *Dusseldorp* (Case

C–203/96) [1998] ECR I–4075). The provisions apply equally to goods manufactured or produced in the EU and to those in 'free circulation' in the EU, regardless of their country of origin. Thus, in *Donckerwolcke and Schou* (Case 41/76) [1976] ECR 1921, where cloth originating from Syria and the Lebanon had been imported into Belgium before being re-imported into France, the ECJ held that Art 34 applied.

14.3 The definition of 'quantitative restrictions'

A 'quantitative restriction' was defined in *Geddo v Ente Nazionale Risi* (Case 2/73) [1973] ECR 865 as 'measures which amount to a total or partial restraint of, according to the circumstances, imports, exports or goods in transit'. This most obviously includes a **quota system** (*Salgoil* (Case 13/68) [1968] ECR 453), but also includes an **outright ban** on imports (*Commission v Italy* (Case 7/61) [1961] ECR 635; *Commission v UK* (Case 40/82) (the French Turkeys case) [1982] ECR 2793). In *R v Henn and Darby* (Case 34/79) [1979] ECR 3795, the ECJ held that s 42 of the UK's Customs Consolidation Act 1876, which made it a criminal offence to be 'knowingly concerned in the fraudulent evasion of the prohibition of the importation of obscene articles', was a quantitative restriction. The ECJ stated:

JUDGMENT

> 'It is clear that [Art 34] includes a prohibition on imports inasmuch as this is the most extreme form of restriction. The expression used in [Art 34] must therefore be understood as being the equivalent of the expression "prohibitions or restrictions on imports" occurring in [Art 36].'

This was contrary to what had been earlier suggested in the Court of Appeal in the same case, by Lord Widgery CJ, that a total prohibition was not a 'quantitative' restriction because the 1876 Act made no reference to quantities of obscene articles ([1978] 3 All ER 1190).

Rosengren & Others (Case C–170/04) [2007] ECR I–4071 concerned Swedish legislation which prohibited individuals from importing spirits, wine or strong beer into Sweden, unless personally transporting it. A number of Swedish nationals had ordered cases of Spanish wine to be imported into Sweden. However, the wine was confiscated by Swedish customs. A legal challenge was brought to recover the wine, which raised a question regarding the legality of the Swedish legislation under EU law. The ECJ held that the Swedish legislation constituted a quantitative restriction on imports.

Generally speaking, it will be positive actions that infringe Arts 34 and 35. However, it will be possible for Member States to infringe Art 34, at least, by omission. This has occurred in two cases:

- *Commission v France (French Farmers)* (Case C–265/95) [1997] ECR I–6959, where the French authorities failed to take action to prevent striking French farmers from blockading ports.
- *Schmidberger v Austria* (Case C–112/00) [2003] ECR I–5659, where the Austrian authorities decided to allow a demonstration by an environmental group to go ahead. The effect was to block a major motorway to heavy goods vehicles.

In both cases the French and Austrian authorities, respectively, were held to have infringed Art 34 – although in *Schmidberger* (2003) the ECJ went on to decide that the authorities' omission was justified (this case is considered below – see section 14.6).

14.4 Defining 'measures equivalent to quantitative restrictions' (MEQRs) in Art 34: the *Dassonville* formula

Nowhere in the TFEU is the phrase 'measures equivalent to quantitative restrictions' (known as MEQRs) defined. The classic formulation was given in *Dassonville* (Case 8/74) [1974] ECR 837, a case involving a provision of Belgian law found to amount to an MEQR.

CASE EXAMPLE

Dassonville (Case 8/74) [1974] ECR 837

Under Belgian legislation, a certificate of origin was required for all imports of a range of goods, including Scotch whisky. Benoît Dassonville, a trader in Belgium, imported a consignment of 'Johnnie Walker' and 'VAT 69' Scotch whisky from France. The French distributor was unable to provide a certificate of origin, which could be issued only by the UK Customs authorities. Despite this, Dassonville went ahead with the transaction, using forged documents. The Belgian authorities discovered the forgery and he was prosecuted. He pleaded Art 34 in his defence, arguing that the certification rule constituted a potential hindrance to trade. The case was referred to the ECJ, which held that the Belgian legislation did infringe Art 34, because it was capable of hindering trade.

The Court stated:

JUDGMENT

'All trading rules enacted by Member States which are capable of hindering, directly or indirectly, actually or potentially, [intra-Union] trade are to be considered as measures having an effect equivalent to quantitative restrictions.'

This definition of an MEQR has been cited in practically every case involving Art 34 ever since. However, in some of the more recent cases, the ECJ has modified the 'formula' slightly, substituting the word 'commercial' for 'trading'.

Note that the 'formula' extends Art 34 to any measure that **might** affect trade (as well as measures that definitely or probably **would** affect trade, or have actually done so). *Dassonville* (1974) therefore gives Art 34 a very wide scope indeed, as the cases examined below illustrate. But there are some limitations. A 'charge having equivalent effect to a Customs duty' cannot also be a measure equivalent to a quantitative restriction – that is, a measure cannot be in breach of both Art 30 **and** Art 34 (*Ianelli & Volpi v Meroni* (1977)). (Article 30 is examined in Chapter 15.)

14.4.1 Distinctly applicable MEQRs

In *Dassonville* (1974), the ECJ did not distinguish between those national rules which only apply to imports (known as 'distinctly applicable' MEQRs), and those national rules which apply both to imports and domestically produced goods (known as 'indistinctly applicable' MEQRs). However, the distinction between the two types of national rules is very important, as it determines whether or not the *Cassis de Dijon* principle (discussed below) applies.

The following are some examples of 'distinctly applicable' MEQRs:

'Buy national' campaigns

Government-sponsored campaigns to encourage consumers to buy domestic products on the basis of their nationality clearly infringe Art 34. See *Commission v Ireland ('Buy Irish' Campaign)* (Case 249/81) [1982] ECR 4005:

CASE EXAMPLE

Buy Irish Campaign (Case 249/81) [1982] ECR 4005

The Irish Goods Council was a semi-public body given the task by the Irish Government of promoting Irish goods on the basis of their Irish origin. The Council was given financial support to launch a major advertising campaign by the Irish Ministry of Industry. The European Commission alleged that the activities of the Goods Council infringed Art 34. It was alleged that, although incapable of passing binding measures, the Council's activities could nevertheless **influence** Irish traders and shoppers into discriminating against imports and thus frustrating free movement. The ECJ agreed.

However, it is **not** contrary to EU law to promote a domestic product by pointing out that it has certain qualities not found in goods from other Member States (*Apple and Pear Development Council v K J Lewis Ltd* (1983)):

CASE EXAMPLE

Apple and Pear Development Council (Case 222/82) [1983] ECR 4083

The Apple & Pear Development Council was set up to promote the consumption of apples and pears grown in England and Wales via television advertising campaigns (using the slogan 'Polish up your English'), research projects and general public relations. This was to be financed by a statutory levy. Several growers, including K J Lewis Ltd, refused to pay the levy and were sued by the Council. In defence they argued Art 34. The case was referred to the ECJ which held that no breach of Art 34 had occurred. The Council was 'under a duty not to engage in any advertising intended to discourage the purchase of products of other Member States or to disparage those products in the eyes of consumers'. Nor was it allowed to 'advise consumers to purchase domestic products solely by reason of their national origin'. The Court concluded that it was permissible to promote a national product by reference to its particular qualities. Hence it was legitimate to point out to consumers that English apples were particularly crisp.

Import licence requirements

Where national legislation insists on importers being licensed, the ECJ has held that such requirements are in breach of Art 34. *Evans Medical & Macfarlan Smith* (Case C–324/93) [1995] ECR I–563 concerned licences to import poppy seeds into the UK. The British Government insisted that importers be licensed, because although poppy seeds can be converted legally into diamorphine, a powerful pain-killing drug widely used in British hospitals, if it falls into the 'wrong hands' it can end up on 'on the street' as a heroin substitute. Article 34 applies even if the granting of the licence would be a mere formality (*Commission v UK (UHT Milk)* (Case 124/81) [1983] ECR 203). This is because the cost and time taken up in having to apply for a licence could act as a barrier to trade (*Franzén* (Case C–189/95) [1997] ECR I–5909).

Similarly, national legislation requiring retailers to be licensed in order to sell a product has also been held to breach Art 34 (*Sandoz* (Case 174/82) [1983] ECR 2445). However, this particular type of licensing system **may** now be regarded, after the decision in *Keck and Mithouard* (Case C–267/91) [1993] ECR I–6097, as a selling arrangement, which is exempt from Art 34.

Hygiene inspections

Hygiene inspections carried out on imported goods (typically food and drugs) may still infringe Art 34 because they involve delay, expense, etc. This was seen in the following cases:

- *Rewe-Zentralfinanz* (Case 4/75) [1975] ECR 843 (German legislation required that imported apples be subject to phytosanitary inspection (to detect the presence of San José Scale)).
- *Commission v France (Italian Wines)* (Case 42/82) [1983] ECR 1013 (French legislation required imported wine from Italy to be subjected to rigorous inspections).

14.4.2 Indistinctly applicable MEQRs

The majority of the cases have involved indistinctly applicable MEQRs, that is, national rules which apply without distinction to imports and to domestically produced goods but which, nevertheless, have the potential to hinder trade.

Origin marking requirements

National laws imposing a requirement that goods be marked with their country of origin could infringe Art 34 for two reasons:

- They impose extra burdens on importers, many of whom will also not even be aware of the national law and so face difficulties in complying with it.
- They may encourage 'latent' nationalistic prejudice in shoppers, who may consciously or subconsciously select domestically produced goods in preference to imports, purely on the basis of their nationality.

In *Commission v UK (Origin Marking)* (Case 207/83) [1985] ECR 1201, the ECJ acknowledges both of these arguments:

CASE EXAMPLE

Commission v UK (Origin Marking) (Case 207/83) [1985] ECR 1201

UK law, the Trade Descriptions (Origin Marking) (Miscellaneous Goods) Order 1981, prohibited the supply or offer of supply of clothing and textiles, domestic electrical appliances, footwear and cutlery in the UK unless marked with, or accompanied by, an indication of origin. Furthermore, the indication had to be clear and legible, and 'not in any way hidden or obscured or reduced in conspicuousness by any other matter, whether pictorial or not'. The Order applied to all goods, UK included. The Commission alleged that this was capable of inhibiting the free movement of goods. The ECJ agreed that a breach of Art 34 had been committed. There were two principal reasons for this decision: (1) the ECJ accepted the argument that origin-marking of goods allowed consumers to assert latent prejudice against foreign goods and (2) the ECJ accepted an argument (put forward by the French Domestic Appliance Manufacturers' Association) that manufacturers of domestic appliances based in other EU Member States who wished to sell their products in the UK would have to mark such products systematically. This was not something they already did and so doing so in order to comply with UK law would increase the cost of the manufacturing process and could disinhibit manufacturers from so doing.

JUDGMENT

'The purpose of origin-marking is to enable customers to distinguish between domestic and imported products and this enables them to assert any prejudices which they may have against foreign products … the Treaty, by establishing a Common Market … seeks to unite national markets in a single market having the characteristics of a domestic market. Within such a market, the origin-marking requirement not only makes the marketing in a Member State of goods produced in other Member States … more difficult, it also has the effect of slowing down economic interpenetration in the [Union].'

Other examples include *Dassonville* (1974) itself and *Commission v Ireland* (*Souvenir Jewellery*) (Case 113/80) [1981] ECR 1625. The *Souvenir Jewellery* case will be discussed below.

Packaging requirements

National laws which relate to how products are packaged may well infringe Art 34, because they increase the costs of manufacturers in other Member States, who will have to develop special packaging processes purely for the importing State. It will also inhibit retailers in the State in question from importing goods that do not comply with the national law. Conversely, it will be much easier for domestic manufacturers to comply with their own national requirements as to packaging. Examples include:

- *Walter Rau v De Smedt* (Case 261/81) [1982] ECR 3961 (Belgian legislation required margarine to be packaged in a cube).
- *Mars* (Case C–470/93) [1995] ECR I–1923 and *Estée Lauder Cosmetics v Lancaster* (Case C–220/98) [2000] ECR I–117 (German legislation prohibited the use of misleading packaging).

Contents and ingredients restrictions

In the following cases, national legislation prescribing or restricting the contents and/or ingredients of various products was held to breach Art 34:

- *Cassis de Dijon* (Case 120/78) [1979] ECR 649: German legislation laid down a minimum alcohol level of 25 per cent per litre for certain spirits.
- *Gilli and Andres* (Case 788/79) [1981] ECR 2071: Italian legislation required all vinegar to be made from wine.
- *Commission v Germany (Beer Purity)* (Case 178/84) [1987] ECR 1227: German legislation prohibited the use of additives in beer.
- *Muller* (Case 304/84) [1986] ECR 1511: French legislation prohibited the use of emulsifying agents in bakery products.
- *Greenham and Abel* (Case C–95/01) [2004] ECR I–1333: French legislation prohibited the sale of any food or drink containing a chemical substance called coenzyme Q10.
- *Commission v Italy (Red Bull)* (Case C–420/01) [2003] ECR I–6445: Italian legislation banned drinks with more than 125 mg per litre of caffeine (such as 'Red Bull', which has a caffeine level double that).

Many of these cases reached the ECJ via requests for preliminary rulings from criminal courts because traders had been prosecuted for selling imported goods that did not comply with the national legislation. Thus:

- Herbert Gilli and Paul Andres were prosecuted in Italy for selling apple vinegar made in Germany.
- Claude Muller was prosecuted in France for selling a cake and pastry mix called 'Phénix', imported from Germany, which contained an emulsifying agent.
- John Greenham and Léonard Abel were prosecuted in France for selling a food supplement, 'Juice Plus', to which had been added Q10. 'Juice Plus' is sold without restriction in the UK, Germany, Italy and Spain.

In all of these cases the ECJ decided that the national rules in question amounted to an indistinctly applicable MEQR, and were thus prohibited by Art 34, unless one of the Art 36 or *Cassis de Dijon* (1979) derogations applied (typically, protection of public health).

Name restrictions

National legislation that reserves particular names to products bearing very specific characteristics is capable of breaching Art 34. For example, in *Smanor* (Case 298/87) [1988] ECR 4489 (French legislation reserved the name 'yoghurt' to fresh produce only, with the result that frozen yoghurt had to be re-named as 'deep-frozen fermented milk') the ECJ decided that Art 34 had been infringed because 'it may none the less make the marketing [of imported frozen yoghurt] more difficult and thus impede, at least indirectly, trade between Member States'.

The same result occurred in the following cases:

- *Fietje* (Case 27/80) [1980] ECR 3839: Dutch legislation made the name 'likeur' compulsory for most alcoholic products of at least 22 per cent proof.
- *Miro* (Case 182/84) [1985] ECR 3731: Dutch legislation prescribed that the word 'Jenever' could only be applied to describe gin that was at least 35 per cent proof.
- *Deserbais* (Case 286/86) [1988] ECR 4907: French legislation restricted the use of the word 'Edam' to describe cheese with a minimum fat content.
- *Guimont* (Case 448/98) [2000] ECR I–10663: French legislation prescribed the contents of 'Emmenthal' cheese very rigidly, in that it had to be 'a firm cheese produced by curing, pressing and salting on the surface or in brine, of a colour between ivory and pale yellow, with holes of a size between a cherry and a walnut [and with a] hard, dry rind, of a colour between golden yellow and light brown'.
- *Commission v Spain* (Case C–12/00) [2003] ECR I–459: Spanish and Italian legislation restricted the use of the name 'chocolate' to products containing only chocolate and no vegetable fats. This affected chocolate products made in the UK, Denmark, Finland, Ireland, Portugal and Sweden, which traditionally contain vegetable fats. These could be sold in Italy and Spain but only under the label 'chocolate substitute'.

Conversely, where national authorities in one Member State ban or restrict the use of a name which is used elsewhere, this could also constitute a breach of Art 34. Thus, in *Clinique Laboratories and Estée Lauder Cosmetics* (Case C–315/92) [1994] ECR I–317, where the German authorities refused to allow the name 'Clinique' to be used for cosmetics, the ECJ held that Art 34 had been infringed.

Prohibitions on use

A complete ban under national legislation on the use of a product is an MEQR. In *Toolex Alpha* (Case C–473/98) [2000] ECR I–5681, Swedish legislation prohibiting the sale, transfer or use, for industrial purposes, of chemical products composed wholly or partially of trichloroethylene was held to breach Art 34 (but was justifiable under Art 36). This case is discussed in detail in the next section.

Three recent cases further illustrate this type of MEQR. In each case the Court held that a complete ban on the use of a product in a Member State breaches Art 34 (even if the product could be lawfully imported and sold) because customers in that State would have little or no interest in buying such a product, if they knew that they could not lawfully use it. Hence the ban creates a potential barrier to trade in that product. Note: in all three cases the legislation, being indistinctly applicable, was at least potentially justifiable using *Cassis de Dijon* principles.

- *Commission v Portugal (Tinted Film for Car Windows)* (case C-265/06) [2008] ECR-I-2245: Portuguese legislation prohibited (with limited exceptions) the 'affixing of tinted film to the windows of passenger or goods vehicles'.
- *Commission v Italy (Motorcycle Trailers)* (Case C-110/05) [2009] ECR I-519: Italian legislation prohibited mopeds and motorcycles from towing trailers.
- *Mickelsson & Roos* (Case C-142/05) [2009] ECR I-4273: Swedish legislation prohibited the use of 'personal watercraft' – jet-skis – except on water designated as a 'general navigable waterway'.

KEY FACTS

MEQRS and the Dassonville formula

Article 34 TFEU prohibits 'measures having an equivalent effect' to quantitative restrictions (MEQRs). This phrase is defined very widely. Any national measure capable of hindering trade – whether directly or indirectly, and whether actually or even potentially – is an MEQR	*Dassonville* (1974)
MEQRS may be distinctly applicable. These are measures which only affect domestic goods OR imports (but not both), such as buy national campaigns, or import inspections	*Commission v Ireland* ('Buy Irish') (1982); *Commission v France* (Italian Wine) (1983)
MEQRS may also be indistinctly applicable. These are measures which affect domestic goods AND imports. Examples include:	
(i) origin-marking rules	*Dassonville; Commission v UK*
(ii) packaging requirements	*Walter Rau v De Smedt* (1982); *Mars* (1995)
(iii) contents and ingredients restrictions	*Cassis de Dijon* (1979), *Gilli & Andres* (1981)
(iv) name restrictions	*Fietje* (1980), *Miro* (1985)
(v) prohibitions on use	*Toolex Alpha* (2000), *Commission v Italy* (Motorcycle Trailers) (2009)

14.5 Article 36 and the derogations from Arts 34 and 35

ARTICLE

'Art 36 The provisions of Articles 34 and 35 shall not preclude prohibitions or restrictions on imports, exports or goods in transit justified on grounds of public morality, public policy or public security; the protection of health and life of humans, animals or plants; the protection of national treasures possessing artistic, historic or archaeological value; or the protection of industrial or commercial property. Such prohibitions or restrictions shall not, however, constitute a means of arbitrary discrimination or a disguised restriction on trade between Member States.'

14.5.1 The grounds under Art 36

The grounds listed are exhaustive and may not be added to. In *Commission v Ireland* (*Souvenir Jewellery*) (1981), the ECJ stated:

JUDGMENT

'The exceptions listed [in Art 36] cannot be extended to cases other than those specifically laid down. In view of the fact that neither the protection of consumers nor the fairness of commercial transactions is included amongst the exceptions set out in [Art 36], those grounds cannot be relied upon as such in connexion with that Article.'

In particular, arguments based on economics have consistently been rejected (*Campus Oil Ltd* (Case 72/83) [1984] ECR 2727; *Evans Medical and Macfarlan Smith* (1995)). Other examples of rejected arguments include:

- consumer protection and/or the fairness of commercial transactions (*Souvenir Jewellery* (1981))
- protection of cultural diversity (*Leclerc* (Case 229/83) [1985] ECR 1).

In that case the ECJ stated that:

JUDGMENT

'Since it derogates from a fundamental rule of the Treaty, [Art 36] must be interpreted strictly and cannot be extended to cover objectives not expressly enumerated therein. Neither the safeguarding of consumers' interests nor the protection of creativity and cultural diversity in the realm of publishing is mentioned in [Art 36].'

However, these two grounds have now been recognised as 'mandatory' or 'overriding' requirements under *Cassis de Dijon* (1979) principles instead (see section 14.6 below). The grounds under Art 36 have also been restrictively interpreted because they operate as exceptions from the fundamental freedom of movement. The burden of proving that an Art 36 derogation has been made out rests with the party seeking to rely upon it, usually the national authorities (*Denkavit Futtermittel* (Case 251/78) [1979] ECR 3369).

In *ATRAL* (Case C–14/02) [2003] ECR I–4431, the ECJ was asked whether a Member State which claims justification under Art36 and/or *Cassis de Dijon* (1979) principles may merely rely on it in the abstract or must specifically demonstrate its genuineness. The ECJ replied (emphasis added):

JUDGMENT

'An exception to the principle of the free movement of goods may be justified under [Art 36] only if the national authorities show that it is necessary in order to attain one or more objectives mentioned in that article and that it is in conformity with the principle of proportionality. *Such justification can only be specifically demonstrated by reference to the circumstances of the case.* The same considerations necessarily apply to exceptions to the free movement of goods based on the overriding requirements recognised by [Union] case-law. The Court adopts an equally specific approach when assessing that category of derogations (see *Cassis de Dijon*).'

Public morality

The protection of public morality was successfully invoked in *R v Henn and Darby* (1979):

CASE EXAMPLE

R v Henn and Darby (Case 34/79) [1979] ECR 3795

UK law, s 42 of the Customs Consolidation Act 1876, provides that it is a criminal offence to be 'knowingly concerned in the fraudulent evasion of the prohibition of the importation of obscene articles'. Maurice Henn and John Darby had imported a consignment of pornographic films and magazines into the UK from Denmark via Rotterdam. The consignment was detected by British Customs. Although the majority of the films and magazines were lawfully produced and marketed in Denmark, the two men were convicted. On appeal they relied on Art 34, while the prosecution invoked public morality under Art 36. The House of Lords referred the case to the ECJ, which held: (1) the 1876 Act imposed a quantitative restriction on imports and was prima facie prohibited by Art 34 and (2) the restriction was justifiable under Art 36.

The ECJ stated:

JUDGMENT

'In principle, it is for each Member State to determine in accordance with its own scale of values and in the form selected by it the requirements of public morality in its territory. In any event, it cannot be disputed that the statutory provisions applied by the UK in regard to the importation of articles having an indecent or obscene character come within the powers reserved to the Member States by the first sentence of Article 36.'

The case was distinguished by the ECJ in *Conegate* (Case 121/85) [1986] ECR 1007 (below). It has since been followed by the UK's Divisional Court, in *R v Wright* [1999] 1 Cr App R 69, a case involving the importation of pornography supposedly to be added to a private collection. The argument advanced was that this was not a fitting subject for the application of the public morality defence. The Divisional Court disagreed (*per* Kennedy LJ):

JUDGMENT

'There is a public morality purpose to be served not only in protecting the innocent but also in protecting the less innocent from further corruption, and the addict from feeding or increasing his own addiction. Furthermore … if a substantial quantity of material is imported for private use there is an obvious risk that it will not be seen only by the importer. There is a potential for distribution which raises the question of public morality.'

Public policy

Despite great **potential** width, this ground has rarely been successfully invoked. It does not provide some general fallback provision for States (*Commission v Italy* (1961)); nor can it be used for purely economic reasons (*Commission v Italy* (Securities for Imports) (Case 95/81) [1982] ECR 2187). It cannot be used to justify measures that really fall within consumer protection (*Kohl v Ringelhan* (Case 177/83) [1984] ECR 3651). It is also no justification that the activities with which the law deals are subject to criminal penalties (*Prantl* (Case 16/83) [1984] ECR 1299). However, the defence was successfully invoked in *R v Thompson* (Case 7/78) [1979] ECR 2247 (involving UK legislation that imposed an export ban on old coins).

CASE EXAMPLE

R v Thompson (Case 7/78) [1979] ECR 2247

UK legislation prohibited the export from the UK of certain goods, including silver alloy coins minted in the UK before 1947, namely sixpences, shillings, florins and half-crowns. In 1975, Ernest Thompson and two other men exported to Germany some 40 tonnes of silver alloy coins. The men were convicted of breaching the UK law. They appealed and the case was referred to the ECJ, which held that (1) the coins were no longer legal tender and could therefore be regarded as 'goods' and (2) the restrictions on exportation were *prima facie* prohibited by Art 35 however, (3) they were justified on public policy grounds, under Art 36, since the State had an interest in protecting its mint coinage. The ban was designed to ensure that there was no shortage of current coins for use by the public.

More controversially, the House of Lords used the public policy derogation in *R v Chief Constable of Sussex, ex p ITF Ltd* [1998] 3 WLR 1260, to justify the Chief Constable's decision to withdraw police officers from the port of Shoreham in Sussex. This had the effect of allowing animal-rights protestors to blockade the port and prevent companies such as ITF Ltd from exporting live animals to other EU Member States. The Lords decided that this decision was justifiable because the Chief Constable had limited police manpower resources and had to deploy his officers throughout the county, not just in one town.

The public policy derogation was successfully invoked by the Finnish Government in *Ahokainen & Leppik* (Case C–434/04) [2006] ECR I–9171. The case involved a provision of Finnish law, under which a licence was required in order to import drinks containing ethyl alcohol over 80 per cent proof, breach of which was a criminal offence. Two Finnish nationals, Jan-Erik Ahokainen and Mati Leppik, were convicted of 'smuggling' – importing without a licence – nearly 10,000 litres of spirits into Finland from Germany and sentenced to prison. On appeal, they argued that the Finnish law amounted to a breach of Art 34. In response, the Finnish Government invoked Art 36 – relying on both public health and public policy. The ECJ agreed, stating that 'Legislation … which has as its objective the control of the consumption of alcohol so as to prevent the harmful effects caused to health and society by alcoholic substances, and thus seeks to combat alcohol abuse, reflects health and public policy concerns recognised by [Article 36]'.

Public security

Again, purely economic reasons will not suffice. However, the presence of an economic justification for national legislation will not be fatal provided that the legislation is also justifiable on public security grounds. The defence was successfully invoked in *Campus Oil* (1984). Irish legislation restricted the importation of petroleum products, ostensibly to reduce the danger of Ireland becoming over-reliant on imports. The effect of the legislation was that petrol companies operating in Ireland were forced to obtain about 30 per cent of their supplies from Ireland's only oil refinery, in Cork. The ECJ stated:

JUDGMENT

'Petroleum products, because of their exceptional importance as an energy source in the modern economy, are of fundamental importance for a country's existence since not only its economy but above all its institutions, its essential public services and even the survival of its inhabitants depend upon them. An interruption of supplies of petroleum products … could therefore seriously affect the public security that [Art 36] allows States to protect … the aim of ensuring a minimum supply of petroleum products at all times is to be regarded as transcending purely economic considerations and thus as capable of constituting an objective covered by the concept of public security.'

Campus Oil (1984) was confirmed in *Commission v Greece (Petroleum Stocks)* (Case C–398/98) [2001] ECR I–7915. The ECJ acknowledged that 'the maintenance on national territory of a stock of petroleum products allowing continuity of supplies to be guaranteed constitutes a public security objective'. However, the Court went on to reject the defence on the facts, finding that the Greek legislation was primarily concerned about protecting the economic freedom of oil refineries rather than Greek public security.

Public security was also raised in *Richardt and Les Accessoires Scientifiques* (Case C–367/89) [1991] ECR I–4621, although this did not involve imports or exports. Instead, it concerned the transit of a machine used in the production of bubble memory circuits from the USA to Russia via Luxembourg. The transit company was prosecuted under Luxembourg law for failing to have acquired the requisite clearance in advance. It challenged the law, and the Luxembourg authorities relied on public security. Bubble memory circuits were a type of computer memory storage that used a thin film of a magnetic material to hold small magnetized areas, known as 'bubbles'. They were widely used in the 1970s and 1980s but eventually fell into disuse with the advent of hard discs. However, bubble memory circuits found uses through the 1980s in computer systems operating in high vibration or harsh environments. It appears that the Luxembourg authorities were concerned that the machine might have been put to military use, and hence invoked the public security derogation. The ECJ stated:

JUDGMENT

'The concept of public security within the meaning of [Art 36] covers both a Member State's internal security and its external security. It is common ground that the importation, exportation and transit of goods capable of being used for strategic purposes may affect the public security of a Member State, which it is therefore entitled to protect pursuant to [Art 36].'

Protection of the health and life of humans, animals and plants

In *Toolex Alpha* (2000), where Swedish legislation prohibited the sale, transfer or use, for industrial purposes, of chemical products composed wholly or partially of trichloroethylene, because of a perceived risk of causing cancer, the ECJ stated that 'the health and life of humans rank foremost among the property or interests protected' by Art 36. Article 36 has been used to justify many measures, typically prohibitions (or at least restrictions) on the import or sale of various foodstuffs, additives, drugs and chemicals; tests and inspections as to quality, etc.

CASE EXAMPLE

Toolex Alpha (Case C–473/98) [2000] ECR I–5681

Swedish law prohibited the sale, transfer or use, for industrial purposes, of chemical products composed wholly or partially of trichloroethylene (TE). Toolex Alpha, a manufacturer of machine parts used in the production of CDs, used TE to remove residues of grease produced during the manufacturing process. Toolex challenged the ban, alleging a breach of Art 34. The Swedish Government relied upon Art 36. It was not contested that TE was a known carcinogenic substance, carrying a risk of cancer in humans and posing a threat to the environment. The Swedish authorities further submitted that TE affects the central nervous system, the liver and the kidneys. The fact that it is highly volatile increases the chances of exposure. Inhaling the substance can cause fatigue, headaches and difficulties with memory and concentration. The case was referred to the ECJ, which held that (1) the Swedish legislation, being an outright ban, was *prima facie* prohibited by Art 34; (2) the Swedish rules were justified under Art 36. The Court noted that concern regarding TE had been mounting in recent years. In particular, the International Cancer Research Agency had produced evidence that TE is a carcinogen. A German case study produced statistics indicating a link between the incidence of renal cancer and exposure to TE. Furthermore, an American epidemiological study indicated that there is an aggravated risk of renal cancer, in particular following exposure to TE at the workplace.

Sometimes the defence is successful. The Dutch restrictions on the sale of vitamin-enhanced muesli bars in *Sandoz* (1983), the Swedish ban on trichloroethylene in case *Toolex Alpha* (2000) and the French ban on 'Red Bull' in *Commission v France* (Case C–24/00) [2004] ECR I–1277 were all upheld. However, sometimes the defence fails. Defences tend be rejected for one of two reasons: (1) lack of evidence of a 'real' health risk or (2) failure to comply with the principle of proportionality (see below).

In general, the ECJ is vigilant to prevent Art 36 from being abused, hence the insistence of evidence of a 'real' risk. However, if the Member State whose legislation is being contested can point to international scientific research supporting them, then the ECJ is far more likely to accept that there was such a risk. In *Greenham and Abel* (2004), the ECJ stated:

JUDGMENT

'Since [Art 36] provides for an exception, to be interpreted strictly, to the rule of free movement of goods within the Union, it is for the national authorities which invoke it to show in each case, in the light of national nutritional habits and in the light of the results of international scientific research, that their rules are necessary to give effective protection to the interests referred to in that provision and, in particular, that the marketing of the products in question poses a real risk to public health.'

Member States may adopt different approaches to the same safety issue. What if there is disputed scientific opinion about whether or not there is a real health risk? In *Sandoz* (1983), the ECJ stated that 'Insofar as there are uncertainties at the present state of scientific research it is for the Member States … to decide what degree of protection of the health and life of humans they intend to assure'. This led the Court to conclude that Dutch rules prohibiting vitamin-enhanced muesli bars were 'justified on principle'.

In *Greenham and Abel* (2004), involving French legislation which prohibited the marketing of food and drink to which a substance called Q10 had been added, the ECJ laid down important guidelines on when the human health derogation would be available in such circumstances. The ECJ stated that:

JUDGMENT

'A decision to prohibit the marketing of a fortified foodstuff, which is in fact the most restrictive obstacle to trade in products lawfully manufactured and marketed in other Member States, can be adopted only if the alleged real risk for public health appears to be sufficiently established on the basis of the latest scientific data available at the date of the adoption of such decision. In such a context, the object of the risk assessment to be carried out by the Member State is to appraise the degree of probability of harmful effects on human health from the addition of certain nutrients to foodstuffs and the seriousness of those potential effects. It is clear that such an assessment of the risk could reveal that scientific uncertainty persists as regards the existence or extent of real risks to human health. In such circumstances, it must be accepted that a Member State may, in accordance with the precautionary principle, take protective measures without having to wait until the existence and gravity of those risks are fully demonstrated. However, the risk assessment cannot be based on purely hypothetical considerations.'

The Court repeated this test in *Commission v Denmark* (Case C–192/01) [2003] ECR I–9693, deciding that Danish rules restricting the marketing of 'enriched' foodstuffs (described as any food to which had been added any substance designed to modify its nutritional value, shelf-life, colour, flavour or taste) were justifiable on human health grounds.

The protection of animal health was invoked by the House of Lords in *R (on the application of Countryside Alliance & Others) v HM Attorney General* [2007] UKHL 52; [2007] 3 WLR 922. The House was asked whether the ban on the hunting with dogs of wild mammals, in particular foxes, imposed under the *Hunting Act 2004,* infringed Art 34 and/or Art 56 (the freedom to provide services). The House accepted that the ban could hinder intra-Union trade. Lord Hope gave as an example horses bred in Ireland for sale to customers in England. However, the House agreed that the ban was justifiable under Art 36. Lord Bingham stated:

JUDGMENT

'I approach the issue of justification on the assumption that Articles 34 and 56 apply, but also on the basis that the measure to be justified is a measure of social reform … In Omega, the German authorities considered, and the ECJ accepted, that "the exploitation of games involving the simulated killing of human beings infringed a fundamental value enshrined in the national constitution, namely human dignity". Parliament considered that the real killing of foxes, deer, hares and mink by way of recreation infringed a fundamental value expressed in numerous statutes and culminating in the 2004 Act. I am of the clear opinion … that the 2004 Act is justifiable in Union law.'

(Note: Art 56 and the Omega case were examined in Chapter 13.)

Protection of national treasures

No case has yet succeeded on these grounds. In any event, it is more likely to apply to measures taken in respect of exports.

Protection of industrial and commercial property

In *Belgium v Spain (Rioja wine exports)* (Case C–388/95) [2000] ECR I–3123, the ECJ upheld provisions of Spanish law requiring *Rioja* wine intended for export to be bottled in the La Rioja region. Although *prima facie* in breach of Art 35, the legislation was justified. This was because *Rioja* wine enjoyed an international reputation for high quality, which might be tarnished if the wine could be transported out of the region in bulk and then bottled elsewhere. The ECJ stated:

JUDGMENT

'Designations of origin fall within the scope of industrial and commercial property rights. The applicable rules protect those entitled to use them against improper use of those designations by third parties seeking to profit from the reputation which they have acquired. They are intended to guarantee that the product bearing them comes from a specified geographical area and displays certain particular characteristics. They may enjoy a high reputation amongst consumers and constitute for producers who fulfil the conditions for using them an essential means of attracting custom. The reputation of designations of origin depends on their image in the minds of consumers. That image in turn depends essentially on particular characteristics and more generally on the quality of the product. It is on the latter, ultimately, that the product's reputation is based.'

14.5.2 The second sentence of Art 36

As well as providing evidence to support the use of one of the six grounds of derogation under Art 36, the Member State in question must also satisfy the Court that no breach of the second sentence of Art 36 has occurred. There are two aspects to this. Any quantitative restriction or MEQR must not:

- discriminate against imports in an 'arbitrary' way or
- be a restriction on imports for economic reasons but 'disguised' using one of the derogations (usually the 'health' derogation).

'Arbitrary discrimination'

National measures which only apply to imported goods (that is, quantitative restrictions in the strict sense, such as import bans; or distinctly applicable MEQRs) may be justified under Art 36. That is, Member States may discriminate against imported goods. An import ban is, by definition, discriminatory against imports. However, national legislation must not discriminate in an 'arbitrary' way. National legislation will be held to be 'arbitrary' if there is no objective basis for making the distinction (*Commission v France* (Case 152/78) [1980] ECR 2299). In *R v Henn and Darby* (1980) (in the context of the 'public morality' derogation) the ECJ said that 'the true function' of the second sentence of Art 36 was:

JUDGMENT

'To prevent restrictions on trade based on the grounds mentioned in the first sentence of [Art 36] from being diverted from their proper purpose and used in such a way as either to create discrimination in respect of goods originating in other Member States or indirectly to protect certain national products.'

In *Henn and Darby* (1980), the ECJ regarded s 42 of the Customs Consolidation Act 1876 as discriminatory, since it prohibited the importation of material which was 'indecent or obscene', whereas domestic (UK-produced) pornography was only illegal under the Obscene Publications Acts 1959 and 1964 if likely to 'deprave or corrupt'. Clearly,

some foreign pornography, unlikely to deprave or corrupt, could still be described as 'indecent or obscene'. However, the ECJ held that, although discriminatory, the UK law was not **arbitrary**, and nor was there a disguised restriction on trade. The UK's anti-pornography laws, **taken as a whole**, did have as their purpose the prohibition (or at least the restraining) of the manufacture and marketing of articles of an indecent or obscene character.

The 1876 Act had, therefore, been genuinely applied for the protection of public morality, and not for the protection of national products, because there was no lawful trade in such goods in the UK. *Henn and Darby* was distinguished on that point in *Conegate* (Case 121/85) [1986] ECR 1007.

CASE EXAMPLE

Conegate (Case 121/85) [1986] ECR 1007

Conegate, a British company, was in the business of importing inflatable rubber dolls, and other articles, into the UK from Germany. A number of consignments of dolls and other articles were seized by Customs at the airport on the grounds that they were 'indecent or obscene' under s 42 of the 1876 Act. However, there was no law preventing the manufacture of such dolls in the UK. Conegate brought an action for recovery of the dolls before the High Court, relying on Art 34. The Customs authorities relied on the 'public morality' defence under Art 36. The ECJ held that (1) there was a *prima facie* breach of Art 34 and (2) Art 36 did **not** apply because, although the sale of sex dolls was **restricted** in the UK, to licensed sex shops, it was not **banned** (unlike the explicit pornography in *Henn and Darby* (1980)). It would therefore constitute 'arbitrary' discrimination to ban the importation of love dolls from Germany when there was already a lawful (albeit restricted) trade in similar, UK-produced, dolls in the UK.

A 'disguised restriction on trade'

A national measure, ostensibly designed to protect human health (for example) may not be protected by Art 36 if, in reality, the measure is 'a disguised restriction on trade'. A good example is provided by *Commission v UK (French Turkeys)* (Case 40/82) [1982] ECR 2793. In 1981 the UK had banned poultry imports, ostensibly because of fears about a health risk. On closer examination, it transpired that the import ban had been imposed for economic reasons. The ECJ stated:

JUDGMENT

'Certain established facts suggest that the real aim of the 1981 measures was to block, *for commercial and economic reasons*, imports of poultry products from other Member States, in particular from France. The UK government had been subject to pressure from British poultry producers to block these imports. It hurriedly introduced its new policy with the result that French Christmas turkeys were excluded from the British market ... The deduction must be made that the 1981 measures did not form part of a seriously considered health policy ... these facts are sufficient to establish that the 1981 measures constitute a disguised restriction on imports of poultry products from other Member States.'

14.5.3 Article 36 and harmonising Directives

Where harmonising Directives in a particular subject (typically human or animal health) have been adopted, Member States may not unilaterally adopt, on their own authority, corrective or protective measures designed to obviate any breach by another State of EU law. Article 36 will not be available. In *Tedeschi v Denkavit* (Case 5/77) [1977] ECR 1555, the ECJ stated:

JUDGMENT

'Where … directives provide for the harmonisation of the measures necessary to ensure the protection of animal and human health and establish [Union] procedures to check that they are observed, recourse to [Art 36] is no longer justified and the appropriate checks must be carried out and the measures of protection adopted within the framework outlined by the harmonising directive.'

The ECJ confirmed this ruling in two cases involving measures taken allegedly in the interests of animal health: *Hedley Lomas (Ireland) Ltd* (Case C–5/94) [1996] ECR I–2553 (conditions in Spanish slaughterhouses) and *Compassion in World Farming Ltd* (Case C–1/96) [1998] ECR I–1251 (live animal exports in crates). In both cases the ECJ held that the measures could **not** be justified using Art 36 because harmonising Directives provided EU-wide protection.

KEY FACTS

The Article 36 derogations

Measures that restrict imports or exports can be justified on six grounds in the TFEU itself:	Article 36 TFEU
1. Public morality	*Henn and Darby* (1979)
2. Public policy	*R v Thompson* (1979); *Ahokainen and Leppik* (2006)
3. Public security	*Campus Oil* (1984)
4. Protection of health and life of humans, animals or plants. Human health protection is the most important ground	*Toolex Alpha* (2000)
Member States are allowed to adopt a precautionary principle, where there is scientific uncertainty	*Sandoz* (1983)
There must be a 'real risk' to human health based on the latest scientific data, and not 'purely hypothetical considerations'	*Greenham and Abel* (2004)
5. Protection of national treasures	
6. Protection of industrial or commercial property	*Belgium v Spain (Rioja wine)* (2000)
The list of grounds in Art 36 is closed and may not be added to	*Commission v Ireland* (Souvenir Jewellery) (1981), *Leclerc* (1985)
There must be no 'arbitrary discrimination' against imports	*Conegate* (1986)
The grounds in Art 36 must not be used as a 'disguised restriction on trade'	*Commission v UK (French Turkeys)* (1982)
Where harmonising directives exist, eg on animal health standards, Art 36 is not available	*Tedeschi v Denkavit* (1977), *Hedley Lomas* (1996), *Compassion in World Farming* (1998)

14.6 The effects of the *Cassis de Dijon* principle

14.6.1 Introduction

By 1979, Art 36 was already 22 years old and, never having been updated, was 'stuck' in 1957. By the late 1970s several Member States (in particular Germany and the UK) had enacted quite sophisticated consumer protection legislation. This legislation was quite capable of restricting the free movement of goods (especially given the wide scope awarded to Art 34 by *Dassonville* (1974)) but was incapable of being justified under Art 36 unless it could be brought under the 'protection of human health' heading. As only the Member States' governments have the power to amend the EC Treaty (and even then they must be unanimous) the wait for Art 36 to be updated was likely to be a very long wait indeed. In 1979, therefore, in *Cassis de Dijon* (Case 120/78) [1979] 649, the ECJ took decisive action. As the ECJ had no power to amend Art 36, it created a parallel set of derogations that Member States could plead as an alternative to Art 36. This is sometimes referred to as the 'rule of reason'.

CASE EXAMPLE

Cassis de Dijon (Case 120/78) [1979] ECR 649

German legislation laid down a **minimum** alcohol level of 25 per cent per litre for certain spirits, including cassis. Rewe-Zentral, a German company, applied to the Federal Monopoly Administration for Spirits for permission to import '*Cassis de Dijon*', a French blackcurrant liqueur about 15–20 per cent proof. Rewe was informed that the French cassis was of insufficient alcoholic strength. Rewe argued that this German law contravened Art 34. The German Government argued that the legislation had been enacted in the interests of public health (by keeping alcohol levels high they were preventing an overall **increase** in alcohol consumption which would follow if the alcoholic content in drinks was lower) and to ensure fairness in commercial transactions (by denying the weaker, and so cheaper, French cassis an advantage over German cassis). The ECJ laid down the 'rule of reason', thereby establishing that national legislation could be justified on such grounds as consumer protection. However, the Court went on to hold that the German rules were not **necessary** to achieve these ends. Other means, less of a hindrance to trade, such as clear labelling, would have been sufficient.

The ECJ held that:

JUDGMENT

'Obstacles to movement within the Union resulting from disparities between the national laws relating to the marketing of the products in question must be accepted in so far as these provisions may be recognised as being necessary in order to satisfy mandatory requirements relating in particular to the effectiveness of fiscal supervision, the protection of public health, the fairness of commercial transactions and the defence of the consumer.'

'Rule of reason': key points

- In *Cassis de Dijon* (1979), the ECJ described the derogations that Member States can plead as 'mandatory requirements'. It has used other, synonymous, expressions too, such as 'objectives of general interest' (*ADBHU* (Case 240/83) [1985] ECR 531). More recently, the ECJ has tended to describe the derogations as 'overriding interests' or 'overriding requirements' (*Familiapress* (Case C–368/95) [1997] ECR I–3689) or 'overriding reason in the general interest' (*Decker* (Case C–120/95) [1998] ECR I–1831).
- In *Cassis de Dijon* (1979), the ECJ gave four examples of 'mandatory requirements' but prefaced its list with the words 'in particular' – thus, there is no limit to the number of mandatory requirements that can be created. This contrasts with Art 36, which is a closed list.

- In subsequent case law the ECJ has added to the list, which now includes the improvement of working conditions (1981), the protection of culture (1985), the protection of the environment (1985), the diversity of the Press (1997), the maintenance of social security systems (1998), road safety (2000), the protection of 'fundamental freedoms' such as the freedom of expression (2003), the protection of children (2008) and the 'fight against crime' (2008).

14.6.2 The 'mandatory requirements'

The protection of public health (1979)

Although generally dealt with under Art 36, in one case at least, public health was dealt with under *Cassis de Dijon* (1979) principles (*Gilli and Andres* (1981)).

The fairness of commercial transactions (1979)

This was successfully argued in *Oosthoek's* (Case 286/81) [1982] ECR 4575. The Dutch Government argued that legislation prohibiting the offering of free gifts as a means of sales promotion was justifiable on grounds of fair trading (and consumer protection). The ECJ agreed. The ECJ held that it was 'undeniable' that offering free gifts 'may mislead customers as to the real prices of certain products and distort the conditions on which genuine competition is based'. In *IDG* (Case 6/81) [1982] ECR 707, the ECJ agreed that Dutch legislation prohibiting the marketing of identical products (known as 'passing off' in English law) was justifiable on grounds of fair trading.

Fair trading was claimed, but rejected, in another 'passing off' case, that of *Prantl* (Case 16/83) [1984] ECR 1299.

CASE EXAMPLE

Prantl (Case 16/83) [1984] ECR 1299

Karl Prantl was prosecuted for importing Italian wine in bottles very similar in shape and design to traditional German bottles, *Bocksbeutele*, protected under German legislation as having a characteristic 'bulbous' shape that designated a particular quality wine. The ECJ acknowledged that the legislation did serve to protect consumers and protect German wine producers from passing off. However, the ECJ went on to conclude that because bulbous wine bottles had been traditionally manufactured in Italy for over a century, 'in accordance with a fair and traditional practice' meant there was no justification for excluding them from Germany.

The Court stated:

JUDGMENT

'National case-law prohibiting the precise imitation of someone else's product which is likely to cause confusion may indeed protect consumers and promote fair trading; these are general interests which … may justify the existence of obstacles to movement within the Union resulting from disparities between national laws relating to the marketing of products.'

The defence of the consumer (1979)

The defence has been successfully raised in some cases, such as *Robertson and Others* (Case 220/81) [1983] ECR 2349, concerning Belgian legislation requiring the hallmarking of silver-plated goods. Another example of the defence being successfully raised is *A-Punkt Schmuckhandels v Schmidt* (Case C–441/04) [2006] ECR I–2093. The case involved an alleged breach by Claudia Schmidt, a jeweller, of the Austrian Trade & Commercial Regulations 1994, which prohibited the sale of silver jewellery to customers in their own homes. Although the Court held that the 1994 Regulations probably amounted to a 'selling arrangement', in which case Art 34 did not apply (see section 14.8 below), the ECJ also considered the possibility that the Regulations breached Art 34 and, if so, whether they could be justified using the consumer protection mandatory requirement. On that point, the Court stated that:

JUDGMENT

'Consumer protection may constitute a justification for the prohibition at issue [taking into account] the specific features associated with the sale of silver jewellery in private homes, in particular the potentially higher risk of the consumer being cheated due to a lack of information, the impossibility of comparing prices or the provision of insufficient safeguards as regards the authenticity of that jewellery and the greater psychological pressure to buy where the sale is organised in a private setting.'

However, the defence has, in the majority of cases, proven to be unsuccessful. It is clear that the ECJ attributes a fair amount of intelligence and sophistication to consumers. Indeed, in *Estée Lauder v Lancaster* (2000) the ECJ held that 'It is necessary to take into account the presumed expectations of an average consumer who is reasonably well informed and reasonably observant and circumspect'.

In *Clinique Laboratories* (1994) and *Mars* (1995) the ECJ rejected the 'consumer protection' defence, which had been advanced by the German Government in order to restrict the marketing of French goods (cosmetics and ice-cream bars, respectively). In *Mars*, the German authorities had objected to the sale of ice-cream bars bearing a '+10%' logo which covered substantially more than 10 per cent of the surface area of the wrapping. The ECJ stated:

JUDGMENT

'It is contended that the measure in question is justified because a not insignificant number of consumers will be induced into believing ... that the increase is larger than that represented. Such a justification cannot be accepted. Reasonably circumspect consumers are supposed to know that there is not necessarily a link between the size of publicity markings relating to an increase in a product's quantity and the size of that increase.'

A consumer protection defence was also rejected in *Clinique Laboratories* (1994):

CASE EXAMPLE

Clinique Laboratories (Case C–315/92) [1994] ECR I–317

German legislation – the Law on Foodstuffs and Consumer Items (1974) – prohibited the sale of cosmetics under misleading names, designations or presentations by which certain properties could be ascribed to products that they did not in fact have. German authorities regarded the name '*Clinique*', a brand of cosmetics produced in France by Estée Lauder, as one such misleading name – it could mislead consumers into thinking that the product had medicinal qualities, as it evoked associations with the word 'clinic'. The consequence of this was that Estée Lauder had to repackage its product for the German market (it was renamed '*Linique*') and advertise it differently to everywhere else, obviously increasing its costs greatly. The German authorities were challenged, alleging a breach of Art 34. The German authorities responded that the law was justifiable on public health and/or consumer protection grounds. The ECJ held that: (1) the German legislation *prima facie* infringed Art 34, because it required the manufacturers to incur expense in re-packaging and re-advertising the product for different markets and (2) as far as consumer protection was concerned, the German rules were not necessary to achieve their objective. First, *Clinique* products were sold everywhere else under that name without causing confusion; second, *Clinique* products were sold in Germany (albeit as 'Linique') exclusively in perfumeries and the cosmetics departments of large stores – never in pharmacies. There was therefore no consumer risk to be protected against.

Often the defence will be rejected because the contested national legislation went beyond what was 'necessary' to protect consumers. Thus, in *Walter Rau v De Smedt* (1982), the ECJ held that the Belgian legislation requiring margarine to be packed in cubes was prohibited by Art 34, despite alleged consumer protection reasons, because Belgian consumers could have been adequately protected by less drastic means, eg clear labelling.

CASE EXAMPLE

Walter Rau v De Smedt (Case 261/81) [1982] ECR 3961

Belgian legislation required margarine to be sold only in cubes. This was ostensibly designed to help consumers distinguish between butter (not sold in cubes) and margarine. The case reached the ECJ after the German margarine producer, Walter Rau, was unable to deliver 30 tonnes of its margarine to the Belgian supermarket chain De Smedt. The supermarket refused delivery because the margarine was packaged in a 'truncated cone' shape, not a cube. When Walter Rau took De Smedt to court, seeking specific performance of the contract of sale, the ECJ held that this legislation was capable of hindering trade and went beyond what was necessary to achieve its alleged consumer protection objective – clear labelling would have achieved the same objective but would have imposed less of an obstacle to trade.

In *Alfa Vita Vassilopoulos* (Cases C–158 & 159/04) [2006] ECR I–8135, the ECJ emphasised that the mandatory requirement involved protection of the consumer, not the promotion of quality. The Court therefore held that the defence was unavailable to justify a provision in Greek law designed to help customers distinguish between fresh bread and 'bake-off' bread – meaning, bread which had previously been frozen – the former, apparently, being superior quality to the latter. The Court stated:

JUDGMENT

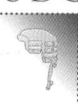

'A national measure which restricts the free movement of goods may not be justified solely on the ground that it aims to promote quality foodstuffs ... such an objective may be taken into account only in relation to other requirements which have been recognised as being imperative, such as consumer or health protection.'

The improvement of working conditions (1981)

The improvement of working conditions was added as a mandatory requirement in 1981 in *Oebel* (Case 155/80) [1981] ECR 1993, concerning German rules preventing bakeries from operating before 4 am. Although this was capable of restricting trade (in that it prevented German bakeries from producing bread early enough for export to pre-breakfast markets just over the border in the neighbouring states of Luxembourg and Belgium), the ECJ held that the restriction was justified. The Court stated that 'It cannot be disputed that the prohibition in the bread and confectionery industry on working before 4 am in itself constitutes a legitimate element of economic and social policy, consistent with the objectives of public interest pursued by the Treaty'.

The protection of the environment (1985)

The European Commission first mentioned this in a Practice Note in 1980. The Commission, ostensibly summarising the list of 'mandatory requirements' at that date, listed 'public health, protection of consumers or the environment, the fairness of commercial transactions, etc'. However, environmental protection was only recognised as a mandatory requirement by the ECJ in 1985 in *ADBHU* (Case 240/83) [1985] ECR 531, involving French legislation restricting the movement of waste oil. The ECJ stated that 'Insofar as such measures ... have a restrictive effect on the freedom of trade ... they must nevertheless neither be discriminatory nor go beyond the inevitable restrictions which are justified by the pursuit of the objective of environmental protection, which is in the general interest'. The best-known case is *Commission v Denmark (the Danish Bottles case)* (Case 302/86) [1988] ECR 4607, where the ECJ stated:

JUDGMENT

'The protection of the environment is one of the Union's essential objectives, which may justify certain limitations of the principle of the free movement of goods … it must therefore be stated that the protection of the environment is a mandatory requirement which may limit the application of [Art 34].'

CASE EXAMPLE

Danish Bottles (Case 302/86) [1988] ECR 4607

Danish legislation required that all beer and soft drinks sold in Denmark had to be packaged in re-usable containers, and that distributors of such products should establish deposit-and-return schemes and recycle the containers in order to protect the environment and conserve resources. The European Commission alleged a breach of Art 34. The ECJ agreed, holding that (1) the Danish rules were *prima facie* prohibited by Art 34, as they would restrict imports of non-recyclable bottles produced in other EU Member States (2) environmental protection was recognised as a mandatory requirement. The deposit-and-return schemes, and the re-use requirements were, theoretically, legitimate under EU law (3) however, the rules had not been shown to be strictly necessary to achieve their objective and therefore infringed the 'proportionality' doctrine (see below).

Environmental protection was also accepted as a defence in *Commission v Belgium (Walloon Waste)* (Case C–2/90) [1992] ECR I–4431, involving Belgian legislation restricting the importation of waste (for recycling purposes) and *Aher-waggon* (Case C–389/96) [1998] ECR I–4473, involving German legislation imposing strict noise levels on aircraft engines. The ECJ rejected an environmental protection defence in *Dusseldorp* (Case C–203/96) [1998] ECR I–4075, involving Dutch legislation restricting the exportation of waste oil filters, but only because the legislation was 'primarily' economic in nature.

Two more cases in which environmental protection was accepted as a defence, at least in principle, are *Commission v Germany (Waste Packaging)* (Case C–463/01) [2004] ECR I–11705 and *Radlberger & Spitz* (Case C–309/02) [2004] ECR I–11763. Both cases involved German legislation providing for a compulsory deposit-and-return scheme for waste packaging, which meant that manufacturers were obliged to charge a deposit for, and accept the return of, waste packaging. Although the Court accepted that the German rules were capable of hindering trade, they were justifiable. The Court stated:

JUDGMENT

'The establishment of a deposit and return system is liable to increase the proportion of empty packaging returned and results in more precise sorting of packaging waste, thus helping to improve its recovery. In addition, the charging of a deposit contributes to the reduction of waste in the natural environment since it encourages consumers to return empty packaging to the points of sale … Inasmuch as those rules thus encourage the producers and distributors concerned to have recourse to reusable packaging, they contribute towards reducing the amount of waste to be disposed of, which constitutes one of the general objectives of environmental protection policy.'

In *Mickelsson & Roos* (Case C-142/05) [2009] All ER (EC) 842, Swedish legislation prohibiting the use of 'personal watercraft' – jet-skis – except on water designated as a 'general navigable waterway' was held to breach Art 34. However, it was justifiable on environmental protection grounds. The Court held that:

JUDGMENT

'A restriction or a prohibition on the use of personal watercraft are appropriate means for the purpose of ensuring that the environment is protected ... Member States cannot be denied the possibility of attaining an objective such as the protection of the environment by the introduction of general rules which are necessary on account of the particular geographical circumstances of the Member State concerned.'

The protection of culture (1985)

This was added to the list in 1985 by *Cinéthèque* (Cases 60 and 61/84) [1985] ECR 2065, concerning French legislation temporarily restricting the availability of films on video, in order to encourage cinema attendance instead. The ECJ held that this policy was justifiable. (It is perhaps not insignificant that this case was heard at a time when cinema attendances were declining across Europe, largely because of the introduction of home video recorders in the early 1980s.)

CASE EXAMPLE

Cinéthèque (Cases 60 and 61/84) [1985] ECR 2065

French legislation prohibited the sale or rental of films on video until 12 months had elapsed since that film's debut at the cinema. This was challenged by the French video retail chain, Cinéthèque, and the case was referred to the ECJ. There it was acknowledged that this rule was capable of restricting trade (other Member States allowing films to be released on video much more quickly than that) but it was justified because it encouraged cinema attendance. The ECJ stated that 'It must be conceded that a national system which, in order to encourage the creation of cinematographic works irrespective of their origin, gives priority, for a limited initial period, to the distribution of such works through the cinema, is so justified'.

In *Torfaen Borough Council v B&Q plc* (Case 145/88) [1989] ECR 3851, which concerned the legality of British Sunday trading legislation, the ECJ first coined the phrase 'socio-cultural characteristics' to describe this mandatory requirement. The ECJ held that the prohibition on Sunday trading, although capable of hindering trade, was justifiable.

The protection of books as 'cultural objects' was recognised as an overriding interest in *Fachverband der Buch- und Medienwirtschaft* (case C-531/07) [2009] 3 CMLR 26. Austrian legislation stipulated a minimum selling price for books. When challenged to justify this legislation, the Austrian Government argued that, in the absence of a pricing system, there would be a drop in prices, which would cause a drop in profits, as a result of which it would become impossible to finance the production and marketing of more demanding but economically less attractive works. Moreover, small booksellers which normally offer a wider choice of specialist books would be driven out of the market by larger booksellers which sell primarily more commercial books. The ECJ accepted that books were 'cultural objects' deserving of protection, although the actual legislation was deemed to go beyond what was necessary to achieve that objective (in other words, it failed the proportionality test).

The diversity of the press (1997)

This was added to the list in 1997 by *Familiapress* (1997), concerning a prohibition in Austrian legislation on newspapers offering cash prizes to competition winners. The ECJ decided that the Austrian legislation was justifiable in the interest of helping smaller publishers to survive against fierce competition from larger publishers (who had the potential to offer bigger prizes), thereby promoting a diverse newspaper industry. The ECJ stated that 'Maintenance of press diversity may constitute an overriding requirement justifying a restriction on free movement of goods. Such diversity helps to safeguard freedom of expression'.

The maintenance of social security systems (1998)

This was added to the list in 1998, in *Decker* (Case C–120/95) [1998] ECR I–1831. D, a Luxembourg national, used a prescription obtained in Luxembourg to purchase a pair of spectacles from an optician in Belgium. When he tried to reclaim the cost from the Luxembourg social security authorities, this was refused as he had not sought prior authorisation. This rule only applied where spectacles were obtained abroad. D argued that this was contrary to Art 34. The ECJ held that the Luxembourg rules were *prima facie* in breach of Art 34, because they encouraged Luxembourg nationals to purchase or have their spectacles assembled in Luxembourg rather than another Member State, such as Belgium. However, the rules were justifiable under *Cassis de Dijon* (1979) principles. The Court stated that, 'the risk of seriously undermining the financial balance of the social security system may constitute an overriding reason in the general interest'.

Road safety (2000)

In *Snellers Autos* (Case C-314/98) [2000] ECR I-8633, the ECJ confirmed that road safety could be added to the list of mandatory requirements. This was confirmed in *Commission v Finland* (Case C–54/05) [2007] ECR I–2473, involving Finnish legislation under which a 'transfer licence' was required before cars registered in other Member States could be imported into Finland. The licence was not automatic but was regarded in practice as a formality. The European Commission alleged a breach of Art 34, and in response the Finnish Government argued that the licensing requirement was justified on the grounds of promoting road safety (licences could be refused to cars not deemed to be roadworthy). The ECJ agreed (in principle, at least), stating that: 'It is not in dispute that road safety does constitute an overriding reason in the public interest capable of justifying a hindrance to the free movement of goods'.

A more recent example is *Commission v Italy (Motorcycle Trailers)* (Case C-110/05) [2009] ECR I-519, involving Italian legislation prohibiting mopeds and motorcycles from towing trailers. The ECJ held that the legislation was capable of hindering trade in such trailers but was justified on grounds of road safety. The Court stated:

JUDGMENT

'In the field of road safety a Member State may determine the degree of protection which it wishes to apply in regard to such safety and the way in which that degree of protection is to be achieved … Member States cannot be denied the possibility of attaining an objective such as road safety by the introduction of general and simple rules which will be easily understood and applied by drivers and easily managed and supervised by the competent authorities.'

The protection of fundamental rights (2003)

In *Schmidberger v Austria* (Case C–112/00) [2003] ECR I–5659, the ECJ stated that the protection of fundamental rights 'is a legitimate interest which, in principle, justifies a restriction of … the free movement of goods.' The case involved a decision made by the Austrian authorities to allow a road to be closed for the purposes of a demonstration. The Court acknowledged that the authorities had been placed in a difficult position, having to balance the right of transport companies to enjoy the free movement of goods under Arts 34 and 35, on one hand, against the rights of the demonstrators to enjoy the freedoms of expression and assembly, under Arts 10 and 11 of the European Convention on Human Rights, on the other. The ECJ held that no breach of EU law had occurred.

CASE EXAMPLE

Schmidberger v Austria (Case C–112/00) [2003] ECR I–5659

The Austrian authorities had permitted an environmental group, Transitforum Austria Tirol, to stage a demonstration designed to raise awareness of traffic pollution. The effect of the demonstration was to block the Brenner motorway in Austria to all traffic for 30 hours and to heavy goods vehicles for even longer. Schmidberger, a German road haulage firm, alleged that this decision constituted a breach of Art 34. The ECJ agreed that this decision had the effect of imposing obstacles (however temporary) to the free movement of goods between Germany, Austria and Italy. However, the ECJ decided that the Austrian authorities were justified by considerations linked to respect of the 'fundamental rights' of the demonstrators to freedom of expression and freedom of assembly, both of which are protected by the European Convention on Human Rights.

The Court stated:

JUDGMENT

'The interests involved must be weighed having regard to all the circumstances of the case in order to determine whether a fair balance was struck between those interests ... the competent authorities enjoy a wide margin of discretion in that regard ... Taking account of the Member States' wide margin of discretion, in circumstances such as those of the present case the competent national authorities were entitled to consider that an outright ban on the demonstration would have constituted unacceptable interference with the fundamental rights of the demonstrators to gather and express peacefully their opinion in public.

Protection of Children (2008)

The case of *Dynamic Medien v Avides Media* (Case C–244/06) [2008] ECR I-505, involved a system under German law of compulsory classification and labelling of DVDs and videos in terms of their suitability for viewing by children. The Court accepted that, although capable of hindering trade, the German rules were justifiable. However, it is not entirely clear whether the Court dealt with the justification as an example of public policy under Art 36, or as a new mandatory requirement. At one point, the Court observed that the European Commission, along with the British, German and Irish Governments, all agreed that 'the rules at issue ... are justified in so far as they are designed to protect young people. That objective is linked in particular to public morality and public policy, which are grounds of justification recognised in [Art 36]'. However, the Court then went on to state that 'the protection of the child is a legitimate interest which, in principle, justifies a restriction on a fundamental freedom guaranteed by the EC Treaty, such as the free movement of goods', which seems to suggest a new mandatory requirement.

Whichever is the true position, the Court accepted that the German rules ensured 'that young people are able to develop their sense of personal responsibility and their sociability. Furthermore, the protection of young people is an objective which is closely related to ensuring respect for human dignity'. The Court accepted that the German rules were 'designed to protect children against information and materials injurious to their well-being' and that, in such a case, in view of the divergence of 'moral or cultural views, Member States must be recognised as having a definite margin of discretion'.

CASE EXAMPLE

Dynamic Medien v Avides Media (2008)

German legislation prohibited the sale in Germany of videos and DVDs via mail order unless they had been examined for their suitability for viewing by young persons – such examination being undertaken by the authorities in Germany itself – and labelled accordingly. Avides Media, a German mail-order company, had imported into Germany from the UK a number of DVDs and videos featuring Japanese 'Anime' cartoons. These had been classified by the British Board of Film Control (BBFC) as suitable for viewing only by those aged 15 years or older. A rival German company, Dynamic Medien, sought to stop Avides from marketing the DVDs and videos in Germany as they had not yet been classified by the authorities in Germany. Avides alleged that the German legislation was in breach of Art 34. The ECJ agreed that the rules were 'liable to make the importation of image storage media ... more difficult and more expensive', with the result that they may dissuade importers. However, the German Government successfully argued that the purpose of the legislation – 'protecting young persons' – was sufficient justification.

The 'fight against crime' (2008)

The 'fight against crime' was added to the list in *Commission v Portugal (Tinted Film for Car Windows)* (case C-265/06) [2008] ECR-I-2245. The Portuguese Government accepted that legislation banning the affixing of tinted film to the windows of cars and other vehicles was capable of hindering trade but argued that it was justified on grounds of public safety and/or road safety. The ban was 'intended to enable the competent authorities to make a rapid external inspection of the interior of motor vehicles without the need to immobilise them, first, in order to ensure that the vehicle's occupants are wearing seat belts and, second, to identify potential criminals for the purpose of combating crime'. The ECJ accepted these arguments, at least in principle, stating that: 'The fight against crime and ensuring road safety may constitute overriding reasons in the public interest capable of justifying a hindrance to the free movement of goods'.

14.6.3 Application to 'indistinctly applicable' measures only?

The traditional position of the ECJ has been that the 'mandatory requirements' are only available when national legislation is 'indistinctly applicable'. In *Gilli and Andres* (1981), for example, the ECJ stated that:

JUDGMENT

'It is only where national rules, which apply without discrimination to both domestic and imported products, may be justified as being necessary in order to satisfy imperative requirements relating in particular to the protection of public health, the fairness of commercial transactions and the defence of the consumer that they may constitute an exception to the requirements arising under [Art 34].'

The ECJ confirmed this in *Commission v Ireland (Souvenir Jewellery)* (1981), rejecting a consumer protection defence on the basis that the contested Irish legislation only applied to imported jewellery.

CASE EXAMPLE

Souvenir Jewellery (Case 113/80) [1981] ECR 1625

Irish legislation, the Merchandise Marks (Restriction on Sale of Imported Jewellery) Order (1971), required imported jewellery which depicted motifs or possessed characteristics which suggested that they were souvenirs of Ireland – such as wolfhounds, shamrocks etc – to bear an indication of their place of origin or the word 'foreign'. The ECJ held that the Irish legislation constituted an unjustifiable infringement of Art 34. Although intended to protect consumers, the legislation was distinctly applicable and therefore the *Cassis de Dijon* (1979) principle was unavailable.

This means that *Cassis de Dijon* (1979) should, logically, never be available in Art 35 cases, because the ECJ has held that national legislation only breaches Art 35 if it is 'distinctly applicable' (*Bouhelier* (Case 53/76) [1977] ECR 197 or if it has as its 'specific object or effect the restriction of patterns of exports' (*PB Groenveld* (Case 15/79) [1979] ECR 3409, discussed below)). However, in two of the cases discussed above the ECJ accepted that *Cassis de Dijon* may apply in the context of Art 35 (*Oebel* (1981) and *Dusseldorp* (1998)).

This area of doubt has now been clarified by the ECJ. *Gysbrechts & Santurel Inter* (case C-205/07) [2008] ECR I-9947 involved Belgian legislation under which it was illegal for Belgian retailers to require any payment from consumers within the seven-day 'cooling off' period allowed for distance-selling contracts. The ECJ accepted that the Belgian legislation had the effect of potentially restricting exports, as it deprived Belgian firms of an effective form of protection against defaulting consumers based in other Member States (given the difficulty of bringing legal proceedings in other jurisdictions). However, the Belgian legislation was held to be justifiable on consumer protection grounds, under *Cassis de Dijon* principles.

The Court stated:

JUDGMENT

'A national measure contrary to [Art 35] may be justified on one of the grounds stated in [Art 36], and by overriding requirements of public interest, provided that the measure is proportionate to the legitimate objective pursued.'

KEY FACTS

The *Cassis de Dijon* principles

The ECJ introduced a parallel set of derogations in 1979. This is a far more flexible, open list of derogations – 'mandatory requirements'– to operate alongside Art 36	*Cassis de Dijon* (1979)
The open list includes: (i) the fairness of commercial transactions	*Oosthoek's* (1982), *Prantl* (1984)
(ii) consumer protection	*Walter Rau* (1982), *Mars* (1994), *Clinique* (1994)
(iii) environmental protection	*Commission v Denmark (Danish Bottles)* (1988), *Radlberger & Spitz* (2004), *Mickelsson and Roos* (2009)
(iv) cultural protection	*Cinéthèque* (1985), *Fachverband* (2009)
(v) road safety	*Snellers Autos* (2000), *Commission v Finland* (2007), *Commission v Italy (Motorcycle Trailers)* (2009)
(vi) the protection of 'fundamental rights'	*Schmidberger v Austria* (2003)
(vii) the protection of children	*Dynamic Medien* (2008)
(viii) and the fight against crime	*Commission v Portugal (Tinted film)* (2008)
It only applies to 'indistinctly applicable' measures, that is, national measures which apply without distinction to imports AND domestic goods	*Gilli & Andres* (1981), *Commission v Ireland (Souvenir Jewellery)*
Except, apparently, for distinctly applicable measures intended to protect the environment	*Commission v Belgium (Walloon Waste)* (1992)
The mandatory requirements can be used in order to derogate from Art 35	*Gysbrechts & Santurel Inter* (2008)

14.7 General rules concerning derogations: proportionality and mutual recognition

14.7.1 Proportionality

The ECJ has consistently held that the purpose of Art 36 is to allow certain national laws and rules to derogate from the free movement provisions only to the extent to which they are 'justified' in order to achieve the objectives in the Article. A measure may be justified provided it does what is **necessary** to achieve the objectives in the first sentence of Art 36, and further that it does **no more than necessary**. If there are other methods capable of achieving that objective which are less restrictive of intra-community trade, then they should be used instead. In *De Peijper* (Case 104/75) [1976] ECR 613, for example, the ECJ said:

JUDGMENT

'National rules or practices which do restrict imports … or are capable of doing so are only compatible with the Treaty to the extent to which they are *necessary* … National rules or practices do not fall within the exemptions specified in [Art 36] if [their objectives] can as effectively be protected by measures which do not restrict intra-Union trade so much.'

Many of the cases where Art 36 is invoked involve national measures introduced to protect against alleged risks to human health. Often, where a particular ingredient or additive has been restricted or prohibited altogether, the ECJ will pose the (rhetorical) question whether human health could still be protected by the simple expedient of requiring manufacturers of products to label the ingredients in their products clearly. Thus, in *Commission v France* (Case C–24/00) [2004] ECR I–1277, for example, the ECJ stated:

JUDGMENT

'It is naturally legitimate … to seek to ensure that consumers are properly informed about the products which they consume. However, appropriate labelling, informing consumers about the nature, the ingredients and the characteristics of fortified foodstuffs, can enable consumers who risk excessive consumption of a nutrient added to those products to decide for themselves whether to use them.'

The same principles apply to attempts by Member States to justify legislation under *Cassis de Dijon* (1979) principles. The best example is perhaps *Walter Rau v De Smedt* (1982), discussed above, where the ECJ stated that 'if a Member State has a choice between various measures to attain the same objective it should choose the means which least restricts the free movement of goods'.

In *Commission v France* (2004), the ECJ summarised the proportionality principle as follows:

JUDGMENT

'The Member States must comply with the principle of proportionality. The means which they choose must therefore be confined to what is actually necessary to ensure the safeguarding of public health or to satisfy overriding requirements regarding, for example, consumer protection, and they must be proportional to the objective thus pursued, which could not have been attained by measures less restrictive of intra-Union trade.'

14.7.2 Mutual recognition

As well as creating the 'mandatory requirements' in *Cassis de Dijon* (1979), the ECJ went on to establish a presumption that, once goods have been 'lawfully produced and marketed in one of the Member States', they may be imported into any other State. This has become known as the 'mutual recognition' principle. The presumption may only be rebutted by evidence that the goods in question pose a threat to one of the heads or Art 36 or one of the 'mandatory requirements'. The net result is to place the burden of proof on the authorities of the Member States seeking to justify their domestic legislation. The best way to rebut the presumption is to identify specific national characteristics (usually involving dietary habits) which would justify different national legislative provisions. In *Muller* (1986), dealing with E475, a baking ingredient allowed in Germany but not in France, the ECJ stated that:

JUDGMENT

'As far as … E475 is concerned, there are serious doubts that it is harmless *in view of the specific eating habits of the French population*. It is clear from a recent survey carried out in France that there is a risk that the daily acceptable intake … will be exceeded in France, particularly in children, *who are major consumers of pastry products* … In the present state of scientific research there is uncertainty as to the critical thresholds of harmfulness since such thresholds vary according to the quantities of additives absorbed with all the food eaten and *thus depend to a large extent on eating habits in the various Member States*.'

Similar principles are seen in these cases:

- *Bellon* (Case C–42/90) [1990] ECR I–4863: French legislation banned certain Italian pastries because they contained sorbic acid. The ECJ held that the legislation was justifiable on health grounds, but only after taking national dietary habits into account.
- *Aher-Waggon* (1998): German legislation set aircraft noise emission levels, which were more restrictive than in other States. The ECJ stated that these rules were justified because Germany 'is a very densely populated State' and therefore 'attaches special importance to ensuring that its population is protected from excessive noise emissions'.
- *Greenham and Abel* (2004): dealing with French legislation that banned, *inter alia*, an ingredient in fruit drinks called coenzyme Q10, the ECJ held that the ban would be permissible on health grounds only if the French authorities could show '*in the light of national nutritional habits* and in the light of the results of international scientific research, that their rules are necessary'.

In practice, rebutting the presumption will not be easy to do. In *Mars* (1995) and *Clinique Laboratories* (1994), German consumer protection arguments were rejected. The ECJ held in each case that the German legislation was in breach of Art 34. As the goods concerned (ice creams and cosmetics, respectively) were lawfully manufactured and marketed in France, the mutual recognition principle applied, and the German Government had failed to show why it needed stricter laws than France. In *Commission v Germany* (the *Beer Purity* case) (1987), concerning German legislation on the additives permitted in beer, the German Government tried to argue that it needed stricter rules on beer purity than other Member States because German nationals tended to drink more beer than nationals of other Member States. However, although not disputing that assertion, the ECJ did not accept that it justified stringent rules which made it practically impossible for French-made beer (containing banned additives) to be sold in Germany. The Court stated:

JUDGMENT

'Some of the additives authorized in other Member States for use in the manufacture of beer are also authorized under the German rules, in particular the regulation on additives, for use in the manufacture of all, or virtually all, beverages. Mere reference to the potential risks of the ingestion of additives in general and to the fact that *beer is a foodstuff consumed in large quantities* does not suffice to justify the imposition of stricter rules in the case of beer.'

CASE EXAMPLE

Beer Purity (Case 178/84) [1987] ECR 1227

German law, specifically Arts 9 and 10 of the *Biersteuergesetz* of 1952 (itself dating back to the *Reinheitsgebot* of 1516), provided that the name 'Bier' could only be used for products brewed using malted barley, hops, yeast and water. The use of other ingredients, such as rice or maize, did not preclude the marketing of a product, but it could not be sold as 'Bier'. The Commission alleged that the *Biersteuergesetz* was in breach of Art 34. The German Government argued that the *Biersteuergesetz* was necessary in order to protect consumers (*Cassis de Dijon* (1979)). The ECJ disagreed. While it was legitimate to seek to 'enable consumers who attribute specific qualities to beers manufactured from particular raw materials to make their choice in the light of that consideration ... that possibility may be ensured by means which do not prevent the importation of products which have been lawfully manufactured and marketed in other Member States'. The Court suggested that 'the compulsory affixing of suitable labels giving the nature of the product sold' would suffice instead. The German Government had argued that, as beer is not necessarily supplied to consumers in bottles or cans capable of bearing the appropriate details, such a system of consumer information was inappropriate. However, this argument was unsuccessful. The *Biersteuergesetz* went on to impose an outright ban on the marketing of all beers containing additives. The rule related to all beers, including those produced in Germany. Here, the German Government argued for the protection of human health (Art 36). However, the additives in question were used in beers lawfully produced in the exporting States, and hence the mutual recognition principle applied. Undaunted, the German Government pointed out that the high beer consumption of German people justified the ban. The ECJ said that, in such cases, the work of bodies such as the World Health Organisation and the Food and Agriculture Organisation of the United Nations, international scientific research, and the dietary habits of the importing State should be referred to. However, the ECJ pointed out that the *Biersteuergesetz* led to a blanket ban on **all** additives, and not just those for which there was concrete justification. This was excessive, particularly given that the same additives were used lawfully in the manufacture of most **soft** drinks in Germany itself. Consequently, although the drinking habits of German people might have justified a ban on some additives in beer, the law as it stood was disproportionate.

KEY FACTS

Proportionality and mutual recognition

Where Art 36 or the *Cassis de Dijon* principles are used, the measures must be the least restrictive option available	*De Peijper* (1976), *Walter Rau v De Smedt* (1982)
The mutual recognition principle is a presumption that goods lawfully produced and marketed in one Member State should be available for sale in all other States	*Cassis de Dijon* (1979)
The mutual recognition principle can be rebutted, by reference to specific national characteristics, eg dietary habits	*Muller* (1986), *Commission v Germany (Beer Purity)* (1987)

14.8 The divisions in *Keck & Mithouard: 'Selling arrangements'*

14.8.1 Introduction

It has been noted already that Art 34 was widely defined in *Dassonville* (1974). However, in 1993, the ECJ acknowledged that the *Dassonville* 'formula' was so wide that it was leading importers and retailers to challenge a whole range of national laws whose likely impact on the free movement of goods was, at most, marginal. In the landmark ruling in *Keck and Mithouard* (1993), the ECJ announced that there was a distinction to be drawn between:

- **Product requirements**: these are laws regulating the goods themselves, which are still governed by Art 34 and the *Dassonville* formula and are prohibited. Such rules are *prima facie* contrary to EU law and require justification, under either Art 36 or *Cassis de Dijon* (1979) principles.
- **Selling arrangements**: these are laws concerning not the goods themselves, but rather how, when and where they are marketed. These rules fall outside of the scope of Art 34 altogether and hence do not require justification. In *Keck*, the ECJ said that these rules were *prima facie* lawful, although they were subject to two pre-conditions.

Strictly speaking, the decision in *Keck* was not entirely unprecedented. In a handful of earlier cases, the ECJ had held that national rules governing 'selling arrangements' are exempt from Art 34. In the earliest cases, *Blesgen* (Case 75/81) [1982] ECR 1211, involving Belgian legislation prohibiting the public consumption of strong alcohol, the ECJ stated that 'Such a legislative measure has no connection with the importation of the products and for that reason is not of such a nature as to impede trade between Member States'. Then, in *Quietlynn v Southend BC* (Case C–23/89) [1990] ECR I–3059, which involved UK law regulating licences for sex shops, the ECJ again ruled that Art 34 did not apply.

The logical conclusion of these developments occurred in *Keck*, which involved French legislation preventing the re-sale of goods at a loss, when the ECJ made a decisive statement on the legality of 'selling arrangements'. The ECJ began by conceding that the French legislation might have an effect on inter-State trade. It considered that such legislation 'may, admittedly, restrict the volume of sales of products from other Member States, insofar as it deprives traders of a method of sales promotion'. However, the ECJ then observed that 'national legislation imposing a general prohibition on resale at a loss is not designed to regulate trade in goods between Member States'. The ECJ concluded that, 'in view of the increasing tendency of traders to seek to avoid non-protectionist national laws' by relying on Art 34, it was necessary to review its position. It went on:

JUDGMENT

> 'Contrary to what has previously been decided, the application to products … of national provisions restricting or prohibiting certain selling arrangements is not such as to hinder, directly or indirectly, actually or potentially, trade between Member States within the meaning of the *Dassonville* judgment, so long as those provisions apply to all relevant traders operating within the national territory and so long as they affect in the same manner, in law and in fact, the marketing of domestic products and of those from other Member States. Where these conditions are fulfilled, the application of such rules to the sale of products from another Member State meeting the requirements laid down by that State is not by nature such as to prevent their access to the market or to impede access any more than it impedes the access of domestic products. Such rules therefore fall outside the scope of [Art 34].'

You will note that the Court overruled any previous conflicting judgments but failed to identify what they are! Since 1993, therefore, there has been considerable discussion about which cases were overruled by *Keck* and which were not.

CASE EXAMPLE

Keck and Mithouard (Case C–267/91) [1993] ECR I–6097

French legislation banned the re-sale of goods at a lower than the purchase price, a form of predatory pricing. Such laws are designed to stop powerful companies from abusing their position and distorting the market by undercutting smaller rivals. Two supermarket managers, Bernard Keck and Daniel Mithouard, were prosecuted under this legislation for re-selling products (coffee and beer, respectively) at lower than their purchase price. The two men argued that the French law hindered trade, and they relied on Art 34. The ECJ introduced the concept of 'selling arrangements'. In the present case, the French rules were held to be 'selling arrangements' and therefore fell outside Art 34. The Court noted that 'National legislation imposing a general prohibition on resale at a loss is not designed to regulate trade in goods between Member States. Such legislation may, admittedly, restrict the volume of sales, and hence the volume of sales of products from other Member States, in so far as it deprives traders of a method of sales promotion. But the question remains whether such a possibility is sufficient to characterise the legislation in question as a measure having equivalent effect to a quantitative restriction on imports'.

14.8.2 Examples of selling arrangements

Sunday trading legislation

Prior to *Keck*, the ECJ's policy was that national legislation regulating the freedom of retailers to trade on Sunday infringed Art 34 because it had the potential to reduce intra-Community trade. One such example was the UK's Shops Act 1950 (subsequently amended by the Sunday Trading Act 1994). In *Torfaen BC v B&Q plc* (1989) (discussed above in the context of the *Cassis de Dijon* principle) and *Stoke-on-Trent CC v B&Q plc* (Case C–169/91) [1992] ECR I–6635 the ECJ held that Art 34 was infringed. However, after *Keck*, the ECJ held that Art 34 did not apply to such legislation at all. This new approach was set down in a series of cases concerning Italian Sunday trading legislation (*Punto Casa and PPV* (Cases C–69 and 258/93) [1994] ECR I–2355, and *Semeraro Casa Uno and Others* (Cases C–418 to 421/93) [1996] ECR I–2975).

Opening hours

In *Tankstation t'Heukske and J B E Boermans* (Cases C–401 and 402/92) [1994] ECR I–2199, concerning Dutch rules on the opening hours of petrol stations, the ECJ stated the rules laid down in *Keck* were satisfied. National licensing legislation (such as that in England and Wales, whereby the normal closing hours for public houses is 11 pm) would also come within this heading.

Sale of goods only through specific outlets

With the benefit of hindsight, the case of *Quietlynn* (1990) (discussed above) falls into this category. UK legislation allowing only licensed retailers to sell alcohol would be classified as a selling arrangement. Another example is *Commission v Greece (Processed Milk)* (Case C–391/92) [1995] ECR I–1621, where Greek legislation prohibited the sale of processed milk for infants except from pharmacies. The ECJ stated that the Greek rules concerned selling arrangements, and not goods themselves, and were therefore exempt from Art 34.

Restrictions on certain forms of sale promotions

In a pre-*Keck* case, *Oosthoek's* (Case 286/81) [1982] ECR 4575, the ECJ ruled that Dutch legislation prohibiting the offering of free gifts as a sales promotion strategy was prohibited by Art 34. Similarly, in *Buet and EBS* (Case 382/87) [1989] ECR 1235, the ECJ ruled that very similar French legislation prohibiting door-to-door canvassing of educational materials could hinder trade. However, it can now be argued that the Dutch and French laws in question were 'selling arrangements'.

For example, in *Burmanjer & Others* (Case C–20/03) [2005] ECR I–4133, three Dutch nationals were accused of breaching Belgian legislation prohibiting the sale of subscriptions to periodicals (such as magazines) on the street without prior authorisation. In their defence they argued that the Belgian law was contrary to Art 34. The ECJ, however, held that the legislation was a selling arrangement and therefore exempt from Art 34. This was because the legislation did not ban the product, or even the sale of it, it simply banned one method of sale.

Restrictions on advertising

In *GB-INNO-BM* (Case 362/88) [1990] ECR I–667, the ECJ was asked to rule on the compatibility of Art 34 with Luxembourg legislation preventing advertising campaigns that made reference to the pre-sale price of a product. The ECJ held that the legislation was prohibited by Art 34 because it was capable of hindering trade. Similarly, in *Aragonesa and Publivia* (1991), the ECJ held that national legislation prohibiting the advertising of alcohol over a certain strength in mass media, on streets and highways, in cinemas and on public transport fell within the *Dassonville* formula.

After *Keck*, it has become clear that national rules imposing partial restrictions on advertising, at least, are not caught by Art 34. In *Hünermund* (Case C–292/92) [1993] ECR I–6787, concerning German legislation preventing pharmacists from advertising on the radio, on TV or at the cinema, the ECJ stated that the conditions in *Keck* were satisfied and the German legislation was therefore exempt from Art 34. The ECJ reached the same conclusion in *Leclerc-Siplec* (Case C–412/93) [1995] ECR I–179, concerning French legislation prohibiting TV advertising by the distribution sector (which included petrol companies) and in *PRO Sieben Media* (Case C–6/98) [1999] ECR I–7599, concerning German legislation on the division of time between programmes and advertising on German television. As will be seen below, however, national rules imposing total prohibitions on advertising are not 'selling arrangements' and continue to be caught by Art 34.

CASE EXAMPLE

Leclerc-Siplec (Case C–412/93) [1995] ECR I–179

French legislation prohibited the advertising on TV of, or by, the following: alcohol over 1.2 per cent proof; literary publications; the cinema; the Press; and the distribution sector. The idea was to get those sectors to advertise in regional newspapers instead, thereby protecting that particular industry. L-S, petrol distributors, were denied access to French TV advertising by TF1 Publicité and M6 Publicité, two advertising companies. L-S argued that the French law was incompatible with Art 34. The ECJ held that Art 34 did not apply: it was a 'selling arrangement'.

Requirements as to how goods are presented in shops

It is well established that national rules imposing packaging requirements on products constitute measures equivalent to quantitative restrictions (*Walter Rau v De Smedt* (1982) being the classic example). However, in *Morellato* (Case C–416/00) [2003] ECR I–9343, the ECJ decided that a requirement under Italian law that bread had to be sold wrapped constituted a selling arrangement. The crucial difference between *Walter Rau* (Art 34 and *Dassonville* applies) and *Morellato* (2003) (*Keck* applies) seems to be that in the former case the onus is placed on the manufacturer, while in the latter situation the onus is placed on the retailer. In *Morellato*, the ECJ stated that the bread could be imported unwrapped and then sold wrapped, with the retailer carrying out the wrapping task. In this way, the wrapping could be regarded as 'a simple transformation process' and was therefore incapable of restricting the free movement of goods.

Price controls

Prior to *Keck*, it had been held that price controls (that is, national rules imposing either maximum or minimum prices on certain products, or rules preventing retailers from selling goods at a loss) could infringe Art 34. However, price controls have now been re-classified as selling arrangements (*Keck* itself is such a case, as is *Belgapom* (Case C–63/94) [1995] ECR I–2467, where *Keck* was applied).

14.8.3 Failure to satisfy the conditions in *Keck & Mithouard*

If a provision of national legislation **appears** to be a 'selling arrangement' but **actually** fails one of the conditions in *Keck*, then the legislation falls to be dealt with under Art 34 as a measure having an effect equivalent to a quantitative restriction.

The first condition

The first condition is that the national rules alleged to constitute a selling arrangement 'apply to all relevant traders operating within the national territory'.

The second condition

The second condition is that those provisions must 'affect in the same manner, in law and in fact, the marketing of domestic products and of those from other Member States'. There have been several cases examining this condition. In *Ortscheit* (Case C–320/93) [1994] ECR I–5243, the ECJ ruled, distinguishing *Keck*, that a prohibition on advertising of all foreign medicinal products was caught by Art 34 (although justifiable on health grounds under Art 36). The second condition was not satisfied.

Similarly, in *De Agostini and TV-Shop* (Cases C–34 to 36/95) [1997] ECR I–3843, concerning Swedish legislation imposing an outright ban on advertising aimed at minors (children less than 12 years of age), the ECJ thought that the legislation might not satisfy the second *Keck* condition. It actually left the final decision on this issue to the Swedish court which had referred the case to the ECJ in the first place. In *Gourmet International Products* (Case C–405/98) [2001] ECR I–1795, involving an absolute prohibition in Swedish legislation on the advertising of alcohol, the ECJ decided that the second condition was definitely not satisfied.

Thus, the Swedish legislation constituted an indistinctly applicable MEQR, *prima facie* prohibited by Art 34 although theoretically justifiable under Art 36 on health grounds.

CASE EXAMPLE

Gourmet International Products (Case C–405/98) [2001] ECR I–1795

Swedish legislation provided that 'In view of the health risks involved in alcohol consumption ... Advertising may not be used to market alcoholic beverages on radio or television. Advertising may not be used to market spirits, wines or strong beers either in periodicals or in other publications ... That prohibition does not, however, apply to publications distributed solely at the point of sale of such beverages'. Gourmet International Products published a magazine entitled '*Gourmet*'. One issue, published in autumn 1997, contained three pages of advertisements for alcoholic beverages, one for red wine and two for whisky. The Swedish authorities applied for an injunction. GIP resisted and the case was referred to the ECJ. There, GIP contended that an **outright** prohibition did not satisfy the criteria established in *Keck*, on the basis that such a prohibition was liable to have a greater effect on imported goods than on those produced in the Member State concerned. The ECJ agreed. The blanket prohibition of all advertising was 'liable to impede access to the market by products from other Member States more than it impedes access by domestic products, with which consumers are instantly more familiar'. The Court observed that, although Swedish law allowed publications containing advertisements for alcoholic beverages to be distributed at points of sale, a company wholly owned by the Swedish State (*Systembolaget AB*), enjoyed a monopoly of retail sales in Sweden, so that the only magazines on sale were those promoting Swedish-made beverages. The Court concluded that the prohibition on advertising was caught by Art 34, although capable of justification on health grounds under Art 36.

The ECJ stated:

JUDGMENT

'In the case of products like alcoholic beverages, the consumption of which is linked to traditional social practices and to local habits and customs, a prohibition of all advertising … is liable to impede access to the market by products from other Member States more than it impedes access by domestic products, with which consumers are instantly more familiar … A prohibition on advertising … must therefore be regarded as affecting the marketing of products from other Member States more heavily than the marketing of domestic products and as therefore constituting an obstacle to trade between Member States caught by [Art 34].'

It should be noted that the UK Parliament has adopted similar legislation in the field of tobacco advertising. Section 2(1) of the Tobacco Advertising and Promotion Act 2002, provides that 'a person who in the course of a business publishes a tobacco advertisement, or causes one to be published, in the UK is guilty of an offence'. Presumably this provision would be dealt with in the same way as that in *Gourmet* (2001) (that is, a *prima facie* breach of Art 34 but justifiable under Art 36 on health grounds).

Gourmet International Products was followed in *Douwe Egberts* (Case C–239/02) [2004] ECR I–7007. Belgian legislation prohibited any references on the labelling of food to the word 'slimming'. Douwe Egberts, a Dutch coffee producer, alleged that various statements, such as 'the absolute breakthrough in weight control' on the labels of 'DynaSvelte Café', a rival brand, infringed this legislation. One issue for the ECJ was whether the Belgian legislation was an MEQR, or whether it was a selling arrangement. The Court confirmed that a total advertising ban could not be categorised as a selling arrangement. The Court stated that 'An absolute prohibition of advertising the characteristics of a product is liable to impede access to the market by products from other Member States more than it impedes access by domestic products, with which consumers are more familiar'. Having categorised the Belgian legislation as an MEQR, the Court went on to consider whether it could be justified, on the grounds of the protection of human health, but rejected that on proportionality grounds.

Similarly, in *Deutscher Apothekerverband* (Case C–322/01) [2003] ECR I–14887, the ECJ again held that the second condition had not been satisfied.

CASE EXAMPLE

Deutscher Apothekerverband (Case C–322/01) [2003] ECR I–14887

German legislation prohibited the Internet sale of most medicines – the practical effect of which was that only pharmacists based in Germany could sell medicines to German customers. 0800 DocMorris, a Dutch Internet pharmacy, offered for sale via its website both prescription and non-prescription medicines to consumers in Germany.., The German Pharmacists Organisation sought an injunction against DocMorris's activities, alleging a breach of the German legislation. The case was referred to the ECJ, which held that the German legislation could not be classified as a selling arrangement because the second Keck condition had not been satisfied. The German rule was 'more of an obstacle to pharmacies outside Germany than to those within it'. The Court stated that although pharmacies in Germany could not use Internet sales either, they were still free to sell the same products over the counter in their dispensaries. However, for pharmacies not established in Germany, that option was not available. For them, the Internet provided 'a more significant way to gain direct access to the German market'. The Court concluded that 'a prohibition which has a greater impact on pharmacies established outside German territory could impede access to the market for products from other Member States more than it impedes access for domestic products'. The German legislation was therefore an indistinctly applicable MEQR and prima facie in breach of Art 34, subject to justification under Art 36 on health grounds.

14.8.4 Academic reaction to *Keck & Mithouard*

Academic reaction to *Keck* has been mixed. Professor Stephen Weatherill has been a particularly outspoken critic. He listed three principal objections ('After *Keck*: Some Thoughts on how to Clarify the Clarification' (1996) 33 CMLR 885):

- the categorisation of some national measures as 'selling arrangements' was 'inappropriately rigid'
- the distinction drawn between 'selling arrangements' and (his words) 'product composition' rules was 'artificial' and 'unworkable'
- the 'selling arrangements' test itself was 'out of line with the objectives of the Treaty'.

Professor Weatherill proposed a different test, based on the question of whether a national measure exerted 'a substantial restriction' on the access of imported goods to the market in that State. He contended that the national measures at issue in *Keck* (1993), *Hünermund* (1993) and *Tankstation t'Heukske* (1994) were not 'selling arrangements' but measures that exercised 'no direct impediment to access to markets of a Member State'.

The 'substantial restriction' test: is it workable?

Professor Weatherill's alternative test has itself been the subject of academic criticism. Peter Oliver ('Some Further Reflections on the Scope of Articles 28–30 (ex Articles 30–36) EC' (1999) 36 CMLR 783) has given three reasons for endorsing the ECJ's implicit rejection of a test based on whether or not a national rule 'substantially' restricts trade:

- 'any measure emanating from any branch of the State and whatever the level of government must be regarded as a matter of inherent importance, and must thus be deemed to have some incidence *per se* on inter-State trade'
- the free movement of goods is 'fundamental', and 'any restriction, even minor, of that freedom, is prohibited'
- 'the practical problems [with the "substantial restriction" test] are very considerable … it would introduce a new element of legal uncertainty and thus make it far harder for national courts to apply [Art 34]'.

Oliver concludes that the *Keck* approach is 'rule based' – by which Oliver means there is a legal formula against which national measures can be tested – and is thus 'far easier for national courts to apply', unlike the 'substantial restriction' approach, which requires 'evaluation of complex economic data'.

KEY FACTS

Keck and Mithouard: Selling arrangements

'Certain selling arrangements' are exempt from Art 34	*Keck and Mithouard* (1993)
Selling arrangements are national rules that regulate the conditions under which goods are sold, not the goods themselves. Examples include: (i) pricing restrictions	*Keck and Mithouard, Belgapom* (1995)
(ii) Sunday trading rules	*Punto Casa and PPV* (1994)
(iii) opening hours	*Tankstation t'Heukske* (1994)
(iv) restrictions on sale outlets/methods	*Commission v Greece (Processed Milk); Burmanjer and others* (2005)
(iv) and partial advertising restrictions	*Hünermund* (1993), *Leclerc-Siplec* (1995)

Selling arrangements must satisfy two conditions. First, they must apply to all relevant traders in the Member State. Second, they must not differentiate – in law or in fact – between the same of domestic goods and imports. A total advertising ban fails the second condition	*Keck and Mithouard, Gourmet International Products* (2001), *Douwe Egberts* (2004)
National rules breaching either or both conditions is an MEQR which will need to be justified using Art 36 or *Cassis de Dijon* principles	*Gourmet International Products, Deutscher Apothekerverband* (2003)

14.9 Article 35 and exports

There are some fundamental differences between the operation of Art 35 and that of Art 34. The case law relating to Art 35 draws an important distinction between distinctly and indistinctly applicable national rules.

14.9.1 'Distinctly applicable' rules

Measures which clearly discriminate against exports will usually be found to be in breach of Art 35. The most obvious examples are export bans, as in:

- *R v Thompson* (1979) – UK law prohibited the exportation of old coins. Held to be a *prima facie* breach of Art 35 (although justifiable under Art 36 on public policy grounds).
- *Hedley Lomas (Ireland) Ltd* (1996) – the Ministry of Agriculture, Fisheries and Food (MAFF) banned live animal exports to Spain. This was held to breach Art 35 (and the ECJ rejected a defence of protection of animal health under Art 36 for lack of evidence).
- *Dusseldorp* (1998) – prohibition in Dutch law on the exportation of waste oil filters. This was held to breach Art 35 (and was not justifiable under *Cassis de Dijon* principles on environmental protection grounds, because the ban was primarily motivated by economic considerations).

The same considerations apply to distinctly applicable MEQRs. Thus, in *Jongeneel Kaas* (Case 237/82) [1984] ECR 483, Dutch law requiring cheese exporters to be in possession of an export licence was held to be in breach of Art 35. Similarly, in *Bouhelier* (Case 53/76) [1977] ECR 197, concerning French rules requiring watchmakers to be licensed for export, ostensibly to ensure quality standards were maintained, the ECJ said that Art 35 had been infringed. The Court drew particular attention to the fact that the rules only applied 'to products intended for export' and were not imposed 'on products marketed within the Member State'. This leads to 'arbitrary discrimination between the two types of products which constitutes an obstacle to intra-Union trade'.

Similarly, in *Belgium v Spain (Rioja wine exports)* (Case C–388/95) [2000] ECR I–3123, Spanish rules on the transportation of Rioja wine drew a distinction between wine intended for export (this wine had to be transported in bottles) and wine intended for distribution to consumers in Spain (this could be transported in bulk). The ECJ held that this rule constituted a breach of Art 35, although justifiable on grounds of protection of commercial property under Art 36.

In *Jersey Potatoes* (Case C–293/02) [2005] ECR I–9543, the ECJ again held that national legislation which only applied to goods intended for export was capable of breaching Art 35. Under the Jersey Potato Export Marketing Scheme Act 2001, potato producers in Jersey were prohibited from exporting potatoes to mainland UK unless they were registered with the Jersey Potato Export Marketing Board. Failure to comply could lead to fines or imprisonment or both. The Jersey Produce Marketing Organisation contended that the provisions in the 2001 Act constituted a breach of Art 35. The Court agreed, stating that 'such legislation is, by its very nature, likely to interfere with the patterns of exports of potatoes grown in Jersey to UK markets'.

(Note: although the UK, the Channel Islands (including Jersey) and the Isle of Man are regarded as one Member State for the purposes of certain aspects of EU law, including the free movement of goods, the Court held that the provisions of the 2001 Act could act as a disincentive to exports of potatoes from Jersey to the mainland UK – and hence could potentially restrict *re-exports* from the UK to other Member States. Thus the provisions of the 2001 Act fell within the ambit of EU law.)

14.9.2 'Indistinctly applicable' rules

Where national rules are 'indistinctly applicable' MEQRs – that is, they do not distinguish between goods intended for the domestic market and goods intended for export – then there is simply no breach of Art 35. In *Groenveld* (1979), concerning Dutch rules banning sausage manufacturers in the Netherlands from using horsemeat (whether the sausages were intended for export or not), the ECJ stated that Art 35 did not apply.

CASE EXAMPLE

Groenveld (Case 15/79) [1979] ECR 3409

Dutch legislation, the Processing and Preparation of Meat Regulation (1973), prohibited, subject to express exceptions, any manufacturer of sausages in the Netherlands from having in stock or processing horsemeat. Groenveld, Dutch sausage manufacturers, brought a challenge to the Dutch authorities against their refusal to allow them to stock horsemeat, alleging a breach of Art 35. The ECJ held that no breach of Art 35 had been committed. The Dutch law made no distinction between domestic sales and exports of sausages.

The Court stated that Art 35 only:

JUDGMENT

'concerns national measures which have as their *specific object or effect* the restriction of patterns of exports and thereby the establishment of a difference in treatment between the domestic trade of a Member State and its export trade in such a way as to provide a particular advantage for national production or for the domestic market of the State in question at the expense of the production or of the trade of other Member States. This is not so in the case of a prohibition … which is applied objectively to the production of goods of a certain kind without drawing a distinction depending on whether such goods are intended for the national market or for export'.

These principles were confirmed in *Jongeneel Kaas* (1984). Dutch law regulated the quality and content of cheese produced in the Netherlands. The ECJ held that, as the national rules drew no distinction between the ultimate destination of the goods concerned, there was no breach of Art 35.

However, this does not mean that an indistinctly applicable measure can never breach Art 35. An example is *Gysbrechts & Santurel Inter* (Case C-205/07) [2008] ECR I-9947, the facts of which were given above. Here, the Court decided that, although a provision of national legislation may be indistinctly applicable in the sense that it applies to all goods, if 'its actual effect is nonetheless greater on goods leaving the market of the exporting Member State than on the marketing of goods in the domestic market of that Member State', then a *prima facie* breach of Art 35 has occurred. Such a measure was, however, capable of justification using *Cassis de Dijon* (1979) principles, such as consumer protection, as well as under Art 36, subject to satisfying the proportionality test.

KEY FACTS

Article 35 TFEU

Quantitative restrictions and distinctly applicable MEQRs on exports are prohibited	Article 35 TFEU
'Quantitative restrictions' involve measures such as export bans	*R v Thompson* (1979), *Hedley Lomas* (1996), *Dusseldorp* (1998)
Distinctly applicable MEQRs are measures which only apply to goods intended for export, eg export inspections or licences	*Bouhelier* (1977), *Jongeneel Kaas* (1984), *Jersey Potatoes* (2005)
Quantitative restrictions and distinctly applicable MEQRs on exports are potentially justifiable under Art 36, subject to satisfying proportionality	*Bouhelier, R v Thompson, Hedley Lomas*
Indistinctly applicable MEQRs – measures which apply to all goods whether intended for export or not – do not, generally speaking, breach Art 35	*Groenveld* (1979), *Jongeneel Kaas*
An indistinctly applicable MEQR whose 'actual effect' is greater on exported goods does breach Art 35	*Gysbrechts & Santurel Inter* (2008)
An indistinctly applicable MEQR is potentially justifiable using Art 36 or *Cassis de Dijon*, subject to satisfying proportionality	*Gysbrechts & Santurel Inter*

ACTIVITY

Applying the law

1. Prompted by developments in the United States, the British Government is considering legislating to tackle the problems created by 'light pollution'. This is defined as the situation which occurs when excessive artificial light is allowed to block the light shining from the stars at night. According to research by pressure groups representing the country's amateur astronomers, light pollution in the UK has been steadily increasing for years and now affects virtually the entire population, even those living in rural areas. Numerous constellations are now effectively invisible to those living in major cities. In addition, some sleep experts have warned of the dangers of light pollution to the human body. Excessive exposure to artificial light can disrupt the body's melatonin levels, which can disrupt sleeping patterns and/or cause hyperactivity, especially in children.

   The Government is considering banning the importation into and/or sale within the UK of all security lights which are unnecessarily powerful or which are not designed in such a way as to prevent light being projected upwards.

   Advise the Government as to the compatibility of the above options with EU law on the free movement of goods.

2. Happihour, a Swedish drinks manufacturer, produces a non-alcoholic sports drink called 'Buzz' and an alcoholic version of the same drink called 'Fuzz'. The ingredients, packaging and taste of both drinks are very similar, the only differences being the names and the presence of alcohol (specifically vodka) in 'Fuzz'. For several years, Happihour has sold both versions to retail outlets throughout Sweden and, six months ago, it also began selling the drinks to British retail outlets – off-licences, supermarkets and public houses. The UK Government became concerned about this, as it envisaged that consumers, particularly in public houses, might easily confuse the two versions.

   Subsequently, the UK Parliament passed legislation, the Alcoholic Drinks Act 2010, which allows the government to regulate the sale of alcoholic drinks in the UK. Using this new legislation, the government prohibited the sale of 'Fuzz' by all retail outlets in the UK, including public houses, with immediate effect. British retail outlets that had been importing 'Fuzz' are now refusing to take new deliveries and Happihour has seen a dramatic slump in trade with outlets in the UK. Last week, Happihour complained that the ban was in breach of EU law on the free movement of goods. A junior minister from the Department for Environment, Food and Rural Affairs (DEFRA) replied, refuting the complaint, and pointing out that a British company which made similar alcoholic and non-alcoholic versions of the same drink was subject to the same ban. The junior minister stated that the ban was still in force although it added that the government was now considering two alternative proposals:

(i) lifting the ban on the sale of 'Fuzz' in the UK, but imposing an absolute ban on all forms of advertising of the product

(ii) allowing the sale of 'Fuzz' in the UK, but only from off-licences.

Advise the government whether its original ban on the sale of 'Fuzz', and whether its alternative proposals, are compatible with EU law on the free movement of goods.

SAMPLE ESSAY QUESTION

According to the ECJ's decision in *Keck* (1993), 'certain selling arrangements' fall outside the scope of Art 34 TFEU. The background to this decision was the 'increasing tendency' of traders to invoke Art 34, which had forced the Court to expand the list of mandatory requirements under *Cassis de Dijon* (1979). Nearly two decades later, however, there is still uncertainty as to which national rules are subject to Art 34 and which are 'selling arrangements'. Arguably, the Court in 1993 should have narrowed the scope of Art 34 in another way: by re-defining the *Dassonville* (1974) formula. Discuss.

Explain scope of Art 34 TFEU:

- Art 34 TFEU prohibits quantitative restrictions and MEQRs on imports
- MEQRs defined as all trading rules enacted by Member States, capable of hindering, directly or indirectly, actually or potentially, intra-Union trade (*Dassonville*)
- Give examples, eg packaging rules (*Walter Rau*); origin-marking requirements (*Dassonville*); buy-national campaigns (*'Buy Irish' Campaign*); import licences (*Evans Medical*); import inspections (*UHT Milk*); contents and ingredients restrictions (*Cassis*); name restrictions (*Smanor, Guimont*); prohibitions on use (*Motorcycle Trailers*)
- Note that Art 34 applies to both 'distinctly' and 'indistinctly' applicable rules; ie even non-discriminatory rules are MEQRs caught by Art 34 if capable of hindering trade
- Observe that Art 34 has been defined very widely.

Explain the introduction of the 'mandatory requirements' in *Cassis de Dijon*:

- In *Cassis* the ECJ authorised exemptions from Art 34 for rules which were necessary to satisfy 'mandatory requirements'
- The list of mandatory requirements is open ended. Give examples, eg consumer protection (*Walter Rau*), environmental protection (*Danish Bottles*), road safety (*Motorcycle Trailers*), cultural protection (*Cinéthèque*); the fight against crime (*Tinted Film*), protection of children (*Dynamic Medien*), etc
- Rules must be 'indistinctly' applicable to benefit under *Cassis* (*Gilli & Andres, Souvenir Jewellery*). Consider why this is the case
- Consider possible exception for environmental protection (*Walloon Waste*).

Explain the meaning and scope of the 'selling arrangements' concept:

- In *Keck*, the ECJ introduced 'selling arrangements', exempt from Art 34
- Explain that selling arrangements are rules which relate to the conditions under which goods are sold, not the goods themselves, although the distinction is blurred (eg *Morellato*)
- Give examples, eg rules on pricing (*Keck*); Sunday trading (*Punto Casa*); shops' opening hours (*Tankstation t'Heukske*); advertising (*Hünermund*); which shops can sell goods (*Processed Milk*); methods of sale (*Burmanjer*)
- Note the two *Keck* conditions. Give examples of cases where one or both were not satisfied eg include total advertising bans (*Gourmet International*), bans on internet sales (*Deutscher Apothekerverband*). Explain why these were not selling arrangements.

Consider how Art 34 could have been re-defined:

- Some academics have criticised *Keck* for being 'rigid' and 'artificial'
- Weatherill proposed a 'substantial restriction' test instead
- Oliver has pointed out that any national legislation has a 'substantial' effect
- Also, the meaning of 'substantial' is uncertain, and would lead to litigation involving decisions based on 'evaluation of complex economic data'.

SUMMARY

- The ECJ defines goods very widely: 'products which can be valued in money, and which are capable, as such, of forming the subject of commercial transactions' (*Commission v Italy*).
- Art 34 TFEU prohibits Quantitative restrictions (QRs) on imports and all measures having equivalent effect (MEQRs). Art 34 is directly effective (*Ianelli & Volpi v Meroni*).
- QRs are 'measures which amount to a total or partial restraint of… imports' (*Geddo v Ente Nazionale Risi*). QRs include import bans (*R v Henn & Darby; French Turkeys, Conegate*).
- The ECJ has defined MEQRs on imports very widely: 'All trading rules enacted by Member States which are capable of hindering, directly or indirectly, actually or potentially, intra-Community trade' (*Dassonville*). As far as establishing an MEQR is concerned, it is irrelevant whether national rules apply only to imports (distinctly applicable measures) or apply equally to domestic goods and imports (indistinctly applicable measures).
- Examples of MEQRs on imports: contents and ingredients restrictions (*Cassis de Dijon, Sandoz, Beer Purity, Muller, Red Bull, Greenham & Abel*); packaging requirements (*Walter Rau v De Smedt, Mars*); prohibitions on the use of goods (*Toolex Apha, Tinted film, Motorcycle trailers, Mickelsson & Roos*); origin-marking requirements (*Dassonville, Souvenir Jewellery*); name restrictions (*Smanor, Guimont*); import inspections (*Commission v France (Italian Wine), Dynamic Medien*).
- Art 35 TFEU prohibits Quantitative restrictions (QRs) on exports and all measures having equivalent effect (MEQRs).
- 'Quantitative restrictions' on exports include export bans (*R v Thompson & Others, Dusseldorp*).
- Distinctly applicable MEQRs on exports are *prima facie* prohibited (*Bouhelier, Jersey Potatoes*). Indistinctly applicable MEQRs on exports only breach Art 35 if they have as their 'specific object or effect' the restriction of exports (*Groenveld; Gysbrechts*).
- Art 36 TFEU allows Member States to justify measures that restrict imports or exports on grounds of public morality, policy or security; protection of health and life of humans, animals or plants; protection of national treasures; protection of industrial and commercial property. It is a closed list. The burden of proof is on the national authorities to show (a) evidence that there is a risk and (b) that the restrictions imposed are 'proportionate' (*ATRAL*).
- Public morality is something for Member States to decide in accordance with their own values (*R v Henn & Darby*).
- Public policy was invoked in *R v Thompson & Others* and *Ahokainen & Leppik*.
- Public security was successfully invoked in *Campus Oil*. It covers both internal and external security (*Richardt & Les Accessoires Scientifiques*).
- Human health protection is the most important derogation under Art 36 (*Toolex Alpha*). Justification 'must be based on a detailed assessment of the risk to public health, based on the most reliable scientific data available and the most recent results of international research' (*Greenham & Abel*). Flexibility is permitted in situations of 'scientific uncertainty' (*Sandoz*).
- Even if a measure is covered by Art 36, it will still be unlawful if it is 'arbitrary', which will be the case if there is already a lawful trade in similar items in the importing State (*Conegate*).
- Member States must not use Art 36 as a 'disguise' for economic protectionism (*French Turkeys*).
- In *Cassis de Dijon*, the Court introduced two key principles. (1) The 'Rule of reason': Member States may maintain or impose trade barriers where 'necessary' to satisfy 'mandatory requirements'; (2) the 'Rule of mutual recognition': a presumption that goods lawfully sold in one Member State should be available in all others. This

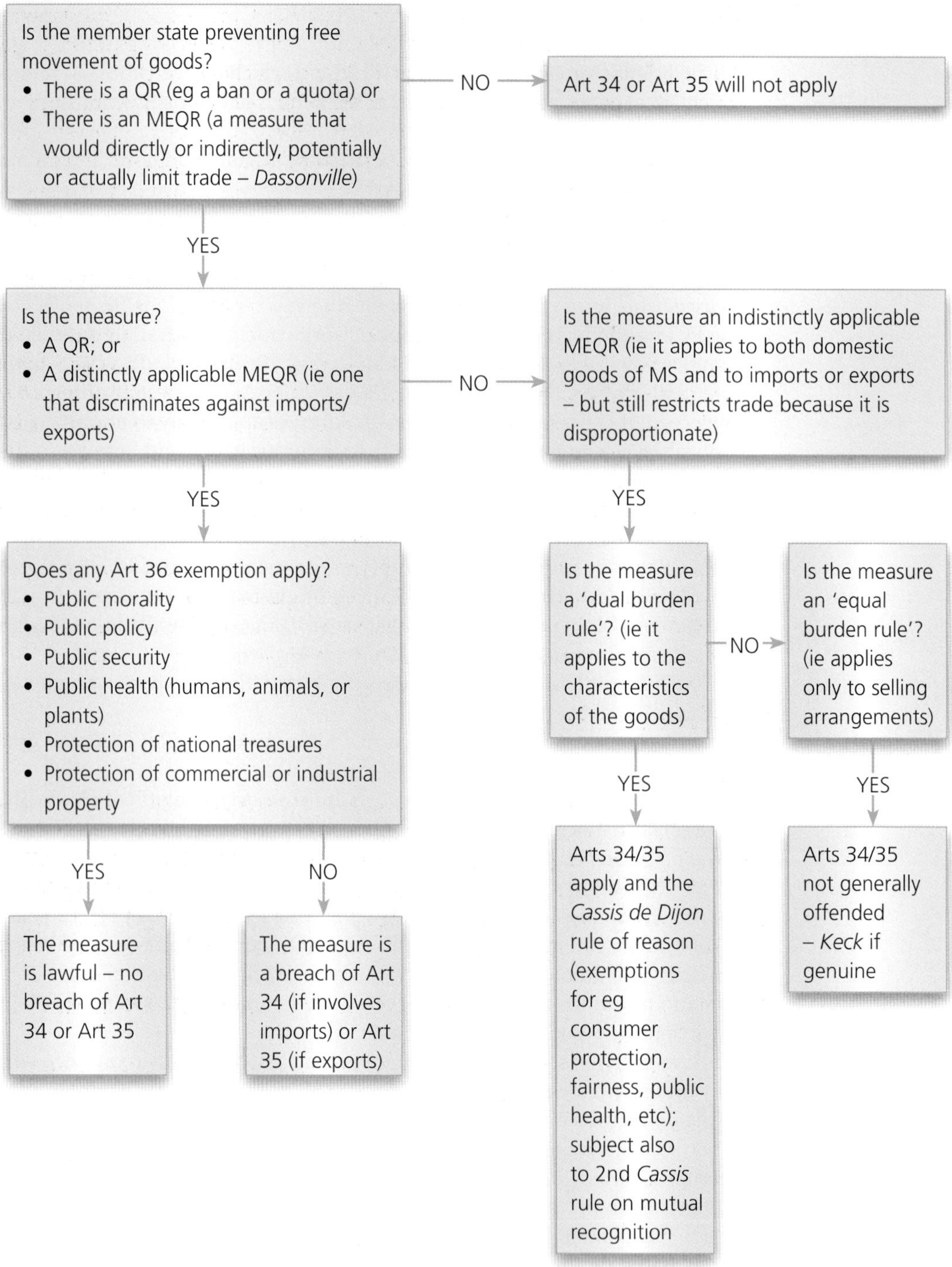

Figure 14.9.2 Flow chart illustrating the means of establishing breach of Art 34

presumption is rebuttable, typically by referring to national characteristics, but the burden of doing so falls on the Member State which is resisting imports. The *Cassis* principles apply to both import and export restrictions (*Dusseldorp, Gysbrechts*).

- The list of mandatory ('imperative') requirements is open ended. Examples include: consumer protection (*Walter Rau v De Smedt*), the success of which depends on the 'presumed expectations' of the 'average… reasonably well-informed… reasonably observant and circumspect' consumer (*Mars, Clinique*); environmental protection (*Danish Bottles, Walloon Waste, Dusseldorp, Aher-Waggon, Radlberger & Spitz,*

Mickelsson & Roos); cultural protection (*Cinéthèque*); protection of fundamental rights (*Schmidberger v Austria*); road safety (*Snellers Autos, Motorcycle trailers*); protection of children (*Dynamic Medien*); the fight against crime (*Tinted film*).

- In principle, the 'Rule of Reason' is limited to 'indistinctly applicable' measures (*Gilli & Andres, Souvenir Jewellery*). However, there is an apparent exception for environmental protection (*Walloon Waste* (import ban) and *Dusseldorp* (export ban)).
- All derogations are subject to a test of 'proportionality'. The test is failed if there is another method (eg clear labelling) capable of achieving the same objective which is less restrictive of trade (*Walter Rau*).
- In *Keck & Mithouard*, the Court decided that 'Contrary to what has previously been decided… certain selling arrangements' were exempt from Art 34.
- Examples include rules on pricing (*Keck & Mithouard, Belgapom*); Sunday trading laws (*Punto Casa*); rules on shops' closing times (*Tankstation t'Heukske*); restrictions on which shops can sell goods (*Processed Milk*); rules on methods of sale (*Burmanjer & Others* – no itinerant sales; *A-Punkt Schmuckhandels* – no door-to-door sales); advertising restrictions (*Hünermund, Leclerc-Siplec*).
- Selling arrangements are exempt from Art 34, provided they 'apply to all relevant traders' and 'affect in the same manner, in law and in fact, the marketing of domestic products and of those from other Member States.'
- Total advertising bans are not selling arrangements because they have a greater impact (in fact) on the marketing of imported goods (*Gourmet International Products, Douwe Egberts*). The same is true of legislation banning internet sales (*Deutsche Apothekerverband*). Such rules are MEQRs on imports, subject to Art 34.

Further reading

Articles

Connor, T, 'Accentuating the Positive: the "Selling Arrangement", the First Decade and Beyond'(2005) 54 ICLQ 127.

Davies, G, 'Can Selling Arrangements be Harmonised?' (2005) 30 EL Rev 370.

Józon, M, 'The Enlarged EU and Mandatory Requirements' (2005) 11 ELJ 549.

Kaczorowska, A, 'Gourmet Can Have His *Keck* and Eat It!' (2004) 10 ELJ 479.

Notaro, N, 'The New Generation Case Law on Trade and Environment' (2000) 25 ELR 467.

Oliver, P, 'Some Further Reflections on the Scope of Articles 28–30 (ex Articles 30–36) EC' (1999) 36 CMLR 783.

Oliver, P & Enchelmaier, S, 'Free Movement of Goods: Recent Developments in the Case Law' (2007) 44 CML Rev 649.

15

Article 28 TFEU and customs tariffs and Art 110 TFEU and discriminatory internal taxation

AIMS AND OBJECTIVES

After reading this chapter you should be able to:

- Understand the law relating to the prohibition of Customs duties and equivalent charges on imports and exports between Member States, in particular Articles 28 and 30
- Understand the law relating to the prohibition of discriminatory internal taxation on products of other Member States, in particular Article 110
- Apply the law to factual situations involving the prohibition of Customs duties and discriminatory taxation

15.1 The Common Customs Policy

In the previous chapter, the provisions of the TFEU dealing with 'quantitative restrictions' and 'measures having an equivalent effect' were examined. Articles 34 and 35 essentially deal with obstacles to trade caused by national legislation regulating the composition and/or packaging of goods. Articles 34 and 35 do not, however, apply to the situation when Customs officers in one Member State impose some form of financial charge on goods because they are crossing the border. Such charges are clearly capable of hindering trade, but they are tackled by different provisions of the TFEU. The key provision is Art 28, which creates the Customs Union. It has two parts:

- A prohibition on Customs duties and charges having equivalent effect. This deals with the imposition of charges on goods moving around the EU from one Member State to another. This prohibition on Customs duties and equivalent charges is reiterated in Art 30.
- A Common Customs Tariff. This deals with the movement of goods into the EU from elsewhere in the world, eg from China or the USA.

15.2 Article 30 and prohibition of Customs duties and charges having equivalent effect

15.2.1 Introduction

Article 30 prohibits Customs duties or charges having equivalent effect on all imports and exports between Member States. The ECJ has clarified that fiscal barriers to trade must be dealt with under Art 30 and not Art 34. In *Compagnie Commerciale de l'Ouest and Others* (Cases C–78 to 83/90) [1992] ECR I–1847, the Court stated:

JUDGMENT

'The scope of [Art 34] does not extend to the obstacles to trade covered by other specific provisions of the Treaty, and that obstacles of a fiscal nature or having an effect equivalent to customs duties which are covered by [Art 30] of the Treaty do not fall within the prohibition laid down in [Art 34].'

A 'Customs duty' is any charge of a fiscal nature that is imposed, directly or indirectly, on goods which cross a border. A simple prohibition of 'Customs duties' *per se* would have allowed Customs authorities to continue to charge importers through less obvious means. Hence, Art 30 also prohibits charges having an effect equivalent to Customs duties (CEE). In *Commission v Italy (Statistical Levy)* (Case 24/68) [1969] ECR 193, a CEE was described as:

JUDGMENT

'Any pecuniary charge, however small and whatever its designation and mode of application, which is imposed unilaterally on domestic or foreign goods by reason of the fact that they cross a frontier, and which is not a customs duty in the strict sense, constitutes a charge having equivalent effect ... even if it is not discriminatory or protective in effect and the product on which the charge is imposed is not in competition with any domestic product.'

In *Commission v Luxembourg and Belgium (Gingerbread)* (Cases 2 and 3/62) [1962] ECR 813, the ECJ emphasised that it is the **effect** of a charge, as opposed to its **name**, which is significant. Otherwise, Member States could disguise charges on imports easily, and use them to destroy any competitive advantage which cheaper imports would otherwise have over domestic products. Such charges need not necessarily be levied at a frontier. The key is whether the charge has been imposed **because the goods were imported** (*Steinike & Weinleg* (Case 78/76) [1977] ECR 595). In *Deutsches Milch-Kontor* (Case C–272/95) [1997] ECR I–1905, the ECJ expressly held that Art 30 applied even though the charges in question were in respect of Customs inspections carried out within Germany on lorries heading for Italy.

Many 'Customs duties' are imposed to make imports relatively more expensive and hence protect the domestic market. But there is no requirement that the charge be levied for protectionist reasons (*Commission v Italy (Statistical Levy)* (1969)). There may even be **no** domestic market in need of protection; but this will not stop the charge from infringing Art 30. This was seen in *Sociaal Fonds voor de Diamantarbeiders v SA Charles Brachfeld & Sons and Chougal Diamond Co* (Cases 2 and 3/69) [1969] ECR 211. Here, Belgian Customs officials imposed a charge on uncut diamonds imported into Belgium. There are obviously no Belgian diamond mines (the diamonds originated in southern Africa) but the ECJ nonetheless held that Art 30 applied.

15.2.2 Derogations from Art 30

Charge for services for the benefit of the importer/exporter

Even if the charge is for a service provided for the **benefit** of the importer or exporter, it may still breach Art 30. A charge for services which benefits the Union in general, eg health inspections or quality control, would not necessarily be compatible with Art 30 either (*Rewe-Zentralfinanz* (Case 39/73) [1973] ECR 1039). To escape Art 30, a charge must be capable of being regarded as a payment for services of tangible benefit to the importer: see *Commission v Italy (Statistical Levy)* (1969). The charge must not exceed the value or cost of the service (*Donner* (Case 39/82) [1983] ECR 19), nor a sum proportionate to the service provided (*Commission v Denmark* (Case 158/82) [1983] ECR 3573). A charge based on the value of the goods is not permissible (*Ford España v Spain* (Case 170/88) [1989] ECR 2305).

Charges for services imposed under EU law

Where the services charged for are imposed under EU law, then a charge could be regarded as a payment for services and therefore it would be permissible for the Member State concerned to require payment for it (*Commission v Italy (Statistical Levy)* (1969)). Similarly, where a service is mandatory under international agreement, a charge could be levied to cover the cost of the service (*Netherlands v P Bakker Hillegom* (Case C–111/89) [1990] ECR I–1735). Where the State is entitled to recover its service costs through a charge, it is only entitled to recover the actual cost of the service, and no more (*Denkavit Futtermittel v Germany* (Case 233/81) [1982] ECR 2933). Where a service is only **permitted** this is insufficient (*Commission v Belgium (Health Inspection Charges)* (Case 314/82) [1984] ECR 1543). It is essential that the service is **imposed** under EU law (*Germany v Deutsches Milch-Kontor* (Case C–426/92) [1994] ECR I–2757).

No other exceptions permitted

There is no correlation with Art 36 or the *Cassis de Dijon* (1979) principles (see Chapter 14). In *Commission v Italy (Export Tax on Art Treasures)* (Case 7/68) [1968] ECR 617, the Italian Government argued, unsuccessfully, that a charge levied on those exporting works of art from Italy was required to protect artistic heritage. In *Diamanterbeiders* (1969), above, the Court rejected any suggestion that the social utility of the Belgian Customs charge provided a defence (it had been argued that any money generated by the import charge on the imported diamonds would be used to provide financial aid for diamond mine workers in Africa). This case was followed in *Kapniki Mikhailidis* (Cases C–441 and 442/98) [2000] ECR I–7415, involving the imposition of charges on exports of tobacco products from Greece, apparently designed to raise money for workers in the tobacco industry. The Court held that this was no justification for breaching Art 30.

15.2.3 Repayment of illegal duties and charges

In several cases examined above it was established that a Customs duty or equivalent charge had been imposed by the customs authorities of a Member State in breach of Art 30. When that happens, then the Member State in question is, in principle, obliged to repay the person subject to the charge, usually the importer or exporter (*San Giorgio* (Case 199/82) [1983] ECR 3595; *Dilexport* (Case C–343/96) [1999] ECR I–579). Moreover, national rules of evidence which have the effect of making it virtually impossible or excessively difficult to secure repayment of charges levied in breach of Art 30 are incompatible with EU law. However, EU law does **not** require the repayment of the duty or charge in circumstances where this would unjustly enrich the person concerned (*Just v Danish Ministry for Fiscal Affairs* (Case 68/79) [1980] ECR 501; *Kapniki Mikhailidis* (2000)). This would occur in a situation, for example, where the burden of the charge has been transferred in whole or in part to other persons. Thus, if an importer had paid the charge, but then passed on the cost to the distributor of the goods in the importing State, then to order the repayment of the charge to the importer would over-compensate that person (*Société Comatelo and others* (Case C–192/95) [1997] ECR I–165).

15.3 The Common Customs Tariff

Article 28 also provides for the creation of a Common Customs Tariff (CCT), which co-ordinates the duties imposed onto all goods imported into the EU. A single tariff 'wall' is erected against imports, which no State is free to breach. The CCT came into operation in July 1968. It lays down common rules on nomenclature; valuation; and origin. CCT duties are fixed by the Council, following proposals made by the European Commission (Art 31).

KEY FACTS

Customs duties and equivalent charges (Art 30)	
• Creates the Customs Union	Article 28
• There are two aspects to this: a prohibition on the imposition of Customs duties and equivalent charges on goods moving from one EU Member State to another, and the Common Customs Tariff, which co-ordinates the imposition of duties on goods entering the EU from elsewhere in the world	
• Member States may not impose Customs duties or equivalent charges on goods when they are being imported or exported. There are very limited derogations from this principle – when charges are imposed to cover the cost (and no more) of a benefit of specific benefit to the importer/exporter, and when charges are imposed to cover the cost of services which are mandatory under EU law itself	Article 30

15.4 Article 110 and the prohibition of discriminatory internal taxation

ARTICLE

'Art 110 No Member State shall impose, directly or indirectly, on the products of other Member States any internal taxation of any kind in excess of that imposed directly or indirectly on similar domestic products.

Furthermore, no Member State shall impose on the products of other Member States any internal taxation of such a nature as to afford indirect protection to other products.'

15.4.1 The scope of Art 110

Article 110 allows Member States the freedom to establish their own taxation system for any given product, provided that there is no discrimination against imports, or indirect protection of domestic products. The purpose of Art 110 is to remove discrimination against imports, not to accord them tax privileges (*Kupferberg* (Case 253/83) [1985] ECR 157). Therefore, internal taxation may legitimately be applied to a particular product even if there is no domestic production of that product, and the tax is effectively levied against imports only. However, this is permitted because the Member State is not **discriminating against** imports. It would only be discriminatory if it was imposing a different rate of tax on similar or competing domestic products, but if there are no similar domestic products, no breach of Art 110(1) can occur, and if there are no competing domestic products, no breach of Art 110(2) can occur either. This was seen in *De Danske Bilimportører* (Case C–383/01) [2003] ECR I–6065. A Danish company had bought and imported a new German-made Audi car. Under Danish law, all new cars must be registered and a 'registration duty' paid. The purchase price of the car was approximately €27,000; the duty came to just over €40,000, bringing the total price to some €67,000. The company could not believe that this was correct and brought a legal challenge. The ECJ decided that no breach of Art 110 had occurred, simply because there were no similar (or even competing) domestic products – Denmark does not manufacture cars. Finally, because Art 110 prohibits discrimination **against** imports, it does not preclude the imposition of higher rates of tax on domestic products than on imports: that is, discrimination **in favour** of imports (known as reverse discrimination) is permitted (*Grandes Distilleries Peureux* (Case 86/78) [1979] ECR 897).

It is very important to remember that internal taxation is only prohibited by Art 110 if it is either discriminatory or has a protective effect. To a very large extent, therefore, the 27 Member States of the European Union are allowed complete discretion whether or not to impose taxes – or 'excise duties' – on a range of goods and, if they do impose such taxes, at what rate. This can lead to significant differences in prices from one Member State to another. For example, in the UK, the most heavily taxed goods are cigarettes, alcohol and petrol. Indeed, the rates at which those products are taxed in the UK has produced some very interesting results:

- In the case of **cigarettes and alcohol**, significant differences in the rate at which those goods are taxed in the UK and France has created the phenomenon of the 'booze cruise' – whereby UK nationals travel across the English Channel by ferry to France in order to buy large quantities of much cheaper alcohol and cigarettes at huge supermarkets in Calais. Under UK law – the Customs and Excise Management Act 1979 – individuals are permitted to bring into the UK alcohol and cigarettes purchased in other EU Member States without having to pay UK excise duty, but only for their own use. HM Revenue & Customs officers are vigilant in seeking to catch people bringing back consignments of those goods which they think may be intended for commercial sale. Anyone caught may face criminal prosecution in a British court for evasion of excise duty, as well as having the goods confiscated.
- In the case of **petrol**, massive disruption was caused to much of the UK in September 2000 when disgruntled lorry drivers (among others) blockaded British oil refineries, preventing fuel delivery trucks from getting in or out and thus causing many petrol stations throughout the country to run dry within a matter of days. The lorry drivers were protesting against the high cost of petrol in the UK, especially compared with petrol prices in much of the rest of the European Union. The lorry drivers eventually backed down when it appeared that public sympathy was beginning to turn against them.

'Products of other Member States'

Despite the clear implication of this phrase, the ECJ has held that the prohibition of discriminatory taxation must apply to goods manufactured or produced **outside** the EU, but which are in free circulation **inside** the EU (*Co-operativa Co-frutta* (Case 193/85) [1987] ECR 2085). Using even more expansive interpretation, the ECJ has held that Art 110 applies to exports, in order to guarantee the neutrality of national systems of taxation (*Larsen* (Case 142/77) [1978] ECR 1543).

15.4.2 Distinguishing Customs duties and taxes

Charges imposed only on imports are clearly contrary to the provisions on Customs duties and are dealt with under Art 30. The position is different where a charge is applied to all goods: domestic products as well as imports. A charge levied indiscriminately on all products of a particular description, in all respects, regardless of the country of origin, is a **tax**, not a **Customs duty**, and should be dealt with under Art 110. The picture can be complicated because many Customs duties are disguised as taxes (eg *Commission v Luxembourg and Belgium (Gingerbread)* (1962)). It is important to distinguish genuine taxes from disguised Customs duties. A 'tax' was defined in *Commission v France (Reprographic Machines)* (Case 90/79) [1981] ECR 283 as one which related to a 'general system of internal duties applied systematically to categories of products in accordance with objective criteria irrespective of the origin of the products'. It follows that a charge which is **apparently** levied on all goods but which is imposed in a different **manner**, and/or which is subject to different **criteria**, for domestic and imported products, would fall to be dealt with under Art 30 (*Marimex* (Case 29/72) [1972] ECR 1309).

Moreover, 'taxes' which actually **benefit** domestic products are, in reality, Customs duties. In *Capolongo* (Case 77/72) [1973] ECR 611, a 'tax' was imposed under Italian law on all cellulose products, such as egg boxes. The proceeds were used to finance the production of paper and cardboard in Italy. The ECJ held that such a 'tax' may fall foul of Art 30 if the proceeds of the charge were used to benefit a domestic product. The Court went on to hold that this applied even where the product on which the charge was levied and the domestic product which benefited from it were **different**.

However, the very wide principle established in *Capolongo* (1973) has subsequently been restricted. In *Fratelli Cucchi* (Case 77/76) [1977] ECR 987, involving an Italian 'tax' on sugar, the ECJ held that a 'tax' would only constitute a CEE in breach of Art 30 if certain criteria were satisfied:

- the tax would need to have 'the sole purpose of financing activities for the specific advantage of the taxed domestic product'
- the taxed product and the domestic product benefiting from the charge must be the same
- taxes imposed on the domestic product would need to be made good in full.

Thus, the charge that was the subject of the *Capolongo* (1973) litigation would not now be found to be in breach of Art 30, because the products involved were different. However, such a charge could very well be regarded as a discriminatory tax instead, in breach of Art 110 (*Co-operativa Co-frutta* (1987), concerning an Italian 'tax' on bananas). The *Fratelli Cucchi* (1977) criteria have been confirmed in a succession of cases subsequently. In *UCAL* (Case C–347/95) [1997] ECR I–4911 and *Fricarnes* (Case C–28/96) [1997] ECR I–4939, involving Portuguese 'taxes' on dairy products and meat respectively, the position was summarised as follows:

JUDGMENT

> 'If the advantages stemming from the use of the proceeds of the contribution in question *fully* offset the burden borne by the domestic product when it is placed on the market, that contribution constitutes a charge having an effect equivalent to customs duties, contrary to [Art 30]. If those advantages only *partly* offset the burden borne by domestic products, the charge in question is subject to [Art 110]. In the latter case, the charge would be incompatible with [Art 110] and is therefore prohibited to the extent to which it discriminates against imported products, that is to say to the extent to which it partially offsets the burden borne by the taxed domestic product.'

15.4.3 Discrimination against imports: Art 110(1)

The ECJ has held that Art 110(1) must be construed broadly, to include all taxation actually and specifically imposed on a particular product. Article 110(1) prohibits the imposition of taxation on domestic products which discriminates against similar imported products. Discrimination may either be direct or indirect and still breach Art 110(1) – the difference is that indirect discrimination may be justified.

Direct discrimination

Discrimination may be 'direct', that is, the discrimination is visible on its face. *Alfons Lütticke* (Case 57/65) [1966] ECR 293 involved German tax legislation that discriminated against the same type of goods – dried milk – purely according to its country of origin. This clearly breaches Art 110(1). Moreover, in *Haahr Petroleum* (Case C–90/94) [1997] ECR I–4085, the ECJ rejected any suggestion that directly discriminatory taxation could be justified.

Indirect discrimination

Where a taxation system is *prima facie* non-discriminatory, but in practice discriminatory against imported products, this is known as indirect discrimination. It will nevertheless amount to a breach of Art 110(1). This is perfectly demonstrated in *Humblot* (Case 112/84) [1987] ECR 1367, a case involving French road tax.

CASE EXAMPLE

Humblot (Case 112/84) [1987] ECR 1367

French road tax operated on a sliding scale depending on engine capacity up to 16 cv, with the top rate being about 1,000 francs. For cars above 16 cv, a flat-rate 'supertax' of about 5,000 francs was payable. Michel Humblot, a French national, imported a 36 cv Mercedes from Germany. He paid the 'supertax' but then sought repayment through the French courts. The ECJ held that the French system amounted to indirect discrimination based on nationality, contrary to Art 110(1). Although *prima facie* applicable without distinction in terms of nationality to all cars, in practice the tax policy discriminated against imported cars, because no cars exceeding 16 cv capacity were manufactured in France. The Court also rejected the French authorities' argument that cars over 16 cv were 'luxury' cars and therefore dissimilar to ordinary cars.

Note: the French franc was abolished when the single European currency, the euro, came into operation in 2002.

Indirect discrimination, unlike direct discrimination, may be justified, provided that the difference in treatment of domestic goods and imported goods is designed to achieve some acceptable outcome. The difference must be based upon objective criteria. In *Commission v France (Tax on Wines)* (Case 196/85) [1987] ECR 1597, sweet wines were taxed at a lower rate than ordinary wines. This was done in order to provide some economic assistance to rural areas in France that were dependent on sweet wine production. The ECJ held that the tax was *prima facie* in breach of Art 110(1) but, as the discrimination was indirect, it was capable of justification.

'Similar products'

It is not necessary that the imported products and the domestic products which are subjected to different rates of taxation are **identical**. They need only be **'similar'**, and in *Commission v France (Taxation of Spirits)* (Case 168/78) [1980] ECR 347, the ECJ held this word should be construed broadly.

CASE EXAMPLE

Commission v France (Taxation of Spirits) (Case 168/78) [1980] ECR 347

Under French legislation, alcoholic beverages distilled from cereals (such as whisky and gin, which were largely imported) were subject to a much higher tax regime than spirits distilled from fruit or wine (such as cognac, armagnac and brandy), of which there was heavy domestic production. The Commission, arguing that all spirits were 'similar', alleged a breach of Art 110(1). The French Government argued that a distinction should be drawn between aperitifs and digestives. The former were drunk, diluted with water, before meals and included all grain-based spirits. The latter were beverages consumed, neat, at the end of a meal, typically spirits obtained from fruit and wine. The French also argued out that cereal-distilled spirits were distinguishable from fruit- and wine-based spirits because of 'a number of organoleptic properties combining taste, aroma and smell'. The ECJ rejected the distinction between aperitifs and digestives. The 'products in question may be consumed before, during or after meals or even completely unrelated to such meals'; moreover, 'according to consumer preference the same beverage may be used indiscriminately as an aperitif or a digestive. Therefore it is impossible to recognise … the objective value of the distinction upon which the French tax practice is based'. The Court also rejected any distinction based on flavour. There was 'no question of denying the reality of and shades of difference in the flavour of the various alcoholic products'. However, it was necessary to realise that this 'criterion is too variable in time and space to supply by itself a sufficiently sound basis for distinction'. The main problem was that the products in question could be consumed in very varied circumstances, either neat or diluted or with a variety of mixers. Hence, 'owing in particular to this flexibility of use' all spirits could be considered as 'similar' or in at least partial competition. The ECJ concluded that it did not need to decide whether the drinks were 'similar' because it was 'impossible reasonably to contest that without exception they are in at least partial competition', and hence Art 110(2) applied instead.

The Court held that:

JUDGMENT

'The first paragraph of [Art 110], which is based on a comparison of the tax burden imposed on domestic products and on imported products which may be classified as "similar", is the basic rule ... This provision ... must be interpreted widely so as to cover all taxation procedures which conflict with the principle of the equality of treatment of domestic products and imported products; it is therefore necessary to interpret the concept of "similar products" with sufficient flexibility ... it is necessary to consider as "similar" products which have similar characteristics and meet the same needs from the point of view of consumers. It is therefore necessary to determine the scope of the first paragraph of [Art 110] on the basis not of the criterion of the strictly identical nature of the products but on that of their similar and comparable use.'

Most cases have arisen in the context of alcoholic drinks, primarily because they are taxed so heavily by most Member States' governments for social and/or revenue-raising reasons. There are also many fine distinctions that can be drawn between different drinks, depending on their raw ingredients, strength, method of manufacture, etc.

- *Commission v Denmark (Tax on Wines)* (Case 106/84) [1986] ECR 833 – wine and fruit wine were 'similar'.
- *John Walker & Sons* (Case 243/84) [1986] ECR 833 – whisky and fruit liqueur wines were not 'similar', because whisky contained twice as much alcohol (40 per cent to 20 per cent).

FG Roders BV (Cases C–367 to 377/93) [1995] ECR I–2229 involved a very thorough examination of the similarity of a number of drinks, including French red wine and champagne, Italian vermouth, Portuguese madeira and Spanish sherry. BENELUX legislation (meaning legislation common to Belgium, Luxembourg and the Netherlands) taxed wines differently according to whether they were still or sparkling, and according to whether they had been made from grapes or from fruit. There were therefore four categories into which wine could fall for tax purposes:

- still grape wine
- still fruit wine
- sparkling grape wine and
- sparkling fruit wine.

Still fruit wine was exempt from tax altogether (provided that it met certain requirements with regard to labelling and packaging) while sparkling fruit wine was taxed at a lower rate than sparkling grape wine. Various importers into the Netherlands of French red wine and champagne, Italian vermouth, Portuguese madeira and Spanish sherry (all of which are made from grapes) argued that their products were 'similar' to domestically produced fruit wine (whether still or sparkling, as the case may be) and should therefore be taxed at the lower rate. The Court made a number of findings, looking at each of the imported drinks in turn.

1. Red **table** wine is 'similar' to still fruit wine. It was in this specific context that the Court made its finding, that 'the two categories of wine possess similar organoleptic properties – in particular taste and alcohol strength – and meet the same needs of

consumers, inasmuch as they can be consumed for the same purposes, namely both to quench thirst and to refresh, and to accompany meals'.

2. Red quality wine may be 'similar' to still fruit wine, but this was a question for the national court, by examining the 'objective characteristics of both categories of beverage, such as their origin, their method of manufacture and their organoleptic properties, in particular taste and alcohol content', and, secondly, by considering 'whether or not both categories of beverage are capable of meeting the same needs from the point of view of consumers'.
3. Vermouth may also be 'similar' to still fruit wine, although again this was a question for the national court. However, the Court did point out two potentially significant differences: 'not only is ethyl alcohol added to grape wine but also a small quantity of mixed herbs which give vermouth its special flavour'.
4. Champagne may also be 'similar' to sparkling fruit wine, although that would be for the national court to decide. Again, the Court pointed out a number of differences between the two drinks: 'champagne is made sparkling by a natural method – by a second alcoholic fermentation in the bottle [but] sparkling fruit wines require the addition of carbon dioxide, a fermentation process which is not natural. Secondly, the organoleptic properties of champagne are not comparable to those of sparkling fruit wines. Thirdly, the two categories of beverage do not meet the same needs of consumers, particularly since the consumption of champagne is usually associated with special occasions.'
5. Finally, sherry and madeira are not 'similar' to still fruit wines. There were two reasons for this, firstly that the imported drinks were 'usually consumed as aperitifs or as dessert wines', and secondly because they had a higher alcohol content (17–18 per cent) than fruit wines (15 per cent).

15.4.4 Indirect protection of domestic products: Art 110(2)

It is unnecessary for the products in question to be 'similar' for the purposes of Art 110(2). Instead, it applies to 'all forms of indirect tax protection in the case of products which, without being similar within the meaning of [Art 110(1)], are nevertheless in competition, even partial, indirect or potential, with each other' (*Co-operativa Co-frutta* (1987)). It is thus much wider than Art 110(1). In several of the cases considered above under Art 110(1), the ECJ found that the products in question were not 'similar'. However, the Court then went on to discuss whether the dissimilar products may, instead, be 'in competition' with each other so that differential levels of taxation may have a protective effect for domestically produced goods. Hence:

- *Commission v France (Taxation of Spirits)* (1980) – brandy and cognac (domestically produced in France) and whisky and gin (imported) were not 'similar' to but were in competition.
- *Commission v UK (Tax on Beer and Wine)* (Case 170/78) [1983] ECR 2265 – beer (domestically produced in the UK) and wine (imported) were not 'similar' but beer was in competition with at least some wines.
- *Commission v Italy (Tax on Fruit)* (Case 184/85) [1987] ECR 2013 and *Co-operativa Co-frutta* (1987) – bananas (imported) were not 'similar' to other fruits (domestically grown in Italy) but were in competition with them.

It should be noted that, just because dissimilar products are in competition with each other, it does not mean that taxing one at a higher rate will have a protective effect on the other. It may be that the imported product is of such a significantly higher quality such that taxing it will have little or no impact on sales. Alternatively, as was the case in *Commission v Belgium (Tax on Wine and Beer)* (Case 356/85) [1987] ECR 3299, if the price differential between the imported product and the dissimilar domestically produced product is already quite substantial, differences in the rates of tax will not serve to protect the domestically produced product.

KEY FACTS

Internal taxation (Art 110)	
• The ECJ will first of all examine different domestically produced and imported products to see if they are 'similar'. This does not mean 'identical'	Article 110(1); *Commission v France* (1980)
• If the answer is yes, then those products must be subject to the same rate of internal taxation or 'excise duty' otherwise there is a breach. This was seen where the Court held that French red table wine was 'similar' to Dutch fruit wine	Article 110(1) *FG Roders BV* (1995)
• The only exception would be if any discrimination was 'indirect', and furthermore capable of objective justification	
• If the same rate of internal taxation is applied to both domestically produced and imported products, but the revenue generated then finds its way back to the domestic producers, such that they are reimbursed in full, then the Article does not apply. Instead, this system would be regarded as imposing a charge equivalent to a Customs duty on imports, which breaches Art 30	Article 110(1)
• If the answer is no the ECJ will examine whether or not the products are in competition with each other and, in addition, whether the differential rates of tax may have a protective effect	Article 110(2)
• This was also seen in *FG Roders BV* (1995) where the ECJ held that Spanish sherry and Portuguese madeira were not 'similar' to Dutch fruit wines, but they were in competition with other	*FG Roders BV* (1995)
• If there is a protective effect then the national legislation must be amended to remove the protective effect, otherwise there is a breach of Art 110(2)	
• Provided that any protective effect is removed, it is not necessary for the rates of tax to be equalised.	

SAMPLE ESSAY QUESTION

The distinction between customs duties and excise duties can be a difficult one to draw, but it is nevertheless a crucial distinction, as the legal implications are very different. Discuss.

Explain the law relating to customs duties:

- Art 30 TFEU prohibits customs duties on imports and exports and all charges having equivalent effect
- Irrespective of its size, name, or purpose, a charge imposed unilaterally on goods crossing one of the EU's internal borders breaches Art 30 (*Commission v Italy (Statistical Levy)*)
- Charges for services which benefit the importer/exporter (*Donner*), or which are imposed under EU law (*Statistical Levy*), may escape Art 30
- Otherwise, no derogations are available (*Sociaal Fonds, Kapniki Mikhailidis*).

Explain the law relating to excise duties:

- Art 110 TFEU prohibits discriminatory internal taxation (excise duties)
- Define taxes (*Commission v France (Reprographic Machines)*)
- Discriminatory excise duties are prohibited whether direct (*Alfons Lütticke*) or indirect (*Humblot*). Direct discrimination cannot be justified (*Haahr Petroleum*), but indirect discrimination is justifiable (*Commission v France (Tax on Wines)*)
- Art 110 (1) prohibits the imposition of a higher rate of excise duty on imported goods *vis-à-vis* 'similar' domestic products. Products are 'similar' if they have 'similar characteristics and meet the same needs from the point of view of consumers' (*Commission v France (Tax on Spirits)*)
- Art 110 (2) prohibits the imposition of excise duties on imported goods which afford 'indirect protection' to domestic goods. Products need not be 'similar' for Art 110 (2) to apply but must be in 'competition, even partial, indirect or potential, with each other' (*Co-operativa Co-frutta*).

Compare/contrast Art 30 with Art 110:

- Art 30 and Art 110 are mutually exclusive
- It is crucial to distinguish between them. Under Art 30, customs duties and equivalent charges are <u>prohibited</u> (subject to certain narrow derogations) but under Art 110, excise duties are <u>permitted</u> (unless they discriminate against similar imported products or afford indirect protection to competing domestic products)
- Examine the cases where a so-called 'tax' was found to be a charge having an effect equivalent to a customs duty instead because it did not satisfy the Court's definition of a 'tax' (*Marimex, Capolongo, Fratelli Cucchi*
- Observe that Art 30 applies when imports are subject to a charge even if there are no competing domestic products (*Sociaal Fonds*). However, for Art 110 to apply, there must be 'similar' or at least competing domestic goods (*De Danske Bilimportører*).

SUMMARY

- Article 30 TFEU prohibits 'Customs duties on imports and exports and Charges having equivalent effect'.
- Equivalent charges are defined very widely. All charges imposed on goods when they cross a national frontier, whether by the importing or exporting State, are prohibited. The size, and the name, of the charge are immaterial (*Commission v Italy (Statistical Levy)*).
- It is irrelevant why a customs duty or equivalent charge has been imposed. It may have been for socially valid reasons (eg raising cash for disadvantaged workers) but this is immaterial (*Sociaal Fonds; Kapniki Mikhailidis*).
- Article 110 TFEU allows Members States to establish their own 'internal taxation' system, in the form of excise duties on goods, but prohibits discrimination against imported products. Discriminatory excise duties are prohibited whether direct (*Alfons Lütticke*) or indirect (*Humblot*). Direct discrimination cannot be justified (*Haahr Petroleum*), but indirect discrimination is justifiable (*Commission v France (Tax on Wines)*). 'Excise duties' are most frequently imposed on tobacco products, alcoholic drinks, and fuel.
- 'Internal taxation' means a 'general system of internal duties applied systematically to categories of products in accordance with objective criteria irrespective of the origin of the products' (*Commission v France (Reprographic Machines)*).
- A so-called 'tax' which is apparently levied on all goods but which is imposed in a different manner, and/or which is subject to different criteria, for domestic and imported products, is therefore not a 'tax' and falls under Art 30 instead (*Marimex*). Similarly, a so-called 'tax' which actually benefits domestic products is not a 'tax' either and falls under Art 30 instead (*Capolongo*). However, the products in question must be the same (*Fratelli Cucchi*).
- Imported goods must not be taxed 'in excess' of the taxation imposed on 'similar' domestic products (Article 110 (1)). 'Similar' products are 'products which have similar characteristics and meet the same needs from the point of view of consumers' *Commission v France (Tax on Spirits)*. Hence products do not have to be identical for Art 110 (1) to apply.
- Where different products are in 'competition' with each other, Member States may impose different excise duties but the level of taxation imposed on imported products must not afford 'indirect protection' to domestic products (Art 110 (2)). Products need not be 'similar' for Art 110 (2) to apply but must be in 'competition, even partial, indirect or potential, with each other' (*Co-operativa Co-frutta*). Beer and wine are not 'similar' products, but they are at least in 'competition' with each other (*Commission v UK (Tax on Beer and Wine)*).
- Art 30 applies when imports are subject to a charge even if there are no competing domestic products (*Sociaal Fonds*). However, for Art 110 to apply, there must be 'similar' or at least competing domestic goods (*De Danske Bilimportører*).

Further reading

Articles

Easson, A, 'Fiscal Discrimination: New Perspectives on Article 95' (1981) 18 CMLR 521; 'The Spirits, Wine and Beer Judgments: A Legal Mickey Finn?' (1980) 5 ELR 318.

Lonbay, J, 'A Review of Recent Tax Cases' (1989) 14 ELR 48.

Plender, R, 'Charges Having an Equivalent Effect to Customs Duties: A Review of the Cases' (1978) 3 ELR 101.

Snell, J, 'Non-discriminatory Tax Obstacles in Community Law' (2007) 56 ICLQ 339.

16

EU competition law

AIMS AND OBJECTIVES

After reading this chapter you should be able to:

- Understand why there are rules regulating anti-competitive practices
- Understand the prohibition under Article 101 TFEU
- Understand the necessary elements for showing a breach of Article 101 TFEU
- Understand the prohibition under Article 102 TFEU
- Understand the necessary elements for showing a breach of Article 102 TFEU
- Understand the enforcement procedures in EU competition law
- Understand the basis of merger control
- Evaluate the effectiveness of EU competition law
- Analyse the relationship between Article 101 TFEU and Article 102 TFEU
- Apply the rules under Article 101 TFEU and Article 102 TFEU to factual situations

16.1 The basis of EU competition law

16.1.1 The purpose of competition law

ARTICLE

Article 2 EC Treaty originally identified the main task of EU law as being '… the promotion of harmonious development of economic activities by the creation of a common market and the progressive approximation of the economic policies of the member states …'. As well as this Art 3(g) also states that the EU must ensure that '… competition in the internal market is not distorted …'.

As a result, the framers of the EU Treaty included very specific rules regarding competition. To have rules on competitive, or rather anti-competitive, behaviour seems at first sight to be inconsistent with the whole idea of economic freedom that is demonstrated in the 'Four Freedoms' and the drive towards a Single Market unfettered by any national barriers to trade. Rules on competition would seem to be a restriction on business efficiency and a restriction on successful businesses and therefore on market forces. This is in fact not the case. The Treaty makers were not trying to restrict businesses from free competition but rather to prevent large powerful businesses from using unfair means to harm small and medium-sized businesses.

The drafters of the Treaty realised that within a newly created Single Market companies would enjoy the benefit of a free and expanded market and might see this as a chance to get round former national policies on anti-competitive activities and operate on a much larger scale to maximise their potential. In other words, the framers of the Treaty recognised the point that unfettered market forces can lead directly on to monopolies. (A monopoly is where a single company or organisation enjoys almost unrestricted trade in a particular product or service.) Monopolies, almost by definition, defeat competition and ultimately, therefore, restrict consumer choice.

As a result, the framers of the Treaty inserted rules in the Treaty aimed at dealing with such practices. In doing so they took the same view as expressed in the Sherman Act of 1890 of the United States of America, that there should be prohibition of 'every contract, combination or conspiracy in restraint of trade' and also 'the monopolization of trade and commerce'. In other words, the rules should prevent the distortion of free competition resulting from either collusion between different businesses or the predominant power of a single business.

Therefore, the framers of the Treaty then drafted in a series of rules with three principal objectives:

- to avoid the possibility of restrictive practices and agreements
- to prevent large businesses from abusing their economic dominance in the market
- to ensure that, within certain limits, the public sector observes the same rules.

Set against the problems foreseen when framing the Treaty, these seem to be quite reasonable controls. Nevertheless, EU competition law has often been criticised in a number of different ways.

Firstly, it has been said that the law is too general in its application. This is because all agreements and practices are treated alike, even if they would actually benefit the consumer.

Secondly, competition law has been criticised on the basis that it in fact only sacrifices equity and efficiency to political goals.

> [The existence of competition law] is 'a perversity' and 'the loud admission of defeat' and 'an admission that the market alone cannot effect competition'.
>
> Another danger, of course, is always that 'member states will continue to promote the national interest over that of the Community, cling rigorously to currency, sovereignty, and intensify economic divergences within the Community'.
>
> I Ward, *A Critical Introduction to European Law* (Butterworths, 2003), p 126

Nevertheless, despite the apparent shortcomings, it is generally accepted that the EU institutions have succeeded in framing a cohesive and consistent set of objectives to be pursued in implementing competition policy. These are all identified in the Commission's Ninth Report on Competition Policy:

- to create an open and unified market which is not partitioned by restrictive and anti-competitive agreements between firms
- to realise an appropriate amount of effective competition in markets, avoiding over-concentration or any abuses exercised by dominant companies
- to achieve fairness in the marketplace, which involves giving support to small and medium-sized firms, measures for the protection of consumers, and the penalising of unlawful State subsidies
- to maintain the competitive position of the Community against its principal rivals in global economy, being mainly the USA and Japan.

16.1.2 The character of competition law

The rules on competition law cover all items capable of forming the subject-matter of commercial transactions. So it includes not only goods and services, but also intellectual property rights. The provisions are actually framed in quite broad terms and as a result have been the subject of much interpretation in the ECJ.

The competition rules can be used against firms regardless of the existence of a registered office in the EU, provided that its actions are capable of affecting trade within the Common Market. This was clearly identified in *The Woodpulp case, Ahlstrom Osakeyhtio and Others v Commission* (Cases 89, 104, 114, 116, 117 and 125–129/85) [1993] ECR I–1307.

The rules are also pragmatic in order to preserve free trade. In this way they are subject to exceptions to preserve market efficiency.

Community law only requires that penalties should apply where the actions of 'undertakings' affect trade between Member States. Nevertheless, this means that they can apply even if the effect is actually quite small, and even if the undertakings involved are in the same Member State.

It is also possible, therefore, for EU competition law and national law to exist alongside each other.

CASE EXAMPLE

Wilhelm v Bundeskartellamt (Case 23/67) [1969] ECR 1

Here, firms were penalised under German law for engaging in an unlawful cartel. They complained, arguing that the German authorities were not in a position to bring such action against them because the matter was the subject of action under EU law also. The ECJ held that the two distinct laws in fact operated in different spheres and for different purposes and therefore that action under both was possible.

Articles 101 and 102 in fact complement each other, in that they pursue common objectives but by focusing on different types of activity in different situations.

It is evident, then, that EU competition law has three main objectives which may at times, nevertheless, appear to be incompatible:

- efficiency
- protection of both consumers and small businesses
- the creation of the Single Market.

It is also true to say that competition law is among the most highly developed of all EU law. In fact, as Josephine Steiner points out:

> 'So pervasive is the influence of EU competition law and so severe are the sanctions for its breach, that business, whatever its size, whether or not their operations are currently confined to their domestic market, cannot afford to ignore Community law.'
>
> J Steiner, *Textbook on EC Law* (2nd edn, Blackstones, 1991), p 106

16.2 Article 101 and provisions on restrictive practices

16.2.1 The scope of Art 101

Article 101 is concerned with restrictive trade practices. It sets out distinctly the nature of the prohibition:

ARTICLE

'The following shall be prohibited as being incompatible with the internal market : All agreements between undertakings, decisions of associations of undertakings and concerted practices which may affect trade between member states and which have as their object or effect the prevention, restriction or distortion of competition within the common market …' are prohibited.

Article 101(1) also goes on to identify specific examples of anti-competitive acts that would fall under the prohibition as anti-competitive practices. These are those which:

- Directly or indirectly fix purchase or selling prices or any other trading conditions: This covers any arrangement that directly or indirectly could hinder intra-Union trade. In this way it can include arrangements whereby undertakings agree on trading conditions applicable to their business dealings such as discounts or credit arrangements. It has, for instance, included a retail price maintenance agreement between Belgian and Dutch booksellers (*VBVB and VVVB v Commission* (Cases 43 and 63/82) [1984] ECR 19.
- Limit or control production, markets, technical development, or investment: This involves agreements where undertakings restrict their own growth in order to raise prices artificially and prevent those outside the agreement from entering the trade, as in the *Quinine Cartel case* [1970] ECR 661 (see below).
- Share markets or sources of supply: This refers to the situation where competitors agree to apportion markets on either a geographical or a product basis. This was in effect what was being done in *Consten and Grundig* [1966] ECR 429 (see below). It might be done in an oligolopical market where competitors appoint each other as exclusive dealers of the other's product or in a particular region of the EU.
- Apply dissimilar conditions to equivalent transactions with other trading parties, thereby placing them at a competitive disadvantage: The object here clearly is to place the competing party at a disadvantage. It might obviously then involve providing advantageous conditions to one purchaser of a product over another.

CASE EXAMPLE

IAZ International Belgium and Others v Commission (Case 96/82) [1983] ECR 3369

A Belgian law meant that only those washing machines and dishwashers conforming to certain Belgian standards could be connected to the mains water supply. The standards had been set in an agreement between the national association of water suppliers and a trade association to which certain major suppliers of washing machines and dishwashers were affiliated. Clearly, this had the effect of disadvantaging those suppliers who were not affiliated to the trade association.

- Make the conclusion of contracts subject to acceptance by the other parties of supplementary obligations which, by their nature or according to commercial usage, have no connection with the subject of such contracts: This refers to situations where in order for a party to enter a contract it is bound to fulfil other obligations which in fact have no real bearing on the contract. A classic example would be requiring a party buying one product or service to buy at the same time a completely unrelated product or service.

Article 101(2) makes all such agreements void. It is then possible for the Commission to grant exemptions in certain cases.

The prohibition under Art 101 has three key elements all of which need to be proved and therefore all of which need to be defined and understood:

- the types of agreements that are prohibited
- the effect on inter-state trade
- the meaning of 'object or effect of preventing, distorting or restricting competition'.

Before looking at these it is important to understand the meaning of the word 'undertaking'.

16.2.2 The concept of 'undertaking'

Both Art 101 and Art 102 are concerned with the anti-competitive activities of 'undertaking'. The term 'undertaking', while used widely, is not defined anywhere in the Treaty and so again we have to look to the case law for interpretation of the term by the ECJ.

In fact, the ECJ has given a broad definition to the term: '… a single organisation of personal, tangible and intangible elements, attached to an autonomous legal entity and pursuing a long term economic aim …' (*Mannesmann v High Authority* (Case 19/61) [1962] ECR 357). The term has also been defined in numerous other cases and in Commission Reports on Competition Law.

As a result, it can be seen that the term covers almost every type of entity regardless of its legal status, from an individual to a multi-national corporation, provided that it has legal capacity and is engaged in an economic activity. Therefore there is a wide spread of disparate economic activities to which the term has been applied over time:

- an opera singer (*Re Unitel* (Commission Decision 78/516) [1978] 3 CMLR 306)
- a sports federation (*Re World Cup 1990 Package Tours* (Commission Decision 92/51))
- a State-owned corporation (*Italian State v Sacchi* (Case 155/73) [1974] ECR 409)
- a public agency (*Höfner v Macrotron* (Case C–41/90) [1991] ECR I–1979)
- a trade association (*FRUBO v Commission* (Case 71/74) [1975] ECR 563)
- banking (*Zuchner v Bayerische Vereinsbank AG* (Case 172/80) [1981] ECR 2021).

It has been held that the definition does not depend on the activity involving a profit motive. Nevertheless, the General Court has recently refined the definition and stated that there must be some form of economic activity, however marginal, for the entity to be regarded as an 'undertaking' for the purposes of competition law.

CASE EXAMPLE

FENIN v Commission (Case T–319/99) [2003] ECR II–357

Spanish hospitals and other health bodies (known collectively as SNS), purchased supplies from FENIN, a Spanish association comprising the majority of firms marketing medical goods and equipment. When SNS delayed payment FENIN complained that this amounted to an abuse of a dominant position under Art 82 (now Art 102 TFEU). The CFI rejected the claim on the ground that SNS was not an undertaking. This was because, even though a purchaser could be classed as an undertaking if the purchases were then used in what amounts to other than an economic activity, then there is no economic activity and no undertaking. SNS, financed by social security contributions, offered a free service to the public and so Art 82 (now Art 102 TFEU) could not apply.

The issue of whether a sporting body can be classed as an undertaking has also been considered. The *Bosman* ruling, of course, suggested that this would only be the case where an economic activity was involved. It could clearly impact upon the law governing free movement of workers for instance where rules of sporting associations limited the numbers of non-national players. However, rules that merely deal with sporting conduct are not within the scope of EU law, and this point has been considered in relation to the International Olympic Committee.

CASE EXAMPLE

Meca-Medina and Majcen v Commission C–519/04P

Two distance swimmers were suspended by the International Olympic Committee after positive drugs tests. They complained that IOC anti-doping rules infringed both EC competition law and the law on provision of services. The Court of First Instance held that purely sporting rules were not covered by EC (now EU) law on either competition or provision of services. The swimmers appealed to the European Court of Justice to set aside the CFI's judgment. The ECJ affirmed the principle that rules of a purely sporting nature have nothing to do with economic activity and therefore are not covered by EC (now EU) law. However, the court also identified that, where the rules concerned penalties as was the case with the IOC's anti-doping rules, then these might indeed have an adverse effect on competition law and so sporting bodies could be classed as undertakings on that basis. However, the swimmers had not complained on the basis of the excessive nature of the penalties so the ECJ rejected their claims.

It is clear in any case that the definition must be taken on a case-by-case basis.

16.2.3 The character of prohibited agreements

There are in fact three distinct types of agreement or restrictive practice which fall within the prohibition in Art 101:

- agreements between undertakings
- decisions by associations of undertakings
- concerted practices.

Agreements between undertakings

An agreement between undertakings must always carry with it some form of collusion. This is inevitably to distinguish it from unilateral acts.

CASE EXAMPLE

AEG Telefunken v Commission (Case 107/82) [1983] ECR 3151

Here, a refusal by a company to admit a trader to its distribution network was in fact seen as an agreement. This was because the refusal formed part of a system of contracts with existing distributors.

However, the agreement must also involve autonomous behaviour by the undertakings. For instance, Art 101 would not be infringed and it could not be classed as an agreement where national law imposed the agreement on the undertakings.

CASE EXAMPLE

Commission and France v Ladbroke Racing Ltd (Joined Cases C–359 and 379/95P) [1998] 4 CMLR 27

Here, French legislation required that companies engaged in off-course totalisator betting should be in the control of the Paris Mutuel Urbain (PMU). Ladbrokes complained that agreements between the companies and PMU were in breach of Art 81 (now Art 101 TFEU). The ECJ identified that this could not be the case since the companies and PMU were operating according to the national law and not of their own initiative.

According to *Tepea v Commission* (Case 28/77) [1978] ECR 1391, it is clear that even informal, oral arrangements can be classed as an agreement for the purposes of Art 101. Indeed, while contractual arrangements would obviously be agreements there is no real requirement that the agreement should be binding for Art 101 to apply. In fact, the leading case has shown that the so-called 'gentlemen's agreements' could still fall foul of Art 101 and in any case the third type, concerted practices, would cover most collusive behaviour.

CASE EXAMPLE

ACF Chemiefarma v Commission (The Quinine Cartel case) (Case 41/69) [1970] ECR 661

Here, firms in France, the Netherlands and Germany agreed to sales quotas and even the prohibition of the manufacture of synthetic quinine. They did so in order to raise the price of the product artificially and this was thus a breach of Art 81 (now Art 101 TFEU).

Decisions of associations of undertakings

Many industries collectively act within trading associations. Usually such associations co-ordinate behaviour and regulate standards in a trade and so incorporate a set of rules by which the members agree to be bound on membership. This is obviously usually beneficial. Nevertheless, when the rules of the association laid down are clearly aimed at harming free competition then they may amount to a breach of Art 101.

The obvious types of decision that could amount to a breach of Art 101 include ones fixing prices, or requiring specific discounts, or requiring collective boycotts of other undertakings, or the inclusion of any kind of restrictive contract clauses.

It has also been held, however, in *NV IAZ International Belgium v Commission* (1983) that even non-binding arrangements might count as a decision leading to a breach of Art 81 (now Art 101 TFEU). Neither does the body concerned have to be involved in commercial activity.

However, there will be no breach of Art 101 where trade associations are genuinely independent of their parent bodies.

CASE EXAMPLE

Germany v Delta Schiffahrts-und Speditionsgesellschaft GmbH (Case C–153/93) [1994] ECR I–2517

Here, both shippers and inland waterway ship operators were represented on freight commissions that were empowered to fix freight charges. These charges were then approved by the Minister of Transport and became compulsory. The shipper claimed that the charges were contrary to Art 81 (now Art 101 TFEU) but the ECJ rejected the claim since it felt that the State was entitled to provide tariffs for inland waterway freight traffic on recommendation from such a body, provided that the body was truly independent and the State still in effect retained control over the decision.

Concerted practices

The term 'concerted practices' has been defined by both academics and the ECJ. Academics have defined it as 'co-ordinated action between undertakings which, without amounting to an agreement, consciously substitutes co-operation for competition'. So the key characteristic of a concerted practice, by contrast with a straightforward agreement, is that it is more disguised or hidden and is generally informal.

In the leading case the ECJ has defined 'concerted practice' as:

JUDGMENT

'... a form of coordination between enterprises that has not yet reached the point where it is a contract in the true sense of the word, but which, in practice, consciously substitutes co-operation for the risks of competition ...'.

CASE EXAMPLE

ICI Ltd v Commission (the Dyestuffs case) (Case 48/69) [1972] ECR 619

This case involved a decision by the major manufacturers of dyestuff, representing in excess of 80 per cent of sales of dyestuff, to raise prices at exactly the same time. The Commission concluded that there had been a concerted practice and imposed fines on the undertakings. The undertakings then challenged this decision, arguing that it was merely parallel behaviour in an oligopoly (similar to a monopoly but where the majority of a market is controlled by a few undertakings rather than a single body). The ECJ held that it was irrelevant that there was no formal agreement because the collusion could be identified in a series of telexes to subsidiary companies and phrased in the same terms. The court identified that:

JUDGMENT

'By its very nature a concerted practice does not have all the elements of a contract but may inter alia arise out of coordination which becomes apparent from the behaviour of the participants. Although parallel behaviour may not by itself be identified with a concerted practice, it may, however, amount to strong evidence of such a practice if it leads to conditions of competition which do not correspond to the normal conditions of the market.'

So the true test of a concerted practice is when the parallel behaviour can be shown to be co-operative such that the undertakings involved appear to be acting with a common design or purpose: *Co-operative Vereniging 'Suiker Unie' v Commission (the Sugar Cartel case)* (Cases 40 to 48, 50, 54 to 56, 111, 113 and 114/73) [1975] ECR 1663.

Horizontal agreements and vertical agreements

Agreements that may offend Art 101 may of course be of two different types: horizontal or vertical.

A **horizontal** agreement is one between undertakings at the same level, so would usually be one between competing manufacturers or distributors. This could, for example, be an agreement to divide up markets; or it could be a price-fixing arrangement as in the *Dyestuffs case (ICI v Commission)* (1972).

A **vertical** agreement, on the other hand, is one reached between undertakings at different levels in the process, for example between the manufacturer and the distributor, or between wholesalers and retailers. These would usually, of course, benefit the consumer because they are likely to streamline the process of trade. However, they may offend Art 101 if they involve exclusive distribution arrangements, or exclusive licensing agreements.

The principles were established in the leading case, commonly referred to as *Consten and Grundig*.

CASE EXAMPLE

Etablissements Consten and Grundig v Commission (Cases 56 and 58/64) [1966] ECR 429

This involved an exclusive dealership under which Consten was appointed sole distributor of Grundig's electrical goods in France in return for which there was a total ban on imports or exports of Grundig's products in any other EU country. Consten complained when another company, UNEF, sold Grundig's goods in France in breach of its exclusive rights. UNEF then complained to the Commission that the dealership was a breach of Art 81 and the Commission issued a decision on this basis. Consten and Grundig argued that the agreement was for the purpose of streamlining distribution of Grundig's products in France where Grundig had competition from other manufacturers and was not an interference with trade. The ECJ identified that vertical as well as horizontal agreements could fall under Art 81 (now Art 101 TFEU) and that this was in fact a breach since it might affect trade between Member States.

16.2.4 The effect on trade between Member States

In order to establish that there has been a breach of Art 101 the Article also requires that the agreement may affect trade between Member States. The important word here is 'may'. In other words, there is no absolute requirement that the agreement has in fact affected trade; merely that it has the potential to do so.

The capacity of the agreement to affect trade is ascertained by reference to the free movement of goods and attainment of a Single Market, the same basic test as that identified in the *Dassonville* formula (see section 14.4).

So an agreement is capable of affecting trade between Member States if it is capable of constituting a threat '… direct or indirect, actual or potential, on the pattern of trade …'.

CASE EXAMPLE

Belasco v Commission (Case 246/86) [1989] ECR 2117

In this case a scheme fixing the price of cement in the Netherlands was held capable of affecting trade between Member States because it strengthened the existing divisions in the market.

In this way there is no need to prove any actual harm, as long as the agreement is likely to prevent, restrict or distort competition to a sufficient degree.

CASE EXAMPLE

Vereeniging van Cementhandelaren v Commission (Case 8/72) [1972] ECR 977

Here, a cartel in the Belgian roofing felt industry was held capable of affecting trade between Member States even though it was argued that there was no actual effect on trade. This was because it was capable of affecting inter-state trade, competitors from outside the cartel being at a potential disadvantage.

16.2.5 The object or effect of preventing, restricting or distorting competition

Article 101 requires also that the agreement must have as its 'object or effect the prevention, restriction or distortion of competition within the common market'.

'Object' and 'effect' in the context of the Article are clearly meant to be alternative tests. On this basis the test has as much to do with the practical outcomes of a business arrangement as it has to do with the intentions of the undertakings that are party to the arrangement.

The key issue then is whether competition has been stifled or affected, rather than whether there has been any actual movement in trade, whether up or down.

CASE EXAMPLE

Etablissements Consten and Grundig v Commission (Cases 56 and 58/64) [1966] ECR 429

As we have already seen, this leading case involved an exclusive distribution agreement between the German electrical goods manufacturer and a retailer/distributor in France. Consten was appointed sole distributor of Grundig's goods in France and also had exclusive rights to use Grundig's trademark. The case arose when another company, UNEF, sold Grundig's goods in France and Consten complained about the breach of its trademark rights. However, UNEF was successful in its counterclaim of breach of Art 81 (now Art 101 TFEU) since the arrangement had the potential to affect trade between Member States.

However, the ECJ nevertheless tries to apply the rules in a way that will not stifle business enterprise and initiative. The concern is not to prevent businesses from operating efficiently and effectively but to prevent a distortion of real competition.

CASE EXAMPLE

Société Technique Minière v Maschinenbau Ulm (Case 56/65) [1966] ECR 337

This involved an exclusive supply agreement which gave STM the sole rights to sell Maschinenbau's heavy earth moving equipment in France. However, unlike in the *Consten & Grundig* case, there were no agreements on exclusive use of the trademark, and neither were there any bans on parallel imports or exports as there were in that case. In other words, the agreement was aimed purely at business efficiency. On an Art 234 (now Art 267) reference to the ECJ the question for the court was whether the agreement was capable of preventing, distorting or restricting competition. The ECJ held that since the agreement was clearly only made because it was necessary to enable a firm penetration of the goods in a new market, it did not breach Art 81 (now Art 101 TFEU).

In the above case the ECJ identified the factors that will need to be taken into account to determine whether or not an agreement is capable of distorting competition:

- The nature and quantity of the product in question – so that the greater the market share of the product concerned, the more likely it is that an agreement may inhibit competition.
- The position and size of the undertakings involved – so that the greater the share of the market that they enjoy, the more there is a possibility of distorting competition.
- The relationship of the agreement to other agreements – so that the more isolated the agreement, the less likely it is to limit competition, but where it forms part of a network of agreements it is more likely to affect competition.
- The extent of the agreement – so that any agreement that extends beyond what is necessary to achieve the desired beneficial risk is likely to limit competition.
- The link with agreements on parallel imports or exports – so that where the agreement also includes bans on parallel imports or exports it will most usually be seen as stifling competition and lead to a breach of Art 101.

Market definition is clearly an important question and is one that the Commission has addressed in the Notice on Definition of the Relevant Market (1997 OJ C372/5). It has also been considered in the case law.

CASE EXAMPLE

European Night Services v Commission (Cases T–374/94 and 375/94) [1998] ECR II–3141

Railway services in France, Germany, the Netherlands and the United Kingdom decided to form European Night Services to provide overnight rail services through the Channel Tunnel between the UK and the other countries. The Commission was concerned that the agreement had the effect of restricting competition but granted it an exemption with strict conditions attached. The CFI (now the General Court) annulled this decision because the court felt that the market share of the parties involved was in fact quite limited. The court stated that, where an agreement does not include any obvious restrictions on competition, then it is necessary to examine the context in which the agreement actually operates, including the economic context.

Traditionally, in any case, the ECJ would apply the *de minimis* rule. The Court would not show interest in agreements which would have a disproportionately minor effect on competition and would only strike down agreements that might affect competition to a noticeable extent.

CASE EXAMPLE

Frans Volk v Establissements Vervaecke Sprl (Case 5/69) [1969] ECR 295

This case involved an agreement between a Dutch electrical goods distributor (Vervaecke) and a German washing machine manufacturer (Volk). The agreement gave the Dutch distributor exclusive distribution rights of the German company's washing machines in Belgium and Luxembourg. In return the agreement was reinforced by a ban on parallel imports of Volk's products by third parties, in other words a total protection. However, in examining the agreement the ECJ acknowledged that Volk only actually produced somewhere between 0.2 per cent and 0.5 per cent of washing machines in Germany and it sold considerably fewer in Belgium and Luxembourg. On this basis the agreement could not be said to have any real effect on competition, the *de minimis* principle applied and there was no breach of Art 81 (now Art 101 TFEU).

In fact, the *de minimis* principle has been introduced by the Commission in the form of Notices on Agreements of Minor Importance. The first of these was in 1986. The most recent is the Commission Notice on Agreements of Minor Importance 2001 (OJ 2001 C368/13).

Under this Notice an agreement will not be in breach of Art 101:

- where the undertakings that are parties to the agreement are actual or potential competitors (in other words, in a horizontal agreement), the aggregate market share of the undertakings concerned does not exceed 10 per cent of the market or
- where the undertakings that are parties to the agreement are not competitors (in other words, in a vertical agreement) the aggregate market share of the undertakings concerned does not exceed 15 per cent of the market.

However, there are qualifications to these basic rules:

- in horizontal agreements the agreement must not contain any restrictions on sale price, limitation of output, or allocation of markets or customers, otherwise the notice will not apply
- in vertical agreements the agreement must not contain restrictions on the minimum re-sale price of goods or on the territory that the goods will be sold in or the consumers that the goods will be sold to, or the notice will not apply.

16.2.6 Exemptions

Not all agreements will be automatically found to be in breach of Art 101. There are in fact different ways of avoiding being caught by Art 101 and until recently these included the granting of exemptions by the Commission. Since 1st May 2004, under the operation of Regulation 1/2003 a different process is in operation involving the Member States.

Sensibly, the Treaty also provided the means by which it could be identified that certain agreements could be exempted from the operation of Art 101. This includes both individual exemptions (which follow individual applications) and block exemptions that can be applied to specific categories of agreement.

Article 101 paragraph 3 specifically creates the criteria for exempting agreements. There are four conditions that must be met in order for exemption to be granted. Two of these are phrased in positive terms and two are phrased in negative terms.

- Firstly, it must be possible to show that the agreement, decision or practice contributes in some way to **improving** the production or distribution of goods or alternatively to **promoting** technical or economic progress.

CASE EXAMPLE

Transocean Marine Paint Association v Commission (Decision 77/454) [1975] 2 CMLR D75

This involved collaboration between a number of marine paint manufacturers with a view to rationalising production. The agreement between them was granted exemption because a global distribution network was created under the agreement which was in fact beneficial to competition.

CASE EXAMPLE

Re Vacuum Interrupters (Decision 77/160) [1977] 1 CMLR D67

Here, a joint venture between manufacturers of switchgear was exempted. This was because the agreement meant that research and development of vacuum interrupters was made possible as a result of the agreement.

- Secondly, a fair share of the resulting **benefit** must pass to the **consumer**. This need not merely be the end consumer.

CASE EXAMPLE

ACEC v Berliet (Decision 68/319) [1968] CMLR D35

This involved an agreement on production of a prototype bus by two French manufacturers. A benefit was gained by intermediaries in a distribution network in consequence of a commercial transaction. This was accepted as sufficient to justify exemption.

- The agreement or practice must not impose any unnecessary **restrictions** that would go beyond the necessary positive aims. An example of a practice that would infringe this negative requirement and therefore mean exemption would be denied is an absolute territorial protection, such as the ban on parallel imports in *Consten and Grundig v Commission* (1966).
- There must not be any possibility of the restrictions **eliminating** competition in respect of a substantial part of the product in question. Obviously, in respect of this requirement the market share of the parties concerned and the level of competition within the specific market will be crucial factors. In *Re Vacuum Interrupters* (1977) (above) the market stretched well beyond the EU because the undertakings faced significant competition from both the USA and Japan. However, where the competition is much more limited the market might be restricted to a single Member State.

Individual exemptions

Prior to 2004 individual exemptions were granted by the Commission under the procedure in Regulation 17/62. Application was by way of a 'notification' of the agreement or practice to the Commission. Individual exemption was then granted in the form of Decisions. These might be for only limited periods and they might also be conditional or depend on the fulfillment of certain criteria or certain obligations identified in the Decision.

Now, under Regulation 1/2003 it is no longer necessary to notify the Commission in order to obtain individual exemption. Article 1(1) of the Regulation instead places the burden on undertakings themselves to identify whether any of their agreements offend Art 101(1) but are in fact exempt under Art 101(3). The national authorities are then responsible for applying the criteria for determining whether a particular agreement is in fact exempt.

Unlike the former system where the Commission had to be notified for exemption to be granted there is no requirement to inform the national authorities in the same way for the exemption to take effect. National authorities will determine whether or not there has been an infringement of Art 101 by the agreement in question.

Block exemptions

Block exemptions were in any case a means of reducing the huge bureaucratic burden on the Commission of applications for individual exemptions. The process was introduced then for the purpose of streamlining competition law.

Inevitably, also, the process of making application for individual exemption left businesses in a state of uncertainty until a Decision was issued. On this basis the use of block exemptions allowed businesses to assess for themselves whether or not a particular type of agreement was exempt. If it was apparent that a particular type of agreement would fall under a block exemption then there would be no need for the businesses concerned to approach the Commission at all. It would only be if there was uncertainty that undertakings would approach the Commission for individual exemption. Nevertheless, the fact that a block exemption existed would not prevent the Commission from stating that particular aspects of individual agreements fell outside the scope of the exemption.

Block exemptions are introduced in the form of Regulations and are granted in respect of specific types of agreements. There are many examples and these have included:

- A block exemption on exclusive distribution agreements in Regulation 1983/83, replaced by Regulation 2790/99 on vertical restraints.
- Another on exclusive purchasing agreements in Regulation 1984/83, also later replaced by Regulation 2790/99 – in fact, Regulation 2790/99 (which came into force in June 2000) replaced exemptions on all vertical agreements with the exception of certain serious restraints.
- One also on patent licensing in Regulation 2349/84, later replaced by an exemption on technology transfer in Regulation 240/96.
- One on motor vehicle distribution in Regulation 123/85.
- Another on know-how licensing in Regulation 556/89.
- Another recent block exemption is that on research and development agreements in Regulation 2658/2000.

Inevitably, the issue of block exemptions is also affected by the introduction of Regulation 1/2003. The new block exemption Regulation 2790/99 creates an exemption for all vertical agreements as a category in their own right. There are limits to its application. There are special rules, for instance in the case of certain sectors such as petrol distribution. It does not apply also to certain types of clause such as non-compete clauses for over five years; those preventing buyers from manufacturing or selling certain goods after the agreement comes to an end; and 'hard core' restrictions, such as those covering re-sale price maintenance or restrictions on re-sale outside exclusive distribution networks. However, it is wider than the Regulations that it replaced, applying, for instance, to unfinished goods.

The new block exemption is applied according to a market share test. In this way it only applies if the buyer or seller has below 30 per cent of the market share. This does not mean that the agreement cannot gain exemption but an individual exemption will have to be applied for. It is on this basis that the new block exemption has been criticised for lacking the certainty of the previous system.

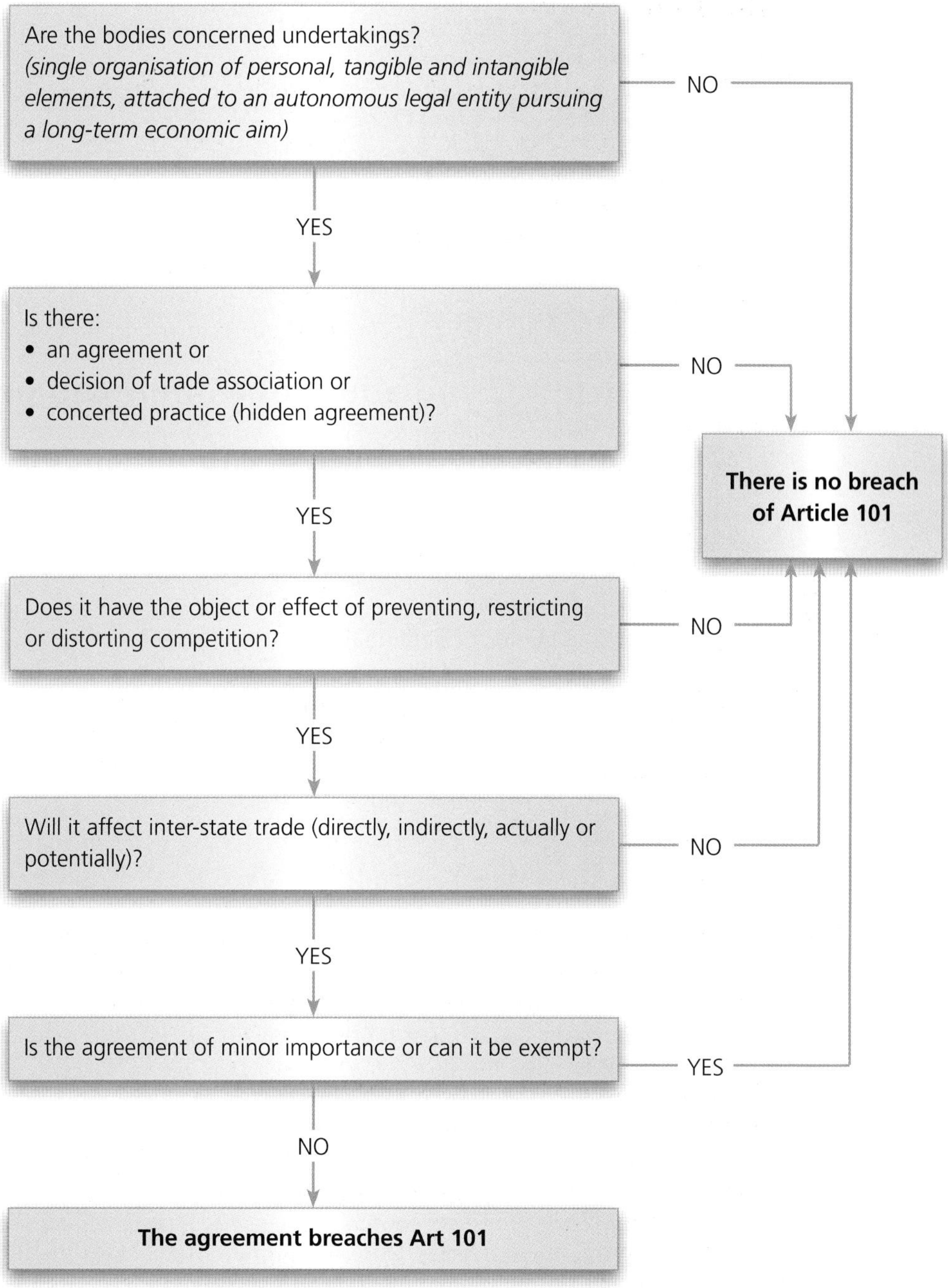

Figure 16.2.6 How a breach of Art 101 is established

ACTIVITY

Self-assessment questions

1. What is the definition of 'undertaking' in EU competition law?
2. What are the 3 main aspects of a claim under Art 101?
3. What 3 types of agreement will the Court of Justice accept amount to an agreement for the purposes of Art 101?
4. What types of agreement are prohibited under Art 101?
5. What was the basis of the decision in *Consten and Grundig v Commission*?
6. What is the difference in the *STM* case?
7. What test is applied in determining the effect on intra-Union trade?
8. What is the effect of the Commission Notice on agreements of minor importance?
9. What exemptions are available to undertakings under Art 101?

16.3 Article 102 and abuse of a dominant position

16.3.1 The concept of abuse of a dominant position

As we have seen, Art 101 concerns some form of collusive behaviour between undertakings that would have an effect on intra-Community trade and that in any case has as its object or effect the prevention, distortion or restriction of competition. Article 102, on the other hand, is usually concerned with the actions of a single undertaking rather than a combination of undertakings.

On this basis Art 102 was introduced to combat the perceived threat to competition posed by the negative effects of large concentrations of economic power in the hands of individual undertakings. It was also traditionally felt that Art 102 could not apply to oligopolies (large concentrations of economic power in the hands of a small number of undertakings). However, this reasoning has been challenged.

CASE EXAMPLE

Re Flat Glass (Decision 89/93) [1992] 5 CMLR 120

Here, the Commission decided that a group of undertakings that held a dominant position within the market for the production of 'flat glass' (between 79 and 95 per cent share) was in fact in a dominant position so that Art 82 (now Art 102 TFEU) could be applied when they engaged in concerted price fixing.

Article 102 is also applicable in the case of mergers and concentrations.

It must be remembered that Arts 101 and 102 are merely different mechanisms for dealing with what is essentially the same problem: the anti-competitive practices. The two Articles are, therefore, not mutually exclusive. Either may be alleged in a specific case and there is some overlap between the two. As a result, the Commission has a discretion how to apply competition law and which Article is in fact breached.

However, while there are overlaps with Art 101, it must also be remembered that there is no possibility of negative clearance in the case of Art 102. Neither are exemptions available (though they are for mergers). Once a breach has been proved then there is no further way of avoiding the consequences of the breach as there is in Art 101.

The basic prohibition is again spelled out in the Article itself. According to Art 102:

ARTICLE

'Art 102 Any abuse by one or more undertakings of a dominant position within the internal market or in a substantial part of it shall be prohibited as incompatible with the internal market insofar as it may affect trade between member states'.

Before moving on to analyse the separate elements of the Article it is important to emphasise that Art 102 does not in any way prohibit the existence of dominant positions. It is plain that the Article is not meant to punish efficient economic behaviour. Its purpose is rather to discourage practices that would cause damage to other undertakings by creating artificial conditions that distort competition. In this way it is the abuse of dominance that is significant more than the dominant position itself.

Looking at the wording of the Article, there are three distinct requirements all of which must be proved in order for there to be a breach of Art 102:

- The undertaking engaging in the practice complained of must have a dominant position in the appropriate market (which can be either the Single Market or a substantial part of it).
- The practice in question must amount to an abuse of that dominant position.
- Trade between Member States is affected as a result of the practice.

16.3.2 The concept of 'undertaking'

Articles 101 and 102 are both concerned with the anti-competitive activities of 'undertakings'. The definition given to the term 'undertaking' then is the same as under Art 101 (see section 16.2.2).

The term is thus defined broadly. Again, it is not defined anywhere in the Treaty, so again we have to look to the case law for interpretation of the term by the ECJ: '… a single organisation of personal, tangible and intangible elements, attached to an autonomous legal entity and pursuing a long term economic aim …'.

Again, it covers almost every type of entity regardless of its legal status, from an individual to a multi-national corporation, provided that it has legal capacity and is engaged in an economic activity. However, as with Art 101, the definition is capable of evolving on a case-by-case basis.

16.3.3 The definition of 'dominance'

'Dominance' is not defined in the Treaty at any point. However, it was originally defined in the ECSC Treaty (European Coal and Steel Community Treaty). The definition given here was that dominance occurs where undertakings hold a position '… shielding them against effective competition in a substantial part of the common market …'.

This is a fairly limited and imprecise definition and so as with other significant terms it has been left to the ECJ to define in the case law. The earliest possibility came in *Continental Can Co v Commission* (Case 6/72) [1973] ECR 215 where the ECJ identified that dominance amounted to:

JUDGMENT

'… power to behave independently without taking into account their competitors, purchasers or suppliers because of their share of the market or … availability of technical knowledge, raw materials or capital, they have power to control production or distribution for significant part of products'.

CASE EXAMPLE

Continental Can Co v Commission (Case 6/72) [1973] ECR 215

In this case Continental Can was a US multinational. Through its European subsidiary company, Europemballage, it possessed an 86 per cent share in another company, Schmalbach. This latter company enjoyed a dominant position in Germany in the market for tins for meat and fish products and also in metal lids for glass containers. When Europemballage proposed to engage in a takeover of another company, Thomassen, a Dutch packaging firm, this was challenged on the basis of being a breach of Art 82 (now Art 102 TFEU). The

Commission held that it did in fact amount to an elimination of potential competition and, therefore, a reduction in consumer choice, and that it was an abuse of a dominant position. The Commission's Decision was, however, overturned by the ECJ on the ground that the Commission had failed to identify the relevant product market and therefore had not proved dominance.

Two clear elements arise from the definition in the above case: the share of the market enjoyed by the undertaking and its ability to act independently. It was not long before the ECJ had the opportunity to review, re-affirm and supplement this definition.

CASE EXAMPLE

United Brands v Commission (Case 27/76) [1978] ECR 207

United Brands was one of the largest producers of bananas in the world, handling 40 per cent of EC trade at the time of the case. The company was alleged to have breached Art 82 (now Art 102 TFEU) and abused its dominant position by implementing a completely different pricing policy in different Member States. The ECJ held that there was such a breach and considered again the definition of dominance.

The ECJ, building on its definition in *Continental Can*, identified that dominance is

JUDGMENT

'… a position of economic strength … which enables it to prevent competition being maintained on the relevant market by giving it the power to behave to an appreciable effect independently of its competitors, and ultimately its consumers …'.

This again emphasises the significance of the ability of the undertaking to act independently without regard to competition. Another significant feature was added by this statement of the ECJ, the importance of the relevant market. In other words the ECJ was acknowledging that market share had to be analysed by reference to the specific market in which the undertaking was competing. In the case there was discussion whether the relevant market was fruit or whether there was a specific market for bananas.

Yet another extension to the definition was provided in the case of *Hoffmann la Roche v Commission* (Case 85/76) [1979] ECR 461:

JUDGMENT

'… such a position does not preclude some competition but enables [it] … if not to determine, at least to have an appreciable effect on the conditions in which that competition will develop, and in any case to act largely in disregard of it …'.

As a result of this gradual development of a definition it is possible to see that there are two critical concepts in determining dominance:

- The relevant market (this will be determined by analysing not only the relevant geographical market but the relevant product market also – other considerations include whether there is in fact a temporal market, and also cross elasticity of supply may be important).
- Calculation of the market share of the undertaking in question.

16.3.4 The relevant market

The relevant product market

Obviously, in terms of defending their position and avoiding a finding of dominance, undertakings will want to argue that the relevant product market should be defined as widely as possible. Inevitably the party complaining that it has been affected by the alleged breach of Art 102 will want the relevant product market to be defined narrowly so there is a greater possibility of dominance being found.

CASE EXAMPLE

United Brands v Commission (Case 27/76) [1978] ECR 207

Here, United Brands was charging different prices in different Member States for the same goods. The company argued that the relevant product market was fresh fruit, in which case it would inevitably have a small market share and dominance could not then be considered. The Commission argued, and it was accepted, that there was in fact a separate product market for bananas themselves. The basis of this argument was that bananas had a very specific market usually being consumed by, according to evidence given, the sick, the aged and the young. They could not therefore be considered merely as a part of a much more general market.

As a result, in identifying what the relevant product market is it must be seen as including not only the specific product itself but also all products which may be perfectly substituted for it. Consequently a key factor for measuring on whether there is a specific market in the specific goods is the concept of 'interchangeability' of the goods in question.

As it was expressed in *Hoffmann la Roche v Commission* (1979) there must be

JUDGMENT

'… sufficient interchangeability between all products forming part of same market insofar as specific use of products is concerned …'.

Relevant product market then is said to depend on 'cross-elasticity of demand' and 'cross-elasticity of supply'. Whether the relevant product market is viewed narrowly or broadly depends on whether there is no perfect substitute for the goods (narrow product market) or whether the goods can easily be substituted by an alternative (broad product market).

Seasonal factors may also be relevant in determining what the relevant product is. With seasonal goods there may be no possible substitute for the goods and therefore the market is likely to be viewed very narrowly. Seasonal fruits, such as the bananas in *United Brands* (1978), are a classic example of a temporal market.

Examples of relevant product market have included:

- **Heavy goods vehicle tyres** (as opposed to tyres generally) in *Michelin NV Nederlandsche Baden-Industrie Michelin v Commission* (Case 322/81) [1983] ECR 3461. Here there was inevitably little to compare the very specific type of tyres concerned with tyres in general. Sheer size alone would have been sufficient to identify the tyres as a distinct product grouping. In any case the client group also differed widely.
- **Cash register parts** supplied by a Swedish firm to a UK firm through its UK subsidiaries, in *Hugin Kassaregister AB v Commission* (Case 22/78) [1979] ECR 1869. Again, these would be seen as very specific goods and not commonly transposed with spare parts generally.
- **Separate cartons for pasteurised and UHT milk** in *Tetra Pak v Commission (No 1)* (Case T–51/89) [1990] ECR II–309. The packaging here would not have been regarded as interchangeable by the consumers.

The relevant geographical market

Geographical market clearly refers to the range of territory within which the goods can expect to be sold. According to Art 102 the undertaking must be dominant 'within the single market or in a substantial part of it'.

In identifying just how far the relevant geographical market does in fact stretch in the context of the particular practice it has been identified that this is '… where the conditions of competition are sufficiently homogenous for the effect of economic power on the undertaking to be evaluated …' (*United Brands v Commission* (1978)). In other words this is where the conditions for competition are the same for all traders in the product.

Clearly, then, while the relevant geographical market is generally assumed to be the whole of the EU, there are obviously other factors to be taken into account. Where there is a high level of cross-elasticity of demand or supply so that consumers have choice because other products can be substituted easily for the product in question then the relevant geographical market can in fact be large, indeed the whole EU.

However, this would depend on factors such as the cost and feasibility of transport arrangements. Producers in busy commercial areas may operate under entirely different conditions to those in remote rural areas, even if they enjoy the same market share. As a result, transport is a critical factor in determining the relevant geographical area.

CASE EXAMPLE

Eurofix and Hilti v Commission (Case T–30/89) [1990] 4 CMLR 602

Here, it was appreciated that transport was much easier and much cheaper in the case of the product in question, nail cartridges, than it would be for instance in the case of perishable foodstuffs. As a result, it was accepted that it would be appropriate to consider the whole of the EU as the relevant geographical market.

Another possibility identified as affecting the relevant geographical market is the pattern and volume of consumption. As a result, in *Suiker Unie* (1975) the relevant geographical market was limited to Belgium and Luxembourg. It has also been identified that if the product or service is only required in a single Member State then the relevant geographical market can even be as narrow as a Member State (*British Leyland plc v Commission* (Case 226/84) [1986] ECR 3263). However, it then has to be considered whether in fact there is an effect on trade between Member States.

16.3.5 Calculation of market share

Once the relevant market is established market share must also be considered in determining whether in fact the undertaking concerned is in a dominant position in that market. We have already seen from the definitions supplied in the *Continental Can* (1973), *United Brands* (1978) and *Hoffmann La Roche* (1979) cases that no particular market share is required in order to prove dominance. The statements of the ECJ in all three cases indicate that the most important element is the ability of the undertaking to act independently from the rest of the market. In *Continental Can Co v Commission* (1973) the subsidiary company owned by Continental Can had a share of nearly 80 per cent of the relevant product market in Germany. This was inevitably seen as a dominant position.

However, the market share does not need to be this large for there to be dominance.

CASE EXAMPLE

United Brands v Commission (Case 27/76) [1978] ECR 207

Here, the market share for bananas enjoyed by the company in Europe was between 40 per cent and 45 per cent. This was still held to be a dominant position. However, as the ECJ noted where the market share is less than 50 per cent other factors must be considered, not least the share of the nearest competitors. In the case the two closest competitors held 16 per cent and 10 per cent of the market. United Brands owned its own fleet and was able to control the volume of other imports. The rest of the market was also highly fragmented. There was reasonably healthy competition in the relevant market but not enough to prevent United Brands being able to act independently of its competitors.

In any case the ECJ has suggested in *Hoffmann la Roche v Commission* (1979) that, while market share is clearly an important factor, it is not absolutely conclusive of dominance. Here, Hoffman La Roche was offering loyalty rebates to purchasers of their vitamins, an obvious enough disadvantage to its competitors. The company enjoyed a market share in the relevant product amounting to more than 80 per cent. Again, this is a fairly obvious position of dominance. Nevertheless, the ECJ identified that there are a number of factors that might be considered apart from market share alone.

These have included:

- Possession of **superior technological knowledge and sales network**. An example would be *Michelin NV Nederlandsche Baden-Industrie Michelin v Commission* (1983) where the tyre company not only possessed the advanced technology but also had the history of supplying such specialist products by contrast to its competitors.
- The **length of time** for which the undertaking has enjoyed its position of dominance. As the ECJ pointed out in *United Brands* (1978), the longer a firm has enjoyed dominance, the more difficult it is for recent competitors to compete in the market.
- **Control of production and distribution**. This was indeed a key feature of the *Hoffmann la Roche* (1979) case.
- **Conduct or performance**. The loyalty rebates in *Hoffmann La Roche* are again a clear example of a 'predatory' policy aimed at stifling competition.

16.3.6 The character of abuse

As has already been identified (see section 16.3.1) it is not the existence of a dominant position which is seen as harmful and therefore prohibited. There is no breach of Art 102 unless an undertaking can be said to have abused its dominant position.

There is in fact no definition of abuse in the Article. So it is once again the ECJ that has supplied the definition, this time in *Hoffmann la Roche v Commission* (1979):

JUDGMENT

'The concept of abuse is an objective concept relating to the behaviour of an undertaking which is such as to influence the structure of the market where, as a result of the very presence of the undertaking in question, the degree of competition is weakened, and which, through recourse to methods different from those which conditions normal competition in products or services on the basis of the transactions of commercial operators, has the effect of hindering the maintenance of the degree of competition still existing in the market or the growth of that competition …'.

In other words, it is behaviour by the undertaking in a dominant position which modifies the structure of the market in such a way that it reduces the level of competition or prevents the growth of competition in the particular market.

Although there is no definition in the Article, there are still several examples of abusive practices identified in it:

- Directly or indirectly imposing unfair purchase or selling prices or other unfair trading conditions, eg:
  - price reduction to kill competition. In *AKZO v Commission* (Case 62/86R) [1986] ECR 1503 a company with a dominant position in the benzole peroxide market cut its prices over a long period of time in order to put a small British competitor out of business
  - differential pricing for different states, as in United Brands (1978)
  - loyalty rebates, as in Hoffmann la Roche (1979).
- Limiting production, markets or technical development to the prejudice of consumers. In *Magill TV Guide and ITP v Commission* (Case C–241/91P) [1995] ECR I–743 a refusal by TV companies to supply information about television listings to a competing producer of a TV guide was an abuse.

- Applying dissimilar conditions to equivalent transactions with other trading parties, thereby placing them at a competitive disadvantage. In *British Leyland v Commission* (1986) different prices were charged for type-approval certificates for left-hand drive cars. There was no objective justification for this discrimination so it was an abuse.
- Making conclusion of contracts subject to supplementary obligations having no connection with the subject of such contracts – eg the 'tying arrangements' in *Tetra Pak International SA v Commission* (Case T–83/91) [1994] ECR II 755. Here, the firm had invented a process for filling cartons that would prolong the shelf life of the foodstuff to six months. It would only sell the machines for the process if customers also bought the cartons 'tetra paks' from its subsidiary company. This additional requirement in the contract was merely an abuse.

16.3.7 Affecting trade between Member States

As with Art 101, there must be an effect on trade within Member States. The effect must be one that is caused by the abuse.

In general the same conditions apply as those in Art 101. The abuse only has to have the potential to affect trade; it need not actually have affected trade. So the test is similar: the abuse of the dominant position is capable of affecting trade between Member States if it is capable of constituting a threat '… direct or indirect, actual or potential, on the pattern of trade…'.

It is generally not hard to show that trade could be affected. In *British Leyland plc v Commission* (1986) the Court stated that specific effects do not have to be shown. It is sufficient to show evidence that trade might be affected.

16.3.8 Exemptions

As has already been stated, unlike Art 101, there are no possible exemptions for breaches of Art 102. What is possible is that it may be shown in the case of some of the abuses above that they are in fact objectively justified. Whether the Court accepts such an argument depends obviously on the facts of the individual case. Many of the factors that have already been seen in section 16.3.4 may be taken into account.

ACTIVITY

Self-assessment questions

1. What is the basic prohibition under Art 102?
2. How is dominance determined under Art 102?
3. What definitions of 'dominance' do the case law provide?
4. What is the significance of the 'relevant product market'?
5. What is the significance of the actual market share under Art 102?
6. What types of activity amount to an abuse of a dominant position?
7. What is the significance of the *United Brands* case?
8. What is the usual relevant geographical market?

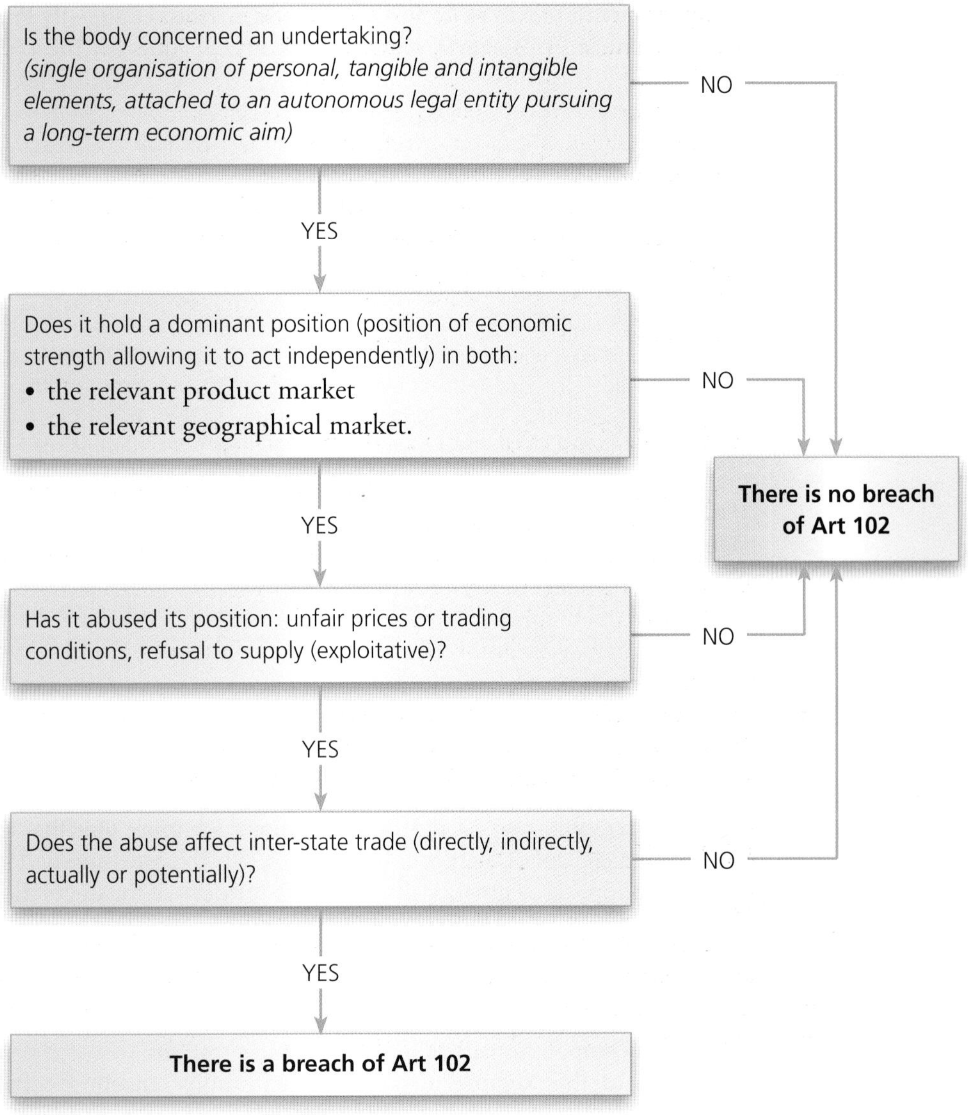

Figure 16.3.8 The means of establishing a breach of Art 102

16.4 Merger control

16.4.1 Merger control under Arts 101 and 102

EU competition law has also been used to control mergers, which in any case would concentrate economic power in fewer hands, and other concentrations of economic power. Both clearly require some form of control because the ultimate logical consequence of mergers and concentrations is to monopolies and by their very nature monopolies are anti-competitive.

Originally, prior to 1990, and the adoption of Regulation 4064/89, only standard competition law was available to deal with mergers and concentrations. The obvious means being an action under Art 102 for an abuse of a dominant position.

In this way it could be argued that Art 102 had been infringed if a dominant undertaking actually strengthened its dominance through a merger so that the only undertakings to remain in the relevant market were those whose behaviour actually depended on the dominant one. This surfaced in the *Continental Can* case (1973) and is identified by

Josephine Steiner in *Textbook on EC Law* (8th edn, Oxford University Press, 2003) p 453 as 'Perhaps the most surprising application of Article 82 [now Art 102 TFEU]'.

CASE EXAMPLE

Europemballage Corporation and Continental Can Co Inc v Commission (Case 6/72) [1973] ECR 215

Here, as we have seen, Continental Can had an 86 per cent share in a German company, Schmalbach, which itself held a dominant position. Continental Can then proposed a take-over of a Dutch Company, Thomassen (the merger or concentration) and that both companies should then be placed under the control of Continental Can's European subsidiary, Europemballage. The Commission issued a decision, identifying the transaction as a breach of Art 82 (now Art 102 TFEU). Continental Can argued that Art 82 (now Art 102 TFEU) was inapplicable because it applied only to activities that were detrimental to consumers and that also there was no abuse because it had not used its dominance to secure the takeover. The ECJ held that it could amount to a breach of Art 82 (now Art 102 TFEU) because a merger could be a way of eliminating competition, and anything affecting the structure of competition could be said to affect consumers. Nevertheless, as we have seen already, the Commission decision was annulled because it had failed to show the relevant product market. However, the application of Arts 101 and 102 to mergers or any other form of concentration was established by the Court.

16.4.2 Merger control under Regulation 4064/89

Inevitably, pressure grew on the EU institutions for more effective legislation for the more effective control of mergers. By the late 1980s this pressure had increased and the EU acted in adopting Regulation 4064/89. The purpose of the Regulation was to identify mergers that were of such a size that they should be controlled by the EU rather than by individual national authorities.

In this way the Regulation identified a broader definition than mere mergers and instead would be applied to '… significant changes in ownership over companies which could distort competition', in other words 'concentrations'.

According to the Regulation, any 'concentrations' meeting certain criteria must be 'notified' to the Commission within one week of the agreement being concluded, provided also that they have a Union dimension. To require notification to the Commission:

- the undertakings concerned must have a combined world turnover of at least 5,000 million euros and
- the total Union-wide turnover of at least two of the undertakings concerned must be in excess of 250 million euros. However, there will be no Union dimension and so no infringement where each of the parties does not derive two-thirds of its business in the EC within a single Member State.

An amendment to these basic requirements was added in Regulation 1310/97. This allowed that there could still be a Union dimension, and so the same controls could apply, where the requirements were not met but:

- the combined turnover of all of the undertakings worldwide is more than 2,500 million euros
- the combined turnover of the undertakings in at least three Member States is more than 100 million euros and
- the combined turnover of at least two of the undertakings in at least three Member States is more than 25 million euros and
- the combined turnover of at least two of the undertakings in the Union as a whole is more than 100 million euros.

Where a concentration falls outside of these two sets of requirements then it is subject to national rather than Union controls. Nevertheless, Member States may ask the Commission to intervene where the concentration would 'significantly impede' competition within its own territory.

16.4.3 Procedure

The test for the Commission is whether the concentration creates or enhances a dominant position that would lead to effective competition being substantially impeded.

Once the Commission has been notified of the concentration then it should take one of three decisions:

- it can decide that the concentration does indeed fall within the scope of the Regulation and that it gives rise to proceedings because it is potentially incompatible with the requirements of a Single Market or
- it can decide that the concentration falls within the scope of the Regulation but that there is no need for proceedings because it does not 'create or strengthen a dominant position as a result of which effective competition would be impeded in the common market or a substantial part of it' or
- it can decide that the concentration does not fall within the scope of the Regulation at all.

The Commission has a month in which to investigate and, if proceedings are initiated, then the Commission must reach a final decision within four months. The Commission can then declare the concentration compatible with the Regulation, or if it declares that it is not then it can be rescinded. The Commission can also fine undertakings which fail to notify a merger.

16.4.4 Reform of procedures on merger control

In 2003 the Commission published a proposal for a new regulation on mergers, reviewing the thresholds and the rules for notification. The underlying theme of the proposal was the same as for enforcement proceedings on Arts 101 and 102 generally, increased co-operation between the Member States.

The original proposal was not introduced immediately since a number of changes to it had to be accepted but the amended proposals have subsequently been introduced as Regulation 139/2004, the Merger Regulation. The Regulation in fact refers to 'concentrations' rather than 'mergers' despite the title given to it. As well as clearing up a lot of the bureaucracy it is also a recognition that national controls may be more effective than Union controls in allowing national industries to compete more effectively in the global market.

The Regulation defines concentrations as:

a) the merger of two or more previously independent undertakings or parts of undertakings or

b) the acquisition, by one or more persons already controlling at least one undertaking, or by one or more undertakings, whether by purchase of securities or assets or by any other means, of direct or indirect control of the whole or parts of one or more undertakings.

The 2004 Regulation allowed for a simplification of the notification proceedings. Where a concentration could be reviewed under national law but this would involve notification in at least three Member States then the Commission can be informed instead. Member States are informed of this and if there is no disagreement within 15 days then the concentration is deemed to have a Union dimension.

The Regulation has also introduced a case referral mechanism by which the case is referred to the most appropriate authority to deal with it. The characteristics of the case and the means of the authority to deal with it should both be considered. There is also a process for 'back referral' to the national authorities. A speedier appraisal system is also introduced, the overriding principle being based on 'compatibility with the common market'.

A simplified procedure has also been introduced for certain types of concentration that experience has shown are rarely in fact anti-competitive. A Commission Notice has identified types of concentration that should fall within this procedure:

- Where undertakings gain joint control of a joint venture that has either no or only negligible activities within the European Economic Area (EEA).
- Where none of the parties are engaged in business in the same product and geographic market (a horizontal relationship), or a product market that is related to that product (a vertical relationship).
- Where, even though the parties are engaged in a horizontal or vertical relationship in a product market and geographic market their combined share of the market is not more than 15 per cent (horizontal) or 25 per cent (vertical).
- Where a party gains total control over an undertaking of which it already has joint control.

16.5 Enforcement procedures and remedies in EU competition law

16.5.1 Introduction

The need for effective enforcement procedures was identified at a very early stage. Until very recently the powers and procedures for enforcement were found in Regulation 17/62. This was subsequently amended but in general the same mechanisms remained intact.

Inevitably, the enforcement procedures gave a great deal of power to the Commission. Inevitably too, it imposed a heavy burden on the Commission and enforcement of Arts 101 and 102 was a lengthy process and subject to lengthy delays. With enlargement looming, the EU felt the need to overhaul the procedures with a view to decentralising the system as far as possible and a Commission proposal was produced. This was then introduced in the main in Regulation 1/2003 which entered into force in May 2004.

Originally the Commission proposal suggested that exemption and notification should cease to be the responsibility of the Commission with national courts and competition authorities given the power to apply Art 101, including Art 101(3) and Art 102. Undertakings would need to take their own advice on whether their activities infringed competition law. The Commission would retain the right to intervene in competition cases being dealt with at a national level. The proposals did create some unrest, with the worry among businesses that national authorities would apply EU competition policy inconsistently.

The Regulation has decentralised enforcement proceedings, and the Commission has changed the focus of its attentions to the detection of serious cartels that are the major threat to competition policy. It has also adopted a 'leniency policy' by which immunity can be granted to undertakings that assist the Commission.

16.5.2 The Commission and enforcement of competition law

The powers of the Commission and Regulation 17/62

The Commission has always had wide powers to deal with actual as well potential infringements of competition law. It could deal with breaches in a variety of ways:

- It could give negative clearance to agreements where Art 101 could be an issue (not in fact an exemption but merely a means of finding out from the Commission whether or not the agreement in fact was in breach of Art 101).
- It could grant individual exemptions under Art 101(3).
- It could create block exemptions from Art 101.
- The Commission might pursue investigations and conclude that there were no grounds to impose a penalty on undertakings following this investigation, although it would usually try to reach an informal conclusion first, for example by the issuing of 'comfort letters'.

In any case, all new agreements were required to be notified to the Commission. This might then prevent the imposition of fines, but of course it would not prevent an agreement which was an infringement from being invalidated by the Commission.

Changes under Regulation 1/2003

Now, under Regulation 1/2003 it is no longer necessary to notify the Commission in order to obtain negative clearance or individual exemption. Article 1(1) of the Regulation instead places the burden on undertakings themselves to identify whether any of their agreements offends Art 101(1) but are exempt under Art 101(3).

This means that the Commission no longer has to examine individual agreements to see if they justify exemption. However, the Commission is still responsible for issuing block exemptions, and can of course investigate anti-competitive agreements on its own initiative or those complained about by parties affected by them. However, its main focus should be on investigating the large price-fixing cartels.

National authorities instead will have the power to demand that a breach is brought to an end, and to order interim measures and accept commitments from undertakings, or indeed to fine or order any other penalty within national law. The Commission can of course issue decisions which are binding on the parties where it does investigate.

The investigative powers of the Commission

Under Regulation 17/62 the Commission could always instigate an investigation either on its own initiative or on the application of a Member State or of any interested parties. The Commission could only then take action after an 'appropriate preliminary investigation' had taken place. If it decided to act it was obliged then to notify the applicants.

In pursuing its investigation the Commission was given extensive powers under the Regulation to obtain information either from the governments of Member States, or their relevant authorities, or indeed from firms. As a result, it had the right to examine books and other business records, take copies or extracts from any of these, request on-the-spot oral explanations, and to enter any premises or transport of an undertaking. Although in *Orkem v Commission* (Case 374/87) [1989] ECR 3283 the ECJ held that while the Commission was entitled to compel an undertaking to reveal all information of which it had knowledge it could nevertheless not compel it to incriminate itself by admitting to breaches of competition rules.

In brief, the Commission was entitled to undertake 'such investigations as are necessary' that would help to reveal a breach of either Art 101 or Art 102.

CASE EXAMPLE

Hoechst AG v Commission (Cases 46 and 227/87) [1989] ECR 2859

Here, the applicant challenged the legitimacy of a 'dawn raid' by the Commission, one that was unannounced and involved a search of his home and that he claimed deprived him of his right to a fair trial. The ECJ disagreed and held that it was for the Commission to decide on the necessity and character of the investigation.

Regulation 1/2003 has not significantly altered the investigative powers identified in Regulation 17/62. The Commission can ask undertakings to provide all relevant information either through a simple request or by a decision. There is also a power to impose fines for misleading information or failing to provide information within the declared time limit. It still has the power to enter undertakings, examine documents and take copies and conduct interviews, although written authorisation must be presented first. The Commission may also ask a national competition authority to conduct the investigation.

The available penalties

The Commission always had the power to impose financial penalties for breaches of Art 101 or Art 102. These were of two types:

- **fines**: ranging from 1,000 to 1 million euros or a larger amount not over 10 per cent of annual global turnover, whichever is the greater. The amount would actually depend on certain criteria:
  - the seriousness and duration of the infringement
  - the economic importance of the undertakings and their market share
  - whether the breaches were deliberate or not
  - whether the undertakings had previously breached competition rules
  - whether the breach involved underhanded behaviour.

  These were later subject to the 1998 Notice on the method of setting fines
- **periodic payments or incentive-led penalties**. The penalty was a specific sum for every day or week that the breach continued and so was an incentive to stop quickly.

Regulation 1/2003 has made only minor changes:

- the Commission must first take advice from a newly constituted Advisory Committee on Restrictive Practices and Dominant Positions
- the fine must not exceed 10 per cent of the undertaking's previous year's turnover
- the Regulation includes an express power for the Commission to grant interim measures.

Review by the General Court

Regulation 17/62 provided that all Commission decisions were reviewable by the court. The method of such review would take the form of either Art 263 or Art 265 actions. So, in effect it is a form of judicial review.

16.5.3 Enforcement of competition law by national authorities

Enforcement of competition law would never have been possible without the assistance of the national authorities in the Member States. As a result, they could be involved in various ways:

- national authorities could initiate an investigation into an anti-competitive practice by making an application to the Commission
- under Art 13 of Regulation 17/62 national authorities could conduct their own investigations, and could also do so at the request of the Commission
- besides this, in any case the national courts could also apply Arts 101 and 102 as well as their own competition rules. However, this was not possible where the Commission was already involved. National courts have this power because Arts 101 and 102 are both directly effective (*BRT v Sabam* (Case 127/73) [1974] ECR 51). Traditionally, only the Commission could issue exemptions, not the national courts, but they can award damages for parties affected by infringements, and also grant injunctive relief.

KEY FACTS

The basis of EU competition law	
States that the EU must ensure that '… competition in the internal market is not distorted'. Three principal objectives of competition rules: • to avoid possibility of restrictive practices and agreements • to prevent large businesses from abusing their economic dominance in the market • to ensure, within certain limits, that the public sector follows same rules. Aim is not to stop good business practice but unfair practice. Rules can be used against firms even if no registered office in EU if their actions could affect trade in the EU. So competition law has three main objectives which may appear at times to be incompatible: • efficiency • protection of both consumers and small businesses • the creation of the Single Market.	Article 3(g)

Article 101 and restrictive practices	
Basic Art 101 prohibition: • Rule prohibits 'agreements between undertakings, decisions of associations of undertakings and concerted practices which may affect trade between member states having as object prevention, restriction or distortion of competition within EU'.	
• Undertakings defined by ECJ as – single organisation of personal, tangible and intangible elements, attached to an autonomous legal entity and pursuing a long-term economic aim.	*Mannesmann v High Authority* (1962)
Commission can grant exemption. **Elements for proving breach of Art 101:** Agreements between undertakings, decisions by associations of undertakings, concerted practices:	
• must involve collusive behaviour • decisions by undertakings are usually by trade associations on, eg fixing discounts, collective boycotts, restrictive contract clauses	*AEG Telefunken v Commission* (1983)
• concerted practices are – a form of co-ordination between enterprises that has not yet reached the point where it is a contract	*ICI v Commission (Dyestuffs case)* (1972)
• Art 101 identifies some prohibited arrangements, eg • price fixing	*VBVB and VVVB v Commission* (1984)
• limiting production • sharing markets or suppliers	*Quinine Cartel case* (1970)
• applying dissimilar conditions to equivalent transactions affecting trade between Member States:	*IAZ International Belgium v Commission* (1983)
• tested by reference to free movement and attainment of Single Market	*Belasco v Commission* (1989)

• must be capable of constituting a threat, direct or indirect, actual or potential, on the pattern of trade • no need to prove harm; just that agreement may prevent, restrict or distort competition sufficiently	*Vereeniging van Cementhandelaren v Commission* (1972)
object or effect of preventing, restricting or distorting competition: • as much to do with practical outcomes as intentions • key issue is whether or not competition is affected	*Consten and Grundig v Commission* (1963)
• ECJ try to apply the rules so as not to stifle enterprise and initiative. **Activities beyond scope of Art 101:** *De minimis* rule: • and Commission Notice on Agreements of Minor Importance. Commercial agents and subsidiaries. Exemption if:	*Société Technique Minière v Maschinenbau Ulm* (1966)
• contributes to improving production or distribution of goods or promoting technical or economic progress	*Transocean Marine Paint Association* (1975)
• consumer gets fair share of benefit	*ACEC v Berliet* (1968)
• no unnecessary restrictions • no risk of eliminating competition Exemptions can be individual or block.	*Consten and Grundig v Commission* (1963)
Article 102 and abuse of a dominant position	
The basic prohibition: Article 102 involves the concentration of economic power in an undertaking Any abuse of commercial dominance is prohibited if it would affect trade between Member States	
Article 102 can also apply to oligopolies	*The Flat Glass case* (1989)
Negative clearance and exemptions are not available Three requirements: • dominant position in market • abuse of dominant position • affects trade between Member States. **Existence of dominance:** • 'Dominance' defined in ECSC Treaty – undertaking holds position shielding it against effective competition	
• ECJ has also defined dominance – power to control production or distribution for a significant part of the products in question	*Continental Can Co v Commission* (1973)

• And a position of economic strength … which enables it to prevent competition being maintained
• Need to consider
  • relevant market
  • market share
	United Brands (1978)

• Relevant product market decided on whether there is sufficient inter-changeability between all products forming part of same market	*Hoffmann la Roche v Commission* (1979)
• So could be, eg separate cartons for pasteurised and UHT milk	*Tetra Pak (No 1)* (1990)
• Geographical market should be whole EU – but can take into account other factors, eg costs and feasibility of transport	*Hilti v Commission* (1979) and (1989)

• Temporal market may involve, eg seasonal; factors	*United Brands* (1978)
• No particular share needed for dominance – eg 40 per cent sufficient	*United Brands* (1978)
• Should consider, eg	
• market share	*Hoffmann la Roche* (1979)
• competitor's share.	*United Brands* (1978)
The abuse:	
• Defined in case law – behaviour which influences structure of market so that competition is weakened, and maintenance or growth of competition is hindered	
• So could include, eg	
• differential pricing for different Member States	*United Brands* (1978)
• 'tying arrangements'	*Tetra Pak II* (1991)
• dissimilar conditions	
• limiting markets, technical development, production.	*Magill TV Guide and ITP v Commission* (1995)
Affecting inter-state trade:	
• must result from the abuse.	

SAMPLE ESSAY QUESTION

'Discuss the ways in which EU competition law actually support the freedoms of the single market.'

Explain the basic prohibitions in Arts 101 and 102:

- against collusive anti-competitive behaviour under Art 101
- against abuses of dominant positions under Art 102.

Explain that in both cases the bodies concerned must be 'undertakings'.

Explain the essential elements of Art 101:

- an agreement between undertakings or a decision of an association of undertakings or a concerted practice
- with the object or effect of restricting, preventing or distorting trade
- which affects trade between MSs 'directly, indirectly, actually or potentially'.

Discuss the type of behaviour that is regulated:

- price fixing, limiting production-sharing markets or supply applying dissimilar conditions; imposing supplementary obligations
- note that the prohibition does not apply in the case of minor agreements, or where there is an exemption.

Explain the essential elements of Art 102:

- the existence of a dominant position – measured against relevant product market, geographical market, temporal market if relevant, and market share
- abuse of that dominance by, eg predatory pricing, differential pricing, tying arrangements, applying dissimilar conditions, imposing supplementary obligations
- affects intra-Union trade directly, indirectly, actually or potentially.

Discuss the effects of Art 102:

- there is no problem with dominance
- it is the abuse of power that is prohibited
- relevant product market can cause debate – so cross elasticity of supply is important
- market share is only one factor.

SUMMARY

- EU competition law is not inconsistent with the freedoms of the Single Market.
- It is not about preventing competition but about preventing unfair competition.
- So it prohibits collusive behaviour and abusive behaviour by large powerful enterprises.
- The basic prohibition under Art 101 concerns agreements between undertakings, decisions of associations of undertakings and concerted practices which may affect trade between member states and have as their object the prevention, restriction or distortion of competition within common market.
- The basic prohibition under Art 102 concerns any abuse by one or more undertakings of a dominant position within the Internal Market or in a substantial part of it insofar as it may affect trade between Member States.
- There are also controls on monopolies and mergers.

Further reading

Books

Furse, M, *Competition Law of the EC and UK* (4th edn, Oxford University Press, 2004).
Rodger, B J and MacCulloch, A, *Competition Law and Policy in the EC and UK* (3rd edn, Cavendish Publishing, 2004), p 399.
Steiner, J, *Textbook on EC Law* (8th edn, Oxford University Press, 2003), Chapters 19–22.
Ward, I, *A Critical Introduction to European Law* (Butterworths, 2003), pp 126–137.

17

Social policy

AIMS AND OBJECTIVES

After reading this chapter you should be able to:

- Understand EU social policy law, in particular the law relating to the protection of workers' health and safety, the protection of pregnant workers and the protection of young workers
- Understand the law relating to working time
- Analyse critically the law relating to social policy in the EU

17.1 Introduction

EU social policy law is designed to protect potentially vulnerable workers through a variety of measures:

- safety and health of workers at work: Directive 89/391
- safety and health at work of pregnant workers: Directive 92/85
- protection of young workers: Directive 94/33
- parental leave: Directive 96/34
- protection for part-time workers: Directive 97/81
- protection for fixed-term workers: Directive 1999/70
- working time: Directive 2003/88 (replacing Directive 93/104).

These measures have dual social and economic aims. They have a **social** aim in that they clearly aim to protect vulnerable workers (those who are most at risk of exploitation – the young; part-time workers). But they also have an **economic** aim in that they are designed to co-ordinate employment policy across the EU. This means that companies in countries run by socialist, Left-leaning governments which would tend to have better worker-protection legislation are not placed at too much of a competitive disadvantage *vis-à-vis* companies in countries run by free-market, Right-leaning governments who would tend to try to maximise the operating freedom of companies. Without such co-ordination, employers might be drawn to setting up their businesses in countries run by Right-leaning governments because of reduced administrative burdens and operating costs (usually referred to pejoratively as 'red tape').

You will note that all of the EU legislation in this area is in the form of Directives, not Regulations. This is not coincidental. Directives allow Member States scope for manoeuvre, to lay down national rules within EU-wide parameters. Regulations, on the other hand, lay down specific EU-wide rules that have to be followed by all Member States. The use of Directives allows for some (but not too much) divergence between different Member States and indeed allows for divergence over time within the same Member

State. To take one example: the maximum average working week, which is set out in Directive 2003/88, the Working Time Directive (WTD), at 48 hours. It must be stressed that this figure is a maximum: Member States are entirely free to set a different figure as long as it does not exceed 48 hours. When this period was established in Directive 93/104, the original WTD, back in 1993, France had a socialist (Left-leaning) government. Consequently, the original implementing legislation opted for a figure far less than the maximum, at 35 hours. However, since then, the political climate in France has shifted to the Right. In 2005, it was reported that France's Right-leaning government had tabled legislation to raise the 35-hour limit in order to help French businesses to become more competitive.

Bearing these dual social and economic aims in mind, the rest of this chapter provides an overview of the main social policy legislation introduced by the EU over the last 20 years.

17.2 Safety and health of workers at work: Directive 89/391

This is a 'framework' Directive which lays down general principles on health and safety of workers (Art 1). It applies to 'all sectors of activity, both public and private (industrial, agricultural, commercial, administrative, service, educational, cultural, leisure, etc.)' (Art 2(1)). Article 2 adds that 'the safety and health of workers must be ensured as far as possible in the light of the objectives of this Directive'. The bulk of the Directive is taken up with imposing obligations on employers to take steps to prevent risks to the safety and health of workers and to provide information and training.

17.3 Safety and health at work of pregnant workers: Directive 92/85

Directive 92/85, widely known as the Pregnant Workers' Directive (PWD), requires Member States to:

- introduce measures to encourage improvements in the safety and health at work of pregnant workers and workers who have recently given birth and are breastfeeding and
- give special protection to women, by prohibiting dismissal during the period from the beginning of their pregnancy to the end of their maternity leave, save in exceptional circumstances unconnected with their condition.

This is legislation which clearly satisfies the dual social/economic aims identified above – the protection of vulnerable workers (pregnant women) combined with the establishment of a level legal playing field for all employers across the EU when faced with pregnant employees. In *Larsson v Føtex Supermarked* (Case C–400/95) [1997] ECR I–2757, the ECJ noted that the PWD had been introduced in view of the 'harmful effects' that the risk of dismissal may have on the 'physical and mental state of women who are pregnant, have recently given birth or are breastfeeding, including the particularly serious risk that pregnant women may be prompted voluntarily to terminate their pregnancy'.

17.3.1 Personal scope

Article 2 of the PWD applies to 'pregnant workers', 'workers who have recently given birth' and 'workers who are breastfeeding'. In each case the woman concerned is required to have informed her employer of 'her condition'.

The meaning of the phrase 'pregnant worker' was examined in *Mayr v Flöckner* (Case C–506/06) [2008] ECR I-1017. The case involved a woman who was undergoing *in vitro* fertilisation but whose fertilised eggs had yet to be implanted in her womb. The Court stated that:

JUDGMENT

'It is clear ... that it is the earliest possible date in a pregnancy which must be chosen to ensure the safety and protection of pregnant workers. However, even allowing, in regard to in vitro fertilisation, that the date is that of the transfer of the fertilised ova into the woman's uterus, it cannot be accepted, for reasons connected with the principle of legal certainty, that the protection [against dismissal] established by Article 10 of Directive 92/85 may be extended to a worker when, on the date she was given notice of her dismissal, the in vitro *fertilised ova had not yet been transferred into her uterus.'*

By 'reasons connected with the principle of legal certainty', the ECJ meant the medical possibility that fertilised ova could be kept *in vitro* for several years, raising the possibility that a judgment in Ms Mayr's favour would protect women in that position from dismissal during that extended period of time.

17.3.2 Material scope

Exposure to risks

Under Art 4, an obligation is imposed on employers to 'assess any risks to the safety or health and any possible effect on the pregnancies or breastfeeding' of workers within Art 2 posed by having to undertake 'activities liable to involve a specific risk of exposure to the agents, processes or working conditions' listed (non-exhaustively) in the Directive itself, and then 'decide what measures should be taken'. The list includes the following:

1. 'Physical agents', in particular (a) shocks, vibration or movement; (b) handling of loads entailing risks; (c) noise; (d) ionising radiation; (e) non-ionising radiation; (f) extremes of cold or heat; (g) movements and postures, travelling, mental and physical fatigue and other physical burdens.
2. 'Biological agents'.
3. 'Chemical agents' including mercury and carbon monoxide.

Note that the Directive does **not** prohibit pregnant workers from carrying out such activities. Under Art 6, however, 'pregnant workers' and 'workers who are breastfeeding' are prohibited from certain activities and are also protected from exposure to various 'agents' listed in the Directive itself. In both cases, the workers may 'under no circumstances be obliged' to perform 'underground mining work', and are protected from exposure to 'chemical agents', specifically 'lead and lead derivatives in so far as these agents are capable of being absorbed by the human organism'. 'Pregnant workers' are further protected from any obligation to work 'in hyperbaric atmosphere, for example pressurized enclosures' and 'underwater diving'. They are also protected from exposure to two 'biological agents', namely toxoplasma and the rubella virus, 'unless the pregnant workers are proved to be adequately protected against such agents by the human organism'.

All of these specific protections are stated to be in addition to the general protections available to all workers under Directive 89/391.

'Night work'

Under Art 7, Member States are required to ensure that all workers listed in Art 2 'are not obliged to perform night work during their pregnancy and for a period following childbirth'. Where this happens, Member States must adopt measures which 'entail the possibility of (a) transfer to daytime work or (b) leave from work or extension of maternity leave where such a transfer is not technically and/or objectively feasible or cannot reasonably be required on duly substantiated grounds'.

'Maternity leave'

Under Art 8(1), pregnant workers are entitled to 'a continuous period of maternity leave of at least 14 weeks allocated before and/or after confinement'. Under Art 8(2), this must include 'compulsory maternity leave of at least two weeks allocated before and/or after confinement'.

The significance of Art 8 was emphasised in *Kiiski* (Case C–116/06) [2007] ECR I-7643, where the ECJ stated that:

JUDGMENT

> 'Pregnancy follows its own inevitable course … It is precisely that inevitable course which the Union legislature took into account when making available to pregnant workers a special right, that is to say a right to maternity leave, which is intended, first, to protect a woman's biological condition during and after pregnancy and, second, to protect the special relationship between a woman and her child over the period which follows pregnancy and childbirth, by preventing that relationship from being disturbed by the multiple burdens which would result from the simultaneous pursuit of employment … The right to maternity leave granted to pregnant workers must be regarded as a particularly important mechanism of protection under employment law.'

Time off for ante-natal examinations

Article 9 guarantees that pregnant workers are entitled to 'time off, without loss of pay, in order to attend ante-natal examinations, if such examinations have to take place during working hours'.

Prohibition of dismissal

Article 10 prohibits the dismissal of pregnant workers and workers on maternity leave.

ARTICLE

> 'Art 10 Member States shall take the measures necessary to prohibit the dismissal of workers, within the meaning of Article 2, during the period from the beginning of their pregnancy to the end of the maternity leave … save in exceptional cases not connected with their condition which are permitted under national legislation and/or practice and, where applicable, provided that the competent authority has given its consent'.

Article 10 has been examined by the ECJ, firstly in *Jiminez Melgar* (Case C–438/99) [2001] ECR I–6915. The Court held that the prohibition on dismissal was directly effective, but the Court also held that the word 'dismissal' did **not** include an employer's failure to renew a short-term contract which had expired under the terms of the contract itself.

Article 10 was again examined in *Paquay* (Case C–460/06) [2007] ECR I-8511. Here the ECJ was asked whether the prohibition of the 'dismissal' of pregnant women covered the *notification of a decision* to dismiss. The Court held that it did, on the ground that a contrary interpretation would deprive Art 10 of its 'effectiveness' and 'could give rise to a risk that employers [could] circumvent the prohibition to the detriment of the rights of pregnant women'. Moreover, the Court held, even the *taking of a decision* to dismiss as well as *taking steps to prepare for* the dismissal, such as searching for and finding a permanent replacement, amounted to conduct caught by Art 10. The only exception would be where the defendant employer was able to prove – to the satisfaction of the national court – that the dismissal (including the decision to dismiss, etc) was totally unconnected to the employee's pregnancy.

When you read Chapter 18 you will find a number of cases which deal with the legality of an employer's decision to dismiss a pregnant worker, either simply because she was pregnant (*Webb v EMO Air Cargo* (Case C–32/93) [1994] QB 718), or because she developed some form of pregnancy-related illness (*Brown v Rentokil Ltd* (Case C–394/96)

[1998] ECR I–4185). These cases were dealt with under the Equal Treatment Directive 76/207 (ETD) because the facts occurred prior to the date of the PWD coming into force (1994). Such cases would now be dealt with under the PWD. The situation in *Hertz v Aldi Marked* (Case 179/88) [1990] ECR I–3979, which deals with the situation when an employer dismisses an employee because of a pregnancy-related illness manifesting itself after the end of her maternity leave, was held to fall outside the scope of the ETD and it would appear to fall outside the scope of the PWD as well.

Employment rights

Article 11 deals with the employment rights of pregnant workers and workers on maternity leave. In particular, Art 11(2) requires that, in the case of workers on maternity leave, the following 'must be ensured': (a) 'the rights connected with the employment contract' of workers within the meaning of Art 2; (b) 'maintenance of a payment to and/or entitlement to an adequate allowance for' workers within the meaning of Art 2.

To a large extent, Art 11(2) has been rendered superfluous by case law developments concerning other provisions of EU legislation. In *Gillespie v Northern Health and Social Services Board* (Case C–342/93) [1996] ECR I–475 and *Boyle v EOC* (Case C–411/96) [1998] ECR I–6401 the ECJ applied Art 157 TFEU (which guarantees equal pay for equal work) to maternity benefits. In *Thibault* (Case C–136/95) [1998] ECR I–2011 the ECJ dealt with the application of the ETD to conditions of employment of pregnant workers. All of these issues are explored in detail in the next chapter of this book.

Notwithstanding the overlap between the PWD and other legislation, the ECJ has handed down some interesting judgments on Art 11(2) itself. In *Kiiski* (2007), the Court was asked to give an interpretation of Art 11(2)(a), in a case involving a pregnant woman who had requested that her employer modify the terms of her pre-arranged child-care leave. After her employer refused, she brought a case and the ECJ upheld her challenge. The Court pointed out that the PWD 'does not exclude from its scope the situation of workers who already enjoy leave such as child-care leave'. The Court held that pregnancy was 'essentially unforeseeable' and hence comparable to events such as serious illness or death. These were all events which meant 'fundamental changes to family life and to relationships ... characterised by the loss of or a substantial diminution in the availability of one of the members of that family, or by the loss of or substantial diminution in the genuine ability of the parent concerned to bring up the child or for it to be brought up. Those events therefore prevent the child from being cared for under the conditions of child-care foreseen at the time when child-care leave was requested'.

In *Lewen v Denda* (Case C–333/97) [1999] ECR I–7243, the Court held that the word 'payment' in Art 11(2)(b) was 'intended to ensure that, during maternity leave, female workers receive an income ... irrespective of whether it is paid in the form of an allowance, pay or a combination of the two'. The case itself involved a disputed Christmas bonus, which the Court held could not be regarded as 'intended to ensure such a level of income' and hence could not be regarded as falling within the concept of 'payment'.

17.4 Protection of young workers: Directive 94/33

This Directive also satisfies the dual social/economic aims of protecting vulnerable workers (this time young workers) while simultaneously providing for a level playing field on which all employers operate.

17.4.1 Work by children

The Directive establishes a general – but not absolute – prohibition on work by 'children' (Art 1(1) and Art 4(1)), defined as persons of less than 15 years of age or who are 'subject to compulsory full-time schooling under national law'. However, Art 5 provides that children may be employed 'for the purposes of performance in cultural, artistic, sports or advertising activities', provided that prior authorisation is given by the 'competent authority' (Art 5(1)) and provided that the activities are not likely to be harmful to the 'safety, health or development of children' and are not such as to be 'harmful to their attendance at school' (Art 5(2)); or if authorised by legislation (Art 5(2)). If Art 5 had not been included in the Directive then it would, for example, have been illegal to recruit the young British cast to play the Hogwarts pupils in the *Harry Potter* film series, most of whom were aged 11 when the first film was released in 2001.

Furthermore, children of at least 14 years of age may perform 'light work', defined as all work not likely to be harmful to their 'safety, health or development' nor such as to be 'harmful to their attendance at school'. Children aged at least 13 may also perform 'light work' for a 'limited number of hours per week' (Art 4(2)).

17.4.2 Work by adolescents

Article 1(2) provides that Member States must 'strictly regulate' all work by 'adolescents'. That term is defined as including any person of at least 15 but less than 18 years of age and who is no longer subject to compulsory full-time schooling under national law.

17.4.3 Work by young people

Article 1(3) provides that 'young people' should have working conditions which 'suit their age' and should be 'protected against economic exploitation and against any work likely to harm their safety, health or physical, mental, moral or social development or to jeopardize their education'. 'Young people' are defined as any persons under 18 years of age. These principles are elaborated upon in Art 7, which provides that Member States must ensure that young people are 'protected from any specific risks to their safety, health and development which are a consequence of their lack of experience, of absence of awareness of existing or potential risks or of the fact that young people have not yet fully matured' (Art 7(1)). A list of prohibited activities is then provided in Art 7(2):

a) work which is objectively beyond their physical or psychological capacity
b) work involving harmful exposure to agents which are toxic, carcinogenic, cause heritable genetic damage or harm to the unborn child or which in any other way chronically affect human health
c) work involving harmful exposure to radiation
d) work involving the risk of accidents which it may be assumed cannot be recognised or avoided by young persons because of their insufficient attention to safety or lack of experience or training
e) work in which there is a risk to health from extreme cold or heat, or from noise or vibration.

17.4.4 Derogations

There are general derogations from the scope of the Directive for 'domestic service in a private household' and for 'work regarded as not being harmful, damaging or dangerous to young people in a family undertaking' (Art 2(2)).

17.4.5 Working time and night work

Article 8 sets out detailed limits on the working time of young people, with an absolute maximum of seven hours per day and 35 hours per week for children (those under 15) and eight hours per day and 40 hours per week for adolescents (those aged 15 or over but not yet 18). Article 10 sets out detailed rules on rest periods, which includes a daily rest period of 14 consecutive hours for children and 12 consecutive hours for adolescents, and a weekly rest period of two days (although this may be reduced 'where justified by technical or organization reasons' but may not be less than 36 consecutive hours). Article 11 also establishes an annual rest period, although it is not subject to any minimum duration. Article 12 also ensures a break of 'at least 30 minutes, which shall be consecutive if possible' where daily working time is more than four and a half hours. Article 12 applies to all young people (children and adolescents).

Article 9 prohibits all work by children between 8 pm and 6 am. With adolescents, Member States have a choice: they may prohibit all work between 10 pm and 6 am or between 11 pm and 7 am. Those restrictions on adolescents working may be relaxed by legislation, although there is an overriding and absolute prohibition on night work between midnight and 4 am.

17.5 Parental leave: Directive 96/34

Directive 96/34, the Parental Leave Directive (PLD), implements the Framework Agreement on Parental Leave concluded between various 'cross-industry organisations' in December 1995. The key provision is cl 2(1) of the Framework Agreement, which provides that a working parent – mother or father – has 'an individual right to parental leave on the grounds of the birth or adoption of a child to enable them to take care of that child, for at least three months, until a given age up to eight years to be defined by Member States and/or management and labour'. The 'conditions of access and detailed rules for applying parental leave' are left to be defined by national law and/or collective agreement.

The scope of the PLD was examined by the ECJ in *Commission v Luxembourg* (Case C–519/03) [2005] ECR I–3067. The case involved a provision of Luxembourg legislation which stated that 'In the event of pregnancy or adoption of a child during parental leave giving entitlement respectively to maternity leave or adoption leave, the latter shall replace parental leave which comes to an end'. The Court agreed with the Commission that this was in breach of the PLD, holding that, as maternity leave and parental leave were designed to achieve different things, one could not simply substitute for the other. The Court stated that:

JUDGMENT

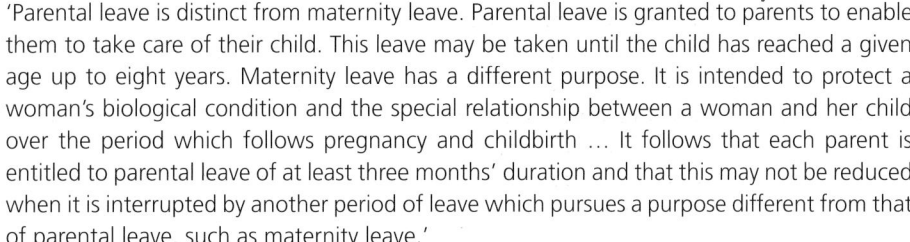

'Parental leave is distinct from maternity leave. Parental leave is granted to parents to enable them to take care of their child. This leave may be taken until the child has reached a given age up to eight years. Maternity leave has a different purpose. It is intended to protect a woman's biological condition and the special relationship between a woman and her child over the period which follows pregnancy and childbirth … It follows that each parent is entitled to parental leave of at least three months' duration and that this may not be reduced when it is interrupted by another period of leave which pursues a purpose different from that of parental leave, such as maternity leave.'

17.6 Protection for part-time workers: Directive 97/81

Directive 97/81 follows the model of the PLD. The Directive implements the Framework Agreement on Part-time Work concluded between various 'cross-industry organisations' in June 1997. The Agreement is designed to 'provide for the removal of discrimination against part-time workers and to improve the quality of part-time work' and to 'facilitate the development of part-time work on a voluntary basis and to contribute to the flexible organisation of working time in a manner which takes into account the needs of employers and workers' (cl 1).

Under cl 2(1) of the Agreement, it applies to 'part-time workers who have an employment contract or employment relationship' as defined by the national laws or collective agreements of practice in each Member State. Under cl 2(2), Member States are entitled to exclude 'part-time workers who work on a casual basis'. This point was addressed in *Wippel* (Case C–313/02) [2004] ECR I–9483, involving an employee of an Austrian company, whose contract of employment was based on a 'work on demand' principle. According to this principle, the employer offers work as and when it is required and the employee is free to accept or reject the offer, in the latter case without having to justify it. There were no fixed hours or fixed income. Eventually Ms Wippel was prompted to bring an action against her employer, and a question was raised as to her entitlement to rely, *inter alia*, on the Framework Agreement. The ECJ held that it was for national courts to determine as a matter of fact whether a particular worker was employed as a 'part-time worker' under cl 2(1) or a 'part-time worker on a casual basis' under cl 2(2).

The key provision is cl 4(1) of the Agreement, which provides that 'part-time workers shall not be treated in a less favourable manner than comparable full-time workers solely because they work part-time unless different treatment is justified on objective grounds'.

17.7 Protection for fixed-term workers: Directive 1999/70

Directive 1999/70 also follows the model of the PLD by incorporating the Framework Agreement on Fixed-term Contracts concluded between various 'cross-industry organisations' in March 1999. A 'fixed-term worker' is defined as 'a person having an employment contract or relationship entered into directly between an employer and a worker where the end of the employment contract or relationship is determined by objective conditions such as reaching a specific date, completing a specific task, or the occurrence of a specific event'. The Agreement on Fixed-term Workers is very similar to the Agreement on Part-time Workers, and again the key provision is cl 4(1), which states that 'fixed term workers shall not be treated in a less favourable manner than comparable permanent workers solely because they have a fixed-term contract or relation unless different treatment is justified on objective grounds'. In *Impact* (Case C-268/06) [2008] ECR I-2483, the ECJ held that cl 4(1) was sufficiently clear and precise to be capable of direct effect.

17.8 Working time: Directive 2003/88

Directive 2003/88, the Working Time Directive (WTD), is in fact the second such Directive. It replaces the original WTD, Directive 93/104. It is a lengthy piece of legislation and space here prevents anything other than an overview of its key provisions:

- **Daily rest (Art 3)** – all workers are entitled to a minimum daily rest period of 11 consecutive hours per 24-hour period.
- **Breaks (Art 4)** – all workers whose working day exceeds six hours are entitled to a rest break.
- **Weekly rest (Art 5)** – all workers are entitled to a minimum uninterrupted weekly rest period of 24 hours. This is in addition to the daily rest period in Art 3.
- **Maximum weekly working time (Art 6(2))** – for all workers, the average weekly working time (including overtime) must not exceed 48 hours. This allows for divergence between the Member States as to the actual maximum period. In the UK's implementing legislation (the Working Time Regulations 1998) the maximum is set at 48 hours, whereas in Austria it is 40 hours and in France it is only 35 hours. For the purposes of calculating the average, a reference period not exceeding four months applies (Art 16). The WTD does not prevent workers from working in excess of the maximum average working week if they agree to do so (Art 22(1)). The same provision states that no worker must be 'subjected to any detriment by his employer because he is not willing to give his agreement to perform such work'.
- **Annual leave (Art 7)** – all workers are entitled to at least four weeks' paid annual leave.
- **Night work (Art 8)** – 'normal hours' for night workers must not exceed eight hours.

17.8.1 Rest periods: Art 3

A question was raised in *Jaeger* (Case C–151/02) [2003] ECR I–8389 regarding the situation of 'on-call' doctors who spent all their 'on-call' time at the hospital itself. The case concerned a doctor in a German hospital who spent part of his working week 'on call'. During this 'on call' time, he was present at the hospital, but was only required to actually carry out his duties when, or indeed if, the need to do so arose. When he was not needed, he was entitled to sleep in a bed in a room in the hospital. Dr Jaeger argued that his entire period 'on call' should be counted towards his average weekly working hours; the defendant authorities argued that periods of inactivity during 'on call' duty should be regarded as 'rest' periods. The case was referred to the ECJ, which agreed with Dr Jaeger, applying the earlier judgment in *SIMAP* (Case C–303/98) [2000] ECR I–7963, considered below. The Court stated:

JUDGMENT

'The objective of [the WTD] is to secure effective protection of the safety and health of employees by allowing them to enjoy minimum periods of rest. That interpretation is all the more cogent in the case of doctors performing on-call duty in health centres, given that the periods during which their services are not required in order to cope with emergencies may, depending on the case, be of short duration and/or subject to frequent interruptions and where, moreover, it cannot be ruled out that the persons concerned may be prompted to intervene, apart from in emergencies, to monitor the condition of patients placed under their care or to perform tasks of an administrative nature.'

The ECJ also dealt with the issue of 'rest periods' in *Commission v UK* (Case C–484/04) [2006] ECR I–7471. The case arose after the UK's Department of Trade & Industry issued guidance on the interpretation of various aspects of the Working Time Regulations 1998, the British legislation implementing the original WTD. The guidance stated, among other things, that 'employers must make sure that workers can take their rest, but are not required to make sure they do take their rest'. The Commission alleged that this did not adequately implement the WTD, and the ECJ agreed. The Court held that, although employers could not 'force' their workers to take rest periods, the guidance nevertheless contravened the WTD, because it threatened to 'render the rights enshrined in Articles 3 and 5 of that directive meaningless'. The Court stated:

JUDGMENT

'Each worker must, inter alia, enjoy adequate rest periods, which must not only be effective in enabling the persons concerned to recover from the fatigue engendered by their work, but also preventive in nature, so as to reduce as much as possible the risk of affecting the safety or health of employees which successive periods of work without the necessary rest are likely to produce.'

17.8.2 Maximum weekly working time: Art 6(2)

An issue concerning the interpretation of Art 6(2) of the WTD arose in *SIMAP* (2000). Litigation between the Spanish public doctors' union (SIMAP) and the Health Ministry in the Valencia region of Spain raised a question regarding whether time spent at home by doctors who were on call counted towards their working time. The Court held that it did not, distinguishing the situation of being on call at the hospital (which did count) and being on call at home (which did not). The Court stated:

JUDGMENT

'The characteristic features of working time are present in the case of time spent on call by doctors where their presence at the health centre is required ... Moreover, even if the activity actually performed varies according to the circumstances, the fact that such doctors are obliged to be present and available at the workplace with a view to providing their professional services means that they are carrying out their duties in that instance ... The situation is different where doctors are on call by being contactable at all times without having to be at the health centre. Even if they are at the disposal of their employer, in that it must be possible to contact them, in that situation doctors may manage their time with fewer constraints and pursue their own interests.'

Article 6(2) was also examined in *Pfeiffer & Others* (Cases C–397 to 403/01) [2004] ECR I–8835, which concerned seven employees of the German Red Cross. The workers all challenged provisions of German legislation implementing the WTD, under which periods of inactivity spent by emergency workers between call-outs was **not** counted towards their average weekly working hours. This was the case even though emergency workers were regarded as being 'on duty' throughout the entire time, whether actually engaged in responding to an emergency or not. The Court held that the German legislation had not correctly implemented the WTD. The Court stated:

JUDGMENT

'The 48-hour upper limit on average weekly working time, including overtime, constitutes a rule of Union social law of particular importance from which every worker must benefit, since it is a minimum requirement necessary to ensure protection of his safety and health and therefore national legislation which authorises weekly working time in excess of 48 hours is not compatible with the requirements of Art 6(2) of the Directive.'

The principles set out in *SIMAP* and *Pfeiffer* have subsequently been applied in the cases of *Dellas & Others* (Case C–14/04) [2005] ECR I–10253 and *Vorel* (Case C–437/05) [2007] ECR I–331, both involving healthcare workers who spent part of their days 'on call'. The Court confirmed that, whenever an employee is required to be physically present at his or her place of employment, and available to do work, then that counted towards their weekly 'working time'. The fact that the employee might have 'some periods of inactivity' during this 'on call' time was 'completely irrelevant'. The ECJ stated, in *Dellas*, that the WTD 'does not provide for any intermediate category between working time and rest periods' and that 'the intensity of the work done by the employee and his output are not among the characteristic elements of the concept of "working time"'.

KEY FACTS

- Time spent 'on call' counts towards 'working time' if the worker is required to be physically present at their place of employment and available to do work. Whether the employee is active throughout this 'on call' time is irrelevant (*SIMAP*, *Pfeiffer*, *Dellas*, *Vorel*).
- Time spent 'on call' but at home does not count towards 'working time' (*Jaeger*).
- There is no intermediate category between 'working time' and 'rest periods' (*Dellas*).

17.8.3 Annual leave: Art 7

One of the first cases to reach the ECJ involving the WTD was *R (on the application of BECTU) v Secretary of State for Trade and Industry* (Case C–173/99) [2001] 1 WLR 2313. This case involved an allegation that the UK legislation implementing the Directive, the

Working Time Regulations 1998, failed to give proper effect to Art 7. Regulation 13(7) of the 1998 Regulations made acquisition of the entitlement to annual leave conditional upon the employee having been continuously employed for 13 weeks by the same employer. The ECJ held that there was nothing in the WTD which allowed Member States to incorporate this provision.

CASE EXAMPLE

R (on the application of BECTU) v Secretary of State for Trade and Industry (Case C–173/99) [2001] 1 WLR 2313

The British trade union BECTU (the Broadcasting, Entertainment, Cinematographic and Theatre Union) represents about 30,000 people in jobs such as sound recordists, cameramen, special effects technicians, projectionists, editors, researchers, hairdressers and make-up artistes. The Union complained that, because the majority of their members were employed under short-term contracts, they tended to work under a series of separate, short-term contracts, either with the same employer or with different employers. Hence, most of the Union's members failed to qualify under Regulation 13 of the Working Time Regulations 1998 and thus did not become entitled to any paid annual leave. The case was referred to the ECJ, which held that the Art 7 had not been properly implemented.

The Court stated:

JUDGMENT

'Legislation of a Member State which imposes a precondition for entitlement to paid annual leave which has the effect of preventing certain workers from any such entitlement not only negates an individual right expressly granted by [the WTD] but is also contrary to its objective. By applying such rules, [those] workers are deprived of any entitlement to paid annual leave … Minimum rest periods are essential for the protection of their health and safety … Furthermore, rules of the kind at issue in the main proceedings are liable to give rise to abuse because employers might be tempted to evade the obligation to grant the paid annual leave to which every worker is entitled by more frequent resort to short-term employment relationships.'

Article 7 was also considered in *Merino Gómez v Continental Industries* (Case C–342/01) [2004] ECR I–2605. The case raised a very interesting question regarding the relationship between annual leave (guaranteed by Art 7 of the WTD) and maternity leave (guaranteed by Art 8 of the PWD, considered above). The complainant worked for a company where all workers took their annual leave at the same time, during a 'factory shutdown' period. This shutdown period coincided with her maternity leave. The question, therefore, was whether she was entitled to take her annual leave at a different time of the year. The ECJ held that she was so entitled. The Court held that Art 7 'must be regarded as a particularly important principle of [Union] social law from which there can be no derogations'. It was designed to provide all workers with a 'rest', and therefore had an entirely different purpose to maternity leave guaranteed by Art 8 of the PWD, which was designed to 'protect women's biological condition during pregnancy and the special relationship that mothers have with their new-born children'. Hence, the requirements of Art 7 of the WTD were not met to the extent that they coincided with a period of maternity leave. Hence, a pregnant worker 'must be able to take her annual leave during a period other than the period of her maternity leave'. It was irrelevant that the maternity leave period coincided with an annual leave period fixed by collective agreement.

CASE EXAMPLE

Merino Gómez v Continental Industries (Case C–342/01) [2004] 2 CMLR 3

María Paz Merino Gómez worked at Continental Industrias del Caucho's tyre factory in Spain. Between May and August 2001, she was on maternity leave. She applied to have her four weeks' annual leave after the end of her maternity leave, in September 2001, but this was refused. Under a collective agreement between Continental and all employees, the latter agreed to take their annual leave in two four-week blocks, one in July and one in August. Every year, six workers were able to take their holiday in September, but priority was given to those who had not exercised this option the previous year. As María had taken her annual holiday in September 2000, she could not choose to do so in 2001. Nevertheless, she argued that the collective agreement was contrary to the WTD. The case was referred the case to the ECJ, which upheld María's claim.

'Rolled up' holiday pay

In *Robinson-Steele v RD Retail Services Ltd* (Case C–131/04); *Clarke & Others* (Case C–257/04) [2006] ECR I–2531, the ECJ was asked to examine the subject of 'rolled up' holiday pay and its compatibility with Art 7. 'Rolled up' holiday pay occurs when holiday pay is paid as part of an employee's normal wages, throughout the year, typically weekly or monthly, rather than paid when the worker is actually on holiday. All the cases involved men employed by companies in the UK. Under the terms of their employment contracts, they were not paid while on holiday; rather, part of their daily/weekly salary for work done throughout the year included a payment for holidays. The ECJ stated that these arrangements were in breach of Art 7 (emphasis added):

JUDGMENT

'The holiday pay required by Article 7(1) is intended to enable the worker *actually to take the leave to which he is entitled*. The term "paid annual leave" in that provision means that, for the duration of annual leave … remuneration must be maintained. In other words, workers must receive their normal remuneration for that period of rest … The directive treats entitlement to annual leave and to a payment on that account as being two aspects of a single right. The purpose of the requirement of payment for that leave is to put the worker, during such leave, in a position which is, as regards remuneration, comparable to periods of work. Accordingly … the point at which the payment for annual leave is made must be fixed in such a way that, during that leave, the worker is, as regards remuneration, put in a position comparable to periods of work.'

Alan Bogg ('The right to paid annual leave in the Court of Justice: the eclipse of functionalism' (2006) 31 EL Rev 892) has argued that 'rolled up' holiday pay has advantages for both employers and employees. Employers may gain in terms of administrative convenience, while employees could gain by 'boosting' their holiday pay through working overtime (at, say, one and a half times their normal hourly rate) and therefore 'securing a premium on the rolled up portion of pay'. However, Bogg acknowledges that there is a 'potentially darker side', in that some workers may not be careful or responsible enough to save their holiday pay throughout the year, so that when their annual leave period arrives they cannot afford to go on holiday. Given that the principles underpinning the WTD are those of workers' health and safety, and that the WTD aims to guarantee that workers get 'rest' (on a daily and weekly basis as well as an annual basis) it is not, therefore, surprising that the ECJ opted to outlaw 'rolled up' holiday pay.

Holiday leave may be carried over … but cannot be 'sold' back

In *Federatie Nederlandse Vakbeweging* (Case C–124/05) [2006] ECR I–3423, the ECJ ruled that some or all of the four-week annual leave guaranteed by Art 7 may be carried over to the next year. But it is still subject to the WTD, and cannot be subsequently 'sold' back to the employer. The case began when the Dutch Ministry of Social Affairs & Employment published an information brochure indicating that employees could, if they wished, save up their holidays for perhaps two years in order to 'undertake a world tour'. It also stated that workers could then 'sell' some of these saved-up days back to their employer for cash, should the need arise (for example for emergency property repairs). The Netherlands Federation of Trade Unions brought a challenge to this, and the ECJ upheld the challenge. The Court explained the reasons behind its decision as follows:

- The minimum annual holiday leave entitlement is intended to have a 'positive effect' on the safety and health of workers.
- Carrying holiday leave over to the next year still contributes to a worker's health and safety, provided it is actually taken, and is therefore compatible with the WTD.
- The possibility of an employee selling their annual holiday leave back to the employer was 'incompatible with the objectives' of the WTD, as it created an 'incentive' not to take leave.

Can a worker claim their annual leave and/or a payment in lieu while on sick leave?

In the joined cases *Schultz-Hoff* (Case C–350/06) and *Stringer & Others v HM Revenue & Customs* (Case C–520/06) [2009] ECR I-179, the ECJ was asked whether a worker on indefinite sick leave still accrued annual leave and/or a payment in lieu of annual leave (in the event that the employment relationship is terminated). The Court ruled as follows:

- Article 7 of the WTD did not preclude national legislation which prevented an employee taking annual leave whilst on sick leave.
- However, the right to take annual leave was accrued during sick leave and could be taken on the employee's return to work. Alternatively, if the employment relationship was terminated before then, the employee was entitled to a payment in lieu of annual leave.

This decision is consistent with that in *Merino Gómez*, discussed above. In that case, you will recall, the ECJ ruled that annual leave and maternity leave served different purposes; basically, a woman on maternity leave is not on 'holiday'. Hence, the fact that an employee had taken time off work on maternity leave did not prevent her from claiming her minimum annual holiday leave on her return to work. Similarly, *Schultz-Hoff and Stringer* decided that a worker off work on sick leave is not on 'holiday' either and is therefore perfectly entitled to take their annual leave once they regain their health and return to work. If they do not regain their health and their employment is terminated, then they are entitled to be compensated for the loss of that leave.

17.8.4 Night work: Art 8

Another issue raised in *SIMAP* (2000) was whether doctors who were regularly on call at night could be regarded as 'night workers'. The ECJ decided that they did not qualify. The WTD itself defines 'night workers' as those who spend at least three hours of their working day during night-time 'as a normal course'. The Court held that on call doctors could not be regarded as working during the night 'as a normal course'.

17.8.5 Derogations

The WTD is subject to numerous derogations. According to Art 17(1), Member States may derogate from their obligations under Arts 3, 4, 5, 6 and 8 when 'the duration of the working time is not measured and/or predetermined or can be determined by the workers themselves', and particularly in the case of:

a) managing executives or other persons with autonomous decision-taking powers
b) family workers
c) workers officiating at religious ceremonies in churches and religious communities.

Art 17(3) provides that Member States may derogate from their obligations in Arts 3, 4, 5 and 8 in several areas, of which the following is a non-exhaustive sample:

- the emergency services
- hospital staff, including doctors
- security guards
- dock and airport workers
- Press, radio, TV, cinematographic production, postal and telecommunication services
- utilities workers (gas, water, electricity production and transmission)
- refuse collection
- agriculture
- regular urban transport services.

Article 18 allows for derogation from Arts 3, 4, 5, and 8 'by means of collective agreements or agreements concluded between the two sides of industry at national or regional level'.

KEY FACTS

Social policy	
• EU social policy law is essentially designed to protect the health and safety at work of all workers in the EU	
• Specific protection is provided for the health and safety at work of pregnant workers. It guarantees pregnant workers a minimum period of maternity leave, and protects pregnant women from the threat of dismissal during their pregnancy and beyond	Directive 92/85
• In addition, young workers, part-time workers and fixed-term workers have specific protection under EU law	
• The Working Time Directive, originally introduced in 1993, is designed to protect workers from the risks associated with long working hours. It guarantees, amongst other things: • A minimum daily rest period of 11 consecutive hours per 24-hour period • A daily rest break for all workers whose working day exceeds six hours • A weekly rest break of at least 24 hours • An average maximum weekly working time of 48 hours (calculated over a four-month period) • At least 4 weeks' paid annual leave	Directive 2003/88
• According to the ECJ this period of annual leave must be in addition to any maternity leave to which the worker is entitled under Directive 92/85. This is because they pursue different objectives. Annual leave provides all workers with a 'rest', while maternity leave protects 'women's biological condition during pregnancy'	*Merino Gómez v Continental Industries* (2004) Directive 2003/88

SAMPLE ESSAY QUESTION

Critically consider the extent to which EU law protects pregnant workers.

Explain what is meant by a 'pregnant worker':

- Directive 92/85 protects 'pregnant workers' plus 'workers who have recently given birth' and 'workers who are breastfeeding'
- 'Pregnant workers' should be protected from the 'earliest possible date in a pregnancy' (*Mayr v Flöckner*)
- Note the position of women undergoing IVF treatment (*Mayr v Flöckner*).

Discuss the provisions of Directive 92/85:

- Employers' obligation to 'assess risks' (Art 4)
- Limitations on night work (Art 5)
- Minimum maternity leave guarantee (Art 8(1)). Explain the dual purpose of maternity leave (*Kiiski*)
- Paid time off for ante-natal examinations (Art 9)
- Protection from dismissal, from beginning of pregnancy to end of maternity leave (Art 10). Note the expansive interpretation of 'dismissal' in *Paquay* but contrast with the more restrictive interpretation in *Jiminez Melgar*
- Protection of contractual rights (Art 11)
- Entitlement to 'adequate' maternity benefits (Art 11).

Consider the application of other EU legislation:

- Although maternity benefits are 'pay' covered by Article 157 (1) TFEU, pregnant workers are not entitled to full pay (*Gillespie, McKenna, Alabaster*)
- Explain why: women on maternity leave are not in a 'comparable situation' with male workers. Note how this can work in women's favour (*Abdoulaye*)
- The refusal to employ a pregnant woman because of her pregnancy is direct sex discrimination contrary to Directive 2006/54 (*Dekker, Mahlburg*). Pregnant women need not inform prospective employers of their pregnancy (*Busch*)
- The dismissal of a pregnant woman because of pregnancy (*Hebermann-Beltermann*, *Webb*), or because of a pregnancy-related illness during maternity leave (*Brown*), or because she is at an 'advanced stage' of IVF treatment (*Mayr v Flöckner*) is direct sex discrimination prohibited by Directive 2006/54
- Employment conditions are protected (Directive 2006/54, Art 15; *Thibault, Sass, Sarkatzis Herrero*)
- Explain and consider the significance of pregnancy-based discrimination being 'direct'. Discuss arguments that it could/should be classed as 'indirect'
- Consider the position of a woman dismissed because of a pregnancy-related illness manifesting itself after the end of maternity (*Hertz*).

SUMMARY

- Directive 89/391 is a 'framework' Directive which lays down general principles on health and safety of workers
- Directive 92/85, widely known as the Pregnant Workers' Directive (PWD), is designed to improve the safety and health at work of pregnant workers. Pregnant workers are entitled to 'a continuous period of maternity leave of at least 14 weeks allocated before and/or after confinement' (Art 8). The dismissal of women from the beginning of pregnancy to the end of their maternity leave, save in exceptional circumstances unconnected with their condition, is prohibited (Art 10). Workers on maternity leave have their contractual rights protected and are also entitled to maternity benefits (Art 11).
- Young workers are protected by Directive 94/33. Children under 15 or in full-time education are prohibited from working, subject to certain exceptions, while children aged 15–17 must have working conditions which 'suit their age' and must be 'protected against economic exploitation and against any work likely to harm their safety, health or physical, mental, moral or social development or to jeopardize their education'.
- Directive 96/34, the Parental Leave Directive (PLD), implements the Framework Agreement on Parental Leave. This provides that a working parent – mother or father – has 'an individual right to parental leave on the grounds of the birth or adoption of a child to enable them to take care of that child, for at least three months'.
- Directive 97/81 implements the Framework Agreement on Part-time Work, which is designed to 'provide for the removal of discrimination against part-time workers' compared to full-time workers.
- Directive 1999/70 incorporates the Framework Agreement on Fixed-term Contracts, which is designed to ensure that fixed-term workers are not discriminated against in comparison to permanent workers.
- Directive 2003/88, the Working Time Directive (WTD), provides that all workers are entitled to: a minimum daily rest period of eleven consecutive hours per 24-hour period (Art 3); a daily rest break if the working day exceeds 6 hours (Art 4); a minimum uninterrupted weekly rest period of 24 hours (Art 5); an average weekly working time (including overtime) not exceeding 48 hours (Art 6(2)); at least four weeks' paid annual leave (Art 7). Night workers' 'normal hours' must not exceed eight hours (Art 8). Time spent 'on call' at the workplace by workers such as doctors counts as working time whereas time spent 'on call' but at home or elsewhere does not (*SIMAP, Jaeger, Pfeiffer, Dellas & Others, Vorel*). The annual leave entitlement contributes towards workers' health and safety. Although it can be carried over, it must actually be taken and cannot be 'sold' back to the employer (*Federatie Nederlandse Vakbeweging*).
- Annual leave (the WTD, Art 7) and maternity leave (the PWD, Art 8) serve entirely different purposes. A pregnant worker 'must be able to take her annual leave during a period other than the period of her maternity leave' (*Merino Gómez*). Similarly, annual leave and sick leave serve entirely different purposes, so that a worker on sick leave does not lose his entitlement to paid annual leave (*Schultz-Hoff; Stringer & Others*).

Further reading

Articles

Barnard, C, 'The Working Time Regulations 1998' (1999) 28 ILJ 61.

Barnard, C, Deakin, S and Hobbs, R, 'Opting out of the 48-Hour Week: Employer Necessity or Individual Choice?' (2003) 32 ILJ 223.

Bogg, A, 'Of Holidays, Work and Humanisation: A Missed Opportunity' (2009) 34 EL Rev 738.
Bond, A, 'The Young Persons Directive' (1995) 24 ILJ 377.
Jeffery, M, 'Not Really going to Work? Of the Directive on Part-time Work, Atypical Work and Attempts to Regulate it' (1998) 27 ILJ 193.
Kilpatrick, C, 'Has New Labour Reconfigured Employment Legislation?' (2003) 32 ILJ 135.
McColgan, A, 'Family Friendly Frolics? The Maternity and Parental Leave, etc, Regulations 1999' (2000) 29 ILJ 125.
Murray, J, 'Normalising Temporary Work' (1999) 28 ILJ 269.
Prechal, S, 'Equality of Treatment, Non-Discrimination and Social Policy' (2004) 41 CMLR 533.
Szyszczak, E, 'Future Directions in European Union Social Policy Law' (1995) 24 ILJ 19; 'The new Paradigm for Social Policy: A Virtuous Circle?' (2001) 38 CMLR 1125.

18

Discrimination law and Art 157

AIMS AND OBJECTIVES

After reading this chapter you should be able to:

- Understand the law relating to the prohibition of discrimination on grounds of sex, in particular Article 157 TFEU and Directive 2006/54
- Understand the law relating to the prohibition of discrimination on grounds of race, in particular Directive 2000/43
- Understand the law relating to the prohibition of discrimination on grounds of age, disability, religion or belief and sexual orientation, in particular Directive 2000/78
- Analyse critically the law relating to discrimination on grounds of age, disability, race, religion or belief, sexual orientation and sex
- Apply the law to factual situations involving discrimination on grounds of age, disability, race, religion or belief, sexual orientation or sex

18.1 Introduction

Article 157 TFEU established the fundamental principle of equality of treatment for men and women. It applies most obviously in employment cases, that is, in disputes between employers and employees. However, it is not limited to that situation and can be used, for example, by individuals to challenge (allegedly) discriminatory national legislation. The principle does not provide that all men and women should be treated alike no matter what the circumstances: a difference in treatment may be permitted so long as it is 'objectively justified'. Following the signing of the Treaty of Amsterdam in 1997, the equal treatment principle has expanded into different areas, and now includes equal treatment regardless of age, disability, race, religion or belief and sexual orientation.

The equality principle takes various forms. The key legislative provisions are:

- equal treatment on grounds of sex in terms of pay for equal work and for work of equal value: Art 157
- equal treatment on grounds of sex in other conditions of employment, including access to and termination of employment: Directive 2006/54
- equal treatment on grounds of sex in matters of social security: Directive 79/7
- equal treatment on grounds of sex for self-employed persons: Directive 86/613
- equal treatment on grounds of race or ethnic origin in employment and certain other areas: Directive 2000/43
- equal treatment on grounds of age, disability, religion or belief and sexual orientation in employment: Directive 2000/78

- equal treatment on grounds of sex in access to and supply of goods and services: Directive 2004/113.

According to the ECJ, the principle of equal treatment for men and women is 'one of the fundamental human rights whose observance the Court had a duty to ensure' (*Defrenne v SABENA* (Case 43/75) [1976] ECR 455).

18.2 'Discrimination'

Discrimination, whether in terms of pay under Art 157, or more generally under one of the various Directives, can be 'direct' or 'indirect'.

18.2.1 'Direct discrimination'

In *Kording* (Case C–100/95) [1997] ECR I–5289, the ECJ defined direct discrimination as 'the application of different rules to comparable situations or the application of the same rule to different situations'. Art 2(1)(a) of Directive 2006/54 (which deals with sex discrimination) defines 'direct discrimination' as occurring 'where one person is treated less favourably on grounds of sex than another is, has been or would be treated in a comparable situation'. Directives 2000/43 and 2000/78 provide similar definitions in the context of the other forms of discrimination. Direct discrimination can rarely be justified.

18.2.2 'Indirect discrimination'

Indirect discrimination may arise in many different ways. Art 2(1)(b) of Directive 2006/54 defines 'indirect discrimination' in the context of sex discrimination as occurring:

ARTICLE

> 'where an apparently neutral provision, criterion or practice would put persons of one sex at a particular disadvantage compared with persons of the other sex, unless that provision, criterion or practice is objectively justified by a legitimate aim, and the means of achieving that aim are appropriate and necessary.'

A typical situation of indirect sex discrimination is where an employer employs both full-time and part-time workers. The former group, comprised exclusively (or mostly) of men, is paid proportionately more than the latter, comprised exclusively (or mostly) of women. Leading cases in this regard are *Jenkins* (Case 96/80) [1981] ECR 911, *Bilka-Kaufhaus* (Case 170/84) [1986] ECR 1607, *Rinner-Kühn* (Case 171/88) [1989] ECR 2743, *Kowalska* (Case C–33/89) [1990] ECR I–2591, *Gerster* (Case C–1/95) [1997] ECR I–5253, *Kording* (Case C–100/95) [1997] ECR I–5289 and *Kachelmann* (Case C–322/98) [2000] ECR I–7505. All bar one of these cases arrived at the ECJ following requests for preliminary rulings from courts in Germany, where it is accepted that the majority of part-time work is carried out by women. Hence, any (direct) discrimination against part-time workers in Germany almost always amounts to (indirect) discrimination against women.

The fact that the adversely affected group contains men and women does not prevent a particular measure from being discriminatory. Otherwise, the fact that there was one man doing the same work as a large group of women would prevent the comparison. This 'might be wholly fortuitous or even, possibly, a situation contrived by an unscrupulous employer' (Nicholls LJ in the Court of Appeal in *Pickstone v Freemans plc* [1989] AC 66).

In *Seymour-Smith and Perez* (Case C–167/97) [1999] ECR I–623, the ECJ gave some helpful advice on when indirect discrimination is established. The applicants in the case,

Nicole Seymour-Smith and Laura Perez, complained that the two-year minimum service requirement (under English law) before which an employee qualified for rights to claim compensation in the event of unfair dismissal indirectly discriminated against women. The Court stated:

JUDGMENT

'In order to establish whether a measure adopted by a Member State has disparate effect as between men and women to such a degree as to amount to indirect discrimination for the purposes of [Art 157], the national court must verify whether the statistics available indicate that a **considerably smaller percentage** of women than men is able to fulfill the requirement imposed by that measure. If that is the case, there is indirect sex discrimination.'

Unlike direct discrimination, indirect discrimination can be justified on 'objective' grounds. This point will be examined below (see section 18.5).

18.2.3 Discrimination based on 'sex'

It is obvious that EU sex discrimination law deals with discrimination on grounds of gender. But does it cover other situations? There are at least two other types of discrimination which might be regarded as falling within the ambit of 'sex' discrimination law:

- discrimination against transsexuals
- discrimination against homosexuals.

However, the ECJ has held that only the former situation amounts to 'sex' discrimination. In *P v S* (Case C–13/94) [1996] ECR I–2143, the ECJ held that the dismissal of a post-operative male-to-female transsexual constituted discrimination based on 'sex'. The Court rejected the British Government's submission that the dismissal was not discriminatory on the ground that the employer would also have dismissed a post-operative female-to-male transsexual. The Court stated that the scope of EU sex discrimination law could not be confined simply to discrimination based on the fact that a person was of one or other sex. It also applied to discrimination arising, as in the present case, from gender re-assignment. Such discrimination was based, essentially if not exclusively, on the sex of the person. A transsexual dismissed because they intended to undergo, or had undergone, gender re-assignment was being treated unfavourably by comparison with persons of the sex to which he or she belonged prior to the re-assignment.

CASE EXAMPLE

P v S (Case C–13/94) [1996] ECR I–2143

In 1991, P, who was male, was employed at a college in Cornwall. In April 1992 he informed S, the Director of Studies in the college, that he intended to undergo 'gender re-assignment', comprising a period of dressing and behaving as a woman, to be followed by surgery to provide the physical attributes of a woman. By September 1992 he had had minor operations. He was then dismissed. He claimed that this was unlawful sexual discrimination, and the ECJ agreed.

More recently, in *KB v National Health Service Pensions Agency* (Case C–117/01) [2004] ECR I–541, the ECJ held that British legislation preventing post-operative transsexuals from marrying in their acquired gender **could** be regarded as a breach of EU 'sex' discrimination law. For a further example of this form of 'sex' discrimination, see the case of *Richards* (Case C-423/04) [2006] ECR I-3585, considered in section 18.8.3 below.

Although the ruling in *P v S* (1996) suggested that the ECJ was prepared to interpret widely the concept of discrimination based on 'sex', when the issue of discrimination against homosexuals came before the Court in *Grant v South West Trains Ltd* (Case C–249/96) [1998] ECR I–621, the ECJ held that EU sex discrimination law did not cover sexual orientation discrimination.

However, sexual orientation discrimination has now been brought under the umbrella of EU discrimination law with the introduction of Directive 2000/78, which will be examined below.

18.2.4 Harassment

'Harassment' on any of the relevant grounds (age, disability, race, religion or belief, sex, or sexual orientation) is also classed as discrimination. 'Harassment' as a form of discrimination prohibited by EU law was first introduced by Directives 2000/43 and 2000/78, and was only later applied to sex discrimination. Harassment on grounds of sex is now prohibited by Directive 2006/54. See Section 18.11.1 below for a more detailed discussion of 'harassment'.

KEY FACTS

Discrimination	
Discrimination takes two forms: direct and indirect	
Direct discrimination occurs where a person is treated less favourably than another person in a comparable situation on grounds of sex, race, age, disability, religion or belief, sexual orientation	Directive 2006/54 (sex); Directive 2000/43 (race); directive 2000/78 (age, disability, religion or belief, sexual orientation)
Indirect discrimination occurs when an 'apparently neutral provision' puts a person at 'a particular disadvantage' because of their sex, race, etc, unless that provision can be justified	
'Sex' discrimination includes discrimination against transsexuals	*P v S* (1996); *KB* (2004)
Harassment is treated as a form of discrimination. It Is defined as 'any form of unwanted conduct' with the 'purpose of violating the dignity of a person'	Directive 2006/54 (sex); Directive 2000/43 (race); directive 2000/78 (age, disability, religion or belief, sexual orientation)

18.3 Article 157 TFEU and equal pay

ARTICLE

'Art 157(1) Each Member State shall ensure that the principle of equal pay for male and female workers for equal work or work of equal value is applied.

(2) For the purpose of this Article, "pay" means the ordinary basic or minimum wage or salary and any other consideration, whether in cash or in kind, which the worker receives, directly or indirectly, in respect of his employment from his employer. Equal pay without discrimination based on sex means:

(a) that pay for the same work at piece rates shall be calculated on the basis of the same unit of measurement;

(b) that pay for work at time rates shall be the same for the same job.

(3) The European Parliament and the Council … shall adopt measures to ensure the application of the principle of equal opportunities and equal treatment of men and women in matters of employment and occupation, including the principle of equal pay for equal work or work of equal value.

(4) With a view to ensuring full equality in practice between men and women in working life, the principle of equal treatment shall not prevent any Member State from maintaining or adopting measures providing for specific advantages in order to make it easier for the under-represented sex to pursue a vocational activity or to prevent or compensate for disadvantages in professional careers.'

In *Defrenne v SABENA* (1976), the ECJ stated that Art 157(1) pursued a 'double aim', one economic and one social. The two aims are:

- **economic aim:** to ensure that employers in States which had already introduced their own principles of equal pay via national legislation did not suffer a 'competitive disadvantage in [intra-Union] competition', compared with employers in other States which had not yet eliminated discrimination against female workers
- **social aim:** to ensure 'social progress and seek the constant improvement of the living and working conditions' of people in the EU.

In *Hill and Stapleton* (Case 243/95) [1998] ECR I–3739, the ECJ elaborated on the social aim identified in *Defrenne* (1976) when it said that the EU's policy in this area is 'to encourage and, if possible, adapt working conditions to family responsibilities'.

Direct effect of Art 157(1)

In *Defrenne v SABENA* (1976), the ECJ made an extremely important ruling. The Court held that Art 157(1) not only satisfied the conditions for direct effect (and hence it could be enforced in the national courts) but, moreover, that it could be enforced not just vertically but also horizontally. The Court stated that the prohibition on discrimination between men and women 'applies not only to the action of public authorities but also extends to all agreements which are intended to regulate paid labour collectively, as well as to contracts between individuals'.

CASE EXAMPLE

Defrenne v SABENA (Case 43/75) [1976] ECR 455

Between 1963 and 1966, Gabrielle Defrenne was employed as an air stewardess with SABENA, the Belgian airline company. Eventually she brought an action against it, claiming that she was being paid less than her male colleagues. At the relevant time, there was no Belgian legislation prohibiting pay discrimination. Gabrielle therefore claimed that Art 157(1) applied. The ECJ agreed that Art 157(1) could be relied upon by individuals in national courts.

Scope of Art 157

The key provisions of 'pay' and 'work' have attracted a large number of preliminary ruling cases over the years, which will be examined below. One important limitation on the scope of Art 157 was identified by the ECJ in *Defrenne v SABENA* (1976) – individuals can only invoke Art 157 to challenge 'unequal pay for equal work which is carried out in the same establishment or service'. In other words, a woman working for company A cannot claim pay equality with a man employed at company B even if they are both doing exactly the same work. This point was confirmed by the ECJ in *Lawrence and Others* (Case C–320/00) [2002] ECR I–7325. The Court ruled that:

JUDGMENT

'Where the differences identified in the pay conditions of workers performing equal work or work of equal value cannot be attributed to a single source, there is no body which is responsible for the inequality and which could restore equal treatment. Such a situation does not come within the scope of [Art 157]. The work and the pay of those workers cannot therefore be compared on the basis of that provision.'

CASE EXAMPLE

Lawrence and Others (Case C–320/00) [2002] ECR I–7325

A number of female workers brought claims against their employers, seeking the same pay as male employees performing work of equal value for North Yorkshire County Council. The female workers had worked for the Council until 1993, preparing school meals for pupils and cleaning schools in the North Yorkshire area. In 1993 the Council tendered out this work to private companies who then became the new employers of the female workers. However, the female workers believed that male employees **retained** by the Council were receiving better pay than themselves, and brought the case. The ECJ held that Art 157 did not apply.

This ruling was confirmed in the similar case of *Allonby v Accrington and Rossendale College* (Case C–256/01) [2004] ECR I–873, where a group of part-time college lecturers (most of whom were female) employed by an agency were unable to claim equal pay with a group of full-time lecturers (most of whom were male) employed by the college itself. Even though the two groups worked in the same place, they had different employers and hence Art 157 did not apply.

18.3.1 The definition of 'pay'

The concept of 'pay' in Art 157(2) is generously worded. You should note that it is explicitly **not** restricted to 'wages' or 'salary'. Nor does it have to be in the form of 'cash'. Rather, it includes 'any other consideration' which the worker receives as a result of his employment relationship. Article 157 has also been generously construed by the ECJ since the 1970s. *Garland v British Rail (Engineering)* (Case 12/81) [1982] ECR 359, for example, concerned special benefits that the employer provided to male employees, although there was no contractual provision to that effect. The ECJ held that it was irrelevant that the benefits were not laid down in the employment contract. Similarly, in *Bötel* (Case C–360/90) [1992] ECR I–3589, the Court stated that remuneration could amount to 'pay' 'irrespective of whether the worker receives it under a contract of employment, by virtue of legislative provisions or on a voluntary basis'. In *Royal Copenhagen* (Case C–400/93) [1995] ECR I–1275, the ECJ was asked whether pay on a 'piece-work' basis – where the level of pay is wholly or partially dependent on the individual employee's output – was covered by Art 157. The Court held that it was. The width of the definition of 'pay' in Art 157 itself, allied to the ECJ's generous interpretation, is of immense practical significance. It means that employers face great difficulty if they try to avoid the provisions of Art 157 by re-classifying some remuneration as something other than 'pay'.

Examples of pay

The following cases demonstrate the breadth of the ECJ's interpretation of the word 'pay':

- **Sick pay:** in *Rinner-Kühn* (1989), the ECJ held that sick pay (that is, continued payment of wages in the event of illness) fell within Art 157.
- **Severance payments:** such payments are designed to help employees who became unemployed involuntarily, for example, following retirement or disability, to adjust

to their new situation. In *Kowalska* [1990] ECR I–2591 the ECJ held that severance pay was within Art 157.

- **Compensation for unfair dismissal:** in *Seymour-Smith & Perez* [1999] ECR I–623, the ECJ held that an award of compensation in the event of unfair dismissal was 'pay' under Art 157. The Court described it as 'a form of deferred pay to which the worker is entitled by reason of his employment but which is paid to him on termination of the employment relationship with a view to enabling him to adjust to the new circumstances arising from such termination'. The Court justified this conclusion by saying that it represented what the worker 'would have earned if the employer had not unlawfully terminated the employment relationship'.
- **Bonuses:** in *Krüger* (Case C–281/97) [1999] ECR I–5127, the ECJ held that an annual Christmas bonus amounted to 'pay'. This was confirmed in *Lewen v Denda* (Case C–333/97) [1999] ECR I–7243, where the ECJ rejected the employer's argument that it was more of a 'goodwill gesture'. The Court stated that 'the reason for which an employer pays a benefit is of little importance provided that the benefit is granted in connection with employment'. Moreover, the Court held that a bonus was still 'pay' whether or not it was regarded as an incentive to future work, or a retrospective reward for services performed. In *Brunnhofer* (Case C–381/99) [2001] ECR I–4961, the ECJ held that a monthly salary supplement, awarded by an employer on an *ad hoc* basis to reflect the quality of individual's work, constituted 'pay'.
- **Payment in lieu:** in *Bötel* (1992), the Court held that compensation payable by an employer in lieu of wages when an employee was required to attend compulsory training, was 'pay' within Art 157.
- **Post-employment benefits:** in *Garland v BRE* (1982) the ECJ held that Art 157 could apply to benefits received by ex-workers, on the basis that it constituted consideration for work done during the employment relationship.
- **Redundancy payments:** in *Barber v Guardian Royal Exchange Assurance Group* (Case 262/88) [1990] ECR I–8889, the ECJ was asked whether money paid by an employer in connection with redundancy was 'pay' within Art 157. The Court held that it was: 'such compensation constitutes a form of pay'. The Court added that redundancy payments helped the worker 'to facilitate his adjustment to the new circumstances resulting from the loss of his employment and which provides him with a source of income during the period in which he is seeking new employment'.
- **Maternity pay:** in *Gillespie v Northern Health and Social Services Board* (Case C–342/93) [1996] ECR I–475, the ECJ held that money paid by an employer to a female employee on maternity leave was based on the employment relationship and therefore constituted 'pay' within Art 157. In *Abdoulaye* (Case C–218/98) [1999] ECR I–5723, the ECJ confirmed that a lump-sum payment to women employees going on maternity leave was 'pay' within Art 157.

An interesting subsidiary question raised in *Gillespie* (1996) was whether a woman on maternity leave was entitled to any pay rises which she would have been awarded had she not been on maternity leave. The Court held that she was. The Court stated that 'to deny such an increase to a woman on maternity leave would discriminate against her purely in her capacity as a worker since, had she not been pregnant, she would have received the pay rise'.

- **Occupational pensions:** the most contentious issue in the context of Art 157 has been whether it applies to occupational pension schemes (as opposed to State old-age pensions). In *Bilka-Kaufhaus* (1986), the ECJ held that **entitlement to join** such a scheme could be regarded as a form of 'pay'. More controversially, in *Barber v Guardian Royal Exchange* (1990) the Court held that **benefits paid** under an occupational pension scheme also constituted 'pay':

CASE EXAMPLE

Bilka-Kaufhaus (Case 170/84) [1986] ECR 1607

Bilka-Kaufhaus (B-K), a large department store chain in Germany employing several thousand people, ran an occupational pension scheme for its employees. B-K employed both full- and part-time workers, each comprising men and women. However, only 10 per cent of the men employed worked part-time, as against 27.7 per cent of the women. Under the pension scheme's rules, workers were only entitled to payment of a pension if they had worked for the company full-time for at least 15 out of the last 20 years. Karin Weber Von Harz, who was employed as a sales assistant full-time between 1961 and 1972 and part-time subsequently, was refused access to the pension scheme. She complained that the pension scheme rules breached Art 157. The ECJ held that the entitlement to join an occupational pension scheme could be regarded as 'pay'.

CASE EXAMPLE

Barber v Guardian Royal Exchange Assurance Group (Case 262/88) [1990] ECR I–8889

Douglas Barber was made redundant, aged 52. He was paid a statutory redundancy payment, but was denied an early retirement pension under his employer's contracted out pension scheme, because such a pension was only available to men made redundant after their 55th birthday. Female employees, meanwhile, were entitled to an early pension, in the same circumstances, aged 50. Barber challenged the legality of this distinction. The ECJ held that Art 157 prohibited the discrimination that Barber had encountered.

These cases also show that the nature of the scheme was irrelevant. Thus, it made no difference whether the employer's scheme was:

- supplementary to the State's retirement pension scheme, as in Bilka-Kaufhaus (1986) or
- designed to replace it (so-called 'contracted out' schemes), as in Barber (1990).

The *Barber* (1990) case provoked a flood of preliminary rulings, mainly from the UK and the Netherlands, seeking further clarification of the extent to which Art 157 applied to occupational pension schemes. The *Barber* (1990) ruling itself was confirmed in *Ten-Oever* (Case C–109/91) [1993] ECR I–4879. In that case, the Court made a further ruling, one which transcends the limited sphere of occupational pension schemes. The Court held that Art 157 still applied even if the pension benefits were paid to someone other than the employee who had earned them, namely the employee's survivor (typically a widow). Such benefits were still 'pay' because they derived from the contract of employment. This ruling was followed in *KB* (2004), considered above.

In *Coloroll Pension Trs v Russell* (Case C–200/91) [1994] ECR I–4389, the Court made another important ruling, again one that transcends its specific factual origins. The Court held that Art 157 still applied even if the scheme benefits, ie the 'pay', were paid by someone other than the employer, namely the pension scheme trustees. Thus, from the unpromising and superficially limited facts of these two judgments come much wider principles, namely that Art 157 applies:

- where 'pay' is provided by the employer **but not to the employee** (*Ten-Oever*) (1993)
- where pay is provided to the employee **but not by the employer** (*Coloroll* (1994)).

Conversely, some of the post-*Barber* (1990) cases imposed limitations on the potential scope of the judgment. In *Neath v Hugh Steeper Ltd* (Case C–152/91) [1993] ECR I–6935, it was held that neither **lump sum payments** nor **transfer payments** were protected by Art 157. The former payments are available as an option under most occupational pension schemes and allow retiring workers to receive part of their pension in a lump sum, with a correspondingly reduced periodic payment. The latter come into effect when a worker changes employment and wishes to transfer their deferred pension entitlement to a new employer, thereby consolidating their pension, for convenience if nothing else. In *Neath* (1993), the Court ruled that lump-sum payments and transfer payments were both calculated using actuarial factors, based on various assumptions about men and women, such as life expectancy, which were intrinsically and unavoidably different between the two sexes. Therefore it was impossible to assert that such payments had to be equal.

18.3.2 Equal work or work of equal value

'Equal work'

Advocate-General Capotorti, in *Macarthys Ltd v Smith* (Case 129/79) [1980] ECR 1275, suggested that 'equal work' was not necessarily confined to identical work. 'Equal work' could include jobs with a high degree of similarity, even if they are not totally identical.

In *Wiener Gebietskrankenkasse* (Case C–309/97) [1999] ECR I–2865, the ECJ held that two groups of employees who were performing 'seemingly identical tasks', but whose **training and/or professional qualifications were different**, were not necessarily to be regarded as doing the 'same work'. This was because of the possibility that different tasks may be assigned to the different groups. The Court concluded that 'two groups of persons who have received different professional training and who, because of the different scope of the qualifications resulting from that training, on the basis of which they were recruited, are called on to perform different tasks or duties, cannot be regarded as being in a comparable situation'. This decision may be criticised as it gives employers an excuse to discriminate between male and female employees – even those doing the same jobs – by pointing to the fact that the different groups of workers have different qualifications. It is submitted that it was wrong for the ECJ to hold that two groups of people doing the same job were not in a 'comparable situation' just because of the possibility that 'different tasks or duties' may be assigned to one of them.

In *Cadman* (Case C–17/05) [2006] ECR I–9683, the ECJ again decided that individual workers' different lengths of experience might justify differential pay rates for otherwise similar jobs, although that was not an automatic conclusion. In particular, it would not be the case 'where the worker provides evidence capable of giving rise to serious doubts as to whether recourse to the criterion of length of service is, in the circumstances, appropriate'. The ECJ stated that (emphasis added):

JUDGMENT

'Rewarding, in particular, experience acquired which enables the worker to perform his duties better constitutes a legitimate objective of pay policy. As a *general rule*, recourse to the criterion of length of service is appropriate to attain that objective. Length of service goes hand in hand with experience, and experience *generally* enables the worker to perform his duties better.'

CASE EXAMPLE

Cadman (Case C–17/05) [2006] ECR I–9683

Mrs Cadman had worked for the Health & Safety Executive (HSE) since 1990, and by 2001 she was head of a Field Management Unit in receipt of an annual salary of some £35,000. However, she complained that four of her male colleagues, who were in the same pay band as herself, were earning between £39,000 and £44,000. All of the male comparators had longer service and this was advanced as justification by the HSE. Nevertheless, Mrs Cadman alleged that this was insufficient of itself and that a breach of Art 157 had occurred. The ECJ decided that the pay differentials were justifiable.

'Work of equal value'

In *Royal Copenhagen* (1995), the ECJ made it clear that it was not for the Court to make decisions on whether different jobs were of equal value. Instead, this was a question of fact for the national court. There have been problems in determining exactly **how** different jobs should be assessed to see if they are of 'equal value'. Article 4 of Directive 2006/54 (the Recast Directive) provides some guidance on this matter. It states that 'where a job classification system is used for determining pay, it must be based on the same criteria for both men and women and so drawn up as to exclude any discrimination on grounds of sex'. Thus, although the directive refers to job classification schemes, it does **not** make them compulsory. However, it is essential that Member States ensure that some system is in place to decide whether work has the same value, whether as the result of a job classification scheme, **or otherwise**.

The use of a job classification system in determining salary levels was considered by the ECJ in *Rummler v Dato-Druck* (Case 237/85) [1986] ECR 210. The ECJ held that such a system 'must be based on criteria which do not differ according to whether the work is carried out by a man or by a woman and must not be organised, as a whole, in such a manner that it has the practical effect of discriminating against workers of one sex'. The Court stressed that it **was** permissible for an employer to use one or more factors that favoured one sex over another, provided that such factors formed part of a package of criteria which, taken as a whole, did not favour one sex over the other. The Court gave as an example 'demand on the muscles'. This would favour men 'since it may be assumed that, in general, they are physically stronger than female workers'. However, it would be permissible for an employer to refer to this criterion provided that it formed part of a package containing other criteria, some of which may favour women. Indeed, in *Rummler* itself, 'muscular effort' was a criterion used to determine salary levels, but it formed part of a package alongside other criteria such as degree of knowledge and training, accuracy and conscientiousness, and responsibility for equipment and/or work.

A similar situation arose in *Royal Copenhagen* (1995), where again muscular strength was a criterion used to determine workers' salaries.

CASE EXAMPLE

Royal Copenhagen (Case C–400/93) [1995] ECR I–1275

Royal Copenhagen, a ceramics producer in Denmark, employed over 1,000 workers. Amongst these were two groups – the automatic machine operators and the blue-pattern painters. The former group, consisting of 26 men, received an average weekly wage of 104 Danish kroner. The latter group, consisting of 155 women and one man, received an average weekly wage of 91 kroner. A trade union brought an action to have the (predominantly female) blue-pattern painters brought up to the value of the (male) automatic machine operators. The ECJ held that it was for the national court to decide whether the work was of equal value. This would have to be done, bearing in mind that the automatic machine operators' job required muscular strength, while the blue-pattern painters' job relied heavily on dexterity; that the operators suffered 'inconveniences from noise and temperature', while the painters had problems caused by 'sedentary and monotonous' work. There were also differences in terms of paid breaks, and the freedom of the workers to organise their own work. Moreover, the Court held that, even if the work was found to be of equal value, the employer would be entitled to try to justify the pay differential. This aspect of the case will be considered below.

ACTIVITY

Applying the law

Apart from 'muscular effort', can you think of any criteria that an employer might decide to use to determine salary levels which would discriminate in favour of one gender and against the other?

Equal pay for work of greater value

In *Murphy* (Case 157/86) [1988] ECR 673, a female factory worker discovered that she – along with 28 other women – was being paid less than a male store labourer in the same factory. When she objected, she was told that because her work was of **greater** value than that of the male labourer, no comparison could be made. Ms Murphy took her claim to court and eventually the case was referred to the ECJ. There, the Court held that although Art 157 referred to the principle of equal pay for equal work, or for work of equal value, but not to work of unequal value, it could nevertheless be applied in Ms Murphy's case. The Court said that to 'adopt a contrary interpretation would be tantamount to rendering the principle of equal pay ineffective and nugatory … an employer would easily be able to circumvent the principle [of equal pay] by assigning additional or more onerous duties to workers of a particular sex, who could then be paid a lower wage'.

KEY FACTS

Equal pay	
Men and women are entitled to equal pay for equal work	Article 157 (1) TFEU
Article 157 (1) TFEU is directly effective	*Defrenne v SABENA* (1976)
In order to claim pay equality, the male and female employees must be working for the same employer	*Lawrence & Others* (2002); *Allonby* (2004)
'Pay' is defined very widely. It includes, but is not restricted to, 'wages' or 'salary'. It includes 'any other consideration' which a worker receives as a result of his or her employment	Article 157 (2) TFEU
'Pay' includes sick-pay, bonuses, and maternity pay	*Rinner-Kühn* (1989), *Krüger* (1999), *Gillespie* (1996)
'Pay' includes post-employment payments such as severance payments, compensation for unfair dismissal, redundancy payments and occupational pensions	*Kowalska* (1990), *Seymour-Smith & Perez* (1999), *Barber* (1990), *Bilka-Kaufhaus* (1986)
Employees performing 'seemingly identical tasks' but whose training, qualifications and/or experience is different may not necessarily be regarded as doing 'equal' work	*Wiener Gebietskrankenkasse* (1999), *Cadman* (2006)
Where a 'job classification system' is used to identify 'work of equal value' it must be based on the same criteria for men and women	Directive 2006/54
However, the ECJ has permitted the use of criteria which favour one sex over another provided the overall package of criteria are gender-neutral	*Rummler* (1986), *Royal Copenhagen* (1995)

18.4 Equal Treatment for men and women in employment – Directive 2006/54

Directive 76/207, widely referred to as the Equal Treatment Directive (ETD), first laid down a general principle for equal treatment in other conditions of employment, other than pay. The ETD was amended by Directive 2002/73 in October 2005, and then repealed in its entirety in August 2009. The principle of equal treatment is now found in Directive 2006/54, known as the 'Recast' Directive. However, some of the case law on the original ETD is still relevant today (see below). Article 1 of the Recast Directive states:

ARTICLE

'Art 1 The purpose of this Directive is to ensure the implementation of the principle of equal opportunities and equal treatment of men and women in matters of employment and occupation.'

To that end, the new directive contains provisions to implement the principle of equal treatment in relation to:

a) access to employment, including promotion, and to vocational training
b) working conditions, including pay
c) occupational social security schemes.

It also contains provisions to ensure that such implementation is made more effective by the establishment of appropriate procedures.

The main substantive provisions of the Recast Directive are as follows:

- Article 3 – allows for 'positive action', defined as 'measures ... with a view to ensuring full equality in practice between men and women in working life'.
- Article 4 – prohibits discrimination in terms of pay. This confirms Art 157 TFEU.
- Articles 5–13 – deal with equal treatment in occupational social security schemes.
- Article 14 – provides for equal treatment as regards access to employment, vocational training, promotion and working conditions (including dismissals).
- Article 19 – sets out the burden of proof in sex discrimination cases.

Article 14(1) provides as follows:

ARTICLE

'Art 14(1) There shall be no direct or indirect discrimination on grounds of sex in the public or private sectors, including public bodies, in relation to:

(a) conditions for access to employment, to self-employment or to occupation, including selection criteria and recruitment conditions, whatever the branch of activity and at all levels of the professional hierarchy, including promotion;
(b) access to all types and to all levels of vocational guidance, vocational training, advanced vocational training and retraining, including practical work experience;
(c) employment and working conditions, including dismissals, as well as pay as provided for in [Art 157 TFEU];
(d) membership of, and involvement in, an organisation of workers or employers, or any organisation whose members carry on a particular profession, including the benefits provided for by such organisations.

18.4.1 Access to employment and vocational training: Art 14(1) (a) and (b)

An example of a case under the original ETD and which would now be dealt with under Art 14(1)(a) is *Meyers v Adjudication Officer* (Case C–116/94) [1995] ECR I–2131. Here, the ECJ held that Family Credit, a British social security benefit intended to supplement the income of low-paid workers who were also responsible for a child, could be regarded as falling within the scope of the ETD. The Court held that it dealt with 'access to' employment because it encouraged people to take low-paid jobs. It followed that a refusal to pay the benefit to a single parent, such as Jennifer Meyers, could amount to indirect discrimination (because the vast majority of single parents in the UK are women).

18.4.2 Employment and working conditions, including dismissals: Art 14(1)(c)

'Working conditions'

This has been given a wide scope by the ECJ. In *Meyers,* the ECJ rejected an argument by the British Government that 'working conditions' only referred to conditions in the contract of employment. Instead, the ECJ stated that 'working conditions' referred to the whole 'employment relationship'.

In *Coote v Granada Hospitality Ltd* (Case C–185/97) [1998] ECR I–5199, the ECJ was asked whether the ETD covered allegedly discriminatory measures occurring after the termination of the employment relationship (in this case, refusal to provide a reference). The ECJ held that it applied here too.

'Dismissals'

The word 'dismissals' is to be interpreted widely. In a case under the original ETD, *Burton* (Case 19/81) [1982] ECR 555, the ECJ said that it extended to any termination of the employment relationship between an employee and his employer, even where this was part of a voluntary redundancy scheme. This was confirmed in *Vergani* (Case C–207/04) [2005] ECR I–7453, where the Court found that provisions of Italian law giving 'tax breaks' on all sums paid on the cessation of the employment relationship, designed to encourage voluntary redundancy, to women aged 50 or over, but which were not available to men until aged 55, breached the ETD.

Perhaps the most significant development in this context was the extension of what is now Art 14(1)(c) of the Recast Directive to cover discriminatory retirement ages in employment contracts. The leading cases are all British. This is because, prior to 1986, British legislation did not prohibit such discrimination. As a result, many British employers adopted a policy of allowing men to work until their 65th birthday whilst female employees had to retire at 60. This blatant discrimination against women could be explained on the basis that the British state pensionable age (that is, the age at which people could claim an old-age pension from the state) was itself discriminatory against men, who only became entitled to a pension at 65 whereas women could claim from 60.

The best-known case is *Marshall* (1986), which has already been examined in Chapter 9. You will recall that Ms Marshall, who was forced to retire shortly after her 60th birthday, brought a successful challenge to her ex-employer's discriminatory retirement age in its contracts of employment, relying upon what is now Art 14(1)(c) of the Recast Directive. The ECJ held that forcing women to retire was tantamount to dismissal and, therefore, in breach of EU law. Following *Marshall* (1986), the UK Parliament passed the Sex Discrimination Act 1986, which prohibited employers from discriminating between men and women in terms of retirement ages. More recently, under the Pensions Act 1995, a new State retirement age for women of 65 has been created, although this only applies to women born after 5th April 1955.

18.4.3 Derogations

Article 14(2) of the Recast Directive provides as follows:

ARTICLE

'(2) Member States may provide, as regards access to employment including the training leading thereto, that a difference of treatment which is based on a characteristic related to sex shall not constitute discrimination where, by reason of the nature of the particular occupational activities concerned or of the context in which they are carried out, such a characteristic constitutes a genuine and determining occupational requirement, provided that its objective is legitimate and the requirement is proportionate.'

Although there is, as yet, no case law on this provision, some of the case law on the original ETD illustrates the type of situations in which Art 14(2) may apply. The ECJ has recognised that sex may be a 'genuine and determining occupational requirement' for posts such as those of:

- armed police officers (*Johnston* (Case 222/84) [1986] ECR 1651)
- prison warders in single-sex prisons (*Commission v France (Civil Service Employment)* (Case 318/86) [1988] ECR 3559)
- midwives (*Commission v UK (Private Households/Midwives)* (Case 165/82) [1983] ECR 3431)
- soldiers in specialist army combat units (*Sirdar* (Case C–273/97) [1999] ECR I–7403).

In *Sirdar*, the ECJ held that the exclusion of women from service in special combat units such as the British Royal Marines was justifiable under what is now Art 14(2). The Marines have a policy of excluding women from service on the ground that their presence is incompatible with the requirement of 'interoperability', that is to say, the need for every Marine, irrespective of his specialisation, to be capable of fighting in a commando unit. The Court ruled that the British Army was entitled 'to come to the view that the specific conditions for deployment of the assault units of which the Royal Marines are composed, and in particular the rule of interoperability to which they are subject, justified their composition remaining exclusively male'.

CASE EXAMPLE

Sirdar (Case C–273/97) [1999] ECR I–7403

Angela Sirdar worked as a chef in the Royal Artillery. In July 1994 she received an offer of transfer to the Royal Marines, who had a shortage of chefs. However, when the Royal Marines became aware that she was a woman (the offer had been made to her in error), they informed Angela that she was ineligible by reason of the policy excluding women. She brought a case alleging sex discrimination, relying on what is now Art 14(1)(a) of the Recast Directive. However, the ECJ held that the organisation of the Royal Marines differed 'fundamentally' from that of other units in the British armed forces, where women are permitted to serve. The ECJ stated that the Marines were the 'point of the arrow head', a 'small force intended to be the first line of attack'. On that basis, the Court held that what is now Art 14(2) of the Recast Directive applied.

Ellis, in 'The Recent Jurisprudence of the Court of Justice in the Field of Sex Equality' (2000) 37 CMLR 1403, was critical of the *Sirdar* judgment. She commented that 'the degree of gender-stereotyping is little short of staggering'. This may be true, but the ECJ has since shown that it is unwilling to allow Member States to exploit similar arguments in order to prevent women serving in the armed forces in any capacity. In *Kreil v Germany* (Case C–285/98) [2000] ECR I–69, the ECJ distinguished *Sirdar* when it ruled that provisions of the German constitution barring women from all army jobs involving the use of arms was contrary to the ETD and could not be saved by what is now Art 14(2) of the Recast Directive. The case came to the ECJ when Tanja Kreil, an electronics expert, was turned down when she applied to join the German army to work with electronic weapons systems. She discovered that women were only allowed to serve in the German army either as medics or musicians. The ECJ held that this went too far. Indeed, the decision in *Kreil* actually supports *Sirdar* – the Court in *Kreil* pointed out that 'derogations remain possible where sex constitutes a determining factor for access to certain special combat units'.

18.4.4 Reversed burden of proof

Article 19(1) of the Recast Directive sets out the following principles relating to the burden of proof:

ARTICLE

'Member States shall take such measures as are necessary, in accordance with their national judicial systems, to ensure that, when persons who consider themselves wronged because the principle of equal treatment has not been applied to them establish, before a court or other competent authority, facts from which it may be presumed that there has been direct or indirect discrimination, it shall be for the respondent to prove that there has been no breach of the principle of equal treatment.'

KEY FACTS

Equal treatment for men and women	
Men and women are entitled to equal treatment in employment. This covers access to employment, working conditions, and dismissals	Directive 2006/54, Article 14(1)
Member States may derogate where a 'difference in treatment' can be justified by reference to 'the nature of the particular occupational activities concerned' provided it 'constitutes a genuine and determining occupational requirement'	Directive 2006/54, Article 14(2); *Johnston* (1986), *Sirdar* (1999)

18.5 Justifications for indirect discrimination

Where indirect discrimination is established, it does not automatically infringe EU law. If the difference in treatment between the two groups can be 'objectively justified', that is, shown to be based in no way on discrimination between the sexes, then EU discrimination law will not be infringed. Article 2(1)(b) of the Recast Directive makes this explicit: there is no breach of EU discrimination law if an indirectly discriminatory 'provision, criterion or practice is objectively justified by a legitimate aim, and the means of achieving that aim are appropriate and necessary'.

In *Bilka-Kaufhaus* (1986), the ECJ stated that discrimination in terms of pay or other work conditions could be justified if the discriminatory measures 'correspond to a real need on the part of the undertaking, are appropriate with a view to achieving the objectives pursued and are necessary to that end'.

18.5.1 'A real need on the part of the undertaking'

Most of the cases involve employers with a mixed staff of men and women, some working full-time (mostly men) and some working part-time (mostly women). Often the full-time staff are paid more (on a *pro rata* basis) than part-time staff and/or receive additional benefits. This constitutes indirect sex discrimination – but can it be justified? The answer is 'yes', if it 'corresponds to a real need'. Over the years, employers have put forward a variety of 'real needs'. A survey of the case law reveals that the ECJ regards the following as acceptable reasons (at least in principle) for indirectly discriminating against women:

- The need to encourage full-time workers – *Jenkins v Kingsgate* (Case 96/80) [1981] ECR 911; *Rinke* (Case C–25/02) [2003] ECR I–8349.
- The need to discourage part-time workers – *Bilka-Kaufhaus* (1986).
- The need to alleviate constraints on small businesses – *Kirsammer-Hack v Sidal* (Case C–189/91) [1993] ECR I–6185.
- The need to reward specific qualities amongst the workforce, eg greater mobility, or extra training – *Danfoss* (Case 109/88) [1989] ECR 3199.
- The need to attract more staff to certain posts – *Enderby v Frenchay HA* (Case C–127/92) [1993] ECR I–5535.

- The need to ensure cost management of public funds – *Jørgensen* (Case C–226/98) [2000] ECR I–2447.
- The need to recruit young workers by encouraging part-time work among older workers – *Kutz-Bauer* (Case C–187/00) [2003] ECR I–2741; *Steinicke* (Case C–77/02) [2003] ECR I–9027.

The employers in *Bilka-Kaufhaus* (1986), a large German department store, admitted that it deliberately operated a policy of discriminating in favour of full-time workers (the majority of which were men) by denying access to its occupational pension scheme to part-time employees (the majority of which were women). The policy was 'intended solely to discourage part-time work, since in general part-time workers refuse to work in the late afternoon or on Saturdays. In order to ensure the presence of an adequate workforce during those periods it was therefore necessary to make full-time work more attractive than part-time work'. The ECJ left it to the national court to decide whether this policy was 'necessary' to meet a 'real need' on the part of the store. The German court, in applying those principles, found that the pay disparities were not actually 'necessary' to attract more full-time workers.

In *Enderby v Frenchay HA* (1993) the Court accepted that the 'state of the employment market' may lead an employer to increase the pay of a particular job in order to attract candidates, and that this may constitute an 'objectively justified economic ground'. In this case, Dr Pamela Enderby was employed as a speech therapist (almost exclusively women) on an annual salary of £10,000. She claimed equality of pay with clinical psychologists (predominantly men) on £12,500, and/or pharmacists (also predominantly men) on £14,000. Dr Enderby claimed that this was indirectly discriminatory. The defendant health authority advanced the justification that the difference in pay was because of a shortage of pharmacists and the need to attract more, suitably qualified, candidates by offering higher salaries. The ECJ accepted this argument.

In *Kutz-Bauer* (2003), the question was whether a retirement incentive scheme run by the City of Hamburg in Germany, designed to free up vacancies for younger workers, could be justified. Under this scheme, full-time employees nearing retirement could apply to work part-time for a period of five years (thus easing their transition from full-time employment to retirement). It was alleged that the scheme indirectly discriminated against women, because all employees (whether male or female) were ineligible once entitled to a full State pension. As the German State pension age was 60 for women and 65 for men, it was much easier for men aged 59 to qualify for the full scheme than it was for women aged 59. The ECJ agreed that, although the scheme indirectly discriminated against women, it was objectively justifiable because its aim was to 'combat unemployment' by offering the 'maximum incentives for workers who are not yet eligible for retirement to do so and thus making posts available'. The Court held that 'it cannot be disputed that the encouragement of recruitment constitutes a legitimate aim of social policy'.

18.5.2 Rejected examples of 'real needs'

In *Gerster* (Case C–1/95) [1997] ECR I–5253, it was argued that extra experience gained by full-time employees justified differential treatment compared with part-time workers. The Court rejected this view. It stated:

JUDGMENT

'It is impossible to identify objective criteria unrelated to any discrimination on the basis of an alleged special link between length of service and acquisition of a certain level of knowledge or experience, since such a claim amounts to no more than a generalisation concerning certain categories of worker. Although experience goes hand-in-hand with length of service, and experience enables the worker in principle to improve performance of the tasks allotted to him, the objectivity of such a criterion depends on all circumstances of each individual case, and in particular on the relationship between the nature of the work performed and the experience gained from the performance of that work.'

This must be right. Otherwise, employers could routinely pay full-time staff (mostly men) more than part-time staff (mostly female) and, when challenged, point out that the full-time staff were 'more experienced'. However, this is obviously not the case: a woman who has worked part-time (say on a 50 per cent contract) for 30 years is clearly far more experienced than a man who has worked full-time for five years.

In *Hill and Stapleton v Revenue Commissioners* (Case C–243/95) [1998] ECR I–3739, the Court ruled that certain provisions of a job-sharing scheme in the Irish civil service were indirectly discriminatory. Under the scheme, workers who shared 50 per cent of a full-time job were automatically credited with only 50 per cent of service time. The Court observed that this automatic feature failed to take account of other factors, such as the quality of work performed, and was capable of amounting to indirect discrimination against women (who made up the majority of the job-sharers). A suggested justification, based on economic grounds, was rejected. The Court stated that 'an employer cannot justify discrimination … solely on the ground that avoidance of such discrimination would involve increased costs'.

KEY FACTS

Justifications for indirect discrimination	
There is no breach of EU discrimination law if an indirectly discriminatory 'provision, criterion or practice is objectively justified by a legitimate aim, and the means of achieving that aim are appropriate and necessary'	Directive 2006/54
Examples of legitimate aims include the need to encourage full-time workers, the need to reward greater mobility or extra training, the need to attract staff to specific posts, the need to recruit young workers	*Jenkins v Kingsgate* (1981), *Danfoss* (1989), *Enderby* (1993), *Kutz-Bauer* (2003)

18.6 Positive action and positive discrimination

Article 157(4) TFEU states that:

ARTICLE

'The principle of equal treatment shall not prevent any Member State from maintaining or adopting measures providing for specific advantages in order to make it easier for the under-represented sex to pursue a vocational activity or to prevent or compensate for disadvantages in professional careers.'

Article 3 of the Recast Directive adds that 'Member States may maintain or adopt measures… with a view to ensuring full equality in practice between men and women in working life'. This policy is known as 'positive action'. However, the ECJ has been very careful to distinguish between 'positive action', which is tolerated (indeed encouraged) and 'positive discrimination', which is contrary to the principle of equal treatment.

18.6.1 Positive action

'Positive action' measures typically involve the removal of obstacles which prevent, or at least restrict, the 'under-represented sex' (which is typically women) from competing on a level playing field with the other sex. A good example of 'positive action' is *Lommers* (Case C–476/99) [2002] ECR I–2891. This case involved an employer's policy of giving women priority in terms of access to nursery places. The Court held that giving women priority in 'certain working conditions designed to facilitate their pursuit of, and progression in, their career, falls in principle into the category of measures designed to eliminate the causes of women's reduced opportunities for access to employment and careers and are intended to improve their ability to compete on the labour market and to pursue a career on an equal footing with men'. The Court did note that such a policy, although designed to help women, might actually 'help to perpetuate a traditional division of roles between men and women', and that it might therefore go beyond what was necessary (that is, it infringed the principle of proportionality). However, on the facts, the ECJ decided that the employer's policy was a justifiable exercise of 'positive action'.

Typically, the 'under-represented sex' for whose benefit positive action measures may be taken will be women. However, Member States are permitted to adopt measures to prevent men from being disadvantaged too. *Schnorbus v Lard Hessen* (Case C–79/99) [2000] ECR I–10997 involved the practical legal training programme in Germany, the first step for those wishing to become judges in that country. If the programme in any given year is oversubscribed, lots are drawn and places allocated or deferred accordingly. However, places are reserved in cases where 'deferment would result in particular hardship'. One example of 'particular hardship' is stated to be the completion of compulsory service in the armed forces, and that, in Germany, was something which could only be done by men. Julia Schnorbus challenged this, but the ECJ held that the measure was justifiable because it was designed to counterbalance the disadvantage suffered by male applicants.

18.6.2 Positive discrimination

'Positive discrimination' measures go further than 'positive action' by actually conferring an advantage on the 'under-represented sex'. This is not tolerated by the ECJ because it essentially substitutes one form of sex discrimination (against women) for another (against men). An example of a prohibited 'positive discrimination' measure is provided by *Kalanke* (Case C–450/93) [1995] ECR I–3051. The case concerned provisions of German law which provided that women who had the same qualifications as men applying for promotion to the same post were to be given priority if women were under-represented in that post. The ECJ held that national laws which guaranteed women absolute and unconditional priority for appointment or promotion went beyond the scope of 'positive action' measures and amounted to prohibited 'positive discrimination'.

Kalanke was followed in *Abrahamsson and Anderson v Fogelqvist* (Case C–407/98) [2000] ECR I–5539. This case concerned provisions of Swedish employment legislation, similar to those in *Kalanke*, which set out positive discrimination for women for teaching posts in higher education. The key provision stated that 'a candidate belonging to an under-represented sex who possesses sufficient qualifications … must be granted preference over a candidate of the opposite sex who would otherwise have been chosen ("positive discrimination") where it proves necessary to do so in order for a candidate of the under-represented sex to be appointed'. The provisions were challenged by a male candidate, Leif Anderson, whose application for the post of Professor of Hydrospheric Sciences at Gothenburg university had been rejected, even though he was the best-qualified candidate. The university had applied the Swedish 'positive discrimination' provisions and appointed Elisabet Fogelqvist instead, despite the fact that she was less well qualified, because of the shortage of female academics in Swedish universities. The ECJ held that the Swedish legislation was another example of 'positive discrimination', following *Kalanke*. Following the ECJ's judgment, the university reconsidered its decision and appointed Mr Anderson.

In *Briheche* (Case C–319/03) [2004] ECR I–8807, the ECJ again found that a provision of national legislation, this time in France, conferred automatic priority on women and thus went beyond positive action and crossed the line into positive discrimination. The French Government had argued that the legislation in issue was adopted 'with a view to reducing actual instances of inequality between men and women, in particular due to the fact that women take on most of the housework'. However, the Court disagreed, finding that the legislation 'automatically and unconditionally gives priority to the candidatures of certain categories of women'. The Court concluded that 'such a provision … cannot be allowed'.

However, *Kalanke* (1995) was distinguished in *Marschall* (Case C–409/95) [1997] ECR I–6363. The ECJ took the view that, where men and women were equally qualified, men tended to be promoted particularly because of prejudices and stereotypes concerning the role and capacities of women in working life. These included, among other things:

- the fear that women would interrupt their careers more frequently
- that view that, because of household and family duties, women would be less flexible in their working hours
- that women would be absent from work more frequently because of pregnancy, childbirth and breastfeeding.

For those reasons, the 'mere fact' that a male and a female candidate were equally qualified did not mean that they had the same chances. Hence, national legislation which gave priority to women could be justified. However, it was crucial that such legislation contained what is typically referred to as a 'saving clause', that is, a provision allowing for men to be appointed nevertheless if the individual circumstances justified it.

CASE EXAMPLE

Marschall v Lord Nordrhein–Westfalen (Case C–409/95) [1997] ECR I–6363

German law provided that, where there were fewer women than men in a particular teaching post in a career bracket, women were to be given priority for promotion in the event of equal suitability, competence and professional performance 'unless reasons specific to an individual male candidate tilt the balance in his favour'. In 1994, Helmut Marschall applied for promotion at his comprehensive school. However, his application was rejected on the ground that there were fewer women than men in that career bracket. An equally qualified woman was promoted instead. He appealed against this but the ECJ distinguished *Kalanke* (1995) on the basis of the saving clause. The German law in this case was permissible.

Marschall was followed in *Badeck* (Case C–158/97) [2000] ECR I–1875, which involved various provisions of German legislation designed to remove obstacles affecting the employment of women in public administration. The stated aim of the law was 'the adoption of advancement plans relating to conditions of access and promotion for women and their working conditions, **with binding targets**' (emphasis added). The use of the phrase 'binding targets' seemed to suggest a degree of rigidity which would bring the legislation within *Kalanke*. However, the ECJ managed to identify a number of saving clauses which instead brought the legislation within *Marschall*. For example, although para 5(4) stipulated that 'more than half of the posts to be filled in a sector in which women are under-represented are to be designated for filling by women', which appeared to be a clear example of unlawful 'positive discrimination', the legislation went on to state that, when a male and female candidate had equal qualifications, then the woman was to be given priority provided that 'no reasons of greater legal weight are opposed'. Hence, the Court ruled that the priority system was 'not absolute and unconditional'.

As a result of these cases it is now possible to distinguish between two types of situation:

- National legislation conferring **automatic priority** on women in employment (known as a **hard** or **rigid quota** system) is prohibited: *Kalanke* (1995); *Abrahamsson* (2000); *Briheche* (2004).
- National legislation conferring priority on women in employment but subject to a '**saving clause**' whereby a male candidate could still be appointed or promoted if

demonstrably the best candidate (known as a **soft** or **flexible quota** system) is tolerated: *Marschall* (1997); *Badeck* (2000).

KEY FACTS

Positive action and positive discrimination	
Positive action involves the removal of obstacles preventing the 'under-represented sex' from competing with the other sex on a level playing field	Article157 (4) TFEU
Positive action is not only permitted but encouraged under EU law	*Lommers* (2002), *Schnorbus* (2000)
Positive discrimination goes beyond positive action by conferring an advantage on the 'under-represented sex', such as prioritising employment or promotion. It is not permitted under EU law	*Kalanke* (1995), *Abrahamsson & Anderson v Fogelqvist* (2000), *Briheche* (2004)
However, positive discrimination measures containing a 'saving clause' are permitted under EU law	*Marschall* (1997), *Badeck* (2000)

18.7 Pregnancy

The application of EU discrimination law on equality between men and women has been somewhat strained when it comes to cases involving pregnancy. As a matter of biological fact, only women can become pregnant. Therefore, any rule which discriminates against someone because of their pregnancy constitutes discrimination against women. This much is not disputed. What has been disputed over the years is whether this form of discrimination constitutes direct discrimination (which is very difficult to justify) or indirect discrimination (which is much easier to justify). This section will deal with the following situations involving pregnant women:

- maternity pay
- refusal to employ a woman on grounds of pregnancy
- dismissal of a woman on grounds of pregnancy
- dismissal of a woman on grounds of pregnancy-related illness
- discrimination in conditions of employment.

18.7.1 Maternity pay and related issues

In *Gillespie* (1996), the ECJ held that benefit paid by an employer to a woman employee on maternity leave was based on the employment relationship, and therefore constituted 'pay' within what is now Art 157 TFEU. However, the Court continued by stating that Art 157 did **not** require 'that women should continue to receive full pay during maternity leave'. Nor did it 'lay down any specific criteria for determining the amount of benefit to be paid to them during that period'. However, the Court did say that 'the amount payable could not, however, be so low as to undermine the purpose of maternity leave, namely the protection of women before and after giving birth'.

The point that pregnant workers on maternity leave are not entitled to full pay was confirmed in *McKenna* (Case C–191/03) [2005] ECR I–7631. Although Margaret McKenna was actually provided with full pay during her maternity leave period (September to December 2000), she spent all of her pregnancy from January to September 2000 on sick leave with a pathological condition linked to her pregnancy. During this time, she was only paid half-pay. She alleged that this constituted direct sex discrimination, but the ECJ disagreed, holding that:

JUDGMENT

'If a rule providing ... for a reduction in pay to a female worker during her maternity leave does not constitute discrimination based on sex, a rule providing ... for a reduction in pay to that female worker who is absent during her pregnancy by reason of an illness related to that pregnancy also cannot be regarded as constituting discrimination of that kind.'

The decision that maternity pay falls within Art 157 has been confirmed in several cases. In *Alabaster v Woolwich plc* (Case C–147/02) [2004] ECR I–3101, the ECJ decided that it was unlawful discrimination not to take account of a woman's pay rise awarded during the course of her pregnancy (but before the commencement of maternity leave) when the level of maternity pay was being calculated. In *Abdoulaye v Renault* (Case C–218/98) [1999] ECR I–5723 the ECJ ruled that a lump-sum payment given to pregnant employees of the French car manufacturers Renault at the commencement of their maternity leave did not breach Art 157. Although the payment was clearly a form of 'pay', the Court held that female workers going on maternity leave were not in a comparable situation with male workers and therefore no discrimination on grounds of sex had occurred. According to the Court, the payment was 'designed to offset the occupational disadvantages' that arise as a result of female workers taking maternity leave. The 'occupational disadvantages' that women on maternity leave may suffer were: possibly being overlooked for promotion; having her period of service reduced by the length of her absence; inability to claim performance-related salary increases; inability to take part in training. Finally, since 'new technology is constantly changing the nature of jobs', the ability of women coming back to work after maternity leave 'becomes complicated'. The Court, therefore, accepted that, 'in this case, male and female workers are ... in different situations, which excludes any breach of the principle of equal pay'.

(Note. Rights to maternity leave and maternity pay are now set out in Directive 92/85, the Pregnant Workers' Directive (PWD), which is examined in more detail in Chapter 17 of this book.)

18.7.2 Refusal to employ a woman on grounds of pregnancy

In *Dekker v Centrum* (Case 177/88) [1990] ECR I–3941, the ECJ stated that refusing to employ a woman because she was pregnant was **direct** discrimination on grounds of sex, and was unjustifiable:

JUDGMENT

'It should be observed that only women can be refused employment on grounds of pregnancy and such a refusal constitutes direct discrimination. A refusal of employment on account of the financial consequences of absence due to pregnancy must be regarded as based, essentially, on the fact of pregnancy ... Such discrimination cannot be justified on grounds relating to the financial loss which an employer who appointed a pregnant woman would suffer for the duration of her maternity leave.'

The company to which Ms Dekker had applied for employment, Centrum, had argued that there were, in fact, no male candidates who were deemed suitable for the job and that, where an employer chooses from exclusively female candidates, that choice cannot be attributable to discrimination on grounds of sex. The ECJ was unimpressed with that argument and held that a refusal to employ a woman because she is pregnant was 'directly linked to the sex of the candidate' and hence unjustifiable.

Professor R Wintemute challenges the conclusion in *Dekker* that discrimination on grounds of pregnancy is automatically direct discrimination. He argues that it is not discrimination because **women have exercised a choice in becoming pregnant**. He writes:

> 'It can be argued that the element of choice that intervenes between "being female" and "being pregnant" breaks the chain of causation with the result that these chosen conditions cease to be legally caused by the person's sex, even though they would not in fact exist "but for" the person's sex. In other words, the discrimination is based on the choice to exercise a physical capacity unique to the chooser's sex, but not on the chooser's sex *per se*.'
>
> Professor R Wintemute, 'When is Pregnancy Discrimination Indirect Sex Discrimination?' (1998) 27 ILJ 23

Wintemute develops this hypothesis further. He poses the following (rhetorical) question: 'Is dismissing a woman because she had an abortion also direct sex discrimination? Or does the element of choice have greater legal significance in the case of abortion, because pregnancy is necessary for the perpetuation of society in a way that abortion is not?'

In *Mahlburg* (Case C–207/98) [2000] ECR I–549 a heart clinic tried to justify its refusal to take on a pregnant woman because of provisions of German legislation, which stated that 'pregnant women must not be assigned to work exposing them to the harmful effects of substances that pose a risk to health'. The clinic took the view that working in an operating theatre would expose Ms Mahlburg to such harmful effects. The ECJ held that such provisions could not be used to justify a refusal to employ Ms Mahlburg. This decision must be correct: after all, a pregnant woman is only pregnant for nine months, but her working life could last 40 years. Employers must take a longer-term perspective.

In *Busch v Klinikum Neustadt* (Case C–320/01) [2003] ECR I–2041, the question for the Court was whether a pregnant woman (who also knew that she was pregnant) was under any obligation to tell a prospective employer of this fact when being interviewed for a job. The ECJ held that it would be direct discrimination to impose this obligation onto a pregnant woman. The Court took the view that, since an employer cannot take the fact of a woman's pregnancy into consideration in deciding whether to employ her, it followed that she was not obliged to inform them that she was pregnant. A woman's pregnancy status becomes immaterial to the decision whether or not to employ her.

The ECJ's firm stance with employers who refuse to employ pregnant women can be applauded for recognising and tackling the difficulties faced by pregnant women in trying to find employment. However, it can be criticised for imposing difficult burdens on employers, particularly small and medium-sized companies, who may struggle to cope financially if forced by law to take on pregnant women. Despite this point, the ECJ has refused to allow employers to derogate from its view that discrimination against pregnant workers is direct sex discrimination.

18.7.3 Dismissal from employment on grounds of pregnancy

Dismissal of a pregnant woman also amounts to unlawful direct discrimination. In *Hebermann-Beltermann* (Case C-421/92) [1994] ECR I-1657, the complainant was sacked from her job as a night nurse in a care home for the elderly when it was discovered that she was pregnant. Her employers claimed that this was necessary under German legislation designed to protect mothers, the key Article of which provided that 'It is prohibited to assign to women who are pregnant or breastfeeding overtime or night-time work between 8 pm and 6 am or work on Sundays or public holidays'. The ECJ held that the complainant had been wrongly discriminated against. This judgment was followed in *Webb v EMO Air Cargo* (Case C–32/93) [1994] ECR I–3567, where the circumstances were rather unusual. However, the ECJ rejected the argument that specific circumstances provided any excuse, confirming that dismissal of a pregnant woman, regardless of the situation, amounts to unjustifiable direct discrimination.

CASE EXAMPLE

Webb v EMO Air Cargo (Case C–32/93) [1994] ECR I–3567

Carole Webb was engaged by EMO Air Cargo, a small organisation with just 16 employees, to replace another employee, Mrs Stewart, who had become pregnant and was due to go on maternity leave. At the time it was envisaged that Mrs Webb's appointment was indefinite, and that she would remain even after Mrs Stewart returned to work. Two weeks after starting, however, she discovered that she was herself pregnant. She was promptly dismissed and brought a claim for unfair dismissal. The ECJ held that the dismissal of a pregnant woman – for the sole reason that she was pregnant – was unjustifiable discrimination on grounds of sex.

Workers on temporary contracts/seasonal workers

In both *Hebermann-Beltermann* and *Webb*, the ECJ explicitly referred to the 'termination of a contract for an indefinite period' because of pregnancy as constituting direct sex discrimination. Did this imply that the termination of a contract for a **definite** period would be treated differently? Contracts for a definite period could refer to workers on a temporary contract, or one held by a seasonal worker (for example someone employed to pick fruit during the summer, or someone employed in a shop during the weeks before Christmas). Would an employer be justified in sacking a woman employed purely for two months if she announced just after starting work that she was six months pregnant? The answer is 'no'. In *Jiminez Melgar* (Case C–438/99) [2001] ECR I–6915 the ECJ held that no distinction should be drawn between pregnant workers on definite, temporary contracts and those on indefinite contracts. This was confirmed in *Tele-Danmark* (Case C–109/00) [2001] ECR I–6993, where the Court stated:

JUDGMENT

'Since the dismissal of a worker on account of pregnancy constitutes direct discrimination on grounds of sex, whatever the nature and extent of the economic loss incurred by the employer as a result of her absence because of pregnancy, whether the contract of employment was concluded for a fixed or an indefinite period has no bearing on the discriminatory character of the dismissal. In either case the employee's inability to perform her contract of employment is due to pregnancy.'

18.7.4 Dismissal from employment on grounds of pregnancy-related illness

Given the principles developed in the above cases – that dismissal of a pregnant women from employment always amounts to unjustifiable, direct discrimination – you may think that the same principles would apply to the situation where a woman is dismissed because she has a pregnancy-related illness. Indeed, if anything, it may seem that the woman's claim is **even stronger**: not only does she have the pregnancy to cope with but she also has the physical illness and (presumably) the mental distress of worrying about the effect of the illness on her child. However, in *Hertz v Aldi Marked* (Case 179/88) [1990] ECR I–3979, the ECJ held that what is now Art 14(1)(c) of the Recast Directive did not **necessarily** preclude dismissal of a pregnant woman on the basis of pregnancy-related illness. The Court held that it depended on when the illness manifested itself. The Court stated:

JUDGMENT

'In the case of an illness manifesting itself after maternity leave, there is no reason to distinguish an illness attributable to pregnancy or confinement from any other illness. Such a pathological condition is therefore covered by the general rules applicable in the event of illness. Male and female workers are equally exposed to illness. Although certain disorders are, it is true, specific to one or other sex, the only question is whether a woman is dismissed on account of absence due to illness in the same circumstances as a man; if that is the case, then there is no direct discrimination on grounds of sex.'

CASE EXAMPLE

Hertz v Aldi Marked (Case 179/88) [1990] ECR I–3979

Birtha Hertz had repeated absences from her part-time cashier job at Aldi caused by an illness which, although connected with her pregnancy and childbirth, occurred some time later. She had been appointed in July 1982, became pregnant in September and gave birth in June 1983. She returned to work on the expiry of her maternity leave in late 1983 but, between June 1984 and June 1985, missed 100 working days. At this point she was dismissed. She appealed. The ECJ held that the dismissal did not discriminate against her on grounds of sex, because it was impossible to distinguish between Ms Hertz's illness and any illness that may be suffered by a man. It was, however, crucially important that the illness Ms Hertz suffered first manifested itself **after** her period of maternity leave ended.

This seemed to strongly imply that, where the illness manifested itself **before or during** maternity leave, then the situation would be different. The ECJ subsequently confirmed that this was the position, in *Brown v Rentokil Ltd* (Case C–394/96) [1998] ECR I–4185. There, the Court stated that:

JUDGMENT

'Where a woman is absent owing to illness resulting from pregnancy or childbirth, and that illness arose during pregnancy and persisted during and after maternity leave, her absence not only during maternity leave but also during the period extending from the start of her pregnancy to the start of her maternity leave **cannot be taken into account** for computation of the period justifying her dismissal.'

The Court noted that pregnancy was a period during which specific disorders and complications may arise, compelling a woman to undergo medical supervision or, in some cases, to rest completely. Such disorders and complications may lead to incapacity for work but, if an employer was to dismiss a woman because of such incapacity, it had to be regarded as 'essentially based on the fact of pregnancy'. As such dismissal could only affect women, it therefore constituted direct (and hence unjustifiable) discrimination on grounds of sex. The Court did, however, confirm the correctness of the decision in *Hertz* (1990), that absence from work because of pregnancy-related illness after the end of maternity leave may be taken into account in deciding whether to dismiss a woman from employment.

The case of *Mayr v Flöckner* (Case C–506/06) [2008] ECR I-1017, which was discussed in Chapter 17 of this book in the context of the Pregnant Workers Directive (PWD), also raised a question regarding the application of the ETD (now the Recast Directive). Sabine Mayr, a waitress, had been dismissed from her job while off sick having undergone *in vitro* fertilisation (IVF) treatment. Although the ECJ ruled that she was not 'pregnant' at the time and, hence, could not claim under the PWD, the Court did hold that it was possible that Ms Mayr's claim could be recognised under what is now Art 14(1)(c) of the Recast Directive, instead (this would ultimately be for a national court to decide). If Flöckner had dismissed her because she was off sick, which in turn was caused by her seeking IVF treatment, specifically the fact that she had just undergone a 'follicular puncture', then that would amount to direct discrimination based on sex. The Court stated that what is now Art 14(1)(c) precluded the dismissal of a female worker who was at 'an advanced stage' of IVF treatment, that is, 'between the follicular puncture and the immediate transfer of the *in vitro* fertilised ova into the uterus', where it can be established that the dismissal is 'essentially based on the fact that the woman has undergone such treatment'.

18.7.5 Discrimination in conditions of employment

In a number of cases under the ETD the ECJ held that it was contrary to that directive for an employer to deny to a woman on maternity leave any employment opportunities that she would have enjoyed had she not been on leave. In the following cases, the ECJ held that the ETD had been breached:

- *Thibault* (Case C–136/95) [1998] ECR I–2011 – Évelyne Thibault had been deprived of the right to an annual assessment of her performance and, therefore, of the opportunity of qualifying for promotion, because she had been away on maternity leave.
- *Sass* (Case C–284/02) [2004] ECR I–11143 – Ursula Sass had been on maternity leave in 1987 for 20 weeks (permitted under East German law prior to reunification, whereas West German law only allowed for eight weeks). After reunification, only the less generous West German rules were carried forward. Mrs Sass' new employer refused to take into account the extra 12 weeks in calculating her length of service, used to assess seniority.
- *Sarkatzis Herrero* (Case C–294/04) [2006] ECR I–1513 – Carmen Sarkatzis Herrero had actually been promoted during her maternity leave but had also been told that her new position would not be formally recognised until she returned to work.

These case law developments have now been incorporated into legislation, in Art 15 of the Recast Directive, which states that:

ARTICLE

'Art 15. A woman on maternity leave shall be entitled, after the end of her period of maternity leave, to return to her job or to an equivalent post on terms and conditions which are no less favourable to her and to benefit from any improvement in working conditions to which she would have been entitled during her absence.'

KEY FACTS

Pregnancy	
Although maternity pay is 'pay' under Art 157 (1) TFEU, women on maternity leave are not guaranteed to receive full pay	*Gillespie* (1996), *Alabaster* (2004), *McKenna* (2005)
This is because women on maternity leave are not in a comparable situation with men	*Abdoulaye* (1999)
A refusal to employ a pregnant woman because of her pregnancy is direct sex discrimination, which is extremely difficult to justify	*Dekker* (1990), *Mahlburg* (2000), *Busch* (2003)
The dismissal of a pregnant woman because of her pregnancy is also direct sex discrimination	*Hebermann-Beltermann* (1994), *Webb* (1994), *Tele-Danmark* (2001)
The dismissal of a pregnant woman because of a pregnancy-related illness is also direct sex discrimination, but only if the illness manifested itself during the pregnancy or maternity leave	*Hertz* (1990), *Brown* (1998), *Mayr* (2008)
It is prohibited for an employer to deny a woman on maternity leave any improvements in working conditions which she would have received had she still been at work	*Thibault* (1998), *Sass* (2004), *Sarkatzis Herrero* (2006)

18.8 Equal treatment in matters of social security: Directive 79/7

Directive 79/7, the Social Security Directive (SSD) establishes a principle of equal treatment 'in the field of social security and other elements of social protection' between men and women (Art 1). Article 2 defines the Directive's personal scope and Art 3 its material scope. Article 4 amplifies on the equal treatment principle established in Art 1.

18.8.1 Personal scope

ARTICLE

> 'Art 2 This Directive shall apply to the working population – including self-employed persons, workers and self-employed persons whose activity is interrupted by illness, accident or involuntary unemployment and persons seeking employment – and to retired or invalided workers and self-employed persons.'

This definition gives the SSD a wide scope but it has been interpreted even more generously by the ECJ.

'The working population'

The ECJ has held that it is irrelevant whether or not the person is regarded under national law as being in 'minor' employment because of the small number of hours worked and/or the low wage earned (*Nolte* (Case C–317/93) [1995] ECR I–4625 and *Megner and Scheffel* (Case C–444/93) [1995] ECR I–4741). These cases involved German law which excluded those who worked less than 15 hours per week and who received less than one-seventh of the average monthly salary from access to the statutory old-age insurance scheme. The ECJ held that the SSD nevertheless applied.

'Persons whose activity is interrupted'

In *Drake v Chief Adjudication Officer* (Case 150/85) [1986] ECR 1995, the Court held that the SSD applies even if a person in employment is forced to interrupt their activity in order to care for a relative. Thus, although the SSD refers to 'persons whose activity is interrupted by illness', the ECJ has interpreted that phrase to include someone else's illness. Thus the claimant, Mrs Drake, who had given up work in order to care for her invalid mother, was entitled to claim invalid care allowance (ICA), a benefit payable under British social security legislation. (It had originally been refused because, under the terms of the legislation, married women were not entitled to the benefit although married men were.) The Court stated:

JUDGMENT

> 'There is a clear economic link between the benefit and the disabled person, since the disabled person derives an advantage from the fact that an allowance is paid to the person caring for him. The fact that a benefit is paid to a third party and not directly to the disabled person does not place it outside the scope of Directive 79/7.'

The same decision was reached in *Johnson v Chief Adjudication Officer (No 1)* (Case C–31/90) [1991] ECR I–3723, where the claimant had given up work in order to look after her disabled daughter. However, in *Achterberg-te Riele* (Case 48/88) [1989] ECR 1963, the ECJ held that the SSD did not apply to a person who had given up work in order to care for children because that was not listed in Art 2. Similarly, in *Züchner* (Case C–77/95) [1996] ECR I–5689, the Court held that the SSD did not apply to someone who was caring for an invalid relative but who had not interrupted an activity in order to do so.

JUDGMENT

'The term "activity" in Art 2 of the directive can be construed only as referring at the very least to an economic activity, that is to say an activity undertaken in return for remuneration in the broad sense.'

It was further argued in *Züchner* (1996) that specialist care provided for an invalid relative could be 'assimilated to an occupational activity'. It was pointed out that such care often required that the carer undergoes training such that the care required a 'degree of competence', and that, if the carer was for some reason unable or unwilling to do it, care would have to be provided in hospital or privately. The ECJ rejected this argument. The Court pointed out that numerous activities call for a 'degree of competence, are of a certain scope and must be provided by an outsider in return for remuneration if there is no-one else, whether or not a member of the family, who will do so without payment'. These included 'the education of children, housework, management of private property or mere incidents of daily life'. Thus, to interpret Art 2 to include all family members who cared for invalid relatives or provided some other activity requiring a 'degree of competence' would 'have the effect of infinitely expanding the scope of the directive'.

CASE EXAMPLE

Züchner (Case C–77/95) [1996] ECR I–5689

Gerhard Züchner, a German national, had been rendered paraplegic following an accident. His wife, Bruna-Alessandra Züchner, looked after him at home providing general nursing care as well as more specific therapeutic treatment. She claimed financial assistance for this, but was not paid in full because of limitations contained in German law. She challenged this, alleging a breach of the SSD on the basis that the majority of home carers were women, and the case was referred to the ECJ. One question was whether or not Bruna-Alessandra belonged to the working population. She admitted that she had not been in employment at the time of Gerhard's accident, but suggested that the care that she provided could be 'assimilated to an occupational activity'. The Court rejected her arguments.

'Persons seeking employment'

Whether or not someone is seeking employment is a matter for the national court to decide. The onus of proof is on the claimant. Relevant evidence could include registration with an employment organisation, sending out job applications and attending interviews. There is no requirement that the person seeking employment must have been in employment previously (*Johnson* (1991)).

18.8.2 Material scope

This is set out in Art 3(1) of the SSD.

ARTICLE

3(1) This Directive shall apply to (a) statutory schemes which provide protection against the following risks:

- sickness,
- invalidity,
- old age,
- accidents at work and occupational diseases,
- unemployment;

  (b) social assistance, in so far as it is intended to supplement or replace the schemes referred to in (a).

(2) This Directive shall not apply to the provisions concerning survivors' benefits nor to those concerning family benefits, except in the case of family benefits granted by way of increases of benefits due in respect of the risks referred to in paragraph (1)(a) ...'

Directive 79/7 had an unusually long implementation period of six years, and so the first cases concerning its interpretation did not appear until the mid-1980s. Initially, the ECJ adopted an expansive interpretation. In *Drake* (1986), the ECJ held that Art 3(1) covered benefits forming either the **whole** or just **part** of a statutory scheme providing protection against one of the specified risks. The Court reiterated this point in *Richardson* (Case C–137/94) [1995] ECR I–3407, adding that any form of 'social assistance having the same objective' as such a scheme was also covered by Art 3(1). In *R v Secretary of State for Social Services, ex p Smithson* (Case C–243/90) [1992] ECR I–467, however, the ECJ did place some limits on the Directive's material scope. The Court held that a benefit must be 'directly and effectively' linked to one of the specific 'risks' listed in Art 3(1) in order to come within the scope of the SSD. Claims for equal entitlement to benefits in which Art 3(1) has been successfully invoked because such a 'direct' link was established include:

- Exemption from prescription charges for women aged 60 plus and men aged 65 plus (*Richardson* (1995)) – fell within Art 3(1) because linked to 'risk' of sickness.
- A winter fuel payment of £20 under UK legislation, the Social Fund Winter Fuel Payment Regulations 1998, which was payable to women aged 60 plus and to men aged 65 plus (*R v Secretary of State for the Home Dept, ex p Taylor* (Case C–382/98) [1999] ECR I–8955) – fell within Art 3(1) because linked to 'risk' of old age.
- Early retirement benefits (*Balestra* (Case C–139/95) [1997] ECR I–549) – fell within Art 3(1) because linked to 'risk' of old age.

In *Smithson* (1992), the ECJ concluded that Art 3(1) did not apply to housing benefit paid under UK legislation to persons on low income – because Art 3(1) did not explicitly refer to (lack of) housing as a 'risk' against which if protection was provided the 'equal treatment' principle would apply. Similarly, in *Hoever and Zachow* (Cases C–245 and 312/94) [1996] ECR I–4895, the Court held that a child-raising allowance was outside the scope of Art 3(1) because the SSD did not explicitly list responsibility for the cost of raising children as a relevant 'risk'.

In *Atkins v Wrekin DC* (Case C–228/94) [1996] ECR I–3633 the ECJ held that entitlement to concessionary travel on British public transport – provided under the Transport Act 1985 – fell outside the scope of Art 3(1). Although the benefit was only available to certain persons (those over the State pension age; persons under 16; those aged 17 or 18 and in full-time education; the blind; the deaf; persons with a disability or injury which seriously impaired their ability to walk; the mentally handicapped; anyone who had been refused a driving licence on medical grounds, those lacking the use of both arms) the Court was not persuaded that that was enough for the SSD to apply. The benefit did not afford 'direct and effective protection against one of the risks listed in Art 3(1)'. The purpose of the benefit was 'to facilitate access to public transport for certain classes of persons who, for various reasons, are recognized as having a particular need for public transport and who are, for the same reasons, less well-off financially and materially. Old age and invalidity, which are among the risks listed in Art 3(1) are only two of the criteria which may be applied to define the classes of beneficiaries of such a scheme'.

In *Jackson and Cresswell* (Case C-63 and 64/91) [1992] ECR I-4737, the Court held that the SSD did not apply because the benefits in question – 'supplementary allowance' and 'income support' – were designed to boost the earnings of low-paid workers (ie people already in employment) and were therefore not directly linked to the 'risk' of unemployment.

KEY FACTS

Benefits to which Art 3(1) has been held not to apply	
• Benefits paid to boost earnings of those in low-paid jobs – not directly linked to unemployment.	*Jackson and Cresswell* (1992)
• Concessionary travel benefits.	*Atkins* (1996)
• Child-raising allowance.	*Hoever and Zachow* (1996)
• Housing benefit.	*Smithson* (1992)

18.8.3 The principle of equal treatment

This is set out in Art 4(1) of the SSD.

ARTICLE

'Art 4(1) The principle of equal treatment means that there shall be no discrimination whatsoever on grounds of sex either directly, or indirectly by reference in particular to marital or family status, in particular as concerns:

- the scope of the schemes and the conditions of access thereto,
- the obligation to contribute and the calculation of contributions,
- the calculation of benefits including increases due in respect of a spouse and for dependants and the condition governing the duration and retention of entitlement to benefits.'

Direct discrimination

The case of *Drake* (1986), considered above, provided a very clear illustration of direct discrimination (invalid care allowance could be claimed by married men but not by married women). The ECJ held that this direct discrimination was contrary to both Arts 1 and 4 of the SSD. Another clear example is provided by *Clarke v Chief Adjudication Officer* (Case 384/85) [1987] ECR 2865. This concerned severe disablement allowance (SDA), a benefit which was payable under British law to both men and women. However, women had to satisfy an additional set of criteria known as the 'household duties test' before the allowance would be paid. The Court held that this was direct discrimination.

A more recent – and unusual – example of direct discrimination occurred in *Richards* (Case C-423/04) [2006] ECR I-3585. Sarah Richards was born, as a man, in February 1942. She was subsequently diagnosed with gender dysphoria, and underwent gender reassignment surgery in May 2001. In February 2002, she applied for a retirement pension, having reached her 60th birthday, the pension age under the Pensions Act 1995 for women born before 6th April 1950. This was rejected, she appealed, and the case was referred to the ECJ. There, the Court held that Ms Richards had suffered discrimination on grounds of sex, in breach of Art 4(1). The Court followed the judgment in *P v S* (Case C–13/94) [1996] ECR I–2143 (considered above in section 18.2.3), and stated that:

JUDGMENT

'The scope of Directive 79/7 cannot thus be confined simply to discrimination based on the fact that a person is of one or other sex. In view of its purpose and the nature of the rights which it seeks to safeguard, the scope of that directive is also such as to apply to discrimination arising from the gender reassignment of the person concerned.'

Indirect discrimination and objective justification

Teuling (Case 30/85) [1987] ECR 2497 provides an example of indirect discrimination. The case concerned Dutch social security benefit supplements; the rules governing entitlement thereto took account of a number of factors including marital status and family situation. Although the rules were superficially gender-neutral, in effect far fewer women than men were entitled to the supplements. This was held to breach Arts 1 and 4 of the SSD. However, the Court went on to hold that, where discrimination was indirect, it was capable of justification, provided that objective grounds (that is, grounds unrelated to sex) could be identified.

The ECJ found that the discrimination in *Teuling* (1987) was justifiable on this basis. In *Ruzius-Wilbrink* (Case 102/88) [1989] ECR 4311, the ECJ found that disability allowances payable under Dutch social security legislation which provided more favourable treatment to full-time workers than to part-time workers were indirectly discriminatory against women (the majority of part-time workers in the Netherlands being female). The Court was unable to find any acceptable justification for this discrimination, however. Similarly, in *De Weerd* (Case C–343/92) [1994] ECR I–571, the ECJ held that Dutch rules making entitlement to incapacity benefit dependent on previous earning levels was indirectly discriminatory against women (men were more likely than women to have earned enough to qualify for the benefit) and was incapable of objective justification.

In *Nolte* (1995) and *Megner and Scheffel* (1995), noted above, the ECJ held that the German rules on entitlement to the old-age insurance scheme (where those in 'minor' employment were excluded) were indirectly discriminatory, because far more women than men were excluded from the scheme. However, the rules also exempted those in minor employment from paying contributions towards unemployment benefit. This led the ECJ to conclude that, overall, the rules were objectively justified. The Court stated that Member States had a broad 'margin of discretion' when it came to implementing social policy.

Increases due in respect of a spouse and for dependants

The leading case here is *Cotter and McDermott* (Case C–377/89) [1991] ECR I–1155. The ECJ established the following propositions:

- Member States can stipulate whatever conditions they wish for entitlement to increases to existing social security benefits, provided that the principle of equal treatment is fully complied with
- spouses do not have to be dependent
- with regard to other persons – 'in particular children' – proof of actual dependency is not required.

18.8.4 Derogation regarding 'the determination of pensionable age'

Article 7 of the SSD provides a number of derogations, by far the most important of which is Art 7(1)(a). This allows Member States to exclude from the scope of the SSD 'the determination of pensionable age for the purpose of granting old-age and retirement pensions and the possible consequences thereof for other benefits'.

This derogation was designed to allow Member States to set differential ages at which men and women would become entitled to claim an old-age pension from the State. Many States had such a system in place, including the UK, where women were entitled to an old-age pension at 60 but men had to wait until 65. The application of Art 7(1)(a) to the differential pension ages in the UK was challenged in *R v Secretary of State for Social Security, ex p Equal Opportunities Commission* (Case C–9/91) [1992] ECR I–4297, but the ECJ dismissed it. In any event, the UK Parliament has amended British law to equalise the pension age for men and women in the Pensions Act 1995, which raises the pension age for women to 65, the same as for men. However, as noted earlier in this chapter, the 1995 Act only applies fully to women born after 5th April 1955.

More recently, in *De Vriendt and Others* (Cases C–377 to 384/96) [1998] ECR I–2105 the ECJ held that Art 7(1)(a) meant that Member States remained entitled to maintain discriminatory pensionable ages for men and women. Moreover, it followed that Member States – in this case, Belgium – were also entitled to discriminate between men and women in terms of the 'method of calculating retirement pensions'. Specifically, differences in the 'length of the period during which persons can contribute to the pension scheme' (45 years for men and 40 years for women) were 'necessarily and objectively linked' to the different pensionable ages.

Derogation concerning 'the possible consequences thereof for other benefits'

Article 7(1)(a) has also been invoked to justify other differential treatment for men and women, provided that it is linked to the State's pensionable age. In *Graham* (Case C–92/94) [1995] ECR I–2521 the ECJ held that British rules which provided for the payment of an invalidity benefit to those workers (male or female) forced to leave work because of ill-health up to the state pension age (60 for women, 65 for men), at which point the benefit would cease and be replaced with the State pension, were allowed under Art 7(1)(a). This was the case even though the effect of the British rules was to penalise women who, potentially, stood to receive more under the invalidity benefit but would lose their entitlement to it five years before men.

Article 7(1)(a) was also successfully invoked in *Hepple and Others* (Case C–196/98) [2000] ECR I–3701, which concerned a British social security benefit called reduced-earnings allowance (REA), paid to workers or ex-workers who had suffered an accident at work or an occupational disease. On reaching the state pension age, REA ceased and was replaced with retirement allowance (RA), calculated at only 25 per cent of the last REA payment. The Court held that there was 'coherence' between the benefit in question and the state's old-age pension scheme, and concluded that 'maintenance of the rules' – which stated that the benefit ceased on the claimant attaining the age of 60 (for women) or 65 (for men) – was 'objectively necessary to preserve such coherence'. Thus, despite the obvious discrimination, it was 'objectively and necessarily linked to the difference between the retirement age for men and that for women, so that it is covered by the derogation for which Art 7(1)(a) provides'. However, in most subsequent cases, the ECJ has limited the scope of the derogation. In *Thomas* (Case C–328/91) [1993] ECR I–1247, the ECJ said that:

JUDGMENT

> 'The scope of the permitted derogation, defined by the words "the possible consequences thereof for other benefits" contained in Art 7(1)(a), is limited to the forms of discrimination existing under other benefit schemes which are necessarily and objectively linked to the difference in pensionable age. That will be the position where such forms of discrimination are objectively necessary in order to avoid disturbing the financial equilibrium of the social-security system or to ensure coherence between the retirement-pension scheme and other benefit schemes.'

This requirement, that benefits must be 'necessarily and objectively linked to the difference in pensionable age' has had the effect of excluding several benefits from the scope of Art 7(1)(a), as the following cases show:

- *Thomas* (1993) – Art 7(1)(a) did not apply to provisions in UK law which prohibited the granting of severe disability allowance and invalid care allowance to those who had reached State retirement age.
- *Richardson* (1995) – Art 7(1)(a) did not apply to provisions in UK law linking exemption from prescription charges to the State retirement age.
- *Taylor* (1999) – Art 7(1)(a) did not apply to provisions in UK law linking entitlement to a winter fuel payment to the State retirement age.

The issue in *Buchner and Others* (Case C–104/98) [2000] ECR I–3625 was different. The ECJ held that Art 7(1)(a) did not apply to Austrian law stipulating discriminatory early retirement ages for men and women (55 for women, 57 for men) on the basis that the law was introduced after the implementation deadline for the SSD (pre-existing Austrian law had set down the same age, 55, for both men and women; the discriminatory law was introduced in September 1996).

18.8.5 Remedies for breach of Directive 79/7

Article 6 of the SSD provides that claimants are entitled to enforce claims by judicial process. The ECJ has interpreted this provision surprisingly narrowly. In *R v Secretary of State for Social Security, ex p Sutton* (Case C–66/95) [1997] ECR I–2163, the Court rejected the claimant's argument that she should be entitled to back-dated interest on her social security benefit which had previously been denied to her in breach of the SSD. The Court distinguished *Marshall v Southampton and South West Hampshire AHA (No 2)* (Case C–271/91) [1994] QB 126, where the Court ordered the payment of interest on compensation awarded for breach of the ETD (now the Recast Directive). In *Sutton* (1997) the Court said that, as social security benefits were in no way compensatory, the principle established in *Marshall (No 2)* (1994) did not apply.

18.9 Equal treatment for self-employed persons: Directive 86/613

All of the above discussion has concentrated on the rights of women (and men) to equality of treatment at work. However, what about the self-employed? It is self-evident that self-employed persons are much less likely to encounter discriminatory treatment than those in employment, as of course there is no chance of being made subject to discriminatory employment practices. However, self-employed persons are vulnerable to discriminatory national legislation, and hence EU measures are required. The legislation is Directive 86/613.

18.9.1 Personal scope

The Directive applies the equal treatment principle to self-employed persons (Art 1). It applies to 'self-employed workers', defined as 'all persons pursuing a gainful activity for their own account' (Art 2(a)). Two examples of 'self-employed workers' are given: farmers and 'members of the liberal professions'. The Directive also applies to 'their spouses, not being employees or partners, where they habitually … Participate in the activities of the self-employed worker and perform the same tasks or ancillary tasks' (Art 2(b)).

18.9.2 Material scope

The Directive eliminates sex discrimination in two areas:

- Member States are to ensure that equal treatment principles operate 'in respect of the establishment, equipment or extension of a business or the launching or extension of any other form of self-employed activity including financial facilities' (Art 4).
- Member States are to ensure that 'the conditions for the formation of a company between spouses are not more restrictive than the conditions for the formation of a company between unmarried persons' (Art 5).

Although there are other provisions, they lack the same level of specificity. For example, Art 7 merely provides that Member States are to 'undertake to examine' how recognition of the work of spouses identified in Art 2(b)) may be 'encouraged'. Similarly, Art 8 simply requires Member States to 'undertake to examine' whether female self-employed workers and the wives of self-employed workers may have access to social services and social security benefits 'during interruptions in their occupational activity owing to pregnancy or motherhood'.

18.10 Equal treatment on grounds of sex in access to and supply of goods and services: Directive 2004/113

The Goods & Services Directive 2004/113 (GSD) establishes a principle of equal treatment on grounds of sex in access to and supply of goods and services (Art 1), while Art 4(1) proscribes both direct and indirect discrimination based on sex in terms of access to and supply of goods and services. Direct discrimination includes 'less favourable treatment of women for reasons of pregnancy and maternity'. The preamble adds that direct discrimination occurs only when one person is treated 'less favourably, on grounds of sex, than another person in a comparable situation'. The preamble gives an example of a situation which is not comparable: a difference in 'the provision of healthcare services, which result from the physical differences between men and women'.

Article 3 defines the scope of the GSD as follows:

ARTICLE

'Art 3(1) ... this Directive shall apply to all persons who provide goods and services, which are available to the public irrespective of the person concerned as regards both the public and private sectors, including public bodies, and which are offered outside the area of private and family life and the transactions carried out in this context.

(2) This Directive does not prejudice the individual's freedom to choose a contractual partner as long as an individual's choice of contractual partner is not based on that person's sex.

(3) This Directive shall not apply to the content of media and advertising nor to education.

(4) This Directive shall not apply to matters of employment and occupation. This Directive shall not apply to matters of self-employment, insofar as these matters are covered by other Community legislative acts.'

Article 4(2) allows for a form of positive action, as it provides that the GSD 'shall be without prejudice to more favourable provisions concerning the protection of women as regards pregnancy and maternity'. Another derogation is set out in Art 4(5), which provides that the GSD 'shall not preclude differences in treatment, if the provision of the goods and services exclusively or primarily to members of one sex is justified by a legitimate aim and the means of achieving that aim are appropriate and necessary'. As yet there is no case law guidance on the interpretation of Art 4(5), but the preamble to the GSD suggests five examples of 'legitimate aims' (with examples of single-sex services that might need to invoke the aim in brackets):

- protection of victims of sex-related violence (shelters);
- reasons of privacy and decency (toilets, changing rooms, wards in private hospitals);
- promotion of gender equality or of the interests of men or women (voluntary bodies);
- freedom of association (private clubs);
- organisation of sporting activities (sports events).

Article 5 deals specifically with 'actuarial factors' (these are factors used by insurance companies, underwriters and pension schemes to calculate insurance premiums and benefits). Prior to the GSD, such factors could be used differentially between men and women (one factor, in particular, is that women's average life expectancy is longer than men's). Article 5 does not completely outlaw the use of such factors but it does state that 'the use of sex as a factor in the calculation of premiums and benefits for the purposes of insurance and related financial services shall not result in differences in individuals' premiums and benefits'.

Article 6 allows for Member States to take positive action in the form of 'specific measures to prevent or compensate for disadvantages linked to sex'. Article 7 confirms that the GSD sets out 'minimum requirements' and that 'Member States may introduce or maintain provisions which are more favourable to the protection of the principle of equal treatment between men and women than those laid down in this Directive'.

18.11 Beyond sex: the EU's new anti-discrimination agenda

In November 2000, the Council of the European Union adopted two Directives under powers conferred on the Council under what is now Art 19 TFEU.

- Directive 2000/43 (the Race Directive): this deals with discrimination on grounds of **race and ethnic origin**. It was implemented into UK law in July 2003 by the Race Relations Act 1976 (Amendment) Regulations 2003.
- Directive 2000/78 (the Framework Directive): this deals with discrimination on grounds of sexual orientation, religion or belief, disability, and age. The provisions on **sexual orientation** were implemented into UK law by the Employment Equality (Sexual Orientation) Regulations 2003. The provisions on **religion or belief** were implemented into UK law by the Employment Equality (Religion or Belief) Regulations 2003. The provisions on **disability** were implemented into UK law by the Disability Discrimination Act 1995 (Amendment) Regulations 2003. The provisions on **age** were implemented into UK law by the Employment Equality (Age) Regulations 2006. Note: the Sexual Orientation Regulations, the Religion or Belief Regulations and the Age Regulations have since been consolidated into the Equality Act 2010.

18.11.1 Common elements

Although differing in certain important respects (which will be dealt with below), the Race and Framework Directives share a number of common elements.

Principle of equal treatment

Article 1 of each Directive establishes that its purpose is to put into effect in the Member States a principle of equal treatment.

Definition of 'discrimination'

Both Directives prohibit direct and indirect discrimination. Each provides a definition of both types of discrimination, in identical terms. Direct discrimination is defined in Art 2(2)(a) of each directive as occurring: 'where one person is treated less favourably than another is, has been or would be treated in a comparable situation' on the grounds or race, religion, sexual orientation, etc. An example of direct discrimination on grounds of age was identified in *Palacios de la Villa* (Case C–411/05) [2007] ECR I-8531. The case involved a provision of Spanish legislation stipulating automatic termination of a worker's employment contract as soon as he or she reached retirement age. The ECJ stated that this 'must be regarded as directly imposing less favourable treatment for workers who have reached that age as compared with all other persons in the labour force'. 'Indirect discrimination' is defined in Art 2(2)(b) of each Directive as follows (this is taken from the Race Directive):

ARTICLE

> 'Art 2(2)(b) Indirect discrimination shall be taken to occur where an apparently neutral provision, criterion or practice would put persons of a racial or ethnic origin at a particular disadvantage compared with other persons, unless that provision, criterion or practice is objectively justified by a legitimate aim and the means of achieving that aim are appropriate and necessary.'

In the Framework Directive the words 'having a particular religion or belief, a particular disability, a particular age, or a particular sexual orientation' appear instead of 'of a racial or ethnic origin'. As an example, an employer providing benefits to married employees (unless national legislation – which has been passed in some Member States – allows for gay couples to marry) could be regarded as indirect discrimination on grounds of sexual orientation. Compulsory HIV testing of employees (or potential employees) could also be regarded as indirect sexual orientation discrimination, given that only 31 per cent of positive diagnoses involve heterosexuals (Terrence Higgins Trust, 2003 figures).

Article 2(2)(a)(ii) of the Framework Directive makes special provision for 'persons with a particular disability'. It states that 'the employer or any person or organisation to which this Directive applies is obliged to take appropriate measures in order to eliminate disadvantages entailed by such provision, criterion or practice'.

'Harassment'

Both Directives also prohibit discrimination in the form of 'harassment'. This is 'deemed' to be discrimination if certain criteria are satisfied. 'Harassment' is defined in Art 2(3) as follows (again, this is taken from the Race Directive):

ARTICLE

'Art 2(3) Harassment shall be deemed to be discrimination … when an unwanted conduct related to racial or ethnic origin takes place with the purpose or effect of violating the dignity of a person and of creating an intimidating, hostile, degrading, humiliating or offensive environment. In this context, the concept of harassment may be defined in accordance with the national laws and practice of the Member States.'

In the Framework Directive the words 'any of the grounds referred to in Article 1' – that is, religion or belief, disability, age or sexual orientation – appear instead of 'racial or ethnic origin'.

The definitions of 'harassment' are wide. They obviously include the situation where, for example, a gay employee is attacked because of his sexuality, or where a black employee is taunted because of her skin colour. But it could also include the situation where a straight employee is attacked because he has gay friends, or where a white employee is taunted because she is married to a black man. In all of these hypothetical cases, there is 'unwanted conduct' which is 'related to' either racial origin or sexual orientation, and thus harassment has occurred.

The definition refers to unwanted conduct which has the 'purpose **or** effect' of violating the dignity of a person etc. Hence, purposeful harassment is one example of discrimination, but 'purpose' is not a precondition. Unintentional harassment is still discrimination – for example, where an employee makes homophobic remarks in front of fellow employees on the mistaken assumption that everyone present is heterosexual. Indeed, the employee may be correct in assuming that all his fellow workers are heterosexual but if the 'effect' of the remarks is (i) to violate the dignity of at least one of them and (ii) to create an intimidating and/or offensive environment, then harassment has occurred.

You will note that the Directives state that 'the concept of harassment may be defined in accordance with the national laws and practice of the Member States'. It will therefore be necessary to consult each Member State's implementing legislation for further information. In the UK, for example, reg 5(1) of the Employment Equality (Sexual Orientation) Regulations 2003 (before it was consolidated into the Equality Act 2010) repeated Art 2(3) of the Framework Directive but reg 5(2) provided in addition that conduct shall be regarded as having the violating and intimidating, offensive, etc effect if 'having regard to all the circumstances, including in particular the perception of [the complainant], it should reasonably be considered as having that effect'.

Thus, in the UK at least, the perception of the complainant is one factor to be taken into account – but it is not decisive. Hence, a racist and/or homophobic remark made by one employee in front of fellow employees could be shrugged off by some of them but be regarded as deeply offensive by the others (or even just one of the others). If one of the latter group takes action, alleging harassment, the tribunal or court dealing with the complaint would have to decide, with 'regard to all the circumstances', whether the remark 'should reasonably be considered' as having violated the complainant's dignity and having created an offensive etc environment.

'Instructions to discriminate'

Both Directives also prohibit 'instructions to discriminate'. Article 2(4) in each Directive simply states that an instruction to discriminate on one of the relevant grounds is 'deemed' to be discrimination contrary to the Directives.

'Positive action'

Both Directives explicitly authorise 'positive action'. Article 5 of the Race Directive and Art 7(1) of the Framework Directive state that 'With a view to ensuring full equality in practice, the principle of equal treatment shall not prevent any Member State from maintaining or adopting specific measures to prevent or compensate for disadvantages' linked to the various grounds on which discrimination may occur within the scope of the two Directives.

'Victimisation'

Article 9 of the Race Directive and Art 11 of the Framework Directive deal with 'victimisation', that is, the possible negative repercussions of bringing a discrimination action. The Directives state that Member States must introduce measures to 'protect individuals from any adverse treatment or adverse consequences as a reaction to a complaint or to proceedings aimed at enforcing compliance with the principle of equal treatment'.

These provisions reflect developments in ECJ and House of Lords case law in the context of sex discrimination to protect those who complain about discrimination from suffering further problems as a result (see *Coote v Granada Hospitality Ltd* (1998), ECJ, and *Relaxion Group plc v Rhys-Harper* [2003] 4 All ER 1113, HL).

Derogation for 'genuine and determining occupational requirements'

Both Directives allow Member States to derogate from the principle of equal treatment established in Art 1 where there is a 'genuine and determining occupational requirement'. Article 4 of the Race Directive states:

ARTICLE

'Art 4 Member States may provide that a difference of treatment which is based on a characteristic related to racial or ethnic origin shall not constitute discrimination where, by reason of the nature of the particular occupational activities concerned or of the context in which they are carried out, such a characteristic constitutes a genuine and determining occupational requirement, provided that the objective is legitimate and the requirement is proportionate.'

In Art 4(1) of the Framework Directive, the words 'any of the grounds referred to in Article 1' appear instead of 'racial or ethnic origin'. This provision was successfully invoked in *Wolf* (Case C-229/08) [2010] 2 CMLR 32.

CASE EXAMPLE

Wolf (Case C-229/08) [2010] 2 CMLR 32

Under German law, the maximum age for recruitment of 'intermediate' firemen (those who would actually be fighting fires, rescuing people and animals, etc) was 30. Colin Wolf had applied for a job as a fireman in Frankfurt. However, his application was rejected because he would be 31 on the date of recruitment. He contended that the German legislation constituted direct discrimination on grounds of age, in breach of the Framework Directive. The Court, however, held that the maximum age limit for firemen was permitted by Art 4(1). The concern to 'ensure the operational capacity and proper functioning of the professional fire service' constituted a legitimate aim. Moreover, the 'possession of especially high physical capacities' may be regarded as a 'genuine and determining occupational requirement' for carrying on the occupation of fireman, at least for those whose tasks include fighting fires and rescuing people. The need to possess full physical capacity to carry on that activity was related to age, since (according to scientific data submitted by the German Government), very few officials over 45 years of age have sufficient physical capacity to perform the fire-fighting part of their activities. Finally, the age limit was appropriate to the objective of ensuring the operational capacity and proper functioning of the professional fire service and was also proportionate to that objective.

Meanwhile, it has been argued that cases where an employer asserts an 'occupational requirement' that employees have a particular 'sexual orientation' may pose considerable practical and theoretical difficulties.

> 'The concept of sexual orientation is in fact a very fluid one. Sexual orientation will often change over time, as people try out different sexual experiences. Although many individuals will clearly define themselves as heterosexual or homosexual, many others may not, and still more will have had experiences in the past that depart from their present sexual identity. On a more theoretical level, the idea of requiring individuals to "label" their own sexuality in this way can be criticized ... Queer theory deconstructs categories of identity as applied to human sexuality. If a queer theory approach is applied, it appears to become impossible to state with any certainty whether a person is of a "particular" sexual orientation.'
>
> Hazel Oliver 'Sexual Orientation Discrimination', (Industrial Law Journal, 2004)

By way of contrast, a person's sex, race, religion (if any), disability (if any) and age should be relatively straightforward to establish. Although a person's sex or religion may change over time (and, obviously, their age will certainly do so), at any given moment these factors can be fixed. Oliver's point is that this is not necessarily the case with a person's sexual orientation, which might be in a state of flux. She goes on to argue that sexual orientation should have been recognised as posing unique issues.

Enforcement

Article 7 of the Race Directive and Art 9 of the Framework Directive provide for the enforcement of the rights established by the new Directives. The provisions state that:

ARTICLE

'Art 7 Member States shall ensure that judicial and/or administrative procedures, including where they deem it appropriate conciliation procedures, for the enforcement of obligations under this Directive are available to all persons who consider themselves wronged by failure to apply the principle of equal treatment to them, even after the relationship in which the discrimination is alleged to have occurred has ended.'

It has been argued that enforcing claims of sexual orientation discrimination raises particular problems because of its 'extremely personal' nature (Hazel Oliver, 'Sexual Orientation Discrimination' Industrial law Journal, 2004). The point is that, while persons claiming to have suffered sex or race discrimination have nothing to 'hide' when making a claim, persons making claims of sexual orientation discrimination might have to reveal extremely private personal details. For this reason, the original UK implementing legislation, the Employment Equality (Sexual Orientation) Regulations 2003, did **not** require complainants to reveal their actual sexual orientation. Oliver writes:

'At first sight, it may seem strange that individuals can bring a claim without even revealing whether or not they are [gay, lesbian or bisexual] ... The importance of this issue lies in the fact that this makes it more likely that individuals may be willing to bring a claim at all. Sexual orientation is unique in being a "hidden" characteristic, which is not generally obvious to an outside observer. Many gay and lesbian employees choose not to be "out" in the workplace, and this may be for a number of reasons, of which fear of discrimination is one ... if individuals experiencing sexual orientation discrimination had to reveal their actual orientation in order to claim protection, clearly this would deter many employees from enforcing their rights. Indeed, for those employees who feared increased problems in the workplace if colleagues were aware of their actual orientation, it would make the right virtually meaningless.'

Hazel Oliver 'Sexual Orientation Discrimination', (Industrial Law Journal, 2004)

Reversed burden of proof

Article 8 of the Race Directive and Art 10 of the Framework Directive both establish a reversed burden of proof in certain circumstances. Specifically, the Directives state that when 'persons who consider themselves wronged because the principle of equal treatment has not been applied to them' are able to 'establish facts from which it may be presumed that there has been discrimination', then the burden of proof is reversed. This is consistent with the principles applicable to sex discrimination claims, set out by Art 19(1) of the Recast Directive, considered above.

Publicity and promotion of the equal treatment principles

Both Directives impose obligations on the Member State to publicise and promote the equal treatment principles. Article 10 of the Race Directive and Art 12 of the Framework Directive require Member States to 'take care that the provisions adopted pursuant to this Directive are brought to the attention of the persons concerned by all appropriate means'.

Article 11 of the Race Directive and Art 13 of the Framework Directive require Member States to 'take adequate measures to promote dialogue' through various means such as 'the monitoring of workplace practices, collective agreements, codes of conduct, through research or exchange of experiences and good practices'. Finally, Art 12 of the Race Directive and Art 14 of the Framework Directive require Member States to 'encourage dialogue with appropriate non-governmental organisations' which have a 'legitimate interest in contributing to the fight against discrimination'.

18.11.2 Race and ethnic origin

Scope

The Race Directive prohibits direct and indirect discrimination based on 'racial or ethnic origin'. These words are not defined and litigation is inevitable to establish exactly what they mean. In terms of scope, the Race Directive is much wider than both the Framework Directive and all EU law on sex discrimination. In particular, it is **not** limited to discrimination occurring in the context of employment. Article 3(1) sets out the Directive's scope as follows:

ARTICLE

'Art 3(1) This Directive shall apply to all persons, as regards both the public and private sectors, including public bodies, in relation to:

(a) conditions for access to employment, to self-employment and to occupation, including selection criteria and recruitment conditions, whatever the branch of activity and at all levels of the professional hierarchy, including promotion;

(b) access to all types and to all levels of vocational guidance, vocational training, advanced vocational training and retraining, including practical work experience;
(c) employment and working conditions, including dismissals and pay;
(d) membership of and involvement in an organization of workers or employers, or any organization whose members carry on a particular profession, including the benefits provided for by such organisations;
(e) social protection, including social security and healthcare;
(f) social advantages;
(g) education;
(h) access to and supply of goods and services which are available to the public, including housing.'

None of these words or concepts is defined in the Directive, and so case law is inevitable. However, some of the words and concepts appear in pre-existing EU legislation, and thus it is possible to predict how the ECJ may interpret them. For example, the word 'pay' in Art 3(1)(c) appears in Art 157 TFEU and it is not unreasonable to expect the ECJ to apply its case law under that provision to the Race Directive. Similarly, the phrase 'social advantages' appears in Art 7(2) of Regulation 1612/68 (which was examined in Chapter 12 of this book).

The first case to reach the ECJ involving the Race Directive was Case C-54/07 *Feryn* [2008] ECR I-5187. The defendant firm, a manufacturer of up-and-over doors in Belgium, had advertised for new employees but, after getting no responses, one of the firm's directors was quoted in a newspaper saying 'Apart from these Moroccans, no one else has responded to our notice in two weeks ... but we aren't looking for Moroccans.' It was alleged that the company had discriminated against potential employees on grounds of race. The ECJ held that the Race Directive had been breached even though there was no specific potential employee who had, or may have had, suffered discrimination. The Court stated:

JUDGMENT

'The objective of fostering conditions for a socially inclusive labour market would be hard to achieve if the scope of Directive 2000/43 were to be limited to only those cases in which an unsuccessful candidate for a post, considering himself to be the victim of direct discrimination, brought legal proceedings against the employer. The fact that an employer declares publicly that it will not recruit employees of a certain ethnic or racial origin, something which is clearly likely to strongly dissuade certain candidates from submitting their candidature and, accordingly, to hinder their access to the labour market, constitutes direct discrimination in respect of recruitment within the meaning of Directive 2000/43. The existence of such direct discrimination is not dependent on the identification of a complainant who claims to have been the victim.'

18.11.3 The Framework Directive

Purpose

Article 1 states that the purpose of the Framework Directive is to lay down a 'general framework for combating discrimination on the grounds of religion or belief, disability, age or sexual orientation as regards employment and occupation'. No definitions of the various grounds is given in the Directive, so case law is inevitable.

Scope

The scope of the Framework Directive (set out in Art 3(1)) is very similar to that of the provisions on sex discrimination in the Recast Directive, essentially covering working conditions and pay, access to employment and vocational training, and dismissal from employment. The Framework Directive's scope is therefore much narrower than that of the Race Directive. There are also no corresponding provisions to Directive 79/7, a point made explicitly in Art 3(3), which states that the Framework Directive 'does not apply to payments of any kind made by state schemes or similar, including state social security or social protection schemes'.

Two recent cases have helped to clarify the scope of the Framework Directive. The case of *Maruko* (Case C–267/06) [2008] ECR I-1757 examined the meaning of the word 'pay'. The case, the first sexual orientation case under the Framework Directive to reach the ECJ, involved a provision of German legislation which provided for (heterosexual) widows and widowers to receive pension benefits, but denied the same benefits to (homosexual) 'life partners'. The Court drew an analogy with the cases under Art 157 TFEU involving similar benefits, such as *Ten-Oever* (1993) and *Coloroll* (1994), and concluded that 'since survivor's benefit ... has been identified as "pay" within the meaning of [Article 157 TFEU it therefore] falls within the scope of Directive 2000/78'.

CASE EXAMPLE

Maruko (Case C–267/06) (2008)

In 2001, Mr Tadao Maruko and his male partner entered into a 'life partnership', a formal relationship recognised under German law for same-sex couples. His partner, a designer of theatrical costumes, had been a member of the German Theatre Pension Institution (the 'VddB') since 1959. The designer died in January 2005, and Maruko applied for a widower's pension. However, this was rejected on the basis that the VddB's scheme rules did not provide pensions to surviving 'life partners', only to spouses (meaning married persons of opposite sex). Maruko challenged this, alleging that the refusal amounted to unlawful discrimination on grounds of sexual orientation. The ECJ agreed.

The case of *Palacios de la Villa* (2008), an age discrimination case, examined the meaning of the word 'dismissal' in the context of compulsory retirement. The ECJ stated that:

JUDGMENT

'[National] legislation ... which permits the automatic termination of an employment relationship concluded between an employer and a worker once the latter has reached the age of 65, affects the duration of the employment relationship between the parties and, more generally, the engagement of the worker concerned in an occupation, by preventing his future participation in the labour force. Consequently, legislation of that kind must be regarded as establishing rules relating to "employment and working conditions, including dismissals and pay".'

'Disability'

As indicated above, there is no definition of 'disability' in the Framework Directive. In *Chacón Navas* (Case C–13/05) [2006] ECR I–6467, the ECJ was asked to provide one. The Court held that the word 'disability' had to be given an 'autonomous and uniform interpretation'. It went on to state that:

JUDGMENT

'The concept of "disability" must be understood as referring to a limitation which results in particular from physical, mental or psychological impairments and which hinders the participation of the person concerned in professional life.'

More specifically, the Court was asked whether the Directive included the case of an employee who has been dismissed by her employer solely on grounds of sickness. Here the Court decided that 'disability' was not synonymous with 'sickness'. The Court stated that:

JUDGMENT

'There is nothing in Directive 2000/78 to suggest that workers are protected by the prohibition of discrimination on grounds of disability as soon as they develop any type of sickness ... a person who has been dismissed by his employer solely on account of sickness does not fall within the general framework laid down for combating discrimination on grounds of disability.'

CASE EXAMPLE

Chacón Navas (Case C–13/05) [2006] ECR I–6467

Sonia Chacón Navas was employed by Eurest, a catering company, in Spain. In October 2003 she was certified as too sick to work (no details are provided in the judgment). In May 2004, Eurest sacked her, without giving reasons but acknowledging that the dismissal was unlawful and offering compensation. She contended that the dismissal was void on the basis of discrimination on grounds of 'disability', contrary to Directive 2000/78. The referring court sought a ruling on the definition of 'disability'; specifically, whether it extended to sickness. The Court held that it did not cover sickness.

In *Coleman v Attridge Law* (Case C–303/06) [2008] ECR I-5603, the Court was asked whether the Framework Directive's provisions on disability discrimination can be invoked, indirectly, by the carer of a disabled child. The case was brought by Sharon Coleman, a former secretary at the London law firm of Attridge Law. In 2002, she gave birth to a son who is disabled and she became his primary carer. In March 2005, she accepted voluntary redundancy but, subsequently, brought a claim for constructive dismissal and disability discrimination against her former employers, arguing that they had treated her less favourably than employees with non-disabled children. For example, she alleged that they called her 'lazy' when she sought to take time off to care for her son. The ECJ held that the Framework Directive applied to the case. The Court stated:

JUDGMENT

'Where it is established that an employee in a situation such as that in the present case suffers direct discrimination on grounds of disability, an interpretation of Directive 2000/78 limiting its application only to people who are themselves disabled is liable to deprive that directive of an important element of its effectiveness and to reduce the protection which it is intended to guarantee.'

General derogations

Article 2(5) of the Framework Directive provides a set of derogations some of which are previously unseen in EU legislation. Curiously, there is no parallel provision to Art 2(5) in the Race Directive. Article 2(5) states:

ARTICLE

'Art 2(5) This Directive shall be without prejudice to measures laid down by national law which, in a democratic society, are necessary for public security, for the maintenance of public order and the prevention of criminal offences, for the protection of health and for the protection of the rights and freedoms of others.'

Article 2(5) – specifically the 'protection of health' derogation – was invoked in *Petersen* (Case C-341/08) [2010] 2 CMLR 31. Domnica Petersen had worked as a dentist in Germany since 1974, but reached her 68th birthday in April 2007, the maximum age permitted under German law. She was told that her entitlement to practise would lapse in June 2007. She complained that this was discrimination on grounds of age. The ECJ held that the maximum age limit for dentists was, in theory at least, permissible under Art 2(5). The Court stated:

JUDGMENT

'It must be accepted that, in the context of Art 2(5), a Member State may find it necessary to set an age limit for the practice of a medical profession such as that of a dentist in order to protect the health of patients. That consideration applies whether the objective of the protection of health is considered from the point of view of the competence of dentists or the financial balance of the national healthcare system.'

Elaborating on the latter point, the Court stated that there was a possibility that a rising number of dentists might lead to an excessive level of expenditure to be borne by the State, and hence the compulsory retirement of the oldest dentists would make it possible to reduce that expenditure.

Article 3(4) creates a further derogation, albeit only in the context of discrimination based on disability and age, in stating that Member States may provide that the Framework Directive shall not apply to 'the armed forces'. That is yet another concept which is not defined in the Directive. It will be up to the ECJ to decide whether the phrase 'the armed forces' means a State's entire military service or whether distinctions can be drawn between, say, fighting units (where physical fitness might be essential) and other units such as transport and catering.

Special provisions regarding disability

'Reasonable accommodation'

Article 5 imposes an extra obligation on employers 'in order to guarantee compliance with the principle of equal treatment in relation to persons with disabilities'. Article 5 states:

ARTICLE

'Art 5 Reasonable accommodation shall be provided. This means that employers shall take appropriate measures, where needed in a particular case, to enable a person with a disability to have access to, participate in, or advance in employment, or to undergo training, unless such measure would impose a disproportionate burden on the employer. This burden shall not be disproportionate when it is sufficiently remedied by measures existing within the framework of the disability policy of the Member State concerned.'

Positive action

Article 7(2) of the Framework Directive contains further provisions with regard to disabled persons. It states that the principle of equal treatment does not prejudice the right of Member States to 'maintain or adopt provisions on the protection of health and safety at work or to measures aimed at creating or maintaining provisions or facilities for safeguarding their integration into the working environment'.

Special derogation regarding churches etc

Article 4(2) provides an additional derogation 'in the case of occupational activities within churches and other public or private organizations the ethos of which is based on religion or belief'. Article 4(2) states that:

ARTICLE

'Art 4(2) A difference of treatment based on a person's religion or belief shall not constitute discrimination where, by reason of the nature of these activities or of the context in which they are carried out, a person's religion or belief constitute a genuine, legitimate and justified occupational requirement, having regard to the organisation's ethos … Provided that its provisions are otherwise complied with, this Directive shall thus not prejudice the right of churches and other public or private organizations the ethos of which is based on religion or belief, acting in conformity with national constitutions and laws, to require individuals working for them to act in good faith and with loyalty to the organisation's ethos.'

Special derogation regarding age

Article 6(1) establishes an additional derogation for Member States in the context of age discrimination. According to Art 6(1), Member States may provide that 'differences of treatment on grounds of age shall not constitute discrimination' if they are 'objectively and reasonably justified by a legitimate aim' and if 'the means of achieving that aim are appropriate and necessary'. Three examples of such 'differences of treatment' are given:

a) the 'setting of special conditions' in the employment context for 'young people, older workers and persons with caring responsibilities in order to promote their vocational integration or ensure their protection'

b) the 'fixing of minimum conditions of age, professional experience or seniority in service for access to employment or to certain advantages linked to employment'

c) the 'fixing of a maximum age for recruitment which is based on the training requirements of the post in question or the need for a reasonable period of employment before retirement'.

The ECJ was asked to interpret Art 6(1)(a) in *Mangold v Helm* (Case C–144/04) [2005] ECR I–9981. The case involved a provision of German legislation which allowed employers to conclude fixed-term contracts if the employee in question was over a certain age (52). Although *prima facie* discriminatory on age grounds, the Court stated that the provision was, at least in principle, 'objectively and reasonably justified by a legitimate aim'. The Court ruled that the purpose of the German legislation was 'plainly to promote the vocational integration of unemployed older workers, in so far as they encounter considerable difficulties in finding work' and that the 'legitimacy of such a public-interest objective cannot reasonably be thrown in doubt'. The Court added that an 'objective of that kind must as a rule, therefore, be regarded as justifying, objectively and reasonably, a difference of treatment on grounds of age' in accordance with Art 6(1)(a).

However, the Court then went on to consider, as required by Art 6(1)(a), whether the 'means of achieving that aim are appropriate and necessary'. The Court started by stating that 'the Member States unarguably enjoy broad discretion in their choice of the measures capable of attaining their objectives in the field of social and employment policy'. However, the Court nevertheless felt unable to support the German legislation:

JUDGMENT

'Application of [the German legislation] leads to a situation in which all workers who have reached the age of 52, may lawfully, until the age at which they may claim their entitlement to a retirement pension, be offered fixed-term contracts of employment which may be renewed an indefinite number of times. This significant body of workers, determined solely on the basis of age, is thus in danger, during a substantial part of its members' working life, of being excluded from the benefit of stable employment … In so far as such legislation takes the age of the worker concerned as the only criterion for the application of a fixed-term contract of employment, when it has not been shown that fixing an age threshold, as such, regardless of any other consideration linked to the structure of the labour market in question or the personal situation of the person concerned, is objectively necessary to the attainment of the objective which is the vocational integration of unemployed older workers, it must be considered to go beyond what is "appropriate and necessary" in order to attain the objective pursued.'

The Court therefore concluded that the German legislation, although justifiable (in principle), went beyond what was strictly necessary (in practice) and therefore was incompatible with the Framework Directive.

Mangold v Helm was distinguished in *Palacios de la Villa* (Case C–411/05) [2007] ECR I-8531. This case involved a provision of Spanish legislation which stated that clauses contained in collective agreements providing for compulsory retirement in the event of workers reaching the Spanish retirement age were lawful. The case was brought by a Spanish national who was told by his employers that he was being compulsorily retired, having reached his 65th birthday. The ECJ held that, although compulsory retirement was tantamount to dismissal and, hence, that a *prima facie* breach of the Framework Directive had occurred, the Spanish legislation was justifiable under Art 6(1)(a), in that it pursued a 'legitimate aim', namely, 'the promotion of full employment by facilitating access to the labour market'. Moreover, the Spanish legislation also satisfied the test of being both 'appropriate and necessary'. On this point the Court emphasised the flexibility built into the Spanish system. The Court stated approvingly that:

JUDGMENT

'The measure cannot be regarded as unduly prejudicing the legitimate claims of workers subject to compulsory retirement because they have reached the age-limit provided for; the relevant legislation is not based only on a specific age, but also takes account of the fact that the persons concerned are entitled to financial compensation by way of a retirement pension at the end of their working life … Moreover, the relevant national legislation allows the social partners to opt, by way of collective agreements – and therefore with considerable flexibility – for application of the compulsory retirement mechanism so that due account may be taken not only of the overall situation in the labour market concerned, but also of the specific features of the jobs in question.'

Three recent cases illustrate the scope of Art 6(1). In *Age Concern England* (Case C-388/07) [2009] ECR I-1569, the Age Concern charity brought a judicial review of the UK legislation implementing the Framework Directive, the Employment Equality (Age) Regulations 2006. It was argued that the UK government had failed to properly implement the directive by providing in the Regulations that it was not unlawful for an employer to impose compulsory retirement on any employee aged 65 or over. The ECJ rejected the charity's argument. The Court held that the legitimate aims and the differences in treatment referred to in Art 6(1) were not exhaustive but were purely illustrative. Moreover, Art 6(1) did not require Member States to draw up, in their implementing legislation, a specific list of the differences in treatment which may be justified by a legitimate aim. Ultimately, it fell to the national court to determine whether and to what extent a provision which allowed employers to dismiss workers who had reached retirement age was justified by 'legitimate' aims within the meaning of Art 6(1). The Court offered the following guidelines:

JUDGMENT

'The aims which may be considered 'legitimate' within the meaning of [Art 6(1)] are social policy objectives, such as those related to employment policy, the labour market or vocational training. By their public interest nature, those legitimate aims are distinguishable from purely individual reasons particular to the employer's situation, such as cost reduction or improving competitiveness, although it cannot be ruled out that a national rule may recognise, in the pursuit of those legitimate aims, a certain degree of flexibility for employers… However, it is important to note that [Art 6(1)] is addressed to the Member States and imposes on them, notwithstanding their broad discretion in matters of social policy, the burden of establishing to a high standard of proof the legitimacy of the aim pursued.'

An Art 6(1) derogation was rejected in *Hütter* (Case C-88/08) [2009] 3 CMLR 35. David Hütter spent two and a half years as an apprentice lab technician at the Technical University of Graz in Austria, between the ages of 16 and 19. He was then recruited by the TUG but his starting salary was significantly lower than that awarded to a female colleague. She had spent exactly the same time as an apprentice but, because she was older, her service record amounted to 28.5 months whereas his was only 6.5 months (ie the period since his 18th birthday). This was because Austrian legislation precluded service completed prior to the age of 18 when calculating salary increments. Hütter challenged this, alleging age discrimination. The Austrian court which referred the case to the ECJ suggested that the legislation was necessary in order to avoid three undesirable situations:

1. placing persons who had obtained a secondary education at a disadvantage
2. discouraging pupils from pursuing secondary education; and
3. making apprenticeship costly for the public sector (and thereby promoting the integration of young apprentices into the labour market).

The ECJ held that the Austrian legislation did discriminate on grounds of age but that the aims of the Austrian legislation were (when looked at individually) legitimate. However, those same aims (when looked at collectively), were mutually contradictory. Aims (1) and (2) were designed to encourage young people to pursue secondary education (rather than vocational education); whereas aim (3) was designed to do the exact opposite. The Court stated that it was therefore 'difficult... to accept that national legislation... can, simultaneously, be of advantage to each of those two groups at the expense of the other' and concluded that the means of achieving the (otherwise legitimate) aims were not 'appropriate and necessary'.

Art 6(1) was also rejected in *Kücükdeveci v Swedex* (Case C-555/07) [2010] 2 CMLR 33. German legislation provided that the notice periods which employers were required to observe on termination of employment were to be increased incrementally with the length of service, but periods of employment before the age of 25 were to be disregarded. For younger employees, employers were only required to observe a basic period of notice. The ECJ held that the German legislation constituted direct discrimination on grounds of age and rejected the purported justification of affording employers greater flexibility by making it easier to dismiss younger workers. The Court held that the German legislation was 'not appropriate' for achieving its purported aim, since it applied to all employees who joined the undertaking before the age of 25, whatever their age at the time of dismissal.

CASE EXAMPLE

Kücükdeveci v Swedex (Case C-555/07) [2010] 2 CMLR 33

Seda Kücükdeveci had worked for a German company called Swedex from June 1996 (when she was aged 18) to December 2006 when she was dismissed. Despite her 10.5 years' service, she was only given one month's notice, corresponding to the three years' service that she had accumulated since her 25th birthday, rather than the four months' notice to which she would have been entitled had her entire employment record been taken into consideration. She alleged a breach of the Framework Directive. One question for the ECJ was whether the German legislation could be justified on the grounds that employers are recognised as having a commercial interest in flexibility as regards staffing – an interest which would be adversely affected by longer periods of notice. Another issue was whether the shorter notice periods given to younger employees vis-à-vis older employees could be justified on the ground that, having regard to their age and/or their lesser social, family and private obligations, the former are assumed to have greater professional and personal flexibility and mobility. The Court rejected the justifications.

KEY FACTS

Directive 2000/43	
Race discrimination (whether direct or indirect, and including harassment) is prohibited	Directive 2000/43
The Directive applies in the public and private sectors and includes discrimination in employment, vocational training, social security, healthcare, education and housing	Directive 2000/43, Article 3
A 'difference of treatment' on race grounds may be justified where, by reason of the nature of the 'particular occupational activities', there is a genuine and determining occupational requirement	Directive 2000/43, Article 4

KEY FACTS

Directive 2000/78	
Discrimination (whether direct or indirect, and including harassment) on grounds of age, disability, religion or belief, and sexual orientation is prohibited	Directive 2000/78
The Directive applies in employment and vocational training	Directive 2000/78, Article 3
A 'difference of treatment' on grounds of age, disability, religion or belief, and sexual orientation may be justified where, by reason of the nature of the 'particular occupational activities', there is a genuine and determining occupational requirement	Directive 2000/78, Article 4; *Wolf* (2010)
'Disability' means a 'limitation' resulting from 'physical, mental or psychological impairments' which hinder 'the participation of the person in professional life'. It does not include sickness	*Chacón Navas* (2006)
Age discrimination may be justified if 'objectively and reasonably justified by a legitimate aim', provided that the means adopted are 'appropriate and necessary'. In principle, this provision allows, eg employers to offer shorter contracts to older workers and for compulsory retirement ages	Directive 2000/78, Article 6; *Mangold v Helm* (2005); *Palacios de la Villa* (2007), *Age Concern England* (2009)

SUMMARY

- Discrimination comes in various forms: direct (which is very difficult to justify), indirect (which can be justified by reference to a legitimate objective) and harassment.
- Article 157 (1) TFEU sets out the principle of equal pay for men and women for equal work. 'Pay' is defined very widely, both in the TFEU itself and in subsequent case law. Article 157 (1) TFEU is directly effective (*Defrenne v SABENA*).
- Positive action is permitted (indeed encouraged) by EU law but positive discrimination is prohibited.
- Directive 2006/54 sets out the principle of equal treatment on grounds of sex in employment (including access to employment and dismissal). There is a derogation for 'genuine and determining occupational requirements'.
- Discrimination against a pregnant woman (including refusal to employ and dismissal of a pregnant woman) constitutes direct sex discrimination.

- Directive 2000/43 sets out the principle of equal treatment on grounds of race and ethnic origin in employment (including access to employment and dismissal) and other areas including education, social services and housing. There is a derogation for 'genuine and determining occupational requirements'.
- Directive 2000/78 sets out the principle of equal treatment on grounds of age, disability, religion or belief and sexual orientation in employment (including access to employment and dismissal). There are general derogations for 'genuine and determining occupational requirements' and special derogations. In particular, age discrimination may be justified by a 'legitimate aim' which is 'appropriate and necessary'.

KEY FACTS

The development of EU discrimination law	
• In 1957, the EC Treaty was signed. It contained the original version of Art 157, which forced Member States to protect the principle that 'men and women should receive equal pay for equal work'. The Article was introduced for economic, as opposed to social, reasons	Article 157 TFEU
• By 1976, however, the ECJ acknowledged that Art 157 pursued a 'double aim', that is, one economic and one social. The Court also elevated sex equality to the status of a 'fundamental right'	*Defrenne v SABENA*
• In the mid-1970s, detailed secondary legislation on sex equality appeared for the first time. The first of these, the Equal Pay Directive, merely expanded the scope of Art 157 to cover work of equal value. The second, the Equal Treatment Directive (ETD), introduced new substantive legal rights of equality in the employment context covering conditions of employment, access to and dismissal from employment. It also introduced provisions allowing for 'positive action', but not 'positive discrimination'	Directive 75/117 Directive 76/207
• At this time, EU sex discrimination legislation still focused exclusively on employment rights. This changed with the introduction in 1979 of a new Directive conferring rights of equality in social security matters	Directive 79/7
• In 1986, the Court held that discriminatory retirement ages in employment contracts were contrary to the ETD. This has had a significant impact on employment rights in the UK in particular	*Marshall*
• In 1990, the ECJ held that discrimination against a pregnant woman constituted direct discrimination and was therefore incapable of justification. This ruling has influenced several subsequent ECJ cases on the topic of pregnancy	*Dekker*
• In 1995, the ECJ held that national 'positive discrimination' legislation breached the ETD	*Kalanke*
• The signing in 1997 of the Treaty of Amsterdam marked a new level for EU discrimination law. Until this point, EU law dealt only with discrimination on grounds of sex. Although the ECJ had been prepared to extend the coverage of the ETD to cover discrimination against transsexuals, the Court refused to extend the scope of Art 157 to tackle sexual orientation discrimination. The Treaty of Amsterdam inserted Art 13 into the EC Treaty (now Art 19 TFEU), authorising the Council of Ministers to combat virtually any form of discrimination	Treaty of Amsterdam *P v S* (1996) *Grant* (1998)

• Two pieces of legislation issued under (what is now) Art 19 TFEU appeared in 2000 The first of these, the Race Directive, tackles race and ethnic origin discrimination. It applies to discrimination in the employment context and beyond, covering matters such as education, housing and social services. The Directive came into force in December 2003	Art 19 TFEU Directive 2000/43
• The second Directive issued under (what is now) Art 19 TFEU, the Framework Directive, tackles discrimination on grounds of age, disability, religion or belief and sexual orientation. It only applies in the context of employment. The provisions on religion and sexual orientation discrimination came into force in December 2003. Member States were given the option of deferring implementation of the provisions on disability and age discrimination by three years 'if necessary'. These provisions came into force in December 2006	Directive 2000/78
• A second equal treatment Directive came into force in October 2005. It updated the original ETD and extended its coverage in certain respects, eg to encompass 'sexual harassment'	Directive 2002/73
Directives 75/117, 76/207 (the ETD), 86/378 and 97/80 are all repealed, replaced by the 'Recast' Directive, in August 2009	Directive 2006/54

SAMPLE ESSAY QUESTION

Critically compare and contrast the protection provided by EU law to victims of 'discrimination' based on 'sex', 'race' and 'age'.

Explain the meaning and scope of 'discrimination' in EU law:

- Define 'direct' discrimination
- Define 'indirect' discrimination
- Explain that 'discrimination' includes 'harrassment' and an instruction to discriminate
- Define 'harrassment'.

Explain the provisions of EU law on 'sex' discrimination:

- Art 157 TFEU prohibits differential pay for men and women doing equal work or work of equal value. 'Pay' is defined widely in the Treaty and in case law. Give examples, eg *Garland, Barber*
- Directive 2006/54 provides for equal treatment of men and women in the workplace
- Directive 2004/113 prohibits sex discrimination in terms of access to/supply of goods and services
- Sex discrimination includes discrimination against pregnant women (*Dekker, Webb, Brown*) and against transsexuals (*P v S*), but not discrimination on grounds of sexual orientation (*Grant v SW Trains*).

Explain the provisions of EU law on 'race' discrimination:

- Directive 2000/43 prohibits discrimination on grounds of 'race' in the workplace
- It also prohibits race discrimination in the context of social security, healthcare, education, 'social advantages' and access to/supply of goods and services available to the public, eg housing
- This is the widest scope of any form of EU discrimination legislation.

Explain the provisions of EU law on 'age' discrimination:

- Directive 2000/78 prohibits discrimination on grounds of 'age' in the workplace
- Derogation is available on grounds of health protection, eg maximum age limits for dentists (*Petersen*)
- Compulsory retirement ages are justifiable (*Palacios de la Villa, Age Concern England*).

Compare/contrast:

- Race discrimination has the broadest scope, covering areas not covered by the others. Age discrimination has the narrowest scope, and is the only one where health grounds may justify discrimination
- In all areas, derogation is permitted on the basis of a 'genuine and determining occupational requirement', eg male only fighting units in the army (*Sirdar*); maximum age limits for fire fighters (*Wolf*)
- All areas provide for 'positive' action, ie the adoption of measures to ensure full equality in practice (*Marschall*), but not 'positive' discrimination (*Kalanke*).

SUMMARY

- EU Law tackles discrimination on grounds of sex, race or ethnic origin, age, disability, religion or belief, and sexual orientation. However, the scope and level of protection varies from one area of discrimination to another. There is also EU law tackling discrimination based on nationality (see Chapters 11, 12 and 13 for discussion).
- Discrimination comes in various forms: direct, indirect, and harassment.
- 'Direct' discrimination occurs when one person is treated less favourably than another person is, has been or would be treated in a comparable situation.
- 'Indirect' discrimination occurs where an 'apparently neutral provision, criterion or practice' gives one person a 'particular disadvantage' compared with another person

because of a difference in age, race, sex, etc., unless that provision, criterion or practice is 'objectively justified by a legitimate aim', and the means of achieving that aim are 'appropriate and necessary'.

- 'Discrimination' includes 'harrassment', where 'unwanted conduct' on grounds of age, race, sex, etc., occurs with the 'purpose or effect of violating the dignity of a person, and of creating an intimidating, hostile, degrading, humiliating or offensive environment'.
- Discrimination includes an instruction to discriminate.
- Indirect discrimination is capable of justification by reference to 'a legitimate aim'. Examples (in the context of sex discrimination) include the need to encourage full-time workers (*Jenkins v Kingsgate*); the need to attract more staff to certain posts (*Enderby*); the need to recruit young workers (*Kutz-Bauer*).
- Discrimination on grounds of 'sex' essentially means discrimination on grounds of gender. It also includes discrimination against transsexuals (*P v S, KB*). Discrimination against pregnant women amounts to direct sex discrimination (*Dekker*).
- Sex discrimination is tackled by several provisions of EU law, the most important of which are Art 157 TFEU and Directive 2006/54 (the 'recast' directive).
- Art 157 (1) TFEU provides for equal pay for men and women doing equal work or work of equal value. This provision is directly effective, vertically and horizontally (*Defrenne v SABENA*). It pursues a 'double aim' – economic and social (*Defrenne*).
- 'Pay' is defined widely in the Treaty, as 'the ordinary basic or minimum wage or salary and any other consideration, whether in cash or in kind, which the worker receives, directly or indirectly, in respect of his employment from his employer' (Art 157 (2) TFEU). It has been broadly interpreted by the Court of Justice, to include post-employment benefits (*Garland*), sick pay (*Rinner-Kühn*), severance payments (*Kowalska*), compensation for unfair dismissal (*Seymour-Smith & Perez*), bonuses (*Krüger*), payments in lieu (*Bötel*), redundancy payments (*Barber*), maternity pay (*Gillespie, McKenna, Alabaster*), membership of occupational pension schemes (*Bilka-Kaufhaus, Barber*).
- Art 157 (1) only applies to pay discrimination that is the responsibility of a single employer. It cannot apply if the alleged pay discrimination involves different employers (*Lawrence, Allonby*).
- 'Equal work' does not mean identical work (*Macarthys Ltd v Smith*). However, employees performing similar tasks but whose level of experience, training and/or qualifications are different should not necessarily be regarded as doing 'equal work' (*Wiener Gebietskrankenkasse*). In particular, rewarding experience which enables a worker to perform his or her duties better constitutes a 'legitimate objective of pay policy' (*Cadman*).
- Whether work is of 'equal value' is ultimately a question of fact (*Royal Copenhagen*). Where a 'job classification system' is used, it must be based on 'the same criteria for both men and women and so drawn up as to exclude any discrimination on grounds of sex' (Directive 2006/54, Art 4). However, individual criteria which favour men or women are permissible provided they form part of an overall package which is gender neutral (*Rummler v Dato-Druck*).
- Directive 2006/54 provides for equal treatment of men and women in the workplace. It prohibits sex discrimination in the context of access to employment, working conditions, promotion, dismissal and vocational training (Art 14). The imposition of different contractual retirement ages for men and women constitutes 'dismissal' and is prohibited (*Marshall*).
- The refusal to employ, or the dismissal of, a pregnant woman because of her pregnancy is direct sex discrimination (*Dekker, Webb*). The same applies to the dismissal of a woman who is at an advanced stage of IVF treatment (*Mayr v Flöckner*), or because of a pregnancy-related illness (*Brown*), but not if the illness manifests itself after the end of the maternity leave period (*Hertz*).

- Women returning to work after maternity leave have their terms and conditions of employment protected (*Thibault*). They are also entitled to benefit from any improvement in working conditions to which they would have been entitled during their absence (Art 15).
- Directive 79/7 prohibits direct or indirect sex discrimination 'in the field of social security and other elements of social protection'. In terms of personal scope, it applies to the 'working population', which is very widely defined, including the self-employed, the retired and the involuntarily unemployed. In terms of material scope, it applies to statutory schemes which provide protection against sickness, invalidity, old age, accidents at work and occupational diseases, and unemployment. There is an important derogation for the 'determination of pensionable age for the purpose of granting old-age and retirement pensions and the possible consequences thereof for other benefits' (Art 7).
- Directive 86/613 prohibits sex discrimination in the context of self-employed persons.
- Directive 2004/113 prohibits sex discrimination in terms of access to/supply of goods and services.
- Directive 2000/43 prohibits discrimination on grounds of 'race and ethnic origin' in the workplace. Race discrimination may be established without the need to prove that there was any specific potential employee who had, or may have, suffered discrimination (*Feryn*).
- It also prohibits race discrimination in the context of social security, healthcare, education, 'social advantages' and access to/supply of goods and services available to the public, eg housing. This gives Directive 2000/43 the widest scope of any form of EU discrimination legislation.
- Directive 2000/78 prohibits discrimination on grounds of 'age', 'disability', 'religion or belief' and 'sexual orientation' in the workplace.
- 'Disability' refers to 'a limitation which results in particular from physical, mental or psychological impairments and which hinders the participation of the person concerned in professional life' (*Chacón Navas*). 'Disability' is not synonymous with 'sickness' (*Chacón Navas*).
- Disability discrimination may occur indirectly, for example when the parent or carer of a disabled child is discriminated against because of the child's disability (*Coleman v Attridge Law*).
- Derogation is available on grounds of public security, public order, crime prevention, health protection, eg maximum age limits for dentists (*Petersen*), and 'for the protection of the rights and freedoms of others'.
- Age discrimination may be justified if 'objectively and reasonably justified by a legitimate aim', provided that the means adopted are 'appropriate and necessary'. In principle, this provision allows, eg employers to offer shorter contracts to older workers and for compulsory retirement ages (*Mangold v Helm, Palacios de la Villa, Age Concern England*).
- In all areas of EU discrimination law, derogation is permitted on the basis of a 'genuine and determining occupational requirement', eg male only fighting units in the army (*Sirdar*); maximum age limits for fire fighters (*Wolf*).
- All areas of EU discrimination law provide for 'positive' action, ie the 'adoption of measure to ensure full equality in practice' (*Lommers, Marschall*).
- 'Positive' discrimination – involving conferring advantages on an under-represented group – is prohibited (*Kalanke, Briheche*).
- EU legislation provides for a reversed burden of proof in discrimination cases. Thus, when a person, who considers themselves to have been the victim of a form of discrimination covered by EU law, is able to establish facts from which it may be presumed that there has been direct or indirect discrimination, it shall be for the respondent to prove that there has been no breach of the principle of equal treatment (see eg Directive 2006/54, Art 19).

Further reading

Articles

Ahtela, K, 'The Revised Provisions on Sex Discrimination in European Law: A Critical Assessment' (2005) 11 ELJ 57.

Barnard, C, 'The Principle of Equality in the Community Context: *P, Grant, Kalanke and Marschall*: Four Uneasy Bedfellows' (1998) 57 CLJ 352.

Barrett, G, '"Shall I Compare Thee To …?" On Article 141 EC and *Lawrence*' (2006) 35 ILJ 93.

Beck, G, 'The State of EC Anti-Sex Discrimination Law and the Judgment in *Cadman*, Or How the Legal can Become the Political' (2007) 32 EL Rev 549.

Bell, M and Waddington, L, 'Reflecting on Inequalities in European Equality Law' (2003) 28 ELR 349.

Burrows, N and Robinson, M, 'An Assessment of the Recast of Community Equality Laws' (2006) 13 ELJ 186.

Caracciolo Di Torella, E and Masselot, A, 'Pregnancy, Maternity and the Organisation of Family Life: an Attempt to Classify the Case Law of the Court of Justice' (2001) 26 ELR 239.

Connelly, M, 'Forced Retirement, Age Discrimination and the Heyday Case' (2009) 37 ILJ 233.

Driessen-Reilly and Driessen, 'Don't Shoot the Messenger: a Look at Community Law relating to Harassment in the Workplace' (2003) 28 ELR 493.

Hosking, D, 'A High Bar for EU Disability Rights' (2007) 36 ILJ 228; 'Great Expectations: Protection from Discrimination Because of Disability in Community Law' (2006) 31 EL Rev 667.

Masselot, A, 'The State of Gender Equality Law in the European Union' (2007) 13 ELJ 152.

Muir, E, 'Enhancing the effects of Community law on national employment policies: the *Mangold* case' (2006) 31 EL Rev 879.

19

The wider social influence of the EU

AIMS AND OBJECTIVES

After reading this chapter you should:

- Have a basic understanding of the wider influence of the EU on Member States

The original EC Treaty was economic in character and while it had a broad range of economic objectives, characterised by the 'Four Freedoms' and the addition of restrictions on anti-competitive practices, as well as a limited form of social policy in the form of Art 141 (now Art 157 TFEU), it was still relatively limited in its focus.

However, a number of different policy areas have become important since the Treaty was first signed in 1957. Social policy has become a significant area in its own right and has been subject to major development (see Chapter 17). Even as early as 1972 discussion between the Member States identified the need for a distinct policy on the environment and environmental protection. As an extension to the 'Four Freedoms' and with a view to making the Single Market more effective a number of developments have also concerned consumer protection.

The SEA and the TEU both included measures to include a wider range of policies now identified as both tasks and as activities (under Art 3). Specifically, the TFEU now includes provisions to include within the legal order of the Community policies on:

- consumer protection – Art 169 TFEU
- the environment – Arts 191–193 TFEU
- transport – Arts 90–100 TFEU
- trans-European networks – Arts 170–172 TFEU
- research and technological development – Arts 179–190 TFEU
- social policy, education, vocational training and youth – Arts 151–161 TFEU
- public health – Art 168 TFEU.

In moves towards closer integration economically, socially and politically it is inevitable that the scope of EU law must grow. It is worth looking briefly at how some of these policies have developed and the extent of EU influence. These are areas that are not normally included in mainstream syllabuses on EU. As a result, this chapter provides only a brief overview of the areas covered for a general understanding of how the EU has developed beyond its early economic programme.

19.1 Protection of consumers

The EC Treaty did not contain any specific provisions for consumer protection because it was felt that the free competition created by the 'Four Freedoms' would inevitably benefit the consumer as well. Indeed, any measures that were introduced had as much to do with protecting free competition as anything else.

In fact, prior to the SEA there were only two specific references in the Treaty to consumer protection. Article 33 (formerly Art 39) identified that under the Common Agricultural Policy (CAP) produce should reach the consumer at what was described as 'fair prices'. Also under Art 101, prohibiting restrictive trade practices, one of the criteria for granting exemptions under Art 101(3) was that the agreement contributed to the improvement of the production or distribution of the goods and that this passed a fair share of the benefit on to the consumer (see section 16.2.3).

The ECJ also of course recognised the importance of protecting the consumer within the so-called 'rule of reason' in the case of *Rewe-Zentral AG v Bundesmonopolverwaltung für Branntwein* (Case 120/78) *(Cassis de Dijon)* [1979] ECR 649 in relation to providing exemption for Member States breaching Art 28 (see Chapter 14).

A Consumer Programme was eventually accepted in 1975 and this set out a plan for implementing five fundamental consumer rights. These were:

- the protection of health and safety
- the protection of the consumer's economic interests
- the right of the consumer to both information and education
- the right of a consumer to redress
- the right of a consumer to representation and participation.

Before the SEA measures concerning consumer protection were introduced under the old Art 100 (now Art 116). In fact, 18 measures were adopted in 1976 under Art 100 covering a range of specific products including for instance motor vehicles. The purpose of the measures was the harmonisation of national laws with the focus very much on avoiding distortion in competition as much as on consumer protection itself. The process was also very slow because it required the unanimous vote of Council.

Probably one of the most significant of the measures introduced by this process was the Product Liability Directive 85/374. This imposed strict liability on producers for all damage caused by defective products. The term 'producer' was defined broadly so that it could include anyone in the chain of supply and distribution, including manufacturers, importers and suppliers. Under the Directive the claimant need only show the defect in the goods, the damage caused and the causal relationship between the two. Although there are a number of defences also available. In the UK the Directive was introduced as Part 1 of the Consumer Protection Act 1987.

A number of other measures were introduced by the same procedure under the old Art 100:

- The Misleading Advertising Directive 84/450: this gives consumers rights of redress when they have entered into contracts on the basis of misleading advertisements. It therefore imposes high standards of business practice on sellers.
- The Doorstep Selling Directive 85/577: this protected consumers by introducing the right to a cooling-off period of seven days for contracts made in their homes or away from the business premises of the seller. A consumer has the opportunity to reflect and cancel the contract.
- The Consumer Credit Directive 87/102.

This provides a range of protections to consumers purchasing goods or services on credit. In fact, UK consumers already enjoyed similar protections under the Consumer Credit Act 1974.

While the SEA did not specifically include provisions for consumer protection it did recognise the need to speed up this process of harmonisation in order to provide greater consumer protection. As a result, it developed the processes already available under the old Art 100a (now Art 114) and made use of qualified majority voting by Council in order to adopt measures.

A number of measures were subsequently introduced by using Art 100a and Art 95 (now Art 114 TFEU). These included:

- The Toy Safety Directive 88/378: this was inevitably aimed at preventing the sale of dangerous toys within the Community by harmonising laws in the Member States. In fact, it introduced a European standards body, the CEN which both introduced a standard for different toys with accompanying certification as well as the requirement for national safety standards to conform to the EC (now EU) model. A further requirement was that all toys supplied in the EC (now EU) should carry a CEN approved mark. In the UK this was implemented as the Toy Safety Regulations 1995.
- The Price Indication Directive 88/314: this required that certain goods, particularly foodstuffs, should be displayed together with their selling price or in some cases with a unit price.
- The Package Travel Directive 90/314: this includes minimum standards of protection in the case of package travel, package holidays and package tours. It has been implemented in the UK as the Package Travel, Package Holidays and Package Tours Regulations 1992. The Regulations following the Directive impose minimum requirements in respect of the information given to consumers prior to contracting and liability for sub-standard or no performance.
- The Unfair Terms in Consumer Contracts Directive 93/13: the basic aim of the Directive is to remove inequalities in consumer contracts that would act as a detriment to the consumer. Any inequality in the contractual terms that would create an imbalance in the respective rights of seller and consumer or any requirement contrary to the requirement of good faith will be seen as unfair and be considered invalid. The Directive applies only to standard terms and not those that are individually negotiated. The Directive is incorporated into English law now as the Unfair Terms in Consumer Contracts Regulations 1999.

The TEU inserted consumer protection as a distinct policy of the EU. In fact Art 153 (now Art 169 TFEU) (Art 129a under the TEU) called for a 'high level of consumer protection'. In fact Art 153 (now Art 169 TFEU) states that:

ARTICLE

'Art 169 In order to protect the interests of the consumer and to ensure a high level of consumer protection, the Community shall contribute to protecting the health, safety and economic interests of consumers, as well as promoting their right to information, education and to organise themselves in order to protect their interests'.

This would be achieved according to the Article by internal market measures under Art 114 TFEU, and also by specific actions using the co-decision procedure. This commitment was carried into the Treaty of Amsterdam.

Significantly, the Article provides for minimum standards so that a higher level of consumer protection within individual Member States is accepted that is still compatible with the provisions of the Treaty.

CASE EXAMPLE

Buet v Ministère Public (Case 382/87) [1989] ECR 1235

Here, French law actually outlawed doorstep selling of educational materials. Directive 85/577, on the other hand, only provided that consumers might withdraw from contracts made at home within a defined period. The ECJ held that the French law did not breach EC (now EU) law under Art 30 but merely offered a greater level of consumer protection which was not inconsistent.

An important measure introduced following the TEU and the inclusion of Art 153 (now Art 169 TFEU) is the Distance Selling Directive 97/7. This is clearly an important development because of the difficulties associated with modern methods of contracting and their potentially international scope. This is a problem already highlighted in the law of many Member States and one of the key purposes of the Directive was the harmonisation of the rules within the Member States. The Directive applies to contracts for the sale of goods and for the provisions of services made by a variety of modern methods, eg:

- telephone
- fax
- Internet shopping
- mail order
- e-mail
- television shopping.

The Directive requires a seller to provide purchasers with certain minimum information, before any contract can be considered to be validly formed. Minimum terms should also be implied into contracts formed in this way for the protection of the consumer including the right to cancel. The Directive is implemented in English law as the Consumer Protection (Distance Selling) Regulations 2000.

Other measures introduced through Art 95 as a result of the new Art 153 (now Art 169 TFEU) include:

- the Timeshare Directive 94/47 and
- the Cross-Border Transfer Directive 97/5.

Recently, the Electronic Commerce Directive 2000/31 (e-commerce) has also been introduced to regulate the formation of contracts by electronic means. Article 11 of the Directive identifies that 'where [a purchaser] in accepting [a seller's] offer is required to give his consent through technological means, such as clicking on an icon, the contract is concluded when the recipient of the service has received from the service provider, electronically, an acknowledgement of receipt of the recipient's acceptance'. This would appear to clear up some of the problems formerly encountered in determining when such agreements are actually complete and a contract is formed.

Directive 2005/29, the Unfair Commercial Practices Directive, introduces an overall ban on misleading trading practices. The Directive identifies a number of practices which are misleading and therefore unlawful. Examples include describing a product as free when there is in fact a hidden charge, and so called 'buy one get one free' (BOGOF) offers.

19.2 Environmental protection

Again, there was no specific provision within the EC Treaty for the protection of the environment. Nevertheless, even before the SEA the Community did adopt three individual Environment Action Programmes. The first two of these were aimed basically at action to remedy existing environmental problems. The third was more proactive, calling for environmental action that would assist economic growth through non-polluting industries. Even before the SEA, then, the EC (now EU) issued numerous Regulations, Decisions and more than a hundred Directives with environmental protection as their purpose.

These were usually introduced under the power given in Art 308 (now Art 352 TFEU) (formerly Art 235). This was a general power allowing the Council following a proposal of the Commission and after consultation to take the appropriate measures to ensure the attainment of a Treaty objective.

The SEA recognised the need for specific measures aimed at environmental protection since pollution, although it may be caused by individual States is even a global problem and certainly the effects of pollution can be felt in more than one State.

As a result, specific environmental policies were introduced in the SEA under Arts 174–176 (now Arts 191–193 TFEU) (formerly Arts 130r–130t). The objectives contained in the former Art 130r were:

- to preserve and improve the quality of the environment
- to contribute towards the protection of human health
- to ensure that there should be both a prudent and a rational use of natural resources.

Under the SEA the EC (now EU) would introduce measures under the old Art 130r on a preventive basis with the provision of removing the source of the problem and making the polluter pay for the damage caused. It was also possible to introduce environmental measures under the old Art 100a (now Art 95) if they could be shown to be associated with the function of the Internal Market.

One limitation of Art 130r was that it was linked to subsidiarity so that EC (now EU) action could only be taken where the problem could not be resolved better by the Member States themselves. Inevitably, the worst polluters were likely to argue against EC (now EU) involvement.

CASE EXAMPLE

Commission v Council (Case C–300/89) (the Titanium Dioxide Directive case) [1991] ECR I–2867

Here, argument focused on the application of Directive 89/48 on titanium dioxide waste. The ECJ accepted that since the Directive was essentially a harmonising Directive it should not have been introduced under the old Art 130r (now Art 191 TFEU) but should have been introduced under Art 95 (ex-Art 100a). As a result, the measure was annulled.

The TEU, on the other hand, specifically included environmental policy as a policy of the EU by inclusion within the amended Treaty. Following the Treaty of Amsterdam the environment is now included within the activities identified in Art 3. The introduction of a specific title covering the environment, Title XIX covering Arts 174–176 (now Arts 191–193 TFEU), means that there is no longer a need to introduce measures by the older more artificial means either of Art 130r or Art 95 (now Art 114 TFEU) (ex-Art 100a).

Article 191 TFEU recognises that introduction of environmental measures must take account of:

- regional variations within the Union
- the availability of scientific and technical data
- the relative costs and benefits of action to be taken or if it is not taken
- the general economic and social development of the Union.

As has been said above, EU environmental policy has been introduced as the result of a series of Environmental Action Programmes. A fourth programme was introduced in 1987 following the SEA. The legislation that has resulted from these programmes tends to have focused on distinct areas:

- Water and air pollution – as a result of which, for instance, Directive 75/324 on the use of CFCs was introduced.
- Noise pollution – an example of this is Directive 80/51 on noise from aircraft.
- Chemical pollution – an example of this is Directive 77/728 which requires labelling of paints to identify pollutants.
- Protection of the natural environment – this is possibly one of the most important but also one of the most controversial areas – one of the earliest measures introduced was Directive 76/160 on bathing water.

Protecting the natural environment is, not surprisingly, controversial. Many of the activities carried out by industry have the potential to affect the environment adversely and many vested interests are therefore at stake in legislating for its protection.

One of the most important of the developments in this field is Directive 85/337 on the use of land. The Directive introduces guidelines under which local planning authorities are supposed to assess in advance the effect of both private and public proposals for the use of land according to the effect that they will have on the environment before they consider any planning applications. The likely impact on the environment should be considered in the light of the size of the project and the nature of the location. Obviously, projects such as the building of power stations or of new transport systems fall within the scope of the Directive but smaller projects must be considered also. In the case of the latter, however, the Member States do have some discretion in terms of introducing the controls. In the UK the Directive was implemented by the Town and Country Planning Regulations 1988.

Other measures introduced with the general objective of protection of the natural environment include:

- Regulation 3258/86 and Regulation 2158/92 concerning the protection of forests both from rain and from fire.
- Directive 96/61 which integrates pollution prevention and control policies and which is mainly concerned with regulating the licensing of industrial appliances.

Enforcement of environmental law is generally against Member States through Art 258 proceedings. One possible problem is that associated with Directives generally, that they may not be directly effective against the bodies causing the pollution. However, the *Francovich v Italy* (Case C–6/90) [1991] ECR I–5357 principle of State liability may be used where the Directive has not been properly implemented or not implemented at all and thus allowing the alleged breaches of EU law.

A fifth Environmental Action Programme was also introduced in 1993 and expired in 2000. This programme focused on five main areas:

- industry
- energy
- transport
- agriculture
- tourism.

One interesting feature of the programme was a change from traditional regulatory practices to measures based on economic benefits such as tax reductions for achieving environmental targets.

19.3 Transport

Transport was actually included in the original EC Treaty. Article 70 (now Art 90 TFEU) (formerly Art 74) simply stated that the objectives of the Treaty should be carried out within the framework of a common transport policy.

Furthermore Art 71 (now Art 91 TFEU) (formerly Art 75) identified how this Common Transport Policy should be provided. This would be by the introduction of:

- the creation of common rules on transport
- the introduction of conditions for carriers who were not resident in the Member State
- the introduction of measures to improve safety within transport
- and also the implementation of any other appropriate measure needed to satisfy these aims.

However, in the early days Council did very little to develop transport policy. A significant development came in the case law of the ECJ. In *Commission v Council* (Case 22/70) [1971] ECR 263 there was disagreement between the Commission and Council over the second European Road Transport Agreement. The first agreement was entered into by five of the original six members of the EC together with some other European States. A second agreement was then proposed because of problems ratifying the first. However,

Council in the meantime had issued a Regulation covering the same areas as the agreement. The Commission was seeking to annul the second agreement but the ECJ held that, because Council was charged with the obligation to create a common transport policy the agreement was valid.

The TEU introduced a number of measures concerning transport including trans-European networks under Title XV and contained in Arts 154–156 (now Arts 170–172 TFEU). Nevertheless, a Common Transport Policy is developing much more slowly than other areas. Following the Treaty of Amsterdam, transport is an area that falls within the co-decision procedure so Parliament may well be more influential in this area. Certainly there is a need to develop a standard safety policy.

19.4 Research and technological development

Again, there was no specific provision for this within the original EC Treaty. There was limited early progress. For instance, guidelines were introduced in 1974 to co-ordinate national policies for the participation in a European Science Foundation and to develop an EC programme for scientific and technological research.

Research was included as a policy within the SEA and this was also retained in the TEU. Following the Treaty of Amsterdam this is now under Title XIX and Arts 179–190 TFEU.

The policy again is aimed at harmonisation and cohesion. Article 181 TFEU states that:

ARTICLE

'Art 181 TFEU The Community and the Member States shall co-ordinate their research and technological development activities so as to ensure that national policies and Community policies are mutually consistent.'

19.5 Education

There was no specific provision for education in the EC Treaty. However, there were still references to education in the Treaty. Article 35 (now Art 41 TFEU) (formerly Art 41) did refer to the co-ordination of vocational training in agriculture. Article 151 (now Art 167 TFEU) (formerly Art 128) also required general principles for the implementation of a Common Vocational Training Policy.

In fact, an Education Action Programme was put in place as early as 1974 and this led on to a number of different studies and reports. This gradually led to the development of an education policy and in 1989 the Commission introduced guidelines for education and training.

In any case, education and training had already been the subject of legislation because of the nature of certain Treaty Articles. Rights of establishment under Art 43 (now Art 49 TFEU) required first harmonisation of professional qualifications through the introduction of a variety of sectoral Directives. Because the process was so slow-moving, Directive 89/48, in the case of three-year degree equivalent qualifications leading to a professional qualification, and Directive 92/51, in the case of vocational qualifications of at least one year, were introduced to simplify matters through the process of mutual recognition. These were later placed under the umbrella of the 'Slim' Directive 2001/19 which increased the factors to be taken into account in assessing qualifications and widened the actual procedural safeguards (see Chapter 13). Now there is Directive 2005/36, the recognition of professional qualifications directive.

Besides this, education was identified as a social advantage in relation to the rights of workers' families under Regulation 1612/68 in relation to the free movement of workers guaranteed by Art 39 (now Art 45 TFEU) (see Chapter 12). More recently, there have also been Directives on the residence rights of students, eg Directive 93/96.

Another aspect of the Community education policy has been the ERASMUS programme which provided for co-operation between universities of different Member States to aid exchange programmes. Later there was the SOCRATES programme which through the LINGUA programme promoted the development of foreign language skills.

The TEU added education as a Community policy, now in Title X under the heading of 'Education, Vocational Training and Youth' in Arts 165–167 TFEU.

19.6 Public health

Public health did have a context in the original EC Treaty as a derogation under Art 39(3) (now Art 45 TFEU), later amplified in Directive 64/221 (replaced by Directive 2004/38), from the free movement of workers under Art 39 (now Art 45 TFEU) (see Chapter 12). The same derogation applies in the case of Art 43 rights of establishment (see Chapter 13). Similarly, there is a public health derogation in Art 36 TFEU from the free movement of goods in Arts 34 and 35 TFEU. Here, however, the derogation is inevitably broader and refers to the health of humans, animals and plants. Such a public health exemption is also accepted within the *Cassis de Dijon* rule of reason (see Chapter 14).

Health is also referred to in Art 153 TFEU under which Member States are required to co-operate in areas such as occupational hygiene and the prevention of occupational diseases and occupational injuries. The so-called 'six pack' of Regulations on health and safety in employment are a result of compliance with EU health and safety law.

Otherwise, the major responsibility still lies with the Member States and this is indicated in Art 168 TFEU. However, the Article does indicate that there should be co-operation between Member States in harmonising standards and that health protection should form a consistent part of the other policies of the EU. Usually EU influence on public health is through recommendations which, of course, while influential, are non-binding.

ACTIVITY

Self-assessment questions

1. What level of consumer protection existed in the EC (now EU) prior to the SEA?
2. How were measures aimed at consumer protection introduced at that time?
3. What changes did the SEA make?
4. In what ways did the TEU alter the area of consumer protection?
5. How did the EC (now EU) impact upon environmental protection prior to the SEA?
6. What effect did the SEA have on environmental protection?
7. In what ways has the TEU altered environmental protection within EU law?
8. What difficulties are associated with the protection of the 'natural environment'?
9. What part did transport play in the original EC treaty?
10. What methods have been used to create a 'Common Transport Policy'?
11. How successful has the transport policy been?
12. How has the TEU affected transport policy?
13. When was research and technological development introduced as a policy of the EC?
14. What methods are used in this area to develop policy among Member States?
15. In what ways does the EU use to support education in the Member States?
16. In what areas of EU law is public health important?
17. To what extent is there an EU public health policy?

KEY FACTS

Consumer protection	Only two aspects in original Treaty: • Art 33 (now Art 39 TFEU) – requirement for 'fair prices' under CAP • possible exemption for breach of Art 81 (now Art 101 TFEU) under Art 81(3). But measures introduced under Art 94'(now Art 115 TFEU) (ex-Art 100) through harmonising Directives: • Product Liability Directive 85/374 • Misleading Advertising Directive 84/450 • Doorstep Selling Directive 85/577 • Consumer Credit Directive 87/102. SEA used Art 95 (now Art 114 TFEU) (ex-Art 100a) through qualified majority voting: • Toy Safety Directive 88/378 • Price Indication Directive 88/314 • Package Travel Directive 90/314 • Unfair Terms in Consumer Contracts Directive 93/13. TEU inserted 'high level of consumer protection' as a policy in Art 153 (now Art 12 TFEU) – to be introduced by co-decision procedure: • Distance Selling Directive 97/7 • Timeshare Directive 94/47 • Cross-Border Transfer Directive 97/5 • Electronic Commerce Directive 2000/31.
Environmental protection	Nothing in Treaty but three Environment Action Programmes before SEA: • and Directives introduced under Art 308 (now Art 352 TFEU) (ex-Art 235). SEA introduced environment as policy: • used Arts 174–176 (now Arts 191–193 TFEU) (formerly Arts 130r–130t) to introduce largely preventive measures • but based on subsidiarity. TEU inserted environment as a distinct policy under Title XIX in Arts 174–176 (now Arts 191–193 TFEU): • Directive 75/324 on the use of CFCs • Directive 80/51 on noise from aircraft • Directive 76/160 on bathing water • Directive 85/337 on the use of land • Regulation 3258/86 and Regulation 2158/92 on protection of forests from rain and fire. Enforcement usually through Art 258 TFEU proceedings.
Transport	Art 70 (now Art 90 TFEU) (formerly Art 74) called for 'Common Transport Policy'. TEU included as Title V in Arts 70–80 (now Arts 90–100 TFEU) and also inserts transEuropean networks under Title XV in Arts 154–156 (now Arts 170–172 TFEU).

Research and technological development	Nothing in original Treaty but guidelines introduced in 1974 to co-ordinate national policies for participation in a European Science Foundation. Included in SEA as policy. Now in TEU under Title XVIII in Arts 163–173 (now Arts 179–190 TFEU). • Art 181 TFEU based on harmonisation so that Member States' policies are 'mutually consistent'.
Education	Only references in original Treaty were: • Art 35 (now Art 41 TFEU) (formerly Art 41) co-ordination of vocational training in agriculture • Art 151 (now Art 167 TFEU) (formerly Art 128) general principles for implementation of Common Vocational Training Policy. • also important in harmonising, then mutual recognition, for Art 49 TFEU. • also social advantage under Regulation 1612/68 for Art 45 TFEU rights. Education Action Programme from 1974. See also ERASMUS, SOCRATES and LINGUA.
Public health	In original Treaty, appears as: • derogation from Art 39 (now Art 45 TFEU) rights under Art 39(3) and Directive 64/221 (replaced by Directive 2004/38) • derogation from Arts 34 and 35 rights under Art 36. Art 153 TFEU requires co-operation on occupational hygiene and health and safety. Art 168 TFEU obligation for public health is on Member States.

SUMMARY

- The programme of the EU is usually associated with the four freedoms and the creation of the single market.
- However, there are other significant areas of legislation deriving from the Treaties as amended.
- These include: consumer protection, environmental protection, transport, research and technological development, education and public health.

Further reading

Books

Kent, P, *Law of the European Union* (3rd edn, Longman, 2001), Chapter 26.

Index

(all references are to page number)